D0138641

Yale Linguistic Series

ADVANCED CHINESE

by John DeFrancis

WITH THE ASSISTANCE OF

Teng Chia-yee and Yung Chih-sheng

SCHOOL OF MISSIONS

New Haven and London, Yale University Press

LIBRARY
LUTHERAN SCHOOL OF THEOLOGY

PL
1121
.C5D4

Copyright © 1966 by Yale University.
Second printing, February 1968.
Set in IBM Documentary and
printed in the United States of America by
The Murray Printing Co., Forge Village, Mass.
All rights reserved. This book may not be
reproduced, in whole or in part, in any form
(except by reviewers for the public press),
without written permission from the publishers.

Library of Congress catalog number: 66–21516

This work was developed pursuant to a contract
between the United States Office of Education
and Seton Hall University and is published with permission
of the United States Office of Education,
Department of Health, Education, and Welfare.

For

Tony, Ann, and Mary

5-5-69, 8.00, ʃɔɹɔɒ ɐɯɐ

PREFACE

The present work forms part of three closely integrated sets of texts in spoken and written Chinese prepared at Seton Hall University. The relationship among them can be seen from the following outline:

CONVERSATION SERIES

Transcription Version	Character Version
Beginning Chinese	Character Text for Beginning Chinese
Intermediate Chinese	Character Text for Intermediate Chinese
Advanced Chinese	Character Text for Advanced Chinese

READING SERIES

Beginning Chinese Reader

Intermediate Chinese Reader

Advanced Chinese Reader

The first two sets are alternate versions of a single series of conversation texts. The two sets are integrated with each other and with the reading series in such a way as to permit the use of the texts in different combinations and sequences. Such flexibility is designed to facilitate the adaption of the texts to various kinds of programs — high school and college, regular and intensive, speaking-oriented and reading-oriented, and so on. Just how this can be done can best be determined for individual programs if the following points are borne in mind regarding each text:

Beginning Chinese presupposes no previous knowledge of the language.
Intermediate Chinese presupposes mastery of Beginning Chinese.
Advanced Chinese presupposes mastery of Beginning Chinese, Beginning Chinese Reader, and Lessons 1–6 of Intermediate Chinese Reader.

Character Text for Beginning Chinese presupposes mastery of Beginning Chinese.
Character Text for Intermediate Chinese presupposes mastery of Beginning Chinese, Intermediate Chinese, and Character Text for Beginning Chinese.
Character Text for Advanced Chinese presupposes mastery of Beginning Chinese, Advanced Chinese, Beginning Chinese Reader, and Lessons 1–6 of Intermediate Chinese Reader.

Beginning Chinese Reader presupposes mastery of Beginning Chinese.

Intermediate Chinese Reader presupposes mastery of Beginning Chinese and Beginning Chinese Reader. Its Lessons 1-6 are correlated with Beginning Chinese, and its Lessons 7-30 with Lessons 1-9 of Advanced Chinese.

Advanced Chinese Reader presupposes mastery of Beginning Chinese, Beginning Chinese Reader, and Intermediate Chinese Reader. Its first twenty lessons are correlated with Lessons 10-24 of Advanced Chinese.

In high school classes it is suggested that the normal sequence of beginning-intermediate-advanced transcription texts be followed. Paralleling these but well behind in time should come the same sequence of readers, with or without the character versions of the conversation texts as supplementary reading matter.

The same sequence can be followed in college courses which emphasize general conversation. In some college programs (especially in accelerated courses with a primary emphasis on reading) it would be possible to defer study of conversation on topics of daily interest, such as preponderate in Intermediate Chinese, until just before the student goes abroad into a Chinese-speaking environment. This does not at all mean that all practice in conversation should be abandoned in favor of reading. Such a course is not recommended because, although the initial progress in reading may seem impressive, the lack of a foundation in the spoken language will weaken the ability to make more rapid progress at a later date.

In anticipation of the fact that different programs may take up the texts in different sequences, the contents of the various texts have been designed so that they are not necessarily mutually exclusive. Depending on just what order is selected for studying the various texts, there may be a certain amount of overlap and repetition. In language texts overlap and repetition is by no means undesirable. When vocabulary is repeated it is usually presented in different contextual situations. Occasionally, especially in the case of grammatical notes, reference will be made to the item in another text so as to reduce the necessity of having to repeat an explanation.

The subject matter of Advanced Chinese is of the sort which most Western students of Chinese are interested in reading about as well as speaking about. Because of this the character version, namely Character Text for Advanced Chinese, can be studied for reading purposes at the same time that the transcription version is studied for speaking purposes. Special efforts have been made to enhance the value of the character version as a reading text to supplement the works specifically prepared as readers. For one thing, the basic transcription text was so compiled that the corresponding character text would provide adequate repetition of new characters, i.e. of those characters, 904 in number, beyond the 480 in Beginning Chinese Reader and the first six lessons of Intermediate Chinese Reader. For another, the relatively rare characters, 69 in all, are accompanied by transcription in every one of their occurrences, so that students do not need to learn these characters at this time but can concentrate on the remaining 835 with the assurance that they are all well worth memorizing.[*] More-

---

[*] Relatively rare characters are those which do not occur either in the first 2,400 characters in the frequency list compiled by Ch'en Ho-ch'in (Yü-t'i-wen ying-yung tzu-hui [Shanghai, 1928]) or in the list of 2,421 characters officially determined as most important for purposes of adult education in mainland China.

over, of these 835 characters, 637 are included in the correlated reading texts—
Intermediate Chinese Reader and Advanced Chinese Reader. Thus the character
text together with the two readers provide an unparalleled amount of reading
matter for a limited number of characters.

The present work is an extension in modified form of a pioneer attempt[*] made
in 1952 to adapt the spoken approach to academic topics. This early effort com-
bined academic lectures with conversation about the lectures. The work was not
wholly successful, in part because the lectures turned out to be too difficult for
students at the level at which they were aimed, in part because, as often happens,
conversations based on lectures tend to be somewhat artificial.

In the attempt to achieve greater realism and authenticity, the present text
seeks a better balance between academic lectures and classroom requirements.
This is achieved by basing the book on two imagined situations, both plausible
and one not only plausible but highly realistic and practical.

In one of the imagined situations Vincent White, an American student who in
Beginning Chinese spent his junior year in China and in Intermediate Chinese
returned to China after an absence of three years, in Advanced Chinese resumes
his studies at Far Eastern University. For the benefit of foreign students like
himself, the University has established a lecture series, one a day for one month,
to provide a general and rather elementary orientation to the Chinese academic
world and to Chinese customs, history, geography, and so on. A teacher is
assigned to each foreign student to prepare him to cope with the lectures by
taking up anticipated points of difficulty. The other imagined situation is the
actual classroom, whether in this country or in China. The teacher introduces
new terms, uses them in conversation, provides illustrative sentences and notes,
and generally lays the groundwork for listening to the lectures and discussing
them.

By thus presenting lectures at a simpler level[†] and dialogue about the lectures in a more realistic setting, the present text has been able to avoid the
shortcomings of the earlier work and to provide a sounder introduction to academic and cultural topics.

The general outline of the lessons is as follows:

1. Dialogue, vocabulary, and illustrative sentences in Chinese
2. Vocabulary list

---

[*] John DeFrancis and Elizabeth Jen Young, Talks on Chinese History, 2 vols.
(New Haven, 1952).

[†] Reducing the level of the lectures was the work of the authors of the present
text and not of the colleagues who were kind enough to provide tape recordings of talks on various topics. The original talks were completely re-
worked by us, in part in order to make each lesson more or less uniform in
length. This necessitated, among other things, a drastic reduction in the
length of most of the lectures. Thus one of the narrowest topics, that having
to do with the celebration of Chinese New Year's, was reduced by more than
fifty per cent from the lecture recorded by Dr. John B. Tsu. In view of such
drastic changes I should like to stress that we alone are responsible for any
sins of omission or commission which may occur in the lectures or elsewhere
in the text.

    3. Grammar drill
    4. Lecture
    5. Recapitulation
    6. Review
    7. Questions
    8. Illustrative sentences (English)
    9. Notes

New vocabulary items are introduced in small batches throughout the dialogue. Related items are grouped together and provided with English definitions (e.g. yīsheng 'doctor,' yīkē 'medical course,' yīxuéyuàn 'medical school'). All of the items are used in the immediately following illustrative sentences and most of them—at least one from each group—occur in the related section of dialogue that follows the illustrative sentences.

The new vocabulary is used and reviewed according to a fixed schedule which has been set up to assure a certain minimum number of repetitions. Within the lesson in which it is first introduced, each item is used at least three times: once in the immediately following illustrative sentences and at least two more times in two separate parts of the same lesson (e.g. dialogue, lecture, review, etc.). Each item occurs again in the next lesson, once more after a gap of one lesson, and again in the final lesson of the unit.

English translations are provided for the illustrative sentences (indicated by the letter T) that are especially difficult or otherwise merit special attention. The English versions, in addition to serving as a check on whether these key sentences are completely clear to the student, can also be used for practice in English-to-Chinese translation.

The material in the grammar drills includes both new patterns and those already introduced in the earlier works, for review purposes. Each new pattern taken up in a grammar drill is reviewed at least once after a gap of one lesson, once more after a further gap of two lessons, and once again in each subsequent unit. If the new vocabulary and illustrative sentences, together with the notes at the end of the lesson, have been thoroughly mastered, the remaining exercises should pose no difficulty. The lectures, from which all points of difficulty have been extracted as the basis for the new terms and illustrative sentences, no longer contain anything new and hence are essentially in the nature of review. Further review of a lecture is provided in the lesson following the lecture in the section entitled Fùshù (Recapitulation). This takes the form of a student summary of the contents of each of the lectures. Miscellaneous review is provided in the section entitled Wēnxi (Review). In addition, each sixth lesson contains a general review of all the material in the preceding five.

The material presented in this text can be studied in various ways depending on what the student brings to the task and what he wants to get out of it. Some students, for example, may already have learned some of the content elsewhere and hence will not need as much practice as others for whom all the material is new. In adapting the text to various programs it is well to bear in mind that all new material is introduced in the illustrative sentences, the exercise entitled Yǔfǎ Liánxi, and the notes at the end of the lesson. This material, together with the lectures themselves, comprise the minimum which all students should study. For those who seek an active and facile command of the material, the dialogues and the section headed Wèntí (Questions) provide an opportunity for additional oral drill. The remaining material can also be used or not depending on whether further practice is desired.

In studying the material particular attention should be paid to the various levels of discourse that have been presented. In all languages, and most especially in Chinese, there are many different styles of speech—the ordinary spoken style in everyday conversation, the somewhat more formal style used by scholars in discussions of academic topics, the still more formal lecture style, which is very close to the modern written style, and so on. Such things as what is being discussed and who is talking to whom require certain choices of words, structures, and other variables of speech. In our material the lectures are in a somewhat formal academic style. The dialogue between Vincent White as a student and Professor Ma as his teacher is less formal than the lectures but more formal (in spots at least) than the conversation of Vincent White with his friends Meiying and Xuexin. Special pains should be taken to avoid, in ordinary speech, forms more appropriate to the formal spoken or written styles. To this end we have used the symbol (W)— standing for written style or wényán— to designate those items which the student might expect to encounter in lectures or in reading but which he would not ordinarily use in his own speech. To give a specific example, the term fùshù, 'recapitulate' or 'recapitulation,' which we have used as the heading for one of the review exercises, has something of the scholarly or pedantic connotation of the English equivalent. In lieu of a better term we have adopted the expression despite the fact that it is not widely used (though it occurs throughout the Modern Chinese Readers, Book One, published in Peking in 1964), but by labeling it with a (W) we warn the student not to use it in ordinary conversation.

I wish to thank the following institutions and individuals for help in making this book possible:

Office of Education, Department of Health, Education and Welfare, for a grant to compile the book.

Seton Hall University, for providing institutional support for my work.

Dr. John B. Tsu, Director of the Institute of Far Eastern Studies, for his energetic concern to make available whatever assistance was needed at all stages of the work.

Mrs. Teng Chia-yee and Mr. Yung Chih-sheng, for their able and painstaking collaboration in writing the book.

The Editorial Committee, consisting of Professors John B. Tsu and Dr. David L. Kuan, of Seton Hall University, Professor Chang Li-tsai, of National Chingchi University in Taiwan, and Mrs. Ho Ti, of the Harvard-Yenching Institute Library, for suggesting many improvements in the text.

The Recording Committee, consisting of Dr. John B. Tsu, Professor Eileen Wei, Mrs. Thomas Ho, and Mr. Fan Wai-tsu, of Seton Hall University, Professor David Kwo, of Upsala College, Mr. James Liang, of the University of Pennsylvania, Professor William S-Y. Wang, of Ohio State University, and Dr. E-tu Zen Sun, of Pennsylvania State University, for providing recordings of lectures as the basis for the material in the book.

Mr. S. C. Peng and Mr. Fan Wai-tsu, for making tape recordings of the revised lectures and other material in the text.*

---

* These recordings are available from the Institute of Far Eastern Studies, Seton Hall University, South Orange, New Jersey.

William Sloane Associates, McGraw-Hill Book Company, and Human Relations Area File, for permission to adapt the maps appearing on pages 68, 111, and 155 respectively.

Mrs. Dorothy de Fontaine, for drawing the maps and charts, and Miss Diana Ma, for doing the remaining illustrations.

My wife, for typing the manuscript.

J. DeF.

Madison, Connecticut
June 1966

CONTENTS

LIST OF ABBREVIATIONS AND SYMBOLS

A, B, C	Miscellaneous noun or verb phrases
AD	Adverb
AT	Attributive
AV	Auxiliary verb
CV	Coverb
IV	Intransitive verb
M	Measure
MA	Movable adverb
N	Noun
NU	Number
O	Object
PR	Pronoun
PW	Place word
RV	Resultative verb
SV	Stative verb
T	Translation in English available
TV	Transitive verb
V	Verb
VO	Verb plus object
W	Wényán, written style
*	Bound form
、	Enumerative comma (See Beginning Chinese Reader, p. 13)
/	or (e.g. shì/wéi = 'shì or wéi')

SETTING THE STAGE

CAST OF CHARACTERS

Bái Wénshān: Vincent White, an American student doing graduate work at Far Eastern University

Mǎ Jiàoshòu :   Professor Ma, a faculty member at Far Eastern University

Huá Xuéxīn :   Friend and fellow student of Vincent White and son of Mr. and Mrs. Hua, at whose home Vincent lives.

Gāo Měiyīng :   Friend and fellow student of Vincent White and daughter of Mr. and Mrs. Gao. Mr. Gao is the manager of the Three Friends Bookstore.

PLACE

A City in China

TIME

September 12 to October 9, the first four weeks of classes at Far Eastern University. (The preceding four days, as reported in Intermediate Chinese, were spent by Vincent White in finding a place to live and getting settled after his arrival in China.)

UNIT I

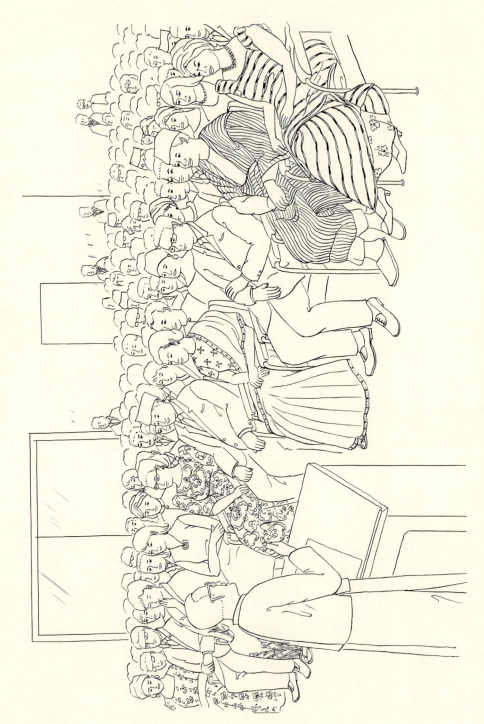

"Yǒu péng zì yuǎn fāng lái bú yì lè hu?"

Dì-Yīkè. Kāishǐ Shàng Kè

Bái: Nín shi Mǎ Jiàoshòu ma?

Mǎ : Shì. Wǒ shi Mǎ Dàwén. Nǐ shi Bái Wénshān ma?

Bái: Shìde.

Mǎ : Nǐ yǐqián zài Yuǎn-Dà niànguo shū, shì bu shì?

5 Bái: Shìde. Wǒ sānnián yǐqián zài zhèr niàn shū. Hòulái wǒ huí guó le.

Mǎ : Nǐ zhèicì shi shénmo shíhou lái de?

Bái: Wǒ zhèicì dào zhèr hái bú dào yíge xīngqī ne.

Mǎ : Zhùzai nǎr? Lí xuéxiào yuǎn bu yuǎn?

Bái: Bù hěn yuǎn. Wǒ zhùzai Běi Hú Lù shíjiǔhào.

10 Mǎ : Oh, Běi Hú Lù shíjiǔhào. Nà bu shi Huá jia ma?

Bái: Shì. Mǎ Jiàshòu rènshi ma?

Mǎ : Rènshi. Wǒmen shi lǎo péngyou.

Bái: Hái yǒu yíwèi Gāo Xiānsheng, shi Sān Yǒu Shūdiànde jīnglǐ. Mǎ Jiàoshòu rènshi bu rènshi?

15 Mǎ : Rènshi, rènshi. Yě shi wǒde péngyou.

Bái: Wǒ zhèicì dào zhèr shi xiān dào de Gāo jia. Wǒ zài Gāo jia zhùle sìtiān. Wǒ zhù Huá jiāde fángzi jiù shi Gāo Xiānsheng jièshao de.

Mǎ : Nǐ hěn zǎo jiu rènshi Gāo Xiānsheng, shì bu shì?

Bái: Wǒ dì-yīcì dào zhèr jiu rènshi. Nèige shíhou Gāo Měiyīng Xiáojie
20 hái zài zhōngxué niàn shū ne.

Mǎ : Hǎo. Xiànzài wǒmen tányitan guānyu wǒmen liǎngge rén zài yíkuàr yánjiu gōngkede wèntí.

Bái: Mǎ Jiàoshòu tài kèqi. Wǒ děi gēn nín qǐngjiào.

Mǎ : Oh, hái yǒu! Shàng kè de shíjiān nǐ dōu zhīdao ma?

25 Bái: Wǒ zhīdao. Wǒ měitiān bādiǎn zhōng shàng Mǎ Jiàoshòude kè. Zài zhèi sānnián lǐtou méi jīhui shuō Zhōngguo huà, kěnéng wàngde tài duō le. Búdàn shàng kè de shíjiān gēn Mǎ Jiàoshòu xué, jiùshi xià kè yǐhòu yě xīwang Mǎ Jiàoshòu duō bāngzhu wo.

Mǎ : Nà méi wèntí. Wǒ bù zhīdào nǐ yǐqián shi zěnmo xuéde. Xiànzài
30 wǒ bǎ wǒde fāngfǎ gēn nǐ shuōyishuō. Wǒmen měitiānde gōngke dōu xiěchulai. Xiànzài gěi ni zhèi jǐzhāng zhǐ, shi wǒmen jīntiande gōngke. Wǒmen xiànzài kàn:

3

1.0.   shēngcí   new word, vocabulary

shēngcí biǎo   word list, vocabulary list

1.1.   Shēngcí biǎoshang dì-sānge cér shi shénmo yìsi?   (T)

1.2.   Shēngcí jiù shi méi xuéguo de cér.   (T)

1.3.   Nǐ wèi-shénmo bu dǒng zhèige cér? . . . Shi shēngcí me.   (T)

2.0.   chéng   (1) be OK, be all right, be satisfactory, (that'll) do; (2) become; (3) postverb meaning 'complete' and 'into, as'

fēnchéng   divide into

2.1.   Wǒmen zhèiyàng zuò chéng bu chéng? . . . Bù chéng, bù chéng! (T)

2.2.   Nǐ nèibén shū xiěchéngle méi yǒu? . . . Hái méi ne.   (T)

2.3.   Měi yìmén gōngke fēnchéng liǎngbùfen.

3.0.   zǔ   group, unit, series   (M)

3.1.   Bǎ zhèi wǔshige shēngcí fēnchéng wǔzǔ.

4.0.   jiěshi   (1) explain; (2) explanation   [untie release]

jiěshi míngbai   explain (something until it is) understood

jiěshide míngbai   explain clearly

4.1.   Nèige cér hěn nán jiěshi.

4.2.   Wǒ xiān bǎ shēngcí gěi nǐmen jiěshi míngbai, ránhòu nǐmen kéyi yòng Yīngwén xiěxialai.

4.3.   Tā jiěshide bù míngbai. Wǒ háishi bù dǒng.

5.0.   jìxu(de)   continue (doing something)   [continue continue]

5.1.   Wǒ méi yǒu qián, bù néng jìxu niàn shū le.

5.2.   Qǐng ni jìxude niànxiaqu.   (T)

Mǎ :   Wǒmen bǎ shēngcí fēnchéng zǔ. Zhè shi dì-yīzǔ. Měi yìzǔli yǒu
       jǐge cér. Zuǒbian shi Zhōngwén, yòubian shi Yīngwén jiěshi.
35   Wǒmen xiān yánjiu dì-yīzǔde cér, ránhòu dì-èrzu, dì-sānzǔ jìxude
       yánjiuxiaqu.

Note: The symbol (T) after a sentence indicates that an English transla-
        tion is available in the section below, entitled Illustrative Sentences.
        An asterisk after an entry indicates that the item is a bound form
        or otherwise restricted in use. The notation (W) means that the
        item belongs to the written, or wényán, style and is not usually
        spoken except in formal speech. For (M) and other letters and sym-
        bols used as references, see the list on p. xv.

Bái: Měicì shàng kè yào xué duōshao shēngcí?

Mǎ : Wǒmen měicì shàng kè zài cér yìfāngmian yánjiu shízǔ zuǒyòu,
      yígòng dàgài yǒu liùshige shēngcí zuǒyòu.

6.0. lìzi   example, sample, illustration

6.1. Nǐ yòng zhèige cér shuō yíge lìzi.

7.0. jǔ   (1) raise, lift; (2) give (an example)

7.1. Shéi huì shéi jǔ shǒu.   (T)

7.2. Wǒ duō jǔ jǐge lìzi, nǐ jiu míngbai le.

8.0. lìjù   illustrative sentence   (W)

8.1. Lìjù jiu shi jǔ ge lìzi de jùzi.

9.0. fānchéng   translate into

9.1. Qǐng nǐ bǎ jiǔ-diǎr-yī zhèige lìjù fānchéng Yīngwén.   (T)

9.2. Qǐng nǐ bǎ bǐjiǎo wén yìdiǎnde shēngcí fānchéng báihuà.   (T)

10.0. fānyì   (1) translate; (2) translation; (3) translator [translate trans-
      late]

10.1. Wǒmende kèwài liànxi měitiān dōu yǒu fānyì.   (T)

10.2. Tā yòng Yīngwén fānyìle yìběn Zhōngwén xiǎoshuō.   (T)

10.3. Tā néng bu néng gěi wǒ dāng fànyì?   (T)

40 Mǎ : Shēngcí yǐwài hái yǒu lìjù. Lìjù jiu shi yòng shēngcí jǔ ge lìzi,
         bǎ ta jiěshi míngbai. Lìjù yǒude wǒmen fānchéng Yīngwén.

    Bái: Lìjù wèi-shénmo yǒude fānyì yǒude bù fānyì ne?

    Mǎ : Bǐjiǎo zhòngyàode hé nán dǒngde yòng Yīngwén fānyì. Róngyide bú
         bì fānyì me.

45 Bái: Zhè duì wǒmen xuésheng xuéqilai hěn fāngbian.

11.0. wēnxi   review (N/V)   [review practice]

11.1. Wǒmen xiān wēnxi wēnxi zuótiande.   (T)

11.2. Wǒmen chúle wēnxi yǐwài hái yǒu yǔfǎ liànxi gēn wèntí.   (T)

12.0. zhùjiě   note, annotation   [annotate untie]

12.1. Wèi-shénmo zhèige yǒu zhùjiě nèige méi yǒu ne? . . . Zhèige bǐjiǎo
      nán yìdiǎr.   (T)

13.0. qīngchu   clear, intelligible (SV and RV postverb) [clear distinct]

13.1. Rúguǒ nǐ hái bù qīngchu wǒ zài jǔ yíge lìzi.   (T)

13.2. Tāde Zhōngwén bú tài hǎo, suǒyǐ tā shuōbuqīngchu.   (T)

14.0. fēicháng   extremely, extraordinarily   [not ordinary]

14.1. Wǒ fēicháng xǐhuan niàn Zhōngwén.

14.2. Jīntian tiānqi fēicháng nuǎnhuo.

14.3. Zhèizhǒng mòshuǐ fēicháng hǎoyòng.

Mǎ : Wǒmen hái yǒu yǔfǎ liànxi, yě yǒu wēnxi, yě yǒu wèntí. Zuìhòu shi
Yīngwén zhùjiě. Wǒ suǒ shuō de nǐ dōu qīngchu la ma?

Bái: Qīngchu le. Oh! Qǐng wèn Mǎ Jiàoshòu, wǒ zěnmo xué ne?

Mǎ : Wǒmen xiān bǎ cér niànyinian. Huìle yǐhòu, zài bǎ lìjù niànyinian.
50   Dōu míngbaile yǐhòu, wǒmen liǎngge rén mǎshàng yòng zhèi jǐge
cér tán huà.

Bái: Zhèige fázi fēicháng hǎo.

15.0. jiǎng   (1) explain, expound, discuss, lecture; (2) speak, say (central
and southern dialects)

15.1. Wǒ yǐ tīng tā shuō "Wǒ huì jiǎng Běijīng huà" jiù zhīdao tā bú shi
zhēnzhèngde Běijīng rén.

15.2. Tā zuótiān jiǎng de shi shénmo tímu?

15.3. Lìjù zhèige cér zěnmo jiǎng?   (T)

16.0. jiǎnghuà   lecture (N/V) [lecture talk]

16.1. Jīntian shi xiàozhǎng duì wǒmen jiǎnghuà.   (T)

16.2. Zhèige xīngqī xiàozhǎng duì wǒmen jiǎngguo liǎngcì huà le.

16.3. Nǐmen néng bu néng bǎ tāde jiǎnghuà fānchéng Yīngwén?

17.0. zhuān(mén)   special(ly) [special door]

17.1. Wǒ zài dàxuéli zhuān xué yǔyánxué.   (T)

17.2. Wǒ dào Zhōngguo lái zhuānmén yánjiu Zhōngguo lìshǐ.

18.0. zhuānjiā   a specialist, an expert   [special house]

18.1. Yánjiu Yuán Cháo lìshǐ tā shi zhuānjiā.   (T)

18.2. Jīntiande jiǎnghuà wǒmen shi qǐngle yíwèi zuì yǒumíngde zhèngzhi-
xué zhuānjiā.   (T)

19.0. zhuāntí   special topic

19.1. Zhuāntíde zhuān shi zhuānménde zhuān. Tí shi tímude tí.   (T)

19.2. Wǒmen měitiān yǒu yícì Zhuāntí Jiǎnghuà.   (T)

Bái: Mǎ Jiàoshòu, wǒ kèwài zěnmo liànxí ne?

Ma: Wǒ gàosu ni. Chúle shàng kè yǐwài, měitiān hái yǒu <u>Zhuāntí Jiǎng-</u>
55   <u>huà.</u>

Bái: Shénmo jiàozuò Zhuāntí Jiánghuà?

Mǎ: Jiùshi jiǎng zhuānménde xuéwen, bǐfang lìshǐ、 dìlǐ、 shèhuì wèntí
     děngděngde.

Bái: Shì bu shi qǐng zhuānjiā lái jiǎng ne?

60 Mǎ: Shìde. Yǒude shi wǒmen xuéxiàode jiàoshòu, yǒude shi cóng wàibiar
     qǐnglái de.

20.0. jiǎngyǎn   lecture (N/V)   [lecture perform]

20.1. Nǐ kéyi yòng Zhōngwén jiǎngyǎn ma?

21.0. yǎnjiǎng   lecture (N/V)   [perform lecture]

21.1. Wáng Jiàoshòu yǎnjiǎngle liǎngge zhōngtóu.

22.0. fùshù   (1) recapitulate, summarize; (2) recapitulation, summary
               (W)   [again narrate]

       lùyīn fùshù   summarize by recording

22.1. Wǒmen gōngkeli <u>fùshù</u> zhèige cér shi bǐjiǎo wén yìdiǎr.

22.2. Wǒ shi lùyīn fùshù ne, háishi xiěxialai ne?   (T)

23.0. qíngxing   situation, condition   [feeling form]

       kàn qíngxing   (1) look at the situation; (2) depending on the situation

23.1. Kàn qíngxing, rúguǒ wǒ yǒu gōngfu wǒ jiù qù.   (T)

24.0. yěxǔ   perhaps   [also permit]

24.1. Wǒ yěxǔ qù, yěxǔ bú qù.

24.2. Wǒ yěxǔ mǎi mòshuǐ gēn běnzi shénmode.

Bái: Wǒ tīngle yǎnjiǎng yǐhòu zuò shénmo?

Mǎ: Nǐ měicì tīngle jiǎngyǎn yǐhòu, qǐng nǐ bǎ tīngguo de yòng lùyīnjī
     nǐ zìjǐ zài liànxí yícì, gěi wǒ tīngyiting, kàn qíngxing yěxǔ yǒude
65   shíhou nǐ bǎ yǎnjiǎng xiěxialai wǒ kànyikan. Kěshi zuì hǎo háishi
     lùyīn fùshù.

Bái: <u>Fùshù</u> shi shénmo yìsi?

Mǎ: Jiù shi nǐ tīngle yǎnjiǎng yǐhòu, nǐ tóngyàngde zài shuō yícì me.
     <u>Fùshù</u> zhèige cér píngcháng shuō huà bù zěnmo yòng. Shūshang、
70   bàoshang cháng yǒu zhèige cér.

25.0. xuéshù   learning, scholarship   [study skill]

25.1. Zhèi liǎngcìde jiǎngyǎn dōu shi xuéshù yìfāngmiànde jiǎngyǎn. (T)

26.0. yǎnjiǎngcí   text of a lecture

26.1. Wǒ xiān niàn yǎnjiǎngcí, ránhòu tīng yǎnjiǎng.

27.0. shìqián   before an event, beforehand   [matter before]

27.1. Wǒ míngtian shídiǎn zhōng tīng xiàozhǎng jiǎnghuà. Shìqián wǒ bǎ xiàozhǎngde yǎngjiǎngcí kànyikan.

28.0. běnxiào   our school, this school   (W)

28.1. Xīwang jiānglái nǐmen háishi dào běnxiào lai jìxùde xué Zhōngwén. (W)

29.0. xuéshi   knowledge (obtained from study)   [study recognize]

29.1. Wǒ gēn Mǎ Jiàoshòu dédào de xuéshi bù shǎo.

Bái: Qǐng wèn Mǎ Jiàoshòu, Zhuāntǐ Jiǎnghuà dōu shi jiǎng něi yìfāng-miànde?

Mǎ: Dōu shi xuéshù yìfāngmiànde. Bǐfang lìshǐ, wénxué, yǔyán děngděng. Yě yǒu shèhuì, dìlǐ, zhèngzhi yìfāngmiànde. Yǐhuěr shi xiàozhǎng duì wàiguo xuésheng jiǎnghuà.

Bái: Xiàozhǎng jiǎnghuàde nèiróng, Mǎ Jiàoshào zhīdao ma?

Mǎ: Shi zhè yàngzi. Suǒyǒude yǎnjiǎngcí shìqián xuéxiào dōu xiān gěi wǒmen xiānshengmen. Wǒmen měicì xiān bǎ yǎnjiǎngcí zài méi jiǎng yǐqián dōu gěi nǐmen jiěshi míngbai, ránhòu nǐmen zài tīng yǎnjiǎng qu.

Bái: Wǒ hěn xǐhuan Mǎ Jiàoshòu jiāode fāngfǎ. Wǒ yídìng yònggōng xuéxiaqu, xīwang duō dédào yìdiǎr xuéshi.

30.0. qīngnián   youth   [blue-green year]

30.1. Mǎ Jiàoshòu shi qīngnián rén háishi zhōngnián rén?

31.0. yōuxiù   superior, first-rate   [superior elegant]

31.1. Zài zhèr niàn shū de wàiguo rén dōu shi yōuxiù qīngnián.

32.0. nǔlì   exert great effort, strive hard   [exert effort]

32.1. Tā niàn shū fēicháng nǔlì.

33.0. xiāngxìn   believe, be convinced that, have trust in   [mutually be-lieve]

33.1. Wǒ bù xiāngxìn tā bú huì yòng Zhōngwén jiǎnghuà.

34.0. dádào   attain   [attain to]

34.1. Wǒ xiāngxìn nǐ yídìng néng dádào nǐ dào Zhōngguo qu niàn shū de mùdì. (T)

35.0. qiú   entreat, seek, aim at

      qiúxué   seek an education

35.1. Zhèijiàn shì wǒ xiǎng qiú biéren bāngzhu wo.

35.2. Wǒ xiāngxìn tā yídìng nénggou dádào tā qiúxué de mùdì.   (T)

35.3. Yàoshi nǐ chūqu wǒ xiǎng qiú nǐ gěi wǒ mǎi mòshuǐ.

Mǎ : Nǐ shi ge yōuxiùde qīngnián.   Nǐ yǒu nǔlì.   Wǒ xiāngxìn nǐ yídìng
       xuéde hěn hǎo.

85 Bái: Wǒ xīwang zhèicì dào Yuǎn-Dà duō xué yìdiǎr dōngxi, bù zhīdào
       néng bu néng dádào zhèige mùdì.

Mǎ : Nǐ yídìng nénggòu dádào nǐ qiúxué de mùdì.

36.0. bāokuò   (1) include; (2) including (especially after a parenthesis)
            [wrap include]

36.1. Wǒ měiyuè yòng sānbǎikuài qián, fángqián、fànqián dōu bāokuò zài
       nèi.   (T)

36.2. Wǒ měi xīngqī shàng shíwǔge zhōngtóude kè (bāokuò Zhuāntí Jiǎng-
       huà zài nèi).

37.0. fànwéi   scope, sphere, bounds, jurisdiction [model surround]

37.1. Zhèicì kǎoshì de fānwéi hěn dà.   Lián kèběn yǐwàide dōu kǎo. (T)

38.0. gè   each, every   (see <u>Intermediate Chinese</u>, p. 222, note 3)

38.1. Jīntiande jiǎnghuà bù zhǐ shi wénxué, shi bāokuòle gèfāngmiàn de.

38.2. Gèwèi tóngxué dōu shi yōuxiù qīngnián.   (W)

38.3. Nèige shūdiàn chūjí、zhōngjí、gāojí gèjíde jiàokeshū tāmen dōu yǒu.
       (T)

38.4. Gèrénde yìjiàn dōu bù yíyàng.

38.5. Wǒ xǐhuan chī zhūròu zuò de gèzhǒng cài.   (T)

39.0. jiǎngtí   (lecture) topic

39.1. Jīntiande jiǎnghuà jiǎngtí shi shénmo?

40.0. zhǔjiǎng   lecture, have the responsibility for a lecture   [chief lec-
             ture]

      zhǔjiǎng(de) rén   lecturer

40.1. Jīntiande jiǎnghuà shi shéi zhǔjiǎng?   (T)

40.2. Shàngcì nèige zhǔjiǎng rén suǒ jiǎng de dōu chūle tímude fànwéi
       yǐwài le.   (T)

Bái: Zhuāntí Jiǎnghùa fànwei hěn dà, bāokuò gèfāngmiànde, shì bu shi?

Mǎ: Dāngrán, yīnwei měi yìtiān yǒu yíge jiǎngtí, yíge yuèli zìrán bāokuò
90   de bù shǎo.

Bái: Zhǔjiǎng rén yě hěn duō ba?

Mǎ: Chúle běnxiào jiàoshòu yǐwài hái qǐngle jǐwèi zhuānjiā zhǔjiǎng.

41.0. kècheng   curriculum   (M: mén)   [lesson progress]

41.1. Wǒmen Zhōngwén zhèimén kècheng fēicháng nán.   (T)

42.0. jìhua   (1) plan, figure out; (2) plan, proposal, plan of action   [reckon
        draw]

42.1. Zhèige fázi shi xiàozhǎng jìhua de, bú shi wǒmen jiāo Zhōngwén
        de jìhua de.   (T)

42.2. Zhèngfǔ duìyu zhòng gōngyè yǒu yíge sānnián jìhua.   (T)

43.0. gǎndào   reach (the conclusion, feeling, opinion)   (W)   [feel to]

43.1. Dàjiā dōu gǎndào zhèizhǒng fāngfǎ fēicháng bù píngděng.   (T)

44.0. mǎn   (1) full (in pattern A B mǎn 'A is full of B'); (2) (postverb)

        mǎnzú   satisfy, meet the demands of   [full enough]

44.1. Diànyǐngryuàn rén mǎn le.   Tāmen bú mài piào le.   (T)

44.2. Wǒ bǎ zhǐ dōu xiěmán le.   (T)

44.3. Dàxué niànmǎnle sìnián cái néng bìyè.   (T)

44.4. Tā niàn Zhōngwén bù mǎn yíge xuéqī jiù bú niàn le.   (T)

44.5. Nǐ zěnmo nǔlì yě mǎnzúbuliǎo tāde xīwang.   (T)

45.0. yīncǐ   because of this, hence, therefore   (W)   [because this]

45.1. Tā dāngle sānshiniánde xiànzhǎng.   Yīncǐ tā duì dìfang xíngzhèng
        hěn yǒu jīngyan.

Bái: Wǒ cóngqián zài zhèr niàn shū de shíhou, wǒmende kècheng méi
      yǒu Zhuāntí Jiǎnghùa.

95 Mǎ: Zhèige fázi shi xiàozhǎng qùnian hé wǒmen jǐge jiāo Zhōngwén de
      xiānsheng jìhua de.   Yuányin shi gǎndào guòqu xuéxiào bù néng
      mǎnzú yǒuxiē xuéshengde xīwang.   Yīncǐ dàjiā wèile zhèige wèntí
      zài yíkuàr tánle jǐcì.

Bái: Jiéguǒ zěnmoyàng?

46.0. zàncheng   approve of, accept, support, be for   [approve become]

46.1. Huìlide rèn dōu zàncheng tígāo dàjiā gōngzuòde shuǐpíng.

47.0. cǎiyòng   adopt, select for use   [pick use]

47.1. Wǒmen néng bu néng cǎiyòng tāmende fāngfǎ?

48.0. juédìng   (1) decide, settle definitely; (2) decision [decide definite]

48.1. Guānyu nèijiàn shì xiànzài néng bu néng juédìng?   (T)

49.0. kāixué   start, open up (school)

49.1. Zhōngguo suǒyǒude dàxué dōu shi jiǔyue kāixué.

50.0. zhūwèi   (1) Gentlemen! Ladies and Gentlemen! (2) you

50.1. Zhūwèi tóngxué jīntian cānjiā wǒmen zhèige huì wǒ fēicháng gāoxìng. (T)

50.2. Jīntiande gōngke jiù dào zhèr.   Xīwang zhūwèi xià kè yǐhòu duō liànxí.   (T)

51.0. dáchéng   attain, achieve   (W)   [attain complete]

51.1. Tāmen xīwang zài shínián lǐtou dáchéng tāmende mùdì.   (W)

100 Mǎ : Jiéguǒ dàjiā dōu zàncheng cǎiyòng zhèige fāngfǎ, suǒyǐ xiàozhǎng jiu juédìng zhèicì kāixué dì-yīge yuèlide kècheng yǒu Zhuāntí Jiǎng-huà zhèimén kècheng.

   Bái : Tīng yǎnjiǎng búdàn duō dé zhīshi, érqiě duì yǔyán yìfāngmiàn yě yǒu hěn dàde bāngzhu.

105 Mǎ : Xuéxiào zhèfāngmiàn shi xīwang zhūwèi wàiguo tóngxué láidào zhèli qiúxué duō xué yìdiǎr dōngxi, cái néng dáchéng dàjiā qiúxué de mùdì.

   Bái : Bú guài wàiguo xuésheng dōu xǐhuan dào Yuǎn-Dà niàn shū. Yuǎn-Dà duì wàiguo xuésheng kècheng yìfāngmiàn fēicháng zhùyì.

52.0. fènzǐ   element, faction, group   (M)   [part element]
    zhīshi fènzǐ   intellectuals

52.1. Zhèxiē qīngnián dōu shi yōuxiù fènzǐ.

52.2. Zhīshi fènzǐ rènwei zhèngfǔde zhèige jìhua zěnmoyàng?   (T)

52.3. Nándào wǒ bú shi guómín yífènzǐ ma?   (T)

53.0. jiātíng   family   [family courtyard]

53.1. Tā cóng xiǎo méi guòguo jiātíng shēnghuó.   (T)

54.0. jìmo   lonesome   [quiet quiet]

54.1. Wǒ yíge rén zài wàiguo fēicháng jìmo.

55.0. kuàilè   happy, joyful   [quick happy]

55.1. Tā yǒu yíge hěn kuàilède jiātíng.

110 Mǎ : Wǒmen jīntiande gōngke jiù dào zhèr. Nǐ duì jīntian suǒ jiǎng de
         yǒu shénmo wèntí méi yǒu? Zhèizhǒng jiāoxuéfǎ chéng bu chéng?

   Bái : Hǎojíle. Méi shénmo wèntí. Mǎ Jiàoshòu jiěshide fēicháng míngbai.
         Wǒ dōu dǒng le.

   Mǎ : Oh, xīngqīliù yǒu ge xuésheng wǎnhuì. Nǐ lái ma?

115 Bái : Shi shénmo huì? Wàiguo xuésheng kéyi lái ma?

   Mǎ : Dāngrán kéyi. Wàiguo xuésheng yě shi Yuǎn-Dà xuéshengde yífènzǐ.
         Yuǎn-Dà měinián zài cái kāixué de shíhou chángcháng yǒu huì.
         Yuányīn shi kǒngpà xuéshengmen yǒude cóng hěn yuǎnde dìfang lái
         de, cái líkai jiātíng, yǒude shíhou yídìng gǎndào jìmo. Rúguǒ dàjiā
120   cháng zài yíkuàr jiànjian miàn xīnli bǐjiǎo kuàilè yìdiǎr.

   Bái : Shìde.   Yìdiǎr yě bú cuò.

56.0. Kǒngzǐ   Confucius

56.1. Kǒngzǐ hé Lǎozǐ dōu shi shēngzai jǐyuánqián.

57.0. zhíyuán   (non-teaching) staff member, official, functionary [office
                  member]

57.1. Zhíyuán、jiàoyuán、gōngren, tāmende gōngzuò bùtóng.   (T)

58.0. jiàozhíyuán   staff-member (teaching and non-teaching) [teach of-
                      fice member]

58.1. Wǒmen xuéxiàode jiàozhíyuán qīngnián rén bǐjǎo duō.

59.0. cānjiā   participate in   [participate add]

59.1. Wǒ bú zàncheng tāmen cānjiā nèizhǒng xuéhuì.

59.2. Zhèicì kāi huì wàiguo xuésheng cānjiāde jiǎo shǎo.   (T)

60.0. gàikuàng   a survey   (W) [résumé situation]

60.1. Tāde jiǎngtí shi "Jīnrì Zhōngguo Gōngyè Gàikuàng."

   Bái : Qǐng wèn, jīnnian xuésheng-huìzhǎng shi něiwèi tóngxué?

   Mǎ : Shi sìniánjíde Kǒng Wénqīng.

   Bái : Shi Kǒngzǐ de Kǒng ma?

125 Mǎ : Jiù shi Kǒngzǐ de kǒng.

   Bái : Xuésheng-huì kāi huì qǐng bù qǐng jiàoshòu hé zhíyuán cānjiā?

   Mǎ : Bù yídìng. Xuésheng-huì yàoshi qǐng wǒmen, wǒmen dāngrán cānjiā.
         Dà duōshù shi xuéshengmen zìjǐ kāi huì. Hěn shǎo qǐng jiàozhíyuán
         de.

130 Bái: Shì bu shi xiānshengmen yě cháng kāi huì?

    Mǎ : Wǒmen chàbuduō měi xīngqī yě yǒu yíge huì, shi wèile kècheng. . . . Xiànzài xiàozhǎng jiǎnghuàde shíjiān dàole.

    Bái: Mǎ Jiàoshòu, míngtian Zhuāntí Jiǎnghuàde tímu shi shénmo?

    Mǎ : Míngtian jiǎng Běnxiào Gàikuàng, jiù shi jièshao běnxiàode qíngxing.

135 Bái: Hǎode. Mǎ Jiàoshòu míngtian jiàn.

    Mǎ : Míngtian zǎochen bādiǎn zhōng jiàn.

SHĒNGCÍ BIǍO

This vocabulary list includes all the new terms introduced above. Run through them quickly and make sure you know each item and can use it in a sentence.

1. shēngcí
   shēngcí biǎo

2. chéng
   fēnchéng

3. zǔ

4. jiěshi
   jiěshi míngbai
   jiěshide míngbai

5. jìxu(de)

6. lìzi

7. jǔ

8. lìjù (W)

9. fānchéng

10. fānyì

11. wēnxi

12. zhùjiě

13. qīngchu

14. fēicháng

15. jiǎng

16. jiǎnghuà

17. zhuān(mén)

18. zhuānjiā

19. zhuāntí

20. jiǎngyǎn

21. yǎnjiǎng

22. fùshù (W)
    lùyīn fùshù

23. qíngxing
    kàn qíngxing

24. yěxǔ

25. xuéshù

26. yǎnjiǎngcí

27. shìqián

28. běnxiào (W)

29. xuéshi

30. qīngnián

31. yōuxiù

32. nǔlì

33. xiāngxìn

34. dádào

35. qiú
    qiúxué

36. bāokuò

37. fànwéi

38. gè

39. jiǎngtí

40. zhǔjiǎng
    zhǔjiǎng(de) rén

41. kècheng

42. jìhua

43. gǎndào (W)

44. mǎn
    mǎnzú

45. yīncǐ (W)

46. zàncheng

47. cǎiyòng

48. juédìng

49. kāixué

50. zhūwèi

51. dáchéng (W)

52. fènzǐ
    zhīshi fènzǐ

53. jiātíng

54. jìmo

55. kuàilè

56. Kǒngzǐ

57. zhíyuán

58. jiàozhíyuán

59. cānjiā

60. gàikuàng (W)

YŬFĂ LIÀNXÍ

A. The topic-sentence construction (see note 1)

1. Jiāo Zhōngwén tā shi hěn yǒu jīngyan de.
2. Zhōnguo xiǎoháizi xiànzài niàn shū hái niàn Qiān Zì Wén ma?
3. Tā niàn shū hěn yònggōng.
4. Shuō Zhōngguo huà yào zhùyì sìshēng.
5. Wǒ zhèicì dào Zhōngguo qù yěxǔ zuò chuán qù.

   B. Single and double use of <u>lái</u> or <u>qù</u> to indicate purpose (see <u>Beginning Chinese</u>, p. 117, note 6 and <u>Intermediate Chinese</u>, p. 26, note 6)

6. Wàn Jiàoshòu dào Yuǎn-Dà lai yǎnjiǎng. Jiǎngtí shi "Kǒngzǐde xuéshuō."
7. Qián Xiàozhǎng bú zài zhèr, tā duì xuésheng jiǎnghuà qu le.
8. Shàng xīngqī wǒ dào Xīdōng Dàxué Yuǎndōng Xuéyuàn qù cānjiā yíge huì qu. Yīnwei wǒ qùwǎn le, rén dōu mǎn le, suǒyǐ wǒ méi yǒu zuòwèi.
9. Zhūwèi dào běnxiào lái niàn shū lai, wǒmen fēicháng huānyíng.
10. Tā bú zànchéng de yuányīn shi tā gǎndào yòng zhèizhǒng jiāoxuéfǎ qù jiāo xuésheng qu yǒu hěn duō duǎnchu.

    C. cái-S_1 jiù/yòu-S_2 (see note 2)

11. Wǒ cái dào xuéxiào Zhuāntí Jiǎnghuà jiù kāishǐ jiǎng le.
12. Xiàozhǎng cái gēn wàiguo xuésheng jiǎngwánle huà, yòu děi hé jiàozhíyuán kāi huì.
13. Wǒ cái bǎ dì-yīkède shēngcí niànhuì le, mǎshàng yòu yào niàn dì-èrkè le.
14. Cái kāixué bú dào yíge xīngqī tā jiù bìng le.
15. Tā cái tīngwánle yíwèi xuézhě jiǎng de Kǒngzǐde xuéshuō, mǎshàng jiù yào niàn <u>Sì Shū</u>.

    D. S_1 cái-S_2 (see note 3)

16. Wǒmen bìděi nǔlì niàn shū, cái néng dédào shízàide xuéwen.
17. Tā gěi wǒ jǔle wǔge lìzi wǒ cái míngbai shēngcí de yòngfǎ.
18. Dàjiā shuōle bàntiān tā cái zànchéng.
19. Wǒ bǎ nèiběn shū kuài yào fānyiwán le cái fāxiàn yǐjing yǒu rén fānyìguo le.
20. Nǐ duō wēnxi jǐcì cái néng míngbai nèige yǎnjiǎngde dàyì.

E. Use of <u>suǒ</u> before verbs (see <u>Beginning Chinese Reader</u>, p. 13)

21. Tā suǒ jiǎngde tímu dōu shi guānyu xuéshu yìfāngmiàn de.

22. Wǒ bǎ xiānsheng suǒ jiāogei wǒ de shēngcí hé lìjù dōu yòng Hànzi xiě-xialai le.

23. Nèiwèi zhuānjiā suǒ jiǎng de hé Mǎ Jiàoshòu suǒ shuō de wánquán yíyàng.

24. Zhuāntí Jiǎngyǎn suǒ bāokuò de yígòng yǒu jǐge tímu?

25. Tīng tā jiǎngyǎn suǒ néng dédào de zhǐ shi wénxué yìfāngmiànde.

F. The enumerative versus the ordinary comma (see <u>Beginning Chinese Reader</u>, p. 13)

26. Wáng Xiānsheng, Wáng Tàitai zài jiā ma?

27. Wáng Xiānsheng、Wáng Tàitai zài jiā ma?

28. Kǒngzǐ、Lǎozǐ dōu shi Zhōngguo gǔdàide dà sīxiǎngjiā.

29. <u>Zhōngguo Jìndài Gōngyè Gàikuàng</u>、<u>Zhōngguo Gōngyè Shǐ</u> dōu shi tā xiěde.

30. Qīngnián rén、zhīshi fènzǐ dōu huānyíng tāde xuéshuō.

JIǍNGHUÀ

Zhūwèi tóngxué:

   Jīntian shi Yuǎndōng Dàxué kāixué de dì-yītiān. Wǒ dàibiǎo quán xuéxiào jiàozhiyuán hé suǒyǒude Zhōngguo tóngxué huānyíng zhūwèi.

   Zhūwèi dōu shi cóng hěn yuǎnde dìfang、bùtóngde guójiā láidào zhèlǐ. Wǒ xiǎng nǐmen zài zhèr bú huì gǎndào jìmo, yīnwei cóng xiànzài qǐ

5 Yuǎn-Dà jiù shi nǐmende dà jiātíng.

   Wǒ jiàndàole zhūwèi xīnli fēicháng gāoxìng. Zhōngguo Kǒngzǐ yǒu yíjù huà: "Yǒu péng zì yuǎn fāng lái bú yì lè hu?"[*] Wǒ xiànzài jiu yòng Kǒngzǐ zhèijù huà lai huānyíng zhūwèi.

   Zhūwèi dōu shi yōuxiùde qīngnián. Dàjiā láidao zhèlǐ dōu yǒu yíge

10 tóngyàngde mùdì, shi qiúxué.

   Zài běnxiàode lìshǐshang, wàiguo xuésheng zài zhèli qiúxué yǐjing yǒu èrshi duō nián le. Zài guòqude èrshi duō nián li, jīngyan gàosu wǒmen wàiguo xuésheng xuéxide xìngqu hé nénglì bǐjiào gāo, kěshi xuéxide qījiān bǐjiào duǎn. Yīncǐ běnxiào jiu bù néng bú yòng tèbiéde fāngfǎ zài jiāo

---

[*] See below, note 4.

15 duǎnde qījiān nèi jiào tóngxuémen nénggòu dédào jiǎo duōde xuéshi, cái

néng mǎnzú dàjiāde xīwang.   Suǒyǐ běnxiào jīnnian zài jiāoxué fāngmiàn

juédìng cǎiyòng yíge tèbié fāngfǎ, jiù shi Zhuāntí Jiǎnghuà.   Běnxiàode

jìhua xiànzài wǒ duì tóngxuémen shuōyishuō:

   Dì-yī.   Bǎ Zhuāntí Jiǎnghuà dàngzuò yìzhǒng kècheng.

20   Dì-èr.   Zài kāixuéde tóu-yīge yuèli měi yìtiān yǒu yíge Zhuāntí
               Jiǎnghuà.

   Dì-sān.   Jiǎngtíde fànwéi dōu shi guānyu Zhōngguo gèfāngmiànde
               qíngxing.

   Dì-sì.   Zhǔjiǎng rén chúle běnxiào jiàoshòu yǐwài hái yǒu jǐwèi
25   zhuānjiā xuézhě.

   Wǒ xiāngxìn zhūwèi duìyu zhèizhǒng fāngfǎ yídìng shi zànchéng de.

   Cóng jīntian qǐ zhūwèi dōu shi Yuǎndōng Dàxuéde yífènzǐ. Zuìhòu,

xīwang nǐmen zài zhèr nǔlì xuéxí, dáchéng nǐmen qiúxué de mùdì.

WĒNXI

1. Zuótian wǒ xuéle hěn duō shēngcí, hái yǒu lìjù.   Dāngshí wǒ jiu bǎ
    shēngcí xiěshang zhùjiě, érqiě fānchéng Yīngwén.   Wànyī wàngle yí kàn
    jiu kéyi dǒng.

2. Shàngcì xuéshù jiǎngyǎn tīng de rén hěn duō. Wǒ yě cānjiā le. Yǎnjiǎng
    de rén shi zhuānmén yánjiu yuánzǐnéng de. Tāde yǎnjiǎngcí hěn cháng,
    shi shìqián xiěhǎo de. Tā shuōle hěn duō yuánzǐnéng yòngfǎde lìzi.
    Zhèige yǎnjiǎng tā yào fēnchéng liǎngcì shuō.   Xiàcì hái yào jìxu jiǎng.
    Tā shi yòng Yīngwén yǎnjiǎng, dāngshí yǒu rén gěi fānyìchéng Zhōngwén.
    Yīnwei wǒ zuòde tài yuǎn yǒude méi tīngqīngchu.

3. Zhōngguode Sì Shū li yǒu yìběn shi Kǒngzǐ xuésheng jìxiale Kǒngzǐ suǒ
    shuō de huà.   Dōu shi wényánde.   Dì-yījù huàde yìsi jiu shi shuō: "Nǐ
    xuéxi de dōngxi yào shícháng wēnxi."

4. Nèige xuéxiàode zhíyuán bǐ jiàoyuán hái duō.

5. Zuótiande jiǎngyǎn rúguǒ jiào wǒ fùshù yícì duōyíbàn wǒ yěxǔ shuōbu-
    shànglái le.

6. Nǐ zuótian wǎnshang lùyīn lùchéngle méi you? . . . Méi yǒu. Jiù lùle yíbàn.

7. Xiānsheng shuō: "Nǐ nián Zhōngwén bù mǎn èrnián jiu néng yòng báihuà
    jiěshi shēngcí, érqiě jiěshide míngbai.   Nǐ zhēn shi hǎo xuésheng."

8. Wàiguode zhīshi fènzǐ xiǎng yào cháng zài Měiguo, Měiguo shì bu shi
    huānyíng? . . . Yǒude huānyíng, yǒude bù huānyíng. Nà jiu yào kàn qíng-
    xing le.

9. Shēngcí biǎo shang dì-sānge cíde yìsi wǒ bù dǒng. Nǐ néng gěi wǒ jiěshi
    míngbai ma?

10. Xiānsheng, shēngcíde zhùjiě wǒ yòng Yīngwén xiě chéng bu chéng?

WÈNTÍ

1. Zài xiàozhǎngde jiǎnghuàli, shuōdào Zhōngguo Kǒngzǐ shuōguo yíjù huà. Zhèijù huà shi shénmo? Shì shénmo yìsi?

2. Yuǎn-Dàde Zhuāntí Jiǎnghuà, jiǎngtíde fànwéi shi zěnmoyàng? Shi jiǎng něi yìfāngmiànde? Shi shénmo rén zhǔjiǎng? Shì zài shénmo shíhou?

3. Yuǎn-Dàde Zhuāntí Jiǎnghuà zhèizhǒng kècheng nǐ zàncheng ma? Wèi-shénmo ne?

4. Fānyì hé fānchéng yǒu shénmo bùtóng? Qǐng nǐ jǔ yíge lìzi lái shuōmíng.

5. Shénmo shi shēngcí? Měi yíkè yǒu duōshao shēngcí? Yíkè shūli de shēngcí fēn jǐzǔ?

6. Mǎ Jiàoshòu duì Bái Wénshān yòng de shi něizhǒngde jiāoxuéfǎ?

7. Qǐng nǐ shuōyishuō shūshang Zhuāntí Jiǎnghuà hé huìhuàli něige jùzi shi bǐjiǎo kèqide jùzi?

8. Qǐng nǐ zài kàn jiǎnghuàlide jùzi. Něige shi wén yìdiǎr de? Zhèige jùzi yàoshi shuō huà yīnggāi zěnmo shuō?

9. Zhèibén shū měi yíkè dōu yǒu shénmo liànxí? Měi yíge liànxíde nèiróng shi shénmo?

10. Nǐ shénmo shíhou gǎndào jìmo, shénmo shíhou gǎndào kuàilè?

ILLUSTRATIVE SENTENCES (ENGLISH)

The following sentences are translations of some of the Chinese sentences introduced in the dialogue at the beginning of the lesson. The sentences selected for translation, those marked with a (T), are limited to those which present special difficulties or otherwise merit special attention. The numbering follows that of the original Chinese sentences.

1.1. What does the third word in the vocabulary list mean?

1.2. The vocabulary consists of words which have not been studied before.

1.3. Why don't you understand this word? . . . It's a new word, don't you see.

   (Note use of me to express the speaker's feeling that he is stating something obvious. See Beginning Chinese, p. 354, note 8.)

2.1. Will it be all right if we do it this way? . . . No, it won't.

2.2. Have you finished writing that book? . . . Not yet.

5.2. Please continue reading.

7.1. Those who know raise your hands.

9.1. Please translate Illustrative Sentence 9.1 [lit. nine dot one] into English.

9.2. Please translate into the spoken style the new words that are somewhat literary.

10.1. We have translation for homework every day.

10.2. He translated a Chinese novel into English.

10.3. Can he translate for me?

11.1. Let's first review yesterday's (work).

11.2. Apart from review we also have grammar drill and questions.

12.1. Why does this have notes and not that? . . . This is a little more difficult.

13.1. If you're still not clear I'll give another example.

13.2. His Chinese isn't too good, so he can't speak clearly.

15.3. What does the term lìjù mean?

16.1. Today the president is lecturing to us.

17.1. I'm specializing in linguistics at the university.

18.1. In the study of the history of the Yuan Dynasty he's a specialist.

18.2. For today's lecture our school has invited a well-known specialist in political science.

19.1. The zhuān of zhuāntí is the zhuān of zhuānmén. Tí is the tí of tímu.

19.2. We have one Special Lecture every day.

22.2. Shall I record the summary, or shall I write it down?

23.1. Depending on the situation, if I have time [then] I'll go.

25.1. These two lectures are both talks in the scholarly area.

34.1. I believe he certainly can attain his objective in going to China to study.

35.2. I'm convinced that he is capable of attaining his scholarly aims [lit. aim in seeking to study].

36.1. I spend $300 a month, including (money for) both food and rent.

37.1. This examination is comprehensive in scope. We're to be examined even on (things) not in the text.

38.3. That bookstore has all levels of textbooks—beginning, intermediate, and advanced.

38.5. I like [to eat] any sort of pork dish.

40.1. Who's giving the lecture today?

40.2. What the last lecturer talked about had nothing to do with the topic.

41.1. This Chinese course of ours is awfully difficult.

42.1. This method was devised by the president, not by us who teach Chinese.

42.2. The government has a three-year plan for heavy industry.

43.1. Everyone feels this procedure is very inequitable.

44.1. The movie's full. They're not selling any more tickets.

44.2. I've filled the paper with writing.

44.3. You can graduate from college after completing four years.

44.4. When he studied Chinese he quit without completing one semester.

44.5. No matter how hard you try you can't satisfy his hopes.

48.1. Is it possible to make a decision now regarding that matter?

50.1. I'm delighted that you [fellow students] are attending this meeting today.

50.2. This is the end of today's lesson. [lit. Today's lesson just to here.] I hope you will practice more after leaving class.

52.2. What do intellectuals think of this plan?

52.3. Can it be that I am not a citizen?

53.1. Since childhood he hasn't experienced any family life.

57.1. Non-teaching staff members, teachers, and workers have different jobs.

59.2. There are comparatively few foreign students attending this meeting.

NOTES

1. In Beginning Chinese (pp. 213–14) examples were given of the topic-comment construction in Chinese. The examples were limited to simple sentences in which a noun was singled out, placed at the beginning, and commented upon by the rest of the sentence. The idea of topic-comment can be extended to include two sentences—one a 'topic sentence' at the beginning and the other a following sentence commenting on the preceding one. For example:

> Tā zuótian dào zhèr lai wǒ yìdiǎr yě bu zhīdào. 'That he came here yesterday was completely unknown to me.'

> Zhèicì kāi huānyíng huì, rìqī shi míngtian. 'As for having this welcoming party, the date is tomorrow.'

Often the topic sentence is without a subject, either because the sentence is impersonal or because the subject is understood or expressed later as the subject of the second sentence:

> Jiāo Hànzì wǒmen yòng zhèige fázi shìyan shìyan. 'In the teaching of Chinese characters we are experimenting with this method.'

If the subject of the topic sentence is the same as that of the following sentence, the topic sentence often occurs after the subject as a sort of insert within the complex sentence:

> Wǒmen jiāo Hànzi yòng zhèige fázi shìyan shìyan. 'In the teaching of Chinese characters we are experimenting with this method.'

2. In the pattern cái-S$_1$ jiù/yòu-S$_2$ the adverb cái 'only, just' occurs in the first of two related sentences the second of which often has jiù 'then' or yòu 'again' or some other element. The construction indicates that the action of the second sentence occurred right after that of the first:

Tā niànle èrniánde Zhōngwén + Tā néng yòng Hànzì xiě dōngxi = Tā cái niànle èrniánde Zhōngwén jiù néng yòng Hànzì xiě dōngxi. 'After having studied Chinese for only two years he was able to write things in Chinese characters.'

In this particular example the two sentences S_1 and S_2 which are joined by cái . . . jiù can stand alone. Often, however, they cannot, as they sometimes appear in the compound sentence with some of their elements omitted or in a form which marks them as dependent clauses. Thus the sentence Xiàozhǎng gēn wàiguo xuésheng jiǎngwánle huà, is an incomplete sentence meaning 'The president having finished the lecture to the foreign students . . .'

3. In the pattern S_1 cái-S_2 the adverb cái 'only then, then and only then' in the second of two related sentences indicates that the action of the second occurs only after that of the first. Very often the first sentence contains the particle le in the dependent clause construction (see Beginning Chinese, p. 175).

Tā jiàngwánle huà wǒmen cái néng zǒu. 'We can leave only after he's finished the lecture.'

4. The lecture style in Chinese is farther from the ordinary conversational style than is the case in most languages. It has many features in common with the modern written style. Some of the lecture style features occur also in more elevated forms of dialogue, as in conversations between scholars. The modern written style in turn is a mixture of various elements, including some derived from the conversational style and some from the classical literary style. The latter tends to be very terse. It also contains many expressions which are now no longer in general use. Some of the ways in which the classical style differs from modern Chinese can be seen in the following analysis of a quotation from Confucius: Yǒu péng zì yuǎn fāng lái bù yì lè hu? 'Is it not also delightful to have friends coming from distant places?'

yǒu	'have'	lái	'come'
péng = péngyou	'friends'	bù	'not'
zì = cóng	'from'	yì = yě	'also'
yuǎn	'distant, far'	lè = kuàilè	'happy'
fāng = dìfang	'place'	hu = ma	(question particle)

A modern spoken equivalent of this sentence might be: Yǒu péngyou cóng hěn yuǎnde dìfang lai, nà bú shi yě hěn kuàilède ma?

Dì-Èrkè. Běnxiào Gàikuàng

Bái: Mǎ Jiàoshòu zǎo.

Mǎ: Zǎo. Zěnmoyàng, zuótian xiàozhǎng jiǎnghuà dōu tīngdedǒng ma?

Bái: Yīnwei shǐqián Mǎ Jiàoshòu bǎ shēngcí dōu yǐjing jiěshiguo le, érqiě xiàozhǎng jiǎngde yě fēicháng qīngchu, suǒyǐ dà duōshù dōu
5 tīngdedǒng. Zuótian wǎnshang wǒ zìjǐ lùle tīngting. Bù chéng. Hěn bu hǎo. Yǒude shíhou shuōde tài màn, yǒu shíhou wénfǎ cuòle, yǒu shíhou bù zhīdào zěnmo shuō. Huòzhě yǐhòu yào hǎo yìdiǎr. Yìhuěr xià kè yǐhòu wǒ gěi Mǎ Jiàoshòu tīngyiting, hǎo bu hǎo?

Mǎ: Hǎo. Wǒ xiāngxìn yǐhòu mànmānde jiu bǐjiǎo róngyi le.

10 Bái: Duìle.

Mǎ: Guānyu cér yìfāngmiàn yǒu wèntí méi yǒu?

Bái: Cér méi yǒu duó dàde wèntí. Kéyi kànkan Yīngwén fānyì hé zhùjiě.

Mǎ: Hǎo. Nènmo xiànzài wǒmen yánjiu jīntiande gōngke. Gěi ni. Zhè shi Běnxiào Gàikuàng lǐtoude shēngcí. Qǐng nǐ xiān kànyikan:

1.0. dào(shi) (1) contrary to expectations, yet, nevertheless; (2) after all, yes of course but . . . , to V all right, but . . . . [inverted is] (see Beginning Chinese, p. 333, note 6)

1.1. Tā suírán niánji xiǎo tā dào hěn zhīdao yònggōng niàn shū.

1.2. Nèi jǐge cérde zhùjiě wǒ kàn dàoshi kànle, kěshi yǒude wǒ háishi bú dà dǒng. (T)

1.3. Wáng Jiàoshòu shuōde huà wǒ méi tīng qīngchu. Tā dàoshi jiào wǒmen bǎ Zhōngwén fānchéng Yīngwén ne, háishi bǎ Yīngwén fānchéng Zhōngwén ne?

2.0. chóng again, re-

zàichóng again, re-

chóngxiū (1) repeat (a course); (2) repair (a house) [repeated self-improvement]

2.1. Nèiběn shū mǎicuò le. Hái děi chóng mǎi. Bái yòngle wǒ wǔkuài qián. (T)

2.2. Nèi jǐge cér wǒ hái méi dǒng. Qǐng Zhāng Jiàoshòu zàichóng jiěshi yícì.

2.3. Yàoshi zhèimén gōngke wǒ niànbuhǎo, míngnian wǒ bìděi chóngxiū. (T)

2.4. Nèisuǒ fángzi děi chóngxiū. (T)

21

3.0. bàn   arrange, manage, handle

      bàn gōng   transact official business

      bàn shì   manage an affair, transact business

      bànhǎo   do, manage (a job satisfactorily) (RV)

      zěnmo bàn?   How manage? What's to be done? What then?

      bànfǎ   way of handling a matter, way to manage

3.1. Tā bú shi gàosuguo nǐ zài bàngōng de shíjiān bù néng suíbiàn tán
      huà ma?

3.2. Tā bù néng bàn shì. Lián nènmo yìdiǎr xiǎo shì tā dōu bànbuhǎo.
      (T)

3.3. Wǒde kànfǎ, zhèijiàn shì yìdiǎr bànfǎ yě méi yǒu. Nǐmen zhūwèi
      shuō, yīnggāi zěnmo bàn ne?   (T)

15 Mǎ : Dì-yīzǔde cér dōu kàn le ma?

    Bái: Kàn dàoshi kànle. Suīrán yǒu Yīngwén jiěshì, kěshi yǒude wǒ hái
          bú huì yòng.

    Mǎ : Zhèi jǐge cér wǒmen xiànzài yánjiu yánjiu.

    Bái: Chóngxiū zhèige cér jiù shi zài niàn de yìsi, shì bu shi?

20 Mǎ : Duìle, zài niàn de yìsi. Chóng zì cháng yòng. Bǐrú chóng xiě jiu
          shi zài xiě de yìsi, chóng zuò jiu shi zài zuò de yìsi. Xiū zì zài
          zhèr shi niànde yìsi. Zhèige zì hěn shǎo yòng.

    Bái: Chóngxiū nà bú shi bǎ yǐqiánde shíjiān dōu bái yòng le ma?

    Mǎ : Kěbushìma! Yāoburán zěnmo bàn? Méi yǒu biéde bànfǎ.

4.0. fǔdǎo   to counsel [auxiliary guide]

4.1. Tāde gōngzuò shi fǔdǎo wàiguo xuésheng.

5.0. zhǔrèn   person in charge, director   [chief duty]

      fǔdǎo zhǔrèn   guidance counsellor, advisor

5.1. Zhèijiàn shì wǒ bù néng zuò zhǔ. Děi wèn zhǔrèn.   (T)

5.2. Xuéxiàolǐde fǔdǎo zhǔrèn tāde gōngzuò shi shénmo?

6.0. liú(xué)   study abroad   [retain study]

      liú Měi   study in America

      liúxuéshēng   person studying abroad, returned student

6.1. Wāng Xiānsheng shi liú Měi de, bú shi liú Yīng de.   (T)

6.2. Bù zhīdào wǒ néng bu néng dádào liúxué de mùdì.

6.3. Gè liúxuéshēng zài wàiguo niàn shū dōu hěn nǔlì.   (W)

7.0. jiàowu   academic affairs, school business [teach matter]

    jiàowuzhǎng   dean (of academic affairs)

7.1. Wǒde gōngzuò shi zài jiàowu yīfāngmiàn.

7.2. Máo Jiàowùzhǎng shi liú Fà de.

8.0. chù*   place, office

    jiàowuchù   dean's office

    bàngōngchù   office

    bànshìchù   office

8.1. Qǐng wèn, jiàowuzhǎng xiànzài hái zài jiàowuchù ma?

8.2. Suǒyǒude jiàozhíyuán dōu zài bàngōngchù jìhua xià xuéqī xuéshengde
      kèchéng. (T)

8.3. Wǒmen jǐge rén dōu zài yíge bànshìchù bàn shì. (T)

8.4. Wǒmen de bàngōngchù tài xiǎo le, yóuqishi jiàowuzhǎng de.

25 Bái: Qǐng wèn Mǎ Jiàoshòu, fǔdǎo zhèige cér shuō huà cháng yòng ma?

    Mǎ : Fǔdǎo jiu shi bāngzhu hé gàosu de yìsi. Píngcháng bù cháng shuō.

    Bái: Yǐqiánde wàiguo liúxuéshēng fǔdǎo zhǔrèn bú shi Zhāng Xiānsheng,
          shi yíwèi Wáng Xiānsheng.

    Mǎ : Zhāng Yǒuzhēn Xiānsheng cóngqián zài jiàowuchù, shi jiàowuzhǎng.
30   Qùnian cái zuò wàiguo liúxuéshēng fǔdǎo zhǔrèn.

9.0. zhì(du)   system   [institution degree]

    dà jiātíng zhìdu   big-family system

    xuézhì   educational system

    xuéfēn-zhì   system based on academic credits

9.1. Wǒ fùqin fēicháng bú zàncheng Zhōngguo nèizhǒng dà jiātíng zhìdu.

9.2. Wǒmen xiànzài yīnggāi juédìng cǎiyòng něizhǒng xuézhì.

9.3. Wǒ rènwei xuéfēn-zhì shi fēicháng hǎode bànfǎ.

10.0. xuénián   school year   (M)

    xuénián-zhì   system based on school years

10.1. Xuénián-zhì yídìng yào niàn jǐxuénián cái néng bìyè.

11.0. chéngji   record of attainment, grade [complete accomplishment]

    chéngji-dān   report card, transcript (of a student's academic record)

11.1. Tā zài dàxué、zhōngxué niàn shū měicì kǎoshì de chéngji dōu hǎo,
       dōu zài jiǔshifēn yǐshàng. Tā shízài shi yíge yōuxiùde qīngnián.

11.2. Chéngji-dān shi měi yíge xuéqī fā yícì.

12.0. jígé   qualify, pass an exam, pass a course   [reach category]

12.1. Tā shū niànde hěn bù hǎo. Gèmén gōngkè dōu bù jígé.

12.2. Wǒ xiāngxìn zhèi xuéqī tāde Zhōngwén yídìng bú huì jígé, yīnwei
       tā wēnxide bú gòu.

13.0. fánshi   whoever (is), whatever (is), etc.

13.1. Fánshi tā xiěde shū wǒ dōu kàn.   (T)

13.2. Zuótian jiàowuzhǎng bàogào shuō fánshi xiǎokǎo chéngji zài bāshiwǔ-
       fēn yǐshàng de bú bì cānjiā dàkǎo.   (T)

14.0. zhǐ yào(shi)   only if, if only, as long as

14.1. Zhǐ yào Máo Jiàoshòu yǎnjiǎng, hěn duō xuésheng dōu qù tīng.

Bái: Mǎ Jiàoshòu, shēngcílǐ yǒu xuézhì zhèige cér, wǒ bù dà qīngchu.

Mǎ : Xuézhì jiu shi měi yíge xuéxiào yǒu yíge xuéxiàode zhìdu. Zhōngxué
      hé dàxué de zhìdu bùtóng. Dàxué duōbàr shi xuéfēn-zhì, yǒude shi
      xuénián-zhì. Zhōngxué dōu shi xuénián-zhì.

35 Bái: Xuénián-zhì jiù shi xuésheng yídìng yào niàn jǐxuénián, shì bu shi?

Mǎ : Duì le. Dànshi yě yào kàn chéngji jígé bu jígé. Xuéfēn-zhì yǒude
      rén sānnián jiù néng bìyè, yǒude rén wǔ-liùnián cái bìyè. Fánshi
      měinián xuéfēn niànde duō de xuésheng jiu kéyi zǎo bìyè, xuéfēn
      niànde shǎo bìyè jiu wǎn.

40 Bái: Dàxué yòng xuéfēn-zhì de duō, shì bu shi?

Mǎ : Shìde, hěn duō dōu cǎiyòng xuéfēn-zhì. Zài Yuǎn-Dà shi zhèiyàng:
      Zhǐ yào niànmǎnle yìbǎi èrshige xuéfēn jiu néng bìyè.

15.0. yī*   medical

       yīsheng   doctor, M.D., Dr.

       yīkē   medical course

       yīyuàn   hospital

       yīxuéyuàn   medical school

15.1. Zhèlǐde yīsheng bú gòu, yīnwei xué yīkē de tài shǎo.

15.2. Míngtian shàngwǔ yīxuéyuàn yuànzhǎng duì yīkē de xuésheng jiǎng-
       yǎn. Jiǎngtí shi shénmo xiànzài wǒmen bu zhīdào.   (T)

16.0. chénglì   establish   [complete set up]

16.1. Wǒmen dàxuéde chūbǎnshè cái chénglì bù jiǔ.   (T)

16.2. Nèige zhuānmén xuéxiào cóng chénglì dào xiànzài bìyè de xuésheng
       yǒu sānqiān duō rén le.

17.0. qǔ   take (out), fetch

       kǎoqǔ   select by examination

17.1. Wǒ qù qǔ mòshuǐ qu.

17.2. Wǒ dào xuéxiào qǔ chéngji-dān qu.   (T)

17.3. Yuǎndōng Dàxué zhèi xuéqī yígòng kǎoqǔle yīqiān wǔbǎige xuésheng.

18.0. yōuliáng   exceptional   [superior good]

18.1. Fánshi chéngji yōuliángde xuésheng bú bǐ cānjiā zhèige kǎoshì.

19.0. xiāngdāng(de)   (1) suitable, suitably; (2) fairly, quite, rather [mutu-
                        ally ought]

19.1. Tā niàn yīkē niànde chéngji xiāngdāng hǎo.

19.2. Nèijiàn shìqing wǒ děi zhǎo yíge xiāngdāngde shíhou zài gàosu ta.
       (T)

Bái: Xuéfēn-zhìde bànfǎ hěn hǎo. Yǒude rén kéyi yìbiār gōngzuò yìbiār
       niàn shū. Xuéfēn gòule jiu kéyi bìyè.

45   Mǎ: Yǒude rén shēng bìng le huòshi yǒu tèbiéde shì bú bǐ lái shàng kè.
       Yàoshi niàn xuénián-zhì kě jiu máfan le.

Bái: Tándào shēng bìng, wǒ xiǎngqilaile. Yuǎn-Dà yīxuéyuàn niàn yīkē
       de xuésheng duō bu duō?

Mǎ: Bù duō, yīnwei shi cái chénglì bù jiǔ. Érqiě yīxuéyuàn zhèi fāng-
50   miàn kǎoqǔ xuésheng de shuǐpíng xiāngdāng gāo, yīnwei yīsheng duì
       bìngren hěn zhòngyào.

Bái: Wǒ shàngcì zài zhèlǐ yě gǎndào yīsheng yě bú gòuyòng.

Mǎ: Shi zhèizhǒng qíngxing: Yīxuéyuàn hěn nán niàn, érqiě bǐ xué biéde
       shíjiān cháng. Hái yǒu, rúguǒ xuéde chéngji tèbié yōuliáng cái
55   nénggou jìxuxiaqu, yàoburán jiu bù néng wǎng xià xué.

20.0. bóshi   doctor of philosophy, Ph.D., Dr.   [learned scholar]

       bóshi lùnwén   Ph.D. thesis

       niàn bóshi   study for a Ph.D.

20.1. Tián Dàwén Bóshi cháng zuò xuéshù yǎnjiǎng.

20.2. Yīnwēi tāde xuéwen hǎo, suǒyǐ tāde bóshi lùnwén xiěde tèbié hǎo.

20.3. Tāde xuéshi hěn hǎo, yǐjing niàn bóshi le.

21.0. xuéwèi   academic degree   [study seat]

21.1. Tā zhèi xuéqī jiu kéyi nádao bóshi xuéwèi.   (T)

22.0. shuòshi   M.A.   [big scholar]

22.1. Zhāng Yìwén niànle wǔnián shuòshi cái nádào shuòshi xuéwèi.

23.0. xuéshi   B.A.   [study scholar]

23.1. Tā dàxué cái bìyè. Tā shi ge xuéshi.

24.0. dān   single, singly

       dānzì   single character

24.1. Wǒmen bǎ cér jiǎngle yǐhòu zài dān jiǎng měi yíge zìde yìsi. (T)

24.2. Yǒude shíhou yíge dānzì yě shi cér.

25.0. cānkǎo   (1) consult, refer to, consider; (2) a basis of reference

       cānkǎo shū   reference work

25.1. Wǒmen yào cānkǎo gè fāngmiànde yìjian.

25.2. Yīxuéyuànde xuésheng dōu yòng Mǎ Dàwén Yīsheng suǒ xiěde shū
       zuò cānkǎo shū.   (T)

25.3. Nǐ yào bǎ tāde yìjian zuò yíge cānkǎo.   (T)

Bái: Mǎ Jiàoshòu, Zhōngwén bóshi、shuòshi zhèi liǎngge cér, wǒ zhīdao
      niànwán dàxué yǐhòu jiu shi xuéshi, ránhòu zài niàn shuòshi xuéwèi,
      niàn bóshi xuéwèi. Bó gēn shuò zhèi liǎngge dānzìde yìsi qǐng Mǎ
      Jiàoshòu gěi wo jiěshi.

60 Mǎ: Bó jiùshi duō de yìsi. Shuò zìde yìsi yě chàbuduō. Dān jiǎng
        zhèige zì jiùshi dà de yìsi. Nǐde bóshi lùnwén kāishǐ xiě le méi
        you?

Bái: Wǒ hái méi xiě ne. Shìqián wǒ děi xiān zhǎo cānkǎo shū.

26.0. fèi   (1) expend; (2) expenses

       fèi shì   (1) expend effort (uselessly); (2) require effort

       xuéfèi   tuition   [study expenses]

26.1. Wǒ fèile hěn duō gōngfu cái bǎ nèiběn shū fānyiwán le.

26.2. Gěi ta jiěshi yíge shēngcí xiāngdāng fèi shì. Zěnmo jiěshi tā yě
       bù dǒng.

26.3. Nèige xuéxiàode xuéfèi xiāngdāng guì.

26.4. Chǎo cài bù hěn fèi shíhou.

27.0. píngjūn   (1) level, even; (2) on the average   [level even]

27.1. Wǒ píngjūn měitiān yào fānyi jǐbǎige jùzi.

28.0. cǐwài   besides this, apart from this   (W)

28.1. Wǒ quánbùde shū dōu zài zhèr. Cǐwài wǒ méi yǒu shū le.   (W)

29.0. juān   donate, give, will

29.1. Wáng Dàifu zài kāixué yǐqián juāngei yīxuéyuàn hěn duō shū.

·Mǎ : Zhǎo cānkǎo shū yě xiāngdāng fèi shíhou.

65 Bái : Yuǎn-Dà túshūguǎnde shū xiànzài wǒ xiǎng yídìng xiāngdāng duō le.

Mǎ : Xiànzàide shū bǐ yǐqián gèng duō, yígòng yǒu shí'èrwànběn shū.
Zài guòqu zhèi èrniánli, píngjūn měi yíge yuè mǎi liǎng-sānqiānběn
shū. Cǐwài gè fāngmiàn juānlai de shū yě bù shǎo.

30.0. jiǎngxuéjīn   scholarship   [encourage study gold]

30.1. Nǐ dédàode jiǎngxuéjīn bāokuò bu bāokuò shēnghuó-fèi zài nèi?

31.0. shēnqǐng   apply, make a request (to a superior)   [extend invite]

31.1. Wǒ shēnqǐng jiǎngxuéjīn jǐcì dōu bu gěi. Wǒ hái yào jìxù shēnqǐng.
Wǒ yídìng yào dádào mùdì.

32.0. jīngji   (1) economical; (2) economics; (3) economy [pass through
            aid]

        jīngjixué   (study of) economics

32.1. Yòng nèizhǒng bànfǎ zài shíjiānshang tài bu jīngji le.

32.2. Tā shi yíwèi liú Měi de jīngjixuéjiā. Tā xiǎng xiě yìběn Zhōngguo
Jīngji Shǐ.

33.0. kùnnán   (1) difficult, troublesome; (2) a difficulty, a trouble, distress
            [distress difficult]

33.1. Zhōngguo huà shuōde bu hěn hǎo de rén yòng lùyīnjī fùshù yǎnjiǎng
nà shi gǎndào xiāngdāng kùnnán de.

Bái : Qǐng wèn Mǎ Jiàoshòu, shēnqǐng de shēn zì shi shénmo yìsi?

70 Mǎ : Shēn shi shuōmíngde yìsi. Shēn zì zài shuō huà de shíhou bù cháng
yòng.

Bái : Zài Měiguo niàn shū shēnqǐng jiǎngxuéjīn bǐděi chéngji hǎo cái néng
shēnqǐng. Rúguǒ shi jīngji kùnnánde dédào de xīwang dà. Bù zhīdào
Zhōngguo shì bu shi yǒu zhèizhǒng bànfǎ?

75 Mǎ : Zài Zhōngguo yě chàbuduō. Chéngji yōuliángde cái néng dé jiǎngxuéjīn.

Bái : Shuōqi jīngji, zài Yuǎn-Dà niàn jīngjixué de yǒu méi yǒu wàiguo liúxuéshēng?

Mǎ : Yǒu. Dànshi rénshù hěn shǎo.

34.0. (xué)xì   course, department (in a college or university)

        xì zhǔrèn   chairman of a department

        yuàn-xì   division (xuéyuàn) and department (xuéxì)

        lìshǐ-xì   history department (similarly for other departments)

34.1. Mǎ Tiānshēng Bóshi shi wǒmen lìshǐ-xìde xì zhǔrèn.

34.2. Běnxiào měi yí yuàn-xì dōu yǒu yuànzhǎng hé zhǔrèn.

35.0. wùlǐ(xué)   physics   [thing principle study]

   wùlǐxuéjiā   physicist   (similarly for some other disciplines)

35.1. Tā shi wùlǐxué bóshi. Tā shi yǒumíngde wùlǐxuéjiā.

36.0. shēngwù(xué)   biology   [life matter study]

36.1. Wùlǐ-xì hé shēngwù-xì dōu zài yíge xuéyuàn ma?

37.0. fǎ*   law

   fǎlǜ   law   [law law]

   fǎxuéyuàn   college of law, law school

37.1. Zhèige dàxuéde fǎxuéyuàn fēnchéng jǐxì?

37.2. Fánshi guómín yífènzǐ dōu yīnggāi dǒngde yìdiǎr běnguó fǎlǜ. (T)

37.3. Nèige dàxuéde yuàn-xì dōu hěn hǎo, yóuqishi fǎxuéyuàn. (W)

80 Bái: Wǒ xiǎng měi yí yuàn-xì dōu bú huì yǒu wǒmen wénxuéyuànde xué-
       sheng duō.

   Mǎ: Yīnwei Zhōngguo shi yíge yǒu sìqiānnián wénhuà de gǔ guó, suǒyǐ
       wàiguo xuésheng duōbàr dào Zhōngguo lái shi xué Zhōngguo wénhuà
       de.

85 Bái: Qǐng wèn Mǎ Jiàoshou, wùlǐ-xì gēn shēngwuxué-xì yǒu wàiguo xué-
       sheng méi yǒu?

   Mǎ: Wǒ zhīdao wùlǐ-xì yǒu liǎngge Rìběn xuésheng. Shēngwù-xì yǒu
       wàiguo xuésheng méi yǒu wǒ bù zhīdào.

   Bái: Hěn duō rén shuō Yuǎn-Dà shēngwù-xì hěn yǒumíng. Xì zhǔrèn shi
90   něiwèi?

   Mǎ: Xì zhǔrèn shi yíwèi hěn yǒumíngde shēngwùxuéjiā. Zhèlǐ gè dàxué
       cháng yǒu rén qǐng ta qu jiǎng shēngwùxuéde zhuāntí yǎnjiǎng.

   Bái: Mǎ Jiàoshòu, qǐng wèn zhèngzhì xuéxì zài něige xuéyuàn?

   Mǎ: Zhèngzhì xuéxì zài fǎxuéyuàn?

95 Bái: Hé fǎlǜ-xì zài yíge xuéyuàn.

   Mǎ: Duìle.

38.0. shǐ*   room

   kèshǐ   classroom

   lùyīnshǐ   recording room, language laboratory

   bàngōngshǐ   office

38.1. Qǐng wèn, xiàozhǎng-shǐ zài nǎr?   (T)

38.2. Jīntiande shēngwù jiǎnghuà bu zài èr-yī-líng kèshǐ, zài èr-yī-èr kèshǐ.

38.3. Máo Xiānsheng dào lùyīnshǐ qu lù yīn qu le.

38.4. Yǐjing liùdiǎn le. Bàngōngshǐli lián yíge rén dōu méi yǒu le.

39.0. dài   (1) belt, strip (M); (2) carry, take, bring

      dàizi   belt

      lùyīndài   (recording) tape

39.1. Tā cóng Měiguo gěi wǒ dàiláile hǎojǐběn wùlǐxuéde cānkǎo shū.
      (T)

39.2. Nèitiáo dàizi shi yòng shénmo zuò de?

39.3. Wǒde lùyīndài dōu lùwán le. Wǒ děi qǐng Zhāng Xiānsheng gěi wǒ
      mǎi.

40.0. pán   (measure for dishes, reels of tape)

      pánzi   dish, plate

      suànpan   abacus   [reckon plate]

40.1. Shéi bǎ pánzilǐde chǎo dòufu dōu gěi chǐwán le?

40.2. Wǒ xiǎng mǎi yíge suànpan. Bù zhīdào zài Měiguo mǎidedào mǎi-
      budào?

40.3. Zhèipán lùyīndài shi Yīngwén dì-sānzǔ dì-jiǔhào, Gāo Měiyīng fùshù
      dì-jiǔcì Yīngwén Zhuāntí Jiǎnghuà.   (T)

    Bái: Mǎ Jiàoshòu, zuótian wǒ dào lùyīnshǐ qu kànkan. Bǐ yǐqián dàde
         duō le. Yǐqián jiù shi zài xiàozhǎng bàngōngshǐ hòubiar nèige xiǎo
         bái fángzili.

100 Mǎ: Shǐ. Xiànzài dà duōle. Yǐqiánde nèige lùyinshǐ xiànzài zuò wùlǐ-
        xǐde kèshǐ le.

    Bái: Mǎ Jiàoshòu, qǐng wèn <u>lùyīndài</u> de <u>dài</u> zǐ shǐ bu shi <u>dàizi</u> de <u>dài</u>?
         Hái yǒu, <u>wǒmen xuéxiào zhèi yídài</u> shǐ bu shi yě shi zhèige <u>dài</u> zǐ?

    Mǎ: Shǐ. <u>Dài dōngxi</u> yě shi zhèige <u>dài</u> zǐ.

105 Bái: <u>Yìpán lùyīndài</u> de <u>pán</u> zǐ shi něige <u>pán</u> zǐ?

    Mǎ: <u>Yíge lùyindài</u> jiàozuò <u>yìpán</u> lùyindài. <u>Chǐ fàn</u> de <u>pánzi</u>、 suànpande
        <u>pán</u> dōu shi nèige <u>pán</u> zǐ.

41.0. zǒng(shi)   always, invariably (together with a negative: never)

      zǒngshù   sum, total amount

41.1. Tā měicì kǎoshǐ, měimén gōngke zǒng zài jiǔshifēn yǐshàng.   (T)

41.2. Xuéxiào kāi huì nǐ wèi-shénmo zǒng bu cānjiā ne?   (T)

41.3. Tā suírán jīngji hěn kùnnán, dànshi tā zǒngshi nènmo hěn kuàilè.

41.4. Wǒ mǎi mòshuǐ zǒngshi mǎi lánde.

41.5. Xuéxiào měi yíge xuéyuàn yǒu duōshao rén wǒ bù zhīdào.   Wǒ jiù
      zhīdao xuésheng zǒngshū yígòng shi sānqiān wǔbǎige rén.

42.0. zǔzhi   (1) organize, form; (2) organization   [organize weave]

42.1. Wǒmen yīnggāi zǔzhi yíge Zhōngguo xuésheng liú Měi tóngxué huì.
      (T)

43.0. guānxi   (1) connection, relationship; (2) relevance, importance

      méi guānxi   (it) doesn't matter

      A duì/gēn B (de) guānxi   connection, importance of A to/with B

      yīnwei . . . de guānxi   because (of) . . .

43.1. Duìbuqǐ wǒ láiwǎn le . . . . Méi guānxi.

43.2. Zhèicìde kǎoshì duì wǒ jiāngláide guānxi hěn dà.

43.3. Wǒ yīnwei zuò fēijī de guānxi suǒyǐ méi dài hěn duō xíngli.

43.4. Tā jīntian yǎnjiǎng huòzhě míngtian yǎnjiǎng dōu duì wǒ méi guānxi.

43.5. Zǒng yǒu yìtiān nèi liǎngge guójiāde guānxi huì hǎo de.   (T)

Bái: Mǎ Jiàoshòu, zǒngshi zhèige cér wǒ bú dà huì yòng.

Mǎ : Zǒngshi jiù shi dōu shì de yìsi. Wǒ shuō liǎngge lìzi. Bǐrú "Wǒ
110   měitian zǒngshi bādiǎn zhōng qǐlai," "Wǒ zǒngshi xiān niàn shū hòu
       xiě zì," "Zhèige zì wǒ zǒng xiěbuhǎo."

Bái: Wǒ dǒng le.

Mǎ : Zǒngshù zhèige cér nǐ míngbai bu míngbai?

Bái: Nèige wǒ míngbai.   Jiù shi suǒyǒude shùmu zài yíkuàr dédào de
115   yíge zǒngshù.

Mǎ : Duìle.

Bái: Mǎ Jiàoshòu, zǔzhi zhèige cér kàn shū de shíhou wǒ zhīdao tāde
       yìsi, kěshi wǒ zìjǐ xiě jiu bú dà huì yòng zhèige cér.

Mǎ : Wǒ zài shuō liǎngge lìzi: "Xuéxiàode xuésheng zǔzhi yíge tóngxué
120   huì." "Nánnǚ jiéhūn yǐhòu zǔzhi yíge xiǎo jiātíng."

Bái: Zhōngguo hái yǒu dà jiātíng, shì bu shi?

Mǎ : Zhōngguo lìlái shi dà jiātíng zhìdu me.   Kěshi jìn jǐshinián lái,
       yīnwei xué xīfáng guójiā de guānxi, suǒyǐ Zhōngguode jiātíng chà-
       buduō dōu shi xiǎo jiātíng le.

44.0. jiàoyu   (1) educate; (2) education   [teach nourish]

Jiàoyu Bù   Ministry of Education

Jiàoyu Bùzhǎng   Minister of Education

44.1. Zhāng Dàwén Bóshi shi yíwèi lǎo jiàoyujiā.

44.2. Zuótian wǒ dào Jiàoyù Bù shēnqǐng chū guó liúxué.

44.3. Xiàozhǎng qǐng Jiàoyù Bùzhǎng dào xuéxiào lái gěi wǒmen jiǎng
       jiàoyu wèntí.

44.4. Suǒyǒu chūjí、zhōngjí、gāojí gèjíde jiàokeshū dōu shi Jiàoyu Bù chū-
       bǎn.   (T)

44.5. Zhōngguo Jiàoyu Bù yìnián yǒu yícì liúxuéshēng kǎoshì.   (T)

45.0. huánjing   environment, circumstances   [ring realm]

45.1. Wǒmen zhèr bú shi niàn shū de huánjing. Měitiān láiwǎng de chē、
       mǎ tài duō le.

46.0. fēnshu   academic grade   [divide number]

46.1. Tā měicì kǎoshì de fēnshu dōu bǐ wǒ gāo.

47.0. yào yǒu   (1) must have; (2) (short for yàoshi yǒu 'if have'. Some-
                  times combined redundantly with rúguǒ)

47.1. Nǐ kǎo nèige dàxué nǐ zhōngxuéde chéngji píngjūn yào yǒu jiǔshifēn
       yǐshàng cái néng cānjiā kǎoshì.   (T)

47.2. Wǒde chéngji rúguǒ yào yǒu nǐ nènmo hǎo wǒ yídìng shēnqǐng jiǎng-
       xuéjīn chū guó liúxué.

125 Bái: Mǎ Jiàoshòu, fǔshang shi dà jiātíng háishi xiǎo jiātíng?

    Mǎ : Zài jiēhūn de shíhou shi xiǎo jiātíng, xiànzài shi dà jiātíng le! Wǒ
          xiànzài yǒu wǔge érnǚ.   Zhè bu shi yíge dà jiātíng ma? Érnǚ
          duōle zhēn bùdeliǎo. Měinián jiàoyu fèi yào hěn duō qián.

    Bái: Zhèlǐde zhōngxué、xiǎoxué dōu yǒu xuéfèi ma?

130 Mǎ : Dōu yǒu. Lián píngmín xuéxiào dōu yǒu xuéfèi. Búguò jiù shi shǎo
          yìdiǎr.

    Bái: Yàoshi jiātíng huánjing bù hǎo de zěnmo bàn ne?

    Mǎ : Nà jiu xiāngdāng kùnnán le.

    Bái: Nínde wǔge háizi dōu niàn xiǎoxué ma?

135 Mǎ : Dōu niàn xiǎoxué. Sānge niàn gāoxiǎo, liǎngge niàn chūxiǎo. Zhèi
          jǐge háizi shū niànde hái dōu búcuò. Měicì kǎoshìde chéngji dōu
          hǎo. Měige háizi píngjūn fēnshu dōu zài bāshiwǔfēn yǐshàng.

    Bái: Niàn shū yào yǒu niàn shū de huánjing. Mǎ Jiàoshòu shi xuézhě,
          nínde háizi yídìng zhīdao yònggōng de.

48.0. hé   (1) be in accord with; (2) merge, pool, put together; (3) to-
                    gether, cooperatively

      hézuò   cooperate   [together work]

      hézuòshè   cooperative (store)   [together work society]

48.1. Wǒ gēn Biān Yǒuwén wǒmen liǎngge rén hémǎile yíge lùyīnjī.

48.2. Tā hé wǒde yìjian bùtóng.   Wǒmen liǎngge rén bù nénggòu hézuò.

48.3. Wǒ xiǎng mǎi lùyīndài.   Bù zhīdào xuéxiàode hézuòshèli yǒu méi
      yǒu.

48.4. Wǒ zhèicì kǎoshì de chéngji bu hé lǐxiǎng.   (T)

49.0. liǎojiě   comprehend   [clear untie]

49.1. Wǒ hé tā shuōle bàntiān tā yě méi liǎojiě wǒde yìsi.

50.0. jìnlì   try one's best   [exhaust strength]

50.1. Wǒ yídìng jìnlì bāngzhu ni.

51.0. jù   basing on, according to

      gēnju   (1) base on; (2) basing on, according to; (3) basis, evidence
                 [root base]

      jùshuō   (1) according to (what they) say; (2) according to

51.1. Jù wǒ suǒ zhīdao de tāde chéngji bu jígé.

51.2. Jùshuō tā shi ge zhuānjiā, kěshi tā jīntian jiǎngyǎnde bu hěn hǎo.

51.3. Jù tā shuō nèijiàn shì tā bànbuliǎo yīnwei kùnnán hěn duō.   (T)

51.4. Jù wǒ kàn zhèi xuéqī Zhāng Dàwénde chéngji yídìng hǎobuliǎo. (T)

51.5. Zhèiyàng bàn shi gēnju fǎlǜshàng něi yìtiáo?   (T)

51.6. Jù wǒ suǒ zhīdao de tāde jīngji qíngxing shi xiāngdāng kùnnán. (T)

52.0. xiángxi   detailed   [detailed fine]

52.1. Nèijiàn shìqing wǒmen zài xiángxide yánjiu yánjiu.   (T)

140 Mǎ : Wǒde háizi tāmen yě bu yídìng zhīdao yònggōng. Nǐ yǒu dìdi mèi-
         mei ma?

    Bái: Yǒu.   Wǒ yǒu yíge dìdi yíge mèimei.

    Mǎ : Xiànzài dōu niàn shū ma?

    Bái: Dōu niàn shū.   Wǒ mèimei shū niànde bú cuò.   Dìdi shū niànde
145   chéngji fēicháng bù hǎo. Duì něimén gōngke dōu méi xìngqu.

    Mǎ : Yīnggāi jìnlì xiǎng fázi liǎojiě tāde xìngqu shi něi yìfāngmiànde.

    Bái: Gēnju guòqude qíngxing wǒ xiǎng tā shi xiǎng xué yìzhǒng zhuān-
         ménde dōngxi. Guò jǐtiān wǒ xiě fēng xiángxide xìn wènwen ta. Wǒ
         zhèige dìdi hé wǒ bù yíyàng.   Bù xǐhuan niàn shū, kěshi biéde
150   shìqing tā gēn wǒ hěn hézuò.

53.0. nóng   agriculture

      nóngren   farmer, peasant

      nóngmín   farmers, peasants (usually collectively)

      nóngyè   agriculture

      nóngtián   agricultural land

      nónggōngyè   agriculture and industry

      nóngyè hézuoshè   agricultural cooperative

      nóngxuéyuàn   college of agriculture

53.1. Wǒ dì-èrge dìdi shi xué nóng de. Tā zài nóngxuéyuàn niàn shū.

53.2. Zhōngguo shi nóngyè guójiā. Duōshùde rénmín shi zhòng tián de.

53.3. Nèi yídàide dì dōu shi nóngtián.

53.4. Nèige guójiā méi shénmo xīwang. Jù shuō zài jīngji yìfāngmiàn hěn
       kùnnán, yóuqishi nónggōngyè yìfāngmiàn hěn bù xíng.

53.5. Zhèlǐde nóngmín dōu shi nóngyè hézuòshède shèyuán.   (T)

53.6. Jùshuō nóngrén píngcháng bu chī chǎo cài.

54.0. gōng(cheng)   construction (job), engineering enterprise   [work
                          journey]

      gōngchengxué   (study of) engineering

      gōngxuéyuàn   college of engineering

54.1. Jù Yuǎn-Dàde Máo Xiānsheng shuō, Yuǎn-Dà yǒu yìdiǎr gōngcheng
       jiào wǒ zuò.

54.2. Xué gōngchengxué yào jǐnián bìyè?   (T)

54.3. Nèige dàxuéde gōngxuéyuàn hěn bu róngyi kǎo.   (T)

55.0. xīn   (1) new; (2) newly, recently

      Xīnhuá   New China (in institutional names)

      xīnwén   news   [new hear]

55.1. Fánshi xīn wùlǐ cānkǎo shū tā dōu yào mǎi.

55.2. Jīntian gěi wǒmen yǎnjiǎng de nèiwèi Zhāng Xiānsheng shi xīn cóng
       Měiguo huílai de.

55.3. Xīnhuá Shūdiàn lí Jiàoyu Bù hěn jìn.

55.4. Jīntián bàozhǐshang yǒu shénmo xīnwén méi yǒu?   (T)

Mǎ : Nǐ dìdi xiànzài niàn zhōngxué ne háishi niàn dàxué ne?

Bái : Tā jīnnián gāozhōng cái bìyè. Suírán shū niànde bù hǎo, kěshi jiā-
       lǐde gèzhǒng dōngxi yàoshi bù hǎoyòng le dōu shi tā shōushi.

Mǎ : Nà zuǐhǎo shi niàn gōngxueyuàn, xué gōngchengxué me.

155 Bái: Wǒ xiǎng tā niànbuliǎo gōngchéngxué. Oh, Mǎ Jiàoshòu, zuótian wǒ
        kàn Zhōnghuá Wǎnbào shangde xīnwén, jìnlái zhèngfǔ ràng rénmín
        zhùzhòng nónggōngyè. Nónggōngyè shi nóngyè gēn gōngyè, shì bu
        shi?

Mǎ : Shì. Jiù shi nóngyè gōngyè jiǎndānde shuōfǎ.   Yīnwei Zhōngguo
160   nóngtián hěn duō, suǒyǐ lìlái shi nóngyè guójiā. Zài zhèige shídài
        bù yīnggāi zhǐ shi zhòng tián, yě yīnggāi zhùzhòng gōngyè.

56.0. lóu   (1) building of two or more stories; (2) (used in names of
                  restaurants and other buildings)

       lóushàng   upstairs

       lóuxià   downstairs

56.1. Nǐ kàn zhèige dìfang wǔnián qián lián yìsuǒ fángzi dōu méi yǒu.
       Xiànzài dōu shi dà lóu le.

56.2. Xīnhuá Lóu shi yíge hěn yǒumíngde fànguǎr.   (T)

56.3. Wǒ lóushàng zhùde nèige xuésheng yònggōng jíle. Tīngshuǒ tā nián-
       nián niàn shū dōu shi jiǎngxuéjīn.   (T)

56.4. Zhèi yídàide fángzi dōu shi gè jīguānde bàngōngshǐ.   (T)

57.0. lǐxuéyuàn   college of science

57.1. Yuǎn-Dàde lǐxuéyuán shi něinián chénglì de?

58.0. jìlù   (1) make a formal written record of, take minutes of; (2) rec-
               ords, minutes   [record record]

58.1. Tāde chéngi hǎo bu hǎo wǒmen méi yǒu jìlù.   (T)

58.2. Měi yícì jiǎngyǎn dōu jiào yíge wàiguo xuésheng jìlù.

59.0. zhéxué   philosophy   [philosophy study]

59.1. Zhèixiē cānkǎo shū dōu shi zhuān wèi yánjiu zhéxué yòng de. (T)

60.0. běntí   this topic, the topic in question   (W)   [root topic]

60.1. Nǐ shuō de huà lí běntí tài yuǎ.. le.

Bái: Xiàndàide guójiā shi yīnggāi zhùzhòng gōngyè de. Mǎ Jiàoshòu,
      shuōdào gōngyè wǒ xiǎngqilai. Shàngcì wǒ zài Yuǎn-Dàde shíhou
      tīngshuō yǒu rén yào juāngěi Yuǎn-Dà yíge dà lóu, zhuān wèi gōng-
165   xueyuàn bàngōng yòng de.

Mǎ : Shìde.   Zhèige dà lóu yě zài zhèi fùjìn, jiù zài lǐxuéyuàn hòubiar.
      Zhèige lóu dà bùfen dōu shi juānlai de. Yǒu yì xiǎo bùfen shi jiào-
      zhiyuán hé xuésheng juān de.   Gēnju jiàowuchùde jìlù, jiàozhiyuán
      hé xuésheng juānle yǒu wǔwàn duō kuài qián. Gōngxueyuàn bàn gōng
170   dà lóu nǐ hái méi kànjian ma?

Bái: Méi yǒu.

Mǎ: Jīntian xiàwǔ wǒmen yíkuàr qu kànkan.

Bái: Hǎojíle. Mǎ Jiàoshòu méi shì ma?

Mǎ: Méi shénmo shì. Wǒ jiù shi dào zhéxué-xì qù yícì, ránhòu jiu méi
175   shì le.

Bái: Jǐdiǎn zhōng qù?

Mǎ: Sāndiǎn zhōng hǎo bu hǎo?

Bái: Hǎo. Wǒ zài nǎr děngzhe nín?

Mǎ: Qǐng nǐ sāndiǎn zhōng hái dào zhèr lái. Wǒmen jīntian tánle hěn
180   duō. Xiànzài yòu gāi shuō běntí le. Shēngcí hái yǒu wèntí méi
    yǒu?

Bái: Méi yǒu shénmo dà wèntí le.

Mǎ: Hǎo. Sāndiǎn zhōng jiàn.

Bái: Sāndiǎn zhōng jiàn.

SHĒNGCÍ BIǍO

1. dào(shi)

2. chóng
   zàichóng
   chóngxiū

3. bàn
   bàn gōng
   bàn shì
   bànhǎo
   zěnmo bàn?
   bànfǎ

4. fǔdǎo

5. zhǔrèn
   fǔdǎo zhǔrèn

6. liú(xué)
   liú Měi
   liúxuéshēng

7. jiàowu
   jiàowuzhǎng

8. chù*
   jiàowuchù
   bàngōngchù
   bànshìchù

9. zhì(du)
   dà jiātíng zhìdu
   xuézhì
   xuéfēn-zhì

10. xuénián
    xuénián-zhì

11. chéngji
    chéngji-dān

12. jígé

13. fánshi

14. zhǐ yào(shi)

15. yī*
    yīsheng
    yīkē
    yīyuàn
    yīxuéyuàn

16. chénglì

17. qǔ
    kǎoqǔ

18. yōuliáng

19. xiāngdāng(de)

20. bóshi
    bóshi lùnwén
    niàn bóshi

21. xuéwèi

22. shuòshi

23. xuéshi

24. dān
    dānzǐ

25. cānkǎo
    cānkǎo shū

26. fèi
    fèi shì
    xuéfèi

27. píngjūn

28. cǐwài (W)

29. juān

30. jiǎngxuéjīn

31. shēnqǐng

32. jīngji
    jīngjixué

33. kùnnán

34. (xué)xì
    xì zhǔrèn
    yuàn-xì
    lìshǐ-xì

35. wùlǐ(xué)
    wùlǐxuéjiā

36. shēngwù(xué)

37. fǎ*
    fǎlǜ
    fǎxuéyuàn

38. shǐ*
    kèshǐ
    lùyīnshǐ
    bàngōngshǐ

39. dài
    dàizi
    lùyīndài

40. pán
    pánzi
    suànpan

41. zǒng(shi)
    zǒngshù

42. zǔzhi

43. guānxi
    méi guānxi
    A gēn/duì B (de) guānxi
    yīnwei . . . de guānxi

44. jiàoyu
    Jiàoyu Bù
    Jiàoyu Bùzhǎng

45. huánjing

46. fēnshu

47. yào yǒu

48. hé
    hézuò
    hézuòshè

49. liǎojiě

50. jìnlǐ

51. jù
    gēnju
    jùshuō

52. xiángxi

53. nóng
    nóngren
    nóngmin
    nóngyè
    nóngtián
    nónggōngyè
    nóngyè hézuòshè
    nóngxuéyuàn

54. gōng(cheng)
    gōngchengxué
    gōngxuéyuàn

55. xīn
    Xīnhuá
    xīnwén

56. lóu
    lóushàng
    lóuxià

57. lǐxuéyuàn

58. jìlù

59. zhéxué

60. běntǐ (W)

YǓFǍ LIÀNXÍ

A. de as a sentence particle (see note 1)

1. Nèige xiǎo xuéxiàode xuéfèi bú huì tài guì de.

2. Yīnwei tā hěn jiǔ méi yǒu gōngzuò, wǒ xiǎng tā jiātíngde huánjing bù kěnéng tài hǎode.

3. Xuéxiào de shìqing fǔdǎo zhǔrèn yídìng néng gàosu wǒmen de.

4. Tā pà nǐ tàitai fèi shǐ. Tā bù néng lǎo shàng nǐ fǔshang qu chī fàn de.

5. Zhāng Xiānsheng yīngdāng míngtian zǒu de.

B. zhǐ yào(shi)-S₁ S₂ (see note 2)

1. Zhǐ yàoshi yǒu guānyu wùlǐxuéde jiǎngyǎn wǒ yào‿hi méi shǐ wǒ yídìng qu tīng.

2. Nǐ kǎo de fēnshu nènmo hǎo, zhǐ yào jiàowuchù néng gěi nǐ xiě yìzhāng chéngji dān, nǐ dāngrán kéyi ná zhèizhāng chéngji dān qu shēnqǐng jiǎngxuéjīn.

3. Zhǐ yào shi bàn gōng de shíjiān wǒ yídìng dōu zài bàngōngchù.

4. Míngtian qu lǚxíng zhǐ yào nǐ zàncheng, biéren yídìng dōu zàncheng.

5. Nèige Měiguo rén yǒu hěn duō cānkǎo shū. Zhǐ yào shi Zhōngwén shū tā dōu xǐhuan mǎi.

C. Use of de in adverbial phrases (see note 3)

1. Wǒ tiāntian hěn yònggōngde niàn Zhōngwén, kěshi wǒ kǎoshì de fēnshu háishi bù hǎo. Nǐ shuō wǒ zěnmo bàn?

2. Nèige xuésheng suírán méi yǒu tiāncái, tā dàoshi hěn nǔlìde xuéxi.

3. Zuótian wǒ qu kàn Mǎ Xiānsheng. Rénjia gàosu wǒ cóng Zhōngshān Lù yìzhíde wàng dōng zǒu, kěshi wǒ zhǎole bàntiān méi bànfǎ zhǎozhao.

4. Wǒ kàn dàoshi kànle, kěshi wǒ hái děi xiángxìde zài kàn yícì.

5. Nǐ jìlù yǎnjiǎng de shíhou hǎohāorde jìlù, bú yào xiě cuò zì.

D. Use of fánshi (see note 4)

1. Fánshi yào dào nèige dàxué niàn bóshi hé shuòshi de, tā dàxuéde chéngji bìděi píngjūn yǒu bāshiwǔfēn yǐshàng cái kéyi.

2. Tā hěn huì bàn shì. Fánshi jiào tā bàn de shì méi yǒu yíjiàn bànbuhǎo de.

3. Xiàozhǎng bàngōngchù lí jiàowuzhǎng bàngōngchù hěn jìn. Fánshi dào jiàowuzhǎng nèr qù de yídìng yào jīngguo xiàozhǎng bàngōngchù.

4. Nèiwèi zhuānjiā yǎnjiǎngde nèiróng chángchang gēn běntí bù hé, suǒyǐ fánshi tāde yǎnjiǎng wǒ dōu bú qu tīng.

5. Tā běnlái shi xué gōngcheng de. Yīnwei huánjingde guānxi tā xiànzài zuò mǎimai le. Tā zài chéng lǐtou yǒu yíge bànshìchù. Tā zuótian gàosu wǒ yǐhòu fánshi zhǎo tāde shíhou zuì hǎo dào tāde bànshìchù.

JIǍNGHUÀ

Zhūwèi tóngxué:

　　Jīntian zhèige shíjiān běnlái shi Zhuāntí Jiǎnghuà. Wǒ xiànzài jièyòng zhèige shíjiān lái shuōyishuo Běnxiào Gàikuàng. Wèi-shénmo yào shuō zhèige tímu ne? Wèideshì xīn tóngxuémen kéyi liǎojiě zhèige xīn huánjing. Zài méi yǒu shuō Běnxiào Gàikuàng yǐqián, wǒ xiǎng gēn zhūwèi

5　tóngxué jièshao jièshao wǒ zìjǐ. Wǒ shi Zhāng Yǒuzhēn. Yǐhòu zhūwèi zhǎo wǒ kéyi zhīdao wǒde míngzi. Wǒ shi běnxiào wàiguo liúxuéshēng fǔdǎo zhǔrèn. Wǒde gōngzuò shi bāngzhu wàiguo liúxuéshēng de. Yǐhòu zhūwèi rúguǒ yǒu shénmo kùnnán kéyi suíshí lái zhǎo wǒ, wǒ yídìng jìnlì bāngzhu zhūwèi.

10   Xiànzài shuōdào běntí, Běnxiào Gàikuàng. Zhūwèi yěxǔ yǐjing kàndao
běnxiào yǒu yìběn xiǎo cèzi, cèzi lǐmian yǒu běnxiàode lìshǐ、zǔzhi děngděng, dōu hěn xiángxi. Dànshi cèzili yǒu yìxiē duì zhūwèi tèbié yǒu
guānxi de, wǒ zài zhèlǐ zài jiǎndānde jièshao jièshao.

        Dì-yī, xiān cóng běnxiàode yuàn-xì shuōqǐ. Běnxiào yǒu dàxué yě yǒu
15 yánjiuyuàn. Wǒmen yígòng yǒu liùge xuéyuàn, jiù shi wénxuéyuàn、fǎxué-
yuàn、lǐxuéyuàn、gōngxuéyuàn、nóngxuéyuàn hé yīxuéyuàn. Biéde xuéyuàn
cóng Yuǎn-Dà chénglì de shíhou jiù yǒu le, zhǐ yǒu yīxuéyuàn zuìjìn cái
chéngli de, chénglìle hái bú dào yìnián ne. Míngnián hái yào chénglì yíge
jiàoyu xuéyuàn.   Zài měige xuéyuànli dōu yǒu bù shǎode xuéxì. Gēnju
20 běnxiào jiàowuchùde jìlù, zhūwèi zài wénxuéyuànde zuì duō, chàbuduō yǒu
zǒngshùde yíbàr duō. Fǎxuéyuàn bǐjiào shǎo, lǐxuéyuàn zuì shǎo, biéde
xuéyuàn xiànzài hái méi yǒu, suǒyǐ wǒ xiànzài jiù shuō wénxuéyuàn、
fǎxuéyuàn、lǐxuéyuàn zhèi sānge xuéyuànde xuéxì.

        Wénxuéyuàn: Yǒu Zhōngwén-xì、wàiwén-xì、zhéxuéxì、lìshǐ-xì、xīnwén-
25   xì、yǔyánxué-xì.

        Fǎxuéyuàn: Yǒu fǎlǜ-xì、zhèngzhi-xì、jīngji-xì、shèhui-xì.

        Lǐxuéyuàn: Yǒu shùxué-xì、wùlǐ-xì、huàxué-xì、shēngwù-xì、xīnlixué-
                xì.

Yǐshàng suǒ shuōde zhèi jǐge yuàn-xì dōu yǒu wàiguo liúxuéshēng.   Hé
30 wàiguo liúxuéshēng méi yǒu guānxi de yuàn-xì wǒ bú bǐ shuō le.

        Dì-èr, yào shuō běnxiàode xuézhì.   Běnxiàode xuézhì cǎiyòng xuéfēn
zhì. Wǒ xiànzài bǎ dàxué hé yánjiuyuàn de xuézhì fēnkai lai shuō:

        Dàxué: Yào yǒu yìbǎi èrshige xuéfēn hé bìyè lùnwén, cái kéyi bìyè,
                jiù kéyi dédào xuéshi xuéwèi.   Měimén gōngke liùshifēn jígé.
35   Rúguǒ bú jígé bìděi chóngxiū.

        Yánjiuyuàn: Shuòshi xuéwèi, yào zài dé xuéshi xuéwèi yǐhòu zài běn-
                xiào yánjiuyuàn yánjiu yìnián, yào yǒu sānshige xuéfēn,
                hái yào xiě shuòshi lùnwén. Bóshi xuéwèi, yào zài dé
                shuòshi xuéwèi yǐhòu zài běnxiào yánjiuyuàn yánjiu èrnián,
40   yào yǒu liùshige xuéfēn, hái yào xiě bóshi lùnwén.

        Dì-sān, jiǎngxuéjīn.   Búlùn zài dàxué、zài yánjiuyuàn, fánshi chéngji
yōuliáng、gèmén gōngke píngjūn fēnshu zài bāshifēn yǐshàng de jiù kéyi
shēnqǐng jiǎngxuéjīn.

Cǐwài hái yǒu guānyu túshūguǎn、 lùyīnshǐ、 cāntīng、 hézuòshè děngděng
45   dōu zài běnxiàode xiǎo cèzi lǐmian xiěde hěn xiángxi.   Zhūwèi kéyi zìjǐ
kànkan, rúguǒ yǒu bù míngbai de dìfang kéyi suíshí wèn wǒ, wǒ yě huāng-
ying hé zhūwèi chángcháng tántan.   Rúguǒ zhūwèi yǒu gōngfu kéyi suíshí
dào wǒ nèr.   Wǒ tiāntiān dōu zài Zǒng Bàngōng Lóu, èrbǎi liùshiyī hào.

FÙSHÙ

Zhèipán lùyīn dài shi Zhōngwén dì-yīzǔ dì-yīhào, Bái Wénshān fùshù
dì-yīcì Zhuāntí Jiǎnghuà.

Zhèicì Zhuāntí Jiǎnghuà shi xiàozhǎng jiǎng de.   Xiàozhǎng xiān shuō
jǐjù kèqi huà huānying wǒmen wàiguo liúxuéshēng.   Tèbié yǒu yìsi de shi
5   tā yòng Kǒngzǐ shuō de yíjù huà huānying wǒmen.   Zhèijù huà shi: "Yǒu
péng zì yuǎn fāng lái bù yì lè hu?"   Zhèijù huà shi wényánwénde.   Yào
bú shi zài jiǎnghuà yǐqián wǒ kànle Yīngwénde zhùjiě, kǒngpà yìdiǎr yě
tīngbudǒng.   Yīnwei zhùjiě jiěshide hěn míngbai, érqiě Mǎ Jiàoshòu yě bǎ
suǒyǒude shēngcí dōu shuō yíge lìzi jùzi, suǒyǐ quánbù jiǎnghuà wǒ dōu
10   dǒng.   Xiànzài wǒ bǎ Kǒngzǐ shuōde huà měi yíge zìde yìsi shuōchulai.

Zhèijù huàli yǒu sìge zì gēn xiànzàide shuōfǎ wánquán yíyàng de.   Zhèi
sìge zì shi <u>yǒu</u>、<u>yuǎn</u>、<u>lái</u>、<u>bù</u>.   Yǒu sānge zì shi jiǎndānde shuōfǎ.   <u>Péng</u>
jiùshi <u>péngyou</u> jiǎndānde shuōfǎ, <u>fāng</u> shi <u>dìfang</u> de jiǎndānde shuōfǎ, <u>lè</u>
shi <u>kuàilè</u> jiǎndānde shuōfǎ.   Yǒu sānge zì gēn xiànzàide shuōfǎ bùtóng.
15   Xiànzài wǒ shuōchulai.   <u>Zì</u> xiànzài shuō <u>cóng</u>.   <u>Yì</u> xiànzài shuō <u>yě</u>.   <u>Hū</u>
xiànzài shuō <u>ma</u>.

Wǒ xiànzài shuōyishuo Zhuāntí Jiǎnghuà.   Yuǎndōng Dàxué duì wǒmen
wàiguo xuésheng hěn guānxīn.   Jù xuéxiào fāngmiàn suǒ zhīdao de, wǒmen
lái qiúxué zài xuéxi yìfāngmiàn shi hěn yǒu xìngqu de, kěshi zài xuéxiàoli
20   niàn shū de shíjiān hěn duǎn, suǒyǐ xuéxiàode gōngke bù nénggou mǎnzú
wǒmen xīwang dédào de.   Qùnian xiàozhǎng gēn jiàoshòumen tándao zhèige
qíngxing, jiu juédìng cǎiyòng zhèige tèbié jiāoxué fāngfǎ.   Zhèige tèbiéde
fāngfǎ jiù shi Zhuāntí Jiǎnghuà.   Shénmo shi Zhuāntí Jiǎnghuà ne?   Jiù
shi qǐng jǐwèi zhuānjiā gěi wàiguo liúxuéshēng yǎnjiǎng.   Jùshuō jiǎnghuà
25   de fànwéi hěn dà, bāokuò dìlǐ、 shèhuì、 lìshǐ、 jīngji、 yǔyán děngděng.   Wǒ
juéde zhèige shi fēicháng hǎode jiàoxuéfǎ.   Wàiguo xuésheng duìyu zhèxiē
tímu dōu hěn yǒu xìngqu, yīnwei kéyi duō zhīdao guānyu Zhōngguode

qíngxing. Zhuāntí Jiǎnghuà shi kèchengde yíbùfen, suǒyǐ wǒmen yě bǐděi

yònggōng xué. Shàng kè de dì-yīge yuè, měitiān yǒu yíge Zhuāntí Jiǎng-

30   huà. Yígòng yǒu èrshicì. Zhǔjiǎngde rén duōbàn shi Yuǎn-Dàde jiàoshòu.

Chúle jiàoshòu yǐwài hái yǒu jǐwèi zhuānjiā shi tèbié qǐnglai de.

    Wǒ tīngwánle xiàozhǎng jiǎnghuà yǐhòu, fēicháng gāoxìng. Wǒ yě zàn-

cheng Zhuāntí Jiǎnghuà zhèizhǒng fāngfǎ. Wǒ xiànzài bǎ xiàozhǎng jiǎng-

huàde dàyì fùshù yícì, zài lùyīnjīli lùxiàlai, wèideshì kéyi tīngting. Wǒ

35   shuōde duì bu duì, huòzhě yǒu shuōde bu hǎode dìfang, wǒ xīwang yǒu

rén gàosu wǒ.

WÉNXI

1. Jīntian Zhuāntí Jiǎnghuà zhǔjiǎng de rén shi Húnán rén. Jiǎng de shi
   xiànzài Zhōngguode nóngmín. Tā yòng Húnán huà jiǎngyǎn. Dāngshí yào
   bú shi yǒu rén fānchéng Guóyǔ, wǒ lián yíjù yě tīngbudǒng.

2. Wáng Xiānsheng shi túshūguǎnde zhíyuán. Tā gǎndào xiànzàide Hànyǔ zi-
   diǎn zhùjiě dōu bu hěn xiángxi. Tā xiǎng biān yìběn zìdiǎn. Tā shuō
   tā yídìng zài liǎngnián yǐnèi dáchéng biān zìdiǎn de mùdì.

3. Zhèige lùyīnshì tài xiǎo, yào tīng lùyīn de rén tài duō. Xiànzài bǎ yào
   tīng lùyīn de rén fēnwéi liǎngzǔ. Dì-yīzǔ zài shídiǎn zhōng tīng lùyīn,
   dì-èrzǔ zài shíyīdiǎn zhōng tīng.

4. Jīntian wǒ qu jiàn jiàowuzhǎng, tā bú zài jiàowuchù. Yǒu yíge jiàowuyuán
   gàosu wǒ, jiàowuzhǎng wǎng lǐxuéyuàn qu le, yěxǔ zài shēngwù-xì xì zhǔrènde bàngōngshì ne. Hòulai wǒ qùdao lǐxuéyuàn, lóushàng、lóuxià wǒ dōu
   zǒudàole yě méi jiàndao jiàowuzhǎng.

5. Túshūguǎn zuìjìn dào de cānkǎo shū xiāngdāng duō. Yǒu wùlǐxuéde, yǒu
   shēngwùxuéde, yǒu jīngjixuéde, yǒu gōngchengxuéde, hái yǒu fǎlǜ hé nóngyè de. Zhèixiē shū tīngshuō dōu shi rénjia juāngěi túshūguǎn de.

6. Zhōngguo Jiàoyu Bù měinián dōu yǒu liúxuéshēng kǎoshì. Kǎoqǔ yǐhòu
   chū guó liúxué. Yǒude liúxuéshēngde xuéfèi dōu shi zhèngfǔ gěi tāmen.

7. Wǒmende kèshì lí lùyīnshì hěn jìn. Wǒ xiàle kè jiù qu tīng lùyīn. Lùyīnshì de lùyīndài hěn duō. Měipán dàizishang dōu yǒu dì-jǐhào shi
   shénmo. Hái yǒu yìběn lùyīndàide mùlù. Búlùn yào tīng něi yìzhǒng lùyīn, zhǐ yàoshi yí kàn mùlù jiù kéyi zhǎodào, yìdiǎr yě bú fèi shì. Lù-
   yīnli yǒu fāyīn liànxí, niàn dānzì, yě yǒu lìjù、huìhuà、gùshi、yǎnjiǎng
   shénmode.

8. Wǒ shi niàn yīkē de. Liǎngnián qián wǒ zài Yuǎn-Dà yīxuéyuàn bìyè.
   Xiànzài wǒ zài Yuǎn-Dàde yīyuàn dāng dàifu.

9. Zhōngguode zhōngxué shi yòng xuénián-zhì. Yǒude guójiāde zhōngxué shi
   yòng xuéfēn-zhì. Nǐ shuō něi yìzhǒng zhìdu hǎo ne?

10. Yǒu yíge Měiguo rén cóng Zhōngguo huílai. Tā zài Zhōngguo mǎile hěn duō dōngxi. Tā mǎide dōngxilǐ yǒu yíge Zhōngguo gǔdàide pánzi, hái yǒu yíge suànpan.

11. Wǒ zài Wáng Xiānshengde bànshìchù kànjian Wáng Xiānsheng le. Wǒ wèn ta: "Wǒ qián jǐtiān qǐng nǐ gěi wǒ bàn de nèijiàn shì bàn le ma?" Wáng Xiānsheng shuō: "Nèijiàn shì bàn shi bàn le, kěshi méi bànhǎo, hái děi chóng bàn. Yàoshi zàichóng bàn hái yào yíge yuède shíjiān." Wǒ xīnli xiǎng "Nǐ bàn shì tài màn le," kěshi wǒ méi shuōchulai.

12. Zhōngguode tǔdì wǒ xiǎng dàgài duōshù shi nóngtián. Rénmín duōshù shi nóngrén, suǒyǐ Zhōngguo shi yíge nóngyè guójiā. Jìnlái Zhōngguo yímiàn zhùzhòng nóngyè, shèlì nóngyè hézuòshè, yímiàn zhùzhòng gōngyè, xīwang chéngwéi yíge nónggōngyède guójiā.

WÈNTÍ

1. Yuǎn-Dà yǒu jǐge xuéyuàn? Dōu shi shénmo míngzi? Shénmo xuéyuàn chénglìde zuì wǎn? Míngnian yào chénglì shénmo xuéyuàn?

2. Yuǎn-Dàde wàiguo liúxuéshēng, něige xuéyuàn zuì duō? Něige zuì shǎo? Něige méi yǒu wàiguo xuésheng? Zhèixiē shùmu shi cóng shénmo dìfang zhīdao de?

3. Liúxuéshēng zài Yuǎn-Dà rúguǒ yǒu kùnnán qù zhǎo shénmo rén bāngzhu? Nèige rén xìng shénmo? Zài shénmo dìfang bàn gōng?

4. Qǐng bǎ Yuǎn-Dà wén、fǎ、lǐ sānge xuéyuàn hé gè xuéxì de míngzi, huà yíge jiǎndānde túbiǎo, zài túbiǎoli yào kànchūlai shénmo xuéxì zài shénmo xuéyuàn.

5. Yuǎn-Dàde xuézhì, dàxué yào yǒu duōshao xuéfēn cái kéyi bìyè? Bìyè de shíhou dédào shénmo xuéwèi?

6. Zài Yuǎn-Dà niàn shū, měimén gōngke duōshao fēn cái kéyi jígé? Bú jígé zěnmo bàn?

7. Zěnmoyàng cái kéyi dédào Yuǎn-Dàde shuòshi xuéwèi? Bóshi xuéwèi? Qǐng fēnbié shuōchulai.

8. Zài Yuǎn-Dà niàn shū de chéngji zěnmoyàng cái kéyi shēnqǐng jiǎngxuéjīn?

9. Qǐng nǐ bǎ dì-èrkè bǐjiǎo wén yìdiǎrde shēngcí fāncheng báihuà.

10. Qǐng nǐ shuōyishuo Měiguo dàxuéde zǔzhi gēn Zhōngguo dàxuéde zǔzhi yǒu shénmo bùtóng?

ILLUSTRATIVE SENTENCES (ENGLISH)

1.2. I've read the explanation of those words, to be sure, but I still don't fully understand a few (of them).

2.1. I made a mistake in buying that book. I have to buy another. I wasted five dollars.

2.3. If I'm not able to do well in this course, I must repeat it next year.

2.4. That house must be repaired.

3.2. He can't manage things. He can't even handle a little task like that.

3.3. As I see it, there's no way of handling that matter. [You all] tell me, what should be done?

5.1. I can't take the responsibility for that matter. We must ask the person in charge.

6.1. Mr. Wang is a returned student from America, not from England.

8.2. The whole staff is in the office planning the students' curricula for next semester.

8.3. We [few people] all work in the same [lit. one] office.

13.1. I read whatever he writes.

13.2. Yesterday the principal announced that all those whose grades on the quiz are over 85 don't need to take the final examination.

15.2. Tomorrow afternoon the dean of the medical school will give a lecture to the medical students. We don't know [now] what the topic is.

16.1. Our university press has been established for just a short while.

17.2. I'm going to school to get my report card.

19.2. I must find an appropriate time to tell him again about that matter.

21.1. He can get his doctorate this semester.

24.1. After we have discussed the terms we also [singly] discuss the meaning of each character.

25.2. The medical students all use the book written by Dr. Ma Dawen as a reference work.

25.3. You should take his views as a basis of reference.

37.2. All those who are citizens should have some slight understanding of the laws of their own country.

38.1. Excuse me, where is the principal's office?

39.1. He brought quite a few reference works on physics from America for me.

40.3. This tape is English unit 3, no. 9, Gao Meiying recapitulating the ninth English Special Lecture.

41.1. Every time he takes an exam in any course he invariably gets over 90.

41.2. (When) the school has a meeting, why do you never participate?

42.1. We should organize an association of Chinese returned students from America.

43.5. There will surely be a day when the relations between those two countries will be good.

44.4. All levels of textbooks, elementary, intermediate, and advanced, are published by the Ministry of Education.

44.5. The Chinese Ministry of Education has one examination a year for students who want to study abroad.

47.1. As regards [your taking the examinations for] that college, only if the average of your middle school grades is over 90 can you take the exam.

48.4. My grade in this exam is not up to my expectations [lit. not in accord with ideal].

51.3. According to what he says, he can't handle that matter because there are a lot of difficulties.

51.4. In my opinion this semester Zhang Dawen's grades certainly can't improve.

51.5. Handling it in this way is in accord with what [item in the] law?

51.6. From what I know his financial [lit. economic] situation is rather difficult.

52.1. Let's investigate that matter a little more in detail.

53.5. The peasants here are all members of the agricultural cooperative.

54.2. If you study engineering, how many years will it take to graduate?

54.3. It's not at all easy to pass the examinations for the college of engineering in that university.

55.4. Is there any news in the paper today?

56.2. The New China Restaurant is a very famous restaurant.

56.3. That student living [my] upstairs is very hard-working. I hear that every year he's on a scholarship.

56.4. The buildings here are all offices of various organs of government.

58.1. We have no record as to whether his grades are good or not.

59.1. These reference works are all [especially] for use in studying philosophy.

NOTES

1. de is used at the end of a sentence, especially one containing a modal auxiliary, with the force of 'the fact is such that' or 'that's the situation':

   Nǐ yīnggāi gàosu ta de.   'You should tell him.'

   Wǒ zǎo jiu zhīdao tā bú huì hǎo de.   'I knew long ago he couldn't get well.'

2. The phrase zhǐ yào means 'only want' if followed by a nominal expression:

   Wǒ zhǐ yào yìběn shū. 'I want only one book.'

   Zhǐ yaò or zhǐ yàoshi used in the first of two related sentences has the force of 'if only . . . then . . .'

   Zhǐ yào nǐ nǔlì niàn shū yídìng kǎodeshàng. 'If only you will study hard you can certainly qualify in the examination.'

   The second sentence often contains an adverb such as jiù 'then,' dōu 'all,' yídìng 'certainly.'

3. The particle <u>de</u> occurs at the end of adverbs and adverbial phrases used to modify a following verb:

> Yìzhíde wàng běi zǒu. 'Go straight north.'

> Wǒmen bùzhībùjuéde zǒule sānlǐ lù. 'Without being aware of it we walked three miles.'

4. The expression <u>fánshi</u> followed by a noun phrase means 'whoever is, whatever is, all (that are),' etc. It is frequently paired with <u>dōu</u> in the following verbal phrase:

> Fánshi wǒde dōngxi dōu nádao nèr qu. 'Whatever things are mine take there.'

> Fánshi tā xiě de dōngxi wǒ dōu yào. 'I want whatever things he's written.'

> Fánshi zàncheng de qǐng jǔ shǒu. 'All those who approve please raise your hands.'

Dì-Sānkè. Jiàoyu

Mǎ : Wénshān, nǐ jīntian bǐ wǒ xiān lái le.

Bái: Zǎo, Mǎ Jiàoshòu.

Mǎ : Zǎo. Wǒ gāngcái dào lùyīnshǐ qu qǔ lùyīndài qu le. Zuótian wǎn-shang wǒ lùle yìpán lùyīndài.

5 Bái: Shi guānyu yǔyánde ma?

Mǎ : Bú shi. Shi guānyu jiàoyude yìxiē wèntí.

Bái: Mǎ Jiàoshòu shi yánjiu jiàoyu de ma?

Mǎ : Wǒ běnlái shi xué jiàoyude. Hòulai wǒ xué wénxué le.

Bái: Xué jiàoyu nán bu nán?

10 Mǎ : Xué shénmo yě bu róngyi. Xué jiàoyu yě shi xiāngdāng nán.

Bái: Guānyu jiàoyu yìfāngmiàn de cānkǎo shū duō bu duō?

Mǎ : Bù shǎo.

Bái: Mǎ Jiàoshòu, zuótian wǒ huíqu yǐhòu wǒ jiu bǎ zuótiande yǎnjiǎng fùshùle yícì, zìjǐ yòu tīngguo liǎngcì. Cuòr hěn duō, yǒude zì yīn
15 yě bú zhèng.

Mǎ : Yěxǔ shi nǐ hěn jiǔ bú yòng de yuánggu. Wǒ dào juéde nǐ fāyīn zhèifāngmiàn hěn hǎo. Gěi ni zhèizhāng shēngcí biǎo. Nǐ xiān kànyikàn.

Bái: Hǎode.

1.0. jīng   a classic

Wǔ Jīng   Five Classics

Sān Zì Jīng   Three Character Classic

1.1. Cóngqián Zhōngguo rén niàn shū, shi xiān cóng Sān Zì Jīng niànqǐ, háishi cóng Wǔ Jīng niànqǐ ne? . . . Dāngrán shi xiān cóng Sān Zì Jīng niànqǐ.   (T)

1.2. Xiàng Qiān Zì Wén、Sì Shū、Wǔ Jīng děng shū, xiànzàide xuésheng duōbàn bú niàn le.   (T)

2.0. bù   a pace, a step   (M)

yíbùyíbù(de)   step by step

jìnbù   (1) advance, progress, take steps toward (VO); (2) pro-gressive

2.1. Wǒmen dì-yībù xiān bǎ dānzì huìle, ránhòu zài xué cér.

45

2.2. Cóng xuéxiào dào yīyuàn de lù hěn jìn. Wǒ yíbùyíbùde zǒu, yìhuěr
jiu zǒudào le.

2.3. Nǐ kànkan wǒde chéngji-dān jiu zhǐdao wǒde gōngke bǐ qùnian jìnbù
le.

2.4. Zài zhèi jǐshinián jiān Zhōngguo zài kēxué yìfāngmiàn yǒu hěn dàde
jìnbù.   (T)

2.5. Zài jìn yíbù shuō, zhèizhǒng xuéshù jiǎnghuà yīnggāi bǎ tímu shuōde
xiángxi yìdiǎr.   (T)

3.0. sī*   private

sīren   private person

sīshú   pre-modern private tutoring school

3.1. Lóushàng shi wǒ sīrende bànshìchù.   Lóuxià shi gōnggòngde bàngōngchù.

3.2. Zhōngguo cóngqiánde xuésheng dōu shi zài sīshúli qiúxué.

4.0. lì*   establish, set up

sīlì   private(ly established)

gōnglì   public(ly established)

guólì   national, state (i.e. established by the state)

shěnglì   provincial (i.e. established by a province)

4.1. Wǒ xiǎoxué shi zài sīlì xiǎoxué niàn de.   Zhōngxué shi gōnglì
zhōngxué.   Dàxué niàn de shi shěnglì dàxué.   (T)

4.2. Wǒ shi guólì Běijīng Dàxué Zhōngwén xuéxì bìyè de.   (T)

5.0. shè*   establish, set up

shèlì   establish, set up

5.1. Zhèige nóngyè hézuòshè shi qùnian shèlì de.

6.0. chéngdu   qualification, degree of achievement   [complete degree]

6.1. Jiàowuchù yào yòng yíge zhíyuán.   Jù jiàowuzhǎng shuō, zhèige
zhíyuán yào yǒu dàxué chéngdu de.   (T)

6.2. Jù wǒ suǒ zhīdaode, tā zhǐ yǒu gāozhōngyīde chéngdu.   (T)

6.3. Zhèrde shēnghuó chéngdu bǐ wǒmen nèr gāode duō.   (T)

20   Bái: Zuótian wǎnshang wǒ zài túshūguǎn kàn shū. Wǒ suíbiàn nále yìběn
Sān Zì Jīng kànkan.   Zhèiběn shū wǒ yǐqián yě kànguo, kěshi wǒ
méi xiángxide kànguo. Zhèiběn shū xiāngdāng hǎo. Yòng jiǎndānde
jùzi cóng rén shuōqǐ yíbùyíbùde shuōdao dìlǐ, lìshǐ děngděngde.

   Mǎ: Zhōngguo yǐqián méi yǒu xuéxiào niàn sīshú de shíhou, xiǎo xué-
25   sheng xiān niàn Sān Zì Jīng, Bǎi Jiā Xìng, Qiān Zì Wén děngděng
nèi jǐběn shū, niánwán yǐhòu cái niàn Sì Shū, Wǔ Jīng.

Bái: Sīshú shi shénmo? Shi sīrén shèlì de xuéxiào ma?

Mǎ : Bú shi sīlì xuéxiào. Sīshú jiu shi sīrén zài jiāli jiāo xuésheng.
       Měi yíge sīshú jiù yǒu yíge xiānsheng. Xiānshengde xuéwen yǒude
30   hěn hǎo, yǒude hěn píngcháng. Xuéshengde chéngdu yě bù yíyàng.
       Yǒude chéngdu hěn gāo. Yǒude shi cái kāishǐ niàn shū de.

7.0.   Qīng   Ch'ing or Manchu period (1644–1911)

7.1.   Zái yī-bā-qī-liù nián Qīng Cháo yǒu sānshige liúxuéshēng dào
       Yīngguo、Fàguo xuéxi gōngyè.

8.0.   kējǔ   select by examination   (W)

8.1.   Zài yī-jiǔ-líng-wǔ nián yǐqián Zhōngguo shi kējǔ zhìdude shídài, yě
       shi dà jiātíng zhìdude shídài.

9.0.   guān   an official, officer

       guānlì   government-established

9.1.   Tā fùqin zai Qīng Cháode shíhou shi zuò guān de. Hòulái bú zuò
       guān le, suǒyǐ tāmende shēnghuó hěn kùnnán.   (T)

9.2.   Zài zhèi yídài yòu shèlìle liǎngge guānlì xiǎo xuéxiào.   (T)

10.0. niánxiàn   time-limit in years

10.1. Zài sīshúli niàn shū méi yǒu yídìngde niánxiàn. Nǐ kéyi suíbiàn
       niàn jǐnián.

11.0. guīdìng   (1) determine, decide, prescribe; (2) decision, provision
                 [rule decide]

11.1. Zhèijiàn shì zài fǎlùshang shi zěnmo guīdìng de?   (T)

12.0. zhāng   chapter, section   (M)

       wénzhāng   essay

12.1. Tāde lùnwén nèiróng xiěde fēicháng hǎo.   Fēnchéng shí'èrzhāng.
       Zìde zǒngshù yǒu shíwàn duō. Rénrén dōu shuō tā zhèige lùnwén
       shi hěn hǎode wénzhāng.

Bái: Mǎ Jiàoshòu, kējǔ shi shénmo yìsi?

Mǎ : Zhōngguo zài Qīng Cháo yǐqián dōu shi kējǔ shídài. Kējǔ shi yìzhǒng
       kǎoshì zhìdu. Kǎoshangde jiu kéyi zuò guān.

35 Bái: Kǎobushàngde zěnmo bàn?

Mǎ : Gāngcái wǒ shuō sīshúde xiānsheng, yǒu xuéwen de duōbàn jiu shi
       nèixiē méi kǎoshangde. Cóngqián niàn shū de rén chúle zuò guān
       yǐwài, tāmende chūlù jiù shi jiāo shū.

Bái: Tīngshuō sīshúde xuésheng yě méi yǒu kǎoshì. Nènmo gēnju shénmo
40   zhīdao xuéshengmende chéngji hǎo bu hǎo ne?

Mǎ : Zài sīshú niàn shū de xuésheng měitiān jiù shi niàn shū xiě zì.
Xuésheng zài sīshú niàn shū de niánxiàn yě bù guīdǐng yào niàn
jǐnián. Měitiān jiù shi niàn shū xiě zì. Niàndao yíge xiāngdāngde
chéngdu jiu xué zuò wén. Shéide wénzhāng zuòde hǎo jiu shi chéngji
45   zuì hǎode xuésheng.

Bái: Měi yíge sīshúlide xuésheng bú huì hěn duō ba?

Mǎ : Bù hěn duō. Jù wǒ suǒ zhīdao de, dàgài měi yíge sīshúli píngjūn
búguò jiù yǒu shíjǐge xuésheng.

13.0. zàojiù   to train

13.1. Nèige dàxuéde yīkē zuì yǒumíng. Zài zhèi jǐshinián jiān zàojiù-
chulai de yīsheng dōu shi hǎo yīsheng.

14.0. qǔxiāo   cancel, call off   [fetch diminish]

14.1. Yǒu yíge nóngyè xuéxiào bànle shínián yě méi bànhǎo. Jiéguǒ
zhèngfǔ bǎ zhèige nóngyè xuéxiào qǔxiāole.   (T)

15.0. táng   (1) hall, room; (2) (measure for classes in school)

kètáng   classroom

xuétáng   school (term used for pre-modern school)

jiǎngtáng   lecture hall

15.1. Jīntian dì-yītáng gōngke, jiàoshòu jiǎngde shi hézuò shìyè, hái jiǎngdào hézuòshè.   (T)

15.2. Yánjiu gōngchéngxué bù yídìng zài kètángli yánjiu. Yǒushí yào dào
yǒu gōngchéng de dìfang qu yánjiu.

15.3. Běi-Dà yuánláide míngzi bú shi dàxué, shi dàxuétáng.

15.4. Nèige xīn jiǎngtáng néng róng duōshao xuésheng?

15.5. Wǒ dào kètáng qu tīng Zhāng Jiàoshòu jiǎng Kǒngzǐde xuéshuō.

16.0. qūshì   trend, tendency   (W)   [hasten tendency]

16.1. Xiànzài mínzhǔ guójiā yuè lái yuè duō. Shídàide qūshì bìděi mínzhǔ
le.   (T)

17.0. zēngjiā   increase   [increase add]

17.1. Jīnnian dàxuéde xuéfèi zēngjiā hěn duō. Xuéfèi yì duōle, jiu yào
yǒu hěn duō xuésheng méi fázi niàn dàxué le.   (T)

18.0. xuékē   course (of study)

18.1. Xiànzài dàxuéde xuékē tài duō. Měi yíge xuésheng dōu gǎndào niàn
shū de shíjiān bú gòu yòng.   (T)

Bái: Mǎ Jiàoshòu, sīshúli yě zàojiù bù shǎode réncái.

50   Mǎ : Shìde. Zhōngguo rén cóngqián qiúxué zhǐ yǒu zài sīshúli.

Bái: Cóngqián hěn zhùzhòng xiě zì, shì bu shi?

Mǎ: Cóngqián yīnwei kējǔde guānxi dōu hěn zhùzhòng xiě zì. Nèige shídài fánshi cānjiā kǎoshì de búdàn wénzhāng děi zuòde hǎo, zì yě yào xiěde hǎo.

55 Bái: Jùshuō xiànzài Zhōngguo rén bù zěnmo zhùzhòng xiě zì le.

Mǎ: Cóng qǔxiāole kējǔ bàn xuétáng yǐlái, shídàide qūshì bìděi zhùzhòng kēxué. Xuéxiàoli zēngjiāle kēxué kèchéng. Xuékē yǐ duō le, xuésheng jiu méi yǒu shíjiān liànxí xiě zì le.

19.0. shēn*   body

        běnshēn   (1) one's own body; (2) (one's) self   [root body]

        qǐshēn   start out, start on a journey   [use body]

        shēn-xīn   body and mind   (W)

19.1. Nèige dàxué běnshēn méi yǒu qián. Tāmende qián dōu shi cóng gè fāngmiàn juānlai de.

19.2. Tā yīnwei yào shàng xué de guānxi, suǒyǐ měitiān zǎoshang bìděi qīdiǎn zhōng qǐshēn.

19.3. Tā xiě xìn gěi ta péngyou, shuō ta zìcóng dào zhèr yǐlái, shēn-xīn dōu bǐ zài jiāli hǎo.

20.0. tǐ*   body

        shēntǐ   body

        dàtǐ   in general, in the main   [large body]

        quántǐ   whole (body)   (W)

        jiǎntǐzì   simplified characters

20.1. Yǒu rén shuō niàn shū rén de shēntǐ méi yǒu nóngrende shēntǐ hǎo.

20.2. Dàtǐshang shuō nèige xuéxiào bànde bú cuò.   (T)

20.3. Xiàozhǎng zài bàngōngshìli duì quántǐ zhíyuán jiǎnghuà ne.

20.4. Wǒmen wénxué xìde xì zhǔrèn zuì bu xǐhuan jiǎntǐzì.

21.0. tuán*   group, organization, organized body

        tuántǐ   group, organization, organized body

        tuányuán   member of a group

21.1. Tā shi qīngnián tuánde tuányuán. Tā shuō tāmen tuántǐlide rén dōu shi yōuxiù qīngnián.

22.0. huá   stroke (of a Chinese character)   (M)

        bǐhuá   stroke   (N)   [pen stroke]

22.1. Qǐng wèn, jìnlìde jìn zì shi duōshao huá? . . . Zhèige jìn zìde bǐhuá shi shísìhuá.   (T)

LIBRARY
LUTHERAN SCHOOL OF THEOLOGY

23.0. shěng   save, economize

23.1. Wèile shěng shíjiān, wǒmen jiǎndān yìdiǎr chī.   (T)

23.2. Wèile shěng shíjiān wǒmen jiù yào ge chǎo dòufu hǎo bu hǎo?

Bái: Mǎ Jiàoshòu, jiǎntǐzìde tǐ, quántǐde tǐ dōu shi yíge tǐ zì ma?

60 Mǎ: Shì. Shēntǐ, tuánti yě shi nèige tǐ.

Bái: Nín duì jiǎntǐzì de kànfǎ zěnmoyàng?

Mǎ: Wǒ rènwei jiǎntǐzì yǒu chángchu yě yǒu duǎnchu. Jiǎntǐzìde chángchu shi bǐhuá shǎo róngyi xiě, érqiě shěng shíjiān.

Bái: Zài xuéxishang yě bǐjiǎo róngyi jì.

65 Mǎ: Duìle. "Wǒde shū ràng tā gěi ná zǒu le" nèige ràng zì yígòng shi
èrshisìhuà. Yàoshi xiě jiǎntǐzì cái wǔhuá.

24.0. shìjiè   world   [world realm]

24.1. Tā shi yíwèi jīngjixué zhuānjiā. Tā duì shìjiè gè guóde jīngji qíngxing fēicháng liǎojiě, yóuqishi duì dōngfāng guójiāde jīngji qíngxing.

24.2. Shìjièshang nǎr yǒu yídìng píng'ānde dìfang?   (T)

25.0. fāzhǎn   (1) develop, expand; (2) development, expansion   [emit un-
           fold]

25.1. Tāde bóshi lùnwén shi Fāzhǎn Nóngyè Bànfǎ.

25.2. Yíwèi wùlǐxuéjiā shuō, xīwang Zhōngguo néng zài zuì duǎnde qījiān
zài kēxué yìfāngmiàn néng yǒu hěn dàde fāzhǎn.   (T)

26.0. zhī (W)   (see note 1)

26.1. Nǐ bǎ xīnshi gàosu wǒ. Wǒmen liǎngge rén zhījiān nǎr yǒu bù néng
shuō de huà ne?   (T)

26.2. Wàiguo liúxuéshēng tīngle xiàozhǎng jiǎnghuà yǐhòu, yǒude shuō
wánquán tīngdedǒng, yǒude shuō néng tīngdǒng bǎifēnzhī bāshí. (T)

26.3. Qǐng nǐ dào Zhāng bóshi jiāli gěi wǒ qǔ nèiběn Zhōngguozhī Zhèngzhi Zhìdu.

26.4. Běi-Dà shi Zhōngguo zuì hǎode dàxuézhī yī.   (T)

27.0. -huà   -ize, -fy

      jiǎnhuà   simplify, reduce

      jiǎnhuà Hànzi   simplified Chinese characters

27.1. Nèige guójiā jìnbùde fēicháng kuài. Búdào sānniánde gōngfu tāmende
nónggōngyè dōu jìndàihuà le.   (T)

27.2. Kǎoqǔ liúxuéshēng de bànfǎ tài fèishì le. Kǎoqǔ de bànfǎ yīngdāng
jiǎnhuà. (T)

27.3. Jùshuō yào bǎ Hànzì jiǎnhuà dào sānqiān zuǒyòu.   (T)

28.0. jīběn   (1) foundation; (2) fundamental   [foundation root]

28.1. Xiǎoxué jiàoyu shi jīběn jiàoyu, suǒyǐ shìjiè gè guó dōu zhùzhòng
      xiǎoxué jiàoyu.

Bái: Jiǎntǐzìde duǎnchu shi shénmo?

Mǎ : Jiǎntǐzìde duǎnchu shi yǐhòu duìyu gǔshūshangde Hànzì dàjiā bú
       rènshi le. Hànzì zài wénhuà fāzhǎnshang suírán shi wǎng jiǎnhuàde
70   lùshang zǒu, dànshi yuánláide Hànzì shi Zhōngguo wénhuàde jīběn,
       yě bù néng bú yòng.

Bái: Nǐnde yìsi shi bù xǐhuan Hànzì jiǎnhuà?

Mǎ : Bú shi. Wǒde yìsi shi shuō, Zhōngguo shi shìjiè wénmíng gǔguózhī
       yī, yuánláide Hànzì běnshēn yǐjing yòngle jǐqiānnián le, suǒyǐ wǒde
75   yìsi shi bù néng zhǐ yòng jiǎntǐzì, bú yòng yuánláide Hànzì le.

Bái: Xiànzài wàiguo rén xué Zhōngwén gèng nán le. Zhèi liǎngzhǒng zì
       dōu yào xué.

29.0. pǔbiàn   general, prevailing, widespread   [universal throughout]

      pǔjí   (make) widespread, (make) universal   [universal attain]

29.1. Zhèizhǒng bìng hěn pǔbiàn. Zhèi yídàide xiǎoháizi chàbuduō dōu
      bìng le. (T)

29.2. Pǔjí jiàoyu zhèizhǒng gōngzuò shi fēicháng kùnnánde.   (T)

30.0. qī*   period

      chángqī   long period

      duǎnqī   short period

30.1. Nǐ zhèicì dào Měiguo shì bu shi chángqī zhùzai nèr? . . . Bù, wǒ
      zhèicì qù shi yíge duǎnqīde lǚxíng.

31.0. tuīxíng   carry out, promote   [push walk]

31.1. Tīngshuō zài nèr tuīxíng jiàoyu de bànfa, fánshi sìsuìde háizi yídìng
      děi dào xuéxiào qu. . . Bú huìde ba. Nǎr yǒu sìsuìde háizi néng
      shàngxué de?

31.2. Pǔjí jiàoyu zài zhèli tuīxíng dàoshi tuīxíngle, kěshi méi shénmo
      chéngji.   (T)

32.0. yìbān(de)   (1) general, in general; (2) average   [one sort]

      yìbān rén   people in general, the average person

      yìbānde shuō   generally speaking

32.1. Kàn yìbānde qíngxing, nèige guójiāde nónggōngyè zài wǔnián lǐtou
      yǒu hěn dàde fāzhǎn.   (T)

32.2. Gēnju yìbān rénde kànfǎ, tā nèige zhèngzhi xuéshuō rénmín bú huì
       huānyíng de.   (T)

32.3. Yìbānde shuō xiànzài Zhōngguode kēxué hái bù néng hé Xīfāng guójiā
       bǐ.

33.0. shòu   receive, suffer, endure

33.1. Dì-yīqíde Měiguo liúxuéshēng huídào Zhōngguo yǐhòu shi bú shòu
       huānyíng de.   (T)

Mǎ : Zhōngguode jiàoyu hái bù pǔbiàn.   Jiǎnhuà Hànzì duìyu pǔjí jiàoyu
       hěn yǒu guānxi.

80 Bái: Wǒ xiǎng búlùn něige guójiā, pǔjí jiàoyu zhèige gōngzuò bú shi
         duǎnqī nénggou dádào de.

    Mǎ : Shìde. Zhōngguo zhèngfǔ xiǎngchu gèzhǒng bànfa jìnlì tuīxíng, kěshi
         hái méi dádào yìbān rénmín dōu néng shòu jiàoyu de mùdì.

    Bái: Búdàn shi Zhōngguo, shìjièshang biéde guójiā yě shi yíyàng. Rénrén
85   néng shòu jiàoyu nà děi yào yíge chángqīde shíjiān.

    Mǎ : Kěshi Xīfāng guójiā hěn zǎo jiu zhùzhòng pǔjí jiàoyu. Zhōngguo
         cóng jìn jǐshí nián cái zhùyi zhèige wèntí. Xiànzài shìjièshang suǒ-
         yǒude guójiā dōu hěn zhùzhòng pǔjí jiàoyu, xīwang méi yǒu yíge rén
         bú shòu jiàoyu de.

34.0. mùbiāo   objective, target   [target sign]

34.1. Tāmende mùbiāo xīwang zài wǔnián lǐtou shèlì wǔge dàxué.   (T)

35.0. xū   require, need (to)

       xūyào   need   (N/V)   [require want]

35.1. Cóng zhèr zuò chuán dào Měiguo qu xū duōshao rìzi?

35.2. Zhèi yídàide háizi hěn duō. Shífēn xūyào zēngjiā jǐsuǒ xiǎo xuéxiào.
       (T)

36.0. luò*   fall

       luòxialai   drop down, land

       luòhòu   fall behind

36.1. Nǐ kàn, nèige fēijī luòzai hǎili le!   (T)

36.2. Yīnwei tiānqi bu hǎo, nèige fēijī zhǎobudào mùbiāo le. Zài tiān-
       shang fēile bàntiān yě méi luòxialai.

36.3. Wǒ cái dào fēijīchǎng fēijī jiu luòxialai le.

36.4. Nèige guójiā shi yíge jīngji luòhòude guójiā.

37.0. shǐ   cause to   (W)

37.1. Zhèige bànfǎ shi shǐ měi yíge rén dōu yǒu jīběn chángshí. (W) (T)

38.0. zǒng'eryánzhi   to sum up, to put it briefly   [sum and say it]

zǒngzhi   to sum up   (W)   [sum it]

38.1. Zǒng'eryánzhi hé zǒngzhi shì bu shi yíyàngde yìsi?

90   Bái: Yào dádào rénrén yǒu jīhui shòu jiàoyu de mùbiāo, wǒ xiǎng zuì
           xūyàode jiu shi yào pǔbiàn shèlì xuéxiào.

     Mǎ : Pǔbiàn shèlì xuéxiào dāngrán shi pǔjí jiàoyu de dì-yībù. Ná Zhōng-
           guo lái shuō, yíge jīngji luòhòude guójiā, shuōqǐlai róngyi, shìshí-
           shang bú shi hěn duǎnde shíjiān nénggou bàndào de.

95   Bái: Zhè dàoshi shízàide qíngxing.

     Mǎ : Zǒng'eryánzhi qīwànwàn rénkǒu de yíge guójiā yàoshi shǐ rénrén
           néng shòu jiàoyu bú shi duǎn shíjiān bàndedào de.

39.0. shēn   deep, profound

gāoshēn   lofty and deep

39.1. Nèitiáo héde shuǐ hěn shēn. Lián dà chuán dōu néng zǒu.

39.2. Wǒmen kàn shū yào shēnshēnde liǎojiě shūde nèiróng. (T)

39.3. Tā suírán méi yǒu shénmo gāoshēnde xuéwen, kěshi tā duì jiàoxué
      yìfāngmiàn shi yǒu xiāngdāngde jīngyan.

40.0. mò   last, end

mònián   last years

40.1. Qǐng nǐ kàn Zhōngguo Dàshì Niánbiǎo shang Míng mò dōu yǒu
      shénmo dàshì? (T)

40.2. Nèiběn xiǎoshuō shi Yuán Cháo mònián yíwèi wénxuéjiā xiě de.

41.0. jiànjiàn(de)   gradually   (MA)

41.1. Yíge luòhòude guójiā búshàng shíniánde gōngfu néng jiànjiànde fāzhǎn
      dào zhèige yàngzi.   (T)

41.2. Xiànzài cóng xiǎoxué dào dàxué, gèjí xuéxiàode chéngdu dōu jiàn-
      jiànde tígāo le.   (T)

42.0. jiù   old (of things)

42.1. Jiù wénxué shi wényánwén, xīn wénxué shi báihuàwén.

43.0. xiāngtóng   (very) similar, almost identical   [mutually like]

43.1. Sīshúde jiàoyu hé xuéxiàode jiàoyu dà bu xiāngtóng.

     Bái: Tándao jiàoyu wèntí, tīngshuō Zhōngguo cóngqián shi nánren shòu
           jiàoyu, nǚren duōshù shi bú shòu jiàoyu.

100 Mǎ : Shì. Nánde kéyi shòu gāoshēnde jiàoyu. Nǔren hěn shǎo tóngyàngde
shòu jiàoyu. Nǔren yǒu bǎifēnzhī jiǔshijiǔ lián yíge zì yě bú rènshi. Zài Qīng Cháo mònián, kējǔ qǔxiāole yǐhòu, jiànjiànde nǔren
yě hé nánren tóngyàngde shòu jiàoyu le.

Bái : Shénmo dàoli cóngqiánde nǔrén bú shòu jiàoyu?

105 Mǎ : Nà shi nánnǔ bù píngděngde yuángu. Yìbān rénde kànfa, nǔren yīnggāi zài jiāli, bú bì yǒu xuéwen.

Bái : Nǔren suírán bù chūqu zuò shì, yě yīnggāi yǒu yìdiǎr xuéwen.

Mǎ : Yìzhí dào xiànzài, zài jiù jiātínglide sīxiǎngshang hái rènwei nǔren
niàn shū shi bú bìyào de.

110 Bái : Shìshíshang xiànzài nánnǔ dōu shòu xiāngtóngde jiàoyu le.

Mǎ : Shì. Xiànzài Zhōngguode jiàoyu shi bù fēn nánnǔ le.

44.0. míngchēng   appellation, designation   [name term]

44.1. Nèige dōngxi suírán yǒu liǎngge míngchēng, kěshi shìshíshang shi
yíge dōngxi.

45.0. yǎnbiàn   (1) develop, unfold; (2) development, unfolding   [perform
change]

45.1. Yīnwei shídàide yǎnbiàn, Zhōngguode jiātíng yě shi xiǎo jiātíng
zhìdu le.

46.0. liú   to flow

cháoliú   current, flow, tide   [tide flow]

héliú   stream, current   [river flow]

46.1. Nèitiáo hélide shuǐ dōu liúdào nèige dà hú lǐtou.

46.2. Yīnwei shídàide cháoliú wǒmen bùdébù yánjiu yuánzǐnéng.   (T)

46.3. Zhōngguo yǒu sāntiáo dà héliú.

47.0. yǐngxiǎng   influence   [shadow resound]

47.1. Yīnwei dàshuǐde guānxi, nóngren duōbàn bù néng zhòng tián.   Jīnniánde nóngyè hěn shòu yǐngxiǎng.

48.0. guòdù   (1) transition; (2) transitional   [pass ferry]

48.1. Nà shi yíge cóng jiù shèhuì yǎnbiàndao xīn shèhuìde yíge guòdù shíqī.

Bái : Mǎ Jiàoshòu, xuétáng gēn xuéxiào zhèi liǎngge míngchēng yǒu
shénmo fēnbié?

Mǎ : Xiànzàide xuéxiào jiu shi cóng cóngqiánde xuétáng yǎnbiàn de. Zài
115   Qīng mò shòule shídài cháoliúde yǐngxiǎng, cóng sīshú yǎnbiàndao
xuéxiào. Zài nèige guòdù shíqī jiào xuétáng, bú jiào xuéxiào.

Bái : Tīngshuō nèige shíhou cái yǒu rén dào gèguó qu liúxué.

Mǎ : Shìde. Wǒ fùqin jiùshi nèige shíhou kǎoqǔ dào Měiguo liúxué. Tā
shi dì-yīqīde liú Měi xuésheng.

49.0. xiūyè   study (at a school)   (W)   [cultivate enterprise]

49.1. Zāi Qīng Cháo mònián de shíhou Mǎ Yǒuwén Xiānsheng jiu zài Běi-Dà xiūyè.

50.0. yòuzhi   young, immature   [young infantile]

       yòuzhiyuán   kindergarten

50.1. Nǐ xiǎngde tài yòuzhi le.   (T)

50.2. Nà shi yíge sīrén bàn de yòuzhiyuán.

51.0. dàtóngxiǎoyì   much alike, not very different   [big same small different]

51.1. Zhèli suǒyǒu zhōngxuéde kècheng dōu shi dàtóngxiǎoyì.

52.0. shǔ*   belong, pertain to

       shǔyu   belong, pertain to

52.1. Zhèige nóngyè hézuòshè shi shǔyu wǒmen Yuǎn-Dà nóngxuéyuàn de ma?

120 Bái: Mǎ Jiàoshòu, <u>xiūyè</u> zhèige cér zài shénmo shíhou cháng yòng?

Mǎ : <u>Xiūyè</u> zhèige cér shi wényánde. Shi zài yǎnjiǎng hé xiě wénzhāng de shíhou yòng de. Shuō huà de shíhou dōu shi shuō "Zài xuéxiào shòu jiàoyu," bù shuō "Zài xuéxiào xiūyè."

Bái: Zhōngguo xiǎo xuésheng kāishǐ shòu jiàoyu, yòuzhiyuán gēn xiǎoxué
125   yígòng jǐnián?

Mǎ : Yòuzhiyuán èrnián, chūxiǎo、 gāoxiǎo yígòng liùnián. Měiguo ne?

Bái: Měiguo xiǎoxué zhìdu hé Zhōngguode zhìdu shi dàtóngxiǎoyì.

Mǎ : Yìbānde shuō wǒ xiǎng xiàndàide jiàoyu zhìdu dàtǐshang dōu chàbuduō.

130 Bái: Zhōngguode yòuzhiyuán dōu shi gēn xiǎoxué zài yíkuàr, shǔyu xiǎoxué yíbùfen ma?

Mǎ : Bù yídìng. Yǒude yòuzhiyuán dān shi yòuzhiyuán, bù yídìng gēn xiǎoxué zài yíkuàr.

Bái: Yòuzhiyuánde xuéfèi guì bu guì?

135 Mǎ : Guānlìde bú guì, sīlìde bǐjiǎo guì yìdiǎr.

53.0. fāngshi   method   [method style]

53.1. Nèige dàxué duì wàiguo liúxuéshēngde jiàoxuéfǎ tāmen shi cǎiyòng něizhǒng fāngshi?

54.0. gǎn   (1) hurry; (2) be in a hurry to finish

       gǎnshang   overtake, catch (up with)   [hurry on]

       gǎnkuài   quickly   [hurry fast]

54.1. Wǒmen zhèibĕn shū néng bu néng zài báyue niànwán? . . . Wǒmen
       gǎnyigǎn, yídìng kéyi niànwán.

54.2. Wǒmen xiànzài mángde hĕn.   Wǒmen gǎn gāojí kèbĕn ne.

54.3. Wǒmen shi gōngyè luòhòude guójiā. Wǒmen bìdĕi nǔlì cái nénggou
       gǎnshang wàiguo.

54.4. Sānniánde gōngfu gōngyè zĕnmo néng gǎnshang Xīfāng guójiā ne?

54.5. Qǐng ni gǎnkuài bǎ nèibĕn Jiǎnhuà Hànzi Kèbĕn gĕi Zhāng Xiānsheng.

54.6. Kuài diǎr zŏu ba.   Yàoburán gǎnbushàng huŏchē le.   (T)

55.0. chōngshí   make abundant, make full   [full solid]

55.1. Wǒde xuéwen bú gòu.   Wǒ bìdĕi duō kàn shū chōngshí zìjǐ.   (T)

56.0. xuǎn   select, choose, vote for

       xuǎnjǔ   select, choose by election   [select lift]

       xuǎnshang   be elected   [elect on]

       xuǎnbá   select   [select pull]

56.1. Yìbānde xuǎnjǔ dōu shi zài dàhuìshang tíchu jǐge rén lai, zài cóng
       zhèi jǐge rénli lái xuǎnbá.   (T)

56.2. Tā bú huì xuǎnshangde, yīnwei dà duōshù rén dōu bu huānyíng ta.
       (T)

57.0. xiàng(zhe)   toward

       xiànglái   hitherto   [toward come]

       fāngxiàng   direction   [place toward]

57.1. Tā bǎ wǒde shū jièqule hǎojǐge yuè le.   Wǒ xiàng ta yàole hǎojǐcì
       tā yĕ bù gĕi wo.   (T)

57.2. Tā zuòqi shì lai xiànglái dōu shi hĕn màilì de.

57.3. Qǐng wèn, dào Yuǎndōng Dàxué yīxuéyuàn qu zhèige fāngxiàng duì
       bu duì?

Mǎ : Wǒ xiànzài yǒu ge wèntí wèn ni. Nǐ juéde xiànzài wǒmende jiāoxué
      fāngshi zĕnmoyàng?

Bái: Wǒ rènwei zhè shi zuì hǎode jiāoxuéfǎ.   Wǒ xiǎng yìbān tóngxué
      dōu xǐhuan zhèige jiāoxuéfǎ.

140 Mǎ : Xuéxiàoli yĕ rènwei zhèizhŏng fāngfǎ hĕn hǎo.

Bái: Wǒ xiāngxìn duì wǒ de bāngzhu hĕn dà.   Jìn jǐnián lai wǒ juéde
      jìnbùde fēicháng màn.   Wǒ yīnggāi gǎnkuàide xiǎng fázi chōngshí
      zìjǐ.

Mǎ : Nǐ yuánláide chéngdu wǒ bù zhīdào, kĕshi wǒ juéde nǐde Zhōngwén
145   xiāngdāng hǎo.

Bái: Nín kèqi. Nín yǒu gōngfude shíhou hái děi qǐng nín gěi wǒ xuǎn jǐběn shū. Wǒ zhèicì méi dào Zhōngguo lái yǐqián, wǒ jiu xiǎng zhèicì dào Zhōngguo dì-yī yào duō mǎi shū.

Mǎ: Hǎo. Wǒ míngtian xiě jǐběn shū míngzi gěi ni. Zài Měiguo mǎi
150   Zhōngwén shū róngyi bu róngyi?

Bái: Zài Měiguo mǎi Zhōngwén shū xiànglái bú dà róngyi. Yīnwei xūyàode shǎo, suǒyǐ shūdiànde Zhōngwén shū bù duō.

58.0. zìrán'érrán(de)   natural(ly), spontaneous(ly), of course

58.1. Nǐ měitiān tīng lùyīn zìjǐ liànxi fāyīn, rìzi jiǔle zìrán'érrán Zhōngguo huà jiu huì jìnbù de.   (T)

59.0. Táng   (1) T'ang period (618–906); (2) (a surname)

59.1. Míng huàjiā Zhāng Dàqiān suǒ huà de měinǔ dōu shi Táng dàide.

59.2. Zuótian Táng Xuélǐ cóng guónèi gěi wo lái xìn shuō: "Qǐng nǐ dài wǒ mǎi gāozhōng wùlǐxué hé jīnqjixué、 shèhuìxué děng shū. Jiàqián duōshao qǐng lái xìn."   (T)

60.0. guòchéng   stage, process   [pass journey]

60.1. Nǐ zhīdao cóng wényánwén yǎnbiàndao báihuàwén de guòchéng ma?

61.0. hǎoxiàng . . . shide   resemble, seem to (see below, Yǔfǎ Liànxi 16–
                              20)

61.1. Kàn tāde yàngzi hǎoxiàng bú dà gāoxìng shide.

62.0. Xiānggǎng   Hong Kong   [fragrant harbor]

62.1. Xiānggǎng shi yíge dà hǎikǎo. Měi yíge guójiāde chuán dōu kéyi dào nèr qù.

63.0. Táiwān   Taiwan, Formosa   [terrace bay]

63.1. Jùshuō Táiwānde rénkǒu zài yī-jiǔ-wǔ-sān nián yǐjing yǒu qībǎi wǔshiwàn rén le.

Bái: Mǎ Jiàoshòu, jīntian wǎnshang qīdiǎn zhōng yǒu ge xuéshù yǎnjiǎng. Wǒ xiǎng qu tīngting.

155 Mǎ: Duì. Nǐ yīnggāi qu tīng. Duō tīng zìrán'érrán huì jìnbù de. Shi shénmo tímu? Shi shéi zhǔjiǎng?

Bái: Shi yíwèi cái cóng Xiānggǎng lái de Máo Hǎitiān Xiānsheng. Jiǎngtí shi "Hàn Táng Wénhuà Jìnbùde Guòchéng."

Mǎ: Máo Hǎitiān zhèige rén hǎoxiang wǒ rènshi shide. Wǒ xiǎngqilai
160   le. Wǒ zài bàozhǐshang kànjianguo tāde míngzi. Tā yǐqián zài Táiwān Dàxué dāng jiàoshòu. Hái yǒu wèntí ma?

Bái: Méi shénmo wèntí. Oh, Mǎ Jiàoshòu, péngyou cóng Xiānggǎng gěi wǒ mǎile liǎngběn shū. Wǒ míngtian nálai nín kànkan.

Mǎ : Shénmo shū?

165 Bái: Yîběn <u>Hànyǔ Yǔfǎ</u>, yîběn shi Xiānggǎng Dàxué chūbǎn de <u>Zhōngguo
Wénhuà Jiǎnghuà</u>.

Mǎ : <u>Hànyǔ Yǔfǎ</u> wǒ yǒu. Nǐ jiù bǎ <u>Zhōngguo Wénhuà Jiǎnghuà</u> nálai wǒ
kànkan déle.

Bái: Hǎode. Míngtian jiàn, Mǎ Jiàoshòu.

170 Mǎ : Míngtian jiàn.

SHĒNGCÍ BIǍO

1. jīng
   <u>Wǔ Jīng</u>
   <u>Sān Zì Jīng</u>

2. bù
   yíbùyíbù(de)
   jìnbù

3. sī*
   sīren
   sīshú

4. lì*
   sīlì
   gōnglì
   guólì
   shěnglì

5. shè*
   shèlì

6. chéngdu

7. Qīng

8. kējǔ (W)

9. guān
   guānlì

10. niánxiàn

11. guīdìng

12. zhāng
    wénzhāng

13. zàojiù

14. qǔxiāo

15. táng
    kètáng
    xuétáng
    jiǎngtáng

16. qūshǐ (W)

17. zēngjiā

18. xuékē

19. shēn*
    běnshēn
    qǐshēn
    shēn-xīn (W)

20. tǐ*
    shēntǐ
    dàtǐ
    quántǐ (W)
    jiǎntǐzî

21. tuán*
    tuántǐ
    tuányuán

22. huá
    bǐhuá

23. shěng

24. shìjiè

25. fāzhǎn

26. zhī (W)

27. -huà
    jiǎnhuà
    jiǎnhuà Hànzî

28. jīběn

29. pǔbiàn
    pǔjí

30. qī*
    chángqī
    duǎnqī

31. tuīxíng

32. yìbān(de)
    yìbān rén
    yìbānde shuō

33. shòu

34. mùbiāo

35. xū
    xūyào

36. luò*
    luòxialai
    luòhòu

37. shǐ (W)

38. zǒng'eryánzhi
    zǒngzhi (W)

39. shēn
    gāoshēn

40. mò
    mònián

41. jiànjiàn(de)

42. jiù

43. xiāngtóng

44. míngchēng

45. yǎnbiàn

46. liú
    cháoliú
    héliú

47. yǐngxiǎng

48. guòdù

49. xiūyè (W)

50. yòuzhi   55. chōngshí   58. zìrán'érrán(de)
    yòuzhiyuán
                      56. xuǎn
51. dàtóngxiǎoyì   xuǎnjǔ   59. Táng
                         xuǎnshang
52. shǔ*   xuǎnbá   60. guòchéng
    shǔyu
                                            61. hǎoxiàng...shide
53. fāngshi   57. xiàng(zhe)
54. gǎn   xiànglái   62. Xiānggǎng
    gǎnshang
    gǎnkuài   fāngxiang   63. Táiwān

YǓFǍ LIÀNXÍ

A. Uses of zhī (see note 1)

1. Nèiběn Hànyǔ Jiàokēshūshangde jiǎntǐzì wǒ niàn shi niànwán le, kěshi wǒ jìzhu de hái bú dào wǔfēnzhī yī ne.

2. Zhèrde guānlì zhōngxué dōu hěn zhùzhòng kēxué. Tāmende xuékē shífēnzhī bā shi kēxué kècheng. Érqiě kècheng dōu hěn shēn.

3. Fēijī luòxialai zhīhòu Mǎ Dàwén tóng Zhāng Yìshān jiu líkai fēijīchǎng le.

4. Zài méi yǒu xuéxiào zhīqián xiǎoxuésheng dōu shi zài sīshú niàn Sān Zi Jīng, Qiān Zì Wén děng shū.

5. Zǒngzhi jiùshi zǒng'eryánzhi jiǎndānde shuōfǎ.

B. Use of zuò and wéi as postverbs (see note 2)

6. Nèige gōnglì xuéxiàode xuésheng fēnwéi liǎngbùfen. Shàng kè yǒude shàngwǔ shàng kè, yǒude xiàwǔ shàng kè.

7. Kǎoshìde shíhou xiānsheng ràng wǒmen xiě kètáng liǎngge zì. Wǒ bǎ táng zì xiěwéi chéng le. Kètáng xiěchéng kèchéng le.

8. Wǒ bǎ sìshēng kàncuòle. Wǒ bǎ yībān niànwéi yíbàn le.

9. Quán shìjièshangde guójiā dōu bǎ nèige guójiā kànzuo shi yíge bù néng jìnbù de guójiā le.

10. Qǐng nǐ bǎ nèi xiēge cér fēnzuò sìzǔ.

C. The pattern ná... lái shuō (see note 3)

11. Ná shēntǐ lái shuō ba, nǐde shēntǐ bǐ wǒ hǎode duō.

12. Nǐ yàoshi hái méi míngbai, wǒ zài yòng yíge lìzi lái gěi ni jiěshi jiěshi.

13. Jīntiande dìlǐ shi jiǎng dà shān gēn héliú. Wǒ xiān cóng héliú lái shuōqǐ.

14. Ná xiě zì lái kàn nǐ jiu bǐ wǒ hǎode duō.

15. Gēnju Jiàoyu Bùde jìlù lái shuō, xuésheng zēngjiāle bǎifēnzhī èrshiwǔ.

D. Use of <u>hǎoxiang</u> . . . <u>shide</u> and <u>hǎoxiang (shi)</u> . . . de yàngzi (see <u>Inter-</u>
<u>mediate Chinese</u>, page 26, note 7)

16. Táng Xiānsheng shuō tā hái yǒu sānge yuè cái dào Zhōngguo qu, kěshi
kàn tāde yàngzi hǎoxiang mǎshàng jiu yào qǐshēn shide.

17. Wǒ jiào tā wǎng nán zǒu, kěshi tā xiàngzhe xīběide fāngxiàng zǒu le.
Tā hǎoxiang méi tīngmíngbai wǒde huà shide.

18. Tāde shēntǐ suírán hěn hǎo, kěshi zuòqǐ shǐ lai hǎoxiang lián yìdiǎr lìqi
yě méi yǒu shide.

19. Nèige tuántǐde quántǐ tuányuán xuǎnjǔ dàibiǎo. Jiéguǒ Zhāng Xiānsheng
xuǎnshang le, kěshi wǒ kàn tā hǎoxiang shi hěn bu gāoxìng dāng dàibiǎo
de yàngzi.

20. Gāo Dàwén zài zhèr zhùle hǎojiǔ le yě méi zǒu. Hǎoxiang shi yào
chángqī zhùzai zhèlǐ de yàngzi.

JIǍNGHUÀ

Shuōdào Zhōngguode jiàoyu, zuìhǎo shi cóng jìn bǎinián lái shuōqǐ,
yīnwei jìn bǎinián lái Zhōngguode jiàoyu yǒu hěn dàde yǎnbiàn. Yǎnbiàn
de yuányīn, yìfāngmiàn shi shòule Xīfāng wénhuàde yǐngxiǎng, yìfāngmiàn
shi shídài cháoliúde qūshǐ, suǒyǐ jiu zìrán'érránde yíbùyíbùde yǎnbiàn.

5 Yǎnbiànde guòchéng kéyi fēnwéi sānge shíqī. Dì-yīqī shi sīshú shíqī, yě
jiu shi jiù jiàoyu shíqī. Dì-èr shi xuétáng shíqī, yě kéyi jiàozuò guòdù
shíqī. Dì-sān shi xuéxiào shíqī, jiu shi xiàndài zhèige shíqī. Xiànzài bǎ
zhèi sānge shíqī fēnbié shuōmíng.

Dì-yī, sīshú shíqī. Zhèige shíqī yě kěyi shuō shi jiù jiàoyu shíqī.

10 Sīshú běnlái shi Zhōngguo cóng gǔshí jiù yǒu de. Zhèlǐ suǒ shuō de sīshú
shíqī jiushi Qīng Cháo mònián jǐshíniánjiān. Dāngshí zhèng shi kējǔ shídài.
Kējǔ shi yìzhǒng kǎoshì zhìdu, yòng ta lái xuǎnbá réncái. Cóng Táng
Cháo yǐlái dào Qīng Cháo mònián dōu shi yòng kējǔ zhìdu. Zhèizhǒng
zhìdu zài kǎoshì de shíhou zhuān kǎo wénxué, suǒyǐ dāngshí niàn shū de

15 rén jiu zhuānmén niàn <u>Sì Shū Wǔ Jīng</u> děngděng wénxuéde shū hé liànxi
xiě wénzhāng. Niàn shū de dìfang jiàozuò sīshú. Sīshú dōu shi sīren
shèlì, bú shi zhèngfǔ shèlì de. Měi yíge sīshú yǒu yíge xiānsheng, yǒu
jǐge huòzhě shíjǐge xuésheng, dōu shi niàn <u>Sì Shū Wǔ Jīng</u> gèzhǒng wénxué.
Zài sīshú niàn shū méi yǒu yídìng niánxiàn, zhǐ yào rènwei zìjǐ kéyi

20 cānjiā kejǔde kǎoshì, jiu qù cānjiā kǎoshì. Kǎoqǔ zhīhòu jiu kéyi
zuò guān. Zhè shi sīshú shíqī jiù jiàoyu qíngxing.

Dì-èr, xuétáng shíqī.   Zhèige shíqī yě kéyi jiàozuò guòdù shíqī, yě
shi zài Qīng Cháo zuìhòude jǐnián.   Dāngshí Zhōngguo duìyu Xīfāng wénhuà
jiànjiànde yǒule rènshi, yě zhīdao kēxuéde zhòngyào le, yòu zhīdao kējǔ
25 zhìdu shi bù hé shídàide xūyào le, suǒyǐ zài yī-bā-jiǔ-bā nián shèlì xuétáng, zài yī-jiǔ-líng-wǔ nián qǔxiāo kējǔ.   Xuésheng zài xuétángli búdàn
yào xuéxi běnguó wénxué, yě yào xuéxi yìdiǎr Xīfāngde kēxué.   Zài gè
xiàn shè xiǎo xuétáng, zài gè shěng shè zhōng xuétáng, zài Běijīng shè
dà xuétáng, guīdìng xuésheng bìyè de niánxiàn.   Zhèixiē xuétáng duōbàn
30 shi zhèngfǔ shèlì, hé yǐqián sīshú jiàoyu dà bù xiāngtóng.   Zhè shi cóng
jiù jiàoyu zǒuxiàng xīn jiàoyude yíge guòdù shíqī.   Zài zhèige guòdù shíqī
de jiàoyu jiu shi xuétáng jiàoyù.

Dì-sān, xuéxiào shíqī.   Zhè shi xiàndài jiàoyude shíqī.   Zhèige shíqī
shi cóng yī-jiǔ-yī-èr nián Mínguó chénglì zhīhòu dào xiànzài.   Zhèige
35 qījiānde jiàoyu fāngshì wánquán shi yòng xuéxiào zhìdu.   Xiànzài bǎ gèjí
xuéxiàode míngchēng hé xiūyède niánxiàn shuōyishuō:

yòuzhiyuán	yìnián huò èrnián
xiǎoxué	liùnián
chūzhōng	sānnián
gāozhōng	sānnián
dàxué	sìnián
yánjiuyuàn	yìnián yǐshàng

Gèjí xuéxiào jiàoyude mùbiāo, zài yòuzhiyuán shíqī shi zhùyì shēn-
xīnde fāzhǎn, zài xiǎoxué shíqī shi xuéxi jīběn zhīshi, zài zhōngxué shíqī
45 shi chōngshí gèzhǒng xuéshi.   Dàxué jiàoyu shi zàojiù zhuānmén réncái,
yánjiuyuàn shi yánjiu gāoshēnde xuéshù.   Zìcóng xuéxiào jiàoyu tuīxíng
yǐlái, shòu jiàoyude rénshù bǐjiǎo yǐqián zēngjiā hěn duō.   Xuéshengde
chéngdu yě dōu xiāngdāngde hǎo.   Dàxuéde xuéshù shuǐpíng yě jiànjiànde
tígāo.   Zhōngguo jiàoyu zài zhèige shíqī shi jìnbù de.

50 Zǒng'eryánzhi, zài zhèi jìn yìbǎinián lái Zhōngguode jiàoyu shi cóng
jiùde jiàoyu zǒudàole xiàndàihuàde jiàoyu.   Gèjí xuéxiàode zhìdu hé Xīfāng
guójiā xuéxiào zhìdu shi dàtóngxiǎoyì.   Xiànzài Zhōngguo jiàoyu zhèng
xiàng liǎngge mùbiāo qiánjìn.   Yíge mùbiāo shi zhùzhòng kēxué.   Yīnwei
cóngqián zài kēxuéshang shi luòhòude, suǒyǐ yào tèbié zhùzhòng kēxué,
55 xīwang gǎnshang Xīfāng guójiā.

Hái yǒu yíge mùbiāo, shi xiǎng yào pǔjí jiàoyu. Yīnwei Zhōngguo rén néng shízì de rén búguò shífēnzhī èr-sān, suǒyǐ yào shǐ měi yíge guómín dōu yào shòuguo xiǎoxué jiàoyu. Kěshi Zhōngguo rénkǎo tài duō, duǎnqīli hái shi bù róngyi shíxiàn de.

FÙSHÙ

Zhèipán lùyīndài shi Zhōngwén dì-yīzǔ dì-èrhào, Bái Wénshān fùshù dì-èrcìde Zhuāntí Jiǎnghuà.

Dì-èrcì Zhuāntí Jiǎnghuàde jiǎngtí shi "Běnxiào Gàikuàng." Zhǔjiǎng-rén shi Yuǎn-Dà wàiguo liúxuéshēng fǔdǎo zhǔrèn Zhāng Yǒuzhēn Xiān-
5   sheng. Zài méi yǎnjiǎng yǐqián, fǔdǎo zhǔrèn Zhāng Xiānsheng jièshào tā zìjǐ. Tā shuō tāde gōngzuò shi bāngzhu wàiguo liúxuéshēng. Tā hái shuō wǒmen rúguǒ zài xuéxiào yùjiàn shénmo kùnnán, wǒmen kéyi suíshí qù kàn ta. Tā gàosu wǒmen tā bàn shì de dìfang shi zài Zǒng Bàngōng Lóu èr-liù-yī hào.

10   Guānyu běnxiào gǎikuàng, Zhāng zhǔrèn shuō gè xuéyuàn dōu yǒu shénmo xuéxì. Tā hái shuō míngnián Yuǎn-Dà yào chénglì yíge jiàoyu xuéyuàn. Yīxuéyuàn shi qùnian xīn chénglì de. Yuǎn-Dà chúle yīxuéyuàn yǐwài, yígòng yǒu wǔge xuéyuàn. Yǒu gōngxuéyuàn、lǐxuéyuàn、fǎxuéyuàn、wénxuéyuàn gēn nóngxuéyuàn. Gōngxuéyuàn hē nóngxuéyuàn méi yǒu
15   wàiguo liúxuéshēng. Zhǐ yóu sānge xuéyuàn yǒu wàiguo xuésheng. Nà jiù shi wénxuéyuàn、fǎxuéyuàn、lǐxuéyuàn. Lǐxuéyuànde wàiguo xuésheng zuì shǎo. Fǎxuéyuànde wàiguo xuésheng yě bù duō. Jiù shi wénxuéyuànde wàiguo xuésheng zuìduō

Zhāng zhǔrèn yòu shuōdào něi yíge xuéxì shǔyu něige xuéyuàn děng-
20   děng. Guāngyu xuéxiào yuàn-xìde zǔzhí zhèi yìdiǎn, yǒude hé Měiguo dàxué bùtóng. Bǐrú Yuǎn-Dà lǐxuéyuàn yǒu shùxuéxì、wùlǐxì、huàxuéxì、shēngwùxì、xīnlǐxì. Zài Měiguo xīnlǐxì bù shǔyu lǐxuéyuàn, shi shǔyú wénxuéyuàn de. Hái yǒu, zài Yuǎn-Dà fǎxuéyuàn, chúle fǎlǜxì yǐwài hái yǒu zhèngzhixì、shèhuìxì hé jīngjixì. Zài Měiguo zhèngzhi、shèhuì hé jīng-
25   jixì bú shi shǔyu fǎxuéyuàn de, shi shǔyu wénxuéyuàn de. Yuǎn-Dà wén-xuéyuànde xuéxì gēn Měiguo wénxuéyuànde xuéxì chàbuduō. Yuǎn-Dà dāngrán yǒu Zhōngwénxì, yě yǒu wàiwénxì、zhéxuéxì、lìshǐxì, hái yǒu xīn-wénxì hé yǔyánxuéxì.

Zhāng zhǔrèn bǎ yuàn-xì jiǎngwánle yǐhòu, yòu tídao xuézhì. Yìbānde
30 xuéxiào yǒu liǎngzhǒng xuézhì. Yǒu xuénián-zhì gēn xuéfēn-zhì liǎngzhǒng.
Xuénián-zhì shi yǒu niánxiàn de. Bǐrú niàn dàxué de xuésheng fánshi
niànmǎnle sìnián chéngji dōu jígé jiu kéyi bìyè, dédào xuéshi xuéwèi.
Xuéfēn-zhì méi yǒu niánxiàn, děi niànmǎn yìbǎi èrshige xuéfēn, yě yào
zuò bìyè lùnwén cái kéyi bìyè. Niàn shuòshi yǎo yǒu sānshige xuéfēn,
35 xiě shuòshi lùnwén, cái néng nádào shuòshi xuéwèi. Niàn bóshi ne, yào
niàn liùshige xuéfēn, xiě bóshi lùnwén. Dāngrán měimén gōngke yào jígé,
bùrán jiu děi chóngxiū.

Zuìhòu Zhāng zhǔrèn yòu shuōdào jiǎngxuéjīnde wèntí. Tā shuō Yuǎn-
Dàde jiǎngxuéjīn shi zhèyàng: Fánshi chéngji yōuliángde xuésheng, fēnshù
40 píngjūn zài bāshifēn yǐshàng, dōu kéyi shēnqǐng jiǎngxuéjīn. Búlùn dàxué
huòshi yánjiuyuàn de xuésheng dōu kéyi shēnqǐng.

WĒNXI

1. Wǒmen xuéxiào chúle yǒu yíge dà jiǎngtáng yǐwài hái yǒu shíjǐge kètáng.

2. Xiànzài Zhōngguode xuéxiàoli xué shùxué dōu bú yòng suànpan le, kěshi
   zuò mǎimai de háishi duōshù yòng suànpan.

3. Xīnhuá Lóu búdàn cài hǎochī, érqiě tāmende pánzi yě xiāngdāng hǎokàn.

4. Zhōngguo cóng kāishǐ bàn xuétáng dào xiànzài yě búguò qīshinián zuǒyòu.

5. Zài shìjièshang hěn duō luòhòude guójiā xiànzài dōu kāishǐ zhùyì kēxué
   le. Kēxué yǐjing chéngle yìzhǒng hěn pǔtōngde xuéwen. Tāmen dōu
   xīwang zài duǎnqīli gǎnshang Xīfāng guójiā.

6. Wǒ jīntiān xiàng zhūwèi tányitán Zhōngguode rénkǒu wèntí.

7. Guólì, shěnglì, sīlì dàxuéde kèchéng yìbānde shuō dōu shi dàtóngxiǎoyì.

8. Nèige tuántǐ yòu kāihuì le. Wèile yào shěng shíjiān nǐ gàosu nèi jǐge
   tuányuán gǎnkuài zuò chē qù.

9. Wǒ juéde tā jìnlái hǎoxiang hěn yònggōng shide. Xiāngxìn tā zhèicì kǎoshìde chéngji yídìng bǐ yǐqián jìnbù.

10. Wǒmen liǎnge rén hé juāngěi Xiānggǎng Hóng Shí Zì Huì fēnhuì sānshikuài
    qián.

11. Gāngcái xuǎnjǔ xuéshenghuì huìzhǎng shi shéi xuǎnshang le?

12. Nèitiáo dàizi tài duǎn, wǒmen yīnggāi chóng mǎi yìtiáo.

13. Qǐng wèn Wàn Jiàoshòu, zǒngzhi, xiūyè gēn shēn-xīn zhei sānge cér shi
    xiě wénzhāng yòng de háishi shuō huà yòng de?

14. Zhōngguode jiàoyu xiànzài xiàngzhe xīnde fāngxiàng zǒu. Jìnlái yòu shèlìle
    hěn duō dà, zhōng, xiǎo xuéxiào hē yòuzhìyuán, xīwang zài zuìjìnde jiāng-
    lái xuéxiào jiàoyu dōu shi xiàndàihuàde.

15. Tā jīnnián yǐjing bāshiwǔsuì le, kěshi tā lǎorénjiāde shēntǐ fēicháng hǎo.
    Zǒuqi lù lai hé qīngniánrén yíyàng.

16. Wǒmen dào fēijīchǎng de shíhou fēijī yǐjing luòxialai bàntiān le.

17. Dàtǐshang shuō tāmende gōngzuò nénglì hěn búcuò le.

18. Tā zìjǐ běnshēn shi yǒumíngde wùlǐxuéjiā, suǒyǐ tā hěn xīwang tāde érzi
    xué kēxué. Tā shuō xiànzàide cháoliú shi tài xūyào kēxué le.

19. Zhōngguo kējǔ zhìdu shi zài Qīng mò de shíhou qǔxiāo de.

20. Yìbān rénde kànfǎ, nèige guójiā jǐnián lǐtou nénggou gǎnshang Xīfāng guó-
    jiā.

WÈNTÍ

1. Jìn bǎinián lái Zhōngguo jiàoyu yǒu hěn dàde yǎnbiàn. Yǎnbiànde yuányīn
   shi shénmo?

2. Jìn bǎinián Zhōngguo jiàoyude yǎnbiàn kéyi fēncheng jǐge shíqī? Měige
   shíqīde míngchēng shi shénmo?

3. Shénmo shi kējǔ zhìdu? Shi cóng něi yíge cháodài kāishǐ de? Něige
   cháodài qǔxiāode?

4. Zhōngguode xuézhì, guīdìng zhōngxuéde niánxiàn shi jǐnián? Zhōngxué
   jiàoyude mùbiāo shi shénmo?

5. Shénmo jiào pǔjí jiàoyu? Zěnmoyàng néng dádào pǔjí jiàoyu de mùdì?

6. Yíge Zhōngguo xiǎoxuéshēng cóng qīsuì qǐ niàn xiǎoxué xuéxi jīběn zhīshi.
   Yàoshi niàndao zhōngxué bìyè de shíhou shi jǐsuì? Niàndao yǒu gāoshēn
   xuéwen déle bóshi xuéwèi de shíhou shi duó dà suìshu?

7. Niàn dàxué hé yánjiuyuàn zài shénmo qíngxing zhīxià cái kéyi shēnqǐng
   jiǎngxuéjīn?

8. Niàn dàxué de shíhou měimén gōngke duōshǎo fēn jígé? Yào niàn duōshao
   xuéfēn cái néng bìyè?

9. Xuéfēn-zhì hé xuénián-zhì yǒu shénmo bùtóng? Něi yìzhǒng zhìdu bǐjiǎo
   hǎo? Zhōngguode dàxué cǎiyòng de shi něi yìzhǒng zhìdu?

10. Sīshú jiàoyu shíqī xuésheng niàn de shénmo shū? Xuéxiào jiàoyude shíqī
    dōu yǒu shénmo gōngke? Něige shíqīde gōngke bǐjiǎo shíyòng ne?

ILLUSTRATIVE SENTENCES (ENGLISH)

1.1.   In the past did Chinese start their studies with the Three Character Clas-
       sic or the Five Classics? . . . They started with the Three Character
       Classic, of course.

1.2.   Such books as the Three Character Classic, the Four Books, and the Five
       Classics are [now] no longer studied by the majority of students.

2.4.   In the past few decades China has made great progress in science.

2.5.   Furthermore [lit. advance a further step and speak], such an academic lecture should treat the topic in somewhat greater detail.

4.1.   My elementary school was [studied in] a private [elementary] school. Middle school was a public [middle] school. College was a provincial university.

4.2.   I graduated in the Chinese department of national Peking University.

6.1.   The Dean's Office wants to engage someone. According to the Dean, this employee should have a college education [lit. qualification].

6.2.   So far as I know, he has only gone through [lit. has only qualifications of] first year of upper middle school.

6.3.   The living standard here is much higher than ours.

9.1.   His father was an official in the Ch'ing period. Later he ceased to be an official, so their life was very hard.

9.2.   In this area they have set up two more public [lit. government-established] elementary schools.

11.1.   How is this matter determined legally?

14.1.   There was one agricultural school, which although in existence for ten years, was poorly run. The result was that the government got rid of it.

15.1.   In the first class today the professor lectured on cooperative enterprises and cooperative stores.

16.1.   There are now more and more democratic countries. The trend [of the times] is toward [lit. requires] democracy.

17.1.   This year college tuition has gone up a great deal. As tuition increases there are bound to be many students who will not have the means to continue in college.

18.1.   There are too many (required) courses in college now. All the students feel that there isn't enough time to study.

20.2.   Generally speaking, that school is well run.

22.1.   May I ask how many strokes there are in the character jìn in jìnlĭ?

23.1.   In order to save time let's have a simple meal.

24.2.   Where in the world is there a really peaceful place?

25.2.   A physicist said that he hoped China would be able in a short period of time to have a great expansion in science.

26.1.   Tell me what's troubling you. Between the two of us how can there be anything that we can't talk about?

26.2.   After the foreign students had heard the president's speech, some said they understood all of it, and some said they were able to understand eighty per cent.

26.4.   Peita is one of China's best universities.

27.1.   That country has advanced very rapidly.   In less than three years' time their agriculture and industry have both been modernized.

27.2.   The method of selecting by examination students who will study abroad is too wasteful of effort.   It should be simplified.

27.3.   They say that Chinese characters will be reduced to about 3,000.

29.1.   This sickness is quite widespread. The children in this area have almost all contracted it [lit. fallen ill].

29.2.   The job of making education universal is extraordinarily difficult.

31.2.   Universal education has been promoted here, to be sure, but nothing has been achieved.

32.1.   All things considered, agriculture and industry have had a considerable development in that country in (the past) five years.

32.2.   Considering the average person's outlook, the people are not likely to welcome his political thought.

33.1.   The first returned students [lit. returned students of the first period] from America were not welcomed when they returned to China.

34.1.   Their objective is [to hope] to establish five colleges within five years.

35.2.   There are a great many children in this area. It is quite necessary to add several elementary schools.

36.1.   Look, that plane has fallen into the sea!

37.1.   This method is to enable [lit. cause] everyone to acquire basic knowledge.

39.2.   In reading we should thoroughly [lit. profoundly] understand the contents of the book.

40.1.   Please look up in Chronology of Outstanding Events in China what were the main events at the end of the Ming dynasty.

41.1.   A backward country was gradually able in less than ten years time to develop to this stage [lit. fashion].

41.2.   Now the standards of every [level of] school from elementary school to college have been gradually raised.

46.2.   The times force us to study atomic energy [lit. because of the current of the times we cannot but study atomic energy].

50.1.   Your thinking is too childish.

54.6.   Let's go a bit faster. Otherwise we won't make [lit. catch up with] the train.

55.1.   I don't know enough. I must read more to make myself more knowledgeable [lit. make self full].

56.1.   Elections generally consist of suggesting a few people in a general assembly and then making a selection from among these people.

56.2.   He's not likely to be elected, because the vast majority of people don't like [lit. welcome] him.

57.1.   It's been quite a few months since he borrowed my book. I requested it of him many times but he hasn't given it to me.

58.1.   If every day you listen to tape recordings and practice pronunciation yourself, after a while your Chinese will naturally make progress.

59.2.   Yesterday Tang Xueli sent me a letter from China [lit. interior of country] saying: "Please buy for me the middle school books on physics, economics, and sociology. Write me how much they cost."

NOTES

1. The literary particle zhī is one of the most important in written Chinese. As a subordinating particle, zhī is equivalent to de in some of its uses and to yǐ in yǐhòu, yǐqián, etc. It also functions as a third-person pronoun in object position after a verb:

> wǔfēnzhī-yī   'one-fifth'   [lit. one of five parts]
>
> méi tīng yǎnjiǎng zhīqián   'before hearing the lecture'
>
> rénzhī chū 'the beginning of man' (opening phrase of the Three Character Classic)
>
> zǒngzhī   'in sum'   [lit. summing it]

The first example indicates the way of expressing fractions in ordinary spoken Chinese. The second example occurs in formal speech such as lectures. Other frequently occurring examples of this usage are zhīhòu 'after'; zhīzhōng, zhīnèi, zhījiān 'in' or 'within'; zhīshàng 'above'; zhīxià 'below'; zhīwài 'outside' or 'beyond.' The third and fourth examples occur only in the written style and in a few frozen expressions taken from it into ordinary speech.

2. The verb zuò 'do' and its more literary equivalent wéi are used as postverbs with the meaning 'as.' They are used in much the same way as chéng in fēnchéng 'divide into,' fānchéng 'translate into.'

> Wǒ bǎ zhēn zì niànzuo zhí le. 'I (mis)read the character zhēn (true) as zhí (straight).'
>
> Tā yǐjing liùshi duō suì le. Wǒ bǎ ta kànwei yíge zhōngnián rén. 'He's already over sixty. I took him to be middle-aged.'

3. The pattern ná . . . lái shuō means 'speak of . . .' or 'speaking of . . . .' In this construction lái is constant, but ná 'take' and shuō 'speak' are replaceable by other verbs. Verbs used in place of shuō include jiǎng 'lecture,' jiěshi 'explain,' kàn 'look.' Verbs used in place of ná include yòng 'use,' cóng 'from,' gēnju 'according to.'

> Ná kǎoshì lái shuō, nǐ měicì kǎode dōu bǐ wǒ hǎo. 'Speaking of exams, you do better than I on every exam.'

Sometimes lái shuō is preceded not by a phrase introduced by a verb such as ná but by adverbial phrases such as jiǎndānde 'simply':

> Jiǎndānde lái shuō, tāde yìjian wǒ bù zàncheng. 'Putting it plainly, I don't approve of his views.'

Zhōng-Měi Dìlǐ Bǐjiào Tú

Dì-Sìkè. Dìlǐ

Bái: Mǎ Jiàoshòu, zǎo.

Mǎ: Zǎo. Jīntian tiānchi hěn hǎo.

Bái: Wǒ dào zhèr zhèi jǐtiān jīntian tiānchi zuì hǎo le.

Mǎ: Zuótian tīng de guānyu jiàoyu de jiǎnghuà yǒu shénmo wèntí méi
5　　yǒu?

Bái: Jiǎngde wǒ dōu dǒng le, méi shénmo wèntí. Kěshi wǒ zhèicìde
　　　fùshù méi yǒu qián liǎngcìde hǎo.

Mǎ: Shénmo yuányīn ne?

Bái: Yīnwei wǒ dōu dǒngle, zài fùshù de shíhou jiu súibiàn shuō, méi
10　　zěnmo zhùyì yòng shēngcí.

Mǎ: Zhǐ yào nǐ dōu míngbai le, jiùshi shēngcí shǎo yě méi duó dà
　　　guānxi. Jiùshi hé zuò wénzhāng yíyàng. Suīrán wénzhāngde tímu
　　　xiāngtóng, dàjiā bù yídìng yào yòng yíyàngde cér xiě wénzhāng.
　　　Zhǔyàode shi yìsi xiāngtóng. Kěshi zài fùshù de shíhou háishi duō
15　　yòng shēngcí bǐjiào hǎo, wèideshi duō liànxi me.

Bái: Duì le. Xiàcì wǒ děi zhùyì zhèi yìdiǎn.

Mǎ: Ná nǐde chéngdu lái shuō, shǐqián bǎ shēngcí duō kàn yìhuěr, zài
　　　lùyīn yǐqián duō xiǎngyixiǎng, zìrán'érránde jiu duō yòng shēngcí
　　　le. Zuótian nèiwèi Zhāng Jiàoshòu jiǎngde zěnmoyàng?

20 Bái: Jiǎngde hǎojíle. Kěshi tā shuō de huà yǒude búshi Guóyǔ, děi hěn
　　　zhùyì tīng cái tīngdedǒng.

Mǎ: Zhāng Jiàoshòu shi Húnán rén. Tīng xuéshù yǎngjiǎng yào zhùyì de
　　　shi tāmen zhǔjiǎngde nèiróng, bú yào zhùyì zhǔjiǎngde yǔyán, shǐ
　　　nǐde yǔyán shòule yǐngxiǎng.

25 Bái: Nín shuōde duì. Wǒmen jīntiande Zhuāntí Jiǎnghuà shi jiǎng Zhōng-
　　　guo dìlǐ, shì bu shi?

Mǎ: Shì. Zhè shi jīntiande shēngcí biǎo.

Bái: Mǎ Jiàoshòu, bùdeliǎo! Zènmo duō shēngcí!

Mǎ: Duō shì hěn duō, kěshi yǒu hěn duō dìlǐ míngzi, hěn róngyi jì.

1.0. xíngróng　　　describe　　[form contain]
　　　xíngróngcí　　adjective

1.1. "Zhāng Xiānshengde shēntǐ hěn hǎo." Zài zhèijù huàlǐ de hǎo zì
　　　shi xíngróngcí, xíngróng Zhāng Xiānshengde shēnti hěn hǎo.　　(T)

69

2.0. dì-dà-wù-bó   large in territory and rich in natural products [land
                     big things vast]

2.1. Zhōngguo hé Měiguo dōu shi dì-dà-wù-bó-de guójiā.

3.0. chǎn   produce

     chūchǎn   (1) produce; (2) product; (3) production [emit produce]

     nóngchǎn   agricultural product

     tǔchǎn   local product   [earth product]

     wùchǎn   product   [thing product]

     chǎnshēng   to produce   [produce bear]

3.1. Zhèrde chūchǎn duō bu duō? Chǎnde zuì duō de shi shénmo?

3.2. Húbiārde nóngtían hěn duō, suǒyǐ nóngchǎn yě hěn duō.

3.3. Yǒu yíge Měiguo rén cóng Zhōngguo huídao Měiguo. Tā shuō
     Zhōngguode wùchǎn tài duō le, tài hǎo le. Tā zhèicì huíguó mǎile
     bù shǎo Zhōngguode tǔchǎn.

3.4. Yǒu rén shuō Zhōngguode báihuàwén shi Wǔsì yǐhòu chǎnshēngde.
     Nǐ shuō duì ma?

4.0. mǐ   (uncooked) rice

4.1. Zhōngguo nóngchǎn zuì duōde shi mǐ.   (T)

5.0. fēngfù   (1) abundant, rich; (2) enrich   [abundant rich]

5.1. Zuótiande Zhuāntí Jiǎnghuà, suǒ jiǎngde tímu shi Zhōngguode
     wùchǎn.   Zhāng Xiānshang bǎ nǎlide chūchǎn fēngfù, nǎli méi yǒu
     chūchǎn gěi wǒmen jiěshide hěn míngbai.

5.2. Wǒmen zhèiběn shū rúguǒ qǐng Wáng Xiānsheng gěi xiě shuōmíng
     nèiróng jiu huì fēngfù.   (T)

6.0. dàzhǐ   in general   [big transmit]

6.1. Zhōngguode yòuzhiyuán hé wàiguode yòuzhiyuán dàzhǐ xiāngtóng.

30 Mǎ : Xíngróng Zhōngguo dà, chūchǎn duō dōu shi yòng "Zhōngguo dì-dà-
          wù-bó" zhèjù huà. Zhè shi shǐshí, yě shi rénrén dōu zhīdao de.

    Bái: Zhōngguo shì bu shi mǐ chūchǎnde zuì duō ne?

    Mǎ : Shì. Mǐ shi nánfāng zuì zhǔyàode nóngchǎn. Nánfāng chūchǎnde zuì
         duō.

35 Bái: Běifāng bù chǎn mǐ ma?

    Mǎ : Běifāng shuǐtián hěn shǎo, suǒyǐ chūchǎn de mǐ bù duō.

    Bái: Nènmo nánfāngde mǐ yídìng bù hěn guì le?

    Mǎ : Nà shi dāngrán le. Chūchǎnde duō jiu bú huì tài guì.

    Bái: Běifāng rén yě chī mǐ ma?

40 Mǎ : Yě chī, búguò jiu shi guì yìdiǎr.

    Bái: Zài dìlǐ shūshang kàn, Zhōngguode wùchǎn hěn fēngfù.

    Mǎ : Dàzhǐ shuō, Zhōngguode wùchǎn <u>shì</u> hěn fēngfù.

    7.0. zāi*   calamity, disaster

          tiānzāi   natural disaster   [heaven disaster]

          shuǐzāi   flood   [water calamity]

          hànzāi   drought   [drought calamity]

    7.1. Shuǐzāi, hànzāi dōu shi tiānzāi. Cǐwài hái yǒu shénmo zāi yě shi
          shǔyu tiānzāi ne?

    8.0. hài   damage, harm   (N/V)

          zāihài   calamity, misfortune   [calamity harm]

          sǔnhài   damage (N)   [damage harm]

    8.1. Shuǐzāi zài Zhōngguo shi yí dà hài. Zhèizhǒng zāihài duìyu rén-
          mínde sǔnhài tài dà le.

    8.2. Zhèicì shuǐzāi shòu hài zuì dà de shi Hénán Shěng.   (T)

    9.0. qū   district, region   (M)

          zìzhìqū   autonomous region   [self govern region]

    9.1. Jīnniánde shuǐzāi, wǒmen nèiqū shòu de zāihài zuì dà.

    9.2. Nèige dìfang shi zìzhìqū. Zìzhìqūlǐde rénmín dōu zài gōnglì xué-
          xiào shòuguo xiǎoxué jiàoyu.

    10.0. yù*   region

           qūyù   region   [district region]

           liúyù   river basin   [flow region]

    10.1. Rúguo bǎ Zhōngguo fēnchéng liǎngge dà qūyù, shi zěnyàng fēnkāi ne?
           (T)

    10.2. Zhōngguo dàde héliú yǒu jǐtiáo? Shénmo héde liúyù cháng yǒu shuǐ-
           zāi?

    11.0. huáng   yellow

           Huáng Hǎi   Yellow Sea

           Huáng Hé   Yellow River

    11.1. Huáng Hé de shuǐ shi huáng yánse. Huáng Hǎi de shuǐ yě shi huáng
           yánsede ma?

    Bái: Zhōngguode chūchǎn xiāngdāngde fēngfù. Kěshi hěn duō rén shēng-
          huó háishi hěn kùnnán.

45 Mǎ : Suīrán yǒu biéde yuányīn, kěshi zhǔyào shi tiānzāi.

Bái: Shénmo jiàozuo tiānzāi?

Mǎ : Jiù shi hànzāi hé shuǐzāi.

Bái: Zāi zì de yìsi shi . . .

Mǎ : Zāi jiu shi zāihài, yě jiu shi shòu sǔnhàide yìsi.

50 Bái: Huáběi zhèige qūyù rénmínde shēnghuó xiāngdāng kùnnán. Shì bu
shi yīnwei Huáng Hé shuǐzāide yǐngxiǎng?

Mǎ : Duōbàn shì. Huáng Hé shuǐzāi xiànglái yě méi zhìhǎoguo. Cóng gǔ
dào jīn duōshao zhuānjiā cǎiyòng gèzhǒng bànfǎ nǔlì qù zhì, dōu bù
xíng.

55 Bái: Zhōngguo wénhuàde kāishǐ shi Huáng Hé liúyù ya.

Mǎ : Nà dào shì.

Bái: Shāndōng、Shānxi、Héběi、Hénán dōu shǔyu Huáng Hé liúyù, shì bu
shi?

Mǎ : Shìde.

12.0. guǎng   extensive, wide

        guǎngdà   vast, profound   [wide big]

        Guǎngdong   Kuangtung   [wide east]

        Guǎnxi   Kuangsi   [wide west]

12.1. Guǎngdong、Guǎngxi liǎngshěng shuǐzāide qūyù tài guǎng le. Guǎngdàde nóngtián dōu shòule sǔnhài.   (T)

13.0. miànji   area   [surface accumulate]

13.1. Běnxiàode miànji yǒu sān fāng Yīnglǐ, bāokuò nóngxuéyuàn zài nèi.

14.0. fēngjǐng   scenery   [wind scenery]

14.1. Guólǐ yīxuéyuànde huánjìng tài hǎo le.   Fēngjǐng fēicháng hǎokàn.

15.0. zhōu   sub-prefecture
        Guǎngzhōu   Canton

15.1. Guǎngzhōu shi yíge shāngyè zhōngxīn.

16.0. (dà)zhōu   continent

        Měi(zhōu)   America(n continent)

16.1. Měizhōude zhōu hé Guǎngzhōude zhōu shì bu shi xiāngtóng ne?. . .
Bù xiāngtóng. Měizhōude zhōu jiǔhuá, gēn dàzhōude zhōu shi yíge
zì. Guǎngzhōude zhōu zhǐ yǒu liùhuá.   (T)

16.2. Shi Nán Měizhōu dà háishi Běi Měizhōu dà?

60 Bái: Guǎng zìde yìsi jiu shi dàde yìsi, shì bu shi?

Mǎ : Búcuò. Wǒ gěi nǐ jǔ ge lìzi: "Wǒmen kǎoshì de tímu bāokuò de
fànwéi hěn guǎng." Guǎngdong, Guǎnxi jiù shi zhèige guǎng zì.

Bái : Guǎngdong、Guǎngxi dōu zài Zhōngguode dōngnánbù. Zhè liǎngshěngde miànji chàbuduō. Kěshi rénkǒu shi Guǎngdong duō háishi Guǎng-
65   xi duō ne?

Mǎ : Zài yī-jiǔ-wǔ-sān-nián Guǎngdong yǒu sānqiān wǔbǎiwàn rén.
Guǎngxi yǒu liǎngqiānwàn rén. Xiànzài yěxǔ yòu zēngjiāle hěn duō.

Bái : Guǎngdong、Guǎngxide fēngjǐng hěn hǎokàn, shì bu shi?

Mǎ : Guǎngxide shānshuǐ shi yǒumíngde.

70 Bái : Oh! Qǐng wèn Mǎ Jiàoshòu, <u>Guǎngzhōude zhōu</u> hé <u>wǔ dàzhōu</u> de
<u>zhōu</u> shi yíge zì ma?

Mǎ : Bú shi.

17.0. Ào(zhōu)   Australia

17.1. Àozhōude miànji dà háishi Měizhōude miànji dà?

18.0. Fēi(zhōu)   Africa

18.1. Fēizhōude wùchǎn yě fēicháng fēngfù ma?

19.0. Ōu(zhōu)   Europe

Ōuhuà   Europeanize

Xī-Ōu   Western Europe

Ōu-Měi   Europe and America

19.1. Yīngguo、Fàguo dōu zài Ōuzhōu, yě dōu zài Xī-Ōu.

19.2. Zài Ōu-Měi de Zhōngguo liúxuéshēng, duōshù xǐhuan Xīfāngde shēnghuó, suǒyǐ yǒu rén shuō Zhōngguo liúxuéshēngde shēnghuó yǐjing
Ōuhuà le.

20.0. Yǎ(zhōu), Yà(zhōu)   Asia

Yǎxiyǎ, Yàxiyà   Asia

Dōngyǎ, Dōngyà   East Asia

20.1. Yǎzhōu zuì dàde guójiā shi Zhōngguo. Zhōngguo zài Yǎxiyǎde dōngbù, suǒyǐ yě kéyi shuō Zhōngguo shi Dōngyǎ zuì dàde guójiā.

21.0. Sūlián   Soviet Union, the U.S.S.R.

Zhōng-Sū   China and the U.S.S.R., Sino-Soviet

21.1. Zhōng-Sū Wénhuà Xuéhuì shi Zhōngguo hé Suliánde zhīshi fènzǐ
zǔzhi de.

22.0. Ē(guo), É(guo), È(guo)   Russia

Ē(wén), É(wén), È(wén)   Russian language

Zhōng-Ē, Zhōng-É, Zhōng-È   China and Russia, Sino-Russian

22.1. Ēguo jiu shi Sūlián cóngqiánde míngchēng. Bǐrú shuō Zhōng-Ē hézuò jiu shi shuō Zhōngguo hé Sūlián liǎngguó hézuò.

Mǎ : Wǔ dàzhōude Yīngwén míngzi dāngrán nǐ huì, yòng Zhōngwén shuō
      nǐ zhīdao zěnmo shuō ma?

75 Bái : Àozhōu、Fēizhōu、Ōuzhōu、Měizhōu、Yǎzhōu.

Mǎ : Duì le.

Bái : Měizhōu yǒu Nán Měizhōu、Běi Měizhōu. Ōuzhōu yǒu Xī-Ōu、Běi-
      Ōu děngděng. Yǎzhōu yǒu shíhou jiào Yǎxiyǎ.

Mǎ : Yě shuō Dōngyǎ.

80 Bái : Ōu-Měi jiu shi Ōuzhōu、Měizhōu zhèi liǎngzhōu jiǎndānde míngchēng,
      shì bu shi? Bàozhǐshang cháng kànjian.

Mǎ : Hái yǒu Ōu-Yǎ、Yǎ-Fēi yě cháng yòng. Guójiā hé guójiā yě cháng
      bǎ liǎngge guójiāde míngchēng hézài yìqǐ. Bǐrú Zhōngguo hé Sūlián
      jiu jiǎndān yòng Zhōng-Sū. Hái you Zhōng-Měi、Zhōng-Yīng、Zhōng-
85   Rì děngděng.

Bái : Zhōng-Sū yě shuō Zhōng-É, shì bu shi?

Mǎ : Yǐqián shi shuō Zhōng-É, yīnwei yǐqián Sūlián jiào Éguo. Xiànzài
      dōu shi yòng Zhōng-Sū le. Dànshi zìdiǎn háishi yòng Zhōng-É
      liǎngge zì, bú yòng Zhōng-Sū zìdiǎn. Niàn shū yě shuō niàn Éwén,
90   bù shuō niàn Sūliánwén.

23.0. wèizhi   position, location [seat establish]

23.1. Xuéxiào yào mǎi nèisuǒ fángzi zuò bàngōngshǐ, yīnwei nèi-
       suǒ fángzide wèizhi jiù zài běnxiàode duìmiàn. Xuéxiào guīdìng zhǐ
       néng zuò jiàozhiyuán bàngōng yòng. (T)

23.2. Zuótian wǒ bìng le, méi cānjiā dìlǐ kǎoshì. Tīngshuō zhǐ yǒu
       liǎngge tímu. Yíge shi Guǎngzhoude wèizhi gēn chūchǎn, yíge shi
       shuōyishuō Yǎzhōude gàikuàng.

24.0. wēn   (1) warm; (2) review (a lesson)

       wēnshū   review   (VO) [review book]

       wēnhé   warm   [warm harmonious]

       wēndài   temperate zone   [warm belt]

24.1. Zuótian wǒ wēnshū de shíhou Mǎ Jiàoshòu lái kàn wǒ. Wǒ yǒu bù
       míngbai de dìfang, dōu shi Mǎ Jiàoshòu gěi wǒ jiěshi míngbai de.

24.2. Wēndàide qìhou shi wēnhéde.

25.0. rè   hot

       rèdài   tropics   [hot belt]

25.1. Àozhōude wèizhi yíbùfen shi zài rèdài, suǒyǐ yǒude dìfang tiānqi
       hěn rè.

26.0. (hǎi)dǎo   island   [ocean island]

       bàndǎo   peninsula   [half island]

26.1. Hǎidǎo shi sìmiàn dōu shi hǎi, bàndǎo shi sānmiàn shi hǎi.

27.0. lù*   land (as opposed to water)

     lùdì   land   [land earth]

     dàlù   mainland   [big land]

27.1. Tāmen zài chuánshang yuǎnyuānde kànjiànle lùdì le. Hòulái tāmen cái zhīdao nà shi yíge xīnde dàlù.

28.0. xìng*   nature, quality, characteristic

     tèxìng   peculiarity, special feature

28.1. Nèi jǐge nóngren tāmen sīren zǔzhíde nèige nóngyè hézuòshè shi chángqīxìngde ma? . . . Shi duǎnqīde. Jiānglái bú zhòngtián de shíhou jiù qǔxiāo le.

28.2. Dàlùxìngde qìhou yǒu shénmo tèxìng, nǐ zhīdao ma?

  Mǎ :   Wǒ xiànzài wèn nǐ jǐge wèntí. Zhōngguode wèizhi shi zài Yǎzhōude nèige fāngxiàng?

  Bái: Zài Yǎzhōude dōngnánbù.

  Mǎ :   Zài wēndài háishi zài rèdai?

95 Bái: Zài běi wēndài.

  Mǎ :   Zhōngguode qìhou zěnmoyàng?

  Bái: Qìhou shi wēnhéde.

  Mǎ :   Duì le. Zhōngguo bú shi hǎidǎo, shi lùdì, suǒyǐ qìhou shi shǔyu dàlùxìngde.

100 Bái: Shì bu shi Zhōngguo gè dìfangde qìhou dōu xiāngtóng?

  Mǎ :   Yìbān de shuō shi chàbuliǎo hěn duō.

29.0. ràng   yield

     ràngbù   yield   [yield step]

29.1. Xuéxiàolide zhíyuán shuō, xiànzài jiǎngtánglide rén mǎn le, shéi dōu bù néng jìnqu le. Wǒ shuōle hěn duō huà tā cái ràng wǒ jìnqu le.

29.2. Nèiběn shū ràng Zhāng Xiānsheng gěi náqu le.

29.3. Nèige tuánli yīnwei xuǎnbá tuányuánde wèntí yǒu yìjian le, liǎngfāngmian dōu bú ràngbù.

29.4. Wǒde mòshuǐ ràng shéi gěi náqu le?

30.0. zhímín   colonize   (W)   [grow people]

     zhímíndì   colony

30.1. Yīngguo cóngqián xiàng Měiguo zhímín.   (W)   (T)

30.2. Zuótiande jiǎngtí shi "Zhímíndì qǔxiāo zhīhòu guòdù shíqīde zhímín
        wèntí."

31.0. shāng*   commerce

        shāngren   merchant

        shāngyè   commerce [commerce enterprise]

31.1. Tā zài shāngyè xuéxiào niàn shū. Tā shi xué shāng de. Jiānglái
        bìyè yǐhòu tā zuò shāngren.

32.0. tōng   go through

        tōngshāng   (have) commercial relations

        tōngxìn   communicate by mail

        tōngguò   (1) pass through; (2) approve, carry (a motion)

32.1. Nèi jǐge dà chéng dōu tōng huǒchē.   (T)

32.2. Zhōngguo hé wàiguo tōngshāng yǐhòu, zuò jìnchūkǒu shēngyi de
        shāngren duōbàr shi yòng tōngxìn de fāngfǎ zuò shēngyi.

32.3. Guānyu Dōngyǎ nèige wèntí, hěn kuàide jiu tōngguòle.

33.0. zhàn   occupy, seize and occupy by force

33.1. Zhèicì xuǎnjǔ tā yídìng xuǎnshang, yīnwei xuǎnjǔ tā de rénshù zhàn
        zǒngshù bǎifēnzhī-bāshí.   (T)

33.2. Cóngqián Táiwān ràng Rìběn gěi zhànqule wǔshinián.   (T)

Bái: Zài dìtúshang kàn, Zhōngguode dà xiǎo hǎidǎo hěn duō. Dànshi zuì
        yǒumíngde shi Xiānggǎng hé Táiwān le. Xiānggǎng xiànzài bù shǔyu
        Zhōngguo le.

105 Mǎ: Xiānggǎng gēn Táiwān zhè liǎngge hǎidǎo dōu yǒu lìshǐxìng. Xiāng-
        xìn nǐ yǐjing zhīdao. Xiān shuō Xiānggǎng. Cóng yī-bā-sì-èr-nián
        rànggěi Yīngguo rén zuò zhímíndì le.

Bái: Tīngshuō Xiānggǎngde shāngyè fēicháng fādá. Shāngren zài nàli
        kéyi hé gèguó tōngshāng.

110 Mǎ: Shìde. Xiānggǎngde hǎishuǐ hěn shēn. Lián zuì dàde chuán dōu
        kéyi jìn hǎikǒu.

Bái: Mǎ Jiàoshòu dàoguo Xiānggǎng ma?

Mǎ: Wǒ zài nèr zhùguo jǐnián. Wǒmen zài shuō Táiwān zhèige hǎidǎo.
        Táiwān zài Zhōngguode dōngnánbiar. Yī-jiǔ-sì-wǔ-nián yǐqián ràng
115   Rìběn zhànle wǔshinián.

Bái: Suǒyǐ Táiwān dāngdì rén dōu huì shuō Rìběn huà ne.

34.0. jiāng*   border, boundary, frontier

        biānjiāng   border, frontier

        Xīnjiāng   Sinkiang [new frontier]

34.1. Jiāng shi tǔdìde yìsi, biānjiāng jiu shi zài biānshangde tǔdì.

34.2. Xīnjiāngde běibiān jiu shi Sūlián.

34.3. Guójiā gēn guójiā shícháng zài biānjiāngshang fāshēng wèntí.   (T)

35.0. biānjiè   frontier between two countries   [frontier realm]

35.1. Zhōngguo zài Qīng Cháo mònián chángcháng hé Ēguo fāshēng biānjiè wèntí. Měicì dōu shi Zhōngguo ràngbù.

36.0. (Xī)zàng   Tibet   [west Tibet]

  Zàngwén   Tibetan language

36.1. Túshūguǎnde Zàngwén shū dōu shi cóng Xīzàng mǎilai de ma?

37.0. Měng(gǔ)   Mongolia

  Nèi Měng(gǔ)   Inner Mongolia

  Wài Měng(gǔ)   Outer Mongolia

  Měng(gǔ)wén   Mongol language

37.1. Qīng Cháode shíhou bǎ Měnggǔ fēnwéi Nèi Měnggǔ、Wài Měnggu. Dōu shi Zhōngguode tǔdì.

37.2. Měng zì zhèizǔli yígòng yǒu jǐge cér? Měi yíge cér dōu yǒu zhùjiě ma?

37.3. Zài Měiguo něige dàxué kéyi niàn Měngwén?

37.4. Wài Měnggǔ shi yíge xīnde guójiā. Tāde wèizhi shi zài Zhōng-Ē zhījiān.   (T)

Bái: Mǎ Jiàoshòu, qǐng jiěshi jiěshi biānjiāng zhèige cérde yìsi.

Mǎ : Biānjiāng jiu shi biānjiède tǔdì. Bǐrú Xīnjiāng、Xīzàng、Měnggǔ dōu shi Zhōngguode biānjiāng.

120 Bái: Wǒ míngbai le. Měnggǔ fēnchéng Nèi Měnggǔ、Wài Měnggǔ. Wǒ zhīdao Wài Měnggǔ bù shǔyu Zhōngguo le. Xiànzài shi Měnggǔ Rénmín Gònghéguó le. Kěshi Nèi Měnggǔ ne?

Mǎ : Nèi Měnggǔ shǔyu Zhōngguo, xiànzài shi zìzhìqū.

Bái: Wǒ yǒu jīhui hái xiǎng xué yìdiǎr Měngwén、Zàngwén.

125 Mǎ : Jiāo Měngwén、Zàngwén de xiānsheng zài zhèr kǒngpà hěn nán zhǎodào.

38.0. jiāojiè   meet at the frontier, be on the frontier   [join realm]

38.1. Zhōngguode dōngběibù hé Sūlián jiāojiè de dìfang yǒu liǎngtiáo hěn dàde héliú.

39.0. Yìndu   India

39.1. Zhōngguo hé Yìndu dōu shi Yǎzhōude gǔ guó.

40.0. Miǎndiàn   Burma

40.1. Miǎndiàn xiànzài shi Yǎzhōude yíge xīnde guójiā.

41.0. kào(zhe)   (1) lean on, depend on; (2) be due to; (3) border on, be lo-
                      cated at; (4) veer in a certain direction

       kěkào   reliable, dependable

       kàodezhù   able to rely on, reliable

41.1. Zhāng Xiānsheng kàozhe xiě xiǎoshuōr guò rìzi.   (T)

41.2. Tā shuō de huà xiànglái shi kàobuzhù de. Nǐ wèi-shénmo shuō tā
       shuō de huà dōu kěkào ne?

41.3. Zài Xiānggǎng zǒu lù dōu shi kào zuǒbian zǒu.

42.0. Qīnghǎi   Chinghai, Kokonor

42.1. Qīnghǎi shi yìshěngde míngzi. Zài zhèishěngli yǒu yíge dà hú jiào
       Qīnghǎi, yīncǐ jiu bǎ zhèishěng jiàozuò Qīnghǎi Shěng.

      Mǎ: Wǒmen xiànzài zài yánjiu yíge wèntí.   Qǐng nǐ shuōyishuō gēn
           Zhōngguo jiāojiè de guójiā dōu shi něi jǐge guójiā?

      Bái: Zài Zhōngguo xībiar gēn xīnánbiar hé Zhōngguo jiāojiède guó shi
130   Yìndu. Nánbiar shi Miǎndiàn gēn Yuènán. Zài běibiarde jiāojiè
           guó shi Sūlián gēn Měnggǔ Rénmín Gònghéguó.

      Mǎ: Dōngbiar ne?

      Bái: Dōngbiar kào hǎi.

      Mǎ: Kào shénmo hǎi?

135   Bái: Huáng Hǎi, Dōng Hǎi, Nán Hǎi. Shuō hǎi wǒ xiǎngqilai yíge wèntí.
           Zài Zhōngguo xīběi bù yǒu yìshěng jiào Qīnghǎi. Wǒ bù míngbai
           wèi-shénmo jiào Qīnghǎi?

      Mǎ: Yīnwei nèishěng yǒu yíge dà hú jiào Qīnghǎi. Dìfang míngzi shi
           gēnju nèige húde míngzi qǐ de.

43.0. Dòngtíng Hú   Tungting Lake

43.1. Dòngtíng Húlide shuǐ rúguǒ tài mǎn le jiu zìrán'érránde liúdào yíge
       dàde héliú qù le.

44.0. Póyáng Hú   Poyang Lake

44.1. Póyáng Hú yídài yǒu shénmo tǔchǎn?

45.0. jiāng   (large) river

       Yángzi Jiāng   Yangtze River

       Cháng Jiāng   Yangtze River   [long river]

Jiāngnán   (1) area south of the Yangtze; (2) Kiangsu and Anhwei

Jiāngxi   Kiangsi

Jiāngsu   Kiangsu

Zhèjiāng   Chekiang

Zhū Jiāng   Pearl River

45.1. Jiāngsu shi zài Cháng Jiāng liúyù. Zhèjiāng bú shi zài Cháng Jiāng liúyù.

45.2. Jiāngxi shi yìshěngde míngzi, kěshi Jiāngnán bú shi yìshěngde míngzi.

45.3. Cháng Jiāng、Zhū Jiāng suírán dōu shi jiāng, kěshi Zhū Jiāng bǐ Cháng Jiāng xiǎo duō le.

46.0. yán(zhe)   skirt, border on, extend along

      yánhǎi   skirt the ocean   (VO)

46.1. Zhèli yánhǎi yǒu yìtiáo gōnglù. Yàoshi zuò chē yánzhe gōnglù zǒu, yòu yǒu shān yòu yǒu shuǐ, fēngjǐng hěn hǎokàn.

47.0. xiāng*   the country (versus the city)

      xiāngxia   the country   [country down]

      tóngxiāng   come from the same place

47.1. Shénmo jiàozuo yú-mǐ-zhī-xiāng ne? Jiu shi yòu yǒu yú yòu yǒu mǐ de dìfang.   (T)

47.2. Wǒ hé Zhāng Xiānsheng shi tóngxiāng. Wǒmen dōu zhùzai xiāngxia.

140 Mǎ : Wǒ xiànzài wèn nǐ Zhōngguo yǒu jǐge dà hú?

    Bái: Yǒu sānge dà hú, jiu shi Dòngtíng Hú、Póyáng Hú gēn Tài Hú.

    Mǎ : Dōu zài nǎr?

    Bái: Zhè sānge hú dōu zài Yángzi Jiāngde liúyù.

    Mǎ : Duì le. Dōu zài Cháng Jiāngde nánbiar. Nǐ zhīdao bu zhīdào zhè
145   sānge hú dōu zài něishěng lǐtou?

    Bái: Dòngtíng Hú zài Húnán. Póyáng Hú zài Jiāngxi. Tài Hú zài Jiāngsu、Zhèjiāng zhījiān.

    Mǎ : Búcuò.

    Bái: Shì bu shi yánhǎi jǐshěng chūchǎn bǐjiǎo fēngfù?

150 Mǎ : Shìde. Jiù ná xiāngxia rénde shēnghuó lái shuō, yánhǎi yídài xiāngxia rénde shēnghuó bǐjiáo hǎo.

48.0. shā   sand

      shāmò   desert   [sand vast]

      Chángshā   Changsha (in Hunan)   [long sand]

48.1. Nǐ rúguó zǒudào shāmò, nǐ yuǎn kàn jìn kàn dōu shi shā.   (T)

48.2. Chángshā zài Húnán Shěng, shi Zhōngguo cóng gǔ shíhou jiu hěn yǒumíngde dìfang.

49.0. běnbù   China Proper   (W)   [root section]

49.1. Qīng mò qǔxiāole kējǔ, zài běnbù shíbāshěngli pǔbiànde shèlì xuétáng.

50.0. dī   low

50.1. Tā zài shěnglì zhōngxué xiūyè yìnián, suǒyǐ tāde chéngdu hěn dī. Tā shuō yào xuǎn jǐběn shū zìjǐ niàn chōngshi chōngshi tā zìjǐ.

51.0. xíngchéng   (1) to form; (2) formation   [form become]

51.1. Nèige xiǎo dǎo shi zěnmo xíngchéng de?

Mǎ: Nǐ zhīdao bu zhīdào Zhōngguode shāmò dìdài zài shénmo dìfang?

Bái: Nèi Měnggǔ hé Xīnjiāng dōu yǒu shāmò.

Mǎ: Zhōngguo běnbù yǒu shāmò méi yǒu?

155 Bái: Zhèige wǒ bú dà qīngchu. Wǒ xiǎng méi yǒu. Shāmò duōbàr zài biānjiāng. Dōu shi zài gāoyuán dìfang, dīde dìfang méi yǒu shāmò.

Mǎ: Nǐ zhīdao shìjiè zuì dàde shāmò zài shénmo dìfang?

Bái: Zài Fēizhōu běibù.

Mǎ: Zài Zhōng Yàxiyǎ yǒu shāmò ma?

160 Bái: Zhōng Yàxiyǎ yǒu, érqiě shāmò hěn dà.

Mǎ: Shāmò shi zěnmo xíngchéngde?

Bái: Shi zìrán huánjìng suǒ xíngchéng de.

52.0. měilì   beautiful   [beautiful elegant]

52.1. Sì Shū shang shuō Kǒngzǐ qù kàn yíge měilìde nǚzǐ, Kǒngzǐde xuésheng zhīdaole zhèjiàn shì, shǐ tāmen hěn bù gāoxìng.

52.2. Wǒ èrnián méi kànjian ta, xiànzài zhǎngchéngle yíge hěn měilìde xiáojie le.   (T)

52.3. Nàlide fēngjǐng zhēn měilì, měilìde jiào wǒ méi fázi xíngróng. (T)

53.0. yǔ   rain   (N)

        xià yǔ   be raining   (see Intermediate Chinese, p. 26, note 8)

53.1. Wǒ cóng jiāli qǐshēn de shíhou jiù xià yǔ. Wǒ zǒuzai lùshang yǔ yuè xià yuè dà. Wǒ kàn zhèige yǔde qūshi shuōbudìng yào xià sāntiān wǔtiān ne.

53.2. Tā zuì xǐhuan chūqu le. Jiùshi xià yǔ tā yě yào chūqu.

53.3. Wǒ xiǎng tā bú huì xià yù tiān qù de.   (T)

53.4. Yīnwei xià yǔ zuótiande huì qǔxiāo le. Něitiān kāi huì zàichóng
      dìng rìzi. (T)

54.0. ní   mud

54.1. Bú xià yǔ de shíhou lùshang yǒu hěn duō tǔ, xià yǔ yǐhòu lùshang
      dōu shi ní. Zǒngzhi zhèitáo lù méi yǒu hǎo zǒude shíhou.

55.0. shí(tou)   stone

55.1. Jīntian dì-yītáng wǒ zài kètángli yǒu rén jiào wǒde xiǎomíng Shítou.

56.0. fādá   (1) develop, advance, prosper; (2) developed, advanced, pros-
              perous; (3) development   [emit attain]

56.1. Yào xiǎng dádào nóngyè fādáde mùdì bìděi gǎnkuài zàojiù nóngyè
      réncái. (T)

57.0. bújiànde   by no means certain, not at all evident

57.1. Yìbān rén suírán niànguo yánjiuyuàn bújiànde dōu yǒu gāoshēnde
      xuéwen.

Mǎ : Zhōngguo shi nóngyè guójiā. Nǐ zhīdao shénmo dìfang chūchǎn zuì
      fēngfù?

165 Bái: Cháng Jiāng、Zhū Jiāng、Huáng Hé liúyù nóngchǎn zuì fēngfù.

Mǎ : Duì le. Yóuqíshi Cháng Jiāng yídài. Dàjiā cháng shuō Jiāngnán
      shi yú-mǐ-zhī-xiāng. Dāngrán shi shuō Jiāngnán chūchǎnde hěn
      fēngfù, yòu yǒu yú yòu yǒu mǐ.

Bái: Fēngjǐng shi nánfāngde měilì, shi běifāngde měilì?

170 Mǎ : Wǒ rènwei nánfāngde fēngjǐng hǎokàn.   Wǒ qiúxuéde shíqī hěn
      xǐhuan lǚxíng. Wǒ suírán zài běifāng niàn shū, kěshi cháng dào
      nánfāng qù.

Bái: Tīngshuō yǒude dìfang lù hěn bù hǎo.

Mǎ : Shì. Běifāngde lù hěn bu hǎo. Shi tǔde. Yàoshi yí xiàyǔ, lùshang
175   dōu shi ní, shízài bù hǎo zǒu. Nánfāng wǒ qùguo de yìxiē dìfang
      lù dōu hěn hǎo, dōu shi shítoude.

Bái: Wǒ yě tīng rén shuōguo, xià yǔ tiān yǒude dìfang jiǎnzhíde bù néng
      chū mén.

Mǎ : Wǒmen zài yánjiu yíge wèntí.   Zhōngguo gōng-shāngyè zěnmoyàng?

180 Bái: Jìn xiē nián lái Zhōngguode gōng-shāngyè hěn fādá. Wǒ xiǎng zuì-
      jìnde jiānglái kéyi gǎnshang Xīfāng guójiā.

Mǎ : Duǎnqī bù néng gǎnshang, yuányīn shi Zhōngguo shi yíge jīngji lò-
      hòude guójiā.

Bái: Yě bújiànde. Jìn xiē nián lái Zhōngguo gèfāngmiànde qíngxing dōu
185   hěn jìnbù.

58.0. yăng   raise, support (family, animals, etc.)

58.1. Tā xĭhuan yăng yú. Tā bă cóng xiăo yú yăngdào dà yú de guòcheng
       hé gèzhŏng yúde tèxìng, dōu shuōde hĕn xiángxì, hĕn yŏu yìsi.

58.2. Wŏ xiànzài niàn shū ne, méi zuò shì. Wŏ bù néng yăng jiā. (T)

59.0. yáng   sheep

       yángròu   mutton, lamb

59.1. Yăng yáng de rén bújiànde dōu yŏu yángròu chī.

60.0. lĕng   cold

60.1. Dàlùxìngde qìhou shi yŏu shíhou hĕn lĕng, yŏu shíhou hĕn rè.

61.0. hányŏu   contain   (W)   [contain have]

61.1. Yángzi Jiāngde shuĭli yĕ hányŏu ní shā ma?

62.0. lìyì   advantage, benefit   (W)   [profit benefit]

62.1. Zuò guān de rén bù yīngdāng zhĭ xiăngdào bĕnshēnde lìyì.

Mă :   Nĭ zhīdao shénmo dìfang kàozhe yăng niú, yăng yáng shēnghuó?

Bái: Mĕnggŭ rén kào yăng niú, yăng yáng shēnghuó.

Mă :   Duì le. Biānjiāng yídài tiānqi hĕn lĕng. Bĭjiăo zuì lĕngde dìfang
       shi năr?

190 Bái: Xīzàng bĭjiăo zuì lĕng. Mă Jiàoshòu, hányŏu zhèige cér qĭng jiĕshi
       jiĕshi.

Mă :   Hányŏu zhèige cér shuō huà bú dà yòng. Jiu shi lĭmiàn yŏu de yìsi.
       Bĭrú "Shuĭli hányŏu ní shā."

Bái: Lìyì zhèige cér shì bu shi jiu shi hăochu de yìsi?

195 Mă : Shìde.

63.0. dìshì   physical feature   [earth tendency]

63.1. Nèibĕn dìlǐ dì-yīzhāng jiăng de shi Zhōngguode dìshì.   (T)

64.0. fāng   square

       sìfāng(de)   square   [four square]

       chángfāng(de) rectangular   [long square]

       fānglĭ   square mile

64.1. Bĕnxiàode dà jiăngtáng shi chángfāngde, xiăo kèshĭ duōbàn shi sì-
       fāngde. Hái yŏu lùyīnshĭ yĕ shi sìfāngde.

64.2. Jiāngnán yídài shuĭtián hĕn duō. Zŏng miànji yŏu dōushao fānglĭ
       ne?

65.0. gōng*   merit

　　　　yǒugōng   have merit, be meritorious   (VO)   (W)

　　　　chénggōng   (1) succeed; (2) success   [become merit]

　　　　zuòchénggōng   achieve success   (RV)

65.1. Tā zài xuéshùshang shi hěn yǒugōngde.   Tā yǒu shénmo gōng ne?
　　　　Tā shi zěnyàng yíbùyíbù chénggōng de ne?

65.2. Rúguǒ zài nàli tuīxíng pǔjí jiàoyu, wǒ xiāngxìn xū èrshiniánde nían-
　　　　xiàn cái néng chénggōng.

65.3. Nèijiān shì tā zuòdechénggōng zuòbuchénggōng?

66.0. shōu   receive, accept, collect

　　　　shōuqilai   set aside, gather up and put away

66.1. Tā gěi wǒ xiě de nèifēng jiǎntǐzìde xìn wǒ shōudào yǐhòu mǎshàng
　　　　jiu shōuqilai le.   Xiànzài zěnmo zhǎo yě zhǎobuzháo le.

67.0. rù   enter   (W)

　　　　rùmén   introduction, primer (in book titles)   [enter door]

67.1. Wǒ jīnnián yào rù dàxué le.

67.2. Guóyǔ Rùmén shi Zhōngguode yǒumíngde yǔyán xuéjiā xiě de.

Mǎ : Zhōngguode dìshì shi shénmo yàngzi?

Bái: Zhōngguode dìshì xīběi gāo dōngnán dī.

Mǎ : Zhōngguode miànji yígòng yǒu duōshao fānglǐ?

Bái: Wǒ bù zhīdào, wǒ jiù zhīdao hé Měiguode miànji chàbuduō.

200 Mǎ : Zhōngguode miànji yǒu jiǔbai liùshi duō wàn fānglǐ.

Bái: Shi Huálǐ shi Yīnglǐ?

Mǎ : Shi gōnglǐ.

Bái: Hái yǒu chénggōng zhèige cér jiu shi chéngle de yìsi ma?

Mǎ : Shìde.   Wǒ jǔ ge lìzi: "Nèijiàn shìqing zuòchéngōng le."

205 Bái: Oh!   Mǎ Jiàoshòu, zuótian yǒu ge péngyou lái fēng xìn.   Tā xiǎng
　　　　xué Zhōngguo huà.   Tā wèn wǒ Guóyǔ Rùmén zhèiběn shū hǎo bu
　　　　hǎo?   Nín shuō nèiběn shū zěnmoyàng?

Mǎ : Nèiběn shū búcuò.   Xiě nèiběn shū de shi yǒumíngde yǔyánxuéjiā.

Bái: Mǎ Jiàoshòu, xièxie nín.   Míngtian jiàn.

210 Mǎ : Míngtian jiàn.   Nǐ shēngcí biǎo hái méi shōuqilai ne.

Bái: Wǒ wàng le.   Míngtian jiàn.

Mǎ : Míngtian jiàn.

SHĒNGCÍ BIǍO

1. xíngrong
   xíngrongcí

2. dì-dà-wù-bó

3. chǎn
   chūchǎn
   nóngchǎn
   tǔchǎn
   wùchǎn
   chǎnshēng

4. mǐ

5. fēngfù

6. dàzhǐ

7. zāi*
   tiānzāi
   shuǐzāi
   hànzāi

8. hài
   zāihài
   sǔnhài

9. qū
   zìzhìqū

10. yù*
    qūyù
    liúyù

11. huáng
    Huáng Hǎi
    Huáng Hé

12. guǎng
    guǎngdà
    Guǎngdong
    Guǎngxi

13. miànji

14. fēngjǐng

15. zhōu
    Guǎngzhōu

16. (dà)zhōu
    Měi(zhōu)

17. Ào(zhōu)

18. Fēi(zhōu)

19. Ōu(zhōu)
    Ōuhuà
    Xī-Ōu
    Ōu-Měi

20. Yǎ(zhōu), Yà(zhōu)
    Yǎ(xiyǎ), Yà(xiyà)
    Dōngyǎ, Dōngyà

21. Sūlián
    Zhōng-Sū

22. Ē(guo), É(guo), È(guo)
    Ē(wén), É(wén), È(wén)
    Zhōng-Ē, Zhōng-É,
      Zhōng-È

23. wèizhi

24. wēn
    wēnshū
    wēnhé
    wēndài

25. rè
    rèdài

26. (hǎi)dǎo
    bàndǎo

27. lù*
    lùdì
    dàlù

28. xìng*
    tèxìng

29. ràng
    ràngbù

30. zhímín (W)
    zhímíndì

31. shāng*
    shāngren
    shāngyè

32. tōng
    tōngshāng
    tōngxìn
    tōngguò

33. zhàn

34. jiāng*
    biānjiāng
    Xīnjiāng

35. biānjiè

36. (Xī)zàng
    Zàngwén

37. Měng(gǔ)
    Nèi Měng(gǔ)
    Wài Měng(gǔ)
    Měng(gǔ)wén

38. jiāojiè

39. Yìndu

40. Miǎndiàn

41. kào(zhe)
    kěkào
    kàodezhù

42. Qīnghǎi

43. Dòngtíng Hú

44. Póyáng Hú

45. jiāng
    Yángzi Jiāng
    Cháng Jiāng
    Jiāngnán
    Jiāngxi
    Jiāngsu
    Zhèjiāng
    Zhū Jiāng

46. yán(zhe)
    yánhǎi

47. xiāng*
    xiāngxia
    tóngxiāng

48. shā
    shāmò
    Chángshā

49. běnbù (W)

50. dī

51. xíngchéng

52. měilì

53. yǔ
    xià yǔ

54. ní

55. shí(tou)

56. fādá

57. bújiànde

58. yǎng

59. yáng
    yángròu

60. lěng

61. hányǒu (W)

62. lìyì (W)

63. dìshì

64. fāng

    sìfāng(de)

    chángfāng(de)

    fānglǐ

65. gōng *

    yǒugōng (W)

    chénggōng

    zuòchénggōng

66. shōu

    shōuqilai

67. rù (W)

    rùmén

YǓFǍ LIÀNXÍ

A. The pattern S₁ S₂ meaning "if . . . then" (see note 1)

1. Zhèicì yǎnjiǎng "Fēizhōu Gàikuàng" shi shéi zhǔjiǎng? Mǎ Jiàoshòu jiǎng wǒ qù tīng. Biéren jiǎng wǒ bù xiǎng qù le.

2. Tā dào le Zhèjiāng Gōnglì Xuéxiào yǐhòu tā jiu bù hé wǒ tōng xìnle. Tā bù lái xìn wǒ bù xiǎng gěi ta xiě xìn le.

3. <u>Sān Zì Jīng</u>, <u>Qiān Zì Wén</u>, <u>Sì Shū</u>, <u>Wǔ Jīng</u>, <u>Zhōng-É Zìdiǎn</u> děng shū wǒ dōu yǒu. Nǐ yào yòng wǒ jiègei ni.

4. Nǐmen zhūwèi dào Dōngyǎ qù lǚxíng zuò chuán háishi zuò fēijī? Zuò chuán wǒ yě qù, zuò fēijī wǒ bú qù.

5. Nèige sīlì xuéxiào gèzhǒng xuékē dōu hǎo, zàojiùle hěn duō réncái. Kěshi hěn nán kǎojìnqù. Xuésheng kǎo nèige xuéxiào, chéngdu gāo tāmen shōu, chéngdu dī tāmen bú yào.

B. The pattern S₁ yě-S₂ (see note 2)

6. Fēijī lùoxialai bàntiān le, tā yě méi xiàlai.

7. Wǒ zuì xǐhuan chī yángròu le. Suíbiàn zěnmo guì wǒ yě děi mǎizhe chī.

8. Nèijiàn shìqing nǐ shuō shénmo tā dōu bú ràngbù.

9. Jiùshi nǐ shuō tā kàodezhù, wǒ yě bù xiāngxìn tā kěkào.

10. <u>Yǒugōng</u> zhèige cér wǒ zěnmo gěi ta jiěshi tā yě bù liǎojiě.

11. Nǐmen shéi shuō Chángshā hǎo, wǒ yě bù xǐhuan nèige dìfang.

12. Wǒ zěnmo shuō Táiwān tǔchǎn hǎo, tā dōu bù xiǎng mǎi.

13. Tāde shìyè nènmo duō, tā háishi bù mǎnzú. Jiùshi nǐ bǎ wǔ dàzhōu gěi le tā, tā dōu bú huì gǎndao kuàilè de.

14. Nèige shāngren zhǐ kàn lìyì zhèi yìfāngmiàn le. Búlùn nǐ zěnmo shuō nèige dìfang bù píngān, tā dōu yào qù.

15. Jīntian yǎnjiǎng zhǐmínde wèntí de nèiwèi Wàn Bóshi gèfāngmiànde xuéshi dōu xiāngdāng hǎo. Suíbiàn jiǎng něi yìfāngmiànde wèntí tā yě bù juéde kùnnán.

C. The pattern <u>yìtiān bǐ yìtiān</u> (see note 3)

16. Yīnwei shídài cháoliúde guānxi, Yǎzhōu rén dào Ōu-Měi liúxué de yìtiān
     bǐ yìtiān duō.

17. Jù yìbān rén shuō, dào Nèi Měnggǔ zìzhìqū qù de rén yìnián bǐ yìnián
     duō.

18. Wǒ tīng nèi jǐge wàiguo xuésheng zài kètángshang yòng <u>Guóyǔ Rùmén</u>
     nèiběn shū xuéxí Guóyǔ, tāmen yíge rén bǐ yíge rén shuōde hǎo.

19. Yíge tóngxiāng cóng Xī-Ōu lái xìn shuō, nàlide nǚháizi yíge bǐ yíge hǎo-
     kàn.

20. Xīwang shòu Huáng Hé zāihài de dìqū zhǐ shuǐ zhìde yìnián bǐ yìnián
     chénggōng.

D. The pattern <u>gè V gède</u> (see <u>Intermediate Chinese</u>, p. 222, note 3)

21. Zhōngguo dì-dà-wù-bó, wùchǎn fēngfù. Gè dìfang yǒu gè dìfangde chūchǎn.

22. Wǒ dào Sūlián lǚxíngle zhīhòu, wǒ gǎndào tāmen měi yíge qūyù yǒu měi
     yíge qūyù fāzhǎnde fāngshì.

23. Nèige tuántǐ de quántǐ tuányuán guānyu Dōngyàde wèntí kāihuì. Yīnwei
     gèrén yǒu gèrénde yìjian, huì kāile sāntiān, yíjiàn shì yě méi tōngguò.

24. Nèi jǐkuài shítou yǒude shi chángfāngde, yǒude shi sìfāngde, gè yǒu gède
     yòngchu.

25. Zǒngzhi guānyu Dōngyàde wèntí wǒmende kànfǎ bùtóng. Tāmen yǒu
     tāmende kànfǎ, wǒmen yǒu wǒmende kànfǎ.

E. The pattern <u>A ná/yòng B bǎ C V</u> (see <u>Intermediate Chinese</u>, p. 52,
    note 4)

26. Qǐng nǐ yòng Zhōngwén bǎ Guǎngdong, Guǎngxi liǎngshěng pǔjí jiàoyu de
     gàikuàng xiěxialai, ránhòu zài fānyìchéng Yīngwén.

27. Yòng shénmo fāngfǎ bǎ Àozhōu chǎnde yáng chūkǒu dào quán shìjiè qu?

28. Jīntian Zhāng Xiānshengde jiǎngtí shi Zhōngguo Wénhuà. Suīrán fànwéi
     hěn guǎng, tā ná hěn jiǎndānde huà bǎ wénhuà fāzhǎn dàzhì qíngxing
     shuōde hěn qīngchu.

29. Tā hěn huì yòng xíngrongcí. Tā yòngle jǐge xíngrongcí bǎ nèige xiāngxia
     nǚháizi xíngrongde fēicháng měilì.

30. Gǔshíhou Měnggǔ rén yòng Měngwén bǎ Zàngwén hé Yìndùwénde míngzhù
     dōu fānchéng Měnggǔwén le.

JIǍNGHUÀ

     Zhōngguo shi yíge dì-dà-wù-bó rénkǒu duō de guójiā. Zhèzhǒng
dì-dà-wù-bó rénkǒu duō de zuì hǎode tiáojiàn shi zěnmo xíngchéngde ne?

Zhè duōbàn shi zìrán huánjing xíngchéng de, yě jiu shi dìlǐde guānxi xíngchéng de. Suǒyǐ yào liǎojiě Zhōngguo, bì xiān míngbai Zhōngguode zìrán
5 huánjing, yě jiu shi shuō bì xiān míngbai Zhōngguode dìlǐ.

Zhōngguode wèizhi zài Yàzhōude dōngnánbù. Dōngbiān shi Huáng
Hǎi、Dōng Hǎi、Nán Hǎi. Běibiān shi Wài Měnggǔ hé Sūlián. Xībiān shi
Zhōng Yàxiyǎ. Xīnán shi Yìndu. Nánbiān shi Yuènán、Miǎndiàn. Quánguóde miànji chàbuduō yǒu sìbǎiwàn fāng Yīnglǐ. Zhàn shìjiè lùdì zǒng miànji
10 shífēngzhī-yī, Yàzhōu sìfēngzhī-yī. Shi Yǎozhōude dì-yīge dà guó.

Zhōngguo guónèide qūyù zài dìlǐshang fēnwéi běnbù hé biānjiāng.
Běnbù yǒu shíbāshěng, biānjiāng yǒu Dōngběi、Měnggǔ、Xīnjiāng、Xīzàng
sìge dìfang. Zài xíngzhèngshang fēnwéi èrshisānshěng, sānge dà zìzhìqū.
Zhè èrshisānshěng chúle běnbù shíbāshěng yǐwài, yǒu Qīnghái Shěng、
15 Táiwān Shěng. Yòu bǎ Dōngběi fēnwéi sānshěng. Yígòng shi èrshisānshěng. Sānge dà zìzhìqū shi Měnggǔ、Xīnjiāng hé Xīzàng.

Zhōngguo běnbùde rénkǒu zhàn zǒng rénkǒude bǎifēnzhī-jiǔshí. Biānjiāngde rénkǒu zhàn bǎifēnzhī-shí. Zài zhè jǐge biānjiāng qūyùlǐ, zhǐ yǒu
Dōngběide tǔdì hěn hǎo, wùchǎn yě duō. Hái yǒu xiàng Měnggǔ、Xīnjiāng、
20 Xīzàng zhèxiě dìfang, nóngtián hěn shǎo. Yǒude shi shāmò hěn duō, yǒude
shi shān tài duō, dāngdìde rén duōbàn kàozhe yǎng niú yǎng yáng guò
rìzi.

Zhōngguode dìshì dōngbù dī, běibù bǐ dōngbù gāo yìxiē. Xībù hé
nánbù duōbàn shi gāoyuán, hái yǒu hěn duō dà shān. Yīnwei dìshì shi
25 xībù bǐ dōngbù gāo, suǒyǐ Zhōngguode héliú duōbàn shi cóng xī wǎng dōng
liú. Zhōngguo zhùmíngde héliú yǒu sāntiáo.

Dì-yī, Cháng Jiāng. Yě jiàozuo Yángzi Jiāng. Zài Zhōngguode
zhōngbù, shi Zhōngguo zuì chángde héliú. Cháng Jiāng liúyù tǔdì hěn hǎo,
nóngchǎn fēngfù, érqiě Cháng Jiāng rù hǎi de hǎikǒu shi Shànghǎi. Shàng-
30 hǎide gōng-shāngyè hěn fādá, shi quánguóde jīngji zhōngxīn. Suǒyǐ Cháng
Jiāng shi gěi Zhōngguo dàilái jīngji lìyì de yìtiáo héliú.

Dì-èr, Huáng Hé. Zài Zhōngguode běibù. Hé shuǐ shi huáng yánsede.
Shuǐlǐ hányǒu ní shā. Huáng Hé chángcháng fāshēng shuǐzāi, měicì shuǐzāi rénmín dōu shòu hěn dàde sǔnhài. Dànshi Zhōngguo zài sānqiānnián
35 qián zuì zǎode wénhuà shi cóng Huáng Hé liúyù kāishǐ, yǐhòu cái jiànjiànde fāzhǎn. Huáng Hé suīrán duì rénmín yǒu hài, kěshi zài Zhōngguo
wénhuàshang shi yǒugōngde.

Dì-sān, Zhū Jiāng.   Zài Zhōngguo nánbù.   Tāde liúyù zhǐ yǒu

Guǎngxi、Guǎngdōng liǎngshěng. Zhū Jiāng liúyù suírán yǒu hěn duō shān,

40 dànshi nóngtián yě bù shǎo.   Zhū Jiāng rù hǎi de hǎikǒu shi Guǎngzhōu,

shi Zhōng-wài tōngshāng zuì zǎode dìfang. Xiànzài shi Zhōngguo nánfāng-

de shāngyè zhōngxīn.

Zài Zhōngguode zhōngbù yǒu sānge dà hú, jiu shi Dòngtíng Hú、

Póyáng Hú、Tài Hú.   Zhèxiē húde sìmiàn nóngtián hěn duō, chūchǎn de

45 mǐ yě hěn duō, húlǐ yòu yǒu hěn duō yú. Yīnwei zhè yídài dìfang dōu zài

Cháng Jiāng yǐnán, suǒyǐ Zhōngguo rén shuō Jiāngnán shi yú-mǐ-zhī-xiāng.

Zhōngguo yánhǎi yǒu yìxiē hǎidǎo. Zuì dàde hǎidǎo shi Táiwān, zài

Dōng Hǎi hé Nán Hǎi zhījiān, lí Zhōngguo dàlù chàbuduō yìbǎi gōnglǐ

zuǒyòu.   Táiwān wùchǎn fēngfù, fēngjǐng měilì, xiànzài shi Zhōngguode

50 yìshěng. Hái yǒu yíge zuì xiǎo yòu zuì zhùmíngde háidǎo shi Xiānggǎng.

Běnlái shi shǔyu Zhōngguo.   Cóng yī-bā-sì-èr nián yǐlái shi Yīngguode

zhímíndì le.

Yīnwei Zhōngguode wèizhi shi zài běi wēndài, suǒyǐ Zhōngguode

qìhou dà bùfen shi wēnhéde. Yòu yīnwei Zhōngguo sānmiàn shi lùdì, zhǐ

55 yǒu yímiàn shi hǎi, suǒyǐ Zhōngguode qìhou yòu shi dàlùxìngde. Dànshi

Zhōngguode dìfang tài dà le, suǒyǐ běibùde qìhou hé nánbù bùtóng, dōng-

bùde qìhou yě hé xībù bùtóng. Dàzhǐ shuōlái, běibù、xībù jiǎo lěng, nánbù

jiǎo rè, dōngbù、zhōngbù wēnhé.

Zǒngzhi, Zhōngguode zìrán huánjìng cóng dàtǐshàng lái kàn shi

60 xiāngdāngde hǎo. Zhōngguo rén yǒu yíjù cháng shuō de huà: "dà hǎo hé

shān," jiu shi xíngrong Zhōngguo zìrán huánjìng hěn hǎo de yìsi.

FÙSHÙ

Zhèipán lùyīndài shi Zhōngwén dì-yīzǔ dì-sānhào, Bái Wénshān fùshù

dì-sāncì Zhuāntí Jiǎnghuà.

Zhècì Zhuāntí Jiǎnghuàde tímu shi Zhōngguo Jiàoyu. Zhǔjiǎng rén

méi yǒu bǎ Zhōngguo jiàoyu cóng gǔ dào jīn dōu jiǎngguo, zhǐshi jiǎng

5 de Zhōngguo jìn yìbǎiniánde jiàoyu. Wèi-shénmo jiù jiǎng jìn yìbǎiniánde

jiàoyu ne? Yīnwei Zhōngguode jiàoyu zài jìn yìbǎinián lǐtou yǒu hěn dàde

yǎnbiàn. Yǎnbiànde zhǔyīn shi shòule wàiguode yǐngxiǎng. Suǒyǐ shídàide

qūshì shi bìděi zhùzhòng xīn jiàoyu.

Zhè yìbǎinián kéyi fēnwéi sānge shíqī. Tóu yíge shíqī shi sīshú

10 shíqī, shi zài yī-bā-jiǔ-bā nián yǐqián. Shénmo jiàozuo sīshú ne? Jiu

shi yíwèi yǒu diǎr xuéwènde rén zài tāde jiā lǐmian shōu jǐge xuésheng.

Zài jiāli kàn xuéshengde chéngdu jiāo tāmen niàn shū. Méi shénmo zǔzhi,

zhǐshi kàn xuésheng chéngdu jiāogei tāmen. Bǐrú cái kāishǐ niàn shū de

jiu jiāogei tāmen Sān Zì Jīng、Bǎi Jiā Xìng shénmode. Yàoshi chéngdu

15 gāo yìdiǎr de jiu niàn Wǔ Jīng, Sì Shū děng shū. Zǒngzhi méi yǒu yídìng-

de kècheng, yě méi yǒu niánxiàn, yě méi yǒu kǎoshì. Sīshú nèige shíqī

jiu shi kējǔ shídài.

Cóng Táng Cháo dào Qīng mò dōu shi kējǔ zhìdu. Nà shi yìzhǒng

kǎoshì de zhìdu. Nèige shídài sīshúde xuésheng rènwei tāmende chéngdu

20 kéyi le, tāmen jiu qù cānjiā kǎoshì. Yàoshi kǎoshang le jiu kéyi zuò guān.

Yǒude rén suīrán tāmen méi kǎoshang, kěshi tāmende xuéwen bújiànde bù

hǎo. Nèixiē rén suīrán méi kǎoqǔ bù néng zuò guān, yǒude zài jiā jìxùde

yánjiu xuéwèn, yǒude tāmende chūlù jiu shi zài jiā shè sīshú jiāo xué-

sheng.

25 Dì-èrge shíqī shi xuétáng shíqī. Cóng yī-bā-jiǔ-bā nián kāishǐ. Yī-

jiǔ-líng-wǔ nián kējǔ qǔxiāo le yǐhòu, xuétáng chénglìde gèng duō le. Xué-

táng gēn xuéxiào chàbuduō, jiù shi míngchēng bùtóng. Xuétáng yǒude shi

guānlìde, yǒude shi sīlìde. Kècheng hé xuésheng xiūyè de niánxiàn dōu

shi zhèngfǔ guīdìng de. Xuétáng shíqī shi xīn jiù jiàoyude yíge guòdù

30 shíqī. Shíjiān bù hěn cháng, búguò yǒu shíwǔnián zuǒyòu.

Dì-sānge shíqī jiu shi xuéxiào shíqī. Xuéxiào shíqī shi cóng Mínguó

chūnián kāishǐ. Xuéxiào hé sīshú dà bú xiāngtóng. Sīshúde xuésheng bù

fēn niánjí. Xuéshengli xiǎoháizi、qīngnián rén、zhōngnián rén dōu yǒu.

Xuéxiàoli fēn niánjí, yǒu yòuzhiyuán、xiǎoxué、zhōngxué、dàxué hái yǒu

35 yánjiuyuàn. Xiàmiàn shuōyishuō jiàoyu de mùbiāo. Zài yòuzhiyuán hé

xiǎoxué shi jiāogei xiǎoxuéshengmen jīběnde zhīshi. Zhōngxué shi ràng

xuésheng duō zhīdao gèzhǒngde xuéshi. Dàxué hé yánjiuyuàn shi zàojiù

zhuānmén réncái.

Zǒng'eryánzhi Zhōngguode jiàoyu shi jiànjiànde tígāo le. Suīrán

40 Zhōngguo xiànzài méi dádào pǔjí jiàoyu zhèige mùbiāo, kěshi xuéshengde

zǒngshù yìtiān bǐ yìtiān zēngjiā. Dàtǐshang shuō, Zhōngguode jiàoyu zhìdu

hé Ōu-Měi shi dà-tóng-xiǎo-yì. Yě kéyi shuō Zhōngguo xiànzàide jiàoyu

zhìdu shi Ōuhuà de.

WÊNXI

1. Qīng Cháode shíhou Zhōng-Ē liǎngguó jiāojiè de dìfang chángcháng fāshēng biānjiè wèntí. Měicì dōu shi Zhōngguo ràngbù, suǒyǐ Zhōngguo yǒu bù shǎode tǔdì jiu ràng Ēguo zhànqu le.

2. Xiànzài shāngren duōbàn yòng tōngxìn de fāngfǎ bǎ dāngdìde tǔchǎn màidao wàiguo qu. Dànshi zhèzhǒng fāngfǎ yǒushí kàodezhù yǒushí bù kěkào. Yǒu yícì zài xìnshang shuō de shi tǔchǎn, kěshi dōngxi dào le wàiguo dōu shi yìxiē dà shítou.

3. Qīnghǎi Shěng suírán yǒu hěn duō shān, kěshi yě yǒu guǎngdàde píngyuán. Zài zhèige píngyuán dìyùde sìmiàn dōu shi shān.

4. Rèdài qìhoude tèxìng shi shícháng xià yǔ, suǒyǐ chǎnshēng de dōngxi duōbàn shi yòu gāo yòu dà. Kěshi yǔ xiàde tài duō le, yě huì chéng le zāihài.

5. <u>Chángfāngde</u>、<u>sìfāngde</u> dōu shi xíngrongcí. Bǐfang shuō "Nèige bàndǎo dàzhì shi chángfāngde," jiu shi xíngrong nèige bàndǎo xiàng shi chángfāngde shide.

6. Dōngyà guójiāde xuésheng dào Ōuzhou qù liúxué, duōbàn zài Xī-Ōu. Tāmen huíguó yǐhòu cháng yǐwéi xuéle bù shǎo dōngxi, duì guójiā hěn yǒugōng. Kěshi yǒude liúxuéshēng chúle zài shēnghuóshang Ōuhuà yǐwài, tāmen zhēnde xuédàole shénmo ne?

7. Zhōngguode Dōngběi lí Ēguo jìn, suǒyǐ yǒu bù shǎo rén dǒngde Ēwén. Yàoshi dàole Zhōngguode nánfāng xiàng Guǎngzhou zhè yídài, yīnwei lí Ēguo tài yuǎn suǒyǐ dǒngde Ēwén de rén jiu hěn shǎo le.

8. Jīnnián Hénán、Shānxi qūyù hěn jiǔ bú xià yǔ, yǐjing chéngle hànzāi. Kěshi yánzhe Cháng Jiāng yídài yǔ xiàde tèbié duō, kàn qíngxing yòu yào yǒu shuǐzāi. Jīnnián bú shi hànzāi jiu shi shuǐzāi, zhēnshi tiānzāi tài duō le.

9. Shìjièshang zuì lěngde dìfang shi zài Sūlián.

10. Huáng Hé shi cóng Shāndong bàndǎo rù hǎi. Zài Zhōngguo lìshǐshang kàn, yǒude shíhou shi cóng bàndǎo nánbiar rù hǎi, yǒude shíhou shi cóng bàndǎo běibiar rù hǎi.

11. Měnggǔ、Xīzàngde rénmín duōshù dōu shi yǎng niú yǎng yáng, suǒyǐ tāmen chī de yě shi niúròu、yángròu.

12. Wèile nèijiàn shì kāile wǔcì huì, yě méi tōngguò. Yuányīn shi dàjiā dōu bú zànchéng.

13. Zìcóng qǔxiāo sīshú yǐhòu, běnlái zài sīshú niàn shū de xuésheng jiànjiānde dōu dào zhèngfǔ lǐ de xuéxiào qù niàn shū le. Zhèngfǔ shèlì xuéxiào, yìfāngmiàn shi wèile xuésheng shēnxīn de fāzhǎn, yìfāngmiàn wèideshì pǔjí jiàoyu. Xiànzài xiàngzhe zhè liǎngge mùbiāo qiánjìn, kàn qíngxing tāmen yídìng kéyi zuòchénggōng de.

14. Nèige liúxuéshēng shi niàn bóshi de. Tā jìnlái gǎn bóshi lùnwén ne. Yǒu rén shuō tā xiě de lùnwén hěn hǎo. Bóshi xuéwèi dàtǐshang shi méi shénmo wèntí, tā kéyi dáchéng dé bóshi de mùdì le. Nèige liúxuéshēng shuō, tā déle bóshi xuéwèi yě bù huíguó, tā xiǎng chángqī zài wàiguo yánjiu xuéwen.

15. Zhāng Xiānsheng zuì xǐhuan mǎi Zhōngguo shū. Búlùn xīn shū huòzhě jiù
shū fánshi Zhōngguo shū zhǐ yàoshi tā xǐhuan de tā jiu mǎi. Qiántian tā
kànjian yìběn Zhōngguo gǔbǎnde shū. Tā běnlái xiǎng jiàqián tài guì le,
tā bù xiǎng mǎi le. Kěshi zuìhòude juédìng háishi mǎi le.

16. Yǒu yíge zhōngxuéshēng zhèng zài jiāli wēnshū. Tā yǒu yíge tóngxiāng
lái kàn ta, tā jiu bǎ shū shōuqilai le. Tāde tóngxiāng shuō jīnnián yánzhe
dà hú de dìyù dōu yǒu shuǐzāi. Húnánde Chángshā gēn Jiāngxide jǐge xiǎo
xiàn shòu de zāihài zuì dà.

WÈNTÍ

1. Zhōngguode wèizhi zài shénmo dìfang? Zhōngguode dōngmiàn shi shénmo
hǎi? Xī, běi, nán sānmiàn dōu yǒu shénmo guójiā?

2. Zhōngguo yǒu jǐtiáo dà hé? Dōu shi shénmo míngzi? Duōbàn wǎng shénmo
fāngxiàng liúqu? Wèi-shénmo wǎng nèige fāngxiàng liúqu?

3. Něitiáo héliú duì Zhōngguo zuì yǒu lìyì? Yǒu shénmo lìyì? Shénmo héliú
duì Zhōngguo yǒu hài? Yǒu shénmo hài? Zhèitiáo yǒu hàide héliú zài
něi yìfāngmiàn shi yǒugōngde?

4. Qǐng nǐ shuō Zhōngguo liǎngge dà hǎikǒude míngzi. Shāndong bàndǎo yǒu
hǎikǒu ma?

5. Zhōngguo yǒu jǐge dà hú? Dōu jiào shénmo míngzi? Dōu zài něitiáo
héliúde liúyù? Zài něishěngli?

6. "Jiāngnán shi yú-mǐ-zhī-xiāng" shi shénmo yìsi?

7. Zhōngguode qìhou zěnmoyàng?

8. Zhōngguo yánhǎi zuì dàde hé zuì xiǎo yòu zuì yǒumíngde hǎidǎo jiào
shénmo míngzi? Xiànzài zhè liǎngge hǎidǎo de qíngxing shi zěnmoyàng?

9. Zhōngguo guónèi fēnwéi jǐge qūyù? Dōu shi shénmo míngchēng? Něige
qūyùde rénkǒu zuì duō?

10. Zhōngguo biānjiāng yǒude dìfang nóngtián hěn shǎo, dāngdì rénmín kào
shénmo shēnghuó?

ILLUSTRATIVE SENTENCES (ENGLISH)

1.1. "Mr. Zhang's health [lit. body] is very good." The word "good" is an adjective describing (the fact) that Mr. Zhang's health is very good.

4.1. The greatest of China's agricultural products is rice.

5.2. If we ask Mr. Wang to write the introduction [lit. explanation] for our book
it will make the whole work more substantial [lit. contents are then
likely to be rich].

8.2. In this flood (the area) that received the greatest damage was Honan Province.

10.1. If we were to divide China into two great regions, how would we do it?

12.1. The flooded areas in Kwangtung and Kwangsi are very extensive. Vast (areas of) agricultural land have suffered damage.

16.1. Are the zhōu of Měizhōu and Guǎngzhōu the same? . . . No. The zhōu of Měizhōu has nine strokes, and is the same character as the zhōu of dàzhōu. The zhōu of Guǎngzhōu has only six strokes.

23.1. The school wants to buy that building as an office, because it is located opposite the school. The school has decided it can only be used as an office for the staff.

30.1. England [formerly] colonized [toward] America.

32.1. Those big cities are all joined by rail.

33.1. He will certainly win [lit. be elected] in this election, because the number of people who will vote for [lit. elect] him comprise eighty per cent of the total.

33.2. [Formerly] Formosa was occupied by Japan for fifty years.

34.3. Problems related to the frontier often arise between countries.

37.4. Outer Mongolia is a new nation. Its location is between China and Russia.

41.1. Mr. Zhang makes his living by writing novels.

47.1. What is "a land of fish and rice"? It is a place that has (a great deal of) both fish and rice.

48.1. If you go to the desert, [looking] far and near all is sand.

52.2. I haven't seen her for two years, and now she's grown into a very beautiful young lady.

52.3. The scenery there is really beautiful, so beautiful that I can't describe it.

53.3. I think he's not likely to go on a rainy day.

53.4. Because of the rain yesterday's meeting was canceled. Another date will be set for the meeting.

56.1. [If one hopes] to achieve [the goal of] a flourishing agriculture it is necessary to train skilled agricultural personnel as soon as possible.

58.2. I'm studying now and haven't been working, (so) I can't support a family.

63.1. The first chapter of that geography book deals with the physical features of China.

NOTES

1. Two sentences S$_1$ and S$_2$ spoken in close sequence often have an 'if . . . then' relationship:

    Jiàqian guì wǒ bù mǎi. '(If) the price is high I won't buy.'

2. In addition to its usual meaning of 'also' the word yě is used interchangeably with dōu in the construction S$_1$ yě/dōu-S$_2$. (See Beginning Chinese, p. 375, note 2.) In this construction the first sentence is concessive in meaning and

the two sentences have the relationship of 'although . . . nevertheless,' 'even though . . . nevertheless' or 'even if . . . still.' The concessive idea is often reinforced by the use of suírán, suíbiàn, jiùshi, lián, or jiùshi lián before the first sentence:

> (Jiùshi) nǐ qù wǒ yě bú qù.   'Even if you go I'm not going.'

Yě is also interchangeable with dōu in a construction in which the first sentence contains a question-word and the two sentences have the relationship of 'no matter . . . still.' Sometimes the relationship is reinforced by the use of búlùn 'regardless of' or suíbiàn 'however one likes':

> (Suíbiàn) nǐ zěnmo zuò tā yě bù gāoxìng.   'No matter what you do (lit. how you do) he's unhappy.'

Note especially carefully the concessive meaning imparted by yě in the second of two sentences without any further markers of the construction:

> Wǒ zhǎolái zhǎoqù yě zhǎobuzháo.   'Although I looked everywhere I couldn't find it.'

> Nǐ qù wǒ yě bu qù.   'Even if you go I'm not going.'

3. The expression yìtiān bǐ yìtiān means 'day by day' or 'one day after another.' Other measures can replace tiān in this construction: yìnián bǐ yìnián 'year by year,' yíge rén bǐ yíge rén 'person after person,' yìsuǒ fángzi bǐ yìsuǒ fángzi 'house after house.'

Dì-Wǔkè.   Rénkǒu

Bái: Mǎ Jiàoshòu, nín jīntian zěnmo zěnmo zǎo jiu lái le?

Mǎ : Wénshān, nǐ láide yě bù wǎn. Xiànzài cái bādiǎn.

Bái: Wǒmen xuésheng yīnggāi zǎo lái. Xiānsheng dào xiān lái le.

Mǎ : Zuótian wǎnshang yǔ xiàde hěn dà.

5 Bái: Kěbushìma! Wǒ wǎnshang tīngjian yǔ xiàzai shítou dìshang de
       shēngyīn fēicháng hǎotīng.

Mǎ : Jīntian zǎoshang jǐdiǎn zhōng qǐlai de?

Bái: Wǒ qǐlai de shíhou hái bú dào liùdiǎn ne.

Mǎ : Zuótian wǎnshang lùyīn le méi yǒu?

10 Bái: Lù le, búguò wǒ juéde háishi bù chéng. Wǒ xiǎng zài lù yícì.

Mǎ : Zěnmo bù chéng? Wǒ xiāngxìn nǐ zìrán'érrán jiu huì jìnbù de.
       Nǐ lù de fùshù Zhōngguo Jiàoyu wǒ tīng le. Dàzhì búcuò, yìdiǎr yě
       tīngbuchūlái shi wàiguo rén lù de yīn.

Bái: Shi zhēnde, nín háishi kèqi ne?

15 Mǎ : Zhēnde. Zuótian dìlǐ jiǎnghuà jiǎngde zěnmoyàng?

Bái: Jiǎngde xiāngdāng hǎo. Zhèiwèi Zhāng Bóshide kǒuyīn shi běifāng
      kǒuyīn. Wǒmen tīngqilai hěn róngyi.

Mǎ : Tā duì dìlǐxué xiāngdāng yǒu yánjiu. Zhèr yǒu hǎojǐge dàxué yòng
      tā xiě de shū zuò dìlǐ cānkǎo shū.

20 Bái: Tā jiǎngde hěn hǎo. Tā xiān cóng Zhōngguode wèizhi gěi wǒmen
       jiǎngqǐ, yòu jiǎng Zhōngguode biānjiāng, zài jiǎng Zhōngguode yánhǎi
       hé jiāojiède guójiā, yíbùyíbùde jiǎngxiaqu. Běnlái dìlǐ zhèimén
       gōngke bù róngyi jiǎngde ràng rén fāshēng xìngqu, kěshi tā jiǎngde
       wǒmen fēicháng xǐhuan tīng.

25 Mǎ : Búlùn něizhǒng xuékē bìděi jiǎngde hǎo, cái shòu rén huānyíng.

Bái: Zhāng Bóshi jiǎng Huáng Hé chángcháng fāshēng shuǐzāi. Suírán
      niánnián zhì shuǐ, kěshi dōu méi zhìhǎo.

Mǎ : Yīnwei Huáng Héde ní shā tài duō le.

Bái: Wǒ jìde zài gǔdàide shíhou yǒu rén zhì shuǐ zhìle shísānnián yě
30   méi huí jiā. Zài zhì shuǐde qījiān tā cóng jiā ménkǒur jīngguo
      sāncì, tā dōu méi jìnqu kànyikàn. Nèicì dàshuǐ shì bu shi yě shi
      Huáng Hé shuǐzāi?

Mǎ : Nèicìde dàshuǐ gēn Huáng Hé yě yǒu guānxi. Zuótian yǎnjiǎng
      nèiróng dōu méi wèntí ma?

35 Bái : Méi shénmo wèntí.

Mǎ : Zhèi shi jiǎng Zhōngguo rénkǒude shēngcí biǎo. Nǐ xiān kànyikàn.

1.0. ān-tǔ-zhòng-qiān   be content in one's native place and consider mov-
                          ing a serious matter (W) [peace earth heavy
                          move]

1.1. Ān-tǔ-zhòng-qiān zhèijù huà shi wényán de, shi "bù suíbiàn líkai
      běntǔ" de yìsi.

2.0. A (yìsi jiu) shi shuō B   A means B

2.1. Ōu-Měi liǎngge zìde yìsi jiu shi shuō Ōuzhou hé Měizhou.

3.0. bān   move, shift

      bānjiā   move, change residence   (VO)

3.1. Yīnwei zhèlǐ shi rèdài, tiānqi tài rè, suǒyǐ tā yào bānjiā. Tā xiǎng
      bāndao tiānqi wēnhé de dìfang qu.

4.0. fēi   not   (W)

      fēi(děi) V (bùkě)   absolutely have to V, insist on V-ing

      chúfēi   unless   [except not]

4.1. Zhōngguo gǔshí yǒu yíwèi zhéxuéjiā shuō "Bái mǎ fēi mǎ." Nǐ
      zhīdao shi shénmo yìsi ma?   (T)

4.2. Míngtian yào kǎo jīngjixué. Wǒ fēiděi wēnshū bùkě.

4.3. Chúfēi yǒu tiānzāi yàoburán tā yìshēng yě bú huì bānjiā.   (T)

4.4. Wǒ bù xiǎng mǎi nèiběn shū. Chúfēi xiānsheng jiào wǒmen mǎi wǒ
      cái mǎi ne.   (T)

5.0. huò   calamity

      rénhuò   man-made calamity

5.1. Huò shi hài de yìsi. Rénhuò jiu shi rén zuòchulai de sǔnhài.

6.0. zhǐ(zhe)   (1) point, point out, indicate, show; (2) refer to,
                          mean that

      zhǐ(zhe) . . . shuō   refer to, speak of, mean that

6.1. Zìzhìqūde yìsi shi zhǐ nèige qūyùlǐde rénmín shi zìzhì de.   (T)

6.2. Yángzǐ Jiāng liúyù shi zhǐzhe Yángzi Jiāngde shuǐ jīngguo de dìfang
      shuō de.   (T)

Bái : Mǎ Jiàoshòu, ān-tǔ-zhòng-qiān zhèige cér wǒ juéde hěn shēng. Wǒ
       háishi dì-yīcì kànjian zhèige cér.

Mǎ : Zhèige cér shi Hàn Shūshangde. Ān-tǔ-zhòng-qiān de yìsi jiu shi
40   shuō rénmen xǐhuan zài yíge dìfang chángqī zhùxiaqu, jué bù suí-
       biànde bānjiā chúfēi shi fāshēng tiānzāi rénhuò, bùdébù bānjiā.

Bái: Jùshuō yǐqián yǒude rén yìshēng yě méi chūguo mér.

Mǎ: Zhè shi shìshi. Yánhǎi yídàide rén bǐjiǎo hǎo yìdiǎr. Cóngqiánde
shāngren dà duōshù shi Shāndong rén, zàibúrán jiu shi Jiāngsū、Zhè-
45   jiāng rén.

Bái: Zhè shi yīnwei dìlǐde guānxi le.

Mǎ: Búcuò. Wǒ shuō ge gùshi. Dāngchū wǒ fùqin hé wǒ mǔqin zài méi
dìng qīnshi yǐqián, wǒ mǔqin jiāli dì-yījiàn shì xiān wèn, wǒ fùqin
jiānglái chūmér bù chūmér.

50 Bái: Nà shi shénmo yìsi ne?

Mǎ: Yàoshi shuō chūmér zhèimén qīnshi tāmen jiu bù xiǎng dìng le.

7.0. zhàn*   war, warfare

zhànzhēng   a war   [war contend]

zhànshì   a war   [war affair]

zhànshí   wartime

zhànqián   before the war, pre-war

zhànhòu   after the war, post-war

nèizhàn   civil war

shìjiè dàzhàn   world war

7.1. Zhàn jiu shi zhànzhēng. Běnguó hé běnguóde zhànzhēng jiàozuo
nèizhàn.

7.2. Zài dì-yīcì shìjiè dàzhànde shíhou, zhànshì gāngyì kāishǐ jiu yǒu
rén xiěle yìběn shū jiào Zhànshì Jīngji.

7.3. Zhànshì Jīngji lǐbiān xiě de yě bāokuò zhànqián、zhànhòude jīngji
wèntí.

7.4. Zhōng-Rì Zhànzhēng shì bu shi dì-èrcì shìjiè dàzhànde kāishǐ?(T)

7.5. Zhèizhāng piānzi shi xíngrong zhànzhēngde kěpà.   (T)

8.0. zhàng   battle, fighting, war

dǎzhàng   fight a battle or war   (VO)

8.1. Zhōngguo hé Rìběn yígòng dǎle bānián zhàng, shi zài yī-jiǔ-sān-qī
nián kāishǐ de.   (T)

8.2. Wai! Lǎo Wáng ma? Nǐ zhīdao bù zhīdào běibiār yòu dǎqi zhàng
lai le?   (T)

9.0. Sìchuān   Szechuan   [four rivers]

9.1. Sìchuān shi Zhōngguode yìshěng. Sìchuān Shěngde xīběi shi Qīnghǎi
Shěng.

10.0. tài*   attitude

      tàidu   attitude   [attitude degree]

      dòngtài   activity, mobility   [move attitude]

      zhuàngtài   situation, status   [condition attitude]

10.1. Fǔdǎo zhǔrènde tàidu duì wǒ hěn bù hǎo.

10.2. Jiàoyu Bùzhǎng duì Jiàoyu Bùde zhíyuán shuō: "Jìnlái liúxuéshēng
      chūguó, huíguó de dōu bù shǎo. Yào bǎ liúxuéshēngde dòngtài xiáng-
      xìde jìlùxialai."

10.3. Wáng Xiàozhǎng duì rénde tàidu hǎojíle, yóuqíshi duì xuésheng.

10.4. Nèi liǎngge guójiā yīnwei biānjiède wèntí hěn kěnéng dǎqilai.   Nǐ
      kàn tāmende yàngzi yǐjing shi yìzhǒng zhànshí zhuàngtài le.   (T)

11.0. zhuàngkuàng   circumstances, state of affairs   [condition situation]

11.1. Jīnnián nóng-gōngyède zhuàngkuàng bǐ qùnián hǎode duō.

Bái: Gāngcái nín shuō tiānzāi rénhuò, rénhuò shi zhǐzhe shénmo shuō
      de?

Mǎ: Duōbàn shi zhǐzhe zhànzhēng shuō de.   Zhōngguo cóng Mínguó
55   chūnián qǐ jiu cháng yǒu nèizhàn. Yǒu yìnián Sìchuān yìshěng yìnián
      jiu dǎle jǐshící zhàng. Rénmín bù néng píng'ānde guò rìzi, tiāntiān
      shi zhànshí zhuàngtài.

Bái: Qǐng wèn, zhuàngtài hé zhuàngkuàng yǒu shénmo fēnbié?

Mǎ: Zhèi liǎngge cérde yìsi chàbuduō, kěshi yòng de shíhou yǒu fēnbié.
60   Bǐrú tándao zhànzhēng wǒmen shuō zhànshí zhuàngtài, tándao jīngji
      wǒmen jiu shuō jīngji zhuàngkuàng.

12.0. yóu*   (1) swim; (2) travel

      shàngyóu   upper reaches (of a stream)

      xiàyóu   lower reaches (of a stream)

12.1. Sìchuān zài Cháng Jiāngde shàngyóu, Jiāngsu zài Cháng Jiāngde
      xiàyóu.

13.0. liánhé   join with, federate with   [unite fit]

      liánhéqilai   join together, ally (with)

      Liánhéguó   United Nations

      Xīnán Liánhé Dàxué   Southwest Associated University (see Inter-
                       mediate Chinese, p. 347, note 4)

      Lián-Dà   (abbreviation for) Southwest Associated Uni-
                       versity

13.1. Liánhéguó zài dì-èrcì shìjiè dàzhàn zhīhòu chénglì de.

13.2. Xī-Ōu guójiā liánhéqilai zǔzhi yíge jīngjixìngde tuántǐ. Zhèizhǒng
       liánhé zǔzhi wèideshì gòngtóng lìyì. (T)

13.3. Zhōngguo gēn Rìběn dǎzhàng de shíhou bǎ běifāngde jǐge yǒumíngde
       dàxué bāndao xīnán, dōu zài yíge dìfang shàngkè. Nà jiu shi Xīnán
       Liánhé Dàxué, yě jiào Lián-Dà.

14.0. guīmó   scope, scale   [rule model]

14.1. Nèige dàxué jìnlái chénglìle nóngxuéyuàn、 gōngxuéyuàn. Lián yuán-
       láide lǐxuéyuàn děngděng yígòng yǒu bàge xuéyuàn. Guīmó hěn dà.

15.0. huàn   change, exchange

       huàn (yí)jù huà shuō   in other words

15.1. Zhōngguo rén ān-tǔ-zhòng-qiān. Huàn yíjù huà shuō jiu shi Zhōng-
       guo rén bù xǐhuan bānjiā, bù xǐhuan huàn dìfang.

16.0. jízhōng   concentrate   [collect middle]

16.1. Xiāngxia shi tǔchǎn chǎnshēng de dìfang. Chénglǐ shi tǔchǎn jízhōng
       de dìfang.

Bái : Sìchuānde fēngjǐng hěn měilì, shì bu shi?

Mǎ : Sìchuānde shānshuǐ hǎokàn jíle. Cóng Sìchuān jiāojiède Húběi zuò
       chuán wǎng Sìchuān qu, chuán zài jiāngli zǒu, liǎngbiānde dà shān
65   zhēn hǎokàn.

Bái : Sìchuān zài Cháng Jiāng shàngyóu, chuán bù hǎo zǒu, shì bu shi?

Mǎ : Shì. Chuán zǒu shàngyóu xiāngdāng bù róngyi, yóuqíshi Sìchuān
       nèitiáo shuǐlù.

Bái : Sìchuānde chūchǎn yě hěn fēngfù, shì bu shi?

70 Mǎ : Shì, Sìchuān chūchǎn fēicháng fēngfù.

Bái : Sìchuān chūchǎn zuì duōde shi shénmo?

Mǎ : Mǐ hé táng.

Bái : Mǎ Jiàoshòu, nín qùguo Sìchuān ma?

Mǎ : Qùguo. Gēn Rìběn dǎzhàng de shíhou wǒ gēn jiāli rén xiān dào
75   Sìchuān. Wǒ niàn dàxué shi zài Xīnán Lián-Dà.

Bái : Xīnán Liánhé Dàxué shi cóng nèidì bāndao xīnánde jǐge xuéxiào
       zǔzhide, shì bu shi?

Mǎ : Shìde.

Bái : Jǐge dàxué zǔzhichéng yíge dàxué dāngrán guīmó hěn dà le.

80 Mǎ : Zài zhànshí zǔzhi de xuéxiào yīnwei huánjingde guānxi dāngrán hěn
       jiǎndānde, guīmó yě bù zěnmo dà. Huàn jù huà shuō, jiu shi dàjiā
       jízhōng zài yíkuàr shàngkè jiu shì le. Kěshi jiàoshòu dōu xiāngdāng
       hǎo, dōu shi hěn yǒumíngde jiàoshòu.

Bái: Tīngshuō zàojiùle bùshǎode réncái.

85 Mǎ: Shìde.

17.0. sūn*   (1) grandchild; (2) (a surname)

sūnzi   grandson

sūnnü(er)   granddaughter

Sūn Zhōngshān   Sun Yatsen

zǐsūn   (1) sons and grandsons; (2) descendants, posterity

duō-zǐ-duō-sūn   (have) many sons and grandsons   (W)

17.1. Sūn Xiānsheng shi wǒde tóngxiāng. Tā wèile yào xià yídàide rén
dōu shòu jiàoyu, suǒyǐ zài xiāngxia bànle yíge xuéxiào.   (T)

17.2. Sūn Zhōngshān Xiānsheng běnlái shi niàn yīkē de. Hòulái tā zài
zhèngzhishang hěn yǒu biǎoxiàn.

17.3. Tāde zǐsūn hěn duō. Tā yǒu sìge érzi, hái yǒu liùge sūnzi báge
sūnnüer. Rénjia shuō tā shi duō-zǐ-duō-sūn.

18.0. chuántǒng   (1) tradition; (2) traditional   [transmit unify]

18.1. Zhōngguo chuántǒngde sīxiǎng shi érzi yīngdāng yǎng fùmǔ.

19.0. yuànyi   be willing (to), like (to)   [willing idea]

19.1. Wǒ yuànyi xué Měngwén、Zàngwén, yīnwei wǒ xiǎng liǎojiě Měnggǔ、
Xīzàngde wénhuà.

20.0. jiézhǐ   limit, regulate, control   [temperate system] ⌡

20.1. Hěn jiǔ bú xià yǔ yào yǒu hànzāi le, suǒyǐ yīngdāng jiézhǐ yòng shuǐ.
(T)

21.0. shēngyù   to bear, rear   [life nurture]

21.1. Fánshi shēngyù tài duō de nǚrén, tāde shēntǐ duōbàn bù hěn hǎo.

Bái: Mǎ Jiàoshòu, duō-zǐ-duō-sūn yìsi jiu shi "érzi duō sūnzi duō," shì
bu shi?

Mǎ: Shìde. Zhōngguo jiùde dà jiātíng zhìdu dōu xīwang zǐsūn duō, érzi
zhǎngdàle jiēle hūn, sūnzi sūnnüer hěn duō, rénkǒu shi yuè duō yuè
90 hǎo.

Bái: Rúguǒ jīngji qíngxing bù hǎode jiātíng, rénkǒu duō bú shi shēnghuó
hěn kùnnán ma?

Mǎ: Zhè shi Zhōngguo lǐlái chuántǒngde sīxiǎng. Búlùn yǒu qián méi
qián jiu shi yuànyi xià yídàide rén duō.

95 Bái: Jìnlái yǒu rén zhǔzhāng jiézhǐ shēngyù. Mǎ Jiàoshòude kànfǎ zěnmoyàng?

Mă :   Wŏ rènwei yīnggāi jiézhĭ shēngyù. Bùrán shìjièshang rénkŏu jiānglái
       bùdéliăo, yóuqíshi Zhōngguo.

22.0. àn   (1) by the . . . ; (2) according to

       ànzhe   according to

       ànzhào   according to

22.1. Tāde gōngqián shi àn yuè jìsuàn, bú shi àn tiān jìsuàn.

22.2. Jiāo shēngwùxuéde jiàoshòu chángcháng bú àn shíhou shàngkè. (T)

22.3. Nĭ shi ànzhe lĭlùn shuō de, wŏ shi ànzhe fălü shuō de.   (T)

22.4. Ànzhào nèiwèi yŭfă zhuānjiāde kànfă, Zhōngwén méi yŏu xíngrongcí.
       (T)

22.5. Ànzhe yìbān rén jiăng lìshĭde fāngfă, yīnggāi xiān cóng yuánshĭ
       shèhuì jiăngqĭ.   (T)

23.0. diàochá   (1) investigate, check up on; (2) investigation [investigate
                     examine]

23.1. Zhōng Yăxiyă hé Dōngyăde rénkŏu yígòng yŏu duōshao, yŏu fázi
       diàochá ma?   (T)

24.0. tŏngjì   (1) statistics; (2) count, obtain statistics on [unify reckon]

       tŏngjixué   statistics (as a study)

24.1. Jùshuō xué tŏngjì hěn nán, shi zhēnde ma?

24.2. Wŏmen yào qĭng yíwèi dŏngde tŏngjixuéde tŏngjì tŏngjì zhèiqūlide
       nóngchăn shùmu.

25.0. yì   hundred million

25.1. Zhōngguo rénkŏu yŏu liùyì duō shi gēnjù yī-jiŭ-wŭ-sān niánde tŏngjì.
       (T)

26.0. quèshí   accurate, correct, true, authentic   [true real]

26.1. Tā suŏ shuō de Àozhōu、Fēizhōu liăngzhōude rénkŏu shùmu shi
       quèshíde ma?

Bái : Mă Jiàoshòu, xiànzài Zhōngguo yŏu duōshao rénkŏu?

100 Mă :   Yī-jiŭ-wŭ-sān nián ànzhào Rénmín Zhèngfŭ diàochá tŏngjìde jiéguŏ,
       yŏu liùyì duō rén. Xiànzài kěnéng yŏu qíyì rén le.

Bái : Nèige shùmu quèshí ma?

Mă :   Zhèige shùmuzì shi bĭjiào kěkào de.

27.0. dù*   degree, extent

       wēndù   temperature   [warm degree]

wēndùbiǎo   thermometer

sùdù   speed, velocity   [speed degree]

27.1. Tāde wēndù zài yìbǎidù yǐshàng le.   (T)

27.2. Wǒ qù kànkan wēndùbiǎo, jīntiande wēndù shi duōshao dù.

27.3. Tā kāi chē de sùdù tài kuài le.

28.0. mì   dense, thick, close

mìdù   density   [dense degree]

28.1. Shuōqilai Zhōngguo rénkǒude mìdù, Shànghǎi shi zuì mìde le.   (T)

29.0. rénkǒuxué   demography

rénkǒuxuéjiā   demographer

29.1. Rénkǒuxuéjiā shuō shìjièshang rénkǒu zēngjiā de sùdù tài kuài le.
Yánjiu rénkǒuxuéde rén rènwei shi yíge dà wèntí.

30.0. shì   municipality

shìzhǎng   mayor   [municipality chief]

chéngshì   town, city   [city municipality]

30.1. Shànghǎi Shì shi Zhōngguo wùchǎn chūkǒu de chéngshì, suǒyǐ
Shànghǎi Shìde shìzhǎng duìyu wùchǎn chūkǒu fēicháng zhùyì.

31.0. xī   sparse, thin, diluted

xīshǎo   few, scarce   (W)   [sparse few]

31.1. Shìjiè rénkǒude mìdù, Ōzhōu zuì mì, Àozhōu zùi xī, shì bu shi?

31.2. Shāmò dìfang rénkǒu xīshǎo.

Bái: Qǐng wèn <u>mìdù</u> zhèige cér zěnmo yòng ne?

105 Mǎ : Běnlái shi wùlǐxuéshang yòng de cér. Rénkǒuxuéjiā zài rénkǒuxué-
shang yě yòng.

Bái: Oh, wǒ míngbai le. "Cháng Jiāng xiàyóu rénkǒude mìdù shi bǐjiǎo
mì de," nín kàn zhènmo shuō yòngde duì bu duì?

Mǎ : Duì, yòngde hěn hǎo. Nǐ zhīdao bù zhīdào Cháng Jiāng xiàyóu měi
110   fāng Yīnglǐ píngjūn yǒu duōshao rén?

Bái: Bù zhīdào.

Mǎ : Píngjūn bābǎi rén dào liǎngqiān rén. Dànshi Shànghǎi Shìde rén
bǐjiǎo gèng duō. Nǐ zhīdao bù zhīdào Zhōngguo shénmo dìfang rénkǒu
zuì xī?

115 Bái: Zhōngguo biānjiāngde rénkǒu zuì xī, píngjūn měi Yīng fānglǐ jiù yǒu
jǐge rén.

32.0. wèi   rank   (M)

32.1. Zhōngguo rénkǒu zuì duō, zhàn shìjiè rénkǒu dì-yīwèi. Něige guójiā
       zhàn dì-èrwèi ne?

33.0. Huáqiáo   overseas Chinese   [Chinese lodge]

33.1. Nèi jǐge Huáqiáo yào zài Miǎndiàn zuò mǎimai. Nǐ shuō zuòdechēng-
       gōng zuòbuchénggōng?

34.0. yídòng   change position, move   [shift move]

       yídòngxìng   mobility

34.1. Něige guójiā rénkǒude yídòngxìng zuì dà? Yídòng de yuányīn nǐ
       zhīdao ma?

35.0. bèi   by, at the hand of   (CV)

35.1. Qīng Cháo shídài Zhōngguo biānjiè yǒu bù shǎode dìfang bèi wàiguo
       zhànqu le. (T)

35.2. Xīnjiāngde zhōngbù yǒu dà shān, suǒyǐ Xīnjiāng bèi dà shān fēnwéi
       nán běi liǎngbù.

36.0. bīpò   press, harass, constrain, force   [force compel]

36.1. Shàngcì shìjiè dàzhàn yǒude guójiā shi bèi bīpò cānjiā de.   (T)

36.2. Tiānzāi rénhuò bīpòde rénmen méi fázi shēnghuó le.   (T)

37.0. xǔ   (1) permit; (2) perhaps

       xǔduō   a great many

       xǔjiǔ   a long time ago

37.1. Fǔdǎo zhǔrèn bù xǔ wǒ líkai tāde bàngōngshǐ.

37.2. Zhāng Xiānsheng shuō tā xǔjiǔ méi yǒu gēn péngyoumen tōngxìn le.

37.3. Wǒ xǔduō rìzi méi chī chǎo niúròu le.

Mǎ : Rénkǒu, Zhōngguo zài shìjièshang kě zhàn dì-yīwèi. Nǐ zhīdao bù
      zhīdào Zhōngguo zài guówàide Huáqiáo yǒu duōshao?

Bái: Jù wǒ tīngshuō de, dàgài yǒu yìqiānwàn zuǒyòu. Zhōngguo rénkǒude
120   yídòngxìng bú dà, shì bu shi?

Mǎ : Wǒmen gāngcái shuō de ān-tǔ-zhòng-qiān yìsi jiu shi shuō Zhōngguo
      rén shi bù yuànyi bānjiā, zài yíge dìfang zhùxiaqu, cónglái bù dǎsuàn
      wǎng biéde dìfang bān de, chúfēi shi fāshēngle tiānzāi rénhuò bèi
      bīpò, zàiburán jiu shi zuòle bù hǎode shì, rénjia bù xǔ tā zhùxiaqu
125   le.

Bái: Xiànzài hé cóngqián bùtóng le.

38.0. (mín)zú   people, nationality, nation

       shǎoshù mínzú   minority nationality, national minority

38.1. Zhè sānzú yígòng yǒu yìqiānwàn rén.

38.2. Zhōngguo shǎoshù mínzú lǐtou, něige mínzúde rénkǒu zuì duō?

39.0. fēnbù   (1) be distributed (over); (2) distribution   [divide spread]

39.1. Shǎoshù mínzú bù yídìng jízhōng zài yíge qūyù.   Tāmen fēnbù zài xǔduō dìfang.

40.0. jǐn   merely, simply, alone   (W)

jǐnjǐn(de)   (1) merely, simply; (2) be merely

40.1. Nèige hǎidǎoshang jǐn yǒu yíge bàoguǎn.   Tāmen chūbǎn de bàozhǐ jǐnjǐn yì xiǎo zhāng, dōu shi běndì xīnwén.   (T)

40.2. Ná wǒ lái shuō, jǐnjǐnde xuéle yìnián tǒngjì, zěnmo kéyi zuò tǒngjì zhǔrèn ne? (T)

40.3. Tā bāndao zhèlǐ jǐn yǒu sāntiān.   Hǎoxiàng yòu yào bānjiā shide. (T)

40.4. Nèicì Huáng Héde shuǐzāi jǐn wǒmen jiā zhè yídài shòu sǔnhài de jiu yǒu liǎngqiān duō jiā.   (T)

41.0. cūn(zi)   village

xiāngcūn   (1) village; (2) rural   [country village]

41.1. Tā zhùzai Jiāngxi Shěngde xiāngcūn.   Nèige cūnzi lí Póyáng Hú hěn jìn, yě shi chǎn mǐde dìfang.

Mǎ : Wǒ xiànzài wèn ni, Zhōngguo mínzú Hànrén zhàn bǎifēnzhī-jǐ?

Bái : Hànrén zhàn bǎifēnzhī-jiǔshijǐ, shǎoshù mínzú yígòng zhàn bǎifēnzhī-wǔ zuǒyòu.

130 Mǎ : Hànrén fēnbù zài shěnmo dìfang?

Bái : Àn rénkǒuxuéjiāde tǒngjì, bǎifēnzhī-jiǔshí yǐshàng dōu zài běnbù, jǐn bǎifēnzhī-shí zuǒyòu fēnbù zài biānjiāng.

Mǎ : Yàoshi ná chéngshì hé xiāngcūnde rénkǒu lái bǐjiǎo, nǎlǐde rénkǒu duō?

135 Bái : Xiāngcūn rénkǒu duō.

Mǎ : Shénmo yuányīn?

Bái : Yīnwei Zhōngguo shi nóngyè guójiā, duōshù rén dōu shi zài cūnzili zhòngtián de.

42.0. dòngluàn   disturbance, upheaval   [move disorder]

42.1. Wǒmen zhèlǐ hěn píng'ān.   Cónglái méi fāshēngguo dòngluàn. (T)

43.0. zhì   (1) arrive, to; (2) most

zhìshǎo   at least

zhìyú   as to

43.1. Qùnián báyuè zhí shí'èryuè wǒ zài Nèi Ménggǔ lǚxíng, zhìshǎo zǒule
       yǒu yìqiān duō lǐ.

43.2. Fánshi nǐ ràng wǒ bàn de shì wǒ yídìng xiǎng bànfǎ bànhǎo. Zhìyú
       zěnmo bàn de, nǐ jiu búbì wèn le.   (T)

44.0. shā   kill, murder

       zìshā   kill oneself, commit suicide

44.1. Ménggǔ rén xǐhuan chī niú-yángròu, suǒyǐ shícháng shā niú, shā
       yáng.

44.2. Tā shi bèi shā háishi zìshā de?   (T)

45.0. sǐ   die   (see Intermediate Chinese, p. 122, note 2)

       shāsi   kill   [kill die]

45.1. Zhèitiáo niú dàoshi yǒu bìng sǐ de ne, háishi bèi rén shāsi de ne?

45.2. Nǐ zhīdao shàngcì dǎzhàng dǎsile duōshao rén?

45.3. Wai! Wai! Nǐ shi Wáng Dàwén ma? Wǒ shi Lǎo Zhāng. Wǒ
       jīntian bú dào nǐ nèr qù le. Wǒ zhèi jǐtian yòu děi niàn shū yòu
       děi zhǎo fángzi bānjiā. Zhēn shi mángsi le.   (T)

45.4. Tā báitiān zài Lián-Dà jiāo shū, wǎnshang zài jiā xiě wénzhāng, yì
       tiān dào wǎn mángde yàosǐ.   (T)

45.5. Nèige xiānsheng bù dǒngde jiāoxuéfǎ, zhǐ shi ràng xuésheng yíkèyíkè-
       de niàn sǐ shū.   (T)

46.0. tíchàng   advocate, promote   [lift advocate]

46.1. Yàzhōu yǒu hěn duō guójiā tíchàng jiézhì shēngyù.

      Bái: Zhōngguo yǐqián shícháng fāshēng nèizhàn. Zài dòngluàn de shíhou
140   xiāngcūn zhòngtián yě hěn shòu yǐngxiǎng le, shì bu shi?

      Mǎ : Dāngrán. Zhìshǎo xiāngxia rén bù néng àn shíhou zhòngdì, yàoburán
            Zhōngguo lǎobǎixìng bú huì nènmo kùnnán.

      Bái: Shìde. Nín cái shuōguo le, jǐnjǐnde Sìchuān yìshěng yìnián jiu dǎle
            jǐshícì zhàng. Búdàn bù néng zhòngtián, érqiě yào shāsi hěn duō
145   rén.

      Mǎ : Suǒyǐ yǒu rén tíchàng jiézhì shēngyù, yǒu rén bú zànchéng. Tāmen
            yǒu tāmende dàolǐ.

47.0. jīngrén   terrifying, dreadful, startling   [alarm man]

47.1. Wǒ shínián méi huí guó le. Jīnnián huí guó yí kàn, nóng-gōngyède
       jìnbù shízài jīngrén.   (T)

47.2. Bàozhǐshang shuō jìnlái zìshā de duōde jīngrén.   (T)

48.0. fùzá   complex, complicated   [complex miscellaneous]

48.1. Jìn bǎinián lái Zhōng-É liǎnguóde wèntí tài duō le, tài fùzá le.

49.0. qīngyì   lightly, unconcernedly

49.1. Yíge guójiāde tǔdì jué bù néng qīngyì bèi biéde guójiā zhànqu.

50.0. niánsuì   (years of) age

50.1. Nǚrén dōu bú yuànyi biéren wèn tāde niánsuì.

51.0. líng   zero   (see <u>Intermediate Chinese</u>, p. 370, note 3)

51.1. Nèige dìfangde wēndù yǒu shíhou shi língxià èrshi duō dù.   (T)

51.2. Zhèlǐde Huáqiáo yǒu liǎngwàn líng bāge rén.   (T)

52.0. xíguàn   (1) be used to; (2) habit, custom, tradition   [practice ac-
          customed]

52.1. Zài zhèr zhù wǒ hěn bu xíguàn.   (T)

52.2. Yíge mínzú yǒu yíge mínzúde shēnghuó xíguàn.

Mǎ :   Cóngqián Zhōngguo měinián yīnwei tiānzāi rénhuò, sǐ de rén hěn
          duō. Yǒu rén shuō Měiguo rén píngjūn huódao qīshisuì, Zhōngguo
150   rén píngjūn huódao èrshijǐsuì. Zhè shi ge jīngrénde shìqing.

Bái :   Zhè shi yīxué bù fādá de wèntí.

Mǎ :   Zhèige wèntí hěn fùzá. Yīlái shi yīxué bù fādá, rénmín yě méi yǒu
          yīxué chángshí, yǒu bìng bù qīngyì qu kàn yīsheng. Èrlái shi gēn
          shēnghuó yě yǒu guānxi. Chīde bú gòu jiu róngyi shēng bìng.

155 Bái :   Xiànzài Zhōngguo rénde niánsuì píngjūn bǐ yǐqián zēngjiāle xǔduō.

Mǎ :   Yǒu rén zhènmo shuō.

Bái :   Shì bu shi zhèlǐde yīsheng bú gòu?

Mǎ :   Shìde. Xué yīkē tài nán, xué de rén yě shǎo. Shuōdao yīsheng,
          jīntian wǒ děi dài xiǎohár qu kàn yīsheng.

160 Bái :   Nǐnde xiǎohár bìngle ma?

Mǎ :   Shìde. Zuótiān wǎnshàng shìshi wēndubiǎo rèdù xiāngdāng gāo, yìbǎi
          líng sān dù.

Bái :   Zhèi jǐtiān tiānqi bù hǎo, róngyi shēngbìng.

Mǎ :   Běnlái zhèige háizi yǒu ge tèxìng shi bù.tīnghuà. Hái yǒu ge xíguàn,
165   tiāntiān zǎoshang dào yuànzi qu wár. Kěshi qiántian fēicháng lěng,
          tā mǔqin bú ràng ta chūqu. Tā fēi qù bùkě.

53.0. jiūjìng   (1) after all, in the end, finally; (2) precisely   [finally ac-
          tually]

53.1. Zhōngguo nóngmínde zǒngshù jiūjìng yǒu duōshao? Shi gēnjù shénmo
          shuō de?   (T)

54.0. xìngzhi   property, attribute, nature   [quality substance]

54.1. Nèige tuántǐ shi shénmo xìngzhi? Shì bu shi xuéshù tuántǐ?

55.0. shíjì   actual, factual, practical   [real interval]

   shíjìshang   as a matter of fact, in fact

55.1. Tā yòng Ēwén xiěle yìběn shū. Shūde nèiróng duōbàn shi shìjiè
      dàzhàn shíjì qíngxing.

55.2. Tā shuō tā juāngěi yíge dàxué hěn duō qián, kěshi shíjìshang tā
      jǐnjǐnde juānle yìbǎikuài qián.

56.0. jué   unquestionably, really, definitely, absolutely (used only be-
                   fore negative verbs)

   juéduì   unquestionably, really, definitely, absolutely   (used before
             positive or negative verbs)

56.1. Yíge rén jué bù yīngdāng zìshā.

56.2. Yǒu rén shuō Zhōng-Sū liǎngguó juéduì bú huì dǎzhàng de. Nǐ shuō
      zhèige huà kàodezhù ma?

57.0. kéyi búbì   not have to

57.1. Nèige wèntí yǐjing kāihuì tōngguò le, wǒmen kéyi búbì zài yánjiu
      le. (T)

Bái: Wǒmen xuéxiàode yīxuéyuàn shèlì de yīyuàn jùshuō xiànzài guīmó
     hěn dà le, jiūjìng zěnmoyàng?

Mǎ : Xiànzài yǒu hǎojǐge yīsheng. Yǐqián nǐ zài zhèrde shíhou cái yǒu
170   yíge yīsheng.

Bái: Měiyīng yě gàosu wǒ le.

Mǎ : Yīshengde tàidu dōu xiāngdāng hǎo, érqiě gěi bìngren kàn bìng yě
     fēicháng rènzhēn.

Bái: Zhèige yīyuàn shi shénmo xìngzhi?

175 Mǎ : Suírán shi xuéxiàode yīyuàn, shíjìshang shi bāngzhu yìbān rén, juéduì
     bù qiú běnshēnde lìyì.

Bái: Nènmo yìbān rén kàn bìng kéyi búbì gěi qián le?

Mǎ : Búbì.

58.0. guāndiǎn   viewpoint   [observe point]

58.1. Guāndiǎnde yìsi jiu shi shuō cóng něi yìfāngmiàn kàn. Bǐfang shuō
      yǒu liǎngge guāndiǎn jiu shi shuō cóng liǎngge bùtóngde fāngmiàn
      lai kàn.

59.0. liàng*   capacity, quantity

   dàliàng   large quantity, large number

59.1. Jìnlái yǒu dàliàng tǔchǎn cóng Shànghǎi chūkǒu le.   (T)

60.0. jiějué   solve (a problem)   [untie decide]

60.1. Yǒu rén shuō tíchàng jiézhǐ shēngyù bújiànde jiu néng jiějué rénkǒu
       zēngjiā de wèntí.

61.0. tuīcè   (1) deduce, infer; (2) deduction, inference   [push guess]

61.1. Ànzhe wǒde tuīcè tāmen liǎngge rén kěnéng hézuò.   (T)

     Bái: Mǎ Jiàoshòu, guāndiǎn shi shénmo yìsi, zěnmo yòng?

180 Mǎ : Jiù shi kànfǎde yìsi.

     Bái: Nín gěi wǒ jǔ ge lìzi.

     Mǎ : "Ànzhào tāmende guāndiǎn, yīnggāi dàliàng chūchǎn cái néng jiějué
           rénmín shēnghuó wèntí."

     Bái: Tuīcè jiu shi cāiyicāide yìsi, shì bu shi?

185 Mǎ : Shi. Bǐrú shuō: "Nèijiàn shì ànzhe wǒde tuīcè . . ."

62.0. yǐjí   and   (W)   [take reach]

62.1. Wǒ niàn dàxuéde shíhou suǒyǒu xuéfèi, fànqián yǐjí mǎi shū děngděng
       dōu shi wǒ zìjǐ xiǎng bànfǎ.

63.0. yè   page   (M)

63.1. Xiānsheng, yídòng zhèige cér zài dì-sānshibáyède dì-jǐháng?   (T)

64.0. dá   to answer

       huídá   answer (that)   [return answer]

       wèndá   question and answer   (N/V)

64.1. Qǐng dàjiā bǎ shū shōuqilai. Wǒ wèn, nǐmen dá.

64.2. Jīntiande tímu tài nán le, yǒu hěn duō wǒmen dábushànglái.   (T)

64.3. Wáng Dàwén, wǒ wèn nǐde wèntí nǐ hái méi huídá wǒ ne.

64.4. Wǒ hěn xǐhuan kàn bàozhǐshangde wénxué wèndá.   (T)

65.0. duǎnwén   short essay

65.1. Zhāng Jiàoshòu cháng zài bàozhǐshang xiě duǎnwén.   (T)

     Bái: Jīntian suǒ jiǎng de fēicháng yǒu yìsi.

     Mǎ : Jīntian hé nǐ suísuibiànbiànde tánle hěn duō. Cóng rénkǒu wèntí
           tándao Zhōngguo chuántǒng sīxiǎng, yòu shuōdao wǒ jiāli yǐjí wǒ
           fùmǔ dìngqīn de gùshi.

190 Bái: Rìzi hěn kuài xīngqīwǔle. Gēn nín xuéxile yíge xīngqī le.

     Mǎ : Wǒmen zhèi yíge xīngqī yánjiule bù shǎode dōngxi. Yīnggāi bǎ suǒ
           xué de dōu wēnxi yící. Zhè shi wēnxikè. Nǐ xiān kàn dì-yīyède
           mùlu, chúle fùshù fāyīn yǐwài hái yǒu wèndá hé duǎnwén.

Bái: Hăode.

195 Mă : Yŏu shénmo wèntí méi yŏu?

Bái: Méi yŏu.

Mă : Wŏ xiăng xīngqītiān qǐng nǐ dào wŏ jiā qu chī wănfàn qu.

Bái: Tài fèishì le.

Mă : Bú fèishì, wŏmen jiănjiandāndānde chī biànfàn. Wŏ bă Mĕiyīng hé
200   Xuéxīn yĕ zhăolai.

Bái: Xièxie nín.

SHĒNGCÍ BIĂO

1. ān-tŭ-zhòng-qiān (W)

2. A (yìsi jiu) shi shuō B

3. bān
   bānjiā

4. fēi (W)
   fēi(dĕi) V (bùkĕ)
   chúfēi

5. huò
   rénhuò

6. zhǐ(zhe)
   zhǐ(zhe) . . . shuō

7. zhàn*
   zhànzhēng
   zhànshì
   zhànshí
   zhànqián
   zhànhòu
   nèizhàn
   shìjiè dàzhàn

8. zhàng
   dăzhàng

9. Sìchuān

10. tài*
    tàidu
    dòngtài
    zhuàngtài

11. zhuàngkuàng

12. yóu*
    shàngyóu
    xiàyóu

13. liánhé
    liánhéqilai
    Liánhéguó
    Xīnán Liánhé Dàxué
    Lián-Dà

14. guīmó

15. huàn
    huàn (yí)jù huà shuō

16. jízhōng

17. sūn*
    sūnzi
    sūnnü(er)
    Sūn Zhōngshān
    zǐsūn
    duō-zǐ-duō-sūn (W)

18. chuántŏng

19. yuànyi

20. jiézhǐ

21. shēngyù

22. àn
    ànzhe
    ànzhào

23. diàochá

24. tŏngjì
    tŏngjixué

25. yì

26. quèshí

27. dù*
    wēndù
    wēndùbiăo
    sùdù

28. mì
    mìdù

29. rénkŏuxué
    rénkŏuxuéjiā

30. shì
    shìzhăng
    chéngshì

31. xī
    xīshăo (W)

32. wèi

33. Huáqiáo

34. yídòng
    yídòngxìng

35. bèi

36. bīpò

37. xŭ
    xŭduō
    xŭjiŭ

38. (mín)zú
    shăoshù mínzú

39. fēnbù

40. jǐn
    jǐnjǐn(de)

41. cūn(zi)
    xiāngcūn

42. dòngluàn	51. líng	58. guāndiǎn
43. zhǐ zhǐshǎo zhǐyú	52. xíguàn 53. jiūjìng	59. liàng* dàliàng
44. shā zìshā	54. xìngzhi	60. jiějué
45. sǐ shāsi	55. shíjǐ shíjǐshang	61. tuīcè 62. yǐjí (W)
46. tíchàng		63. yè
47. jīngrén	56. jué	64. dá
48. fùzá	juéduì	huídá wèndá
49. qīngyì		
50. niánsuì	57. kéyi búbì	65. duǎnwén

YǓFǍ LIÀNXÍ

A. Reduplicated stative verbs (see note 1)

1. Tāde chéngji zài fǎxuéyuànli bú shi zuì hǎode, shi píngpingchángchángde.

2. Tā chéngji-dānshangde fēnshu míngmingbáibǎide dōu bú jígé, kěshi tā duì tāde fùqin shuō dōu jígé le.

3. Wǒ dào fǔshang chī fàn, nǐ qiānwàn bú yào fèishì. Wǒmen chī de dōngxi yào jiǎnjiandāndānde.

4. Yīsheng shuō nèige bìngren suírán méi yǒu hǎole de xīwang, kěshi xiànzài qiānqianwànwàn bu yào gàosu ta.

5. Tāde bóshi lùnwén wǒ yǐjing xiángxiangxìxìde kànguo le, bú yòng zài chóng kàn le.

6. Liú Měide xuésheng zài Měiguo dōu shi kuàikuailèlède niàn shū.

7. Zhōngguode nóngren duōshù shi lǎolaoshíshíde.

8. Bàngōngshǐli zěnmo néng róngdexià zhènmo xǔuduōduōde rén?

9. Wǒ shíshizàizàide gàosu ni, nǐ shēnqǐng de jiǎngxuéjīn shi méi yǒu xīwang le.

10. Nèipán lùyīndài shi wǒ suísuibiànbiàn lù de.

B. děi + N/S (see Intermediate Chinese Reader, lesson 3, note 1)

11. Cóng Cháng Jiāng shàngyóude Sìchuān zuò chuán děi qītiān cái kéyi dào Shànghǎi.

12. Fǔdǎo zhǔrèn gēn wàiguo xuésheng fēnbié tán huà. Gēn tāmen dōu tángguo le. Xiànzài gāi wǒ le.

13. Jiàowùzhǎng méi jiào wǒmen liǎngge rén qu. Nǐ bú yào qu. Yīnggāi wǒ
    yíge rén qu.

14. Yīnwei nǐ shi Lián-Dà xuéshenghuìde huìzhǎng, nèijiàn shìqing bǐděi nǐ
    qù cái néng bànhǎo.

15. Wǒ xiǎng niànwán zhèibǎn tǒngjixué zhìshǎo xūyào sānge yuè.

C. bù/méi V biéde (N) jiù V N ⎫
   shénmo yě bù/méi V jiù V N ⎬ 'to V nothing but N' (see note 2)
                              ⎭

16. Wǒ jiu xǐhuan niàn fǎlǜ, bù xǐhuan niàn biéde.

17. Wǒ měicì zài lùyīnshì lùyīn bú lù biéde jiù lù wǒ fùshù de Zhuāntí Jiǎng-
    huà.

18. Wàiguo liúxuéshēng fǔdǎo zhǔrèn bú zuò biéde shì, tā jiù shi bāngzhu
    wàiguo xuésheng.

19. Zuótian Zhuāntí Jiǎnghuàde nèiwèi zhuānjiā tā shénmo yě méi jiǎng jiù
    jiǎng Zhōng-Sū biānjiède qíngxing.

20. Tā bàngōng de shíhou bú bàn biéde shì zhǐshi jìsuàn xuéshengde fēnshu.

D. Expressions of duration of time (see note 3)

21. Xiānggǎng shi Yīngguode zhímíndì yǐjing yǒu yìbǎi duō nián le.

22. Zhāng Xiānshengde bóshi lùnwén xiěle búdào liǎngnián jiu xiěwán le.

23. Tā zài Ōuzhōu búguò liǎngtiān. Tā zěnmo nénggou zhīdao Ōuzhōude
    shāngyè qíngxing ne?

24. Wǒ líkai Táiwān méi yǒu sāntiān, wǒ nèiren jiu cóng Táiwān lái xìn jiào
    wǒ huíqu.

25. Tā zài Nèi Měnggǔ hé Wài Měnggǔ yígòng yǒu èrshi duō tiān, zài Éguo
    zhǐ yǒu liǎngtiān.

E. yī V$_1$ jiu V$_2$ 'as soon as V$_1$ then V$_2$' (see Beginning Chinese, p. 352,
   note 1)

26. Tā zài chuánshang hǎoxiàng shi yǒubìng shide. Yí dào lùdì tāde bìng jiu
    hǎo le.

27. Wǒ zuì bù xǐhuan rède dìfang. Yí qù rèdài wǒ jiu shēngbìng.

28. Wǒ yí tīngshuō wǒde chéngji jígé wǒ jiu mǎshàng gěi wǒ fùqin xiě xìn.

29. Zhèitiáo lù hěn dī. Yí xià dà yǔ jiu méi fázi zǒu le.

30. Rénjia gàosu wǒ nèige hézuòshè yǒu hěn duō tǔchǎn. Wǒ dào nèr yí kàn,
    yuánlái dōu shi Rìběnde tǔchǎn.

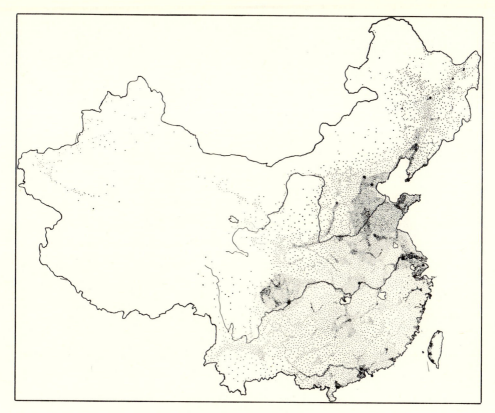

Zhōngguode Rénkǒu

JIǍNGHUÀ

Zhōngguo shi yíge rénkǒu zuì duōde guójiā. Zhōngguode rénkǒu duō
dào shénmo chéngdu ne? Rúguǒ ná shìjiè rénkǒu zǒngshù lái bǐjiǎo, Zhōngguode rénkǒu chàbuduō zhàn shìjiè rénkǒu zǒngshù sìfēnzhī-yī.   Yòu
chàbuduō zhàn Yǎzhōu rénkǒu zǒngshù èrfēnzhī-yī.   Suǒyǐ Zhōngguode
5   rénkǒu zài shìjièshang shi dì-yīwèi. Nènmo Zhōngguo rénkǒu jiūjìng yǒu
duōshǎo ne? Gēnjù Zhōngguo zhèngfǔ yī-jiǔ-wǔ-sān nián nèicìde diàochá
tǒngjì, yǒu liùyì líng yìbǎi jiǔshisānwàn bāqiān líng sānshiwǔge rén. Nèicì
diàochá de shùmu jù gèguó rénkǒuxué zhuānjiāde kànfǎ shi xiāngdāng
kěkàode, xiāngdāng quèshíde.   Xiànzài lí nèicì diàochá yòu yǒu bù shǎo
10   nián le, yǒuxiē zhuānjiāmen rènwei Zhōngguo rénkǒu shíjìshang xiànzài
zhìshǎo yǒu liùyì wǔqiānwàn zuǒyòu.

Zhè liùyì duō rénkǒu fēnbù de zhuàngkuàng shi zěnmoyàng ne?
Wǒmen kéyi cóng liǎngge guāndiǎn lái kàn.   Dì-yī, ànzhào dìyù lái kàn,
Zhōngguo dà bùfen rénkǒu shi jízhōng zài sān dà héliúde liúyù. Zhè sān
15   dà héliú zài shàngcì yǐjing jiǎngguo, jiu shi Cháng Jiāng、Huáng Hé gēn

Zhū Jiāng. Zhè sān dà héliúde liúyù dōu shi Zhōngguode běnbù. Běnbù rénkǒu zhàn quánguó rénkǒu zǒngshù bǎifēnzhī-jiǔshí, bǎifēnzhī-shí shi fēnbù zài biānjiāng qūyù yě jiu shi Dōngběi、Měnggǔ、Xīnjiāng、Xīzàng děng dìfang. Dì-èr, ànzhào dìfangde xìngzhi lái kàn, yě jiu shi ànzhào

20 chéngshì hé xiāngcūn lái kàn, xiāngcūn rénkǒu zhàn bǎifēnzhī-bāshí, chéng- shì rénkǒu zhǐ zhàn bǎifēnzhī-èrshí. Zhè shi yīnwei Zhōngguo shi nóngyè guójiā, suǒyǐ xiāngcūnde rénkuǒ zhàn duōshù. Kěshi jìnlái Zhōngguo zhèng zài tíchàng gōngyè. Gōngyè duōbàn shèzai chéngshì qūyù yǐnèi. Rúguǒ gōngyè fādá, chéngshì rénkǒu yídìng yìtiān bǐ yìtiān duō le.

25   Wǒmen dōu zhīdao Zhōngguode tǔdì hěn dà. Xiànzài jiu yánjiu zhè liùyì duōde rénkǒu zài zhèikuài hěn dàde tǔdìshang, shi dì shǎo rén duō ne, háishi rén duō dì shǎo ne? Huàn yíjù huà shuō, yě jiu shi yánjiu rénkǒude mìdù. Wǒmen xiān kàn shìjiè rénkǒude mìdù. Shìjiè rénkǒude mìdù shi píngjūn měi fāng Yīnglǐ yǒu liùshí rén. Zhōngguo rénkǒu píngjūn

30 měi fāng Yīnglǐ yǒu èrbǎi rén. Kějiàn Zhōngguo rénkǒude mìdù shi bǐjiào mìde. 'Zài kànkan Zhōngguo guónèi gèdì shénmo dìfang rénkǒu gèng mì? Shénmo dìfang rénkǒu xīshǎo ne? Jù diàochá, Cháng Jiāng shàngyóu rénkǒu bǐjiào shǎo, xiàyóu yídài rénkǒu zuì mì. Píngjūn měi fāng Yīng- lǐ cóng bābǎi rén zhǐ èrqiān rén. Běifāng píngyuán píngjūn měi fāng

35 Yīnglǐ yǒu liùshíwǔge rén. Zhìyú Xīzàng、Měnggǔde rénkǒu, píngjūn měi fāng Yīnglǐ jǐn yǒu yì-liǎngge rén.

    Xiànzài yào shuōyishuo Zhōngguo rénkǒude dòngtài. Dòngtàide yìsi jiu shi zhǐzhe rénkǒu yídòng de zhuàngtài. Yìbān lái shuō Zhōngguo rén- kǒude yídòngxìng bú dà. Zhōngguo rénde xíguàn shi "ān-tǔ-zhòng-qiān."

40 Shénmo jiào "ān-tǔ-zhòng-qiān" ne? Yìsi jiu shi shuō hěn yuànyi píng- ping'ānānde zài lǎo jiā guò rìzi, juéduì bù qīngyìde bāndao biéde dìfang qu, chúfēi shi yīnwei zhànzhēng、shèhuìshangde dòngluàn, huòzhě shi shuǐzāi、hànzāi tāmen cái bùdébù zǒu, bùdébù huàn yíge dìfang qù zhǎo fàn chī. Wǒmen kéyǐ jǔchū jìndài liǎngge lìzi lái shuō. Yíge lìzi shi

45 Míng Cháo mòniánde dòngluàn, zài Zhōngguo xībù Sìchuān Shěngde rén duōbàn bèi rén shāsi le. Hòulái cóng Guǎngdong、Húběi qù Sìchuānde rén hěn duō. Yòu yíge lìzi shi Shāndong Shěngde rén yīnwei shuǐzāi dàliàng dào Dōngběi qu. Zhè dōu shi shòule huánjìngde bīpò bùdébù yídòng. Yánhǎi yídài yǒu bù shǎo rén dào wàiguo qu. Zhè jiu shi Huáqiáo. Zhōng-

50   guo zài guówàide Huáqiáo yuē yǒu yìqiānwàn rén zuǒyòu. Kěshi zhèizhǒng

yídòng bìng bú shi zhèngfǔ yǒu jǐhuade dà guīmóde jiào rénmín yídòng.

Rúguǒ zài jìn yíbù yánjiu yánjiu Zhōngguo rénkǒu zēngjiā de qūshì,

ànzhào xiànzàide qíngxing lái tuīcè, zēngjiā de sùdù shi jīngrénde, suǒyǐ

jìnlái yǒu rén tíchàng jiézhǐ shēngyù. Kěshi Zhōngguo rén yǒu yíge chuán-

55   tǒngde sīxiǎng shi xīwang duō-zǐ-duō-sūn de, suǒyǐ Zhōngguo rénkǒu shi

yíge hěn fùzáde wèntí, yě shi yíge hěn bù róngyi jiějué de wèntí.

Cǐwài wǒmen yīnggāi zhīdao zhè liùyì duō de rénkǒu shi shǔyu

shénmo mínzú, yǒu duōshao ge mínzú, něige mínzúde rénkǒu zuì duō,

yǐjí gège mínzúde qíngxing shi zěnmoyàng? Zhèxiē wèntí děngdao xiàcì

60   jiǎngdao Zhōngguode mínzúde shíhou zài xiángxide jiǎng.

FÙSHÙ

Zhèipán lùyīndài shi Zhōngwén dì-yīzǔ dì-sìhào Bái Wénshān fùshù

dì-sìcìde Zhuāntí Jiǎnghuà.

Zuótian wǒ tīngle dìlǐ jiǎnghuà yǐhòu, wǒ juéde Zhōngguode zìrán

huánjing fēicháng hǎo. Zhōngguo yǒu yíjù huà shuō, "dà hǎo shān hé,"

5   xíngrong Zhōngguode dìfang hǎo. Wǒ xiànzài bǎ jiǎnghuàde dàyì fùshù

yícì.

Zhōngguo shi Yǎzhōu dì-yīge dà guó, wèizhi zài Yǎzhōude dōngnán

bù, shi dì-dà-wù-bó rénkǒu duōde guójiā. Zhōngguode miànji hé Měiguode

miànji chàbuduō. Dōngbiār shi Huáng Hǎi、Dōng Hǎi, nánbiār shi Nán

10   Hǎi, běibiār shi Wài Ménggǔ gēn Sūlián, xī'nánbiār shi Yìndu, nánbiār

shi Yuènán gēn Miǎndiàn.

Zhōngguo běnbù yǒu sāntiáo dà hé. Zuì chángde yào suàn shi Cháng

Jiāng le. Cháng Jiāng liúyùde tǔdì hǎojíle. Cháng Jiāng nánbiār yǒu

sānge dà hú, yǒu Tài Hú、Dòngtíng Hú、Póyáng Hú. Húbiārshang yǒu

15   nóngtián, chūchǎn de mǐ xiāngdāng fēngfù, húlǐde yú yě hěn duō. Yàoshi

yǐ shuō "yú-mǐ-zhī-xiāng" jiu zhīdao shuōde shi Jiāngnán. Cháng Jiāng

rù hǎide dìfang shi Shànghǎi. Shànghǎi shi hé shìjiè gèguó tōngshāng de

dà hǎikǒu, shi Zhōngguo jīngji zhōngxīn. Cháng Jiāng duì Zhōngguo shi

yǒu lìyì de.

20   Zhōngguo dì-èrtiáo dà hé shi Huáng Hé, zài Zhōngguode běibù.

Jǐqiān nián yǐqián Zhōngguo wénhuà kāishǐ shi zài Huáng Hé liúyù, dànshi chángcháng fāshēng shuǐzāi.   Yán Huáng Hé yídài zhùde rénmín niánnián shòu Huáng Héde zāihài.   Huáng Héde shuǐli hányŏu ní shā, suŏyǐ shuǐ shi huángsède.

25   Dì-sāntiáo hé jiu shi Zhū Jiāng.   Zhū Jiāng zài Zhōngguo nánbù. Guăngdong、Guăngxī zhèi liăngshěng shŭyu Zhū Jiāng liúyù.   Zhū Jiāng liúyù yŏu hěn duō shān, nóngtián yě hěn duō, nóngchăn yě xiāngdāng fēngfù. Zhōngguo hé wàiguo tōngshāng zuì zăode yíge hăikŏu shi Guăngzhōu. Guăngzhōu jiu shi Zhū Jiāng rù hăide hăikŏu.

30   Zhōngguo běnbù yígòng yŏu shíbāge shěng.   Zhōngguo biānjiāngde dìfang shi Dōngběi、Měnggŭ、Xīnjiāng、Xīzàng.   Dōngběide chūchăn hěn duō.   Měnggŭ、Xīnjiāng yŏu shāmò, dāngdì rén duōbàn shi kàozhe yăng niú yăng yáng shēnghuó.   Xīzàng yŏu hěn duō shān.

      Zhōngguo qìhou shi dàlùxìngde qìhou.   Tāde wèizhi shi zài běi wēndài.

35 Búguò běifāng bǐjiăo lěng, nánfāng bǐjiăo rè, xībiān gèng lěng yìxiē.

      Zhōngguo yánhǎi yŏu bù shǎode hǎidǎo.   Zuì dàde dǎo shi Táiwān. Zuì yŏumíngde xiǎo dǎo shi Xiānggǎng, dànshi Xiānggǎng zhèige xiǎo dǎo zài yī-bā-sì-èr nián zài Qīng Cháode shíhou rànggěi Yīngguo, shi Yīngguo rénde zhímíndì le.

WÉNXI

1. Zhāng Dàwén shi yíwèi shìzhǎng, yě shi yíwèi xuézhě. Tā duì rénde tàidu fēicháng kèqi. Tā zuì xǐhuan kàn shū. Tā shuō wèile zēngjiā xuéshi fēiděi duō kàn shū bùkě. Tā yòu shuō cóngqián tā zài Měiguo nián bóshide shíhou, zŏngshi jìnlì duō măi cānkǎo shū, zhǐ yàoshi kéyi zuòwéi cānkǎo yòng de, tā dōu măi. Măi shū suírán fèile hěn duō qián, kěshi yě dédào xǔduō xuéshi.

2. Wŏmen xuéxiàode zŏng bānshìchù shi yìsuǒ jiù lóu, jīnnián chóngxiū le. Chóngxiū de jìhua shi ànzhào xiàozhǎngde yìsi, qǐng gōngchéngxuéde jiào-shòu huàde tú. Zhèiwei jiàoshòu shìqián yě jiào jǐge xué gōngchéngde xuésheng cānjiā. Tā ànzhe shíjìshangde xūyào bǎ yuánláide xiàozhǎng shǐ、jiàowuzhǎng shǐ、fŭdǎo zhŭrèn shǐ dōu gěi bānle jiā le, dōu bāndao lóushàng. Zhìyú lóuxià cóngqián yŏu liăngge kèshǐ hé hézuòshè yě dōu bānzŏu le. Xiànzài wánquán shi ge yuàn-xìde bàngōngshǐ. Gè yuànde yuànzhǎng、gè xuéxìde xì zhŭrèn dōu jízhōng zài lóuxià bàngōng.

3. Xiànzài Zhōngguode jiàoyu zhìdu yǐjí xuézhì duōbàn shi cǎiyòng Xīfāng guójiāde zhìdu. Zhōngxué、xiǎoxué cǎiyòng xuénián-zhì, dàxué duōbàn shi xuéfēn-zhì. Xuénián-zhì, fēiděi niànmǎn guīdìng de xuénián bùkě. Xuéfēn-zhì kéyi búbì yídìng niàn duōshao nián. Zhǐ yàoshi bǎ guīdìng de xuéfēn niànmǎn jiu kéyi le.

4. Tā shi lùyīnshǐde zhǔrèn, suǒyǒu lùyīndài dōu shi tā shōuqilai. Yǒu rén
   wèn ta yígòng yǒu duōshǎo pán. Tā shuō. "Xiànzài yǐjing lùyīn de jǐnjǐn
   yǒu shíjǐ pán.   Zhǐyú lù de shi shénmo, nǐ kànkan zhèizhāng dānzi jiu
   zhīdao le."

5. Tā shi xué tǒngjixué de. Zài dàxué de shíhou chéngji jiu tèbié yōuliáng,
   déle xuéshì hé shuòshì xuéwèi. Hòulái zài yíge jīguānli dāng tǒngjì zhǔrèn. Xiànzài tā yòng kǎoshì de fāngfǎ xuǎn dǒng tǒngjìde zhíyuán. Yǒu
   rén wèn tā yào qǔ jǐge rén? Tā shuō yào qǔ yíge rén, yěxǔ qǔ liǎngge
   rén.

6. Wǒmen dàxué yǒu jǐwèi yǒumíngde jiàoshòu. Yíwèi shi wùlǐxuéjiā, yíwèi
   shi shēngwùxuéjiā. Tāmen liǎngwèide niánsuì dōu shi wǔshi suì zuǒyòu.
   Cǐwài hái yǒu yíwèi jiāo zhéxuéde jiàoshòu, chàbuduō yǒu liùshisuì le.

7. Yǒu yíge wàiguo xuésheng wèn wo, Zhōngguode pánzi hé suànpan shì bu
   shi yíyàngde dōngxi? Wǒ gàosu ta bú shi yíyàngde.   Pánzi shi chī fàn
   yòng de, suànpan shi jìsuàn shùmu yòng de.

8. Sūn Xiānshengde jiā běnlái zài Guǎngzhōude xiāngxia, shi zài yíge shān-
   xiàde xiǎo cūnzili. Zhèige cūnzilǐ rénkǒu xīshǎo, fēngjǐng měilì. Tāmen
   píngping'ānānde shēnghuó zài nèige huánjìngli. Dànshi jìn jǐnián lái tiānzāi rénhuò bīpòde tāmen bùdébù bān jiā. Tāmen bāndàole Guǎngzhōu Shì.
   Tāmen juéde chéngshi yòu méi yǒu hǎo fēngjǐng, rénkǒu yòu mì, tā tiāntiān xiǎng huídao xiāngxiade lǎo jiā, kěshi bù néng huíqu. Yǒu yìtiān tā
   hěn bù gāoxìngde shuō: "Búdàn wǒ bù néng huídao xiāngxia qu, jiu shi
   jiānglái wǒde zǐsūn yě bù yídìng néng huídao xiāngxia."

9. Nǐ zhīdao bù zhīdào Ménggǔde shāmò yǒu duōshǎo fāng Yīnglǐ? Nàlǐde
   tiānqi shì bu shi hěn lěng? Báitiānde wēndù yǒu duōshao dù? Wǎnshangde
   wēndù shì bu shi gèng dī? Zài shāmò qūyù shì bu shi rénkǒu xī? Tāmen
   kàozhe shénmo shēnghuó? Shì bu shi shícháng yídòng? Háiyǒu, shāmò
   dàoshi zěnmo xíngchéng de?

10. Dìdi wèn wǒ shénmo shi bàndǎo? Shénmo shi lùdì? Dàlù hé lùdì yǒu méi
    yǒu fēnbié? Wǒ gàosu ta: "Zhèixiē dōu shi dìlǐshangde chángshí. Nǐ
    xiān kànkan dìlǐ jiàokēshū. Nǐ yàoshi kànbumíngbai wǒ zài gàosu ni."

11. Zài dì-èrcì shìjiè dàzhàn yǐqián yǒu hěn duō guójiā dōu xiàng Fēizhōu
    zhímín, suǒyǐ Fēizhōu yǒu bù shǎo dìfang dōu shi zhímíndì. Dàole zhàn-
    hòu, zhèixiē zhímíndì dōu shi xīnde guójiā le. Tāmen duì yuánlái guójiā
    yǐjīng méi guānxi le.

12. Yī-jiǔ-sān-qī nián Chángshā Shì fāshēng zhànshì, hěn duō rénmín dōu
    bānzǒu le. Dàole zhànhòu yòu jiànjiànde bānhuilai. Yǒu rén diàochá
    Chángshā zhànshì rénkǒu dòngtài, bǎ zhànqián hé zhànshì yǐjí zhànhòu
    rénkǒude shùmu diàochádé fēicháng xiángxi.

13. Cóngqián Zhōngguo rén chúle niàn shū de yǐwài hái yǒu nóng、gōng、shāng
    sānzhǒng rén, lián niàn shū de rén yígòng yǒu sìzhǒng rén. Zài zhèi
    sìzhǒng rénli niàn shū rén de dìwei zuì gāo.

14. Yī-liù-bā-jiǔ nián Zhōng-É biānjiè fāshēng wèntí. Hòulái Éguo ràngbù
    le. Zhè shi Zhōngguo duì wàiguode guānxi zuì chénggōngde yícì. Dāng-
    shí Zhōngguo bàn zhèijiàn shìde rén duìyu guójiā zhēn shi yǒugōng le.

15. Wǒ zhèng zài niàn Ēwén Rùmén Lù Xiānsheng lái wèn wo, cóng Zhōng-
    guode Dōngběi dào Ēguo, tōng huǒchē ma? Wǒ gàosu ta kéyi zuò huǒchē.

16. Wǒ jiù zhǐdao Sūn Zhōngshān Xiānsheng shēngzai Guǎngdong Shěng Zhōng-
    shān Xiàn. Zhìyú Zhōngshān Xiàn shì bu shi zài Zhū Jiāng shàngyóu nà
    wǒ kě bù zhǐdào le.

17. Xīnhuá Nóngyè Hézuòshède shèzhǎng cóngqián shi Yīngguo liúxuéshēng.
    Tāde rìcháng shēnghuó yǐjing Ōuhuà le. Yǒu yìtiān tā kànjian tāde sūnzi,
    sūnnüer dōu zài wēnxi gōngke. Tā shuō: "Niànguo de shū dāngrán fēi
    chóng wēn bùkě, kěshi xīn shū yě yào duō kàn. Zuìjìn yǒu yìběn xīn xiǎo-
    shuō Huáng Hǎi shi Ōuzhōu yǒumíngde xiǎoxhuō, nǐmen kéyi kànkan."

18. Xiě wénzhāngde shíhou qiānwàn zhùyì bú yào líkai běntí. Rúguǒ líkai
    běntí, xiěde fànwéi tài guǎng. Nà jiu yídìng bù shi hǎo wénzhāng le.

19. Wǒ yào mǎi chē. Wǒ jiějie xiǎng gēn wǒ hé mǎi. Wǒ shuō: "Wǒ yòng
    chē de shíhou duō, wǒ yào zìjǐ dān mǎi, wǒ bù gēn nǐ hé mǎi."

20. Zhèicì shuǐzāi shòu hàide dìfang fēicháng guǎngdà. Shuǐzāi qūlide xiāng-
    cūn, nóngtián fánshi dìshi bù gāode dìfang dōu shi dàshuǐ. Nèi yídàide
    rénmín jùshuō yě sǐle bù shǎo. Zhèiyàng dàde shuǐ shi cóng nǎlǐ láide
    ne? Yǒu rén shuō shi jiānglǐ chūláide shuǐ, yǒu rén shuō shi xià yǔ
    xiàde tài duō le, suǒyǐ chéngle shuǐzāi.

21. Tā xiěle yìběn Kēxué Wèndá. Quán shū yígòng yǒu sānbǎi liùshiyè, bāokuò
    bābǎi duō ge wèntí. Měi yíge wèntí hòumiàn dōu yǒu hěn xiángxide huídá.
    Shi yìběn hěn hǎode cānkǎo shū.

22. Xuéle xǔduō shēngcí zhīhòu, jiu yào yòng zhèixiē shēngcí liànxi xiězuò.
    Liànxi xiězuò de fāngfǎ zuì hǎo shi xiān liànxi xiě duǎnwén. Duǎnwén
    liànxihǎo le, jiu zìrán'érránde néng xiě chángde wénzhāng le.

23. Zhāng shìzhǎng jiào wǒ bǎ shǐlǐ zài zhànqián hé zhànhòude rénkǒu zuò
    yíge bǐjiào. Wǒ wèn ta: "Nǐ shuō de zhànshǐ shi zhǐzhe shìjiè dàzhàn
    shuō de háishi zhǐzhe shàng yícì nèizhàn shuō de?" Zhāng shìzhǎng
    shuō: "Jiù àn shàngcì nèizhànde qiánhòu zuò yíge bǐjiào jiu kéyi le."

24. Zhāng Xiānsheng shi cóngqiánde Xīnán Liánhé Dàxuéde jiàoshòu. Tā shuō:
    "Cóngqián Sūn Zhōngshān Xiānsheng shuōguo, Zhōngguo yào liánhé shìjiè-
    shang duì Zhōngguo hǎode guójiā gòngtóng nǔlì. Zhèijù huà shuōle méi
    yǒu xǔjiǔ, hòulái zài shìjiè dì-èrcì dàzhàn zhīhòu jiu yǒule Liánhéguó.
    Liánhéguóli yǒu xǔduō guójiā dàjiā dōu hěn hézuò."

25. Wǒmen zài shàngkède shíhou cháng yǒu wèndá. Yǒu yìtiān Zhāng Xiān-
    sheng yǒu yíge wèntí wèn wǒmen néng bu něng dá? Tā shuō: "Xiānzài
    xǔduō guójiā dōu zhǔzhāng bù dǎzhàng. Kěshi jiānglái shì bu shi zhēnde
    bù dǎzhàng le ne? Shéi néng zhǐdao?" Wǒmen shuō: "Zhèige wèntí méi
    fázi huídá."

WÈNTÍ

1. Gēnjù Zhōngguo zhèngfǔ yī-jiǔ-wǔ-sān nián diàochá de Zhōngguo rénkǒu
   zǒngshù, shi duōshao rén? Zhàn shìjiè rénkǒu zǒngshùde jǐfēnzhī-jǐ?
   Nènmo shìjiè rénkǒu zǒngshù yǒu duōshao ne?

2. Zhōngguo rénkǒude fēnbù, shénmo dìfang zuì mì? Píngjūn měi fāng Yīnglǐ
   yǒu duōshao rén? Xiāngcūn rénkǒu zhàn zǒngshù jǐfēnzhī-jǐ? Wèi-shénmo
   xiāngcūnde rénkǒu duō?

3. Zhōngguo rénkǒude dòngtài hěn xiǎo shi shénmo yuányīn ne? Zhōngguo
   rén zài shénmo qíngxing zhīxià cái bùdebù bānjiā?

4. Qǐng jiāng Zhōngguo jìndài rénkǒu yídòng de liǎngge lìzi xiángxi shuōshuo.

5. Zhōngguo rénkǒu zēngjiā de sùdù jīngrén. Zhè hé Zhōngguo yìzhǒng chuántǒng de sīxiǎng hěn yǒu guānxi. Zhèizhǒng sīxiǎng shi shénmo?

6. Zhōngguo rénkǒu dà bùfen fēnbù zài něi jǐtiáo héliúde liúyù? Zhàn rénkǒu
   zǒngshù bǎifēnzhī-jǐ?

7. Shénmo shi Huáqiáo? Huáqiáo fēnbù zài shénmo dìfang? Yǒu duōshao
   rén? Něi yìshěngde rén zuì duō?

8. Shénmo jiào nèizhàn? Nèizhàn duì rénkǒu yǒu shénmo yǐngxiǎng?

9. Jiézhì shēngyù duìyú rénkǒude quānxi shi zěnmoyàng?

10. Qǐng nǐmen huídá rénkǒu hé zhànzhēng de guānxi.

ILLUSTRATIVE SENTENCES (ENGLISH)

4.1. In ancient China there was a philosopher who said: "A white horse is not a
     horse." Do you know what that means?

4.3. Unless there's a calamity [otherwise] he's not likely to move during his
     whole lifetime.

4.4. I don't plan to buy that book. I won't buy it unless the teacher tells us to.

6.1. [The meaning of] 'autonomous region' means that the people of that region
     govern themselves.

6.2. The Yangtze River basin refers to the area through which the Yangtze River
     flows [lit. water of the Yangtze River passes].

7.4. Was the Sino-Japanese War the beginning of World War II?

7.5. This movie depicts the frightfulness of war.

8.1. China and Japan fought a total of eight years beginning in 1937.

8.2. Hello! Wang? Do you know that fighting has broken out in the north again?

10.4. It's quite possible that those two countries will come to blows because of
      the border problem. [You see that] they are already on [lit. their appear-
      ance already is] a sort of wartime footing.

13.2. The Western European countries joined together to organize a group which
      was economic in nature. This joint organization was for the common in-
      terest.

17.1. Mr. Sun is from the same place as I. Because he wants everyone in the
      next generation to receive an education, he has started a school in the
      countryside.

20.1. Since it hasn't rained for a long time there's bound to be a drought, so we should limit the use of water.

22.2. The professor of biology often fails to go to class on time.

22.3. You spoke on the basis of theory, I spoke on the basis of law.

22.4. In the view of that linguist [lit. language specialist], Chinese has no adjectives.

22.5. According to the way the average person lectures on history, one should start from primitive society.

23.1. Is there any way of investigating the total population of Central and Eastern Asia?

25.1. (The fact that) China's population is in excess of six hundred million is based on statistics of the year 1953.

27.1. His temperature is over a hundred.

28.1. Speaking of the density of population in China, (that of) Shanghai is the densest.

35.1. In the Ch'ing Dynasty there were quite a few areas on China's frontiers which were occupied by foreign countries.

36.1. In the last world war some countries were forced to join.

36.2. The people harassed by natural and man-made calamities had no way to survive.

40.1. There is only one newspaper office on that island. The paper they publish is simply a small one containing nothing but local news.

40.2. In my case, having studied statistics for just one year, how can I be the chief statistician?

40.3. It's only three days since he moved here. It seems as if he's going to move again.

40.4. In that Yellow River flood those who suffered losses in the area of our family alone numbered over two thousand families.

42.1. It's very tranquil here. There has never been any disturbance.

43.2. I'll certainly think of a way to take care of anything that you ask me to handle. As to how I do it, you don't need to inquire.

44.2. Was he killed or did he commit suicide?

45.3. Hello! Hello! Is this Wang Dawen? This is Zhang. I won't be going to your place [there. These few days] I have to study and also find a house to move to. I'm terribly busy.

45.4. In the daytime he taught at Southwest Associated University, and in the evening he wrote essays. He was awfully busy all day until late.

45.5. That teacher doesn't know anything about teaching methods. He simply has the students read dull [lit. dead] books lesson by lesson.

47.1. I hadn't been back to my own country for ten years. On returning home this year I saw that the progress in agriculture and industry was really startling.

47.2. The newspapers say that recently the number of suicides has increased alarmingly [lit. those who have killed themselves are dreadfully numerous].

51.1. The temperature in that area is sometimes more than twenty degrees below zero.

51.2. There are 20,008 overseas Chinese here.

52.1. I'm not at all accustomed to living here.

53.1. What after all is the total number of Chinese peasants? What are you basing your statements on?

57.1. That question has already been settled [lit. passed] in the meeting, and we don't have to go into it any further.

59.1. Recently large quantities of local products have been exported from Shanghai.

61.1. It is my guess that those two will be able to cooperate.

63.1. Teacher, in what column on page thirty-eight is the word yídòng?

64.2. Today's topic is too difficult. There are a good many (questions) that we can't answer.

64.4. I love to read the questions and answers on literature in the newspaper.

65.1. Professor Zhang often writes short essays for [lit. on] the newspapers.

NOTES

1. A two-syllable stative verb of the form AB may be reduplicated as AABB, generally with the addition of de and with restoration of tone on the second syllable if it was neutral, the result being an intensified adverbial or adjectival modifier.

> qīngchu 'clear' → qīngqīngchǔchǔ(de) 'very clear(ly)'

2. The sentence Wǒ jiù chī Zhōngguo fàn, bù chī biéde fàn 'I eat Chinese food, I don't eat other food' can be reversed to Wǒ bù chī biéde (fàn), jiù chī Zhōngguo fàn and can be translated somewhat more idiomatically as 'I eat nothing but Chinese food.' The general underlying pattern is bù/méi V biéde (N), jiù V N 'to V nothing but N.' Variations on the basic pattern include sentences in which the verbs and nouns are different. (See Sentence 20 in Yǔfǎ Liànxí.) Also, a frequently used alternative pattern is:

> shénmo yě bù/méi V, jiù V N

The following is an example of this pattern:

> Tā shénmo yě bu zuò, jiù niàn shū. 'He does nothing but study.'

3. Expressions of duration of time follow the sentence to which they refer, with or without an intervening verb:

Tā zài zhèr yìtiān   'He was here for a day'

Tā zài zhèr yŏu yìtiān   'He was here for a day'

Tā zài zhèr méi yŏu yìtiān   'He was here for less than a day'

Tā zài zhèr búdào yìtiān   'He was here for less than a day'

Tā zài zhèr búguò yìtiān   'He was here for only a day'

Dì-Liùkè.   Wēnxi

FÙSHÙ

Zhèipán lùyīndài shi Zhōngwén dì-yīzǔ dì-wǔhào, Bái Wénshān fùshù dì-wǔcìde Zhuāntí Jiǎnghuà.

Zhèicì Zhuāntí Jiǎnghuà jiǎng de shi Zhōngguo rénkǒu wèntí. Zhǔjiǎng rén shi yíwèi rénkǒuxué zhuānjiā. Zhèiwèi zhuānjiā shuō shìjièshang 5 rénkǒu zuì duōde guójiā shi Zhōngguo. Zhōngguo rénkǒu zhàn shìjiè rénkǒu zǒngshùde sìfēnzhī-yī, zhàn Yàzhōude èrfēnzhī-yī. Zhōngguo rénkǒu yǒu liùyì líng yìbǎi duō wàn rén. Zhèige shùmu shi gēnju Zhōngguo zhèngfǔ zài 1953 nián nèicì diàochá tǒngji de jiéguǒ. Kěshi nà shi hěn jiǔ yǐqiánde jìlù, xiànzài shíjìshang kěnéng yǒu qīwànwàn le.

10 Zhèiwèi zhuānjiā jiēzhe yòu jiǎng Zhōngguo rénkǒu fēnbù zhuàngkuàng. Tā shuō zhèige wèntí kéyi yòng liǎngge guāndiǎn lai kàn. Xiān ànzhào dìfangde qūyù lai shuō. Yǒu bǎifēnzhī-jiǔshí shi jízhōng zài Cháng Jiāng、Huáng Hé、Zhū Jiāng sānge liúyù de. Cǐwàide bǎifēnzhī-shí shi zài Dōngběi hé biānjiāng děng dìfang. Tā yòu shuō, rúguǒ ànzhe dìfang 15 xìngzhi lai shuō, yìsi jiù shi shuō ná chéngshì gēn xiāngcūn lai shuō, chéngshì rénkǒu jǐnjǐnde zhàn bǎifēnzhī-èrshí, xiāngxiade rénkǒu zhàn bǎifēnzhī-bāshí. Tā shuō xiāngxiade rénkǒu wèi-shénmo zhènmo duō ne?

Yīnwei Zhōngguo shi nóngyè guójiā, dà duōshùde rénmín shi nóngren.

Búguò jìnnián yǐlái yīnwei tíchàng gōngyè, suǒyǐ chéngshìde rénkǒu yìtiān

20   bǐ yìtiān duō le.

Shuōdao zhèli tā yòu shuō Zhōngguo shénmo dìfangde rénkǒu zuì duo,

shénmo dìfangde rénkǒu xīshǎo. Tā shuō nà shi rénkǒu mìdùde wèntí.

Zhōngguo rénkǒude mìdù zuì mìde dìfang shi Cháng Jiāng xiàyóu yídài,

píngjūn měi fāng Yīnglǐ cóng bābǎi rén dào èrqiān rén. Rénkǒu zuì xīde

25   dìfang shi Xīzàng, píngjūn měi Yīng fānglǐ zhǐ yǒu yì-liǎngge rén. Běifāng

píngyuán píngjūn yǒu liùshiwǔge rén zuǒyòu.

Zhèiwèi zhuānjiā jiēzhe yòu jiǎng rénkǒude dòngtài. Tā shuō Zhōng-

guo rén shi ān-tǔ-zhòng-qiān, yìsi jiu shi shuō Zhōngguo rén bù xíguàn

suíbiàn yídòng, suǒyǐ rénmínde yídòngxìng bú dà. Yíbānde rén dōu xǐhuan

30   zài lǎo jiā píngpíng'ānānde guò rìzi, juéduì bù qīngyì bānjiā, chúfēi yǒule

tiānzāi rénhuò bèi bīpò bānjiā. Shénmo shi tiānzāi ne? Jiù shi shuǐzāi、

hànzāi. Rénhuò ne? Jiù shi zhǐzhe zhànzhēng hái yǒu shèhuìshangde

dòngluàn shénmode.

Zài Dōngběi yǒu hěn duō Shāndong rén. Yīnwei dāngchū Shāndong

35   Shěng yǒule tiānzāi, hěn duō rén dào Dōngsānshěng qu le. Sìchuān yě

yǒu hěn duō rén shi cóng Guǎngdong、Húběi bānqu de. Nà shi yīnwei

Míng Cháo mònián Sìchuānde dòngluàn, rénmín duōbàn bèi shāsi le, suǒyǐ

Sìchuān rénkǒu tài shǎo le. Yīncǐ Guǎngdong、Húběide rén bāndao Sìchuān

qu le. Kěshi zhèizhǒng yídòng bú shi zhèngfǔde jìhuà ràng rénmín dà

40   guīmóde yídòng, nà shi rénmín zìjǐ jiànjiànde bānqu de.

Zuìhòu shuōdao Zhōngguo rénkǒu yìtiān bǐ yìtiān duō. Zēngjiā de

sùdù shi hěn jīngréndė. Zhè shi yīnwei Zhōngguo rén chuántǒngde sīxiǎng,

xīwang zǐsūn duō, yě jiu shi yuànyi duō-zǐ-duō-sūn. Yàoshi yǒu rén

tíchàng jiézhì shēngyù lai jiějué rénkǒu zēngjiā de wèntí, lǎobǎixìng duōshù

45   bú dà zàncheng.

NOTE ON SUBSTITUTION FRAMES

The following exercise entitled Wèndá (Questions and Answers) consists of
sentences in the form of substitution frames followed by lists of expressions
which can be used to fill in the blank space in the sentences. These expressions
are listed in the order of the lessons in which they occurred so as to facilitate
their review either after the lesson of first occurrence or in the present lesson.

The exercises can be used in various ways. One of the best is for the teacher to ask questions using the listed expressions and for the students to give one or more appropriate answers. It is not necessary to limit oneself to a simple question and answer. These can often be expanded into an exchange of several sentences.

WÈNDÁ

I. Nǐ wèi-shénmo . . . ?

(dì-yīkè)

bú cānjiā zhèige huì
cǎiyòng zhèige fázi
bù fānchéng Yīngwén
bù yào jiǎngyǎn
juédìng bú qù
bù zàncheng
bù nǔlì xuéxí
niàn zhèige kècheng
bù xiāngxìn ta

(dì-èrkè)

shuō méi bànfǎ
bú niàn bóshi
chéngji nènmo hǎo
bìděi chóngxiū
niàn gōngchengxué
shuō méi guānxi
méi dài qián
bù liú Měi qu
fèi nènmo duō shí
bù juān qián

(dì-sānkè)

bù gǎnkuài zǒu
xiě jiǎnhuà Hànzì
mǎi Wǔ Jīng
bú zuò guān
mǎi jiù shū
jīntian qǐshēn
bú dào jiǎngtáng qu
xūyào nènmo duō qián
méi xuǎnshang
bù xiě wénzhāng
chángqī zài nèr
xūyào mòshuǐ

(dì-sìkè)

méi chénggōng
shuō tā bù kěkào
dào Chángshā qu
bú zuò shāngren
gēn tā bù tōngxìn
bù wēnshū
zài xiāngxia zhù

yǎng yáng
zhànzai nèr
mǎi huáng zhǐ
niàn Zàngwén
bú ràngbù
názhe shítou
niàn Ēwén
bù xǐhuan Àozhōu
dào Yìndu qu
líkai Táiwān
shuō Guǎngdong huà

(dì-wǔkè)

bān jiā
fēi qù bùkě
niàn rénkǒuxué
qù kàn shìzhǎng
dào Sìchuān qu
bú yuànyi qu
shuō tā bèi shā le
bú zhù cūnzili
huàn qián
shuō wēndù bú gòu
juéduì bù shuō
shuō tā sǐle

II. . . . shi shénmo?

(dì-yīkè)

shēngcí
lìjù
wēnxi jùzi

zhùjiě
fùshù
wǔnián jìhua
dà jiātíng

jiǎnghuà
yǎnjiǎngcí
shēngcí biǎo
jīntiande jiǎngtí

(dì-èrkè)

bóshi lùnwén

chéngji-dān

bàngōngchù

bànshìchù

hézuòshè

jiǎngxuéjīn

nóngyè hézuòshè

kèshǐ

lùyīnshǐ

bàngōngshǐ

shuòshi lùnwén

yīyuàn

pánzi

suànpan

xuénián-zhì

cānkǎo shū

(dì-yīkè)

zhǔjiǎng rén

jiàozhíyuán dōu

(dì-èrkè)

jiàowuchù

Jiàoyu Bùzhǎng

xì zhǔrèn

Xīnhuá Lóu

yīsheng

fǔdǎo zhǔrèn

wǒde dàizi

gōngxuéyuàn

nǐde suànpan

(dì-sānkè)

Qǐng Cháode guódū

---

dānzi

xuéfèi

(dì-sānkè)

jiǎnhuà Hànzì

kējǔ

sīlì xuéxiào

pǔji jiàoyu

sīshú

jiǎntǐzì

yòuzhiyuán

xuétáng

Sān Zì Jīng

kètáng

(dì-sìkè)

nóngchǎn

fēngjǐng

hǎidǎo

III. . . . zài nǎr?

yòuzhiyuán

shēnglì dàxué

(dì-sìkè)

Shāndong bàndǎo

Huáng Hǎi

Huáng Hé

Dòngtíng Hú

Póyáng Hú

Xiānggǎng

Yángzi Jiāng

Jiāngnán

Jiāngxi

Jiāngsu

Zhèjiāng

Zhū Jiāng

Guǎngxi

---

zìzhìqū

rèdài

Guóyǔ Rùmén

tǔchǎn

bàndǎo

shāmò

xíngrongcí

yángròu

hànzāi

zhímíndì

biānjiāng

shuǐzāi

(dì-wǔkè)

mìdù

rénkǒuxué

sùdù

chéngshì

tǒngjixué

shìjiè dàzhàn

Guǎngdong

Guǎngzhou

Xīnjiāng

Xīzàng

Měnggǔ

Nèi Měnggǔ

Wài Měnggǔ

Miǎndiàn

Sūlián

Yìndu

Ēguo

Xī-Ōu

Dōngyǎ

Qīnghǎi

(dì-wǔkè)   Sìchuān   shìzhǎng

Shànghǎi Shì   Huáng Héde shàngyóu   nǐde sūnnüer

IV. . . . báihuà zěnmo shuō?

(dì-yīkè)   (dì-èrkè)   běnbù

běnxiào   běntǐ   chǎnshēng

gǎndào   cǐwài   hányǒu

lìjù   lìyì
                                   (dì-sānkè)
yīncǐ   míngchēng   měilì

zhūwèi   zǒng'eryánzhi   dì-dà-wù-bó

dáchéng   jiànjiànde

gàikuàng   zǒngzhi   (dì-wǔkè)

                                   (dì-sìkè)   ān-tǔ-zhòng-qiān

                                                                 duō-zǐ-duō-sūn

V. Nǐ zěnmo zhīdao . . . ?

(dì-yīkè)   shi wǒ zhǔjiǎng de

zhèicì kǎoshìde fànwéi   bǐděi fùshù zhèige zhuāntí

tā shi yōuxiù fènzǐ   bāokuò wǒ zài nèi

tā fēicháng jìmò
                                   (dì-èrkè)
tā yào jiǎng de zhuāntí   tā bàn nèijiàn shì

tā jiěshide qīngchu   wǒde bàngōng dìfang

tā xīnli mǎnzú le   tā hěn néng bàn shì

shénmo shíhou kāixué   wǒ yǐjing bànhǎo le

Kǒngzǐde shēngri   yào chénglì fǎxuéyuàn

tā hěn kuàilè   yào zàichóng xiě yícì

rén mǎn le   nà shi gēnjù fǎlǜ

nèige qīngnián hěn hǎo   wǒde fēnshu

wǒde jiātíng qíngxing   tā shi fǔdǎo zhǔrèn

tā lai qiú wo   tāmende guānxi

tā shìqián bù zhīdào   tā shi xué gōngchéng de

tā yǒu zhuānmén xuéshì   tā jiāo gōngchéngxué

tā yěxǔ bù lái   tā gēn wǒ yǒu guānxi

tā shi zhíyuán   wǒmen néng hézuò

tā shi zhuānjiā   nèige huánjìng bù hǎo

tā jiǎngde bù qīngchu   shi tā jìlù de

wǒmen dōu shi dì-yīzǔ

jiàowuzhǎng yào zǒu le

Jiàoyu-Bù yǒu duōshao rén

tā zài lǐxúeyuàn

wǒ bu liǎojiě ni

nèisuǒ lóu shi wǒde

lóushàng lóuxià dōu méi rén

tā shi nóngren

nóng-gōngyède qíngxing

wǒde píngjūn fēnshu

tā shēnqǐng liúxué

tā xǐhuan shēngwù

tā jiāo shēngwùxué

wǒ mǎile xīn chē

tā déle xuéshì xuéwèi

tā yào yǒu bìng

tā zài yīxuéyuàn

Zhōngguo shi dà jiātíng zhìdu

zǒngshù shi duōshao

tā yǒu jǐpán lùyīndài

tā shi nóngmín

   (dì-sānkè)

tāde wénzhāng jìnbù le

wǒde chéngdu gǎnshang tā le

tāmen jiǎngde shi dà-tóng-xiǎo-yì

fāzhǎn de fāngshì

yǎnbiàn de guòchéng

shi shéi guīdìng de

nà shi guòdù shíqī

nà shi guólì dàxué

shěnglì xuéxiào yǒu duōshao ne

tāde sīxiǎng luòhòu le

fēijī yào luòxialai le

yǐhòude qūshì ne

nèige tuántǐ qǔxiāo le

shèlǐ xuétángde guòcheng

hé shuǐ bù shēn

tā yǒu gāoshēnde xuéwen

tāde shēnxīn dōu hěn hǎo ne

tā shòule wǒde yǐngxiǎng

nà shi shǔyu sīrende

Táng Cháo jiu yǒu kējǔ le

tāde shēntǐ hěn hǎo

quántǐ bù cānjiā

jiǎntǐzì yǒu duōshao

wǒmende kànfǎ xiāngtóng

chuán zǒu de fāngxiang

tā xiūyè bú dào yìnián

xuǎnjǔ de rìqi

tā méi xuǎnshang

yào zēngjiā xuéfèi

nà shi cháoliúde qūshì

dì-èrtáng méi yǒu kè

zěnyàng fāzhǎn nóngyè

tā niàn wǔge xuékē

bǐhuáde xiānhòu

tā shi yíbùyíbù xuéde

tāde gōngzuò shi duǎnqī de

   (dì-sìkè)

dàlùde chūchǎn hěn duō

Zhōngguode wùchǎn fēngfù

shāngyè hěn fādá

tā kàodezhù

tā kàozhe xiě shū shēnghuó

yǒu hěn dàde sǔnhài

shi shéi zhì shuǐ yǒugōng

Zhū Jiāng liúyù tiānqi bù
    lěng

Cháng Jiāng cóng nǎli rù hǎi

Xiānggǎngde miànji

tōngshāng yǒu lìyì

Jiāngnán qìhou wēnhé

shāmo shi zěnmo xíngchéng de

wǒmen shi tóngxiāng

niánnián yǒu tiānzāi

Měnggǔ yǒu guǎngdàde shāmò

wǒ huì Měngwén

shi wǒ ràng tā lái de

Xīzàng bù chǎn mǐ

shuǐli yǒu ní shā

nèijiàn shǐ méi tōngguò

tāde shēnghuó Ōuhuà le

méi zàojiù réncái

nà shi tā běnshēnde shì

(dì-wǔkè)

shi ànzhào shíjì shuō de

tā shi bèi bīpò de

wǒ yuànyi zhùzai xiāngcūn

diǎocháde hěn quèshi

wǒmende guāndiǎn bùtóng

Huáqiáode zhuàngkuàng

nèige tuántǐde xìngzhi

Àozhōu rénkǒu xīshǎo

shi tā tíchàng de

shi zhǐzhe tā shuō de

nà shi chuántǒng sīxiǎng

wèntí tài fùzá

méi fázi jiějué

jǐn yǒu yíge rén

zhèr jiézhǐ shēngyù

Sūn Zhōngshānde xuéshuō

tāmen yào dǎzhàng

yìbān rénde xíguàn

tāde zǐsūn duō ne

tā juéduì bú zàncheng

tāmen liánhéqilai le

tā zìshāle ne

yào jiézhǐ yòng shuǐ le

VI. Nǐ shénmo shíhou . . . ?

(dì-yīkè)

jìxù gěi wǒ jiǎng

gěi wǒ jǔ yíge lìzi

qù tīng xuéshù yǎnjiǎng

gǎndao zuì jìmò

bǎ zhùjiě xiěhǎo

cái kéyi zuòwán

(dì-èrkè)

cái kéyi chóng xiě

dào fǎxuéyuàn qu

xuéde jiàoyu

yǒu kùnnán

yánjiu de jīngji

xiǎng jiàn xì zhǔrèn

gěi wǒ xiángxi shuōshuo

kāishǐ yánjiu zhéxué

yánjiu de gèguó xuézhì

zǔzhide zhèige xuéhuì

mǎide zhèiběn cānkǎo shū

(dì-sānkè)

cái kéyi gǎnshang ta

xuǎnde zhèiběn shū

shòule tāde yǐngxiǎng

lìde zhèige mùbiāo

xiěde wénzhāng

jiǎng Zhōngguode héliú

(dì-sìkè)

kāishǐ gēn tā tōngxìn

yánzhe hébiān zǒu de

dàoguo yán hǎide dìfang

qùguo Jiāngxi

líkaile Jiāngsu

zài Zhèjiāng niàn shū

dào Yǎzhōu lǚxíng

bǎ shū shōuqilai de

shōu de xìn

dào Ōuzhōu qù

dàoguo Zhōng-È biānjiè

mǎide zhèixie shítou

(dì-wǔkè)

huànde chē

kànjian wǒde tàidu bù hǎo

tǒngjìde rénshù

xiěde Zhànshí Jiàoyu

qùguo Liánhéguó

zài Xīnán Liánhé Dàxué niàn
shū

líkaile Lián-Dà

xǔ tā chū guó

dà guīmóde qǐng kè

jiào tā bān jiā

wēnxi duǎnwén

huídá wǒ

kàn wèndáde jùzi

kàndao zuìhòu yíyè

jiàngguo Sūn Xiáojie

dào Sìchuān qù

FĀYĪN

The following pairs of terms are distinguished in speech solely by differences in tone. Define each item, use in a sentence, or otherwise indicate that you know the difference in meaning of the terms.

1. dáchéng, dà chéng

2. dádào, dàdāo

3. jìhua, jǐhuá

4. jìgé, jǐge

5. kèshǐ, kěshi

6. wùlǐ, wǔlǐ

7. yīkē, yíkè

8. yīyuàn, yìyuán

9. zhǔrèn, zhǔren

10. dān zǐ, dānzi

11. jīběn, jǐběn

12. sīlì, sìlǐ

13. sīshú, Sì Shū

14. xiànglái, xiǎng lái

15. yòuzhi, yǒu zhǐ

16. dìshì, dì-shí

17. jízhōng, jǐzhǒng

18. shìzhǎng, shízhǎng

19. shíjì, shí jǐ

20. xuéxì, xuéxi

HUÌHUÀ

Měi: Wai.

Bái: Wai. Měiyīng ma?

Měi: Oh, Wénshān, zěnmoyang? Gōngke máng bu máng?

Bái : Mángde bùdeliǎo. Lián gěi nǐ diànhuà de shíjiān dōu méi yǒu.

5 Měi: Tīngshuō nǐmen zhè xuéqī yǒule Zhuāntí Jiǎnghuà. Zhuāntí Jiǎnghuà jiūjìng yǒu yìsi méi yìsi? Dōu shi shǔyu něizhǒngde tímu?

Bái : Hěn yǒu yìsi. Wǒmen zhèige xīngqī yǒu wǔge bùtóngde tímu.

Měi: Jiǎng de dōu shi hé něizhǒng xuékē yǒu guānxi de?

Bái : Nǐ tīng wǒ gàosu ni. Xiàozhǎng jiǎnghuà、xuéxiào gàikuàng、Zhōng-
10   guo jiàoyu、Zhōngguo dìlǐ hái yǒu Zhōngguo rénkǒu.

Měi: Nǐmen yíge xuéqī xué hěn duō dōngxi ya.

Bái : Dōngxi dàoshi xuéde bù shǎo, kěshi mángde yàosǐ.

Měi: Oh! Mǎ Jiàoshòu hòutiān qǐng wǒmen sānge rén dào tā jiā qu chī
fàn qu. Nǐ gēn Xuéxīn yídìng zǎo jiù zhīdaole ba?

15 Bái : Wǒ jiù shi wèi zhèige dǎ diànhuà gěi ni. Hòutiān sāndiǎn zhōng
wǒ dào fǔshang lai. Wǒmen yíkuàr qu.

Měi: Xuéxīn shì bu shi gēn wǒmen yíkuàr qu ne?

Bái : Tā gēn wǒmen yíkuàr qu. Búguò tā dào fǔshang láide wǎn yìdiǎr.

Měi: Wénshān, Mǎ Tàitai cài zuòde hǎojíle. Mǎ Tàitai shi Sìchuān rén,
20   zuò Sìchuān cài. Wǒ zuì xǐhuan chī tā zuò de cài, yóuqíshi tā
chǎo de cài.

Bái : Mǎ Tàitai shuō huà kǒngpà wǒ yào tīngbudǒng.

Měi: Nǐ yídìng tīngdedǒng. Yīnwei tā shòule Mǎ Jiàoshòude yǐngxiǎng,
tāde Sìchuān kǒuyīn bu tài zhòng le.

25 Bái : Mǎ Jiàoshòu shi zài Sìchuān jiē de hūn ma?

Měi: Shìde. Hé Rìběn dǎzhàng yǐhòu Mǎ Jiàoshòu shi zài Sìchuān jiē
de hūn.

Bái : Mǎ Jiàoshòu bú shi zài Xīnán Lián-Dà niàn de shū ma?

Měi: Jiēhūn gēn niàn shū yǒu shénmo guānxi?

30 Bái : Wǒde yìsi shi Xīnán Lián-Dà bú zài Sìchuān.

Měi: Nèige shíhou tā jiā zài Sìchuān. Tā zài Sìchuān rènshide Mǎ
Tàitai.

Bái : Oh. Yuánlái shi zènmo huí shì.

Měi: Mǎ Tàitai rén hǎojíle.

35 Bái : Mǎ Tàitai zuò shì ma?

Měi: Tā zài yíge sīlìde yòuzhiyuán dāng jiàoyuán. Nèige yòuzhiyuán
shi zhuān wèile huí guó Huáqiáode xiǎoháizi bàn de.

Bái : Guīmó dà bu dà?

Měi: Yìbānde yòuzhiyuán guīmó dōu bú dà. Zhèi yídài hěn xūyào yòu-
40   zhiyuán, bìxū duō bàn jǐge. Yǒu xǔduō xiǎoháizi zài jiāli, bù néng
rù xuéxiào. Jǐnjǐn zhèi yídài zhǐshǎo yǒu liǎngbǎi xiǎoháizi méi
shàngxué.

Bái : Pǔjí jiàoyu dì-yījiàn shì shi děi duō shèlì xuéxiào.

Měi : Nǐ shuōde hěn duì.

45 Bái : Hǎo. Hòutiān sāndiǎn zhōng jiàn le.   Qǐng xiàng Gāo Xiānsheng
      Gāo Tàitai wèn hǎo.

Měi : Hǎode, xièxie ni.   Hòutiān jiàn . . .

(Wénshān dàole Gāo jiā)

Měi : Wénshān, nǐ zhēn ànzhe shíhou lái le.

Bái : Gēn xiáojie dìng shíjiān nǎli nénggou bú àn shíhou ne? Zuò shénmo
50   ne, Měiyīng?

Měi : Kàn shū ne.

Bái : Zhēn yònggōng.

Měi : Xuéwèn bú gòu děi gǎnkuài zìjǐ chōngshí zìjǐ me.

Bái : Nǐ xiànglái shi nènmo nǔlì.

55 Měi : Nǎr a, nǎr yǒu nǐ nènmo nǔlì ya.

Bái : Bié tí le. Wǒ zài zhèi sānnián lǐtou jiǎnzhí bǎ Zhōngwén dōu gěi
      wàng le. Wǒmen kèchéngli yǒu Zhuāntí Jiǎnghuà. Měicì tīngwánle
      yǐhòu fēiděi fùshù bùkě, wǒ gǎnjué xiāngdāngde nán.

Měi : Shénmo jiàozuo fùshù? Zhèige míngchēng hěn tèbié. Yě shi yìmén
60   gōngke ma?

Bái : Jiu shi tīngle yǎnjiǎng zhīhòu àn yuánláide yǎnjiǎng ná lùyīnjī bǎ
      nèige yǎnjiǎng zìjǐ zài shuō yícì.

Měi : Mǎ Jiàoshòu jiāo shū dāngrán jiāode búcuò le.   Tā duì xuésheng
      de tàidu zěnmoyàng?

65 Bái : Tā rén hǎojíle, tā quèshí shi ge hǎo xiānsheng. Gēn tā xuéxi wǒ
      juézhe fēicháng jìnbù.

Měi : Hěn duō rén shuō tāde jiàoxuéfǎ xiāngdāng hǎo, yóuqíshi duìyu
      wàiguo xuésheng.

Bái : Shìde. Tā cǎiyòng de jiàoxuéfǎ hěn hǎo. Tā bú shi yòng yìzhǒng
70   niàn sǐ shū de jiàoxuéfǎ. Tāde jiàoxuéfǎ shi yòng hěn píngchángde
      huà mànmānde yíbùyíbùde jiǎngdao běntí. Tā shi yòng hěn róngyi
      dǒng de huà jiěshì hěn gāoshēnde xuéwèn.

Měi : Xiānshengde jiàoxuéfǎ hǎo, xuésheng zìrán'érránde jìnbù.

Bái : Zǒngeryánzhi Mǎ Jiàoshòu xuéguo jiàoyu, suǒyǐ tā liǎojiě jiāoxué
75   de fāngfǎ.

Měi : Dàtǐshang shuō wǒmen Yuǎn-Dàde jiàoshòu dōu búcuò. Duìyu xué-
      shengde kèchéng dōu xiāngdāng rènzhēn.

Bái : Biéde jiàoshòu wǒ dōu bú rènshi ne, xiànzài zhǐ rènshi Mǎ Jiào-
      shòu, hái yǒu wàiguo xuésheng fǔdǎo zhǔrèn, yīnwei jiànmiàn de
80   jīhui bǐjiào duō yìdiǎr.

Měi : Nǐmen Zhuāntí Jiǎnghuà shǐ bu shi bāokuò gèzhǒng xuékēde tímu?

Bái : Shìde. Wǒmen měitiān yíge tímu, suǒ jiǎng de dōu shi bù xiāng-tóng de xuékē.

Měi : Dōu shi Mǎ Jiàoshòu yíge rén jiāo a?

85 Bái : Shì. Zhǐ shi Mǎ Jiàoshòu yíge rén jiāo wo.

Měi : Mǎ Jiàoshòu shi yíwèi wànnéng jiàoshòu.

Bái : Mǎ Jiàoshòude xuéwen 'shì hěn hǎo.

Měi : Wǒ fùqin gēn tā shi tóngxué. Jù fùqin shuō Mǎ Jiàoshòu zài Xīnán Lián-Dà sìnián, chéngji dōu hǎo, měi xuéqī dōu kǎo dì-yī. Wǒ
90 fùqin shuō tā wénzhāng xiěde fēicháng hǎo. Shuō tā zuò xuésheng de shíqī, yǒu yícì bàozhǐshang yào xuǎn yíge zuì hǎode lùnwén, tímu shi "Zěnyàng Tuīxíng Pǔjí Jiàoyu." Zìshù zhìshǎo yào xiě sānwàn zì. Jiéguǒ Mǎ Jiàoshòude wénzhāng xuǎnshang le.

Bái : Wǒmen xià xīngqī yào xiě lùnwén le.

95 Měi : Shénmo tímu?

Bái : "Zhōngguo Wěnzìde Yǎnbiàn." Wǒ hái méi xiǎngchulai zěnmo xiě ne.

Měi : Zhèige tímu kànqilai hěn jiǎndān, xiěqilai hěn fūzá.

Bái : Guīdìng wǒmen zhìshǎo yào xiě wǔqiān zì. Wǒ děi qǐngjiào nǐ le.

100 Měi : Kèqi. Nǐ yuánlái hái shi wǒde shùxué lǎoshī ne.

Bái : Xiànzài nǐ shi wǒde Zhōngwén lǎoshī le.

Měi : Xiě lùnwén xiān bǎ tímu liǎojiěle yǐhòu, zài yǒu yíge zhōngxīn sīxiǎng jiu róngyi le. Zuò wénde mùdì shi yào bǎ nǐde sīxiǎng gàosule biéren.

105 Bái : Wǒ xiěhǎole yǐhòu qǐng nǐ gěi wǒ kànyikàn.

Měi : Nǐ bié kèqi le . . . Wàimian yǒu rén jiào mén. Dàgài shi Xuéxīn.

Bái : Wǒ qu kāi. Shéi ya?

Xué : Wǒ. Wénshān!

Bái : Nǐ bú shi shuō sìdiǎn zhōng jiu lái ma?

110 Xué : Wǒmen lìshǐ nèige huì kāi wǎn le.

Měi : Xuéxīn!

Xué : Měiyǐng! Máng ba?

Měi : Bù máng. Wǒmen sānge rén lǐtou wǒ xiāngxìn zuì mángde shi Wénshān.

115 Xué : Zhè dào shi zhēnde. Měitiān wǎnshang tā yònggōng dōu shi dào yìdiǎn zhōng.

Bái : Yīnwei xǔjiǔ méi niàn Zhōngwén le, gǎnjué yǒu diǎr kùnnán, zǒng děi yòng diǎr gōng.

Xué: Wǒ rènwei nǐmende gōngkeli zuì máfande shi Zhuāntí Jiǎnghuà.
120   Búdàn yào xué cér yào tīng jiǎng, yòu děi fùshù. Érqiě jiǎng de
       tímu yě hěn duō. Yíge xīngqī jiǎng jǐge tímu?

Bái: Wǒmen yíge xīngqī yào jiǎng wǔge tímu.

Xué: Shàng xīngqī dōu jiǎng shénmo?

Bái: Chúle xiàozhǎng jiǎnghuà hé fǔdǎo zhǔrèn bàogào xuéxiào gàikuàng
125   yǐwài, zhǐ yǒu sānge zhuāntí yǎnjiǎng. Jiǎng de shi Zhōngguo
       jiàoyu、rénkǒu yǐjí dìlǐ.

Xué: Měi yícìde jiǎngyǎn yīnwei shíjiān hěn duǎn bù néng bǎ quánbùde
       dōngxi dōu jiǎngwánle ba?

Bái: Zhǐ shi jiǎng yíge dàgàide qíngxing.   Huàn ju huà shuō jiù shi
130   jiǎngde hěn jiǎndān. Bǐrú shuō, jiǎng Zhōngguo jiàoyu jiù shi jiǎng
       kējǔ zhìdu gēn sīshú, hái yǒu guòdù shíqīde xuétáng hé xiàndài de
       xuéxiào, yǐjí zěnyàng tuīxíng pǔjí jiàoyu děngděng.

Měi: Guānyu rénkǒu wèntí jiǎng xiē shénmo ne?   Yě jiǎng mínzú ma?

Bái: Zhǐ jiǎng Zhōngguo rénkǒu zhàn shìjiè dì-yīwèi, yě jiǎngdao Zhōng-
135   guo suīrán jīngji luòhòu, shēnghuó zhuàngkuàng búlùn zěnmo bù
       hǎo, dànshi dōu bú zàncheng tíchàng jiézhi shēngyù, yìsi jiu shi
       shuō yuànyi duō-zǐ-duō-sūn.

Měi: Zhè shi Zhōngguo chuántǒng de sīxiǎng.   Lǎo xiānsheng、lǎo tài-
       taimen dōu xǐhuan xià yídài rénkǒu duō. Yàoshi gēn biéren jiàn-
140   miàn xiān shuō tā yígòng yǒu duōshao sūnzi、sūnnüer.

Bái: Zhōngguo chuántǒng de sīxiǎng yě yǒu tāmende dàolǐ.

Xué: Nènmo nǐ zànchéng duō-zǐ-duō-sūn le.

Bái: Zhōngguo dà jiātíng hěn yǒu yìsi.

Xué: Xiàng ge xiǎo tuántǐ.

145 Měi: Érzi、sūnzi hǎoxiàng tuányuán.

Xué: Lǎo xiānsheng、lǎo tàitai jiu shi tuánzhǎng.

Měi: Dàjiā dōu shuō Zhōngguo yǒu liùyì duō rén. Zhèige shùmu quèshí
       bú quèshí?

Bái: Zhè shi gēnju rénkǒuxuéjiā shuō de.   Zài yī-jiǔ-wǔ-sān nián de
150   shíhou diàochá tǒngjì de jiéguǒ shi liùyì rén. Tāmende tuīcè xiàn-
       zài yǒu liùyì wǔqiān wàn rén le. Zhōngguo rénkǒu zēngjiā de
       sùdu zhēn shi jīngrén.

Xué: Tā shuō Zhōngguo rénkǒude dòngtài zěnmoyàng?

Měi: Xuéxīn, wǒmen xiànzài shi kǎo Wénshān ne.

155 Bái: Tā shuō Zhōngguo rén zài xíguànshang shi jué bù qīngyì bānjiā
       de, suǒyǐ yídòngxìng hěn xiǎo.

Měi: Xiàng zhùzai chéngshìde rén yǒu shíhou hái bānjiā. Xiāngcūnde
       rén yìshēng yě bù zhīdào shénmo jiàozuo bānjiā.

Xué: Zhōngguo rénkǒu zènmo duō, nǎrde rénkǒu z ˀ mǐ ne?

160 Bái: Shuōqi Zhōngguo rénkǒude mìdù, Cháng Jiāng xiàyou rénkǒu zuì mǐ.

Měi: Cháng Jiāng shàngyóu ne?

Bái: Yìbānde shuō, héliúde shàngyóu rénkǒu dōu bǐ xiàyóu xī, yīnwei shàngyóu duōbàn shi gāo shān, rénkǒu zìránde xīshǎo.

Xué: Rénkǒu hé zhànzhēng yǒu shénmo guānxi?

165 Bái: Shìjièshang búlùn shi shénmo dìfang zhǐ yàoshi yǒule zhànshì jiu yǒu dàliàngde rénmín bèi shāsǐ, suǒyǐ búlùn shi nèizhàn huòzhě shìjiè dàzhàn juéduì bù yīnggāi zài fāshēng le.

Měi: Ànzhào xiànzàide tuīcè shì bu shi yídìng nénggou méi yǒu zhàn-zhēng ne?

170 Bái: Hěn nán shuō. Yīnwei dàjiā yǐjing zhīdao zài zhànshí shòu de sǔnhài tài dà, hái yǒu shídài cháoliúde qūshì, suǒyǐ jìnlái guójiā hé guójiā fāshēng wèntí duōbàn shi dàjiā zài Liánhéguó xiǎng fázi jiějué. Zhìyú shíjìshang néng bu néng bù dǎzhàng néng jiějué wèntí, nà jiu hěn nán shuō le.

175 Xué: Zǒng'eryánzhi zhànzhēng jiu shi rénhuò.

Měi: Búcuò. Zhànzhēng shi rénhuò. Wǒ shuō yíge shìshí. Cóngqián wǒ fùqin yǒu yíwèi péngyou dāngguo shìzhǎng. Yīnwei lǎo le, quán jiā bāndao xiāngxia yíge xiǎode cūnzi qu zhù. Yǒu yìnián yīnwei nèizhàn dìfangshang yǒule dòngluàn. Běnlái hěn yǒuqián, hòulai

180 pǎodao biéde dìfang lián fàn dōu chībushàng le.

Bái: Nǐmen liǎngwèide guāndiǎn shi zhǐzhe shòu sǔnhài yìfāngmian shuō de. Kěshi zài guòqu yǒude rénkǒuxuéjiā rènwei zhànzhēng néng jiějué rénkǒu zēngjiā de wèntí, suǒyǐ shuō zhànzhēng hé rénkǒu hěn yǒu guānxi.

185 Měi: Rénkǒuxuéjiā zhèizhǒng shuōfǎ wǒ bú zàncheng.

Bái: Xiànzài shi yuánzǐ shídài le, zhànzhēng yě yǎnbiàndao yuánzǐ zhàn-zhēng. Yàoshi zài fāshēng zhànzhēng de shíhou gěi rén de zāihài gèng dà le.

Xué: Zuótian wǒ cānjiāle yíge yǎnjiǎng huì. Jiu shi jiǎng yuánzǐnéng.

190 Měi: Nǐ cānjiā de nèige huì shi shénmo xìngzhi de? Shi xuéshùxìngde háishi zhèngzhixìng de ne?

Xué: Shi xuéshùxìng de.

Bái: Nǐ zài nǎr tīng de yǎnjiǎng?

Xué: Zài xuéxiào kètángli.

195 Bái: Tīng de rén duō bu duō?

Xué: Yǒu sānbǎi duō ren.

Měi: Kètáng róngdexià ma?

Xué: Zài èrbǎi líng wǔhào nèige dà jiǎngtáng.

Bái : Jiǎngde hǎo bu hǎo?

200   Xué: Hǎo. Zhǔjiǎngde shi yíwèi guólì dàxué wùlǐxué jiàoshòu. Niánsuì jiù yǒu sānshi zuǒyòu. Wǒ cóngqián tīngguo xǔduōcì yuánzǐnéng jiǎngyǎn, dōu shi dàtóngxiǎoyì. Zhèicì tā jiǎng de hé biéren dà bù xiāngtóng. Wǒ tīngle yǐhòu cái zhīdao tā zhēn yǒu gāoshēnde xuéshi.

205   Měi: Nǐ shi yánjiu lìshǐ de. Tīng yuánzǐnéng zuò shénmo?

Xué: Zhè shi chángshì a.

Bái : Xiànzài gāi wǒ kǎokao nǐmen le.

Xué: Hǎo. Nǐ chū tímu ba.

210   Bái : Rén dōu shi yuànyi yìshēng zài zìjǐ lǎojiā píng'ān guò rìzi, bù xǐhuan suíbiàn bānjiā. Zhèi liǎngjù huà yàoshi yòng wényán zěnmo shuō?

Xué: Shuō huà wèi-shénmo yào yòng wényán ne?

Měi: Yòng wényán lai shuō shì bu shi "ān-tǔ-zhòng-qiān"?

215   Bái : Duìle, wǒ yě shi zuótian cái xué de. Zhèijù huà shi shénmo shū-shang de?

Měi: Shi Hàn Shū shang de.

Xué: Měiyīng shi gǔ-jīn wénxué dōu dǒng.

Měi: Nǎlǐ.

Bái : Zhōngguo cóngqian yǒude rén zhēn shi jǐbǎi nián bù bānjiā de.

220   Měi: Cóngqiánde rén chúfēi bèi bīpò cái bānjiā.

Xué: Shíjiān bù zǎo le. Wǒmen gāi wàng Mǎ Jiàoshòu nèr qù le.

Bái : Měiyīng, zuò chē qù ne, háishi zǒuzhe qù ne?

Xué: Bù hěn yuǎn. Kéyi búbì zuò chē.

Bái : Měiyīng bù xíng ba.

225   Měi: Shéi shuō de? Wǒ tiāntiān dào xuéxiào dōu shi zǒu lù.

Bái : Gāo Xiānsheng cóngqián hěn xǐhuan zǒu lù. Tā háishi nèige xíguàn ma?

Měi: Wǒ fùqin háishi nèige lǎo máobing. Xià yǔ tā yě chūqu. Tā shuō zǒu lù duì shēnxīn dōu yǒu hǎochu.

230   Bái : Gāo Xiānsheng měitiān zǎoshang jǐdiǎn zhōng qǐlai?

Měi: Zǎoshang wǔdian zhōng jiu qǐlai.

Bái : Guàibude Gāo Xiānsheng shēntǐ nènmo hǎo ne.

Xué: Wénshān, wǒmen xià xīngqī shàng shān, hǎo bu hǎo?

Bái : Hǎo a.

235   Měi: Wǒ yě cānjiā.

Xué: Rúguǒ tiānqi bù hǎo yàoshi xiàyǔ jiu qǔxiāo, zàichóng dìng rìzi.

Bái: Xīngqīliù jǐdiǎn zhōng zài nǎr jiànmiàn?

Xué: Xià xīngqīliù zǎoshang bādiǎn zhōng zài Shènglì Gōngxuéyuàn ménkǒur jiàn.

240 Bái: Shènglì Gōngxuéyuàn zài nǎr? Hǎoxiàng zài Běi Hú Lù shide.

Měi: Duìle.

Xué: Shuōzhe huà zǒu lù bùzhībujué yǐjing yào dào le.

Bái: Mǎ Jiàoshòu jiā wǒ hái méi qùguo ne.

Měi: Nǐ kàn nèige xiǎo hóng lóu jiù shì.

DUǍNWÉN

1. Wǒ xiǎo de shíhou zài yíge sīshúlǐ niàn shū. <u>Sān Zì Jīng</u>、<u>Bǎi Jiā Xìng</u> dōu niànwán le. Yòu niàn <u>Sì Shū</u>. Xiānsheng shuō <u>Sì Shū</u> niànwán zhīhòu jiù niàn <u>Wǔ Jīng</u>. Hòulai zhèli shèlǐle yíge gōnglì xuéxiào. Yǒu yìtiān wǒ dào gōnglì xuéxiào qu jiàn xiàozhǎng. Wǒ shuō xiǎng dào xuéxiào lai niàn shū. Xiàozhǎng shuō ànzhe wǒde chéngdu kéyi niàn chūzhōngèr. Wǒ zhōngxué jiu shi zài nèige gōnglì xuéxiào bì de yè.

2. Zhōngguo cóng Táng Cháo yǐlái dào Qīng Cháo mònián xuǎnbá réncái dōu shi yòng kējǔ kǎoshì zhìdu. Rúguǒ xiǎng zuò guān bìxū jīngguo zhèizhǒng kǎoshì.

3. Xīnán Liándà shi zhànshí cái chénglì de, bú shi zhànqián jiu yǒu de. Nàli zàojiùle bù shǎo réncái. Mǎ Xiānshengde tǒngjìxué jiu shi zài nàli niàn de.

4. Nèige dìfang cóng zhànhòu gōng-shāngyè fēicháng fādá. Zuìjìn nàlide gōng-shāngyè liánhéqilai zǔzhíle yíge lǚxíng tuán. Tāmende mùbiāo shi fǎngwèn Ōuzhōu.

5. Zhōngguo zì yǒude bǐhuá hěn duō, yǒude yǒu sānshijǐ huá. Jìnlái yǒu rén tíchàng yòng jiǎntǐzì, jiu shi bǎ fùzáde Hànzì jiǎnhuà le. Xiěqilai kéyi shěng shíjiān.

6. Zhèlide jǐge zhōngxué liánhé bànle yíge píngmín xuéxiào, mùdì shi xīwang pǔjí jiàoyu. Xuéxiàode míngchēng shi Píngmín Shìzì Xuéxiào. Cóng kāixué dào xiànzài jǐn yǒu jǐbǎige rén lai. Tāmende kǒuhào shi shǐ rénrén yǒu shū niàn, shǐ rénrén yǒu jīběn chángshì.

7. Cóngqián zài sīshúli niàn shū méi yǒu xiūyè de niánxiàn, bù fēn chūjí、gāojí. Cóng xiǎoxué zhì zhōngxué chéngdu dōu yǒu.

8. Nèige dìfang shǔyu wēndài. Qìhou bú tài lěng, yě bú tài rè. Wēndù zǒng-shi zài liùshidù zuǒyòu.

9. Nèitiáo héde shuǐ shi xiàng dōng liú, dōu shi liúdao nèige dà húli. Jùshuō nèitiáo héde shuǐ bù hěn shēn.

10. Sūn Zhōngshān Xiānsheng shi Guǎngdong Shěng Zhōngshān Xiàn rén. Shēngzai gōngyuán yī-bā-liù-liù nián shíyíyuè shí'èrrì. Sǐzai Zhōnghuá Mínguó shísìnián sānyuè shí'èrrì.

11. Zài dì-yīqīde <u>Rénkǒuxué Yuèbàoshang</u> dì-yīzhāng shi Sūn Xiānsheng xiě
de wénzhāng. Tímu shi "Huáqiáode Fēnbù hé Dòngtài." Dàyì shuō yīnwei
Měiguo cóngqián xūyào dàliàng gōngren, suǒyǐ Huáqiáo dào Měiguo lái de
hěn duō. Huáqiáo zài Měiguo yìbānde shuō dōu shi jízhōngzai dà chéng-
shìli.

12. Liánhéguó jīntian zǎoshang jiǔdiǎn zhōng kāihuì. Wáng Xiānsheng gǎnzhe
kāihuì qu. Tā zìjǐ kāi chē qu de. Kěshi tā bú rènshi lù, zài lùshang
yòngle hěn duō shíhou. Tā xiǎng yídìng gǎnbushàng kāihuì le. Méi fázi.
Tā wèn biéren. Biéren zhǐzhe dìtú gàosu tā, jiào tā huàn ge fāngxiàng
zǒu. Tā cái zhǎozháole mùbiāo.

13. Zhāng Xiānsheng

      Zuótian wǒ chūqu mǎi shū, huílai yǐhòu jiu juéde shēnshang hěn nán-
guò. Wǒ yòng wēndubiǎo shìshi wēndù, yǒu yìbǎi líng sìdù, suǒyǐ jīntian
bù néng dào xuéxiào shàng kè qu le. Zhù
Hǎo!

                                    xuésheng
                              Mǎ Dàshān shàng
                                sānyue èrshiwǔrì

14. Dì-Èrcì Shìjiè Dàzhàn cái wán, shìjièshangde guójiā hǎoxiàng yǒu xiàngzhe dàzhànde lùshang zǒu. Yǒude guójiā yòu shi zhànshíde zhuàngtài le.
Suīrán chénglìle Liánhéguó, jìnlì yòng gèzhǒng fāngshì xīwang bú zài
fāsheng zhànzhēng, kěshi gèguó yǒu gèguó de dǎsuàn, jiūjìng néng bu néng
méi yǒu zhànzhēng háishi méi fázi tuīcè.

15. Zhōngguo shi nóngyè guójiā. Shénmo jiàozuò nóngyè guójiā ne? Yìsi jiu
shi shuō Zhōngguo rénmín bǎifēnzhī-bāshijǐ shi zhòngdì de. Yīnwei duōshù
rén zhòngdì, suǒyǐ shi nóngyè guójiā. Zhōngguo rén duōshù chī mǐ, érqiě
chǎn mǐ de qūyù hěn guǎng. Fánshi Huázhōng、Huánán dà hé liúyùde xiàyóu dìqū dōu chǎn mǐ.

16. Zhǐ shi cháng yòng de dōngxi. Shèhuì yuè wénmíng yòng de zhǐ yuè duō.
Jù Liánhéguóde tǒngjì, shìjièshang měirén měinián yòng de zhǐ zài Měizhōu shi Měiguo rén zhàn dì-yīwèi, zài Yàzhōu shi Rìběn rén zhàn dì-
yīwèi, zài Ōuzhōu shi yíge xiǎode guójiā zhàn dì-yīwèi, Yīngguo rén zhàn
dì-èrwèi. Zhìyú Fēizhōu yòng zhǐ jiu bǐjiǎo shǎo le.

17. Jùshuō Zhōngguo liúxuéshēng zài chūguó zhīqián bìděi jīngguò liúxué kǎoshì. Rúguǒ chéngdu dī, jiu bù néng kǎoqǔ. Jiùshi kǎoqǔ le yě yǒu hěn
duō wèntí. Cóng kāishǐ shēnqǐng zhǐ chūguó, zǒngshi yào fèi xiāngdāngde
shíjiān. Zhè shi zhǐzhe yǐqián shuō de. Xiànzài chūguó bǐ yǐqián róngyi
duō le, kéyi búbì fèi nènmo hěn duō shíjiān le.

18. Zhāng Xiānsheng shi nóngxuéyuàn yuànzhǎng. Jìnlai tā zài jiàowu fāngmiàn tuīxíng yìzhǒng xīn bànfǎ. Zhèizhǒng xīn bànfǎ shi ànzhào xiànzài
shíjì xūyào yòu cānkǎo xǔduō wàiguo dàxué de bànfǎ cái guīdìng de.

19. Yǒu yíge dàxué yào xuǎnbá jǐge zài wùlǐ fāngmiàn yǒu tiāncáide xuésheng.
Yǒu rén zhǔzhāng kéyi zài měi xuénián chéngji zuì hǎode xuésheng dāng-
zhōng xuǎnbá. Yǒu rén shuō tiāncái hé chéngji shi liǎnghuí shì. Yǒu
tiāncáide xuésheng bù yídìng chéngji yōuliáng, huàn yíjù huà shuō chéngji
yōuliángde xuésheng bújiànde jiu yǒu tiāncái.

20. Yǒu yíwei rénkǒuxuéjiā xiěle yìběn shū jiào <u>Rénkǒu hé Shǎoshù Mínzú</u>. Tā shuō shǎoshù mínzú zài rénkǒude shùmushang suīrán jiào shǎo, kěshi ànzhe zhèixiē mínzúde běnshēn lai shuō gè yǒu gède shēnghuó xíguàn, gè yǒu gède chuántǒng sīxiǎng. Yīnwei yǐshàng zhǒngzhǒng yuányīn tāmen bù néng qīngyì jiu bèi biéde mínzú tónghuà de.

21. Zài Dōngyǎ yǒu yíge xiǎo dǎo, miànji hěn xiǎo, rénkǒu hěn mǐ. Dǎoshang-de rén suǒ yòng de shuǐ quán kàozhe xià yǔ. Rúguǒ bú àn shíhou xià yǔ huòzhě yǔ xiàde shǎo le, dàjiā jiu méi yǒu shuǐ yòng. Yǒu yícì dǎoshang yǒule zhànshì, érqiě xǔjiǔ méi xià yǔ, shèhuìshang fāshengle dòngluàn, dǎoshangde rén zǒule hěn duō. Zǒu de yuányīn shi wèile zhànzhēng, dōu shi bèi huánjing bīpò de. Jǐnjǐnde zài yíge yuèli zǒu de rénshù zhēn shi jīngrén. Dàole zhànhòu yǒu rén bǎ zhànqián hé zhànshí yǐjí zhànhòu de rénkǒude dòngtài xiángxi tǒngjì bǐjiào, cái zhīdao zài zhèi yícì zhànzhēng zhōng zǒu de rénkǒu quèshíde shùmu.

22. Yíge guójiā rúguǒ gēn biéde guójiā méi yǒu zhànzhēng, guónèi yě méi yǒu nèizhàn, rénmínde shēnghuó zìrán'érrán biàn huì hěn hǎo de, zhìshǎo shi píngpíng'ānānde. Qián jǐtiān yǒu yíge lǎoniánrén shuōdao zhànzhēng, tā biàn xíngrong shòu zhànzhēngde sǔnhài. Tā shuō yǒu yìnián dǎzhàng, tāmen nèige xiǎo cūnzili jiu sǐle yìbǎi líng wǔge rén. Tā yǒu yíge zuì xǐhuande sūnzi, niánsuì hái bú dào èrshi, yě bèi dǎsǐ le. Suǒyǐ tā shuō zhàng shi bù néng zài dǎ de le, bù néng lǎo ràng rénmín shòu hài.

23. Zhāng Xiānsheng shi Lián-Dàde jiàoshòu. Tā měitiān dōu kàn shū, wèideshì chōngshí zìjǐde xuéshi. Tā shuō tā kàn shū yǒu liǎngzhǒng fāngfǎ. Yìzhǒng shi dàtǐde kànyikan, zhǐ yào dǒngde dàyì jiu kéyi le. Zhèizhǒng fāngfǎ kéyi zài duǎnqī nèi duō kàn yìxiē shū, yǒude shíhou yìtiān néng kàn jǐshíyè dào jǐbǎiyè. Hái yǒu yìzhǒng kànfǎ shi bǎ měizhāng měijù dōu xiángxide kàn, yào shēnshēnde liǎojiě shūde nèiróng. Zhèi liǎngzhǒng fāngfǎ gè yǒu gède hǎochu. Zhìyú něizhǒng shū yòng něizhǒng fāngfǎ kàn, zhèige wèntí hěn nán huídá. Zǒngzhi měitiān kàn shū búlùn yòng něizhǒng fāngfǎ dōu shi yǒu hǎochu de.

24. Zhèicì xuǎnjǔ huìzhǎng bù zhīdào shi zěnmo xuǎn de. Jùshuō zài xuǎnjǔ de guòchéngli fāshēngle hěn duō wèntí. Cái bǎ huìzhǎng xuǎnchulai jiu yǒu rén zhǔzhāng yīngdāng chóng xuǎn. Yìbānde kànfǎ yě rènwei yīngdāng chóng xuǎn.

25. Zài tiānqi rè de shíhou, wǒ xǐhuan dào hǎibiān qu. Nèige hǎibiān yǒu yìtiáo xiǎo hé, zài nàli liúdao hǎili. Hǎi shuǐ、 hé shuǐ dōu shi wēnde, hǎibiānshang yǒu shā. Wǒ yǒushi zài shāshang huà zì, yǒushi zài hǎili zuò xiǎo chuán, yìzhí dào wǎnshang hái bù xiǎng huí jiā qu.

26. Zài zhèige chéngli yǒu liǎngge fànguǎn. Yíge shi Zhōnghuá Lóu, yíge shi Xīnhuá Lóu. Yǒu yìtiān yǒu rén yào qǐng wǒ chī Zhōngguo fàn, tā wèn wo: "Dàoshi chī Zhōnghuá Lóu háishi chī Xīnhuá Lóu ne?"

27. Yǒu yìtiān wǒ zuòzai chuánshang, chuán zǒude hěn kuài. Wǒ wǎng lùshang yí kàn, hǎoxiàng shi lùdì zài yídòng shide. Wǒ xīnli xiǎng, suīrán lùdì méi yǒu yídòngxìng, kěshi wǒ wèi-shénmo kàn lùdì hǎoxiàng zài yídòng ne?

28. Chángfāngde jiu shi liǎngbiān shi chángde, liǎngbiān shi duǎnde. Sìfāngde jiu shi sìbiān dōu shi yíyàng chángde, yě jiào fāngde. Bǐrú shuō yìfānglǐ jiu shi sìbiān dōu shi yíyàng cháng, dōu shi yìlǐ cháng, jiu jiàozuo yìfānglǐ.

29. Zài Zhōngguo lìshǐshang měige cháodàide mònián duōbàn shi gè dìfang
yǒule dòngluàn, rénmín méi fázi shēnghuó. Yìzhí dào xīnde cháodài chūxiàn, rénmín cái kéyi dédao píng'ānde shēnghuó.

30. Cóngqián Zhōng-È jiāojiè yǒu hěn duō dìfang rénkǒu hěn xī, yòu yīnwei
biānjiè bú dà qīngchu de guānxi, suǒyǐ liǎngguóde shāngren hé lǚxíng de
rén, chúfēi yǒu tèbiéde yuányīn, hěn shǎo yǒu rén dào nèixiē dìfang qu.

31. Tā shi qiántiān cóng Měiguo qǐshēn dào Rìběn qu de. Tā xiǎng zài Rìběn
niàn dàxué. Shìqián yǒu rén gàosu ta Rìběn dàxué yìbān lai shuō dōu hěn
hǎo, bìyè de niánxiàn duōbàn shi sìnián, yě yǒu cǎiyòng xuéfēn-zhì de.

32. Jù zuìjìnde tǒngjì, fēnbùzai gèguó de Huáqiáo yǒu yìqiān liùbǎi wǔshí wàn
rén. Xiànzài wǒ bǎ fēnbù de qíngkuàng xiězai xiàmian:

Yàzhōu	yìqiān liùbǎi wàn
Měizhōu	sìshísì wàn
Ōuzhōu	èrwàn
Fēizhōu	sìwàn

33. Zuótian wǒ zài túshūguǎn kàn shū, fāxiànle yìběn xīn shū. Shū míngzi shi
Zài Yàzhōu de Zhímín Wèntí. Kāishǐ shi duǎnwén. Hòutou shi huìhuà.
Wǒ kāishǐ bù xiǎng kàn. Kànle yìhuěr hěn yǒu yìsi. Yòng wèndá fāngfǎ
bǎ zhímín wèntí jiěshìde fēicháng xiángxi.

34. Yǒu rén wèn wǒ shēntǐ zěnmoyàng? Wǒ shuō: "Wǒde shēntǐ cóngqián bú
dà hǎo. Jìnlái bǐ yǐqián hǎode duō le."

35. Yǒu yíge liúxuéshēng, suǒyǒu xuéfèi yǐjí chī fàn zhù fángzi de qián dōu
shi péngyou gěi ta de. Tā yǒu shíhou xiǎng: "Yàoshi péngyou jiānglái
bù gěi wǒ qián wǒ zěnmo bàn? Wǒ yīngdāng zǎo yìdiǎr zìjǐ xiǎng bànfǎ."

UNIT II

Hànzú

Zàngzú

Měngzú

Wéiwú'ěrzú

Yízú

Miáozú

Cháoxiǎnzú

Mínzú

Dì-Qīkè. Mínzú

Bái: Mǎ Jiàoshòu zǎo.

Mǎ: Zǎo. Zuótian dào jiā hěn wǎn le ba?

Bái: Bù wǎn. Wǒmen xiān sòng Měiyīng huíqu. Dào jiā de shíhou hái
bú dào shídiǎn zhōng. Zuótian wǒmen zài fǔshang chīde hǎo, tánde
5 gāoxìng, jiùshi tài máfan Mǎ Tàitai le. Zuótian Mǎ Tàitai lèi le
ba?

Mǎ: Nǐmen dào wǒ jiā qu wǒ nèiren fēicháng gāoxìng.

Bái: Mǎ Tàitai cài zuòde zhēn hǎo, érqiě cài yě tài fēngfù le. Nèige
hóngshāo yángròu gēn chǎo dòufu tài hǎochī le.

10 Mǎ: Nèige chǎo dòufu shi Sìchuān zuòfǎ. Nǐ xǐhuan chī ma?

Bái: Wǒ hěn xǐhuan.

Mǎ: Wǒ nèiren yángròu zuòde dàoshi búcuò shi yīnwei wǒ xǐhuan chī
de yuángu. Zài wǒmen cái jiēhūnde shíhou tā bù xǐhuan chī yángròu.
Yīnwei wǒ xǐhuan, tā mànmānde xíguàn le, yě xǐhuan le.

15 Bái: Shì bu shi běifāng rén xǐhuan chī yángròu?

Mǎ: Shìde. Yīnwei Zhāngjiākǒu chūchǎn de yáng hǎochī, suǒyǐ běifāng
rén xǐhuan chī yángròu. Yóuqíshi Měnggǔ rén, tāmen dōu shi chī
niú-yángròu. Wǒ nèige nán háizi yǒu ge tèxìng. Měitiān chī fàn
bù chī biéde jiù zhuānménde chī niú-yángròu. Hái xǐhuan chī táng.

20 Bái: Niú-yángròu duì shēntǐ dàoshi yǒu hǎochu.

Mǎ: Yěxǔ. Nǐ kàn tāde shēntǐ duómo hǎo.

Bái: Mǎ Jiàoshòu, fǔshang de fángzi hěn hǎo.

Mǎ: Wǒ yě hěn xǐhuan nèisuǒ fángzi. Shi yíge tóngxiāngde. Zhèisuǒ
fángzi tā mǎile búguò yìnián tā dào biéde dìfang qù le, jiù bǎ zhèisuǒ
25 fángzi màigei wǒ le. Wǒ zuì xǐhuan de shi yǒu yíge sìsifāngfāngde
dà yuànzi. Tiānqi nuǎnhuode shíhou háizimen kéyi zài wàitou wár.

Bái: Nín zài nèr zhù duōshao nián le?

Mǎ: Wǒ zài zhèr zhù hái búdào èrnián ne.

Bái: Dìfang zhēn búcuò. Sìmiànde huánjing hǎode hěn. Qiánmiàn yǒu
30 shuǐ, hòumiàn yǒu shān. Fēngjǐng xiāngdāng měilì.

Mǎ: Guò jǐtiān zài qǐng nǐmen dào wǒ jiā qu chī hóngshāo jī hé hóngshāo
shīzi tóu qu.

Bái: Nǎr néng lǎo ràng nín qǐng kè? Xiàcì gāi wǒmen qǐng nín hé Mǎ
Tàitai le.

35 Mǎ: Háishi nǐmen dào wǒ nèr. Jī shi wǒ nèiren zìjǐ yǎng de. Yǎngle
hái méi yǒu yìnián ne, xiànzài xiǎo jī zhǎngchéng dà jī le.

141

Bái: Yǒu rén shuō zìjǐ yǎng de jī bǐ mǎi de jī hǎochī.

Mǎ: Yěxǔ. Zìjǐ yǎng jī shi gěi mǐ chī. Zhèr mǎi de jī yībān dōu shi xiāngxia rén yǎng de, rén dōu hěn shǎo chī mǐ. Jī nǎr nénggou
40   chī mǐ ne?

Bái: Zhè dàoshi zhēnde.

Mǎ: Jīntiande jiǎnghuà shi Zhōngguode Mínzú. Xiànzài kāishǐ yánjiu yánjiu zhèixiē cér.

Bái: Hǎo ba. Wǒ xiān kànkan.

1.0. (zōng)jiào   religion, religious denomination   [ancestor teaching]

   Kǒngjiào   Confucianism

1.1. Zhōngguo rén bǎ Kǒngjiào kànzuò shi zōngjiàozhī yī.   (T)

2.0. qíshí   actually, as a matter of fact   [its real]

2.1. Yǒu rén shuō Zhū Jiāng shi Zhōngguo sān dà héliúzhī yī, qíshí Zhū Jiāng bú tài cháng.

2.2. Zhāng Xiānsheng gěi wǒ mǎile hěn duō táng.   Qíshí wǒ bù xǐhuan chī táng.

3.0. bìng   really (before negative)

3.1. Nèige dìfang zuò mǎimai yídìng zuòbuchénggōng, yīnwei nàlǐde shāngyè bìng bù fādá.

4.0. huángdì   emperor   [emperor emperor]

4.1. Xiànzài Ōuzhōu hé Yǎzhōude guójiā hái yǒu yǒu huángdì de ma? (T)

45 Bái: Mǎ Jiàoshòu, yìbānde rén cháng shuō Zhōngguo yǒu sān dà zōngjiào, bǎ Kǒngzǐde xuéshuō yě suàn shi yìzhǒng zōngjiào. Qíshí Kǒngzǐde xuéshuō bìng bú shi yìzhǒng zōngjiào.

Mǎ: Kǒngzǐ shi yíwèi zhéxuéjiā、jiàoyujiā、wénxuéjiā, yě kéyi shuō shi zhèngzhijiā. Kǒngzǐ hěn zhùzhòng wénxué. Tā yǒu hěn duō xué-
50   sheng. Kǒngzǐde jiàoyu guāndiǎn tèbié zhùzhòng pǔjí jiàoyu.

Bái: Nèige shídài Zhōngguode jiàoyu yě bù pǔbiàn ma?

Mǎ: Zài Kǒngzǐ nèige shídài yǒu zhèngfǔ shèlì de xuéxiào, zhǐ shōu zuò guān de érzi, bù shōu píngmín. Kěshi Kǒngzǐ shuō rénrén kéyi shòu jiàoyu. Tā bǎ wénhuà jiàoyu gēn xuéshù zhīshi dōu jiāogěi yìbān
55   rén. Búlùn xuésheng shi cōngmingde háishi bènde, Kǒngzǐ dōu xiǎng fázi jiāo. Hòulái Zhōngguode shèhui dōu ná Kǒngzǐde xuéshuō zuò zhōngxīn, suóyǐ shuō Kǒngzǐde xuéshuō shi Kǒngjiào.

Bái: Kǒngzǐde xuéshuō yǐngxiǎng Zhōngguo yìzhí dào xiànzài, shì bu shi?

Mǎ: Shì. Zhōngguo lìdài huángdì dōu rènwei Kǒngzǐde xuéshuō néng zhì
60   guó.

5.0. Fó   Buddha, Buddhism

Fójiào   Buddhism

Fóxué   Buddhist studies

5.1. Zhōngguo rén shuō Fó shi cóng xīfāng lái de.   (T)

5.2. Miǎndiàn xìn Fójiào de rén hěn duō, kěshi yánjiu Fóxué de rén bìng bu duō.

5.3. Tāmen jiā jǐdài dōu shi xìn Fó de.   (T)

6.0. qǐyuán   beginning, origin, source   [rise source]

6.1. Zhōngguo wénhuàde qǐyuán zài Huáng Hé liúyù.

7.0. chuán   pass on, hand on, transmit

chuánxialai   hand down

chuánshuō   (1) rumor (N/V); (2) hearsay; (3) it is said; (4) transmit by tradition   [transmit say]

7.1. Zhōngguode Fójiào shi cóng Yìndu chuánlai de.

7.2. Kējǔ zhìdu shi cóng Táng Cháo chuánxialai de.

7.3. Tīng biéren chuánshuō de shìqing, yǒude kàodezhù, yǒude shi bù kěkàode.

8.0. Lǎma   Lama (priest)

Lǎmajiào   Lamaism

8.1. Měnggǔ rén hé Xīzàng rén dōu xìn Lǎmajiào. Cóngqián nánren yǒu sānfēnzhī-yī dāng Lǎma.

9.0. Mǎn(zhōu)   Manchu, Manchuria, Manchurian

Mǎnzú   Manchu nationality

9.1. Mǎnzú qǐyuán zài Zhōngguode dōngběibù. Nèige dìfangde míngzi jiào Mǎnzhōu.

10.0. tǒngzhì   control, dominate   [unify, manage]

10.1. Táiwān cóngqián bèi Rìběn tǒngzhìle wǔshi nián, cóng yī-bā-jiǔ-wǔ nián dào yī-jiǔ-sì-wǔ nián.

Bái: Zhōngguo rén duōshù shi xìn Fójiàode. Fójiàode qǐyuán shi zài Yìndu. Wǒ bù zhīdào shi shénmo shíhou chuándao Zhōngguo de?

Mǎ : Fójiào shi qián Hàn shíqī chuándao Zhōngguo de.

Bái: Hěn duō rén yánjiu Fóxué. Fóxuéde shū jù shuō hěn bù róngyi dǒng, shì bu shi?

Mǎ : Shì. Hěn nándǒng, érqiě yě hěn duō.

Bái: Lǎmajiào yě shi shǔyu Fójiào de ma?

Mǎ : Shì. Lǎmajiào yě shi Fójiào. Shi Xīzàngde Fójiào. Lǎma shi Xīzàng huà.

70 Bái: Zhōngguo nǎlǐ yǒu Lǎmajiào? Pǔbiān bù pǔbiān? Shi quánguóxìngde
          ma?

     Mǎ: Búshi.   Zhǐ shi zài Xīzàng、Qīnghǎi hé Nèi-Měnggǔ、Wài-Měnggǔ
          yídài dìfang.   Zìcóng Mǎnzhōu rén tǒngzhì Zhōngguo yǐlái (jiu shi
          Qīng Cháo) hěn zhùzhòng Lǎmajiào.

     11.0. Huí(hui)   Mohammedan, Moslem

            Húizú   Chinese Moslem nationality

            Huíjiào   Moslem religion

     11.1. Zhōngguo rén yǒushí bǎ Húizúde rén jiàozuò Huíhui.

     11.2. Zhōngguo běnbù hé yánhǎi yídài xìn Huíjiào de rén bù duō.

     12.0. Wéiwú'ěr(zú)   Uighur (nationality)

     12.1. Qīnghǎi Shěng yě yǒu Wéiwú'ěrzúde rén ma?

     13.0. Yúnnán   Yunnan Province   [clouds south]

     13.1. Yúnnánde wèizhi shi zài wēndài, suǒyǐ qìhou wēnhé. Érqiě fēngjǐng
            yě hěn piàoling.

     14.0. yuē   approximately

            dàyuē   probably, most likely   [big approximately]

     14.1. Nèige hǎidǎode miànji yuē yǒu bābǎi duō fānglǐ.

     14.2. Zhōngguo hé wàiguo tōngshāng dàyuē yǒu yìbǎi duō nián le.

     14.3. Cóng Sānfánshì dào Niǔyuē dàyuē yǒu duōshao Yīnglǐ?

     15.0. Gānsu   Kansu Province

     15.1. Gānsu Shěngde dìshì shi xībù gāo, dōngbù dī.

     16.0. tuánjié   (1) cohere, unite; (2) be closely knit, united   [group bond]

     16.1. Yǒu rén shuō cóngqián Zhōngguo rén bù zhīdào tuánjié. Xiànzàide
            Zhōngguo rén zhīdao tuánjié le.

75 Bái: Xìn Huíjiào de chúle Huízú yǐwài hái yǒu biéde mínzú ma?

     Mǎ: Chúle Huízú yǐwài hái yǒu Wéiwú'ěrzú yě xìn Huíjiào.

     Bái: Zài Zhōngguo nèidì xìn Huíjiào de rén dàbàn dōu zài něi jǐshěng?

     Mǎ: Shānxi、Sìchuān、Héběi dōu yǒu. Zài nánbiārde Guǎngdong、Yúnnán
          yě yǒu rén xìn.

80 Bái: Jùshuō Huíhui xiāngdāng tuánjié.

     Mǎ: Shì.   Yǒu zhènmo yì shuō.

     Bái: Zhè liǎngge mínzú fēnbù de dìqū dōu zài nǎr?

     Mǎ: Huízú, dà bùfen zài xīběibù, bǐrú Xīnjiāng、Qīnghǎi、Gānsu yídài.

Bái: Tāmende rénkǒu yǒu dōushao?

85 Mǎ: Dàyuē yǒu sānbǎi wǔshi wàn rén.

Bái: Wéiwú'ěrzú ne?

Mǎ: Wéiwú'ěrzú fēnbùzai Xīnjiāng.   Rénkǒu yě yǒu sānbǎi duō wàn.

Bái: Zhè liǎngge mínzú yǒu shénmo fēnbié ne?

Mǎ: Zài yǔyánshang yǒu fēnbié.   Huízú rén shuō Zhōngguo huà.   Wéi-
90   wú'ěrzú yǒu tāmen zìjǐde yǔyán.

17.0. Yí(zú)   Yi nationality

17.1. Nèige qūyùde rénmín, Yízú zhàn bǎifēnzhī-bāshí. Qíyúde shi Hànrén.

18.0. Zhuàng(zú)   Chuang nationality

18.1. Zhuàngzú zìzhìqūnèi nóngchǎn fēngfù, biéde tǔchǎn yě duō.

18.2. Bǎ suǒyǒu fēnbù dào biéde dìfangde Zhuàngzú suànzài yìqǐ yǒu liùbǎi
       duō wàn rén ne.   (T)

19.0. Miáo(zú)   Miao nationality

19.1. Nǐ zhīdao Miáozúde tèdiǎn hé fēnbù zài shénmo dìfang ma?   (T)

20.0. Zhòngjiā   Chungchia nationality

20.1. Zhòngjiā shi shǎoshù mínzúzhī yī.   Dàyuē yǒu yìbǎi duō wàn rén.

21.0. Xīkāng   Sikang

21.1. Xīkāng zài Xīzàngde dōngmiàn.   Zhèige dìyù dà shān hěn duō.

22.0. Guìzhōu   Kweichou Province

22.1. Guìzhōu chūchǎn táng ma?

Bái: Zhōngguo yǐqián zhǐ shuō wǔzú, xiànzài bǎ suǒyǒude mínzú dōu
     suànzài yíkuàr yǒu liùshi duō ge mínzú.   Bǐrú Yízú, Zhuàngzú,
     Miáozú, Zhòngjiā dōu zài Zhōngguo něibùfen?

Mǎ: Yízú zài Yúnnán, Xīkāng jiāojiè.   Zhuàngzú fēnbù zài Guǎngxi háiyǒu
95   Guǎngxi fùjìn yídài dìfang.   Miáozú zài Guìzhōu hé Húnán.   Zhòngjiā
     fēnbù zài Guìzhōu xīnán yídài.

Bái: Zhèixiē mínzú dōu shi gè yǒu gède yǔyán ma?

Mǎ: Chúle Huízú yǐwài gè mínzú yǒu gè mínzúde yǔyán.

23.0. pīn   spell out, represent speech-sounds in writing

       pīnyīn   (1) spell out (VO); (2) spelling

       Hànyǔ Pīnyīn   Chinese Phonetic Alphabet

23.1. Nèixiē Zhōngguo zì, nǐ néng yòng Hànyǔ Pīnyīn pīnchulai ma?   (T)

23.2. Zhèige zì zěnmo pǐn? Shì bu shi wǒ pīncuò le?

23.3. Zhèiběn shū shi yòng Hànyǔ Pīnyīn xiěchulai de.

24.0. Měng(gǔ)zú   Mongol nationality

24.1. Cóngqián Mǎnzú rénde shēnghuó hěn xiàng Měnggǔzú. Hòulai hěn
      xiàng Hànrén le.

24.2. Nèi Měng zìzhìqū de rénkǒu, jiù yǒu qīfēnzhī-yī shi Měngzú rén.

25.0. gǎi   change, revise, correct

      gǎi V   change to V-ing

      gǎiyòng   change to using

      gǎigé   reform (N/V)

25.1. Nèi jǐge jùzi dōu hǎo. Búyòng gǎi.

25.2. Zhōngguo cóngqián dōu shi yòng suànpan. Jìnlai yě yǒu gǎiyòng
      jìsuànjī de le.   (T)

25.3. Tā cóngqián xué Zàngwén, xiànzài gǎixué Měngwén le.   (T)

25.4. Zhōngguo wénzì gǎigéde guòchéng nǐ zhīdao ma?   (T)

26.0. qítā   the rest, the others (PR)

26.1. Jiù shi wǒ yíge rén huì Hànyǔ Pīnyīn. Qítāde rén dōu bú huì.

  Bái: Zhōngguo shǎoshù mínzúde wénzì yǒu méi yǒu yòng pīnyīn zì de?

100 Mǎ : Yǒu. Xiàng Měngzú yǐjing bǎ wénzì gǎigé le. Tāmen yǐjing gǎiyòng
          pīnyīn zì le. Qítā mínzú yě yǒu yòng pīnyīn zì de. Wénshān, wǒ
          zhīdao zài Měiguo dàxuéli yǒu rén yánjiu Měngwén hé Zàngwén de.
          Yǒu méi yǒu yánjiu Mǎnwén de?

  Bái: Yǒu shi yǒu, kěshi bú tài duō. Jùshuō Sānfánshì gēn Niǔyuēde dàxué
105   yǒu.

27.0. Cháoxiǎn   Korea

      Cháoxiǎnzú   Korean nationality

27.1. Zài Zhōngguo Dōngběi hé Cháoxiǎn jiāojiède dìfang yǒu yíge Cháo-
      xiǎnzú zìzhìqū.

28.0. Hànzú   Chinese nationality

28.1. Zài Qīng Cháode chūnián Mǎnzú rén bù néng hé Hànzú rén jiēhūn.

29.0. gònghé   (1) united (in purpose); (2) republican [together harmonious]

29.1. Zhōngguo zài Mínguó chūnián de shíhou shi yíge wǔzú gònghéde guó-
      jiā.

29.2. Yǎzhōu yǒu duōshao guójiā shi gònghéguó?

30.0. fēngsú   customs, practices, usages   [custom vulgar]

30.1. Zhōngguode fēngsú hé Ōu-Měide fēngsú bǐjiǎoqilai dà bu xiāngtóng.
(T)

30.2. Shǎoshù mínzú zài shēnghuóshang gè yǒu gède fēngsú xíguàn.   (T)

31.0. tónghuà   assimilate   [same transform]

31.1. Jìnlái Měnggǔzú yě yǒu bùshǎode rén hé Hànzú tónghuà le.

32.0. Zàngzú   Tibetan nationality

32.1. Zàngzúde rén bù qīngyì líkai Xīzàng.

Mǎ : Wǒ xiāngxìn nǐ zhīdao Cháoxiǎn zài nǎr, kěshi wǒ xiànzài yào ràng
nǐ shuōyishuō.

Bái : Cháoxiǎn zài Rìběn Hǎi hé Huáng Hǎi zhījiān.   Shi yíge bàndǎode
guójiā.   Cháoxiǎnzú yǒu yíbùfen zài Zhōngguo Dōngběi yídài dìfang.

110 Mǎ : Duìle.

Bái : Zhōngguo zuì dàde mínzú shi Hànzú.   Mínguó chūniánde shíhou dōu
shuō Hàn、Mǎn、Měng、Huí、Zàng wǔzú gònghé.   Zài fēngsú xíguànshang zhèi wǔge mínzú yíyàng bu yíyàng?

Mǎ : Bǐrú Mǎnzú bèi Hànzú tónghuà le.   Fēngsú xíguàn shi dàtóngxiǎoyì
115   le.   Qítā jǐge mínzú xiàng Měngzú、Zàngzú shénmode jiù bù xiāngtóng le.

33.0. zhěng   (1) all, entire, whole (before nouns and measures); (2)
                  exactly, precisely (before numerals or verbs)

zhěnggè(r)   all, the whole (of)

zhěngtiān   the whole day

33.1. Zuótian zhěngtiān dōu xià yǔ.

33.2. Zuótian wǒ dào shūdiàn mǎi dōngxi.   Mǎide shū hé běnzi yígòng
wǔkuài qián.   Wǒ zhěng yǒu wǔkuài qián, dōu gěi shūdiàn le.

33.3. Cóngqiánde Fēizhōu zhěnggèr shi zhímíndì.

33.4. Zhěnggèr shuōqilai, mínzú gēn mínzú zǒng shi yǒu wèntí de.   (T)

33.5. Shì bu shi Fēizhōu zhěnggèr dàochù dōu yǒu shīzi?

34.0. zhēngduó   seize   [contend snatch]

34.1. Nèi liǎngge guójiā yīnwei dōu yào zhēngduó nèige zhímíndì jiu dǎqi
zhàng lái le.   (T)

35.0. ér   and, and yet, while on the other hand (see p. 160, note 1)

35.1. Tā wèile yánjiu Lǎmajiào ér qù dāng Lǎma.   (T)

35.2. Tā dào Měiguo bú shi liúxué ér shi zuò mǎimai.   (T)

35.3. Zhōngguode Fójiào shi cóng Yìndu ér lái.   (T)

36.0. kuòzhǎn   develop, expand   [enlarge unfold]

36.1. Nèige shāngren xiǎngyào kuòzhǎn tāde shēngyi. Tā xiǎng zài Niǔyuē、
       Sānfánshì dōu shè yíge fēnhào.

37.0. lǐngtǔ   territory   [lead earth]

37.1. Nèige dìfang shì bu shi Sūliánde lǐngtǔ?

37.2. Nèi liǎngge guójiā wèile zhēngduó lǐngtǔ qǐle zhànzhēng.   (T)

Bái: Zhōngguo zhěnggède shuōqilai shi hěn duō mínzú zǔzhiqilai de. Shì
      bu shi yǒude shíhou wèile zhēngduó tǔdì ér zhànzhēng?

Mǎ: Zài guòqu lìshǐshang zhèizhǒng shìqing shi shícháng fāsheng de.
120   Bǐrú biéde mínzú yào zhàn Hànzúde tǔdì, huòzhě Hànzú yào kuòzhǎn
      tāmen lǐngtǔ.

Bái: Měi yíge guójiā, mínzú hé mínzú dōu shi yǒu wèntí de.

Mǎ: Yóuqíshi Zhōngguo, lìlái shi zhànzhēngde guójiā. Cóng gǔ dào jīn
      búlùn shi gēn biéde mínzú huòzhe shi nèizhàn shícháng dǎzhàng.
125   Lǎobǎixìng méi yǒu píngping'ānānde hǎohāorde guò rìzi, dōu shi zài
      zhànzhēngde huánjingli shēnghuó.

38.0. (dǐ)kàng   resist   [resist resist]

       Kàngzhàn   War of Resistance (i.e. anti-Japanese War of 1937-1945)

38.1. Qīqī shi Zhōngguo duì Rìběn Kàngzhànde rìzi. Rìběn lái dǎ Zhōng-
       guo, Zhōngguo bùdébù dǐkàng.   (T)

38.2. Yíge rénde lìqi nénggou dǐkàng shīzi ma?

39.0. kuòdà   enlarge, widen, expand   [enlarge big]

39.1. Qīqī yǐhòu Zhōngguo hé Rìběnde zhànshì jiu kuòdà le.

40.0. línjìn   (draw) near, nearby   [neighbor near]

40.1. Tā jiā zài Jiāngxi, línjìn shi Póyáng Hú.

41.0. shìjì   (1) century; (2) age, period   [world order]

41.1. Èrshi shìjìde Zhōngguo rén shēnghuó hěn duō Ōuhuà le.   (T)

41.2. Zhōng shìjìde shíhou Ōuzhōu gè dìfang cháng yǒu dòngluàn.   (T)

Bái: Zuótian wǒ zài túshūguǎn kànle yìběn shū shi guānyu Zhōngguo Kàng-
      zhàn shíqīde gùshi.

Mǎ: Xiěde hǎo bu hǎo?

130 Bái: Xiěde búcuò. Dàzhǐ xiě de shi Zhōngguo dǐkàng Rìběn, zhànshì jiàn-
        jiànde kuòdà dào Dì-Èrcì Shìjiè Dàzhàn. Guānyu nèicì Rìběn hé
        Zhōngguo dǎzhàng, Rìběn zhǔyàode mùdì shi shénmo?

Mǎ: Rìběn zhǔyàode mùdì shi yào zhàn Zhōngguode lǐngtǔ.

Bái: Zài lìshǐshang kàn, lìlái liǎngguó shícháng fāsheng zhànzhēng.

135 Mǎ: Yīnwei liǎngguó shi línjìnde guójiā, érqiě Rìběn zhèige guójiā yòu
xǐhuan zhàn rénjiade tǔdì. Zài shíjiǔ shìjìde shíhou bǎ Táiwān zhàn
le. Zài yī-jiǔ-sān-yī nián zhàn Dōngsānshěng. Yī-jiǔ-sān-qī nián
dǎdào Zhōngguo nèidì.

42.0. Dé(guo)   Germany

Déwén   German language

42.1. Tā shi Jiāngsu rén. Zài Déguo liúxué. Déwén hǎojíle.

43.0. Yìdàlì   Italy

43.1. Zài Zhōngguo yǒu yíge Ōu-Měi tóngxuéhuì. Wǒ zuì xǐhuan dào huìli
qu chī Yìdàlì fàn.

44.0. jiāotōng   communications   [join communicate]

44.1. Shāmò dìdài jiāotōng bú dà fāngbian.

44.2. Yīnwei jiāotōng bú biàn nàlǐde shāngyè bù hěn fādá.

45.0. qícì   next, second(ly)   [its occasion]

yòuqícì   third(ly)   [again its occasion]

45.1. Yàzhōu guójiā rénkǒu zuì duōde shi Zhōngguo. Qícì shi Yìndu.
Yòuqícì shi Rìběn.

45.2. Wǒmen zhèi yìshěng zhǔyàode chūchǎn shi mǐ, qícì shi chǎn táng.

46.0. hépíng   peace   [harmonious level]

46.1. Liánhéguó duìyu shìjiè hépíng shi yǒugōngde.

Bái: Yǒu rén shuō Zhōng-Rì zhànzhēng shi Dì-Èrcì Shìjiè Dàzhànde
140   kāishǐ. Rìběn kāishǐ shi xiān dǎ Zhōngguo. Ránhòu gēn Déguo、
Yìdàlì liánhéqilai le. Zhōngguo gēn Fàguo、Yīngguo、Sūlián hé
Měiguo yě liánhéqilai le. Zhèicìde zhànzhēng yígòng bānián.

Mǎ: Nèige shíhou wǒ zhèng zài Yúnnán. Yǒude shíhou dào Sìchuan qu
kànkan fùmǔ.

145 Bái: Nèige shíhou tīngshuō jiāotōng hěn bù fāngbian.

Mǎ: Shìde. Zhōngguo zài Kàngzhànde shíhou, búdàn yīnwei zhànzhēng sǐle
bù shǎo rén, érqiě chē、chuán chūshì yě sǐle hěn duō rén.

Bái: Cháng tīngshuō dào Sìchuan qù de lù fēicháng kùnnán.

Mǎ: Dào Sìchuan qu jiù kàozhe zuò chuán gēn zǒu gōnglù. Suīrán yǒu
150   fēijī kěshi fēijī tài shǎo.

Bái: Nèige shíhou chē、chuán cháng chūshì de yuányīn shi shénmo?

Mǎ: Dì-yī shi rén duō, chē、chuán tài shǎo. Bǐrú zhǐ róng yìqiān rén
de chuán yào zuò liǎngqiān rén. Tài zhòng le jiù děi chūshì. Gōng-

155
       lùshangde chē yě shi yíyàng. Qícǐ shi Xīnán shānlù duōbàn jiāotōng
       bú biàn. Gōnglù bù zěnmo hǎo.

Bái: Xīwang jiānglái shìjièshang shi yíge hépíngde shìjiè, bú yào zài dǎ-
      zhàng le.

47.0. xìtǒng   system   [system unify]

47.1. Měngwén hé Zàngwén dà bù xiāngtóng. Gè yǒu gède yǔwén xìtǒng.

48.0. lìrú   for example   [example like]

48.1. Dà jiāng、dà hé rù hǎi de hǎikǒu, shāngyè bújiànde dōu hěn fādá.
      Lìrú Huáng Hé rù hǎi de dìfang shāngyè bìng bù fādá.

49.0. jìng*   boundary

      biānjìng   boundary   [frontier boundary]

49.1. Shìjiè zuì gāode shān shi zài Zhōngguo hé Yìndude biānjìng.

49.2. Cháoxiǎnzú zìzhìqū shi zài Zhōngguo jìngnèi, zài Zhōngguode Dōng-
      běi hé Cháoxiǎnde biānjìng.   (T)

50.0. bǐcǐ   mutual(ly), reciprocal(ly), one another, between <u>or</u> among them-
            selves, yourselves, ourselves   [that this]

50.1. Wǒ hěn zǎo jiù xiǎng kànjian ni . . . Bǐcǐ, bǐcǐ.

50.2. Tā bǎ wǒ kànzuò dìdi yíyàng . . . Nà shi nǐ duì tā hǎo. Zhè shi
      bǐcǐ liǎngfāngmiànde shìqing.   (T)

51.0. fēnxi   (1) analyze; (2) analysis   [divide analyze]

51.1. Wáng Jiàoshòu jiǎng "Shìjiède Jiāotōng," fēnxide hěn xiángxi.

Bái: Mǎ Jiàoshòu, wǒ zài túshūguǎn zhǎo cānkǎo shū de shíhou, kàndaole
      yìběn lìshǐ xiěde xiāngdāng qīngchu. Xiěde hěn yǒu xìtǒng. Lìrú
160   Zhōngguo biānjìngde guójiā hé Zhōngguo lìlái bǐcǐ de guānxi yǒu hěn
      xiángxide jiěshi, ér bǎ měi yíge cháodài dōu xiě yíge biǎo. Fēnxide
      hěn míngbai.

Mǎ: Nèiběn lìshǐ jiào shénmo míngzi?

Bái: <u>Zhōngguo Lìshǐ Yánjiu.</u>

165 Mǎ : Nèiběn lìshǐ shi yíwèi Zhāng Dàwén Xiānsheng xiěde. Tā shi yǒu-
      míngde lìshǐjiā. Zhǐ yàoshi yánjiu lìshǐ de rén dōu zhīdao ta.

52.0. qí(zi)   flag (M: ge, miàn)

      guóqí   national flag

      wǔsèqí   five-color flag (used in 1912 by the Republic of China)

52.1. Zhèi liǎngmiàn qízi, yímiàn shi xīnde, yímiàn shi jiùde.

52.2. Nǐ zhīdao Yìdàlìde guóqí shi shénmo yàngzi ma?

52.3. Zhōnghuá Mínguó cóngqiánde guóqí shi wǔsèqí.

52.4. Wǔsèqí hěn piàoliang. Tā yǒu wǔzhǒng yánse shi hóng, huáng, lán, bái, hēi.

52.5. Nèige qízishang wèi-shénmo yǒu yíge shīzi?

53.0. chuàngzào   create, originate   [create make]

53.1. Nǐ zhīdao Zhōngguode wénzì shi shéi chuàngzào de ma?

53.2. Zhèiběn shūshang yǒu yíkè "Chuàngzào wénzì gēn wénzì gǎigé." (T)

54.0. yílǜ   uniformly, all the same   [one law]

54.1. Mínzhǔ guójiāde rénmín zài fǎlǜshang yílǜ píngděng.

55.0. gēnběn   (1) fundamental, underlying; (2) fundamentally, basically; (3) after all   [root root]

55.1. Wǒ tài bèn le. Gēnběn bù míngbai nèige xíngróngcí zěnmo yòng.

Bái: Zhōngguo guà wǔsèqí de shíhou nín kànjianguo ma?

Mǎ : Zài wǒ chūshēng yǐhòu jiù bú guà wǔsèqí le, kěshi wǒ niàn xiǎoxué de shíhou Guówénshang yǒu yíkè "Hóng huáng lán bái hēi." Xiān-
170   sheng gàosu wǒmen nà shi cóngqián guóqíde yánse.

Bái: Nà wǔzhǒng yánsè hěn piàoliang. Dāngchū chuàngzào Zhōnghuá Mínguó de shíhou guīdìng de guóqí hǎoxiang jiu shi wǔsèqí shide.

Mǎ : 'Shì wǔsèqí. Shuōqi guóqí lai hěn yǒu yìsi. Zài Mínguó shíqīniánde shíhou Nánjīngde zhèngfǔ dàole Běijīng ràng rénmín zài ménshang
175   yílǜ dōu yào guà guóqí. Zhōngguode lǎobǎixìng gēnběn bù zhīdào guóqíde zhòngyàoxìng, guóqí gēn guójiāde guānxi. Nèicìde guóqí guàde zhēn yǒu yìsi. Qíqiguàiguàide shénmo yàngzide qízi dōu yǒu.

56.0. guānniàn   concept, conception, idea   [observe ponder]

56.1. Xiànzàide Zhōngguo rén duìyu guójiāde guānniàn hé yǐqián bùtóng le.

57.0. yìshi   consciousness   [idea recognize]

57.1. Shāngrende yìshi duōbàn dōu zài běnshēnde lìyì.

57.2. Zài nèixiē rénde yìshili gēnběn méi yǒu tuánjié.   (T)

58.0. biàn   change, alter, become

       gǎibiàn   change, alter   [change alter]

       biàngēng   change, alter   [change alter]

58.1. Guòle yìhuěr wēn shuǐ biàn le lěng shuǐ le.

58.2. Yíge rénde shēnghuó xíguàn bù róngyi gǎibiàn.

58.3. Tāmende jìhua biàngēng le. Wǔnián jìhua gǎiwéi qīnián le.

59.0. ruògān   (1) quite a number (of), quite an amount (of), a certain (number of); (2) how much? how many?

59.1. Zài ruògān nián yǐqián Zhōngguo yě fāmíngle bù shǎode dōngxi. (T)

Bái: Mǎ Jiàoshòu, yǒu rén shuō Zhōngguo rén jiù yǒu jiātíng guānniàn, méi yǒu guójiā guānniàn. Zhè shi shízàide ma?

180 Mǎ: Zài yìshishang Zhōngguo rén duì jiātíng de guānniàn shēn.

Bái: Xiànzài zhèizǒng sīxiǎng shì bu shi yǐjing gǎibiàn le?

Mǎ: Zhè shi ruògān nián chuántǒng de sīxiǎng, yìshí gǎibiànbuliǎo.

60.0. hùzhù   render mutual assistance   [mutually help]

60.1. Rén hé rén yīngdāng hùzhù.

61.0. (xiāng)chù   get along (with someone)

(xiāng)chùbulái   unable to get along (with someone) (RV)

61.1. Zhōng-É biānjìngde rénmín xiāngchùde hǎo bu hǎo?

61.2. Wǒmen suírán dōu zài yíge dàxué niàn shū, kěshi wǒmen xiāngchùbulái. Wǒmen liǎngge rén chángcháng fāsheng yìjian, bǐcǐ zhěngtiān bù shuō huà.   (T)

62.0. děngyú   equivalent to   [grade at]

62.1. Tā zài Měiguo liúxué bìng bù yòngxīn niàn shū, shénmo yě méi xuédào, děngyú méi qù liúxué.

63.0. bù   (measure for sets of books, movies, etc.)

63.1. Nèibù wénxuéshǐ yígòng yǒu sìběn.   (T)

64.0. jiégòu   structure   [knot construct]

64.1. Zhōngguo Yǔfǎ Jiégòu nèiběn shū hěn hǎo. Bǎ yǔfǎde jiégòu fēnxide fēicháng qīngchu.   (T)

65.0. jī(ji)hū   nearly, almost, practically, virtually

65.1. Shàngcì tā bìngde jījihū sǐle. Yīsheng gēnběn yánjiubuchūlái tā shi shénmo bìng.   (T)

65.2. Nèige rén zài méi fázi shēnghuó de shíhou jīhū yào zìshā.

65.3. Wǒ jīhū méi gǎnshang huǒchē.   (T)

65.4. Wǒ xiǎo érzi tài bèn le, érqiě hái zhěngtiān wár. Měimén gōngke dōu shi liùshifēn. Jījihū jīnnián gāozhōng méi bìyè.

Bái: Qǐng wèn Mǎ Jiàoshòu, hùzhùde yìsi shi shénmo?

Mǎ: Hù shi bǐcǐde yìsi. Zhù jiù shi bāngzhu. Bǐrú "Péngyou zài yíkuàr
185   xiāngchù jiu yào hùzhù."

Bái: Wǒ míngbai le.

Mǎ: Hái yǒu shénmo wèntí méi yǒu?

Bái: Méi yǒu le. Jīntian děngyú niànle yíbù <u>Zhōnghuá Mínzú-shǐ</u>. Míngtian jiǎng shénmo tímu?

190 Mǎ: Míngtian jiǎng shèhuìde jiégòu. Oh. Wǒ jǐjihū wàng le. Jiǎnghuà, jīntian yào wǎn yíge zhōngtou, yīnwei jīntian jiǎnghuàde zhǔjiǎng rén shi wàibian qǐnglai de.

Bái: Hǎode.

SHĒNGCÍ BIǍO

1. (zōng)jiào
Kǒngjiào
2. qíshí
3. bìng
4. huángdì
5. Fó
Fójiào
Fóxué
6. qǐyuán
7. chuán
chuánxialai
chuánshuō
8. Lǎma
Lǎmajiào
9. Mǎn(zhōu)
Mǎnzú
10. tǒngzhì
11. Huí(hui)
Huízú
Huíjiào
12. Wéiwú'ěr(zú)
13. Yúnnán
14. yuē
dàyuē
15. Gānsu
16. tuánjié
17. Yí(zú)
18. Zhuàng(zú)

19. Miáo(zú)
20. Zhòngjiā
21. Xīkāng
22. Guìzhōu
23. pīn
pīnyīn
Hànyǔ Pīnyīn
24. Měng(gǔ)zú
25. gǎi
gǎi V
gǎiyòng
gǎigé
26. qítā
27. Cháoxiǎn
Cháoxiǎnzú
28. Hànzú
29. gònghé
30. fēngsú
31. tónghuà
32. Zàngzú
33. zhěng
zhěngè(r)
zhěngtiān
34. zhēngduó
35. ér
36. kuòzhǎn
37. lǐngtǔ

38. (dǐ)kàng
Kàngzhàn
39. kuòdà
40. línjìn
41. shìjǐ
42. Dé(guo)
Dé(wén)
43. Yìdàlì
44. jiāotōng
45. qícì
yóuqícì
46. hépíng
47. xìtǒng
48. lìrú
49. jìng*
biānjìng
50. bǐcǐ
51. fēnxi
52. qí(zi)
guóqí
wǔsèqí
53. chuàngzào
54. yílǜ
55. gēnběn
56. guānniàn
57. yìshi

58. biàn   60. hùzhù   63. bù
    gǎibiàn   61. (xiāng)chù
    biàngēng   (xiāng)chùbulái   64. jiégòu
59. ruògān   62. děngyú   65. jī(ji)hū

YŬFĂ LIÀNXÍ

A. The uses of er (see note 1)

1. Tā shi yīnwei hé tā jiějie xiāngchùbulái ér líkai jiā de.

2. Guānyu Cháoxiǎnzú shi cóng nǎli ér lái de nà shi yíge hái méi jiějué de wèntí.

3. Tā dào zhèli lái bú shi zhuānmén wèile lǚxíng ér lái de. Zhǔyàode shi dào zhèli lái kāihuì. Qícì cái shi lǚxíng ne.

4. Wǒ wèi tāde shìqing ér biàngēngle wǒ suǒyǒude jìhua.

5. Zhèicìde zhànzhēng shi cóng xībĕide biānjìng ér dǎdào Zhōngguo jìngnèi de.

6. Nèige tuántǐ shi hěn duō dānwèi zǔzhí ér chéng de.

7. Nèibĕn xiǎoshuō yuánwén bú shi Yīngwén ér shi cóng Déwén fānyi de.

8. Tā bìng bú shi xìn Fó de, ér shi yánjiu Fóxué de.

9. Fójiào shi cóng Yìndu lái de, ér Lǎmajiào shi cóng Xīzàng lái de.

10. Kàngzhànde shíhou tā wèi guó ér sǐ le.

B. jiù N (see note 2)

11. Wǒmen wǔge rén lǐtou jiù tā yíge rén shi Mǎnzhōu rén.

12. Zhèi sānmiàn qízi jiù yímiàn shi bĕnguó de.

13. Tā dào nèr dàyuē jiù sāntiān.

14. Jù wǒ suǒ zhīdao jiù Mǎnzú nèi yíge mínzú bèi Hànzú gĕi tónghuà le.

15. Jīnnián gèshĕng dōu yǒu hànzāi. Jiù Guǎngdong yìshĕng méi yǒu.

C. yī M yī M (de) (see note 3)

16. Qǐng nǐ bǎ nèi jǐge Hànzì yígèyígède dōu jiāogei tā zĕnmo pīn.

17. Fēngsú xíguàn dōu shi yídàiyídàide cóng shànggǔ chuánxialai de.

18. Nèi liǎngguó biānjìngshangde zhànshì, kàn qíngxing yìdiǎryìdiǎrde yào kuòdà le.

19. Hànyǔ Pīnyīn zĕnmo jiāo ta, tā yĕ bú huì. Yícìyícíde lǎoshi wèn wǒ.

20. Nǐ bǎ tā xiĕ de zì yíge zì yíge zì xiángxide kànyikàn. Yàoshi yǒu cuò zì, qǐng nǐ gǎiyigǎi.

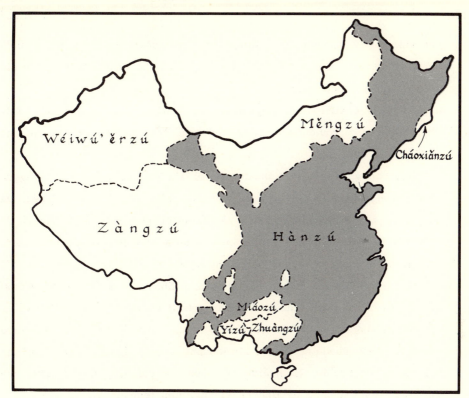

Zhōngguo Mínzú Fēnbù Tú

JIǍNGHUÀ

Zhùwèi tóngxué:

    Jīntian jiǎng de tímu shi Zhōngguode mínzú. Jiǎng zhèige tímu běnlái yīnggāi cóng mínzúde qǐyuán jiǎngqǐ, kěshi nà jiu děngyú yào jiǎng yíbù mínzú-shǐ. Zài zhèige hěn duǎnde shíjiānli dāngrán jiǎngbuwán. Suǒyǐ

5 zhǐ hǎo cóng xiàndài yě jiu shi cóng Mínguó chūnián jiǎngqǐ.

    Zài Mínguó chūniánde shíhou, Zhōngguode guóqí shi wǔseqí. Shénmo shi wǔseqí? Shi shénmo yàngzi ne? Wǔseqí shi yíge chángfāngde, shàngmian yǒu wǔzhǒng yánse, fēnwei wǔtiáo. Tóu-yìtiáo shi hóngsè, dì-èrtiáo shi huángsè, yǐxià shi lánsè、báisè、hēisè yígòng yǒu wǔzhǒng yánse. Zhèi

10 wǔzhǒng yánse shi shénmo yìsi ne? Shi dàibiǎo Zhōngguo wǔge mínzú de. Hóngsè dàibiǎo Hànzú, huángsè dàibiǎo Mǎnzú, lánsè dàibiǎo Měngzú, báisè dàibiǎo Huízú, hēisè dàibiǎo Zàngzú. Cóng zhèimiàn guóqí kànlai jiu zhīdao dāngshí duì Zhōngguo mínzú de shuōfǎ shi yǒu wǔzú de. Nèige shíhou Zhōngguo rén cháng shuō, Zhōngguo shi wǔzú gònghé、wǔzú píng

15 děngde guójiā. Dànshi shìshíshang zài Zhōngguo tǔdìshang de mínzú bù

zhǐ shi wǔge, chàbuduō yǒu liùshi duō ge, suǒyǐ hòulái zhèige shuōfǎ
biàngēng le.   Yàoshi shuōdao Zhōngguo mínzú, bù shuō shi wǔzú ér shi
shuō yǒu hěn duōde mínzú.

 Xiànzài fēnxifēnxi Zhōngguode mínzú jiūjìng yǒu duōshao le.   Měi
20 yíge mínzú dàgài yǒu duōshao rén? Fēnbù zài shénmo dìfang? Yǒu shénmo
tèdiǎn?

 Xiān cóng rénshù zuì duōde Hànzú shuōqǐ.   Hànzú zhàn Zhōngguo
rénkǒu zǒngshù bǎifēnzhī-jiǔshisì, yuē yǒu wǔyì sìqiān duō wàn rén. Dà
bùfen shi zài Zhōngguode nèidì, zài Dōngběi gè dì hé Xīnjiāng gè dà
25 chéngshì de yě bù shǎo.   Hànzú chuàngzàole Zhōngguode wénhuà.   Zài
Zhōngguo lìshǐshang, duōshù shíqī shi Hànzú tǒngzhì Zhōngguo.

 Qícì shuō Mǎnzú.   Mǎnzú běnlái zhùzai Zhōngguode dōngběibù. Gōngyuán yī-liù-sì-sì nián Mǎnzú zuòle Zhōngguode huángdì, jiu shi Qīng Cháo,
tǒngzhì Zhōngguo yǒu èrbǎi liùshi duō nián, suǒyǐ yǒu hěn duō Mǎnzhōu
30 rén dàole Zhōngguode nèidì, zài yǔwénshang fēngsú xíguànshang jiànjiànde
bèi Hànzú tónghuà le.   Xiànzàide Mǎnzhōu rén suīrán yuē yǒu èrbǎi duō
wàn rén, kěshi duōshù hé Hànrén yíyàng, jīhū fēnbuchūlái le.

 Yòu qícì shuō Měngzú.   Dà bùfen zài Nèi-Měnggǔ hé línjìnde dìfang.
Gōngyuán yī-èr-bā-lǐng nián Měngzú zuòle Zhōngguode huángdì, jiu shi
35 Yuán Cháo, búdàn tǒngzhìle Zhōngguo, érqiě guótǔ kuòzhǎndao Ōuzhōu
dōngbù, chéngle gǔ-jīn Zhōng-wài dì-yíge dà guó.   Xiànzài Měngzú yuē
yǒu yìbǎi sìshi duō wàn rén. Tāmen xìn de zōngjiào shi Fójiàode Lǎmajiào,   Tāmen shuō Měnggǔ huà, yě yòng Měnggǔde wénzì, kěshi xiànzài
Měnggǔ wénzì yǐjing gǎigé, gǎiyòng pīnyīn wénzì le.

40 Xiànzài shuō Huízú. Huízú shi Táng Cháo shíhou láidao Zhōngguode
xīběi, xiànzài dà bùfen zài Zhōngguo xīběibù de Xīnjiāng、Qīnghǎi、Gānsu
yídài. Zài nèidìde běibù、xīnánbù yě yǒu bù shǎo Huízú. Yígòng yuē yǒu
sānbǎi wǔshi duō wàn rén. Tāmende tèdiǎn shi dōu xìn Huíjiào.

 Zàngzú, dà bùfen zài Xīzàng、Qīnghǎi yídài hé línjìnde dìfang.   Yuē
45 yǒu èrbǎi qīshi duō wàn rén.   Tāmende tèdiǎn yě shi dōu xìn Fójiàode
Lǎmajiào.   Tāmen yòng de wénzì shi Zàngwén.   Xīzàngde yǔyán gēn
Zhōngguo yǔyán shi yíge xìtǒng, kěshi wénzì shi zài qī shìjì cong Yìndu
lái de.

Yǐshàng suǒ shuō de shi rénshù jiào duōde wǔge mínzú dàgàide qíng-
50 xing.   Chúle zhèixiē mínzú yǐwài, hái yǒu ruògān qítā rénshù jiào shǎo
de mínzú.   Xiànzài bǎ rénkǒu zài yìbǎi wàn yǐshàng de shǎoshù mínzú
shuōyishuō:

Miáozú, fēnbùzai Zhōngguo xīnán、zhōngnán yídài.   Zài Guìzhōu hé
Húnàn xībù de zuì duō.   Yígòng yuē yǒu sānbǎi èrshí duō wàn rén.

55 Wéiwú'ěrzú, fēnbùzai Xīnjiāng jìngnèi, yígòng yuē yǒu sānbǎi duō wàn
rén.   Yǒu Wéiwú'ěrde wénzì.   Xiànzài Wéiwú'ěrde wénzì yǐjing gǎigé le,
gǎiyòng pīnyīn wénzì le.

Yízú, dà bùfen zài Yúnnán、Xīkāng jiāojiè.   Yuē yǒu sānbǎi sìshi duō
wàn rén.

60 Zhuàngzú, fēnbùzai Guǎngxi hé línjìnde dìfang.   Yuē yǒu liùbǎi wǔshi
wàn rén.

Zhòngjiā, zài Guìzhōude xīnán yídài.   Yuē yǒu yìbǎi bāshi duō wàn
rén.

Cháoxiǎnzú, fēnbùzai Zhōngguode Dōngběi hé Cháoxiǎn jiāojiè yídài.
65 Yuē yǒu yìbǎi yīshi duō wàn rén.   Tāmen yòng de shi Cháoxiǎn yǔwén.

Cǐwài hái yǒu yìxiē shǎoshù mínzú, dōu shi rénkǒu bú tài duō de,
jiu bú bǐ yígèyígède shuō le.   Zài zhèixiē shǎoshù mínzúli, yīnwei dìlǐ
gēn jiāotōng bú fāngbiàn de guānxi, tāmende jīngji、wénhuà yǒude bǐjiǎo
luòhòu, zài shēnghuó xíguànshang yě hé Hànzú dà bù xiāngtóng.   Zhōngguo
70 zhèngfǔ xiànzài zài zhèixiē shǎoshù mínzúde zhǔyào qūyù shèli mínzú
zìzhìqū.   Zìzhìqū yǒude hěn dà, yǒude hěn xiǎo.   Lìrú Xīnjiāng shi yíge
zuì dàde zìzhìqū.   Yǒu liùshí sānwàn duō fāng Yīnglǐ, bǐ Déguo、Yìdàlì、
Fàguode zǒng miànji hái dà.

Zuìhòu shuōdao Zhōngguo mínzú bǐcǐde guānxi.   Zài Zhōngguode
75 lìshǐshang lái kàn, Hànzú shi Zhōngguo mínzúde zhōngxīn.   Hànzú gēn
qítā mínzú yǒushí hépíng xiāngchù, yǒushí dǎqi zhàng lai, kěshi dǎzhàng
de yuányin qíshí bìng bú shi wánquán wèile mínzú wèntí.   Yíbàn shi wèile
biéde mínzú yào zhēngduó Hànzúde tǔdì, Hànzú bùdébù dǐkàng.   Yě yǒushíhou shi Hànzú yào kuòdà lǐngtǔ, jiu qù dǎ biéde mínzú.   Zhè dōu shi
80 guòqude shì le.   Xiànzàide Zhōngguo gè mínzú zhījiān de guānniàn dōu
gēnběn gǎibiàn le.   Dàjiāde xiǎngfǎ shi zài dìwèishang yílǜ píngděng.
Zhěnggè mínzú yìshi shi xiàngzhe hùzhù tuánjiéde lùshang zǒu.

WĒNXI

1. Yǒu yíge wàiguo rén zài Zhōngguo lǚxíng. Tā shi cóng Xiānggǎng qù de Zhōngguo dàlù, xiān dào Guǎngzhou, yòu dào Chángshā, yòu dàoguo Dòng-tíng Hú, ránhòu yánzhe Cháng Jiāng dàole Shànghǎi. Tā lǚxíng zhěng liùge yuè. Tā shuō: "Jiāngnán yídài shānshuǐ tài měilì le. Shānshuǐ měilìde jiào wǒ méi fázi xíngrong."

2. Shuǐzāi, hànzāi dōu shi tiānzāi. Měicì tiānzāi duìyu rénmín de sǔnhài dōu shi hěn dà. Wǒ jìde wǒmen xiāngxia yǒu yícì fāshēng shuǐzāi, lùdìshang jījihū dōu shi dàshuǐ, búdàn sǐle hěn duō rén, lián yǎng de niú, yáng yě sǐle bù shǎo. Nèicì shuǐzāi shòu hài tài dà le.

3. Cóngqián Zhōngguode dà jiātíng rénkǒu hěn duō. Jiālide rén yǒude xiāng-chùde hěn hǎo, yǒude xiāngchùbulái, kěshi dàjiā zài biǎomiànshang hái děi kèkeqīqīde zhùzai yíkuàr.

4. Gǔ shíhoude shèhuì jiégòu bǐjiǎo jiǎndān. Jīngguole ruògān niándàide yǎn-biàn, xíngchéngle xiànzàide shèhuì. Xiànzàide shèhuì jiégòu zhēn shi tài fùzá le.

5. Zài gāng fāxiàn Měizhōu yǐhòu, yīnwei tǔdì guǎngdà, rénkǒu xīshǎo, suǒyǐ xǔduō Ōuzhōu guójiā yǐ tīngshuō le jiu dōu xiàng Měizhōu zhímín. Fánshi Ōuzhōu rénmín, zhǐ yàoshi zìjǐ yuànyi qù Měizhōu, jiù kěyi suíbiànde qù.

6. Tā shénmo yě bù xǐhuan, jiù xǐhuan dào rèdàide hǎishang lǚxíng, qícì shi rèdàide lùdì yǒu shān de dìyù, yòu qícì shi Yàxiyà yídàide xiǎode guójiā.

7. Yǒu rén shuō Zhōngguo dà héde shuǐ duōbàn hányǒu ní shā, zhǐ yǒu Yángzi Jiāngde shuǐ bǐjiǎoqilai yòu méi yǒu ní yòu méi yǒu shā.

8. Wǒ zhèng kàn dìtú yǒu rén wèn wǒ Huáng Hǎi zài Yàzhōude shénmo dìfang? Wǒ zhǐzhe dìtú gàosu ta, Huáng Hǎide wèizhi zài Dōngyà, rúguǒ cóng Shāndong zuò chuán wǎng Cháoxiǎn qù, yídìng yào zǒu Huáng Hǎi.

9. Zhāng Xiānsheng yǒu yíwèi cóng biānjiāng lái de péngyou shi Huíhui. Zhāng Xiānsheng shuō Huíhuide tèdiǎn shi hěn tuánjié, háiyǒu zhǐ chī niú-yángròu, bù chī zhūròu.

10. Wǒ jiāo dìdi xué Hànyǔ Pīnyīn. Wǒ gàosu ta: "Hànyǔ shi yídàiyídài chuán-xialai de. Pīnyīn shi zuìjìn yánjiuchulai de. Nǐ yào yòngxīn xué, wǒ gěi nǐ yìběn shū yòu yǒu Hànzì yòu yǒu pīnyīn. Nǐ yào zhùyì yīn shi zěnmo pīn. Rúguǒ chàbuduō huì pīn le, jiu bǎ shū shōuqilai zìjǐ liànxízhe pīn, ránhòu zài bǎ shū náchulai chóng kàn yícì, yǐhòu hái yào chángcháng wēnshū. Zhèiyàng xuéxi nǐ yídìng huì chénggòng de."

11. Wǒ kànjian Wáng Xiānsheng niàn <u>Yīngyǔ Rùmén</u>, wǒ wèn ta: "Wèi-shénmo yào niàn Yīngwén ne?" Tā shuō: "Yīngwénde yòngchu hěn guǎng. Xiànzài wǔ dàzhōuli yòng Yīngwén de guójiā tài duō le, suǒyǐ wǒ xué Yīngwén."

12. Dìdi wèn wǒ <u>fāng</u> zì zěnmo jiǎng? Wǒ gàosu ta: "<u>Fāng</u> zì shi xíngróngcí. Lìrú 'Nèizhāng zhǐ shi sìfāngde' shi xíngrong zhǐde yàngzi shi sìfāngde."

WÈNTÍ

1. Zhōngguo zài Mínguó chūniánde shíhou yòng de guóqí jiàozuo shénmo qi? Shi shénmo yàngzi? Yǒu jǐzhǒng yánse? Dōu shi shénmo yánse? Měi yìzhǒng yánse dàibiǎo de shi shénmo ne?

2. Zhōngguo mínzú zài shìshíshang yǒu duōshao zú? Něi yíge mínzúde rénshù zùi duō?

3. Zhōngguo lìshǐshang yǒu shǎoshù mínzú tǒngzhìguo Zhōngguo ma? Shi shénmo mínzú? Shi shénmo cháodài? Tǒngzhìle duōshao nián?

4. Zhōngguo shénmo mínzú xìn Lǎmajiào? Xìn Lǎmajiào de mínzú duōshù fēnbùzai shénmo dìfang? Kǒngjiào shi zōngjiào ma?

5. Huízú shi shénmo shíhou láidao Zhōngguo? Fēnbùzai shénmo dìyù? Tāmen dàyuē yǒu duōshao rén? Tāmende tèdiǎn shi shénmo?

6. Zàngzúde yǔyán shi shǔyu shénmo yǔyán xìtǒng? Zàngwén shi zài zhénmo shíhou cóng shénmo dìfang lái de?

7. Zhōngguode shǎoshù mínzú rénkǒu zài yìbǎi wàn yǐshàngde shi shénmo zú? Qǐng nǐ shuōchu wǔge huòzhě shi liùge shǎoshù mínzúde míngchēng.

8. Zhōngguode shǎoshù mínzú duōbàn chénglìle zìzhìqū. Zuì dàde zìzhìqū zài shénmo dìfang? Tāde miànji yǒu duō dà? Bǐ Ōuzhōu něi sānge guójiāde zǒng miànji hái dà?

9. Zhōngguo mínzúde zhōngxīn shi něige mínzú?

10. Hànzú zhàn Zhōngguo rén zǒngshù bǎifēnzhī-jǐ? Yuē yǒu duōshao rén? Dà bùfen fēnbùzai shénmo dìfang?

ILLUSTRATIVE SENTENCES (ENGLISH)

1.1. Chinese consider Confucianism as one of the religions.

4.1. Are there countries in Europe and the Americas [now] which still have kings?

5.1. The Chinese say Buddha came from the West.

5.3. Their family has believed in Buddhism for several generations.

18.2. If we reckon together (the members of)the Zhuang nationality who are dispersed among other areas, there are over six million.

19.1. Do you know the special features of the Miao nationality and where it is dis-distributed?

23.1. Can you write [lit. spell] those characters in Chinese pīnyīn?

25.2. Formerly in China everyone used the abacus. Recently there are some (people) who have gone over to the use of computing machines.

25.3. He used to study Tibetan. Now he has changed over to the study of Mongol.

25.4. Do you know the course of writing reform in China?

30.1. Chinese customs and those of Europe and America [compared] are quite different.

30.2. Each of the minority nationalities has its own customs and habits [in life].

33.4. Generally speaking, problems invariably arise between peoples.

34.1. The two countries came to blows because they both wanted to take over that colony.

35.1. He became a Lama priest in order to study Lamaism.

35.2. He's going to America not to study but to engage in business.

35.3. Chinese Buddhism came from India.

37.2. Those two countries went to war over the seizure of some territory.

38.1. "Seven-seven" is the day of (the beginning of) the Chinese War of Resistance against Japan. Japan [came and] attacked China, and China was forced to resist.

41.1. The life of many Chinese in the twentieth century has become Europeanized.

41.2. During the Middle Ages there were frequent disturbances all over Europe.

49.2. The autonomous region of the Korean nationality is within Chinese territory, on the border between [China's] Manchuria and Korea.

50.2. He treats me like a younger brother . . . That's because you are well disposed toward him. It's mutual [lit. a mutual matter].

53.2. In this book there's a lesson (entitled) "Creating a Script and Script Reform."

57.2. Fundamentally there is no (thought of) unity in the minds [lit. consciousness] of those people.

59.1. Some years ago China also invented quite a few things.

61.2. Although we both study at the same university, we can't get along together. The two of us often clash [lit. give rise to opinions] and don't talk to each other all day long.

63.1. That history of literature comprises four volumes in all.

64.1. That Syntactical Structure of Chinese is excellent. Its analysis of syntactical structure is extremely clear.

65.1. [Last time] he was so sick that he almost died. The doctors simply could not find out what his illness was.

65.3. I almost didn't make the train.

NOTES

1. The particle ér has a variety of meanings (and, but, whereas, while on the other hand) and is used in several different but related ways. It is frequently paired with the words cóng 'from,' wèi(le) and yīnwei 'because (of)':

Nèige yīyuàn shi jǐge yīsheng zǔzhí ér chéng de. 'That hospital was organized and brought into being by several doctors.'

Nèige xuéxiào bu shi zhèngfǔ shèlì de, ér shi sīren shèlìde. 'That school was not established by the government, but [was established] by private persons.'

Tā shi yīnwei yào yánjiu Zàngwén ér yào dào Xīzàng qu. 'He wants to go to Tibet because he wants to study Tibetan.'

Tā shi wèi guó ér sǐ de. 'He died for his country.'

The last example is a written rather than spoken form, and the others, while speakable, convey a rather literary flavor. Students are advised not to use ér in speech unless similar utterances have actually been heard in appropriate situations.

2. The word jiù, which usually functions as an adverb before a verb, is also used in the meaning 'only' before nominal expressions:

Tā zài zhèr niàn shū jiù liùge yuè. 'He studied here for only six months.'

Jiù tā yíge rén huì shuō Zhōngguo huà. 'Only he can speak Chinese.'

3. Measures reduplicated in the pattern yī M yī M(de) mean 'one M after another' or 'M by M':

Nà shi yídàiyídàide chuánxialai de. 'That was handed down generation after generation.'

Nǐ bǎ nèi jǐge jùzi yígèyígède niàngei wǒ tīngting. 'Read those sentences to me one by one.'

Sometimes a noun is inserted after the measure:

Qǐng nǐmen yíge zì yíge zì de kànyikàn. 'Please look at it character by character.'

Note that yíge recovers the original fourth tone on the second syllable when it occurs in yígèyígède, and that numbers other than yī 'one' can also be used:

Nǐmen liǎngge liǎnggede jìnlai. 'Come in by twos.'

Dì-Bākè. Shèhuì Jiégòu

Bái : Mǎ Jiàoshòu zǎo.

Mǎ : Zǎo, zǎo. Wǒ jīntian qǐlai wǎn le. Lián zǎofàn dōu méi chī.

Bái : Nín yào bu yào xiān qu chī zǎofàn?

Mǎ : Búbì. Wǒ zǎofàn chī bu chī dōu méi shénmo dà guānxi.

5　Bái : Wǒ jīntian zǎoshang biǎo bù zǒu le. Wǒ jiéguǒ qǐlaide dào zǎo le.
Wǒ qǐlai dàyuē yǒu bànge zhōngtóu Xuéxīn cái qǐlai.

Mǎ : Nǐ hé Xuéxīn nǐmen liǎngge rén yíkuàr dào xuéxiào lai ma?

Bái : Shìde. Wǒmen liǎngge rén zǎoshang yíkuàr chī zǎofàn. Wǒmen
liǎngge rén xiāngchǔde fēicháng hǎo.

10　Mǎ : Rúguǒ zhùzai yíkuàr dàjiā xiāngchǔbulái hěn méi yìsi.

Bái : Shìde. Wǒ gēn Xuéxīn wǒmen liǎngge rén niánsuì chàbuduō. Gè
fāngmiànde xìngqu hé xíguàn dōu xiāngtóng.

Mǎ : Nǐ hé Huá Xiānsheng hěn shǎo jiànmiàn ba?

Bái : Shìde. Yǒushíhou zhěngtiān kànbujiàn, yǒushíhou zài chī wǎnfàn de
15　shíhou cái néng kànjian tāmen. Huá Xiānsheng hé Huà Tàitai duì
rén de tàidu fēicháng hǎo. Duì wǒ hǎojíle. Huàn ju huà shuō bǎ
wǒ dàngzuo zìjǐ jiāli rén yíyàng.

Mǎ : Zhè yě shi bǐcǐ liǎngfāngmiànde shìqing.

Bái : Zhè shi Huá Xiānsheng、Huá Tàitai duì rén hǎo.

20　Mǎ : Shuōqi rén hé rén xiāngchǔ de wèntí, wǒ gěi nǐ shuō ge gùshi. Zài
Kàngzhàn shíqī wǒ zài Xīnán Lián-Dà niàn shū de shíhou, wǒ jiu
zài xuéxiào fùjìn zhǎo de fángzi, fángdōng shi ge méi zhīshi de
zhōngnián nǔren. Cóng wǒ bānjinqu zhīhòu tiāntian máfan wǒ, bú
shi shuō wǒ huílaide tài wǎn le jiù shi shuō wǒ qǐlaide tài zǎo le.
25　Kāishǐ wǒ gēn tā kèqi. Hòulai wǒ jiu bù lǐ ta le. Jǐnjǐnde zhùle
yíge yuè, wǒ shízài zhùbuxiàqù le, fēi bānjiā bùkě le. Zhǐhǎo zhǎo
ge fángzi bān le. Nèisuǒ fángzi lí xuéxiào hěn jìn. Wǒ zhēn bú
yuànyi bān.

Bái : Rén méi yǒu yíyàngde.

30　Mǎ : Shì. Yǒude rén duì rén hěn hǎo. Yǒude rén jiu bù xíng.

Bái : Qíshí rén dōu yīngdāng hùzhù.

Mǎ : Yǒude rén yě bù xīwang biéren bāngzhu ta, ér tā yě bú yuànyi
bāngzhu biérén.

Bái : Xiànzàide rén zhěnggèr sīxiǎng chàbuduō dōu biàn le.

35　Mǎ : Shídàide qūshì yíqiè dōu biàn le. Yuè biàn yuè jìnbù.

Bái: Shuōdao jìnbù, zhèi liǎngnián lai zhèli zhēn shi jìnbùle bù shǎo. Jiù
ná jiāotōng lai shuō ba, cóngqián zhèr dōu shi xiǎolù. Xiànzài chàbuduō dōu shi dàlù le.

40
Mǎ: Shìzhǎng yǒu yíge sānnián jìhua. Tā xiǎng zài sānnián yǐ'nèi bǎ
zhèige chéngshìde lù yílù gǎicheng dàlù.

Bái: Shíhou dào le. Mǎ Jiàoshòu nín qu chī zǎofàn ba. Wǒ zìjǐ xiān bǎ
shēngcí kànyikàn.

Mǎ: Suànle, wǒ bù chī le, yìhuěr jiu chī zhōngfàn le. Wǒ nèiren zhōngwǔ
zuò jiǎozi.

1.0. suǒwèi   called, so-called   [actually say]

1.1. Suǒwèi Kǒngjiào qíshí shi Kǒngzǐ xuéshuō. Bù néng suàn shi zōngjiào.

2.0. jiējí   class, rank   [step grade]

2.1. Xiànzài rénrén píngděng. Jué bù yīngdāng zài yǒu jiējíde guānniàn.

3.0. shìdàfū, shìdàifū   gentry   [scholar big man]

3.1. Shìdàfū jiējí shi zhǐzhe niàn shū hé zuò guān rén shuō de.   (T)

4.0. yíxiàng   hitherto, habitually, always (in the past)   [one toward]

4.1. Měngzú, Zàngzú yíxiàng dōu xìn Fójiào ma?

5.0. xiǎonóng   small peasant

5.1. Wai! Wǒ shi Zhāng Yǒushān. Zuótian wǒ qǐng nǐ qu diàochá nèige
xiāngcūnli jiūjìng yǒu duōshao xiǎonóng, nǐ diàochá le ma?   (T)

45
Mǎ: Wénshān, nǐ duì Zhōngguo gǔshíhoude shèhuì hěn yǒu yánjiu. Suǒwèi
liǎng dà jiējí dōu bāokuò něi liǎngzhǒng rén?

Bái: Suǒwèi liǎng dà jiējí dì-yī shi shìdàfū, jiu shi zhīshi fènzǐ, dà dìzhǔ gēn zuò guān de. Qícì jiu shi nóngmín jiējí. Shìdàfūli yě bāokuò
niàn shū de, bǎ shū niànhǎo yǐhòu qu zuò guān. Tāmen jiu shi
50
tǒngzhì jiējí le. Zhōngguo yíxiàng bǎ niàn shū rén kànde zuì gāo.
Niàn shū de zuòle guān dāngrán shi zuì gāo jiējí le.

Mǎ: Nóngmín jiējí shi zhǐzhe něizhǒng nóngmín shuō de ne?

Bái: Shi zhǐzhe xiǎonóng shuō de.

6.0. diànnóng   tenant farmer   [lease farming]

6.1. Sūn Zhōngshān zhǔzhāng zhòng dì de rén dōu yào zìjǐ yǒu tǔdì, nà
jiu shi shuō kéyi búbì yǒu diànnóng le.   (T)

7.0. hù   household   (M)

dàhù   great family, rich family

xiǎohù   poor family   [small household]

7.1. Míng Cháo mònián dàochu dōu yǒu dòngluàn. Rénmín sǐde hěn duō. Sìchuān yǒu yíge xiāngcūn yǒu èrbǎi duō hù, yǒude rén bèi shāsǐ le, yǒude rén zìshā le, quán cūnde rén dōu sǐ le.

7.2. Shàngcì zhànzhēng, chénglǐde dàhù, xiǎohù dōu bèi bīpòde bānzǒu le. (T)

8.0. qióng   poor, impoverished

      qióngren   a poor person

8.1. Nèige rén bìng bu qióng. Zhìshǎo xiànzàide shēnghuó shi méi wèntí de.   (T)

8.2. Zhèige cūnzili dōu shi qióngren, jiù yǒu Wáng jia shi yǒuqiánde.

9.0. fù   rich

      fùguì   (1) rich and distinguished; (2) riches and honor

      fùren   a rich person

9.1. Huáqiáode jīngji zhuàngkuàng bìng bù xiāngtóng. Yǒude hěn fù, yǒude hěn qióng.

9.2. Tāmen suírán bú shi fùguì jiātíng, kěshì yě bú shi qióngren. Shuōde- shàng shi fùren.

10.0. jiā   family   (see note 5)

      rénjiā   a home

10.1. Zhōngguo rén duìyu jiā de guānniàn yíxiàng hěn shēn.   (T)

10.2. Guìzhōu shān duō rén xī. Yíge xiāngcūn yěxǔ jiù yǒu jǐjiā rénjiā. (T)

10.3. Rénjiade érzi nènmo cōngming, wǒde érzi zhènmo bèn.

10.4. Wǒmen jiā lìdài shi diànnóng, dōu shi zhòng dàhù rénjiāde tiándì. (T)

10.5. Wáng Xiànzhǎng bǎ nèi yíxiàn zhìde hěn hǎo. Lǎobǎixìng jiājiā dōu yǒu fàn chī.   (T)

Bái: Mǎ Jiàoshòu, qǐng wèn <u>diànnóng</u> zhèige cér wǒ bú dà dǒng.

55 Mǎ: Diànnóng jiu shi zhòng dàhù rénjiā tiándì de.

Bái: Diànnóng zìjǐ dōu méi yǒu dì ma?

Mǎ: Méi yǒu. Diànnóng yǒude shi qióngren, yǒude bìng bú tài qióng, kěshi yě bù hěn fù, dōu shi xiǎohù rénjiā. Yībānde cūnzili dàhù bù hěn duō, zhǐ yǒu liǎng-sānjiā. Qíyúde dōu shi ruògān xiǎohù. Huàn
60   ju huà shuō jiu shi qióngren duō fùren shǎo.

11.0. shì*   form, style

      Zhōngshì   Chinese style

Xīshì   Western style

jiùshì   old style

xīnshì   new style

11.1.   Nèige dàxué guīmó hěn dà, jiùshìde hé xīnshìde fángzi dōu yǒu.

11.2.   Zhāng Xiānsheng jiāli yòng de dōngxi jījihū quán shi Xīshìde, méi
yǒu Zhōngshìde.

11.3.   Liánhéguó mén wàitou guàzhe gèshì gèyàngde qízi.   (T)

12.0.   rènhé   any (used attributively)

12.1.   Rènhé xìngzhide tuántǐ tā dōu bú yuànyi cānjiā.   (T)

13.0.   fúcóng   obey, follow obediently   [submit follow]

13.1.   Jiùshìde jiātíng duìyu jiāzhǎng suǒ shuō de huà yào juéduì fúcóng.
(T)

14.0.   jià   marry (of a woman)

chūjià   (leave home to) get married

jiàchū   (leave home to) get married

14.1.   Zhāng Xiáojie jiàle yíge Déguo rén. Chūjià yǐhòu tāmen xiāngchǔde
hěn hǎo.

14.2.   Zhōngguo rén cháng shuō: "Jiàchūde nǚer jiu shi rénjiade rén le."

14.3.   Nǐ wèi-shénmo shuō nǐ jiějie jiàbuchūqù le?   (T)

15.0.   yóu   from, by (W)

yóuyu   because, since, thanks to, as a result of [from at]

yóu(yu) A (ér) V   (1) to V from A, to V because of A; (2) be V'd by A

15.1.   Zhōngguode Wànlǐ Chángchéng shíjìshang jǐn yǒu qīqiān duō lǐ, yóu
Héběi Shěng zhì Gānsu Shěng.

15.2.   Yóuyu rénkǒu zēngjiā de sùdù jīngrén, hěn duō rén tíchàng jiézhi
shēngyù.

15.3.   Yóuyu biānjìngde chéngshì dōu chéngle zhànshí zhuàngtài, suǒyǐ gè
gōngshāngyè dōu shòule yǐngxiǎng le.   (T)

15.4.   Nèige dìfangde rénmín yóuyu tiānzāi rénhuò ér bānjiā, bìng bú shi
zìjǐ yuànyi yídòng de.

16.0.   yíqiè   all (of), the whole lot   [one cut]

16.1.   Tiāntiān kàn bàozhǐ, kéyi zhīdao shìjièshang yíqiè dòngtài.

Bái: Shì bu shi zhǐ yǒu dàhù shi dà jiātíng zhìdu?

Mǎ :   Dāngrán le.

Bái: Tīngshuō cóngqián Zhōngguo jiùshì dà jiātíngli rènhé shìqing dōu
yào fúcóng jiāzhǎng. Bǐrú érzi jiēhūn, nǚer chūjià dōu děi yóu fùmǔ
65   zuòzhǔ.

Mǎ : Búdàn shi érnǚ qīnshì, yíqiè dōu děi tīng jiāzhǎng de.

Bái: Hànzú﹐ Mǎnzú dōu shi zhèizhǒng fēngsu xíguàn ma?

Mǎ : Wǒ xiǎng chàbuduō.

17.0. zǔ*   ancestor

       zǔfù   father's father, grandfather

       zǔmǔ   father's mother, grandmother

       zǔxiān   ancestors   [ancestor first]

17.1. Tāde zǔfù﹐ zǔmǔ shuō zài tāmen niàn zhōngxué de shíhou guóqí shi
       wǔsèqí. Zài jìniànrì jiājiā dōu yào guà qízi.   (T)

17.2. Wǒ jiā shi ge dà jiātíng. Zǔfù﹐ zǔmǔ tāmen dàjiā shícháng bǐcǐ
       fāshēng yìjian, ér dàjiā yǒule yìjian jiu děi hǎojǐtiān shéi yě bù gēn
       shéi shuō huà le. (T)

18.0. dìxiong   (older and younger) brothers

       xiōngdì   (older and younger) brothers

       xiōngdi   younger brother   (note neutral tone)

18.1. Wǒ jiāde dìxiōng hěn duō. Wǒ shi lǎodà. Wǒ yǒu sānge xiōngdi.

18.2. Wǒ zuì xiǎode xiōngdi zuì xǐhuan chī táng le, ná táng dāng fàn chī.

18.3. Shǎoshù mínzú bǐcǐ hùzhù xiàng xiōngdì yíyàng.   (T)

18.4. Tāmen dìxiong sānge rén chī fàn dōu shi ná zuǒshǒu yòng kuàizi.

19.0. jiěmèi   (older and younger) sisters

19.1. Tāmen jiěmèi wǔge dōu huì Déwén.   (T)

19.2. Zǐmèi sānge rénde gāngbǐ zǐ, xiěde dōu nènmo piàoliang.

20.0. pūren, púren, pǔren   servant (W) [servant man]

20.1. Tā jiā cóngqián yǒu yíge hěn lǎode pūren, niánsuì hé tāde zǔfù
       chàbuduō.

21.0. jīchǔ   foundation, base   [foundation foundation]

21.1. Nèige dàxué gōngke hěn nán. Chúfēi nǐ zài zhōngxué de gōngke yǒule
       hǎode jīchǔ yàoburán yídìng gēnbushàng.   (T)

21.2. Wǒ sìshēng bù zhǔn shi yīnwei fāyīnde jīchǔ bù hǎo.   (T)

22.0. shēngchǎn   (1) produce; (2) production   [bear produce]

22.1. Yào xiǎng fāzhǎn jīngji bìděi zēngjiā shēngchǎn.   (T)

Mǎ : Guānyu Zhōngguo dà jiātíng wǒ shuō yíge shìshí gěi nǐ tīng. Dāngchū
70   wǒ jiāli jiu shi yíge dà jiātíng. Wǒ jìde wǒ xiǎode shíhou jiāli yǒu
       zǔfù﹐ zǔmǔ﹐ fùqinde dìxiōng jiěmèi děngděng lián nánnǚ pūren yǒu
       sìshijǐkǒu rén. Tāmen dōu zài jiāli, shéi yě bù chūqu zuò shì. Shū

yě niànde bú tài duō. Dàgài dōu shi gāozhōngde chéngdu. Jiù shi
wǒ fùqin dàxué bìyè le chūguó liúxué qu.

75 Bái: Dàjiā dōu bu zuò shì, qián cóng nǎlǐ lái ne? Zěnmo shēnghuó ne?

Mǎ: Dà jiātíngde jīngji jīchǔ dōu shi xiāngdāng hǎode. Yīnwei jiāli yǒu
fàn chī, shéi yě bù xiǎng qu shēngchǎn. Dōu kàozhe jiātíng shēnghuó.

Bái: Rénrén dōu bu gōngzuò, dōu kào jiātíng shēnghuó, dà jiātíng hěn
80 róngyi qióng le.

Mǎ: Shìde. Yǒude dà jiātíng mànmārde jiu yuè lái yuè qióng. Ér dàjiā
yǒule yìjian jiu děi fēnkāi.

Bái: Zhōngguo jiātíng zěnmoyàng fēn jiā ne?

Mǎ: Yàoshi yǒu wǔge érzi, jiu bǎ dōngxi fēngei wǔge érzi.

85 Bái: Nènmo nǚer hé sūnzi, sūnnüer ne?

Mǎ: Zhōngguo rénde fēngsu xíguàn bù fēngei jiàchūde nǚer. Sūnzi,
sūnnüer shi shǔyu érzi de, suǒyǐ yě bù fēngei tāmen.

Bái: Zhèiyàngde jiātíng dōu shi fùguì rénjiā, shì bu shi?

Mǎ: Dāngrán le, yào bu shi fùguì rénjiā yě jiu méi yǒu dōngxi fēngei
90 érzi le.

23.0. cítáng   ancestral hall

23.1. Hànzú rénjiā duōbàn yǒu cítáng. Qítā mínzú lìrú Miáozú, Zhòngjiā,
Yízú, Wéiwǔ'erzú děngděng shì bu shi yě yǒu cítáng ne?

24.0. zǔzong   ancestor   [ancestor ancestor]

24.1. Tā jiā yǒu bù shǎo gǔshū, dōu shi tā zǔzong chuánxialai de.

25.0. miào   temple

Kǒngmiào   Confucian temple

25.1. Zhōngguo gè dìfang dōu yǒu miào. Quánguóde miào duōde méi fázi
tǒngjì. (T)

25.2. Běijīng yǒu Kǒngmiào yě yǒu Lǎmamiào. Kǒngmiào gēn Lǎmamiào
ménkǒur dōu yǒu liǎngge dà shítou shīzi.

26.0. hòudài   succeeding generations, descendants   [rear generations]

26.1. Xiànzàide Měiguo rén duōbàn shi Déguo, Yīngguo, Fàguo, Yìdàlìde
hòudài.

Bái: Qǐng nín gěi wǒ jiěshi jiěshi cítáng zhèige cérde yìsi shi shénmo?

Mǎ: Cítáng jiu shi jìniàn zǔzong de dìfang. Děngyu miào yíyàng. Miào
nǐ dāngrán zhīdao le.

Bái: Zhīdao. Fójiào dōu yǒu miào. Cǐwài hái yǒu Kǒngmiào. Zhōng-
95 guo rén, jiājiā dōu yǒu cítáng ma?

Mǎ : Cítáng bìng bú shi jiājiā dōu yǒu de. Fánshi yíge zǔxiān chuánxialai de hòudài dàjiā zhǐ yǒu yíge cítáng.

27.0. zé(ren)   responsibility, duty

27.1. Nèijiàn shì méi bànhǎo. Wǒmen yào fēnxi fēnxi nà shi shéide zéren.
(T)

28.0. fù*   assume, shoulder, bear

      fùzé   assume responsibility

      fù zéren   assume responsibility

28.1. Nèige dìfang shi yóu tā tǒngzhì de, suǒyǐ yīngdāng tā fùzé.

28.2. Rúguǒ tā bú fù zéren, qǐng wèn, zhèige zéren yīngdāng shéi fù?
(T)

29.0. (zōng)zú   clan   [ancestor clan]

      tóngzú   be of the same clan

      zúzhǎng   clan head

29.1. Zōngzú shi Zhōngguo gǔshí shèhuì jiēgòude zhōngxīn.

29.2. Tóngzúde rén yīngdāng tuánjié. Yàoburán jiu duìbuqǐ zǔxiān le.
(T)

29.3. Wǒmen zhèi yìzúde zúzhǎng shi yíwèi lǎonián rén, tā duì tóngzú rén
de tàidu fēicháng héqi.

30.0. (yàoshi) . . . de huà   if

30.1. Zhōngguo rén suírán shi ān-tǔ-zhòng-qiān, kěshi yàoshi yǒu tiānzāi
rénhuò de huà tāmen háishi yào yídòng de.

30.2. Nǐ jīntian néng lái de huà, wǒ jiu zài jiā děng ni le.

30.3. Yàoshi wǒ érzi bú bèn de huà, tā dàxué zǎo jiu bìyè le.

31.0. shènzhì(yu)   even to, even as far as to, culminating in   [very to at]

31.1. Nèige héde shàngyóu qìhou tài lěng le. Yǒushíhou wēndù shi líng
xià shídù, shènzhìyu shi líng xià èrshi duō dù.

31.2. Tā bù shízì. Shènzhì lián tā zìjǐde míngzi yě bú rènde.

32.0. wú   not have, lack (W)

      wúlùn   no matter (= búlùn)   [lack discuss]

      wúsuǒwèi   be of no importance, make no difference, not matter [lack
                  actually say]

32.1. Yǒu rén tuīcè wúlùn dào shénmo shíhou yě bú huì yǒu Dì-Sāncì
Shìjiè Dàzhàn fāshēng de. Nǐ shuō zhèige huà kěkào ma?

32.2. Wúlùn něige bàoshangde shèlùn dōu shuō, nèi liǎngge guójiā wèile
biānjìng língtǔde wèntí yào fāshēng zhànshì.   (T)

32.3. Zhōngguo rén duìyu guònián, yǒu rén rènwei hěn zhòngyào, yǒu rén rènwei wúsuǒwèi.

32.4. Yǒu yíge Zhōngguo rén zài wàiguo guò yīnlìnián. Tā shuō: "Wǒ zài wàiguo wúsuǒwèi guònián, zhǐ shi chī yìdiǎr hǎochīde dōngxi jiu suàn guònián le."

Bái: Zhōngguode cítáng shi shéi fùzé ne?

Mǎ: Ànzhào chuántǒngshangde bànfǎ shi dàjiā xuǎn zōngzúlide yíge zú-
100 zhǎng lai fù zéren.

Bái: Zúzhǎng shi shénmo yìsi?

Mǎ: Zúzhǎng jiu shi tóngzú rén zài běnzú rénli xuǎnchū de. Yàoshi běnzú yǒu shì de huà dōu zhǎo ta.

Bái: Shénmo shì dōu zhǎo ta ma?

105 Mǎ: Wúlùn dàshì xiǎoshì, shènzhìyu tóngzú rén fāshēng yìjian yě qù zhǎo zúzhǎng gěi shuōhé. Zúzhǎng yàoshi běnzú yǒu shì hǎoxiàng shi tāde zéren shide.

Bái: Zúzhǎng shì bu shi xuǎnchū yǐhòu yóngyuǎn dāngxiaqu ne?

Mǎ: Yě bu yídìng.

33.0. zìgēngnóng, zìjīngnóng   peasants who farm their own land   [self plow farming]

33.1. Zìgēngnóngde yídòngxìng hěn xiǎo, yīnwei tāmen zìjǐ yǐjing yǒule tǔdì, jiu bù qīngyì bānjiā le.

34.0. wéichí   maintain, keep up, hold together   [maintain hold]

34.1. Liánhéguó quèshí shi zài xiǎng fázi wéichí shìjiè hépíng.

34.2. Wǒ yíge yuè cái wǔshikuài qiánde gōnggian. Zěnmo néng wéichí yìjiā rén de shēnghuó ne?   (T)

35.0. kǔ   bitter (literally and figuratively), hard

kǔgōng   (1) hard physical labor; (2) laborer, worker (engaged in hard physical labor)

chīkǔ   suffer, stand a great deal   (VO)   [eat bitter]

35.1. Yíge rén yàoshi bù néng chīkǔ de huà, tāde shìyè bù róngyi chénggōng de.

35.2. Néng zuò kǔgōng de rén bù yídìng zuì kǔ, bù néng zuò kǔgōng de rén, yěxǔ shi zuì kǔde rén.

35.3. Nèixiē kǔgōngde shēnghuó yìnián bǐ yìnián nán.   (T)

36.0. jiēshòu   receive, accept   [receive receive]

36.1. Tā shuō de tiáojiàn wǒmen dōu bù néng jiēshòu.   (T)

37.0. fǎnduì   oppose   [reverse toward]

37.1. Zài Qīng Cháo mònián, Hànzú fǎnduì Mǎnzú tǒngzhì Zhōngguo.

37.2. Cóngqián wǒ niàn shū de shíhou wǒde lǎoshī fǎnduì wǒ yòng gāngbǐ
       xiě Zhōngguo zì.

37.3. Wǒ zǔfù fǎnduì wǒmen yòng qiānbǐ xiě zì, tā jiào wǒmen yòng máobǐ.

110 Bái: Mǎ Jiàoshòu, shénmo jiào zìgēngnóng?

    Mǎ : Zìjǐ yǒu dì zhòng de. Bú shi dà dìzhǔ ér shi dìzhǔ hé diànnóng
           zhōngjiàn de.

    Bái: Wǒ zhīdao le. Jiu shi tāmen zìjǐ zhòng zìjǐde tiándì wéichí yìjiā
           rénde shēnghuó.

115 Mǎ : Duìle.

    Bái: Zìgēngnóng hé diànnóng shì bu shi dōu shi shǔyu xiǎonóng?

    Mǎ : Dōu shi xiǎonóng.

    Bái: Zhōngguo nóngren yìbānde shuōqilai hěn kǔ, shì bu shi?

    Mǎ : Kǔde bùdéliǎo. Guònián cái shā zhū. Píngcháng gēnběn chībuzháo
120   ròu.

    Bái: Jìnlai yǒu rén tíchàng yòng xiàndài xīnshìde fāngfǎ zhòngtián. Bù
           zhīdào nóngren yuànyi bu yuànyì jiēshòu zhèizhǒng fāngfǎ?

    Mǎ : Wǒ xiǎng yǒu rén fǎnduì, yǒu rén zànchéng.

38.0. shì   scholar (W)

38.1. Shì shi yǒu xuéshi de rén. Zài cóngqián Zhōngguode shèhuìli, shìde
       dìwèi bǐ nóng、gōng、shāng dōu gāo.   (T)

39.0. cúnzài   exist, survive, continue   [exist be at]

39.1. Zhōnghuá Mínguóde guóqí zuìchū shi wǔsèqí. Hòulái biàngēng le.
       Xiànzài wǔsèqí yǐjing bu cúnzài le.

40.0. pǔtōng   common, ordinary

       pǔtōnghuà   common speech, general speech   [universal communi-
                    cate]

40.1. Zhōngguo jìnlái bǎ shuō Guóyǔ jiàozuo shuō pǔtōnghuà. Jùshuō xiàn-
       zài pǔtōng rén duōbàn huì shuō pǔtōnghuà le.

40.2. Nǐ tīng nèige piàoliang xiáojiede pǔtōnghuà shuōde zhēn hǎo.

41.0. dú   (1) read; (2) study

       dúshū   study (VO)   [read book]

41.1. Dúshū zuì zhǔyàode shi liǎojiě dàyì.

41.2. Wǒmen jiā jǐdài dōu shi dúshū de.   (T)   (see note 3)

41.3. Rúguǒ nǐ xiǎng zuò wényánwén zuìhǎo shi duō dú gǔshū.

42.0. díquè   really and truly, certainly

42.1. Zài yǔyánxuéjiāde guāndiǎn kànlai rènwei Hànyǔ pīnyīn zài xuéxí Hànyǔshang díquè yǒuyòng.

42.2. Tā díquè xǐhuan chī jiǎozi, tā yǐ chī jiǎozi jiu děi chī wǔshíjǐge.

Bái: Mǎ Jiàoshòu, zài yǐqiánde shèhuìli bǎ rénde jiējí fēnde hěn qīngchu,
125   bǎ rén fēnwei sìge jiējí, suǒwèi shì、nóng、gōng、shāng. Zhèizhǒng guānniàn xiànzài yǐjing bù cúnzài le ba?

Mǎ: Biǎomiànshang zhèizhǒng guānniàn xiànzài shi wánquán gǎibiàn le. Zài shíjìshang zhèizhǒng sīxiǎng dào xiànzài hái cúnzài. Ná pǔtōng yībān rénjiā dǐng qīnshì lai shuō, yǒude rén hái xīwang hé dúshū
130   de huòzhě hé zuò guān de dǐng qīnshì.

Bái: Chuántǒng sīxiǎng díquè bù róngyi gǎi.

43.0. dì   hand over, pass to

chuándì   transmit, pass on (W) [transmit pass to]

43.1. Qing nǐ bǎ <u>Rénkǒuxué</u> hé <u>Tǒngjìxué</u> nèi liǎngběn shū dìgei wǒ.

43.2. Nèixiē shítou shi yóu gōngren yíge chuán yíge chuándìdao lóushang lai de.   (T)

43.3. Qǐng nǐ bǎ qiānbǐ hé gāngbǐ dōu dìgei wǒ.

44.0. gōngyòng   function, use   [accomplishment use]

44.1. Cháng Jiāng xiàyóu bù cháng yǒu shuǐzāi duōbàn shi Dòngtíng Húde gōngyòng.   (T)

45.0. gōng(ji)   supply (with assistance), help   [supply give]

45.1. Wǒ gōng ta liúxué.   (T)

45.2. Tāde xuéfèi yǐjí shēnghuófèi dōu shi yóu wǒ gōngji.   (T)

45.3. Wǒ děi gōngji wǒ liǎngge érnǚ niàn dàxué.   (T)

45.4. Wǒ xiànzài yǒu liǎngge yìjian gōng zhūwèi cānkǎo.   (T)

46.0. tiānrán   natural   [heaven is]

46.1. Zhèlide fēngjǐng shi tiānrán de, nǐ kàn duómo piàoliang a.

47.0. lèi   (1) kind, sort, category (M); (2) used as suffix, e.g. <u>tāng-lèi</u> 'soups' (in a menu)

rénlèi   mankind

zhǒnglèi   variety, type, species

47.1. Tā xiě de shū fēn liǎnglèi. Yílèi shi kèběn, yílèi shi cānkǎo shū.

47.2. Zhànzhēng gěi rénlèi dàilaile hěn dà sǔnhài.   (T)

47.3. Yú yǒu hěn duō zhǒnglèi. Nǐ xǐhuan chī něi yìzhǒng ne?

47.4. Càidārshang tānglèi、ròulèide zhǒnglèi tèbie duō, zěnmo méi yǒu diǎnxinlèi ne?

Bái: Mǎ Jiàoshòu, dān yòng dǐ zhèige cér wǒ zhīdao, lìrú "Dǐ wǒ yìbēi chá," "Dǐ wǒ nèiběn shū." Kěshi chuándǐ zěnmo yòng ne?

Mǎ: Chuándǐ jiu shi yǒu hěn duō rén zài zhèr yào bǎ yíge dōngxi cóng
135   dǐ-yīge rén chuándao zuì hòu yíge rén, yíge-rén-yíge-rénde chuán-
        guoqu jiàozuo chuándǐ. Dǐ shi shuō de. Chuándǐ shuō huà shíhou
        hěn shǎo yòng. Yǎnjiǎngcíli huòshi xiězuò cháng yòng chuándǐ.

Bái: Háiyǒu gōngyòng zhèige cér zěnmo yòng ne?

Mǎ: Bǐrú yìzhǒng dōngxi suǒ néng gōngji wǒmen de hǎochu jiàozuo gōng-
140   yòng. Jǔ ge lǐzi lai shuō, niú tiānrán duì rénlèi yǒu hǎochu. Tāde
        gōngyòng shi bāng rén zhòng tián.

48.0. jiàngrén   skilled worker, artisan, craftsman   [artisan man]

       mùjiang   carpenter   [wood artisan]

48.1. Yǒu yíge xiǎoxuéshēng shuō tā jiānglái yuànyi zuò jiàngrén, gèng yuànyi dāng mùjiang.

49.0. jìshu   (1) technique, skill; (2) technology   [skill skill]

49.1. Měige guójiā dōu xūyào yǒu zhuānmén jìshude réncái.

49.2. Zhèibù kēxué jìshu zìdiǎn shi Wáng Jiàoshòu biān de.   (T)

50.0. móu   (1) to plan, scheme; (2) seek

       móushēng   make a living, eke out an existence

50.1. Zài lìshǐshang kàn cháng yǒu rén móu shā huángdì.

50.2. Yǒu zhuānmén jìshu de rén móushēng yídìng róngyi.   (T)

51.0. fúlì   welfare, security   [fortune profit]

51.1. Zhèngfǔ yīngdāng gěi rénmín móu fúlì.

52.0. bǎozhàng   safeguard (N/V)   [protect obstacle]

52.1. Zuò duǎngōng de rén rúguǒ méi yǒu gōngzuò jiu méi yǒu gōngqian, suǒyǐ zài shēnghuóshang shi méi yǒu bǎozhàng de.

53.0. zhǐhuī   (1) lead, guide, command, conduct; (2) guidance, command;
                 (3) conductor   [point wield]

53.1. Tā bú huì zhǐhuī rén, yě bú shòu rén zhǐhuī.   (T)

Bái: Mǎ Jiàoshòu, jiàngrén hé gōngren yǒu fēnbié ma?

Mǎ: Jiàngrén shi yǒu jìshu de, lìrú mùjiang, yě shi gōngren de yìzhǒng.

Bái: Zhèli gōngren móushēng róngyi ma? Tāmende fúlì zěnmoyàng?

145 Mǎ: Tāmen móushēng bù hěn nán, fúlì yě hěn hǎo, érqiě shēnghuó hěn
yǒu bǎozhàng. Jiù ná shēng bìng lai shuō ba. Suīrán bú zuò gōng
kěshi yíyàng gěi tāmen gōngqián, suǒyǐ zhèlǐde gōngren zài gōng-
zuòshang fēicháng rènzhēn, érqiě yě hěn tīng zhǐhuī.

Bái: Shì, wǒ kàn bàozhǐshang cháng lùndao wèi gōngren móu fúlì de wèntí.

150 Mǎ: Shì, zhèli tèbié zhùyì gōngrende shēnghuó.

54.0. shī   poem, poetry

shīren   poet

54.1. Wáng Xiānsheng xǐhuan zuò shī, shī yě zuòde hěn hǎo, suǒyǐ dàjiā
dōu shuō tā shi shīren.

54.2. Jùshuō zài Niǔyuēde Zhōngguo rén yǒu hěn duō huì zuò shī de.

55.0. zhào(zhe)   according to

zhàoyàng   (1) follow a pattern exactly (VO); (2) as usual

55.1. Yīnwei tā shi shǐzhǎng, wǒmen yīnggāi zhào tāde yìsi qu zuò.

55.2. Chuàngzào yíjiàn xīnde dōngxi shi hěn nán de. Rúguǒ zhàoyàng zuò
yíjiàn dōngxi, jiu bǐjiào róngyi le.   (T)

56.0. zázhì   magazine, periodical   [miscellaneous record]

56.1. Zài zhèli gèguóde zázhì dōu kéyi mǎidedào.

57.0. zhōukān   a weekly   [cycle print]

57.1. Wǒ yào mǎi yìběn zuìjìnde Kēxué Zhōukān.   (T)

58.0. piān   (1) section, chapter, book (e.g. Book I) (M); (2) (measure for
articles and essays)

58.1. Gāo Xiānsheng xīn xiěli yìpiān wénzhāng shi Duō-zǐ-duō-sūn.   (T)

58.2. Nèiběn shūli fēnwei sānpiān. Dì-yīpiān yǒu sānwàn duō zì, dì-èrpiān
yǒu liǎngwàn duō zì, dì-sānpiān jiù yǒu yíwàn duō zì.

59.0. tōngsú   popular, common   [through vulgar]

59.1. Lù Xiānsheng xiě de xiǎoshuō yǒu hěn duō zhǒnglèi. Yǒu yìzhǒng
shi báihuà xiǎoshuō, nánnü lǎoshào dōu xǐhuan kàn. Yǒu rén shuō
nà shi tōngsú xiǎoshuō.

Bái: Mǎ Jiàoshòu, nín huì zuò shī ma?

Mǎ: Huì shi huì, kěshi wǒ zuòde bù hǎo.

Bái: Zuò shī nán bu nán? Zhōngguo shī shì bu shi yǒu hěn duō zhǒnglèi?

155 Mǎ: Zhōngguo shī yǒu wényánde, yǒu báihuàde. Wényán shī xiāngdāng
nán. Báihuà shī bǐjiào róngyi.

Bái : Yàoshi xué zuò báihuà shī yīnggāi zěnmo xué?

Mǎ : Kāishǐde shíhou xiān niàn biéren xiě de báihuà shī. Niànde duōle
        jiu kéyi zhàoyàng zuò le.

160 Bái: Zuò shī xiān yào zhùyì de shi shénmo?

Mǎ : Zuò shī jiu shi shuō huà, jiu shi yào shuōmíng nǐde yìsi. Yìsi hǎo,
        jùzi hǎo, jiu shi hǎo shī. Zuò shī zuì hǎo shi yòng tōngsúde huà
        xiěchulai, ràng rénrén kàndedǒng.

Bái: Wǒ zuótian kànjian yìběn zázhìshang yǒu piān wénzhāng tídào xiě
165   shī, xiěde hěn xiángxi.

Mǎ : Shénmo zázhìshang?

Bái : Wénxué Zhōukān.

60.0. zhīchi   (1) support(oneself or others); (2) aid, back up   [prop hold]

60.1. Tā dàilai de xuéfèi jǐnjǐnde néng zhīchi yìnián.   (T)

61.0. zhǔchí   have charge (of), have authority (over)   [chief hold]

61.1. Měicì kāi huì dōu shi yóu jiàowu zhǔrèn zhǔchí. Kěshi zhèicì kāi
        huì shi yóu xiàozhǎng zìjǐ zhǔchí de.   (T)

62.0. gòngtóng   mutual, common (W)   [lit. together same]

62.1. Xī-Ōu guójiá jīngji hézuò shi wèile gòngtóng lìyì.   (T)

63.0. yúshi(hū)   (1) thereupon; (2) therefore

63.1. Cháng Jiāng xiàyóu tǔdì hǎo, qìhou hǎo. Yúshihū rénkǒude mìdù bǐ
        biéde dìfang mìde duō le.

63.2. Cóngqián chuántǒngde sīxiǎng shi bú yào líkai jia. Yúshi dào wàiguo
        qù de rén jiu hěn shǎo le.

Bái: Qǐng wèn zhīchí hé zhǔchí yǒu shénmo fēnbié?

Mǎ : Zhīchí yǒu liǎngge yìsi. Bǐrú "Zhèicìde xuánjǔ wǒmen yídìng zhīchí
170   tā chénggōng." Hái yǒu "Wǒde qián zhǐ néng zhīchí yìnián de shēng-
        huó."

Bái: Zhǔchí ne?

Mǎ : Zhǔchí jiu shi zuòzhǔ de yìsi. Bǐrú hěn duō rén gòngtóng zuò yíjiàn
        shì, bìděi yǒu yíge rén lai zhǔchí, yìsi shi yàoshi yǒu rén zuòzhǔ
175   yúshi dàjiā kěyi ànzhào tāde yìsi qu zuò.

64.0. zìyóu   (1) free; (2) freedom   [self by]

64.1. Zài fǎlǜ fànwéi zhīnèi rénrén kéyi zìyóu.   (T)

65.0. zhǔyì   principle, idea, theory, ism   [chief meaning]

        mínzú zhǔyì   nationalism

zìyóu zhǔyì   liberalism

Sānmín Zhǔyì   Three People's Principles (of Sun Yatsen)

65.1. Yǒu rén wèn shénmo jiàozuo zhǔyì? Yǒu rén huídá shuō: "Fánshì yíge xuéshuō yǐjing shíxíngle jiu jiàozuo zhǔyì."

65.2. "Mínzú zhǔyì" shi Sānmín Zhǔyì de yíbùfen.   (T)

65.3. Tāmen cóngqián bù zhīdào shénmo shi zìyóu zhǔyì.

66.0. yuánwén   original text, actual text   [source writing]

66.1. Tā zhèicì xiě de bù gēn yuánwén yíyàng le. Yǒu hěn duō jùzi dōu gǎi le, hái yǒu bù shǎode zì yě huàn le.

67.0. pīping   (1) criticize; (2) criticism   [criticize judge]

67.1. Tā xiěle yìběn shū shi Wénxué Pīping. Duìyu gǔ-jīn Zhōng-wài yǒumíngde wénxué dōu yǒu pīping.

67.2. Zhèiběn shū shi wǒ dìdi xiě de. Qǐng nǐ pīping pīping.

Bái: Wǒ jìde Zhōngshān Xiānsheng zài Sānmín Zhǔyìshang shuōguo zìyóu zhèige cér shi wàiguo chuánlai de. Nándào Zhōngguo méi yǒu zhèige cér ma?

Mǎ : Yǒu. Táng Cháo yǒu yíwèi shīren xiě de shīshang jiu yǒu zìyóu
180   zhèi liǎngge zì. Dànshi nèige shíhou rénde sīxiǎngshang duì zhèi liǎngge zì shi bu shi xiànzài zhèige yìsi ne? Nà wǒmen jiu bù zhīdào le.

Bái: Zài Sānmín Zhǔyìshang zěnmo shuō de wǒ yě wàng le.

Mǎ : Wǒmen zài kànkan Sānmín Zhǔyì shi zěnmo shuō de . . . Zài dì-
185   bāshísìyèshang . . . Zhǎozhao le ma?

Bái: Zhǎozhao le.

Mǎ : Qǐng nǐ xiān kànkan, ránhòu bǎ dàyì shuōyishuō.

Bái: Hǎo . . . Dàyì shì: Ōuzhōu liǎng-sānbǎi nián lái de zhànzhēng chàbu-
        duō dōu shi wèile zìyóu, suǒyǐ Ōu-Měi xuézhě duìyu zìyóu kànde
190   hěn zhòngyào, yìbān rénmín dōu hěn liǎojiě zìyóu shi shénmo yìsi.
        Dànshi zhèige cér jìnlai chuánjìn Zhōngguo, zhǐ yǒu yìbān xuézhě
        dǒngde shénmo jiào zìyóu. Zhìyú pǔtōng rénmín, xiàng zài xiāng-
        cūn huòzhě lùshang de rén, rúguǒ wǒmen shuō zìyóu, tāmen yídìng
        bù dǒngde. Sānmín Zhǔyìde yuánwén shi: "Wàiguo rén pīping
195   Zhōngguo rén shuō Zhōngguo rénde wénmíng chéngdu zhēn shi tài
        dī, sīxiǎng tài yòuzhì, lián zìyóude zhīshi dōu méi yǒu."

Mǎ : Nǐ duì Sānmín Zhǔyìshang wàiguo rén duì Zhōngguo rén guānyu zì-
        yóu de pīping yǒu shénmo yìjian?

Bái: Yǒude wàiguo rén tāmende zhīshi bú gòu. Tāmen bù liǎojiě Zhōng-
200   guo rén, yě bù zhīdào Zhōngguode lìshǐ, suǒyǐ tāmen bù liǎojiě
        Zhōngguo rén chuántǒngde sīxiǎng shi yuànyi zìyóu. Yěxǔ zìyóu
        zhèige cér Zhōngguo rén bú dà zhùyì, kěshi rénrén yào zìyóu, wèi-
        shénmo shuō Zhōngguo rén méi yǒu zìyóude zhīshi ne?

Mǎ : Nǐ shuō de hěn duì . . . Shíjiān dào le. Míngtian jiàn.

205 Bái : Míngtian jian.

SHĒNGCÍ BIĂO

1. suǒwèi

2. jiēji

3. shìdàfū

4. yíxiàng

5. xiǎonóng

6. diànnóng

7. hù
   dàhù
   xiǎohù

8. qióng
   qióngren

9. fù
   fùguì
   fùren

10. jiā
    rénjiā

11. shì*
    Zhōngshì
    Xīshì
    jiùshì
    xīnshì

12. rènhé

13. fúcóng

14. jià
    chūjià
    jiàchū

15. yóu (W)
    yóuyu
    yóu(yu) A (ér) V

16. yíqiè

17. zǔ*
    zǔfù
    zǔmǔ
    zǔxiān

18. dìxiong
    xiōngdì
    xiōngdi

19. jiěmèi

20. pūren (W)

21. jīchǔ

22. shēngchǎn

23. cítáng

24. zǔzong

25. miào
    Kǒngmiào

26. hòudài

27. zé(ren)

28. fù*
    fùzé
    fù zéren

29. (zōng)zú
    tóngzú
    zúzhǎng

30. (yàoshi) . . . de huà

31. shènzhì(yu)

32. wú (W)
    wúlùn
    wúsuǒwèi

33. zìgēngnóng, zìjīngnóng

34. wéichí

35. kǔ
    kǔgōng
    chīkǔ

36. jiēshòu

37. fǎnduì

38. shì (W)

39. cúnzài

40. pǔtōng
    pǔtōnghuà

41. dú
    dúshū

42. díquè

43. dì
    chuándì (W)

44. gōngyòng

45. gōng(ji)

46. tiānrán

47. lèi
    rénlèi
    zhǒnglèi

48. jiàngrén
    mùjiang

49. jìshu

50. móu
    móushēng

51. fúlì

52. bǎozhàng

53. zhǐhuī

54. shǐ
    shǐren

55. zhào(zhe)
    zhàoyàng

56. zázhì

57. zhōukān

58. piān

59. tōngsú

60. zhīchi

61. zhǔchí   64. zìyóu   zìyóu zhǔyì
                                                          Sānmín Zhǔyì
62. gòngtóng (W)   65. zhǔyì   66. yuánwén
63. yúshi(hū)   mínzú zhǔyì   67. pīping

YÚFǍ LIÀNXÍ

A. Resultative verbs with de/bu + lái (see note 1)

1. Wǒ xiōngdi suīrán bǐ wǒ xiǎo shísuì, kěshi wǒmen liǎngge rén hěn tándelái.

2. Jiào wǒ shuō pǔtōnghuà wǒ shuōdelái, Guǎngdong huà wǒ kě shuōbulái.

3. Yàoshi yòng kuàizi chī fàn de huà nǐ yòngdelái yòngbulái?

4. Wǒ suīrán hěn xīwang yǒu gōngzuò, kěshi nèi yílèide shì wǒ zuòbulái.

5. Suīrán wǒ Zhōngwén shū dúle bù shǎo, kěshi Zhōngguo zì lián yíge yě xiě-
   bulái.

B. zhǐ yǒu N/S cái V (see note 2)

6. Zhèige zéren zhǐ yǒu Zhāng Xiānsheng cái néng fù.

7. Zhǐ yǒu Mǎ Xiānsheng zhīchi wǒ, cái néng bǎ nèijiàn shìqing zuòchénggōng.

8. Fēi wǒ zǔfù zuò zúzhǎng tāmen cái bu fǎnduì.

9. Zhǐ yǒu wǒ qù zuò gōng cái néng wéichí yìjiā rén de shēnghuó gēn gōng
   wǒ liǎngge háizi niàn shū.

10. Wǒ jiějie shuō yàoshi tā jiēhūn de huà, fēi Máo Xiānsheng tā cái jià.

C. V N de (see note 3)

11. Tā shi zuò shī de, tā shi yíge hěn yǒumíngde shīren.

12. Nǐmen dúshū de dōu kéyi cānjiā nèige kǎoshì.

13. Zuò mùjiang de hěn chīkǔ.

14. Tā bú shi dà dìzhǔ, shi diànnóng, shi zhòngdì de.

15. Wáng Xiānsheng bìng bú shi fùren, tā hěn qióng. Yīnwei tā shi ge jiāo-
    shū de, suóyǐ tā gōngjibuliǎo tā érzi niàn dàxué.

D. bǐ QW dōu (see note 4)

16. Zhāng Dàwén díquè shi bǐ shéi dōu cōngming. Shàng kè xiānsheng jiǎng
    de biéren hái méi dǒng ne, tā wánquán dōu huì le.

17. Wǒ zài Sānfánshì mǎi de nèiběn Hàn Yīng Zìdiǎn bǐ rènhé yìběn dōu
    xiángxi.

18. Wǒmen jiā nèi yídài zhǐ yǒu liǎng-sānjiā rénjiā. Chē shǎo rén yě shǎo,
    bǐ nǎr dōu hǎo.

19. Tā shuō nèibĕn xiăoshuō bĭ nĕibĕn xiăoshuō
    xiĕde dōu hăo, hĕn tōngsú. Wúlùn nĭ yŏu xué-
    wen méi xuéwen dōu kàndedŏng.

20. Zhōngguo rénmín bĭ nĕiguóde rénmín dōu néng
    chīkŭ.

JIĂNGHUÀ

Gèwèi Tóngxué:

   Jīntian wŏ suŏ jiăng de tímu shi Zhōngguode shèhuì jiégòu. Zhōngguo shèhuì zài zhèi
jĭshí niánli yŏu hĕn dàde găibiàn. Yào dŏngde
5 xiànzàide shèhuì, bìdĕi xiān míngbai cóngqiánde
shèhuì. Wŏmen jīntian jiu jiăng cóngqiánde
shèhuì jiégòu. Xiànzài yào shuō de yŏu liăngdiăn. Dì-yī yào shuō Zhōngguo shèhuìlide jiēji shi zĕnmoyàng? Dì-èr yào shuō Zhōngguo
10 shèhuìde zhōngxīn shi shénmo?

   Zhōngguo shèhuìlide jiēji kéyi fēnwei sìjí,
jiu shi shì, nóng, gōng, shāng. Shì jiu shi zhīshi
fènzĭ, shi dì-yījí, dìwèi zuì gāo. Nóng yīnwei
nóngyè shi Zhōngguo jīngjide jīchŭ, suŏyĭ bă
15 nóngmín jiu fàngzai dì-èrwèi. Gōng-shāng liăng-
jí zài chuántŏng sīxiăngli zuì dī le. Zhèli suŏ
shuō de <u>gōng</u> bìng bú shi xiàng Mĕiguo suŏwèi
gōngren, ér shi shŏugōngyède jiàngren. Gōngde
dìwei hái bĭ shāngrén gāo yìdiăr. Shāngren dì-
20 wei zuì dī, yīnwei chuántŏngde kànfă rènwei
shāngren zìjĭ shénmo yĕ bú zuò, yóu măimàili
ér dédao lìyi, bú shi zhēnzhèng shēngchăn de
rén. Zhōngguo shāngren gēn Xīfāng guójiāde
shāngren yĕ yŏu bùtóngde dìfang. Zhōngguo
25 shāngren yàoshi yŏule qián jiu qu măi tŭdì, jiu
yào biàncheng yíge dìzhŭ jiēji.

   Zhōngguo shèhuìli zuì zhŭyàode kéyi shuō
shi liăng dà jiēji. Dì-yī shi shìdàfū, bāokuò

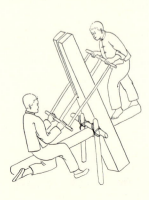

suǒyǒu zhīshi fènzǐ, dìzhǔ hé zuò guān de. Zhǐ yǒu zhīshi jiēji cái kéyi
30 zuò guān. Dì-èr jiu shi nóngmín jiēji. Zhè shi zhǐ xiǎonóng shuō de.
Zhèi liǎngge jiējide shēnghuó dà bu xiāngtóng. Shìdàfū jiēji shi yóu dúshū
ér zuò guān, hòulai jiu chéngle tǒngzhì jiēji. Zhèige jiēji yě shi chuándì
Zhōngguo wénhuà de yíge jiēji, yīnwei zhǐ yǒu shìdàfū jiēji yǒu xiāngdāngde
zhīshi gēn shíjiān lai yánjiu xuéwen, yánjiu Zhōngguode lìshǐ, yánjiu
35 Zhōngguode wénhuà, shènzhìyu zuò shǐ, xiě wénzhāng, huà huàr déngděng
yílèide shìqing. Nóngmín jiēji ne? Wǒmen shuō nóngmín jiēji shi zhǐ
xiǎo zìgēngnóng huòzhě shi diànnóng lai jiǎng. Yàoshi yíge nóngmín biànchéngle dà dìzhǔ yǐhòu, tā zìjǐ jiu bú zhòngtián, tā jiu bú shi nóngmín,
tā biàncheng dìzhǔ jiēji le. Tāde érzi yě kéyi niàn shū, shū dúhǎo cānjiā
40 kējǔde kǎoshì, yúshi chéngle shìdàfū jiēji, zuò guān qu le. Nóngmín jiēji
yíxiàng shi zhàn rénmínli zuì dàde yíbùfen. Xiǎo zìgēngnóng gēn diànnóng
jiù shi bèi tǒngzhì de jiēji.

Xiànzài shuō Zhōngguo shèhuì zǔzhide zhōngxīn shi shénmo? Zhōngguo shèhuì shi yíge ná jiātíng hé zōngzú zuò zhōngxīn de shèhuì. Shénmo
45 jiàozuo dà jiātíng hé zōngzú zhìdu ne? Dà jiātíng jiu shi zǐsūn duōde
jiātíng. Yíhù bāokuò liǎngdài yǐshàngde rén. Zài zhèizhǒng jiātíng rénkǒu
bǐjiǎo duō. Yǒu fùqin, mǔqin, yǐjing jiēhūn de érzi, háiyǒu méi chūjià de
nǚer, yǒu xǔduō sūnzi, sūnnǚer hái yǒu pūren děngděng. Zài zhèizhǒng
dà jiātíngli yíqiè shì dōu yóu jiāzhǎng lai zhǔchí. Dàjiā wèile wéichí
50 zhèige jiātíng ér fúcóng jiāzhǎng. Nènmo shénmo shi zōngzú ne? Zōngzú
shi yíge zǔzong chuánxialai de, bāokuò hěn duō hù, kěnéng yǒu dàhù,
kěnéng yǒu xiǎohù. Zhèi xǔduō hù dōu shi yíge zǔzongde hòudài. Tóngzúde rén yǒude shi fùguì rénjiā, yǒude shi qióng rénjiā, kěshi dàjiā gòngtóng yǒu yíge cítáng. Yǒule wúlùn rènhé dàshì de huà yǒngyuǎn yào tīng
55 yíge zúzhǎngde zhǐhuī. Zhèi jiu shi dà jiātíng hé zōngzú zhìdu de dàgài
qíngxing.

Yǒu rén shuō zhèizhǒng dà jiātíng zhìdu zài shèhuì díquè yě yǒu
yìzhǒng gōngyòng, tā néng gěi rén yíge jīngji bǎozhàng, tóngshí yǒu hǎoxiàng shi gěi rén yìzhǒng tiānránde shèhuì fúlìde bǎozhàng. Yìsi jiu shi
60 shuō rén yàoshi méi fázi zìjǐ móushēng de huà, dà jiātíng yào fùzé gōngji
tāde shēnghuó. Zhèizhǒng shuōfǎ hǎoxiàng yě yǒu yìdiǎr dàoli. Qíshí
zhèizhǒng dà jiātíng shi bǐjiǎo fùde rénjiā. Zhōngguo tōngsú yǒu yíjù huà

shi "dàhù rénjiā." Zhè jiu shi shuō zhèijiā rén bú shi qióngren, xiāngdāngde yǒuqián. Nénggou zhīchí yíge dà jiātíng xǔduō niándài de shēnghuó,
65   duōbàn shi shìdàfū jiējí hé yǒuqiánde shāngren. Yàoshi nǐ dào xiāngcūnli
qu kàn yìbān xiǎo zìgēngnóng, bù nénggou yǒu zhèizhǒng dà jiātíng.
Pǔtōngde nóngren jiāli rénkǒu bìng bù tài duō. Zhèizhǒng jiùshì dà jiātíng
hé zōngzú zhìdu, dàole èrshi shìjǐ yīnwei shòule Xīfāng wénhuàde yǐngxiǎng, jiu méi fázi zhàoyàng cúnzài le.   Yìbān qīngnián rén yóuyu jiē-
70   shòule Xīfāng wénhuàde zìyóu zhǔyì, dōu fǎnduì zhèizhǒng jiùde zhìdu le.

FÙSHÙ

Zhèipán lùyīndài shi Zhōngwén dì-yīzǔ dì-liùhào, Bái Wénshān fùshù
dì-liùcìde Zhuāntí Jiǎnghuà.

Zhèicì Zhuāntí Jiǎnghuàde zhǔjiǎngrén shi lìshǐxìde Biān Jiàoshòu.
Tā jiǎng de shi Zhōngguo mínzú.   Tā shuō yīnwei shíjiānde guānxi bù
5   nénggou bǎ zhěnggèr Zhōnghuá mínzú cóng kāishǐ jiǎngqǐ, zhǐ néng cóng
Mínguó chūnián jiǎngqǐ.   Tā shuō zài Mínguó chūnián de shíhou Zhōngguode guóqí hé xiànzàide bùtóng.   Nèige shíhou shi wǔsè guóqí, jiu shi
yìmiàn guóqíshang yǒu wǔzhǒng yánse—hóng, huáng, lán, bái, hēi. Zhèi
wǔzhǒng yánse shi dàibiǎo wǔge mínzú, wǔzú gònghé.   Kěshi zài shíjì-
10   shang bù zhǐ shi wǔge mínzú.   Dàgài yǒu liùshijǐge mínzú.   Jiēzhe yòu
gěi wǒmen fēnxi měi yíge mínzúde tèdiǎn gēn tāmen fēnbù zài shénmo
dìfang.   Tā kāishǐ xiān shuō Hànzú, qícì shuō biéde mínzú.

Tā shuō Hànzúde rénshù zhàn zhěnggèr Zhōnghuá mínzúde bǎifēnzhī-
jiǔshisì.   Tā yòu shuō Hànzú dà bùfen zài Zhōngguo nèidì.   Xīnjiāng、
15   Dōngběi yě yǒu Hànzú.   Yòu shuōdao Mǎnzú.   Qīng Cháo jiu shi Mǎnzhōu
rén zuò huángdì tǒngzhì Zhōngguo. Tāmen tǒngzhìle Zhōngguo èrbǎi liùshi duō nián.   Mǎnzú hòulai bèi Hànzú tónghuà le, suǒyǐ zài wénhuà hé
fēngsu xíguàn děngděng fāngmiàn dōu hé Hànzú yíyàng le.   Suīrán xiànzài hái yǒu èrbǎi duō wàn Mǎnzhōu rén, tāmen hé Hàn rén méi duō dàde
20   fēnbié le.

Yòu shuōdao Měngzú.   Měnggú rén yě zuòguo Zhōngguode huángdì,
jiu shi Yuán Cháo. Zhōngguo tǔdì kuòzhǎn zuì dàde yào suàn Yuán Cháo
le. Tāmen yǐjing dǎdao Ōuzhōude dōngbù qu le. Nèige shíhou Yuán Cháo
kéyi shuō shi zuì dàde guójiā. Měnggǔ rén xìn Lǎma jiào, yě shi Fójiào-

25   de yìzhǒng. Měnggǔ yǒu Měnggǔde wénzì. Tāmen xiànzài bú yòng yǐqiánde

wénzì le, yīnwei xiànzài tāmende wénzì gǎigé le, yòng pīnyīn zì le.

Huízú shi cóng Táng Cháo láidao Zhōngguo de. Huízú dà bùfen zài

Zhōngguode xīběibù, xiàng Xīnjiāng, Gānsu, Qīnghǎi děng dìfang. Tāmen

yǒu tāmende zōngjiào. Tāmen xìn Huíjiào. Huízú rén hái yǒu ge míngzi

30   jiào Huíhui.

Zàngzú zài Xīzàng, Qīnghǎi yídài. Tāmen yǒu èrbǎi qīshi wàn rén.

Tāmen yǒu wénzì, shi Zàngwén. Tāmende zōngjiào yě shi Lǎmajiào.

Yǐshàng suǒ shuō de shi rénkǒu duō de mínzú. Yòu shuōdao rénkǒu

shǎode mínzú. Tā shuō rénkǒu zài yìbǎi wàn yǐshàngde shǎoshù mínzú,

35   zài xīnán yǒu Miáozú, Zhòngjiā, Yízú, Zhuàngzú; xīběi yǒu Wéiwǔ'ér;

Dōngběi yǒu Cháoxiǎnzú. Chúle shàngmian suǒ shuō de mínzú yǐwài, hái

yǒu yìxiē shǎoshù mínzú yīnwei jiāotōng bù fāngbian de guānxi, tāmende

wénhuà luòhòu, shēnghuó hé fēngsu xíguàn gēn Hànzú yìdiǎr yě bù yíyàng.

Xiànzài zhèngfǔ zài shǎoshù mínzú dìdài shèlìle mínzú zìzhìqū.

40   Zuìhòu Biān Jiàoshòu shuō, ànzhào zhěnggè Zhōngguo lìshǐ lai shuō,

Hànzú chuàngzàole Zhōngguode wénhuà, Hànzú shi Zhōnghuá mínzúde

zhōngxīn. Hòulai yòu shuō mínzú bǐcǐ xiāngchǔ de qíngxing. Tā shuō

yǐqián wèile zhēngduó tǔdì shícháng dǎzhàng. Xiànzài dàjiāde sīxiǎng dōu

gǎibiàn le. Gè mínzú dōu xīwang bǐcǐ hépíng xiāngchǔ le.

WĒNXI

1. Jù rén chuánshuō, biānjìngde zhànshi yǐjing kuòdà, línjìnde chéngshì dōu
   chéngle zhànshi zhuàngtài. Zhìyú shíjì qíngxing jiūjìng shi zěnmoyàng, fēi
   děngdào biānjìng láile rén cái néng zhīdao.

2. Yǒu yíwèi yǔyánxuéjiā jìnlái yánjiu Zhōngguo yǔyán xìtǒng. Yǒu rén wèn
   tā Zhuàngzú, Huízúde yǔyán shi shǔyu něi yíge xìtǒng? Yòu wèn tā Cháoxiǎnzú suǒ shuō de Cháoxiǎn huà shi bu shi Zhōngguo yǔyán xìtǒng? Tā
   huídá shuō, Huízú yǔyán jiu shi Zhōngguo huà, Cháoxiǎnzúde yǔyán bu shi
   Zhōngguo yǔyán xìtǒng. Zhuàngzú yǔyán shi něi yíge xìtǒng, xiànzài zhèng
   yánjiu ne.

3. Yǒu yíwèi rénkǒuxuéjiā zài yìběn zázhìshang xiěle yìpiān wénzhāng shi
   "Dōngfāng shǎoshù mínzúde zōngjiào." Yǒu rén wèn tā xìn Lǎmajiào de
   Lǎma, xìn Huíjiào de Huíhui dōu fēnbùzai shénmo dìfang? Jízhōng zài
   shénmo dìfang? Tāmende dòngtài zěnmoyàng? Yǒu méi yǒu hé Hànzú
   tónghuà de? Tā shuō: "Qǐng nǐ kànkan wǒ xiě de nèipiān wénzhāng, nà
   jiu shi gěi nǐmen míngbai zhèige wèntí de."

4. Zài zhōng shìjì de shíqī yǒu xiē guójiā chángcháng wèile zhēngduó lǐngtǔ
   qǐle zhànzhēng, měi yíge guójiā suǒ shòu de sǔnhài jiǎnzhí méi fázi tǒngjì.

5. Zhāng Xiānsheng shi <u>Hànyǔ Zhōukānde</u> biānzhě. Tā shuō: "Xuéxi Hànyǔ
   yào xiān xué pīnyīn. Yīn huì pīnle yǐhòu, qícì xué huìhuà. Yòu qícì xué
   rènzì. Wǒ zuìjìn kànjian yìběn Hànyǔ kèběn, yǒu sìbǎi duō yè, shūde
   nèiróng jiu shi zhèiyàng xiě de."

6. Yàoshi yǒu rén lái dǎ wo, wǒ shì bu shi yào dǐkàng ne? Rúguǒ bù dǐkàng,
   bú shi bèi rénjia dǎle ma? Rúguǒ dǐkàng de huà, nà bú shi wǒ yě dǎ rén
   le ma?

7. Shāmò dìdài yīnwei shuǐ shǎo suǒyǐ rénjia yě hěn xīshǎo. Rúguǒ yǒu yíge
   dìfang yǒu dàliàngde shuǐ, nènmo hěn kuài jiu yǒu hěn duō rénjiā le. Yǒu
   yícì wǒ zài shāmò lǚxíng, zǒule yuē yǒu yìbǎi duō lǐ cái kànjian yìjiā rénjiā. Zhèijiā rénjiā yǒu yíge xiǎoháizi. Wǒ wèn ta: "Nǐ zhīdao shénmo
   shi hǎi ma?" Tā hǎoxiang bù dǒng wǒde huà shide. Zhèi háizide yìshili
   gēnběn méi yǒu hǎi.

8. Zhōngguo zài Mínguó chūnián shi wǔzú gònghéguó. Yǒu rén shuō gònghé
   zhìdu shi Zhōngguo gǔshí jiu yǒu le, bú shi cóng wàiguo chuánlai de.

9. Kàngzhànde shíhou wǒ zài Sìchuān Dì-Sì Zhōngxué niàn shū. Hěn duō
   tóngxué yào dào Xīkāng qu lǚxíng. Tāmen wèn wǒ qù bu qù. Wǒ shuō
   wǒ wúsuǒwèi, qù bu qù dōu kéyi. Wǒmen zhèixiē qīngnián rén dào Xīkāng
   de mùdì yě jiu shi shàng shān qu.

10. Zhōngguo zhèngfǔ zài yī-jiǔ-wǔ-sān nián diàochá Zhōngguode rénkǒu yǐjing
    yǒu liùyì yìbǎi jiǔshí duō wàn rén le. Àn yìbān rén de kànfǎ xiànzài
    yǐjing yǒu qīyì rén le.

11. Sūn Zhōngshān Xiānsheng tíchàng <u>Sānmín Zhǔyì</u>. <u>Sānmín Zhǔyìli</u> yǒu
    "mínzú zhǔyì." Cóngqián yǒu rén pīping "mínzú zhǔyì." Wǒ zuìjìn kàndao
    "mínzú zhǔyi" de yuánwén, wǒ rènwei méi yǒu shénmo kéyi pīping de.

12. Wǒ zǔmǔ duì wǒ shuō: "Wǒ zài méi jiàchū de shíhou wǒ jiālide dìxiong
    jiěmèi hěn duō. Wǒ jǐge xiōngdi dōu yào xué pǔtōnghuà, wǒmen jiāli jiu
    qǐngle yíwei jiāo pǔtōnghuà de xiānsheng, tiāntiān lai jiāo pǔtōnghuà. Zhèi-
    wèi jiāo pǔtōnghuà de xiānsheng hòulai jiù shi nǐde zǔfù."

13. Nèige mùjiang jìshu hěn hǎo. Zhōngshìde, Xīshìde dōngxi tā dōu huì zuò.
    Tā shuō zài tāde xiǎngfǎ wúsuǒwèi Zhōngshì, Xīshì dōu shi yíyàngde zuò.

14. Rénlèi wèi-shénmo shícháng yǒu zhànzhēng? Rúguǒ rénlèi méi yǒu zhàn-
    zhēng, shìjiè wénmíng yídìng gèng jìnbù le.

15. Yǒu rén wèn wǒ Zhōngguo wèi-shénmo yǒu hěn duō miào? Yòu wèi-shénmo
    yǒu Kǒngmiào? Wǒ shuō zhèige wèntí hěn fùzá, bú shi yì-liǎngjù huà jiu
    néng huídá de.

16. Yǒu yíge wáiguo rén shuō: "Zhōngguo rén chī dōngxi de shíhou yòng de
    yìzhǒng dōngxi hǎoxiàng shi liǎngzhī qiānbǐ. Nèizhǒng dōngxi jiào shénmo
    míngzi?" Yǒu rén gàosu ta nà jiào kuàizi, yòu gàosu tā wàiguo rén yòng
    kuàizi chī dōngxi hěn bù róngyi, yàoshi yòng kuàizi chī jiǎozi gèng bù
    róngyi.

WÈNTÍ

1. Zhōngguo cóngqiánde shèhuî fēnwei jǐge jiēji? Dōu shi shénmo jiēji?
   Něige jiēji shi dî-yīwèi? Dî-èrwèi ne? Shénmo jiēji zuî dī? Wèi-shénmo
   zuî dī?

2. Zhōngguo cóngqiánde shèhuî suǒwèi gōngrén hé xiànzài Měiguode gōngren
   shi yíyàng ma? Rúguǒ bù yíyàng Zhōngguo gōngren shi shǔyu něi yílèi de?

3. Zhōngguo cóngqiánde shèhuî zuî zhǔyàode liǎngge jiēji shi shénmo jiēji?
   Zhèi liǎngge jiējide shēnghuó shi yíyàng ma? Rúguǒ bù yíyàng de huà,
   tāmende shēnghuó shi zěnmoyàng de?

4. Zhōngguo cóngqiánde shèhuî jiégòu shi ná shénmo zuò zhōngxīn? Shénmo
   jiàozuo dà jiātíng zhìdu? Dà jiātíng zhìdu yǒu shénmo gōngyòng? Wèi-
   shénmo xiānzài bù néng cúnzài le?

5. Shénmo shi zōngzú? Tóngzú rénde jīngji zhuàngkuàng dōu xiāngtóng ma?
   Tōngzúde rén yào tīng shénmo rén zhǐhuī?

6. Nóngmín jiēji shi zhǐzhe něizhǒng nóngren shuō de? Nóngmín zìjǐ bú
   zhòng tián tā jiu biàncheng shénmo jiēji le?

7. Zhōngguo cóngqiánde shèhuî shénmo rén shi tǒngzhì jiēji?

8. Shénmo shi diànnóng? Shénmo shi xiǎo zìgēngnóng? Shénmo shi xiǎonóng?

9. Dà jiātíng yíqiède shì dōu yóu shéi zhǔchí? Dà jiātínglide rén duìyu jiāzhǎng yīnggāi zěnmoyàng? Wèi-shénmo ne?

10. Shénmo jiàozuo dàhù? Shénmo shi xiǎohù? Dàhù rénjiā duōbàn shi shénmo
    jiēji? Xiāngcūnli yě yǒu dàhù ma? Dàhù hé dà jiātíng yǒu fēnbié ma?
    Yǒu shénmo fēnbié?

ILLUSTRATIVE SENTENCES (ENGLISH)

3.1. The gentry class refers to scholars and officials.

5.1. Hello! This is Zhang Youshan. (About) my asking you yesterday to go find
     how many small peasants there are in that village, did you make the study?

6.1. Sun Yatsen advocated that those who till the land should all have their own
     land, that is to say, that there should be no tenant farmers.

7.2. In the last war the rich and the poor families were all forced to move away.

8.1. That man isn't poor. At least there's no question about his present liveli-
     hood.

10.1. The Chinese concern for the family has always been very deep.

10.2. In Kweichou there are many mountains and few people. A village may have
      only a few families.

10.4. Our family has been tenant farmers for generations. We've always worked
      the land of the great families.

10.5. Mr. Wang has administered that district very well.   Every family [of the people] has food to eat.

11.3. There are all sorts of flags hanging outside [the door of] the United Nations.

12.1. He's not willing to belong to any kind of organization.

13.1. Old-style families absolutely had to go along with everything that the head of the family said.

14.3. Why do you say your older sister can't get married?

15.3. Owing to the fact that the cities along the frontier are all in [lit. have all become] a wartime situation, all industrial and commercial enterprises have been affected.

17.1. His grandfather and grandmother said that when they were in middle school the national flag was the five-color flag.   On commemorative days every family had to hang up a flag.

17.2. Ours is a big household.   Grandfather, grandmother, and everyone often quarreled [lit. mutually developed views], and when they did they invariably wouldn't speak to each other for days.

18.3. The national minorities help each other like brothers.

19.1. All five sisters know German.

21.1. The courses in that university are very hard. Unless you have had a good foundation [in the courses] in middle school [otherwise] you certainly won't be able to keep up.

21.2. (The reason why) my tones are inaccurate is that [lit. because] my grounding in pronunciation wasn't good.

22.1. In order to expand the economy it is necessary to increase production.

25.1. There are temples everywhere in China.   There are so many temples throughout the country that it is impossible to count them.

27.1. That matter wasn't attended to properly. We must make an analysis as to whose responsibility that was.

28.2. If he won't assume the responsibility, please tell, who should assume it?

29.2. People of the same clan should join firmly together.   Otherwise they couldn't face their ancestors.

32.2. The editorials in every newspaper say those two countries will go to war because of the frontier territory.

34.2. In one month I (have) wages of only $50. How can I support [the livelihood of] a family?

35.3. The life of those workers grows more difficult year by year.

36.1. None of us can accept the conditions he has stipulated [lit. spoken].

38.1. A shì [scholar] is a learned person. In the Chinese society of the past the scholar's position was higher than that of the peasants, artisans, and merchants.

41.2. All of our family for several generations have been scholars.

43.2. Those stones were handed up to the second floor from one worker to another.

44.1. The lower reaches of the Yangtze River do not often suffer from flood. For the most part this is due to [lit. is the function of] Tungting Lake.

45.1. I provide him assistance to study abroad.

45.2. His tuition and living expenses are all provided by me.

45.3. I must help my two daughters to obtain a college education.

45.4. Now I have two ideas to give you for your consideration.

47.2. War brings great harm to mankind

49.2. This dictionary of science and technology was compiled by Professor Wang.

50.2. People who have a specialized skill certainly find it easy to make a living.

53.1. He can't lead people, and he can't accept leadership from (other) people.

55.2. To create a new thing is very difficult. If one follows a pattern in making something, it is comparatively easy.

57.1. I'd like to buy a copy of the latest Science Weekly.

58.1. Mr. Gao has recently written a novel Many Sons, Many Grandsons.

60.1. The tuition (money) he's brought can barely maintain him for a year.

61.1. Every time there's a meeting it is run by the dean. But this meeting was run by the president himself.

62.1. Economic cooperation among the West European countries is for the benefit of all.

64.1. Within the scope of the law everyone can be free.

65.2. 'Nationalism' is one part of the Three People's Principles.

NOTES

1. The verb lái (lit. 'come') is used with de and bu to form the positive and negative potential forms of resultative verbs. The form without de and bu does not occur:

> chǐdelái   'able to eat'

> chǐbulái   'unable to eat'

2. The pattern zhǐ yǒu S cái V means 'only if S then V':

> Zhǐ yǒu nǐ duō gěi ta qián tā cái néng màigei ni.   'He'll be able to sell it to you only if you give him more money.'

In the pattern zhǐ yǒu N cái V the phrase zhǐ yǒu N means 'only N.' The noun in question is grammatically related to the following sentence as subject, object, etc.

Zhǐ yōu Wáng Xiānsheng cái néng jiào nǐmen. 'Only Mr. Wang can teach you.'

Zhèibĕn shū zhǐ yŏu Wáng Xiānsheng wŏ cái gĕi. 'I'll give this book only to Mr. Wang.'

In this pattern zhǐ yŏu is replaceable by fēi.

3. The pattern V N de means 'one who V's.' Some of the phrases are so well established that they function as names of occupations:

Tā shi ge yăn diànyĭngr de. 'He's a movie actor' (lit. one who acts in movies.)

Zuò măimai de yĕ kéyi zuò guān ma? 'Can (those who are) merchants become officials?'

Tā shi măimài fángzi de. 'He [is one who] buys and sells houses.'

4. The pattern bǐ QW dōu SV means 'more SV than any other . . . ,' the blank being filled by some expression appropriate to the question-word:

bǐ shéi dōu hăo   'better than any other person'

bǐ shénmo dōu guì   'more expensive than anything else'

bǐ nĕibĕn shū dōu yŏu yòng   'more useful than any other book'

bǐ năr dōu rè   'hotter than any other place'

The word rènhé 'any' followed by a noun is used in the same pattern in place of a question word:

bǐ rènhé rén dōu hăo   'better than any other person'

5. In addition to its use as a noun meaning 'house,' 'home' or 'family,' the word jiā also functions as a measure word for homes, families, branches of stores, and other establishments, as in yìjiā fànguăr 'a restaurant.' It also enters into two combinations rénjiā 'a home' and rénjia 'people' or 'other people' which need to be carefully distinguished. The following are examples of the use of these terms:

Rénjia dōu shuō ta shi hăo rén. 'Everyone says he's a nice person.'

Nèr dōu shi shāmò. Yìjiā rénjiā dōu méi yŏu. 'It's all desert there. There isn't a single house.'

Dì-Jiǔkè. Fāmíng

Bái: Mǎ Jiàoshòu zǎo.

Mǎ: Zǎo. Zuótian wǎnshang xià yǔ le. Jīntian zǎoshang xiāngdāng lěng.

Bái: Kěbushìma! Zuótian wǎnshang Gāo Xiānsheng jiào wǒ dào tā fǔshang qu chī wǎnfàn. Chīwán fàn wǒ cái dào jiā jiu xiàqi yǔ lai le.

5   Mǎ: Gāo Xiānsheng tāmen dōu hǎo ma?

Bái: Dōu hǎo. Gāo Xiānsheng, Gāo Tàitai hái tídao nín le. Tāmen shuō guò jǐtiān yào dào nín fǔshang qu kàn nín qu.

Mǎ: Wǒ yě shi lǎo méi gōngfu qù kàn tāmen.

Bái: Gāo Xiānsheng jìnlái yòu zuò shī ne.

10 Mǎ: Lǎo Gāo yíxiàng jiu xǐhuan xiě zì zuò shī.

Bái: Gāo Tàitai hěn yǒu běnshi. Jiāli yíqiè de shìqing dōu yóu Gāo Tàitai zhǔchí. Gāo Xiānsheng zài jiā méi shì, yě jiu shi xiěxie zì, zuò-zuo shī.

Mǎ: Zuótian de Zhuāntí Jiǎnghuà nǐ lùyīn le ma?

15 Bái: Lù le. Zuótian suǒ jiǎng de shi Zhōngguode shèhuì jiégòu. Wǒ tīngguo yǐhòu, liǎojiěle liǎngjiàn shìqing. Yíge shi shénmo shi shì-dàfū. Yíge shi shénmo shi dà jiātíng hé zōngzú zhìdu. Yǐqián wǒ bú da liǎojiě zhè liǎngge wèntí. Xiànzài dōu qīngchu le.

Mǎ: Hǎojíle. Jīntian jiǎng Zhōngguode fāmíng. Zhèicìde jiǎnghuà nèiróng
20 gēn cér dàoshi méi shénmo. Wǒ xiāngxìn nǐ méi yǒu hěn duō bù dǒng de. Nǐ xiān kànyikàn, wǒmen zài yánjiu.

Bái: Wǒ xiǎng wǒ háishi bù dǒng de duō.

Mǎ: Bù dǒng de wǒmen jiu yánjiu.

1.0. sī   (raw) silk

1.1. Yòng sī zuòde dōngxi, duōbàn shi fùren yòng de.

2.0. chóu(zi)   silk cloth

2.1. Nǐ zhīdao yóu sī zěnmo zuò chóuzi ma?

3.0. duàn(zi)   satin

     chóuduàn   silk and satin

3.1. Xiǎonóng jiējí hěn shǎo mǎi duànzi.

3.2. Xǐhuan mǎi chóuduàn de rén duōbàn shi shìdàfū jiējí.

4.0. zhī   weave

4.1. Tā jiā cónglái jiu kàozhe zhī chóuduàn wéichí shēnghuó.

5.0. pǐn*   goods, stuff, article

rìyòngpǐn   article of daily use

sīzhīpǐn   article made of silk

5.1. Nǚ-háizi chūjià de shíhou, dōu mǎi bù shǎo rìyòngpǐn gēn sīzhīpǐn
      shénmode.

5.2. Cóngqiánde sīzhīpǐn yàoshi jīngguo niándài tài jiǔ le jiù biàn yánse
      le.

Bái: Mǎ Jiàoshòu, zuótian jiēdào wǒ mǔqinde xìn shuō péngyoude nǚer
25   yào chūjià le, tā shuō xiǎng mǎi Zhōngguo sīzhīpǐn sònggei nèiwèi
      xiáojie. Wǒ yòu děi qù máfan Měiyīng le.

Mǎ : Zhōngguo sīzhīpǐn zhǒnglèi hěn duō. Mǎi zhèilèide dōngxi bǐděi tài-
      tai xiáojiemen. Nǐ mǔqin xǐhuan Zhōngguo chóuduàn ma?

Bái: Tā tài xǐhuan le. Qián jǐtian wǒ hái gěi ta mǎile yíjiàn, yě shi
30   Měiyīng gěi xuǎn de.

Mǎ : Zhōngguo duànzi 'shí hǎo. Dōu shi zhēn sīde.

Bái: Búdàn shi zhēn sīde, érqiě zhǐde yě hǎokàn.

6.0. chóngzi   insect

6.1. Tiánli zhòng de dōngxi dōu bèi chóngzi chǐ le. Wúlùn diànnóng,
      zìgēngnóng jīnniánde shēnghuó dōu chéng wèntí le.

7.0. cán   silkworm

7.1. Zhōngguo jiāngnán de rénjiā wúlùn dàhù, xiǎohù dōu xǐhuan yǎng
      cán.

8.0. tǔ   spit (out)

tù   vomit, spew forth

8.1. Nǐ bú yào wàng dìxia tǔ dōngxi.

8.2. Wǒ zuì xiǎo de xiōngdi bù zhīdào chǐle shénmo dōngxi, cái chǐwán
      fàn jiu tù le.

Bái: Tù sī de nèizhǒng chóngzi jiào shénmo míngzi? Wǒ wàng le.

Mǎ : Jiào cán. Sān Zì Jīngshang yǒu yíjù "Cán tù sī." Cán kànjianguo
35   méi you?

Bái: Wǒ méi kànjianguo. Měiguo gēnběn méi yǒu. Shàngcì zài zhèli yě
      méi jīhui kànjian zhèizhǒng dōngxi.

Mǎ : Wǒ yǒu ge péngyou xǐhuan yǎng cán. Wǒmen kéyi dào tā nèr qu
      kànkan qu.

9.0.   réngōng   (1) human labor; (2) man-made, artificial

9.1.   Xī Húde shānshuǐ shi tiānránde, bú shi réngōng de.

10.0. xiàn   thread

       sīxiàn   silk thread

       wúxiàndiàn   radio   [lack thread electricity]

10.1. Bǎ sī zuòchéng xiàn jiàozuo sīxiàn. Zuò sīxiàn yě shi yìzhǒng jìshu.
       Bìděi yǒu jiàngrén cái néng zuò.   (T)

10.2. Xiànzài yǒu wúxiàndiànde rénjiā tài duō le, shènzhìyú xiāngxia rénjiā
       yě yǒu le.

11.0. yīfu   clothing   [clothing garment]

11.1. Nèige rén yīfude yàngzi shi jiùshì de.

12.0. chuān   wear

12.1. Tāmen xiōngdì dōu xǐhuan chuān Xīshìde yīfu.

13.0. lìngwài   in addition, additionally, besides   [besides outside]

13.1. Tóngzúde rén dōu shi yíge zǔxiānde hòudài.   Zhǐ yǒu yíge cítáng.
       Méi yǒu lìngwài zài yǒu yíge cítáng de.

14.0. yòngtú   usage, use   [use road]

14.1. Rènhé dōngxi dōu yǒu tāde yòngtú.

14.2. Kuàizide yòngtú jiù shi chī dōngxi.

40 Bái: Cán tùle sī yǐhòu bú yòng réngōng qu zuò, zìrán jiu shi sīxiàn ma?

    Mǎ: Bù.   Cán yuánlái shi yíge hěn xiǎode chóngzi. Tiānqi yì nuǎnhuo
          tā jiu zhǎngdà le, yóu xiǎo chóngzi biànchéng dà chóngzi, zhǎngdàle
          yǐhòu jiu tù sī. Cán tù de sī jīngguo réngōng chéngle sīxiàn, yòng
          sīxiàn zài zhīchéng sīzhīpǐn.

45 Bái: Sīzhīpǐn chúle zuò yīfu chuān, lìngwài hái yǒu yòngtú ma?

    Mǎ: Bù zhǐ shi zuò yīfu chuān, yě yǒu rén zài sīzhīpǐnshang xiě zì, huà
          huàr.

    Bái: Shì bu shi duōbàn dōu shi ná chōuduàn zuò yīfu?

    Mǎ: Shìde. Búguò duōbàn shi yǒuqián rén chuān. Qióngren kě chuānbuqǐ
50   chóuduàn.

15.0. zào   make, build

15.1. Tā shi něizhǒng jiàngren? . . . Tā shi yíge mùjiang. Tā gěi rénjia
       zàole bù shǎode fángzi.

16.0. bǎoshǒu   (1) protect, defend, conserve, preserve; (2) conservative
                  [protect guard]

16.1.   Shídài shi jìnbù de.   Tā zhǐ zhīdao bǎoshǒu, zěnmo nénggou gēn-
shang shídài ne!

17.0.   mìmi   secret   (N/SV)   [secret close]

17.1.   Zhōngguo gǔdàide rén fāmíng hěn duō dōngxi dōu bǎoshǒu mìmi, bú
ràng biéren zhīdao, yúshihū yǒu hěn duō dōngxi bù néng chuándào
xiànzài.

18.0.   Luómǎ   Rome

        Luómǎzì   romanization

        Guóyǔ Luómǎzì   National Language Romanization

18.1.   Luómǎ yǒumíngde shīrén shi shéi?

18.2.   <u>Guóyǔ Rùmén</u> shi yòng Guóyǔ Luómǎzì xiě de.

18.3.   Yǒu rén fǎnduì yòng Luómǎzì xué Guóyǔ.

19.0.   jīn(zi)   gold

        huángjīn   gold   [yellow gold]

        Měijīn   U.S. currency

19.1.   Měiguode qián jiàozuo <u>Měijīn</u>.

19.2.   Yīnwei jīnzi shi huáng yánsede suǒyǐ yě jiàozuo <u>huángjīn</u>.

19.3.   Nèige guójiā yòng huángjīn huàn yuánzǐnéng jìshushangde mìmi.

20.0.   (yǒu) duóma SV (a)!   how SV!

20.1.   Nǐ kàn nèixiē kǔgōngde shēnghuó yǒu duóma kǔ a!

Bái: Chuánshuō Zhōngguo yuánlái yǎng cán zào sī de fāngfǎ shi bǎoshǒu
mìmi de.   Kěshi hòulái wàiguo zěnmo zhīdao zhèige fázi le ne?

Mǎ: Yīnwei dāngshí tíchàng dàjiā yǎng cán zào sī, yǎng cán zào sīde rén
yí duō le dāngrán jiu méi fázi bǎoshǒu mìmi le.

55   Bái: Dàole Hàn Cháo yòu bǎ sīzhīpǐn chuándao Luómǎ.

Mǎ: Shuōqǐ Luómǎ hěn yǒu yìsi.   Chuánshuō dāngchū Luómǎ shi yòng
huángjīn huàn Zhōngguode sīzhīpǐn.   Nǐ xiǎng Zhōngguode sīzhīpǐn
shi duóma piàoliang a!   Wàiguo rén duóma xǐhuan!

21.0.   zhuā   (1) scratch; (2) grasp, seize

21.1.   Zài cóngqiánde shihou rénmín rúguǒ bù fúcóng zhèngfǔde zhǐhuī,
zhèngfǔ jiu bǎ rénmín zhuāqilai.

22.0.   shǐ   use (V)

        shǐyòng   use (V)   (W)

22.1.   Wàiguo rén duōshù bú huì shǐ kuàizi.

22.2.   Zài Rìběn mǎi dōngxi, kéyi shǐyòng Měijīn ma?

22.3. Wǒ zǔfù bú huì shǐ gāngbǐ gēn qiānbǐ xiě zì. Tā lǎorénjiā jiù huì yòng máobǐ.

23.0. Zhōu   Chou (Dynasty) (ca. 1027-221 B.C.)

23.1. Kǒngzǐ shi Zhōu Cháo shíhoude rén.

24.0. zhú(zi)   bamboo

24.1. Nèige dōngxi shi yòng zhúzi zuò de.

25.0. mùtou   wood

25.1. Měiguo hěn duō fángzi shi yòng mùtou zào de.

26.0. chā(zi)   fork

   dāochā   knife and fork

26.1. Chīfàn de shíhou rúguǒ yòng dāochā shi zuǒ shǒu ná chāzi ne, háishi yòng yòu shǒu ná chāzi ne?

Bái: Zài yuánshǐde shíhou rénlèi chī dōngxi dōu shi yòng shǒu zhuāzhe
60   chī. Bù zhīdào zài shénmo shíhou Zhōngguo rén fāmíng shǐ kuàizi
      le?

Mǎ : Jùshuō zài jǐyuánqián sān shíjǐ rén jiu shǐ kuàizi chī fàn le. Nà
      jiu shi Zhōu Cháode shíhou.

Bái: Kuàizi shi yòng zhúzi zuò de háishi yòng mùtou zuò de?

65 Mǎ : Yìbānde kuàizi dōu shi zhúzi zuò de. Bǐjiǎo hǎo yìdiǎrde shi mùtou
      zuò de.

Bái: Dāngchū wǒ yì kāishǐ yòng kuàizi hěn bù hǎo yòng. Nèige shíhou
      wǒ juéde dāochā chī dōngxi zuì róngyi.

Mǎ : Nǐ chī Zhōngguo fàn yòngguo dāochā ma?

70 Bái: Méi yǒu. Wǒ cóng kāishǐ yì chī Zhōngguo fàn jiu shǐ kuàizi, jué
      bú yòng dāochā.

27.0. yào   medicine, drug

   chī yào   take medicine   [eat medicine]

   huǒyào   gunpowder   [fire medicine]

27.1. Yǒude dìfang, qióngrén shēng bìng bù chī yào, yīnwei tāmen méi qián mǎi yào.

27.2. Huǒyào yǒu shénmo yòngtú, nǐ zhīdao ma?

28.0. pàozhang   firecracker, fireworks   [firecracker battle]

   fàng pàozhang   shoot off firecrackers, set off fireworks

28.1. Tāmen jǐge xiōngdì dōu xǐhuan fàng pàozhang. Shícháng zhǎo wǒ lái fàng pàozhang, suóyǐ wǒ mǎile hěn duō pàozhang. (T)

28.2. Huǒyàode yòngtú hěn duō. Wǎng dàde fāngmiàn jiǎng, kéyi yòngzai jūnshìshang. Wǎng xiǎode fāngmiàn jiǎng, kéyi zuò pàozhang. **(T)**

29.0. bàozhú   firecracker, fireworks (w)   [explode bamboo]

29.1. <u>Bàozhú</u> jiu shi <u>pàozhang</u>. Zhōngguo rén guò niánde shíhou dōu mǎi bàozhú.

30.0. wǔqì   military equipment   [military implement]

30.1. Nèige guójiāde wǔqì dōu shi xīnshì de.

31.0. jìnzhǐ   forbid   [prohibit stop]

31.1. Cóngqián huángdì zuò de shì jìnzhǐ pīping.

31.2. Nèige diànyǐngyuàn jìnzhǐ shí'èrsuì yǐxiàde xiǎo háizi jìnqu kàn diàn-yǐng.

Bái: Jù lìshǐshang shuō huǒyào shi Zhōngguo rén lǎozǎo fāmíng de.

Mǎ : Huǒyào fāmíng zài dì-liù shìjì. Zài nèige shíhou huǒyào zhǐ shi zuò pàozhang yòng de. Hòulái rénlèi ná huǒyào zuò wǔqì yòngzai zhàn-
75   zhēngshang le.

Bái: <u>Bàozhú</u> jiu shi <u>pàozhang</u>, shì bu shi?

Mǎ : Shìde. <u>Bàozhú</u> shi xiě de. Pǔtōng shuō huà jiàozuo <u>pàozhang</u>.

Bái: Pàozhang shi zhǐ gēn huǒyào zuò de, gēn zhúzi yǒu shénmo guānxi? Wèi-shénmo yòu jiào <u>bàozhu</u> ne?

80 Mǎ : Gǔdài bàozhu shi yòng zhúzi zuò de, suǒyǐ jiào <u>bàozhu</u>.

Bái: Zhōngguode pàozhang měinián chūkǒu bù shǎo a.

Mǎ : Shìde. Jiu shi zài guówàide Huáqiáo měinián háishi fàng pàozhang. Cóngqián zhèngfǔ jìnzhǐ rénmín guònián fàng pàozhang, kěshi zhèi-zhǒng chuántǒngde fēngsú wúlùn zěnmo jìnzhǐ yě jìnzhǐbuliǎo.
85   Rénmín háishi zhàoyàng fàng.

32.0. yìn   to print

  yìnshuā   (1) to print; (2) printing   [print brush]

  yìnshuāsuǒ   printing works, print-shop

32.1. Rúguǒ yìn shū zuì hǎo dào Dà Huá Yìnshuāsuǒ, yīnwei Dà Huá yìnde yòu hǎo yòu kuài.   **(T)**

32.2. Wáng Xiānsheng kāi yíge yìnshuāsuǒ. Tā shi zuò yìnshuā shēngyi de.

33.0. zhèngquè   accurate, precise

33.1. Tā suǒ shuōde shēngchǎn shùmuzì bú dà zhèngquè.   **(T)**

34.0. mùbǎn   (1) wooden board; (2) wooden block engraved for printing [wood board]

34.1. Zhōngguo fùguì rénjiāde fángzi, hěn shǎo shi yòng mùbǎn zào de.

35.0. kē   carve, engrave

     kē zì   engrave characters

35.1. Tā néng zài mùbǎnshang kē zì, érqiě kēde hěn hǎo.

36.0. Sòng   Sung (Dynasty) (960-1127)

36.1. Nèige chénglide Kǒngmiào, jùshuō shi cóng Sòng Cháo jiu yǒu le.

37.0. huózì   movable type   [live type]

37.1. Zhōngguo yòng huózì yìnshuā shi cóng Sòng Cháo kāishǐ ma?   (T)

Bái: Mǎ Jiàoshòu, Zhōngguo fāmíng yìnshuā shi zài shénmo shíhou?

Mǎ : Ànzhe zhèngquède shuōfǎ shi zài gōngyuán liùbǎi niánde shíhou.

Bái: Kāishǐ shi yòng mùbǎn kē zì yìnshuā, shì bu shi?

Mǎ : Shìde. Kāishǐ shi yòng yíkuài mùbǎn, shàngmian kē hěn duō zì.
    Hòulai dào Sòng Cháo cái jìnbùdao huózì yìnshuā.

Bái: Shénmo jiào huózì yìnshuā?

Mǎ : Jiu shi bǎ měi yíge zì kēzai yíkuài mùtoushang. Yàoshi yìn dōngxi
    de shíhou xūyào něige zì jiu ná něige zì.

38.0. zhēn   needle

    dǎzhēn   inoculate   (VO) [hit needle]

    zhǐnánzhēn   compass   [point south needle]

38.1. Yàoshi dǎzhēn de huà zuì hǎo qǐng yīsheng, bú yào zìjǐ dǎzhēn.

38.2. Zhǐnánzhēnde zhēn shi yǒu tèxìng de, yǒngyuǎn zhǐzhe nán-běide
    fāngxiàng.   (T)

39.0. kōng   empty, unoccupied

    kōnghuà   empty talk

39.1. Nèige fángzili méi yǒu rén, yě méi yǒu dōngxi, wánquán kōng le.

39.2. Tā shi lǎoshi rén, yíxiàng bù shuō kōnghuà de.   (T)

40.0. háng   (1) sail; (2) aeronautics, aeronautical

    hángkōng   aviator, aerial navigation   [sail empty]

    hángkōngxìn   airmail

    hánghǎi   navigate, sail   [sail sea]

40.1. Tā zuì xǐhuan hánghǎi, suóyǐ tā zài chuánshang zuò shì.

40.2. Xiànzài hángkōng shìyè fēicháng fādá. Cóngqián xǐhuan hánghǎi
    lǚxíngde rén dōu gǎi hángkōng lǚxíng le.   (T)

40.3. Yóu hángkōng chuándì de xìn shi hángkōngxìn.   (T)

41.0. jūn*   army

       jūnren   servicemen, military personnel

       jūnguān   military officer

       jūnshì   military matter

       Měijūn   U.S. army

41.1. Wǒmende zúzhǎng cóngqián shi gāojí jūnguān.   (T)

41.2. Jūnren shi guójiāde bǎozhàng. Méi yǒu jūnren, guójiā jiu méi yǒule
       bǎozhàng.

41.3. Yǒude jūnren bù yídìng dǒngde jūnshì.

41.4. Zài guówàide Měijūn yǒu duōshao, nǐ zhīdao ma?

41.5. Jūnrenmen yídìng yào tīng jūnguānde zhǐhuī.

       Bái: Tīngshuō zhǐnánzhēn zài shànggǔde shíhou jiu fāmíng le. Zhèige
95   huà kěkào bu kěkào?

       Mǎ : Quèshí zài shénmo shídài fāmíng de wǒmen yě méi fázi zhīdao. Yě
             yǒu rén shuō zài Nán Běi Cháode shídài cái yǒu de.

       Bái: Nènmo yě yǒu yìqiān wǔbǎi nián zuǒyòu le.

       Mǎ : Zhǐnánzhēn shi yǒngyuǎn zhǐzhe nán-běi de. Zhǐnánzhēn zài háng-
100   kōng, hánghǎi hé jūnshìshangde gōngyòng hěn dà.

       Bái: Wǎng xiǎode yìfāngmiàn jiǎng, wǒmen lǚxíng yě yǒu yòngchu.

42.0. Shāng   Shang (Dynasty) (ca. 1500–1028 B.C.)

42.1. Shāng Cháode wénzì shi Zhōngguo zuì gǔde wénzì.

43.0. tóng   copper, brass, bronze

       tóngqì   article made of bronze (M: jiàn)

43.1. Nèige dōngxi shi tóngde háishi jīnde?

43.2. Zhōngguo cóng shénmo shídài kāishǐ yǒu tóngqì?

44.0. tiě   iron

       tiěqì   article made of iron

44.1. Hěn duō wǔqì shi yòng tiě zào de.

44.2. Wǒ xiǎng zhǎo yíge huì zuò tiěqìde jiàngrén.

45.0. bǎocún   preserve, keep safely [protect exist]

45.1. Zǔzong liúxia de dōngxi, yīngdāng yóu hòudài fùzé bǎocún.   (T)

46.0. zhèngmíng (1) prove; (2) proof [proof clear]

46.1. Nǐ shuō zhèngfǔ gěi rénmín móu fúlì, yǒu shǐshi kéyi zhèngmíng
      ma?   (T)

47.0. gǔwù   artifact   [ancient object]

47.1. Bǎocún xīn fāxiàn de gǔwù shi zhèngfǔde zérèn. Bù yīngdāng jiào
      sīren fù zérèn.

Bái: Shāng Cháo、Zhōu Cháo dōu shi tóngqì shídài. Zhìyú tiěqì shídài
      wǒ zhīdao Ōuzhōu shi zài jìyuánqián yìqiān niánde shíhou, Zhōngguo
      bǐjiǎo wǎn yìdiǎr. Shi zài shénmo shíhou?

105 Mǎ: Zhōngguo kāishǐ shǐyòng tiěqì shi zài jìyuánqián wǔbǎi nián zuǒyòu
      de shíhou.

Bái: Zài wǒmen xuéxiào lìshǐ yánjiuyuàn yídìng bǎocúnle bù shǎo Shāng、
      Zhōu shídàide tóngqì hé tiěqì ba.

Mǎ: Dāngrán yánjiu lìshǐ yào yòng gǔwù lái zhèngmíng, suǒyǐ bìděi yǒu
110   yìxiē gǔwù.

48.0. túzhang   a seal   [illustration seal]

48.1. Tā shi kào kē túzhang móushēng de.

48.2. Tā huì kē túzhang hái bú suàn, bìngqiě yǒu hěn duō gǔdàide túzhang
      ne. (T)

48.3. Wǒ mǎi túzhang bìng bú shì wèile yòng, shi wèile wár.   (T)

49.0. céng(jīng) V (guo)   already V'd

49.1. Zhōngguo céngjīng yòngguo Sānmín Zhǔyì zuò zhì guó de jīchǔ ma?
      (T)

49.2. Wǒ céngjīng shuōguo Zhōngguode dà jiātíng zhìdu yǐjing bù cúnzài
      le.

49.3. Wǒ zài Měiguo céngjīng chīguo Zhōngguo jiǎozi.

50.0. jiéshěng   (1) economize on, save (on); (2) frugal, economical   [tem-
                  perate save]

50.1. Wǒmen jiāli méi yǒu duōshao qián le. Cóng xiànzài kāishǐ yíqiè
      dōu yào jiéshěng.

51.0. bìngqiě   moreover   [side-by-side moreover]

51.1. Tā búdàn huì shuō Zhōngguo pǔtōnghuà, bìngqiě dúguo Sì Shū、Wǔ
      Jīng.

51.2. Tā búdàn bù xǐhuan niàn shū, bìngqiě cháng zuò huàishì.

52.0. yín(zi)   silver

52.1. Nèixiē dāochā shi yòng yínzi zuò de.

Bái: Mǎ Jiàoshòu, xuéxiào fùjìn yǒu kē túzhang de ma? Wǒ xiǎng kē yíge.

Mǎ: Nǐ shi kē pǔtōng de háishi kē hǎo yìdiǎr de?

Bái: Pǔputōngtōngde kē yíge jiu kéyi.

115 Mǎ: Yàoshi kē pǔtōng de bú bǐ zhǎo rén kē, wǒ gěi ni kē yíge.

Bái: Nín néng kē túzhang? Wǒ tài bù hǎo yìsi máfan nín.

Mǎ: Wǒ duì kē zì hěn yǒu xìngqu. Wǒ niàn gāoxiǎode shíhou kē zì kěde wǒ lián shū dōu bú niàn. Wǒ mǔqin wèile wǒ kē túzhang﹑ bú niàn shū céngjīng dǎguo wo.

120 Bái: Kē túzhang nán bu nán?

Mǎ: Shítoude bù nán kē, tóngde bǐjiǎo nán kē yìdiǎr.

Bái: Qiú nín kē túzhangde duō bu duō?

Mǎ: Kāishǐ kē de shíhou rén bù duō, hòulai yǒu hěn duō rén zhǎo wǒ kē. Huì kē túzhang le yǐhòu fèile hěn duō qián, wǒ bǎ jiéshěngchulai de
125   qián dōu mǎile shítou. Yàoshi yǒu rén zhǎo wǒ kē túzhang, gěi rénjia kē hái búsuàn bìngqiě hái gěi rénjia mǎi shítou.

Bái: Yìnzi yě kéyi kē ma?

Mǎ: Kéyi. Yìnzi hěn róngyi kē.

53.0. bì   currency

zhǐbì   paper currency

Gǎngbì   Hongkong currency

Rénmínbì   currency of the Chinese People's Republic

Táibì   currency of the Republic of China on Taiwan

53.1. Suǒwèi bì jiu shi dàibiǎo qián de yìsi.   (T)

53.2. Xiānggǎngde zhǐbì jiàozuo Gǎngbì.

53.3. Zhèibǎn Hànyǔ Jiàokeshū Rénmínbì duōshao qián?

53.4. Guómín zhèngfǔ zài Táiwān yòngde zhǐbì jiàozuo Táibì.

54.0. hé   equivalent to (in currency)

54.1. Měijūn dào Táiwān yě yòng Měijīn. Yíkuài Měijīn chàbuduō hé sìshi-kuài Táibì.

54.2. Zài Xiānggǎng mǎi nèiběn zìdiǎn, yào hé Měijīn sānkuài qián. Yàoshi àn Gǎngbì suàn shi shíbākuài qián zuǒyòu.   (T)

55.0. réngrán   still, yet, continuing   [still so]

55.1. Yǒude rén suírán nénggou chīkǔ, réngrán bù néng wéichí yìjiā rénde shēnghuó.

55.2. Ōuzhōu yǒude dìfang shì bu shi xiànzài réngrán yǒu xiē Měijūn?

56.0. ǒurán   by chance, occasionally   [pair so]

ǒurán(de) yíge jīhui   by a chance encounter, (on) an unexpected occasion

56.1. Yǒu rén shuō duìyu qióngrén ǒurán bāngzhu ta yìxiē qián shi kéyi
de, bù yīngdāng chángcháng gōngji ta.

56.2. Nèige xiáojie zài ǒuránde yíge jīhuili rènshi yíge jūnren, hòulái jiu
jiàgěi nèige jūnren le.

57.0. lìyòng   (1) use for one's own ends, make a tool of; (2) utilization
[profit use]

57.1. Hěn duō dìfang lìyòng tiānránde shuǐlì fādiàn.   (T)

Bái: Shì bu shi kě túzhang yǒude jiàqián xiāngdāng guì?

130 Mǎ : Shì. Yàoshi kěde hǎo de jiu xiāngdāng guì le, dàgài kě yíge túzhang
yào hé Měijīn sān-sìshikuài qián ne.

Bái: Yàoshi àn Gǎngbì suàn shi duōshǎo qián?

Mǎ : Yíkuài Měijīn hé Gǎngbì chàbuduō liùkuài qián. Dàgài yào èrbǎi
duō kuài Gǎngbì le. Suīrán guì, réngrán yǒu hěn duō rén kě. Qíshí
135   túzhang yǒu yíge jiu gòu yòng le. Yǒude rén bìng bú shi wèile yòng,
shi wèi wár. Gèshì gèyàngde túzhang dōu yǒu. Qián jǐtiān ǒurán
yíge jīhui jiànzhaole yiwèi lǎo xiānsheng. Tánqi túzhang lái, tā shuō
tā yǒu sānbǎi duōge túzhang.

Bái: Nín tiāntiān jiāo shū hái yǒu shíjiān kě túzhang ma?

140 Mǎ : Wǒ dōu shi lìyòng xīngqīliù huòshi xīngqīrì méi shì de shíhou.

58.0. gēge   older brother

58.1. Wǒ gēge xǐhuan tán zìyóu zhǔyì、mínzú zhǔyì, kěshi tā bìng bù zhēn
dǒngde zhèi liǎngge zhǔyìde yìsi.   (T)

59.0. zhēngfú   conquer, subjugate   [attack submit]

59.1. Hěn duō nánrén bèi nǚrén zhēngfú le.

60.0. jiē   (1) receive; (2) connect

jiēzhe   continuing, going on   (AD)

60.1. Dì-yī Zhōngxué xiàozhǎng zìcóng Mǎ Dàwén jiēle yǐhòu, xuéxiàolide
dàshì、xiǎoshì dōu shi yóu Mǎ Dàwén yíge rén zhǔchí.   (T)

60.2. Wǒ zhèng zài dú shū, láile yíge péngyou. Hòulái péngyou zǒule, wǒ
yòu jiēzhe dú shū.   (T)

61.0. jǐn   (1) tight; (2) urgent; (3) close, near

jǐn jiēzhe   following closely (in time)

61.1. Wǒ zhèi jǐtiān shǒuli méi qián, hěn jǐn.   (T)

61.2. Qián jǐtiān shi Zhāng Xiānshengde shēngri, jǐn jiēzhe yòu shi Zhāng
Tàitaide shēngri.

62.0. guāng   (1) only (AD); (2) finished, completed (postverb)

62.1. Nèige shānshang guāng yǒu yíge miào. Méi yǒu rénjiā.

62.2. Wǒde qián dōu yòngguāng le.   (T)

Bái: Shēngcí biǎoshang dì-sìháng cóng shàngmian wǎng xià shǔ dì-liù-
qīge cér wǒ kàn bu dà qīngchu.

Mǎ : Nǐ shuō de shi gēge hé zhēngfú zhōngjiānde nèi liǎngge cér, yìn de
bú dà qīngchu ma?

145 Bái: Bú dà qīngchu. Kànbuchūlái shi shénmo.

Mǎ : Shi jǐn gēn jǐn jiēzhe.

Bái: Jǐn jiēzhe zhèige cér wǒ huì yòng, yàoshi dān yòng yíge jǐn zì zěnmo
yòng ne?

Mǎ : Wǒ jǔ ge lìzi: "Wǒ shàngge yuè bìng le, biéde bú suàn, guāng chī
150   yào dǎzhēn jiu yòngle èrbǎi Měijīn, suǒyǐ zhèige yuè wǒ jǐnde bùdéliǎo."

Bái: Wǒ míngbai le.

63.0. gòngxiàn   (1) contribute, offer; (2) contribution, offering [offer con-
tribute]

63.1. Yíge rén duì guójiā shèhuì zǒng yào yǒu yìdiǎr gòngxiàn.   (T)

64.0. huā(r)   flower

huāyuán   (flower) garden

64.1. Xiànzài huāyuánde huār zhèng zài kāizhe ne.   (T)

65.0. mò   (1) ink-stick (M: kuài); (2) Chinese ink

mòshuǐ   Western-style ink   [ink water]

mòzhī   Chinese-style ink   [ink juice]

65.1. Wǒ yào mǎi yìzhī máobǐ, yíkuài mò.   (T)

65.2. Tā yòng gāngbǐ xiě zì de shíhou xǐhuan yòng hóng mòshuǐ.

65.3. Sān Yǒu Shūdiàn mài de mòzhī tèbié hǎo.

Mǎ : Wǒmen jiēzhe wǎng xià yánjiu. Qǐng nǐ yòng gòngxiàn shuō yíge
jùzi.

155 Bái: "Jù kǎogǔjiā zhèngmíng, Zhōngguo hěn zǎo jiu zhīdao yǎng cán zào
sī. Zhè yě shi zài fāmíngshang zuì dà gòngxiàn zhī yī."

Mǎ : Yòngde hěn hǎo. Nǐ shuō nà shi fāmíngshang zuì dà gòngxiàn zhī yī yìdiǎr yě búcuò. Zhōngguode chóuduàn zhēnshi zhíde hǎokàn. Shàngmiàn zhī de huār piàoliang jíle.

160 Bái: Zhōngguo shi shénmo shíhou yǒu mòshuǐ de?

Mǎ : Zhōngguo hěn zǎo jiu yǒu le mò. Zhōngguo bú jiào mòshuǐ, jiào mòzhī. Yòng gāngbǐ xiě zì de jiào mòshuǐ, yòng máobǐ xiě zì de jiào mòzhī.

SHĒNGCÍ BIǍO

1. sī

2. chóu(zi)

3. duàn(zi)
   chóuduàn

4. zhī

5. pín*
   rìyòngpǐn
   sīzhīpǐn

6. chóngzi

7. cán

8. tǔ
   tù

9. réngōng

10. xiàn
    sīxiàn
    wúxiàndiàn

11. yīfu

12. chuān

13. lìngwài

14. yòngtú

15. zào

16. bǎoshǒu

17. mìmi

18. Luómǎ
    Luómǎzì
    Guóyǔ Luómǎzì

19. jīn(zi)
    huángjīn
    Měijīn

20. (yǒu) duōma SV (a)!

21. zhuā

22. shǐ
    shǐyòng (W)

23. Zhōu

24. zhú(zi)

25. mùtou

26. chā(zi)
    dāochā

27. yào
    chī yào
    huǒyào

28. pàozhang
    fàng pàozhang

29. bàozhú (W)

30. wǔqì

31. jìnzhǐ

32. yìn
    yìnshuā
    yìnshuāsuǒ

33. zhèngquè

34. mùbǎn

35. kē
    kē zì

36. Sòng

37. huózì

38. zhēn
    dǎzhēn
    zhǐnánzhēn

39. kōng
    kōnghuà

40. háng
    hángkōng
    hángkōngxìn
    hánghǎi

41. jūn*
    jūnren
    jūnguān
    jūnshì
    Měijūn

42. Shāng

43. tóng
    tóngqì

44. tiě
    tiěqì

45. bǎocún

46. zhèngmíng

47. gǔwù

48. túzhang

49. céng(jīng) V
    (guo)

50. jiéshěng

51. bìngqiě

52. yín(zi)

53. bǐ
    zhǐbǐ
    Gāngbǐ
    Rénmínbì
    Táibì

54. hé	59. zhēngfú	63. gòngxiàn
55. réngrán	60. jiē	64. huā(r)
56. ǒurán	jiēzhe	huāyuán
ǒurán(de) yíge jīhui	61. jǐn	65. mò
57. lìyòng	jǐn jiēzhe	mòshuǐ
58. gēge	62. guāng	mòzhī

YǓFǍ LIÀNXÍ

A. bǐ QW dōu V   (see note 1)

1. Nǐ kàn Zhāng Xiáojie chuān de nèijiàn duànzi yīfu duómo piàoliang a! Tā shuō zhèijiàn yīfu bǐ nèijiàn tā dōu xǐhuan.

2. Tāmen jiāde huāyuán bǐ shéi jiāde dōu dà, érqiě huār yě duō.

3. Nǐ kě bié dào nèige yìnshuāsuǒ qu yìn dōngxi. Bǐ něijiā yìnde dōu guì.

4. Guònián de shíhou wǒ bǐ shéi dōu xǐhuan fàng pàozhang.

5. Zhèiběn Guóyǔ Luómǎzìde kèběn wǒ bǐ něiběn dōu xǐhuan.

B. SVqilai (see note 2)

6. Jìnlái Měiguo xuésheng dào Zhōngguo liúxué de bǐ yǐqián duōqilai le.

7. Shìjiè dàzhàn yǐhòu gèdìde shēnghuó shuǐpíng dōu gāoqilai le.

8. Yīnwei rìyòngpǐn dōu guìqilai le, suǒyǐ shēnghuó gèng kùnnán le.

9. Cóng shíjiǔ shìjǐ yǐlái Zhōngguo shòu Xīfang wénhuàde yǐngxiǎng jiu dàqilai le.

10. Wǒ dìdide píngjūn fēnshù jígé le. Tāde chéngji bǐ yǐqián hǎoqilai le.

C. The coverb jiù   (see note 3)

11. Jiù wǒ suǒ zhīdao de, tā gēge lái de bù shi hángkōngxìn.

12. Jiù wǒde kànfǎ, rìyòngpǐn yào yìtiān bǐ yìtiān guì.

13. Jiù tā suǒ shuō de, tā yǐjing ná Táibì bǎ dōngxi dōu mǎilai le.

14. Jiù jīntiande jiàqián lái shuō, Měijīn yíkuài hé Gǎngbì wǔkuài qī.

15. Jiù tāde guòqu lái kàn, tā zhèicì shuō de kěnéng háishi kōnghuà.

D. SV + V   (see <u>Beginning Chinese</u>, p. 100, note 1)

16. Nǐ yùbei de mòzhī bú gòu yòng.

17. Wúxiàndiànlǐde bàogào yǒu shíhou hěn nán dǒng.

18. Nèige chāzi shi tiěde, hěn bù hǎo yòng.

19. Zhōngguo mò zài Měiguo róngyi mǎi ma?

20. Nèizhǐ gāngbǐ hǎo shǐ ma? Rúguǒ hǎo shǐ jiè wǒ shǐyishǐ.

JIǍNGHUÀ

Zhōngguo shi yíge wénmíng gǔguó, suǒyǐ zài gǔshíhou yǒu hěn duōde fāmíng. Xiànzài xiān bǎ jǐzhǒng zhòngyàode shuǒyishuō.

Sīde fāmíng zuì zǎo. Gēnju kǎogǔxuéjiā zài yǐjing fāxiàn de gǔwùli suǒ dédào de zhèngmíng, zài Shāng Cháo yǐqián jiu yǒule sī. Lìngwài hái
5　yǒu yìzhǒng shuōfǎ, jùshuō sīde fāmíngde jīngguò shi zhèiyàngde: Gǔshíhou yǒu rén zài huāyuánli ǒurán kànjian yíge chóngzi zài nàlǐ tù sī, érqiě zhèizhǒng sī shi hěn cháng hěn cháng yìtiáo yìtiáode. Yúshi tā jiu xiǎng fázi yǎng zhèige chóngzi, nà jiu shi cán, jiēzhe yòu xiǎng fázi bǎ cán tùchulai de sī yòng réngōng zuòchéngle sīxiàn. Yòu yòng sīxiàn zhīchéngle chóuduàn
10　děngděng sīzhīpǐn.

Sīzhīpǐn hěn měilì, yòngtú yě hěn duō. Kéyi zài shàngmian xiě zì huà huàr．Hòulái búdàn yòngzai Zhōngguo, yě màigei wàiguo rén. Zài Hàn Cháode shíhou céng bǎ sīzhīpǐn chuándao Luómǎ. Nà shíhou Luómǎ shi yòng huángjīn huàn sīzhīpǐn. Luómǎ huángdì wèile jiéshěng huángjīn, suǒyǐ
15　jìnzhǐ chuān sīzhīpǐnde yīfu. Dāngchū duìyu yǎng cán zào sīde fázi hěn bǎoshǒu mìmi. Hòulái yǎng cán zào sī de rén duōqilai le, jiu bǎ zhèizhǒng fázi chuāndàole Rìběn, Yìndu yǐjí quán shìjiè.

Chá zài Zhōngguo yěxǔ hěn zǎo jiu yǒu le, kěshi dàole gōngyuán sān shìjìde shíhou cái yǒu rén tídàole chá. Xiān shi zài Zhōngguo nánbù
20　fāxiàn, hòulái běibù yě yǒu le, dàole Táng Cháo yǐhòu cái pǔbiànle quán Zhōngguo. Hòulái gōngyuán yī-èr-líng-líng nián yǐhòu Rìběn yě yǒule chá, shíqī shíjì Ōuzhōu yě yǒu hěn duō rén hē chá. Jùshuō chá duìyu rénde shēntǐ hěn yǒu hǎochu, suǒyǐ hē chá de rén hěn duō.

Zhǐnánzhēnde fāmíng, ànzhe Zhōngguo lǐláide chuánshuō, shi zài hěn
25　zǎo yǐqián jiu yǒu le. Dànshi quèshíde zhèngmíng, shi zài gōngyuán wǔ shìjì Nán Běi Cháode shíhou cái yǒule zhǐnánzhēn. Hòulái dàole gōngyuán yī-yī-yī-jiǔ nián yǒu rén xiěle yìběn shū shuōdao zhǐnánzhēn duìyu hánghǎide yòngtú. Zhǐnánzhēnde tèxìng shi yǒngyuǎn zhǐzhe nán-běide fāngxiàng, suǒyǐ zài hánghǎi, hángkōng hé hěn duō biéde fāngmiàn dōu
30　lìyòng ta, cái néng zhīdao zhèngquède fāngxiàng.

Zhōngguode Fāmíng

Huǒyàode fāmíng hěn zǎo. Dàole gōngyuán liù shìjìde shíhou jiu yǒu rén yòng huǒyào zuò bàozhú. Dāngshí bìng méi yǒu biéde yòngtú. Hòulái dàole shí'èr shìjì cái kāishǐ bǎ huǒyào yòngzai zhànzhēngshang. Yǐhòu dàole Yuán Cháo zhēngfú Ōu-Yà, jiu shi lìyòng huǒyào zuò wǔqì, suǒyǐ
35 Yuán Cháo zài jūnshì shǐyòng de huǒyào zuì duō.

Zhǐde fāmíng shi zài gōngyuán yìbǎi nián zuǒyòu Hàn Cháode shíhou. Zhǐde yòngtú hěn guǎng. Yóuqíshi zài wénhuàshangde gōngyòng gèng dà. Zìcóng fāmíngle zhǐ yǐhòu, xiě shū dōu yòng zhǐ le. Suǒyǐ yǒu hěn duō gǔ shū yǒude yīnwei shi xiězai zhǐshang, jīngguo niándài tài jiǔ le jiu méi
40 fázi bǎocún le. Yòng zhǐ zuòchengde zhǐbì shi cóng Táng Cháo mònián kāishǐ de.

Yìnshuāde fāmíng dàyuē shi zài gōngyuán liùbǎi nián zuǒyòu. Zhōngguo rén zài hěn zǎo yǐqián jiu yǐjing yǒule zhǐ, yě yǒule mò. Yòu zhīdao kē túzhāng le, yě zhīdao zài tóngshang hé shítoushang kē zì, bìngqiě cóng
45 tóngshang hé shítoushang yìnxialai. Hòulái jiu fāmíng yìnshuā. Zài fāmíng yìnshuā kāishǐde shíhou shi xiān yòng mùbǎn kē zì ránhòu 'zài yìnshuā. Dàole Sòng Cháo cái yòng huózì yìnshuā. Xīfāng guójiā zài shíwǔ shìjì Déguo cái yǒu yìnshuā, bǐ Zhōngguo wǎnle hěn duō nián le.

Kuàizi pǔtōng yòng de dōu shi zhúzi gēn mùtou zuò de, shi Zhōngguo
50 rén chī dōngxi shíhou shǐyòng de. Zài gōngyuánqián sān shìjì Zhōngguo lìshǐ shūshang tídao kuàizi, kějiàn zài gōngyuánqián sān shìjì Zhōu Cháode shíhou huòzhe bǐ zhèige shíhou hái zǎo kuàizi jiu fāmíng le. Shìjièshangde rénlèi yuánshǐ shíqī chī dōngxi de shíhou dōu shi yòng shǒu zhuā. Hòulái yǒude rén shǐ kuàizi. Xīfang rén zài shíliù shìjì cái kāishǐ yòng dāochā.
55 Jùshuō xiànzài shìjièshangde rén yǒu sānfenzhī-yī yòng dāochā, yǒu sānfenzhī-yī yòng kuàizi, háiyǒu sānfenzhī-yī réngrán yòng shǒu zhuā.

Cóng yǐshàng suǒ shuō de jǐzhǒng fāmíng lái kàn, Zhōngguo rén zài fāmíngshang duōma yǒu gòngxiàn a!

FÙSHÙ

Zhèipán lùyīndài shi Zhōngwén dì-yīzǔ dì-báhào, Bái Wénshān fùshù dì-bácì Zhuāntí Jiǎnghuà.

Zuótiān xuéxiào qǐnglai yíwèi shèhuìxué zhuānjiā jiǎng Zhōngguo shèhuì, tímu shi Zhōngguode shèhuì jiégòu. Tā shi xiān cóng jiùde shèhuì

5 zhìdu jiăngqĭ. Tā shuō rúguŏ yào liăojiĕ Zhōngguo xiàndàide shèhuì, bĭ-
děi cóng xiānqiánde shèhui jiăngqĭ. Tā shuōle liăngdiăn. Dî-yī shi shuō
Zhōngguo shèhuìde jiēji, dì-èr shuō de shi Zhōngguo shèhuìde zhōngxīn.

Tā shuō Zhōngguode shèhuì yĭqián fēncheng sìge jiēji, jiu shi shì、
nóng、gōng、shāng. Shénmo jiàozuò <u>shì</u> ne? Jiu shi niàn shū de zhīshi
10 fènzĭ. Zài Zhōngguo guòqu niàn shū rén jiu shi zhīshi fènzĭ, dìwei kànde
hěn gāo. Qícì shi nóng. Yīnwei Zhōngguo shi nóngyè guójiā nóngyè shi
Zhōngguode jīngji jīchŭ, suŏyĭ nóngren shi dì-èrwèi. Yòu qícì shi gōngren,
jiu shi jiàngrén. Gōngren hé jiàngrén yŏu diar fēnbié. Gōngren shi yòng
lìqi, jiàngrén shi yŏu jìshu de. Zuìhòu cái shi shāng. Zhōngguo yĭqiánde
15 kànfă, gōngrén hé shāngrende dìwei dī, yóuqíshi shāngren. Guòqu rènwei
shāngren bú shi shíjĭ nénggou shēngchănde rén.

Tā yòu shuō Zhōngguode shèhuì yŏu liăng dà jiēji. Yíge shi shìdàfū
jiēji. Yíge shi nóngmín jiēji, shi zhĭzhe xiăonóng shuō de. Zhèi liăngge
jiēji yŏu hěn dàde fēnbié. Shìdàfū jiēji shi niàn shū ránhòu zuòle guān,
20 jiù shi tŏngzhì jiēji. Shìdàfū jiēji duì Zhōngguo wénhuà yìfāngmiàn tāmen
hěn yŏugōng. Tāmen tiāntiān bú shi xiě wénzhāng、zuò shī、huà huàr jiu
shi yánjiu <u>Wŭ Jīng</u>、<u>Sì Shū</u> gēn shĭxué děngděngde.

Zài shuō nóngmín jiēji, jiu shi bèi tŏngzhì de jiēji, jiu shi xiăo zìgēngnóng gēn diànnóng. Huàn jù huà shuō shi zìjĭ méi yŏu tiándì de nóngmín.
25 Tāmen zhòng de dì dà duōshù shi dìzhŭde. Zhèizhŏng nóngren yàoshi
măile tiándì tāmen yě jiu shi dìzhŭ le. Tāmende érzi yě kéyi cānjiā kējŭ
kăoshì, yúshi yě jiu biànchéngle shìdàfu jiēji zuò guān le.

Zài shuō Zhōngguode shèhuì zhōngxīn. Zhōngguode shèhuì shi ná
jiātíng hé zōngzú zuò zhōngxīn. Zhōngguo yĭqián shi dà jiātíng zhìdu.
30 Shénmo shi dà jiātíng ne? Nà jiu shi jiāli yŏu jĭdài rén dōu zhùzai yíkuàr.
Yŏu zŭfù、zŭmŭ、fùqin、mŭqin、méi chūjià de xiáojie、jiēle hūnde érzi
háiyŏu sūnzi sūnnüer děngděngde. Dà jiātíng dōu shi yŏuqiánde. Dāngrán
nánnü yòngren yě bù shăo le. Yíge jiātíng nánnü lăoshào dàdà xiăoxiăo
yŏu jĭshikŏu rén. Dà jiātíngli rènhé shìqing dōu shi yóu jiāzhăng zuò
35 zhŭ. Érnü dìng qīnshi yĭjí jiātíng shēnghuóshangde dà-xiăo shìqing dōu
shi jiāzhăng zhŭchí, biéren dōu děi fúcóng ta. Zhōngguo rén cháng shuō
"dàhù rénjiā," jiu shi zhĭzhe zhèizhŏng jiātíng shuō de. Zhèizhŏng dà
jiātíng dōu shi dà shāngren huòzhě shi zuò guān de.

Zōngzú jiu shi yíge zǔzong chuánxialai yíxìngde rén. Suīrán shi yíge
40   zǔzong chuánxialai de, kěshi duōshao dài yǐhòu zhèixiē tóngzú rén yǒude
hěn fù, yǒude hěn qióng. Suīrán jīngji huánjìng bùtóng, kěshi dàjiā gòngtóng yǒu yíge cítáng.   Cítáng hǎoxiàng yíge miào, shi jìnian zǔzongde
dìfang. Yīnwei cítáng shi dàjiāde, bìděi yǒu yíge rén fùzé zhèige cítáng.
Zhè jiu shi zúzhǎng.   Tóngzú rén yǒu shì dōu děi tīng zúzhǎng de.
45   Dà jiātíng yǒu dà jiātíngde hǎochu. Rúguǒ zìjǐ bù néng móushēng de
huà, yíqiè shēnghuó dà jiātíng dōu néng gōngji. Zhèizhǒng dà jiātíng zài
zhè èrshi shìjǐ shòule Xīfāng wénhuàde yǐngxiǎng, yǐjing bù cúnzài le.

WĒNXI

1. Xiàozhǎng duì yíge xiě zì de rén shuō: "Nǐ suǒ xiě de zì shi zhào yuánwén xiě de ma? Zěnmo wǒ kàn hǎoxiang hé yuánwén bù yíyàng? Qǐng
   nǐ bǎ yuánwén dìgei wo, wǒ kànkan yuánwén.   Zàiburán wǒmen liǎngge
   rén gòngtóng kànyikàn."

2. Wǒ jìde wǒ xiǎode shíhou, wǒ jiāli cháng lái yíwèi wàiguo kèren. Zhèiwèi
   wàiguo rénde xìngmíng wǒ bú jìde. Wǒ dāngshí jiào ta "Xiè Xiānsheng."
   "Xiè" bú shi tāde xìng, nǐ yìhuěr jiu míngbai le.   Xiè Xiānsheng zuìchū
   shi wǒ zǔfùde péngyou, hòulái gēn wǒ zǔfù xué zuò shī.   Xiè Xiānsheng
   yóu péngyou ér biàn xuésheng, dàjiā gèng cháng láiwǎng le. Tā huì shuō
   Guóyǔ, xǐhuan chuān Zhōngshì yīfu.   Tā lái de shíhou, pūren gěi tā kāi
   mén, tā yídìng shuō "Xièxie." Yǒushí gēn wǒmen dìxiōng jiěmèi shuōwán
   huà, yě shuō "Xièxie." Zǔmǔ gěi ta zuò diǎnxin chī, tā shuō de "Xièxie"
   gèng bù zhīdào yǒu duōshǎo cì le. Yóuyu tā cháng shuō "Xièxie," wǒ jiu
   gěi tā qǐ ge wàihào jiào "Xiè Xiānsheng."

3. Zài yìběn zázhìshang yǒu yìpiān wénzhāng shi "Shuō Zìyóu Zhǔyì." Wénzhāngde dàyì shuō: Yǒude rén shífēn xūyào zìyóu. Yǒude rén wúsuǒwèi,
   zìjǐ yǐwéi méi yǒu shénmo bú zìyóu, yīncǐ duìyu zhèizhǒng zhǔyì bìng bù
   zěnmo guānxīn.

4. Yǒu yíge wàiguo liúxuéshēng zài Zhōngguo yánjiu Zhōngguode fēngsú. Tā
   shǒuli méi yǒu qián.   Yǒu rén yào gōng ta xuéfèi yǐjí shēnghuófèi.   Tā
   bù jiēshòu. Tā shuō tā zìjǐ xiǎng bànfǎ.   Tā xiǎng gěi yíge Yīngwén
   zhōukān xiě wénzhāng, zhuānmén xiě Zhōngguo fēngsú zhèi yíleìde wénzhāng. Tā yě kéyi xiě xiǎoshuō.   Tā yǐjing xiěle yìpiān Jiàchu de Nǚer.
   Tā xiǎng tā kéyi zìjǐ zhīchi zìjǐde xuéfèi hé shēnghuó.

5. Yǒu rén shuō: "Tàibì, Gǎngbì, Rénmínbì yǐjí Měiguo rénmín shǐyòng de
   qián dōu shi cóng yìnshuāsuǒli yìnchulai de zhǐbì, wèi-shénmo Měiguo qián
   bú jiào Měibì ér jiào Měijīn ne?"   Yǒu rén shuō: "Zhè yěxǔ shi yīnwei
   Měiguode zhǐbì cóngqián kéyi xiàng zhèngfǔ huàn jīnzi, suóyǐ jiu jiào
   Měijīn le."

6. Yǒu yíge jūnren tā shēng bìngde shíhou yě bù chī yào yě bù dǎzhēn, guāng
   zài fángzilǐ bù chūlai. Tā shuō: "Rén yǒu bìng de shíhou, gè yǒu gède
   zhìfǎ. Wǒde zhìfǎ shi bù chū fángzi, guò liǎngtiān bìng jiu hǎo le."

7. Wǒde péngyou gěi Měijūnde jūnguān dāng fānyi. Měitiān yígeyígede gěi
tāmen fānyi. Tā shuō shìqing tài máfan le, tā bù xiǎng zuòxiaqu le.

8. Nèixiē gǔwù shi tiěqì shídài kāishǐ shíhoude dōngxi. Jiù lìshǐ yánjiusuǒde
suǒyuán néng qù kàn.

WÈNTÍ

1. Zhōngguo zài shénmo shíhou jiu yǒule sī? Fāmíng sīde jīngguò shi zěnmoyàng? Hòulái yòng sī zuòcheng shénmo?

2. Sīzhīpǐn yǒu shénmo yòng? Sīzhīpǐn shi zài shénmo shíhou chuándao
shénmo dìfang? Shénmo dìfang jìnzhǐ chuān sīzhīpǐnde yīfu? Wèi-shénmo
jìnzhǐ?

3. Zài Zhōngguo shénmo shíhou cái yǒu rén tídao chá? Xiān zài shénmo
dìfang fāxiàn? Shénmo shíhou cái pǔbiàn quán Zhōngguo? Rìběn zài
shénmo shíhou yě yǒule chá? Ōuzhōu ne?

4. Fāmíng zhǐnánzhēn yǒu quèshí zhèngmíng shi zài shénmo shíhou? Zhǐnánzhēn yǒu shénmo tèxìng? Duìyu shénmo fāngmiàn zuì yǒu yòng?

5. Zhōngguo shénmo shíhou fāmíngle huǒyào? Dāngshi zuò shénmo yòng?
Hòulai yòu yòngzai shénmoshang? Shi zài shénmo shíhou kāishǐ yòng de?
Zhōngguo něi yì cháodài yòng de huǒyào zuì duō? Wèi-shénmo yòng de
zuì duō?

6. Zhǐ shi shénmo shíhou fāmíng de? Zài něi yìfāngmiàn zhǐde gōngyòng
zuì dà? Gǔ shū wèi-shénmo bù róngyi bǎocún? Yòng zhǐ zuòcheng zhǐbǐ
shi cóng něi yì cháodài kāishǐ de?

7. Yìnshuāde fāmíng dàyuē shi zài shénmo shíhou? Zhōngguo rén zài méi
yǒu fāmíng yìnshuā yǐqián, xiān yǒu shénmo zài yìnshuāshang hěn xūyào
de dōngxi?

8. Kāishǐ fāmíng yìnshuāde shíhou xiān yòng shénmo kē zì? Shénmo shíhou
cái yòng de huózì? Xīfāng guójiā zài shénmo shíhou cái yǒu yìnshuā?

9. Zhōngguo rén chī fàn huòzhě chī dōngxide shíhou cháng yòng shénmo?
Zài shénmo shíhou cái yǒu rén yòng kuàizi? Kuàizi shi shénmo yàng,
shi shénmo zuò de?

10. Rénlèi yuánshǐ shíqī chī dōngxide shíhou dōu yòng shénmo dōngxi? Dàole
shénmo shíhou Xīfāng rén cái kāishǐ yòng dāochā? Xiànzài shìjièshang
yǒu jǐfēnzhī-jǐ yòng kuàizi? Jǐfēnzhī-jǐ yòng dāochā? Yòng shǒude zhàn
jǐfēnzhī-jǐ? Nǐ chī dōngxide shíhou yòng shénmo ne?

ILLUSTRATIVE SENTENCES (ENGLISH)

10.1. Thread made from silk [lit. take silk make thread] is called 'silk thread.'
The making of silk is also a craft. It requires an artisan [and only then
is it possible to make].

28.1. They [several brothers] all like to shoot off firecrackers. They often invite [lit. seek] me to come and shoot off firecrackers, so I've bought quite a few [firecrackers].

28.2. There are many uses for gunpowder. A major one [lit. speaking toward the big side] is that it can be used in warfare. A minor one is that it can be used to make fireworks.

32.1. If you are printing a book it would be best to go to the Great China Printing Office, because Great China's printing is good and also fast.

33.1. The production figures he quoted are not very accurate.

37.1. Did Chinese use of movable type begin in the Sung Dynasty?

38.2. A compass needle has the peculiarity of always pointing north-south.

39.2. He's a forthright person, never given to empty talk.

40.2. The aviation industry has undergone an extraordinary expansion [now]. Those who formerly liked to travel by boat [lit. navigation] have now changed over to air travel.

40.3. Letters transmitted by air [lit. aviation] are airmail letters.

41.1. The head of our clan was formerly a high-ranking military officer.

45.1. Later generations should assume the responsibility of preserving things left by their ancestors.

46.1. Do you have any facts to prove your statement that the government is concerned with the welfare of the people?

48.2. Apart from his being able to carve seals, he has a great many ancient ones.

48.3. I buy seals not to use, but for the fun of it.

49.1. Has China used the Three People's Principles as the foundation for governing the country?

53.1. 'Currency' refers to the representation of money.

54.2. To buy that dictionary in Hongkong will require the equivalent of $3.00 in American currency. Figured in Hongkong currency, this is about $18.00.

57.1. Many places make use of natural water power to produce electricity.

58.1. My older brother likes to talk about liberalism and democracy, but he doesn't really understand the meaning of these [two] ideas.

60.1. Since Ma Dawen succeeded (to the post of) principal of Number 1 Middle School, all school matters of major and minor importance are managed by him alone.

60.2. Just as I was reading, a friend came. After a while the friend left and I went on reading.

61.1. These past few days I haven't had any money at hand. (Things are) very tight.

62.2. My money is all used up.

63.1. A person should [invariably] make some small contribution to society [of the state].

64.1. The flowers in the garden are just opening now.

65.1. I'd like to buy one brush-pen and one ink-stick.

NOTES

1. In the pattern <u>bǐ QW dōu SV</u> the stative verb can be replaced by other appropriate verbs:

   > Tā bǐ shéi dōu yuànyi lǚxíng.   'He's more willing to travel than anyone else.'

2. The pattern <u>SVqilai</u> means 'to become more SV':

   > Tiānqi lěngqilai le.   'The weather has become colder.'

3. Besides being used in the meaning of 'then' and 'only' the word <u>jiù</u> also functions as a coverb meaning 'from, on the basis of, according to':

   > Jiù tā suǒ shuō de tā míngtian bu lái.   'According to what he says he's not coming tomorrow.'

   > Jiù tāde guòqu lai kàn, tā shi kàobuzhù de.   'Considered from his past, he can't be depended on.'

Dì-Shíkè.　Guònián

Bái: Mǎ Jiàoshòu, zǎo.

Mǎ: Zǎo.

Bái: Zuótian tiānqi hěn lěng. Wǒ zhěngtiān méi chū mér. Jīntian gèng lěng. Qíshí hái bú dào lěng de shíhou ne.

5　Mǎ: Zhèlide tiānqi jiù shi zhèige yàngzi. Tiānqi hǎo jiu nuǎnhuo, tiānqi bù hǎo jiu lěngde bùdeliǎo. Nǐ chuān de tài shǎo le.

Bái: Méi guānxi. Wǒ dàoshi bù zěnmo pà lěng.

Mǎ: Zuótian Zhuāntí Jiǎnghuà, jiǎng Zhōngguode fāmíng. Bù zhīdào jiǎng- de zěnmoyàng?

10　Bái: Jiǎngde búcuò. Tā hái dàilaile yìxiē gǔwù lai zhèngmíng tā suǒ jiǎng de.

Mǎ: Dàilai de shénmo gǔwù?

Bái: Tā dàilaile yíjiàn tóngqì shídàide tóngqì, hái yǒu Shāng Cháo fāxiàn de wénzì. Tā hái dàilai yìdiǎr méi jīngguo réngōng de cán tǔ de
15　sī, jiào wǒmen kàn. Wǒ hěn xǐhuan Shāng Cháode wénzì. Piàoliang jíle.

Mǎ: Zhèiwèi zhǔjiǎngrén shi yíwèi zuì yǒumíngde shǐxuéjiā.

Bái: Zhōngguode fāmíng zhēn bù shǎo.

Mǎ: Shìde. Xiàng yìnshuā, huǒyào, zhǐnánzhēn zhèixiē dōngxi yòngqilai
20　hěn fāngbiàn, kěshi kāishǐ fāmíng shi hěn bù róngyi.

Bái: Shízài shi bù róngyi.

Mǎ: Jīntian Zhuāntí Jiǎnghuà, jiǎng Zhōngguo rén guònián. Wǒmen liǎngge rén tántan guònián de wèntí. Zhèixiēge dōu shi guòniánde cér:

1.0.　Xīnnián　New Year's

1.1.　Zhōngguo rén zài Xīnnián de shíhou fàng pàozhang zhè shi chuán- tǒngde xíguàn.　(T)

2.0.　lǐ*　　　calendar　(see note 3)

　　　rìlǐ　　　calendar　[day calendar]

　　　yīnlǐ　　lunar calendar

　　　yánglǐ　　solar calendar

　　　jiùlǐ　　old (lunar) calendar

　　　xīnlǐ　　new (solar) calendar

2.1. Wǒ mǎile yíge rìlì, yòngle Měijīn liǎngkuài.

2.2. Yīnlì nián (jiu shi yīnlìde Xīnnián) dàyuē zài yánglìde èryueli. (T)

2.3. Tā gēgede shēngri shi jiùlì liùyue èrshiqī rì . . . Xīnlì yīnggāi shi jǐyue jǐrì ne?

3.0. zhēngyue   first lunar month   [chief month]

3.1. Yīnlìde zhēngyue qíshí jiu shi yīnlìde yíyue.

4.0. chū   beginning of the lunar month   (see note 4)

4.1. Zhōngguo rén tídao yīnlì de shíhou, duìyu měiyuède qián shítiān dōu yòng yíge chū zì. Lìrú sānyue wǔrì yīngdāng shuō sānyue chūwǔ.

5.0. chúxī   New Year's Eve

5.1. Guòle chúxī jǐnjiēzhe jiu shi Xīnnián.

25 Bái: Mǎ Jiàoshòu, shì bu shi yīnlì yě jiào jiùlì, yánglì yě jiào xīnlì?

Mǎ : Shì.

Bái: Yīnlì Xīnnián shi zhēngyue chūyī. Wǒ jìde yìnián zuì hòude yìtiān bú jiào sānshí, lìngwài yǒu yíge míngzi, wǒ wàngle zěnmo shuō le?

Mǎ : Jiào chúxī.

30 Bái: Duìle, nín yì shuō wǒ xiǎngqilai le. Háiyǒu, shì bu shi yīnlì Xīnnián dōu shi zài yánglìde èryue? Shi zài èryue jǐhào?

Mǎ : Bù yídìng. Chàbuduō dōu shi zài èryue qián shítian lǐtou.

Bái: Wǒ shàngcì zài zhèr kànjian Zhōngguo péngyoumen jiāli guònián hěn yǒuyìsi.

35 Mǎ : Xiāngxia rén guònián gèng yǒuyìsi le. Jiājiā shā zhū, xiǎoháizi chuān xīn yīfu, fàng pàozhang, mǎi táng chī.

Bái: Zhōngguo dìfang dà, gè dìfang guòniánde fēngsu yě bù xiāngtóng ba?

Mǎ : Suīrán gè dìfang yǒu xiē bùtóng de fēngsu, kěshi dàzhì dōu chàbuduō.

Bái: Mǎnzú gēn Hànzúde fēngsu yíyàng ma?

40 Mǎ : Dàzhì dōu chàbuduō.

6.0. chūn*   spring

chūntian   spring   [spring day]

6.1. Yìnián lǐtou zuì hǎode shíhou shi chūntian. Wǒ yuànyi yìniánli dōu shi chūntian.

7.0. dēng   lamp, light

kāi dēng   turn on a light   [open light]

7.1. Dēngde yòngchu shi zài wǎnshang. Xiànzài háishi báitian. Wèi- shénmo yào kāi dēng?

8.0. jié   festival

     guòjié   celebrate a festival   (VO)

     Chūnjié   Spring Festival

     Dēngjié(r)   Lantern Festival

     jiérì   festival, holiday (W)   [festival day]

8.1. Yīnli zhēngyuèlǐde jiérì tèbié duō. Cái guòle Chūnjié jiēzhe jiu shi
     Dēngjié.   (T)

8.2. Nǐ zhǐdao yīnlì báyue shíwǔrì shi shénmo jié? Guòjié de shíhou
     fàng bàozhú bu fàng?

9.0. Xiǎonián(r)   Little New Year's

9.1. Yíge jūnguān shuō: "Míngtiān jiu guò Xiǎoniánr, kěshi niánniánde
     Xiǎoniánr wǒ dōu bù néng zài jiāli."

10.0. qīnqi   relatives   [related relative]

10.1. Wǒ yǒu yíge qīnqi huì zhī chóuzi, yě huì zhī duànzi.   (T)

11.0. bài   (1) bow to; (2) call on; (3) worship

      bàinián   pay New Year's calls   (VO)

      bàishén   worship the gods   (VO)

11.1. Guòniánde shíhou yǒu rén dào qīnqi jiāli qu bàinián, yǒu rén dào
      miàoli qu bàishén. Wǒ shi shénmo yě bú bài.   (T)

Bái: Chūnjié shi jiùlì Xīnnián. Dēngjié hé Chūnjié yǒu shénmo guānxi?

Mǎ : Chūnjié shi guònián, Dēngjié shi Chūnjié zuìhòude yíge rìzi.

Bái: Dēngjié shi zài něi yìtiān?

Mǎ : Dēngjié shi zhēngyue shíwǔ. Zhōngguo guòniánde rìzi kě cháng le.
     Cóng guò Xiǎoniánr kāishǐ yìzhí děi dàole zhēngyue shíwǔ cái suàn
     bǎ nián guòwán le.

Bái: Guòniánde shíhou, qīnqi, péngyou dàjiā bǐcǐ bàinián, guò Xiǎoniánr
     bìng bú bàinián, shì bu shi?

Mǎ : Yīnwei Xiǎoniánr shi zài guò Xīnnián yǐqián, suǒyǐ bú bàinián.

12.0. hùxiāng   mutual(ly), reciprocal(ly)   [mutually mutually]

12.1. Yǒu rén shuō shèhuìshangde rén duōbàn shi hùxiāng lìyòng.   (T)

13.0. gōngxǐ   congratulate (VO)   [respectful glad]

13.1. Zài guòniánde shíhou rúguǒ yǒu xiāngchǔbuláide rén dàjiā jiànle
      miàn bǐcǐ yě shuō "Gōngxǐ" ma?

14.0. fācái   become rich   [emit wealth]

14.1. Tīngshuō nèige mài pàozhang de rén fācái le.

14.2. Nǐ rúguǒ qu kàn yíge mǎimairén, zhèng shi tā dì-yītiān kāishǐ zuò
mǎimai, nǐ kéyi duì tā shuō: "Gōngxǐ fācái."   (T)

15.0. jílì   lucky, auspicious   [lucky profit]

15.1. Zhōngguode fēngsu rènwei zài guòniánde shíhou chī yào dǎ zhēn shi
bù jílìde.

16.0. kētóu   to kowtow   [tap head]

16.1. Zhōngguo cóngqián zuò guān de jiànle huángdì bìděi kētóu.   (T)

50 Bái: Zài guòniánde shíhou qīnqi péngyoumen jiànmiàn dàjiā hùxiāng shuō:
"Gōngxǐ fācái." Shuō zhèijù jílì huà de fēngsu yìshi dào xiànzài
hái yǒu Zhìyú kētóu zhèige fēngsu xiànzài hái yǒu ma?

Mǎ : Xiànzài guònián kētóu de hěn shǎo le. Kěnéng zài xiāngxia hé jiùshì
jiātíngli hái yǒu.

17.0. yú   (1) remainder, the rest; (2) be left (over)

qíyú(de)   the remainder, the remaining, the leftover

duōyú   surplus, superfluous   [much remainder]

17.1. Biānjìngde zhànshì yìtiān bǐ yìtiān kuòdà. Rénmín chàbuduō dōu zǒu
le. Suǒ yú de búguò jǐbǎi rén.   (T)

17.2. Zhèixiē zhúzi、mùtou nǐ kéyi náqu yíbàn qu zào fángzi. Qíyúde wǒ
lìngwài yǒu yòngtú.

17.3. Wǒ jiù yǒu zhèi yímiàn guóqí, méi yǒu duōyúde. Wǒ zěnmo néng
jiègei ni ne?

18.0. xí *   banquet

jiǔxí   banquet   [wine banquet]

zhǔxí   chairman   [chief banquet]

18.1. Mǎnzhou rén jiǔxí hé Huízúde jiǔxí dōu hé Hànrénde jiǔxí bù yíyàng.
(T)

18.2. Tā shi Fóxué yánjiuhuìde zhǔxí, suǒyǐ tā xìn Fójiào.

19.0. guǎn   (1) control, take care of; (2) (coverb in <u>guǎn A</u>
<u>jiào B</u> 'to designate A as B')

bùguǎn   (1) not have charge of; (2) disregard, pay no attention to; (3) regardless of whether, no matter

zhǐguǎn V   only take care of V-ing (see note 6)

zhǐguǎn V hǎo le   go ahead and V

19.1. Nèige háizi yòng shǒu zhuā nǐ. Tāde fùmǔ zěnmo bù guǎn ne?

19.2. Nèige tàitai bùguǎn yǒu qián méi qiǎn, tā yídìng yào chuān chóuzi、
duànzide yīfu.

19.3. Zhāng Xiānsheng zhǐguǎn xiě shū, bùguǎn yìn shū.

19.4. Nǐ zhǐguǎn shuō hǎo le, bú yào pà.   (T)

19.5. Tā zhǐguǎn shuō tāde, wǒ zhǐguǎn mǎi wǒ de.   (T)

19.6. Běifāngde xiǎoháizi guǎn bàozhú jiào pàozhang.

20.0. duōchulai   be in excess (of an expected amount)   [much exit
                        come]

      (duō)yúchulai   (1) be left over, be superfluous; (2) have as surplus

20.1. Wǒ shǔyishǔ wǒde Gǎngbǐ, bù zhīdào zěnmo duōchulai yíkuài qián.

20.2. Wǒ mǎi dōngxi yǐhòu duōyúchulai de qián dōu gěi wǒ dìdi le.

21.0. tóngyīn   have the same sound

      tóngyīnzì   homonym   [same sound character]

21.1. Zhōngguo zì tóngyīnde hěn duō.

21.2. Tóngyīnzì suírán shi tóngyīn, kěshi yìsi bù tóng.

55 Bái: Mǎ Jiàoshòu, gōngxǐ zhèijù huà shēng háizi, jiéhūn de shíhou dōu
          kéyi yòng. Zhìyú fùguì yǒuyú zhèijù huà zhǐ shi guònián cái néng
          yòng, shì bu shi?

    Mǎ : Fùguì yǒuyú shi guònián zhuān yòng de cér. Zhōngguo jiātíng zài
          chúxī wǎnshangde jiǔxíshang, bùguǎn xǐhuan chī yú bù xǐhuan chī yú,
60   dōu yào zuò yìtiáo yú.

    Bái: Nà shi shénmo yìsi?

    Mǎ : Fùguìde yìsi nǐ shi zhīdao de. Yǒuyúde yú hé yìtiáo yúde yú tóngyīn,
          suǒyǐ yǒuyúde yìsi jiu shi duōchulaide yìsi, nà jiu shi shuō fùguì
          lǎo yě bù wán.

22.0. zào   stove

22.1. Zhōngguo běifāng xiāngxia yòng de zào duōbàn shi yòng ní zuò de.
      (T)

23.0. jì   offer sacrifices (to)

      jìzào   make offerings to the Kitchen God   (VO)

23.1. Zhōngguo rén zài guò Xiǎoniár de shíhou chúle jìzào yǐwài hái jì
      shénmo?

24.0. yé *   old gentleman

      shàoye   (your) son (polite form)

      lǎoye   old gentleman (polite form)

      zàowangyé   Kitchen God   [stove king old gentleman]

24.1. Měnggǔ rén hé Xīzàng rén shì bu shi yě dōu jì zàowangyé?

24.2. Cóngqián duì rén jiào <u>lǎoye</u> děngyu xiànzài duì rèn jiào <u>xiānsheng</u>.

24.3. Wǒ dàizhe wǒmen xiǎo shàoye dào gōngyuán qu kàn shīzi.

25.0. làyue   twelfth lunar month

25.1. Zhōngguo rén yí dàole yīnlìde làyue jiu yùbei guònián.

65   Bái: Guò Xiǎoniánr jiu shi jìzào, shì bu shi?

     Mǎ: Shìde. Nǐ zhīdao jìzào shi shénmo yìse ma?

     Bái: Jìzào jiu shi jì zǎowangyé.

     Mǎ: Nǐ zhīdao bù zhīdào Zhōngguo rén zài shénmo shíhou jìzào?

     Bái: Shì bu shi zài làyue èrshisān?

70   Mǎ: Shìde

26.0. shén   spirit, deity, god

     jiēshén   welcome the gods (VO)

     zàoshén   Kitchen God (W)

     shénhuà   myth [god speech]

26.1. Miáozúde rén xìn shénmo shén?

26.2. Zhōngguo rén zài guòniánde shíhou shì bu shi jiājiā yílǜ jiēshén?

26.3. Shìjiè gèguó shànggǔde lìshǐ duōbàn shi shénhuàde.

26.4. Zàoshén jiu shi zàowángyé.

27.0. shāo   (1) burn; (2) roast

27.1. Qiántian dà huǒ nèige yìnshuāsuǒ jījihū dōu shāoguāng le.   (T)

28.0. xiāng   perfume, incense

28.1. Jiēshén de shíhou bìxū shāo xiāng.

29.0. shàng tiān   ascend to heaven

29.1. Guò Xiǎoniánrde wǎnshang sòng zàoshén shàng tiān.   (T)

     Bái: Qǐng wèn, jìzào zěnmo jì ne?

     Mǎ: Jùshuō zàowangyé zài làyue èrshisān nèitiān wǎnshang shàng tiān, suǒyǐ zài èrshisān wǎnshang gěi zàowangyé gòng shuǐguǒ、diǎnxin, shāo xiāng, sòng zàowangyé shàng tiān.

75   Bái: Shénmo shíhou zàowangyé zài huílai ne?

     Mǎ: Děngdao chúxī wǎnshang jiēshén de shíhou zàowangyé yòu huílai le.

30.0. pái(zi)   (1) signboard; (2) trademark; (3) brand, make; (4) playing cards, dominoes, mahjong pieces zhǐpái   playing cards

wán(r) pái   play (cards, mahjong, etc.)

30.1. Nǐde chē hěn hǎo. Shi shénmo páizi de? (T)

30.2. Zhāng dàifude ménkǒu yǒu yíge páizi. Wǒ yí kànjian nèige páizi cái zhǐdao shi Zhāng dàifu kàn bìng de dìfang.

30.3. Tāmen chīguo wǎnfàn jǐnjiēzhe jiù wár zhǐpái.

30.4. Zhōngguo zhǐpái zài shénmo shíhou yǒu de, nǐ zhīdao ma?

31.0. májiàng   mahjong

dǎ májiàng   play mahjong

31.1. Zhōngguo zài kàngzhànde shíhou, zhèngfǔ jìnzhǐ rénmín dǎ májiàng.

31.2. Tā bǎ zhèige yuède gōngqian, dǎ májiàng dōu dǎguāng le.   (T)

32.0. fùnǚ   women, womankind   [woman female]

32.1. Cóngqián Zhōngguo Jiāngnánde fùnǚ dōu huì yǎng cán.

33.0. jǐshí   (1) when; (2) some time or other   [how many time]

33.1. Nǐ jǐshí xué de Déwén? Shì bu shi zài Déguo xué de?

33.2. Nǐ jǐshí yǒu gōngfu wǒmen yíkuàr wár pái.   (T)

34.0. xiāoqiǎn   (1) pastime, hobby, pleasurable activity; (2) engage in a pleasurable activity

34.1. Dǎ májiàng、tīng wúxiàndiàn、kàn diànyǐngr, nǐ yàngyàng dōu bu xǐhuan. Nènmo nǐ zuò shénmo xiāoqiǎn ne?

34.2. Wǒ měitiān chúle gōngzuò yǐwài yào xiāoqiǎn xiāoqiǎn.

Bái: Tīngshuō guònián、guòjié Zhōngguo rén dōu xǐhuan wár pái, shì bu shi?

Mǎ: Duōshù shi fùnǚ zài jiā méi shì, dàjiā zài yíkuàr wárwar pái.

80 Bái: Shi dǎ májiàng ne, háishi wár zhǐpái ne?

Mǎ: Yǒu wár zhǐpái de, yě yǒu dǎ májiàng de.

Bái: Nín huì dǎ májiàng ma?

Mǎ: Wǒ huì shi huì, kěshi wǒ bù xǐhuan.

Bái: Wǒ hái méi kànjianguo dǎ májiàng de.

85 Mǎ: Wǒmen yǒu yìjiā qīnqi tāmen jiāli hěn xǐhuan dǎ. Jǐshí wǒmen dào tā jiā qu kàn tāmen dǎ. Qíshí lǎorén zài yíkuàr dǎ májiàng xiāoqiǎn xiāoqiǎn dào kéyi, wǒ bú zànchéng qīngniánrén cháng dǎ.

35.0. rènao   hustling, busy, lively, entertaining, sociable   [hot noisy]

35.1. Tā bù xǐhuan rènao. Tā xǐhuan yíge rén zài huāyuánli kàn huār. (T)

35.2. Guòniánde shíhou, yàoshi rén duō cái néng rènao. Wǒ jiā rén shǎo,
rènaobuqǐlái.   (T)

36.0. dàren   an adult   [big person]

36.1. Dēngjiéde wǎnshang, dàren、 xiǎohár dōu qu kàn dēng.

37.0. wū(zi)   room (in a house)   (M: jiān)

37.1. Nèijiān wūzi cónglái méi rén jìnquguo. Ǒurán yǒu yíge jīhui wǒ
jìnqu yí kàn, yuánlái shi kōng de.

38.0. yùbei   prepare, get ready   [beforehand prepare]

38.1. Wǒ yào xiě dà zì. Qǐng nǐ xiān gěi wǒ yùbei bǐ hé mòzhī.

39.0. bù   cotton cloth

39.1. Tā yào yòng bù zuò yímiàn wǔsèqí. Biéde yánsede bù dōu yǒu le,
jiù méi yǒu lán yánsede bù.

40.0. gōngsī   company, corporation   [public control]

bǎihuò gōngsī   department store   [hundred goods company]

40.1. Nèige gōngsī ménqiánde páizi shi tóngde ne háishi tiěde ne?

40.2. Yǒu yìjiā bǎihuò gōngsī dōngxi hěn duō. Búdàn yǒu rìyongpǐn, bìngqiě lián zhòngtián de tiěqì dōu yǒu.

Mǎ : Cóngqián wǒ xiǎode shíhou, yīnwei jiāli shi dà jiātíng, rénkǒu duō,
yí dàole guònián de shíhou tèbié rènao. Jiālide dàrenmen měi yíge
90   rén dōu mángde bùdéliǎo. Yǒude shōushi wūzi, yǒude mǎi dōngxi.

Bái : Guònián dōu mǎi shénmo dōngxi ne?

Mǎ : Mǎi chī de、 chuān de、 yòng de. Guònián yǐqián yě yào mǎi hěn duō
cài, bǐrú jī、 yú、 ròu shénmode, yào zài guònián yǐqián yùbeichulai
yíge xīngqīde cài lai. Jiāli tàitaimen dào bǎihuò gōngsī qu mǎi
95   rìyòngpǐn、 chóuduàn gēn bù shénmode.

41.0. shuì(jiào)   to sleep   (VO)

41.1. Gāo Xiānsheng zài yìnshuāsuǒ zuò shì. Nèige yìnshuāsuǒde gōngzuò
hěn duō. Tā shuō tā cóng zuótian mángdào xiànzài, hái méi shuìjiào
ne.

42.0. yè   night   (M)

bànyè   midnight   [half night]

42.1. Zuótian yèli wǒ hé Zhāng Xiānsheng tándao zōngjiào hé Kǒngjiào.
Wǒmen tándao bànyè yǐhòu cái shuìjiào.

43.0. jīngshen   (1) spirits, energy; (2) be energetic, have energy [essence
spirits]

43.1. Shēntǐ bù hǎo de rén jīngshen yě yídìng bù hǎo.

44.0.   gòng   (1) offering; (2) make offerings (to); (3) make offerings (of)

        gòngshén   make offerings to the gods (VO)

        shànggòng   make offerings (VO)

        gòng cài   make offerings of food (VO)

44.1.   Zhōngguo rénde jiāli zài guònián de shíhou yǒu rén gòngshén, yǒu
        rén bú gòng.

44.2.   Guòniánde shíhou jiājiā dòu yào gěi shén shànggòng.

44.3.   Zhōngguo rén shànggòng de shíhou dōu gòng cài.

Bái: Mǎ Jiàoshòu, nín fǔshang shi xiǎo jiātíng, guònián háishi nènmo
        rènao ma?

Mǎ :   Xiànzài bú rènao le, yīlái rén shǎo, èrlái wǒ nèiren bú yuànyi wèile
        guònían yòng hěn duō qián.

100 Bái: Nín fǔshang hái jìzào ma?

Mǎ :   Xiànzài méi yǒu mài zàowangyé de le.

Bái: Zěnmo, zàowangyé hái děi mǎi ma?

Mǎ :   Nǐ dàgài méi kànjianguo zàowangyé. Wǒ lǎojiā nèr yí dàole làyue
        jiu yǒu mài zàowangyé de le. Yàoshi qu mǎi zàowangyé bù néng
105   shuō mǎi, děi shuō qǐng zàowangyé.

Bái: Zàowangyé shénmo yàngr?

Mǎ :   Jiù shi yìnchulai de yìzhāng huàr, shi yíge gǔdài rénde yàngzi.
        Wǒmen jiā xiànzài bú jìzào, kěshi guò Dēngjiér. Yīnwei háizimen
        xǐhuan dēng, suǒyǐ mǎi hěn duō yòng zhǐ zuò de dēng guàqilai.

110 Bái: Chúxī wǎnshang nín fǔshang shuìjiào bu shuì?

Mǎ :   Bú shuì. Yīnwei Zhōngguo chuāntǒng shuō, rúguǒ zài chúxī yèli shuì-
        jiào yìnián jiu bù jīngshen.

Bái: Nín fǔshang gòngshén bú gòng a?

Mǎ :   Wǒ nèirén bu xìn Fó, tā shénmo yě bú gòng.

115 Bái: Jiùshi xìn Fó de gòng shén ma?

Mǎ :   Shìde.

45.0.   lǐ   gift, present

        sònglǐ   send a gift (VO)

45.1.   Wǒ hé Tián Xiānsheng xiāngchùde hěn hǎo. Měinián guònián de
        shíhou tā gěi wǒ sònglǐ, wǒ yě sònglǐ gěi ta.

45.2.   Tā gěi wǒ sòng de lǐ tài duō le.

45.3.   Wǒ gěi Wàn Xiānsheng sòng guòjié lǐ qu.

46.0. rénqíng   (1) human feeling; (2) favor, kindness   [man emotion]

46.1. Bǐcǐ hùxiāng sònglǐ shi biǎoshì rén hé rén zhījiān de rénqíng. (T)

47.0. rénmen   people

47.1. Bú yuànyi bèi rén zhēngfú de rénmen yīnggāi tuánjiéqilai.

48.0. bìmiǎn   avoid, circumvent   [avoid avoid]

48.1. Hánghǎi yòng zhǐnánzhēn kéyi bìmiǎn zǒucuò fāngxiàng.

49.0. jiǎ   false

      jiǎhuà   falsehood   [false speech]

      jiǎrú   if   [false like]

49.1. Tā cháng shuō jiǎhuà, suǒyǐ zhèicì tā shuō de huà yídìng yě shi
      jiǎde.

49.2. Jiǎrú nǐ línjìnde guójiā lai zhēngduó nǐde lǐngtǔ, nǐ shì bu shi yào
      dǐkàng ne?

Bái: Zhōngguo rén guòjié、 guònián shì bu shi dōu yào sònglǐ?

Mǎ : Zhèi shi yìzhǒng rénqíng. Suírán jìnlái yǒu rén tíchang guònián、
      guòjié bú yào sònglǐ, kěshi hái bìmiǎnbuliǎo rénmen sònglǐ de fēngsu
120   xíguàn.

Bái: Yìbānde sònglǐ, dōu sòng shénmo?

Mǎ : Bù yídìng. Yǒu sòng diǎnxin、 shuǐguǒ de, yě yǒu sòng yú、 ròu de,
      hái yǒu sòng rìyòngpǐn de.

Bái: Sònglǐ shi hěn nánde yíjiàn shì. Jiǎrú wǒ gěi rénjie sònglǐ, wǒ
125   gēnběn jiu bù zhīdào gěi rénjia mǎi shénmo.

50.0. zhāodài   entertain, be hospitable to   [recruit treat]

      zhāodàishì   reception room, waiting room

50.1. Wǒ zài zhāodàishì děngle liǎngge zhōngtóu bìng méi yǒu rén chūlai
      zhāodài wo.

50.2. Rúguǒ tā dào Sānfánshì lai, wǒ děi hǎohāo zhāodai zhāodai ta.

51.0. jì(shi)   since, because (W)

      jìrán   since, because

51.1. Tā jìshi bú xìn Lǎmajiào wèi-shénmo shícháng qu Lǎma miào?

51.2. Nǐ jìrán láile jiu zài zhèli duō zhù jǐtiān ba.   (T)

52.0. huài   bad (see note 5)

      huàihuà   slander (N)   [bad speech]

      qìhuài   be terribly angry

huàirén   an evil person, a bad egg

huàishì   evil deed

52.1. Nèige lùyīnjī huài le, bù néng yòng le.

52.2. Yíge rén bú yào lǎo shuō biéren de huàihuà, yě bú yào zuò huàishì.
(T)

52.3. Nèige háizi bù tīng dàrende huà, bǎ tā mǔqin qìhuài le.   (T)

52.4. Nǐ shuō tā jiā méi yǒu hǎo rén, děngyu shuō tā yě shi huàirén le.

Mǎ: Shuō sònglǐ wǒ xiǎngqilai, xià xīngqīliù yǒu ge péngyoude shàoye
     jiēhūn.

Bái: Jiēhūn sònglǐ dōu sòng shénmo?

Mǎ: Duōshù shi sòng qián, yě yǒude sòng dōngxi.   Sòng dōngxi duōbàn
130 shi chuān de, yòng de. Zhèige péngyou shi Huíhui. Tāmen nèitiān
     yòng Huíjiào jiǔxí zhāodài qīnqi péngyou.

Bái: Huíjiào jiǔxí shì bu shi jiù shi méi yǒu zhūròu?

Mǎ: Duìle, jiù shi méi yǒu zhūròu, qíyúde cài gēn wǒmende chàbuduō.

Bái: Nín zhèiwèi péngyou shi wǒmen xuéxiàode ma?

135 Mǎ: Shìde, tā shi fǎxuéyuànde Biān Yòuwén, Biān Xiānsheng.

Bái: Oh, Biān Xiānsheng wǒ rènshi.

Mǎ: Jìrán rènshi nǐ yě cānjiā, hǎo bu hǎo?

Bái: Hǎo.   Wǒ sòng shénmo lǐ ne?

Mǎ: Nǐ sòng sìkuài qián ba.

140 Bái: Zài nǎr? Shi zài tā jiāli ma?

Mǎ: Bú shì, zài Dàhuá Lù Zhōnghuá Fàndiàn.

Bái: Zhōnghuá Fàndiàn hěn yǒumíng.

Mǎ: Shì, Zhōnghuá Fàndiànde dìfang hǎo, érqiě cài yě bú huài, suǒyǐ
     jiēhūn de dōu xǐhuan zài nèr.

53.0. bīng   soldier

53.1. Cóngqián Zhōngguo rén bú zhòngshì dāng bīng de, suǒyǐ cháng shuō:
"Hǎo nán bù dāng bīng." Kěshi xiànzài guānniàn gǎibiàn le, bú
rènwei dāng bīng bù hǎo le, suǒyǐ yòu shuō: "Hǎo nán yào dāng
bīng" le.   (T)

54.0. jù   gather, get together

tuánjù   collect together (W)   [group gather]

54.1. Wǒ xīwang wǒmen jǐge rén yǒu jīhui zài jùyijù.   (T)

54.2. Tāde érzi zài Yìdàlì niàn shū, yǒu wǔnián méi huíjiā. Xiànzài huíjiā lai le, yìjiā rén tuánjù le.   (T)

55.0. bìxū   need, require   [must must]

55.1. Rénmen xiāngchù bìxū hùzhù.   (T)

56.0. mìnglìng   order, command (N/V)   [command order]

56.1. Jūnrén bìxū fúcóng mìnglìng.

57.0. kū   cry, weep

57.1. Tīngshuō nèige rén sǐ le, ruògān rén dōu kū le.

145 Mǎ : Biān Xiānsheng zài Kàngzhànde shíhou, tā érzi gāng shēngchulai tā
          jiù qu gěi Měijūn dāng fānyì.

    Bái : Kàngzhàn de shíhou, Měiguo bīng zài Zhōngguo de duō bu duō?

    Mǎ : Zhèige wǒ bú dà qīngchu. Dǎwánle zhàng yǐhòu tā yòu dào Luómǎ
          qu le. Tā shuō líkai jiā hěn jiǔ cái gēn jiāli rén tuánjù.

150 Bái : Tā zěnmo bù xiǎng fázi zǎo diǎr huíjiā kànkan ne?

    Mǎ : Dāng jūnren bìxū fúcóng mìnglìng, bù néng suíbiàn huíjiā. Biān
          Xiānsheng yǒu yícì gēn wǒ shuōqilai le. Tā shuō tā nèige shíhou
          yīnwei xiǎng jiā xiǎngde zhēn xiǎng kū.

58.0. cìxu   (proper) sequence, scheduled order of events   [occurrence
                series]

58.1. Tā bǎ rénmíngcèshang rénmíngde cìxu xiěcuò le.   (T)

59.0. shīwàng   (1) lose hope; (2) be disappointed

59.1. Tā kǎo dàxué méi kǎoshang. Tā hěn shīwàng.

59.2. Wǒ zhèici bù néng dào Niǔyuē qu. Wǒ fēicháng shīwàng.

60.0. yùnqi   (1) luck (good or bad); (2) lucky   [transport air]

60.1. Rénrén dōu xīwang yǒu hǎo yùnqi, kěshi rénrén bù yídìng dōu yǒu
       hǎo yùnqi.

    Bái : Wǒ fùqin cóngqián shi jūnren. Tā shuō cóngqián jūnren zài wàiguo
155   de shíhou, zhèngfǔ shi ràng tāmen ànzhe cìxu huí jiā de. Tā yǐ
          tīngshuō yǒu rén yào huíjiā le, yàoshi méi yǒu tāde míngzi, tā jiu
          hěn shīwàng.

    Mǎ : Nà dāngrán le, shéi bù xiǎng huíjiā ne?

    Bái : Wǒ fùqin yǒu yícì gēn wǒmen shuōde hěn yǒu yìsi. Tā shuō nèige
160   shíhou tā bǐ shéi dōu xiǎng huíjiā, yīnwei tā cái gēn wǒ mǔqin jiéhūn
          bù jiǔ, dànshi zhèngfǔ bù guǎn nǐ xīn jiéhūn bù xīn jiéhūn. Kěshi
          tāde yùnqi hǎo, méi yǒu hǎojiǔ zhèngfǔ jiù ràng tā huíguó le.

61.0. yóuxì   (1) play, have fun; (2) game, entertainment, amusement [travel
                play]

61.1. Yǒude xuésheng zhǐ xǐhuan yóuxì, bù xǐhuan niàn shū.

61.2. Zhèizhǒng yóuxì zài Měiguo yě yǒu ma?

62.0. zuò(r)   seat

　　　　shàngzuò(r)   seat of honor   [upper seat]

62.1. Wǒ jiā yǒu sānkǒu rén. Chī fàn de shíhou yǒu sānge zuòr. Fùqin zǒngshi zuò shàngzuò.

63.0. wèi, wèr   taste, flavor, odor

63.1. Wǒ xǐhuan chī Zhōngguo fàn, yīnwei Zhōngguo fànde wèr hǎo.

63.2. Zhèr zěnmo zhènmo dàde huǒyào wèr ne? Shì bu shi gāngcái nǐ fàng pàozhang le?

63.3. Lǎo Zhāng yìdiǎr rénqing wèr yě méi yǒu. Wǒ bìngle jǐge yuè tā yě méi lái kànkan wǒ.   (T)

64.0. bāo   (1) to wrap; (2) package, bundle   (M)

　　　　zhǐbāo(r)   package   [paper package]

64.1. Qǐng nǐ bǎ wǒ mǎi de shū bāoqilai.   (T)

64.2. Zhōngguo běifāng rén zài guònián de shíhou duōban bāo jiǎozi chī. (T)

64.3. Nǐ nèige zhǐbāor lǐtou shi shénmo dōngxi?

Mǎ : Jīntian xiàwǔ sì-wǔdiǎn zhōng nǐ yǒu gōngfu ma?

Bái : Wǒ xiǎngyixiǎng . . . Méi shénmo shì.

165 Mǎ : Dì-yī zhōngxué yǒu ge huì, wǒ nèi liǎngge háizi yě cānjiā biǎoyǎn. Lìngwài hái yǒu xiǎoháizimen yóuxì. Nǐ yào bu yào qù?

Bái : Hǎo. Wǒ qù. Xuéshengmen biǎoyǎn, xiǎoháizimen yóuxì dōu hěn yǒu yìsi.

Mǎ : Tīngshuō qù de rén hěn duō, wǒmen děi zǎo diǎr qù, yàoburán jiù
170   méi zuòr le. Nǐ sìdiǎn zhōng zuǒyòu dào wǒ jiā qu chī diǎr diǎnxin, ránhòu wǒmen yíkuàr qù.

Bái : Tài máfan Mǎ Tàitai le.

Mǎ : Méi shénmo.

Bái : Wǒ wàng le shuō le, shàngcì Mǎ Tàitai zuò de cài wèr zhēn hǎo.

175 Mǎ : Yàoshi nǐ xǐhuan chī de huà, kéyi cháng dào wǒ ner chī biànfàn qu.

Bái : Xièxie nín.

Mǎ : Jīntian hěn lěng. Wǒmen qù děi chuān hòu yìdiǎrde yīfu.

Bái : Duìle. Nènmo xiàwǔ jiànle.

Mǎ : Xiàwǔ jiàn. Zhèige zhǐbāor shì nǐde ma?

180 Bái : Shì wǒde. Wǒ wàngle.

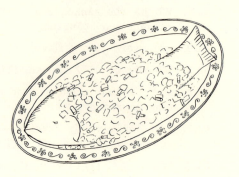

Guònián

SHĒNGCÍ BIǍO

1. Xīnnián

2. lǐ *
   rìlǐ
   yīnlǐ
   yánglǐ
   jiùlǐ
   xīnlǐ

3. zhēngyue

4. chū

5. chúxī

6. chūn *
   chūntian

7. dēng
   kāi dēng

8. jié
   guòjié
   Chūnjié
   Dēngjié(r)
   jiérì (W)

9. Xiǎonián(r)

10. qīnqi

11. bài
    bàinián
    bàishén

12. hùxiāng

13. gōngxǐ

14. fācái

15. jílǐ

16. kētóu

17. yú
    qíyú(de)
    duōyú

18. xí *
    jiǔxí
    zhǔxí

19. guǎn
    bùguǎn
    zhǐguǎn V
    zhǐguǎn V hǎo le

20. duōchulai
    (duō)yúchulai

21. tóngyīn
    tóngyīnzì

22. zào

23. jì
    jìzào

24. yé *
    shàoye
    lǎoye
    zàowangyé

25. làyue

26. shén
    jiēshén
    zàoshén (W)
    shénhuà

27. shāo

28. xiāng

29. shàng tiān

30. pái(zi)
    zhǐpái
    wán(r) pái

31. májiàng
    dǎ májiàng

32. fùnǚ

33. jǐshí

34. xiāoqiǎn

35. rènao

36. dàren

37. wū(zi)

38. yùbei

39. bù

40. gōngsī
    bǎihuò gōngsī

41. shuìjiào

42. yè
    bànyè

43. jīngshen

44. gòng
    gòngshén
    shànggòng
    gòng cài

45. lǐ
    sònglǐ

46. rénqíng

47. rénmen

48. bǐmiǎn

49. jiǎ
    jiǎhuà
    jiǎrú

50. zhāodài
    zhāodàishǐ

51. jì(shi) (W)
    jìrán

52. huài
    huàihuà
    qǐhuài
    huàirén
    huàishì

53. bǐng

54. jù
    tuánjù (W)

55. bìxū

56. mìnglìng

57. kū

58. cìxu

59. shīwàng

60. yùnqi

61. yóuxì

62. zuò(r)
    shàngzuò(r)

63. wèi, wèr

64. bāo
    zhǐbāo(r)

YǓFǍ LIÀNXÍ

A. Reduplication of measures (see <u>Beginning Chinese</u>, p. 397, note 3)

1. Tā shuō de huà jùjù shi kōnghuà.

2. Xiànzài shi chūntian. Tiāntiān dōu hěn nuǎnhuo.

3. Tāmen zhāodài kèrén yòng de chāzi, gègè shi yín de.

4. Wǒ shǒulide Táibǐ, zhāngzhāng dōu shi wǔkuài qián de.

5. Tiáotiáo dà lù tōng Luómǎ.

B. <u>yī</u> in the meaning "the whole of" (see <u>Beginning Chinese</u>, p. 419, note 1)

6. Tā kāi chē cónglái bù xiǎoxīn. Yǒu yícì zài bànyè chūshì le, yì chēde rén dōu sǐ le.

7. Wǒ dàole bǎihuò gōngsī yí kàn, yì gōngsī dōu shi Rìběnde dōngxi.

8. Yì xuéxiàode xuésheng gègè dōu shi Cháoxiǎn rén.

9. Yǒu rén shuō Wéiwú'ěrzúde jiǔxí, yì jiǔxí dōu shi niú yáng ròu.

10. Yì wūzi rén zuótian dǎle yíyède májiàng, suǒyǐ jīntian báitiān tāmen shuìle yìtiānde jiào.

C. V$_1$ hǎo V$_2$ (see note 1)

11. Nǐ bǎ zhǐpái bāoshang, hǎo náhui jiā qu gěi shàoye wár.

12. Nǐ xiān dào zhāodàishǐ qu kāi dēng, hǎo ràng kèrén zài nàli děng wo.

13. Wǒ qù mǎi yuèbing, hǎo gěi rénjia sòng guòjié lǐ.

14. Qǐng nǐ niànyiniàn zhèi jǐge pīnyīn jùzi, hǎo zhīdao nǐ huì bu huì Luómǎzìde pīnyīn.

15. Guònián de shíhou jiājiā zuò hěn duōde cài hǎo gěi zǔxiān gēn shén shànggòng.

D. méi yǒu N kě V (de) (see note 2)

16. Wǒ duìyu jūnshì gǎigé méi yǒu shénmo kě shuō de.

17. Tāde péngyou méi yǒu yíge kěkào de.

18. Wǒmen méi yǒu lù kě zǒu le.

19. Wǒmen lái wǎn le, méi yǒu zuòr kě zuò le.

20. Wǒ dàole bǎihuò gōngsī yí kàn, méi yǒu shénmo dōngxi kě mǎi.

JIǍNGHUÀ

Gèwèi tóngxué:

Jīntian tántan Zhōngguode guònián. Zhōngguo guònián shi zuì rènaode, yě shi zuì néng biǎoxiàn rénqíng wèr de. Měinián yí dào yīnlì làyuè (jiu

shi shí'èryuè), jiājiā jiu kāishǐ yùbei guònián—mǎi bù zuò xīn yīfu la,

5 shōushi wūzi la, mǎi guònián yòng de dōngxi la, qīnqi péngyou hùxiāng

sòng lǐ la, yìzhí mángdao làyuè èrshisān jiù guò Xiǎoniár le. Guò Xiǎo-

niár shi jìzào de rìzi. Shénmo jiào jìzào ne? Jìzào jiu shi shāo xiāng,

shànggòng, sòng zàoshén shàng tiān. Zhōngguo shénhuà shuō zàoshén

(pǔtōng jiào zàowangyé, jiu shi guǎn zào de shén) zài làyuè èrshisān shàng

10 tiān, làyuè sānshí chúxī wǎnshang zài huílai. Jùshuō yìjiā rén suǒ zuò

de shì, wúlùn shi hǎoshì huòzhe shi huàishì, zàoshén dōu jìxialai. Dàole

guò Xiǎoniár de zhèi yìtiān wǎnshang, zàoshén shàngle tiān, yào xiàng

tiānshàngde shén bàogào zhèi yìjiā rén zài zhèi yìnián lǐtou suǒ zuò de

shì. Suǒyǐ jiājiā zài zhèi yì wǎnshang jìzào, qǐng tā shàng tiān zhīhòu

15 duō shuō hǎo huà.

Guòle Xiǎoniár yǐhòu, jiēzhe jiu shi chúxī. Chúxī shi làyuè zuìhòu
yìtiānde wǎnshang, yě shi yìnián zuì hòu yìtiānde wǎnshang, jiào chúxī.
Zhè yì wǎnshang zuì zhùyì de yíjiàn shì shi quán jiā tuánjù. Fánshi jiārén
zài yuǎnde dìfang bùguǎn shi zuò shì de huòshi niàn shū de, rúguǒ kěnéng
20 de huà dōu yào huídao jiāli, dàjiā zài yíkuàr chī chúxīde wǎnfàn. Jiǎrú
jiāli yǒu rén bù néng huílai guònián de huà, jiāli rén jiu huì hěn shīwàng.
Rúguǒ quán jiā tuánjùle, dàjiā dāngrán dōu hěn kuàilède zài yíkuàr. Háizi,
dàren dōu bìmiǎn shuōchu bù jílìde huà, xiǎoháizi yě bù xǔ kū.

Zhèige shíhou dàjiā chī hěn hǎode wǎnfàn. Wǎnfàn bìxū yǒu yìtiáo yú.
25 Yīnwei Zhōngguo rén guònián dōu yào shuō jílì huà, suǒyi yǒu yíjù huà
shi "Fùguì yǒu yú." Yú jiù shi duōyú de yìsi. Yǒuyúde yìsi jiu shi xīwang jīnniánde qián duōchulai de yìsi. Yīnwei chī yú de yú gēn duōyú de
yú shi tóngyīnzì, suǒyǐ guònián yídǐng yǒu yìtiáo yú.

Chīwánle wǎnfàn dàole bànyè, quán jiā dōu dào yuànzilǐ jiēshén, nà
30 jiu shi shāo zhǐ, shāo xiāng, kētóu, fàng pàozhang. Jùshuō shén kéyi gěi
rénmen hǎode yùnqi. Jiēguòle shén dàjiā huídao wūzili qǐng lǎonián rén
zuò shàngzuò, jiārén ànzhe cìxu gěi lǎorén kētóu bàinián. Lǎonián rén
duì měige rén shuō xiē jílìde huà, gěi háizimen yíge hóng zhǐbāo, lǐmiàn
shi qián. Dàrenmen yǒude dǎ mǎjiàng, yǒude wár zhǐpái, duōbàn zhēngyè
35 bú shuìjiào, yìsi shi yǒu jīngshen. Jiù zhèiyàng rèrenāonàode yóu chúxī
dàole Xīnnián.

Xīnnián shi zhǐzhe zhēngyue chūyī shuō de. Zhè shi Xīnnián de dì-
yītiān. Zhè yītiān jiājiā yào bǐcǐ bàinián. Měige rén jìrán yào chūqu
gěi qīnqi、péngyou、tóngzúde rén bàinián, yòu yào zài jiāli zhāodài lái
40 bàiniánde rén, suǒyǐ jiājiā mángde bùdéliǎo, chàbuduō zuìshǎo máng wǔ-
liùtiān cái kéyi bàiwán nián. Zài bàinián de shíhou dàjiā jiànmiàn dì-
yījù huà yào shuō: "Gōngxǐ fācái." Rénjia rúguǒ yǒu xiǎoháizi yě yào
gěi xiǎoháizi qián. Háizimen jùzai yíkuàr yóuxì huòzhě fàng pàozhang.
Dàole zhēngyue shíwǔ qiánhòu yě yǒu jǐtiān rènaode rìzi jiàozuo Dēngjié.
45 Jiājiā guàzhe hěn hǎokànde dēng. Dēngjié wánle zhīhòu cái suàn guòwánle
nián.

Yǐshàng suǒ shuō de guònián qíngxing xiànzài yǒude yě gǎibiàn le.
Bǐfang shuō xiànzài hěn shǎo yǒu rén kētóu le. Guò yīnli nián běnlái shi
Zhōngguo rén duōnián chuántǒngde xíguàn. Zài Mínguó chūnián zhèngfǔ
50 mìnglìng rénmín yào guò yánglì nián. Dànshi zhè shi yìzhǒng xíguàn,
hěn bù róngyi gǎibiàn. Hòulai zhèngfǔ zhǐ hǎo bǎ yīnlì nián jiàozuo Chūnjié, hǎo jiào rénmín zhàoyàngde guò zhèige yīnlì nián. Jiěguǒ xiànzài
Zhōngguo rén zài yìnián zhīnèi yào guò liǎngge nián, yīnlì nián hé yánglì
nián.

FÙSHÙ

Zhèipán lùyīndài shì Zhōngwén dì-yīzǔ dì-jiǔhào, dì-jiǔcìde lùyīn, shi
Bái Wénshān fùshù Zhōngguode fāmíng.

Wǒmen xuéxiào cóng wàibiar qǐnglai yíwèi hěn yǒumíngde shǐxuéjiā,
gěi wǒmen jiǎng Zhōngguode fāmíng. Kāishǐ xiān jiǎng sīde fāmíng. Tā
5 shuō Zhōngguo zài Shāng Cháo yǐqián jiù yǐjing fāmíngle sī. Tā yòu shuō
hěn gǔde shíhou yǒu rén ǒurán zài yuànzili kànjian chóngzi tǔ sī (jiu shi
cán tǔ sī), yúshì tā jiu yǎng cán tǔ sī, bǎ cán tǔde sī zuòchengle xiàn,
ránhòu yòu yòng sīxiàn zhīchéng sīzhīpǐn, lìrú chóuzi、duànzi děngděng.
Sī zhī de dōngxi dōu hěn piàoliang, sīzhīpǐn búdàn néng zuò yīfu érqiě yě
10 kéyi yòng ta xiě zì gēn huà huàr. Tā hái shuō nèige shíhou rénmen bǎ
fāmíng zhī chóuduàn de fázi bǎoshǒu mìmi, kěshi zhī de rén yì duō le
jiu méi fázi bǎoshǒu mìmi le. Zài Hàn Cháo de shíhou bǎ chóuduàn
chuándàole Luómǎ. Luómǎ zhèige guójiā yòng huángjīn lai mǎi Zhōngguode chóuduàn. Luómǎ huángdì yí kàn yòng jīnzi huàn chóuduàn zuò

15 yīfu, tā bú yuànyi bǎ Luómǎde jīnzi dōu liúdao Zhōngguo qu, suǒyǐ tā jiu

kāishǐ jìnzhǐ chuān chóu duàn zuò de yīfu.

Zhǐnánzhēn yě shi Zhōngguo fāmíng de. Shìshí zhèngmíng zhǐnánzhēn

zài Nán Běi Cháode shíhou jiu yǒu rén yòng le. Zhǐnánzhēn duì hángkōng,

hánghǎi dōu yǒu yòngchu. Tāde tèxìng shi tā lǎo zhǐzhe nán běi. Tā zhǐ

20 de xiāngdāng zhèngquè, juéduì bú huì cuò de.

Zhōngguo hái fāmíng zào zhǐ. Zài Hàn Cháode shíhou jiu yǐjing fāmíng

le. Zài nèige shíhou zhǐde yòngchu hěn dà, yīnwei nèige shíhou shū dou

shi rén yòng zhǐ xiěchulai de.

Yìnshuā yě shi Zhōngguo gǔdài fāmíng zhī yī, yě shi hěn zǎo jiu

25 fāmíng le. Dàyuē zài gōngyuán liùbǎi nián de shíhou jiu zhīdao zài tóng-

shang huòzhě shítoushang kē zì, tóngshí yě huì kē túzhāng le. Nèige

shíhou jiù zhīdao zài tóngshang hé shítoushang de zì yòng zhǐ hé mò bǎ

ta yìnxialai. Zhè kéyi shuō shi yìnshuāde kāishǐ. Fāmíng yìnshuā shi

xiān yòng mùbǎn bǎ zì kēshangqu zài yìnxialai. Dào Sòng Cháo de shíhou

30 jiu yǒule huózì yìnshuā le. Děngdao shíwǔ-liù shìjì de shíhou, Déguo cái

yǒu yìnshuā. Zhè kéyi zhèngmíng Xīfāngde yìnshuā bǐ Zhōngguo wǎn.

Hē chá yě shi Zhōngguo rén kāishǐ de. Zài gōngyuán sān shìjì jiu

yǒu rén tídao hē chá. Zài Táng Cháo zhīhòu hē chá de xíguàn cái pǔbiàn

le.

35 Yòu shuōdao kuàizi. Zhōngguo rén chī dōngxi dōu shi yòng kuàizi.

Kuàizi zài gōngyuánqián sān shìjì jiu yòng le. Yīnwei nèige shíhou jiu

yǒu rén tídao yòng kuàizi, shuōbudìng Zhōu Cháo yǐqián jiu bú yòng shǒu

ér yòng kuàizi chī dōngxi le. Xīfāng rén shíliù shìjì cái yòng dāo chā,

nènmo Zhōngguo rén yòng kuàizi bǐ Xīfang rén yòng dāo chā zǎole chàbu-

40 duō liǎngqiān nián. Jùshuō xiànzài shìjièshangde rén hái yǒu sānfēnzhī-yī

réngrán yòng shǒu zhuāzhe chī ne.

WĒNXI

1. Chūntian shi yìnián lǐtou zuì hǎode rìzi. Tiānqi bù lěng yě bú rè. Jiǎrú
yǒu gōngfu, zhènghǎo qu lüxíng. Zài guòqu jǐniánde chūntian, wǒ dōu dào
yǒu shān yǒu shuǐ de dìfang zhù jǐtiān. Zhǐ yǒu zài yǒu shān yǒu shuǐ
de dìfang cái néng shēnshēnde gǎndao chūntian de měi.

2. Jīntian guòjié wǒ zhèng zài jiāli bāo jiǎozi, hūrán yǒu jǐge péngyou lai
kàn wo. Wǒ duì tāmen shuō: "Wǒ méi yǒu shénmo kéyi zhāodài nǐmen

de, jiù zài wǒ jiā guòjié chī jiǎozi ba. Nǐmen chī jiǎozi chīdelái ma?"
Yǒu yíge péngyou shuō: "Chīdelái." Yòu yǒu yíge péngyou shuō: "Wǒ
búdàn chīdelái, yàoshi yǒu duōyúde wǒ hái yào ná jǐge huí jiā qu ne."

3. Yǒu yíge yánjiu Zhōngguo mínzú de wàiguo rén. Tā shuō zài Zhōngguo
zhěnggèr mínzúli bāokuò yǒu liùshi duō ge shǎoshù mínzú. Zhèixiē shǎoshù mínzúde míngchēng tài bù róngyi jì. Xiànzài bǎ zhǔyàode mínzú hé
dàyuēde rénshù xiězai xiàbian:

Hànzú	wǔyì sìqiān duō wàn rén.
Mǎnzú	èrbǎi duō wàn rén
Měngzú	yìbǎi sìshi duō wàn rén
Huízú	sānbǎi wǔshi duō wàn rén
Zàngzú	èrbǎi qīshi duō wàn rén
Miáozú	sānbǎi èrshi duō wàn rén
Wéiwú'ěrzú	sānbǎi duō wàn rén
Yízú	sānbǎi sìshi duō wàn rén
Zhuàngzú	liùbǎi wǔshi duō wàn rén
Zhòngjiā	yìbǎi bāshi duō wàn rén
Cháoxiǎnzú	yìbǎi yīshi duō wàn rén

4. Yǒu jǐge xuésheng yào dào hěn gāode shānshang qù huà huàr qu, hái xiǎng
zài shānshang zhù jǐtiān. Tāmen zhīdao shānshang méi yǒu rénjiā, bìděi
zìjǐ zuò fàn chī. Tāmen yòu xiǎngdao shānshang yídìng méi yǒu zào,
zěnmo zuò fàn ne? Hòulai yǒu yíge xuésheng shuō: "Wǒmen kéyi zài
shānshang yòng tǔ zuò yíge zào." Dàjiā shuō: "Hǎo."

5. Zhōngguo rén zài jiérì duōbàn yào jìshén hé bàishén. Jìshén hé bàishén
yǒu shénmo fēnbié ne? Yǒu rén shuō jìshén yídìng yào shànggòng, yào
gòng cài gēn shuǐguǒ shénmode. Dāngrán yě yào shāo xiāng kētóu. Bàishén bù yídìng shànggòng, zhǐ shi shāo xiāng kētóu jiù kéyi le.

6. Zhōngguo rén cóngqián guò Xīnnián de shíhou jiājiā gòngshén. Xiànzài
yǒude gòngshén yǒude bú gòngshén le.

7. Zhōngguo xiāngcūnde rénmen píngcháng bù néng ná wán zhǐpái zuòwei
xiāoqiǎn, rènwei wán zhǐpái shi huàishì. Kěshì yí dàole guònián kě jiù
suíbián wán zhǐpái le.

8. Mǎ Xiānsheng yǒu yíge tóngqì. Jù chuánshuō shi cóng Zhōu Cháo chuánxialai de, lí xiànzài yuē yǒu jǐqiān nián le. Yǒu huàirén shuō Mǎ Xiānshengde huàihuà, shuō nèige tóngqì shi jiǎ de. Mǎ Xiānsheng shuō:
"Bùguǎn shi zhēnde shi jiǎde wǒ yào hǎohāode bǎocún zhèige tóngqì."

9. Yīnlì làyue chūwǔ shi Wáng zhǔxíde shēngri. Tā xiǎng yùbei jiǔxí zhāodài qīnqi péngyou. Kěshì tā wèile bìmiǎn dàjiā sònglǐ, tā zài shìqián bú
jiào rénjia zhīdao shi tāde shēngri.

10. Yǒu liǎngge xuésheng shi tóngxìng, tāmende míngzi yòu shi tóngyīnzì,
suǒyǐ dàjiā jiàoqi tāmen liǎngge rénde míngzi hěn nán fēnbié. Tāmen

tīngle yǒu rén jiào, yě bù zhīdào shi jiào shéi? Hòulái yǒu yíge xuésheng bǎ tā míngzi dì-èrge tóngyīnde zì gǎi le. Dàjiā jiàoqilai cái fāngbiàn le.

11. Rén bù yīngdāng shuō jiǎhuà.   Rúguǒ shuōle yícì jiǎhuà, xiàcì shuō huà rénjia bù xiāngxìn le.   Yǒu yícì, yǒu yíge rén yǒu yíge tóngde chāzi, tā shuō shi jīnde, dàjiā zhīdao tā shi shuō jiǎhuà.   Hòulái tā zhēnde yǒule yíge huángjīn de chāzi, tā yòu duì dàjiā shuō shi jīnde chāzi. Tā cái yì shuō dàjiā jiù yǐwei tā yòu zài shuō jiǎhuà le.

12. Rén zài shèhuìshang duìyu qítāde rén yào hùxiāng bāngzhu. Bú yào zhǐguǎn zìjǐ, bùguǎn biéren.

13. Yòng qián yīngdāng jiéshěng. Zuì hǎo néng zài yǒu qiánde rìzi xiǎngdao jiānglái méi yǒu qián de rìzi. Qiānwàn bú yào dàole méi qián de shíhou, cái xiǎngqi dāngchū yǒu qiánde shíhou.   Nà jiù wǎn le.

14. Yǒu yíwèi zhǔxi cháng shuō dàhuà.   Yǒu rén shuō: "Shuō dàhuà jiu shi shuō jiǎhuà."   Yòu yǒu rén shuō: "Dàhuà shi dàhuà, jiǎhuà shi jiǎhuà, bìng bù wánquán xiāngtóng."   Xiànzài wǒ qǐng wèn ni, dàhuà hé jiǎhuà shì bu shi xiāngtóng? Qǐng nǐ xiángxì fēnxifēnxi.

15. Xīkāng shi Zhōngguo xiànzàide yíge shěng.   Xīkāng Shěng jìngnèi yǒu yíbùfen tǔdì zuìchū shi yóu Xīzàngde Lǎma tǒngzhì, hòulái biànwei yóu zhèngfǔ tǒngzhì le. Zhèizhǒng biàngēng duì guójiā rénmín dōu yǒu hǎochu.

16. Zhōngguode zhǐbì qǐyuán zài Táng Cháo. Dāngshí shi gōngyuán qī-bā shìjì.   Táng Cháode lǐngtǔ yìtiān bǐ yìtiān kuòzhǎn, duìwàide jiāotōng yě yìtiān bǐ yìtiān duōqilai le. Yuánlái suǒ yòng tóng、 tiě zuò de qián, dàiqilai hěn bù fāngbiàn, suǒyǐ jiu zìrán'érránde gǎiyòng zhǐ zuò de qián. Nà jiu shi zhǐbì.

17. Wǒ duì dìdi shuō: "Bàoshang yǒu yìpiān wénzhāng xiě de zuì hǎo, wǒ yí kàn zhèipiān wénzhāng jiu zhīdao shi Zhāng Xiānsheng xiě de." Dìdi wèn wo: "Zhāng Xiānshengde wénzhāng hǎo zài shénmo dìfang ne?" Wǒ shuō: "Zhāng Xiānshengde wénzhāng dì-yī shi yǒu chuàngzàoxìng. Qícì shi wénzhāngde jiégòu hǎo, yǒu xìtǒng." Dìdi shuō: "Zhāng Xiānsheng yìtiān bú zuò biéde jiù xiě wénzhāng, tāde wénzhāng dāngrán hǎo le."

18. Yǒu yíge rén xué Hànyǔ Pīnyīn. Tā wèn wǒ gònghéde hé zì zěnmo pīn? Tā yòu wèn gònghéde hé gēn hépíngde hé Hànzì shì bu shi yíge zì?

19. Yǒu rén wèn wo duōshao Rénmínbì hé yíkuài Měijīn? Wǒ shuō wǒ méi kànjianguo Rénmínbì, wǒ bù zhīdào.

20. Yǒu yíge yàofànde jǐn gēnzhe yíge rénde hòubian, yìbiān zǒu yìbiān shuō: "Lǎoye gěi wo yìdiǎr qián ba!" Zhèige yàofànde yòu shuō: "Xiānsheng bāngbang máng ba." Nèige rén jiu gěi tā yìdiǎr qián. Kěshi xīnli xiǎng: "Zhèige yàofànde wèi-shénmo jiào wǒ lǎoye yòu jiào wǒ shi xiānsheng ne? Huòzhě tā shi yíge jiù shídàide rén, suǒyǐ tā duì rén hái jiào lǎoye. Hòulái tā yěxǔ juéde zài zhèige xīn shídài duì rén yīngdāng jiào xiānsheng, suǒyǐ yòu jiào wǒ shi xiānsheng le."

21. Zhāodàishìli zuòzhe hǎojǐwèi kèrén. Zuòzai zhōngjiànde yíge lǎonián rén, jùshuō shi Qīng Cháo shíhou zài Gānsu Shěng zuòguo guān.   Cóngqián dàjiā dōu jiào tā shi Zhāng lǎoye. Jīntiān lái jiàn zhèlide zhǔrén, tā shuō: "Cóngqián wǒ hé zhèlide zhǔrén cháng jùzai yíkuàr. Kěshi jīntiān

wǒ lái de shíhou zhèlide zhǔrén búdàn méi chūlai jiē wo, yòu jiào wǒ zài
zhāodàishǐ děngle dà bàntiān. Zhè gāi jiào rén duómo nánguò a, zhēn
bǎ rén qìhuài le."

22. Wǒ yǒu yíge péngyou shi Měijūnde yīsheng. Yǒu yìtiān tā lái kàn wo,
wǒmen tánle yìhuěr. Zài tā yào zǒu de shíhou hūrán fāxiàn tāde chē huài
le, méi fázi zǒu le. Wǒ duì tā shuō: "Chē jìshi huài le, nǐ jiu búbì zǒu
le. Jiù zài wǒ zhèli chīguo wǎnfàn zài zǒu ba." Tā shuō: "Wǒ yídìng
yào mǎshang jiu zǒu, yīnwei wǒ hái yào gěi yíge rén qu mǎi yào ne."

23. Yǒu yíge wàiguo rén wèn wo: "Zhōngguo rén chī fàn shíhou de zuòwei
nǎlǐ shi shàngzuò? Nǎlǐ shì zhǔren zuò de dìfang? Shì bu shi gēn wàiguo rénde xíguàn yíyàng?" Wǒ gàosu tā bú shi yíyàng de.

24. Zài qīngnián rènde yìshìlǐ zuì hǎo néng yǒu chuàngzàoxìng. Nénggòu
chuàngzào cái nénggou jìnbù.

25. Yǒu sānge xuésheng shícháng zài yíkuàr zuò fàn chī. Yǒu yíge rén shuō:
"Qián jǐcì zuò fàn dōu shi nǐmen mǎi de dōngxi. Wǒ jìshi cháng zài zhèli
chī fàn, zhèicì zuò fàn gāi wǒ mǎi dōngxi le."

WÈNTÍ

1. Zhōngguo rén kāishǐ yùbei guònián shi zài yīnlì něi yíge yuè? Zěnmo
   yùbei?

2. Shénmo shi guò Xiǎonián? Guò Xiǎonián yào zuò shénmo?

3. Shénmo jiào jìzào? Wèi-shénmo yào jìzào? Zàoshén yào dào nǎlǐ qu?
   Shénmo shíhou huílai?

4. Yīnlì làyue zuìhòu yìtiānde wǎnshang jiàozuo shénmo rìzi? Zài zhèi wǎnshang zuì zhùzhòngde yíjiàn shì shi shénmo?

5. Chúxīde wǎnfàn bìxū yǒu shénmo cài? Wèi-shénmo yào yǒu nèige cài
   ne?

6. Yīnlìde zhēngyue qíshi shi jǐyue? Zhēngyue shíwǔ shi shénmo jié? Wèi-
   shénmo jiào zhèige míngchēng ne?

7. Bàinián de shíhou dàjiā jiànmiàn dì-yījù huà duōban yào shuō shénmo?
   Zhèijù huà chúle zài bàinián shíhou shuō hái zài shénmo shíhou kéyi shuō
   ne?

8. Zhēngyue chūyī shi Xīnniánde dì-yītiān. Jiājiā wèi-shénmo dōu hěn máng?
   Dàyuē yào máng jǐtiān?

9. Chúxī wèi-shénmo yào jiēshén? Shi zěnmoyàngde jiē?

10. Wèi-shénmo Zhōngguo rén zài yìniánli yào guò liǎngcì nián? Yīnlì nián
    wèi-shénmo yòu jiào Chūnjié?

ILLUSTRATIVE SENTENCES (ENGLISH)

1.1. It is a traditional custom for Chinese to set off [lit. let go] firecrackers
     at New Year's.

2.2. In general the lunar year (i.e. the lunar New Year) is in February in the solar calendar.

8.1. In the first month of the lunar year in particular there are a lot of holidays. Right after the Spring Festival has been celebrated the Lantern Festival comes along.

10.1. I have a relative who can weave silk and satin.

11.1. In celebrating New Year's some people go to the homes of relatives to pay New Year's calls, and some go to the temples to worship the gods. I don't do either.

12.1. Some people say that most people [in society] make use of each other.

14.2. If you go see a merchant right on the first day that he begins to do business you can say to him: "Best wishes [lit. congratulations] for your prosperity."

16.1. Formerly in China officials had to kowtow when they saw the emperor.

17.1. The fighting on the frontier is spreading day by day. Almost all the people have left. Those who remain don't exceed a few hundred.

18.1. Manchu and Mohammedan banquets are different from those of the Chinese.

19.4. Go ahead and talk, don't be afraid.

19.5. Say whatever you like, I'll buy whatever I want.

22.1. The stoves used in the country in North China are for the most part made of (dried) mud.

27.1. In yesterday's big fire that print shop was almost completely burned down.

29.1. In the evening when celebrating Little New Year's they see the Kitchen God off to heaven.

30.1. Your car's very nice. What make is it?

31.2. He squandered the whole of his wages for this month playing mahjong.

33.2. Sometime when you have time let's play cards together.

35.1. He doesn't like socializing. He likes to look at the flowers by himself in the garden.

35.2. When celebrating the New Year's it can only be lively if there are a lot of people. My family is small so it can't be (as) lively.

46.1. Giving gifts to each other is an expression of (good) feeling among people.

51.2. Since you've come, stay a few more days here.

52.2. A person should not constantly slander other people nor should he do evil deeds.

52.3. That child doesn't obey adults and has infuriated his mother.

53.1. In the past the Chinese didn't have a high regard for soldiering, so they frequently said: "Good men [lit. male] don't become soldiers." But now the outlook has changed, and soldiering is no longer considered unworthy [lit. bad], so they say: "Good men should become soldiers."

54.1. I hope we [few people] will have an opportunity to get together again.

54.2. His son studied in Italy and hadn't returned home for five years. Now he's returned home, and the whole family has gathered together.

55.1. People living together should help each other.

58.1. He wrote the names in the wrong order in the roster.

63.3. Zhang has no human sympathy. I was sick for several months but he didn't come to see me.

64.1. Please wrap up the books I bought.

64.2. Most Northern Chinese make [lit. wrap] dumplings to eat when celebrating New Year's.

NOTES

1. The word hǎo 'good' used between two verbal phrases means 'so as to, in order to':

> Wǒ xiǎng mǎi yìpán lùyīndài hǎo lù yīn. 'I'd like to buy a tape so as to do some recording.'

2. The construction méi yǒu N kě V (de) means 'not have any N that one can V':

> Tā méi yǒu huà kě shuō de. 'He didn't have anything to say' or 'There was nothing that he could say.'

3. Before 1912 the Chinese used a lunar calendar consisting of twelve months of twenty-nine or thirty days each. A thirteenth month was added from time to time to keep the lunar year abreast of the solar year. The first month of the lunar year began about February first in the solar calendar. The lunar and solar calendars are called yīnlì and yánglì respectively. The first syllables of the names refer to the yīnyáng dualism of moon versus sun, dark versus light, female versus male, even numbers versus odd numbers, and so on.

4. The first ten days of the lunar month are designated by the numbers one to ten preceded by chū 'beginning':

> chūyī   'first day of the lunar month'
>
> chūshí   'tenth day of the lunar month'

5. The stative verb huài 'bad, spoiled' also functions as a postverb. As a postverb it has in some cases its original meaning; in others it functions as an intensifier:

> Tā bǎ pánzi dōu dǎhuài le. 'He smashed all the dishes.'
>
> Tā bǎ xiǎoháizi dǎhuài le. 'He gave the child an awful beating.'

6. The expression zhǐ guǎn is used in a variety of ways, some of which can be illustrated by the following sentences:

> Tā zhǐ guǎn zuò fàn. 'He just takes care of the cooking.'

Nǐ zhǐ guǎn shuō. or Nǐ zhǐ guǎn shuō hǎo le. 'Just go ahead and say (what you have in mind' (i.e. don't mind others).

Nǐ zhǐ guǎn shuō nǐde. Wǒ zhǐ guǎn zuò wǒde. 'Just go ahead and talk. I'll do just what I want.'

Tā zhǐ guǎn shuō tāde. Wǒ bù lǐ ta. 'He just talked. I didn't pay any attention to him.'

Guòjié

Dì-Shíyīkè. Guòjié

Bái: Mǎ Jiàoshòu zǎo.

Mǎ : Zǎo. Zuótian jiǎng guònián, duìyu cér hé suǒ jiǎng de nèiróng yǒu shénmo wèntí méi yǒu?

Bái: Méi yǒu shénmo wèntí.

5 Mǎ : Lùyīn fùshù le ma?

Bái: Zuótian wǎnshang lùguo le. Wǒ zìjǐ tīngting bǐ yǐqián jǐcì shuōde bǐjiǎo jìnbù le.

Mǎ : Nà hǎojíle.

Bái: Zuótian jiǎng de guò Zhōngguo nián hěn yǒu yìsi—jìzào、jiēshén、
10   guò Dēngjié shénmode.

Mǎ : Nǐ yì shuō guònián wǒ jiu hěn xiǎng wǒde lǎojiā. Zài lǎojiāde shíhou tóngzúde rén hé qīnqi péngyou duō, suǒyǐ yí dàole guònián nà shi xiāngdāng rènao.

Bái: Nà duómo yǒu yìsi a. Mǎ Jiàoshòu, zuótian wǒ jiēdào wǒ mǔqin
15   lái xìn shuō, wǒ dìdi kǎoshang dàxué le.

Mǎ : Nǐ dìdi yě niàn dàxué le?

Bái: Bié tí le. Wǒ zhèige dìdi ya, wèile niàn shū bú yònggōng bǎ wǒ fùmǔ gěi qìhuài le. Fùmǔ dōu rènwei tā bù kěnéng niàn dàxué, méi xiǎngdào tā kǎoshang le.

20 Mǎ : Tā suīrán bú yònggōng wǒ xiāngxìn tā yídìng hěn cōngming. Kěshi kǎoshì yě yǒude shíhou kào yùnqi.

Bái: Wǒ shuō tā shi shǔyu dì-èrzhǒng de, shi kào yùnqi le.

Mǎ : Nǐ dìdi jīnnián duó dà le?

Bái: Shíbāsuì le. Shuōqi tā niàn shū lai zhēn yǒu yìsi. Tā yǒu yíyàng
25   hǎochu—jiāli shénmo dōngxi huàile tā dōu huì shōushi. Báitiān wár, wǎnshang hěn zǎo jiu shuìjiào, cónglái bú yùbei gōngke, fēiděi dàkǎo cái kàn shū.

Mǎ : Tā niàn něixì?

Bái: Niàn gōngchéng.

30 Mǎ : Tā yídìng shùxué hěn hǎo le?

Bái: Yě bújiànde. Wǒ xiǎng xīngqīliù yǒu gōngfu gěi ta xiě fēng xìn, gàosu tā niàn dàxué bù yào xiàng niàn zhōngxué nènmo bú yònggōng, yào yǒu hǎode chéngji bìděi nǔlì xuéxi.

Mǎ : Tā jìrán jìnle dàxué zìrán'érránde jiu zhīdao yònggōng le.

1.0. dēng   mount, ascend

dēng shān   ascend a mountain

dēnggāo   ascend to a high place

1.1. Wǒ zuì xǐhuan dēng shān, yīnwei zài shānshang kéyi kàndao hěn
     yuǎnde dìfang.

1.2. Qǐng nǐ kànkan rìlì, míngtian rúguǒ shi yīnlì jiǔyue chūjiǔ wǒ xiǎng
     gēn nǐ yíkuàr qu dēnggāo.

2.0. shù   tree (M: kē)

shùlínzi   forest, woods

2.1. Wǒmen nèige cítáng ménqián yǒu hěn duō shù, dōu shi wǒmen zú-
     zhǎng zhòng de.

2.2. Nèi jǐge háizi tiāntiān zài shùlínzili yóuxì.

3.0. kē   (measure for trees and plants)

3.1. Nèikē dà shù xiàbiān yǒu yíge xiǎo miào.   Miàoli bù zhīdào shi
     shénmo shén, tiāntiān yǒu rén lái bài.

4.0. wèi*   not yet (W)

wèilái(de)   future

4.1. Jùshuō shén néng zhīdao wèiláide shì.

5.0. nàn   distress, disaster, difficulty

nànmín   refugee [disaster people]

zāinàn   calamity, disaster [calamity disaster]

5.1. Shuǐ、huǒde gōngyòng suírán hěn dà, kěshi yǒushíhou yě gěi rénlèi
     dàilai hěn dàde zāinàn.   (T)

5.2. Yīnwei zhànzhēng méi fázi zhòng dì. Fánshi nóngmín, wúlùn dìzhǔ、
     zìgēngnóng、diànnóng dōu biànchéng nànmín le.

6.0. zhī   (measure for animals and various objects)

6.1. Wǒ zài yánglì xīnnián chīle yìzhī jī, wèr hěn hǎo.

35 Bái: Mǎ Jiàoshòu, yòu kuài dào dēnggāo de shíhou le.

Mǎ : Hái yǒu liǎngge xīngqī ne.

Bái: Nín dào nǎr dēnggāo qu?

Mǎ : Yě wúsuǒwèi dēnggāo le.   Yàoshi xīngqīliùde huà, dàizhe xiǎohár
     dēng shān qu, zhǎo yíge shùlínzi zài nèr chīchi dōngxi, wárwar.
40   Yěxǔ zhǎo liǎngge péngyou yíkuàr qu.

Bái: Dēnggāo yě shi shìdàfu jiējide yìzhǒng xiāoqiǎn.

Mǎ : Duìde. Yàoshi méi yǒu fàn chī shéi hái qù dēnggāo?

Bái: Mǎ Jiàoshòu, zhèige fēngsu shi cóng shénmo shíhou yǒu de?

Mǎ : Jù chuánshuō shi zài Dōng Hànde shíhou yǒu yíge rén, tāde lǎoshī
45   zhīdao wèiláide shìqing. Yǒu yìtiān gàosu ta, jiǔyue chūjiǔ nèitiān
        tāmen yìjiā rén dōu yǒu zāinàn, nèitiān bǐděi dào gāo shānshang
        qu. Dàole jiǔyue chūjiǔ nèitiān, tāmen yìjiā rén jiu dào shānshang
        qu le. Děngdào wǎnshang huílai yi kàn, zhēnde yǒule zāinàn, jiā-
        lide jī˴ yā yìzhī yě méi huó, dōu sǐ le.

7.0. jié   festival

      Wǔyuejié   Dragon-Boat Festival [five month festival]

      Bāyuejié   Mid-Autumn Festival [eight month festival]

      Qīngmíng(jié)   Festival of the Tombs [clear bright festival]

      Chóngyáng(jié)   Ninth Month Festival (see note 5)

      Duānyáng(jié)   Dragon-Boat Festival (see note 5)

7.1. Zhōngguo rén zài Wǔyuejié˴ Bāyuejié guòjiéde shíhou hùxiāng sòng-
      lǐ. (T)

7.2. Jùshuō měiniǎnde Qīngmíngjié duōbàn shi xià yǔ.

7.3. Hěn duō shīren dōu xǐhuan zài Chóngyángjié dēnggāode shíhou zuò
      shī.

7.4. Yǒude mùjiang zài Duānyángjié guòjié zhèi yìtiān háishi zhàoyàng
      zuò gōng.

8.0. láiyuán   source, place of origin   [come source]

8.1. Nǐ jǐshí yǒu gōngfu qǐng nǐ gěi wǒ jiǎngyijiǎng Zhōngguo jiùlǐ hé
      xīnlǐde láiyuán. (T)

9.0. Qū Yuán   (name of a Chou Dynasty figure)

9.1. Jiǎrú Qū Yuán duìyu dāngshíde zhèngzhi bù shīwàng, yěxǔ tā bú
      huì zìshā de.

10.0. Chǔ   (name of a kingdom of the Chou period)

10.1. Zhōngguo gǔ shíhoude Chǔ Guó jiu zài xiànzàide Húnán˴ Húběi
       liǎngshěngde dìfang.

11.0. tóu*   throw, cast

       tóujiāng   throw oneself into a river

11.1. Jīntian zǎoshang yǒu rén tóujiāng. Yàobúshi wǒ kànjian de huà tā
       yídìng sǐ le.

50 Mǎ : Zhōngguo zuì dàde jiérì yǒu jǐge, nǐ zhīdao ma?

    Bái : Zhōngguo yǒu sāngde dà jié, chúle guònián jiù shi Wǔyuejié hé
           Bāyuejié.

    Mǎ : Nǐ zhīdao Wǔyuejié hái yǒu yíge míngzi jiào shénmo?

Bái: Jiào Duānyángjié.

55 Mǎ : Nǐ zhīdao Duānyángjiéde láiyuán ma?

Bái: Shi jìniàn Qū Yuán.

Mǎ : Qū Yuán shi shénmo shíhoude rén?

Bái: Shi liǎngqiān duō nián yǐqián Chǔ Guó rén. Tā shi Chǔ Guóde guān.

Mǎ : Nǐ zhīdao Chǔ Guó shi xiànzài shénmo dìfang?

60 Bái: Cóngqián Húnan、Húběi dōu shǔyu Chǔ Guóde fànwéi.

Mǎ : Nǐ zhīdao Qū Yuán zěnmo sǐ de ma?

Bái: Tóujiāng sǐ de.

12.0. zòngzi   dumpling made of glutinous rice

12.1. Wǔyuejié jiājiāhùhù chī zòngzi shi Zhōngguode fēngsu. (T)

13.0. ài   love, love to, like

         àiguó   love one's country, be patriotic (VO)

13.1. Xiǎoháizimen zuì ài tīng rénjia jiǎng gùshi.   (T)

13.2. Guójiā jìshi rénmínde bǎozhàng, suǒyǐ rénmín yīngdāng àiguó.

14.0. bài   be defeated (also used as postverb)

         dǎbài   (1) defeat; (2) be defeated (RV) [hit defeat]

         shībài   be defeated, fail [lose defeat]

14.1. Yǒu liǎngge háizi dǎqilai le. Nèige xiǎode háizi dǎbài le, kū le.

14.2. Nèige guójiāde shēngchǎn jìhua shībài le. (T)

15.0. rēng   throw (away)

15.1. Wǒ zài zhōngxué dúshū de shíhou dúguo de shū jiu suíbiàn rēng le.

Bái: Duānyángjié chī zòngzi shi jìnian Qū Yuán, shì bu shi?

Mǎ : Shìde. Qū Yuán hěn àiguó. Chǔ Wáng tīngle biérénde huàihuà, suǒ-
65   yǐ Qū Yuánde zhèngzhi jìhua shībài le. Tóu jiāng sǐle yǐhou, rén-
       men bǎ zòngzi rēngzai jiāngli jǐ ta. Hòulái biànchéngle yíge fēng-
       su, niánnián wǔyue chūwǔ zhèi yìtiān, jiājiāhùhù chī zòngzi.

Bái: Qū Yuánde shī zài wénxuéshang yě zhàn hěn zhòngyàode dìwei.

Mǎ : Qū Yuán zuò de shī, jīběn tèdiǎn shi ài guó ài rénmín.

16.0. lóng   dragon

         lóngchuán   dragon-boat

16.1. Nèitiáo chuánde yàngzi xiàng yìtiáo lóng, suǒyǐ jiàozuo lóngchuán.

17.0. sài   compete (in)

sài chuán   (1) to race boats; (2) a boat race

sàibuguò   unable to compete successfully with   (RV)

17.1. Yǒu jǐge dàxué měinián sài chuán. Zài sài de shíhou yǒu yíge dàxué zǒngshi sàibuguò rénjia.

18.0. huá   to row

18.1. Wǒ zuì xǐhuan yèli zài húli huá chuán.   Yǒushí huádao bànyè, yuè
huá yuè yǒu jīngshen.

19.0. páng   (1) other, others; (2) side; (3) from the sidelines, as a
                        spectator

páng bian(r)   side

pángren   other people

pángmén   side door

pángtīng   audit (a course), sit in as an auditor

19.1. Zuótian Wáng jia tóngzúde rén zài zúzhǎngde wūzili kāihuì. Chī
fàn de shíhou méi yǒu pángren, dōu shi Wáng jia běnzú rén, suǒyǐ
ràng zúzhǎng zuòzai shàngzuòr.

19.2. Zhāng Xiānsheng jiēhūn qǐng kè. Chī jiǔxíde shíhou, wǒ pángbiar
nèige zuòrshang zuòle yíwèi piàoliang xiáojie.

19.3. Nèige bǎihuò gōngsīde mén hěn duō. Wǒ shi cóng xībiande pángmén jìnqu de.

19.4. Zuótian yǒu rén yòng pǔtōnghuà duì Zhōngguo xuésheng jiǎng Sānmín Zhǔyì, yǒu jǐge wàiguo xuésheng yě lái pángtīng.

20.0. mùdidì   objective, destination [target place]

20.1. Wǒmen zhèicì lǚxíng shi yǐ Kǒngmiào wéi mùdidì.   (T)

21.0. shèng   (1) victorious; (2) victory

shènglì   (1) victorious; (2) victory [victory profit]

dǎshèng   fight and win   (RV)

21.1. Cóngqián Déguo hé Fàguo cháng yǒu zhànzhēng. Yǒushí shi Déguo
shèng le, yǒushí shi Fàguo shèng le.

21.2. Jìn bǎinián lái, Zhōng-Rì zhànzhēng yǒu liǎngcì. Yícì shi Rìběn
dǎshèng le, yícì shi Zhōngguo shènglì le.

70 Mǎ : Nǐ kànjianguo sài lóngchuán de ma?

Bái: Méi you. Wǒ tīngshuōguo.

Mǎ : Sài lóngchuán yě shi zài Duānyángjié zhèi yìtiān.

Bái: Sài lóngchuán dōu shi zài nánfāng, shì bu shi?

Mǎ : Shì. Sài lóngchuán dōu shi zài yǒu shuǐ de dìfang.

75   Bái: Sài lóngchuán yídìng hěn rènao ba?

Mǎ : Duìle. Měinián Duānyángjiē zhǐ yàoshi sài lóngchuán jiu xiāngdāng
rènao. Hǎibiar gēn hébiar rén dōu zhànmǎn le.

Bái: Wéi-shénmo jiào lóngchuán ne?

Mǎ : Shi mùtou zuò de, chuánde yàngzi xiàng yìtiáo lóng. Huá chuánde
80   rén zuòzai chuánde liǎng pángbiar. Měi yìbiār zuò shíge rén huò
shíwǔge rén, chuānzhe hěn piàoliangde yīfu. Gēn hěn duō biéde
chuán bǐsài, shéi xiān dào mùdidì shéi jiu shèng le.

22.0. qiū*   autumn

qiūtian   autumn

qiūshōu   harvest [autumn collect]

Zhōngqiūjié   Mid-Autumn Festival

22.1. Zhōngguo suǒwèi xiǎonóng jiu shi zhòngtián bu duōde nóngmín.
Tāmen zuì dàde xīwang jiu shi yǒu hǎode qiūshōu.   (T)

22.2. Qiūtianli yǒu liǎngge jié, yíge shi Zhōngqiūjié, yíge shi Chóngyángjié.

23.0. gǎnjué   (1) feel that; (2) feelings [feel feel]

23.1. Méi yǒu jìshude rén gǎnjué móushēng hěn bù róngyi.   (T)

24.0. bǐng   flat wheat cake, bread, biscuit

yuèbing   moon-cake

24.1. Wǒ yǒushíhou chī fàn, yǒushíhou chī bǐng.   (T)

24.2. Zhōngguo rén guò Bāyuèjié de shíhou jiājiā chī yuèbing.

25.0. tù(r)   rabbit, hare (M: zhī)

tùryé   moon-rabbit [rabbit old gentleman]

25.1. Nèige háizi zuì xǐhuan tùr, suǒyǐ tā dàole Bāyuèjié yídìng mǎi yíge
tùryé.

26.0. shǐzhōng   (from) beginning to end, the whole course of an affair

26.1. Jīnnian cóng chūntian yǐlái shǐzhōng méi xià yǔ.   Yídìng yào yǒu
hànzāi le.

26.2. Wǒ shǐzhōng bù xǐhuan chī jiǎozi.

27.0. yáng   (1) ocean; (2) from beyond the ocean, foreign

yángren   a foreigner

Xīyáng   the West [west ocean]

Dàxīyáng   Atlantic Ocean [great west ocean]

27.1. Cóngqián Zhōngguo rén guǎn wàiguo rén jiào yángren.

27.2. Zhōngguo cóng shíbā、shíjiǔ shìjì cái jiēshòu Xīyáng wénmíng.

27.3. Tāde zǔxiān cóngqián shi yóu Yīngguo zuò chuán jīngguo Dàxīyáng láidao Měiguo de.

Bái : Cóngqián yǒu yíwèi péngyou gàosu wǒ tā céngjīng dàoguo Zhōngguo běifāng, tā qù de shíhou zhèng shi Zhōngqiūjié. Tā shuō guòjié yǒu yìsi jíle.

85

Mǎ : Tā duì Zhōngqiūjiéde shénmo shìqing zuì gǎnjué xìngqu?

Bái : Tā shuō tā ài chī yuèbing, tā yě xǐhuan tùryé. Tā hái bǎ tùryé mǎile yíge dàihui guó qu gěi tāmende háizi.

Mǎ : Wǒ zài qī-bāsuìde shíhou hái zài běifāng ne, fánshi kànjian tùryé wǒ jiu yào mǎi.

90

Bái : Wǒ shǐzhōng méi kànjianguo tùryé shénmo yàngzi.

Mǎ : Shi yòng ní zuò de tùr, chuānzhe gǔdài rénde yīfu. Hěn hǎokàn. Zài běifāng hěn duō yángren mǎi tùryé. Tāmen juéde hěn hǎo wár.

28.0. shǎng   (1) reward, grant, bestow; (2) enjoy, appreciate

shǎngqián   (1) bestow money   (VO); (2) a tip

shǎngyuè   enjoy the moon

28.1. Yàoshi yǒu rén jiào tāde pūren lái gěi ni sònglǐ, nǐ bìxū gěi pūren shǎngqián.

28.2. Zhōngguo rén zài Zhōngqiūjiéde wǎnshang, wúlùn qióngren、fùren dōu yíyàng shǎngyuè.

28.3. Yǒu rén gěi nǐ kāi chē mén, nǐ shǎng bù shǎng qián?

29.0. yuèliang   (1) moon; (2) moonlight [moon light]

29.1. Zhèiběn zázhìshang yǒu yìpiān guānyu yuèliangde shénhuà shi Zhāng Xiānsheng xiě de.   (T)

30.0. zhuō(zi)   (1) a table; (2) (measure for banquets)

30.1. Tāmen xiǎng dǎ májiàng, kěshi méi yǒu zhuōzi.

30.2. Wǒmen jǐge rén zài Dà Huá Fàndiàn chīle yìzhuō jiǔxí.   (T)

30.3. Dàjiā dōu zuò nèr yào chī fàn le, kěshi zhuōzishang méi kuàizi.

31.0. bǎi   display, arrange, spread out

31.1. Zhèige zhuōzi tài xiǎo. Néng bǎi jiǔxí ma?

Bái : Mǎ Jiàoshòu, shǎngyuè shì bu shi gòng yuèliang?

95 Mǎ : Bù. Shǎngyuè shi kàn yuèliang, gòng yuèliang shi jì yuèliang, shi liǎnghuí shì. Shǎngyuè shi zài bāyue shíwǔ Zhōngqiūjié. Zhèitiān

wǎnshang dàjiā zài yuànzili, yìbiār kàn yuèliang, yìbiār chīzhe yuèbing ，hēzhe chá, dàjiā hěn gāoxìngde tán huà.

Bái: Zhōngguo guòjié guònián dōu hěn yǒu yìsi.

100 Mǎ: Díquè shi yǒu yìsi, yóuqíshi xiǎoháizimen.

Bái: Zěnmoyàngr gòng yuèliang ne?

Mǎ: Duìzhe yuèliang fàng yìzhāng zhuōzi, bǎishang shuǐguo 、yuèbing.
Hǎoxiang guònián gòngshén yíyàng.

32.0. sǎo   to sweep

dásao   to sweep [hit sweep]

32.1. Yuànzili luòxialai de huār tài dūo le. Zěnmo méi yǒu rén sǎo ne?

32.2. Jīntian yào lái hěn duō kèren.   Nǐ qù bǎ zhāodàishǐ dásao dásao
hǎo zhāodai kèren.

33.0. zhàngfu   husband

33.1. Yǒu rén shuō nǔren chūjià zhīhòu yíqiède shì dōu yào fúcóng zhàngfu.

34.0. cháng-shēng-bù-lǎo   (1) be immortal; (2) immortality [long life not
old]

34.1. Zhēngyuè chūyī shi wǒ zǔmǔde shēngri. Wǒ duì zǔmǔ shuō: "Xīwang nín cháng-shēng-bù-lǎo!"

35.0. jí   (1) hurried, hasty, urgent; (2) worried, excited, upset

jímáng   worried, flustered [hurried busy]

zháojí   worried, flustered [catch worried]

35.1. Wǒde xiōngdi píngcháng duìyu kǎoshì de fēnshu duōshǎo dōu wúsuǒwèi. Hòulai dàkǎo bù jígé, tā cái jí le. Kěshi yě wǎn le.

35.2. Tā duì rènhé shìqing yixiàng bù zháojí de.

35.3. Nèi jǐge háizi zhèng wár zhǐpái, kànjian dàren lái le jímáng bǎ
zhǐpái shōuqilai le.

36.0. dú   alone

dúlì   independent [alone stand]

dúzì   alone, independently, by oneself [alone self]

36.1. Zhèizhǒng shù shi Rìběn dú yǒu de. Biéde guó dōu méi yǒu. (T)

36.2. Nèige dìfang bù fúcóng zhèngfǔde mìngling, děngyu dúlì le.

36.3. Chúxīde yèli tā dúzì zài wūzili, yě bù shuō huà yě bù kāi dēng.
Dàjiā yǐwei tā shuìjiào le.

36.4. Nèige guójiā zǒng yǒu yìtiān shi yào dúlì de.

37.0. táo   escape (from)

táozǒu   escape, flee   [escape go]

táonàn   flee from calamity   [escape disaster]

37.1. Nèige mùjiang wèi-shénmo táozǒule ne? . . . Yǒu rén shuō tā běn-
       lái jiu shi huàiren, cóngqián zài biéde dìfang zuòguo huàishì, cái
       táodào zhèli lái de.

37.2. Měicì dǎzhàng, hěn duō lǎobǎixìng dōu děi táonàn.

Bái: Huá jiade Wáng Mā shàng xīngqiliù dásao wǒ wūzide shíhou gěi wǒ
105   jiǎng yuèliangde gùshi.

Mǎ :   Niánji dà diar de lǎo tàitaimen dōu zhīdao yuèliangde shénhuà.

Bái: Wáng Mā shuō yuèliangli yǒu yíge hěn piàoliangde nǚren, yīnwei
       chīle tā zhàngfu zuò de cháng-shēng-bù-lǎo yào, tā zhàngfu shēngqì
       le, nèige nǚren yi zháojí jiu dúzì yíge rén táodao yuèliang lǐtou qu
110   le.

Mǎ :   Hái yǒu yíge shuōfa, shi tùryé zài yuèliangli zuò yào.

38.0. fén   grave (M: ge, zuò)

       féndì   graveyard, cemetery

38.1. Tāmen yì jiā rén dōu shàng fén qu le.   (T)

38.2. Nèige shānshang duōbàn shi yǒuqián rénjiāde féndì.

39.0. mù*   tomb, grave

       fénmù   tomb, grave [grave grave]

       sǎomù   sweep the graves (of one's ancestors)

39.1. Qīngmíngjié jiājiā qù sǎomù. Sǎomù jiu shi bǎ fénmù dáosao dáo-
       sao.

40.0. yíbiàn(r)   once (see note 6)

       yìhuí   once

       yíxià(r)   once

       yìshēng(r)   once

40.1. Qǐng nǐ bǎ zhèi jǐge tóngyīnzì yígeyígede zài niàn yíbiàn.

40.2. Jiùshìde jiātíng fǎnduì háizimen qù kàn diànyǐng, shènzhìyu zhǐ kàn
       yìhuí yě bù xíng.

40.3. Qǐng nǐ bǎ dēng kāi yíxiàr.

40.4. Nǐ jìrán zhīdao tā shi huàiren, cháng shuō jiǎhuà, nǐ wèi-shénmo
       bu xiān gàosu wǒ yìshēng?   (T)

40.5. Qǐng nǐ gàosu mǔqin yìshēngr wǒ qù mǎi gāngbǐ gēn qiānbǐ qu.

41.0. zhuāng*   style of dress

Zhōngzhuāng   Chinese-style dress

Xīzhuāng   Western-style dress

yángzhuāng   foreign-style dress

41.1. Tā jiā dìxiong hěn duō. Zhǐ yǒu tā chuān Zhōngzhuāng, qíyúde
       xiōngdì dōu xǐhuan chuān Xīzhuāng.

41.2. Nèige Zhōngguo xiáojie chuānshang yángzhuāng gèng hǎokàn le.

42.0. chéngrèn   admit, acknowledge, confess [receive recognize]

42.1. Yǒu rén gàosu wǒ, Zhāng Yǒuwén shuō wǒ huàihuà. Wǒ qù wèn
       Zhāng Yǒuwén, tā bu chéngrèn yǒu zhèizhǒng shì. (T)

Bái: Mǎ Jiàoshòu, Qīngmíngjié zhòngyào bú zhòngyào?

Mǎ: Hěn zhòngyào. Shi dào féndì qu de rìzi.

Bái: Sǎomù zhèige cér wǒ bú dà dǒng.

115 Mǎ: Sǎo jiu shi dásao. Mù jiu shi fénmù. Yìsi jiu shi zǐsūn yīnggāi
         dào zǔxiānde fénmùshang dásao yíxiàr. Érqiě yě zài fénmùde sì-
         biārshang zhòngzhong shù.

Bái: Yě shāo zhǐ kētóu ma?

Mǎ: Dāngrán děi shāo zhǐ kētóu le.

120 Bái: Niánnián zhǐshi zài Qīngmíngjiéde shíhou qù ma?

Mǎ: Bù. Qíyuè shíwǔ、shíyue chūyī yǒude shíhou yě děi dào féndì qu.
      Dànshi Qīngmíngjié shi yídìng yào qu de.

Bái: Shàng fén qu, chuānzhe pǔtōng yīfu kéyi ma?

Mǎ: Biéren jiā wǒ bù zhīdào. Wǒmen jiā shi yíge jiùshì jiātíng. Shàng
125   fén de shíhou bìděi chuān Zhōngzhuāng.

Bái: Nín píngcháng bù chuān Zhōngzhuāng ma?

Mǎ: Wǒ zài qī-bāsuì xiǎoháizide shíhou jiu chuān Xīzhuāng le. Yǒu yícì
      Qīngmíng qù shàng fén yǐqián, wǒ yào chī táng wǒ mǔqin bù xǔ wǒ
      chī, wǒ bù gāoxìng le. Jiāli jiào wǒ huàn Zhōngzhuāng dào fén-
130   shang qu, wǒ bú huàn. Zǔfù shuō: "Nǐ yàoshi bú huàn yīfu wǒ bù
      chéngrèn nǐ shi wǒde sūnzi."

43.0. hūrán   suddenly, unexpectedly [suddenly thus]

43.1. Wǒ kāi chē kāidao bànlùshang, chē hūrán huài le. Wǒ xiūle bàntiān
       yě méi xiūhǎo. Zhēn bǎ wǒ qìhuài le.

44.0. jú*   office, bureau

       diànbàojú   telegraph office

44.1. Tā zài diànbàojú gěi rénjia sòng diànbào. Shēnghuó hěn kǔ.

45.0. tì   as a substitute for, on behalf of   (CV)

45.1. Nǐ zhíguǎn zǒu hǎo le. Rúguǒ yǒu shénmo zéren wǒ tì nǐ fù.   (T)

46.0. shǒuxu   procedure [hand continue]

46.1. Chūguó liúxué yǒu zhǒngzhǒng shǒuxu dōu yào shìqián bànhǎo. (T)

47.0. kěn   be willing (to)

47.1. Nèige bǎihuò gōngsī bù kěn mài wàiguo dōngxi.

Bái : Mǎ Jiàoshòu, wǒ hūrán xiǎngqilai le, wǒ xiān gēn nín shuō yìshēngr.

Mǎ : Shénmo shì?

Bái : Míngtian zǎoshang wǒ láide wǎn yìdiǎr. Wǒ děi xiān dào diànbào-
135   jú qu dǎ diànbào.

Mǎ : Wǎng jiāli dǎ ma?

Bái : Bú shi. Wǎng Yīngguo dǎ. Yǒu yíge péngyou tā yào dào zhèr lái
     niàn Zhōngwén, tā ràng wǒ tì tā wènwen zhèr dàxuéde shǒuxù.

Mǎ : Tā xiànzài jiu yào lái ma?

140 Bái : Shìde. Suǒyǐ wǒ děi gěi ta dǎ diànbào, yàoburán shíjiān tài wǎn le.

Mǎ : Tā wèi-shénmo bu zǎo diar bàn shǒuxu ne?

Bái : Tā mǔqin jiu yǒu tā yíge érzi, bú ràng tā líkai jiā. Xiànzài hé tā
     mǔqin shuōhǎo le, tā mǔqin kěn le.

Mǎ : Wǒ hěn liǎojiě fùmǔ duì érnǚde ài.

145 Bái : Yīnwei nín shi yǒule érnǚ de rén le.

48.0. mǒu(mǒu)   a certain, so-and-so, such-and-such

      mǒurén   a certain person

48.1. Mǒumǒu huìde zhǔxì bù guǎn huìyuánde fúlì, zhǐ guǎn xiàng huìyuán
      yào qián. (T)

48.2. Mǒurénde jiěmèi jiàchu zhīhòu, bù jiǔ jiu líhūn le.

49.0. jiù   save, rescue

      jiùrén   (1) save a person; (2) Help!

49.1. Tā dàshēng jiào "Jiùrén! Jiùrén!" kěshi méi yǒu rén lái jiù ta.

50.0. dǎng   political party (N/M)

      Guómíndǎng Kuomintang [country people party]

50.1. Mínzhǔ guójiāde rénmín zài zhèngzhishang kéyi zìyóu zǔzhi yíge
      dǎng.

50.2. Guómíndǎng shi zài shénmo shíhou chénglì de?

51.0. pài   faction, party, group (M)

      dǎngpài faction, party

51.1. Zài yíge dǎng lǐtou, yǒushíhou fēnchéng ruògān pài.

51.2. Yǒu rén shuō tā shi wú dǎng wú pài de, yě jiu shi shuō tā shi bù shǔyu rènhé dǎngpài de. (T)

52.0. xiāoxi   information, news

52.1. Zhèige xiāoxi nǐ shi cóng nǎli tīnglai de? Quèshí ma?

53.0. yōuchóu   worried, distressed, grieved, sad [worried worry]

53.1. Tā yīnwei bù néng wéichi shēnghuó, suǒyǐ tiāntiān yōuchóu.

Mǎ : Wǒ jìde wǒ zài Lián-Dà niànshū de shíhou wǒ mǔqin zài Jiùguó Rìbàoshang kànjian Yúnnán mǒu dàxuéde xuésheng yǒu dǎngpài. Wǒ mǔqin zhīdao zhèige xiāoxi jíde bùdeliǎo. Nèige shíhou wǒ gěi wǒ mǔqin zēngjiāle bù shǎode yōuchóu.

150 Bái: Mǎ Jiàoshòu nín shi něi yìdǎng?

Mǎ : Wǒ shénmo dǎng yě bú shì.

54.0. qiáng   (1) powerful; (2) preferable, better

qiángguó   (1) strengthen a country, make a country powerful (VO); (2) a powerful country

54.1. Xiànzài shìjièshang yǒu jǐge qiángguó, něiguó zuì qiáng, nǐ zhīdao ma?

54.2. Zhèicì kǎoshì nǐde chéngji bǐ wǒ qiángde duō. (T)

55.0. wěiyuán   committee member [depute member]

wěiyuánhuì   committee [depute member meeting]

55.1. Tián Xiānsheng shi dìfang zìzhì wěiyuánhuìde wěiyuán. (T)

56.0. shì*   look at

zhòngshì   give attention to, regard with esteem [heavy look]

diànshì   television [electricity look]

56.1. Cóngqián Zhōngguode shèhuì zhòngshì shìdàfu jiēji.

56.2. Tā yǒu yíge xīnshìde diànshì, néng kàndao hěn duō dìfangde xīnwén.

57.0. qiántú   prospects for the future [front road]

57.1. Nèige xuésheng shū niànde hěn hǎo. Tāde qiántú hěn yǒu xīwang.

58.0. tóngqíng   (1) sympathetic (to); (2) sympathy [same feelings]

58.1. Yǒu yíge jiàngrén hěn néng chīkǔ. Báitiān wǎnshang dōu zuò gōng. Yǒude shíhou wǎnshang hái niàn shū. Dàjiā hěn tóngqíng ta.

Bái: Mǎ Jiàoshòu, wǒ zhèi jǐtián kàn Qiángguo Rìbàoshangde xiǎoshuō "Wáng Wěiyuánde Jiātíng," xiěde zhēn hǎo. Jiānglái yàoshi yìnchéng shū wǒ mǎi yìběn, yǒu gōngfu zài kàn yìhuí.

155 Mǎ : Wǒ yě kàn le. Tīngshuō yào yòng zhèige gùshi yǎn yíbù diànyǐngr ne.

Bái : Wǒ xiāngxìn zhèibù piānzi yídìng hěn hǎokàn.

Mǎ : Kěnéng diànshìshang yě yào biǎoyǎn zhèige gùshi.

Bái : Xiě zhèige xiǎoshuōde rén nín rènshi ma?

160 Mǎ : Wǒ bú rènshi. Tīngshuō tā niánji hěn qīng. Tā hěn yǒu qiántú. Jùshuō tā jiāli yuánlái hěn qióng. Tā gēnběn bù kěnéng niàn shū. Tā jiu xiǎng zuò yìdiǎr kǔgōng, dé diǎr qián niàn shū. Kěshi tā niánji tài xiǎo, méi rén yòng ta. Hòulai yǒu yíge péngyou tóngqíng ta, gōngji tā niàn shū. Nèiwèi péngyou yìzhí gōng ta dàxué bìle yè.

165 Bái : Zhèiwèi péngyou tài nándé le.

59.0. pò   break, broken, worn out (also used as postverb)

    dǎpò   smash (RV) [hit break]

    pòhuài spoil, destroy (literally and figuratively), slander   [break bad]

59.1. Wǒ yǒu yíjiàn bù yīfu yǐjing pò le, bù néng chuān le, zhǐhǎo zài zuò yíjiàn.

59.2. Xīn qīngnián yīngdāng dǎpò jiù xíguan.

59.3. Nǐ zànchéng tāmen líhūn jiu děngyú pòhuài tāmende jiātíng.

60.0. lüè   (1) outline; (2) a little, somewhat

    dàlüè in outline, in general [big outline]

60.1. Nǐ búbi shuō yuánwén, jiù bǎ dàyì lüè shuōyishuō.

60.2. Wǒ bǎ mínzú zhǔyì hé zìyóu zhǔyì dōu dàlüè hé nǐmen shuōyishuō.

61.0. xìnren   to trust [believe duty]

61.1. Yóuyu tā cóngqián cháng shuō jiǎhuà, suǒyǐ dàjiā dōu bú xìnren ta le.

62.0. yì*   discuss, criticize

    huìyì   (1) conference; (2) hold a conference [meeting discuss]

    yìyuán   member of a parliament or congress [discuss member]

    yìyuàn   parliament, congress [discuss institution]

    huìyìshǐ conference room

62.1. Yìyuán zài huìyì de shíhou suǒ shuō de huà shi dàibiǎo rénmín shuō de. (T)

62.2. Jīntian yìyuàn kāihuì, suǒyǒu yìyuán dōu dào le.

62.3. Xiàozhǎng hé quánxiào jiàoyuán dōu zài huìyìshǐ kāihuì ne. (T)

63.0. jiē   street

Zhōngguojiē   Chinatown

63.1. Zài Niǔyuē hé Sānfánshî dōu yǒu Zhōngguojiē, yě jiào Zhōngguo-chéng. Jiēshangde rén duōbàn shi Zhōngguo rén.

63.2. Wǒ zài Zhōngguojiē kànjian liǎngwèi Zhōngguo xiáojie, dōu hěn hǎokàn. Gè yǒu gède měi. (T)

64.0. suǒyǐ   the reason why (see note 4)

64.1. Wǒ suǒyǐ bú qù Rìbén niàn dàxué shi yīnwei wǒ bú huî Rìwén, yě bù xiǎng xué Rìwén.

Bái: Mǎ Jiàoshòu, pòle hé pòhuài zhèi liǎngge cér yǒu shénmo fēnbié?

Mǎ: Wǒ jǔ liǎngge lîzi nǐ tīng. "Wǒde yīfu pòle, děi mǎi yíjiàn xīnde le." "Tā lǎo zài xiàozhǎng miànqián pòhuài wo."

Bái: Pòhuài jiu shi duî mǒu yíge rén shuō lìngwài yíge rénde huàihuà,
170   pòhuài rénjia, shî bu shi?

Mǎ: Kéyi pòhuài yíge rén, yě kéyi pòhuài yíjiàn shîde chénggōng. Hǎo. Jīntiande cér, dàlüède dōu yánjiu le.

Bái: Hái yǒu yíge cér xìnren, jiu shi "Wǒ bú xìnren ta," huòzhě "Wǒ hěn xìnren ta."

175 Mǎ: Duî. Yìhuěr nǐ qu tīng Zhuāntí Jiǎnghuà. Wǒ hái děi dào huîyìshî qu kāihuî qu.

Bái: Wǒ zuótian jiu zhîdao jīntian xuéxiào kāihuî.

Mǎ: Nǐ zěnmo zhîdao de?

Bái: Zuótian wǒ zài jiēshang kànjian Biān Jiàoshòu le. Tā shuō jīntian
180   dào xuéxiào lái kāihuî.

Mǎ: Tā hěn shǎo dào xuéxiào lái. Tā suǒyǐ bú dào xuéxiào lái shi tā yíge xīngqi bù yídìng yǒu yìtáng kè.

Bái: Míngtian jiàn.

Mǎ: Míngtian jiàn.

SHĒNGCÍ BIǍO

1. dēng
   dēng shān
   dēnggāo

2. shù
   shùlínzi

3. kē

4. wèi* (W)

wèilái(de)

5. nàn
   nànmín
   zāinàn

6. zhǐ

7. jié
   Wǔyuejié

Bāyuejié
Qīngmíng(jié)
Chóngyáng(jié)
Duānyáng(jié)

8. láiyuán

9. Qū Yuán

10. Chǔ

11. tóu*
    tóujiāng

12. zòngzi

13. ài
    àiguó

14. bài
    dǎbài
    shībài

15. rēng

16. lóng
    lóngchuán

17. sài
    sài chuán
    sàibuguò

18. huá

19. páng
    pángbian(r)
    pángren
    pángmén
    pángtīng

20. mùdidì

21. shèng
    shènglì
    dǎshèng

22. qiū*
    qiūtian
    qiūshōu
    Zhōngqiūjié

23. gǎnjué

24. bǐng
    yuèbing

25. tù(r)
    tùryé

26. shǐzhōng

27. yáng
    yángren
    Xīyáng

    Dàxīyáng

28. shǎng
    shǎngqián
    shǎngyuè

29. yuèliang

30. zhuō(zi)

31. bǎi

32. sǎo
    dásao

33. zhàngfu

34. cháng-shēng-bù-lǎo

35. jí
    jímáng
    zháojí

36. dú
    dúlì
    dúzì

37. táo
    táozǒu
    táonàn

38. fén
    féndì

39. mù*
    fénmù
    sǎomù

40. yíbiàn(r)
    yìhuí
    yìxià(r)
    yìshēng(r)

41. zhuāng*
    Zhōngzhuāng
    Xīzhuāng
    yángzhuāng

42. chéngrèn

43. hūrán

44. jú*
    diànbàojú

45. tì

46. shǒuxu

47. kěn

48. mǒu(mōu)
    mǒurén

49. jiù
    jiùrén

50. dǎng
    Guómíndǎng

51. pài
    dǎngpài

52. xiāoxi

53. yōuchóu

54. qiáng
    qiángguó

55. wěiyuán
    wěiyuanhuì

56. shì*
    zhòngshì
    diànshì

57. qiántú

58. tóngqíng

59. pò
    dǎpò
    pòhuài

60. lüè
    dàlüè

61. xìnren

62. yì*
    huìyì
    yìyuán
    yìyuàn
    huìyìshǐ

63. jiē
    Zhōngguojiē

64. suǒyǐ

YǓFǍ LIÀNXÍ

A. yào SV   (See note 1)

1. Tiānránde shānshuǐ bǐ réngōng zuòde yào hǎokàn.

2. Zhèicì táonàn de nànmín bǐ shàngcìde hái yào duō.

3. Xīshìde chuán bǐ Zhōngshìde chuán yào dàde duō.

4. Qǐng nǐmen bǎ měi yíge zì xiěde yào qīngchu yìdiǎr.

5. Zhuōzi yào xiǎo yìdiǎr cái hǎo.

 B. V le yòu V (See note 2)

6. Lǎoye, shàoye dōu bàishén. Yì tiān dào wǎn bàile yòu bài. Jiūjìng yǒu shénmo yòngchu ne?

7. Nèige háizi chīle yòu chī. Tā jiūjìng yào chī duòshao ne?

8. Yì yǒule zhànshì lǎobǎixìng dōu táonàn, dōu chéngle nànmín. Tāmen táole yòu táo, dàoshi táodao nǎlǐ ne?

9. Měinián làyue èrshisānrì dōu jìzào, niánnián jìle yòu jì, zàowangyé gěi rénmen shénmo hǎochu le ne?

10. Tā shuōle yòu shuō. Tā yǐwéi wǒ hái méi tīngmíngbai ne!

 C. lián V dōu/yě bù/méi V (See note 3)

11. Tā jiāli yǒu liǎngge diànshì, tā lián kàn dōu bu kàn.

12. Tāmen zōngzúde rén dōu zài cítánglì tuánjù. Jiù tā yíge rén lián qù dōu bu qù.

13. Rénjia gěi ta sòng lǐ, tā lián shǎngqián yě bu shǎng.

14. Jiūjìng duōchulái duōshao qián tā lián wèn dōu méi wèn.

15. Tāde háizi qù chī shànggòng de gòngcài, tā lián guǎn yě bù guǎn.

 D. suǒyǐ V shì/wéi (See note 4)

16. Wǒ suǒyǐ bú qù gěi ta bàinián shi yīnwei tā méi xiān lái gěi wǒ bàinián.

17. Tā suǒyǐ bù huí jiā guò xiǎoniánr shi tā tài máng.

18. Nèige wàiguo rén lái bàiniánde shíhou suǒyǐ bù shuō "Gōngxǐ fācái" shi yīnwei tā bú huì shuō Zhōngguo huà.

19. Zhāng Xiānsheng suǒyǐ jímáng huí jiā shi tā jiāli láile yíge qīnqi.

20. Guòniánde shíhou suǒyǐ yào chī yúde yuányīn shi yīnwei yú shi jílì de yìsi.

JIǍNGHUÀ

 Zhōngguo rén zài yìnián lǐtou zuì zhòngyàode jiérì shi guònián, qícì shi guòjié. Guānyu guòniánde qíngxing, shàngcì yǐjing dàlüède jiǎngguo, jīntian jiǎngjiang Zhōngguode guòjié. Zhōngguo rén yìniánlide jiérì hěn duō. Bǐjiào zhòngyàode shi Wǔyuèjié hé Bāyuèjié. Cǐwài jiu shi Qīng-
5 míngjié hé Chóngyángjié.

 Wǔyuèjié shi zài yīnlì wǔyue wǔrì, yě jiàozuo Duānyángjié. Zhèi

yìtiān jiājiā dōu chī zòngzi, yě yào kàn sài lóngchuán. Wèi-shénmo chī
zòngzi, sài lóngchuán ne? Qǐyuán shi zhèiyàng de: Zài gōngyuánqián sì
shìjìde shíhou Zhōngguo Chǔ Guó yǒu yíge hěn yǒu xuéshìde rén jiào Qū
10 Yuán. Tā běnlái zài Chǔ Guó zuò guān, xiǎng bǎ Chǔ Guó zhìde hěn hǎo.
Kěshi Chǔ Guó mǒu yíge dǎngpàide rén zài Chǔ Wáng miànqián pòhuài
tā shuō Qū Yuánde huàihuà. Chǔ Wáng yúshì bù kěn xìnren Qū Yuán.
Qū Yuán wèile guójiāde qiántú xīnli hěn yōuchóu. Tā jiu líkaile Chǔ
Wáng, shícháng dúzì yíge rén zài jiāngbiān, yìbiān zǒu yìbiān zuò shī,
15 bǎ tāde xīnshì dōu zài shīli xiěchulai. Suǒyǐ hòulaide rén shuō tā shi
àiguóde shīren. Yǒu yìtiān shi wǔyue wǔrì Qū Yuán hūrán tóujiāng zìshā
le. Dāngshíde rén hěn tóngqíng ta. Yǒude rén zuò chuán qu zhǎo ṭa,
xiǎng yào jiù ta, yòu zuò zòngzi rēngzai jiāngli wèideshì gěi ta chī.
Zhèixiē shì hòulai jiu biànchengle fēngsu. Měinián dàole Wǔyuejié dàjiā
20 jiu chī zòngzi、 sài lóngchuán, wèideshì jìnian zhèige àiguóde shīren.

Bāyuejié yě jiàozuo Zhōngqiūjié, shi zài yīnli bāyue shíwǔrì. Zhè
shíhou zhèng shi qiūtian, bù lěng bú rè, yòu shi nóngmín qiūshōude shíhou, suǒyǐ dàjiā duìyu zhèige jié fēicháng gāoxìng, fēicháng zhòngshì. Zài
Bāyuejiéde wǎnshang, jiājiā dōu yào shǎngyuè、 chī yuèbing. Yuèbing yǒu
25 hěn duō zhǒnglèi, duōshù rén dōu xǐhuan chī.

Zhōngguo rén duìyu yuèliang yǒu yíge chuánshuō. Jùshuō yuèliangli
yǒu yíge nǚren. Tā chīle cháng-shēng-bù-lǎo-de yào suǒyǐ néng cháng
zài yuèliangli. Yòu shuō yuèliangli yǒu yìzhī tùr, shi zài nàli zuò yào.
Yīncǐ Zhōngguo běifāng dàole Bāyuejié jiu yǒu rén yòng ní zuòcheng tùr,
30 zài jiēshang mài. Xiǎoháizimen dōu xǐhuan mǎi yíge lái wár, guǎn ta
jiào tùryè. Yǒude rénjiā bǎ tùryé bǎizài zhuōzishang, yě bǎi xiē shuǐguǒ、
yuèbing lái bài tùryé.

Chúle Wǔyuejié gēn Bāyuejié zhīwài, hái yǒu Qīngmíngjié hé Chóngyángjié. Qīngmíngjié yǔ biéde jiérì yǒu yíge bùtóngde dìfang, shi méi
35 yǒu yídìngde rìzi. Qīngmíngjié duōbàn shi zài yīnli sānyue lǐtou. Jiūjìng shi něi yìtiān, shi niánnián bùtóngde. Měiniánde Qīngmíngjié dōu zài
yīnlìde rìlishang yǒu guīdìng. Qīngmíngjié zhèng shi chūntian, jiājiāhùhù
dōu qù sǎomù. Shénmo jiào sǎomù ne? Jiu shi dào yǐjing sǐle de qīnrén
fénmùshang qù jìyijì dásao dásao zhòngzhong shù. Shi bú wàng zǔxiān de
40 yìsi.

Chóngyángjié shi zài yīnlì jiǔyue chūjiǔ, shi yíge dēnggāo de rìzi.
Rénrén suǒyǐ zài zhèi yìtiān dēnggāo shi yīnwei zài Dōng Hàn shíhou
yǒu yíge rén, tāde lǎoshī gàosu ta jiǔyue jiǔrì tā jiā yào yǒu zāinàn, zhǐ
yǒu nèitiān dào gāo shānshang qu cái kéyi táoguo zhèicì zāinàn. Zhèige
45 rén jiu zài jiǔyue jiǔrì jímáng dàile quánjiāde rén dōu shàng shān le.
Dàole wǎnshang huí jiā yi kàn, jiālide niú, yáng, zhū, jī dōu sǐ le. Tāde
lǎoshī duì ta shuō zhèixiē niú, yáng, zhū, jī shi tìle tāmen yìjiā rén shòu
zāinàn le. Suǒyǐ hòulaide rén měinián jiǔyue jiǔrì dōu qù dēnggāo, jùshuō
kéyi bìmiǎn wèiláide zāinàn.

FÙSHÙ

Zhèipán lùyīndài shi Zhōngwén dì-yīzǔ dì-shíhào, Bái Wénshān fùshù
dìshícìde Zhuāntí Jiǎnghuà. Jiǎngtí shi Zhōngguo Guònián.

Zhèicì xuéxiào Zhuāntí Jiǎnghuà shi yóu běnxiàode Wén Yǒushān
Jiàoshòu gěi wǒmen jiǎng guānyu Zhōngguo rén guòniánde yíqiè fēngsu
5 xíguan.   Wǒ fùshù yicì, suīrán wǒ shuōde bù hǎo, dànshi fùshù yě shi
kèchéngde yíbùfen.   Měicì tīngwánle jiǎng, dōu děi fùshù.   Wǒ shuō jù
xiàohua ba.   Fùshù jiǎnzhí shi yìzhǒng bìmiǎnbuliǎode zāinàn.   Hǎole,
xiànzài shuō běntí.

Wén Jiàoshòu shi cóng guò Xiǎoniánr shuōqǐ de. Tā shuōde xiāng-
10 dāng yǒu yìsi. Zhōngguo rén jiùlìde shí'èryue bú jiào shí'èryue jiào làyue. Wén Jiàoshòu shuō Zhōngguo rén guònián bù guāng shi rènao, érqiě
yě yǒu yìzhǒng rénqíng wèr zài lǐtou.   Tā shuō Zhōngguo rén yí dàole
làyue chū, jiu kāishǐ mángzhe guònián. Guònián máng de shi dásao wūzi,
mǎi guòniánde cài gēn guònián yòng de dōngxi. Fùnǚmen mǎi bù zuò xīn
15 yīfu, yùbei guònián chuān, yě mángzhe gěi qīnqi péngyou sòng lǐ.

Guò Xiǎoniánr shi zài làyue èrshisān nèitiān. Jùshuō shi zàowangyé
shàng tiān de rìzi. Zhōngguo běifāng jiājiā dōu gòngzhe yíge zàowangyé.
Zàowangyé hái yǒu yíge míngzi jiào zàoshén. Pǔtōng guǎn tā jiào zàowangyé.   Shuō shi zàowangyé shàng tiān yǐhòu, bǎ zhèijiāde shìqing dōu
20 bàogào gěi tiānshàngde shén. Suǒyǐ rénmen jiājiāhùhù dōu děi zài zàowangyé shàng tiān de zhèitiān jìzào, xīwang zàowangyé dào tiānshang duō
shuō hǎo huà. Xiǎoniánr guòle yǐhòu, jǐnjiēzhe méi jǐtiān jiu guò Xīnnián le.

Xīnniánde tóu yìtiān wǎnshang yě yǒu yíge míngzi jiàozuo chúxī.
25 Chúxī zhèitiān wǎnshang dàjiā zhěngyè bú shuìjiào.   Zhèitiān wǎnshang
fēicháng rènao. Dàjiā dōu bù chūqu le. Rúguǒ yǒu rén zài yuǎnde dìfang
zuò shìqing, yàoshi kěnéngde huà yào zài chúxī yǐqián huílai. Yìjiā rén
zài Xīnnián dōu yào zài yíkuàr tuánjù de.

Zài chúxīde wǎnshang yě jiu shi sānshíde wǎnshang le, jiājiā dōu
30 zuò hěn duō cài, bìděi yǒu yìtiáo yú.   Chúxī wǎnshang yào shuō jílì huà.
Chúxīde wǎnshang búdàn yào gěi shén shànggòng,   yě yào gěi zǔxiān
shànggòng.   Gòng de dōngxi dōu shi chī de.   Chúxī wǎnfàn zhèitiáo yú
shi bìxū yǒu de, shi fùguì yǒuyú de yìsi.   Chī yúde yú hé yǒuyú de yú
shi tóngyīnzì. Yìsi jiu shi jīnnián qián búdàn gòu yòng érqiě hái nénggou
35 duōyúchulai.   Zhè yě shi jílì huà.

Jiēshén yě shi zài chúxīde wǎnshang.   Jiēshénde shíhou yào shāo
zhǐ、 shāo xiāng gěi shén hé zǔxiān kētóu.   Ránhòu ànzhe cìxu gěi zǔfù
zǔmǔ hé fùmǔ bàinián, xiǎohár gěi dàren kētóu bàinián, ér dàrenmen bìděi gěi háizimen qián, dōu shi yòng hóng zhǐ bāozhe. Zhōngguo rén yòng
40 hóng yánse dàibiǎo jílì.   Sānshí wǎnshang díquè shi hěn yǒu yìsi.

Zhēngyue chūyī shi Xīnnián le.   Qīnqi、 péngyou dàjiā hùxiāng bàinián, yìzhí bàidao chūliù. Zài zhèi jǐtiānli rénrén mángde bùdéliǎo. Cóng
Xīnnián zhèitiān qǐ, gēn rénjia jiànmián dì-yíjù huà bìděi shuō "Gōngxǐ
fācái." Dào rénjia jiāli bàinián, yǒu xiǎoháizi de yě děi gěi xiǎoháizi
45 qián. Guònián zuì gāoxìngde shi xiǎoháizimen. Chī hǎo dōngxi, fàng pàozhang, hái yǒu rén gěi qián.

Nián guòwánle hái yǒu Dēngjié.   Dēngjié shi zài zhēngyue shíwǔ,
yě hěn rènao. Jiājiā dōu guàqilai hěn hǎokànde dēng.

Zài Mínguó chūniánde shíhou zhèngfǔ yǒu yíge mìngling shuō rén-
50 mín yīngāi yílǜ guò yánglì nián. Suírán zhèngfǔ yǒu mìngling, kěshi rénmín réngrán zhàoyàng guò yīnlì nián.   Zhèngfǔ kànchu ruògān niánde
xíguan bú shi duǎn shíjiān kéyi gǎi de, zhèngfǔ méi fázi, bǎ yīnlì nián
gǎi ge míngzi jiào Chūnjié.

Wén Jiàoshòu hái shuō xiànzài hěn shǎo yǒu rén zài guònián shí-
55 hou kētóu le. Guānyu kētóu zhèige fēngsu mànmān jiu méi yǒu le.

WÉNXI

1. Jùshuō zài Měiguo Dúlì Zhànzhēngde shíhou, yǒu yige rén pà dāng bīng, yào táozǒu. Dāngshí yǒu rén duì tā shuō: "Zhèicì zhànzhēng búdàn shi wèile wǒmen zhèi yídài, yě shi wèile wǒmende hòudài. Cānjiā zhànzhēng shi wǒmende zérèn. Rénrén dōu yào fùqi zhèige zérèn, bù néng xīwang bìmiǎn. Zhǐ yǒu gòngtóng nǔlì gòngtóng zhīchí cái néng gòngtóng cúnzài." Yúshihū nèige rén jiu bù xiǎng táo le.

2. Mǎ Xiānsheng shi yíwèi zìyóu zhǔyìde xuézhě. Tā zhǔchí yíge zhōukān. Zuìjìn tā zài zhōukānshang pīping xiàndàide dǎngpài zhèngzhi. Tā pīping shìjièshang zhèngzhi dǎngpài. Bùguǎn shi xīfāng guójiā huòshi dōngfāng guójiā, tā rènwei dōu bù yīngdāng cúnzài. Tā yòu shuō zǒng yǒu yìtiān yào dǎpò dǎngpài zhèngzhi, hǎo jiào nèixiē kào dǎngpài móu zìjǐ lìyide rén méi fázi zài lìyòng dǎngpài.

3. Sòng zàoshén shàng tiān shi Zhōngguode shénhuà. Jùshuō xiāngxia rén zài sòng zàoshén zhèi yìtiān wúlùn dàhù、 xiǎohù dōu zài zàode qiánbian shāo xiāng kētóu, wèideshì qǐng zàowángyé shàng tiān zhīhòu duō shuō hǎo huà. Xiàng zhèilèide shénhuà, xiǎo háizimen zuì ài tīng, lǎo tàitaimen zuì ài jiǎng, jiu suàn shi jiǎde kěshi tīng de jiǎng de dōu juéde hěn yǒu yìsi.

4. Yǒu yíge zài xiāngxia zhù de diànnóng zài qiūshōu zhīhòu zuòle yìxiē bǐng, nádào chénglǐ qu sònggěi tāde dìzhǔ. Zhèixiē bǐng běnlái shi yòng zhǐ bāo de. Dàole chénglǐ zhǐbāor pòle. Zhèige diànnóng hěn zháojí, juézhe hěn bùhǎoyìsi. Tā duì dìzhǔ shuō: "Zhǐbāor suīrán pòle, kěshi bǐng shi hěn hǎode." Dìzhǔ shuō: "Zhǐbāor pòle nǐ bú yòng jí. Nǐ yóu xiāngxia lái zhènmo yuǎnde lù ér sòng bǐng gěi wǒ, zhè shi rénqíng, wǒ hěn gāoxìng."

5. Mǒu rén ài dǎ májiàng, bǎ tā zǔzong liúxia de tiándì、 fángzi dōu dǎ májiàng dǎguāng le. Suǒyúde zhǐ shi yíbù chē. Zhèibù chēde páizi dào bú shi pǔtōngde páizi, shi yíge yǒumíngde páizi. Yǒu yìtiān tā dào mǎimài qìchēde gōngsīli yào mài zhèibù chē. Gōngsīlide rén shuō: "Zhèibù chē yǐjing jiù le, zhǐ néng zhào yuánjià shífēnzhī-yī gěi qián." Tā shuō: "Hǎo." Tā bǎ zhèibù chē màile nádàole qián, yòu hé jǐge rén jùzai yíkuàr dǎ májiàng qu le.

6. Zhōngguo zì tóngyīnde hěn duō. Yǒu yìtiān Gāo Xiānsheng bǎ suǒyǒude tóngyīnzì xiě yìzhāng biǎo, ràng xuésheng kàn. Gāo Xiānsheng ràng xuésheng ànzhe zuò de cìxu cóng qiánbiān yígeyígede chuàndìzhe kàn.

7. Yǒu yìniánde Duānyángjié wǒ qù kàn sài chuán. Nèicì yǒu wǔzhī lóngchuán, sàile sāncì. Yǒu yìzhī guàzhe huáng qíde lóngchuán, měicì dōu shi dì-yī. Biéde chuán jiǎnzhí shi sàibuguò ta. Yǒu rén shuō nèizhī chuán suǒyǐ dé dì-yī shi yīnwei chuánshang zhǐhuī de rén zhǐhuīde hǎo, érqiě zhǐhuī de rén shìqián duì huá chuán de rén shuō rúguǒ déle dì-yī tā lìngwài gěi shǎngqián, měirén shǎng shíkuài qián. Yúshìhū dàjiā dōu nǔlì. Búdàn měicì dōu dé dì-yī, érqiě chuánde sùdù dǎpò cóngqiánde jìlu.

8. Mínguó chūnián mǒumǒu shěng bù tīng zhèngfǔ zhǐhuī, děngyú dúlì. Dāngshí àiguóde rén dōu shuō: "Bìxū bǎ zhèizhǒng dúlì zhuàngtài qǔxiāo, guójiā qiántú cái yǒu xīwang."

WÈNTÍ

1. Zhōngguo rén zài yìnián lǐtou zuì zhòngyàode rìzi shi guònián, qícì shi shénmo?

2. Zhōngguo rén zài yìnián lǐtou yǒu sìge zhòngyàode jié. Qǐng nǐ bǎ zhèi sìge jiéde míngchēng shuōyishuō.

3. Wǔyuejié yòu jiào shénmo jié? Zài zhèi yìtiān jiājiā dōu yào chī shénmo? Hái yào qù kàn shénmo?

4. Chī zòngzi、sài lóngchuánde qǐyuán shi zěnmoyàng? Qǐng nǐ lüè shuō-yishuō.

5. Zhōngguo rén wèi-shénmo zhòngshi Bāyuejié? Bāyuejié yào chī shénmo bǐng?

6. Zhōngguo rén guānyu yuèlianglide shénhuà, qǐng nǐ lüè shuōyishuō.

7. Zhōngguo rén zài shénmo jié qù sǎomù? Sǎomù shi shénmo yìsi?

8. Chóngyángjié shǐ bu shi zài qiūtian? Zài zhèi yìtiān wèi-shénmo yào dēngshān?

9. Qīngmingjié shǐ bu shi zài chūntian? Duōbàn shi zài yīnlìde jǐyuè?

10. Zhōngguode jiérì niánnián dōu shi yǒu yídìngde rìzi, zhǐ yǒu Qīngmíng-jié měiniánde rìzi bùtóng. Nènmo zěnyàng cái néng zhīdao něi yìtiān shi Qīngmingjié ne?

ILLUSTRATIVE SENTENCES (ENGLISH)

5.1. Although water and fire are very useful, nevertheless at times they [also] bring mankind great disaster.

7.1. Chinese send each other presents at the time of [celebrating] the Dragon-Boat Festival and Mid-Autumn Festival.

8.1. Sometime when you have time please explain to me the origin of the old and new calendars in China.

12.1. It is a Chinese custom for everyone [lit. all families and households] to eat glutinous dumplings at the Dragon-Boat Festival.

13.1. Children dearly love to listen to people tell stories.

14.2. That country's production plan has failed.

20.1. This trip of ours has the Confucian temple as its objective.

22.1. The so-called small peasants of China are farmers who don't till much land.

23.1. Unskilled workers [lit. people] feel that it is not at all easy to make a living.

24.1. Sometimes I eat rice, sometimes wheat cakes.

29.1. This journal has an article on myths about the moon written by Mr. Zhang.

30.2. We [few people] had a banquet at the Great China Restaurant.

36.1. This kind of tree exists only in Japan.   No other country has it.

38.1. The whole family has gone to (visit) the grave.

40.4. Since you knew he is no good and always tells lies, why didn't you tell me?

42.1. Someone told me that Zhang Youwen had slandered me.   I went and asked Zhang Youwen, but he wouldn't acknowledge it [lit. that there was any such matter].

45.1. Just go ahead and leave. If anything comes up [lit. if there's any responsibility] I'll take care of it for you.

46.1. In going abroad to study there are all sorts of procedures which must be taken care of beforehand.

48.1. The chairman of a certain organization is not concerned with the welfare of the members, but simply demands money of them.

51.2. People say that he is of no party or faction, that is to say, that he belongs to no party.

54.2. Your grade on this exam is a lot better than mine.

55.1. Mr. Tian is a member of the local self-governing committee.

62.1. What the member of parliament said at the conference was said as a representative of the people.

62.3. The principal and all the [lit. whole school's] teachers are holding a meeting in the conference room.

63.2. I saw two young Chinese ladies in Chinatown, both very beautiful, each in her own way.

NOTES

1.   Stative verbs when used in a comparative meaning are often preceded by yào or hái yào.   Generally they are equivalent to gèng 'more,' but sometimes they retain some of their literal meaning and can be translated as 'should':

> Nǐ bǐ wǒ hái yào gāo. 'You're even taller than I.'

> Nǐ guò lù yào xiǎoxin yìdiǎr. 'You should be a bit more careful in crossing the street.'

2.   The construction V le yòu V means 'to keep on V-ing' or 'to V over and over again':

> Wǒ xiěle yòu xiě. Háishi xiěde bu hǎo. 'I wrote it over and over again but still wrote it badly.'

3.   The pattern lián V dōu/yě bù/méi V means 'not even V':

> Tā lián chī dōu bù chī le. Yídìng huóbuliǎo. 'He doesn't even eat. He certainly can't survive.'

4. In addition to meaning 'therefore,' suǒyǐ is used as a noun meaning 'reason why' in the pattern N suǒyǐ V shi . . . 'the reason why N V is . . .' In the written style, shi is often replaced with wéi, and the subordinating particle zhǐ is used between N and suǒyǐ.

> Wǒ suǒyǐ méi lái shi wǒ méi gōngfu.   'The reason I didn't come is that I didn't have time.'

The end of the suǒyǐ phrase is sometimes marked by de yuányin:

> Wǒ suǒyǐ méi lái de yuányin shi wǒ méi gōngfu.

5. The Chinese festival which involves climbing up to a high place occurs on the 9th day of the 9th lunar month.   Odd numbers in Chinese are referred to as yáng numbers (and even numbers as yīn), so that one of the names for this festival is Chóngyángjié, literally 'the festival of the repeated odd number.'   The name Duānyángjié for the Dragon-Boat Festival on the 5th day of the 5th month is derived from the fact that the number five is exactly (duān) in the middle of the odd numbers from one to nine.

6. The expressions yíbiàn, yìhuí, yíxià, and yìshēng are used after a verb in the meaning 'once':

> Zài niàn yíbiàn.   'Read it once more.'

> Nǐ wèn yìshēng.   'Make an inquiry.'

> Nǐ děng yíxiàr.   'Wait a moment.'

Others numbers can be used:

> Tā jiàole liǎngshēng jiu yǒu rén tīngjian.   'People heard him after he shouted a couple of times.'

> Nǐ dǎ ta jǐxiàr.   'Hit him a few times.'

Dì-Shí'èrkè. Wēnxi

FÙSHÙ

Zhèipán lùyīndài shi Zhōngwén dì-yīzǔ dì-shíhào, Bái Wénshān lùyīn fùshù de Zhuāntí Jiǎnghuà "Guòjié."

Zhèicìde Zhuāntí Jiǎnghuà shi Wén Jiàoshòu gěi wǒmen jiǎng de.
Tā shuō Zhōngguo rénde jiérì hěn duō, zuì zhòngyàode jié shi Duānyáng-

5 jié (jiu shi Wǔyuejié) hé Zhōngqiūjié (jiu shi Bāyuejié). Qícìde shi Qīngmingjié hé Chóngyángjié. Wén Jiàoshòu shuō Qīngmingjié duōbàn shi zài
chūntian sānyueli. Měinián dōu shi bùtóngde rìzi, bú xiàng Wǔyuejié gēn
Bāyuejié yǒu yídìngde rìzi. Qīngmingjié jiājiā qu sǎomù, sǎomù de yìsi
jiu shi bú wàng zǔxiān. Měinián dào fénmù qu dásao dásao, zhòngzhong

10 shù.

Wǔyuejié shi zài yīnlìde wǔyue chūwǔ. Zhèi yìtiān jiājiā chī zòngzi, kàn sài lóngchuán de. Wén Jiàoshòu shuō kàn lóngchuán chī zòngzi de
láiyuán shi zhèiyàng: Zài gōngyuánqián sì shíjì de shíhou Chǔ Guó yǒu

yíge hěn yǒu xuéwen de rén jiào Qū Yuán.   Tā běnlái shi zài Chǔ Guó

15 zuò guān de.   Tā hěn xīwang Chǔ Guó qiáng le.   Tā xiǎng bāngzhu Chǔ

Wáng bǎ Chǔ Guó zhìhǎo.   Kěshi zài nèige shíhou Chǔ Guó lìngwài yǒu

yìxiē zuò guān de gēn Chǔ Wáng shuō Qū Yuánde huàihuà, yúshi Chǔ Wáng

jiu bú xìnren Qū Yuán le.   Qū Yuán kànle zhèizhǒng qíngxing, xīnli shífēn

yōuchóu, tā jiu líkai Chǔ Wáng.   Qū Yuán shī zuò de hěn hǎo, shícháng

20 bǎ xīnlide shìqing yòng shī xiěchulai.   Yìzhí dào xiànzài rénmen hái shuō

tā shi àiguó shīren.   Yǒu yìtiān shi wǔyue chūwǔ, tā xiǎng guójiā shi méi

xīwang le, tā xīnli yǐ nánguò jiu tóujiāng zìshā le.   Dāngshíde rén duōshù

dōu tóngqíng ta, yǒu rén zuò chuán zài jiāngli zhǎo ta, xiǎng jiù ta, yòu

zuò zòngzi rēngzài jiāngli yìsi shi gěi tā chī.   Suǒyǐ hòulai chéngle yíge

25 fēngsu le.

Wén Jiàoshòu shuō Bāyuejié shi zài yīnlì bāyue shíwǔrì.   Zhèng shi

qiūtiande shíhou, tiānqi bù lěng bú rè, yě shi nóngmín qiūshōude shíhou,

suǒyǐ dàjiā dōu fēicháng zhòngshì.   Bāyuejié zài bāyue shíwǔde wǎnshang,

jiājiā dōu shǎngyuè chī yuèbing.

30 Zhōngguo rén duì yuèliang yǒu ge gùshi, shuō yuèliangli yǒu yíge

nǚrén, yīnwei chīle cháng-shēng-bù-lǎo de yào suǒyǐ nénggou cháng zài

yuèliangli.   Hái yǒu yíge shuōfa, shuō yuèliangli yǒu tùr.   Zài Zhōngguo

běifāng Bāyuejiéde shíhou yǒu rén yòng ní zuò tùryé zài jiēshang mài.

Shénmo jiào tùryé ne? Jiu shi yòng ní zuò de tùr. Xiǎoháizimen dōu xǐ-

35 huan.

Tā yòu jiǎng Chóngyángjié.   Tā shuō Chóngyángjié shi zài jiǔyue

chūjiǔ nèitiān, qǐyuán shi zài Dōng Hànde shíhou.   Yǒu yíge rén yǒu yì-

tiān tāde lǎoshī gàosu ta, jiǔyue jiǔrì ta jiāli yǒu zāinàn, ràng tā jiǔyue

chūjiǔ quánjiā dōu dào yíge gāo shānshang qù, jiu kéyi táole zhèicìde zāi-

40 nàn.   Tā jiǔyue chūjiǔ zhēnde dàile jiāli rén dào shānshang qù le. Dàole

wǎnshang huíjiā yí kàn, jiālide jī, yā dōu sǐguāng le, lián yìzhǐ yě méi

huó.

WÈNDÁ

I. Nǐ wèi shénmo . . . ?

(dì-qīkè)

niàn Déwén   xìn Fójiào gǎibiàn guānniàn   biàngēng jìhua

bù néng dǐkàng   méi yǒu zōngjiào

shuō jiāotōng bú biàn   zhěngtiān bú niàn shū

xué yǔfǎ jiégòu

(dì-bākè)

fǎnduì tāde yìjian   shuō nǐ bú zìyóu

bù dú shū   bù shuō pǔtōng huà

xǐhuan zuò mùjiang   bù fúcóng ta

niàn <u>Sānmín Zhǔyì</u>   bù tīng ta zhǐhuī

zuò kǔgōng   bù gōngjì ta niàn shū

kàn zázhì   bú zhàoyàng xiě

(dì-jiǔkè)

tīng wúxiàndiàn   gěi ta huángjīn

chuān xīn yīfu   mǎi zhǐnánzhēn

lǎo shuō kōnghuà   zhuā ta

tiāntiān mǎi huār   zào fángzi

bù xǐhuan jūnren   bù chuān duànzi

tiāntiān dǎ zhēn   mǎi sīxiàn

xiě hángkōngxìn   tùle

jìnzhǐ tā qù   mǎi mùbǎn

(dì-shíkè)

chúxī bu huí jiā   bànyè cái huílai

kū   shuō cìxu bú duì

bu shuìjiào   bìxu qù

shāo xiāng   shīwàng le

dào zhāodàishǐ qu   bú jì zào

sòng ta lǐ   bù xiāoqiàn xiāoqiǎn

méi jīngshen   bìmiǎn gēn tā jiànmiàn

shuō nǐ bù guǎn   guǎn ta jiào lǎoshī

shuō yánglì hǎo

(dì-shíyīkè)

qiūtian huí guó	rēngzai shuǐli
mǎi diànshì	sàibuguò ta
shǐzhōng bù xǐhuan ta	bù huá chuán
mǎi tùryé	zài shuō yíbiàn
zháojí	zhànzai pángbiar
zuòzai zhuōzishang	pángtīng
shuō tā shi nànmín	nènmo yōuchóu
bù bǎ kuàizi bǎihǎo	jiù qù yìhuí
shuō mǒurén bù hǎo	bù xìnren ta
dúzì yíge rén qù	dǎ ta yíxiàr
mǎi zhèikē shù	tóngqíng ta
bù yǎng jī	

II.   Shénmo jiào . . . ?

(dì-qīkè)

Yízú	Lǎmajiào
Kàngzhàn	rénmín gònghé guó
gǎigé	yǔyán xìtǒng
Zhòngjiā	Guómíndǎng

(dì-bākè)

zǔzong	shèhuì fúlì
hòudài	zōngzú
zìgēngnóng	tōngsú xiǎoshuō
mínzú zhǔyì	

(dì-jiǔkè)

gǔwù	zhǐbì
wǔqì	réngōng
chóuduàn	jūnshì
túzhang	

(dì-shíkè)

Xīnnián	chūnjié
Dēngjié	zàowangyé
jiérì	yóuxì
tóngyīnzì	mìngling
shénhuà	guò Xiǎoniár

(dì-shíyīkè)

tùryé	Qīngmingjié
lóngchuán	Chōngyángjié
cháng-shēng-bu-lǎo	wěiyuanhuì
dúlì guójiā	dǎngpài
Duānyángjié	qiángguó
Zhōngqiūjié	Zhōngguojiē

III. . . . zài nǎr?

(dì-qīkè)

Cháoxiǎn	Yìdalì
Déguo	Yúnnán
Gānsu	Mǎnzhou
Guìzhou	Huáng Hé qǐyuán
Xīkāng	

(dì-bākè)

nǐde xiōngdi	Wáng jiade cítáng
Kǒngmiào	nǐ zuò de shī
yuánwén	zúzhǎng
zǔfù zǔmǔ	pūren
nèipiān wénzhāng	

(dì-jiǔkè)

Luómǎ	wúxiàndiàn
wǒde yīfu	chāzi
nǐ gēge	yìnshuāsuǒ

nǐ mǎide huār	zhúzi
sīzhīpǐn	dāochā
chóuduàn	Měijūn

(dì-shíkè)

nǐ qīnqi	wǒmende bīng
zhǐpái	Wáng Zhǔxí
wǒde zhǐbāor	qíyúde rén
shàngzuòr	

(dì-shíyīkè)

Chǔ Guó	zhuōzi
mùdidì	nǐde féndì
tùr	diànbàojú
Xīyáng	pángmén
Dàxīyáng	huìyishǐ
yuèliang	wǒde pò yīfu

IV. . . . yǒu shénmo tèdiǎn?

(dì-qīkè)

Cháoxiǎnzú	Wéiwú'ěrzú
Hànzú	Zàngzú
Huízú	wǔsè qí
Mǎnzú	

(dì-bākè)

mùjiang	xiǎonóng
shìdàfu	

(dì-jiǔkè)

huózì	Guóyǔ Luómǎzì
sīzhīpǐn	Shāng Cháo
cán	Zhōu Cháo
zhǐnánzhēn	Sòng Cháo

(dì-shíkè)

jiùlî   bǎihuò gōngsī
xīnlî

(dì-shíyīkè)

Qū Yuán xiěde shī   guò Zhōngqiūjié
guò Wǔyuejié

V.   Nǐ zěnmo zhǐdao . . . ?

(dì-qīkè)

tāmen xiāngchǔbulái   tāmen bù tuánjié
zhèige děngyu nèige   tā yào tǒngzhi shìjiè
huángdì sǐle   línjìn méi yǒu rén
tā xìn Kǒngjiào   yílǜ píngděng
tā shi lǎma   tā bìng bú xìn Fó
tā gǎibiàn le   shi tā chuàngzào de
tā jīhu sǐ le   zhèrde fēngsu bù hǎo
wǒ pīncuò le   tāmen bèi tónghuà le
Zhuàngzú bù duō   tā gēnběn méi qù
zhànshì yào kuòdà le

(dì-bākè)

tā shi qióngren   tā shi shīren
zhè shi Xīshìde   tā pīping wǒ
tā bu huì fùzé   tā zhǔchí nèige huì
tāmen shì tóngzú   tā jìshù hǎo
tā néng chī kǔ   tā jīchǔ bù hǎo
rénlèi méi xīwang   nèige jiàngrén hěn bèn
móushēng hěn nán

(dì-jiǔkè)

chóuzi guì   tā céngjīng qùguo
fángzi shi kōngde   tāde gòngxiàn hěn dà
tā huì kē zì   tā lìyòng wo

yòngtú hěn dà   tā lìngwài yǒu qián

tā xǐhuan hánghǎi   tā shuōde bú zhèngquè

tā réngrán zài zhèr   tā hěn jiéshěng

huǒyào hěn guì   bù jiēzhe shuō

tā yǒu zhèngmíng

(dì-shíkè)

tāde yùnqi hǎo   wǒ bù guòjié

tā shuō nǐ huàihuà   tāmen bǐcǐ sònglǐ

tā fācái le   tā jīngshen bù hǎo

míngtian shi chūyī   gòng shén yào gòng cài

rìlì bú duì   tā cháng zuò huàishì

tā shi huàirén

(dì-shíyīkè)

tāmen shi nànmín   tā bù néng jiù guó

Qū Yuán shi shīren   jiēshang méi rén

tā dǎbài le   tā hěn yǒu qiántú

tā hěn àiguó   tā pòhuài wǒ

tā tóujiāng le   tā bú shi wěiyuán

tāmen shi yìdǎng   chī yuèbingde láiyuán

tā chéngrèn cuò le   tā yídìng shībài

tā hūran sǐ le   wǎn shi tā dǎpòde

shǒuxu bànhǎo le   tāmen huìyì ne

tā bù kěn qù   tā bù kěn yòng kuàizi

VI. Nǐ shénmo shíhou . . . ?

(dì-qīkè)

xiǎng xué Fóxué   yánjiu Huíjiào

guà qízi   jiǎng shèhuì jiégòu

dào Jiāotōng Bù qu   yòng Hànyǔ Pīnyīn

gǎiyòng pīnyīn   mǎi nèibù shū

(dî-bākè)

fù zhèige zéren   mǎi xīnshì fángzi
qù jiàn zǔfù

(dî-jiǔkè)

dǎ zhēn   dào huāyuánr qu
yòng dāochā   bǎoshǒu mìmi
mǎi huār   huàn Měijīn
yòng Gāngbî   yòng mùtou
gěi wǒ kē túzhang   kē zî
fàng pàozhang   mǎi rîyòngpǐn
chuān Zhōngshî yīfu   shǐyòng dāochā
chī yào

(dî-shíkè)

zuò zhǔxî   shāo xiāng
zuò shàngzuòr   bàinián
shuîjiào   shuō gōngxǐ
wár zhǐpái   jiē shén
kētóu   zhāodài tāmen
kāi dēng   gòng shén
dǎ májiàng   yùbei fàn
sòng lǐ   shànggòng
dào bǎihuò gōngsī qu

(dî-shíyīkè)

tî ta qù   chī zòngzi
dēng xī shān   sài chuán
dásao wūzi   shǎngyuè
mǎi tùryé   sǎomù
chī yuèbing   gǎnjué jîmo
dēng shān   kàn diànshî

VII. . . . gen . . . yǒu shénmo fēnbié?

(dì-qīkè)

qízi, guóqí   tǔdì, lǐngtǔ

yíbù shū, yìběn shū   Miáozú, Hànzú

hùzhù, bāngzhu   chuánshuō, lìshǐ

Hànzì, pīnyīn   Huíjiào, Huízú

Hànzú, Huízú

(dì-bākè)

diànnóng, xiǎohù   jiěmèi, dìxiong

jiēhūn, chūjià   zhōukān, yuèbào

jiàngren, gōngren

(dì-jiǔkè)

mòshuǐ, mòzhī   yìnshuā, chūbǎn

tiěqì, tóngqì   cán, chóngzi

Táibì, Rénmínbì   jīnzi, yínzi

Luómǎzì, pīnyīn

(dì-shíkè)

jiǔxí, jiāchángfàn   rènao, máng

bīng, jūnguān   zhēngyue, yīyue

wūzi, fángzi   làyue, shí'èryue

fùnǚ, nǚrén   bù, chóuzi

qīnqi, zǔxiān   dàren, xiǎoháizi

(dì-shíyīkè)

jiē, lù   fénmù, féndì

wúxiàndiàn, diànshì   Wǔyuejié, Bāyuejié

chūntian, qiūtian   táonàn, táozǒu

shù, shùlínzi   xiāoxi, xīnwén

dēnggāo, dēngshān   jímáng, zháojí

VIII. . . . de lìngwài yíge shuōfǎ shi shénmo?

(dì-qīkè)

qítā	qícì
lìrú	dàyuē
jīhū	zhěnggèr
Hànzú	Měngzú

(dì-bākè)

yíqiè	pūren
fùren	dú shū
chūjià	yúshi
fùzé	wúlùn

(dì-jiǔkè)

bìngqiě	céngjīng
réngrán	bàozhú
shǐ	

(dì-shíkè)

jiǎrú	huài
yīnlì	zàoshén
yánglì	

(dì-shíyīkè)

yángzhuāng	pángren
dàlüè	Xīzhuāng
yángrén	zāinàn

IX. . . . de duìmiàn shi shénmo?

(dì-qīkè)

biānjiāng	hépíng

(dì-bākè)

qióngren	fǎnduì
pūren	diànnóng

fùren   qióng

dàhù   jiùshì

(dì-jiǔkè)

gēge   jìnzhǐ

kōng

(dì-shíkè)

yīnlì   yánglì

jiǎhuà   lǎoye

jiùlì   kū

shàoye   bìxū

dàren   xīnlì

huài   jiǎde

(dì-shíyīkè)

wèiláide   Zhōngzhuāng

dǎshèng   zhòngshì

zhàngfu   shènglì

FĀYĪN

(See page 128)

1. shìjì, shíjǐ   11. jǐshi, jìshi

2. rénjiā, rénjia   12. zhòngshì, Zhōngshì

3. xiōngdì, xiōngdi   13. shǎngyuè, shàngyue

4. zhǔyì, zhúyi   14. Chǔ Guó, chū guó

5. jiùshì, jiùshi   15. bàinián, bǎinián

6. huār, huàr   16. qíshí, qīshí

7. zhēngfú, zhèngfǔ   17. guò jiē, guò jié

8. Gāngbì, gāngbǐ   18. yìshēng, yīsheng

9. jílì, jīlǐ   19. yìkē shù, yíkè shū

10. dàren, dǎ rén   20. yìyuàn, yìyuán, yīyuàn

HUÌHUÀ

Bái : Xuéxīn zǎo.

Xué: Zǎo. Nǐ zuótian wǎnshang hěn zǎo jiu shuì le.

Bái : Yīnwei méi shénmo gōngke yùbei, suǒyǐ jiu shuìde zǎo yìdiǎr. Nǐ ne?

5 Xué: Wǒ kànle yìhuěr diànshì, shíyīdiǎn zhōng shuì de. Wǒ yíxiàngde xíguan dōu shi shíyīdiǎn zuǒyòu shuìjiào. Rènhé shìqing dōu bù néng yǐngxiǎng wǒ shuìjiào de shíjiān.

Bái : Zuótian wǎnshang nǐ kàn de shi shénmo?

Xué: Shi diànyǐngr. Shi yíbù dì-yícì shìjiè dàzhànde piānzi. Zhèizhāng
10 piānzide gùshi shi fēnwéi liǎngfāngmiànde. Yìfāngmiàn shi xíngrong zhànzhēngde kěpà, yìfāngmiàn yǒu xǔduō nànmín táonàn de qíngxing. Lìng yìfāngmiàn hái yǒu jūnrén dàochu pòhuài. Bǐrú tāmen dǎdào mǒu yíge dìfang, jiu bǎ nèige dìfang lìdài bǎocúnxialai de lìshǐxìngde gǔwù dōu bǎ ta pòhuài le.

15 Bái : Wǒ yě xǐhuan kàn zhèi yílèide piānzi.

Xué: Kàn zhèizhǒng piānzi kéyi zhīdao hěn duō jūnshìshangde chángshi hé cóngqiánde jūnshì mìmi.

Bái : Shíhou chàbuduō le. Wǒmen gāi dào shènglì gōngxuéyuàn ménkǒur qù děng Měiyīng qu le.

20 Xué: Jīntian wǒmen qù dēng shān. Hái yǒu liǎngge xīngqī jiu gāi dēnggāo le.

Bái : Jīntian shi yánglì jiǔyue èrshisì.

Xué: Yīnlì shi bāyue èrshijiǔ. Hái yǒu zhěng shítiān jiu shi Chóngyáng-jié.

25 Bái : Nǐ Chóngyángjié dào nǎr dēnggāo qu?

Xué: Wǒ mǔqin qiántian gēn wǒ fùqin shuō, dēnggāo nèitiān qǐng Gāo Xiānsheng、Gāo Tàitai、Měiyīng háiyǒu nǐ、wǒ dàjiā yíkuàr qu shàng shān zài yíkuàr wárwar.

Bái : Hǎojíle. Chóngyángjié shì bu shi dàjiā dōu hěn zhòngshì?

30 Xué: Méi yǒu Wǔyuejié gēn Bāyuejié nènmo zhòngshì.

Bái : Chóngyángjié yǐhòu jiēzhe méi yǒu shénmo jié le ba?

Xué: Jiu shi jiùlì Xīnnián le. Kěshi hái zǎozhe ne, hái yǒu jǐge yue ne.

Bái : Fǔshang guò nián, shi guò yīnlì nián háishi guò yánglì nián?

Xué: Wǒmen jiā duì guònián shi wúsuǒwèi de.

35 Bái : Yǒude rénjiā guò liǎngcì nián, shì bu shi?

Xué: Jùshuō guò jiùlì nián zhèngfǔ dāngchū céngjīng jìnzhǐguo, kěshi lǎo-bǎixìng bù lǐ, háishi guò. Jiéguǒ shi yìnián guò liǎngcì nián.

Bái : Nǐ guònián fàng pàozhang ma?

Xué : Xiǎode shíhou fàng. Yí dàole guònián jiu mǎilai hěn duō zhǒnglèide
40   pàozhang, tiāntiān fàng. Wǒ mǔqin bú ràng wǒ fàng, wǒ shi jué bù
         tīng de. Tā zhǐguǎn shuō tāde, wǒ háishi fàng wǒde, bǎ wǒ mǔqin
         gěi qìhuài le.

Bái : Zhèngfǔ bú shi jìnzhǐ fàng pàozhang ma?

Xué : Guònián nèi jǐtiān méi guānxi. Zhōngguode pàozhang měinián chū-
45   kǒu hěn duō. Jù wǒ zhīdao de, zài Měiguo Zhōngguojiē Huáqiáomen
         guònián dōu fàng pàozhang. Jùshuō hěn duō yángrén yí dào guò
         Zhōngguo nián dōu shàng Zhōngguojiē qu kàn rènao.

Bái : Shì. Yǒu yícì wǒ dào Niǔyuēde Zhōngguojiē qù chī fàn, yí dàole
         nèr jiu yǒu hěn dàde huǒyào wèr, tīngshuō shi gāng fàngwánle pào-
50   zhang.

Xué : Huǒyàode fāmíng yuánlái bìng bú shi xiǎng yònglai shā rén de, kě-
         shi hòulai rénmen jiu lìyòng ta zuò shā rén de wǔqì le.

Bái : Fāmíng yìzhǒng dōngxi zuì nán. Wǒ rènwéi gǔrén bǐ wǒmen cōng-
         míngde duō.

55 Xué : Wǒ yě shi zhènmo xiǎng. Bǐrú zhǐnánzhēn, yìnshuā, kē zì shén-
         mode, dōu shi gǔrén fāmíng de. Kéyi zhèngmíng gǔrén hěn cōng-
         míng. Wénshān, nǐ zài zhèr děngzhe Měiyīng. Wǒ qù mǎi wǒmen
         chī de dōngxi.

Bái : Hǎo. Wǒ děng ta . . . .

60 Měi : Wai, Wénshān.

Bái : Měiyīng, zǎo.

Měi : Wǒ hěn yuǎn jiu kànjian nǐ le. Xuéxīn ne?

Bái : Tā gēn wǒ yíkuàr chūlai de. Tā qu mǎi chīde dōngxi, yìhuěr jiu
         lái.

65 Měi : Qiántian nǐ zài diànhuàli shuō ràng wǒ tì nǐ mǎi sīzhīpǐnde lǐwù,
         wǒ yǐjing mǎihǎo le.

Bái : Xièxie ni, zhēn máfan ni.

Měi : Bié kèqi. Dōngxi hěn piàoliang. Shi tiānrán sī de, bìngqiě jià-
         qian yě bú guì.

70 Bái : Duōshao qián?

Měi : Shíjiǔkuài qián.

Bái : Zhēn bú guì.

Měi : Zài méi mǎi zhīqián běnlái wǒ xiǎng, nǐ shénmo shíhou yǒu gōngfu
         wǒmen liǎngge rén yíkuàr qu mǎi. Kěshi yòu pà nǐ tài máng, méi
75   shíjian.

Bái : Wǒ díquè méi shíjian, tiāntiān mángde yào sǐ, shènzhìyu yǒude shí-
         hou lián chī fàn de gōngfu dōu méi yǒu. Háiyǒu, zhèizhǒng dōngxi
         jiù nǐ néng mǎi. Wǒ qùle yě méi yòng.

Měi : Nǐ wèi-shénmo zhènmo máng ne?

80 Bái : Wǒ shuōgei nǐ tīngting. Jiù ná lùyīn lái shuō. Tīngle Zhuāntí Jiǎnghuà jiu děi lùyīn fùshù, fēiděi lù yì-liǎngcì zìjǐ tīngzhe kéyi le, cái
bú lù le. Yǒude shíhou yào lù hǎojǐcì, jiu yào fèi hǎojǐge zhōngtóude
shíjian.

Měi : Zhào nǐ zhènmo yì shuō nǐ zhēnshi tài máng le. Nǐ xiān bǎ ta shuō
85   jǐcì dōu shuōhǎo le, zài lùyīn bú shi jiéshěng yìdiǎr shíjian ma?

Bái : Duìle. Wǒ tài bèn le. Háishi nǐ bǐ wǒ cōngming.

Měi : Wǒ xiǎng Xuéxīn bú tài máng ba.

Bái : Tā yě hěn máng. Tā hěn yònggōng, shi yíge hěn yǒu qiántúde qīngnián.

90 Měi : Wénshān, nǐ míngtian yǒu gōngfu ma? Wǒ fùqin jiào wǒ gàosu ni,
nǐ ràng tā xiě de zì yǐjing xiěhǎo le. Tóngshí hǎojǐtiān yě méi
kànjian ni le. Shuō qǐng nǐ dào wǒmen jiā qu chī biànfàn.

Bái : Hàode. Wǒ yídìng lái.

Měi : Wǒ mǔqin mǎile hěn duō zhūròu shuō míngtian hǎo zuò shīzi tóu
95   gěi ni chī.

Bái : Gāo Tàitai tài fèi shì le. Gāo Xiānsheng shūdiàn máng bu máng?

Měi : Shūdiàn dào bù máng. Tā zuìjìn zài yìnshuāsuǒ yòu fù yìdiǎr zérèn,
suǒyǐ bǐjiǎo máng yìdiǎr. Wǒ mùqin qián jǐtiān ǒuránde bìngle yícì,
qǐngle dàifu dǎ zhēn chī yào, xiànzài yǐjing wánquán hǎo le.

100 Bái : Shì ma! Nǐ yě méi gàosu wo. Yě méi qù kànkan Gāo Tàitai.

Měi : Wǒ běnlái xiǎng gàosu ni, wǒ mǔqin shuō nǐ cái kāixué yídìng hěn
máng, bú ràng wǒ shuō.

Bái : Nǐ yīnggāi gàosu wo. Nǐ kàn Xuéxīn huílai le.

Měi : Kěbushìma. Nǐ kàn ta shǒuli názhe nènmo duō dōngxi.

105 Xué : Měiyǐng, nǐ cái lái ma?

Měi : Wǒ cái lái. Nǐ mǎi zhènmo duō chī de, wǒmen sānge rén chīdeliǎo
ma?

Xué : Méi guānxi. Chībuliǎo náhuilai. Nǐ kàn jīntian tiānqi yǒu duómo
hǎo a.

110 Měi : Wǒmende yùnqi hǎo.

Xué : Wǒmen cóng dàlù zǒu, háishi cóng xiǎolù zǒu?

Bái : Wǒ sānnián méi zǒu zhèi liǎngtiáo lù le. Dàgài gǎibiànle bù shǎo.

Měi : Xiǎolùshangde xiǎo shù xiànzài yìkēyìkēde dōu zhǎngde hěn gāo le,
biànchéng dà shù le. Dàlù méi shénmo gǎibiàn. Jìde wǒmen cóng
115   zhèr zǒu méi yǒu hěn yuǎn bú shi yǒu yíge dà shùlínzi ma? Hé
yǐqián yíyàng.

Bái : Xuéxīn, wǒmen cóng zhèr dào mùdidì yào duōshao shíhou?

Xué : Yào liǎngge zhōngtóu. Měiyǐng, zěnmozhe? Xiànzài gǎi zhúyi hái
kéyi.

120 Měi: Wèi-shénmo yào gǎi zhúyi? Nǐ zhēn kànbuqǐ wo.

   Xué: Nǐ shi nǚ háizi a.

   Měi: Nǐ shi qīngnián rén, yě bú shi lǎotóur. Zhèizhǒng sīxiǎng bù yīng-
         gāi cúnzài le.

   Bái: Xuéxīn, wǒ jǐtiān yǐqián jiu xiǎng wèn nǐ dōu wàng le. Měiyīng
125   shuō lǎotóur ràng wǒ xiǎngqilai le. Jùshuō lìshǐ xǐ yǒu Shāng,Zhōu
         shídàide gǔwù. Nǐ jǐshí dài wǒ qu kànkan, hǎo bu hǎo?

   Xué: Hǎo. Shénmo shíhou dōu kéyi, wǒ wúsuǒwèi. Nǐ jǐshí yǒu gōngfu?

   Bái: Xià xīngqitiān xiàwǔ sāndiǎn zhōng hǎo bu hǎo?

   Xué: Kéyi. Nèixiē gǔwùli yǒu Shāng Cháode wénzi yě yǒu tóngqì shídài
130   gēn tiěqì shídài zào de tóngqì gēn tiěqì.

   Bái: Shàngmiàn yě kēzhe dōngxi ma?

   Xué: Shàngmiàn kēzhe zì. Háiyǒu Sòng Cháo fāmíng de huózì yìnshuā,
         suǒ kē de zì yígeyígede dōu shi mùtou kē de.

   Bái: Yòng mùtou kē de zì yìzhí bǎocún dào xiànzài zhēn bù róngyi.

135 Xué: Shízài bū róngyi.

   Bái: Shuō kē zì wǒ xiǎngqilai le. Qiántian wǒ qǐng Mǎ Jiàoshòu gěi wǒ
         jièshao yíge kē túzhangde dìfang, kē yíge túzhang. Mǎ Jiàoshòu
         shuō tā huì kē, tā shuō gěi wǒ kē yíge.

   Měi: Wǒ tīng wǒ fùqin shuō tā búdàn huì kē, érqiě kēde hěn hǎo.

140 Bái: Mǎ Jiàoshòu shuō tā hěn xǐhuan kē túzhang.

   Xué: Wǒmen zǒule yǒu yíbàn le.

   Bái: Nǐmen kàn zuǒbiār nèige dà huāyuán zhēn dà. Lǐbiār hái yǒu yíge
         dà shítou shīzi.

   Měi: Nà jiu shi Qián jia huāyuánr. Yí dàole chūntian huār kāile de shí-
145   hou, yòu xiāng yòu piàoliang.

   Bái: Wǒ xǐhuan tiānránde fēngjǐng, xiàng dà shān le, dà hǎi le. Réngōng
         zào de fēngjǐng wǒ bù xǐhuan.

   Xué: Gè yǒu gède měi.

   Bái: Zìránde fēngjǐng hǎoxiang yíge nǚháizi shide—bù chuān chóuduàn yīfu,
150   jiu chuānzhe pǔtōng bù yīfu, kěshi tā yǒu nèizhǒng zìránde měi.
         Yǒude nǚháizi běnlái zhǎngde bú piàoliang, kěshi lǎo shi chuānzhe
         chóuzi duànzide yīfu. Měiyīng shǔyu wǒ xiān shuō de nèi yílèide.

   Měi: Bié shuō wo, hǎo bu hǎo?

   Xué: Wénshān, nǐ shuōde zhēn duì.

155 Měi: Nǐmen kàn, nèige xiǎo hébiārshang dōu shi zhúzi. Wǒ zuì xǐhuan
         zhúzi le.

   Bái: Guàibude nǐ jìnlái huà de huàr zhāngzhāng shi zhúzi.

   Měi: Shì. Wǒ jìnlái guāng huà zhúzi le.

Bái : Huà zhúzi dōu shi yòng mò huà ma? Wǒ kàn nǐ suǒ huà de zhúzi
160   méi yǒu yìzhāng shi yòng yánse huà de.

Měi : Yě yǒu yòng yánse huà de. Búguò yòng mò huà zhúzi yàoshi huàde
       hěn hǎo, nà shi xiāngdāng nánde. Nǐ kàn wǒmen jiā kètīng guàzhe
       de nèizhāng gǔrén huà de zhúzi hǎoxiang zhēnde yíyàng.

Xué : Wǒmen xiān dào nèikuài dà shítoushang zuò yìhuěr, hǎo bu hǎo?

165 Bái : Wǒ zàncheng. Wǒ kàn Měiyǐng hǎoxiang lèile de yàngzi.

Měi : Shéi shuō de? Wǒ kě bú lèi!

Xué : Xiànzài jǐdiǎn le?

Bái : Shídiǎn bàn.

Měi : Lí zhèr hái yǒu búdào èrlǐ lù jiu yào shàng shān le.

170 Xué : Hǎo, wǒmen xiànzài zài jìxù zǒu.

Měi : Jīntian yǒu něige xuéxiàode xuésheng lái lǔxíng ba? Nǐmen kàn yí-
       lùshangde xuésheng bù shǎo me.

DUǍNWÉN

1. Yǒu yíge guójiā zìcóng mǒunián zài jūnshìshang shībàile zhīhòu, jiu chéng-
    le lìngwài yíge guójiāde zhímíndì. Hòulai zài mǒu yìnián dúlì le, búshàng
    shíniánde gōngfu yǐjing biànchéng dì-yīděng qiángguó le.

2. Zuótian zài shūdiàn kàn shū. Kànle bàntian yě méi shū kě mǎi. Hòulai
    kànjian yìběn xiǎoshuō Wèiláide Shìjiè, lǐmiàn yǒu jǐpiān hěn yǒu yìsi.
    Xiànzài wǒ bǎ nèiběn xiǎoshuō kànle yíbiàr le, wǒ hái xiǎng zài kàn yì-
    huí.

3. Jù bàozhǐshang mǒurén xiě de shèlùn, dàlüè shi: Mǒumǒu dìfang, yīnwei
    mǒu yíge guójiā yào kuòzhǎn tāmende lǐngtǔ ér zhànle línjìn guójiāde tǔ-
    dì. Liǎngguó bǐcǐ zhēngduó nèikuài dìfang, yǐjing yǒu qītiān le. Jù běn-
    guó jūnshì wěiyuánhuìde yíwei jūnguān fēnxi, zhèige zhànzhēngde qūshì
    kěnéng kuòdà. Suīrán Liánhéguó shi wéichi shìjiè hépíngde dìfang, ér
    shìjiè gèguó yě gòngtóng zhīchí ta, kěshi fāshēngle shìqing rúguǒ yào yóu
    Liánhéguó lái jiějué shi xiāngdāngde màn le.

4. Zuótian wǒ dào hángkōng gōngsī qu mǎi dào Sānfánshì de fēijī piào. He!
    Zhèige ǒuránde jīhui kě zhēn shi nándé. Wǒ kànjian cóng Luómǎ lái de
    liǎngwèi zuì yǒumíngde diànyǐng nǚ míngxīng. Tāmen yě shi lái mǎi fēi-
    jī piào de.   Tāmen bìng méi chuān yángzhuāng, chuān de Zhōngzhuāng,
    piàoliang jíle. Wǒ zhànzai tāmen pángbiār, yìzhí kànzhe tāmen mǎiwánle
    piào. Tāmen yě gǎnjué dao wǒ zài kàn tāmen, tóngshí tāmen yě zài kàn
    wo. Bìng búshi yīnwei wǒ zhǎngde hǎokàn tāmen kàn wo. Wǒ xiǎng tā-
    men kàn wo dàgài shi yīnwei wǒ chuān de Xīzhuāng tài pò le.

5. Wǒ gēge zuìjìn cóng Dàxīyáng hánghǎi ér lái de. Tā shuō chuán zǒudao
    bànlùshang zhèng shi bāyue shíwǔ Zhōngqiūjiéde shíhou. Tā zài chuán-
    shang kànjianle yuèliang jiu shífēn xiǎng jiā. Tā xīnli jiu xiǎng, yàoshi
    zài jiāli chī yuèbing shǎng yuè hé jiāli rén tuánjù shi duómo yǒu yìsi
    ya. Kěshi jīntian zài chuánshang kànjian de shi Xīyáng rén, chī de shi

wàiguo fàn. Tóngshí tā yòu kànjian yíge Yìdàlì rén chī de dōngxi, hǎoxiàng jiǎozi shide. Tā gèng xiǎng jiā le.

6. Zài Duānyángjié nèitiān, wǒ hé wǒde nǚ péngyou wǒmen liǎngge rén dào
húlǐ qu huá chuán. Wǒmen yìbiār huázhe chuán, yìbiār kàn fēngjǐng. Kāishǐ wǒmen liǎngge rén hé huá yìzhī chuán. Hòulai tā yào gēn wǒ sài
chuán kàn shéi huáde kuài, suǒyǐ tā lìngwài huá yìzhī. Běnlái wǒ xiǎng
tā shi nǚháizi, yídìng huábuguò wo. Jiéguǒ wǒde chuán lǎoshi gēnzài tā
chuán hòutou, shǐzhōng sàibuguò ta.

7. Wáng Xiānsheng zài yìyuànli gōngzuò.   Tāde gōngzuò yìdiǎr yě bú lèi.
Chúfēi shi yìyuánmen huìyì, tā bìděi shìqián dào huìyìshǐ qu, yàoburán
yìyuànli tā lián qù dōu búbì qù.

8. Yǒu yíge guójiā zài zhèngzhìshang fēnwéi liǎng dà dǎng, měi yíge dǎng
yòu fēn hěn duō pài.   Yǒu rén shuō, rúguǒ yíge guójiā dǎngpài tài duō
le, duìyu guójiā yě yǒu hǎochu, yě yǒu huàichu.   Hǎochu shi biǎoxiàn
zhèige guójiāde zìyóu hé mínzhǔ. Huàichu shi yǒu shíhou yíge hěn zhòngyàode wèntí, dǎngpài duō, yìjian bùtóng, yìshí juédìngbuliǎo.

9. Yǒu jǐge xiǎoháizi zài yíkuàr wár. Yǒu yíge xiǎoháizi yìshí bù xiǎoxin,
bǎ lìngwài yíge xiaoháizide tóu yòng shítou dǎpò le. Biéde háizi dōu pǎo
le, zhǐ yǒu yíge niánji zuì xiǎode háizi méi pǎo. Tā xiǎng bāngzhu zhèige
háizi, kěshi yě méi fázi. Tā jíde bùdéliǎo. Zhèige shíhou pángbiār yíge
rén yě méi yǒu. Tā hūrán xiǎngqilai le, yīnggāi dàshēng jiào. Yúshi tā
jiu jiào "Jiùrén na! Jiùrén na!" Tā cái jiàole liǎngshēng jiu yǒu rén
tīngjian le, jímáng bǎ nèige xiǎoháizi sòngdao yīyuàn qu le.

10. Wǒ shi Yuǎn-Dà yǔyán xuéxǐde yíge pángtīngshēng. Zuótian zài túshūguǎn
kànjian yìběn guānyú Zhōngguo yǔyánxuéde shū, shi yòng Guóyǔ Luómǎzì
xiě de.   Xiěde hěn qīngchu, dàyì shi shuō yǔyánxué hé yǔyánde fēnbié.

11. Wǒ zǔfù 、 zǔmǔ fēicháng ài wo.   Yàoshi wǒ yǒu cuòr le huòshě bù tīng
huà mǔqin yào dǎ wǒde shíhou, zǔmǔ yídìng bù xǔ tā dǎ wo.   Wǒ jìde
yǒu yícì mǔqin jiào wǒ xiě zì wǒ bù kěn xiě, mǔqin jí le, yào dǎ wo,
zǔmǔ yòu shuō bù xǔ dǎ, kěshi mǔqin yīnwei tài shēngqì le, méi tīng zǔmǔde huà, hái shuō "Nín bú yòng guǎn," jiu dǎle wǒ le. Zǔmǔ shuō wǒ
mǔqin: "Nín bú yào dǎ ta. Nǐ dǎ wǒ ba."   Mǔqin búdàn bù néng zài dǎ
wo, hái děi xiàng zǔmǔ chéngrèn tā cuò le. Wǒ yòu shènglìle yícì! Xiànzài xiǎngqǐ dāngshí mǔqinde xīnlǐ shi duómo nánguò ya!

12. Yíwèi lǎo xiānsheng cónglái méi yòng dāozi 、 chāzi chīguo fàn. Yǒu yícì
rénjia qǐng ta chī wàiguo fàn, dāngrán shi yòng dāochā le.   Tā cónglái
méi yòngguo, zìrán shi bú huì shǐ le.   Chī de shi jī.   Zài chī fàn de
shíhou, jī yě fēi le, érqiě tā ná dāochā de yàngzi hěn kěxiào. Pángrén
xiǎng xiào kěshi yòu bù hǎoyìsi.

13. Zuótian jiēdao wǒ mǔqinde hángkōngxìn. Xiànzài wǒ niànchulai, gěi nǐmen tīngting:

Dàwén ér:
    Nǐ sānhàode xìn shōudào le. Nǐ shuō nǐ suǒyǐ bù cháng wǎng jiāli
láixìn shi yīnwei gōngke tài máng le. Tóngshí zhīdao nǐ shi quánxiào
gōngke zuì hǎode xuésheng. Zuò fùmǔ de zuì gāoxìngde shi érnǚ shū niànde hǎo.

Wǒmen Qīngmingjié dào féndî qu sǎomù, zài féndîshang yòu zhòngle jǐkē shù.

Wǒmen jiāde fángzi ràngchū yíbùfen gěi Wáng jia zhù le. Fángzi suǒyǐ yào rànggěi Wáng jia zhù de yuányīn shi nǐ fùqin shuō wǒmen jiā rén shǎo, yòngbuliǎo zhènmo duōde fángzi, Wáng jia zhùzai zhèr duî wǒmen yě mái yǒu shénmo bù fāngbian, tāmen zǒu pángmén.

Nǐ dîdi kǎoshang Zhōng-Dà le, shǒuxu dōu yǐjing bànhǎole.

Qiántian jiēdào Mǎ Xiānsheng diànbào. Tāmen quánjiā shíhào zuò fēijī dào zhèr lai, ràng wǒmen gěi tāmen dìng lǚguǎn, yě xīwang wǒmen dào fēijīchǎng qu jiē tāmen. Wǒmen dāngrán děi qù jiē tāmen le. Nǐ fùqin dào diànbàojú huíle tāmen yíge diànbào, shuō yídìng qu jiē tāmen. Tāmen dào zhèr lai wǒmen hěn gāoxìng. Duōshao niánde lǎo péngyou duōnián bú jiàn le, yīnggāi dàjiā jùyijù.

Yǐshàng shi jìnlai jiālide qíngxing. Xīwang duō wǎng jiāli xiě xîn. Tīngshuō nèibiārde tiānqi bù hǎo. Duō zhùyì shēntǐ, nǔlî qiúxué. Mòshuǐ gēn gāngbǐ qiānbǐ hái yǒu yîbāo táng, dōu shōudàole ma?

Zhù

Jìnbù   Mǔ
                                        sānyue shíliùrî

14. Zuótian wǎnshang wúxiàndiàn bàogào xīnwén, guānyu jînlaide zhànshî tāmen dàlüè shuōle yìdiǎr. Tāmen shuō Měijūn zuìjìn zài mǒu dìfang hé mǒujūn fāshēng zhànshì, jiéguǒ Měijūn dǎshèng, mǒujūn shībài. Zhèige xiāoxi yě bù zhīdào zhèngquè bu zhèngquè.

15. Wǒ mèimei jīnnian dàxué yào bìyè le. Wǒ děi sòng ta yìdiǎr dōngxi zuò jìniàn. Rúguǒ mǎi yìdiǎr bǐjiào guìde dōngxi, kěshi wǒ xiànzài shǒubiār hěn jǐn. Yàoshi mǎi rìyòngpǐn, yě méi shénmo yìsi. Yǒu le! Wǒ xiǎngqilai le. Wǒ qǐng kē zî de Máo Dàwéi Xiānsheng kē yíge túzhang sònggei ta. Suīrán duî tā méi yǒu shénmo yòngtú kěshi mèimei cónglái méi kànjianguo. Tóngshí wǒ zhīdao mèimei hěn ài xiǎo yáng. Wǒ xiǎng mǎi kuài shítou, shàngmian kēzhe xiǎo yáng, xiàmian kēshang tāde míngzi. Wǒ xiāngxìn tā yídìng xǐhuan.

16. Zuótian Wáng Jiàoshòu gěi wǒmen jiǎng de yǎng cán zào sî. Jiǎngwán zhīhòu tā dàizhe wǒmen dào yîjiā yǎng cán de rénjiā qu kàn. Wǒmen kànjian hěn duō dà chóngzi, nà jiu shi cán, tóngshí yǎng cán de zhǔrén bǎ yǐqián cán tù de sî náchulai gěi wǒmen kàn. Yòu bǎ sīxiàn chóuzi děngděng dōu náchulai gěi wǒmen kàn. Wǒmen wèn ta měinián cán shēngchǎn de sî duō bù duō? Zhèiwèi zhǔrén shuō bù shǎo. Tā hái gàosu wǒmen tāmen zhèixiē yǎng cán de rénjiā dōu yào gōngji shāngren chūkǒu, měinián huànlái de qián hé Měijīn yǒu jǐshíwàn ne.

17. Wǒ zài qīsuìde shíhou fùqin jiu sî le, kàozhe mǔqin gěi rénjia zuò yīfu shēnghuó. Zhèizhǒng shēnghuó yìdiǎr bǎozhàng yě méi yǒu, érqiě yě kǔde bùdeliǎo. Měiyuè chúle fángqián gēn chī fàn zhīwài, duōbuchūlái jǐge qián le. Suǒyǐ wǒ zhǐ yǒu chūzhōngde chéngdu. Xiànzài zhǎodàole yíge gōngzuò, shi xué kē zî, shi xué zài mùbǎnshang kē zî. Zài xuéxi de qījiān, měiyuè gěi de gōngqián hé Gāngbì èrshikuài qián. Yàoshi hé Měijīn hái bú dào sîkuài qián ne. Suīrán gōngqián shǎo, kěshi guònián, guòjié hái yǒu yìdiǎr shǎngqián.

18. Zhāng Xiānsheng yǒu yíge jiějie, jīnnián kuài sìshí le hái méi jiàchuqu ne. Suǒyǐ jiàbuchūqù de yuányīn shi zhǎngde tài nánkàn le, méi yǒu rén xǐhuan ta. Suírán zhǎngde bú piàoliang, kěshi hěn xǐhuan chuān yáng-zhuāng. Zhāng Xiānshengde fùqin sīxiǎng hěn gǔlǎo, fēicháng bǎoshǒu, suírán bú zànchéng dànshi yě méi fázi, guānbuliǎo ta.

19. Wàn Yǒuwénde shēngyi shi mǎimài jīnzi hé huàn qián. Bǐrú biéde dìfang rén dào zhèr lái lǚxíng, tāmen dài de qián zài dāngdì bù néng mǎi dōng-xi, jiu xiān dào ta nèr qu huàn. Suǒyǐ tā tiāntiān kànjian bù shǎode huángjīn、yínzi、zhǐbì gèshì gèyàngrde tā dōu kànjianguo, bǐrú Měijīn、Gǎngbì、Táibì、Rénmínbì shénmode.

20. Shànggǔ shídài dōu shi yòng tóng zào wǔqì, hòulai jìnbù dào yǐ tiě zào wǔqì. Dāngrán shi yòng tiě zào wǔqì de kéyi zhēngfúle yòng tóng zào wǔqì de le.

21. Yíge rénde xíguan hěn bù róngyi gǎiguolai. Wǒ fùqin shi zài Yìndu zhǎng-dà de. Yīnwei Yìndu rén chī dōngxi shi yòng shǒu zhuāzhe chī, suǒyǐ wǒ fùqin cóng xiǎo jiu yǎngchéngle zhèizhǒng xíguan le. Tā yǐjing líkāi Yìn-du sānshínián le, kěshi tā yǒu shíhou chī dōngxi réngrán yòng shǒu zhuā.

22. Lǎo Zhāng lǎo shuō kōnghuà. Jiànzhe rén jiu shuō yào qǐng rénjia chī fàn. Rìzi jiǔ le tā lǎo nènmo shuō, hòulai méi rén xiāngxìn ta le. Yǒu yícì tā zhēnde yào qǐng rénjia chī fàn le. Tā hé jǐge rén dōu shuō le, èryue shíwǔhào qǐng rénjia dào tā jiā chī wǎnfàn. Tā tàitai mángle hǎo-jǐtiān, zuòle hěn duō cài, jiéguǒ lián yíge rén dōu méi qù.

23. Wǒ jiā yǒu yíge tóng pánzi. Jùshuō shi zài yìqiān duō nián yǐqiánde dōngxi, shi cóng wǒde zǔxiān yídài yídài chuándào xiànzài de.

24. Wǒ zǔmǔ zuótian wǎnfàn zhīhòu gěi wǒmen shuō gùshi. Tā lǎorénjiā shuō de yě shi shìshí. Tā shuō dàyuē zài bāshi duō nián yǐqián wǒmen hái shi yǒuqiánde rénjiā, yě shi shìdàfu jiēji, yòu shi dà jiātíng. Zìcóng Qīng Cháo mònián hé wàiguo dǎzhàng, wǒmen jiā cóng lǎojiā táozǒule yǐhòu, jiu mànmānrde biànchéng zhèizhǒng gōngren jiējide jiātíng le.

25. Qiántian xuéxiào kāi wǎnhui. Yǒu yíge yóuxì shi ná yíge dōngxi dàjiā hù-xiāng rēngzhe chuándì. Nǐ dìgěi wǒ, wǒ zài dìgěi tā, zhèi yàngzide bǐcǐ chuándì.

26. Kuàizide gōngyòng shi chī fàn de. Suírán Zhōngguo rén chī fàn rénrén dōu shi yòng kuàizi, kěshi shéi yě méi yánjiu kāishǐ shǐyòng kuàizi shi zài shénmo shíhou.

27. Zài yíge guòniánde wǎnshang, jiājiāhùhù zhèngzai fàng bàozhúde shíhou, yíge jūnguān hé tàitai gēn háizimen zhèngzai jiā guò nián ne, hūrán yǒu rén lái gàosu tā shuō: "Zhèicìde zhànzhēng kěnéng shi wǒmen dǎbài le." Tā bú xìn, tā shuō xiāoxi bú zhèngquè. Zhèng zài zhèige shíhou jiēzhe jiu lái yíge diànhuà shuō rénjiade bīng yǐjing dǎdào mǒumǒu dìfang le. Zhèihui tā cái zháojí le, jímáng cóng jiāli zǒu le. Tā zǒu de shíhou yě méi shuō yìshēngr shàng nǎr qu, jiù lián tā tàitai yě bù zhīdào tā zhàng-fu shi dào nǎr qu le.

28. Zuótian Gāo Xiānsheng dǎ diànhuà gěi wǒ shuō qǐng wǒ wǎnshang dào tā jiāli qù chī wǎnfàn. Zuótian wǎnshang liùdiǎn zhōng dào tā jiāli yí kàn, zhuōzishang bǎile hǎojǐ dà pánzi cài, hái yǒu yí dà pánzi bǐng. Zhèixiē

cài dōu shi Gāo Tàitai yíge rén zuò de. Chīwánle fàn yǐhòu Gāo Xiānsheng sòng wǒ sìběn guānyu wénzìxué de shū. Gāo Xiānsheng shuō zhèi
sìběn shū yígòng wǔkuài qián, měiběn cái hé yíkuài duō qián. Wǒ gēn
Gāo Xiānsheng shuō bú yào sònggei wo, wǒ bǎ qián gěi ta, tā bù kěn,
yídìng yào sònggei wo.

29. Wǒ dào zhèige dàxué niàn shū chàbuduō yìnián le. Wǒ shi yíge wàiguo
xuésheng, yīnwei chéngdu bú gòu suǒyǐ zài zhèige dàxué shi yíge pángtīngshēng. Zuótian yǒu yíge tóngxué gàosu wo: "Rúguǒ nǐ yí jìn xuéxiào
shi pántīngshēng jiānglái nǐ bú zuò pángtīngshēng de shíhou zài shǒuxu-
shang shi fēicháng máfan." Kěshi wǒ wèile qiántú búlùn zěnmo máfan yě
děi xiǎng fázi. Wǒ hěn zǎo jiu xiǎng qu jiàn jiàowuzhǎng qǐng tā tì wǒ
xiǎngxiang fázi, kěshi shǐzhōng yě méi shíjiān qu kàn ta.

30. Zuótian wǎnfàn zhīhòu wǒ dúzì yíge rén zài jiēshang zǒuzou, yùjian Zhāng
Jiàoshòu le. Wǒ hěn jiǔ méi kànjian Zhāng Jiàoshòu le. Hé tā zài lùshang shuōle jǐjù huà. Zhāng Jiàoshòu gàosu wǒ jiào wǒ gēn Wáng Wénhuá shuō yíxiàr jiào Wáng Wénhuá míngtian zǎoshang dào tā shūfáng qu.
Zhāng Jiàoshòu shi hěn yǒumíngde wénxuéjiā. Tā yǒu yíge tèxìng, zài
tā yánjiu xuéwènde shíhou lìlái shi yuànyi yǒu xuésheng zài tā pángbiār,
yàoshi fāxiàn yǒuyìside wèntí jiu mǎshàng gēn xuéshengmen tǎolùn, bìngqiě ràng xuésheng dōu ná bǐ jìxialai.

UNIT III

"Jīntian jiāli yīngyīngyànyàn, rènao jíle."

Dì-Shísānkè.　Xuéxí Zhōngguo Huà

Bái:　Mǎ Jiàoshòu zǎo.

Mǎ:　Zǎo.　Nǐ zǎo lái le?

Bái:　Wǒ yě gāng lái.　Nín zhèi liǎngtiān shàng nǎr wár qu le ma?

Mǎ:　Wǒ zhèi liǎngtiān yīnwei jīngshen bù hǎo, zuótian zài jiā shuìle yì-
5　　tiānde jiào, nǎr yě méi qù.　Nǐ hé Xuéxīn Měiyǐng shàng shān qu
　　le, shì bu shi?

Bái:　Shìde.　Xīngqiliù wǒmen qu shàng shān.　Zuótian shi Gāo Xiānsheng
　　shēngri, dào Gāo jia qu le.

Mǎ:　Duìle.　Zuótian shi Lǎo Gāode shēngri.　Hái yǒu biéren qù ma?

10 Bái:　Yǒu yíwèi Wáng Lǎo Tàitai shi Gāo Tàitaide qīnqi, hái yǒu Měiyǐng-
　　de liǎngge nǚ tóngxué.　Shìqián wǒ bù zhīdao shi Gāo Xiānsheng
　　shēngri.　Děngdao chī fàn de shíhou wǒ cái tīngshuō, wǒ yě méi
　　sòng yìdiǎr lǐ.

Mǎ:　Nà dào wúsuǒwèide.

15 Bái:　Zài chī fànde shíhou, wǒ duì Gāo Xiānsheng Gāo Tàitai shuō "Gōngxǐ
　　gōngxǐ." Nín shuō kéyi ma?

Mǎ:　Guò shēngri shuō "Gōngxǐ" yě kéyi.

Bái:　Wǒmen jǐge rén tánde hěn rènao.　Nèitiān Gāo Tàitai yùbei de cài
　　zhēn fēngfu, jiǎnzhí hǎoxiang yìzhuō jiǔxí, érqiě měi yíge càide wèr
20　　dōu hěn hǎo.

Mǎ:　Nǐ duì Zhōngguo cài něi yíyàngr dōu chǐdelái ma?

Bái:　Dōu chǐdelái.　Méi yǒu yíyàngr wǒ chǐbulái de.　Zuótian chī fàn de
　　shíhou wǒmen hái hēle yìdiǎr jiǔ.

Mǎ:　Lǎo Gāo píngcháng bù hē jiǔ de, shì bu shi?

25 Bái:　Shìde.

Mǎ:　Tā jìnlai zuò shénmo xiāoqiǎn ne?

Bái:　Wǒ kàn tā jiu shi ná xiě zì dàng xiāoqiǎn.　Měitiān xiěle yòu xiě.

Mǎ:　Tīngshuō Lǎo Gāode zì yìtiān bǐ yìtiān xiěde hǎo.

Bái:　Tā tiāntiān xiě me!

30 Mǎ:　Jǐshí wǒ děi qiú tā gěi wǒ xiě yìzhāng.

Bái:　Nín méi yǒu Gāo Xiānshengde zì ma?

Mǎ:　Méi yǒu.　Tā kěn bù kěn gěi biéren xiě ya?

Bái:　Gāo Xiānsheng zuì gāoxìngde jiu shi yǒu rén qiú ta xiě zì le.　Nín
　　gēn tā shi lǎo péngyou, xiāngxìn gèng méi wèntí le.

281

35 Mǎ : Měiyīngde huàr, huàde yě búcuò le ba?

    Bái: Nín méi kànjianguo ma? Huàde hěn hǎo.

    Mǎ : Měiyīng zhèi háizi hěn tèbié, tāde huàr cónglái bú jiào rén kàn.

    Bái: Gāo Xiānsheng shūfángli guà de nèi yìzhāng jiu shi tā huà de. Nà
         shi yìtiān Gāo Xiānsheng zhèng zai xiě zì de shíhou, Měiyīng bǎ tā
40   huàxialai de.

    Mǎ : Měiyīng díquè shi hěn cōngming de.   Nǐ duì huà huàr yǒu xìngqu
         méi yǒu?

    Bái: Wǒ hěn xǐhuan, kěshi wǒ méi yǒu huà huàrde tiāncái.

    Mǎ : Nǐ bìng bú shi méi yǒu tiāncái. Nǐ shi zhuānmén xiàng wénxué yì-
45   fāngmiàn fāzhǎn le.

    Bái: Wǒ shízài shi méi yǒu tiāncái.   Yǒude rén shi duō fāngmiànde.

    Mǎ : Nǐ zhènmo cōngming zài biéde fāngmiàn yòng yìdiǎr gōngfu yídìng
         chéngji yě bú huài. Zěnmoyàng? Shàng yíge xīngqī suǒ xué de yǒu
         wèntí méi yǒu?

50 Bái: Dàzhì méi shénmo wèntí. Qǐng wèn nín jīntiande jiǎngtí shi shén-
         mo? Shi guānyu něi yìfāngmiàn de?

    Mǎ : Jīntian jiǎng Xuéxí Zhōngguo Huà. Cóng jīntian qǐ zhèi yíge xīng-
         qī dōu shi jiǎng Zhōngguo yǔwén zhèi fāngmiànde.   Míngtian jiǎng
         Zhōngguode wénzì.

55 Bái: Zhèi yíge xīngqīde tímu nín dōu zhīdao ma?

    Mǎ : Zhīdao. Hòutian xīngqīsān jiǎng cānkǎo shū. Xīngqīsì jiǎng Zhōng-
         guo yǔyán. Xīngqīwǔ jiǎng Zhōngguo wénxué.

1.0. shǒuxiān   first of all, in the first place [head first]

1.1. Guòniánde shíhou shǒuxiān yào gěi zǔfù zǔmǔ kētóu bàinián.

2.0. liúlì   fluent [flow sharp]

2.1. Tā jìrán Zhōngguo huà shuōde nènmo liúlì le, wèi-shénmo hái yào
      xué?

3.0. jīlěi   accumulate, pile up [accumulate accumulate]

      rìjīyuèlěi   (1) gradually; (2) build up gradually (MA) [day accumu-
                   late month accumulate]

3.1. Wǒ bìngle yíge duō yuè, bù néng gōngzuò, suǒyǐ wǒde gōngzuò dōu
      jīlěiqilai le.   (T)

3.2. Wǒ suīrán méi xuéguo Zhōngguo huà, kěshi wǒ hé Zhōngguo rén
      cháng zài yíkuàr, rìjīyuèlěi wǒ jiu xuéhuìle hěn duō.

4.0. yǎngchéng xíguan   develop a habit

4.1. Tā yǎngchéng xíguan le bànyè bìxū chī dōngxi.   (T)

Bái: Wǒ shàngcìde lùyīn nín tīngguo le ma?

Mǎ: Tīngguo le. Hěn hǎo, fùshùde fēicháng wánquan. Nǐ shǒuxiān shuō
60   de nèi jǐjù huà yě hěn hǎo.

Bái: Wǒ tīngzhe máobing tài duō, érqiě shuōde yě bù liúlì.

Mǎ: Wǒ tīngzhe dào bú shi bù liúlì, jiu shi shuōde màn yìdiǎr. Nà dōu
shi nǐ píngcháng rìjǐyuèlěi yǎngchéng de xíguan.

Bái: Wǒ rènwei háishi shuōde bù hǎo, méi yǒu Zhōngguo rén shuō de
65   nènmo zìrán.

Mǎ: Shuōde zìrán dāngrán shi zuì hǎo le. Xué wàiguo yǔyán, shǒuxiān
háishi děi shuōchulai yào biéren tīngle hěn míngbai, zhīdao nǐ shuō
de shi shénmo.

5.0. (xiǎo)yàn(r)   swallow (bird) [little swallow]

5.1. Nǐ kàn zěnmo wūzili fēijinlai yìzhī xiǎoyànr a?

6.0. huángyīng   oriole [yellow oriole]

yīngyīngyànyàn   animated (like a flock of swallows and orioles)

6.1. Huángyīng jiào de shēngyīn fēicháng hǎotīng.

6.2. Dēngjié wǒmen jiā láile hǎojǐwèi xiáojie, yīngyīngyànyànde, hěn
rènao.

7.0. niǎo(r)   bird

7.1. Jīntian zǎoshang wǒmen ménkǒu nèikē dà shùshang yǒu hěn duō xiǎo
niǎor, fēilái fēiqù, hǎoxiang zài zuò yóuxì.   (T)

8.0. bǐyu   (1) metaphor; (2) compare metaphorically [compare allegory]

8.1. Shīren zuò shīde shíhou chángcháng yòng bǐyu.

9.0. yùnyòng   put to use, apply, carry out [revolve use]

9.1. Nèige shāngren hěn huì yùnyòng tāde qián. Zuòle sānnián mǎimai
jiu fācái le.

9.2. Nǐ néng yùnyòng zhèixiē zì xiě yìpiān dōngxi ma?

10.0. shīyì   poetic quality, lyricism [poem meaning]

10.1. Yǒu rén shuō Zhōngguo yǔyán yǒu shīyì, zhèi shi zhēnhuà ne, hái
shi jiǎhuà ne?

Bái: Yīngyīngyànyàn zhèige cér shi xíngrongcí ma? Bù zhīdào zài shén-
70   mo shíhou kéyi yòng?

Mǎ: Yīng shi huángyīng. Yàn shi xiǎoyànr. Shi liǎngzhǒng niǎorde míngzi. Zhèi liǎngzhǒng niǎor jiào de shēngyīn dōu hěn hǎotīng. Rúguǒ
yǒu jǐwèi niánqīngde xiáojiemen zài yíkuàr, jiu yòng zhèige cér lái
xíngrong tāmen. Yàoshi yǒu jǐwèi lǎo tàitai zài yíkuàr kě qiānwàn

bù néng yòng. Rúguǒ ná <u>yīngyīngyànyàn</u> lái bǐyu lǎo tàitai, jiu kěxiào le, chúfēi nǐ shi gùyìde shuō xiàohua.

Bái: Suǒyǐ cér yàoshi yòngde bù hǎo, jiù huì chū xiàohua de.

Mǎ: Zhōngguo yǔyánde nánchu jiu shi xíngróngcí nán yùnyòng

Bái: Shuō Zhōngguo yǔyán yǒu shíyì yě jiu shi zhèige yuányīn.

11.0. gǎnqíng   emotion, sentiment, feeling [feel emotion]

   rèqíng   (1) enthusiasm, ardor, warmth of feeling; (2) be warm to-
            ward a person [warm emotion]

11.1. Bùguǎn nǐ zěnmo gēn tā xiāngchù, tā duì nǐ yìdiǎr gǎnqíng yě méi
      yǒu.

11.2. Wǒ jīnnian zhēngyue tóu yícì hé tā jiànmiàn, jiu juéde tā hěn rè-
      qíng.

12.0. hánxu   (1) restrained, reserved; (2) restraint [contain store]

12.1. Tāmen liǎngge rén, yíge shi yǒu huà jiu shuō, yíge shi shuō huà
      bǐjiǎo hánxu. (T)

12.2. Wáng Xiānsheng shuō huà xiāngdāng yǒu hánxu, érqiě shénmo duō-
      yúde huà yě bù xǐhuan shuō.

13.0. jìshǐ   even if, supposing (W) [then cause]

13.1. Wǒ bù xiāngxìn yǒu zàowángyé. Jìshǐ yǒu wǒ yě bù xiāngxìn tā huì
      shàng tiān.

14.0. fǒu   (1) no, not so; (2) is not (W)

   fǒurèn   deny, refuse to acknowledge

   shìfǒu   is or is not (W)

   néngfǒu   can or cannot (W)

14.1. Rénjia dōu shuō Mǎ Yǒuzhēn yǒu nǚ péngyou le, kěshi tā zìjǐ fǒu-
      rèn.

14.2. Nǐ chángcháng bài shén. Nǐ shìfǒu kànjianguo shén? (W)

14.3. Nǐ néngfǒu zài xīnlǐ niánde shíhou bǎ yǐqián nǐ jiè wǒ de qián gěi
      wǒ yíbùfen, qíyúde jiùlì nián zài gěi wǒ? (W) (T)

14.4. Wáng Zhǔxí jīnrì lái fǒu? (W) (T)

15.0. liǎn   face

   liǎn hóng   flush, blush [face red]

15.1. Tā liǎnshang dàizhe bù gāoxìngde yàngzi shuō: "Wǒ bú qù!" (T)

15.2. Wǒ dào tā jiā qù de shíhou tā zhèng zài wár zhǐpái ne. Tā yí kàn-
      jian wǒ láile liǎn dōu hóng le.

15.3. Lǎo Wáng gēn biéren shuō Lǎo Zhāng huàihuà, bǎ Lǎo Zhāng qì-
      huài le, liǎn dōu qìhóng le. (T)

80 Bái: Zhōngguo nǚháizi zài gǎnqíng fāngmiàn, méi yǒu Měiguo nǚháizi
          nènmo rèqíng.

    Mǎ : Bù. Zhōngguo nǚháizi zài zhèi fāngmiàn shi bǐjiǎo hánxu. Bǐrú
          yíge nǚháizi kànjian yíge nánháizi, jué bú huì xiān hé nèige nán-
          háizi shuō huà.

85 Bái: Wǒ tīngshuō Zhōngguo nǚháizi rúguǒ tā yǒule hěn yàohǎode nán
          péngyou tā yě bùhǎoyìsi chéngrèn.

    Mǎ : Duìle. Yàoshi yíge Zhōngguo nǚháizi tā yǒu yíge gēn tā hěn hǎode
          nán péngyou, yàoshi nǐ wèn shì bu shi yǒu nènmo yìhuí shì, tā yí-
          dìng liǎn hóng shènzhìyú fǒurèn.

16.0. yǐbiàn   so as to (W) [take convenient]

16.1. Wǒmen yīngdāng wènyiwèn fēijī shénmo shíhou dào, yǐbiàn dào zhāo-
       dàishì qu fǎngwèn ta. (W)

17.0. sùchéng   advance quickly, accelerate [rapid accomplish]

       sùchéngkē   accelerated course (of study)

17.1. Zhèlǐ xīn chénglìle yíge Guóyǔ sùchéngkē. Tāmen yùbei zài wǔge
       yuèli jiu kéyi bǎ Guóyǔ sùchéng.

18.0. wéiyǒurúcǐ   only thus (W) [only have like this]

18.1. Wéiyǒurúcǐ cái néng bú ràng rén shīwàng. (W)

19.0. diào   (1) fall, drop; (2) fall to, fall into; (3) (postverb); (4) lose (by
               dropping from clothes, etc.)

19.1. Nǐ kàn nǐde chē páizi yào diàoxialai le.

20.0. kèfú   conquer, subdue [overcome submit]

20.1. Nǐ bú yào yōuchóude tiāntiān kū. Nǐ yīnggāi xiǎng fázi kèfú zhèige
       bù hǎode huánjing.

90 Bái: Mǎ Jiàoshòu, yǐbiàn zhèige cér zěnmo yòng? Qǐng nín gěi wǒ jǔ
          ge lìzi.

    Mǎ : "Nèijiàn shìqing nǔlì qu zuò yǐbiàn sùchéng."

    Bái: Wéiyǒurúcǐde yìsi jiu shi "zhǐ yǒu zhèige yàngzi," duì bu duì?

    Mǎ : Duìle. Lìrú "Yào xiǎng kèfú zhǒngzhǒng de kùnnán wéiyǒurúcǐ qu
95   zuò."

    Bái: Wǒ míngbai le.

    Mǎ : Diào zìde yòngfǎ nǐ zhīdao ma?

    Bái: Wǒ zhīdao. Jiu shi dōngxi diàoxialai de diào.

21.0. cuòwù   a mistake [wrong error]

21.1. Búdàn shi háizi jiu shi dàren yě shícháng yǒu cuòwù.

22.0. yǐ   take (CV) (W) (see note 1)

22.1. Wǒ měitiān yǐ zuò kǔgōng wéi shēng.   Nǎr yǒu duōyúde qián ne?
      (W) (T)

23.0. bǎngyàng   (human) example, model, pattern [example kind]

23.1. Tā shi ge huàirén, nǐ bù néng ná ta zuò bǎngyàng.

24.0. pèng   to knock, bump

      pèngjian   meet with, run into [bump see]

24.1. Zuótian yèli wǒde chē bèi biérende chē gěi pènghuài le.

24.2. Zuótian wǒ zài bǎihuò gōngsī mǎi bù, pèngjian Zhāng Xiáojie le.

Bái: Mǎ Jiàoshòu, wǒ xiě dōngxide shíhou cháng fāshēng de cuòwù jiu
100   shi yǒu shíhou hěn nán fēnbié yíge cér shi shuō de háishi xiě de.
       Hái yǒu shíhou yíge cér yě bù zhīdào zài shuō huà de shíhou shì-
       fǒu kéyi yòng? Wǒ xiànzài shuō ge lìzi: "Yǐ Wáng Xiānsheng zuò
       bǎngyàng." Nín shuō duì rén shuō huà de shíhou zhèige yǐ zì néng
       yòng ma?

105 Mǎ: Zài Zhōngguo rén, bù yánjiu yǔyánde rénmen yě bù néng juéduìde
       fēnde hěn qīngchu.   Pǔtōng shuō huà de shíhou dōu shi shuō "Ná
       Wáng Xiānsheng zuò bǎngyàng." Yàoshi yǎnjiǎng de shíhou kéyi shuō
       "Yǐ Wáng Xiānsheng zuò bǎngyàng."

Bái: Yǒu shíhou pèngjian yíge shēngcí, wǒ zhēn bù gǎn juédìng tā yīnggāi
110   shi shǔyu něi yílèi de.

25.0. wéiyī(de)   exclusive, only, sole [only one]

25.1. Wǒ wéiyīde xīwang shi néng zhǎodào yíge gōngzuò yǒu diǎr qián
      jiānglái hǎo niàn dàxué. (T)

26.0. miǎn   avoid, save the trouble of V-ing

      miǎnde   (so as) to avoid, lest

26.1. Shuō wàiguo huà bùguǎn shuōde zěnmo hǎo yǒu shíhou yě nán miǎn
      yǒu cuòr. (T)

26.2. Wǒmen zǎo diǎr qù miǎnde méi zuòr le.

27.0. jiēchǔ   come in contact with, encounter [join touch]

27.1. Tā suǒyǐ Zhōngwén nènmo hǎo shi yīnwei tā jiēchǔ de rén dōu
      yònggōng, dàjiā shícháng hùxiāng yánjiu. (T)

28.0. hūlüè   disregard, neglect, be forgetful of [neglect somewhat]

28.1. Guòjié gěi péngyou sòng lǐ shi rénqíng, nǐ bié hūlüè le. (T)

Bái: Wǒ xiànzài wéiyīde xīwang shi yào bǎ huà shuō hǎo, cér hé yǔfǎ
       yòng duì le, miǎnde shuōchu huà lai bú zìrán.

Mǎ : Ànzhào xiànzài nǐde chéngdu zhè bìng bù nán. Nǐ cháng hé Zhōngguo tóngxué jiēchǔ cháng shuō, zìrán jiu huì jìnbù de.

115 Bái: Hé tóngxuémen zài yíkuàr tánhuà, dàjiā dōu hěn kèqi. Jǐshǐ cuòle
rénjia yě bùhǎoyìsi shuō.

Mǎ : Kěshi nǐ yào zhùyì pángren shuō, bú yào hūlüè tāmende yǔfǎ.

29.0. diū   lose

diūdiào   lose [lose drop]

diū liǎn   lose face, be embarrassed

29.1. Zài Dēngjiéde wǎnshang, wǒmen chūqu kàn dēng de shíhou jiā lǐtou
diū dōngxi le. (T)

29.2. Wǒ chūcì zài Zhōngguode shíhou wǒ diūdiào yíge hěn hǎode xuéxí
Guóyǔ de jīhui.

29.3. Xiānsheng jiào wǒ xiě zàowangyé sānge zì. Wǒ lián yíge yě méi
xiěshanglai. Nǐ shuō duómo diū liǎn.

29.4. Zuótian zài fànguǎnr chī fàn de shíhou, yí suàn zhàng cái fāxiàn
wǒde qián diū le.

30.0. duàn(r)   segment, section, paragraph, period   (M)

30.1. Zhèikè shū yígòng fēn liǎngduànr. Tóu yiduànr jiǎng jiérì, hòu yiduànr jiǎng Zhōngguode shénhuà.

31.0. hòuhuǐ   regret, feel remorse [rear repent]

31.1. Wǒ hěn hòuhuǐ yǐqián wǒ cónglái bú zuò shì, lǎo wár májiàng.

32.0. zhǎngwò   (1) have in one's grasp, have under control;   (2) control
[palm grasp]

32.1. Tā yìdiǎr yě bù qióng. Tā shuō de dōu shi jiǎde, tā shǒuli zhǎng-
wòle jǐshiwàn ne.

32.2. Zhèige jīhui hěn nán dé. Nǐ yào zhǎngwòzhù. (T)

33.0. búduàn(de)   uninterrupted(ly) [not break]

33.1. Tā jīngji qíngxing tài huài le. Wǒ búduànde bāngzhu ta.

Bái: Nín gāngcái shuō, xué Zhōngguo yǔyán yīnggāi duō hé Zhōngguo tóngxué jiēchǔ. Zhèige shi duìde. Wǒ cóngqián zài zhèrde shíhou, yǒu
120   yíge Měiguo tóngxue, běnlái yǒu hěn duō jīhui kéyi hé Zhōngguo tóngxué shuō huà. Dànshi tā zìjǐ juéde Zhōngguo huà shuōde bù hé lǐxiǎng, pà shuōcuòle diū liǎn, suǒyǐ jiu bìmiǎn duō shuō Zhōngguo
huà. Jiéguǒ shi niànle hǎojǐniánde Zhōngwén, jiànle Zhōngguo rén
bùgǎn shuō Zhōngguo huà. Tā xiànzài xiǎngqilai guòqu nèi yíduàn
125   shíjiān hěn hòuhuǐ.

Mǎ : Yǒule jīhui jiu yīnggāi zhuāzhù, bù yīnggāi hūlüè.

Bái: Shì a. Yǒu jīhui yīnggāi zhǎngwòzhù búduànde liànxi.

34.0. línghuó   lively   [spirit live]

34.1. Nǐ kàn nèige diànyǐng míngxīngde shēntǐ yǒu duómo línghuó.

35.0. dáyì   make one's meaning clear   [attain idea]

        cí bù dáyì   words do not make one's meaning clear

35.1. Nǐ kàn zhèipiān guānyu tóngyīn gēn tóngyīnzi de wénzhāng xiěde tài huài le.   Cí bù dáyì, bù zhīdào shuō de shi shénmo.   (T)

36.0. chúncuì   (1) pure, unadulterated; (2) purely, simply [pure essence]

36.1. Zhèige cài zhēn xiāng, chúncuì shi běifāng wèr.

37.0. tōng   comprehensible, communicable   (also used as RV suffix)

37.1. Yányǔ bù tōng bànqǐ shì lai zhēn máfan.   (T)

37.2. Tā xiě de wénzhāng bàn tōng bàn bù tōngde.   Bù zhīdào tāde yìsi shi shénmo.   (T)

37.3. Wǒ gēn tā shuōle bàntiān yě shuōbutōng.   (T)

38.0. mófǎng   imitate   [model imitate]

38.1. Tā mófǎng Mǎ Lǎoshī jiǎnghuà de yàngzi tài xiàng le.   Chà yìdiǎr bǎ wǒ gěi xiàosi.   (T)

Mǎ :   Guānyu yǔyán yìfāngmiàn nǐ méi yǒu shénmo dà wèntí.   Zhǐshi zài xiězuò yìfāngmiàn, yòng cér hé wénfǎ yǒu shíhou bù zěnmo zìrán.
130   Nà jiu shi yùnyòngde bù línghuó.

Bái :   Shìde.   Wǒ gǎnjuédào zìjǐ suǒ xiě de dōngxi chángcháng cí bù dáyì.

Mǎ :   Zìjǐ kàndechulai zìjǐde máobìng jiu néng jìnbù.   Xiězuò chúncuì shi yìzhǒng jīngyan.   Yào duō kàn biérénde xiězuò, zhùyì biérénde yǔfǎ hé yòng cér, yǐjí jùzide jiégòu děngděng.

135 Bái :   Yǒu shíhou kànkan zìjǐ xiě de dōngxi hěn kěxiào, bàn tōng bàn bù tōngde.

Mǎ :   Jiǎrú shi kāishǐ xué xiězuò dōu děi mófǎng biérén de.   Ná nǐ xiàn-zàide chéngdu lái shuō jiu bú bì le.

39.0. gē(r)   song

39.1. Zài yánglì xīnnián nèitiān wǒmen qu kàn diànyǐngr.   Nèige piānzilǐ yǒu yíge gēr zhēn hǎotīng.

40.0. chàng   sing

       chàng gē(r)   sing songs

40.1. Zài yīnlì xīnnián nèi yìtian wǒmen dìxiong jiěmèi jùzai yíkuàr chàngle bàntiān gēr.

41.0. zhǔxiū   to major in a subject   [chief self-improvement]

       zhǔxiūkē   major   (course of study)

41.1. Wǒ mèimei zhǔxiū xīnlǐxué.

41.2. Tāde zhǔxiūkē shi něimén gōngkè?

42.0. bǎoguì   precious, valuable [treasure expensive]

42.1. Wǒmen zài zhèi chūntiande shíhou yīnggāi duō nǔlì xuéxí, bú yào
bǎ bǎoguìde shíjiān báibáide guòqu.   (T)

42.2. Xièxie ni gěile wǒmen yíge bǎoguìde yìjian.   (T)

43.0. chízǎo   sooner or later   [late early]

43.1. Tā chē kāide nènmo kuài chízǎo yào chūshì de.

Mǎ : Tīng Gāo Xiānsheng shuō, nǐ Zhōngwén hé Zhōngguo huà dōu nènmo
140   hǎo shi yīnwei nǐ niàn gāozhōng jiu xuǎnle Zhōngwénde kēmù.

Bái: Shìde.

Mǎ : Zài Měiguo niàn shū de huánjìngli, nǐ zěnmo huì duì Zhōngwén fāshēng xìngqule ne?

Bái: Wǒ suǒyǐ yǒu xìngqu niàn Zhōngwén de yuányīn shi zhèiyàng. Wǒ
145   cóng xiǎo jiu xǐhuan tīng wàiguo rén shuō huà. Wǒ tīng rénjia shuō
wàiguo huà wǒ jiu juéde hěn yǒuqùr. Yóuqíshi Zhōngguo huà, wǒ
tīngzhe hǎotīng jíle, xiàng chàng gēr shide. Wǒ niàn gāozhōng běnlái shi zhǔxiū kēxué, kěshi wǒ yě xuǎnle yìmén Zhōngguo yǔyán.
Měi xīngqī zhǐ yǒu wǔge zhōngdiǎn. Wǒ xiǎng zhèige bǎoguìde shí-
150   jiān wǒ yào hǎohǎor lìyòng ta, tóngshí wǒ xiǎng chízǎo wǒ yào dào
Zhōngguo qu.

44.0. jìnrù   enter (W) [enter enter]

44.1. Wǒmen xuéxí Zhōngwén kèchéng yǐjing jìnrù dì-èrge xīngqī le. (W)
(T)

45.0. xuéyè   (advanced) education (W) [study occupation]

45.1. Nǐ zhèici dào Zhōngguo qu, zhù nǐ yílù píngān, xuéyè jìnbù.   (W)

46.0. yǒu xiào   effective [have efficacy]

46.1. Tāde bìng zhìbuhǎo le, chīle hěn duō yào yě méi yǒu xiào.

Mǎ : Wǒmende kèchéng yǐjing jìnrù dì-sānge xīngqī le. Wǒmen suǒ tǎolùn de dōngxi bù shǎo, dànshi xué de rén néngfǒu zhēnde liǎojiěle
ne?

155 Bái: Wǒ gèrén juéde zhèi liǎngge xīngqī quèshi zhīdao bù shǎode dōngxi.

Mǎ : Yǒu shíhou wǒ xiǎng, qīngniánrén zài qiúxué de shíhou, rúguǒ xuéyè
bú jìnbù yīnggāi yòng shénmo yǒu xiào de fāngfǎ shǐ ta jìnbù?

Bái: Niàn dàxué le, yóuqíshi xiànzài yǐjing shi yánjiushēng le, bìxū yào
kào zìjǐ qu nǔlì le. Yàoshi zìjǐ lián yánjiu dōu bù yánjiu dāngrán
160   dédàode jiu hěn shǎo le.

47.0. yǔ   and (W)

47.1. Wǒ zuótian mǎile yìběn shū, míngzi shi Fùnǚ yǔ Jiātíng.

48.0. quē   (1) lack, be without; (2) scarce

48.1. Wǒde shūfángli shénmo dōu yǒu, jiu quē yíge rìlì.

49.0. tuì   withdraw, retire, move back, retreat, return

tuìbù   withdraw, retire, retreat [withdraw step]

49.1. Jìshi bú màigěi wǒ le qǐng nǐ bǎ qián tuìhuilai. (T)

49.2. Zài nèige gōngsī mǎi dōngxi yàoshi mǎicuò le tāmen bú tuì yě bú huàn. (T)

49.3. Wǒ sānnián méi shuō Zhōngguo huà le. Xiànzài shuōde bǐ yǐqián tuìbù le.

50.0. xiūxi   rest (N/V) [rest rest]

tuìxiū   retire, cease work [retreat rest]

50.1. Jūnguān mìnglìng nèixiē bīng zuòzài dìxia xiūxi xiūxi. (T)

50.2. Tā yǐjing qīshi duō suì le, zǎo jiu yīnggāi tuìxiū le. (T)

51.0. shòu   thin (of people)

51.1. Zuòzai shàngzuòr hěn shòude nèiwèi lǎo xiānsheng shi shéi ya?

52.0. pàng   fat, stout

pàngzi   a fat person

52.1. Nǐ kàn wǒmen liǎngge rén shéi pàng shéi shòu?

52.2. Wǒmen lǎoyé shi ge dà pàngzi.

Bái: Mǎ Jiàoshòu, yǒu yíwèi Jiǎn Yìduō Xiānsheng xiě de Xīn Wénxué yǔ Jiù Wénxué zhèiběn shū xiànzài hái yǒu mài de ma?

Mǎ : Zhèige wǒ bú dà qīngchu. Kěshi zuòzhě shi wǒ lǎoshī. Nǐ yào mǎi nèiběn shū ma?

165 Bái: Zhèiběn shū běnlái wǒ yǒu, zài liǎngnián yǐqián wǒ gěi diū le. Zhèiběn shū duì wǒ yǒu hěn dàde bāngzhu, fēicháng yǒu yòng. Wǒ yòu dào shūdiàn qu mǎi, kěshi zhèiběn shū hěn quē, suǒyǐ něige shūdiàn yě mǎibuzháo. Biérén xiě de dōu méi yǒu nèiběn hǎo.

Mǎ : Zhǐ yǒu Jiǎn Xiānsheng cái néng xiěchu nèiyàngr hǎo wénzhāng.
170   Cóng tā tuìxiū yǐhòu, bù zěnmo xiě dōngxi le.

Bái: Wèi-shénmo bù xiěle ne?

Mǎ : Yīnwei tā shēntǐ bú tài hǎo. Tā cháng shuō tā zìjǐ tuìbù le.

Bái: Nín cháng jiànzhe ta ma?

Mǎ : Yīnwei wǒ gēn ta niàn shū de shíhou tā hěn xǐhuan wo, suǒyǐ wǒ
175   gēn ta bǐjiào qīnjìn.

Bái : Jǐshí nín dài wǒ qu bàifang bàifang Jiǎn Xiānsheng.

Mǎ : Děng wǒ gēn ta dìng yíge shíhou, wǒ xiǎng tā yídìng huānyíng nǐ qu gēn ta tántan. Zhèiwèi lǎo xiānsheng hěn shòu. Wǒmen xué- xiàode Wáng Jiàoshòu bú shi hěn shòu ma? Gēn Jiǎn Xiānsheng
180   bǐqilai hái shi ge pàngzi ne!

53.0. zǐmèi   sisters [elder-sister younger-sister]

53.1. Zǐmèi liǎngge dōu shi làyue sānshíde shēngri.   (T)

54.0. zǎorì   at an early date (W) [early day]

54.1. Lǎo Zhāng: Xīwang nǐ zǎorì huíguó.   (W)

55.0. huāngluàn   be in confusion, be in disorder, be upset [flustered con- fused]

55.1. Tā jiēdào tā mǔqinde xìn shuō tā fùqin bìng le. Tā shuō tā zhèi jǐtiān xīnli hěn huāngluàn.

56.0. xīnyì   (1) thoughts; (2) ideas, aims; (3) (token of) appre- ciation [heart idea]

xīnhuāngyìluàn   flustered, upset [heart confused ideas disordered]

56.1. Zhèige zhǐbāorde dōngxi qǐng nín shōuxia. Zhè shi wǒ yìdiǎr xīnyì. (T)

56.2. Wǒ zhèi jǐtiān bù zhī wèile shénmo xīnhuāngyìluànde, shénmo shì yě zuòbuxiàqù.   (T)

57.0. biǎoshì   show, express, make clear [express show]

57.1. Zhōngguo rén guònián, jiē shén﹑ shāo xiāng﹑ shāo zhǐ, gòng cài shénmode shi biǎoshì rénmen duì shénde xīnyì.   (T)

58.0. yúkuài   (1) happy, pleased, contented [contented quick]

58.1. Máo Xiānsheng gēn tā tàitai wèile gòng shén de wèntí liǎngge rén yǒu yìjian le. Zhèi jǐtiān xīnli dōu bu yúkuài.   (T)

Mǎ : Wǒ gēn nǐ shuōshuo wǒ hé Jiǎn Lǎoshǐde yíduàn gùshi. Jiǎn Lǎo- shǐ hé wǒ fùqin běnlái yě shi péngyou. Tā shi niàn gǔshū de. Tāde sīxiǎng hěn jiù. Yǒu yícì gěi wǒ fùqin xiě xìn, xìnshangde dàyì shi: "Nǐde shàoye shū niàn de xiāngdāng hǎo, jiānglái yídìng yǒu qiántú.
185   Wǒde nǚér xiànzài dōu yǐjing bù xiǎo le. Zài zhèizhǒng huāngluàn shíqī xīwang tāmen zǐmèi zǎorì jiàchū. Wǒ xīwang hé nǐmen jiā dìng yìmén qīnshi, bù zhīdào nǐde xīnyì zěnmoyàng?"

Bái : Zhè zěnmo bàn ne?

Mǎ : Wǒ fùqin jiēdàole xìn hěn nán biǎoshì tāde yìsi.

190 Bái : Jiǎn Xiáojie nín jiànguo ma?

Mǎ : Wǒ méi kànjiànguo.

Bái: Zěnmo huídá de?

Mǎ : Wǒ fùqin dàgài shuō, xiànzài érnǔ qīnshi wǒmen bù néng zuòzhǔ le.

Bái: Jiǎn Xiānsheng yídìng hěn bù yúkuài le.

195 Mǎ: Wǒ juéde tā dào méi yǒu, yìzhíde hé wǒmen láiwǎng.

59.0. zhēnquè   true, actual, valid (also used as RV suffix) [real
                            true]

       qiānzhēnwànquè   completely authentic [1000 real 10,000 true]

59.1. Bìng bú shi nènmo yìhuí shì. Tā shuō de yìdiǎr yě bù zhēnquè. (T)

59.2. Tā shuō de shi qiānzhēnwànquède yíge shìshí.

60.0. yùzhù   wish (someone well) (W) [beforehand congratulate]

60.1. "Yùzhù nǐ fācái huíjiā" zhè shi duì chūmén zuò mǎimai de rén shuō
       de yìzhǒng jílì huà.

61.0. xiàng   (1) article, section (of a document); (2) item, matter (M)

61.1. Qǐng nǐ bǎ gōngsīlide zhàng yíxiàngyíxiàngde ànzhe cìxu suànyisuàn.
       (T)

61.2. Wǒ měi yíxiàng dōu suàn le. Háishi duōchulai wǔkuài qián. (T)

62.0. tǎolùn   discuss (formally) [seek discuss]

62.1. Yǒu shénmo wèntí nǐmen zhǐguǎn tǎolùn hǎo le.   (T)

62.2. Zuótian Guómíndǎng kāi huì, tǎolùn de dōu shi dǎnglide wèntí.

63.0. tóufa   hair (on the head)

63.1. Zhāng Xiáojiede tóufa shi huángde. Hǎoxiàng wàiguo rén yíyàng.

Mǎ : Xiànzài wǒmen hái yǒu liǎngge cér.

Bái: Zhēnquè, yùzhù.

Mǎ : Zhèi liǎngge cér wǒ xiǎng nǐ dōu huì yòng.

Bái: Yùzhù jiu shi xīwang de yìsi. Bǐrú "Yùzhù nǐ chénggōng. Yùzhù nǐ
200   kǎo dì-yī." Zhēnquè gēn shízàide yìsi chàbuduō.

Mǎ : Hǎo. Jīntiande cér yíxiàngyíxiàngde dōu tǎolùnwán le. Oh! Míng-
       tian wǎnshang qīdiǎn zhōng xuésheng zhōngxīn qǐng Wáng Dàwén
       Xiānsheng jiǎng Zhōngguo wénxué. Nǐ yǒu gōngfu kéyi qu tīngyi-
       tīng. Méi gōngfu búbì qù.

205 Bái: Wǒ qù. Nándéde jīhui.

Mǎ : Bù zhīdào Měiyīng yào bu yào tīng.

Bái: Měiyīng jìnlái hěn máng. Tā bú huì qù ba?

Mǎ : Huòzhě nǐ qù tā yě qù le.

Bái: Bú huì de. Wǒ qù tā yě bu yídìng qù, búguò wǒ wènwen ta. Wáng
210   Dàwén Xiānsheng shi něige dàxuéde?

Mǎ : Yǐqián zài Zhōng-Dà zuòle shíjǐniánde jiàoshòu, jīnnian yǐjing qīshi-
jǐ le, tóufa dōu bái le, háishi dàochu qu yǎnjiǎng. Jiù xǐhuan hé
qīngniánrén tán xuéwen. Xuésheng zhōngxīn nǐ zhǎodezháo ma?
Yào bú yào wǒ gēn nǐ yíkuàr qù?

215 Bái: Xièxie nin. Xuésheng zhōngxīn wǒ qùguo. Nín yě hěn máng. Wǒmen gè qù gède ba. Nín shénmo shíhou dào xuésheng zhōngxīn?

Mǎ : Wǒ qīdiǎn yǐqián dào.

SHĒNGCÍ BIǍO

1. shǒuxiān	21. cuòwù	zhǔxiūkē
2. liúlì	22. yǐ (W)	42. bǎoguì
3. jīlěi	23. bǎngyàng	43. chízǎo
rìjīyuèlěi	24. pèng	44. jìnrù (W)
4. yǎngchéng xíguàn	pèngjian	45. xuéyè (W)
5. (xiǎo)yàn(r)	25. wéiyī(de)	46. yǒu xiào
6. huángyīng	26. miǎn	47. yǔ (W)
yīngyīngyànyàn	miǎnde	48. quē
7. niǎo(r)	27. jiēchǔ	49. tuì
8. bǐyu	28. hūlüè	tuìbù
9. yùnyòng	29. diū	50. xiūxi
10. shǐyì	diūdiào	tuìxiū
11. gǎnqíng	diū liǎn	51. shòu
rèqíng	30. duàn(r)	52. pàng
12. hánxu	31. hòuhuǐ	pàngzi
13. jìshǐ (W)	32. zhǎngwò	53. zǐmèi
14. fǒu (W)	33. búduàn(de)	54. zǎorì (W)
fǒurèn	34. línghuó	55. huāngluàn
shìfǒu (W)	35. dáyì	56. xīnyì
néngfǒu (W)	cí bù dáyì	xīnhuāngyìluàn
15. liǎn	36. chúncuì	57. biǎoshì
liǎn hóng	37. tōng	58. yúkuài
16. yíbiàn (W)	38. mófǎng	59. zhēnquè
17. sùchéng	39. gē(r)	qiānzhēnwànquè
sùchéngkē	40. chàng	60. yùzhù (W)
18. wéiyǒurúcǐ (W)	chàng gē(r)	61. xiàng
19. diào	41. zhǔxiū	62. tǎolùn
20. kèfú		63. tóufa

YŬFĂ LIÀNXÍ

A. yǐ 'take' as a coverb   (see note 1)

1. Tā měitian yǐ dǎ májiàng wéi xiāoqiǎn.

2. Tā sānge yuè méi zuò shì le, yǐ shénmo zuò shēnghuófèi ne?

3. Tā zài něige dàxué niàn shū, yǐ něimén gōngkè zuò zhǔxiūkē ne?

4. Nǐ lián guònián de cài dōu méi mǎi, wǒ yǐ shénmo zuò chúxī shànggòng
de cài ne?

5. Wǒmen dìxiōng sìge rén dōu yǐ wǒ gēge zuò bǎngyàng.

B. Rhetorical questions   (see note 2)

6. Zhèipán lùyīndài yídìng bú shi tā lù de.   Tā zěnmo néng shuō zhènmo
liúlìde Zhōngguo huà ne?

7. Tā nènmo bèn, zěnmo néng niàn sùchéngkē ne?

8. Wǒ xīn lǐtou nǎr yǒu nǐ xīn lǐtou nènmo yúkuài ne?

9. Shéi yǒu nènmo hǎode yùnqi ne?

10. Wǒde tóufa nǎr bǐdeshàng nǐde tóufa nènmo hēi ne!

JIĂNGHUÀ

Zhūwèi tóngxué:

Jīntian wǒmen yào tǎolùn de shi "Xuéxí Zhōngguo Huà." Zhūwèi dào
Zhōngguo lái yánjiu xuéwen huòzhě shi xué Zhōngguo wénxué, huòzhě shi
yánjiu Zhōngguo lìshǐ, huòzhě shi xuéxí qítā kēmu. Búlùn zhūwèide zhǔ-
5 xiū kēmu shi shénmo, zuì jīběnde, yě shi zuì zhǔyàode, shi xiān yào bǎ
Zhōngguo huà xuéhǎo. Yàoshi nǐ shàngkè de shíhou tīngbudǒng xiānsheng
shuō de huà, kàn shūde shíhou sùdù yě bú gòu kuài, hé Zhōngguo rén
láiwǎng de shíhou bù néng hùxiāng liǎojiě, nènmo, zhūwèide xuéyè búdàn
bù néng xiàng lǐxiǎng nèiyàngde jìnbù, érqiě zhūwèi zài Zhōngguo liúxué
10 de zhèiduàn qījiānli, jīngshenshang yě yídìng bú huì yúkuài.

Zhūwèi tīngle wǒ shuō de zhèixiē huà yěxǔ huì shuō: "Wǒmen dào
Zhōngguo lái yǐqián dōu yǐjing xuéguo liǎngnián huò sānniánde Zhōngguo
huà le, suīrán wǒmen shuō de bù néng xiàng Zhōngguo rén yíyàngde liú-

lǐ, kěshi wǒmen xiànzài yǐjing láidàole Zhōngguo, zhǐ yàoshi měitiān liàn-
15 xí hái yǒu shénmo wèntí?" Zhèixiē huà duìjíle.   Zhǔwèi yǐjing jìnrùle
Zhōngguo shèhuì, yǔ Zhōngguo rén zài yìqǐ xiāngchù hé xuéxí, yǔyánde
kùnnán chízǎo zǒngshi kéyi kèfú de.   Búguò, zhǔwèi dà duōshùde jìhua
shi zài Zhōngguo liúxué yíge duǎn shíqī, bǐfang shuō yìnián, liǎngnián
huòzhě shi sānnián. Yào xiǎng zài zhèige zuì duǎn qījiānli sùchéng zhǔ-
20 wèi yǔyánde nénglì, yǐbiàn jìxù yánjiu gèxiàng zhuānmén kēmu, zhè jiu
shi xiànzài yíge hěn yàojǐnde wèntí. Jīntian wǒ zhǔyào yào tán de jiùshi
zhèige "Xuéxí Zhōngguo Huàde Wèntí."   Wǒ xiànzài tíchu jǐge yìbān rén
xuéxí wàiguoyǔ shícháng hūlüè de dìfang gōng zhǔwèi cānkǎo.

Dì-yī, dàjiā dōu zhīdao yǔyán shi rìjīyuèlěide yìzhǒng xíguan. Zhèi-
25 zhǒng xíguan yǎngchéng róngyi, gǎibiàn nán. Yíge xiǎoháizi xué shuō huà,
cóng méi yǒu yǔyán xíguan kāishǐ ér yǎngchéng yìzhǒng yǔyán xíguan,
nà shi bǐjiǎo róngyi de.   Zhǔwèi cóng yǐjing yǒule běnguó yǔyánde xíguan, zài gǎichéng wàiguo yǔyánde xíguan jiu nánde duō le.   Yào xiǎng
kèfú zhèizhǒng kùnnán, wéiyī yǒu xiào de bànfǎ jiu shi yǐ xiǎoháizi xué
30 shuō huà zuò bǎngyàng, búduànde lìyòng jīhui qù tīng, qù mófǎng. Xiànzài zhǔwèi láidào Zhōngguo, xuéxí yǔyánde huánjing shi yǒu le, kěshi zhǔwèi néngfǒu chénggōng yǐjí néngfǒu zǎorì chénggōng jiu quán kào zhǔwèi
néngfǒu mófǎng xiǎoháizi xué shuō huà de fázi.   Huàn jù huà shuō, jiu
kàn zhǔwèi néngfǒu zhǎngwò zhèige xuéxí de huánjing le.

35 Wǒ zhīdao yǒu hěn duō Zhōngguo xuésheng dào wàiguo qu liúxué,
zài wàiguo niànle sānnián shènzhi wǔniánde shū, jiéguǒ duìyu wàiguode
yǔyán háishi méi xuéhǎo. Měicì hé wàiguo rén jiēchù, shuō huà de shíhou bù shi xīnhuāngyìluàn jiu shi cí bù dáyì, jìshǐ "dáyì" shuōchulai de
huà háishi miǎnbuliǎo yǒu cuòwù, zǒng shi bàn tōng bàn bù tōngde, yòu
40 xiàng wàiguo huà yòu xiàng Zhōngguo huà.   Zhèi bìng bú shi shuō zhèixiē Zhōngguo xuésheng méi yǒu yǔyán tiāncái, ér shi yīnwei tāmen méi
yǒu hǎohāode lìyòng tāmende xuéxí huánjing. Tāmen chúle shàngkè yǐwài
jiu shi hé qítāde Zhōngguo tóngxué jùzài yíkuàr, yòng Zhōngguo huà tán
tiān, jiu bǎ xuéxí wàiguo yǔyán de jīhui diūdiào le.

45 Zhǔwèi láidao Zhōngguo líkai běnguó hěn yuǎn, yěxǔ líkai běnguó
hěn jiǔ, rǔguǒ pèngjian yíge shuō zìjǐ guójiā yǔyánde rén, zìrán bù miǎn
yào qīnjìn qīnjìn.   Kěshi zhǔwèi yào jìzhu, zhǔwèi yào shǒuxiān qīnjìn

zhèige bǎoguìde xuéxí huánjing, yào zhǎngwò zhèige huánjing, bú yào jiào
ta pǎo le. Wéiyǒurúcǐ zhūwèide Zhōngguo huà cái néng jìnbùde hěn kuài,
50   yě wéiyǒurúcǐ zhūwèi jiānglái cái bú huì hòuhuǐ.

  Dì-èr, zhūwèi xiànzài dàgài dōu rènshi liǎng-sānqiānge Zhōngguo
zì. Zhè shi hěn bù xiǎode yíge shùmu. Yìbān lái shuō, Zhōngguo rén
rìcháng yòng de zìshù yě búguò sān-sìqiānge, kěshi, wèi-shénmo zhūwèi
shícháng yǒu "yǒu huà shuōbuchūlái" de gǎnjué ne? Huòzhě jiu shi shuō-
55   chulaile yě juéde bú gòu zìrán hé yǒu wèr ne? Wǒ xiǎng zhè kěnéng shi
zěnyàng yùnyòng de wèntí, yě jiu shi hái bù néng línghuó yùnyòng. Děi
zěnyàng cái nénggòu línghuó yùnyòng ne? Zhè děi xiān zhùyì Zhōngguo
huàde tèdiǎn. Yǒu rén shuō Zhōngguo huà shi yǒu shīyì de. Wǒmen xiān
búbì shuō zhèijù huà shìfǒu zhèngquè, kěshi yǒu yìdiǎn shi qiānzhēnwàn-
60   quède, nà jiu shi Zhōngguo rén shuō huà yòng bǐyu de shíhou fēicháng
duō. Bǐfang shuō yǒu yìtiān nǐde zǐmèi qǐngle hěn duōde nǚ tóngxué dào
jiāli lái wár, nǐ kéyi shuō: "Jīntian jiāli yīngyīngyànyàn, rènao jíle." Nǐ
dāngrán yě kéyi shuō: "Jiāli láile hěn duō nǚ xuésheng, dōu hěn piàoliang,
yǒu cháng tóufa de yě yǒu duǎn tóufa de, yǒu pàngde yě yǒu shòu yìdiǎr
65   de, rènao jíle." Zhèi liǎngzhǒng shuōfǎ suírán yìsi chàbuduō, kěshi qiántoude shuōfǎ bǐ hòutoude shuōfa jiu hǎo duō le. Zhèizhǒng bǐyu de shuōfǎ, zài Zhōngguo huàli duōjíle. Zhūwèi zài xuéxí xīnde cíde shíhou rúguǒ
zhùyì dao zhèixiē yǒuqù de yòngfǎ, búdàn néng zēngjiā xuéxí de xìngqu,
bìngqiě jiānglái zhūwèide Zhōngguo huà yě yídìng shi zhēnzhèngde Zhōng-
70   guo wèr.

  Dì-sān, wǒ yào qǐng zhūwèi zhùyì xuéxí Zhōngguode fēngsu xíguan.
Wǒ tídào fēngsu xíguan kě bú shi shuō zhūwèi yídìng yào xǐhuan chī
Zhōngguo fàn, xǐhuan hē Zhōngguo chá, cái néng bǎ Zhōngguo huà xuéhǎo. Wǒ suǒ yào shuō de, zhūwèi yào zhùyì hé Zhōngguo huà yǒu guān-
75   xide Zhōngguo fēngsu xíguan. Bǐfang shuō, yǒu yìtiān nǐ zài péngyou jiāli
pèngjianle yíwèi hěn měi hěn cōngmingde Zhōngguo xiáojie. Tánle yìhuěr
yǐhou, nǐ juéde tā hěn héqi érqiě shuō huà hěn yǒu yìsi. Nǐ xiǎng gēn tā
shuō: "I like you very much. We must get together again soon." Zhèijù huà
yòng Yīngwén shuō, dāngrán méi yǒu shénmo bú duìde dìfang. Kěshi
80   rúguǒ yòng Zhōngguo huà lái shuō, nǐ shuō: "Wǒ zhēn xǐhuan ni. Wǒmen
zuìjìn yídìng yào zhǎo ge jīhui jùyijù." Zhèiwèi Zhōngguo xiáojie yídìng

juéde hěn qíguài, bù zhīdào nǐ shuō de huà shi shénmo yìsi. Tā yěxǔ yào liǎn hóng, hái kěnéng hěn shēngqì. Zhè shi wèi-shénmo ne? Zhè shi yīnwei zài Zhōngguode fēngsu xíguanshang shi bù néng zhèiyàng shuō de,

85 yīnwei Zhōngguode fēngsu xíguan nánnǚ zhījiānde gǎnqing réngrán shi bǐjiǎo hánxu de. Yíge nánrén duì yíwèi xiáojie rúguǒ shuō "Wǒ xǐhuan nǐ" de shíhou, píngcháng zhèijù huàde yìsi bǐ Yīngwénde "I like you" duō yìdiǎr, děngyú shuō "Wǒ ài nǐ." Zhūwèi xiǎngxiang, rúguǒ duì yíwèi cái jiànmiàn de xiáojie jiù shuō "Wǒ ài nǐ" nènmo nèiwèi Zhōngguo xiáojie

90 yídìng bú ài nǐ de.   Yàoshi nǐ dǒngde Zhōngguode fēngsu xíguan nǐ duì nèiwèi xiáojie shuō: "Gēn nǐ tánhuà zhēn yǒu yìsi. Wǒmen děi zhǎo jīhui duō tántan." Tīngle zhèijù huàde nèiwèi Zhōngguo xiáojie yídìng hěn gāoxìng, nènmo, yěxǔ nèiwèi xiáojie jiù gēn ni zuò péngyou le.

    Jīntian wǒ suíbiàn tíchūle shàngmiànde jǐdiǎn gěi zhūwèi cānkǎo.

95 Wǒ yùzhù zhūwèi zài Zhōngguo liúxué zhèiduàn qījiānli xuéyè jìnbù, shēnxīn yúkuài, bìngqiě yùzhù zhūwèi shuō de Zhōngguo huà shi chúncuìde Zhōngguo wèr.

WĒNXI

1. Wáng Xiānsheng zhèicì bāngle wǒ hěn dàde yíge máng, suǒyǐ wǒ mǎile yìdiǎr dōngxi sònggěi tā biǎoshì yìdiǎr xīnyì. Wáng Xiānsheng hěn kèqi érqiě hěn rèqíngde duì wǒ shuō: "Yǐhòu yǒu shénmo kùnnánde shìqing zhǐguǎn gàosu wǒ hǎo le, qiānwàn bú yào sòng lǐ."

2. Zuótian bànyèli wǒ fāxiàn shūfángde dēng hái kāizhe ne. Jīntian zǎoshang wǒ wèn wǒ dìdi, tā fǒurèn. Tā shuō, "Zuótian wǎnshang gēnběn wǒ méi dào shūfáng qù, wǒ zěnmo huì kāi dēng ne?" Qíshí qiānzhēnwànquè dēng shi tā kāi de, yīnwei zài shuìjiào yǐqián, wǒ fēnmíng kànjian tā zài shūfángli kàn shū ne.

3. Zhāng Xiáojie zài Yuàn-Dà niàn kēxué. Tā zhǔxiūkē shi shēngwù. Tóngshí tā yě niàn yìmén Zhōngguo wénxué, tā shuō miǎnde jiānglái bǎ Zhōngwén dōu wàng le.

4. Wǒ jiāde jīngji zhuàngkuàng bù hěn hǎo, rúguǒ yào mǎi shū shi xiāngdāng kùnnánde yíjiàn shì. Zuìjìn wǒ zài shūdiàn fāxiànle yìběn shū, shi Zhōngguo Wénxué Pīpíng. Wǒ xiǎng měitiān shǎo chī yìdiǎr diǎnxin, jīlěi yìdiǎr qián, jǐtiān yǐhòu wǒ jiu kéyi mǎi zhèiběn shū le.

5. Zhèlǐ yǒu hěn duō fùnǚ bù shízì. Yīnggāi chénglì yíge shízì sùchéngkē, shǐ zhèixiē fùnǚ kéyi yǒu yige shízì de jīhui.

6. Qiú xuéwen shi yīnggāi búduànde yánjiuxiàqu. Yàoburán jiù yào tuìbù de.

7. Wǒde xiǎo érzi tài gěi wǒ diūliǎn le. Zuótian hé Wáng Xiānsheng tāmen yíkuàr qu jìnchéng, tā kànjian shénmo yào mǎi shénmo. Tā kànjian mài

niǎor de, xiàng huángyīng, xiǎoyànr, tā dōu kūzhe yào mǎi. Jiéguǒ Wáng Xiānsheng dōu gěi ta mǎi le. Nǐ shuō yǒu zhèiyàngr érzi duómo diūliǎn.

8. Yíge huì chàng gēr de xiáojie tāde gēr chàngde xiāngdāng hǎo, hěn shòu rén huānyíng. Zuìjìn hūrán bìng le. Tāde bìng hěn qíguài. Hǎole zhīhòu gēr chàngbuchūlái le, érqiě huà yě shuōbuqīngchǔ le. Nǐ tīng tā shuō de huà yìdiǎr yě tīngbuzhēnquè. Jù yīsheng shuō tā xiūxi yìnián yěxǔ huì hǎo de.

9. Wǒ xiǎo nüerde zìdiǎn diū le. Wǒ gěi tā qián ràng tā zìjǐ dào shūdiàn qu mǎi. Jiéguǒ tā mǎicuò le. Yúshi wǒ gēn tā yìtóng dào shūdiàn qu huàn. Mài shū de rén liǎnshang fēicháng bù gāoxìngde yàngzi shuō: "Wǒmen shūdiànde shū, màichuqu zhīhòu bú tuì yě bù huàn."

10. Wǒ zǎoshang dào xuéxiào qu de shíhou, fēnmíng cóng jiāli názhe sìběn shū, dàole xuéxiào yǐhòu, yí kàn shū quēle yìběn, yídìng shi diàozai lùshang le. Chūqu yánzhe wǒ zǒu de nèitiáo lù, zhǎole bàntiān yě méi zhǎozháo.

11. Wǒ zài zhōngxué niàn shū de shíhou diūdiàole yíge xuéxi Zhōngwénde jīhui. Xiànzài xiǎngqilai hěn hòuhuǐ.

12. Wǒ fùqin lǎo le, xiànzài tuìxiū le. Měiyuè yuánlái zuò shì nèige jīguān gěi de qián, zhǐ gòu wǒ fùqin yíge rén chī fàn de, suǒyǐ wǒ bìděi xiǎng fázi zhǎo gōngzuò lái wéichī shēnghuó.

WÈNTÍ

1. Yǔyán shi rìjīyuèlěide yìzhǒng xiguan. Wèi-shénmo xiǎo háizi cóng yì kāishǐ xuéxi jiu bǐjiǎo rǒngyi, ér yǐjing huìle běnguo yǔyánde rén xuéxi wàiguoyǔ jiu nánde duō le ne?

2. Zài wàiguo liúxué de xuésheng wǎngwǎng yǒu liúxué sān-wǔnián duìyu wàiguo yǔyán háishi bàn tōng bàn bù tōng. Shi shénmo yuányīn ne?

3. Nǐmen dào Zhōngguo lái yánjiu xuéwen zuì jīběn, zuì zhǔyàode shi shénmo?

4. Yǐjing rènshi liǎng-sānqiān Zhōngguo zì de wàiguo xuésheng wèi-shénmo hái yǒu "yǒu huà shuōbuchūlái" de gǎnjué ne?

5. Zhōngguo huà xǐhuan yòng bǐyu. Qǐng nǐ shuōchu yíge lìzi lái.

6. Nǐ zài péngyou jiāli pèngjiànle yíwèi hěn měi hěn cōngmingde Zhōngguo xiáojie, wèi-shénmo bù néng shuō: "Wǒ xǐhuan ni. Wǒmen zuìjìn yídìng yào zhǎo ge jīhui jùyijù?" Yīngdāng zěnyàng shuōfǎ ne?

7. Qǐng nǐ yòng báihuà jiěshi cí bù dáyì hé rìjīyuèlěi zhèi liǎngge cíde yìsi.

8. Qǐng nǐ yòng liúlì, zhǎngwò zhèi liǎngge cér gè zuò yíge jùzi.

9. Zhōngguo cháng yòng de zì dàgài yǒu duōshǎo? Zài xuéxi xīn cíde shíhou zěnyàng cái néng zēngjiā xuéxi de xìngqu, shuōchu huà lái cái néng shi zhēnzhèngde Zhōngguo wèr?

10. Zài běnkè jiǎnghuà lǐtou yīngyīngyànyàn shi zhǐzhe shénmo shuō de? Rúguǒ yòng biéde shuōfǎ, yīngdāng zěnmo shuō?

ILLUSTRATIVE SENTENCES (ENGLISH)

3.1. I've been sick for over a month and haven't been able to work, so my work has piled up.

4.1. He's developed the habit of eating something in the middle of the night.

7.1. This morning over that tree at our gate there were a lot of small birds flying about as if they were playing.

12.1. [Those two men,] one speaks up immediately if he has anything to say, and one is rather reserved in speaking.

14.3. Can you give me at the time of the solar new year part of the money which you borrowed from me before, and give me the rest of it at the lunar new year?

14.4. Is Chairman Wang coming today or not?

15.1. He said, with a displeased expression on his face, "I'm not going."

15.3. Wang slandered Zhang to others, enraging Zhang, whose face became flushed with anger.

22.1. Every day I do hard work for a living. How could I have any extra money?

25.1. My sole desire is to be able to find a job and have a little money so that in the future I'll be able to go to college.

26.1. No matter how well one speaks a foreign language, it's hard to avoid making mistakes.

27.1. The reason why his Chinese is so good is that the people he's in contact with are all studious and everyone is always helping each other studying.

28.1. Giving presents to friends when celebrating festivals is a matter of sentiment. Don't neglect it.

29.1. During the evening of the Lantern Festival, while we were out looking at the lanterns some things were stolen [lit. lost] from our home.

32.2. This is a rare opportunity. You must seize it [firmly].

35.1. [You see that] this article on homonymy and homonyms is very badly written. The ideas don't get across. I don't know what it's talking about.

37.1. If people can't communicate with each other it's hard to get things done.

37.2. The essays he writes are only semi-intelligible. I don't know what he's trying to say.

37.3. I talked with him for a long time but couldn't get across to him.

38.1. His take-off of Teacher Ma lecturing is very close. It almost makes me die laughing.

42.1. During this spring period we should work harder at studying. We shouldn't let this precious time go by uselessly.

42.2. Thanks for giving us your valuable opinion.

44.1. Our course in [studying] Chinese has already entered the second semester.

49.1. Since you won't sell it to me please return my money.

49.2. In buying things at that store if you make a wrong purchase they won't take it back or exchange it.

50.1. The officers ordered the soldiers to sit on the ground and rest.

50.2. He's already over seventy and should long since have retired.

53.1. Both sisters have their birthday on the thirtieth of the twelfth lunar month.

56.1. Please accept the thing in this package. It's a small token of my appreciation.

56.2. The past few days, I don't know why, I've been very upset and can't do [lit. continue doing] anything.

57.1. When Chinese celebrate New Year's, they welcome the gods, burn incense and paper, and make offerings of food. This shows their feelings toward the gods.

58.1. Mr. Mao and his wife had a quarrel over the question of making offerings to the gods. The past few days they've both been upset.

59.1. There's no such thing. What he says is not at all true.

61.1. Please check [lit. reckon] the store accounts item by item [in order].

61.2. I've checked every item. It's still five dollars over.

62.1. If there's a problem just discuss it.

NOTES

1. The literary expression yǐ 'take' occurs frequently as a coverb, especially in the construction yǐ N$_1$ zuò/wéi N$_2$ 'take N$_1$ as N$_2$.' The spoken equivalent is yòng/ná N$_1$ zuò N$_2$. The following sentences all mean 'They take the Four Books as a textbook':

>   Tāmen ná Sî Shū zuò kèběn.

>   Tāmen yǐ Sî Shū zuò kèběn.   (W)

>   Tāmen yǐ Sî Shū wéi kèběn.   (W)

2. Chinese makes frequent use of rhetorical questions like English 'How would I know?' Nǎr 'where' is used in situations in which English uses where? or how? For example:

>   Nǎr yǒu wàiguo rén huî shuō nènmo hǎode Zhōngguo huà? 'Where is there a foreigner who can speak such excellent Chinese?'

>   Wǒ nǎr néng chî nènmo duō fàn ne? 'How can I eat so much food?'

Dì-Shísìkè. Zhōngguode Wénzì

Bái: Mǎ Jiàoshòu zǎo.

Mǎ: Zǎo. Jīntian zǎoshang hěn lěng a. Hái méi dào Chóngyángjié ne, jiu zhènmo lěng.

Bái: Shì a! Zuótian yèli jiu lěngqilai le.

5 Mǎ: Zuótian méi jīhui wèn ni, Zhāng Jiàoshòu jiǎng de Xuéxí Zhōngguo Huà jiǎngde zěnmoyàng?

Bái: Zhāng Jiàoshòu jiǎngde hǎojíle. Wǒmen tīngle juéde hěn yǒuqùr. Jíshǐ nǐ duì yánjiu yǔyán méi xìngqu, tīngle Zhāng Jiàoshòu jiǎng de yě juéde yǒu yìsi.

10 Mǎ: Tā shi yíwèi hén yǒu qiántúde yǔyánxuéjiā. Tā búdàn shi yǔyánxuéjiā tā gēr chàng de yě xiāngdāng búcuò. Lùguo yīn le ma?

Bái: Zāogāo, wǒ wàng le dàilai le.

Mǎ: Nǐ zuótian wǎnshang yòu qù tīng yǎnjiǎng, kǒngpà méi gōngfu lù.

Bái: Wǒ yǐjing lù le.

15 Mǎ: Nǐ shénmo shíhou lù de?

Bái: Wǒ xià kè yǐhòu xiān lùyīn, ránhòu chīle diar dōngxi jiu qu tīng yǎnjiǎng. Zuótian wǎnshang Jiǎn Xiānsheng jiǎng de, wǒ zhǐ liǎojiě shífènzhì-bā. Yìlái shi bǐjiǎo shēnde xuéshù yǎnjiǎng, èrlái shi Jiǎn Xiānsheng shuō huà kǒuyīnde guānxi, yǒude huà wǒ tīngbudǒng.

20 Mǎ: Jiǎn Xiānsheng shi Guǎngxi rén, tā Guǎngxi kǒuyin hěn zhòng. Wǒ cháng gēn tā zài yíkuàr tántan, yǒushí tā shuō de huà wǒ yě tīngbudǒng.

Bái: Tā xuéwen zhēn búcuò.

Mǎ: Tā xīn-jiù wénxué dōu hǎo. Jiǎn Xiānsheng zhùzuò hěn duō. Wǒ-
25 men dào tā nèr qù de shíhou nǐ yí kàn jiu zhīdao tā shi yíge xué-zhě.

Bái: Nín hé Jiǎn Xiānsheng shuōle ma? Wǒmen qu bàifǎng ta.

Mǎ: Gēn tā shuōguo le. Tā fēicháng gāoxìng. Tā shuō yíbàntiān dǎ diànhuà gěi wo, dìng yíge shíjiān. Tā hái shuō qǐng wǒmen zài tā
30 nèr chī fàn.

Bái: Chūcì qu bàifǎng Jiǎn Xiānsheng nà bù hǎoyìsi ba?

Mǎ: Méi shénmo. Tā lǎo xiānsheng fēicháng xǐhuan qīngnián péngyou.

Bái: Wǒ shì bu shi yīnggāi gěi ta lǎorénjiā mǎi diar shénmo?

Mǎ: Búbì. Wǒ yě bú dài dōngxi.

35 Bái: Dì-yícì qù bùhǎoyìsi ba?

Mǎ : Nènmo nǐ mǎi diar shuǐguǒ. Jiǎn Xiānsheng xǐhuan chī shuǐguǒ.

Bái: Hǎo.

Mǎ : Jiǎn Xiānsheng cóng niánqīngde shíhou jiu yǎngchéng yíge hěn hǎode
       xíguan, zǎo shuì zǎo qǐ. Tā lǎorénjiā měitiān wǔdiǎn zhōng jiu
40   qǐlai sǎo yuànzi, zìjǐ shōushi tāde shūfáng, ránhòu sòng ta sūnzi
       sūnnüer qu shàngxué.

Bái: Tīngshuō Jiǎn Xiānsheng jiāole jǐshiniánde shū le.

Mǎ : Lǎo xiānsheng yímiàn jiāo shū yímiàn xiězuò yǒu sìshinián le.

Bái: Lǎo xiānshengde jīngyan xiāngdāng fēngfù le.

45 Mǎ : Kěbushìma. Jīntiande Zhuāntí Jiǎnghuà shi Zhōngguode Wénzî. Zhèi
       liǎngzhāng shēngcí biǎo nǐ xiān kànyîkàn ránhòu wǒmen zài yánjiu
       yánjiu.

1.0. jiǎ*   (1) armor, shell; (2) first (in a series)

     jiǎyú   turtle, tortoise [armor fish]

     jiǎ, yǐ, bǐng, dǐng   A, B, C, D   (see note 3)

1.1. Jùshuō chī jiǎyú duì shēntǐ hěn hǎo.

1.2. Nèi sîge rén wǒmen bù zhīdào tāmen xìng shénmo, jiào shénmo
     míngzi. Wǒmen yòng jiǎ, yǐ, bǐng, dǐng sîge zî dàibiǎo tāmen sîge
     rén.

2.0. gǔ*   bone

     gútou   bone (note tone)

     jiǎgǔ   tortoiseshells and bones

     jiǎgǔwén   inscriptions on tortoiseshells and bones

2.1. Yīnwei gútou bù róngyi huài suǒyǐ Shāng Cháo shídàide jiǎgǔ wénzî
     dào xiànzài hái yǒu.

2.2. Tā shi zhǔxiū kǎogǔ de, tā xiànzài yánjiu jiǎgǔwén ne.

3.0. guī   tortoise, turtle (M: zhī)

     guījiǎ   tortoiseshell

3.1. Zài Xiānggǎng gōngyuánli yǒu yìzhī dà guī, jùshuō yǒu liǎngqiān-
     nián yǐshàng le.

3.2. Nèige guījiǎshangde jiǎgǔwén quēle hěn duō zî.   (T)

4.0. bèi   the back

4.1. Cóng dìli fāxiàn nèikuài guī bèi shi Shāng Cháode ma?

5.0. xiàngxíng   (1) pictograph; (2) pictographic [resemble form]

     xiàngshēng   phonetic character [resemble sound]

5.1. Jùshuō zuì zǎode wénzî dōu shi xiàngxíng wénzî.

5.2. Yǒude Hànzì měi yíge zì fēn liǎngbùfen. Yībùfen shi xiàngxíng, yíbùfen shi xiàngshēng. (T)

6.0. liào*   materials

zīliào   materials [resources materials]

mùliào   lumber [wood materials]

6.1. Qǐng nǐ tì wǒ zhǎo yìdiǎr guānyu xiě lùnwénde zīliào.

6.2. Zhèixiē mùliàode láiyuán shi shénmo dìfang?

6.3. Zuótian wǒ qù mǎi mùliào yí suàn zhàng wǒde qián bú gòu le.

Bái: Mǎ Jiàoshòu, shénmo jiào guījiǎ?

Mǎ : Guījiǎ jiu shi guī bèi. Zài sānqiān duō nián yǐqián Zhōngguode wénzì
50   yǒude shi xiězai guījiǎ hé niú gútoushang.

Bái: Shì bu shi jiu shi jiǎgǔwén?

Mǎ : Shìde.

Bái: Jiǎgǔwén shi xiàngxíng wénzì ma?

Mǎ : Shi xiàngxíng wénzì.

55 Bái: Nín néng xiě ma?

Mǎ : Wǒ jiu néng mófǎngzhe xiě jǐge, xiěde yě bù hǎo. Wǒ cóngqián yǒu
        yíge hěn hǎode jīhui kéyi xué jiǎgǔ wénzì, kěshi bǎ zhèige jīhui gěi
        diūdiào le. Yǒu yìnián wǒ lǎoshī tā shi yíwèi hěn yǒumíngde kǎo-
        gǔjiā. Tā dào zhèr lái zhǎo cānkǎo zīliào jiu zhùzai wǒ jiāli. Tā
60   shuō xīwang wǒ bǎ jiǎgǔwén xiěhǎo. Dànshi wǒ méi xìngqu. Yǒu
        yícì lǎoshī gēn wǒ shuō: "Nǐ hǎohāor bǎ jiǎgǔwén xuéhǎo wǒ sǐle
        yǐhòu nǐ kéyi jìxùde xiě ya."

Bái: Nín xiě méi yǒu?

Mǎ : Méi yǒu. Wǒ duì jiǎgǔwén bù gǎnjué yǒu xìngqu. Wǒ juéde hěn
65   nánxiě.

Bái: Qǐng wèn Mǎ Jiàoshòu, jiǎgǔ de jiǎ gēn jiǎyú de jiǎ Hànzì shi tóng
        yíge zì ma?

Mǎ : Shi tóng yíge zì. Dōu shi jiǎ, yǐ, bǐng, dīng de nèige jiǎ zì.

7.0. Liù Shū   Six Categories of Characters

7.1. Liù Shū de shū bu shi zhèibě́n shū de shū de yìsi. Shi zào Zhōngguo zì de liùzhǒng fázide míngchēng.

8.0. zhǐshì   simple ideograph [indicate matter]

8.1. Zhǐshì shi Liù Shūlide míngchēng zhī yī.

9.0. huìyì   compound ideograph [assemble meaning]

9.1. Míng zì zài Liù Shūli shi huìyìde zì. Yíge zìli bāokuòle liǎngge zì.
Bǐrú míng zì shi rì 、 yuè liǎngge zì zǔzhīchéng de, jiùshi huìyì. (T)

10.0. jiǎjiè   phonetic loan [false borrow]

10.1. Jiǎjiè jiu shi jièlái yòng yíxiàr de yìsi, yě shi Liù Shū zhī yī. (T)

11.0. xíngshēng   radical-phonetic compound [form sound]

11.1. Fángzi de fáng, zhòng dì de zhòng dòu shi xíngshēng zì.

12.0. zhuǎn   (1) revolve, evolve, change; (2) pass on

     zhuǎnzhù   (1) derive; (2) derivative character [evolve
                               note]

     zhuǎnchéng   change, evolve into [evolve become]

     zhuǎn bài wéi shèng   change defeat into victory

12.1. Qǐng nǐ bǎ zhèifēng xìn zhuǎngei Mǎ Wěiyuán.

12.2. Zhuǎnzhù jiu shi cóng yíge zì zhuǎnchéng lìngwài yíge zì. (T)

12.3. Gēnjù bàozhǐshangde xiāoxi, wǒ jūn zhuǎn bài wéi shèng.   (T)

Bái: Zhōngguode wénzì xiāngdāng nán. Bù shuō biéde jiu ná Liù Shū
70   lái shuō, wàiguo rén yánjiuqilai hěn nán le.

Mǎ : Búdàn wàiguo rén, Zhōngguo rén xuéqilai yě hěn nán. Nǐ néng bǎ
      Liù Shūde míngzi shuōchulai ma?

Bái: Wǒ shìshi kàn a . . . Xiàngxíng、 zhǐshì、 huìyì、 jiǎjiè、 xíngshēng、
      zhuǎnzhù.

75 Mǎ : Bǎ Liù Shūde míngzi nénggou shuōchulai hěn bù róngyi le.   Liù
      Shūde yìsi nǐ dōu míngbai me?

Bái: Wǒ dōu míngbai.

13.0. xíngzhuàng   (1) appearance; (2) form, shape; (3) condition [form
                    condition]

13.1. Zuótian wǒmen qu dēng shān. Zài dà shānshang kànjian yíkuài dà
      shítou, tāde xíngzhuàng hǎoxiàng yíge rén zài nàli zhànzhe shide.

14.0. dútè   particular, special (W) [alone special]

14.1. Zhōngguo zì měi yíge zì yǒu měi yíge zì dútède xíngzhuàng.   (T)

15.0. gòu*   construct

     gòuzào   (1) construct; (2) construction [construct make]

     gòuchéng (1) construct, form; (2) formation [construct become]

15.1. Nǐ kàn wǒ duómo diūliǎn. Wǒ bǎ liǎngge jùzide gòuzào dōu xiěcuò
      le.

15.2. Nèige cér shi yòng sānge zì gòuchéng de.

16.0. tào   set (of books, clothes, etc.) (M)

16.1. Zuótian wǒ zuòle yítào xīzhuāng. Jiàqián suīrán bú guì, kěshi zuòde
      hěn zāogāo.   (T)

16.2. Nǐ kàn Mǎ Xiáojie chuān de nèitào yángzhuāng duó piàoliang.

16.3. Tāde yǎnjiǎng lǎo shi nèi yítào, wǒ bù xiǎng tīng le.   (T)

Bái: Zhōngguo zì měi yíge zì yǒu měi yíge zì dútède xíngzhuàng.

Mǎ : Búcuò. Zhōngguode fāngkuàrzì měi yíge zì gòuzào shi bùtóngde.

80 Bái: Zhōngguo zì xuéqilai suírán hěn nán, kěshi zài wǒ gèrénde kànfa,
        wǒ rènwéi shi wéiyī zuì hǎokànde wénzì le, bǐ shìjièshang něiguóde
        wénzì dōu hǎokàn.

Mǎ : Nǐ xǐhuan Zhōngguo zì wǒ yǒu yítào shū zhuānmén shuō xiě zì de.
      Míngtian wǒ dàilai gěi nǐ kànkan.

85 Bái: Xièxie nin.

17.0. dānyīn   single sound

      dānyīnzì   monosyllabic character

      dānyīnjié   monosyllable

      duōyīnjié   polysyllable

17.1. Zhōngguo zì shi dānyīnzì. Měi yíge zì dōu shi dānyīn de.

17.2. Zhōngguo zì dōu shi dānyīnjié. Yīngwén duōshù shi duōyīnjié.

18.0. yōudiǎn   good point, advantage, merit

18.1. Zhāng Xiānsheng xiě de wénzhāng zuì dàde yōudiǎn shi jiǎndān míng-
      bai. (T)

19.0. juédàduōshù   greatest majority

19.1. Juédàduōshūde cuòwu dōu shi tā zuò de, kěshi tā bù kěn chéngrèn.

20.0. Shuōwén   (book title. See note 6)

20.1. Niàn wénzìxuéde shíhou bìděi yǒu Shuōwén zhèibù shū zuò cānkǎo.

21.0. shì   clan name (see note 4)

      Xǔ Shì Shuōwén   (book title) (see note 4)

21.1. Zhōngguo cóngqián yàoshi Lǐ Xiáojie hé Zhāng Xiānsheng jiéle hūn,
      tā jiu shi Zhāng Lǐ Shì le. (T)

21.2. Xǔ Shì Shuōwén yígōng yǒu shísìpiān.   (T)

Bái: Zhōngguo zì shi dānyīnzì, měi yíge zì dōu shi dānyīn de. Wǒ rèn-
      wei zhè shi wénzìde yōudiǎn. Zhǐyú cér ne, suírán yě yǒu dānyīn
      cér, yíge zì jiu shi yíge cér, dànshi juédàduōshù bú shi dānyīnde.
      Chàbuduō dōu shi liǎng-sānge dānzì zǔzhīchéng de.

90 Mǎ : Duìde. Lìrú wǒmen zhèizhāng shēngcí biǎoshangde cér, yígòng yǒu
      liùshí jǐge, kěshi hái bú dào shíge shi dānyīn de.

Bái: Shìde. Mǎ Jiàoshòu, yǒu shíhou wǒ xiě guānyú wénzì yìfāngmiànde
      dōngxi, wǒ kàn <u>Xǔ Shì Shuōwén</u> duōshù kànbudǒng. Shàngmian dōu
      shi yòng wényán jiěshì de. Wǒ yòngle xiāngdāng chángde shíjiān
95   kàn, shǐzhōng kànbudǒng. Rúguǒ <u>Shuōwén</u> yǒu fānchéng báihuà de,
      nà duì wàiguo rén jiu fāngbiànde duō le.

Mǎ : Duìle, wǒ yě zài zhènmo xiǎng ne.

22.0. xiàngshì   simple ideograph [resemble matter]

22.1. <u>Xiàngshì</u> jiu shi <u>zhǐshì</u> de lìngwài yíge shuōfa.

23.0. zìxíng   form of a character

       zìyīn   sound of a character

       zìyì   meaning of a character

23.1. Zhōngguo zìxíng yǔ Xīyáng wénzì bùtóng, yǒu tā dútède xíngzhuàng.
       (W)

23.2. Zhōngguo zìde zìyīn shi dānyīnzì. Yíge zì yǒu yíge yīn.

23.3. Shénmo jiàozuo <u>zìyì</u> na? Jiu shi zìde yìsi.

24.0. yùn   (1) rhyme; (2) final (sound)

       shīyùn   (1) rhyme in poetry; (2) (book title)

       yùnshū   rhyming dictionary

       yīnyùn   pronunciation, phonology

       yīnyùnxué (study of) phonology

24.1. Zuò shī bìděi zhǎo shīyùn.

24.2. Zuò shī gēn xiě wénzhāng bùtóng. Zuò shī bìděi dǒng yīnyùn.

24.3. Zhāng Xiānsheng duìyú yīnyùnxué hěn yǒu yánjiu.

24.4. Nǐ yǒu yùnshū ma? Jiè wǒ kànkan.

25.0. shēng   initial (sound)

25.1   Yíge zìde fāyīn bāokuò liǎngzhǒng dōngxi. Qiánbiānde yīn shi <u>shēng</u>,
       hòubiānde yīn shi <u>yùn</u>.

Bái: Mǎ Jiàoshòu, <u>xiàngshì</u> zhèige cér qǐng nín jiěshì yíxiàr.

Mǎ : <u>Xiàngshì</u> yě shi Liù Shū zhī yī, yě jiào <u>zhǐshì</u>. Yìsi jiu shi hěn
100   míngbaide zhǐchu yíjiàn shì lai. Nǐ yí kàn tāde xíngzhuàng jiu
      míngbai zìde yìsi shi shénmo. Bǐrú <u>shàng</u> 上、<u>xià</u> 下.

Bái: Yánjiu wénzìxué hěn yǒu yìsi.

Mǎ : Wǒ niàn dàxué yìniánjí de shíhou shi xiān niàn wénzìxué. Wénzì-
      xué shi Zhōngguo dútède yìzhǒng xuéwen.

105 Bái: Niàn wénzìxué nín kāishǐ xiān xué shénmo?

Mǎ : Wǒ nèige shíhou yánjiu zìxíng ﹑ zìyīn ﹑ zìyì.   Wénzìxué shi yìzhǒng
     hěn fùzáde xuéwen.

Bái : Háiyǒu, shénmo jiàozuo <u>yùn</u> ne?

Mǎ : Zhōngguo zì měi yíge zì dōu shi dānyīnzì.   Fánshi yíge zìde qián
110   yíbùfen jiàozuo <u>shēng</u>, hòu yíbùfen jiàozuo <u>yùn</u>.

Bái : Yánjiu Zhōngguo wénzì shì bu shi yào zhùyì yīnyùn?

Mǎ : Dāngrán yào zhùyì.   Nǐ duì yīnyùnxué yǒu xìngqu ma?

Bái : Wǒ xiǎng yánjiu yánjiu, dànshi bù zhīdào yīnggāi kàn shénmo shū?

Mǎ : Zhōngguode yùnshū hěn duō.   Zuò shī de rén cháng yòng de <u>Shīyùn</u>
115   yě shi yùnshūde yìzhǒng.

26.0. jiǎnbǐzì   simplified character [simple pen character] (see note 7)

26.1. Hànzì <u>huānglànde</u> <u>làn</u> ﹑ <u>dǎngpàide</u> <u>dǎng</u> dōu yǒu jiǎnbǐzì.

27.0. dǐ   (1) bottom; (2) end (after <u>nián</u> 'year,' <u>yuè</u> 'month')

      dǐxia   (1) underneath; (2) next in order [end below]

      dàodǐ   (1) to the end; (2) finally, after all [to end]

27.1. Wǒ fùqin jīnnián niándǐ jiu yīngdāng tuìxiū le, dànshi tā bù kěn tuì-
      xiū.

27.2. Nǐde dìlǐ jiàokèshū zài zìdiǎn dǐxia ne.

27.3. Zuò shī yào zuò dàodǐ, bú yào zuò yíbàr jiu bú zuò le.

27.4. Nǐ yíhuěr shuō qù, yíhuěr shuō bú qù.   Nǐ dàodǐ qù bu qù ya?

28.0. yìyì   meaning, purport, significance [idea meaning]

      běnyì   basic meaning [root meaning]

      biéyì   secondary meaning [other meaning]

      yí-zì-yí-yì one-character one-sound (W)

28.1. Tā xiě de nèipiān wénzhāng wǒ cóng tóu dàodǐ dōu kàn le, kěshi
      wǒ bù míngbai tāde yìyì shi shénmo? (T)

28.2. <u>Běnyì</u> shi <u>Shuōwén</u>shangde dì-yíge yìsi.   (T)

28.3. <u>Biéyì</u> shi lìngwàide yíge yìsi. Bǐrú <u>yuán</u> zìde běnyì shi <u>kāishǐ</u>, bié-
      yì shi <u>cháodàide</u> <u>míngzi</u> gēn <u>yíkuài</u> <u>qián</u>.   (T)

28.4. Yí-zì-yí-yì jiu shi "yíge zì yíge yìsi."

29.0. jiǎnshǎo   reduce [diminish few]

29.1. Shènglì yǐhòu zhèlide nànmín yìtiān bǐ yìtiān jiǎnshǎo le.

30.0. dàzhòng   the masses [big multitude]

30.1. Shídài bùtóng le. Xiànzài yīnggāi yǐ dàzhòngde yìjian wéi yìjiàn. (T)

31.0. nòng   do (see note 5)

31.1. Zhōngqiūjié Máo Xiānsheng qǐng wǒ dào tā jiā qu chǐ fàn, Máo Tàitai nòngle hěn duō cài.

31.2. Qíshí wǒ měitiānde gōngzuò bìng bú tài duō, kěshi tiāntiān bǎ wǒ nòngde hěn máng. (T)

31.3. Zuótian wǒ dào huǒchēzhàn, chē zǎo jiu kāi le, yuánlái wǒ bǎ zhōng-diǎr gěi nòngcuò le. (T)

Bái: Qǐng wèn Mǎ Jiàoshòu, jiǎnbǐzî gēn jiǎntǐzî dàodǐ yǒu shénmo fēn-bié ne?

Mǎ : Jiǎnbǐzî jiu shi bǎ zî xiěde bǐhuá jiǎndān le. Cóng hěn zǎo yǐqián jiu yǒu zhèizhǒng xiěfa. Jiǎntǐzî me, shi jìnlái Zhōngguo dàlùshang

120   tuīxíng wénzî gǎigé de dì-yībù, bǎ fùzáde Hànzî dōu gěi ta jiǎnhuà le. Yìyî shi yiyàng, xiě de shíhou shěng shíjiān.

Bái: Jiǎnhuà Hànzî bìng bù zhǐshi bǎ měige Hànzî jiǎndānhuàle, shì bu shi?

Mǎ : Bǎ Hànzîde shùmu yě yào jiǎnshǎo yìxiē. Jiǎnhuà Hànzî shi wénzî

125   gǎigéde yíbùfen.

Bái: Wénzî gǎigéde mùdi shi wénzî yào dàzhònghuà, yě yào jiǎndānhuà, shì bu shi?

Mǎ : Shìde.

Bái: Zhèicî wǒ nòngqīngchu le.

32.0. fǎzé   rule, pattern [law principle]

32.1. Tāmen zuò shì méi yǒu yídìngde fǎzé.   Huàn jù huà shuō jiu shi yìdiǎr yě bù kēxué.

33.0. biǎodá   to express [express attain]

33.1. Yǔyán shi biǎodá yìsi de.

34.0. zhǔn   permit, allow, grant

34.1. Zāogāo, wǒ zhèicî shēngqǐng jiǎngxuéjīn méi zhǔn. (T)

35.0. bèi   learn by heart

       bèi shū   (1) learn the contents of a book by heart; (2) recite from memory

35.1. Jīntian xiānsheng yàoshi ràng wǒmen bèi shū wǒ yídìng bèibuxià-lái. (T)

36.0. lîwài   (1) exception; (2) be an exception [example outside]

36.1. Jīntian zhèige huìyî shi lîwài de, yīnwei Zhāng Wěiyuán yào zǒu le, dàjiā bìděi zài yíkuàr kāi huî tǎolùn tǎolùn. (T)

130 Bái: Mǎ Jiàoshòu, yí-zî-yí-yî jiu shi yíge zî yǒu yige zîde yìsi, shì bu shi?

Mǎ : Duìle.

Bái: <u>Fǎzé</u>、<u>fāngfǎ</u> yìsi shi yíyàng ma?

Mǎ : Yǒu diǎn bù yíyàng.

Bái: Wǒ shícháng yǒu zhèizhǒng qíngxing. Xiěle dōngxi zìjǐ kànkan zǒng-
135   shi juéde xiěchulaide méi nénggou bǎ xīnli xiǎng shuō de huà biǎo-
         dáchulai.

Mǎ : Duō kàn shū, cér zhīdaode duō le, zìrán'érránde jiu huì yùnyòng
        le, nǐ xīn lǐtou xiǎng shuō shénmo dōu néng yòng wénzì biǎoshì-
        chulai.

140 Bái: Wǒ xiǎng wǒ jìnbùbuliǎo le.

Mǎ : Bú huì de. Nǐ duō kàn shū yídìng néng jìnbù.

Bái: Wǒ xiǎng wǒ shi lìwài le. Zài yě jìnbùbuliǎo le.

Mǎ : Zhōngguo rén yǐqián niàn shū dōu děi bèixialai. Wǒ dào juéde nèige
        fázi hěn hǎo. Wǒ xiǎode shíhou niàn de shū xiànzài hái néng bèi-
145   chulai, jiu shi yīnwei dāngshí dōu bèixialai. Wǒmen niàn shū de
        shíhou rúguǒ bèibuxiálái, lǎoshī bù zhǔn huí jiā chī fàn.

Bái: Wǒ dàoshi zànchéng bèi shū.

37.0. sù   plain, not fancy

       yīnsù   basic sound, phoneme

       yàosù   essential element

37.1. Tā niánji nènmo qīng lǎoshi chuān sù yīfu.

37.2. Nǐ zhīdao cháng-shēng-bù-lǎo zhèige cér yígòng yǒu jǐge yīnsù?

37.3. Shìyè néng chénggōng wéiyīde yàosù shi nǔlì.

38.0. shí   (1) eat; (2) food   (W)

       liángshi   provisions, food

38.1. <u>Chī fàn</u> de <u>chī</u> yàoshi yòng wényán xiě jiu xiě <u>shí</u>.

38.2. Zhèli chūchǎn de liángshi zhǐ gòu dāngdì rén chī de. (T)

39.0. xíng   walk, go, travel (W)

       xíngdòng   movement, action [walk more]

39.1. Zhōngshān Xiānsheng shuō yī、shí、zhù、xíng shi rénshēng sì dà
        yàosù. (T)

39.2. Wǒ tàitai lǎo guǎnzhe wo. Wǒde xíngdòng yìdiǎr bú zìyóu.

40.0. yǐnshēn   (1) amplify; (2) infer, derive (W)

40.1. <u>Yǐnshēn</u> jiu shi cóng yuánláide yìsi yòu shuōdào gèng shēn gèng
        dàde yíge yìsi. (T)

41.0. kěxī   be unfortunate, too bad (that. . .) [can pity]

41.1. Wǒ jiāde diànshì hěn qīngchu, kěxī ràng wǒ dìdi gěi nònghuài le.
        Xiànzài yìdiǎr yě kànbuqīngchu le.

Bái: Mǎ Jiàoshòu, yīnsù wǒ míngbai, yàosù zhèige cér wǒ bù zhīdào zěn-
      mo yòng.

150 Mǎ: Yàosù jiu shi "yàojǐnde tiáojiàn" de yìsi. "Yī, shí, zhù, xíng" shi
         rénmen shēnghuóde sì dà yàosù.

Bái: Hái yǒu yǐnshēn zhèige cér. Wǒ bù dǒng shi shénmo yìsi.

Mǎ: Yǐnshēn shi xiě wénzhāng yòng de cér. Shi bǎ běnláide yìsi yòu
     wǎng dà yìdiǎr lái shuōyishuō jiàozuo yǐnshēn.

155 Bái: Jīntiande cér, wényánde hěn duō. Kěxī wǒ méi niànguo wényánwén,
         suǒyǐ hěn duō dōu bù dǒng.

42.0. zōngkuò   (1) bring together; (2) generalize; (3) comprehensive
                      [synthesize include]

       zōngkuò yíjù   to sum up in a word

42.1. Zōngkuò guónèide qíngxing lái kàn, zhèicìde zhànzhēng wǒmen yídîng
       dǎshèng. (W) (T)

42.2. Dàjiā suírán yǒu hěn duō yìjian, zōngkuò yíjù dàjiā dōu zànchéng
       dúlì.

43.0. huìhé   join together, come together, merge [meeting join]

43.1. Bàoshangde xiāoxi mǒu jūn hé mǒu jūn zài Shāndong huìhé. Dàjiā
       dōu hěn zhòngshì zhèijiàn shì. (T)

44.0. duì   a group (M)

       jūnduì   army, troops

44.1. Nǐ kàn jiēshang yǒu yíduì bīng cóng zhèr lùguò.

44.2. Zhèlǐde gōnglù yǐqián céngjīng bèi mǒu guó jūnduì gěi pòhuài le. (W)

45.0. yīndiào   (1) tune; (2) intonation [sound tune]

45.1. Nǐ tīngting zhèige gērde yīndiào duómo fùzá. Yǒu gāo, yǒu dī, yǒu
       kuài, yǒu màn.

Bái: Qǐng wèn, zōngkuò de yìsi shi shénmo?

Mǎ: Jiu shi "zhěnggèr dōu bāokuò zài lǐmiàn" de yìsi.

Bái: Huìhé zhèige cér wǒ zhīdao, kěshi xiě wénzhāng de shíhou wǒ bú
160   huì yòng.

Mǎ: Jiu shi "jùzai yíkuàr" de yìsi. Bǐrú "Mǒu jūn hé mǒu jūn zài nàlǐ
     huìhé dǐkàng mǒu guó jūnduì, mǒu jūn jiu zhuǎn bài wéi shèng le."

Bái: Běnyì hé běnláide yìsi yíyàng ma?

Mǎ: Chàbuduō yíyàng. Běnyì jiu shi běnláide yìyì. Yìyì jiu shi yìsi.

165 Bái: Biéyì jiu shi biéde yìsi.

Mǎ: Duìle.

Bái: Yíyì zhèige cér niàn de shíhou dōu yǒu yīn ma?

Mǎ : Dōu yǒu yīn, dōu shi sìshēng.

Bái: Wǒ shuō huà zuì dàde máobing shi yīndiào yìfāngmiàn. Búlùn zěn-
170   mo shuō, zǒngshi bùrú Zhōngguo rén nènmo zìran.

46.0. lì*   profit

      yǒulì   beneficial, advantageous

      búlì   not beneficial, harmful

46.1. Zhèicìde dàzhàn wǒmen jūnduì tuìdao yǒulì dìdài.

46.2. Nǐ zhèiyàngde zuòxiaqu, duì nǐde qiántú hěn búlì.

47.0. Lādǐng   Latin

      Lādǐngwén   Latin language

      Lādǐnghuà   (1) Latinize; (2) Latinization

47.1. Jùshuō niàn yīkē de bìděi xué Lādǐngwén, yīnwei hěn duō yàode
       míngzi shi Lādǐngwén.

47.2. Yǒu rén tíchàng Guóyǔ Lādǐnghuà.   (T)

48.0. zhōngyāng   (1) center, middle part; (2) central   [middle center]

48.1. Niǔyuē sìshí'èr jiēde huǒchēzhàn yàoshi fānyìchéng Zhōngguo huà
       shi "dà zhōngyāng chēzhàn."   (T)

48.2. Zhōngyāng běnlái shi dāngzhōngde yìsi.   Zhōngyāng zhèngfǔ jiǎn-
       dānde shuōfa yě jiào zhōngyāng.

49.0. xìnyòng   credit, trust (N)   [believe use]

49.1. Tā cónglái méi yǒu xìnyong, suǒyǐ méi rén xìnren ta.   (T)

49.2. Nèige gōngsīde xìnyong bù hǎo, zùi hǎo shǎo dào nèr qu mǎi dōng-
       xi.

50.0. quèdìng   (1) certain, sure; (2) ascertain for sure [true definite]

50.1. Zhōngyāng Yánjiuyuàn yào yǒu yícì huìyì, rìqī yǐjing quèdìng zài
       běnyuè shíwǔrì. (W)   (T)

Mǎ : Xué wàiguo yǔyán yào xiǎng xuéde hǎo shi zuì kùnnánde yíjiàn shì-
      qing. Jiù ná xué Zhōngguo huà lái shuō, jìshǐ nǐ fāyīn sìshēng dōu
      hěn zhèngquè le, yě bújiànde bǎ huà shuōde hěn hǎo. Lǎoshi shuō
      zài wǒ rènshi de wàiguo xuéshēngli zài yǔyán yìfāngmiàn nǐ shi zuì
175   hǎode yíge le.

Bái: Wǒ chàde hěn yuǎn ne.

Mǎ : Kàn nǐ shuō Zhōngguo huà de chéngji zhènmo hǎo, nǐ shi yíge hěn
      yǒu yǔyán tiāncáide rén. Nǐ xuéguo jǐzhǒng wàiguo yǔyán le?

Bái: Chúle Zhōngwén yǐwài wǒ hái xuéguo Déwén、Fàwén gēn Lādǐngwén.

180 Mǎ : Nǐ zhùzai Huá jia zài xué Zhōngguo huà fāngmiàn duì nǐ shi hěn
          yǒulì de.

    Bái : Nà dàoshi shízàide. Měitiān píngjūn zhìshǎo yě yào gēn Xuéxīn tán
           yì-liǎngge zhōngtóu. Wǒ hái wàngle gēn nín shuōle ne.

    Mǎ :   Shénmo shì?

185 Bái : Huá Xiānsheng shuō zuìjìn zhōngyāng jìhuàzhe zài dōngbù zào yìtiáo
           gōnglù. Zhīdao Huá Xiānsheng zuò shì yǒu xìnyong. Běnlái Huá
           Xiānsheng duì gōnglù zhèizhǒng gōngchéng méi xìngqu. Kěshi zhèng-
           fǔ juéde zhèige gōngchéng yídìng děi qǐng Huá Xiānsheng qu.

    Mǎ :   Lǎo Huá zuò bu zuò zhèige gōngchéng?

190 Bái : Tā dàgài zuò. Kěshi shénmo shíhou kāishǐ, hái méi quèdìng ne.

    51.0. tún*   village

           túnzi   village

    51.1. Yòu yào dǎzhàng le. Wǒmen nèi yì túnzide rén yòu gāi táonàn le.
           Zhēn zāogāo.

    51.2. Kǎogǔjiā zài Hénán Shěng Ānyáng Xiàn Xiǎotún Cūn dì dǐxia fāxiànle
           Shāng Cháode wénzì. (T)

    52.0. jué   dig out

    52.1. Zhāng Xiānsheng nèikuài dì xiǎng yào zào fángzi. Gōngrén yì jué
           dì, juéchu hěn duō huángjīn lai.

    53.0. Cāng Jié   (name of legendary inventor of writing)

    53.1. Jù gǔshūshang shuō Zhōngguo zì shi Cāng Jié zào de.

    54.0. zhèngshì   formal(ly), official(ly)   [orthodox form]

    54.1. Wáng Tàitai hé tā zhàngfu sānnián bú zài yíkuàr shēnghuó le, kěshi
           hái méi zhèngshì líhūn ne.

    Bái : Qǐng wèn tún zì zěnmo yòng ne?

    Mǎ :   Yǒude dìfang xiǎo cūnzide míngzi jiào túnzi. Dìmíng cháng yòng
           tún. Bǐrú Wáng Jiā Tún, Liùlǐ Tún. Kǎogǔjiā zài dìlǐ juéchulái
           jiǎgǔde dìfang míngzi jiào Xiǎotún Cūn.

195 Bái : Wǒ kàn lìshǐshang Cāng Jié zào zì nà bú shi bǐ jiǎgǔwén zǎo yì-
           qiānnián le ma?

    Mǎ :   Zhōngguo zì zǎo jiu yǒu le, kěshi yīnwei méi yǒu quèshíde gēnjù,
           suǒyǐ yìbān xuézhě rènwei bù néng zhèngshì chéngrèn.

    55.0. yīn'ér   (and) hence (W)

    55.1. Tā jiēdào jiāzhōng diànbào zhīdao tā fùqin zài shēng bìng, yīn'ér
           xīnzhōng shífēn huāngluàn. (W)

56.0. guāngmíng   bright, brilliant, splendid [light bright]

56.1. Nǐ zhèicì dào Yīngguo qu liúxué yùzhù nǐ qiántú guāngmíng, xīwang nǐ zǎorì huí guó. (W)

57.0. kuàiji   accounting

57.1. Wǒ gēge zài diànbàojú dāng kuàiji zhǔrèn yǐjing yǒu wǔnián le.

58.0. shěnghuì   provincial capital [province meeting]

shānghuì   chamber of commerce [commerce meeting]

58.1. Jīntian Wáng Xiànzhǎng dào shěnghuì qu cānjiā yíge zhòngyàode huìyì.

58.2. Qǐng wèn, zhèlǐde shānghuì chúle huìzhǎng yǐwài hái yǒu shéi fùzé?

59.0. guǐ   spirit, ghost, devil

yángguǐzi   foreign devil

59.1. Hěn duō rén shuō nèisuǒr dà fángzili yǒu guǐ.

59.2. Yǒu rén shuō guǐ zuì pà guāngmíng. (T)

59.3. Zhōngguo rén jiào wàiguo rén shi yángguǐzi nǐmen zhīdao zhèige láiyuán ma?

59.4. Wǒ xiǎode shíhou zuì xǐhuan tīng rénjia shuō guǐ gùshi.

Bái: Mǎ Jiàoshòu, yīn'ér zhèige cér shuō huà bú dà yòng, shì bu shi?

200 Mǎ : Shì. Duōshù xiě wénzhāng yòng.

Bái: Guāngmíngde yìsi shi shénmo?

Mǎ :   Yǒu shíhou yòng ta xíngróng yíge rén yǒu qiántú: "Tāde qiántú hěn guāngmíng."

Bái: Kuàiji 會計 bù néng niàn huìji ma?

205 Mǎ : Bù néng. Qíshí Hànzì dōu shi yíge zì. Bù zhīdào wèi-shénmo bǎ huìji niànchéng kuàiji. Bǐrú gōnghuì、shānghuì、kāihuì dōu shi huìde yīn.

Bái: Yángguǐzi xiǎng shuō Zhōngguo huà zhēn bù róngyi. Xiàng zhèizhǒng dìfang chángcháng nòngchu xiàohua lai. Suǒyǐ rénjia shuō:

210   "Tiān bu pà, dì bu pà, jiù pà yángguǐzi shuō Zhōngguo huà."

Mǎ :   Nǐ zhèige yángguǐzi dàoshi lìwài.

60.0. mài(zi)   wheat

60.1. Màizi yě shi liángshide yìzhǒng, Hénán Shěng chūchǎnde zuì duō.

60.2. Wǒmen zhèr bù chūchǎn màizi, suǒyǐ dōu chī mǐfàn. (T)

61.0. dùn   (measure for meals)

61.1. Wǒ yìtiān suǒ dé de gōngqián zhǐ gòu wǒ chī liǎngdùn fàn de.

62.0. má   hemp

62.1. Mǎ Xiáojiede yīfu shi yòng má bù zuò de.   (T)

63.0. chǎng*   factory (M: jiā)

gōngchǎng   factory

mùchǎng   lumber yard

63.1. Nèige rénzào sī gōngchǎngde guīmó xiāngdāng dà, yǒu yìqiān duō
gōngren zài nèr zuò gōng.

63.2. Nèige dà shùlínzi shi shǔyu nèige mùchǎng de.

64.0. mà   scold, rail at, curse, revile

64.1. Shànghǎi rén mà niánji dà yìdiǎr de nánrén shi "zhèige lǎo jiǎyú." (T)

Bái: Zhōngguo nánfāng chǎn mǐ, běifāng chǎn màizi. Jiù wǒ suǒ zhīdao
de běifāng rén bú dà chī mǐ, shì bu shi?

Mǎ : Nánfāng rén měidùn fàn dōu chī mǐ. Běifāng rén yǒude rénjiā wǔ-
215   fàn chī mǐfàn, yǒude rénjiā wǎnfàn chī mǐfàn.

Bái: Má shì bu shi běifāng chūchǎn de?

Mǎ : Má zhèizhǒng dōngxi duōshù shi zài nánfāng chūchǎn de. Wǒmende
cér xiànzài dōu shuōwán le. Shíjiān yě chàbuduō le. Nǐ qù tīng
jiǎng. Wǒ děi dào mùchǎng qu mǎi diar mùliào qu.

220 Bái: Nín mǎi mùliào zuò shénmo?

Mǎ : Wǒmende háizi duō, dōngxi yě duōqilai le, suǒyǐ fángzi bú gòu yòng
le. Xiǎng zài hòuyuànr zào yìjiān mùtou fángzi. Wǒ tàitai shuōle
hǎojiǔ le, jiào wǒ mǎi mùliào, yàoshi zài bù mǎi gāi mà wo le.

Bái: Mǎ Jiàoshòu yuánlái pà tàitai ya.

225 Mǎ : Wǒ bú pà. Tā zhǐ shi mà wo, hái méi dǎguo wo ne!

SHĒNGCÍ BIǍO

1. jiǎ*
jiǎyú
jiǎ, yǐ, bǐng, dǐng

2. gǔ*
gútou
jiǎgǔ
jiǎgǔwén

3. guī
guījiǎ

4. bèi

5. xiàngxíng
xiàngshēng

6. liào*
zīliào
mùliào

7. Liù Shū

8. zhǐshì

9. huìyì

10. jiǎjiè

11. xíngshēng

12. zhuǎn
zhǎnzhù
zhuǎnchéng
zhuǎn bài wéi
shèng

13. xíngzhuàng

14. dútè (W)

15. gòu*
gòuzào

gòuchéng   yí-zî-yí-yì (W)   búlî

16. tào   29. jiănshăo   47. Lādīng
                                                                      Lādīngwén
17. dānyīn   30. dàzhòng   Lādīnghuà
    dānyīnzî
    dānyīnjié   31. nòng   48. zhōngyāng
    duōyīnjié
                              32. făzé   49. xìnyong
18. yōudiăn
                              33. biăodá   50. quèdìng
19. juédàduōshù
                              34. zhŭn   51. tún*
20. Shuōwén   túnzi
                              35. bèi
21. shî   52. jué
    Xŭ Shî Shuōwén   36. lîwài
                                                                53. Cāng Jié
                              37. sù
22. xiàngshî   yīnsù   54. zhèngshî
                                  yàosù
23. zìxíng   55. yīn'ér (W)
    zìyīn   38. shí (W)
    zìyì   liángshi   56. guāngmíng

24. yùn   39. xíng (W)   57. kuàiji
    shīyùn   xíngdòng
    yùnshū   58. shěnghuì
    yīnyùn   40. yīnshēn (W)   shānghuì
    yīnyùnxué
                              41. kěxī   59. guĭ
25. shēng   yángguĭzi
                              42. zōngkuò
26. jiănbĭzî   zōngkuò yíjù   60. mài(zi)

27. dĭ   43. huìhé   61. dùn
    dĭxia
    dàodĭ   44. duì   62. má
                                  jūnduì
                                                                63. chăng*
28. yìyì   45. yīndiào   gōngchăng
    běnyì   mùchăng
    biéyì   46. lî*
                                  yŏulî   64. mà

YŬFĂ LIÀNXÍ

A. V N de V N (see note 2)

1. Nèixiē yánjiu jiăgŭwén de lăo xiānsheng kàn guī bèi de kàn guī béi, kàn
   niú gútoude kàn niú gútou.

2. Nèi jĭwèi shīrén zài Duānyángjiéde shíhou dàjiā zài yíkuàr zuò shī. Tán
   zìyīn de tán zìyīn, tán zìyì de tán zìyì.

3. Jiă、yĭ、bĭng、dīng sìge rén gè yŏu gède shìqing. Dásao wūzi de dásao
   wūzi, băi yuèbing de băi yuèbing.

4. Nèige jūnduìde bīng zài guò Wŭyuèjié de shíhou yŏu yìtiānde xiūxi. Tāmen huá chuán de huá chuán, chī zòngzi de chī zòngzi.

5. Nèi jǐwèi yìyuán zhèicì kāi huì nòngde hěn máng. Zài huìyìshǐli kāi huì
   de shíhou, tǎolùn de tǎolùn, jìlù de jìlù.

   B. hǎo 'good, better' and disjunctive questions (see <u>Beginning Chinese</u>,
       p. 84 note 12; p. 324 note 13; p. 354 note 5)

6. Nǐ shuō nèijian shìqing zhènmo bàn hǎo ne, háishi nènmo bàn hǎo ne?
   . . . Zǒngkuò yíjù zěnmo bàn yě bànbuhǎo le. (W)

7. Wǒ yào dào wàiguoyǔ sùchéngkē niàn yìmén wàiguo yǔwén. Nǐ shuō wǒ
   niàn Lādīngwén hǎo, háishi niàn Fàwén hǎo? . . . Nǐ suíbiàn niàn něimén
   dōu hǎo.

8. Nǐ shuō zhèijiàn shìqing shi ànzhe dàzhòngde yìsi hǎo ne, háishi jǐge
   rén kāi huì juédìng hǎo? . . . Háishi kāi huì juédìng hǎo.

9. Máo Xiānsheng shuō yíbàntiān qǐng wǒ chī fàn. Tā zhèidùn fàn wǒ dàodǐ
   chī hǎo ne, háishi bù chī hǎo ne? . . . Wǒ shuō nǐ háishi chī hǎo.

10. Lǎo Zhāng jiēhūn, wǒ chuān Zhōngzhuāng hǎo, háishi chuān yítào Xīzhuāng
    hǎo ne? . . . Wǒ shuō nǐ háishi chuān Xīzhuāng hǎo.

    C. Rhetorical questions (see <u>Intermediate Chinese</u>, p. 155, note 3)

11. Wáng Xiānsheng cái mǎile yíge dà tùryé ràng tā érzi gěi nònghuài le.
    Nǐ shuō duóma kěxī.

12. Tā tài méi xìngyong le. Jiè wǒ nèiběn <u>shǐyùn</u>de shíhou shuō xīngqīsān
    yídìng gěi wǒ sònglai. Jiéguǒ dào jīntian tā yě méi gěi wo. Nǐ kàn wǒ
    yīnggāi zěnmo bàn?

13. Nèige rénzào sī gōngchǎng měitiān gōngren yào gōngzuò shíyī xiǎoshí.
    Nǐ shuō tāmen duóma nǔlì shēngchǎn.

14. Nèige hóngshāo jiǎyú dōu ràng wǒ gěi chīguāng le. Nǐ xiǎng wǒ duóma
    ài chī ba.

15. Nèiběn guǐ gùshide xiǎoshuō tā shuō nà shi qiānzhēnwànquède shìshí. Nǐ
    shuō ta duóma yòuzhi.

JIǍNGHUÀ

Zhūwèi tóngxué:

   Jīntian jiǎnghuà de tímu shi Zhōngguode Wénzì. Zhèige tímu bāokuò de fànwéi hěn dà, jīntian suǒ jiǎng de zhǐ shi bǎ Zhōngguo wénzìde
qǐyuán hé zìxíng、zìyīn、zìyì yǐjí jīnláide gǎigé dàlüède tányitán.

5   Zhōngguo wénzì shi zài shénmo shídài chuàngzào de? Lí xiàndài
yǒu ruògān nián? Zuìchūde wénzì shi shénmo yàng? Zhèige wèntí yìzhí
dào xiànzài hái méi fázi quèdìng. Wǒmen xiànzài suǒ néng kàndedào de
Zhōngguo zuì gǔde wénzì, zhǐ yǒu jiǎgǔwén. Jiǎgǔwén shi sānqiān duō

nián yǐqián Shāng Cháo shídài shǐyòng de wénzì. Jiǎgǔwénde fāxiàn shi
10 zài liùshi duō nián yǐqián. Zài Hénán Shěng Ānyáng Xiàn Xiǎotún Cūn
yǒu rén cóng dìxia juéchulai hěn duō guījiǎ hé niú gǔ, zài zhèixiē guījiǎ
hé niú gǔshang dōu yǒu wénzì. Hòulai jīngguo Zhōng-wài xuézhě yánjiu
rènwei shi Shāng Cháo shídàide wénzì. Yīnwei zhèixiē wénzì dōu kēzai
jiǎgǔshang, suǒyǐ jiu jiàozuo jiǎgǔwén. Zhè shi wǒmen xiànzài quèshí
15 néng kàndedào de Zhōngguo zuì gǔde wénzì le.

Zài jiǎgǔwén yǐqián kěnéng hái yǒu gèng gǔde wénzì. Bǐfang shuō
zài Zhōngguo gǔshūli shuō: "Cāng Jié zào zì yǒu guǐ yè kū." Yìsi shi
shuō shànggǔde shíhou dàyuē zài sìqiān duō nián yǐqián yǒu yíge rén
míngzi jiào Cāng Jié tā zàochule wénzì. Zài tā zàochu wénzìde shíhou
20 yǒu yìxiē guǐ zhīdao rénlèi fāmíngle wénzì jiu yào yìtiān bǐ yìtiān wénmíng, jiānglái duìyu guǐ yídìng búlì de, suǒyǐ guǐ zài yèli kūqilai le.
Yīnwei zhèizhǒng shuōfa hǎoxiang shénhuà, bìng méi yǒu kěkàode zhèngmíng, suǒyǐ jiǎgǔwén jiu suàn Zhōngguo zuì gǔde wénzì le.

Shìjièshang wúlùn něi yìzhǒng wénzì tāde gòuchéng dōu yào yǒu
25 sānge "yàosù," jiu shi "zìxíng, zìyīn hé zìyì." Zhōngguo wénzì yě bù néng
lìwài. Xiànzài shǒuxiān jiǎng Zhōngguo wénzìde zìxíng. Zhōngguo wénzìde zìxíng shi fāngkuàide. Zhèizhǒng fāngkuài zì bú xiàng pīnyīn wénzì.
Pīnyīn wénzì shi yòng zìmǔ huò duō huò shǎo pīnchéngle yíge zì. Zhōngguo fāngkuài zì shi yòng ruògān bùtóngde bǐhuá xiěchéngle yíge zì. Suǒyǐ
30 Zhōngguo zì měige zì yǒu měige zìde dútède zìxíng. Yīnwei zìxíng tài
fùzá le, zài xuéxíshang jiu bǐjiǎo kùnnán. Qíshí zhèizhǒng zìxíng duìyu
xuéxíshang shi yǒu bāngzhu de. Zhè huà zěnmo jiǎng ne? Wǒmen kéyi
jǔchu lìzi lái shuō. Wǒmen zhīdao Zhōngguo zìde gòuzào shi yǒu liùge
jīběn fǎzé, zhèi liùge fǎzé jiàozuò Liù Shū. Liù Shū shi xiàngxíng、zhǐ-
35 shì、huìyì、jiǎjiè、xíngshēng、zhuǎnzhù.

Zài Liù Shūli dì-yíge fǎzé shi xiàngxíng. Shénmo jiào xiàngxíng
ne? Jiu shi suǒ zàochulai de zì shi zhàozhe yíge dōngxide xíngzhuàng
huàchulai de. Xuéxí de rén yí kànjian zhèige xíngzhuàng jiu kéyi rènshi
zhèige zì le. Bǐrú rì 日、yuè 月、shān 山、chuān 川、mén 門 děngděng.
40 Dì-èrge fǎzé shi xiàngshì, yě jiàozuo zhǐshì. Zhǐshìde yìsi shi
míngbai zhǐchu yíjiàn shì. Wǒmen yí kànjian zhèige zhǐshì de xíngzhuàng
jiu kéyi zhīdao shi shénmo zì le. Bǐrú shàng 上、xià 下 zhèi liǎngge zì

mǎ	xué
tóu	huà
ràng	hàn
马	学
头	画
让	汉
馬	學
頭	畫
讓	漢
馬	學
頵	畫
讓	漢

shi xiān xiě yíge $\underline{yī}$ — zì. Zhèige $\underline{yī}$ zì shi
biǎoshì zhōngyāngde yìsi.   Zài $\underline{yī}$ zì shàng-
45 tou yǒu bǐhuáde jiu shi $\underline{shàng}$ zì, zài $\underline{yī}$ zì
xiàmian yǒu bǐhuáde jiu shi $\underline{xià}$ zì.

     Dì-sān shi $\underline{huìyì}$. $\underline{Huìyì}$ shi yíge zìli
bāokuò yǒu liǎngge zì, kàn zhèi liǎngge zìde
yìsi jiu kéyi zhīdao zhèi yíge zì shi shénmo
50 zì le. Lìrú $\underline{xìn}$信 zì shi $\underline{rén}$人、$\underline{yán}$言 liǎngge zì zǔzhichéng de.   Rén、yán jiu shi "rén
shuō huà."   Rén shuō huà yīngdāng yǒu xìn-
yong. $\underline{Xìnyong}$ jiu shi $\underline{xìn}$.   Yòu bǐfang $\underline{míng}$
明 zì shi $\underline{rì}$日 hé $\underline{yuè}$月 liǎngge zì zǔzhichéng
55 de.   Rì hé yuè zài yíkuàr yídìng tèbié guāng-
míng, suǒyǐ nà jiu shi $\underline{guāngmíngde}$ $\underline{míng}$ zì.

     Dì-sì shi $\underline{xíngshēng}$, shi yíge zìli bāo-
kuò liǎngge zì, yíge shi xiàngxíng de, yíge
shi xiàngshēng de.   Lìrú $\underline{kǎo}$烤 zì shi huǒ-
60 $\underline{chē}$de huǒ火 hé $\underline{kǎoshìde}$ kǎo考 liǎngge zì zǔ-
zhicheng de. $\underline{Huǒ}$火 zì shi xiàngxíng, $\underline{kǎo}$考
zi shi xiàngshēng, hézài yíkuàr jiu shi $\underline{kǎo}$
$\underline{yāzide}$ kǎo zì.

     Dì-wǔ shi $\underline{zhuǎnzhù}$, shi cóng yíge zì
65 zhuǎnchéng lìngwài yíge zì.   Jiu xiàng $\underline{lǎo}$-
$\underline{rénde}$ lǎo老 zì zhuǎnzhùchéng $\underline{kǎoshìde}$ kǎo考
zì.

     Dì-liù shi $\underline{jiǎjiè}$, jiu shi jièyòng biéde
zì.   Lìrú gǔshí $\underline{màizide}$ $\underline{mài}$ zì dāngshíde xiě-
70 fa gēn xiànzài $\underline{lái}$ $\underline{qù}$ de $\underline{lái}$ zì shi yíyàng de.
Yīnwei dāngshí hái méi yǒu $\underline{lái}$ zì, jiu jiǎjiè
yuányǒu $\underline{mài}$ zìde xiěfa dàngzuò $\underline{lái}$ zì le,   jièyòng rìzi jiǔle jiu zhèngshì suànshi $\underline{lái}$ zì le.

     Zhèi liùzhǒng fǎzéde zìxíng zài Zhōng-
75 guo zìli zhàn juédàduōshù, suǒyǐ Zhōngguo
zìxíng duìyú wénzìde xuéxíshang shi hěn yǒu
bāngzhu de.

Qícì yào jiǎng de shi zìyīn. Zhōngguo zìde zìyīn shi dānyīnzì, yě

jiu shi dānyīnjié, yí-zì-yì-yīn. Bú xiàng pīnyīn wénzì zài yíge zìlǐ yěxǔ

80 yǒu hǎojǐge yīnjié. Zhōngguo wénzì suīrán shi dānyīnjié, kěshi rúguǒ

jìnyíbù yánjiu bǎ měige zìyīn zài fēnxi yíxià, nènmo měige zìyīnli kéyǐ

fēnchéng qiánhòu liǎngbùfen, yě jiu shi yǒu qiánhòu liǎngge yīnsù. Zài

qiánde yíbùfen jiàozuo sheng, zài hòude yíbùfen jiàozuo yùn. Fánshi yíge

zìyīn dōu shi yóu shēng、yùn pīnchéng de. Lìrú mā zìde zìyīn shi m、a

85 liǎngge yīnsù pīnchéng de. M jiu shi shēng, a jiu shi yùn.

Zhōngguo gǔshí duìyu yīnyùn jiu hěn zhùyì. Yǒu rén xiě de xiàng

yùnshū yílèide shū hòulai zài yánjiu yīnyùnxuéshang hěn yǒu yòngchu. Cǐ-

wài Zhōngguo zìyīn hái yǒu yíge tèdiǎn yào tèbié zhùyì de, jiu shi měi

yíge zìyīn fēnwéi sìshēng. Zhè shi ànzhào yīndiàode gāo、dī、cháng、duǎn

90 fēnchulai de. Zhè sìshēng jiu shi dì-yīshēng, dī-èrshēng, dì-sānshèng, dì-

sìshēng. Lìrú mā shi dì-yīshēng, má shi dì-èrshēng, mǎ shi dì-sānshēng,

mà shi dì-sìshēng. Měige zìyīn yīnwei niànchu de shēng de bùtóng, yīn'ér

nèige zìde yìsi yě jiu bùtóng le.

Xiànzài shuōdào zìyì. Zìyì jiu shi měi yíge zìde yìsi. Zìyì zài

95 wénzì sān yàosùli shi zuì zhòngyàode yìzhǒng, yīnwei zìde zhǔyào zuò-

yong shi zài biǎodá yìsi. Rúguǒ zhǐ néng rènshi zìxíng, shènzhìyú yě

néng niànchu zìyīn, kěshi bù zhīdào zìyì, nà háishi méi yǒu yòngchu.

Zhōngguo zìde zìyì yǒu běnyì yǒu biéyì. Běnyì jiu shi běnláide yìsi.

Shénmo shi běnláide yìsi ne? Jiu shi zhèige zìde yìsi yào hé zhèige zìde

100 zìxíng yǒu guānxi huòzhě ànzhào Xǔ Shì Shuōwén suǒ dìng de yí-zì-yì-yì.

Zhè dōu shi běnyì. Shénmo shi biéyì ne? Jiu shi cóng běnyì yǐnshēn-

chulai huòzhě jiǎjièchuqu de. Huàn ju huà shuō jiu shi chúle běnyì yǐ-

wài lìngwàide yìsi. Wǒmen zhīdao Zhōngguo zì yíge zì wǎngwǎng yǒu

hěn duō yìsi, shènzhìyú zài yìzhǒng dìfang yǒu yìzhǒng jiǎngfǎ. Lìrú huì

105 會 zì, běnyì shi huìhé de yìsi, dànshi tāde biéyì—jiu shi lìngwàide yìsi—

hěn duō. Jiù xiàng: (1)"huì bú huì guóyù" de huì; (2)"kāihuì" de huì; (3)

"shěnghuì、shānghuì" de huì; shènzhìyú "kuàiji" de kuài. Tā suǒ dàibiǎo

de yìsi dōu shi bù xiāngtóng de. Suǒyǐ yǒu rén rènwei Zhōngguo wénzìde

zìyì tài duō, zhè yě shi bù róngyi xuéxí de yuányīn zhī yī.

110 Zǒngkuò lái shuō, Zhōngguo wénzì zài zìxíng、zìyīn、zìyìshang yǒu

tāde yōudiǎn yě yǒu tāde quēdiǎn. Yǒu rén rènwei rúguǒ gēn pīnyīn wén-

zì lái bǐjiǎo, Zhōngguo wénzì shi bǐjiǎo nánxué, yě bù róngyì xiě. Suǒyǐ
jìnlái yǒu hěn duō rén zhǔzhāng wénzì gǎigé. Zhǔzhāng wénzì gǎigé de
bànfa dàzhì kě fēnwéi liǎngzhǒng. Yǒu yìzhǒng zhǔzhāng bǎ Zhōngguo
115 yuánláide wénzì jiǎnhuà. Bǐfang shuō yuánlái wénzì bǐhuá tài duōde kéyi
bǎ tā jiǎndānhuà. Zhèizhǒng zhǔzhāng, búdàn zài zhèngfǔ fāngmiàn tíchàng. Jiu shi zài shèhuìshang yě yīnwei shìshíshangde xūyào, zìrán'érránde xíngchéngchulai yìzhǒng jiǎnbǐzì, rìzi jiǔle dàjiā yě jiu dōu shǐyòng
le. Cóng zhèi yìdiǎn kànlai, Zhōngguo wénzì yīngdāng gǎigé jiǎnhuà, zhè
120 shi dàzhòngde xūyào. Cǐwài lìng yǒu yìzhǒng zhǔzhāng shi bǎ Zhōngguo
wénzì gǎiyòng pīnyīn wénzì, bú yòng Hànzì, zhǐ yòng Lādīng zìmǔ, zhè
jiu shi suǒwèi "Zhōngguo wénzì Lādīnghuà." Kěshi zhèizhǒng zhǔzhāng
yīnwei hé Zhōngguo chuántǒng de sīxiǎngshang bù hé, suǒyǐ néng bù néng
shíxíng háishi yíge wèntí.

FÙSHÙ

Zhèipán lùyīndài shi Zhōngwén dì-yīzǔ dì-shíyīhào. Bái Wénshān
fùshù dì shíyīcì Zhuāntí Jiǎnghuà.

Zuótiande Zhuāntí Jiǎnghuà shi yóu běnxiào yǔyán xuéxìde xì zhǔrèn
Zhāng Guāngmíng Jiàoshòu suǒ jiǎng de "Xuéxí Zhōngguo Huà." Zhāng
5 Jiàoshòu shi Běijīng rén, suǒyǐ tā shuō de shi hěn chúncuìde Běijīng huà.
Xiànzài wǒ dàlüède fùshù yícì.

Zhāng Jiàoshòu shuō rúguǒ yào yánjiu Zhōngguode wénxué huòshi
yánjiu Zhōngguo lìshǐ, zuì yàojǐnde shi yào bǎ Zhōngguode yǔyán xiān
xuéhǎo. Yàoshi bù dǒng huà, zěnmo yánjiu Zhōngguode xuéwèn ne? Hái-
10 yǒu, rúguǒ bù dǒng Zhōngguo huà zěnmo néng tīng biéren yǎnjiǎng ne?
Jiu shi hé Zhōngguo péngyou jiēchǔ yě bìděi liǎojiě Zhōngguo huà.

Tā shuō dàjiā yǐjing jìnrùle Zhōngguo shèhuì, yàoshi yǔyánshang
yǒu kùnnán yídìng hěn róngyi kèfú. Tā yòu shuō tā bǎ xué wàiguo yǔyán
róngyi hūlüè de yìxiē shìqing tā gěi wǒmen jiǎngyijiǎng.

15   Zhāng Jiàoshòu yòu shuō wǒmen shi cóng hěn yuǎn bùtóngde guójiā
láidao Zhōngguo, yěxǔ lí jiā hěn jiǔ le. Pèngjian yíge shuō běnguó yǔyánde rén yídìng gāoxìngde bùdéliǎo, miǎnbuliǎo dàjiā yào qīnjìn qīnjìn
chángcháng zài yíkuàr tántan. Zhè dāngrán shi fēicháng yúkuàide shì le,
kěshi bǎ xuéxí yǔyán bǎoguìde jīhui jiu guòqu le. Suǒyǐ yídìng yào zhǎng-

20 wòzhe jīhui búduànde liànxi, cái néng hěn kuàide jìnbù. Yàoburán búdàn
    bú jìnbù, érqiě hái yào tuìbù.   Zuì yǒu xiào de fāngfa háishi yǒu jīhui
    jiu shuō, lìyòng jīhui duō shuō Zhōngguo huà.

         Zhāng Jiàoshòu shuō wǒmen rènshi liǎngqiān dào sānqiānge zì le.
    Zhè shi xiāngdāng bù shǎo le.   Zhōngguo zì chángyòng de yě búguò shi
25 sān-sìqiān zì. Kěshi yǒude rén, xīnli xiǎng shuō de huà shuōbuchūlái, jí-
    shǐ shuōchulai yě bú zìrán, bú xiàng Zhōngguo rén shuōde nènmo yǒu
    wèr, nènmo liúlì.   Zhāng Jiàoshòu yòu shuō, huà shuō de méi wèr, nà
    shi yùnyòngde bù línghuó. Tā hái shuō rúguǒ xiǎng bǎ Zhōngguo huà shuō
    de hěn zìrán, bìděi zhùyì Zhōngguo huàde tèdiǎn. Yǒu rén shuō Zhōngguo
30 huà hěn yǒu shīyì. Zhèige huà duì bú duì ne? Zhèige huà yǒu diar duì.

         Zhōngguo rén shuō huà chángcháng yòng bǐyù. Zhāng Jiàoshòu yòng-
    le yíge hěn yǒuyìside lìzi.   Tā shuō yàoshi nǐ jiāli zìmèi qīnglaile hěn
    duō nǚ tóngxué, nǐ gàosu biérén shuō: "Wǒmen jiā láile hěn duō xiáojie,
    nèixiē xiáojie dōu hěn piàoliang, yīngyīngyànyàn rènao jíle." Dāngrán yě
35 kéyi shuō: "Nèixiē xiáojie hěn hǎokàn, yǒude cháng tóufa, yǒude duǎn
    tóufa, yǒu pàngde yǒu shòude, rènao jíle." Nǐ kàn zhèi liǎngge shuōfǎ shì
    bu shi dì-yíge shuōfǎ bǐjiǎo shēngdòng ne? Shuō huà yòng bǐyù zài Zhōng-
    guo huàli hěn duō. Yàoshi dàjiā duō zhùyì zhèixiē yě néng zēngjiā shuō
    Zhōngguo huàde xìngqu.

40   Zhāng Jiàoshòu shuō yě yào zhùyì Zhōngguo rénde fēngsu xíguan.
    Tā shuō bìng bú shi ràng wǒmen měi yíge rén ài chī Zhōngguo fàn hē
    Zhōngguo chá, shi yào liǎojiě hé Zhōngguo yǔyán yǒu guānxide Zhōngguo
    fēngsu xíguan. Tā shuō bǐrú wǒmen pèngjian yíwèi Zhōngguo xiáojie, zhèi-
    wèi xiáojie hěn piàoliang yě hěn huì shuō huà. Nǐ gēn tā tánle yíhuěr, nǐ
45 xīwang yǐhòu zài hé tā jiàn miàn, nǐ duì tā shuō: "Wǒ hěn xǐhuan ni, wǒ
    xiǎng zài yǒu jīhui hé nǐ jiàn miàn." Zhèiwei xiáojie kěnéng shēngle qì
    le, yěxǔ liǎn jiu hóng le. Nǐ zhīdao zhè shi shénmo yuányīn ma?   Zhè
    jiu shi Zhōngguo rén hé wàiguo rén fēngsu xíguande bùtóng.   Zhōngguo
    rén nánnǚde gǎnqíng shi hánxu de. Yíge nánháizi bù néng hé yíge chūcì
50 jiàn miàn de nǚháizi shuō "Wǒ xǐhuan ni." Háiyǒu, zài Zhōngguo huàli
    "Wǒ xǐhuan ni" hé "Wǒ ài ni" de yìsi chàbuduō. Nǐ gēn yíwèi tóucì jiàn
    miàn de xiáojie jiu shuō xǐhuan ta, tā dāngrán hěn bùhǎoyìsi. Zhāng
    Jiàoshòu shuō rúguǒ dǒngde Zhōngguo rénde xíguan, duì nèiwèi xiáojie

shuō: "Hé nǐ zài yíkuàr tántan hěn yǒuyìsi, xīwang jiānglái wǒmen hái
55 yǒu jīhui tántan." Nèiwèi xiáojie tīngle nǐ zhèi liǎngjù huà yídìng hěn gāoxìng.

Zhāng Jiàoshòu yòu shuō yǔyán shi rìjīyuèlěi de yìzhǒng xíguan.
Yào xiǎng kèfú xué Zhōngguo huàde kùnnán, yǒu xiào de bànfa shi lìyong
jīhui duō tīng duō jiǎng.   Zhāng Jiàoshòu hái shuō xuéxí yǔyán néngfǒu
60 chénggōng nà jiu děi kàn nǐ néng bu néng zhǎngwò xuéxí de huánjìng. Tā
zuìhòu yòu shuō yǒu yìxiē Zhōngguo xuéshēng dào wàiguo qu liúxué, yǒude
suīrán yǐjing niànle sānnián wǔniánde shū le, kěshi hái bù néng gēn wàiguo rén shuō huà. Hé rénjia yì tán huà, bú shi cí bù dáyì jiùshi xīnhuāng
yìluàn de. Shuōchu de huà miǎnbuliǎo fāshēng hěn duō cuòwu.   Tā shuō
65 zhè bú shi tāmen méi yǒu yǔyán tiāncái, zhè shi tāmen méi hǎohāorde
lìyong jīhui.   Tāmen shàngkè yǐwài dōu shi gēn Zhōngguo tóngxué zài
yíkuàr shuō Zhōngguo huà le.   Wǒ rènwei Zhāng Jiàoshòu shuō de hěn
yǒu dàolǐ. Jiù ná wǒmen wàiguo rén zài Zhōngguo xué yǔyán lái shuō
ba, yě bù yīnggāi yángguǐzi gēn yángguǐzi lǎoshi zài yíkuàr tán huà.

WÈNXÍ

1. Wǒ jiā fángzide pángbiār yǒu yìkē shù. Yǒu shíhou wǒ dúzì zuòzai shù-
    xià, kànjian jǐge xiǎoyànr fēilái fēiqù.   Wǒ xīnli xiǎng, zhèixiē yànr bǐ
    rén dōu qiáng, yànrde shēnghuó duóma zìyóu, zhǐ yǒu kuàilè méi yǒu yōu-
    chóu.

2. Chóngyángjié dēnggāo jùshuō kéyi bìmiǎn zāinàn.   Kěshi rénlèi wèiláide
    zāinàn hěn duō. Jìshǐ tiāntiān dēnggāo, dēngdao zuì gāode dìfang, shìfǒu
    néng bìmiǎnle zāinàn ne?

3. Yǒu yíge liúxuéshēng huíguó de shíhou zhèng shi qiūtian. Tāde jǐge péng-
    you qǐng ta guò Bāyuejié shǎngyuè.   Yǒu yíge péngyou wèn ta wàiguode
    qíngxing. Tā shuo: "Wǒ liúxué de dìfang shi zài Dàxīyángde xībiān, shi
    yíge qiángguó, rénmín dōu zhīdao àiguó, juéduì bú zuò duì guójiā búlìde
    shì. Rénmín yě yǒu tóngqíng xīn, gèng yǒu rèqíng bāngzhu pángrén. Zài
    zhèngzhishang zhēnzhèng mínzhǔ, yǒu yìyuàn dàibiǎo rénmínde yìsi. Zài
    jīngjishang zhùzhòng shēngchǎn.   Jiù ná liángshi lái shuō, shífēn fēngfù
    . . ." Zhèige liúxuéshēng yìbiār shuō yìbiār chī yuèbing.   Hūrán yǒu
    yíge péngyou duì tā shuō: "Yǒude liúxuéshēng shuō yángrén shénmo dōu
    hǎo, lián wàiguode yuèliang dōu bǐ běnguóde dà, shi zhēnde ma?" Zhèige
    liúxuéshēng shuō: "Nà búguò shi shuō guānyú liúxuéshēngde yíduàn xiào-
    hua. Nǎlǐ huì shi zhēnde ne?"

4. Qīngmíngjié jiājiā qù sǎomù, wèideshì bú wàng zǔxiān. Duānyángjié chī
    zòngzi chùchù sài lóngchuán, wèideshì jìnian tóujiāng de Chǔ Guó Qū
    Yuán.   Zhè dōu shi Zhōngguode fēngsu xíguan, jué bu róngyi dǎpò de.

5. Qùnián sàichuán, wǒmen zhèitiáo chuán sàibuguò biéde chuán, shībài le. Jīnnián yòu yào sài chuán. Wǒmen jímáng liànxí. Dàole bǐsài zhèi yìtiān wǒmen yòu qu cānjiā. Zhèi yìhuí bǐsài de chuán gèng duō. Zài kāishǐ bǐsài de shíhou, wǒmende chuán shi zǒuzai hòubiān, yòu yào shībài. Kěshi nǔlì de jiéguǒ hòulai wǒmende chuán shǒuxiān dàole mùdìdì. Wǒmen zhuǎn bài wéi shèng le.

6. Shuōwén zhèi yíbù shū shi yíge xìng Xǔ de zuò de, suǒyǐ bǎ zhèibù shū jiàozuo Xǔ Shì Shuōwén. Zài zhèibù shūli suǒwèi "gǔwén" yǒu rén shuō shi zhǐ Cāng Jié suǒ zào de zì.

7. Yǒu rén wèn wo: "Zhōngguo zì shì bu shi dānyīnjié? Zhōngguo Liù Shū lǐtou yǒu yíxiàng shi xíngshēng. Xíngshēng shi shénmo yìsi?" Wǒ shuō: "Zhèi liǎngge wèntí qǐng nǐ kànkan běnkè de Zhuāntí Jiǎnghuà, nǐ jiu kéyi míngbai le."

8. Wǒ zuì ài kàn Zhōngwén bàozhǐ. Cóngqián bǎ měitiān kànguo de bàozhǐ dōu shōuqilai. Kěshi rìzi jiǔle jīlěide tài duō le, suǒyǐ wǒ jìnlai kàn Zhōngwén bàozhǐ kànguo yǐhòu jiu rēng le.

9. Nóngmín wéiyīde xīwang shi qiūshōu. Qiūshōu zhǔyàode dōngxi shi liáng-shi. Měinián dàole qiūtian, cóng nóngmínde liǎnshang jiu kéyi kànchū tāmende qiūshōu shi zěnmoyàng. Rúguǒ tāmende liǎnshang shi xiào de yàngzi, nà yídìng shi qiūshōu hěn hǎo.

10. Zhāng Xiānsheng jiālide féndì zài yíge xiǎo shānshang, zhàn de dìfang hěn dà, kěshi fénmù bìng bù duō. Tā shuō lǐbiān yǒu yíge zuì dàde fén, shi tāmen zǔxiānde. Tāmende zǔxiān shi gēn wàiguo dǎzhàng de shíhou dǎbàile sǐ de. Hòulai zhèngfǔ jiu bǎ zhèikuài dì gěile tāmende zǔxiān zuò féndì le.

11. Wǒ zài dàxué niàn shū de shíhou, zuìchū shi pángtīng, hòulai cái zhuǎn-chéng zhèngshì xuésheng. Yóu pángtīng zhuǎnchéng zhèngshì xuésheng de shǒuxù dào hěn jiǎndān. Zhǐyào kǎoshì jígé jiù kéyi zhuǎn le.

12. Cóng wǒ jiā huāyuánde pángmén jìnlaile yìzhī xiǎo tùr, kànjianle wo hǎoxiàng yào táozǒu. Wǒ rēngle yíkuài bǐng, wǒde xīnyì shi xiǎng gěi ta chī, kěshi tā yǐwéi wǒ yào dǎ ta. Tā dōng pǎopao xī pǎopao, zháojíde bùdéliǎo. Hòulai tā zhǎodao pángménde xiàbiār yǒu yìdiǎr huàile de dìfang, tā jiu cóng nàli táochuqu le.

13. Hěn duō nián yǐqián wǒ zài Zhōngguo běifāng lǚxíng, zǒudao Hénán Shěng-de yíge dìfang yǒu yíge nóngrén názhe jǐkuài gútou yào màigei wo. Wǒ xiǎng zhèixiē dōngxi méi yǒu yòngchu, wǒ jiu méi mǎi. Hòulai wǒ cái zhīdao nà jiu shi guījiǎ hé niú gǔ, shàngmian dōu yǒu zì, jiu shi jiǎgǔ-wén. Wǒ hěn hòuhuǐ dāngshí méi mǎi, kěshi hòuhuǐ yě wǎn le.

14. Wǒ xiǎng xuéxí xiě Zhōngguo zì, kěshi méi yǒu zhuōzi. Lǎo Zhāng zhī-dao le jiu jiègěi wǒ yíge, bìngqiě hái jiào rén sònglai. Sònglai de shí-hou wǒ gěile sòng zhuōzi de rén wǔkuài qiánde shǎngqian. Wǒ jiu kāishǐ liànxi xiě Zhōngguo zì. Kěshi wǒ xiǎng Zhōngguo zì bú shi yíxiàr jiu huì xuéhǎo de, chízǎo wǒ zǒng děi zìjǐ mǎi yige zhuōzi.

15. Wǒ yǒu yìběn jiù shū suīrán shi pòle kěshi jù biérén shuō zhèiběn shū bú zài chūbǎn le, zài shūdiànli jué mǎibudào le. Yǒu yìtiān Zhāng Xiān-sheng yào jièqu kàn, wǒ bùhǎoyìsi bú jiè, zhǐhǎo jiègei ta. Kěshi hǎojiǔ

le yě méi sònghuílai. Wǒ jiu xiě xìn qu yào. Zhāng Xiānsheng huíxìn
shuō, zhèiběn shū bù zhī zěnmo zhǎobudào le, yě bu zhī diūzai shénmo
dìfang le, jiào wǒ gàosu ta shénmo dìfang mài, yǐbiàn gěi wǒ mǎi yìběn.
Tā yòu shuō wéiyǒurúcǐ méi yǒu biéde fázi.

16. Wáng Jiàoshòu gěi xuésheng jiǎng guówén. Yàoshi yǒu bù róngyi dǒng de
jùzi, tā dōu shi yòng bǐyù lái jiěshì gěi xuésheng tīng. Érqiě yě shícháng
ràng xuésheng bèi shū, fánshi kèwén shi wényánwénde tā dōu ràng xuésheng bèi. Tā shuō bèiguo de dōngxi shi yǒngyuǎn bú huì wàngji de.

WÈNTÍ

1. Wǒmen quèshí néng kàndedào de Zhōngguo zuì gǔde wénzì shi shénmo
   wénzì? Zhèizhǒng wénzì shi zài shénmo cháodài yòng de? Lí xiànzài
   yǒu ruògān nián le? Zài shénmo shíhou shénmo dìfang fāxiàn de?

2. Jù chuánshuō zài jiǎgǔwén yǐqián yǒu shénmo rén zào zì? Tā zào zì de
   shíhou yǒu yìxiē guǐ wèi-shénmo kū le?

3. Shìjièshang wúlùn něi yìzhǒng wénzìde gòuchéng dōu yǒu sānge yàosù.
   Sānge yàosù shi shénmo? Zhōngguo wénzìde zìxíng shi shénmo yàng de?

4. Xuéxí Zhōngguo wénzì wèi-shénmo bǐjiào kùnnán? Zhōngguode zìxíng duìyu xuéxí shang yǒu méi yǒu bāngzhu?

5. Zhōngguo zìde gòuzào yǒu jǐge fǎzé? Zhèixiē fǎzéde zǒngmíngchēng jiàozuo shénmo? Měizhǒng fǎzéde míngchēng qǐng nǐ shuōyishuō.

6. Shénmo shi xiàngxíng? Shénmo shi zhǐshì? Qǐng nǐ gè jǔ yíge lìzi fēnbié shuōmíng.

7. Zhōngguode zì, měi yíge zì yǒu jǐge yīnjié? Yīnjié hé yīnsù yǒu shénmo
   bùtóng?

8. Zhōngguo wénzì, zài yíge zìyīnli yǒu jǐge yīnsù? Zài qiánde yīnsù jiàozuo shénmo? Zài hòude yīnsù jiàozuo shénmo? Nǐ néng jǔ lìzi shuōmíng
   ma? Zhōngguo zìyīnde tèdiǎn shi sìshēng. Qǐng nǐ jǔ ge lìzi shuōmíng
   sìshēng.

9. Shénmo jiào zìyì? Shénmo jiào běnyì? Shénmo shi biéyì? Nǐ néng jǔ ge
   lìzi shuōmíng ma?

10. Zhōngguo wénzì wèi-shénmo yào gǎigé? Gǎigé de bànfa dàzhì yǒu jǐzhǒng?
    Něizhǒng shòu rén huānyíng? Něizhǒng hái yǒu wèntí? Wèi-shénmo yǒu
    wèntí?

ILLUSTRATIVE SENTENCES (ENGLISH)

3.2. The [tortoiseshell and bone] inscription on that tortoiseshell is lacking
     quite a few characters.

5.2. Some Chinese characters [each character] can be divided into two parts.
     One part is a pictograph, one part is a phonetic.

9.1. In the Six Categories of Characters the character _míng_ is a compound ideograph. The one character includes two characters, that is, it is made up of the two characters for <u>sun</u> and <u>moon</u>.

10.1. 'Phonetic loan' means to borrow and use, and is also one of the Six Categories of Characters.

12.2. A 'derivative character' is one which is derived from another.

12.3. According to the [news in the] newspaper, our army has changed defeat into victory.

14.1. Each Chinese character has its own particular form.

16.1. Yesterday I made a Western-style suit. Although it wasn't expensive, I made quite a mess of it.

16.3. His lectures are always the same [lit. that set], and I don't want to hear them any more.

18.1. The chief merit of the essays that Mr. Zhang writes is that they are simple and clear.

21.1. Formerly in China if Miss Li married Mr. Zhang she became (known as) Zhang née Li.

21.2. There are altogether fourteen chapters in <u>Mr. Xu's Shuowen</u>.

28.1. That essay he's written I've read from beginning to end, but I don't understand what he means (to say).

28.2. The 'basic meaning' is the first meaning in <u>Shuowen</u>.

28.3. The 'secondary meaning' is an additional meaning. For example, the basic meaning of <u>yuán</u> is 'begin,' the secondary meanings are 'name of a dynasty' and 'dollar.'

30.1. Times change. Now the opinion of the people should be paramount [lit. take opinion of the people as the opinion].

31.2. Actually each day's work isn't too much, but it keeps me busy every day.

31.3. Yesterday when I got to the railroad station the train had long since departed. [Actually] I had made a mistake in the time.

34.1. Darn, my application for a scholarship this time was not granted.

35.1. If the teacher asks us to recite from memory today I certainly won't be able to do so.

36.1. The meeting today is exceptional. Since Committee Member Zhang is leaving, everyone must meet together for a discussion.

38.2. The food produced here is just enough for the local people [to eat].

39.1. Sun Yatsen has said that clothing, food, habitation, and travel are four great essentials of life.

40.1. <u>Yǐnshēn</u> means that from the original meaning one reaches to [lit. speaks to] a deeper and greater meaning.

42.1. Considering the general situation in the country, we will certainly attain victory in this war. (W)

43.1. The news in the paper is that certain armies are coming together in Shan-
tung. Everyone attaches much importance to this matter.

47.2. Some people advocate the Latinization of the National Language.

48.1. The railroad station on Forty-Second Street in New York is translated into
Chinese as 'great central station.'

49.1. He's never inspired any confidence, so no one trusts him.

50.1. The Central Research Institute intends to hold a conference. The date has
already been set for the fifteenth of the present month.   (W)

51.2. Archaeologists discovered some Shang Dynasty writing at [under the ground
of] Xiaotun Village in Anyang District in Honan Province.

59.2. Some people say that spirits are most fearful of the light.

60.2. We don't produce wheat here, so everyone eats rice.

62.1. Miss Ma's clothing is made of hemp cloth.

64.1. The people of Shanghai revile an older person as "this old turtle."

NOTES

1.   In the term liù shū the character shū 'book' has the derived meaning 'writing' and hence the term means 'six writings.' It refers to the six categories
into which Chinese characters are traditionally divided. These are:

a. xiàngxíng 'pictograph' (lit. resemble form). Example: 馬 mǎ 'horse.'

b. zhǐshì 'simple ideograph' (lit. indicate matter). These characters
consist of simple diagrammatic indications of ideas. Thus ⊥ and ⊤
originally represented the ideas now expressed by 上 shàng 'up' and
下 xià 'down.'

c. huìyì 'compound ideograph' (lit. assemble meaning). Example: 明 míng
'bright,' formed by combining 日 rì 'sun' and 月 yuè 'moon.'

d. jiǎjiè 'phonetic loan character' (lit. false borrow). This involves
representing a word by borrowing a character of the same sound but
originally different meaning. Thus in ancient Chinese a character
designating a kind of wheat was borrowed to represent the homoph-
onous word 'come' (in modern Chinese 來 lái).

e. xíngshēng 'radical-phonetic compound' (lit. form sound). This is a
character made up of two parts, a radical element which indicates
the meaning and a phonetic element which indicates the sound. Because of historical shifts in meaning and pronunciation, the two parts
often give only very approximate clues in these areas. Example: 住
zhù 'live' made up of the 'man radical' and 主 zhǔ as the phonetic.

f. zhuǎnzhù 'derivative character' (lit. evolve note). This involves
changing one character into another by a slight modification in the
writing. E.g. 老 lǎo 'old' and 考 kǎo 'examine.'

2. The pattern $V_1 N_1$ de $V_1 N_1$, $V_2 N_2$ de $V_2 N_2$ means 'some did $V_1 N_1$, some did $V_2 N_2$':

    Kàn bào de kàn bào, xiě zî de xiě zî. 'Some read newspapers, some wrote characters.'

3. The terms jiǎ, yǐ, bǐng, dǐng are used much like A, B, C, D in English to designate items in a series or subdivisions in an outline.

4. Shî 'clan name' is used in place of xiānsheng 'Mr.' in formal writing. It is used also in reference to married women when both the maiden name and husband's name are given: Wáng Máo Shî 'Mrs. Wang, née Mao.'

5. The verb nòng is a generalized verb of doing which is best translated into English by a verb appropriate to the context. Thus nòng fàn is to 'cook food,' nòngde hěn máng is 'make very busy.' It is often followed by a resultative verb complement: nòngcuò 'make a mistake,' nònghuài 'spoil, put out of order.'

6. The basic etymological dictionary of Chinese is Shuōwén (lit. discussing writing) by Xǔ Shèn (Hsü Shen; died about 120 A.D.). It is often referred to as Xǔ Shî Shuōwén 'Mr. Xu's Shuowen.' The dictionary analyzes 9553 characters.

7. The term jiǎnbǐzi 'simplified characters' refers to characters which are written in abbreviated form without necessarily having official sanction. Jiǎntǐzi refers to the simplified characters which have been officially put into use in mainland China.

Dì-Shíwǔkè.   Cānkǎo Shū

Bái: Mǎ Jiàoshòu zǎo.

Mǎ : Zǎo.

Bái: Duìbuqǐ wǒ láiwǎn le.   Chǐ zǎodiǎn de shíhou Xuéxīn wèn wǒ yíge
        wèntí, hé ta duō shuōle jǐjù huà, yǐ kàn biǎo bǐ měitiān chū mén-
5   kǒur wǎnle shífēn zhōng.

Mǎ : Méi guānxi.   Zuōtiande Zhuāntí Jiǎnghuà fùshù le méi yǒu?

Bái: Fùshù le.

Mǎ : Oh.   Shàngcì wǒ wàngle gàosu ni.   Shàngcìde fùshù cóng tóu dào
        dǐ shuōde dōu hǎo, kěxī yǒu jǐge zìde zìyīn bù hěn zhǔn.   Yǐhòu
10   zhùyì zhèi yìdiǎn.

Bái: Shìde.   Lùhǎole yǐhòu zìjǐ yě tīngchulai le.   Běnlái xiǎng zài chóng
        lù yícì, kěshi cái tīngwán, yīwèi tóngxué jiu lái le.   Yìzhíde tándào
        shíyīdiǎn cái zǒu.

Mǎ : Zuótiande Zhuāntí Jiǎnghuà yǒu shénmo wèntí ma?

15 Bái: Guānyú Zhuāntí Jiǎnghuà dàoshi méi shénmo wèntí.   Búguò wǒ fù-
        shù de hěn zāogāo, háishi bù rú lǐxiǎng.

Mǎ : Nǐ zuìjìnde lùyīn zhǐshi zài zìyīn hé sìshēng yǒu diar xiǎo máobing,
        zài biéde fāngmiàn dōu hǎo.

Bái: Wǒ xīwang yícì bǐ yícì jiǎnshǎo fāyīn hé sìshēngshangde cuòwu.   Wǒ
20   yǐqián fùshù dōu shi bǎ yuánwén ʰèixialai ránhòu zài lù, xiànzài wǒ
        shi bǎ zìjǐ suǒ jìluxialai de dàzhì shuōyishuō.

Mǎ : Zhèi jiu shi jìnbù le.

Bái: Jīntiande Zhuāntí Jiǎnghuà shi jiǎng "Cānkǎo Shū" ma?

Mǎ : Shìde.   Hǎo, xiànzài wǒmen tǎolùn tǎolùn zhèixiē cér.

25 Bái: Hǎode.

1.0. xì   a play

       tīng xì   listen to Chinese opera

       kàn xì   see a (spoken) play

       jīngxì   Peking opera   [capital opera]

       chàng xì   act [lit. sing] in an opera

1.1. Wàiguo rén yě yǒu xǐhuan kàn Zhōngguo xì de.

1.2. Běijīng rén duōbàn xǐhuan tīng xì.   Běijīng rén guǎn kàn jīngxì
        jiào "tīng xì."

1.3. Zuótian Wáng Xiānsheng qǐng wǒ kàn xì, wǒ méi qù.

1.4. Yǎn jīngxìde rén yǒushi bǎ liǎn yòng yánse huàshang. (T)

1.5. Wǒ yǒu yíge péngyou shi yǒumíngde chàng xì de. (T)

2.0. jù*   drama

     xìjù   drama, play

     huàjù   (spoken) drama

     jùběn   text of a play, script of a play

2.1. Jìnlái yǒu hěn duō hěn yǒumíngde xìjù dōu shi huàjù.

2.2. Nèige huàjùde jùběn shi yíge wénxuéjiā xiě de, hěn yǒu jiàoyude yìyì. (T)

3.0. duǎnpiān xiǎoshuō   short story

     chángpiān xiǎoshuō   novel

3.1. Tā bǎ gōngrén zài gōngchǎng chī kǔ de qíngxing xiěchéng yìpiān duǎnpiān xiǎoshuō.

3.2. Nèiběn chángpiān xiǎoshuō xiě de dōu shi shénhuà.

4.0. xuǎnjí   selected works [select collect]

     quánjí   complete works [whole collect]

4.1. Wǒ yào mǎi yíbù Zhōngguo Gǔwén Xuǎnjí. Bù zhīdào yǒu méi yǒu zhèi yílèide shū?

4.2. Tīngshuō yǒu yíbù shū shi Zhōngshān Quánjí. Nǐ kànguo méi yǒu?

5.0. yìshu   the arts [art skill]

     yìshupǐn   art objects

5.1. Fánshi yìshu dōu hányǒu měide yìsi. (T)

5.2. Nèixiē tóngqì dōu shi gǔdàide yìshupǐn.

Bái: Mǎ Jiàoshòu, xià xīngqī yǒu ge Zhōngguo péngyou qǐng wǒ qu kàn xì qu.

Mǎ : Kàn shénmo xì? Jīngxì háishi huàjù ne?

Bái: Huàjù. Jùshuō jùběn shi hěn yǒumíngde yíwèi zuòjiāde quánjíli xuǎnchulái de yìpiān chángpiān xiǎoshuō. Yǎnyuán yě shi hěn yǒumíngde. Mǎ Jiàoshòu xǐhuan kàn huàjù ma?

Mǎ : Wǒ xǐhuan tīng jīngxì, wǒ yě rènshi jǐge yǒumíngde chàng xì de. Duìyú huàjù zhèizhǒng yìshu bú dà yǒu xìngqu. Nǐmen xīngqījǐ qù?

Bái: Xīngqīliù.

Mǎ : Piào mǎihǎole ma?

Bái: Nèiwèi péngyou yǐjing bǎ piào mǎihǎo le.

Mǎ : Wǒ tīngshuō zuìjìn měitiān kàn xî de rén hěn duō. Xīngqīliù rén
        yídìng gèng duō le.

6.0. xuǎnzé   choose, select [select select]

6.1. Nǐ yào mǎi mùliào yīngdāng dào mùchǎngli qu xuǎnzé.

7.0. huì*   collection

      zìhuì   list of characters, vocabulary

      cíhuì   word-list, vocabulary

      huìbiān   compendium

7.1. Zìhuì yǒu liǎngzhǒng. Yǒu yìzhǒng shi yǒu zìyî de. Yǒu yìzhǒng
      shi zhǐ yǒu zì ér bù jiěshì zìyî de. (T)

7.2. Zhōngguode cíhuì yǒu hǎojǐzhǒng, nèiróng dōu chàbuduō.

7.3. Wǒ nèibèn Xiàndài Hànyǔ Huìbiān zài nǐ nèr ma?

8.0. chá   look up (in a dictionary)

      chákàn   look into (a matter), investigate

8.1. Nǐ rúguǒ yǒu bú rènshi de zì, kéyi qu chá zìdiǎn.

8.2. Tā cóngqián zuòguo bù hǎode shì, suǒyǐ jìnlái zhèngfǔ shícháng
      jiào rén lái chákàn tāde xíngdòng.

9.0. bù   radical of a character   (M)

      bùshǒu   radical of a character [section head]

9.1. Qǐng wèn, Cāng Jiēde cāng zì zài chá zìdiǎn de shíhou, yīngdāng
      chá něi yíbù? (T)

9.2. Tā bǎ zìdiǎnde bùshǒu dōu bèixialai le.

9.3. Zài zìdiǎnde bùshǒuli yǒu gútoude gǔ zhèi yíbù ma? (T)

9.4. Nǐ yào mǎi ànzhe bùshǒu chá de zìdiǎn, háishi yào mǎi ànzhe pīn-
      yīn chá de zìdiǎn? (T)

10.0. qiè   cut

      fǎnqiè   (1) traditional Chinese system of spelling; (2) to spell by the
      fǎnqiè system [reverse cut] (see note 5)

      Qièyùn   (title of book on phonology written in the Sui Dynasty)

10.1. Nǐ xuéguo fǎnqiè, nǐ zhīdao guī zì shi zěnmo qiè ma? (T)

10.2. Qièyùn shi yùnshūde yìzhǒng. Tāde nèiróng suǒ shuō de dōu shi
      zìde yīnyùn, shi yánjiu yīnyùnxuéde yìzhǒng cānkǎo shū.

10.3. Wǒmen zài zìdiǎnli kéyi kàndao jiā zìde yīn shi yòng jīběnde jī hé
      yāzide yā fǎnqiè de. (T)

10.4. Fǎnqiède fāngfǎ shi yòng liǎngge zì. Dì-yīge zì qiè yīn, dì-èrge zì
      qiè yùn. (T)

11.0. hàomǎ(r)   a mark, a number   [mark figure]

sîjiǎo hàomǎ(r)   four-corner system   (see note 4)

11.1. Túshūguǎnde shū dōu biānzhe hàomǎr.   (T)

11.2. Wáng Yúnwǔ biān de sìjiǎo hàomǎr zìdiǎn wǒ jiù zhīdao yíge dàgài, wǒ hái bú huî yòng.   (T)

Bái: Mǎ Jiàoshòu, wǒ yào mǎi yîběn zìdiǎn.   Nín shuō něizhǒngde hǎo
40   ne?

Mǎ : Kàn nǐ xūyào něizhǒng.   Gè yǒu gède yōudiǎn.   Dào shūdiàn qu kànyikàn zîjǐ xuǎnzé yíxiàr.

Bái: Wǒ shi xiǎng yào mǎi yîběn cídiǎn.   Wǒ suîrán yǐqián mǎiguo liǎngběn cíhuî, dōu méi yǒu xiángxîde jiěshî, méi yǒu yîběn kěyòngde.

45   Mǎ : Nǐ shi yào Zhōng-Yīngwénde, háishi zhǐ shi Zhōngwénde ne?

Bái: Wǒ yào Zhōngwénde, yào ànzhe bùshǒu chá de nèi yîzhǒng de.

Mǎ : Zìdiǎnde zhǒnglèi tài duō le.   Xiàng zìdiǎn、zîhuî、cídiǎn、cíhuî
děngdengde.

Bái: Shî bu shi suǒyǒude cíhuî、zîhuî dōu méi yǒu jiěshî?

50   Mǎ : Zìdiǎn、cídiǎn cái yǒu jiěshî.   Zîhuî gēn cíhuî juédàduōshù shi méi
yǒu jiěshî de.

Bái: Yǐqiánde dà zìdiǎn yào zhīdao zìyīn, zhǐshi yòng fǎnqiè.   Wàiguo
rén yòng fǎnqiè nèizhǒng fázi xiāngdāng kùnnán.

Mǎ : Fǎnqiè kéyi shuō shi Zhōngguo pīnyīnde yìzhǒng lǎo fāngfǎ.

12.0. yùgào   advance notice   [before inform]

12.1. Yùgào jiu shi "shíqián gàosu" de yìsi.

13.0. fēnlèi   classify, put into categories   [divide category]

13.1. Nǐ zhīdao Shuōwénlide zì shi zěnmo fēnlèi de ma?

14.0. liú   (1) keep, reserve, hold on to; (2) leave behind, keep behind,
detain; (3) transmit

liúxia   put aside, put by

liúxīn   pay attention to   [detain heart]

liúyì   give attention to   [detain idea]

14.1. Nǐ yídìng yào zǒu, wǒ jiu bù liú nǐ le.   (T)

14.2. Yǒu yíduì jūnrén bǎ wǒmen cūnzilide liángshi dōu názǒu le, jiù liú-
xiale yìdiǎr màizi.

14.3. Zuò huǒchēde shíhou, nǐ yào liúxīn zìjǐde dōngxi.

14.4. Tāde tóufa liúde hěn cháng.   (T)

14.5. Tā shuō de bǐyù wǒ méi liúyì, suóyǐ wǒ shuōbushànglái.

15.0. bàodǎo   (1) announce, report; (2) announcement, report   [report
       guide]

15.1. Nèiběn zázhìde nèiróng duōbàn shi bàodǎo Guómíndǎngde shìqing de.

16.0. jiǎnjiè   a brief introduction, a notice

16.1. Jiǎnjiè jiu shi "jiǎndān jièshao" de yìsi.

55   Mǎ : Yǒu yíbù Guóyǔ Chángyòng Cí Huìbiān. Bù zhīdào nǐ yǒuyòng méi
            yǒu. Nǐ kéyi dào shūdiàn qu kànkan.

     Bái: Yǒude shíhou xiǎng mǎi xīn shū, kěshi bù zhīdào zěnmo qu zhǎo.

     Mǎ : Nǐ zuì hǎo cháng kàn túshū mùlù. Shàngmian dōu yǒu yùgào. Bìng-
            qiě mùlùshangde shū dōu yíxiàngyíxiàngde fēnlèi.   Zhìyú mǎi xīn
60   shū, nǐ liúyì xīn shū bàodǎo huòzhě xīn shū jiǎnjiè.

     Bái: Wǒ yě cháng kàn túshū mùlù. Suīrán wǒ xiànzài shǒubiān yǒude
            shū hái kànbuwán ne, kěshi yǒude shíhou wǒ yào zhǎo cānkǎo zī-
            liào.

17.0. Cíyuán   (book title) [words source]

17.1. Guānyú zì hé cí de cānkǎo shū, yìbān rén dōu yòng Cíyuán huòzhe
       shi Cíhǎi.

18.0. shāowēi   slightly, somewhat [somewhat tiny]

18.1. Qǐng nǐ bǎ zhèige zìde yīndiào niànde shāowēi qīng yìdiǎr.

19.0. suǒyǐn   (1) index; (2) list of contents

19.1. Shūli suǒyǐnde yòngtú shi jiào nǐ hěn kuài jiu zhīdao nǐ yào zhǎo
       de zài shūlide shénmo dìfang huòzhě shi dì-jǐyè.

     Bái: Mǎ Jiàoshòu, Cíyuán 、 Cíhǎi zhèi liǎngběn cídiǎn nèiróng dàtóng-
65   xiǎoyì, wèi-shénmo yào yǒu liǎngběn ne?

     Mǎ : Zhèi liǎngběn dà zìdiǎn gēnběn chàbuduō. Yīnwei bú shi yíge dì-
            fang chūbǎn de, suóyǐ yòng liǎngge míngchēng.

     Bái: Zhèi liǎngběn cídiǎn, wǒ xǐhuan chá Cíhǎi. Shāowēi jiǎndān yìdiǎr.
            Bùshǒu suǒyǐn yě bǐjiǎo róngyi.

20.0. Kāngxī   (reign-title, 1662-1723)

20.1. Kāngxī shi Qīng Cháo huángdìde niánhào. Zhèiwèi huángdì jiào rén
       biānle yíbù zìdiǎn jiào Kāngxī Zìdiǎn.

21.0. shìyòng   (1) sufficient for use, answers the purpose, usable, appli-
                 cable, applied; (2) application, applicability [suitable use]

21.1. Qīng Cháode fǎlù, dàole Mínguó jiu bú shìyòng le.

22.0. juàn   (1) document, records; (2) chapter, section (M)

kāi-juàn-yǒu-yì   there is profit in opening a scroll—i. e. in reading
books

22.1. Zhōngguo Wénxuéshǐ yígòng yǒu shàng﹑zhōng﹑xià sānjuàn.

22.2. Kāi-juàn-yǒu-yì zhèijù huà shi ràng rén duō kàn shūde yìsi. Tāde
yìsi shi shuō zhǐyào dǎkāile shūběn qu kàn, shi juéduì yǒu hǎochu
de.

23.0. yuèdú   to read (W) [read read]

23.1. Wǒ zuì xǐhuan yuèdú wénxué míngzhù, wǒ yǐjing dúguo shíjǐbù. (W)

24.0. suíbǐ   miscellaneous jottings [follow pen]

24.1. Suíbǐ jiu shi "suibiàn yòng bǐ xiěchulai" de yìsi.

70   Bái: Mǎ Jiàoshòu, nín yǒu Kāngxī Zìdiǎn ma?

Mǎ : Yǒu. Zhèibù shū xiànzài bú dà shìyòng le.

Bái: Nèiróng gēn Xǔ Shì Shuōwén yíyàng ma?

Mǎ : Bù yíyàng. Zhèi liǎngbù shū dōu gè yǒu gède dútède yōudiǎn.

Bái: Kāngxī Zìdiǎn zhèibù shū hěn dà ba?

75   Mǎ : Zhèibù zìdiǎn yǒu sìshi'èrjuàn. Zài cóngqián zhèibù zìdiǎn shi zuì
wánquánde le. Yígòng yǒu sìwàn duō zì.

Bái: Zuótian zài túshūguǎn zhǎo cānkǎo zīliào kànjiàn yìběn Yuèdú Suíbǐ. Wénzhāng xiěde zhēn hǎo.

25.0. értóng   children (W) [child child]

25.1. Xiě értóng yòng de shū yào dǒngde értóng xīnlǐ.

26.0. dúwù   reading matter (W) [read thing]

26.1. Értóng dúwù duōbàn shi yǒu túhuà de.

27.0. zuòpǐn   a work (of literature, art, etc.) (W) [do article]

27.1. Shǐjì shi yǒumíngde lìshǐ zuòpǐn, yě shi zuì hǎode wénxué zuòpǐn.

28.0. gāncuì   (1) direct, unequivocal, clear-cut; (2) would be best if . . .

28.1. Tā xué Lādīngwén, xuéle hǎojǐge yuè yě bú jìnbù. Tā shuō: "Wǒ
wèi-shénmo bìděi xué Lādīngwén ne? Gāncuì bù xué le."

29.0. dìng   (1) order merchandise; (2) subscribe to a periodical

29.1. Wǒ yào dìng zázhì. Bù zhīdào shi dìng yìnián hǎo ne háishi dìng
bànnián hǎo? (T)

30.0. cóngshū   collectanea, collection of books published in a set [thicket
book]

30.1. Wǒ yào mǎi yíbù értóng gùshi cóngshū.

30.2. Zài <u>Shìjiè Zhīshi Xiǎo Cōngshūli</u>, yǒu méi yǒu guānyu wùlǐ huàxué
      de? (T)

Bái: Qián jǐtiān yǒu yíge zài Měiguo de Zhōngguo péngyou gěi wǒ láixìn,
80   ràng wǒ zài zhèr gěi tāmende xiǎoháizi mǎi jǐběn "értóng dúwù."
          Zhèige kě bǎ wǒ gěi nánzhù le.   Wǒ bù zhīdào bā-jiǔsuìde xiǎo-
          háizi yīnggāi kàn shénmo shū.

Mǎ : Xiǎoháizi kàn de shū hěn duō.   Yìxiē zuòpǐn dōu bú cuò. Gāncuì
          nǐ gěi ta dìng yítào <u>Xiǎo Péngyou</u>. Nà shi xiǎoháizi zuì xǐhuan kàn
85   de zázhì. Nǐ zài gěi ta mǎi jǐběn <u>Shìjiè Zhīshi Xiǎo Cōngshū</u>.

31.0. yóujì   travel journal [travel record]

31.1. Yǒu hěn duō yóujì zài wénxuéshang hěn yǒu jiàzhi.

32.0. zhuàn   biography

       zhuànjì   biography [biography record]

       zìzhuàn   autobiography   [self biography]

32.1. Wǒ zuì xǐhuan kàn <u>Shǐjìlide</u> zhuàn.   (T)

32.2. Zhuànjì shi xiě mǒu yíge rén yìshēngde shìqing.   Zìzhuàn shi zìjǐ
       xiě zìjǐ guòqude shìqing.

32.3. Tā zài zìzhuànli shuō tā xiǎode shíhou zuì bù xǐhuan bèi shū.   (T)

33.0. niánjiàn   yearbook [year mirror]

33.1. Tā yǒu yìběn yī-jiǔ-liù-wǔ-nián <u>Xiānggǎng Jīngji Niánjiàn</u>.

34.0. sǎnwén   (1) prose; (2) essay [loose writing]

34.1. Zhāng Xiānsheng shi ge shīrén.   Tāde zuòpǐn dōu shi shī.   Tā jué
       bù xiě sǎnwén.

Bái: Mǎ Jiàoshòu, yóujì zhèizhǒng wénzhāng shi shénmo xìngzhi de?

Mǎ : Shi yìzhǒng lǚxíng xìngzhi de, jiu shi bǎ lǚxíng de shíhou suǒ kàn-
          jian de huòzhě suǒ xiǎng de xiěchulai de wénzhāng. Yǒu shíhou xiě
          sǎnwén, yǒude shíhou yě zuò shī.

90 Bái: Zhuànjì shì bu shi zìzhuàn?

Mǎ : Zìzhuàn shi xiě zìji, zhuànjì shi xiě biérén.

Bái: Niánjiàn ne?

Mǎ : Niánjiàn shi jìlù yìniánde gèzhǒng dàshì gēn tǒngjì děng, mùdì shi
          róngyi chákàn.

35.0. fǒuzé(de huà)   otherwise, or else

35.1. Nǐ yǐhòu bù zhǔn mà rén, fǒuzéde huà wǒ yào dǎ ni le.

36.0. kuòhú   parentheses, brackets [include arc]

36.1. Zài shùxuéshang yào xiān jìsuàn kuòhúlide shùmù.   (T)

37.0. zìpáng(r)   (1) side of a character; (2) side radical

      zìtóu(r)   (1) top of a character; (2) top radical

37.1. Zài zìdiǎnli yào chá fànwéide fàn 範 zì shi chá chē zìpáng háishi
      chá zhú zìtóu ne?   (T)

38.0. chúdiào   exclude, except, remove [deduct drop]

38.1. Míng 明 zì chúdiào rì zì jiu shi yíge yuè zì.   (T)

39.0. wēixiǎn, wéixiǎn   dangerous [perilous danger]

39.1. Hē jiǔ de rén kāi chē shi hěn wéixiǎnde yíjiàn shì.

95 Bái: Fǒuzéde huà zhǐ yòng fǒuzé yě kéyi, shì bu shi?

   Mǎ : Kéyi. Nǐ kàn cíbiǎoshang fǒuzé(de huà), (de huà) yǒu kuòhú, biǎo-
        shi kéyi zhǐ yòng fǒuzé.

   Bái: Gāncuìde cuì 脆 yàoshi bǎ ròu zìpáng chúdiào jiu shi wéixiǎnde
        wéi 危, shì bu shi?

100 Mǎ : Duìle.

   Bái: Shuō wéixiǎn wǒ gàosu nín yíjiàn shì. Qiántian hé yíge tóngxué zuò
        chē qu wár, zǒuzai gōnglùshang hūrán duìmiàn láile ge chē kāide
        tài kuài le, chà yìdiǎr jiu chū shì, zhēn wéixiǎn

   Mǎ : Yǒu rén jiù xǐhuan kāi kuài chē. zhēnshi bù míngbai tāmende xīn-
105   lǐ.

40.0. shuāng   double, pair (M)

      Shuāngshíjié Double Tenth (i. e. Oct. 10, national day of Republic
                    of China)

40.1. Shuāng shi "yíyàngde dōngxi yǒu liǎngge" de yìsi. Bǐfang shuō "yì-
      shuāng kuàizi."

40.2. Shíyue shírì shi Zhōnghuá Mínguóde Shuāngshíjié.

41.0. zhǔnbèi   prepare, get ready [regulate prepare]

41.1. Xià xīngqī yào dàkǎo le, wǒ bìděi zhǔnbèi wǒde gōngke le.

42.0. pù(zi)   store (N)

42.1. Wǒ zài Běijīngde shíhou, cháng dào mài jiù shūde pùzili qu kàn jiù
      shū.

42.2. Nèige pùzi mài de dōngxi dōu shi yìshupǐn.

43.0. qùwei   interest (N)

43.1. Yǒu rén juéde chàng xì shi hěn yǒu qùwei de.

44.0. fēng   wind   (N)

dàfēng   (1) big wind; (2) typhoon

fēngzāi   windstorm [wind disaster]

fēnglì   force of the wind   [wind strength]

44.1. Jīntian hĕn rè, lián yìdiăr fēng dōu méi yŏu.

44.2. Yánhăi yídài shícháng yŏu dàfēng.

44.3. Yŏude dìfang cháng yŏu fēngzāi, sŭnhài hĕn dà.

44.4. Yīnwei fēnglìde guānxi, chuán zŏude tài màn le.

45.0. shāng   (1) injure, wound; (2) injury, wound

shòushāng   be wounded, be injured   [receive injury]

shāngfēng   (1) catch cold (VO); (2) a cold [wound wind]

sĭshāng   (1) die and be wounded; (2) dead and wounded

45.1. Huŏchē chū shì le, shòushāng de rén hĕn duō.

45.2. Wŏ jīntian méi dào xuéxiào qu, yīnwei wŏ shāngfēng le.

45.3. Mĕicì zhànzhēng lăobăixìng dōu yŏu sĭshāng.

Bái: Zhèlĭ yŏu yíge cér shi Shuāngshíjié.

Mă : Hái yŏu wŭtiān jiu shi shíyue shíhào. Wŏ xiăode shíhou zuì xĭhuan
      Shuāngshíjié zhèi yìtiān, yīnwei shíyue shíhào shi wŏ fùqinde shēng-
      ri. Fùqin shēngri zhèitiān jiāli hĕn rènao, érqiĕ xuéxiào yòu fàng-
110   jià.

Bái: Nín yòu gāi zhŭnbèi gĕi nín fùqin sòng shēngri lĭ le.

Mă : Zuótian dào pùzi qu kànleyikàn, bù zhīdào măi shénmo hăo. Kànle
      bàntiān méi dōngxi kĕ măi. Wŏ fùqin shuōguo, zuì yŏu qùweide
      shìqing shi kàn shū.

115 Bái: Nín măi yìbĕn shū sòng ta.

Mă : Tāde shū duōde bùdeliăo. Wŏ yĕ bù zhīdào yīnggāi măi shénmo
      shū. Zhèixiē shìqing mĕinián dōu shi wŏ nèiren qu bàn. Zhèi jĭ-
      tiān tā shāngfēng le, suŏyĭ jiu dĕi wŏ qù le. Wŏ zuì pà măi dōng-
      xi.

46.0. láo-ér-wú-gōng   work to no avail   (W) [toil and lack accomplish-
                                            ment]

46.1. Zuò gōng de rén rúguŏ bú zhàozhe zhŭrénde yìsi qu zuò shi láo-
      ér-wú-gōng de.   (T)

47.0. căo   (1) grass; (2) cursive (in reference to characters)

căozì   running hand characters

47.1. Wŏ fángzide qiánbiān yòu yŏu huā yòu yŏu căo, shífēn hăokàn.

47.2. Tāde zì xiěde tài cǎo le, wǒ kànbuqīngchu.

47.3. Wǒ búdàn bú huì xiě cǎozì, érqiě yě bú rènshi cǎozì.

48.0. yuánzé   principle [source principle]

48.1. Jiǎ, yǐ, bǐng, dīng sìge rén dōu lái qiú wǒ xiě zì. Wǒ duì tāmen shuō: "Nǐmen jiào wǒ xiě zì, nà hěn róngyi, kěshi wǒ yǒu yíge yuánzé, zhǐ xiě dà zì bù xiě xiǎo zì."

49.0. hēibǎn   blackboard

49.1. Hēibǎnshang shi shéi xiě de zì? Xiěde hěn hǎo a!

50.0. jiǎnyào   (1) sketch, compendium; (2) concise, sketchy (W) [brief important]

50.1. Nèiběn shūde yǒudiǎn hěn jiǎnyào míngbai, suǒyǐ yǒu hěn duō rén dōu shuō nèiběn shū hǎo. (T)

120 Bái: Mǎ Jiàoshòu, láo-ér-wú-gōngde láo 劳 zì, yǒude rén xiě cǎo zìtóur. Cǎo zìtóur gēn huǒ zìtóur shi yíyàng ma?

    Mǎ : Shi yíge zì. Cǎo zìtóur shi jiǎnxiě de.

    Bái: Shì bu shi yǒu zhèiyàngr yíge yuánzé: fánshi huǒ zìtóu, jiǎnxiě kéyi yòng cǎo zìtóu, zhú zìtóude zì, jiǎnxiě jiu bù néng yòng cǎo zì-
125   tóu?

    Mǎ : Bù yídìng. Nǐ kàn hēibǎnshang jiǎnyàode jiǎn 简 zì jiu bù néng yòng cǎo zìtóur. Kěshi děngjíde děng 等 yě kéyi xiě cǎo zìtóur.

    Bái: Mǎ Jiàoshòu, hēibǎnshangde zì shi nín xiě de ma?

    Mǎ : Shìde.

130 Bái: Nín zì xiěde zhēn hǎo. Zhèixiēge zì gèger dōu nènmo hǎo.

51.0. mínsú   popular customs, folkways (W) [people common]

    súyǔ   common saying, maxim, proverb [common speech]

51.1. Mínsú jiu shi mínjiānde fēngsu. Yíge guójiā yǒu yíge guójiāde mín- sú, yíge shídài yǒu yíge shídàide fēngsu.

51.2. Súyǔ jiu shi yìbān rén chángcháng shuō de hěn yǒu dàolǐ de huà. Bǐfang shuō "Xíguan chéng zìrán" jiu shi yíge súyǔ. (T)

52.0. páiliè   arrange in a series (W) [line up rows]

52.1. Yīngwén zìdiǎnde zì shi àn Yīngwén zìmǔde cìxu páiliè de. Zhōng- wén zìdiǎnde zì shi àn bùshǒu páiliè de.

53.0. tíshǒu(r)   'lifting hand' (radical)

53.1. Zài Liù Shūli zhǐshìde zhǐ 指 zì zuǒbiār shi yíge tíshǒur.

54.0. qiáo   look at

    qiáojian   see

54.1. Nǐ jiào wǒ wǎng tiānshang qiáo. Wǒ zěnmo shénmo yě méi qiáojian
ne? (T)

Mǎ : Nǐ shuō mínsú gēn súyǔ yǒu shénmo bùtóng?

Bái : Súyǔ shi rénmen chángcháng shuō de yìzhǒng huà. Mínsú shi mínjiānde fēngsu, bǐfang guònián guòjié shénmode.

Mǎ : Duìle.

135 Bái : Shuō mínsú zhèige cér wǒ xiǎngqilai le. Zhèlǐ yǒu méi yǒu chūbǎn
de guānyu mínsúde gùshi shū?

Mǎ : Yǒu. Wǒ qián jǐtiān zài Dà Huá Shūdiàn qiáojian yìběn Mínsú Gùshi Xuǎnjí, nǐ kéyi qu kànkan.

Bái : Mǎ Jiàoshòu, páiliè de pái shì bu shi tíshǒu?

140 Mǎ : Shìde.

55.0. lìrér   'standing man' (radical)

       dānlìrér   'single standing man' (radical)

       shuānglìrér   'double standing man' (radical)

55.1. Xíngdòngde xíng 行 zuǒbiār shi shuānglìrér. Lìwàide lì 例 zuǒbiār
shi dānlìrér.

56.0. biānji   (1) edit, put together; (2) editor   [edit edit]

56.1. Tā shi Wénxué Zhōukānde biānji.

56.2. Chángshí Cōngshū shi wǒmen sānge rén gòngtóng biānji de.

57.0. jiǎshè   (1) if, supposing that; (2) hypothesis [false establish]

57.1. Jiǎshè shìjiè rénlèi dōu shuō yìzhǒng yǔyán, bǐcǐde yìsi jiu gèng
róngyi biǎodá le.

58.0. chónggǎi   revise [again change]

58.1. Zhèige gērde yīndiào bú tài hǎo, néng bu néng chónggǎi yíxià?

59.0. sāndiǎn shuǐ   'three-dot water' (radical)

       liǎngdiǎn shuǐ   'two-dot water' (radical)

       sìdiǎn huǒ   'four-dot fire' (radical)

59.1. Juédìngde jué 决 zì shi liǎngdiǎn shuǐ, yǒu shíhou yě xiě sāndiǎn
shuǐ.

59.2. Kāngxīde xī 熙 、hēibǎnde hēi 黑 xiàbiàn dōu shi sìdiǎn huǒ.

59.3. Nǐ rúguǒ dǒngde sāndiǎn shuǐ、liǎngdiǎn shuǐ děngděng bùshǒude
cér, nǐ jiu kéyi gàosu biérén zěnmo qu chá zìdiǎn le. (T)

Bái : Mǎ Jiàoshòu, wǒ yǐqián chá zìdiǎnde shíhou chá yìtiáo chuánde tiáo

條 zî, zǒng rènwei shi zài rén bù ne, zěnmo chá yě zhǎobuzháo. Zhèige zì yuánlái shi zài mù bù. Kěshi shíhoude hòu 候 zài rénbù, suànshi lîrér.

145 Mǎ : Wǒ yě bù qīngchu yuánlái biānji zîdiǎnde shíhou dàodǐ shi gēnju shénmo fǎzé. Jiǎshè xiànzài yǒu rén yào chóng biān zîdiǎnde huà, yídìng yào chónggǎi.

Bái : Wǒ hái yǒu yíge wèntí, yǒu "sāndiǎn shuǐ" zhèige cér, yǒu méi yǒu "liǎngdiǎn shuǐ" ya?

150 Mǎ : Yǒu. Tiānqi hěn lěngde lěng 冷 zì jiu shi liǎngdiǎn shuǐ ya.

60.0. tōngxùn   (1) send news; (2) news (W) [go through news]

       tōngxùnshè   (1) press agency; (2) Associated Press

       tōngxùn bàodǎo   news report, news reporting

60.1. Xiànzài tōngxùn de fāngfǎ bǐ gǔdàide kuài duō le.

60.2. Bàozhǐshang yǒu yíduàn "Huáběi Tōngxùn," nǐ kànguole méi yǒu? (T)

60.3. Nèige tōngxùnshède tōngxùn bàodǎo bǐjiǎo quèshi.

61.0. yú   in, at (W) (see note 1)

61.1. Wáng Jiàoshòu yú wǔyuè liùrî yào dào mǒu dàxué qu jiǎngyǎn. (W)

62.0. rú   (1) be like; (2) for example; (3) such as (W)

       rúhé   how? be like what? (W) [like what]

62.1. Qiúxué rú zǒu lù, bìxu yíbùyíbùde wǎng qián zǒu.

62.2. Nǐ bù nǔlì xuéxí rúhé néng jìnbù? (W)

63.0. lîhai   severe [severe harm]

63.1. Tā jiēdao tā jiějiede diànbào, shuō tā mǔqin bìngde hěn lîhai.

64.0. guā   blow (V)

       guā fēng   be windy (VO)

64.1. Zuótian guā dàfēng, bǎ wǒ jiāde fángzi guāhuài le. (T)

Bái : Mǎ Jiàoshòu, zuìjìn Huánán yánhǎi yǒu fēngzāi, shì bu shi?

Mǎ : Shìde. Wǒ zuótian kàn Dà Huá Rîbàoshang yǒu yíduàn "Huánán Tōngxùn" shuōdào zhèicî yánhǎi fēngzāide qíngxing, dàyì shi: "Yú běnyuè wǔrî Huánán yánhǎi hūrán dàfēng, rénmín suǒ shòu de sǔn-
155   shī xiāngdāng dà, sǐshāngle bù shǎo rén. Zhǐyú sǔnshī ruògān, xiángxìde qíngxing rúhé, xiànzài hái méi fázi tǒngjì."

Bái : Fēngzāi zěnmo zhènmo lîhai ne. Tīngshuō Xiānggǎng、Táiwān yě shícháng guā dàfēng, shì bu shi?

Mǎ : Shìde. Yǒu yìnián Xiānggǎng guā dàfēng, bǎ hǎilǐde dàchuán gěi
160   guādao lùdìshang qu le. Nǐ kàn fēnglî yǒu duōma dà.

SHĒNGCÍ BIǍO

1. xì
   tīng xì
   kàn xì
   jīngxì
   chàng xì

2. jù*
   xìjù
   huàjù
   jùběn

3. duǎnpiān xiǎoshuō
   chángpiān xiǎoshuō

4. xuǎnjí
   quánjí

5. yìshu
   yìshupǐn

6. xuǎnzé

7. huì*
   zìhuì
   cíhuì
   huìbiān

8. chá
   chákàn

9. bù
   bùshǒu

10. qiè
    fǎnqiè
    Qièyùn

11. hàomǎ(r)
    sìjiǎo hàomǎ(r)

12. yùgào

13. fēnlèi

14. liú
    liúxia
    liúxīn
    liúyì

15. bàodǎo

16. jiǎnjiè

17. Cíyuán

18. shāowēi

19. suǒyǐn

20. Kāngxī

21. shìyòng

22. juàn
    kāi-juàn-yǒu-yì

23. yuèdú (W)

24. suíbǐ

25. értóng (W)

26. dúwù (W)

27. zuòpǐn (W)

28. gāncuì

29. dìng

30. cōngshū

31. yóujì

32. zhuàn
    zhuánjì
    zìzhuàn

33. niánjiàn

34. sǎnwén

35. fǒuzé(de huà)

36. kuòhú

37. zìpáng(r)
    zìtóu(r)

38. chúdiào

39. wēixiǎn, wéixiǎn

40. shuāng
    Shuāngshíjié

41. zhǔnbèi

42. pù(zi)

43. qùwei

44. fēng
    dàfēng

fēngzāi
fēnglì

45. shāng
    shòushāng
    shāngfēng
    sǐshāng

46. láo-ér-wú-gōng

47. cǎo
    cǎozî

48. yuánzé

49. hēibǎn

50. jiǎnyào (W)

51. mínsú (W)
    súyǔ

52. páiliè (W)

53. tíshǒu(r)

54. qiáo
    qiáojian

55. lìrér
    dānlìrér
    shuānglìrér

56. biānji

57. jiǎshè

58. chónggǎi

59. sāndiǎn shuǐ
    liǎngdiǎn shuǐ
    sìdiǎn huǒ

60. tōngxùn (W)
    tōngxùnshè
    tōngxùn bàodǎo

61. yú (W)

62. rú (W)
    rúhé (W)

63. lìhai

64. guā
    guā fēng

YǓFǍ LIÀNXÍ

A. V + yú (see note 1)

1. Wǒmen yīngdāng duō zuò yǒulìyú dàzhòng de shì.

2. Nǐ nèiběn zìhuì yàoshi bù jíyú xūyào de huà wǒ zài jièyòng jǐtiān.

3. Yīnwei tā mángyú dào tōngxùnshè qù, suǒyǐ tā bú dào zhèr lái le.

4. Zhèicì dàfēng rénmín suǒ shòu de sǔnshī dàyú shàngcì.

5. Zhèiběn cíhuì hěn hǎo. Lǐmiànde cér duōyú nèiběn.

6. Wǒ xiě de zhèiběn xuǎnjí zǎoyú nèibù chángpiān xiǎoshuō.

7. Tā jíyú yào zhǎo nèi jǐkuài guījiǎ, wèideshì yánjiu jiǎgǔwén.

8. Wǒ zài shānghuì zuò kuàiji, dàole měiyuède yuèdǐ mángyú suànzhàng, yìdiǎn gōngfu dōu méi yǒu.

9. Yǒu rén shuō, zài jiātíngli tàitaide dìwei gāoyú yíqiè.

10. Pò yīfu qiángyú méi yǒu yīfu.

B. SV + dào (see note 2)

11. Nèiběn cídiǎn guìdào jiǔshikuài qián yìběn, háishi yǒu rén mǎi.

12. Zhèicì dàfēng dàdào bù néng zài dà le.

13. Zuótiande xì zhēn hǎo. Kàn xì de rén tài duō, duōdào méi yǒu zuò de dìfang le.

14. Nèige tōngxùnshède bàodǎo zāogāodào méi rén xiāngxìn le.

15. Nǐ nèipiān tōngxùn bàodǎo de zì xiěde tài cǎo, cǎodào jiǎnzhíde kànbuchūlái le.

C. NV → VN (see note 3)

16. Wǒ zhèng yào qu tīng xì hūrán jiāli láile rén.

17. Tā niánji nènmo xiǎo jiu zài jūnduìli zuò shì, yuányīn shi hěn zǎo tā jiu sǐle fùqin le.

18. Zhāng Dàwén zhēn méi xìnyong. Tā bǎ wǒ xìjùde kèběn jièqu le, shuō shàng xīngqī jiu gěi wo. Dào jīntian yě méi gěi wo, zhēn qìsi wo le.

19. Wǒmen lóuxià zhùle yíwèi lǎo tàitai, yīnwei niánji tài lǎo le yìtiān sāndùn fàn dōu bù néng zìjǐ zuò le.

20. Zhèlide qìhou hěn bù hǎo, suǒyǐ jìnlai bìngle hěn duō értóng. (W)

JIǍNGHUÀ

Zhūwèi tóngxué:

Shàngcì jiǎng de shi "Zhōngguode Wénzì." Wǒ xiǎng zhūwèi tīngle

zhīhòu duìyú Zhōngguo wénzì yǐjing zhīdao yíge dàgài. Jīntian yào jiǎng
de shi "Cānkǎo Shū."

5   Zhūwèi mùqián zuì xūyàode cānkǎo shū yǒu liǎngzhǒng.   Yìzhǒng
shi guānyu zì hé cí de, yìzhǒng shi guānyu yǔwén chángshì de. Zài xuǎnzé zhèi liǎngzhǒng shū zhīqián yào yǒu yíge yàojǐnde yuánzé, yào xuǎn
jiǎnyàode.   Huàn yíjù huà shuō jiu shi yào xuǎn zuì yǒuyòngde, fǒuzéde
huà shi láo-ér-wú-gōng de.

10   Zì hé cí de cānkǎo shū dàjiā dōu zhīdao shi zìdiǎn hé cídiǎn、zìhuì
hé cíhuì děngděng. Zài zhèixiē shūli yǒude shi Zhōngwén de, yě jiu shi
zhǐ yǒu Hànzì de. Yǒude shi Zhōng-wàiwénde, yě jiu shi yòu yǒu Zhōngwén yòu yǒu wàiwén de, xiàng Zhōng-Yīngwénde、Zhōng-Fàwénde、Zhōng-
Éwénde、Zhōng-Déwénde、Zhōng-Rìwénde děngděng.   Guānyú Zhōng-wài-
15 wén zài yíkuàr de zìdiǎn, zhūwèi yěxǔ yǐjing huì shǐyòng le, xiànzài jiǎngjiang zěnyàng chá Zhōngwénde zìdiǎn.   Chá Zhōngwén zìdiǎn xiān yào
dǒngde de shi "bùshǒu." Zhèixiē bùshǒu yígòng yǒu èrbǎi shísìge, dōu
yìnzai zìdiǎnde zuì qiánmian. Tāmende páiliè cìxu shi bǐhuá shǎo de zài
qián, bǐhuá duō de zài hòu.   Zài zhèixiē bùshǒuli suīrán dōu shi Hànzì,
20 kěshi yǒude bùshǒude niànfǎ shi hěn tèbié de. Bǐrú wǒ zài hēibǎnshang
xiě de zhèige bùshǒu 氵 shi shuǐ bù, kěshi niàn de shíhou cháng shuō
shi "sāndiǎn shuǐ." Wǒ zài xiě yíge bùshǒu 亻 shi rén bù, niàn de shíhou niànzuo "lìrér." Yòu rú 彳 jiàozuo "shuānglìrér," 扌 jiàozuo "tíshǒu," 艹 jiàozuo "cǎo zìtóu."

25   Bǐfang shuō yào chá yíge bú rènshi de zì, jiu yào xiān kàn zhèige
zì shǔyú shénmo bùshǒu. Jiǎrú yào chá pù 鋪 zì, wǒmen kàndào pù zìde
zuǒbiān yǒu yíge jīn 金 zì, nà jiu shi shuō pù zìde bùshǒu shi jīn. Ránhòu zài shǔyishǔ pù zìde bǐhuá yǒu duōshao? Kěshi zài shǔ bǐhuáde shíhou, yào bǎ bùshǒu jīn de bǐhuá chúdiào, zhǐ shǔ qíyúde bǐhuá. Wǒmen
30 yǐ shǔ pù zìde bǐhuá, chúle jīn yǐwài hái yǒu qīhuá. Wǒmen jiu dǎkāi
zìdiǎn, huòzhě zài Cíhǎili qu zhǎo jīn bùde qīhuá, nà yídìng zhǎodào pù
zì le.

       Zhǎodào pù zì zhīhòu, wǒmen kéyi kàndao yǒu yíge kuòhú 〔, zài
kuòhúli xiě de shi jiǎ 甲. Zài hòubiān yòu yǒu yíge kùohú, lǐmian xiě
35 de shi yǐ 乙. Nà jiu shi gàosu wǒmen zhèige pù zì yǒu jiǎ、yǐ liǎngge
yīn, yě yǒu liǎngzhǒng yìsi.

Yòu bǐfang shuō wǒmen yào chá <u>shāng</u> 傷 zì, wǒmen xiān kàn <u>shāng</u>
zìde zuǒbiān shi yíge "lìrér," wǒmen jiu zhīdao zhèige <u>shāng</u> zìde bùshǒu
shi "rén" bù. Wǒmen zài shǔyishǔ <u>shāng</u> zìde yòubiān yígòng yǒu shíyī-
40 huá.   Wǒmen jiu zài <u>Cíhǎi</u>li qu zhǎo "rén" bù shíyīhuá, yídìng zhǎodào
<u>shāng</u> zì le. Ránhòu zài kàn <u>shāng</u> zìde xiàmian xiězhe "shī yāng qiè."
Nà jiu shi shuō zhèige <u>shāng</u> zì shi yòng <u>shī</u>、<u>yāng</u> liǎngge zì pīnchéng
de. <u>Qiè</u> jiu shi <u>fǎnqiè</u>. Shénmo jiào <u>fǎnqiè</u> ne?

Fǎnqiè shi Zhōngguo gǔdàide pīnyīn fāngfǎ.   Zhèizhǒng fǎnqiè shi
45 yòng liǎngge zì héchéng yíge yīn. Xiànzài bǎ fǎnqiè de fázi jiǎndān shuōyishuō. Shàngcì jiǎnghuà céngjīng jiǎngguo Zhōngguo zì měi yíge zì kéyi
fēnwéi qiánhòu liǎngge yīnsù. Qiánmiànde jiàozuo <u>shēng</u>, hòumiànde jiàozuo <u>yùn</u>.   Fǎnqiè jiu shi bǎ qiántou zhèige zìde <u>shēng</u> hé hòutou zhèige
zìde <u>yùn</u> hézài yíkuàr jiu chéngle yíge xīnde zìyīn. Jiu xiàng <u>shāng</u> 傷
50 zì shi 詩央切. 詩 zì shi <u>shī</u>, 央 zì shi <u>yāng</u>. Zài fǎnqiè de shíhou shi yòng <u>shī</u> zì qiánbiānde shēng <u>sh</u> ér bú yòng tāde yùn <u>ī</u>, yòu yòng
<u>yāng</u> zì hòubiānde yùn <u>āng</u> ér bú yòng tāde shēng <u>y</u>. Yúshi bǎ <u>sh</u> hé <u>āng</u>
liǎngge yīn hézài yìqǐ jiu shi <u>shāng</u> le. Wǒmen zài kàn <u>shī yāng qiè</u> de
xiàbiān xiězhe 音商. Nà jiu biǎoshì zhèige <u>shāng</u> 傷 zìde yīn hé <u>shāng</u>
55 商 zì yíyàng. Ránhòu zài wǎngxià kàn xiě de shi ㊀㊁㊂…㊅.
Nà jiu shi shuō zhèige <u>shāng</u> 傷 zìde zìyī yǒu liùge, yě jiu shi yǒu liùzhǒng yìsi.

Guānyú chángshìde cānkǎo shū, ànzhe zhūwèi mùqiánde Zhōngwén
chéngdu lái shuō, hái bù jíyú xūyào tài shēnde cānkǎo shū.   Dànshi bù
60 néng bù xiān zuò yíge zhǔnbèi, yě bù néng bù zhīdào rúhé qu xuǎnzé cānkǎo shū.   Xiànzài jiǎshè yǒu yìběn túshū mùlù fàngzai wǒmende miànqián, wǒmen dǎkai mùlù yěxǔ shǒuxiān kàndao mùlù suǒyǐn. Zài suǒyǐnli yídìng bǎ gèzhǒng túshū fēnlèi xiěchulai. Bǐfang shuō zài zìdiǎnlèi wǒmen kéyi xuǎn xiàndài shìyòng de <u>Xuéshēng Zìdiǎn</u>、<u>Zhōnghuá Dà Cídiǎn</u>、
65 <u>Cíhǎi</u>、<u>Cíyuán</u> yǐjí gǔdài bǐjiào yǒu jiàzhide <u>Kāngxī Zìdiǎn</u> hé <u>Xǔ Shì Shuō-</u>
<u>wén</u>.   Cǐwài hái yǒu xiàndài xuézhě biānji de yìzhǒng sìjiǎo hàomǎ xīn
cídiǎn. Tóngshí zài suǒyǐnshang hái kéyi xuǎn gèzhǒng niánjiàn、niánbiǎo
děngděng.   Zài cōngshūlèili wǒmen kéyi xuǎn <u>Xiàndài Zhōngguo Wénxué</u>
<u>Míngzhù Cōngshū</u>、<u>Qīngnián Zhīshi Cōngshū</u>.   Zài xiǎoshuōlèili zuì hǎo
70 xuǎnzé duǎnpiānde báihuà xiǎoshuō. Cǐwài guānyú yóují zhuànjì、míngrén

zuòpǐn xuǎnjí huò quánjí、sǎnwén suíbǐ、mínjiān gùshi、huàjù jùběn, yǐjí
tōngxùn bàodǎo、zázhì huìbiān, dōu yào liúyì xuǎnzé yuèdú. Yǐshàng suǒ
shuō de dōu shi pǔtōng yìbānde dúwù. Dànshi zhūwèi zài zhèli zhǔxiū de
kēmu bìng bù xiāngtóng. Yǒude yánjiu yǔwén, yǒude yánjiu lìshǐ, háiyǒu
75 yánjiu yìshu、mínsú、kǎogǔ、xìju, shènzhìyú gǔdiǎn wénxué、értóng xīnlǐ...
Nènmo měige rén suǒ xūyào de cānkǎo shū yě jiu bù yíyàng le, dōu yīnggāi shi shǔyú zhuānmén xìngzhi de le. Yào xiǎng xuǎnzé zhèixiē zhuānmén
xìngzhide cānkǎo shū, zhǐyǒu cháng liúxīn gèzhǒng zhuānmén xìngzhi de
shūbào, shènzhìyú yào zhùyì xīn shū yùgào、xīn shū jiǎnjiè, nènmo duìyú
80 suǒ yào yánjiu de kēmu yídìng yǒu hěn dàde bāngzhu.

      Zǒng'éryánzhi yánjiu xuéwen chúle kèběn zhīwài yào duō kàn cān-
kǎo shū. Kàn cānkǎo shū kàn de rìzi jiǔ le zìrán'érrán yǎngchéng yìzhǒng kàn shū de qùwei. Zhōngguo yǒu yíjù súyǔ "kāi-juàn-yǒu-yì." Yìsi
jiu shi shuō zhǐyào dǎkāi shūběn zǒng shi yǒu hǎochu de. Xīwang dàjiā
85 duōduō kàn shū!

FÙSHÙ

      Zhèipán lùyīndài shi Zhōngwén dì-yīzǔ dì-shí'èrhào, dì-shí'èrcìde
fùshù, shi yóu Bái Wénshān fùshù de "Zhōngguode Wénzì."

      Zhèicìde Zhuāntí Jiǎnghuà shi yóu Jiǎn Jiàoshòu jiǎng de. Tímu
shi Zhōngguode Wénzi. Jiǎn Jiàoshòu shi wǒmen wénzìxuéde lǎoshī. Tā
5 jiǎngde fēicháng xiángxì. Yīnwei tā jiāo wǒmen, suǒyǐ tā hěn liǎojiě wǒmen xūyào zhīdao de shi shénmo.

      Jiǎn Jiàoshòu shuō Zhōngguode wénzì yǐjing yǒu sānqiān duō niánde
lìshǐ le. Tā shuō zài liù-qīshinián yǐqián yǒu rén zài Hénán Shěng yíge
dìfang cóng dìli juéchulai guījiǎ、niú gútou, shàngmian yǒu zì, nà jiu shi
10 Shāng Cháo shíqīde jiǎgǔwén. Zhè shi zhǐzhi yǒu shízàide zhèngmíng shuō
de.

      Jiǎn Jiàoshòu shuō Zhōngguo hěn zǎo jiu yǒule wénzì. Bǐrú gǔshū-
shang shuō "Cāng Jié zào zì guǐ dōu kū le." Zhè dāngrán shi shénhuà le.

      Jiǎn Jiàoshòu yòu shuōdao Liù Shū. Tā gěi wǒmen jiěshìde hěn
15 qīngchu. Tā yòu shuō wénzìde zǔzhi yǒu sānge jīběn yàosù, nà jiu shi
zìxíng、zìyīn hé zìyì.

      Jiǎn Jiàoshòu yòu shuō Zhōngguo zìxíng tài fùzá, xuéqilai shízài

kùnnán, suǒyǐ jìnlái yǒu rén tíchàng Zhōngwén yòng zìmǔ xiě.   Qíshí zhèige duì wàiguo rén xué Zhōngguo yǔyán dàoshi fāngbiàn le.   Wǒ
20 xiǎng Zhōngguo rén yídìng yǒu hěn duō rén bú zànchéng.   Jiǎn Jiàoshòu
yòu shuōle yìdiǎn guānyú wénzì gǎigé de wèntí.   Tā shuō Zhōngguo zìde
gòuzao wǎngwǎng yíge zì yǒu sānshíjǐhuá, rènqilai xiāngdāng kùnnán, xiěqilai yě xiāngdāng fèi shíhou.   Rúguǒ jiǎndānhuà le, xiěqilái yòu shěng
shíjiān yòu róngyi xiě.

25   Jiǎn Jiàoshòu gěi wǒmen jiěshì Liù Shū.   Wǒ juéde zhè shi xué
wénzìxuéde jīchǔ, yǐqián dōu hūluèle zhè shi yīnggāi jìzhu de.   Tā xiān
shuō xiàngxíng, yīnwei xiàngxíng wénzì shi Zhōngguo zuì kāishǐ de wénzì.   Shénmo jiàozuo xiàngxíng ne?   Jiù shi yíge zì huà de shi yuánláide
dōngxi.   Bǐrú rì、yuè、shān、chuān、mén děng.

30   Zhǐshì jiu shi bǎ yìsi zhǐchulai, lìrú shàng, xià.   Nǐ yí kàn jiu
míngbai nèige zìde yìsi le.

Tā shuō huìyì shi yóu liǎngge zì héqilái, nǐ yí kàn jiu míngbai tāde
yìsi.   Yíge zì yǒu zuǒyòu liǎngbùfen, bǐrú xìnyongde xìn zì zuǒbiān shi
rén, yòubiān shi yán.

35   Tā shuō xíngshēngde yìsi shi liǎngge zì hézài yíkuàr, yìbiān shi
zìxíng, yìbiān shi zìyīn.   Bǐrú shuō kǎo yāzi de kǎo yìbiān shi huǒchēde
huǒ, yìbiān shi kǎoshì de kǎo.   Huǒ shi xíng, kǎo shi shēng.

Zhuǎnzhù yìsi shi cóng jiǎ zhuǎnchéng yǐ, bǐrú lǎorénde lǎo zhuǎnchéng kǎoshì de kǎo.

40   Jiǎjiè jiu shi jièyòng de yìsi.   Jiǎn Jiàoshòu bìngqiě jǔle yíge lìzi.
Tā shuō gǔshíhou màizide mài dāngchūde xiěfǎ hé xiànzài lái qù de lái
shi yíyàngde xiěfǎ.   Nèige shíhou méi yǒu lái zì, jiu bǎ mài zì jièyòng
dàngzuo lái zì.   Jièyòng de rìzi yǐ duō le, jiu yǒngyuǎn ná ta dàngzuo
lái zì yòng le.

45   Wǒ běnlái duì Liù Shūde rènshì bú dà qīngchu.   Jiǎn Jiàoshòu gěi
wǒmen jiǎngle zhèige Zhuāntí Jiǎnghuà yǐhòu, wǒ cái zhēnzhèngde míngbaile Liù Shū shi shénmo.

WĒNXI

1. Wáng Xiānsheng xǐhuan yánjiu yǔyīnxué.   Tā shuō Yìn-Ōuyǔde zìyīn shi
duōyīnjié.   Zhōngguoyǔde zìyīn shi dānyīnjié, suǒyǐ Zhōngguo zì yě kéyi
shuō shi dānyīnde, yòu kéyi shuō shi dānyīnzì.   Kěshi rúguǒ bǎ dānyīnzì

zài fēnxī yíxià, měi yíge zî yòu kéyi fēnchéng qiánhòu liǎngge yīnsù. Qiánbiānde yīnsù jiàozuo <u>shēng</u>, hòubiānde yīnsù jiàozuo <u>yùn</u>. Zhōngguode yùnshū hěn duō. <u>Qièyùn</u>、<u>Shīyùn</u> dōu shi yǒumíngde yùnshū.

2. Zhōngguo xiàndài xuézhě Wáng Yúnwǔ Shì biānle yìzhǒng zìdiǎn shi sìjiǎo hàomǎ zìdiǎn. Zhèizhǒng zìdiǎn zài chá zî de shíhou yào ànzhe zîde sìge jiǎorde hàomǎ chákàn. Yīnwei Zhōngguo zî měige zîde gòuzào shi yòng bǐhuá gòuchéng de, dōu shi sìfāngde, dōu yǒu sìge jiǎo. Jiǎode xíngzhuàng gòng yǒu shízhǒng. Zhèi shízhǒng xíngzhuàng jiu yòng shíge hàomǎ lái dàibiǎo, suóyǐ chá zhèizhǒng zìdiǎn yào chá zîde sìjiǎo hàomǎ.

3. Yánjiu Zhōngguo wénzì bǐděi zhīdao Liù Shū. Liù Shūde míngchēng yǒu liǎngzhǒng bùtóngde shuōfǎ. Yìbān chángyòngde shuōfǎ jiu shi xiàngxíng、zhǐshì、huìyì、xíngshēng、zhuǎnzhù hé jiǎjiè. Zhìyú lìng yìzhǒng shuōfǎ shi bǎ zhǐshì jiàozuo xiàngshì, xíngshēng jiàozuo xiàngshēng. Zhè búguò shi míngchēngshangde bùtóng. Yìsi shi yíyàngde.

4. Yǒu rén wèn wo: "Zhōngguode zî yǒu běnyì yǒu biéyì. Zhè shi shuō yíge zî yǒu hǎojǐge yìsi. Wèi-shénmo nǐ shuō Zhōngguo zî shi yì-zî-yì-yì ne?" Wǒ shuō: "yì-zî-yì-yì shi zhǐzhe běnyì shuō de. Zhìyú biéyì wúlùn yǒu jǐge, dōu shi cóng běnyì yǐnshēnchulai de."

5. Mǒu yìshěngde shěnghuì guā dàfēng. Zhōngyāng zhèngfǔ jiào rén dào nàli qu chákàn. Chákàn de rén huílái shuō, shěnghuìlide fēngzāi hěn lìhai. Hěn duō pùzi dōu méi kāi mén. Yǒu yìjiā tōngxùnshède fángzi hé yìjiā mài yìshupǐnde pùzi de fángzi dōu guāhuài le. Fángzili yǒu hěn duō rén dōu shòule shāng. Lìngwài shòushāng de rén yě bù shǎo.

6. Zài Zhōngguo huàli rú <u>jiǎyú</u> hé <u>guī</u>, yòu rú <u>yāzi</u> hé <u>niú</u> dōu shi mà rén cháng yòng de cí.

7. Tīngshuō Wáng Xiānsheng yǒu bìng le, érqiě hěn wéixiǎn, wǒ jiu dào yīyuàn qù qiáo ta. Dào yīyuàn yǐhòu wèn ta zěnmo dé de bìng? Tā shuō: "Qián jǐtiān shāowēi yǒu diar shāngfēng, wǒ yě méi zhùyì, hòulai yuè bìng yuè lìhai, zhuǎnchéng hěn zhòngde bìng. Kěshi xiànzài hǎo yìdiǎr le." Wǒ yòu wèn ta: "Shénmo shíhou kéyi wánquán hǎo le?" Tā shuō: "Líkai yīyuànde rìzi xiànzài hái bù néng quèdìng."

8. Yǒu yíge rén zuì xǐhuan tīng xì. Tā dǒngde de xì hěn duō, yóuqíshi jīngxì tā dǒngde de gèng duō. Zuìjìn tā cóng jīngxìli xuǎnchulai yìxiē biānchéng yìběn shū jiàozuo <u>Jīngxì Huìbiān</u>. Xiàyuè jiu kéyi chūbǎn. Wǒ yě dìngle yìběn.

9. Zhāng Xiānsheng shuō: "Wǒ xiǎode shíhou jiāli méi yǒu qián. Wǒ niàn zhōngxuéde shíhou jiu yìmiàn zuò gōng yìmiàn niàn shū. Zuìchū zhǐ shi zuò bàntiānde gōng, hòulai gāncuì bǎ quántiānde shíjiān dōu zuò gōng le, zhǐ néng zài wǎnjiān niàn shū. Dàole niàn dàxué de shíhou yěshi yíyàng. Zǒngkuò yíjù huà wǒ shi kào zìjǐ gōngzuò cái néng niàn shū." Yǒu rén shuō: "Nǐ jiānglái xiě zìzhuàn de shíhou, yīnggāi bǎ zhèizhǒng qíngxing xiěchulai."

10. Yǒu yíge wàiguo rén shuō: "Cóngqián Zhōngguo rén yǒu rén jiào wǒ shi yángguǐzi, yǐn'ér wǒ zìjǐ yě cháng shuō wǒ shi yángguǐzi." Yǒu rén shuō: "Nà nǐ bú shi zhèngshì chéngrènle ma?" Nèige wàiguo rén shuō: "Nà yǒu shénmo guānxi? Zhèige míngzi yě hěn yǒu yìsi ya."

11. Zhōngguo rén chuánshuō guǐ shi zài yèli chūxiànde, tā shícháng duì rén
    búlì. Zhèizhǒng shuōfǎ nǐ xiāngxìn ma?

12. Cóngqián yǒu rén shuō Zhōngguo wénzì jiǎshè Lādīnghuà, nà jiu róngyi
    xué le, suǒyǒu xiànzàide shuānglìrén、. . . zìpáng děngdeng bùshǒude cér
    jiu dōu méi yòng le.

13. Shuāngshíjiéde shuāng zì hé guāngmíngde guāng zì, háiyǒu huìhéde hé zì
    shi yòng shénmo zì qiè de, nǐ néng shuōchulai ma?

14. Májiàngde má zì、gōngchǎngde chǎng zì háiyǒu yīnsùde sù zì、túnzide tún
    zì、zōngkuòde kuò zì zài chá zìdiǎn de shíhou yīngdāng chá shénmo bù-
    shǒu, nǐ zhǐdao ma?

15. Jùshuō cóngqián zài Hénán Shěng yige xiǎo túnzide dì dǐxia juéchulai hěn
    duō guǐjiǎ hé niúde gútou. Dāngshi méi yǒu rén zhùyì. Hòulái jīng kǎo-
    gǔxuéjiā yánjiu, cái fāxiànle jiǎgǔwén.

WÈNTÍ

1. Wǒmen mùqián yào yòng de cānkǎo shū dàzhǐ kéyi fēnzuò něi liǎngzhǒng?
   Xuǎnzé zhèi liǎngzhǒng cānkǎo shū de yuánzé shi shénmo?

2. Chá Zhōngwén zìdiǎn xiān yào dǒngde shénmo? Yǒu duóshao bùshǒu?
   Duōbàn yìnzai zìdiǎnde shénmo dìfang? Zěnyàng páiliè?

3. Chá Zhōngwén zìdiǎn cháguo bùshǒu zhīhòu hái yào zuò shénmo?   Lián
   bu lián bùshǒu zài nèi?

4. Chá Zhōngwén zìdiǎn rúguǒ yǒu 甲 乙 nà shi gàosu wǒmen shénmo?

5. Shénmo jiào fǎnqiè? Qǐng nǐ jiǎndānde shuōshuo fǎnqiè de fāngfǎ.

6. Qǐng nǐ shuō jǐzhǒng xiàndài chángyòngde hé gǔdài yǒumíngde zìdiǎn huò
   cídiǎnde míngchēng.

7. Wǒmen yào yuèdú pǔtōng yìbānde dúwù, yīngdāng xuǎnzé shénmo?

8. Yào xuǎnzé zhuānmén xìngzhi de cānkǎo shū yīngdāng liúxīn shénmo?

9. Láo-ér-wú-gōng shi shénmo yìsi? Qǐng nǐ yòng báihuà shuōmíng. Kāi-
   juàn-yǒu-yì shi shénmo yìsi?

10. Yánjiu xuéwèn chúle kèběn zhīwài yào duō zuò shénmo?

ILLUSTRATIVE SENTENCES (ENGLISH)

1.4. Sometimes actors in the Peking opera apply color to their faces.

1.5. I have a friend who's a famous opera singer.

2.2. [The text of] that drama was written by a literary personage. It has great
     educational significance.

5.1. All art includes the idea of beauty.

7.1. There are two kinds of lists of characters. One kind includes the meaning [of the characters].   Another kind only contains characters and does not explain the meaning [of the characters].

9.1. Could you tell me, in looking up the character cāng of Cang Jie in the dictionary, what radical should one look up?

9.3. Among the radicals in the dictionary is there the radical gǔ of 'bone'?

9.4. Do you want to buy a dictionary arranged [lit. look up] by radical, or [do you want to buy a dictionary arranged] by spelling?

10.1. You've learned the traditional Chinese system of spelling.   Do you know how the character guī is spelled [lit. cut]?

10.3. From the dictionary we can see that the sound of the character jiā is spelled by using the jī of jīběn and the yā of yāzi.

10.4. The traditional Chinese system of spelling uses two characters. The first spells the initial [lit. cuts off round], the second spells the final [lit. cuts off rhyme].

11.1. All library books are marked [lit. edited] by numbers.

11.2. The four-corner-number dictionary compiled by Wang Yunwu I just know about in general.   I still don't know how to use it.

14.1. If you insist on leaving, I won't detain you.

14.4. He let his hair grow long.   [lit. His hair was left very long.]

29.1. I'd like to subscribe to a journal.   I don't know whether it would be better to subscribe for a year or for half a year.

30.2. Is there anything on physics and chemistry in the Small Collection of World Knowledge?

32.1. I like most of all to read the 'biographies' in the Historical Records.

32.3. He said in his autobiography that when he was young he very much disliked memorizing.

36.1. In mathematics one must first compute the figures in parentheses.

37.1. In looking up the fàn of fànwéi does one look up the side-radical 'cart' or the top-radical 'bamboo'?

38.1. The character 'bright' with the character 'sun' eliminated is the character 'moon.'

46.1. People who work labor in vain if they don't follow the wishes of their superiors.

50.1. The merit of that book is that it is very concise and clear, so a lot of people say it is really good.

51.2. A maxim is an apt saying which is commonly used by people [in general].   For example, "Practice makes perfect" [lit. Practice becomes natural] is a maxim.

53.1. You ask me to look up at the sky.   How come I don't see anything?

59.3. If you understand such terms for radicals as 'three-dot water' and 'two-dot water' you can tell other people how to consult a dictionary.

60.2. The [news] reporting of that news agency is comparatively accurate.

64.1. Yesterday there was a typhoon.   It destroyed my house.

NOTES

1. The combination of verb plus yú, a literary word meaning 'at,' encompasses several constructions which are limited for the most part to the written style.   In some cases the combination is equivalent to verb plus zài 'at' in the spoken style:

    Tā shēngyu Zhōngguo, zhǎngyu Rìběn.   'He was born in China but grew up in Japan.'

    The combination of SV + yú when followed by a verbal expression generally describes the state under which the following activity is performed:

    Tā mángyú dào huǒchēzhàn qu.   'He is in a hurry to go to the railroad station.'

    Tā jíyú xūyào yìběn Zhōng-Yīng zìdiǎn. 'He urgently needs a Chinese-English dictionary.'

    Here the combination SV + yú is equivalent to SV + zhe in the spoken style:

    Tā mángzhe dào huǒchēzhàn qu.

    Tā jízhe xūyào yìběn Zhōng-Yīng zìdiǎn.

    In the construction A SV + yú B the stative verb often has a comparative sense, i. e. A is more SV than B:

    Nèige xuéxiào nǚ xuésheng duóyú nán xuésheng.   'In that school there are more girl students than boy students [lit. girl students are more numerous than boy students].'

    Here the written construction A SV yú B is equivalent to the spoken construction A bǐ B SV:

    Nǚ xuésheng bǐ nán xuésheng duō.

2. A stative verb followed by dào 'to' means 'SV to such-and-such amount or degree':

    Zhèiběn shū běnlái shi èrshikuài qián.   Xiànzài guìdao bāshikuài qián.   'This book originally was $20. Now it has increased to [lit. become expensive to] $80.'

    Zhèiběn shū guìdao xuésheng dōu mǎibuliǎo.   'This book has become so expensive that students can't afford to buy it.'

3. The change of NV to VN indicates a shift from definite to indefinite N:

    Sānge rén lái le.   'The three men came' or 'Three of the men came.'

    Láile sānge rén.   'Three men came' or 'There came three men.'

    Sometimes the shift of N from subject position to object position involves a change in meaning from 'N did V' to 'X caused N to V' or 'X had NV.'

    Wǒ hěn zǎo jiu sǐle mǔqin le.   'My mother died when I was very young'—more literally, something like 'I had my mother die on me when I was very young.'

    Tā qìsi wo le.   'He makes me very angry.'

4. The "four-corner system" is a numerical scheme of classifying Chinese characters devised by Wang Yunwu, the author of several dictionaries utilizing the system. In this scheme the numbers 0 to 9 are assigned to ten classes of strokes. For example, a line written from left to right is 1, a line written from top to bottom is 2, a dot is 3. The strokes at the four corners of a character are assigned a number in the order top left corner, top right corner, bottom left corner, bottom right corner. Thus the character hé 'river' is designated by the number 3112.

5. The term fǎnqiè 'reverse cut' refers to a system of indicating pronunciation which utilizes the pronunciation of two characters to represent the sound of a third. The system can be illustrated by the following typical entry from the Cíhǎi dictionary for the character shāng 'wound':

詩央切

This is to be read as shī yāng qiè, i. e. 'shī yāng cut.' The 'reverse cut' system requires cutting off the initial (shēng) of the first character, giving sh, and the final (yùn) of the second character, giving āng, and then combining the two, giving shāng.

Dì-Shíliùkè.　Zhōngguode Yǔyán

Bái: Mǎ Jiàoshòu zǎo.

Mǎ: Zǎo.

Bái: Mǎ Tàitai shāngfēng hǎo le ma?

Mǎ: Xièxie ni, tā shāowēi hǎo le yìdiǎr.　Tā zhèici shāngfēng shāngde
5　　hěn lìhai.　Zěnmoyàng, cānkǎo shūde jiǎnghuà méi wèntí ma?

Bái: Dàzhì méi wèntí.　Jiǎng zhèige tímu duì wǒmen hěn yǒuyòng.　Wǒ
běnlái bù dǒng shénmo jiào fǎnqiè.　Tīngle zhèicìde jiǎnghuà, wǒ
wánquán liǎojiě le.　Xiànzài wǒ zhīdao fǎnqiè de fāngfǎ shi yòng
liǎngge zì lái pīnyīn, dì-yīge zì qiè yīn, dì-èrge zì shi qiè yùn.

10　Mǎ: Nǐ lùyīn le ma?

Bái: Lù le.　Wǒ dàilai le.　Yíhuěr nín tīngting.　Zuótian Huá Xiānsheng、
Huá Tàitai hé Xuéxīn yǒu rén qǐng tāmen chī fàn, jiù wǒ yíge rén
zài jiā lùyīn.　Wǒ lùle yòu lù, lùle hǎojǐcì.　Zìjǐ tīngzhe bǐ yǐqián
lùde yào hǎode duō.

15　Mǎ: Nǐ búduànde liànxi, zìrán'érránde jiu huì chénggōng de.　Xuéwèn
shi yíbùyíbù mànmān jìnbù de.

Bái: Péngyou ràng wǒ mǎi értóng dúwù.　Zuótian xià bàntiān dōu gěi ta
bànhǎo le.

Mǎ: Mǎi de shénmo shū?

20　Bái: Wǒ méi mǎi shū, jiu gěi ta dìng de <u>Xiǎo Péngyou</u>.　<u>Xiǎo Péngyou</u>
wǒ zài shūdiàn kànlekan, díquè shi búcuò, chúncuì shi xiǎohár kàn
de shū.　Lǐmiàn yíduànyíduànde bāokuò hěn duō guānyú xiǎoháizi
zēngjiā zhīshide zuòpǐn.　Lǐmiàn hái yǒu yíduàn chángpiān xiǎoshuō
shi yíqīyíqíde jiēzhe xiěxiaqu de.

25　Mǎ: Duìle.　Tā shi zhōukān, měi xīngqī chūbǎn yìběn.

1.0.　Yuè　　monosyllabic name for Kwangtung

　　　Yuèyǔ　Cantonese dialect　(W)

1.1.　Yuè jiu shi Guǎngdōng Shěng, zài Zhōngguode dōngnánbù.

1.2.　Zài Měiguode Huáqiáo duōshù shuō Yuèyǔ.

2.0.　Xiāng　　monosyllabic name for Hunan

　　　Xiāngyǔ　Hunan dialect　(W)

2.1.　Xiāng shi Húnán Shěngde jiǎndān míngchēng.　Xiāngyǔ jiu shi Húnán huà.

3.0.　Fújiàn　Fukien

　　　Fúzhōu　Foochow

3.1. Fújiàn Shěngde shěnghuì shi Fúzhōu.

4.0. Wú   (1) name of a dynasty (229-280); (2) monosyllabic name for
              Kiangsu

      Wúyǔ   Wu dialect (W)

4.1. Wú shi Zhōngguo gǔshíhoude yíge guómíng, zài xiànzài Jiāngsu yí-
      dài.   (T)

4.2. Wúyǔ jiu shi Jiāngsude fāngyán.

5.0. Mǐn   monosyllabic name for Fukien

      Mǐnyǔ   Fukien dialect (W)

      Mǐnběiyǔ   Northern Fukien dialect (W)

      Mǐnnányǔ   Southern Fukien dialect (W)

5.1. Mǐn shi Fújiàn Shěng. Fújiàn rén shuō de huà jiàozuo Mǐnyǔ.

5.2. Mǐnyǔ fēnwéi liǎngzhǒng, yìzhǒng shi Mǐnnányǔ, yìzhǒng shi Mǐn-
      běiyǔ.

6.0. Gàn   monosyllabic name for Kiangsi

      Gànyǔ   Kan dialect (W)

6.1. Nǐ zhīdao Gàn shi něi yìshěng ma?

6.2. Gànyǔ jiu shi Jiāngxi huà. Nǐ huì shuō Jiāngxi huà ma?

Bái: Mǎ Jiàoshòu, Yuè jiu shi Guǎngdōng ma?

Mǎ : Shìde, Yuè jiu shi Guǎngdōng. Zhōngguode jǐshige shěngli chàbuduō
      dōu yǒu zhèizhǒng jiǎndān míngchēng de.

Bái: Xiāng shi Húnán ma?

30   Mǎ : Duìle. Hái yǒu Wú jiu shi Jiāngsū, Mǐn jiu shi Fújiàn, Gàn jiu shi
      Jiāngxī.

Bái: Zhèi jǐshěngde yǔyán shì bu shi yìdiǎr yě bù yíyàng?

Mǎ : Bù yíyàng. Yàoshi yíge Guǎngdōng rén gēn yíge Běijīng rén shuō
      huà, tā lián yíjù yě tīngbudǒng.

7.0. Xiàmén   Amoy (in Fukien)

7.1. Xiàmén shi Fújiàn Shěng yánhǎide yíge shì.

8.0. fēnqū   (1) divide into regions (VO); divided into regions; (3) region

      dìqū   region, area [earth region]

8.1. Wǒ yào mǎi yìzhāng Shànghǎi Shì fēnqū dìtú.

8.2. Nǐ zhīdao zhèige dìqūli fēn duōshao qū?

9.0. shēngdiào   (1) tones; (2) tune [sound tune]

9.1. Xué Hànyǔ yào liúyì shēngdiào.　Rúguǒ shēngdiào yǒu cuòwu yěxǔ jiu yào cǐ bù dáyì le.

10.0. jùlí　　distance　[distance separate]

10.1. Nèige hēibǎnshangde zì yīnwei jùlí tài yuǎn wǒ kànbuqīngchu.

35　Bái : Mǎ Jiàoshòu, qǐng wèn zài Mǐnyǔ lǐtou Fúzhōu huà hé Xiàmén huà yǒu hěn dàde fēnbié ma?

　　Mǎ : Suírán Fúzhōu hé Xiàmén dōu zài Fújiàn Shěng, kěshi tāmende yǔyán fēn liǎngqū. Mǐnnán huà yòng Xiàmén huà zuò dàibiǎo. Mǐnběi huà yòng Fúzhōu huà zuò dàibiǎo.

40　Bái : Wǒ tīngshuō gè dìfang yǔyánde shēngdiào yǒu hěn dàde jùlí.

　　Mǎ : Shìde.

　　Bái : Nènmo hé Guóyǔde chābié gèng dà le.

　　Mǎ : Chābié hěn dà. Jìshǐ nǐ yǒu yǔyán tiāncái yě bù róngyi tīngdǒng le.

11.0. Chéngdū　　Chengtu (in Szechuan)

11.1. Tāde zǐmèi dōu zài Chéngdū.　Tā chízǎo yào dào Chéngdū qù yícì.

12.0. Kūnmíng　　Kunming (in Yunnan)

12.1. Wǒ cóng Kūnmíng lǚxínghuílai xiěle yìběn Kūnmíng Lǚxíng Suíbǐ.　(T)

13.0. Yángzhou　　Yangchow (in Kiangsu)

13.1. Hěn qíguài tā fǒurèn qùguo Yángzhou, kěshi wǒ zài Yángzhou qiānzhēnwànquède kànjianguo ta.

14.0. Shěnyáng　　Mukden (in Manchuria)

14.1. Shěnyángde shěn 瀋 zì zuǒbiān shi sāndiǎn shuǐ, bú shi liǎngdiǎn shuǐ.

15.0. yǔyīn　　　sound, phonetics　[language sound]

　　　yùyīnxué　　(study of) phonetics

15.1. Zhāng Xiānsheng shi yǔyīnxué zhuānjiā, búdàn duì yǔyīn hěn yǒu yánjiu, jiùlián niǎor jiào de shēngyin tā dōu néng xué. Tā xué xiǎoyànr hé huángyīng jiào de shēngyīn xiàngjíle.

45　Bái : Mǎ Jiàoshòu, nín qùguo Chéngdū ma?

　　Mǎ : Qùguo.　Kàngzhànde shíqī wǒ fùqin zài Chéngdū Huáxī Dàxué jiāo shū.

　　Bái : Chéngdū huà yě shi shǔyú pǔtōnghuà fànwéi yǐnèi de ma?

　　Mǎ : Shìde.　Pǔtōnghuàde qūyù bāokuò fànwéi hěn dà.　Kūnmíng huà、
50　　Chéngdū huà、Hànkǒu huà、Nánjīng huà、Běijīng huà dōu shi pǔtōnghuà.

Bái : Shì bu shi Yángzhou huà yě suàn pǔtōnghuà?

Mǎ : Yángzhou huà kéyi dàibiǎo Zhōngguode nánfāngde pǔtōnghuà.

Bái : Wǒ tīng Dōngběide Shěnyáng huà hé Běijīng huà chàbuliǎo tài duō.

55   Mǎ : Yǒu diar fēnbié, zài yǔyīnshang yǒu yìdiǎr bùtóng.

16.0. Shànggǔ Hànyǔ   Archaic Chinese   (Chou Dynasty)

       Zhōnggǔ Hànyǔ   Ancient Chinese   (about 600 A.D.)

16.1. Cóng zhèiběn shūli kéyi zhīdao yìdiǎr Shànggǔ Hànyǔ hé Zhōnggǔ
       Hànyǔ, kěshi suǒ néng zhīdao de zhǐ shi yǔyīn.

17.0. Shī Jīng   Book of Odes

17.1. Shī Jīng yǒu sānbǎi duō piān, hěn duō piān shi yòng bǐyù de.

18.0. Shàng Shū   Book of History

18.1. Cóngqián yǒu rén sònggei wǒ yíbù Shàng Shū, wǒ méi yào. Xiànzài
       xiǎngqilai hěn hòuhuǐ.   (T)

19.0. gòucífǎ   method of word-formation, morphology   [construct word
                  method]

19.1. Yánjiu yìzhǒng yǔyán, bìděi yánjiu zhèizhǒng yǔyánde gòucífǎ. Fǒu-
       zéde huà shi láo-ér-wú-gōng de.

20.0. Suí   Sui Dynasty (581-618 A.D.)

20.1. Suí Cháo zhīhòu jiu shi Táng Cháo.

Bái : Qǐng nín bǎ cíbiǎoshangde Shànggǔ Hànyǔ gēn Zhōnggǔ Hànyǔ jiě-
       shi jiěshi.

Mǎ : Xuézhěmen bǎ jìyuánqián liùbǎinián zuǒyòude Shī Jīng hé Shàng Shū
       jiàozuo Shànggǔ Hànyǔ.   Yòu bǎ Suí Táng shídàide yùnshū Qièyùn
60   rènwéi shi zhōnggǔde yǔyīn, suóyǐ jiàozuo Zhōnggǔ Hànyǔ.

Bái : Shénmo jiào gòucífǎ?

Mǎ : Jiu shi bǎ měige dānzì zàochéng cérde fāngfǎ.   Yě jiu shi zǔzhí
       cérde fázi.

Bái : Wǒ míngbai le.

21.0. míngcí   (1) name; (2) expression   [name word]

21.1. Yǒu rén wèn wǒ: "Liǎnhóng de liǎn hé diū liǎn de liǎn shì bu shi
       míngcí?" Wǒ shuō: "Zhèi liǎngge liǎn zì dōu shi míngcí."

22.0. yǔzú   language family   [language clan]

       Hàn-Zàng yǔzú   Sino-Tibetan language family

       Yìn-Ōu yǔzú   Indo-European language family

22.1. Yìndu hé Xīzàng suīrán jùlí hěn jìn, kěshi tāmende yǔzú bùtóng. Yíge shi Yìn-Ōu yǔzú, yíge shi Hàn-Zàng yǔzú.

23.0. bīncí   object (of a sentence) [guest word]

zhǔcí   subject (of a sentence) [chief word]

23.1. Zài "Wǒ kàn shū" zhèige jùzili, něige shi zhǔcí něige shi bīncí?

24.0. biàndiào   change in tone, tone sandhi

24.1. Biàndiào jiu shi shēngdiào biàn le. Lìrú Hànyǔli rúguǒ yǒu liǎng- ge dì-sānshēng, nènmo qiántoude dì-sānshēng jiu yào biànchéng dì- èrshēng le.

25.0. mái   bury

25.1. Nǐ bǎ nèige sǐ niǎor mái le, miǎnde yǒu wèr.

26.0. zàng   bury

máizàng   bury

26.1. Rén sǐle zhīhòu yào máizàng. Zàng de dìfang jiào féndì.

65 Mǎ : Jīntian tǎolùn de zhèixiē cér duōbàn shi yǔyánxuéshangde míngcí. Xiànzài wǒ zài wèn nǐ yíge wèntí. Hàn-Zàng yǔzúli jùzide gòuzào shi zěnmoyàng de?

Bái: Hàn-Zàngyǔli yǒu yíge tèdiǎn, shi zhǔcí zǒngshi zài yíge jùzide qiántou.

70 Mǎ : Duìle. Hái yǒu biàndiào shi zěnmo yìhuí shì?

Bái: Fánshi liǎngge dì-sānshēng zài yíkuàr shuō de shíhou, tóu-yíge zì- yīn jiu huì biān de. Bǐrú "Wǒ yòng qián mǎi mǎ" de <u>mǎi</u> gēn "Mǎ sǐ le mái mǎ" de <u>mái</u> tóngyīn le.

Mǎ : Duìle.

27.0. chóngdié   (1) piled one on another; (2) reduplicated [duplicate re- peated]

27.1. Nèige dìfang fēngjǐng zhēn hǎo. Yuǎn shān chóngdié, hǎoxiang huà de shide. (W) (T)

28.0. dòngcí   verb [move word]

28.1. Zhōngguo huàde jùzili yǒu shíhou méi yǒu dòngcí. Bǐrú shuō "Tā sānsuì" zhèiju huàli jiu shi méi yǒu dòngcí.

29.0. fùcí   adverb [secondary word]

29.1. Nǐ yánjiu yǔfǎ yǐjing jìnru dì-bāge yuè le, zhīdao de yǐjing bù shǎo le. Qǐng nǐ shuōyishuō shénmo shi fùcí, zhǔcí gēn bīncí?

30.0. wěi(ba)   tail

jùwěi   end of a sentence

30.1. Wěi shi hòubiānde yìsi. Jùwěi jiu shi yíjù huàde hòutou.

30.2. Tā xiàng wǒde wěiba shide. Lǎo gēnzhe wo.

31.0. cítóu   prefix [word head]

cíwěi   suffix [word tail]

31.1. Cítóu shi yíge cí qiánbiārde zì. Cíwěi shi yíge cíde hòubiārde zì.

75 Mǎ : Chóngdiéde yìsi nǐ dǒng ma? Qǐng nǐ jǔ ge lìzi.

Bái: Chóngdié zài dòngcí yìfāngmiàn yǒu "kànkan, shuōshuo," zài míngcí
yìfāngmiàn yǒu "gēge, dìdi, jiějie, mèimei." Chóngdié cí zài dòngcí yìfāngmiàn bǐjiǎo duō, zài míngcí yìfāngmiàn bǐjiǎo shǎo.

Mǎ : Xíngróngcí ne?

80 Bái: Dàngzuo fùcí yòng. Bǐfāng mànmārde, hǎohāorde. Zhōngguo yǔ-
yánlide cítóu bìng bù duō, shì bu shi?

Mǎ : Zhōngguo yǔyánde cítóu hěn shǎo. Jiù yǒu dì, chū, lǎo. Rú "dì-yī,
dì-èr, dì-sān; chūyī, chūèr, chūsān; Lǎo Wáng, lǎoshī, lǎoye."

Bái: Cíwěi bǐjiǎo duō yìdiǎr?

85 Mǎ : Shìde. Wǒ shuō jǐge jiǎnyào de, bǐrú zhuōzi, pánzi, kuàizi, wěiba
děngděngde.

32.0. dàimíngcí   pronoun [substitute name word]

rénchēng dàimíngcí   personal pronoun

32.1. Zài "Tā shòushāng le" zhèiju huàli, něi yíge zì shi dàimíngcí? Shì
bu shi rénchēng dàimíngcí?

33.0. yíwèn   question, doubt [doubt ask]

yíwèncí   question particle

yíwèn dàimíngcí   question pronoun

yíwènshì   question form (of a sentence)

33.1. Zhèige zìzhuàn shìfǒu tā zìjǐ xiě de zhēn shi ge yíwèn. (W)

33.2. Shénmo gēn nǎlǐ dōu shi yíwèncí. Shéi shi yíwèn dàimíngcí.

33.3. "Nǐ qù ma?" Zhèige jùzi shi yíwènshì.

33.4. Yàoshi duì cér yǒu yíwèn zuìhǎo kànkan zhèiběn Chángyòng Cí
Huìbiān.

34.0. xùshù   narrate, describe [narrate relate]

xùshùshì   affirmative form (i. e. non-negative)

34.1. Tā gěi tāde péngyou xiě de zhuàn, xùshùde hěn xiángxi. (W) (T)

34.2. "Tā xǐhuan yánjiu Zhōngwén" zhèige jùzi shi xùshùshì de.

35.0. fǒudìng   (1) not so; (2) uncertain; (3) negation [not definite]

fǒudìngshì   negative form (of a sentence)

35.1. <u>Bù</u> gēn <u>méi</u> dōu shi fǒudìngde cér.

35.2. "Nǐ kàn zhèibén shū bú kàn?" zhè shi yíwènde jùzi, bú shi fǒu-dìngshì.

Bái : Mǎ Jiàoshòu, dàimíngcí gēn rénchēng dàimíngcí yǐjí xíngróngcí hái-yǒu yíwèn dàimíngcí wǒ dōu dǒng le. Qǐng wèn nín yíwènshì shi zěnmo huí shì?

90 Mǎ : Jiu shi xùshùshì gēn fǒudìngshìde liǎngge jùzi hézài yíkuàr, jiu chéngle yíwènshì le. Wǒ jǔ ge lìzi. Yǒu yíge xùshù jùzi shi "Tā chī fàn" tóngshí hái yǒu yíge fǒudìngshìde jùzi shi "Tā bù chī fàn," zhèi liǎngge jùzi hézài yíkuàr jiu biànchéngle yíge yíwènde jùzi "Tā chī bu chī fàn?" Zhè jiu shi yíwènshì.

36.0. cídiào   (word) tone [word tone]

36.1. Zài Hàn-Zàng yǔzúli yǒu cídiào. Zài biéde yǔzúli shi bu shi yě yǒu cídiào ne?

37.0. zhí   worth

zhíqián   valuable [worth money]

zhíde   worth, worthwhile

jiàzhi   price, value

37.1. Tā bǎ ta wéiyī zhíqiánde dōngxi, gāngbǐ, gěi diū le.

37.2. Wèile yìdiǎr xiǎoshì nǎr zhíde shēngqì ne?

37.3. Niàn sùchéngkē yǒushí xuébudào shénmo, bù zhíde qu niàn.

37.4. Tāde zuòpǐn zài wénxuéshang hěn yǒu jiàzhi.   (T)

38.0. fùhé   compound, complex, composite [complex join]

fùhéjù   composite sentence

38.1. "Tā yīnwei méi yǒu qián, suǒyǐ bú niàn shū le," xiàng zhèizhǒng jùzi shi bu shi fùhéjù?

39.0. zàojùfǎ   syntax [construct sentence method]

39.1. Yánjiu Zhōngwén yào xiān rèn zì, zài xué cér, ránhòu zài xué zào-jùfǎ.

40.0. xiǎnzhù   obvious [prominent prominent]

40.1. Tāde xuéyè jìnlai yǒu xiǎnzhùde jìnbù.

95 Mǎ : Qǐng nǐ shuōyishuō, shénmo jiàozuo <u>cídiào</u>?

Bái : Cídiào jiu shi shēng, yě jiu shi zìde sìshēng. Sìshēng zài pǔtōng-

huàli hěn yǒu yánjiu de jiàzhi. Cídiào yàoshi bù zhǔn, shuōchu huà
lai hěn nántīng.

Mǎ : Háiyǒu, fùhéjù shi shénmo yìsi?

100 Bái: Fùhéjù yě shi yîzhǒng zàojùfǎ. Jiu shi yíge jùzili bù zhǐ bāokuò
yíge jùzi. Wǒ jǔ gé lîzi, bǐrú: "Wǒ méi xiūxi, chīle fàn jiu zuò
shì." Fùhé jùzi yǒude bù róngyi liǎojiě. Bǐrú "Tā qù wǒ bú qù,"
kāishǐ xué Zhōngguo huà de rén hěn bù róngyi kànchulai zhèijù
huàde yìsi jiu shi shuō "Yàoshi tā qù wǒ jiu bú qù." Rúguǒ yòng
105   hòumian zhèige shuōfa, jiu hěn xiǎnzhùde míngbai shi shénmo yìsi.

41.0. liàngcî   measure word

41.1. "Wǒ jiā láile liǎngwèi kèren" zài zhèiju huàli wèi zî jiu shi liàngcî.

42.0. gé   case (in inflected languages)

zhǔgé   nominative case [chief case]

bīngé   accusative case [guest case]

42.1. Zài Yìn-Ōuyǔ jùzilide cí yǒu zhǔgé yǒu bīngé. Bǐfāng shuō "Wǒ
kàn tā" wǒ shi zhǔgé, tā shi bīngé.

43.0. érhuàyùn   retroflex sound [r-ized rhyme]

43.1. Zhǐ yǒu Běijīng huàli yǒu érhuàyùn.

44.0. qīngyīn   neutral tone [light sound]

44.1. Qīngyīn jiu shi yíge zî niànchu de shēngyin qīng yìdiǎr, bú yào
niànzhòngle de yìsi.

45.0. qiàqiǎo   (1) just at that moment, precisely (then), just; (2) accidentally, by coincidence

45.1. Zuótian Wáng Xiānsheng lái kàn wǒ qiàqiǎo wǒ bú zài jiā. Tā gěi
wo liúxia yîfēng xìn, xìnli shuō míngtian tā chàng xì, qǐng wǒ qu
kàn xì.

Mǎ : Háiyǒu, shénmo shi liàngcí?

Bái: "Yîběn shū, liǎngkuài qián" de běn gēn kuài dōu shi liàngcî.

Mǎ : Qǐng nǐ zài kàn shēngcí biǎoshangde gé zî. Zhōngguo huàli yǒu
géde biànhuà méi yǒu?

110 Bái: Zhōngguo huàli méi yǒu géde biànhuà. Mǎ Jiàoshòu, érhuàyùn shì
bu shi jiu shi Běijīng huà lǐtou yǒu?

Mǎ : Shìde. Érhuàyùn shi Běijīng huàli dú yǒu de, yǒude shíhou yùnwěi
yào jiāshang ér. Kěshi érde yīn bù néng niànzhòng le, bìděi bǎ ta
niànchéng qīngyīn, érqiě yào gēn cérde yùnwěi liánhéchéngle yíge
115   yīn. Bù néng shuō nǎ-er, bìděi shuō nǎr. Guānyú érhuàyùn wǒ
shuō ge gùshi. Wǒ yǒu ge qīnqi shi Shànghǎi rén, tā xuézhe shuō

Běijīng huà.   Yǒu yícî péngyou qǐng ta chī fàn tā méi qù.   Hòulai
tā kànjian nèige péngyou tā shuō: "Duìbuqǐ, wǒ suǒyǐ méi lái chī
fàn-er shi yīnwei wǒ qiàqiǎo yǒu yàojǐnde shìqing-er." Dàjiā dōu
120   xiào le, yīnwei zhèi liǎngjù huà bìng búshi érhuàyùnde yùnwěi.

Bái: Wǒ yě juéde érhuàyùn hěn nán.

Mǎ : Bù róngyi. Yǒude rén bǎ érde yīn niànde hěn zhòng, jiu hěn nántīng le.

Bái: Zhǐ yǒu Běijīng rén yòng de zìran.

125 Mǎ : Súyǔ shuō "Xíguàn chéng zìran." Děi duō shuō duō yòng.

Bái: Búcuò.

46.0. guīnà   (1) inductive (reasoning); (2) generalize, consolidate

guīnàfǎ   inductive method

46.1. Zhǔxî shuō: "Xiànzài wǒ bǎ dàjiā zhǒngzhǒngde yìjian guīnàwéi
liǎngge yìjian yǐbiàn tǎolùn." (W) (T)

46.2. <u>Guīnàfǎ</u> shi lùnlǐxuéde míngcî. Zhèizhǒng fāngfǎ shi yóu zhǒngzhǒng
tèshūde shî guīnàchulai yíge yuánzé.   (T)

47.0. biànqiān   change, variation, vicissitudes [change move]

47.1. Huáng Hé rù hǎi de dìfang, jùshuō zài jìn wǔbǎiniánli biànqiānle
hěn duō cî.

48.0. biànhuà   (1) transform, change; (2) transformation, change [change
transform]

48.1. Tā zuótian shuō de huà jīntian jiu biànhuà le.

49.0. zuǐ   mouth

zuǐba   (1) mouth (Shanghai dialect); (2) cheek

dǎ zuǐba   slap the cheeks

49.1. "Tāde zuǐ hěn huì shuō huà" jiu shi shuō "Tā hěn yǒu kǒucái" de
yìsi.

49.2. Bái Xiānsheng dìdide zuǐ yě nènmo huì shuō, hé Bái Xiānsheng yíyàng. (T)

49.3. Zhāng Tàitai bǎ háizi guǎnde hěn lìhai. Háizi yàoshi bù tīng huà tā
jiu dǎ tāmen zuǐba.   (T)

Bái: Zhōngguo yǒu jǐqiānniánde lìshǐ le, zài yǔyán zhèi fāngmian yǒu hěn
dàde yǎnbiàn ba?

Mǎ : Guīnàqilai shuō, yīnwei shídàide biànqiān suǒyǐ yǔyán dāngrán yǒu
130   hěn dàde biànhuà. Bǐrú <u>Shī Jīng</u>、<u>Shàng Shū</u> jùshuō shi gǔrén zuǐli
suǒ shuō de huà.   Nǐ kàn xiànzài nǎr yǒu rén shuō nèizhǒng huà
ne?   Xiànzài wǒmen ná <u>Shī Jīng</u>、<u>Shàng Shū</u> lái kàn lián dǒng dōu
bù dǒng, shènzhiyú xiānsheng gěi jiǎngle hái bù míngbái.

50.0. císù   smallest meaningful element, morpheme [word element]

50.1. Císù jiu shi gòuchéng cíde jīběn dānwèi. (T)

51.0. chéngfèn   element, constituent, ingredient [become element]

51.1. Zài wùlǐxuéshang suǒwèi jiùshi duō zhǒng chéngfèn nǐ zhīdao ma?

52.0. qūzhé   (1) bent; (2) inflection [bent bend]

52.1. Lādīngwénde qūzhé bǐ Yīngwénde fùzáde duō.

53.0. fùjiā   (1) add, affix, supplement; (2) addition, affixing   [attached add]

53.1. Yǒude fànguǎr zài suàn zhàngde shíhou chúle fànqian yǐwài hái yào fùjiā xiǎofèi.

Bái: Mǎ Jiàoshòu, shì bu shi yǒude yǔyánxuéjiā rènwéi Shàng Shū, Shī
135   Jīng bú shi zuǐli shuō de huà, shi nèige shíhou xiě de wényán?

Mǎ : Yě yǒu zhènmo shuō de. Wǒ xiànzài zài wèn nǐ shénmo jiào císù?

Bái: Jiu shi zǔzhi cérde chéngfèn jiàozuo císù. Bǐrú máizàng zhèige
        cér mái gēn zàng jiu shi císù.

Mǎ : Qūzhé zhèige cér nǐ míngbái tāde yìsi ma?

140 Bái: Qūzhé de běnyì jiu shi "bù zhí" de yìsi, zài yǔyánxuéli géde biàn-
        huà jiu shi qūzhé. Qǐng wèn fùjiā shi kǒuyǔ ma?

Mǎ : Fùjiā shi xiě de. Bǐrú xiě xìn: "Wǒ suǒyǐ méi mǎi nèisuǒr fáng-
        zide yuányīn shi chúle fángzi jiàqian zhīwài xū lìngwài fùjiā wǔbǎi
        yuán."

54.0. liánchuàn   string together [join string]

      yìliánchuàn(de)   continuously, one after the other

54.1. Nǐ néngfǒu bǎ zhèi jǐge cí liánchuàn zài yìqǐ zuòchéng yíge jùzi?

54.2. Tāde chē zài lùshang chū shì le, yìliánchuànde pèngle sānge rén.

54.3. Tā yìliánchuàn xiěle sānpiān zhuànjìxìngde xiǎoshuō. (T)

55.0. nǎozi   brains

      huàn nǎozi   switch to another subject, take up something else
                    [change brains]

55.1. Wǒde nǎozi tài bù hǎo le. Shénmo yě jìbuzhù le. Zhèige zì běnlái
        shi shuānglìrér, wǒ xiěchéng lìrér le.

55.2. Wǒ kàn shū kàn de tài jiǔ le. Wǒ xiǎng tīngting lùyīn huànhuan
        nǎozi. (T)

56.0. tài*   grand

      Tàiguó   Thailand

      Tàiyǔ   Thai language (W)

56.1. Tián Xiānsheng shi Zhōngguo rén.   Zài Tàiguó yòng Tàiyǔ jiǎng-
       yǎn, jiǎng de yòu liúli yòu shēngdòng.

56.2. Zhōngguo hé Tàiguó bǐcǐ zhījiān yǒu láiwǎng ma?   (T)

57.0. lèisì   similar, alike, like [category resembling]

57.1. Tā xiě de wénzhāng lèisì xiǎoxuésheng xiě de, suǒyǐ bǐděi chóng-
       gǎi.

145 Mǎ : Wǒmen yìliánchuànde yánjiule hěn duō yǔyánxuéde cér.   Xiànzài
          huànhuan nǎozi tántan biéde.   Zuìjìn yǎn yíbù Tàiguo diànyǐng, jù
          shuō hěn yǒu yìsi.

    Bái : Nín xiǎng kàn ma?

    Mǎ : Wǒ xiǎng qu kànkan.

150 Bái : Piānzishangde duìhuà shi yòng Tàiguo huà ma?

    Mǎ : Shì.   Tàiguo huà yě shi bāokuò zai Hàn-Zàng yǔzú zhīnèi de.

    Bái : Wǒ yě xiǎng qù kànkan.   Wǒ bú dà liǎojiě Tàiguode qíngxing.   Wǒ
           jiu zhīdao Tàiguode sīzhīpǐn bú cuò.

    Mǎ : Shìde, xiànzài yǒu yìzhǒng Tàiguo chóu, tàitai、xiáojiemen dōu yòng
155   Tàiguo chóu zuò yīfu.

    Bái : Tàiguo chóu shénmo yàngzi?   Wǒ méi kànjianguo.

    Mǎ : Lèisì Shāndong zhī de chóuzi.

    Bái : Oh, Shāndong chóu wǒ zhīdao.   Zài Měiguo yǒu mài de.   Yǒu yícì
           wǒ mǔqin mǎile yíduàn Shāndong chóu.

160 Mǎ : Jùshuō zhèi liǎngzhǒng chóuzi kànshangqu chàbuduō.   Bù zhīdào shi
          Shāndōng chóu mófǎng Tàiguo chóu ne, háishi Tàiguo chóu mófǎng
          Shāndōng chóu ne?

58.0. qiángdiào   emphasize [strong tune]

58.1. Tā qiángdiàode shuō: "Wǒ yídìng yào kèfú zhèige kùnnan."

59.0. guǎngbō   broadcast (N/V) [broad spread]

59.1. Wǒ jīntian tīng wúxiàndiànde guǎngbō, shuō míngtian yào guā dà-
       fēng.

59.2. Wǒ zuì xǐhuan tīng wúxiàndiànli zhèiduàn guǎngbō xìjù.   (T)

60.0. chéngwei   become, be

60.1. Fánshi xīn shūde jiǎnjiè, tā kànwán zhīhòu dōu liúzhe.   Rìjīyuèlěi
       jílěile hěn duō, kéyi chéngwei yíbù xīn shū jiǎnjiè huìbiān le. (W)

61.0. yōuyuè   superlative, excellent [superior exceed]

61.1. Zhōngguo zài dìlǐshang yǒu zhǒngzhǒng yōuyuède tiáojiàn.

62.0. wènhuà   (1) pose questions; (2) a question sentence

62.1. "Nǐ yúkuài ma?" zhèijù huà shi yíjù wènhuà.

Bái: Wǒ zuótian tīng wúxiàndiàn guǎngbō xīnwén shuō yǒu yíge guójiāde
      rénmín kāi quántǐ dàhuì qiángdiàozhe shuō tāmende guójiā zài zuì-
165   jìnde jiānglái yídìng chéngwei shìjièshang dì-yīděng qiángguó, yīnwei
      tāmen yǒu tiānránde yōuyuè tiáojiàn.

Mǎ : Shuōde yǒu dàoli. Tiānránde tiáojiàn dāngrán shi zhǐzhe dìlǐ shuō
      de.   Búguò rénmín yě yǒu zérèn.   Quángwó rénmín yìzhíde nǔlì,
      zhòng dì de zhòng dì, yánjiu kēxué de yánjiu kēxué, yě shi qiáng-
170   guó zuì yàojǐnde chéngfèn.

Bái: Yìhuěr tīngwán le Zhuāntí Jiǎnghuà, xiàozhǎng hái yào wènhuà ne.

Mǎ : Měinián kāixué yǐhòu xiàozhǎng duì měi yíge wàiguo liúxuéshēng
      yào dāndú wènhuà yícì.

Bái: Wǒ yǐqián zài zhèr niàn shū yě shi zhèiyàngr. Xiàozhǎng duì wǒ-
175   men wàiguo xuésheng chùchù biǎoshì guānxīn.

SHĒNGCÍ BIǍO

1. Yuè
    Yuèyǔ (W)

2. Xiāng
    Xiāngyǔ (W)

3. Fújiàn
    Fúzhōu

4. Wú
    Wúyǔ (W)

5. Mǐn
    Mǐnyǔ (W)
    Mǐnběiyǔ (W)
    Mǐnnányǔ (W)

6. Gàn
    Gànyǔ (W)

7. Xiàmén

8. fēnqū
    dìqū

9. shēngdiào

10. jùlí

11. Chéngdū

12. Kūnmíng

13. Yángzhou

14. Shěnyáng

15. yǔyīn
     yǔyīnxué

16. Shànggǔ Hànyǔ
     Zhōnggǔ Hànyǔ

17. Shī Jīng

18. Shàng Shū

19. gòucífǎ

20. Suí

21. míngcí

22. yǔzú
     Hàn-Zàng Yǔzú
     Yìn-Ōu Yǔzú

23. bīncí
     zhǔcí

24. biàndiào

25. mái

26. zàng
     máizàng

27. chóngdié

28. dòngcí

29. fùcí

30. wěiba
     jùwěi

31. cítóu
     cíwěi

32. dàimíngcí
     rénchēng dàimíngcí

33. yíwèn
     yíwèncí
     yíwèn dàimíngcí
     yíwènshì

34. xùshù
     xùshùshì

35. fǒudìng
     fǒudìngshì

36. cídiào

37. zhí
     zhíqián
     zhíde
     jiàzhi

38. fùhé
     fùhéjù

39. zàojùfǎ

40. xiǎnzhù	48. biànhuà	huàn nǎozi
41. liàngcî	49. zuǐ	56. tài*
42. gé	zuǐba	Tàiguó
zhǔgé	dǎ zuǐba	Tàiyǔ (W)
bīngé	50. císù	57. lèisî
43. érhuàyùn	51. chéngfèn	
44. qīngyīn	52. qūzhé	58. qiángdiào
45. qiàqiǎo	53. fùjiā	59. guǎngbō
46. guīnà	54. liánchuàn	60. chéngwei
guīnàfǎ	yìliánchuàn(de)	61. yōuyuè
47. biànqiān	55. nǎozi	62. wènhuà

YŬFĂ LIÀNXÍ

(See note at end of lesson)

1. Wǒmende Zhōngwén xiānsheng zhēn lîhai. Búshi shuō wǒmende shēngdiào
   bú duì, jiushi shuō wǒmen shuō de bù liúli, zàiburán jiu shuō wǒmende
   yǔyīn bù qīngchu.

2. Nèiwèi yánjiu yǔyīnxué de yàoshi pèngjian ni, búshi duì nǐ shuō Wúyǔ
   jiushi shuō Gànyǔ, zàiburán jiushi shuō Yuèyǔ.   (W)

3. Nǐ bié máng. Wǒ tīngwánle zhèiduàn guǎngbō xìjù jiu zǒu.

4. Wǒ niànwánle <u>Qiān Zî Wén</u> jiu niàn <u>Shī Jīng</u>.

5. Tāmen liǎngge rén jīngguo Wáng Xiānshengde jièshao jiu chéngwei hǎo
   péngyou le.

6. Wǒ mǎile yìběn <u>Yuèyǔ Yǔfǎ</u> kànle bàntiān yě bù dǒng. Jīngguo Wáng
   Xiānsheng gěi wo jiěshî wǒ cái dǒng le.

7. Tā shàngge yuè jiu líkai Tàiguó zuò chuán wǎng zhèr lái le, ànzhe rìzi
   lái suàn tā zǎo jiu yīnggāi dào le.

8. Ànzhe jùlí lái suàn tā Shuāngshíjié kéyi dào zhèr le.

9. Tā búdàn duì yǔyīnxué yǒu xìngqu, duìyu yìshu yě yǒu xìngqu.

10. Wáng Xiānsheng búdàn yánjiu Wúyǔ hé Xiāngyǔ, yě yánjiu Wú、Xiāng liǎng-
    ge dìfangde mínsú.   (W)

11. Tā zuìjìn búdàn xiěle hěn duō sǎnwén hái xiěle yìběn shū guānyu Yìn-
    Ōuyǔ géde biànhuà (xiàng zhǔgé、bīngé shénmode).

12. Nèige wàiguo rén búdàn yánjiu Mǐnyǔ、Yuèyǔ, hái dǒngde Gànyǔ.   (W)

13. Zhāng Xiānsheng zuótian búdàn qǐng wǒmen chī fàn, yòu qǐng wǒmen tīng
    de xì.

14. Tā bǎ nèi jǐge Hànzî dōu xiěcuò le. Búdàn bǎ shuānglîrér xiěchéng tí-
    shǒur le, yòu bǎ <u>Hàn Cháo</u>de <u>hàn</u> zì xiěchéng yán zîpáng le.

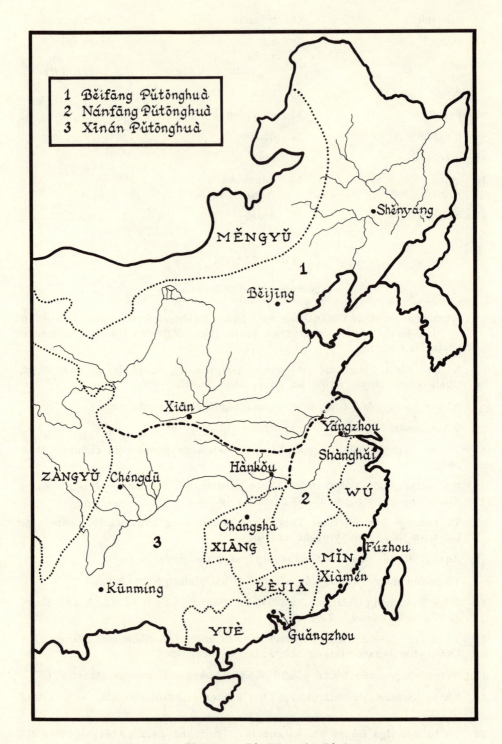

1 Běifāng Pǔtōnghuà
2 Nánfāng Pǔtōnghuà
3 Xīnán Pǔtōnghuà

MĚNGYǓ

1

· Shěnyáng

· Běijīng

· Xiān

· Yángzhou

· Shànghǎi

ZÀNGYǓ · Chéngdū

· Hànkǒu

2

WÚ

· Chángshā

3 XIĀNG

MǏN

· Fúzhou

· Kūnmíng

KÈJIĀ

· Xiàmén

YUÈ

· Guǎngzhou

Zhōngguo Dà Fāngyán Dìqū

15. Tā děngdao bǎ tā fùqin zàngle zhīhòu zài dào Xiàmén qu.

16. Zhāng Xiānsheng shuō děngdao tāde Fúzhou xì xuéhǎo yǐhòu zài dào Yáng-zhou qu yánjiu Yángzhoude dìfang xì.

17. Děng dàfēng guāwán le, wǒmen diàochá yígòng yǒu duōshao rén sǐshāng.

18. Děng wǒ cóng Tàiguó huílai wǒmen xiángxì tǎolùn zhèige shēngyì zhíde bù zhíde qu zuò.

19. Nǐ tuìxiūle yǐhòu nǐ yàoshi líkai Kūnmíngde shíhou qiānwàn gàosu wo yì-shēngr.

20. Yàoshi nǐ qiáojian Máo Xiānshengde shíhou, nǐ wèn ta wǒde yìběn Tōng-xùn Bàodǎo gēn xīn chūbǎn de Guǎngdong Shěngde fēnqū dìtú tā kànjian-le méi yǒu?

21. Wǒ xiān jiěshì zhǔcí gēn bīncí, zài shuō cítóu gēn cíwěi.

22. Wǒmen xiān qu chī fàn, zài dào chéng lǐtou qu kàn xì.

23. Zhè shi hěn xiǎnzhùde shìshi. Tā wèile yánjiu jīngxì cái xué Běijīng huà.

24. Mǎ Xiānsheng wèile dào Shěnyáng tōngxùnshè gōngzuò cái dào Dōngběi lái de.

25. Nèiwèi xiáojie kànzhe hǎoxiang duì rén hěn rèqíng. Qíshí yìdiǎn gǎnqíng yě méi yǒu.

26. Wǒ wǔnián méi dào zhèr lái le. Xiànzài kànzhe hǎoxiang yǒu hěn dàde biànhuà shide.

27. Wàn Xiānsheng shuō zuì yǒu qùweide shì shi yánjiu fāngyán le. Tā shuō ta zài méi yǒu yánjiu yǔyánxué yǐqián tā jiù huì Mǐnnán huà gēn Mǐnběi huà le.

28. Tā zài méi yǒu xiě zhèiběn zhuànjìxìngde xiǎoshuō yǐqián yìliánchuànde xiěguo hěn duō shū le.

29. Bīncí zài jùzili yǒushíhou yě xiàng zhǔcí yíyàng kéyi fàngzai dòngcí qián-bian.

30. Jīn Xiānshengde érzi yě xiàng Jīn Xiānsheng、Jīn Tàitai yíyàng shi ge pàngzi. Érqiě zuì yě nènmo huì shuō.

JIǍNGHUÀ

   Zhōngguode yǔyán shi shìjièshang zhòngyào yǔyán zhī yī. Wèi-shén-mo néng chéngwéi zhòngyào yǔyán zhī yī ne? Yǒu hǎojǐge yuányīn. Dì-yī, Zhōngguo dì dà rén duō, rénkǒu zhàn shìjiè zǒngshùde sìfenzhī-yī. Zài xiànzài hé jiānglaide qūshì, shuō Zhōngguo huà de rén bǐ shuō rènhé yì-

5 zhǒng yǔyánde rén dōu yào duō. Dì-èr, Zhōngguo wénhuà yǐjing yǒule hǎojǐqiānniánde lìshǐ, shi zuì fēngfù zuì yōuyuè de. Chú cǐ zhīwài, hái yǒu liǎngge tèdiǎn shi yǔyánxuéjiā suǒ zhùyì de. Yíge shi yǒu cídiào, yíge

shi méi yǒu qūzhé. Yīnwei yǒu yǐshàng zhèi jǐge yuányīn· suǒyǐ cóng rénlèi zǔzhi hé sīxiǎng xuéwènde guāndiǎn lái kàn, Zhōngguo yǔyán shi hěn
10 yǒu yánjiu jiàzhi de.

Xiànzài wǒmen xiān lái tántan Zhōngguo yǔyán lìshǐde yǎnbiàn. Wǒmen zhīdao Zhōngguo huà shi shǔyú yíge fànwéi hěn guǎngde yǔzú, jiu
shi Hàn-Zàng Yǔzú. Hàn-Zàng Yǔzú chúle Zhōngguoyǔ yǐwài hái bāokuò-
zhe Tàiyǔ、Miǎndiànyǔ、Xīzàngyǔ děngděng. Dàibiǎo Zhōngguo yǔyán zuî
15 zǎode wénzì shi jiǎgǔwén. Guānyú jiǎgǔwén shàngcì yǐjing jiǎngguo, zhèli
bú bì zài jiǎng. Yǒuxiē xuézhě shuō Shī Jīng、Shàng Shū děngděng shuō
shi jìyuánqián liùbǎi nián zuǒyòude Hànyǔ, jiàozuo Shànggǔ Hànyǔ, yòu
bǎ Suí Táng shídàide yùnshū Qièyùn rènwéi shi Suí Táng shídàide yǔyīn. Suí Táng shídài shi jìyuánhòu liù-qīshìjì, suǒyǐ jiu jiàozuo Zhōnggǔ
20 Hànyǔ. Xiànzàide Zhōngguo pǔtōnghuà zìrán shi xiàndài Hànyǔ le. Cóng
Shànggǔ Hànyǔ dào xiànzàide Zhōngguo huà yǐjing yǒule sānqiānnián zuǒyòude lìshǐ hé biànhuà.

Qícì wǒmen yào tán de shi Zhōngguo yǔyánde fēnqū. Xiànzài Zhōngguo huà kéyi fēnchéng liùge dà fāngyán dìqū. Zuî zhòngyàode zìrán shi
25 pǔtōnghuà. Zhōngguo rén shuō pǔtōnghuà de zhàn rénkǒu zǒngshù sìfēnzhī-sān. Pǔtōnghuà yòu kéyi fēnchéng sān dà lèi. Běifāng huà kéyi yòng
Běijīng huà lái dàibiǎo. Nánbùde pǔtōnghuà kéyi yòng Yángzhou huà lái
dàibiǎo. Xīnánbù pǔtōnghuà kéyi yòng Chéngdū huà lái dàibiǎo. Shuō pǔtōnghuà de qūyù hěn guǎng. Búlùn bǐcǐ jùlí duó yuǎn, kěshi yǔyánde
30 chābié bìng bú tài dà. Yíge cóng Yúnnán Kūnmíng dìqū lái de rén gēn
yíge cóng Dōngběi Shěnyáng dìqū lái de rén bǐcǐ zhījiān de huà bìng bù
chéngwéi wèntí.

Qíyúde jǐge fāngyán shi Yuèyǔ, kéyi yòng Guǎngzhou huà lái dàibiǎo; Wúyǔ, kéyi yòng Sūzhou huà lái dàibiǎo; Xiāngyǔ, kéyi yòng Cháng-
35 shā huà lái dàibiǎo. Gànyǔ hé Kèjiā huà hěn xiāngjìn, kéyi guīnàzai yíge
fāngyán qūyùli, pǔtōng jiàozuo Kèjiā huà. Hái yǒu yíge jiu shi Mǐnyǔ.
Mǐnyǔ fēn nánběi liǎngqū. Mǐnnán huà kéyi ná Xiàmén huà zuò biāozhǔn.
Mǐnběi huà kéyi ná Fúzhou huà zuò biāozhǔn. Zhèixiē dà fāngyán qū bǐjiǎoqilai, jìrán yǐ pǔtōnghuàde fāngyán qū wéi zuî dà, nènmo wǒmen jiu
40 tántan pǔtōnghuà, yě jiu shi Běijīng huà.

Běijīng huàli rúguǒ bú suàn shēngdiào yǒu sìbǎi duō ge yīnjié.
Měige yīnjié fēn sìshēng, hái yǒu qīngyīn hé biàndiào. Sìshēng jiu shi

dì-yīshēng, dì-èrshēng, dì-sānshēng, dì-sìshēng, zài qiáncì céngjīng jiǎngguo.   Qīngyīn biàndiào shi shénmo ne?   Qīngyīn shi cóng sìshēng jīběn
45 shēngdiàoli biànchulai de. Jǔ ge lìzi: "Mǎimai dōu bù hǎo." Zài zhèige
lìzili mǎi hé mài běnlái shi liǎngge bùtóngde dòngcí. Kěshi yàoshi wǒmen shuō "Mǎimai dōu bù hǎo," bǎ mài zì shuōchéng qīngyīn, nà jiu bǎ
mǎimai shuōchéngle yíge míngcí, gēn shēngyi de yìsi chàbuduō le. Biàndiào jiu shi dāng liǎngge dì-sānshēng zài yìqǐde shíhou, qiántoude dì-sān-
50 shēng yào biànchéng dì-èrshēng. Bǐrú shuō zuò mǎimai de mǎi gēn máizàng de mái běnlái shi bùtóng shēngdiào de, kěshi zài "Mǎi mǎ" zhèige
jùzili jiu biànchéng tóngyīn de, dōu shi dì-èrshēng le. Suǒyǐ yàoshi yǒu
rén shuō "Mái mǎ" wǒmen gēnběn jiu méi fázi zhīdao, tā shi yào bǎ mǎ
mǎilai ne, háishi yào bǎ mǎ máizai dìli.

55   Zài Běijīng huà yīnyùnshang hái yǒu yìdiǎn zhíde zhùyì de, jiu shi
yìbān suǒwèi de érhuàyùn. Érhuàyùn jiu shi zài yǒuxiē yīnjiéde hòumian
jiāshang yíge xiàng ér yàngde shēngyin. Bǐfang shuō yìzhāng huà kéyi
shuōchéng yìzhāng huàr, chūqu wán kéyi shuōchéng chūqu wár, hǎohǎode
kéyi shuōchéng hǎohǎorde.

60   Xiànzài shuōshuo Zhōngguo huàlide cí shi zěnyàng gòuchéng de, zhè
jiu shi gòucífǎ. Yìn-Ōu yǔyánde gòucífǎ yǒude shíhou shi bǐ Zhōngguo
yǔyán gòucífǎ fùzá. Bǐfāng shuō Yīngwén jùzili yǒu "One book is expensive.   Two books are expensive." Zài zhèige lìzilide míngcí gēn dòngcí
dōu shòu "shùmu" de yǐngxiǎng ér shuōfǎ bùtóng. Kěshi zài Zhōngguo
65 huàli jiu méi yǒu zhèiyàngde biànhuà, zhǐ shi shuō "Yìběn shū guì" hé
"Liǎngběn shū guì" jiu kéyi le. Míngcí hé dòngcí dōu méi yǒu biànhuà.
Yòu bǐrú Yīngwénlide "I like him" hé "He likes me" de rénchēng dàimíngcí dōu shi yǒu géde biànhuà. Zhōngguo huàli jiu méi yǒu zhèige
biànhuà. Zhōngguo huà shuō "Wǒ xǐhuan tā" hé "Tā xǐhuan wǒ." Zhèlide
70 rénchēng dàimíngcí dōu shi yíyàng de. Yīnwei Zhōngguo huàde gòucífǎli
méi yǒu lèisì Yìn-Ōu yǔyánzhōngde nèiyàng qūzhé, suǒyǐ guòqu yǒu hěn
duō rén yǐwéi Zhōngguo huàli méi yǒu yǔfǎ. Zhèizhǒng shuōfǎ zìrán yě
shi bù hé shìshí de.

Zài Zhōngguo huàli yǒu hěn duō císù kéyi chóngdié, lìrú dòngcí
75 zǒuzou, kànkàn, dǎtīng dǎtīng. Xíngróngcí chóngdié cháng dàngzuo fùcí
yòng, bǐfang shuō kuàikuāide, gāogāoxìngxìngde. Míngcí chóngdié de bǐ-

jiǎo shǎo, dànshi yě yǒu yìxiē lìrú <u>gēge</u>、<u>dìdi</u>、<u>jiějie</u>、<u>mèimei</u> děng. Yǒu hěn duō néng zuò liàngcide míngcí yě shi cháng chóngdié de, lìrú <u>nián-nián</u>、<u>jiājiā</u>、<u>tiāntiān</u> děng.

80   Hái yǒu yíge cíde fùhé fāngfa, jiu shi "fùjiā chéngfèn." Zhōngguo huàlide suǒwèi cítóu hěn shǎo, zhǐ yǒu <u>dì</u>、<u>chū</u>、<u>lǎo</u> děng, lìrú <u>dì-yī</u>、<u>dì-èr</u>; <u>chū-yī</u>、<u>chū-èr</u>; <u>Lǎo Zhāng</u>、<u>lǎoshī</u>. Kěshi cíwěide fùjiā dào fēicháng duō. Gāngcái tánguo de érhuàyùn kéyi suànshi cíwěide yìzhǒng. Hái yǒu hěn duō biéde cíwěi, xiàng jiāzai míngcí hòutoude <u>zi</u>, lìrú <u>zhuōzi</u>、<u>érzi</u>、

85   <u>nǎozi</u>; huòzhě fùjiā yíge <u>tou</u> zì xiàng <u>shítou</u>、<u>wàitou</u>、<u>gútou</u>; huòzhě fùjiā yíge <u>ba</u> zì xiàng <u>wěiba</u>、<u>zuǐba</u> děng.

Zhōngguo huàli hái yǒu yíge tèdiǎn jiu shi liàngcí. Bǐfāng shuō <u>yì-běn shū</u>、<u>liǎngzhī qiānbǐ</u>, <u>běn</u> hé <u>zhī</u> dōu shi liàngcí, bù néng bú yòng.

Bǎ cí liánchuànzai yìqǐ, biànchéng jùzi, zhè jiu shi zàojùfǎ. Zhōng-

90   guo huàde zàojùfǎ zǒngshi zhǔcí zài qián, bīncí zài dòngcí zhīhòu. Kěshi yě yǒu shíhou wèile yào qiángdiào mǒu yíge chéngfèn bǎ bīncí fàngdao qiánmian.   Lìrú "Shū, wǒ méi màiwán" zhè jiu shi bǎ bīncí tíqián le.

Zai biǎoshì wènhuà de shíhou yǒu sānge bànfǎ. Dì-yī shi yòng yí-wèn dàimíngcí, bǐfang shuō <u>shéi</u>? <u>shénmo</u>? <u>nǎr</u>? <u>jǐge</u>? <u>zěnmo</u>? Dì-èr

95   shi yòng jùwěi yíwèncí, xiàng <u>ma</u>、<u>ba</u> děngděng, lìrú "Nǐ qù ma?" Dì-sān shi yíwènshì, shi bǎ xùshùshì hé fǒudìngshì liánzài yìqǐ chéngwéi yíge yíwènshì, lìrú "Tā mǎi shū" "Tā bù mǎi shū" liánzài yìqǐ biàn-chéng "Tā mǎi bù mǎi shū?" de yíwèn jùzi.

Yǐshàng suǒ shuō de búguò shi zài Zhōngguo yǔyánzhōng tíchu jǐge

100   bǐjiāo xiǎnzhùde lìzi, tèbié shi gēn <u>Yìn-Ōu</u> yǔzú bǐjiāo bùtóngde, shāo-wēi shuōmíng zuòwéi zhūwèide cānkǎo.

FÙSHÙ

Zhèipán lùyīndài shi Zhōngwén dì-yīzǔ dì-shísānhào, shísāncìde fù-shù Zhuāntí Jiǎnghuà. Shi yóu Bái Wénshān fùshù de.

Zhèicìde Zhuāntí Jiǎnghuà shi tán "Cānkǎo Shū." Hái shi yóu Jiǎn Jiàoshòu gěi wǒmen jiǎng˜ de. Wǒmen búlùn xué něizhǒng kēxué dōu lí-

5   bukāi cānkǎo shū. Suǒyǐ Jiǎn Jiàoshòu gěi wǒmen jiǎng de guānyú cān-kǎo shū zhèige tímu shi xiāngdāng zhòngyào de. Tā búdàn jièshaole hěn duō shū gěi wǒmen, érqiě bǎ rúhé chá zìdiǎn de fāngfǎ hěn xiángxide gàosu wǒmen. Zhèige hěn bǎoguìde zīliào wǒmen bù yīnggāi hūlüè le.

Jiǎn Jiàoshòu shǒuxiān gàosu wǒmen de shi cānkǎo shūde zhǒnglèi.
10 Tā shuō yǒu liǎngzhǒng.   Yìzhǒng shi guānyú zì hé cí de, yìzhǒng shi
guānyú chángshí de. Jiǎn Jiàoshòu shuō xuǎnzé cānkǎo shū zuì yàojǐnde
yuánzé shi yào xuǎn zuì shìyòngde.

.   Tā yòu shuō guānyú zì hé cíde cānkǎo shū yǒu liǎngzhǒng. Yǒude
shi liǎngzhǒng yǐshàngde wénzì xiàng Zhōng-Yīng、Zhōng-Fà、Zhōng-Dé、
15 Zhōng-Rì de. Yǒude zhǐshi Zhōngwén de. Zì hé cíde cānkǎo shū dōu yǒu
xiē shénmo shū ne? Nà jiu shi cídiǎn、zìdiǎn hé zìhuì、cíhuì.

Jiǎn Jiàoshòu gěi wǒmen jiǎng zìdiǎnde bùshǒu. Tā shuō Zhōngwén
zìdiǎn yígòng yǒu èrbǎi yìshísìge bùshǒu.   Bùshǒu suǒyǐn páiliè de cìxu
dōu shi ànzhe bùshǒude bǐhuá duōshǎo páilièqilai de.   Jiǎn Jiàoshòu gěi
20 wǒmen jǔ ge lìzi yīnggāi zěnmoyàng chá zìdiǎn. Tā shuō yàoshi wǒmen
bú rènshi <u>pùzide pù</u> zì, wǒmen chá zìdiǎnde shíhou bìděi xiān zhīdao <u>pù</u>
zìde bùshǒu shi shénmo.   Wǒmen zhīdao bùshǒu shi <u>jīn</u>, jiu shi <u>jīn</u> zìpáng le.   Wǒmen zài shǔshu jīn zì jǐhuá, jīn zì yígòng shi bāhuá. Hǎo
le, wǒmen xiān kàn bùshǒu suǒyǐn, zài suǒyǐnli zhǎo jīn zì.   Zhǎodàole
25 jīn zì zhīhòu, zài kànkan jīn zì xiàmiande shùmuzì, nà jiu shi zìdiǎnde
dì-jǐyè, wǒmen jiu zhīdao zài něi yīyèshang.   Zài kàn <u>pù</u> zì yígòng shi
jǐhuá, dànshi yào jìzhu yígòng shi jǐhuá bù bāokuò bùshǒu, děi bǎ bùshǒude bǐhuá chúdiào.   <u>Pù</u> zì chúdiàole bùshǒu jīn zì hái yǒu qīhuá le,
wǒmen jiu zài jīn bùde qīhuáli qu zhǎo. Yàoshi wǒmen chá de shi <u>Cíhǎi</u>,
30 pù zì zài <u>Cíhǎi</u>li zhǎodàole, tóu-yīge zì shi <u>pù</u> zì, jǐnjiēzhe shi yíge kuòhú, zài kuòhúli shi yíge <u>jiǎ</u> zì, xiàmian jiu shi yīn. Bǎ zìde yìsi jiě-
shiwánle zhīhòu yòu yǒu yíge kuòhú, lǐmian shi ge <u>yǐ</u> zì, yǐsi jiu shi
shuō pù zìde niànfǎ yǒu jiǎ、yǐ liǎngge yīn, tóngshí yě yǒu liǎngzhǒng
yìsi.

35   Háiyǒu, wǒmen wàiguo rén chá Zhōngwén zìdiǎn shi jìzhu bùshǒude
cìxu, jiu shi shùmuzì. Bǐfang shuō chá rén bù shi bùshǒu 9, shuǐ bù jiu
shi 85, jīn zì shi 167. Zhèige fāngfǎ bǐjiào kuàide duō. Zhè kě bú shi
Jiǎn Jiàoshòu jiǎnghuà lǐmian de, shi wǒ gèrén chá zìdiǎnde jīngyàn.

Jiǎn Jiàoshòu yòu gěi wǒmen jiǎng zìdiǎnde fǎnqiè. Tā shuō fǎnqiè
40 jiu shi gǔshíhou Zhōngguode pīnyīn fāngfǎ.   Yīnwei Zhōngguo gǔshíhou
méi yǒu zìmǔ pīnyīn, nà jiu shi gǔrén fāmíng de yìzhǒng pīnyīn de fázi.
Jiǎn Jiàoshòu shuō Zhōngguo zì měi yíge zì duōbàn shi liǎngge yīnsù,

qiánmiande yīnsù jiàozuo <u>shēng</u>, yě jiàozuo <u>yīn</u>, hòumiande yīnsù jiàozuo <u>yùn</u>. Fǎnqiè jiu shi yíge shēng hé yíge yùn hézài yíkuàr fāchulai de
45   yīn. Rú <u>shāng</u> zî zài zìdiǎnli chádàole yǐhòu, <u>shāng</u> zìde xiàmian yídìng
xiězhe sānge zî "<u>shī</u> <u>yāng</u> qiè." Yìsi gàosu wǒmen shāng zìde yīn shi yóu
<u>shī</u> gēn <u>yāng</u> pīnchulai de. Tā shuō <u>shī</u> zî yòng qiánbiande shēng ér bú
yòng tāde yùn. <u>Yāng</u> zî yòng hòubiànde yùn ér bú yòng tāde shēng. Zhèiyàng héqilai de yīn jiu shi qièchulai de zìyīn.

50   Jiǎn Jiàoshòu yě gàosu wǒmen guānyú chángshíde cānkǎo shū. Tā
shuō wǒmen mùqián suīrán bú bì jíyú kàn bǐjǐao shēnde cānkǎo shū, dànshi yào zhǔnbèi jiānglái xūyào de shíhou yīnggāi zěnmoyang qu xuǎnzé
qu. Jiǎn Jiàoshòu shuō kàn túshū mùlu de shíhou shǒuxiān kàn mùlu
suǒyǐn. Suǒyǐnli bǎ túshū dōu fēnlèi, yíxiàngyíxiàngde xiěchulai. Lìrú
55   zìdiǎn、xiǎoshuō、gèzhǒng cōngshū, dōu yīyīde fēnkāi.

      Jiǎn Jiàoshòu yòu shuō wǒmen zài wénxué yìfāngmiànde cōngshūli
zuì hǎo shi xuǎn duǎnpiān báihuà xiǎoshuō、xuǎnjí、quánjí、zázhì, huàjù
jùběn děng. Fánshi zhèixiē shū dōu kéyi kànkan.

      Zuìhòu Jiǎn Jiàoshòu shuō Zhōngguo yǒu jù súyǔ "kāi-juàn-yǒu-yì."
60   Zhèiju huà hěn yǒu dàolǐ, zhǐyào shi shū, wǒmen kànle dōu duì wǒmen
zēngjiā zhīshi, érqiě yě yǎngchéngle wǒmen yǒu yìzhǒng yuèdú de xíguàn.

WÉNXI

1. Yǒu yícî wǒ lǚxíng, zǒule Mǐn、Gàn、Yuè sānshěng. Zài lǚxíng qījiān wǒ
suíshí gěi wǒ jiāli xiě xìn, gàosu jiāli wǒ kàndao de yíqiè shìqing. Kěshi wǒ hěn jiǔ méi jiēdao jiālide huíxìn. Dāngshí wǒ xīnli yǒu liǎngge
yíwèn. Dî-yī, shî bu shi wǒ jiāli fāshēngle shénmo shìqing? Dî-èr, shî
bu shi wǒ qù de xìn dōu diū le? Wǒ yuè xiǎng yuè xīn-huāng-yì-luàn de.
Hòulai guòle hěn duō rìzi cái jiēdào jiālide huíxìn, xìnli shuō jiào wǒ
zǎorì huí jiā. Dāngshí wǒde xīnyî yě dǎsuàn zǎo diar huíqu kànkan de,
yúshi wǒ jiēdao jiā xìn yǐhòu jiu qǐshēn huí jiā le.

2. Zài fēnxi yíge Lādīngwénde jùzide shíhou, bǐděi zhùyî něige cí shi zhǔgé?
Něige cí shi bīngé? Wéiyǒurúcǐ cái kéyi zhīdao něige shi zhǔcí něige
shi bīncí.

3. <u>Kāngxī Zìdiǎn</u> shi zài Qīng Cháo Kāngxī wǔshiwǔnián yě jiu shi gōngyuán
yī-qī-yī-liù nián biānchéng. <u>Cíyuán</u> shi gōngyuán yī-jiǔ-yī-wǔ nián chūbǎn. Wáng Yúnwǔ Shî biānzhù de sîjiǎo hàomǎ zìdiǎn shi Zhōnghuá Mínguó shíjiǔnián chūbǎn.

4. Xiáojiemen zài yìqǐ duōbàn xǐhuan shuō huà. Zuótian yǒu wǔ-liùwèi xiáojie jùzai yíkuàr zhēn shi yīngyīngyànyàn rènao jíle.

5. Wáng Xiānsheng huì xiě cǎozì. Tā xiě de shíhou tāde yìzhī bǐ yùnyòngde shífēn línghuó, zhēnshi yòu kuài yòu hǎo. Kěshi yǒu rén shuō tā xiěde tài cǎo le, jiǎnzhí shi rènbochulái. Bǐfang shuō, sìdiǎn huǒ běnlái shi
   sìge diǎr, kěshi tā zhǐ xiě yìhuá, lèisì yíge yī zì.

6. Wǒ gāng xuéhuì kāi chē, suǒyǐ wǒ kāi chē de shíhou měicì kànjian biéde
   chē, wǒ xīnli jiu miǎnbuliǎo yǒu diar huāngluàn. Yǒu rén gàosu wo zuì
   yàojǐnde shi zhǎngwò zìjǐde chē, bú bì pà biérénde chē.

7. Yǒu yíge wàiguo rén chá Zhōngguo zìdiǎn bǐ shéi dōu kuài. Tā shuō:
   "Wǒ bǎ zìdiǎnli bùshǒude hàomǎ dōu jìzhu le. Zài chá zìdiǎn de shíhou
   zhǐ yào chákàn něige zì shi shénmo zìpáng huòzhě shi shénmo zìtóur jiu
   zhīdao shi shǔyú shénmo bùshǒu. Ránhòu ànzhe bùshǒude hàomǎ qu chá,
   hěn kuài jiu chádào le."

8. Yǒu yíwèi wénxuéjiā shuō huà de shíhou zuǐli zǒngshi xǐhuan shuō wényán. Yǒushíhou shuō de huà hái dài yìdiǎr shīyì. Tā shuō: "Jiǎrú dàjiā cháng shuō wényán, zài wénxuéshang yídìng néng jìnbu de." Yǒu yìtiān yǒu rén wèn zhèiwèi wénxuéjiā: "Nǐ zànchéng bú zànchéng báihuàwén?" Tā zhǐ shuōle yíge zì, shi fǒudìngcílide fǒu zì.

9. Yíge jūnren zài dǎzhàng de shíhou shòushāng le. Yǒu rén shuō: "Zhèige
   jūnren wèile guójiā ér shòule shāng. Tā shi jūnrénde hǎo bǎngyàng."

10. Fāng Xiānsheng cóngqián zài dàxué zhǔxiū de kēmu shi xīnwén. Wèile
    sùchéng, niàn de shi sùchéngkē. Xiànzài tā gěi wàiguo bàozhǐ xiě tōng-
    xùn. Měicì tōngxùn xùshùde yòu xiángxi yòu zhēnquè. Fāng Xiānsheng
    shuō tā shi yǐ yìzhī bǐ xiě tōngxùn wéi shēnghuó.

11. Zuótian wǒ zài shūdiàn mǎile yíbù Zhōngguo Gǔwén yǔ Jīnwén yígòng shi
    sānshiliùběn. Dāngshí wǒ méi xiángxide kàn, jīntian wǒ cái fāxiàn quēle
    yìběn shi juàn liù de, nèiróng dàgài shi guānyú qiè yīn de. Yìběn shū
    suīrán zhíbuliǎo duōshao qián, kěshi quēle yìběn zhèibù shū jiu bù wán-
    quán le.

12. Wǒ qu mǎi lùyīnjī. Mài lùyīnjī de rén shuō: "Wǒmen mài de lùyīnjī shi
    yǐ hǎoyòng gēn jiàqián dī wéi mùdì de, rúguǒ bù hǎoyòng kéyi tuìhuilai,
    dànshi tuìhuilai de yǒu xiào qījiān shi zài yíge yuè yǐnèi."

13. Zhāng Xiáojie zuì ài tāde tóufa, yòu hēi yòu cháng. Yǒu yìtiān tā fāxiàn
    tāde tóufa diàole hěn duō. Tā hěn nánguò, kūqilai le.

14. Wǒ yǒu yíge tóngxué yào dào wàiguo qu liúxué. Zài tā líkai běnguóde shí-
    hou, wǒmen jǐge rén qu sòng ta, dàjiē duì ta shuō: "Yùzhù nǐ xuéyè
    chénggōng."

15. Zuótian wǒmen yǔyánxué yǒu yíge kǎoshì yígòng shi liǎngge tímu. Dì-
    yīge tímu shi Zhōngguo yǒu jǐge dà fāngyán qū, gè fāngyán qū shì bu shi
    yǒu yǔyán bùtōng de kùnnan? Hái yǒu yíge tímu shi yíwèn dàimíngcí gēn
    yǔwěi yíwèncí, háiyǒu yíwènshì dōu yǒu shénmo bù tóng?

16. Jīntian kāi huì, zhǔxí bǎ hěn duōde wèntí guīnà chéngwéi liǎngge, jiào
    dàjiā tǎolùn.

WÈNTÍ

1. Zhōngguo yǔyán wèi-shénmo néng chéngwéi shìjiè zhòngyào yǔyán zhī yī?

2. Zhōngguo yǔyán shǔyú shénmo yǔzú? Zhèige yǔzǔ chúle Zhōngguo yǔyán yǐwài hái yǒu shénmo yǔyán?

3. Zhōngguo zuì zǎode wénzì shi shénmo? Yǒu xiē xuézhě bǎ shénmo shū rènwei shi Shànggǔ Hànyǔ? Shénmo shū rènwei shi Zhōnggǔ Hànyǔ? Dà-yuē dōu zài shénmo shíhou?

4. Zhōngguo yǔyán kéyi fēnchéng jǐ dà fāngyán qū? Měige fāngyán dìqūli yòng shénmo dìfangde huà zuò biāozhǔn?

5. Běijīng huà rúguǒ bú suàn shēngdiào yǒu duōshao yīnjié? Shénmo jiào qīngyīn? Shénmo jiào biàndiào? Jǔ ge lìzi shuōmíng.

6. Shénmo jiàozuo gòucífǎ? Zhōngguo yǔyán gòucífǎ hé Yìn-Ōu yǔyán gòu-cífǎ yǒu shénmo bùtóng? Qǐng nǐ jǔ ge lìzi shuōmíng.

7. Zhōngguo huàlide císù kéyi chóngdiéde yòng. Nǐ néng jǔ jǐge lìzi ma?

8. Shénmo shi cítóu? Shénmo shi cíwěi? Shénmo shi érhuàyùn? Shénmo jiào liàngcí? Qǐng nǐ fēnbié jǔ lìzi shuōmíng.

9. Zhōngguo huàde zàojùfǎ shénmo zài qián? Shénmo zài hòu? Zài shénmo shíhou kéyi bǎ bīncí xiězai qiánbian?

10. Zhōngguo huà zài biǎoshì wènhuà de shíhou yǒu něi sānzhǒng bànfa? Nǐ néng jǔ lìzi shuōmíng ma?

ILLUSTRATIVE SENTENCES (ENGLISH)

4.1. Wu is the name of a state in ancient China. It is in the present-day area of Kiangsu.

12.1. On returning from a trip to Kunming I wrote a book Jottings on a Trip to Kunming.

18.1. Some time ago someone sent me a copy of the Book of History, but I didn't accept it. Thinking about it now I'm very regretful.

27.1. The scenery in that place is really nice.   The far mountains are piled up one on another, like a painting.   (W)

34.1. He narrated in great detail the biography of [lit. which he wrote for] his friend.

37.4. Is a sentence such as "Because he doesn't have any money, he's no longer studying" a composite sentence?

46.1. The chairman said: "Now I'll consolidate the various views [of everyone] into two ideas for convenience in discussion."   (W)

46.2. 'Inductive method' is a term in logic. This method generalizes a principle from a diversity of [special] things.

49.2. Mr. Bai's younger brother is also such a good speaker, like Mr. Bai.

49.3. Mrs. Zhang handles her children very strictly. If the children don't obey she slaps them on the cheek.

50.1. A morpheme is a unit in the formation of words.

54.3. He wrote three biographical novels one after the other.

55.2. I've been reading too long. I think I'll listen to some recordings for a change.

56.2. Have China and Thailand hitherto had relations [between themselves]?

59.2. I very much enjoy listening to this [broadcast] play on the radio.

NOTES

In this lesson the thirty sentences in Yŭfǎ Liànxí review a number of miscellaneous constructions. These, together with the number of the sentences illustrating them, are listed below:

1 – 2. búshi A jiùshi B yàoburán C 'either A or B or C'

3 – 4. V_1 le jiu V_2 'to V_2 after having V_1'

5 – 6. jīngguo A jiu V 'to V after A'

7 – 8. ànzhe A lai suàn 'calculate according to A'

9 – 10. búdàn A yě B 'not only A but also B'

11 – 12. búdàn A hái B 'not only A but also B'

13 – 14. búdàn A yòu B 'not only A but also B'

15 – 16. děngdao A zài B 'to B after A'

17 – 18. děng A B 'to B after A'

19 – 20. yàoshi A de shíhou 'if and when A'

21 – 22. xiān V_1 hòu V_2 'first V_1 then V_2'

23 – 24. wèile V_1 cái V_2 'to V_2 in order to V_1'

25 – 26. kànzhe hǎoxiàng V 'seems as if V'

27 – 28. zài méi yǒu V yǐqián 'before V-ing'

29 – 30. A yě xiàng B yíyàng V 'A, like B, V'

Dì-Shíqīkè. Zhōngguode Wénxué

Bái: Mǎ Jiàoshòu zǎo.

Mǎ : Zǎo. Yìliánchuànde xiàle liǎngtiānde dà yǔ, jīntian lùshang dōu shi ní, hěn bù hǎozǒu.

Bái: Kěbushìma! Zuótian tīng guǎngbō tiānqì bàogào, yǔ hái yào jìxùde
5   xià ne.

Mǎ : Zài Měiguo rénrén yǒu chē, zài zhèr jiu děi zǒu lù le.

Bái: Qíshí zǒu lù duì shēntǐ dào hǎo. Búguò cóng wǒ nèr dào xuéxiào lái yílùshang dōu shi zào fángzi de, lùshang hěn duō shítou、mùliào shénmo de, hěn bù hǎo zǒu.

10 Mǎ : Jīnnian yǔ xiàde tài duō le, hěn duō dìfang yǒu shuǐzāi. Míngnian chūntian liángshi yídìng yào guì de.

Bái: Shuǐzāide dìfang hěn duō ma?

Mǎ : Jù shuō Hénán Shěng gēn Húnán Shěng zuì lìhai.

Bái: Hénán chūchǎn màizi, shì bu shi?

15 Mǎ : Shìde.

Bái: Bǐrú liángshi guìle de huà, yào guìdao shénmo chéngdu ne?

Mǎ : Guìdao yíge rén zuò gōng de gōngqián gōngbuliǎo quánjiā wǔ-liùkǒu rén chī fàn.

Bái: Wǒ kàn bàozhǐshang shuō Zhōngguo zhèngfǔ jíyú xiǎng fázi mǎi wài-
20   guode mǐ ne.

Mǎ : Húnán yě yǒu shuǐzāi, nà shi chǎn mǐ de qūyù.

Bái: Nín shuō Húnán, wǒ xiǎngqi zuótiande jiǎngyǎn. Jiǎn Jiàoshòu bǎ hěn duō shěngde míngzi dōushi yòng yíge zì dàibiǎo. Húnán tā yòng Xiāng, Jiāngxī tā yòng Gàn.

25 Mǎ : Zhōngguo měishěng dōu yǒu jiǎndānde míngchēng. Xiàng Fújiàn shi Mǐn, Guǎngdong shi Yuè.

Bái: Hěn yǒu yìsi.

Mǎ : Zuótian wǎnshang lùyīnle ma?

Bái: Zuótian wǎnshang wàimian xiàzhe yǔ, wǒ zài wūzili lùde yīn. Yǔ
30   xià de shēngyin hěn dà. Suǒyǐ lù de yīn hǎoxiang méi yǒu yǐqián lù de nènmo qīngchu shide. Tóngshi wǒ yě yímiàn tīngzhe yímiàn yòng Hànzì bǎ ta xiěxialai le. Yíhuèr nín kànkan.

Mǎ : Hǎojíle. Yìhuěr wǒmen tǎolùnwánle shēngcí yǐhòu wǒ kànkan.

374

1.0. mèng   a dream

zuòmèng   to dream   (VO) [make dream]

mèngjian   see in one's dream, dream that

Hóng Lóu Mèng   Dream of the Red Chamber

1.1. Wǒ zuótian wǎnshang zuòle yíge mèng, hěn kěpà. Mèngjianle yíge
guǐ.

1.2. Hóng Lóu Mèng shi yíbù yǒumíngde chángpiān xiǎoshuō.

2.0. rú*   (1) scholar; (2) Confucian

Rújiā   scholar of the Confucian School

Rúlín Wàishǐ   The Scholars [Confucian forest outside history]

2.1. Zhōngguo rén cóngqián bǎ niàn shū de rén jiàozuo rú.

2.2. Nǐ zhǐdao Rújiāde xuéshuō zhǔzhāng de shi shénmo ma? (T)

2.3. Rúlín Wàishǐ shi yíbù xùshù zhīshi fènzǐ gùshide xiǎoshuō. Yǒude
dìfang zhēn kěxiào. Wǒ kàn de shíhou bǎ wǒ xiàosi le.   (T)

3.0. cán*   (1) remnant; (2) crippled

cánfèi   crippled, partly incapacitated [crippled abolish]

Lǎo Cán Yóujì   Travels of Mr. Derelict

3.1. Tā cóngqián zài jūnduìde shíhou yīnwei dǎzhàng shòushāng le, xiànzài tā chéng yíge cánfèi rén le.

3.2. Lǎo Cán Yóujì shi yíbù yǒumíngde báihuà xiǎoshuō. Cháng kàn
zhèizhǒng xiǎoshuō duìyú xué báihuàwén duōshǎo yǒu xiē bāngzhu.
(T)

4.0. xīnshǎng   appreciate, like [joy bestow]

4.1. Yǒu rén xīnshǎng Máo Dùn xiě de xiǎoshuō, yǒu rén xīnshǎng Lǔ
Xùn xiě de xiǎoshuō.   (T)

5.0. fěngcì   ridicule, satirize [satirize pierce]

5.1. Bā Jīn、Lǎo Shè xiě de xiǎoshuō duōbàn shi fěngcì jiù shèhuì de.
(T)

Mǎ : Hóng Lóu Mèng、Rúlín Wàishǐ gēn Lǎo Cán Yóujì zhèi sānbù shū
35   nǐ dōu kànguo ma?

Bái : Wǒ dōu kànguo le.

Mǎ : Nǐ zuì xīnshǎng něibù?

Bái : Wǒ xǐhuan Rúlín Wàishǐ.   Bìng bú shi mà rén, nà shi yíbù fěngcì
zhīshi fènzǐde zhùzuò.

40   Mǎ : Lǎo Cán Yóujì gēn Hóng Lóu Mèng ne?

Bái : Wǒ duì Hóng Lóu Mèng hěn yǒu xìngqu. Wǒ rènwei shūshang měi
yíge rénde kǒuqi dōu shi xiàndàide yǔfǎ.

6.0. jiézuò   masterpiece [hero do]

6.1. Xǔ Shì Shuōwén zài Zhōngguo wénzìxuéli shi yíbù jiézuò.

7.0. tǐcái   style of literature, genre [body cut]

7.1. Hú Shì xiě de nèipiān wénzhāng shi shénmo tǐcái? Shi sǎnwén hái
      shi shī? (T)

8.0. zhízhèng   (1) administer, be in charge; (2) administration [grasp
                   government]

8.1. Zhízhèng shi zhǎngwò zhèngzhìde yìsi.

9.0. jīngcǎi   excellent, refined and elegant (W)

9.1. Zuótian wǎnshangde xìju jīngcǎi jíle. (W)

10.0. chuàngzuò   (1) create, originate; (2) literary or artistic work
                    [create do]

10.1. Máo Zédōng zuì yǒumíngde chuàngzuò shi shénmo, nǐ zhīdao ma?

Mǎ : Lǔ Xùn gēn Lǎo Shè zhèi liǎngge rénde wénzhāng nǐ xǐhuan něige
      rén de?

45 Bái: Wǒ duì Lǎo Shè de zhùzuò bǐjiǎo yǒu xìngqu. Suīrán Lǎo Shè gēn
        Lǔ Xùn xiě de tǐcái bù yíyàng, kěshi liǎngge rén xiě de dōu shi
        fěngcì mà dāngshí zhízhèng de wénzhāng. Liǎngge rénde zuòpǐn gè
        yǒu gède yōudiǎn.   Lǔ Xùn xiě de dōngxi jiào rén kànle hèn, Lǎo
50   Shè xiě de jiào nǐ kànle xiào. Lǎo Shè xiě de zuì jīngcǎide dìfang
        shi tā xíngróng yíge rén, xíngróngde hǎoxiang nǐ kànjianle nèige rén
        le shide.

Mǎ : Wǒ niàn zhōngxuéde shíhou rénjia sòng wǒ yìběn Lǎo Shède chuàng-
      zuò zhēnshi yíbù jiézuò, wǒ kànle yǐhòu bǎ wǒ xiàode yàosǐ. Wǒ-
      men tōngxuéde chàbuduō nèige shíhou měi yíge rén shǒuli dōu yǒu
55   yìběn.

Bái: Lǎo Shède zhùzuò shi yìzhǒng dàzhòng wénxué. Rénrén dōu néng
      xīnshǎng.

11.0. yùndong   (1) to exercise; (2) movement [transport move]
      Wǔsì Yùndong   May Fourth Movement

11.1. Wǔsì Yùndong shi tíchàng xīn wénxué de yùndong.

12.0. Xīn Qīngnián   La Jeunesse

12.1. Xīn Qīngniánshangde wénzhāng dōu shi báihuàwén.

13.0. dēng   publish
      dēngzǎi   publish (W) [publish contain]

13.1. Tāde zuòpǐn xiànglái shi zài zázhìshang dēngzǎi, juéduì bù dēngzài
      bàoshang. (W)

14.0. kānwu   publication [print thing]

14.1. Nǐ zài shénmo kānwushang kànjianguo Chén Dúxiùde zuòpǐn le? (T)

15.0. wényì   literature and art

15.1. Tā shi xǐhuan wényìde rén, tā yuànyi zuò wényì gōngzuò.

Bái: Hú Shì shi xiàndài hěn yǒumíngde xuézhě, shi yíge fǎnduì jiù wén-
        xué de. Tā shi Wǔsì shídài tíchàng báihuàwén hěn yǒulìde yífènzǐ.

60   Mǎ :   Zài Wǔsì Yùndong yǐqián Hú Shì Xiānsheng xiěle yìpiān yào gǎigé
        jiù wénxuéde wénzhāng shi zài <u>Xīn Qīngnián</u> zázhìshang dēngchulai
        de. Zài nèipiān wénzhāngshang, tā yígòng tíchule báge yuánzé lai.
        Zài nèige shíhou yǒude rén zànchéng wénxué gémìng, yǒude rén hěn
        fǎnduì.

65   Bái: Tīngshuō Wǔsì shídài hěn duō kānwu dōu shi tíchàng báihuàwén de?

     Mǎ :   Shìde. Yīnwei yìbān qīngnián shòule Xīyáng wényìde yǐngxiǎng, dà-
        jiā dōu fǎnduì wényánwén.

16.0. Qín   Ch'in Dynasty (221-206 B.C.)

     Xiānqín   pre-Chin

16.1. Qín Cháode niándài suīrán hěn duǎn, dànshi zài lìshǐshang shi hěn
      zhòngyàode yíge cháodài.

16.2. Fāng Xiānsheng zuótian jiǎngyǎn de tímu shi "Xiānqín Wénxué."

17.0. bǔcí   divination test [divine word]

17.1. Guō Mòruò Shì duìyu jiǎgǔwénde bǔcí zuì yǒu yánjiu.   (T)

18.0. Zhànguó   (1) Warring States; (2) Warring States Period (403-321
        B.C.)

     <u>Zhànguócè</u>   Records of the Warring States

18.1. Zài Qín Cháo yǐqián yǒu yíge shíqī jiàozuo Zhànguó.   <u>Zhànguócè</u>
      zhèi yíbù shū xiě de jiu shi Zhànguó shídàide shìqing.

19.0. Chūnqiū   (1) Spring and Autumn Period (770-475 B.C.);   (2) <u>Spring
        and Autumn Annals</u>

19.1. Zài Zhōu Cháo mònián yǒu yíge shíqī jiàozuo Chūnqiū.

20.0. <u>Zuǒ Zhuàn</u>   Tso Chuan

20.1. <u>Zuǒ Zhuàn</u> shi gǔshūde míngzi, shi Zhōu Cháo yíge xìng Zuǒ de
      zuò de.

Bái: Qǐng wèn Xiānqín wénxué shi shénmo?

Mǎ :   Jiu shi Qín Cháo yǐqiánde wénxué.

70   Bái: Zhōngguo zuì zǎo shíqīde wénxué shi shénmo ne?

Mǎ :   Jiu shi jiǎgǔwénshangde bǔcí.

Bái: <u>Zhànguócè</u> shi Zhànguó shíhou xiě de ma?

Mǎ :   Shîde. Nà shàngmian shi bǎ Zhànguó dāngshi dǎzhàng guójiāde shî-
       qing jìxialai le. <u>Shǐ Jì</u> yǒu yíbùfen jiu shi gēnjù nèiběn shū xiě de.

75 Bái: <u>Chūnqiū</u> zhèige cér shi shū míngzi yě dàibiāo shídài, shì bu shi?

Mǎ :   <u>Chūnqiū</u> shi Kǒngzǐ zuò de shū. Yǒude shíhou yě dàibiāo nèige shí-
       dài. Kǒngzǐ zuò <u>Chūnqiū</u>de shíqī jiu jiàozuo "Chūnqiū Shídài."

Bái: <u>Zuǒ Zhuàn</u> hái yǒu biéde míngzi ma?

Mǎ :   Yǒu. <u>Zuǒ Zhuàn</u> yě jiào <u>Zuǒ Shì Chūnqiū</u>. Guānyú zhèi yílèide gǔ-
80   shū nǐ dōu kànguo ma?

Bái: Wǒ kànguo dàoshi kànguo, kěshi nèiróng tài shēn le, yǒude dìfang
       wǒ kànbudǒng.

21.0. Mèngzǐ   Mencius

21.1. Mèngzǐde xuéshuō shi zhùzhòng mínzhǔ de.

22.0. Zhuāngzǐ   Chuang Tzu

22.1. Zhuāngzǐ shi Zhànguó shídàide xuézhě.   Tā xiě de shū yě jiào
       <u>Zhuāngzǐ</u>.

23.0. Mòzǐ   Mo Tzu

23.1. Mòzǐde xuéshuō lèisî Fójiàode xuéshuō ma?

24.0. zǔzhǐ   impede, obstruct, stop [obstruct stop]

24.1. Tāde xíngdòng méi yǒu shénmo rén kéyi zǔzhǐ de.   (T)

Bái: Kǒngzǐ gēn Mèngzǐde xuéshuō wǒ zhīdao.   Zhuāngzǐ gēn Mòzǐ shì
       bu shi tóng yíge zhǔzhāng?

85 Mǎ : Mòzǐ shi zhǔzhāng ài zìjǐ yě ài biérén, zǔzhǐ rénlèide zhànzhēng.
       Zhuāngzǐde xuéshuō hé Lǎozǐ yíyàng.   Zài <u>Zhuāngzǐ</u>li yǒu yíduàn
       hěn yǒu yìside wèndá. Yǒu yícì Zhuāngzǐ gēn yíge zuò dà guān de
       yíkuàr zǒudao hébiārshang. Zhuāngzǐ shuō: "Yú zài héli láiláiqùqùde
       zhēn kuàilè ya." Nèige dà guān shuō: "Nǐ bú shi yú, zěnmo zhīdao
90   yú kuàilè ne?" Zhuāngzǐ shuō: "Nǐ yě bú shi wǒ, nǐ zěnmo zhīdao
       wǒ bù zhīdào yú kuàilè ne?"

25.0. shīgē   poems and songs

25.1. Yǒu yíge wàiguo rén yánjiu Zhōngguo wénxué.   Tā zuì xīnshǎng
       Zhōngguo gǔdàide shīgē.

26.0. <u>Lúnyǔ</u>   <u>Analects</u> [discuss speech]

26.1. <u>Lúnyǔ</u> shi <u>Sì Shū</u>de yíbùfen. Shi Kǒngzǐde xuésheng jìlù de Kǒngzǐ
       suǒ shuō de huà.

27.0. Chǔcí   Ch'u Poetry

27.1. Chǔcí shi Chǔ Guó Qū Yuán suǒ chuàngzuò de.

28.0. zǒngjí   comprehensive collection, general collection

28.1. Zhōngguo gǔshíhou shīgēde zǒngjí shi Shī Jīng.

29.0. Yì Jīng   Book of Changes

29.1. Yì Jīng zài gǔshíhou shi zuò shénmo yòng de, nǐ zhīdao ma? (T)

Bái: Mǎ Jiàoshòu, Shī Jīng zhèiběn shū shi gǔrén zuò de shīgē ma?

Mǎ : Shìde. Jùshuō yě jiu shi nèige shídàide yǔyán. Lúnyǔshang yǒu yí-
       jù huà, yìsi shi rúguǒ bú niàn Shī Jīng jiu bú huì shuō huà.

95 Bái: Shī Jīng gēn Chǔcí yǒu shénmo fēnbié méi yǒu?

Mǎ : Zhèi liǎngběn shū dōu shi shī gēn gēde zǒngjí. Tāmende fēnbié shi
       Chǔcí suǒ shōu de zuòpǐn shi Cháng Jiāng liúyù de, kéyi shuō shi
       nánfāng wénxué. Shī Jīng suǒ shōu de zuòpǐn shi Huáng Hé liúyù
       de, shi běifāng wénxué. Háiyǒu, Chǔcí měi yíjù huà yǒu sìge zì de,
100   liùge zì de, qīge zì de. Ér Shī Jīng dà bùfen shi měi yíjù huà dōu
       shi sìge zì de.

Bái: Yì Jīng ne?

Mǎ : Yì Jīng shi Zhōu Cháo shídài biān de. Duōshù shi bǔcí.

30.0. yuèfǔ   folksongs (generally with five characters to a line)

30.1. Yuèfǔ shi cóng Hàn Cháo kāishǐ yǒu de.

31.0. Wèi   Wei (kingdom, period: 386-535 A.D.)

31.1. Nèipiān gǔwén shi Wèi Cháode shíhou yíge yǒumíngde xuézhě zuò
       de.

32.0. Jìn   Tsin (kingdom, period: 265-420 A.D.)

32.1. Jìn Cháo zì gōngyuán èr-liù-wǔ-nián zhì sì-èr-líng-nián, gòng yǒu
       yìbǎi wǔshíliùnián. (W)

33.0. chéngshú   mature, ripe [become ripe]

33.1. Dàole qiūtian nóngrén zhòng de dōngxi dōu chéngshú le.

34.0. huà   demarcate

       huàfēn   demarcate [demarcate divide]

34.1. Zìcóng Mínguó chénglì, Zhōngguo zài zhèngzhishang yǒu huà shídài
       de gǎigé. (T)

34.2. Bǎ nèige dìfang huàfēnwéi wǔge qūyù shi gēnjù shénmo huà de?
       (T)

35.0. xióngzhuàng   vigorous, powerful, heroic [heroic strong]

35.1. Nǚrén chàng xióngzhuàngde gēr yídìng biǎodábuchūlái nèizhǒng
       xióngzhuàngde shēngyin.

Bái: Mǎ Jiàoshòu, shénmo jiàozuo yuèfǔ?

105 Mǎ : Yuèfǔ yě shi shī, shi chàng de. Yǒude shi cóng bǎixìng zuǐli shuōchulai de, yǒude shi cóng wénrén shǒuli xiěchulai de, yílǜ jiàozuo
yuèfǔ.

Bái: Yuèfǔ shi cóng shénmo shídài yǒu de?

Mǎ : Yuèfǔ shi cóng Hàn Dài jiu yǒule de. Jīngguòle Wèi Jìn liǎngcháode
110   fāzhǎn dádào xiāngdāng chéngshú le. Zài Wèi Jìnde shíqī huàfēnwéi liǎngge, yíge shi nánfāng yuèfǔ, yíge shi běifāng yuèfǔ. Tāmen
gè yǒu bùtóngde tèdiǎn. Nánfāngde yuèfǔ shi hěn wēnhé ér yǒu
gǎnqíng de, běifāngde yuèfǔ shi yìzhǒng hěn xióngzhuàng ér yǒu lìliang de.

36.0. cí   poem of unequal lines with fixed tonal pattern

36.1. Zài Zhōngguo wénxuéshǐshang Sòng Cháode cí shi zuì zhùmíngde.

37.0. yùnwén   rhyming literature

37.1. Wǒ xǐhuan sǎnwén, bù xǐhuan yùnwén.

38.0. qǔ(zi)   (classical) song

gēqǔ   (modern) song

38.1. Yuán Cháode qǔzi, zài Zhōngguo wénxuéshǐshang zuì zhùmíng.

38.2. Yǒu rén xǐhuan tīng gǔdàide qǔzi, yǒu rén xǐhuan tīng xiàndàide gēqǔ.

39.0. tèshū   (1) special; (2) a characteristic [special unique]

39.1. Tèshū jiu shi tèbiéde yìsi.

40.0. fù   poetic essay

Hànfù   Han poetic essay

40.1. Zài Hànfùli něi yìpiān fù nǐ zuì xǐhuan?

41.0. xiàn   limit (N/V)

xiànyu   limited to, limited in (W)

xiànzhi   impose a limitation [limit system]

yǒuxiàn   be limited [have limit]

41.1. Mǎ Jiàoshòu jiào wǒ xiě yìpiān wénzhāng, xiàn sāntiān xiěwán. (T)

41.2. Wáng Jiàoshòu jīntian jiǎng wénzìxué, yīnwei xiànyu shíjiān zhǐ
jiǎng zìxíng, méi jiǎng zìyīn hé zìyì. (W)

41.3. Yǒu yíge guójiā xiànzhi běnguó rén chūguó, dànshi liúxuéshēng shi
lìwài.

41.4. Wǒ shǒulide qián yǒuxiàn, bù néng suíbiàn yòng.

41.5. Nèige xuéhuìde huìyuán yǐ dàxué jiàoshòu wéi xiàn. (T)

115 Bái : Cí hái yǒu lìngwàide yíge yìsi, yě shi wénxuéde yìzhǒng ma?

Mǎ : Cíde běnyi shi biǎoshi yìzhǒng guānniàn. Lìngwàide yíge yìsi jiu
shi yùnwénde yìzhǒng, shi cóng Táng Cháo kāishǐ de. Cí zhèizhǒng
yùnwén shi cóng yuèfǔ yǎnbiànchulai de. Shi yìzhǒng tèshū tǐcái.

Bái : Shì bu shi yě kéyi dàngzuo qǔzi?

120 Mǎ : Cíde tǐcái gēn yuèfǔ bǐjiǎoqilai suírán yǒu diar tèshū, kěshi yě kéyi
dāng qǔzi chàngchulai.

Bái : Fù shi zěnmoyàngde yìzhǒng tǐcái?

Mǎ : Fù nǐ kànqilai hǎoxiang sǎnwén. Jùzi yǒude cháng, yǒude hěn duǎn.
Yīnwei fù yě zhùzhòng shēng, yě yǒu yùn, suǒyǐ gēn shīde tǐcái
125   chàbuduō. Fù zài jùzishang kàn fēicháng měilì. Zài yìpiān fùli
wǎngwǎng méi yǒu xiànzhi de yòng xíngróngcí.

42.0. piàntǐwén   literature characterized by balanced sentences [paired
         body writing]

42.1. Piàntǐwén dōu shi sìge zì gēn liùge zìde jùzi.

43.0. tuō   (1) disrobe; (2) get away from

43.1. Tā shi gōngchǎngde kuàiji. Yàoshi gōngchǎngde zhàng yǒu cuòwu,
         tā jiu tuōbulái zérèn.   (T)

44.0. Xīn Cháo   New Tide

44.1. Zài Xīn Cháoli yìliánchuàn yǒu jǐpiān wénzhāng dōu shi tǎolùn xīn
         shī hé gēqǔ de.

45.0. géxīn   (1) to reform, change; (2) innovation [remove new]

45.1. Nèige guójiā juédàduōshùde rénmín xīwang zhèngzhi géxīn.

Bái : Piàntǐwénde tèdiǎn shi shénmo?

Mǎ : Piàntǐwénde tèdiǎn shi "sì liù jùzi." Bǐfang shàng yíjù huà shi sìge
zì, xià jù huà yě děi yòng sìge zì. Rúguǒ dì-yījù huà shi liùge zì,
130   dì-èrjù huà yě děi yòng liùge zì. Ná xiě xìn lái shuō ba, yìfēng xìn cóng
tóu dào wěi de jùzi dōu shi "sìge zì hé liùge zìde jùzi," tóngshí yě
zhùzhòng shēngdiào. Cóngqián niàn shū xuésheng dōu děi bèi shū,
xiàng piàntǐwén gèng yào bèixialai le.

Bái : Xiànzài hái yǒu rén yòng piàntǐwén xiě wénzhāng huòzhě xiě xìn
135 ma?

Mǎ : Xiě xìn xiànzài hěn shǎo rén yòng piàntǐwén le, kěshi xiě wénzhāng
hái yǒu rén yòng. Dànshi dōu shi yìxiē niàn gǔshūde lǎo xiānshengmen, tāmen zǒng tuōbuliǎo xiě zhèizhǒng wénzhāngde xíguan.

Bái : Tīngshuō yǒu yìzhǒng wénxué kānwu jiào Xīn Cháo, nèiróng xiě de
140   dōu shi guānyu wénxué géxīn de wénzhāng. Xiànzài hái mǎidedào
ma?

Mǎ : Xiànzài kǒngpà hěn nán mǎidedào le.

46.0. zuòtánhuî   conference [sit converse meeting]

46.1. Zuótian zài zuòtánhuîshang tán de dōu shi yǔyīn wèntí.

47.0. piàn   sheet, slice (M)

dǎchéng yípiàn   become one, form a group [lit. become one sheet]

47.1. Tā zài chuánshang kànjian yuǎnyuǎnde yǒu yípiàn lùdî.

47.2. Dǎchéng yípiàn jiu shi "dàjiā hézuò, bù fēn bǐcǐ" de yìsi. (T)

47.3. Cóng dìxia juéchulai de guījiǎ shi yípiàn yípiànde, duōbàn shi hěn
      xiǎo de. (T)

48.0. Guóyǔ   Discourses of the States

48.1. Guóyǔ shi shūmíng, shi gǔshi Zhōu Cháo yǒu yíge xìng Zuǒ de zuò
      de.

49.0. Gòngchǎndǎng   Communist Party [together property party]

      Guó-Gòng   Kuomintang and Communist parties

49.1. Zài Zhōngguo duì Rìběn Kàngzhàn qījiān Guó-Gòng shi hézuò de.
      Hòulai Gòngchǎndǎng jiu dúzì xíngdòng le.

49.2. Tā shi Guómíndǎng, bú shi Gòngchǎndǎng. (T)

50.0. gōngjù   tool [work instrument]

50.1. Yǔyán shi biǎodá yìside gōngjù. (T)

51.0. tuīdòng   impel forward, promote [push move]

51.1. Báihuàwén shi zài shénmo shíhou tuīdòng de?

Bái : Zuótian wǎnshang zài Zhōngguo wénxué zuòtánhuîshang dàjiā tǎolùn
      yǒu liǎngge duō zhōngtóu.

145 Mǎ : Cānjiā zuòtánhuî de tóngxué duō bu duō?

Bái : Bù shǎo. Zhōngguo tóngxué、wàiguo tóngxué dōu yǒu. Dàjiā tánlái-
      tánqù, dōu hěn tándelai. Wǒmen dàjiā jiǎnzhí dǎchéng yípiàn le.

Mǎ : Zuótian tǎolùn de shi shénmo wèntí?

Bái : Dōu shi guānyu xīn-jiù wénxuéde zhīshi. Tándao Guóyǔ wǒ cái zhī-
150   dao Guóyǔ shi yìzhǒng lìshǐ xìngzhide shū.

Mǎ : Shi Zhōu Cháode xuézhě xiě de. Shàngmian shi jìlù měige guójiāde
      shìqing.

Bái : Xīn wénxué yìfāngmiàn tándao jìndàide jǐwèi wénxuéjiā.

Mǎ : Dōu tándao něi jǐwèi?

155 Bái : Tándao Chén Dúxiù、Guō Mòruò、Bā Jīn、Máo Dùn hé tāmen měi
      yíge rén zuòpǐnde tèdiǎn. Dàjiā yě tándao Gòngchǎndǎng duìyu wén-
      xuéde guāndiǎn gēn wénzì gǎigé de wèntí. Yòu tándao Máo Zédōng
      duì wénxué de kànfǎ, wénxué shi zhèngzhi gēn jiàoyude gōngjù.

Mǎ : Suǒyǐ xiànzài dàlùshangde xuézhě dōu zhǔzhāng xiě bàogào wén-
160 xué.

Bái : Zuìhòu hái tǎolùndao pǔjí jiàoyu. Yǒu yiwèi tóngxué shuō, fánshi
wǒmen zhīshi fènzǐ duì pǔjí jiàoyu zhèi yìfāngmian yīnggāi fù yìdiǎr zérèn, qu tuīdòng pǔjí jiàoyu.

Mǎ : Zhè shi hěn yǒu yìyi de.

52.0. Yán'ān   Yenan (in Shensi Province)

52.1. Yán'ān shi dìfangde míngzi, zài Zhōngguode xīběibù.

53.0. zhǎnkāi   open out, open up (W) [unfold open]

53.1. Wǔsì Yùndong zhǎnkāile xīn wénxuéde yùndong.

54.0. quánmiàn   total(ly), overall   [all sides]

54.1. Zhōngguo zài shénmo shíhou duì Rìběn zhǎnkāile quánmiàn Kàngzhàn? (T)

55.0. jiùguó   (1) save the nation; (2) national salvation

55.1. Tā wèi-shénmo bu cānjiā jiùguó yùndong?

56.0. díren   enemy [opponent man]

56.1. Wǒmen yào zhīdao shéi shi wǒmende díren.

165 Bái : Yán'ān yǒu yige shíqī shi Gòngchǎndǎngde zhèngzhi zhōngxīn ma?

Mǎ : Shìde. Gòngchǎndǎng ná Yán'ān zuò zhèngzhi zhōngxīn cóng Kàngzhàn yǐqián dào yī-jiǔ-sì-bā nián.

Bái : Shì bu shi zài Kàngzhàn shíqī Guó-Gòng yòu hézuò le?

Mǎ : Shìde. Zhōngguo zài zhǎnkāi quánmiàn duì Rìběn Kàngzhàn de shí-
170 hou, dàjiā wèile jiùguó gòngtóng dǐkàng díren yòu hézuòle yíge duǎn
shíqī.

57.0. Chuàngzào Zhōukān   Creation Weekly

57.1. Yǒu rén shuō Chuàngzào Zhōukānde mùdì shi zài tuīdòng xīn wénxué.

58.0. shǐmìng   task, mission [cause command]

58.1. Chuàngzào Zhōukān hé Xīn Cháo dōu shi tuīdòng xīn wénxué de.
Tāmende shǐmìng méi shénmo liǎngyàng. (T)

59.0. bèijǐng   (1) background; (2) ulterior motive [back scenery]

59.1. Xīnshǎng wénxué yào xiān zhīdao dāngshíde shídài bèijǐng.

60.0. sīcháo   flood of ideas [idea tide]

60.1. Sīcháo jiu shi sīxiǎngde cháoliú, yě jiu shi sīxiǎngde qūshì.

Bái: Mǎ Jiàoshòu, <u>Chuàngzào Zhōukān</u> yě shi Wǔsî shídàide kānwu ma?

Mǎ : Shìde. Nà shi dāngshí fùzhe yìzhǒng gǎigé wénxué shǐmìngde kānwu.

175 Bái: Xiàng <u>Xīn Cháo</u> ，<u>Xiǎoshuō Yuèbào</u> dōu shi yǒu shídài bèijǐngde kānwu ma?

Mǎ : Shì. Yīnwei shòu Xīfāng wényì sīcháode yǐngxiǎng, jiu ná zhèi xiēge
kānwu lái tuīdòng báihuàwénde yùndong.

Bái: Shì bu shi dāngshí yě yǒu rén fǎnduì báihuàwén ne?

180 Mǎ : Dāngshí dāngrán yǒu hěn duō rén fǎnduì. Yǒu rén rènwei báihuàwén
bìng bú shi wénxué. Qíshí báihuàwén bìng bù róngyi xiě.

Bái: Wǒ tīngshuō wényánwén xiěde hǎo, bìng bù yídìng xiědelái báihuàwén.

Mǎ : Nà dàoshi shízài de.

61.0. fēnshuǐlǐng   watershed [divide water range]

61.1. Zài Qīnghǎi yǒu yíge dà shān shi Huáng Hé hé Cháng Jiāngde fēnshuǐlǐng.

62.0. wàishǐ   historical novel [outside history]

62.1. Wàishǐ suǒ xiě de shi lìshǐ yǐwài bú dà zhòngyào de shìqing.

63.0. yóucǐ   from this (W)

63.1. <u>Yóucǐ</u> shi <u>cóng zhèli</u> de yìsi. Lìrú "yóucǐ wǎng nán" jiu shi "cóng
zhèli wǎng nán."

185 Bái: Mǎ Jiàoshòu, <u>fēnshuǐlǐng</u> shi shénmo yìsi?

Mǎ : Rúguǒ huàfēn liǎngge héliúde shíhou yòng shān lái fēn, zhèige shān
jiàozuo <u>fēnshuǐlǐng</u>.

Bái: Háiyǒu, <u>wàishǐ</u> gēn <u>lìshǐ</u> yǒu shénmo fēnbié ne?

Mǎ : Wàishǐ bu shi zhèngshìde lìshǐ. Zài lìshǐshang xiě mǒu yíge huáng-
190   dìde lìshǐ yǐwài, yòu yǒu rén bǎ nèige huángdì rìcháng shēnghuóde
shìqing lìngwài xiěchu yìběn shū lai jiu shi wàishǐ le.

Bái: Háiyǒu, <u>yóucǐ</u> zhèige cér zài kǒuyǔshang bù cháng yòng, shì bu shi?

Mǎ : "Yóucǐ kànlai," "yóucǐ kějiàn" dōu shi bù cháng shuō de, shi xiě
de shíhou yòng de.

SHĒNGCÍ BIĂO

1. mèng
   zuòmèng
   mèngjian
   Hóng Lóu Mèng

2. rú*
   Rújiā
   Rúlín Wàishǐ

3. cán*
   cánfèi
   Lǎo Cán Yóujì

4. xīnshǎng

5. fěngcì

6. jiézuò

7. tǐcái

8. zhízhèng

9. jīngcǎi (W)

10. chuàngzuò

11. yùndong
    Wǔsì Yùndong

12. Xīn Qīngnián

13. dēng
    dēngzǎi (W)

14. kānwu

15. wényì

16. Qín
    Xiānqín

17. bǔcí

18. Zhànguó
    Zhànguócè

19. Chūnqiū

20. Zuǒ Zhuàn

21. Mèngzǐ

22. Zhuāngzǐ

23. Mòzǐ

24. zǔzhǐ

25. shīgē

26. Lúnyǔ

27. Chǔcí

28. zǒngjí

29. Yì Jīng

30. yuèfǔ

31. Wèi

32. Jìn

33. chéngshú

34. huà
    huàfēn

35. xióngzhuàng

36. cí

37. yùnwén

38. qǔ(zi)
    gēqǔ

39. tèshū

40. fù
    Hànfù

41. xiàn

xiànyu (W)
xiànzhi
yǒuxiàn

42. piàntǐwén

43. tuō

44. Xīn Cháo

45. géxīn

46. zuòtánhuì

47. piàn
    dǎchéng yípiàn

48. Guóyǔ

49. Gòngchǎndǎng
    Guó-Gòng

50. gōngjù

51. tuīdòng

52. Yán'ān

53. zhǎnkāi (W)

54. quánmiàn

55. jiùguó

56. dìren

57. Chuàngzào Zhōukān

58. shǐmìng

59. bèijǐng

60. sīcháo

61. fēnshuǐlǐng

62. wàishǐ

63. yóucǐ (W)

YǓFĂ LIÀNXÍ

A. dōu V QW   (see note 1)

1. Zhāng Xiānsheng xǐhuan kàn sǎnwén gēn duǎnpiān xiǎoshuō. Zhāng Tàitai dōu xǐhuan kàn shénmo shū?

2. Wǒ dào shūdiàn jiu mǎi yìběn Hóng Lóu Mèng. Nǐ dōu mǎi shénmo?

3. Nǐ zhèicì lǚxíng dōu dào nǎr? Dōu gēn shéi qù? Quèdìngle méi yǒu?

4. Fújiàn dōu yǒu shénmo dìfangde fēngjǐng shi yǒumìngde?

5. Tā zài zuòtánhuìshang dōu shuō shénmo huà le?

B. S shi N (see note 2)

6. Nǐ bù xiǎng cānjiā zhèizhǒng àiguóde yùndong shi shénmo yuányīn?

7. Wǒ bù xǐhuan kàn Lǔ Xùnde wénzhāng shi yīnwei tāde wénzhāng tài shēn le.

8. Tā lǎo zǔzhǐ wo, bù zhǔn wǒ cānjiā nèige zuòtánhuì shi yīnwei nèige huìli suǒ tǎolùn de gēnběn méi shénmo jiàzhi.

9. Tā bù cānjiā Wǔsì Yùndong shi zěnmo yìhuí shì?

10. Wǒ bú kàn fěngcì xiǎoshuō shi yīnwei duōbàn dōu shi mà rén de.

C. Series (see note 3)

11. <u>Rúlín Wàishǐ</u>、<u>Hóng Lóu Mèng</u> zhèi liǎngbù shū dōu shi chángpiān xiǎoshuō ma?

12. Hú Shì、Chén Dúxiù zhèi liǎngge rén dōu shi tíchàng xīn wénhuà yùndong de xuézhě ma?

13. <u>Xīn Qīngnián</u>、<u>Xīn Cháo</u> gēn <u>Chuàngzào Zhōukān</u> zhèi sānzhǒng kānwu dōu shi Wǔsì shídài tuīdòng xīn wénxuéde kānwu.

14. Máo Xiānsheng、Máo Tàitai huì chàng wǔshěngde gēqǔ. Yīnwei tāmen dàoguo Guǎngdong、Guǎngxī、Húnán、Fújiàn、Jiāngxi zhèi wǔshěng, suǒyǐ tāmen huì chàng zhèi wǔshěngde gēqǔ.

15. Wǒ niànguo Lādīngwén、Fàwén gēn Yīngwén zhèi sānzhǒng wénxué.

JIǍNGHUÀ

Zhūwèi tóngxué:

    Jīntian yào jiǎng de tímu shi Zhōngguode Wénxué. Zhèige tímu hěn dà, yīnwei xiànyu shíjiān, zhǐhǎo xuǎnzé jǐge yàodiǎn lái gēn zhūwèi shuōshuo. Zhōngguo wénxué cóng tǐcáishang lái shuō kéyi fēnwéi liǎng dà

5 lèi, yílèi shi yùnwén, yílèi shi sǎnwén. Shénmo shi yùnwén? Shénmo shi sǎnwén ne? Fánshi shī、cí、gē、fù děngděng yǒu yùnde zuòpǐn dōu shi yùnwén. Chúle yùnwén yǐwài qíyúde kéyi shuō dōu shi sǎnwén.

    Zài Zhōngguo wénxuéshǐshang, cóng gǔshí dào xiàndài měige shídài yǒu měige shídàide tèshūde wényì. Wǒmen xiān cóng gǔdài shuōqǐ. Gǔ-

10 dài wénxué yě jiàozuo Xiānqín wénxué, yìsi jiu shi shuō zài Qín Cháo yǐqiánde wénxué. Zhōngguo zài Qín Cháo yǐqián zuì zǎoqǐde wénxué jiu shi Shāng Cháo jiǎgǔwénshangde bǔcí. Lìngwài jiu shi Zhōu Cháo shíhou

biāndìng de <u>Yì Jīng</u>, qícì jiu shi <u>Shī Jīng</u>. <u>Shī Jīng</u> běnlái shi gōngyuánqián liùshíjì yǐqiánde rén suǒ zuò de shī, yóu Kǒngzǐ xuǎnchu sānbǎi duō

15 piān jiu jiàozuo <u>Shī Jīng</u>, kéyi shuō shi gǔdài shīgēde zǒngjí. Hòulai dàole
Chūnqiū Zhànguó shídài, zài yùnwén fāngmian yǒu Qū Yuán děng chuàng-
zuò de <u>Chǔcí</u>, zài sǎnwén fāngmian yǒu <u>Zuǒ Zhuàn</u>、<u>Guóyǔ</u>、<u>Zhànguócè</u> hé
<u>Lúnyǔ</u>、<u>Lǎozǐ</u>、<u>Mèngzǐ</u>、<u>Mòzǐ</u>、<u>Zhuāngzǐ</u> děng dōu shi hěn yǒu wénxué jià-
zhide zuòpǐn.

20   Qín Cháo zhīhòu dàole Hàn Cháo.   Hàn Cháo wénxué zuì tèchūde
shi Hànfù、yuèfǔ hé zhuànjì wénxué.   Zài zhuànjì wénxuéli xiàng <u>Shǐ Jì</u>、
<u>Hàn Shū</u> dōu shi zuì jīngcǎide sǎnwén.   Hàn Cháo yǐhòu dàole Wèi Jìn Nán
Běi Cháo yǒu piàntǐwén.   Yòu yǐhòu xiàng Táng Cháode shī、Sòng Cháode
cí、Yuán Cháode qǔ yǐjí Míng、Qīng liǎngcháode xiǎoshuō, qízhōng Qīng

25 Dàide xiǎoshuō xiàng <u>Hóng Lóu Mèng</u>、<u>Rúlín Wàishǐ</u> yǐjí <u>Lǎo Cán Yóujì</u>
dōu shi wénxuéshangde jiézuò.

        Gōngyuán yī-jiǔ-yī-qī nián qiánhòu yīnwei Xīyáng wényì sīcháode
yǐngxiǎng hé Zhōngguó guónèi zhèngzhi géxīn yùndongde shídài bèijǐng,
jiu zài yī-jiǔ-yī-jiǔ nián chǎnshēngle Wǔsì Yùndong.   Zhè shi Zhōngguó

30 wénxuéshang huà shídài de yíge fēnshuǐlǐng. Yìbān yǒu xīn sīxiǎngde xuézhě xiàng Hú Shì、Chén Dúxiù děng tāmen dōu qǐlai tuīdòng xīn wénhuà
yùndong, xiě báihuàwén zuò báihuà shī xiě báihuà xiǎoshuō bàn báihuà
zázhì xiàng <u>Xīn Qīngnián</u>、<u>Xīn Cháo</u>、<u>Xiǎoshuō Yuèbào</u>、<u>Chuàngzào Zhōu-</u>
<u>kān</u> děngděng.   Dāngshí yě yǒu xǔduō rén duìyu tāmende báihuàwén hé

35 báihuà yùndong fēicháng fǎnduì. Tāmen dōu rènwei báihuà bú shi wénxué,
suǒyǐ tāmen bàn de kānwu jué bù dēngzǎi báihuàwén de. Báihuàwén suīrán shòu xǔduō rénde fǎnduì hé pīping, dànshi yīnwei nèige shídài yǐjing
chéngshú le, méi yǒu rén kéyi zǔzhǐ le, suǒyǐ xīn wénhuà yùndong jiu
quánmiàn zhǎnkāi. Zìcóng yī-jiǔ-yī-qī dào yī-jiǔ-èr-qī zhèi shínián jiān

40 zài "Guó-Gòng hézuò" de shíhou jiu chǎnshēngle xǔduō tóngqíng dàzhòng
pīping jiù shèhuìde wénxuéjiā xiàng Lǔ Xùn、Máo Dùn、Guō Mòruò děng.
Tāmen xiěle xǔduō wénzhāng hé chángpiān、duǎnpiānde xiǎoshuō zài bàoshang fābiǎo, hěn shòu yìbān rénde huānyíng.

        Cóng yī-jiǔ-èr-bā nián dào Zhōngguó duì Rìběn Kàngzhànde shíqī,

45 yǒu xǔduō wénxuéjiā xiàng Lǎo Shě、Bā Jīn tāmende zuòpǐn dōu shi dàile
yìzhǒng fěngcì jiù shèhuì tóngqíng dàzhòngde wénzhāng. Yóuqíshi zài

Kàngzhàn shíqī suǒyǒude zuòpǐn dōu tuōbuliǎo dài diar Kàngzhàn jiùguó
de jīngshen.

    Shuōdao zhèli zhūwèi yěxǔ yǒu rén yào wèn, xiànzài dàlùde wénxué
50 qíngxing shi zěnmoyàng? Zhèige wǒmen kéyi kàn Máo Zédōng zài Yán'ān
wényì zuòtánhuìshang fābiǎo de tánhuà, wǒmen jiu kéyi zhīdao. Tāde zhǔzhāng shi wénxué gēn zhèngzhì、jiàoyu yīnggāi shi dǎchéng yípiàn.   Tā
shuō wénxué shi zhèngzhi gēn jiàoyude gōngjù, suǒyǐ zài zhèizhǒng yuánzé
zhīxià, Gòngchǎndǎng zhízhèng dǐxiade wénxuéjiā yīnggāi fùzhe xīnde wén-
55 xué shǐmìng. Zhèige xīnde wénxué shǐmìng jiu shi bǎ wénxué dàngzuo yìzhǒng gōngjù lái tuīdòng dádao zhèngzhìde mùdì. Suǒyǐ dàlù yìbān wénxuéjiā zài dàlù jīntian qíngxing zhīxià, tāmen dōu zài nàlǐ tuīdòng suǒwèi
"bàogào wénxué."

    Yóucǐ kějiàn wǒmen yánjiu wénxué yídìng děi zhīdao tāde shídàixìng,
60 zhīdao tāde bèijǐng、zhèngzhide qíngxing、shèhuìde qíngxing, ránhòu wǒmen
cái néng liǎojiě cái néng xīnshǎng tāmende zuòpǐn.

FÙSHÙ

    Zhèipán lùyīndài shi Zhōngwén dì-yīzǔ dì-shísìhào, shísìcìde fùshù
Zhuāntí Jiǎnghuà, "Zhōngguode Yǔyán," shi yóu Bái Wénshān fùshù de.

    Zhèicìde jiǎnghuà shi yóu Jiǎn Jiàoshòu gěi wǒmen jiǎng de tímu
shi "Zhōngguode Yǔyán." Yīnwei Zhōngguo shi yíge wénhuà gǔguó, yǒu
5 jǐqiān niánde lìshǐ le, tāde wénhuà shuǐpíng dāngrán shi hěn gāo le. Ér
Zhōngguo yǔyán yě yǒu liǎngzhǒng tèdiǎn, yíge shi yǒu cídiào, yíge shi
méi yǒu qūzhé. Zhōngguo huà shi shìjièshang zhòngyàode yǔyán zhǐ yī.
Àn xiànzài hé jiāngláide qūshì lai shuō, yánjiu Zhōngguo huàde rén jiānglái yuè lái yuè duō. Ànzhào yǐshàngde zhǒngzhǒng yuányīn lai fēnxì,
10 Zhōngguo huà yǒu bìděi yánjiu de jiàzhi.

    Jiǎn Jiàoshòu shǒuxiān gěi wǒmen jiǎng Zhōngguo yǔyánde fēnqū.
Tā shuō xiànzàide Zhōngguo huà kéyi fēnwéi liùge dà fāngyán dìqū. Zuì
zhòngyàode shi pǔtōng huà. Shuō pǔtōng huàde zhàn Zhōngguo rénkǒu
zǒngshùde sìfēnzhī-sān. Ér pǔtōng huà yòu fēnchéng sān dà lèi. Běifāng
15 huà shi yòng Běijīng huà dàibiǎo, nán fāngde pǔtōng huà shi yòng Yángzhōu huà dàibiǎo, xī'nánde pǔtōng huà shi yòng Sìchuānde Chéngdū huà
dàibiǎo.

Tā shuō zhěnggèr Zhōngguo shuō pǔtōng huàde qūyù hěn guǎng. Bùguǎn bǐcǐ lízhe de jùlí yǒu duó yuǎn, yàoshi shuō pǔtōng huà fēnbié bìng
20 bú tài dà.   Bǐfang yíge Kūnmíng rén gēn yíge Shěnyáng rén chūcì jiànmiàn, zài yǔyánshang bìng méi yǒu duō dàde wèntí.

Jiǎn Jiàoshòu jiēzhe yòu gěi wǒmen jiǎng Zhōngguode jǐzhǒng fāngyán.   Tā shuō Yuèyǔ shi yòng Guǎngzhōu huà dàibiǎo. Wúyǔ yòng Sūzhōu
huà dàibiǎo.   Xiāngyǔ shi yòng Chángshā huà dàibiǎo, Gànyǔ lèisî Kèjiā
25 huà. Mǐnyǔ yòu fēnwéi nánběi liǎngqū. Mǐnnán huà yòng Xiàmén huà zuò
biāozhǔn, Mǐnběi huà yòng Fúzhōu huà zuò biāozhǔn.

Jiǎn Jiàoshòu shuō zhèixiē dà fāngyánli, zìrán shi yòng pǔtōng huàde
fànwéi zuì dà le. Suǒyǐ Jiǎn Jiàoshòu xiān gěi wǒmen jiǎng de shi pǔtōng
huà, yě jiu shi Běijīng huà.

30 Jiǎn Jiàoshòu jiǎng Běijīng huàli chúle shēngdiào yǐwài yígòng yǒu
sìbǎi duō ge yīnjié. Měige yīnjié yǒu sìshēng. Hái yǒu yíge qīngyīn hé
biàndiào. Qīngyīn shi cóng sìshēng jīběn shēngli biànhuachulai de. Bǐrú
<u>mǎimai</u> de <u>mài</u> zì děi niàn qīngyīn. Jiǎn Jiàoshòu yòu jiǎngdao biàndiào.
Tā shuō rúguǒ yíge cérde císù shi liǎngge dì-sānshēng, tóu-yíge císù zài
35 niàn de shíhou yào biànchéng dì-èrshēng. Bǐrú <u>zuò</u> <u>mǎimai</u> de <u>mǎi</u> gēn
<u>máizàng</u> de <u>mái</u> běnlái bú shi tóng yíge shēngdiào. Rúguǒ nǐ shuō "mái
mǎ" tīng de rén yàoshi bù- zhīdào shàngxiàwén jiu bù zhīdào shi yào yòng
qián bǎ mǎ mǎilai, háishi yào bǎ sǐ mǎ máizai dìli.

Jiǎn Jiàoshòu yòu gěi wǒmen jiǎngdao Běijīng huàli tèyǒude érhuà-
40 yùn. Rú "chūqu wán" Běijīng huà shuō "chūqu wár," "hǎohāode" Běijīng
huà jiào "hǎohāorde," cíwéishang yǒu <u>érde</u> yīn.

Jiǎn Jiàoshòu yòu jiǎng Yìn-Ōuyǔli yǒu géde biànhuà zài Zhōngguo
huàli shi méi yǒu de. Tā yòu shuōdao guānyu cítóu hé cíwěi. Tā shuō
Zhōngguo huàli cítóu hěn shǎo, kěshi cíwěi dàoshi hěn duō. Érhuàyùn yě
45 shi cíwěi zhī yìzhǒng. Lìngwài hái yǒu hěn duō cíwěi. Cér hòutoude <u>zi</u>
bǐrú "érzi、nǎozi" háiyǒu "gútou、shítou、wàitou" de <u>tou</u> zì yě shi cíwěi.

Jiǎn Jiàoshòu yòu gàosu wǒmen Běijīng huàli biǎoshì wènhuàde shíhou yǒu sānge fāngfa. Dì-yī shi yòng yíwèn dàimíngcí, bǐrú "shéi? shén-
50 mo? nǎr?" Dì-èr shi jùwěi yòng yíwèncí "ma、ba" bǐrú "Nǐ qù ma?"
"Nǐ qù ba?" Dì-sān shi yíwènshì, shi bǎ fǒudìngshì gēn xùshùshì hézài

yíkuàr, jiu chéngle yíge yíwènshì. Bǐrú "Tā mǎi shū" "Tā bù mǎi shū" zài yíkuàr jiu biànchéngle "Tā mǎi bù mǎi shū?" de yíge yíwèn jùzi le.

   Zuìhòu Jiǎn Jiàoshòu shuō tā shuō de zhǐshi jǔchu jǐge xiǎnzhùde

55 lìzi, tèbié shi gēn Yìn-Ōuyǔ bùtóng de, ràng wǒmen zuò ge cānkǎo.

WÉNXÍ

1. Wàn Xiānsheng cóngqián yánjiu Mòzǐ xuéshuō, xiànzài tā zài Tàiguó xuéxí Tàiyǔ. Tā shuō: "Mòzǐde zhǔzhāng yǒu xiē dìfang lèisì Fóxué. Tàiguó shi yíge Fójiào guójiā, suǒyǐ wǒ dào Tàiguó xué Tàiguo huà hǎo yánjiu Fóxué." Tā yòu shuō Tàiguo yǔyán qiàqiǎo hé Hànrénde yǔyán dōu shi shǔyu Hàn-Zàng yǔzú, suǒyi xuéxí Tàiyǔ bǐjiào róngyi.

2. Jiǎ Yǐ Bǐng Dīng sìge rén yánjiu Zhōngguo wénzìde qǐyuán. Jiǎ shuō: "Zhōngguo gǔshūshang shuō: 'Cāng Jié zào zì' nà jiu shi Zhōngguo zuì zǎode zì." Yǐ shuō: "Zhèizhǒng shuōfa yǒu shénmo quèshi zhèngmíng ma?" Bǐng shuō: "Gǔshū jiu shi zhèngmíng." Dīng shuō: "Nà zhǐ shi gǔshūshang shuō de. Méi yǒu shénmo yuánshǐ kěkàode zīliào kéyi zhèngmíng. Rúguǒ ànzhe yuánshǐ kěkàode zīliào lái shuō, zhǐ yǒu jiǎgǔwén cái suànshi zuì zǎode wénzì, yīnwei jiǎgǔwén shi kèzài yípiàn yípiàn guījiǎde bèishang hé yíkuài yíkuài niú gútoushangde zì. Zhèixiē guījiǎ gēn niú gútou dōu shi Shāng Cháo de, jìndài cái cóng dìxia juéchulai de."

3. Yǒu yíge xué Zhōngwén de wàiguo xuésheng duì wǒ shuō: "Wǒ suǒ zhīdao de Zhōngwén hěn yǒuxiàn. Qǐng nǐ gàosu wo shénmo shi Liù Shū?" Wǒ gàosu ta: "Xiàngxíng、zhǐshì、huìyì、jiǎjiè、xíngshēng hé zhuǎnzhù jiu shi Liù Shū." Tā yòu wèn wo: "Yǒu rén hái shuōguo <u>xiàngshì</u>、<u>xiàngshēng</u>. Shì bu shi yě shi Liù Shū zhǐ yī ne?" Wǒ yòu gàosu ta: "<u>Xiàngshì</u> jiu shi <u>zhǐshì</u>. <u>Xiàngshēng</u> shi zhǐzhe <u>xíngshēng</u>lide yíbùfen shuō de."

4. Wǒmen zài xué yǔyīnxuéde shíhou, guānyu cháng yòng de gèzhǒng cí lìrú yǔyīn、yīnsù、dānyīn、dānyīnzì、dānyīnjié、duōyīnjié、yīndiào děngděngde dōu yào yánjiu míngbái.

5. Jiǎyú gēn guī kànqilai yàngzi hěn xiāngtóng, kěshi yǒu rén shuō yǒu fēnbié.

6. Xiānsheng duì xiǎo xuésheng shuō: "Nǐmen kāishǐ xué xiě zì zuì hǎo bú yào xiě jiǎnbǐzì." Yǒu yìtiān yǒu yíge xiǎo xuésheng yìliánchuàn xiěle liù-qīge jiǎnbǐzì. Xiānsheng kànjianle wèn ta wèi-shénmo yídìng yào xiě jiǎnbǐzì? Xiǎo xuésheng shuō: "Jiǎnbǐzìde bǐhuá shǎo, kéyi jiǎnshǎo xiě zì de shíjiān. Qǐng wèn xiānsheng, dàodǐ wèi-shénmo yào xiànzhi wǒmen, bú jiào wǒmen xiě jiǎnbǐzì ne?"

7. Gòucífǎ hé zàojùfǎ yǒu shénmo bùtóng? Gòucífǎ shi yánjiu yíge cí shi zěnyàng gòuchéng de. Zàojùfǎ shi yánjiu yíge jùzi shi zěnyàng gòuzào de.

8. Rénde shēnghuó yǒu sì dà yàosù jiu shi yī、shí、zhù、xíng. Zài zhèi sì dà yàosùli něi yìzhǒng zuì yàojǐn? Yǒu rén shuō: "Shí zuì yàojǐn, yīnwei rén měitiān duōbàn chī sāndùn fàn. Rúguǒ jǐtiān bù chī dōngxi, zěnmo néng huó ne?"

9. Yǒu Jiǎ Yǐ liǎngge Yìndu xuésheng, zài yíge Zhōngguo yǔfǎ zuòtánhuìli tīngjian biéren tándao míngcí、 dòngcí、 fùcí、 dàimíngcí hé rénchēng dàimíngcí. Yòu tīngdao zhǔcí、 bīncí děngděng. Jiǎ duì Yǐ shuō: "Zhōngguo yǔfǎli cíde fēnlèi hé wǒmen yǔfǎli cíde fēnlèi shì bu shi dàtóngxiǎoyì?" Yǐ shuō: "Zhōngguo yǔyán gēn Yìndu yǔyán bìng bú shi yíge yǔzú, gè yǒu dútède yǔfǎ. Bǐfang shuō zài Yìndu yǔfǎli yǒu zhǔgé、 bīngé, zài Zhōngguo yǔfǎli zhùyì de shi cídiào. Zǒngkuò lai shuō shi bù xiāngtóng de."

10. Kǒngzǐ、 Mèngzǐde xuéshuō dōu shi Rújiā xuéshuō. Yǒu rén shuō: "Rújiā xuéshuō duìyu rénmín yǒude shi yǒulìde, yě yǒu búlìde."

11. Yǒu yíge wàiguo rén néng shuō Zhōngguo Yuè、 Mǐn liǎngshěngde fāngyán. Tā yòu néng shuō Jiāngsu huà. Jiāngsu gǔshí shi Wú Guó, suǒyǐ tā yòu suànshi néng shuō Wúyǔ.

12. Shěnyáng shi Zhōngguo Dōngběi yíge shěngde shěnghuì. Yī-jiǔ-sān-yī nián jiǔyue shíbārìde yèli Rìběnde jūnduì jìnru Shěnyáng. Rìběn jūnduì qiángdiàode shuō, shi Zhōngguo jūnduì shǒuxiān duì Rìběn jūnduì yǒu búlìde xíngdòng, suǒyǐ Rìběn jūnduì cái jìnrù Shěnyáng. Kěshi zhèizhǒng huà shéi néng xiāngxìn ne? Zhè jiu shi Zhōngguo lìshǐshang suǒ shuō de Jiǔ Yī Bā.

13. Zài Zhōngguo lìshǐshang, Suí Cháode niándài bǐjiǎo duǎn, Qín Cháode niándài gèng duǎn. Suí Cháo yǒu sānshíjiǔnián, Qín Cháo zhǐ yǒu shíwǔnián.

14. Hàn Dài wénxuéde zhǔyào dàibiǎo shi fù, suǒyǐ hòulai jiàozuo Hànfù.

15. Shàng Shū shi gǔdàide shū, cóng zhèiběn shūli kéyi zhīdao gǔdàide yǔyán, suǒyǐ yánjiu shànggǔ Hànyǔ de rènwei Shàng Shū shi bìyào yánjiu de gǔshū zhī yī.

16. Táng Cháo yǒu yíge shīren, yǒu yìtiān wǎnshang zuòle yíge mèng, mèngjian tā zuò shī yòng de bǐ shēngchu huā lai le. Hòulai tāde shī jiu yuè zuò yuè hǎo, chéngle yíge yǒumíngde shīren.

17. Wǒ zuì bu xǐhuan niàn Lādīngwén, kěshi xiānsheng yídìng jiào wǒ niàn. Méi yǒu fázi, zhǐhǎo niàn le. Yǒu yìtiān yǒu rén wèn wo: "Lādīngwén shì bu shi yí-zì-yí-yì, háishi yě yǒu biéyì?" Wǒ shuō: "Wǒ suīrán niàn Lādīngwén kěshi Lādīngzì wǒ rènshi de dōu yǒuxiàn ne."

18. Yǒu rén shuō guǐ zuì pà guāngmíng, suǒyǐ guāngmíng shi guǐde dírén. Jiǎshè shìjièshang dàochu dōu shi guāngmíng, nènmo guǐ jiu méi fázi cúnzài le.

19. Dìdi tài yònggōng le. Niànle sìge zhōngtóude shū yě méi xiūxi. Wǒ shuō: "Dìdi, nǐ yīnggāi huànhuan nǎozi, tīngting lùyīn le." Dìdi shuō méi yǒu shénmo kéyi tīng de. Wǒ shuō: "Nǐ tīngting Zhāng Xiānsheng lù de gēr ya." Dìdi shuō: "Tā chàng de gēr wǒ bù xiǎng tīng, dōu shi nèi yítào, bùzhíde tīng." Wǒ shuō: "Nǐ bú shi zuì xǐhuan tīng xióngzhuàngde gēr ma? Zhāng Xiānsheng zhèicì lù de dōu shi xióngzhuàngde gēr." Dìdi shuō Zhāng Xiānshengde chàngfǎ yídìng biǎodábuchulai shi xióngzhuàngde gēr.

20. Yǒu yìjiā mùchǎng shēngyì bù hěn hǎo, xìnyong yě bú dà hǎo. Mùchǎngde zhǔren xiǎng qǐng shānghuì zhīchí. Tā shuō: "Rúguǒ méi rén zhīchí, dàole niándǐ wǒ jiu bù néng wéichi le." Shānghuìde rén shuō: "Nǐde chǎng běnlái shēngyi hěn hǎo. Búdàn chénglǐde rén cháng mǎi nǐde dōngxi, jiu

shi lí chéng bù yuǎnde dà xiǎo túnzide rén yě cháng lai mǎi nǐde dóngxi.
Nènmo hǎode shēngyì zěnmo xiànzài zhènmo zāogāo ne? Zhēn tài kěxī
le."

21. Zhōngguo cóngqián niàn shū de rén duōbàn yǐwéi tā bǐ biéren yǒu yìdiǎr
yōuyuè. Dāngshíde shèhuì bǎ niàn shū de rén jiàozuo _shì_, yě jiàozuo _rú_,
yěshi yǒu yìdiǎr zhòngshi de yìsi. Hòulai shídài biànqiān le, nóngren、
gōngren、 shāngren zài shèhuishang dàjiā dōu píngděng, yíyàng shòudao
zhòngshì, méi yǒu shénmo rén lìwài.

22. Zhōngyāng zhèngfǔ zuìjìn yǒu zhèngshi mìnglìng zài guówàide rénmín xiànyu sānge yuè yǐnèi huí guó, guòle sānge yuè jiu bù zhǔn tāmen huí guó
le.

23. Yǒu rén wèn: "_Fùhéjù_ hé _guīnàfǎ_ zhèi liǎngge cér zài shénmo xuékēli
cháng yòng?" Wǒ shuō: "_Fùhéjù_ zài yǔyánxuéli cháng yòng. _Guīnàfǎ_ zài
lùnlǐxué hé shùxuéshang dōu cháng yòng."

24. Rén huózai shìjièshang hǎoxiang zuòle yíge mèng. Shíjiān shi hěn yǒuxiàn de, zuì duō búguò yìbǎi nián zuǒyòu. Wǒmen yīnggāi lìyong jīhui
zuò diar shìqing huòzhě shi yánjiu yánjiu xuéwen.

25. _Shénmo_ zhèige cér shícháng yòngzai wènhuàli, lìrú "Nǐ shénmo shíhou
zǒu?" Kěshi yǒushíhou yě bú yòngzai wènhuàli. Bǐrú "Tā shénmo yě bù
zhīdào" zhè jiu bú shi wènhuà le.

26. Wǒ zuótian wǎnshang zuòle yíge mèng, mèngjian wǒ xiǎode shíhou zài
yíge sīshúli niàn shū. Lǎoshī jiào wǒ bèi shū, wǒ bèibuxiàlái, lǎoshī jiu
dǎle wǒ yíge zuǐba. Wǒ kūzhe jiu huí jiā le.

WÈNTÍ

1. Zhōngguo wénxué cóng tǐcáishang lai shuō kéyi fēn jǐ dà lèi? Shī、cí、
gē、fù shǔyú něi yílèi?

2. Chūnqiū Zhànguó shídài zài yùnwén fāngmiàn yǒu shénmo chuàngzuò? Shi
shéi chuàngzuò de? Zài sǎnwén fāngmiàn yǒu shénmo yǒu wénxué jiàzhide zuòpǐn?

3. Shénmo rén tuǐdòng xīn wénhuà yùndong? Dāngshí yǒu shénmo kānwu?
Zài zhèixiē kānwushang dēng de zuòpǐn shi wényánwén háishi báihuàwén?
Wèi-shénmo méi yǒu rén kéyi zǔzhǐ xīn wénhuàde fāzhǎn?

4. Lǔ Xùn、Máo Dùn、Guō Mòruòde wénzhāng wèi-shénmo shòu rén huānyíng?
Lǎo Shè、Bā Jīnde zuòpǐn dàiyǒu yìzhǒng shénmo jīngshen?

5. Zài Yán'ān wényì zuòtánhuìshang Máo Zédōng duì wénxué yǒu shénmo
zhǔzhāng? Gòngchǎndǎng zhízhèng dǐxiade wénxuéjiā fùzhe shénmo shǐmìng?

6. Shénmo yùndong shi Zhōngguo wénxuéshǐshang huàfēn shídàide fēnshuǐlǐng?
Zhèige yùndong shì bu shi bǎ zhèngzhi géxīn hé xīn wénhua yùndong liánchuàn zài yìqǐ?

7. Hàn Cháo wénxué zuì tèchūde yùnwén shi něi jǐzhǒng? Chúle yùnwén zhīwài hái yǒu shénmo jīngcǎide sǎnwén?

8. Nánběi Cháo shídàide wénxué shi piàntǐwén. Sòng Cháo, Yuán Cháo shídàide wénxué shi yǐ shènmo wéi zuî zhùmíng ne?

9. Shénmo xiǎoshuō shi Qīng Dài zhùmíngde xiǎoshuō? Qǐng nǐ jǔchu sānge
   xiǎoshuōde míngzi lái.   Yě qǐng nǐ shuōshuo rú gēn Rújiā shi shénmo
   yìsi?

10. Qǐng nǐ yòng "quèdìng, chóngdié, fǒudìng, huíhé, fùjiā, zhuǎnchéng, zǒng-
    kuò" měi yíge cér shuō yíge duǎn jùzi.

ILLUSTRATIVE SENTENCES (ENGLISH)

2.2. Do you know what was advocated by [the theories of] the Confucianists?

2.3. The Scholars is a novel which tells the story of some intellectuals.   In
     some places it is really funny.   When I read it I die laughing.

3.2. Travels of Mr. Derelict is a famous novel in the vernacular. The constant
     reading of such novels is quite [lit. more or less somewhat] useful in
     studying vernacular literature.

4.1. Some people like the novels written by Mao Dun, others those by Lu Hsün.

5.1. Most of the novels written by Pa Chin and Lao She satirize the old society.

7.1. What is the genre of the piece of writing by Hu Shih? Is is prose or poetry?

14.1. In what publication did you see the work by Ch'en Tuhsiu?

17.1. Mr. Kuo Mojo has done a lot of research on divination texts in the oracle
      bone writing.

24.1. His actions can't be stopped by anybody.

29.1. What was the Book of Changes used for in ancient times, do you know?

34.1. Since the establishment of the Republic, in the political area China has had
      some reforms ushering in a new period.

34.2. On what basis was that area divided into five regions?

41.1. Professor Ma told me to write an essay and limited me to five days to fin-
      ish writing it.

41.5. The members of that scholarly organization are limited to college profes-
      sors.

43.1. He's the factory accountant. If there are mistakes in the factory accounts,
      he can't duck the responsibility.

47.2. Dǎchéng yípiàn means "everyone cooperates without divisions among our-
      selves."

47.3. The tortoiseshells which were dug up from the ground were in fragments.
      Most of them were very small.

49.2. He's (a member of) the Kuomintang, not the Communist Party.

50.1. Language is a tool for expressing ideas.

54.1. At what time did China open up the all-out War of Resistance against Ja-
      pan?

58.1. Creation Weekly and New Tide both promoted the new literature. Their
mission was the same [lit. did not have any two kinds].

NOTES

1. The adverb dōu 'all' generally refers to something which has already been
mentioned, in the same sentence or in a previous sentence. It can, however, refer to something following, provided that the something is a question
word or is preceded by a question word:

> Nǐ dōu mǎi shénmo shū? 'What books are you buying?' (Note that
> without dōu the sentence might mean either 'What book are you buy-
> ing?' or 'What books are you buying?'

> Nǐ dōu dào nǎr qu? 'Where are you going?'—in the sense of 'What
> places are you going to?'

2. In the pattern S shi N the copula shi joins a sentence with a noun:

> Nǐ bú qù shi shénmo yuányin? 'What is the reason (why) you aren't
> going?'

3. Items in a series are often recapitulated by a number expression at the end
of the series. Such recapitulation is especially helpful when inadequate
punctuation or other typographical aids make it difficult to determine how
many items are being listed:

> Zài Zhōngguo lìshǐshang Zhōu、Hàn、Táng、Míng、Qīng zhèi wǔge
> cháodài shi bǐjiǎo chángde. 'In Chinese history [the five dynasties
> of] Chou, Han, T'ang, Ming, and Ch'ing were comparatively long.'

4. In this lesson reference is made to a number of leading figures, mostly
writers, in modern China, namely Hú Shì (Hu Shih), Chén Dúxiù (Ch'en
Tuhsiu), Lǔ Xùn (Lu Hsün), Máo Dùn (Mao Tun), Lǎo Shè, Bā Jīn (Pa
Chin), Guō Mòruò (Kuo Mojo), and Máo Zédōng (Mao Tsetung).

Dì-Shíbākè.　Wēnxi

FÙSHÙ

Zhèipán lùyīndài shi Zhōngwén dì-yīzǔ dì-shíwǔhào, dì-shíwǔcìde Zhuāntí Jiǎnghuà.　Jiǎngtí shi "Zhōngguode Wénxué," yóu Bái Wénshān fùshù.

Jiǎn Jiàoshòu zhèicì jiǎng de shi "Zhōngguode Wénxué." Tā suǒ
5　jiǎng de, qián yíduàn shi shǔyu lìshǐxìngde wénxué zhīshi, yě jiu shi jiù wénxué. Hòu yíduàn jiǎng de shi jìndài wénxué. Xiànzài wǒ bǎ Jiǎn Jiàoshòu suǒ jiǎng de fùshù yícì.

Jiǎn Jiàoshòu kāishǐ shuō Zhōngguo wénxué zhèige tímu bāokuò de fànwei hěn dà, xiànzài zhǐ xuǎn zhòngyàode jiǎngyijiǎng. Tā shuō Zhōng-

10 guo wénxué cóng gǔ dào jīn měige shídài yǒu měige shídài tèshūde wényì zuòpǐn. Tā shuō zài gǔdài Xiānqín wénxué, yǒu Shāng Cháode "bǔcí,"
yǒu Zhóu Cháode Yì Jīng、Shī Jīng děngděngde. Jiǎn Jiàoshòu shuō Shī
Jīng běnlái shi gōngyuánqián dì-liùshíjì yǐqián rénmen zuò de shīgē, hòulai jīngguo Kǒngzǐ zài nèixiē shī lǐmian xuǎnchulaile sānbǎi duō piān jiu
15 jiàozuo Shī Jīng. Shī Jīng shi shīgēde zǒngjí. Jiǎn Jiàoshòu jiēzhe yòu
shuōdao Chūnqiū Zhànguó shídài, zài yùnwén yìfāngmian yǒu Qū Yuánde
Chǔcí. Zhìyú sǎnwén yìfāngmiàn yǒu Zuǒ Zhuàn、Guóyǔ、Zhuāngzǐ、Mòzǐ、
Mèngzǐ、Lúnyǔ、Zhànguócè, dōu shi xiāngdāng yǒu jiàzhide shū.

Jiǎn Jiàoshòu yòu shuō Hàn Cháo wénxué zuì tèchūde jiu shi fù gēn
20 yuèfǔ. Hái yǒu Hàn Shū、Shǐ Jì dōu shi zuì yǒu jiàzhide sǎnwén. Děngdao Wèi、Jìn、Nán Běi Cháo yòu yǒu piàntǐwén. Yǐhòu jiù shi Táng
Cháode shī、Sòng Cháode cí、Yuán Cháode qǔ、Míng Cháo gēn Qīng Cháode
xiǎoshuō. Jiǎn Jiàoshòu shuō Qīng Cháo zuì yǒumíngde xiǎoshuō shi Hóng
Lóu Mèng、Rúlín Wàishǐ、Lǎo Cán Yóujì děng. Guānyu zhèi jǐbù xiǎoshuō
25 wǒ dōu kànguo. Hóng Lóu Mèng shi xiě yíge dà jiātínglide yìxiē shìqing.
Lǎo Cán Yóujì shi yìzhǒng lǚxíng rìjìde tǐcái, érqiě yě xiěchulaile Qīng
Cháo zuò guān de zěnmo huài. Rúlín Wàishǐ lǐmiàn shi fěngcì dāngshí
wénrén de.

Jiǎn Jiàoshòu jiēzhe yòu jiǎng cóng yī-jiǔ-yī-qī nián de shíhou yīn-
30 wei Zhōngguo shòule Xīfāng guójiāde yǐngxiǎng, hái yǒu Zhōngguo zhèngzhi gǎigé de bèijǐng, suǒyǐ jiu zài yī-jiǔ-yī-jiǔ nián fāshēngle wénxué
géxīn, jiu shi Wǔsì Yùndong. Nà shi Zhōngguo wénxué huà shídài de
yíge shíqī. Zài nèige shíhou, Hú Shì、Chén Dúxiù tamen dōu fǎnduì jiù
wénxué, tíchàng xīn wénxué, jiu shi tíchàng báihuàwén. Tāmen xiě bái-
35 huà de wénzhāng, bàn báihuàwénde zázhì, xiàng Xīn Qīngnián、Xīn Cháo、
Xiǎoshuō Yuèbào shénmode. Tāmen lìyòng zázhì wéi gōngjù tuīxíng báihuàwén.

Jiǎn Jiàoshòu shuō dāngshí yǒu yìbān xuézhě fēicháng fǎnduì tíchàng
báihuàwén zhèizhǒng yùndong. Tāmen rènwei báihuàwén bìng bú shi wén-
40 xué. Suírán yǒu rén fǎnduì, dànshi shídàide qūshì, rènhé lìliang shi zǔ-
zhǐbuliǎo zhèizhǒng yùndong de.

Jiǎn Jiàoshòu jiēzhe yòu shuō zài Guó-Gòng hézuò de shíhou jiu
yǒu hǎojǐwèi tóngqíng dàzhòng, fǎnduì jiù shèhuìde wénxuéjiā, xiàng Lǔ

Xùn、Máo Dùn、Guō Mòruò zhèi xiēge xuézhě. Tāmen xiě de dōngxi hěn
45 shòu lǎobǎixìngde huānyíng. Hòulai yòu yǒu hěn duō wénxuéjiā chūxiàn,
xiàng Lǎo Shè、Bā Jīn. Tāmende zuòpǐn dōu shi zhànzai rénmín fāngmiànde yìzhǒng wénzhāng, dāngrán shòudào dàzhòngde huānyíng le.

Jiǎn Jiàoshòu yòu shuōle yìdiǎr xiànzài dàlùshang duì wénxué de
kànfa. Tā shuō Máo Zédōng dāngchū zài Yán'ān zuòtánhuìshang shuōguo,
50 wénxué gēn zhèngzhi hé jiàoyu yīnggāi dǎchéng yípiàn, wénxué shi zhèngzhi gēn jiàoyude gōngjù. Gēnjùle zhèizhǒng yuánzé, suǒyi xiànzài dàlùshangde wénxuéjiā, tāmen shi fùzhe shǐmìng de. Tāmen xiànzài tuīdòng-
zhe yìzhǒng "bàogào wénxué."

WÈNDÁ

I. Nǐ wèi-shénmo. . . ?

(dì-shísānkè)

bù xǐhuan yànr	mófǎng ta
nènmo hánxu	hūlüè le zhèijiàn shì
fǒurèn shi nǐ xiě de	yǎngchéng zhèige xíguan
hòuhuǐ méi qù	gēn tā shuōbutōng
shǒuxiān suàn zhàng	zhǔxiu yīnyùnxué
tuìbù le	biǎoshi bú qù

(dì-shísìkè)

bù mǎi <u>Xǔ Shì Shuōwén</u>	yòng zhèige fǎzé
shuō ta shi lìwài	bù xǐhuan bèi shū
mǎi guījiǎ	xíngdòng bú zìyóu
bù zhǔn ta lái	

(dì-shíwǔkè)

bù xǐhuan yìshupǐn	shuō méi you liǎngdiǎn shuǐ
yào mǎi <u>Qièyùn</u>	bú niàn yìshu
chúdiào tāde míngzi	mǎi <u>Xìju Jiǎnyào</u>
bù xǐhuan kàn xì	duì xìju méi xìngqu
xiān kàn dì-èrjuàn	xuǎnzé zhèige jùběn

(dì-shíliùkè)

yánjiu Shànggǔ Hànyǔ   qiángdiào zhèijiàn shì

dǎ tāde zuǐba

(dì-shíqīkè)

fěngcì shèhuì   mǎi zhènmo duō kānwu

bú niàn Yì Jīng   yào xiànzhi tā yòng qián

jiù xǐhuǎn xiě cí   bú kàn Hóng Lóu Mèng

II. . . . shi shénmo?

(dì-shísānkè)

sùchéngkē   pàngzi

zhǔxiūkē   huángyīng

(dì-shísìkè)

jiǎyú   jūnduì

mùliào   yīndiào

dānyīnzì   shānghuì

yīnsù   shēnghuóde yàosù

(dì-shíwǔkè)

jīngxì   Shuāngshíjié

sìjiǎo hàomǎr   hēibǎn

suǒyǐn   súyǔ

dúwù   tōngxùn bàodǎo

yóujì   shuānglìrér

niánjiàn   sāndiǎn shuǐ

kuòhú   tíshǒu

(dì-shíliùkè)

Shī Jīng   yíwèn dàimingci

Shàng Shū   cídiào

fùcí   fùhéjù

(dì-shíqīkè)

jiézuò	zuòtánhuì
chuàngzuò	fēnshuǐlǐng
Wǔsì Yùndong	sīcháo
bǔcì	gōngjù
yuèfǔ	<u>Xīn Qīngnián</u>
Hànfǔ	<u>Zhànguócè</u>
piàntǐwén	

III. . . . shi shénmo yìsi?

(dì-shísānkè)

yīngyīngyànyàn	qiānzhēnwànquè
cì bù dáyì	rìjīyuèlěi
xīnhuāngyìluàn	

(dì-shísìkè)

jiǎ, yǐ, bǐng, dīng	zōngkuò yíjù
yí-zì-yí-yì	huìyì gēn jiǎjiè

(dì-shíwǔkè)

kāi-juàn-yǒu-yì	fǒuzéde huà
láo-ér-wú-gōng	

(dì-shíliùkè)

yìliánchuànde	yōuyuè
yíwèn dàimíngcí	xùshùshì
zàojùfǎ	huàxuéde chéngfēn

(dì-shíqīkè)

dǎchéng yípiàn	huàfēn dìqū
piàntǐwén	Chūnqiū
<u>Chǔcí</u>	shídài bèijǐng

IV. . . . zài năr?

(dì-shísānkè)

nĭde zĭmèi   nèiwèi pàng tàitai

(dì-shísìkè)

nèitào shū   má
Shuōwén   zhōngyāng zhèngfŭ
wŏde yùnshū   xīn shū yùgào
shěnghui

(dì-shúwŭkè)

Kāngxī Zìdiăn   nĭde túshū jiănjiè
tōngxùnshè   Guóyŭ Huìbiān

(dì-shíliùkè)

Fúzhōu   Yángzhōu
Xiàmén   Shěnyáng
Chéngdū   Tàiguó
Kūnmíng

(dì-shíqīkè)

Yán'ān   nĭ nèibĕn Yì Jīng

V. . . . báihuà zĕnmo shuō?

(dì-shísānkè)

shìfŏu   jìnrù
néngfŏu   yŭ
yìbiàn   zĭmèi
wéiyŏurúcĭ   zăorì
chízăo   yùzhù

(dì-shísìkè)

zhuăn-bài-wéi-shèng

(dì-shíwǔkè)

értóng   mínsú
yuèdú

(dì-shíqīkè)

yóucǐ   dēngzǎi
Xiānqín

VI. Nǐ zěnmo zhīdao . . . ?

(dì-shísānkè)

wǒde shū diūdiào le   wǒ ná tā zuò bǎngyàng
tāde cuòwu hěn duō   fēijī diàoxialai le
wǒde chē pènghuài le   tā shuōde bù zhēnquè
tā shuōde bù liúlì   tā gōngke tuìbù le
tā hěn rèqíng

(dì-shísìkè)

juédàduōshù zànchéng   tā hěn yǒu xìnyong
nèige jùběn bù hǎo   biǎo shi tā nònghuài de
tā zhǎo zīliào   nèige shānde xíngzhuàng
tā yuèdǐ huílai   tā yánjiu shīyùn ne

(dì-shíwǔkè)

míngtian yào guā fēng   bùshǒu shi rén zi páng
sìdiǎn huǒ bú duì   tā shāowēi shòu le
bùshǒu shi lìrér   nèiběn shū bu shìyòng
sǐshāng de rén hěn duō   yuánzéshang kéyi le
tāmen yào yòng fēnglì   tā huì chàng xì

(dì-shíliùkè)

Yīngwén qūzhé bù nán   tāde shēngdiào bú duì
tā chéngwéi huàjiā le

(dì-shíqīkè)

Gòngchǎndǎng shi dǎngpài   Guó-Gòng yào hézuò

tāmen dǎchéng yípiàn   dàzhàn zhǎnkāi le

tā zuòmèngle   tā xǐhuan chàng gēqǔ

VII. Nǐ shénmo shíhou . . . ?

(dî-shísānkè)

liǎn hóng   xīuxi

chàng gēr   yùnyòng bǐyu

xīnhuāngyìluàn   gēn tāmen jiēchǔ

tuîxiū   néng wánchéng xuéyè

(dî-shísîkè)

shuō: "Zāogāo!"   bèi shū

zhèngshî jiǎngyǎn

(dî-shíwǔkè)

qù tīng xi   chónggǎi wénzhāng

chá zîdiǎn   dào pùzi qū mǎi yā

dìng zázhî   zhòng cǎo

shāng fēng le

(dî-shíliùkè)

xué Mǐnnán huà   xǐhuan huàn nǎozi

yòng guīnàfǎ   fùjiā érhuàyùn

(dî-shíqīkè)

zuòmèng   kāishǐ niàn Zuǒ Zhuàn

yùndong yùndong   mǎi de Zhànguócè

VIII. . . . gēn . . . yǒu shénmo bùtóng?

(dî-shísānkè)

pèngjian, yùjian   niǎo, jī

tǎolùn, shuō huà   shēng, yùn

tóufa, máo   gǎnqíng, rèqíng

(dì-shísìkè)

xiàngxíng, xiàngshēng

běnyì, biéyì

yángguǐzi, wàiguo rén

jiǎgǔwén, jiǎnbǐzì

Liùshū, liùběn shū

yīnyùnxué, yǔyánxué

yōudiǎn, tèdiǎn

gōngchǎng, mùchǎng

mà rén, shuō rén

màizi, liángshi

zìxíng, zìyì

yìwǎn fàn, yídùn fàn

gútou, jiǎ

dàzhòng, lǎobǎixìng

zìyīn, zìyì

Lādīngwén, Lādīnghuà

zìyì, zìxíng

huìhé, pèngjian

(dì-shíwǔkè)

xuǎnjí, quánjí

zìhuì, cíhuì

Cíyuán, Cíhǎi

zhuànjì, zìzhuàn

fēngzāi, shuǐzāi

cǎozì, jiǎntǐzì

cóngshū, quánjí

fǎnqiè, pīnyīn

bùshǒu, zì

huàjù, jīngxì

(dì-shíliùkè)

Hàn-Zàng yǔzú,
   Yìn-Ōu yǔzú

míngcí, dòngcí

liàngcí, míngcí

dàimíngcí, rénchēng
   dàimíngcí

yǔyīnxué, yǔyánxué

biàndiào, qīngyīn

gòucífǎ, zàojùfǎ

xùshùshì, fǒudìngshì

císù, yīnsù

Shànggǔ Hànyǔ, Zhōnggǔ
   Hànyǔ

cítóu, cíwěi

(dì-shíqīkè)

yùnwén, sǎnwén

lìshǐ, wàishǐ

Rújiā, xuézhě

díren, péngyou

Guóyǔ, Guóyǔ

quánjí, zǒngjí

zhízhèng, zhèngzhì

IX. . . . de duìmiàn shi shénmo?

(dì-shísānkè)

pàng   quē
shǒuxiān   shòu
diū

(dì-shísìkè)

yǒulì   dǐxia
duōyīnjié   dānyīnjié
jiǎnshǎo   búlì

(dì-shíwǔkè)

értóng   yǒu qùwei
duǎnpiān xiǎoshuō   liúyì

(dì-shíliùkè)

cítóu   bīngé
bīncí   cíwěi
zhǔgé   zhǔcí
zhíde

(dì-shíqīkè)

zǔzhǐ

X. . . . shi shéi?

(dì-shísānkè)

nèige pàngzi   chàng gēr de

(dì-shísìkè)

Cāng Jié   nèiwèi kuàiji

(dì-shíwǔkè)

dìng zázhì de   shòu shāng de
pùzide zhǔren   biānji nèiběn shū de

(dì-shíliùkè)

nèiwèi Fújiàn rén   nèige Tàiguo rén

huì shuō Mǐnběi huà de   guǎngbō xīnwén de rén

(dì-shíqīkè)

Hú Shì   Bā Jīn

Chén Dúxiù   Máo Zédōng

Lǔ Xùn   Mèngzǐ

Máo Dùn   Zhuāngzǐ

Guō Mòruò   Mòzǐ

Lǎo Shè

XI. . . . de lìngwài yíge shuōfǎ shi shénmo?

(dì-shísānkè)

cuòwu   yúkuài

diūliǎn   búduànde

huāngluàn

(dì-shísìkè)

zhǐshì   yīn'ér

guī   xiàngshì

túnzi

(dì-shíwǔkè)

liúxīn   jiǎshè

zhǔnbèi   rúhé

qiáojian   fǒuzé

(dì-shíliùkè)

Yuèyǔ   Gànyǔ

Xiāngyǔ   Tàiyǔ

Wúyǔ   lèisì

Mǐnyǔ

(dì-shíqīkè)

xīnshǎng   tèshū

wényì

XII.   Shénmo shi . . . de?

(dì-shísānkè)

shēngdòng   zuì bǎoguì

yǒu shíyì   línghuó

chúncuì   yǒuxiào

(dì-shísìkè)

kěxī   yǒu yìyi

yǒulì   dútè

guāngmíng

(dì-shíwǔkè)

wēixiǎn   lìhai

(dì-shíliùkè)

chóngdié   fùhé

yǒu jiàzhi   zuì zhíqián

(dì-shíqīkè)

jīngcǎi   quánmiàn

xióngzhuàng   rénlèi chuàngzào

yǒuxiàn

FĀYĪN

Distinguish the following pairs by defining each item, using each in a sentence, or otherwise indicating that you know the difference in meaning of the terms.

1. shíyì, shíyī   4. shígē, shíge

2. yíbiàn, yìbiān   5. liàngcì, liǎngcì

3. búlì, bùlǐ   6. zǔzhǐ, zǔzhi

7. bèijǐng, Běijīng

8. jīlěi, jīlèi

9. <u>Yì Jīng</u>, yǐjing

10. huìhé, huì hē

11. dǐxia, dìxia

12. zhǐshì, zhīshi

13. shǐyòng, shìyòng

HUÌHUÀ: BÁI WÉNSHĀN GĒN GĀO MĚIYĪNG

Měi: Wénshān lái le. Hǎo jiǔ bú jiàn.

Bái: Hǎo jiǔ bú jiàn, hǎo ma? Gāo Xiānsheng, Gāo Tàitai dōu hǎo ma?

Měi: Wǒmen dōu hǎo.

Bái: Tāmen liǎngwèi zài jiā ma?

5 Měi: Tāmen qu kàn xì qu le. Liùdiǎn zhōng jiu huílai le. Nǐ máng bu máng?

Bái: Zhèi yíge xīngqī díquè máng. Nǐ ne?

Měi: Wǒ bù zěnmo máng. Búguò qián jǐtiān shāngfēng shāng de hěn lì-hai, zhèi liǎngtiān cái hǎo.

10 Bái: Méi zhǎo dàifu kànkan ma?

Měi: Xiǎo máobing bù zhíde zhǎo yīsheng. Zìjǐ mǎile yìdiǎr yào chī le, xiūxi xiūxi jiu hǎo le. Zhèixiē rìzi nǐmende Zhuāntí Jiǎnghuà dōu shi shénmo tímu?

Bái: Jiǎngle wǔge tímu, tīng wǒ gàosu ni: Tántan Zhōngguo Huà, Zhōng-
15 guode Wénzì, Cānkǎo Shū, háiyǒu Zhōngguode Yǔyán gēn Zhōng-guode Wénxué.

Měi: Dōu shi guānyu yǔyán gēn wénxué zhèi fāngmiàn de.

Bái: Shìde.

Měi: Xiàcì děi huàn tímu le ba?

20 Bái: Wèi-shénmo?

Měi: Děi huànhuan nǎozi ya.

Bái: Wǒ xiànzài hái bù zhīdào xiàcì jiǎng shénmo ne.

Měi: Nǐ chúle tīng jiǎng yǐwài hái zuò shénmo ne?

Bái: Wǒ ya, zhǎozhao zīliào, kànkan kèwàide shū shénmode.

25 Měi: Zhēn yònggōng. Nǐ kèwài dōu kàn shénmo shū?

Bái: Wǒ kàn <u>Zuǒ Zhuàn</u> gēn <u>Yì Jīng</u> ne. Suīrán zhèi liǎngbù shū hěn nándǒng, kěshi súyǔ shuō "kāi-juàn-yǒu-yì."

Měi: Dāngrán yònggōng shi duìde le, kěshi xiàng nǐ zhèiyàng yě tài kǔ le.

30 Bái: Wǒ yàoshi bù duō yòng diar gōng, zài liǎngnián lǐtou nábudào xué-wèi, nà jiu zāogāo le, gāi hòuhuǐ le.

Měi : Jìshǐ nǐ bú zhèiyàngr yònggōng, wǒ xiāngxìn nǐ zài liǎngnián lǐtou
       yídìng nádedào bóshi xuéwèi de.

Bái : Nǐ zhīdao yángguǐzi niàn Zhōngwén bu néng gēn Zhōngguo rén bǐ
35   ya?

Měi : Yángguǐzi gēn yángguǐzi bùtóng. Nǐ shi lìwài de. Nǐ gēn Zhōngguo
       rén méi shénmo liǎngyàng.

Bái : Zài xuéwen yìfāngmiàn jiu yǒu fēnbié le.

Měi : Nà shi nǐ kèqi.

40 Bái : Zhēnde. Zuótian wǎnshang wǒ liǎngdiǎn bàn cái shuìjiào.

Měi : Wèi-shénmo yào shuì nènmo wǎn ne?

Bái : Chá Cíyuán.

Měi : Zěnmo chá zhènmo jiǔ?

Bái : Wǒ bù zhǐshi chá yì-liǎngge zì, wǒ shi chá yìxiē cérde yòngfa gēn
45   jiěshì.

Měi : Guàibude, yīnwei Cíyuán、 Cíhǎishangde jiěshì dōu shi wényánwén, nà
       dāngrán yào fèi hěn duō shíjiān le.

Bái : Wǒ xiànzài xiǎngqilai yíge zì wǒ yào qǐngjiào ni. Nǐ shuō juédìngde
       jué yīnggāi xiě sāndiǎn shuǐ háishi liǎngdiǎn shuǐ ne?

50 Měi : Jué zì sāndiǎn shuǐ shi zhèngxiě. Pǔtōng xiěfa shi liǎngdiǎn shuǐ.
       Shi yíge zì, xiě něige dōu kéyi.

Bái : Xièxie ni.

Měi : Bú kèqi.

Bái : Oh, wǒ hái wàngle yíjiàn shì. Huá Tàitai shuō xià xīngqīwǔ qǐng
55   Gāo Xiānsheng、 Gāo Taìtai gēn nǐ dào Huá jia chī wǔfàn, ránhòu
       dàjiā yìqǐ dào nǎr wárwar qu.

Měi : Hǎode. Děng yíhuèr wǒ fùqin、 mǔqin huílai, wǒ gàosu tāmen.

Bái : Huá Tàitai jìnlai bǐ yǐqián jīngshen hǎode duō le, yě bǐ yǐqián shāo-
       wēi pàngle yìxiē.

60 Měi : Dàgài bú xiàng yǐqián nènmo xiǎng tāde èr érzi le.

Bái : Jiànle miàn zuǐli háishi búduànde tíqi tāde èr érzi. Yǒu yícì Huá
       Tàitai bǎ èr érzi zài méi sǐ yǐqián lùyīn lù de chànggēr náchulai
       tīng, hái méi tīngwán ne tā jiu kūqilai le.

Měi : Huá jia èr érzi sǐle zhēn kěxī. Shū niànde hǎo, duì péngyou rè-
65   qíng. Zhēnshi qīngniánrénde hǎo bǎngyàng. Tā huózhe de shíhou,
       gēn Xuéxīn dìxiong liǎngge rénde gǎnqíng xiāngdāng hǎo.

Bái : Xuéxīn yě cháng gēn wo tídào ta dìdi.

Měi : Xuéxīn jìnlai zěnmoyàng?

Bái : Tā jìnlai duì huà huàr hěn yǒu xìngqu. Zài yíge yìshu xuéyuànde
70   sùchéngkē xué huàr ne. Wǒ kàn ta duì huà huàr hěn yǒu qùwei.

Měi: Tā dōu huà shénmo?

Bái: Huà shānshuǐ huàr. Měiyǐng, nǐ yǒu Hóng Lóu Mèng gēn Lǎo Cán Yóujì zhèi liǎngbù xiǎoshuō ma?

Měi: Rúlín Wàishǐ wǒ yǒu, Hóng Lóu Mèng gēn Lǎo Cán Yóujì wǒ méi
75   you. Nǐ wèishénmo yào kàn zhèi liǎngběn shū ne?

Bái: Zhèi liǎngběn shū wǒ kàn dàoshi kànguo le. Zhèicì wǒmende jiǎng-huà yòu tídao zhèi jǐběn shū. Wǒ xiǎng zài chóng kànyikàn.

Měi: Hóng Lóu Mèng zhèibù zuòpǐn suírán yǐjing yǒu èrbǎi nián le, kěshi tā shàngmiande yǔfǎ gēn wǒmen xiànzàide yǔfǎ méi yǒu duō dàde
80   jùlí.

Bái: Shìde. Zhèibù shū duì wǒ xué yǔyán, duōshǎo yǒu yìxiē bāngzhu. Nǐ xǐhuan zhèibù shū ma?

Měi: Wǒ duì Hóng Lóu Mèng méi duō dà xìngqu.

Bái: Nǐ shi ge nǚháizi, zěnmo bù xǐhuan kàn Hóng Lóu Mèng ne?

85 Měi: Shi nǚháizi dōu děi xǐhuan kàn Hóng Lóu Mèng ma? Qíshí wǒ mǔ-qin zuì ài kàn Hóng Lóu Mèng. Tā kànle bù zhīdào yǒu duōshao biàn le. Dàgài tā dōu bèixialai le. Wǒ mǔqin hěn huì bèi shū. Tā yǐqián niàn de Lúnyǔ、Mèngzǐ、Shī Jīng、Chǔcí tā xiànzài hái jìde ne.

90 Bái: Gāo Tàitai xīn-jiù wénxué yídìng dōu búcuò le.

Měi: Tā wényánwén xiěde hěn hǎo.

Bái: Gāo Xiānsheng zì xiěde hǎo, Gāo Tàitai wénxué hǎo, nǐ huàr huàde hǎo. Fǔshang shi yòu yǒu wénxuéjiā yòu yǒu yìshujiā.

Měi: Nǐ shuōde tài hǎo le.

95 Bái: Měiyǐng, wǒmen sìdiǎn zhōng dào xuésheng zhōngxīn qu hǎo bu hǎo?

Měi: Shì bu shi yǒu ge wénxué zuòtánhuì?

Bái: Shì. Nǐ yǒu xìngqu méi yǒu?

Měi: Qù, qù. Tīngle kéyi zēngjiā zhīshi. Jīntian tǎolùn shénmo, nǐ zhī-dao ma?

100 Bái: Jīntian tǎolùn Lǔ Xùn、Lǎo Shè、Máo Dùn tāmen měi yíge rén zuò-pǐn de tèdiǎn. Jīntian yīnwei xiànyu shíjiān de guānxi kǒngpà měi yíge rén shuō huà de shíjiān kěnéng bù duō.

Měi: Nǐ cháng cānjiā zuòtánhuì ma?

Bái: Wǒ měige xīngqī dōu qù. Cānjiā de tóngxué dōu hěn tándelái, dàjiā
105   néng dǎchéng yípiàn qu yánjiu xuéwen. Fēicháng yǒu yìsi.

Měi: Zhèige zuòtánhuì yǒu shénmo bèijǐng méi you?

Bái: Juéduì méi you.

Měi: Shàng xīngqī tǎolùn shénmo tímu?

Bái: Zhōngguo Liù Shū.

110 Měi: Xiànzài wǒ kǎokao ni. Nǐ shuōshuo Liù Shū dōu shi shénmo míngzi?

Bái: Yěxǔ bǎ wo kǎozhù le. Wǒ shìshi: Xiàngxíng、xiàngshēng、zhǐshì、
huìyì、jiǎjiè、zhuǎnzhù.

Měi: Yìbǎi fēn.

Bái: Wǒ shàngcì xiě de nèipiān dōngxi nǐ kànguole méi you? Yǒu hěn
115   duō dìfang yào chónggǎi yícì ba?

Měi: Wǒ kànguo le. Méi you shénmo dà máobing. Jùzide gòuzào hǎo,
wénfǎ yòngde duì, wénzhāng yě hěn liúli. Jiùshi yǒude jùzi nǐ xīnli
xiǎng shuō de, jùzishang bù nénggou biǎodáchulai. Zhèizhǒng qíngxing dàoshi bú tài duō. Yǒu yíge zì túshū jiǎnjiè de jiǎn nǐ xiěchéng
120   cǎo zìtóur le.

Bái: Nǐ méi gěi wo gǎiyigǎi ma?

Měi: Wǒ dōu ná hóng bǐ yòng kuòhú huàshang le.

Bái: Xièxie lǎoshī.

Měi: Nǐ cái shi lǎoshī ne. Kuài dào sìdiǎn le. Wǒmen gāi zǒule ba?

125 Bái: Yàoshi zǒu lù jiu gāi zǒu le. Zuò chē de huà, hái zǎo yìdiǎr. Zuòtánhuì wánle yǐhòu wǒmen dào nǎr qu wárwar ne? Kàn diànyǐngr,
hǎo bu hǎo?

Měi: Zhèi jǐtiān měige diànyǐngryuàn dōu méi you hǎo piānzi. Gāncuì
wǒmen qu kàn huàjù.

130 Bái: Wǒ yě tīngshuō zhèi jǐtiān yǒu yíge huàjù xiāngdāng hǎo, jùběn shi
Bā Jīn xiě de. Jiù pà mǎibuzhuó piào.

Měi: Mǎibuzhuó piào wǒmen tīng jīngxì qu. Nǐ duì jīngxì yǒu xìngqu méi
you?

Bái: Jīngxì chàng de wǒ bú dà dǒng. Kěshi wǒ hěn xǐhuan kàn. Biǎoyǎn
135   de duōbàn shi lìshǐ gùshi.

Měi: Nǐ kàndedǒng ma?

Bái: Wǒ yǐqián zài zhèr kànguo liǎngcì. Yícì kàn de shi Sān Guóshangde
gùshi, yícì shi Zhuāngzǐde gùshi. Wǒ dōu kàndedǒng.

Měi: Jīntian wǎnshang shi Zhōnghuá Xìjù Xuéxiào xuésheng chàng de.
140   Tīngshuō xiāngdāng jīngcǎi.

Bái: Jīngxì jǐdiǎn zhōng kāishǐ?

Měi: Qīdiǎn zhōng.

Bái: Shì bu shi tīng xì qu děi xiān dìng zuòr?

Měi: Bú bì dìng zuòr. Dànshi děi xiān mǎi piào qu.

145 Bái: Wǒmen zuòtánhuì wánle jiu qu mǎi piào.

HUÌHUÀ: BÁI WÉNSHĀN GĒN HUÁ XUÉXĪN

Xué: Wénshān zǎo.

Bái: Zǎo.

Xué: Nǐ zuótian huílaide hěn wǎn, shì bu shì?

Bái: Shíèr'diǎn bàn le. Wǒ hé Měiyīng kàn xì qu le.

5 Xué: Shì bu shi kàn huàjù?

Bái: Bú shi, shi jīngxì.

Xué: Jīngxì nǐ dōu dǒng ma?

Bái: Yǒude dǒng. Bù dǒng de jīngguo Měiyīng yi jiěshì jiu míngbai le.
       Hěn yǒu yìsi. Zài xìjùlide yǎnyuán yǒude bǎ liǎn yòng yánse huà-
10   shang.

Xué: Nà shi biǎoshì hǎorén gēn huàirén.

Bái: Xìjù duì jiàoyu hěn yǒu guānxi.

Xué: Shì. Xìjù、xiǎoshuō duì yìbān rénmín hěn yǒu guānxi. Zuótian wǎn-
       shang nǐmen kàn de shi shénmo xì?

15 Bái: Zuótian wǎnshang yǎnle liǎngge xì. Yíge shi Zhànguó shídàide gù-
       shi, yíge shi gēnjù Yuán qǔ biān de. Wǒ hěn xīnshǎng. Yǒu yíge
       yǎnyuán biǎoyǎn yíge cánfèi rén zǒu lù. Nèige gùshi wǒ dǒng, shi
       yǒu yìdiǎr fěncìxìng.

Xué: Nǐ shuō fěngcì wǒ xiǎngqilai le. Wǔsì shídàide kānwu nǐ yào kàn
20   ma?

Bái: Dāngrán yào kàn le. Nǐ yǒu ma?

Xué: Zuótian wǒ dào péngyou jiā qù, kànjian péngyoude fùqin yǒu Wǔsì
       Yùndong shíqīde zázhì <u>Xīn Qīngnián</u> gēn <u>Xīn Cháo</u>. Yàoshi nǐ kàn
       wǒ míngtian qu jièlai. Tā shénmo shū dōu yǒu, lián <u>Kāngxī Zìdiǎn</u>
25   dōu yǒu. Tāde shū dōu biānzhe hàomǎr, wèideshi zhǎo de shíhou
       róngyi. Tā shuō tā yě huānyíng biéren jiè.

Bái: <u>Xīn Qīngnián</u> gēn <u>Xīn Cháoshang</u> yǒu Chén Dúxiù gēn Guō Mòruòde
       zuòpǐn ma?

Xué: Duìbuqǐ, nèiróng wǒ méi kàn.

30 Bái: Nǐ qu jiè de shíhou wènwen nèiwèi xiānsheng yǒu méi you <u>Chuàng-
       zào Zhōukàn</u>.

Xué: Hǎo. Wǒ wènwen kàn. Xiàng zhèixiē zázhì dōu shi Wǔsì Shídài
       tuīdòng báihuàwénde yìzhǒng gōngjù. Xiànzài yě bu shìyòng le. Nǐ
       jiè ta zuò shénmo?

35 Bái: Zhè dōu shi wǒ zhǔnbèi zuò lùnwén de bǎoguì zīliào. Wǒ yào xiě
       Zhōngguo wénxuéshǐ. Yīnwei Wǔsì shi huàfēn xīn-jiù wénxuéde fēn-
       shuǐlǐng, nà shíhou xīn sīcháo chéngshú le, wǒ yào kànkan nèige
       shíhou géxīnde wényì zuòpǐn dōu shi shénmo tǐcái de.

Xué: Wǒ míngtian yídìng qu jiè.   Shì bu shi dāngshí nèixiē tíchàng xīn
40   wénxué yùndong de lìyong nèixiē kānwù zuò jiùguóde xuānchuán?

Bái : Yě bù dōu shì. Búguò Wǔsì nèige shídàide bèijǐng shi ná jiùguóde
        kǒuhào lái tuīdòng wénxué gémìng. Wénzhāng yídìng dōu shi xīnde
        chuàngzuò.

Xué: Wǒ bǎ tāde shū duō ná diar, nǐ zìjǐ xuǎnzé yǒu yòng de jiu liúxia.

45 Bái : Shàngcì nǐ shuō yào túshū bàodǎo, shì bu shi?

Xué: Shìde.

Bái : Wǒ qiántian shōudàole shūdiànlide xīn shū yùgào, shàngmian yǒu
        hǎojǐzhǒng xīn shū. Wǒ ye xiǎng mǎi jǐběn qu.

Xué: Wǒmen yíkuàr qu mǎi qu.

50 Bái : Hǎo ba.

DUǍNWÉN

1. Wǒ líkai jiā yǐjing yǒu liùnián le.   Zài wǒ gāng dào zhèrde shíhou, wǒ
    érzi cái liùsuì, jīnnian tā yǐjing shí'èrsuì le. Zuótian wǒ jiēdao wǒ nèi-
    ren láixìn shuō zhèi háizi yǐjing rènshi hěn duō zì, pǔtōngde értóng dú-
    wù dōu néng kàn le. Yǒushí xiě duǎnde báihuàwén, dōu néng bǎ zìjǐ yào
    shuō de yìsi biǎodáchulai, méi you cí bù dáyì de dìfang.   Wǒ kànwánle
    zìn zhīhòu, xīnli yúkuài de jiǎnzhí shi xíngrongbuchulái. Wǒ zǎo jiu xiǎng
    zài zhèli gěi wǒde érzi mǎi jǐběn értóng kànle yǒu qùwei yě shìyòng de
    cóngshū.   Qiàqiǎo yǒu yíge tóngxiāng zhèi jǐtiān jiu yào huí jiā, wǒ jiu
    mǎile yítào értóng cóngshū qǐng zhèiwèi tóngxiāng gěi wǒ érzi dàiqu.

2. Zuótian Lǎo Wáng gěi wǒ láile yìfēng xìn.   Xìnli shuō tāmen nèige dì-
    fang shi yíge xiǎo hǎidǎo.   Qián jǐtiān guā dàfēng, fēnglǐ hěn lìhai, sǐ-
    shāngle bu shǎo rén, niú mǎ yě yǒu hěn duō shòushāng de, lián hǎilide
    chuán dōu guādao lùdìshang lái le.   Xìnli yòu shuō tā chízǎo yào líkai
    nèige dìfang, fǒuzé zài yǒu dàfēng jiu bùdéliǎo le. Kěshi tā dàodǐ shén-
    mo shíhou líkai, xìnli méi shuō. Wǒ hěn xīwang ta zǎorì líkai nèr.

3. Zhāng Xiānsheng shi yíge xuézhě. Tāde shū hěn duō. Guānyu gǔshū tā
    yǒu Shàng Shū、Yì Jīng、Shī Jīng、Zuǒ Zhuàn、Guóyǔ、Zhànguócè、Mèngzǐ,
    hái yǒu Wèi、Jìn yǐjí Suí、Táng děng cháodàide míngren zhùzuò.   Zhìyú
    jìndàide shū yě bu shǎo.   Cǐwài guānyu zìdiǎn、cíhuì、zìhuì gèngshi duōde
    bùdéliǎo.   Tā shuō: "Zài jiù wénxuéli wǒ zuì xǐhuan shīgē, suǒyǒu shī、
    cí、gē、fù wǒ dōu ài kàn. Zài xīn wénxuéli wǒ cháng kàn Hú Shìde zuò-
    pǐn." Tā méi shì de shíhou bǎ suǒyǒude shū fēnlèi páiliè, yòu ànzhe bǐ-
    huáde cìxu biānle yíge túshū suǒyǐn. Tā jiā zhēn xiàng yíge túshūguǎn.

4. Mǎ Xiānsheng cháng gěi yíge tōngxùnshè xiě tōngxùn bàodǎo.   Tā shuō:
    "Xiě tōngxùn bàodǎo chángcháng shi láo-ér-wú-gōng de, yīnwei búlùn
    bàodǎo xiěde zěnyàng hǎo, jiǎshè bàodǎo de shìshí yǒu yìdiǎr yíwèn, nà
    jiu yíge qián yě bù zhí le."

5. Wǒ zuótian wǎnshang zuòle yíge mèng, mèngjian hǎoxiang zài Kàngzhàn
    de shíhou, Guó-Gòng hézuò duì Rìběn zhǎnkāi quánmiàn dǐkàng. Wǒ hé
    wǒ fùqin yě cānjiā zhànzhēng. Jiéguǒ wǒ bèi díren dǎshāng le, chéngle

cánfèi le. Wǒ zhèng zài nánguò, tīngjian fùqin jiào wo. Yuánlái shi yíge mèng.

6. Zài Chūnqiū Zhànguó shídài Chǔ Guó yǒu yíge rén yīnwei guówáng yào shā ta, tā jiu táozǒu le, táodao Chǔ Guóde biānjìng. Nàli yǒu hěn duō Chǔ Guóde jūnduì, tā méi fázi táochu guó qu, tā jiu zài péngyoude jiāli xiǎng bànfǎ. Péngyou gàosu ta yào děng jīhui, děngdao jīhui chéngshú zài xíngdòng. Tā xiǎngle yíyè, yòu zháoji yòu yōuchóu. Dì-èrtiānde zǎoshang, tāde tóufa dōu biàncheng báide le.

7. Gòngchǎndǎng zài Yán'ānde shíhou shi Máo Zédōng zhízhèng. Tāmen shēnghuó fēichángde kǔ, kùnnán yě hěn duō, kěshi tāmen dōu zhèiyàng shuō: "Wèile dáchéng shǐmìng, rènhé kùnnán dōu bú yào pà, érqiě yídìng yào bǎ kùnnán kèfú."

8. Hú Shì shi Zhōngguo yíge tèshūde réncái. Tā liúxué Měiguo, Zhōng-Xī wénxué dōu hěn hǎo. Wǔsì Yùndong shíqī tā tíchàng báihuàwén. Tā zài Xīn Qīngniánshang fābiǎole yìpiān wénzhāng duìyu wénxué yǒu bāxiàng zhǔzhāng. Yǒu rén shuō nà shi Hú Shìde jiézuò.

9. Gāo Xiānsheng yǒu sānge nǚer. Zǐmèi sānge dōu hěn cōngming. Dà nǚer xué wénxué, èr nǚer xué huà huà, sān nǚer zài dàxué zhǔxiū jiāzhèng. Yǒu yìtiān zǐmèi sānge rén tánqi xué shénmo zuì yǒuyòng? Dà nǚer shuō shi wénxué, èr nǚer shuō shi huà huà, zhǐ yǒu sān nǚer bù shuō huà. Hòulai dàjiā wèn ta wèi-shénmo bù shuō huà ne? Sān nǚer shuō: "Zuì yǒuyòngde shi jiāzhèng, zhè shi zuì xiǎnzhùde shìshí."

10. Yíge wàiguo xuéshēng shuō: "Wǒ juéde xué Zhōngguo yǔwén zuì kùnnánde shi yǔyīn, yě jiu shi měige zìde zìyīn. Zhōngguo yǔwén suīrán měige zì shi dānyīn, dànshi zài shuō huà de shíhou yào bǎ zhèixiē dānyīn lián-chuànqilai, jiu gǎnjuézhe fēicháng bù róngyi."

11. Wǒ zài yíge mài jiù shū de pùzili kànjian yìběn Yuèdú Suíbǐ, shi yíge wénxuéjiā xiě de. Zhèiběn suíbǐli bǎ Xǔ Shì Shuōwénde zìyì yǒu hěn duō yǐnshēn de jiěshì, bìngqiě duì yuánláide jiěshì tíchule xǔduō yíwèn. Yòu duì Liù Shūlide huìyì、xíngshēng、jiǎjiè、zhuǎnzhù yǐjí měige zìde xíng-zhuàng hé gòuchéng yě yǒu hěn duō yìjian. Lìngwài hái yǒu yíduàn shi guānyu yīnyùnxué de. Tā duìyu gǔdài yùnshū rú Shīyùn děngděng zài yīn-yùnshang yě dōu yǒu yìjian. Zǒngkuò lái shuō zhèiběn suíbǐ duìyu gǔshū shi bú dà xiāngxìn de. Qiàqiǎo wǒ zhèng zài yánjiu zhèixiē wèntí, suǒyǐ wǒ yuè kàn yuè juéde yǒu xìngqu. Wǒ jiu bǎ zhèiběn shū mǎilai le.

12. Yǒu yíge rén yánjiu Zhōngguo mínsú. Tā shuō: "Cóngqián Zhōngguo yǒu-de dìfang rúguǒ rén sǐ le, duōbàn děi guòle hěn duō tiān, shènzhì guòle sān-sìshitiān, cái máizàng. Guānyu máizàng de dìfang yě tèbié xuǎnzé. Jìnlai zhèizhǒng fēngsu jiànjiànde méi yǒu le."

13. Zuò shì miǎnbuliǎo yǒu kùnnán. Bìděi zhǎngwò jīhui kèfú kùnnán cái kéyi wánchéng, fǒuzéde huà shi bu huì chénggōng de.

14. Xīn Cháo děng de zuòpǐn, yǐ báihuàwén wéi xiàn. Zài zhèixiē zuòpǐnli yǒude shi bàodǎo xīn wénxuéde fāzhǎn, yǒude shi zhǔzhāng zhèngzhi géxīn.

15. Zài Hàn-Zàng yǔzúli zài biǎoshì wènhuà de shíhou yòng yíwèncí huòzhě yòng yíwènshìde jùzi. Zài Yìn-Ōu yǔzúli yě shi yíyàng.

16. Zài Zhōngguo duì Rìběn Kàngzhàn de shíhou, yǒu bu shǎo jiùguóde tuántǐ, dōu shi rénmín wèile jiùguó cái zǔzhi de.

17. Yǒu rén gàosu wo, biānjìngde zhànshì cháng yǒu biànhua,   jiānglái néng
bu néng shènglì xiànzài hái méi fázi quèdìng.

18. Jiǎ wèn Yǐ: "Gútoude gǔ zì, yào chá zìdiǎn yīnggāi chá chénmo bùshǒu?
Shì bu shi chá yuè zì bù?" Yǐ shuō: "Bú shi." Jiǎ yòu shuō: "Zàiburán
shi ròu zì bù? Yīnwei ròu zì yǒushí yě xiěde xiàng yuè zì." Yǐ yòu
shuō: "Bú shi." Jiǎ shuō: "Dàodǐ shi něi yíbù ne?" Yǐ shuō: "Gǔ zì
běnshēn jiu shi bùshǒu, yīnggāi chá gǔ zì bù."

19. Wǒ niànwán zhōngxué, wǒ fùqin jiu ràng wǒ niàn dàxué gōngkē. Wǒ zhīdao fùqinde xīnyì, búdàn yuànyi wǒ niàn gōngkē érqiě hái xīwang sùchéng.
Wǒ jiu niànle gōngkēde sùchéngkē. Niànle yìnián wǒ xiǎng zhuǎn yīkē,
yòu xiǎng zhuǎn wénkē. Jiéguǒ dōu méi zhuǎnchéng, wǒ xiànzài réngrán
shi niàn gōngkēde sùchéngkē.

20. Yǒu yíge rén, shēnghuó hěn kǔ. Měitiān zhǐ chī yídùn fàn. Tā xiǎng zài
gōngchǎng zhǎo gōngzuò, gōngchǎngde rén gàosu ta: "Měiyuède yuèdǐ
kěnéng yǒu jīhui. Kěshi zhǎo gōngzuò de rén hěn duō, àn shēnqǐng de
cìxu páiliè, nǐ shi dì-sānmíng. Nǐ xiān liúxia yíge tōngxùn de dìfang, yǒu
jīhui de huà wǒ xiě xìn gěi ni."

21. Zhāng Xiānsheng xǐhuan yánjiu Zhōngguo fāngyán. Tā yǐjing yánjiule
Xiāng、Yuè、Mǐn、Gàn sìshěngde fāngyán, xiànzài tā zhèng yánjiu Wúyǔ.
Wúyǔ jiu shi Zhèjiāngde fāngyán.

22. Nèi liǎngtiáo hé huìhé yǐhòu jiu biànchéng yìtiáo dà hé. Cóng dà héde
zhèi yìbiān kàn duìmiànde nèi yìbiān, shénmo yě qiáobujiàn. Nǐ shuō
zhèitiáo dà hé liǎngbiānde jùlí gāi yǒu duómo yuǎn ne?

23. Yǒu yíge sì-wǔsuìde xiǎoháizi xǐhuan zài hǎibiān nòng hǎi shuǐ wár. Yàoshi hǎi shuǐ tuì le, tā jiu nòng ní shā wár. Tā yǒude shíhou wárde gāo-
xìngle gāncuì bǎ yīfu tuō le. Yǒu rén gàosu ta, hǎibiānde rén hěn duō,
bù kéyi tuō yīfu.

24. Yǒu yíge rén yánjiu Lādīngwén. Yǒu rén wèn ta jiǎshè Zhōngwén Lādīnghuà shì bu shi jiu róngyile ne? Tā shuō: "Yàoshi Lādīnghuà le kěnéng
bǐjiào róngyi xué le."

25. Zhāng Xiānsheng shi yíge hěn yǒu xìnyongde rén. Yǒu rén shuō Zhāng
Xiānshengde xìnyong zhǐ xiànyu zài tā zhù de nèige túnzili, chūle túnzi
jiu méi rén xìnren ta le.

26. Rénrén dōu shuō nèisuǒ fángzili yǒu guǐ, suǒyǐ méi yǒu rén zhù. Yǒu
yíge rén shuō: "Shìjièshang yǒu shéi zhēnde kànjianguo guǐ? Jìrán méi
kànjianguo, nǎlǐ huì yǒu guǐ? Wǒ yíge rén qu zhù nèisuǒ yǒu guǐde fángzi,
yàoshi zhēnde yǒu guǐ lái, wǒ yuànyi hé guǐ tántan. Rúguǒ guǐ shuō de
huà yǒu diar jiàzhi, wǒ yěxǔ gěi guǐ zuò yíge zhuàn ne!"

27. Wǒ cóng dìxia juéchulai yípiàn shítou, shítoushang hǎoxiang yǒu jǐge zì,
kěshi kàn bu tài qīngchu, zhǐ kànchulai yǒu xiàng shuāng zì de, háiyǒu
xiàng biànqiān de qiān zì shide. Yòu yǒu yíge xiàng kuòhú xíngzhuàng
de. Hái yǒu yíge zì yòu xiàng Qín Cháode Qín zì, yòu xiàng Tàiguode
tài zì, yīnwei zhèige zìde zìtóu hěn qīngchu, zìde xiàbiān jiu bù qīngchu
le. Zhè shi yíkuài shénmo shítou? Dào xiànzài yě méi fázi zhīdao.

28. Zuótian kāi huì de shíhou, dàjiā jiǎngle hěn duō huà. Zuìhòu yóu huìzhǎng bǎ dàjiāde yìjian guīnà yíxià. Dà duōshùde yìjian shi fǒudìng de,
suǒyǐ nèijiàn shì zài huìyìli jiu méi fázi tōngguò le.

UNIT IV

Yìshu

Dì-Shíjiǔkè. Yìshu

Bái: Mǎ Jiàoshòu zǎo.

Mǎ : Zǎo. Shàngge xīngqī dào nǎr qùle méi yǒu?

Bái: Kàn jīngxì qu le.

Mǎ : Nǐ yíge rén qù de ma?

5 Bái: Bú shi. Wǒ gēn Měiyīng liǎngge rén yìqǐ qù de.

Mǎ : Zài nǎr kàn de? Shì bu shi kàn de Zhōngguo Xìjù Xuéxiào xuésheng
biǎoyǎn de?

Bái: Shìde. Hěn hǎo, hěn yǒuyìsi. Chàng de shēngdiào hěn hǎotīng. Xìli
shuō huà yě shi yǒu qiāngdiào de, wǒ tīngbudǒng. Nín xǐhuan tīng
10   jīngxì ma?

Mǎ : Xǐhuan. Wǒ niàn zhōngxué de shíhou céngjīng qǐng rén jiāoguo wo.

Bái: Nènmo nín chàngde yídìng búcuò le.

Mǎ : Huì shi huì yìdiǎr, kěshi yǐjing hěn duō nián bu chàng le.

Bái: Zuótian xì lǐtou yǒu yíge xiǎoháizi biǎoyǎn de yàngzi hěn kě xiào,
15   kěshi tā chàng de qǔzi gēn shuō de huà wǒ dōu bù dǒng. Měiyīng
shuō tā chàng de shi Yángzhōu shēngdiào, shuō de huà shi Yángzhōu
huà.

Mǎ : Zuótian kàn xì de rén duō bu duō?

Bái: Duō. Wǒ xiān qu mǎi piào, kěshi piào dōu màiwán le. Qiàqiǎo yǒu
20   yíge rén tuì piào, zhènghǎo shi liǎngzhāng piào, wǒ jiu mǎi le. Nín
shàngge xīngqī dào nǎr qùle ma?

Mǎ : Wǒ běnlái bù dǎsuan dào nǎr qu de, jiu zài jiāli kànkan shū. Wǒ
zhèngzai kàn shū ne, wǒ nèiren shuō: "Yìliánchuàndde kànle wǔtiānde
shū le, yīnggāi huànhuan nǎozi le. Hái bu chūqu zǒuzou qu?" Wǒ
25   xiǎng wǒ tàitai duì wǒ zhēn hǎo. Wǒ shuō: "Hǎo, wǒ chūqu yìhuěr."
Tā jiēzhe yòu shuō le. Nǐ cāi ta shuō shénmo? Tā shuō: "Háizimen
zài jiā wǒ bù néng zuò shì, nǐ bǎ háizi yě dàichuqu ba." Wǒ cái
míngbai yuánlái shi jiào wǒ bǎ háizi dàichuqu.

Bái: Wǒ chà yìdiǎr wàng le, zuótian Měiyīng﹑Xuéxīn shuōle xià xīngqī
30   wǒmen sānge rén qǐng nín gēn Mǎ Tàitai chī wǎnfàn.

Mǎ : Wǒ shuō qǐng nǐmen chī hóngshāo jī﹑shīzi tóu hái méi qǐng ne.

Bái: Bù. Wǒmen hái méi qǐngguo Mǎ Tàitai ne. Wǒmen sānge rén yánjiu
le qǐng Mǎ Tàitai qu chī Sìchuān guǎnzi, bù zhīdào ta xǐhuan bu xǐhuan?

35 Mǎ : Tā shénmo cài dōu xǐhuan chī. Yàoshi nǐmen qǐng ta chī Sìchuān
cài tā gèng gāoxìng le.

417

Bái: Hǎojíle. Nènmo wǒmen xià xīngqiliù xiàwǔ sìdiǎn zhōng dào fǔshang qu jiē nǐmen, yíkuàr xiān dào nǎr wárwar qu, ránhòu zài qu chī fàn.

Mǎ: Hǎo. Xièxie nǐmen. Xiànzài wǒmen bǎ shēngcér yánjiu yánjiu.

1.0. liǎnpǔ   (facial) make-up

1.1. Zài jīngxìli yòng liǎnpǔ lai biǎoshì yíge rén shi hǎoren huòzhě shi huàiren.

2.0. huā   fancy, colored, figured (cloth, etc.)

huāliǎn   (1) painted face (of actors in general); (2) non-white painted face (representing a heroic character)

báiliǎn   white-painted face

2.1. Tā xǐhuan chuān huā yīfu, wǒ xǐhuan chuān sù yīfu.   (T)

2.2. Zài jīngxìli yǒude rén yòng yánse bǎ liǎn huàchéng huāliǎn.

2.3. Nèige yǎnyuán wèi-shénmo huà báiliǎn?   (T)

3.0. rénwu   person, personage   [man thing]

3.1. Zhāng Xiānsheng shi shèhuìshang yǒumíngde rénwu.

4.0. jiānzhà   crafty   [traitorous dishonest]

4.1. Yǒu rén shuō tā bú shi hǎoren, yīnwei tā hěn jiānzhà.

5.0. yīngyǒng   brave, gallant, martial   [brave brave]

5.1. Zài nèiběn értóng dúwùli yǒu bù shǎo értóng yīngyǒngde gùshi.

40 Bái: Qǐng wèn nín, liǎnpǔ shi shénmo?

Mǎ: Liǎnpǔ jiu shi xìjùli zài yǎnyuán liǎnshang huà huāliǎnde gèzhǒng yàngshi.

Bái: Zhōngguo xìjùlide yǎnyuán wèi-shénmo yǒude yào bǎ liǎn huàchéngle huāde ne?

45 Mǎ: Huà huāliǎn shi biǎoshì xìjùlide rénwu shi hǎoren háishi huàiren. Jiānzhàde rén jiu huàchéng báiliǎn. Yīngyǒngde huàchéng huāliǎn.

Bái: Shì bu shi kàn xì de rén yí kàn jiu kéyi cóng liǎnshang kànchulai shi hǎoren háishi huàiren?

Mǎ: Shì. Hěn xiǎnzhùde kéyi kànchulai.

6.0. Xuānhé   (reign-title, 1119-1125)   [proclaim harmony]

6.1. Xuānhé shi něicháo huángdìde niánhào?

7.0. huàpǔ   book of paintings   [painting treatise]

7.1. Tā cái xuéle sāntiānde huàr jiu yào mǎi yìběn zuì guìde huàpǔ. Yǒu rén shuō zhíde, yǒu rén shuō bù zhíde.

7.2. Wǒ jiā yǒu yìběn huàpǔ shàngmiàn yǒu Táng Cháo Wáng Wéi huà de shānshuǐ huà. (T)

8.0. huìhuà   (1) draw and paint; (2) drawing and painting   (W)   [draw draw]

8.1. Wǒ zài xuéxiào xué huìhuàde shíhou jiù xǐhuan huà mǎ. (W)

9.0. huāhuì   flowers and plants (as a branch of painting)   [flower plant]

9.1. Tā xǐhuan huà huāhuì, bù xǐhuan huà shānshuǐ.

10.0. shū(fǎ)   calligraphy   [writing method]

10.1. Qián Xiānshengde shūfǎ shi zuì yǒumíngde.

11.0. gāodù   high-grade, superior

11.1. Zhèiběn shū zài kēxuéshang shi yǒu gāodùde kēxué jiàzhi de.

50   Bái: Xuānhé shi Sòng Cháo huángdìde niánhào, shì bu shi?

     Mǎ: Duìle. Xiànzài cháng tídào Xuānhé Huàpǔ, yīnwei Xuānhé Huàpǔ shi hěn yǒumíngde. Zhèibù huàpǔli yígòng yǒu liùqiān sānbǎi duō zhāng huàr.

     Bái: Huà huàr hé huìhuà shì bu shi yíyàng?

55   Mǎ: Xiě wénzhāng duōshù shi xiě huìhuà, kǒuyǔshang shuō huà huàr.

     Bái: Tīng Měiyīng shuō Mǎ Tàitai yòu néng xiě yòu néng huà.

     Mǎ: Tā xiǎo zì xiě de hái búcuò, huàr bù zěnmoyàng. Jiù huì huà yìdiǎr huāhuì. Tā méi zhèngshìde xuéguo, jiù shi zìjǐ kànzhe huàpǔ xuézhe huà.

60   Bái: Zhōngguo zì yě shi yìshu, bǐrú zìhuàr.

     Mǎ: Shūfǎ gēn huàr shi bù néng fēnkāi de. Shūfǎ jiu shi xiě zì. Zhōngguode zì gēn huàr dōu yǒu zuì gāodùde yìshu jiàzhi.

12.0. Dūnhuáng   Tunhuang (in Kansu Province)

12.1. Yīnwei Wáng Xiānsheng jiā zhùzai Dūnhuáng Xiàn, suǒyǐ shícháng yǒu hěn duō yìshujiā dào ta jiāli qu zhù.

13.0. bìhuà   wall-painting

13.1. Dūnhuáng bìhuà yǒude shi Wèi Jìn shíhou liúxialai de, yǒude shi Táng Cháo rén huà de.

14.0. shíkū   stone cave

14.1. Yǒu rén shuō zài nèige shíkūli yǒu bù shǎo bìhuà.

15.0. qiáng   a wall

15.1. Shi shéi wǎng qiángshang xiě zì le? (T)

16.0. shíkè   stone engraving

16.1. Nèixiē shíkè shi Sòng Cháo rén kè de.

Mǎ : Xiànzài wèn nǐ yíge wèntí, nǐ zhīdao Dūnhuáng bìhuà zài shénmo dìfang fāxiàn de?

65 Bái: Shi zài Gānsu Shěng Dūnhuáng Xiàn. Nàlǐ yǒu hěn duō shíkū. Bìhuà jiu shi shíkūli qiángshangde huàr.

Mǎ : Duìle, yīnwei shíkū shi shítou de. Shàngmiàn shi shíkè de Liù Cháo gēn Táng Cháode yìshu.

Bái: Wǒ zài yíwèi Zhōngguo péngyou jiāli kànjian yìzhāng huàr, huàle yíge
70   měiren hǎoxiàng fēiqilaile shide. Péngyou shuō nà shi ànzhe Dūn- huáng bìhuàde yàngzi huàxialai de.

17.0. diāokè   (1) carve, sculpt, engrave; (2) carving, engraving, sculpture
       [carve carve]

17.1. Fúzhōude diāokè zuì chūmíng. Wǒ měicì dào Fúzhōu dōu mǎi jǐjiàn
       diāokè de dōngxi.

18.0. jiànzhu   (1) construct; (2) construction, architecture   [erect build]

18.1. Zhèixiē fángzi dōu shi zuì xīnshìde jiànzhu.

19.0. qí   ride (astride)

19.1. Wǒ xǐhuan qí mǎ, bù xǐhuan qí niú.

20.0. (yīn)yuè   music   [sound music]

       yīnyuèhuì   concert

       yīnyuèjiā   musician

       yīnyuèxì   music school, music department

       (yīn)yuèduì   orchestra, band

       yuèqì   musical instrument   (M: jiàn)

       guóyuè   Chinese music

       Xīyuè   Western music

20.1. Wáng xiānsheng zuì xǐhuan yīnyuè. Tā zǔzhile yíge yīnyuèduì, měi-
       yuè kāi yícì yīnyuèhuì. Rénjia dōu shuō ta shi ge hǎo yīnyuèjiā.

20.2. Guóyuède yuèqì gēn Xīyuède yuèqì dà bù xiāngtóng. Wǒmen yīnyuèxì
       yǒu guóyuè yě yǒu Xīyuè.

21.0. wǔ*   dance

       tiàowǔ   dance (N/V)   [jump dance]

       wǔdǎo   dance (N)   [dance tread]

       wǔtái   stage, theater (literal and figurative)   [dance platform]

       wǔtáijù   stage play

       gēwǔ   (1) sing and dance; (2) singing and dancing

21.1. Mǎ Xiáojie xuéguo wǔdǎo, suǒyǐ tiàowǔ tiào de hěn hǎo.   (T)

21.2. Zài wǔtáishang biǎoyǎn gēwǔde rén yígòng yǒu èrshige.

21.3. Zuótian wǒ kàn de bú shi diànyǐngr, shi wǔtáijù.

Bái: Shíkè yě shi diāokè de yìzhǒng ma?

Mǎ :   Shìde. Fánshi zài jīnzi、 shítou huòshi mùtoushang kēshang gèzhǒng
       dōngxi dōu jiào diāokè.

75 Bái: Shíkè shi bu shi cóng Shāng Cháo jiu yǒu le?

Mǎ :   Suírán zài Hénán Ānyáng juéchulai yǒu Shāng Cháode shíkè, dànshi
       Zhōngguo zuì chūmíngde shi Hàn Cháode shíkè. Jùshuō shi zài
       Shāndong yíge cítáng fāxiàn de. Nèige cítáng shi zài jǐyuán yìbǎi
       sìshiqī nián zuǒyòu jiànzhu de. Cítáng xiànzài suírán yǐjing méi
80   yǒu le, zài cítáng yuánláide dìfang fāxiàn hěn duō shítou, shàngmiàn
       diāokèzhe zuò chē de gēn qí mǎ de, hái yǒu yuèduì、 wǔdǎo gèzhǒng
       tú.

22.0. lǐ*   etiquette

       lǐjié   etiquette, formality   [etiquette section]

       lǐyuè   etiquette and music

22.1. Bàinián shi Zhōngguo rén zài guònián de shíhou de yìzhǒng lǐjié.

22.2. "Zhōngguo yǐ lǐyuè zhì guó" zhèijù huà shi biǎoshì Zhōngguo rén
       zhòngshì lǐyuède yìsi.   (T)

22.3. Chūnqiū shídài Kǒngzǐ shi yǐ lǐyuè jiàoyu rénmín.   (T)

23.0. shèng   flourishing, prosperous, glorious

23.1. Zhōngguo gǔdàide gēwǔ yǐ Táng Cháo wéi zuì shèng. (W)   (T)

24.0. fánróng   flourishing, prosperous   [complicated glory]

24.1. Yíge guójiā yàoshi méi yǒu zhànshì, jīngji jiu fánróng le.

25.0. gēwǔ shēngpíng   live a peaceful life full of song and dance   [song
                        dance rise peace]

25.1. Guójiā zài tàipíng shíqī, rénmín gāoxìngde yòu gē yòu wǔ, zhè jiu
       jiàozuo gēwǔ shēngpíng.

26.0. yǐ A wéi zhǔ   take A as the main thing, concentrate on A   (W)

26.1. Nǐ zhīdao Zhōngguo jīngxì yòng de yuèqì yǐ shénmo wéi zhǔ ma?
       (W)

27.0. fǎnyìng   (1) reflect; (2) reflection   [reverse reflect]

27.1. Lǎo Shěde xiǎoshuō duōbàn shi fǎnyìng qióngrende shēnghuó de.

27.2. Cóng rénmínde shēnghuóshang jiu kéyi fǎnyìngchulai nèige guójiāde
       jīngji qíngxing.   (T)

Bái: Zhōngguo lìlái shi ná lǐyuè zhì guó, dāngrán shi zhòngshì lǐjié hé
yīnyuè le. Jiù wǒ suǒ zhīdao de, Zhōngguo yīnyuè zuì shèngde shíqī
85   yào suàn Táng Cháo le.

Mǎ: Shìde. Yīnwei Táng Cháo shi yíge tàipíng shíqī, suǒyǐ jīngji hěn
fánróng, dàjiā shēnghuó hǎo, dāngrán jiu xǐhuan yánjiu yīnyuè、tiào-
wǔ zhèi yílèide yìshu le.

Bái: Mǎ Jiàoshòu, gēwǔ shēngpíng zhèige cér shi kǒuyǔshang yòng de
90   ma?

Mǎ: Bú shi. Shi xiě de shíhou yòng de. Yǎnjiǎng de shíhou xíngrong
guójiā tàipíng yě kéyi shuō.

Bái: "Zhèicìde yīnyuèhuì yǐ dōngfāng yīnyuè wéi zhǔ" zhèijù huà shi xiě
de, shì bu shi?

95 Mǎ: Duìle, shi xiě de.

Bái: Fǎnyìng zhèige cér ne?

Mǎ: Kǒuyǔ gēn xiě wénzhāng dōu kéyi yòng.

28.0. Mínghuáng   Illustrious Emperor (ruled 713~756) [bright emperor]

28.1. Nèige dìfang-xì yǎn de shi Táng Mínghuángde gùshi.   (T)

29.0. lí   pear

líyuán   pear garden

líshù   pear tree

29.1. Zhōngguo běifāng chūchǎn de lí bǐ nánfāng chūchǎn de duō.

29.2. Líyuán yǒu liǎngge yìsi. Yíge shi yǒu líshùde yuánzi, yíge shi zhǐzhe xué chàng xì de dìfang shuō de.   (T)

30.0. zǐdì   sons and younger brothers, sons and heirs, one's juniors (W)

30.1. Měige jiātíng dōu xīwang tāde háizi hǎo. Huàn yíjù huà shuō, jiu
shi měi yíge jiātíng dōu xīwang yǒu hǎo zǐdì.

31.0. xùnliàn   drill, practice, train   [instruction drill]

31.1. Tā zài Shěnyáng xùnliàn jūnduì de shíhou jiào jūnren bù xǔ máfan
lǎobǎixìng.

31.2. Tāmen xùnliànle jǐshíge nánnǚ qīngnián, yùbèi jiānglái zuò yǎn xīn
xìde yǎnyuán.   (T)

Bái: Zài Táng Cháode shíhou Táng Mínghuáng hěn xǐhuan gēwǔ gēn xìjù,
shì bu shi?

100 Mǎ: Duìle. Tā zài líyuán xùnliàn hěn duō nánnǚ xuéxí chàng gē、wǔdǎo,
suǒyǐ yìzhí dào xiànzài jiào Zhōngguo xìjùde yǎnyuán shi "Líyuán
zǐdì."

Bái: Wǒ cháng zài bàozhǐshang kàn xìjù xiāoxi yǒu <u>líyuán</u> zhèi liǎngge
zì. Xiànzài wǒ míngbai le. Líyuán jiushi zhòng líshù de yuánzi,
105 shì bu shi?

Mǎ : Shìde.

32.0. biānzi   a whip

32.1. Nǐ qí mǎ de shíhou bú yào wàngji ná biānzi.

33.0. xiàngzhēng   (1) symbol; (2) symbolize   [appearance recruit]

33.1. Zài jīngxìli yǒushíhou yòng yíkuài bù xiàngzhēng yíge chéng.   (T)

34.0. dòngzuò   action, movement   [move do]

34.1. Tā zài wǔtáishang yìliánchuàn yǒu jǐge dòngzuò dàjiā dōu shuō biǎo-
yǎnde hěn hǎo.

35.0. zīshi   carriage, deportment, bearing, manner   [posture tendency]

35.1. Nǐ kàn nèige yǎnyuán shǒuli názhe biānzi, wǔdǎode zīshi duōma
hǎokàn.

36.0. qiāngdiào   (1) tune; (2) intonation; (3) stylized operatic sing-song
[tune tune]

36.1. Tā chàng de qiāngdiào hěn tèbié, biéren chàngbushànglái.

Bái: Zài jīngxì lǐtou, wǒ kànjian yǎnyuán shǒuli názhe biānzi. Kàn tāde
yàngzi hǎoxiàng shi shàng mǎ、xià mǎ、dǎ mǎ.

Mǎ : Jīngxì shi yìzhǒng xiàngzhēngshìde yìshu. Yíqiède dōngxi chàbuduō
110 dōu shi yòng dòngzuò biǎodáchulai. Bǐrú kāi mén, wǔtáishang gēnběn
méi yǒu mén, jiu shi yòng shǒu zuò kāi mén de zīshi. Qí mǎ de
shíhou jiu yòng yíge biānzi, biǎoshìchulai qí mǎ de zhǒngzhǒng dòngzuò.

Bái: Zhōngguo xìjù dōu shi gēnjù lìshǐ biān de ma?

115 Mǎ : Jīngxì gēn dìfang-xì chàbuduō dōu shì. Suírán bújiànde dōu shi shìshi dànshi zǒngshi xiē lìshǐxìngde gùshi. Zhìyú huàjù, jiu yǒu hěn
duō shi bǎ Xīfāngde wǔtáijù fānyìchéng Zhōngwén lái biǎoyǎn.

Bái: Jīngxìde duìhuà dōu yǒu qiāngdiào de, bìng bú xiàng pǔtōng rén shuō
huà yíyàng.

120 Mǎ : Jīngxì suírán míngzi jiào jīngxì kěshi jīngxìde qǐyuán shi Húběi
Shěng. Shi Húběi Shěngde yīnyùn, yǒude dìfang lèisì Húběi huà.

Bái: Suǒyǐ wǒ tīng jīngxì de shíhou tāmen shuō huà huòzhě chàng wǒ
yìdiǎr yě tīngbudǒng.

37.0. zòu*   perform (music)

hézòu   play music together   [together perform]

yǎnzòu   perform music   (W)

yǎnzòuhuì   concert   [perform music meeting]

37.1. Nèige yīnyuèduì měicì yǎnzòu dōu yǒu yìbǎi duō rén hézòu.

37.2. Jīntian yǎnzòuhuì suǒ yòng de yuèqì dōu shi Zhōngguo zuò de.

38.0. guócuì   essence of a nation   [country essence]

38.1. Yǒu yíge dùi gǔshū yǒu xìngqu de rén shuō: "Gǔshū shi Zhōngguode
         guócuì."

39.0. nǎpà   (1) why fear?; (2) even (if), even though, no matter if, never
         mind how

39.1. Zhǐyào nǔlì niàn shū nǎpà kǎoshì bu jígé?   (T)

39.2. Nǎpà méi yǒu rén lái tīng, tā háishi yào kāi yīnyuèhuì.   (T)

40.0. liúchuán(xialai)   hand on, transmit

40.1. Wǒ jiā yǒu jǐjiàn yuèqì shi wǒ zǔfù liúchuánxialai de.

41.0. fāyáng   extend   [emit raise]

41.1. Mǎ Jiàoshòu zài wàiguo dàxué jiāo Zhōngwén, wèideshì fāyáng Zhōng-
         guo wénhuà.

42.0. zuòqǔ(zi)   write songs   (VO)

         zuòqǔfǎ   song-writing technique

42.1. Tā chàng de nèige gēr shi shéi zuò de qǔzi, nǐ zhīdao ma?

42.2. Nǐ zhīdao wàiguode zuòqǔfǎ hé Zhōngguo jiù yǒu de zuòqǔfǎ yǒu
         shénmo bùtóng?   (T)

        Mǎ : Biǎoyǎn jīngxì yòng de yuèqì nǐ kànjianguo méi yǒu?

125 Bái: Wǒ kànjianguo.   Wǒmen xuéxiào yīnyuèxì yǒu guóyuè, shì bu shi?

        Mǎ : Yǒu.   Dàgài zài guò liǎng-sānge xīngqī tāmen yào kāi yícì guóyuè
              yǎnzòuhuì.

        Bái: Zhōngguo yīnyuè hézòuqilai hěn hǎotīng.

        Mǎ : Rúguǒ nǐ méi shì jiu qù tīngting.

130 Bái: Wǒ hěn xǐhuan tīng. Nǎpà wǒ nèitiān méi gōngfu wǒ yě xiǎng fázi
              qù tīng qu. Jùshuō Zhōngguo rén xiànzài dōu hěn zhòngshì Zhōng-
              guo yīnyuè.

        Mǎ : Shìde.   Yīnwei yánjiu Zhōngguo yīnyuè de rén rènwei shi gǔren
              liúchuánxialai de, shi Zhōngguode guócuì, búdàn yào bǎocún, hái yào
135   tíchàng fāyáng.

        Bái: Xiànzài yánjiu Xīyuède yě yìtiān bǐ yìtiān duō le.

        Mǎ : Zhè shi yīnwei shídàide cháoliú. Hěn duō rén xǐhuan Xīyuè, yě yòng
              Xīyáng zuòqǔfǎ zuò qǔzi. Yòng de yuèqì yě dōu shi Xīyángde yuèqì.
              Hái yǒu zhōng-xiǎoxuéde yīnyuè kèchéng dōu shi xué Xīyáng yīnyuè
140   le.

43.0. měishù   fine arts   [beautiful skill]

43.1. Tā huà de huàr hěn hǎo. Hěn duō rén shuō tā yǒu měishùde tiāncái.

44.0. tícái   topic, subject   [subject material]

44.1. Tā xiě de shī duōbàn yǐ qióngrende shēnghuó wéi tícái. (W)

45.0. jiàocái   teaching materials

45.1. <u>Shī Jīng</u> bú shi xiǎoxuéde jiàocái.

46.0. xìnggé   disposition, temperament   [quality frame]

46.1. Xiě xiǎoshuō yào bǎ rénwude xìnggé xiěchulai.

47.0. jìqiǎo   (1) ingenious, skillful, expert; (2) skill, expertness   [skill
        skillful]

47.1. Yǒu rén néng zài yíkuài xiǎo shítoushang kē yìpiān gǔwén, nà shi
        yìzhǒng jìqiǎo.

48.0. fēngqi   fashion, style   [custom air]

48.1. Xiànzàide qīngnián xǐhuan chàng nèizhǒng xīn gēr, chéngle yìshíde
        fēngqi. (T)

Bái: Qǐng wèn, xiànzài yìbān xué měishù de, ná huà huàr lái shuō ba,
      tāmen suǒ huà de tícái dōu shi něi yìzhǒng de? Shì bu shi yǒu
      guīdìng de jiàocái?

Mǎ : Bù yídìng, děi ànzhe měi yíge xuéshengde xìnggé gēn tāmende xìngqu
145   lái dìng.

Bái: Huà huàr shi yìzhǒng tiāncái. Yǒu zhèizhǒng měishù tiāncái cái
      nénggou xuéde hǎo. Tóngyàngde xué huàr, yǒude rén huàde hěn yǒu
      jìqiǎo, yǒude rén huàde hěn píngcháng.

Mǎ : Shì. Wǒ yǒu ge qīnqi tā niàn shū bǐ shéi dōu cōngming, kěshi xué
150   huà huàr a, huà shénmo bú xiàng shénmo.

Bái: Jìnlái yǒu hěn duō rén xué huàr, yóuqíshi tàitai、 xiáojiemen.

Mǎ : Zhè yě shi yìshíde fēngqi.

49.0. jìzǎi   record   (N/V)   [record contain]

49.1. Gēnjù Zhōngguo lìshǐde jìzǎi Táng Mínghuáng shi zuì xǐhuan gēwǔ
        de.

50.0. fēi(zi)   imperial concubine

       guìfēi   imperial concubine of the first or second rank   [honorable
                 concubine]

50.1. Cóngqián Zhōngguode huángdì dōu shi yǒu hěn duō fēizi de.

50.2. <u>Guìfēi</u> shi fēizide yìzhǒng míngchēng.

51.0. gōng(tíng)   palace   [palace courtyard]

51.1. Gōngtíng lǐbiārde lǐjié hěn fùzá.

51.2. Nèige fēizi hěn xiǎo jiu jìn gōng le.   (T)

52.0. xíngshì   (1) form, figure, model; (2) aspect, appearance, externals
      [shape form]

52.1. Xíngshì jiu shi xíngzhuàng hé yàngzi. Bǐfang shuō nèisuǒ fángzide
      xíngshì xiàng yíge miào.

52.2. Tāmen jiāo xiǎoháizi yòng gèzhǒng xíngshìde jiàoxuéfǎ.   (T)

53.0. yíshì   ceremony   [rite form]

53.1. Zhōngguo jiùshìde jiéhūn yíshì hěn máfan.

Bái: Jù lìshǐ shūshang jìzǎi, lìdàide huángdì dōu yǒu hěn duō fēizi. Zhèi-
     xiē fēizi jìn gōng de shíhou shi yòng shénmo fāngshì?

155 Mǎ: Jùshuō xiān cóng mínjiān xuǎnchu hěn duō piàoliang nǚháizi, bǎ
        tāmen dàijìn gōng qu, zài cóng zhèi hěn duō nǚháizili zài xuǎnchu
        jǐshige lái, liúzai gōngli. Zài xíngshìshang shi gěi huángdì xuǎn
        fēizi, shìshíshang jùshuō yǒude fēizi yìshēng lián huángdì dōu méi
        jiànzhaoguo.

160 Bái: Xuǎn fēizi hái yǒu shénmo yíshì ma?

    Mǎ: Wǒ xiǎng xuǎn fēizi yídìng yě yǒu yíge yíshì le.

54.0. zhúqì   articles made of bamboo

      mùqì   articles made of wood

      shíqì   articles made of stone

54.1. Yòng zhúzi zuò de dōngxi jiàozuo zhúqì.

54.2. Tā jiāli yòng de mùqì dōu shi xīnshì de.

54.3. Zài lìshǐshang yǒu yíge shíqī jiàozuo shíqì shídài, yīnwei nèige shí-
      hou rénlèi huì shǐyòng shítou zuò gōngjù le.

54.4. Líshù duì rén hěn yǒu yòng. Lí shi shuǐguǒ, ér líshù yòu kéyi zuò
      mùqì.

55.0. táo   pottery

      táoqì   pottery   [pottery vessel]

55.1. Táoqì shi yòng yìzhǒng tèbiéde tǔ zuò de. Zuòhǎo zhīhòu, zài yòng
      huǒ shāo, jiu chéngle táoqì le.

56.0. yù   jade   (M: kuài)

      yù(qì)   jade object

56.1. Yù shi yìzhǒng zuì hǎode shítou. Yòng yù zuò de dōngxi jiàozuo
      yùqì.

57.0. chún   pure(ly)

57.1. Nǐ zhǐdao shénmo shi chún wénxué ma?

Bái: Zhōngguode táoqì hěn zǎo jiu yǒule ma?

Mǎ : Zhōngguo mínzú cóng xīn shíqī shídài jiu yòng táoqì le. Érqiě zuò
       táoqìde jìshu bǐ tóng yíge shíqī biéde guójiā zuòde dōu hǎo.

165 Bái: Zhúqì gēn mùqì shi jìndàide dōngxi ba?

Mǎ : Mùqì xiànzài yòngde hěn pǔbiàn. Zhìyú zhúqì, jiu yǒu diar dìfang-
       xìng le. Zài Zhōngguo dà bùfen shi nánfāng rén yòng, yīnwei zhúqì
       shi yòng zhúzi zuò de, zhúzi chūchǎn zài nánfāng.

Bái: Yù shi shítou yílèide dōngxi, shì bu shi?

170 Mǎ : Shi shítou yílèi de, kěshi bǐ shítou zhíqián. Dànshi tāde jiàzhí bìng
       bu yíyàng. Yǒude hěn zhíqián, yǒude bù hěn guì.

Bái: Yù shi něizhǒngde zuì hǎo ne?

Mǎ : Zuì bǎoguìde shi yìzhǒng chún báisède.

58.0. pànduàn   (1) judge, give a judgment, determine; (2) judgment,
                      decision   [judge break]

       xià pànduàn   reach a conclusion

58.1. Nèi liǎngguóde zhànshi jiānglái shéi shèng shéi bài xiànzài méi fázi
       pànduàn.

58.2. "Zuìhòu shènglì yídìng shi wǒmen" zhè shi wǒmen zìjǐ xià de
       pànduàn.   (T)

59.0. zhuǎnbiàn   change (N/V)   [revolve change]

59.1. Jìnlái tāde sīxiǎng yǒu diar zhuǎnbiàn le.

60.0. zhújiàn   gradually, little by little   [pursue gradual] (W)

60.1. Tā zài Tàiguo yǒu sānnián le. Tā duì Tàiguode fēngsu zhújiàn liǎo-
       jiěle bu shǎo.

61.0. mìqiè   closely connected   [close close]

61.1. Zhōng-Rì liǎngguó zài dìlǐshang、lìshǐshang dōu yǒu mìqiède guānxi.

62.0. yìchéng   translate into   [translate become]

62.1. Qǐng nǐ bǎ zhèiběn Zhōngwén xiǎoshuō yìchéngle Yīngwén.

Bái: Pànduàn shì bu shi yǒu juédìng de yìsi?

175 Mǎ : Yǒu yìdiǎr fēnbié. Wǒ jǔ ge lìzi: "Néng bu néng fāshēng dì-sāncì
       shìjiè dàzhàn, yào kàn jiānglái shìjièshangde zhuǎnbiàn. Xiànzài
       hěn nán pànduàn."

Bái: Zhújiàn jiu shi jiànjiànde yìsi?

Mǎ: Duìle. Mìqiè zhèige cér wǒ xiǎng nǐ huì yòng.

180 Bái: "Wǒmen liǎngge rénde guānxi hěn mìqiè."

Mǎ: Duì. Jīntiande cér dōu tǎolùnwán le. Wǒ xiǎng zhèicìde yǎnjiǎng nǐ tīngle yǐhòu qǐng nǐ bǎ yǎnjiǎngcí yìchéngle Yīngwén wǒ kànyikàn.

Bái: Hǎo. Wǒ shìshi kàn.

Mǎ: Wǒmen míngtian jiàn le.

185 Bái: Míngtian jiàn.

SHĒNGCÍ BIĂO

1. liǎnpǔ

2. huā
   huāliǎn
   báiliǎn

3. rénwu

4. jiānzhà

5. yīngyǒng

6. Xuānhé

7. huàpǔ

8. huìhuà (W)

9. huāhuì

10. shū(fǎ)

11. gāodù

12. Dūnhuáng

13. bìhuà

14. shíkū

15. qiáng

16. shíkè

17. diāokè

18. jiànzhu

19. qí

20. (yīn)yuè
    yīnyuèhuì
    yīnyuèjiā
    yīnyuèxì
    (yīn)yuèduì

yuèqì
guóyuè
Xīyuè

21. wǔ*
    tiàowǔ
    wǔdǎo
    wǔtái
    wǔtáijù
    gēwǔ

22. lǐ*
    lǐjié
    lǐyuè

23. shèng

24. fánróng

25. gēwǔ shēngpíng

26. yǐ A wéi zhǔ (W)

27. fǎnyìng

28. Mínghuáng

29. lí
    líyuán
    líshù

30. zǐdì (W)

31. xùnliàn

32. biānzi

33. xiàngzhēng

34. dòngzuò

35. zīshi

36. qiāngdiào

37. zòu*
    hézòu
    yǎnzòu (W)
    yǎnzòuhuì

38. guócuì

39. nǎpà

40. liúchuán(xialai)

41. fāyáng

42. zuòqǔ(zi)
    zuòqǔfǎ

43. měishù

44. tícái

45. jiàocái

46. xìnggé

47. jìqiǎo

48. fēngqi

49. jìzǎi

50. fēi(zi)
    guìfēi

51. gōng(tíng)

52. xíngshì

53. yíshì

54. zhúqì
    mùqì
    shíqì

55. táo
    táoqì

56. yù	58. pànduàn	60. zhújiàn (W)
yù(qì)	xià pànduàn	61. mìqiè
57. chún	59. zhuǎnbiàn	62. yìchéng

YǓFǍ LIÀNXÍ

(See note 1)

1. Suírán lí hěn guì, kěshi tā hěn xǐhuan chī. Nǎpà wǔkuài qián yíge, tā yě mǎizhe chī.

2. Nèige háizi jiù xǐhuan zài qiángshang xiě zì. Nǎpà tā mǔqin tiāntiān mà ta, tā háishi zhàoyàng zài qiángshang xiě.

3. Wáng Xiānsheng jiǎng Zhōngguo shūfǎ hǎoxiang niàn shū.

4. Nèiwèi lǎo xiānsheng niàn <u>Shī Jīng</u> hǎoxiang chàng gēr.

5. Jiǎ guó gēn Yǐ guó dǎzhàng le. Jiǎ guóde jūnduì suírán dōu hěn yīngyǒng, kěshi tāmen dǎbuguò Yǐ guóde jūnduì.

6. Suírán wǒ yě yánjiule bù shǎo rìzide yǔyīnxué, kěshi wǒde chéngji hái bǐbuguò nǐ.

7. Wǒ zuìjìn xiǎng dào Gānsu qu kàn Dūnhuáng bìhuà. Qiàqiǎo zhèi jǐtiān hěn máng. Wǒ xiǎng guò yìtiān liǎngtiān zài zǒu.

8. Wǒmen xuéxiào lìshǐxì yǒu hěn duō Táng Dài gēn Míng Dàide táoqì. Wǒ kàn zuì shǎo yě yǒu sānshijiàn wǔshijiàn de.

9. Gēwǔ shi shénmo ne? Jiu shi chàng gē gēn tiàowǔ de zǒng míngchēng jiu jiàozuo gēwǔ.

10. Shíkè jiu shi bǎ túhuà huòzhě shi wénzì diāokè zài shítoushang jiu jiàozuo shíkè.

11. Nǐ kàn nèige huāliǎnde liǎn huà de hǎo kěpà ya!

12. Nǐ kàn wǔtáishang tiàowǔ de nèi jǐge xiáojie hǎo piàoliang a!

13. Shàngkè de shíhou xiānsheng wèn wo <u>xià pànduàn</u> shi shénmo yìsi, shi dòngcí háishi míngcí? Wǒ zěnmo yě xiǎngbuqǐlái le.

14. Wǒ yǒu yìběn hěn bǎoguìde huàpǔ ràng Lǎo Wáng gěi jièqu le. Wǒ zěnmo yě gēn ta yàobuhuílái le.

15. Míngtian báitiān wǒ qǐng nǐ qu kàn wǔtáijù "Yáng Guìfēi," hǎo bu hǎo? . . . Xièxie nǐ le, wǒ měitiān mángde yào sǐ. Nǎr lái de shíjiān qu kàn xì?

16. Nǐ zhēnshi shuō xiàohuar ne. Wǒ nǎr lái de qián mǎi yù ne?

17. Nèige yīnyuèjiā cái lái bù jiǔ yòu yào dào Xiàmén qu le.

18. Tā cái mǎile huàpǔ bù jiǔ yòu yào mǎi huàpǔ.

19. Tā xué huà huāhuì cái yǒu liǎngge xīngqī jiu huà de zhènmo hǎo.

20. Wǒmen xuéxiào yīnyuèxì shàngkè cái yǒu yíge duō yuè jiu yào kāi yīnyuèhuì le.

JIĂNGHUÀ

Zhūwèi tóngxué:

Jīntian jiǎnghuà de tímu shi Zhōngguode Yîshu. Yîshu shi fǎnyìng yíge guójiāde wénhuà de. Zhōngguo shi wénmíng gǔguó, yìshu fādáde zuî zǎo, gǔshíhoude yìshupǐn liúchuánxialai de xiāngdāngde duō. Wǒmen xiàn-

5   zài kéyi kàndedào de yǒu shíkè、tóngqì、táoqì、yùqì děngděng. Hái yǒu zhúqì、mùqì、diāokè、jiànzhu yǐjí wényì、shīgē、yīnyuè、wǔdǎo hé xìjù dōu shi yǒu gāodù yîshu jiàzhi de.

Yîshude fànwéi bāokuòde hěn guǎng. Yǒu rén bǎ xiàndài yìshu fēnwei bālèi: Dî-yī shi wénxué, dî-èr shi yīnyuè, dî-sān shi huìhuà, dî-sî shi

10   xìjù, dî-wǔ shi jiànzhu, dî-liù shi diāokè, dî-qī shi wǔdǎo, dî-bā shi diàn-yǐng. Zhèi bāzhǒng yìshu rúguǒ yìzhǒng yìzhǒng xiángxìde jiǎng, zài zhèi duǎnduǎnde shíjiānli dāngrán jiǎngbuwán. Xiànzài zhǐ shuōyishuō yīnyuè、wǔdǎo、huìhuà hé xìjù.

Xiànzài xiān shuō yīnyuè hé wǔdǎo. Zhōngguo shi yǐ lǐyuè zhì guó.

15   Lǐ shi lǐjié hé yíshì. Yuè jiu shi yīnyuè. Gǔshí gōngtíng hé mínjiān zài yíshìli duōbàn líbukāi yīnyuè gēn gēwǔ, suǒyǐ yīnyuè gēwǔ zài Zhōngguo wénhuàshang xiànglái yǒu hěn gāode dìwei. Dàole Táng Cháode shíhou yīnwei guójiā hěn tàiping, suǒyǐ jīngji hěn fánróng, kéyi shuō shi yíge gēwǔ shēngpíngde shídài. Táng Mínghuáng shi xǐhuan yīnyuè hé gēwǔ de,

20   tā shèlì Líyuán zhuānmén xùnliàn yīnyuè gēwǔde réncái. Nèige shíhoude yuèqì jiu yǒu yìbǎi duō zhǒng, hézòu de shíhou yào yòng jǐbǎi rén yǎnzòu. Nèige shíhou wǔdǎo yě hěn fādá, Yáng Guìfēi hé Líyuán zǐdìde gēwǔ dōu shi hěn yǒumíngde. Zhè dōu zài gǔshūshang yǒu jìzǎi de, suǒyǐ wǒmen kéyi shuō Zhōngguo gǔdàide yīnyuè wǔdǎo zài Táng Cháo shi zuî shèngde

25   shíqī.

Dàole jìndài yīnwei shòule Ōu-Měi wénhuàde yǐngxiǎng, Zhōngguo yíqiè yìshu dōu yǒule xīnde zhuǎnbiàn. Zài zhōngxué、xiǎoxuéde yīnyuè kèchéng, duōbàn yǐ Xīyáng yīnyuè wéi zhǔ, jiāng xǔduō Ōu-Měi gēqǔ yì-chéng Zhōngwén zuòwei jiàocái. Dàxuéde yīnyuèxì yě fēnle Xīyuè hé guó-

30   yuè liǎngxì. Zhōngguo bu shǎode yīnyuèjiā yòng Xīyángde zuòqǔfǎ zuò qǔ huòzhě shi yòng Xīyángde yuèqì yǎnzòu, huò zhǐhuī yuèduì. Zhìyú wǔdǎo fāngmiàn gèng yǒu bu shǎo qīngnián nánnǚ xǐhuan xué Xīyángde tiàowǔ, chéngle yìshíde fēngqi.

Qícì shuōdao huìhuà. Huìhuà jiu shi huà huàr. Yǒu rén shuō Zhōng-
35 guode huìhuà shi yìshulide yìzhǒng chún měishù. Zhèijù huà hěn yǒu dàoli.
Zhōngguo gǔdàide huàr, yǐ Táng、Sòng liǎngcháo wéi zuì shèng shíqī. Táng
Cháo yǒumíngde huàjiā Wáng Wéi, tā huà de shānshuǐ zuì chūmíng. Hái
yǒu zài jìndài fāxiàn de Dūnhuáng shíkū, shíkūli yǒu hěn duō bìhuà, dōu
shi Táng Cháo huàjiāde zuòpǐn. Sòng Cháo yǒu yíbù <u>Xuānhé Huàpǔ</u>, zài
40 zhèibù huàpǔli yǒu liùqiān sānbǎi duō zhāng huàr, dōu shi yánjiu Zhōngguo
huàde bǎoguì zīliào. Cǐwài Zhōngguo huàr yǒu yíge tèdiǎn, shi hé "shū"
yǒu mìqiè guānxi. <u>Shū</u> shi <u>shūfǎ</u>, yě jiu shi <u>xiě zì</u>. Zài Zhōngguo huàr-
shang búdàn dōu yào xiěshang hé huàr yǒu guānxide zì, érqiě xiě zì yě
néng dúzì chéngwei yìzhǒng yìshupǐn. Wǒmen cháng kànjian Zhōngguo
45 rénde jiāli yǒu huà de huàr, yǒu xiě de zìhuàr. Yīnwei shū hé huàr zài
chuàngzuò de guòchéng zhōng suǒ yòng de jìqiǎo shènzhìyú gōngjù shi
wánquán xiāngtóngde, suǒyǐ shū hé huàr shi zǐmèi yìshu. Zhōngguo huàrde
tícái yǒu rénwu、shānshuǐ、huāhuì děng lèi. Zhè dōu shi zhǐzhe Zhōngguo
yuányǒude huìhuà shuō de.

50   Zìcóng Xīfāng wénmíng chuándaole Zhōngguo, Zhōngguode huìhuà yě
shòule yǐngxiǎng. Jīnhòu Zhōngguo huàrde qūshì huì zěnmoyàng? Xiànzài
xià yíge pànduàn háishi tài zǎo.

Xiànzài shuōdao xìjù. Zhōngguode xìjù, wúlùn jīngxì huòzhě shi dìfang-xì, dōu yǒu jǐzhǒng tèdiǎn:

55   Dì-yī, fánshi xìlide shēngyīn chàbuduō dōu shi yǐ chàng de fāngfǎ
biǎoyǎn. Lìrú xìlide rén shuō huà de qiāngdiào gēn píngcháng rén shuō
huà jiu bùtóng.

Dì-èr shi suǒyǒude dòngzuò dōu shi wǔdǎode zīshi. Lìrú xìlide rén
zǒuqi lù lai de zīshi yě lèisì wǔdǎo, hé píngcháng rén zǒu lù de zīshi
60 bùtóng.

Dì-sān shi wǔtáishang yòng de dōngxi shi xiàngzhēng de, bìng bu yòng
zhēnde dōngxi. Lìrú yòng biānzi xiàngzhēng qí mǎ.

Dì-sì shi yòng liǎnpǔ biǎoxiàn rénwude xìnggé. Lìrú báiliǎn biǎoshì
jiānzhà, huāliǎn biǎoshì yīngyǒng. Zhè dōu shi zhǐzhe Zhōngguo yǐqiánde
65 xìjù shuō de.

Mínguó yǐlái yīnwei shòule Xīyáng xìjùde yǐngxiǎng, chǎnshēngle yìzhǒng xīnde xìjù xíngshì. Zhèizhǒng xīnde xìjù shi yǐ duìhuà wéi zhǔ, hé

Zhōngguo yuánlái yǐ gēwǔ wéi zhǔ de dà bù xiāngtóng, suǒyǐ zhèizhǒng jiàozuo huàjù yě jiàozuo xīn xì.

70   Zǒngkuò lái shuō, Zhōngguode yīnyuè﹑ wǔdǎo﹑ huìhuà hé xìjù suírán zhújiàn yǒu xīnde fāzhǎn, dàn dàduōshùde rén réngrán xǐhuan jiù yǒu de. Yóuqíshi jìnlái dàjiā tíchàng fāyáng Zhōngguo guócuì, suǒyǐ Zhōngguo jiù yǒu de yīnyuè﹑ wǔdǎo﹑ huìhuà hé xìjù búdàn néng bǎocún érqiě shi tiān-tiān zài jìnbù.

WÈNXI

1. Zhōngguode Yuè﹑ Xiāng﹑ Mǐn﹑ Gàn sìshěng dōu shi zài Zhōngguode nánbù. Zhèi sìshěng bǐcǐde jùlí bìng bú tài yuǎn, wèi-shénmo Yuèyǔ﹑ Xiāngyǔ﹑ Mǐnyǔ hé Gànyǔ dà bù xiāngtóng ne? Yīnwei zhèi sìshěngde jùlí suírán bù yuǎn, kěshi zhèi jǐshěngde biānjìng dōu yǒu dà shān. Yīnwei shòule zìrán huánjìngde yǐngxiǎng, suǒyǐ zhèi sìshěng jiu gè shuō gède fāngyán le.

2. Wáng Jiàoshòu shi Jiāngsu rén, tā jiù huì shuō Jiāngsu huà, jiu shi Wúyǔ. Yǒu yìtiān yǒu yíge xīn lái de xuésheng qu tīng Wáng Jiàoshòu jiǎngyǎn. Yīnwei Wáng Jiàoshòu shuō de shi Jiāngsu huà, zhèige xuésheng yìzhí tīngdao wán yíjù yě méi tīngdǒng. Yuánlái zhèige xīn xuésheng shi xīn cóng Fújiàn lái de, tā jiù dǒng Mǐnnányǔ, suǒyǐ tā tīngbudǒng. Hòulái tā wèn biéde tóngxué, shi bu shi jiù tā yíge rén tīngbudǒng. Biéren gàosu ta, biéren yě tīngbudǒng.

3. Tián Xiānsheng zài duì Rìběn Kàngzhàn de shíhou, cóng Shěnyáng dàole Yángzhōu, hòulái yòu cóng Yángzhōu dàole Chéngdū. Zài Chéngdū zhùle yìnián, yòu dàole Kūnmíng. Tā shuō: "Zhèicì Kàngzhàn jiù Dōngběi rén bèi Rìběn rén hàide tài kǔ le. Wǒ cóng Dōngběi jiù yíge rén táochulai, zǒule hěn duō shěng. Měi dào yíge dìfang jiu yòngxīn yánjiu nèige dì-qūde yǔyīn. Hòulái wǒ xiěle yìběn shū, zài shūli huàle yìzhāng Zhōngguo yǔyīn fēnqū tú. Yǒu shíhou wǒ xīnli xiǎng yào bú shi Kàngzhàn yěxǔ wǒ bú huì zǒu zhènmo duō shěng, gèng bú huì xiě zhèiběn shū."

4. Zuótian wǒ qu kàn Mǎ Xiānsheng, Mǎ Xiānsheng zhèng zài jiāli kàn shū. Wǒ wèn ta jìnlái kàn shénmo shū? Tā shuō: "Zuìjìn kàn Shàng Shū hé Shī Jīng, hái yào kàn xiē guānyu yīnyùnde shū." Wǒ wèn ta wèi-shénmo kàn zhèixiē gǔshū ne? Tā shuō: "Wèideshì yánjiu Shànggǔ Hànyǔ hé Zhōnggǔ Hànyǔ."

5. Yǒu yíwèi yǔyánxuéjiā xiěle yìběn shū, shūli duìyu Hànyǔde shēngdiào﹑ biàndiào yǐjí qīngyīn, érhuàyùn dōu xiěde hěn xiángxì. Tā shuō zhè shi Hàn-Zàng Yǔzúlide tèdiǎn, zài biéde yǔzú xiàng Yìn-Ōu Yǔzúli shi méi yǒu de, suǒyǐ tā tèbié xiěchulai.

6. Zài yánjiu gòucífǎ zhīqián yào xiān dǒngde shénmo shi dòngcí, shénmo shi fùcí, yě yào dǒngde shénmo shi míngcí﹑ dàimíngcí.

7. Yǒ yíge wàiguo xuésheng kāishǐ xué Zhōngwén. Xiānsheng gàosu ta yào zhùyì zàojùfǎ, yòu gàosu ta shénmo shi fùhéjù, shénmo shi xùshùshì hé

yíwènshìde jùzi, yīngdāng zěnyàng yòng yíwèncí hé yíwèn dàimíngcí cái
kéyi biǎoshìchulai shi wènhuà, hái yǒu fǒudìngshìde jùzi yào yòng shénmo
cí lai biǎoshì fǒudìng . . . Zhèige xuésheng shuō: "Xièxie nín yìliánchuàn
shuōle zhèixiē wèntí. Wǒde nǎozi shízài jìbuzhù zhènmo duō. Qǐng nín
děng yìhuěr zài shuō. Wǒ xiān qu dào wàibian huànhuan nǎozi. Wǒ huílai
nín zài shuō."

8. Yǒu yíge wàiguo xuésheng shuō: "Wǒ zài niàn Zhōngguo gǔ shǐde shíhou
zhídao Táng Mínghuángde gōngli yǒu fēizi sānqiān rén, wǒ rènwei zhè shi
yíge yíwèn." Yǒu rén gàosu ta: "Nà búguò shi shǐrende yìzhǒng shuōfǎ,
xíngrong Táng Mínghuángde fēizi tài duō le, bìng bú shi yídìng yǒu sān-
qiānge fēizi."

9. Yǒu yíge wàiguo xuésheng xǐhuan kàn Zhōngwén xiǎoshuō Hóng Lóu Mèng.
Tā shuō: "Hóng Lóu Mèngli yǒu yíwèi zhǎngde zuì měide xiáojie, shī yě
zuòde zuì hǎo. Zhèiwèi xiáojiede míngzide dì-yíge zì wǒ bú rènde, dì-
èrge zì shi yíge yù zì, wǒ jiu guǎn ta jiào "shénmo Yù Xiáojie" ba.
Zhèiwèi "shénmo Yù Xiáojie" de xìnggé hěn tèbié. Tā céng bǎ luòzai
dìshangde huā máizai tǔli. Tā shuō: "Xiànzài huā luòle yǒu wǒ lai zàng
huā. Jiānglái wǒ sǐle, bù zhídào shi shéi lái máizàng ne?"

10. Zuìjìn yǒu yíge guówáng zài gōngtíngli kāi yīnyuèhuì. Tā bǎ yǎnzòu de
yīnyuè yòng wúxiàndiàn guǎngbō dào wàimiàn qu. Tā shuō: "Jiù wǒ yíge
rén tīng hěn méi yìsi. Jiào rénmín yě yǒu jīhui tīngting gōngtíngli yīnyuèhuìde yǎnzòu."

11. Wěi shi hòubiānde yìsi, jùwěi jiu shi yíge jùzi hòubiānde zì.

12. Zhèicì wǒ dào Tàiguo jiù sāntiān. Wǒ bù dǒng Tàiguo huà, yě bu rènshi
Tàiguo zì. Wǒ kàn Tàiguode bàozhǐ, dōu shi yǒu rén gěi wǒ yìchéng
Zhōngwén. Hòulái wǒ mǎile yìběn Tàiyǔ Huìhuà Kèběn, kànle bàntiān lián
yíge zì yě méi dǒng.

13. Xiānsheng jiào xuésheng fēnxi nǚháizi zhèige cérde chéngfèn. Xuésheng
shuō: "Zhèige cér yǒu sānge císù. Nǚ hé hái hái yǒu zi dōu shi císù.
Zi zì shi cíwěi. Nǚ zì shì bu shi cítóu, wǒ bu dà qīngchu."

14. Zài Dōng Hànde shíhou yǒu yíge xìng Kǒng de xiǎoháizi, tā zài sìsuìde
shíhou hé tā jiālide rén zài yíkuàr chī lí. Tā nále yíge zuì xiǎode lí lái
chī. Yǒu rén wèn ta wèi-shénmo bù ná yíge dàde lí ne? Tā shuō: "Wǒ
niánji zuì xiǎo, yīngdāng ná xiǎode." Yǒu rén shuō zhèige háizi zhēn hǎo,
jiānglái dàqilai yídìng shi ge bùdéliǎode rénwu.

15. Yǒu rén xǐhuan kàn wǔtáijù. Yǒu rén xǐhuan zìjǐ zài wǔtáishang gēwǔ
jiào biéren kàn. Hái yǒu rén yìtiān dào wǎn jiù xǐhuan gēn nǚren tiàowǔ.

16. Qǐng nǐ shuō shénmo shi rénchēng dàimíngcí? Shénmo shi liàngcí?
Shénmo jiào cídiào? Shénmo jiào qiángdiào? Zuì hǎo nǐ néng fēnbié jǔchu
lìzi lai.

17. Zài Yìn-Ōu Yǔzúde yǔfǎli yǒu zhǔgé hé bīngé. Zài Hàn-Zàng Yǔzúde
yǔfǎli yǒu zhǔcí hé bīncí. Zhǔgé hé zhǔcí, bīngé hé bīncí shì bu shi
yíyàng? Rúguo bú shi yíyàng yǒu shénmo fēnbié?

18. Nèige guójiā suóyǐ chéngwei qiángguó shi yīnwei tā zài dìlǐshang yǒu yōuyuède tiáojiàn.

19. Wŏ zài yìbĕn huàpŭshang kànjian yìzhāng huàr jùshuō shi Suí Cháo rén
    huà de. Huàde tícái shi shān. Yŏu jìnde shān, yŏu yuănde shān. Yuănde
    shān yĭwài hái yŏu gèng yuănde shān. Nèixiē shān kànqilai yuè kàn yuè
    duō, yuè kàn yuè yuăn. Yŏu rén shuō zhèizhāng huàr jiàozuo "Yuăn Shān
    Chóngdié."

20. Zài Yīn-Ōu Yŭzúli dòngcíde biànhuà hĕn duō. Yŏu rén xiăng bă gèzhŏng
    biànhuà guīnàwei jĭge yuánzé.

21. Yŏu yíge rén hĕn xĭhuan shuō huà. Búlùn nèijiàn shì gēn ta yŏu guānxi
    méi guānxi, tā dōu yào pīping pīping. Yŏu yícì bù zhīdào shi shénmo
    shìqing, tā bă huà shuōcuò le, rénjia dă tā yíge zuĭba, érqiĕ hái wèn ta:
    "Nĭde zuĭ yĭhòu hái duō shuō huà bu duō shuō huà le?"

22. Bă jĭge cí liánchuànzai yìqĭ jiu shi yíge jùzi. Hĕn duō jùzi liánchuànzai
    yìqĭ jiu shi yìpiān wénzhāng.

23. Yŏu rén shuō Hànyŭlide míngcí méi yŏu qūzhé de. Zhèige qūzhéde yìsi
    shi shuō méi yŏu hĕn duōde biànhuà.

24. Wŏ zuótian zài fànguăr chī fàn, fànqián shi sānkuài qián, fùjiā sānmáo
    qián shi xiăofèi, yígòng yòngle sānkuài sān.

25. Cónggián Zhōngguo rén niàn shū, duōshù niàn <u>Shī Jīng</u>、<u>Yì Jīng</u>. Yīnwei
    shídàide biànqiān, xiànzài chàbuduō méi rén niàn le.

26. Yŏu yíge wàiguo xuésheng zài Zhōngguo xué Zhōngwén. Zuìchū tā shuō
    hĕn nán. Hòulai tāde Zhōngwén chéngdu gāoqilai le, tā yòu shuō niàn
    Zhōngwén bìng bù hĕn nán le. Zuìjìn tā néng yòng Zhōngwén bă wén-
    zhāng xiĕde hĕn hăo. Tā shuō xué Zhōngwén yuè xué yuè yŏu yìsi.

WÈNTÍ

1. Xiànzài yìshu fēnwei duōshao lèi? Qĭng nĭ shuōyishuō.

2. Zhōngguo shi yĭ lĭyuè zhì guó. Shénmo shi lĭyuè? Lĭyuè wèi-shénmo
   zài wénhuàshang yŏu hĕn gāode dìwei?

3. Táng Cháode shíhou gēwŭ shēngpíng. Táng Mínghuáng zuì xĭhuan yīnyuè
   gēwŭ. Tā zài shénmo dìfang xùnlian gēwŭ réncái? Shénmo rén gēwŭ
   zuì yŏu míng?

4. Shénmo shi yìshulide chún mĕishù? Zhōngguo gŭdàide huà yĭ nĕi liăngcháo wéi zuì shèng?

5. Táng Cháo yŏumíngde huàjiā shi shéi? Jìndài fāxiàn de shíkū lĭmiàn
   yŏu Táng Cháode bìhuà shi zài shénmo dìfang?

6. <u>Xuānhé Huàpŭ</u> shi nĕi yìcháodài de? Zhèibĕn huàpŭ yōu duōshao zhāng
   huàr?

7. Shénmo shi shūfă? Shūfă hé huà huàr wèi-shénmo jiàozuo 'zĭmèi yìshu?'

8. Shénmo jiàozuo <u>jīngxì</u>? Yăn jīngxì de shíhou suŏ yòng de dōngxi yŏushí
   shi xiàngzhēng de. Nĭ zhīdao yòng biānzi xiàngzhēng de shi shénmo?

9. Jīngxìlide liānpǔ yǒu shénmo yòng? Báiliǎn biǎoshì shénmo yàngde rén? Huāliǎn ne?

10. Zhōngguo xìjù zìcóng Mínguó yǐlái chǎnshēngle yìzhǒng xīn xíngshì. Nèizhǒng xīn xíngshìde míngchēng shi shénmo?   Shì bu shi yǐ duìhuà wéi zhǔ?

ILLUSTRATIVE SENTENCES (ENGLISH)

2. 1. She likes to wear figured dresses, I like to wear plain dresses.

2. 3. Why has that actor painted his face white?

7. 2. I have a book of paintings at home that includes a landscape by Wang Wei of the T'ang Dynasty.

15. 1. Who wrote on [lit. toward] the wall?

21. 1. Miss Ma has studied dancing, so she dances very well.

22. 2. The sentence "(In) China (they) ruled the country with rites and music" signifies that the Chinese looked upon rites and music as important.

22. 3. In the Spring and Autumn Period Confucius used rites and music to teach the people.

23. 1. Ancient China's song and dance flourished most in the T'ang Dynasty [lit. took T'ang Dynasty as most flourishing].

27. 2. From the people's livelihood it is possible to see [lit. to reflect out] the economic conditions of that country.

28. 1. What that local play depicts is the story of the Illustrious Emperor of T'ang.

29. 2. Líyuán has two meanings.   One is "a garden with pear trees," the other refers to a place for studying [singing] opera.

31. 2. They trained several dozen youths of both sexes, preparing them [in the future] to be actors in the new drama.

33. 1. In the Peking opera they sometimes use a piece of cloth to symbolize a city.

39. 1. As long as you study hard why fear that you won't pass the exam?

39. 2. Even if no one comes to listen he still wants to hold the concert.

42. 2. Do you know the difference between the foreign song-writing technique and the old Chinese technique?

48. 1. Young people of today like to sing that kind of song, which has become the rage of the moment.

51. 2. That concubine entered the palace when she was quite young.

52. 2. In teaching elementary school pupils they use various kinds [lit. forms] of teaching methods.

58. 2. "The final victory will be ours." This is a conclusion that we have reached ourselves.

NOTES

1. The following miscellaneous usages are illustrated in the exercise Yǔfǎ
   Liànxí in this lesson:

   a (1-2).   nǎpà 'even (if)' in the first two clauses is generally followed by
   dōu or yě in the second:

   > Tāde gǔwén hěn hǎo.   Nǎpa Shī Jīng, Shāng Shū, Zuǒ Zhuàn tā
   > dōu néng bèidexiàlái. 'His (knowledge of) ancient literature is ex-
   > cellent.   Even the Book of Odes, the Book of Lord Shang, and the
   > Tso Chuan he can recite them all from memory.'

   Nǎpà is sometimes followed, redundantly, by jiùshi:

   > Nǎpà jiùshi xià yǔ wǒ yě děi qù. 'Even if it rains I have to go.'

   b (3-4).   V₁ hǎoxiang V₂ 'to V₁ as if V₂'

   > Tā xiě zìzhuàn hǎoxiang xiě xiǎoshuōr   'He wrote his autobiog-
   > raphy as if he were writing a novel.'

   c (5-6).   V + guo form a resultative verb compound, usually with the meaning 'surpass in V-ing':

   > Tā zì suírán xiěde hǎo, kěshi tā hái xiěbuguò nǐ. 'Although he
   > writes characters well, he can't write better than you do.'

   d (7-8).   A few fixed combinations consisting of the same measure with
   two different numbers are used to express the idea of 'one or two' or 'a
   few.' The most commonly used pairs of numbers are yī... liǎng, sān...
   liǎng, sān... wǔ, shí... bā:

   > Wànlǐ Cháng Chéng bìngbú shi sānnián liǎngniánde gōngchéng.
   > 'The Great Wall was not constructed in [lit. a construction of] just
   > a few years.'

   e (9-10).   A jiu shi B jiu jiàozuò A 'A is B.'   Here jiu jiàozuò A 'is
   called A' is used redundantly:

   > Máizàng jiu shi rén sǐle yǐhòu bǎ ta máizai dì lǐtou jiu jiàozuo
   > máizàng 'Máizàng is burying a person in the ground after he has
   > died.'

   f (11-12). hǎo SV! 'How SV!':

   > Tāde érzi nènmo cōngming, sǐle hǎo kěxī! 'His son was so bright.
   > What a pity that he died!'

   g (13-14). Zěnmo yě bū V. This is short for zěnmo V yě bù V 'nohow V.'
   For example:

   > Zhōngguo fàn wǒ zěnmo zuò yě zuòbushàngléi or Zhōngguo fàn
   > wǒ zěnmo yě zuòbushànglái. 'I can't make Chinese food nohow.'

   h (15-16). nǎr láide N V 'where would one find the N to V?'

   > Tā bìng gāng hǎo. Nǎr láide lìqi bān nènmo dàde dōngxi? 'He
   > just recovered from his illness. Where would he find the strength
   > to move such a large thing?'

i (17-18). cái V bu jiǔ 'V'd a short while ago':

> Tā cái tuìxiū bu jiǔ yòu yǒu rén yào qǐng ta zuò shì.'He retired only a short time ago and now he's been asked again to take a job.'

j (19-20). V$_1$ cái yǒu TW jiù V$_2$ 'to V$_2$ after having V$_1$ for only TW':

> Tā xiě nèige jùběn cái yǒu liǎngge xīngqī jiu wánle 'He finished that play after [writing] only two weeks.'

2. This and subsequent lessons contain further examples of the construction yǐ A wéi B 'take A as B' which was introduced in Lesson 13. (See note 1 of that lesson.)

> yǐ A wéi zhǔ 'take A as the chief (thing)'

> yǐ A wéi shèng 'take A as the most flourishing' or, more freely 'A was the most flourishing'

Dì-Èrshikè. Sīxiǎng hé Zōngjiào

Bái: Mǎ Jiàoshòu, nín láide zhēn zǎo.

Mǎ: Wǒ liùdiǎn bàn jiu lái le.

Bái: Nín wèi-shénmo lái zhènmo zǎo a?

Mǎ: Qián xiē rìzi yǒu yìběn kānwù ràng wǒ gěi tāmen xiě yìdiǎr wényìde dōngxi. Tāmen xiàn wǒ zài zhèige xīngqī bìděi gěi tamen.
Wǒ shi yìtiān mángdào wǎn, báitiān gēnběn méi shíjiān xiě.

Bái: Nènmo nín dōu zài shénmo shíhou xiě ne?

Mǎ: Wǒ dōu shi zài wǎnfàn yǐhòu.

Bái: Nín xīngqīliù gēn xīngqī bu xiě dōngxi ma?

Mǎ: Wǒ xīngqīliù gēn xīngqī, yìtiān dào wǎn dōu děi bāngzhu wǒ tàitai
kàn háizi. Nǎr lái de gōngfu xiě dōngxi ne?

Bái: Nín xiě wénzhāngde nèiběn kānwù, shénmo shíhou chūbǎn?

Mǎ: Dàgài zài yǒu liǎngge xīngqī jiu kéyi chūbǎn le.

Bái: Nèige shíhou kéyi kànjian nínde jiézuò le.

Mǎ: Nǐ yǐhòu yě kéyi zài wǒmen xuéxiàode Xuésheng Tōngxùnshang xiě
diar dōngxi.

Bái: Wǒ zěnmo gǎn zài kānwùshang xiě dōngxi ne?

Mǎ: Zuòjiāmen hái bu dōu shi yìdiǎr yìdiǎr, mànmārde liànxichulai de?

Bái: Wǒ duì xiězuò chàde tài yuǎn ne.

Mǎ: Bújiànde. Nǐ kèqi ne. Zuótian wǒ gěi nǐ nèipiān dōngxi nǐ yìchéng
Zhōngwén le ma?

Bái: Wǒ cái fānyìle yíbàn. Yǒude jùzi hěn nán, yǒu shíhou hěn bu róngyi
zhǎodào yíge Zhōngwén jùzi, gēn Yīngwénde yìsi wánquán yíyàngde.

Mǎ: Fānyì dōngxi yǒude shíhou jiu huì fāshēng zhèizhǒng kùnnán.

Bái: Shìde. Yàoshi yòng cér yòngde bú tài hǎo, bǎ yuánwénde wèr jiu
biǎodábuchūlái.

Mǎ: Kěbushìma! Fānyì wénzhāng hěn bù róngyi. Shàng xīngqīde Yuǎn-
Dà Zhōukānshang yǒu yíwèi wàiguo tóngxué fānyìle yìpiān "Gǔ Luómǎde Měishù" nǐ kànguo méi yǒu?

Bái: Wó kàn le, fānyìde búcuò.

Mǎ: Suóyi wǒ ràng nǐ yě xiě diar shìshi. Jīntian wǎnshang xuéxiào yǒu
yīnyuè yǎnzòuhuì nǐ lái bu lái?

Bái: Bù yídìng, yěxǔ lái, yào kàn wǒde shíjiān zěnmoyàng.

Mǎ : Yǒu guóyuè yě yǒu Xīyuè. Zhǐhuī Xīyuède shi yíwèi hěn yǒumíng-
35   de yīnyuèjiā.

Bái: Tīngshuō hěn duō xuéxiào yòng tā zuò de qǔzi dāng jiàocái.

Mǎ : Suǒyǒude zhōng xiǎoxué, shífēnzhī-jiǔ shi yòng tā zuò de qǔzi. Wǒ-
        men xiànzài tǎolùn tǎolùn jīntian jiǎnghuà lǐmiànde cér.

Bái: Hǎode.

1.0. Jīdūjiào   (1) Christianity; (2) Protestantism [Christ religion]

1.1. Zhōngguo rén xìn Fójiàode duōyu xìn Jīdūjiào de.   (W)

2.0. Tiānzhǔjiào   Catholicism [heaven master religion]

2.1. Tā xìn Tiānzhǔjiào yǒu èrshi duō nián le.

3.0. Jǐngjiào   Nestorian Christianity, Nestorianism [luminous reli-
                         gion]

3.1. Táng Cháo shíhou de Jǐngjiào jiù shi Jīdūjiào.

4.0. xìnjiào   have a religious belief, believe in a religion (VO)[believe
                    religion]

        chuánjiào   preach religion, proseletyze (VO) [transmit religion]

4.1. Nǐ xìn shénmo jiào?

4.2. Qīng Cháo yǒu yīge shíqī xiànzhi wàiguó rén lái chuánjiào. (T)

5.0. shénfù   (Catholic) priest [deity father]

5.1. Cóngqián Zhōngguo rén zuò shénfù de hěn yǒuxiàn, hòulái jiānjiānde
        duō le.

6.0. Lì Mǎdòu   Matteo Ricci

6.1. Lì Mǎdòu dàole Zhōngguo yǐhòu, Tiānzhǔjiàode chuánjiào gōngzuò
        jiu zhǎnkāi le.

40 Mǎ : Nǐ zhīdao bu zhīdào, Jīdūjiào zài shénmo shíhou fēn xīn-jiù liǎng-
             pài?

     Bái: Dàgài shi zài shíqī shíjìde shíhou.   Jiùde jiào Tiānzhǔjiào, xīnde
             jiào Jīdūjiào.

     Mǎ : Kāishǐ chuándào Zhōngguode shíhou jiào shénmo míngzi?

45 Bái: Jiào Jǐngjiào. Wǒ wàngle shì bu shi zài Táng Cháode shíhou chuán-
             dào Zhōngguo lái de?

     Mǎ : Shì zài Táng Cháode shíhou chuándào Zhōngguo de.   Jùshuō Suí﹑
             Tángde shíhou chuánjiào céngjīng tíngzhǐguo yíge shíqī.

     Bái : Hòulái shénmo shíhou tāmen yòu dào Zhōngguo lai chuánjiào ne?

50 Mǎ : Děngdào Míng Cháode shíhou yòu yǒu Yìdàlì shénfù Zhōngguo míng-
             zi jiào Lì Mǎdòu zài dào Zhōngguo lai chuánjiào.

7.0. chuánrù   (1) transmit; (2) penetrate into   (W) [transmit enter]

7.1. Fójiào zài shénmo shíhou chuánrù Zhōngguo de, nǐ zhīdao ma?

8.0. tú*   disciple, apprentice (frequently affixed to names of religions)

      xìntú   believer, disciple [believe disciple]

8.1. Zhèige chéngli Jīdūjiàode xìntú bǐ Fójiàotú shǎode duō.   (T)

9.0. mùshi   (Protestant) minister, pastor [pasture teacher]

9.1. Nèi wàiguo mùshi zài Zhōngguo chuánjiào yǒu èrshi duō nián le.

10.0. shìli   strength, power, influence [tendency strength]

10.1. Zài Mínguó chūnián gè dìfang jūnrende shìli dàyu zhōngyāng zhèng-
     fǔ.   (W)

Bái: Jīdūjiào zài Zhōngguo zuì shèngde shíqī shi Táng Cháo ma?

Mǎ: Jīdūjiào suírán shi Táng Cháo chuánrù Zhōngguo de, kěshi dāngshí
     xìn de rén bìng bù duō.   Cóng Míng mò dào Qīng Cháode shíhou
55   xìntú cái zhújiànde zēngjiā, Mínguó yǐlái xìn de rén jiu hěn duō le.

Bái: Wǒ xiǎng kāishǐ de shíhou shénfù gēn mùshimen chuánjiào yídìng
     xiāngdāng kùnnán.

Mǎ: Nà shi miǎnbuliǎo de.   Yào zhuǎnbiàn rénde sīxiǎng gēn zōngjiào
     bìng bú shi yíjiàn róngyide shìqing.

60 Bái: Zài Zhōngguo shi Tiānzhǔjiàode shìli dà ne, háishi Jīdūjiàode shì-
     li dà ne?

Mǎ: Zhèige hěn nán shuō.

11.0. guānliáo   officials, bureaucracy [official bureaucrat]

11.1. Zài Mínguó chūnián, tā fùqin shi yíge dà guānliáo.

12.0. zūn   to honor

     zūnzhòng   honor, respect (N/V) [honor heavy]

     zūnchóng   to worship, reverence, respect [honor honor]

12.1. Gǔdàide shíhou zūn huángdì hǎoxiang shi shén.   (T)

12.2. Xiànzài Guó-Gòng liǎngfāngmiàn dōu zūnzhòng Sūn Zhōngshān Xiān-
     sheng.

12.3. Zhōngguo niàn shū de rén xiànglái shi zūnchóng Kǒngzǐde xuéshuō.

13.0. dàodé   morality, virtue [way virtue]

     Dàodé Jīng   Morality Classic

13.1. Nèige rén yòu yǒu xuéwen yòu yǒu dàodé.

13.2. Dàodé Jīng shi wényánde.   Hěn duō rén kànbudǒng.

14.0. zhuānzhì   despotic, autocratic [specialized system]

14.1. Zhōngguo zhèngzhì cóngqián shi zhuānzhì de. Xiànzài shì bu shi mínzhǔ de?

Bái: Jùshuō zài Míng Cháode shíhou yǒu jǐge guānliáo yě xìnjiào le.

Mǎ : Nà shi shòule Lǐ Mǎdòude yǐngxiǎng. Lǐ Mǎdòu búdàn Zhōng-Xī
65   wénxué hǎo, érqiě tā tiānwén、dìlǐ、shùxué shénmo dōu dǒng. Yīn-
        wei zūnzhòng Lǐ Mǎdòude dàodé xuéwèn, suǒyǐ yǒu jǐge zuò guān
        de yě xìnjiào le.

Bái: Zài zhuānzhì shídài zuò guān de kéyi xìn yíge wàiguode zōngjiào
        ma?

70 Mǎ : Kéyi. Lǐ Mǎdòu suǒyǐ gēn Míng Cháode dà guān dǎchéng yípiàn
        zhǔyào mùdì shi wèile zài Zhōngguo chuánjiào.

15.0. xìn-shǎng-bì-fá   foster a belief in rewards and make a certainty of
                        punishments (W) [believe reward must penalize]

15.1. Xìn-shǎng-bì-fá de yìsi jiu shi: "Shuōle shǎng, jiu yídìng shǎng.
        Yīnggāi fá de, jiu yídìng yào fá."

16.0. yǐ-fǎ-zhì-guó   rule the country by means of law (W) [use law rule
                        country]

16.1. Yǐ-fǎ-zhì-guó shi yòng fǎlù zhìlǐ guójiā.

17.0. Fǎjiā   legalist(s)

        Mòjiā   Mohist(s)

17.1. Fǎjiā、Mòjiāde xuéshuō dōu shi Zhànguó shídàide xuéshuō.

18.0. Hán Fēi(zǐ)   Han Fei (Tzu) (died 233 B.C.)

18.1. Hán Fēizǐ hé Mèngzǐ dōu shi Zhànguó shídàide sīxiǎngjiā.

19.0. jūn   (1) ruler, sovereign, lord; (2) gentleman; (3) Lord, Mr.

        jūnzǐ   gentleman

        Shāng Jūn   Lord Shang

19.1. "Wáng Jūn、Lǐ Jūn" jiu shi "Wáng Xiānsheng、Lǐ Xiānsheng" de
        yìsi. Dōu shi xiě de shíhou cái yòng jūn.

19.2. Jūnzǐ shi hǎorénde yìsi.

19.3. Shāng Jūn zài Qín Guó zuò guān, tā shíxíng yǐ-fǎ-zhì-guó. (W)

Bái: Mǎ Jiàoshòu, xìn-shǎng-bì-fá shi shénmo gǔshūshang de?

Mǎ : Shi Hàn Shūshang de. Wǒ xiànzài wèn nǐ jǐge wèntí. "Yǐ-fǎ-zhì-
        guó" shi shénmo yìsi?

75 Bái: Zhè shi Fǎjiāde dàolǐ, yìsi shi ná fǎlù zhìlǐ guójiā.

Mǎ : Zhōngguo gǔshíhou zuì yǒu míngde liǎngge Fǎjiā shi shéi?

Bái: Hán Fēizǐ gēn Shāng Jūn.

Mǎ : Dōu shi shénmo shíhoude rén?

Bái: Dōu shi Zhànguó shíhoude rén.

80   Mǎ : Qíshí Hán Fēizǐ běnlái jiào Hán Fēi. Tā xiě de shū jiào Hán Fēi-
       zǐ, kěshi hòulái rénmen jiu bù fēn le. Shū yě jiào Hán Fēizǐ, rén
       yě jiào Hán Fēizǐ le.

20.0. jiān'ài universal love [equal love]

20.1. Jiān'ài zhǔyì shì bu shi ài zìjǐ yě ài díren? (T)

21.0. gōngji attack (N/V) [attack strike]

21.1. Yǒu rén xīnshǎng Lǎo Cán Yóujì, shuō shi xiěde hěn hǎo. Yě yǒu
      rén gōngji Lǎo Cán Yóujì, shuō shi xiěde bù hǎo.

22.0. dào   The Way

      Dàojiā   Taoist(s)

      Dàojiào   Taoism

22.1. Dàojiā suǒwèi dào hé Rújiā suǒ shuō de dào shì bu shi xiāngtóng?

22.2. Zhōngguo rén xìn Fójiàode zuì duō. Qícì jiu shi xìn Dàojiào de.
      Yě yǒu yòu xìn Fójiào yòu xìn Dàojiào de.

23.0. shǐzǔ   first ancestor, founder, founding father

23.1. Fójiàode shǐzǔ shi něiguó rén, nǐ zhīdao ma?

24.0. qīngjìng   quiet, silent [clear quiet]

24.1. Wǒ jiā zhùzai xiāngcūn. Huánjìng hěn qīngjìng.

25.0. wúwéi   (1) do nothing, remain passive; (2) inaction, quietism [not
                do]

      qīngjìng wúwéi   quiescence and inaction (W)

      wúwéi ér zhì   govern by doing nothing (W) [not do and rule]

25.1. Dàojiāde zhǔzhāng shi "wúwéi." Zhèizhǒng xuéshuō nǐ zànchéng ma?

25.2. Rúguǒ rénrén dōu "qīngjìng wúwéi" shì bu shi zǔzhǐle shèhuìde
      jìnbù?

25.3. Qǐng nǐ yòng "wúwéi ér zhì" shuō yíge xiě de jùzi. (T)

Bái: Mòjiā jiu shi Mòzǐde xuéshuō me?

Mǎ : Shìde. Qǐng nǐ shuōyishuō Mòzǐde zhéxué shi ná shénmo zuò jīchǔ?

85   Bái: Mòzǐde zhéxué ná jiān'ài zuò jīchǔ. Jiān'àide yìsi jiu shi ài zìjǐ
      yě ài biéren.

Mǎ : Dùile. Yīnwei Zhànguóde shíhou shèhuìshang yǒu hěn dàde dòngluàn, rén gēn rén、guó gēn guó dōu shi hùxiāng gōngji, Mòzǐ gǎn-
juédao rúguǒ yào wéichi rénlèi hépíng, bìxū ài zìjǐ yě ài biéren.
90 Yàoshi kàn biéren hǎoxiang shi zìjǐ yíyàng, jiu bu huì duì biéren
bù hǎo le. Yàoshi kàn biéde guójiā hǎoxiang shi zìjǐde guójiā, yě
jiu bú huì dǎzhàng le.

Bái : Chuàngzào Dàojiàode shi Lǎozǐ ma?

Mǎ : Bìng bú shi Lǎozǐ chuàngzào de, kěshi Dàojiā dōu ná Lǎozǐ dàng
95 shǐzǔ.

Bái : <u>Dàodé Jīng</u> jiu shi Lǎozǐde zhùzuò, shì bu shi?

Mǎ : Duì. <u>Dàodé Jīng</u> yígòng yǒu wǔqiānjù huà, rénmen cháng shuō "dàodé wǔqiān yán," jiu shi zhǐzhe zhèiběn <u>Dàodé Jīng</u> shuō de.

Bái : "Qīngjìng wúwéi," "wúwéi ér zhì" shi Lǎozǐde zhéxué ma?

100 Mǎ : Shìde. <u>Qīngjìng</u> jiu shi méi yǒu gèzhǒng máfan. <u>Wúwéi</u> jiu shi
xīnli méi yǒu shénmo shìqing. <u>Wúwéi ér zhì</u> jiu shi bú yào jìhua
zěnyàng zhì guó, yào chún zìránde zhìlǐ.

26.0. lún*   human relationship

wǔlún   five human relationships

26.1. <u>Wǔlún</u> jiu shi rén gēn rénde wǔzhǒng guānxi.

27.0. chén   (imperial) minister, official

jūnchén lords and ministers

27.1. <u>Chén</u> shi zhuānzhì shídài zuò guān de míngchēng.

27.2. Fánshi mínzhǔ guójiā méi yǒu jūnchén ma?   (T)

28.0. fùzǐ   father and son

28.1. Tāmen fùzǐ liǎngge rén dōu shi shèhuìshang yǒumíngde rénwu.

29.0. fūfù   husband and wife

29.1. Zài wǔlúnli, fūfùde guānxi shì bu shi zuì mìqiè de?

30.0. fēngjiàn   feudal [enfief erect]

30.1. Tāde jiā shi yíge fēngjiànde jiātíng. Jiālide yíqiè shìqing dōu děi
tīng tā fùqinde mìnglìng.

Mǎ : Zhōngguo rén hěn zhùzhòng wǔlún. Qǐng nǐ shuōshuo shi něi wǔlún?

105 Bái : Jūnchén、fùzǐ、xiōngdì、fūfù、péngyou.

Mǎ : Duìle. Yìsi jiu shi zhèi wǔzhǒng guānxi yàoshi wéichíhǎole jiu shi
hǎoren.

Bái : Zhè shi fēngjiàn shídàide dàodé guānniàn.

Mǎ: Zhè yě kéyi shuō shi Zhōngguo rén yìzhǒng chuántǒngde dàodé
110   guānniàn.

31.0. zhū-zǐ-bǎi-jiā   all classes of philosophers   [various philosophers
                              hundred families]

31.1. Zhū-zǐ-bǎi-jiā shi xíngrong Zhànguó shíhou gè jiāde xuéshuō tài
         duō le de yìsi.

32.0. zhǔtǐ   main thing, pivot, theme [chief body]

32.1. Zhèibén Shīgē Zǒngjíli yǐ Shī Jīng wéi zhǔtǐ.   (W) (T)

33.0. rén 仁 (1) human, humane; (2) humanity, human-heartedness

33.1. Rén shi shénmo?   Shi shénmo xuéshuōde zhǔzhāng?

34.0. shèng(rén) a sage [holy man]

34.1. Zhōngguo zūn Kǒngzǐ wéi shèngrén shi cóng Hàn Cháo kāishǐ de.
         (W) (T)

Mǎ: Zài Chūnqiū Zhànguóde shíhou, zhū-zǐ-bǎi-jiā gè yǒu gède sīxiǎng
         gēn tāmende xuéshuō. Nǐ zhīdao Rújiā ná shéide xuéshuō zuò zhǔ-
         tǐ?

Bái: Ná Kǒngzǐde xuéshuō zuò zhǔtǐ.

115 Mǎ: Kǒngzǐde xuéshuō, zhōngxīn shi shēnmo?

Bái: Shi rén.

Mǎ: Duìle. Rén shi duì rénlèide tóngqíng. Qǐng nǐ shuōyishuō Kǒngzǐde
         zhèngzhi sīxiǎng shi shénmo?

Bái: Shi yòng lǐyuè lái jiàoyu rénmin, zhìlǐ guójiā. Qǐng wèn Mǎ Jiào-
120   shòu, wèi-shénmo jiào Kǒngzǐ shi shèngrén?

Mǎ: Shèngrénde yìsi jiu shi yíge rénde xuéwen、dàodé yíqiè dōu bǐ pǔ-
         tōng rén gāode duō. Yīnwei Zhōngguo wénhuàde xíngchéng gēn fā-
         zhǎn shòu Kǒngzǐde yǐngxiǎng zuì dà, suǒyǐ zūn Kǒngzǐ shi shèng-
         rén.

35.0. fèng   to honor (W)

35.1. Zhōngguo xìjù yǎnyuán fèng Táng Mínghuáng wéi shǐzǔ. (W) (T)

36.0. sì   temple, monastery (Buddhist)

36.1. Sì jiu shi miàode yìsi. Fójiàode miào duōshù jiàzuò sì.

36.2. Cháng Shēng Sì li yǒu hěn duō líshù.

37.0. Fójīng Buddhist scriptures

37.1. Zhōngguo yǒu yíbù zhùmíngde xiǎoshuō, xiě de shi yíge rén dào
         Xīfāng qu qiú Fójīngde gùshi. (T)

38.0. chuàngshǐ (1) initiate, begin; (2) beginning (W) [create first]

38.1. Zhōngguode lǐjié duōbàn shi Zhōu Cháo chuàngshǐ de. (W)

39.0. chǎnwù product, production (W) [produce object]

39.1. Xīn Cháo hé Chuàngzào Zhōukān dōu shi xīn wénxué xīn sīxiǎngde chǎnwù.

125 Bái: Mǎ Jiàoshòu, qǐng wèn fèng shi shénmo yìsi?

    Mǎ : Fèng zhèige cér yàoshi shuō huà jiu shi zūn de yìsi. Bǐrú "Dàojiā fèng Lǎozǐ wéi shǐzǔ" yìsi jiu shi Dàojiā zūn Lǎozǐ shi shǐzǔ.

    Bái: Sì jiu shi miào ma?

    Mǎ : Sì jiu shi miào. Wǒmen fùjìnde Cháng Shēng Sì nǐ méi qùguo ma?

130 Bái: Qùguo le. Shàng xīngqītiān wǒ gēn Měiyīng yíkuàr qù de. Nèige miào hěn dà, lǐmiàn yǒu hěn duō Fójīng. Nín qùguo méi yǒu?

    Mǎ : Nǐ shuō wǒ duō máng ba! Cháng Shēng Sì lí wǒ jiā zhènmo jìn, wǒ lián qù dōu méi qùguo.

    Bái: Chuàngshǐ shi xiě wénzhāng yòng de ma?

135 Mǎ : Shì. Shuō huà bu yòng chuàngshǐ, kǒuyǔshang shi yòng kāishǐ chuàngzào.

    Bái: Qǐng wèn, chǎnwù shi shénmo yìsi?

    Mǎ : Shuō huà de shíhou jiu shi "chǎnshēng de dōngxi." Wǒ gěi nǐ jǔ ge lìzi yīnggāi zěnmo yòng, xiàng "Nà shi yìzhǒng wénxué chǎnwù."

40.0. tiánchǎn landed property (W) [field produce]

40.1. Tā méi yǒu tiánchǎn, jiu yǒu yìsuǒ fángzi.

41.0. fánrǎo (1) annoy, disturb, unsettle; (2) annoyance, disturbance (W) [troublesome disturb]

41.1. Tā xiězuò de shíhou jiu pà yǒu rén lái fánrǎo. (W)

42.0. wúyíde unquestionably, doubtless (W)

42.1. Jù kǎogǔjiāde pànduàn, nèijiàn yùqì wúyíde shi Táng Cháode dōngxi. (W)

43.0. yǒngjìn inundate, enter like a flood (W) [inundate enter]

43.1. Zuótian kāi yīnyuèhuìde shíhou hěn duō méi yǒu piàode rén cóng chūkǒude mén yǒngjìnlai le.

44.0. cháoshuǐ tide [tide water]

44.1. Nèige hǎibiān měitiān wǎnshang cháoshuǐ hěn dà. Wǒ cháng qu kàn.

45.0. zhuǎnlìdiǎn, zhuǎnlièdiǎn turning point [revolve twist point]

45.1. Nèige guójiā biànchéng qiángguó de zhuǎnlǐdiǎn shi shíxíngle mín-
       zhǔ.   (T)

140 Bái: Tiánchǎn shi shénmo yìsi?

    Mǎ : Tiánchǎn jiu shi kéyi zhòngtián de tǔdì jiào tiánchǎn. Xiànzài qǐng
         nǐ yòng fánrǎo shuō yíge xiě de jùzi.

    Bái: "Wǒ jiā zhù de dìfang hěn qīngjìng, méi yǒu chē mǎ zhī fánrǎo."

    Mǎ : Zhèige jùzi yàoshi shuō huà yīnggāi zěnmo shuō?

145 Bái: Yàoshi shuō huà jiu shi: "Wǒ jiā zhù de nèige dìfang fēicháng
         qīngjìng, yòu méi yǒu chē, yòu méi yǒu mǎ, yìdiǎr shēngyīn yě
         méi yǒu."

    Mǎ : Duìle.

    Bái: Wúyíde jiu shi kǒuyǔshang méi wèntí de huòzhě shi yídìng de.

150 Mǎ : Shì.

    Bái: Yǒngjìn yě shi xiě de ba?

    Mǎ : Shì xiě de. Wǒ jǔ ge lìzi: "Nèige zhǔyì xiàng cháoshuǐ shide yǒng-
         jìnle nèige guójiā."

    Bái: Zhuǎnlǐdiǎn zěnmo yòng?

155 Mǎ: Zhuǎnlǐdiǎn zài kǒuyǔshang shuō shi "zhuǎnbiàn de nèige shíhou."
         Wǒ jǔ ge lìzi: "Jiǎ、Yǐ liǎngge guójiā dǎqi zhàng lai le. Kāishǐ
         shi Jiǎ guó dǎbài le, Yǐ guó dǎshèng le. Hòulai Jiǎ guó yòu zhuǎn
         bài wéi shèng." Nèige zuìchūde zhuǎn bài wéi shèng de shíhou jiu
         shi zhuǎnlǐdiǎn.

160 Bái: Wǒ míngbai le.

46.0. dǎdǎo   (1) knock down, overturn; (2) Down with . . . ! [hit topple]

      dǎdǎo Kǒng jiā diàn!   Down with Confucianism! (See note 2)

46.1. Yào géxīn zhèngzhi bǐděi dǎdǎo guānliáo.

46.2. "Dǎdǎo Kǒng jiā diàn!" jiu shi bú zànchéng Kǒngzǐ xuéshuò de yìsi.

47.0. jūnfá   militarist, warlord [army clique]

47.1. Cóngqián Zhōngguo jūnfáde shìli hěn dà. Xiànzài méi yǒu jūnfá le.

48.0. huódong   (1) movable; (2) active; (3) flourishing; (4) activity [live
                move]

48.1. Tā cónglái bù cānjiā zhèngzhi huódong.

49.0. fǎnkàng   (1) oppose; (2) opposition [reverse resist]

49.1. Fǎnkàng jiu shi fǎnduì hé dǐkàng de yìsi.

50.0. mínzhǔ zhǔyì   democracy

shèhuì zhǔyì   socialism

gòngchǎn zhǔyì   communism

50.1. Mínzhǔ zhǔyìde guójiā shi yǐ duōshù rénmínde yìsi wéi zhǔ.   (W)
(T)

50.2. Xiànzài yǒu duōshao guójiā shi shèhuì zhǔyìde guójiā?

50.3. Gòngchǎn zhǔyì shì bu shi cóng wàiguo chuánrù Zhōngguo de?

Bái: Cóngqián xuéshengmende àiguó yùndong cháng yòng "dǎdǎo" zhèige
cér, shì bu shi?

Mǎ : Nà shi Wǔsì yǐhòu xuéshengmen àiguó yùndong chángcháng yòng de
cér.

165 Bái: Tīngshuō jūnfá shídài xuésheng zuò zhèngzhi huódong, yǒu bù shǎode
xuésheng sǐ le.

Mǎ : Shìde. Wǒ fùqin yǒu yíge tóngxué, tā jiu shi yíge xǐhuan zuò zhèngzhi huódong de rén. Tā bǎ gōngke fàngzai yìbiār, zhěngtiānde dōu
shi chūqu xuānchuán jiùguó. Jiéguǒ dāngshí zhízhèng de shuō ta
170   fǎnkàng zhèngfǔ, hái shuō ta shi Gòngchǎndǎng, xuānchuán gòngchǎn
zhǔyì, bǎ ta gěi shā le. Qíshí tā bìng bú shi.

51.0. xīshōu   absorb [whole receive]

51.1. Zài Sānmín Zhǔyìli yě xīshōule Xīfāngde xīn sīxiǎng.

52.0. Mǎkesī   Marx

52.1. Yǒu rén shuō Mǎkesī shi gòngchǎn zhǔyìde shǐzǔ.

53.0. Lièníng   Lenin

53.1. Nǐ yánjiuguo Lièníng suǒ xiě de gòngchǎn zhǔyī ma?

54.0. gémìng   (1) to revolt; (2) revolution [change fate]

54.1. Fàguo dà gémìng shi lìshǐshangde yíjiàn dàshì.

55.0. lǐngxiù   leader [collar sleeve]

55.1. Lièníng shi Sūlián gémìng de lǐngxiù.

Mǎ : Zhōngguo rén zài shénmo shíhou jiu xīshōule Mǎkesī gēn Lièníng
zhǔyì?

Bái: Zhōngguo zài Wǔsì Yùndong qiánhòu jiu xīshōule zhèige zhǔyì.

175 Mǎ : Zhōngguo Gòngchǎndǎng zài Yán'ān de shíqī gémìng lǐngxiù shi shéi?

Bái: Shi Máo Zédōng.

Mǎ : Gòngchǎndǎng zhèngfǔ yuánlái zài shénmo dìfang?

Bái: Yuánlái zài Yán'ān.

56.0. wéiwùlùn   materialism [only object ism]

56.1. Wéiwùlùn shi gòngchăn zhŭyî zhŭyàode lĭlùn zhī yī.

57.0. Shĭdàlín   Stalin

57.1. Shĭdàlín bĕnlái shi yánjiu zōngjiào de. Hòulai yòu chéngle Măke-
      sīde xìntú le.

58.0. zuòfēng   behavior, style of work [do wind]

58.1. Wŏmen yīngdāng xuéxi mínzhŭ zuòfēng. (T)

59.0. biàndong   (1) to change, alter; (2) change, re-arrangement; (3) ex-
      citement [change move]

59.1. Xīn xiàozhăng láile yĭhòu, xuéxiàoli yíqiè méi yŏu hĕn dàde biàn-
      dong.

      Mă : Nĭ zhīdao bu zhīdào shéi shi wéiwùlùn zhèizhŏng xuéshuōde xìntú?
180 Bái: Măkesī、 Lièníng gēn Shĭdàlín dōu shi zhèizhŏng xuéshuōde xìntú.

      Mă : Shĭdàlín zài shénmo shíhou zuò Sūliánde zhèngzhi lĭngxiù?

      Bái: Shĭdàlín zài yī-jiŭ-èr-wŭ niàn zuŏyòu dào yī-jiŭ-wŭ-sān nián shi
            Sūliánde zhèngzhi lĭngxiù.

      Mă : Tāde zhèngzhi zuòfēng gēn xiànzài gòngchăndăng zhèngzhi lĭngxiù
185   shì bu shi xiāngtóng?

      Bái: Yŏu rén shuō tāmen zhèngzhi yuánzé méi yŏu shénmo găibiàn, yĕ
            yŏu rén shuō yŏu hĕn dàde biàndong.

60.0. shèngxíng   (1) flourishing; (2) practice extensively (W) [flourishing
      walk]

60.1. Yùnwén zài Wèi Jìn liăngcháo hĕn shèngxíng. (W)

61.0. shūrù   import (N/V) (W) [transport enter]

61.1. Nèixiē Xīshì mùqî dōu shi zài bĕndì zuò de, bú shi cóng wàiguo
      shūrù de. (W)

62.0. chùlĭ   (1) dispose (of), deal with; (2) disposition [dispose arrange]

62.1. Chùlĭ nèijiàn shìqingde bànfă tā xiăngde bĭ wŏ hái yào hăo. (T)

      Bái: Shèngxíng zhèige cér shi shuō de ma?

      Mă : Duōshù shi xiĕ de. Wŏ jŭ ge lìzi. "Jìnlái shèngxíng yìzhŏng qí-
190   guàizhī tiàowŭ."

      Bái: Shūrù yĕ shi xiĕ de ma?

      Mă : Shìde. Bĭrú "Jīdūjiào shūrù Zhōngguo zài shénmo shíqī?" Yàoshi
            shuō huà shi "Jīdūjiào chuándào Zhōngguo lai shi zài shénmo shí-
            hou?"

32.1. This <u>Comprehensive Collection of Poems and Songs</u> centers around the <u>Book of Odes.</u>

34.1. China's honoring Confucius as a sage started in the Han Dynasty.

35.1. Chinese [play] actors honor the Illustrious Emperor of T'ang as a founding father.

37.1. There's a famous novel in China which tells the story of a man going to the western regions in search of the Buddhist scriptures.

45.1. The turning point in that country's becoming a great power was its putting democracy into practice.

50.1. Countries (based on the principle) of democracy place the greatest emphasis on the opinions of the majority of the people.

58.1. After the new principal came there were no great changes in the school.

62.1. He thought of a better way than I to handle that matter.

NOTES

1. In the expression <u>rénzhě rén yě</u>, which is written in the classical literary style, the pattern is "A zhě B yě," meaning "A is B." This pattern is used frequently in definitions. The thing defined is signaled by a following zhě, which can be considered as somewhat equivalent to quotation marks or italics. The definition is signaled by a following ye, which in the literary style functions as a final particle. Thus <u>rénzhě rén yě</u> may be rendered as "<u>rén</u> is man," or, more freely, "The term <u>rén</u> means 'man.'"

2. One of the slogans of the May Fourth Movement was Dǎdǎo Kǒng Jiā diàn! "Down with Confucianism!" <u>Kǒng Jiā diàn</u> is a contemptuous reference to Confucianism; it literally means 'the shop of the Kong family.'

3. The following miscellaneous usages are illustrated in the exercise <u>Yǔfǎ Liànxí</u> in this lesson:

   a (1-2). N_1 méi yǒu N_2 bù/méi V 'There isn't any N_2 that N_1 doesn't/hasn't V':

   > Tā méi yǒu yíge dìfang méi qùguo. 'There isn't any place he hasn't been to.'

   b (3-4). dàole . . . cái V 'didn't V until . . . ':

   > Dàole Qīng Cháo mònián cái yǒu Zhōngguo rén dào wàiguo liúxué. 'Chinese didn't go abroad to study until the last years of the Ch'ing Dynasty.'

   c (5-6). yào dào . . . cái V 'will not V until . . . ':

   > Yào dào míngnian wǒ cái néng dào Zhōngguo qu. 'I won't be able to go to China until next year.'

   d (7-8). yào xiān V_1 cái néng V_2 'One can only V_2 after V_1':

   > Nǐ yào xiān zuò gōngke cái néng qu wár. 'You can't go out to play until you've done your lessons.'

e (9-10). zènmo Vqilai 'in so V-ing, V-ing in this way, from what is V'd':

Zènmo xuéqilai nǐ hěn kuài jiu huì le. 'By studying in this way you will master it very quickly.'

f (11-12). xiàng N$_1$ V de N$_2$ 'an N$_2$ who/which V's like N$_1$':

Xiàng tā nènmo néng zuò shì de rén hěn shǎo. 'People who can handle things like him are rare.'

g (13-14). Vde xiàng N$_1$ SVde N$_2$ 'an N$_2$ who/which V's as SV as V':

Shuōde xiàng tā nènmo hǎode wàiguo xuésheng hěn shǎo. 'There are very few foreign students who can speak as well as he does.'

h (15-16). lái N 'bring N, cause N to come' (See Intermediate Chinese, p. 122, note 3):

Zài lái yìwǎn fàn. 'Bring another bowl of rice.'

i (17-20). SV + V (e. g. hǎo chī 'good to eat,' hǎo mǎi 'easy to buy'):

Wǒde qián bú gòu yòng. 'I don't have enough money [to use].'

Dì-Èrshiyīkè. Jīngji

Bái: Mǎ Jiàoshòu zǎo.

Mǎ: Zǎo. Jīntian hěn rè.

Bái: Kěbushìma! Jīntian kěnéng yǒu jiǔshijǐdù. Qián jǐtiān nènmo lěng, zhèi liǎngtiān yòu zhènmo rè.

5 Mǎ: Wǒ nèiren qiántian bǎ rè tiānde yīfu dōu shōuqilai le, zuótian yòu dōu náchulai le.

Bái: Wǒ yě shì. Wǒ yǐwei bú huì zài rè le, bǎ rè tiān chuān de yīfu yě dōu shōuqilai le. Jīntian zǎoshang wǒ chuānle Xuéxīn yíjiàn yīfu.

10 Mǎ: Xuéxīn jìnlái zěnmoyàng?

Bái: Xuéxīn hěn hǎo. Huá jia zhèi liǎngtiān dōu bú zài jiā. Tāmen yǒu yíge qīnqi jiēhūn qǐng tāmen quán jiā qù le. Qīnqi jiāli lí zhèr hěn yuǎn, suǒyǐ tāmen děi zài nèr zhù jǐtiān.

Mǎ: Jiù nǐ yíge rén zài jiāli hěn qīngjìng, zhèng hǎo yònggōng.

15 Bái: Qīngjìng dàoshi hěn qīngjìng, búguò yǒu diar jìmo.

Mǎ: Zhèi liǎngtiān dōu kàn shénmo shū le?

Bái: Wǒ kànle diar lìshǐ. Wǒ kàn <u>Zhōngguo Xiàndài Shǐ</u>.

Mǎ: Kànwánle ma?

Bái: Kànwán le. Wǒ shi xiàng kàn xiǎoshuō shide kànle yíbiàn.

20 Mǎ: Nǐ shi cóng nǎr kànqi de?

Bái: Cóng Wǔsì xuésheng àiguó yùndong, fǎnkàng jūnfá, xuésheng bèi shā, yìzhí dào guómín zhèngfǔ zài Nánjīng chénglì.

Mǎ: Zhèi jǐtiān wǒ yě zài jiā kàn shū.

Bái: Nín kàn de shi guānyu něi yìfāngmiànde shū?

25 Mǎ: Wǒ kàn de shi yíge péngyou xiě de, shi guānyu Zhōngguo wénhuà yìfāngmiàn de. Wǒ dàilai le. Nǐ méi shì de shíhou kéyi kànkan.

Bái: Zhèiběn shū duì wǒ xiě lùnwén, guānyu wénhuà yìfāngmiàn yídìng yǒu hěn duō cānkǎo de zīliào.

Mǎ: Tā xiě de hěn xiángxì. Tā bǎ Zhōngguo rén yuányǒude dàodé gēn
30 zōngjiào、sīxiǎng dōu xiě le.

Bái: Nín zhèiwei péngyou xiànzài zài nǎr ne?

Mǎ: Tā zài Rìběn ne. Qián jǐtiān jiēdào tāde xìn, tā shuō tā zuìjìn dào Ōuzhōu qu lǚxíng qu, kěnéng bù jiǔ dào zhèr lái cānguān gè dàxué.

Bái: Jiānglái xīwang yǒu jīhui jiànzhe ta.

459

35 Mǎ : Tā láile wǒ yídìng gěi nǐ jièshao.

    Bái : Hǎode. Jīntian Zhuāntí Jiǎnghuà jiǎng jīngji, shì bu shì?

    Mǎ : Shìde. Zhèizhāng shēngcí biǎo gěi ni. Wǒmen bǎ cér yánjiu yán-
         jiu.

    Bái : Zhèicìde cér yídìng yǒu hěn duō wǒ bù dǒng de. Wǒ xiǎng guānyu
40   jīngji yìfāngmiànde zhuānmén míngcí, yídìng yǒu hěn duō.

    Mǎ : Yě bújiànde nǐ bù dǒng.

    1.0. péngzhàng   (1) swell, expand, inflate; (2) expanded, swollen [swol-
                       len distended]

    1.1. Rènhé dōngxi yǐ rè de shíhou yídìng yào péngzhàng de.

    2.0. tōnghuò   money, currency (W) [penetrate commodity]

          tōnghuò péngzhàng   (1) (currency) inflation; (2) undergo inflation

    2.1. Zhèngfǔ fāxíng de zhǐbì rúguǒ méi yǒu xiànzhi jiu yào fāshēng
          tōnghuò tài duō de wèntí le.

    2.2. Tōnghuò tài duō zài jīngjixuéshang jiu jiàozuo <u>tōnghuò péngzhàng</u>.

    3.0. huòbì   currency (W) [commodity currency]

    3.1. Cóngqiánde huòbì duōshù shi jīn、yín hé tóng. Xiànzàide huòbì dà
          duōshù shi zhǐbì. (W)

    4.0. wùjià   commodity prices [article price]

    4.1. Yīnwei wùjià yìtiān bǐ yìtiān gāo suǒyǐ shēnghuó yìtiān bǐ yìtiān
          kùnnán.

    5.0. zhǎng   swell, distend

          zhǎngjià   increase in price (N/V) [swell price]

          gāozhǎng   (1) rise, surge up; (2) a rise, an upsurge (W) [high swell]

    5.1. "Shuǐ zhǎng chuán gāo" shi Zhōngguo yíjù súhuà, yìsi shi shuō,
          shuǐ rúguǒ zhǎngde hěn gāo, zài shuǐshangde chuán yě jiu gāoqilai
          le.

    5.2. Zhèi jǐtiān rìyòngpǐn quándōu zhǎngjià le.

    5.3. Yǔ xiàde tài dà le, suǒyǐ héshuǐ gāozhǎng. (W)

    Bái : <u>Péngzhàng</u> zhèige cér shi wùlǐxuéshang yòng de cér, shì bu shi?

    Mǎ : Zài jīngjishang yě cháng yòng. Bǐrú "tōnghuò péngzhàng."

    Bái : <u>Tōnghuò</u> shi shénmo?

45 Mǎ : <u>Tōnghuò</u> shi <u>huòbì</u>, jiu shi qián. Bàozhǐshang guānyu jīngjide xiāo-
         xi cháng yǒu "jìnlái tōnghuò péngzhàng, wùjià gāozhǎng."

    Bái : Shìde. Wǒ zài <u>Dà Huá Rìbào</u>shang guānyu jīngjide nèi yíyèshang
         kànjianguo zhèixiē jùzi.

6.0. wěndìng   stable, stabilized [steady definite]

6.1. Zhànshíde wùjià duōbàn shi bù wěndìng de.

7.0. fùdān   (1) bear a burden; (2) a burden [bear load]

7.1. Wǒ jiāde rénkǒu hěn duō. Jiù wǒ yíge rén gōngzuò yǎng jiā. Wǒde fùdān tài zhòng le.

8.0. hǔnluàn   confusion, chaos [mix disordered]

8.1. Jìn Cháo mònián shi Zhōngguo lìshǐshang zuì hǔnluànde shíqī.

9.0. bēngkuì   collapse (N/V) [collapse break down]

9.1. Tōnghuò búduànde péngzhàng wúyìde jīngji jiu yào bēngkuì le. (W) (T)

Bái: Mǎ Jiàoshòu, cóng Mínguó yǐhòu, Zhōngguo zài jīngji yìfāngmiàn
50   shénmo shíhou zuì wěndìng?

Mǎ : Wǒ jìde cóng Mínguó chūnián dào Kàngzhàn yǐqián, wùjià yìfāng-
     miàn hái suàn wěndìng. Zhǐyú zhěnggède jīngji bù wěndìng. Zài
     Kàngzhàn de shíhou, zhèngfǔ zēngjiāle fùdān bùdébù duō yìn piàozi,
     suǒyǐ dōngxi nòngde yuè lái yuè guì le, wùjià yě bù wěndìng le.

55 Bái: Zhōngguo nèizhànde shíqī tīngshuō jīngjide qíngxing fēicháng hǔn-
     luàn.

Mǎ : Suǒyǐ hòulái jīngji bēngkuì le.

10.0. cáizhèng   finances, administration of finances [wealth politics]

10.1. Cáizhèng hé jīngji yǒu mìqiède guānxi.

11.0. guóji   international [country interval]

11.1. Wǒ kàn bàozhǐ xiān kàn guóji dàshì.

12.0. màoyì   trade, commerce [commerce change]

12.1. Xiàndài guójiā dōu hěn zhùyì duì wàiguode màoyì.   (T)

13.0. zhèngcè   (administrative) policy [politics policy]

13.1. Yǒu hěn duō rén gōngji xiànzàide jiàoyu zhèngcè.

14.0. zīběn   capital [resources capital]

     zīběnjiā   capitalist

     zīběn zhǔyì   capitalism

14.1. Zhāng Xiānsheng shi yíge dà zīběnjiā, zài hěn duō shíyè gōngsīli
     dōu yǒu tāde zīběn.

14.2. Yǒude zīběn zhǔyi guójiā jīngji fāzhǎn de jiéguǒ shi gōngren hěn
     kǔ, zīběnjiā dédào hěn dàde lìyì.

Bái: Wǒ zài túshūguǎn kànjian yìběn <u>Cáizhèng yǔ Jīngji Wèntí</u>.

Mǎ: Shi shéi biān de?

60   Bái: Shūshang yìnzhe "Zhōu Dàwéi biānzhù."

Mǎ: Nèiróng nǐ kànle ma?

Bái: Méi yǒu. Wǒ jiù kànle mùlù le. Yǒu "Zhōngguo Guóji Màoyi zhī Zhèngcè, Zīběn Zhǔyì Guójiāde Gōng-Shāngyè Gàikuàng" děngděng.

Mǎ: Zhōu Dàwéi Jiàoshòu shi xiànzài yǒumíngde jīngjixuéjiā. Tā zhèi-
65   běn shū yǒu hěn duō yánjiu jīngji de názhe zuò cānkǎo.

Bái: Wǒ cóng túshūguǎn jièlái le. Yǒu shíjiān kànyikàn.

Mǎ: Súyǔ shuō "kāi-juàn-yǒu-yì."

Bái: Yào chōngshí zìjǐ, gèfāngmiànde zhīshi dōu yīnggāi xīshōu.

15.0. hángyè   shipping industry [sail enterprise]

15.1. Fāzhǎn hángyè shi Zhōngguo jīngji zhèngcè zhī yī. (T)

16.0. huīfu   recover, revive [recover return]

16.1. Wǒ xiànzài tiāntiān hé xuéshengmen zài yìqǐ, wǒ yòu huīfu xué-sheng shídàide shēnghuó le.

17.0. huòwu   (articles of) merchandise [commodity article]

17.1. Qùnián zhèli chūkǒu de huòwu bǐ jìnkǒu de duō.

18.0. shìchǎng   market, marketplace [market arena]

18.1. Yīnwei yǒu dàliàng huòwu yǒngjìn shìchǎng, suǒyǐ wùjià jìnlái bù zhǎng le. (W)

19.0. jīxiè   (1) machinery; (2) mechanical, machine

19.1. Yǒude guójiā zài nóngyè fāngmiàn hái yòng rénlì, yǒude guójiā yǐ-jing jīxièhuà le. (T)

Mǎ: Nǐ zhīdao bu zhīdào, zài Yǎzhōude guójiāli, něige guójiāde hángyè
70   zuì fādá?

Bái: Rìběnde hángyè zuì fādá. Kěshi zài dì-èrcì dàzhàn yǐhòu, yǒu yíge duǎn shíqī bù xíng, dànshi bù jiǔ yòu huīfu le.

Mǎ: Rìběn zhànhòu búdàn hángyè huīfu le, jìnlái jīngji yě fánróngde bù-déliǎo.

75   Bái: Rìběnde huòwu chūkǒude hěn duō, shì bu shi?

Mǎ: Shì. Nǐ kàn bàozhǐshangde Shāngyè Tōngxùn, shìjiè gèguóde shì-chǎngshang dōu yǒu Rìběn huò.

Bái: Jùshuō Rìběn zài jīxiè yìfāngmiàn yě hěn fādá.

Mǎ: Rìběnde zhòng gōngyè、qīng gōngyè dōu bù luòhòu.

20.0. kuàng   (1) a mine; (2) ore

kuàngyè   mining industry

kuàngchǎn   mineral product, mineral production

20.1. Shānxi Shěng shénmo kuàng zuì duō, nǐ zhǐdao ma?

20.2. Yòu méi yǒu shuǐ, yòu méi yǒu diàn, zhèlide kuàngyè zěnmo néng fāzhǎn?

20.3. Zhōngguo dì-dà-wù-bó, dìlǐ yǒu hěn duō kuàngchǎn.

21.0. shíyóu   petroleum [store oil]

21.1. Gānsu Shěng chūchǎn shíyóu shi jìnlái fāxiàn de ma?

22.0. méi   coal

22.1. Méide yòngchu hěn duō, yóuqíshi zài gōngyè fāngmiàn.

23.0. gāngtiě   iron and steel [steel iron]

gāngtiěchǎng   iron and steel mill

23.1. Zhōngguo Dōngběi yǒu yíge dà gāngtiěchǎng, měinián shēngchǎn de gāngtiě zhàn quánguóde dì-yīwèi.

24.0. kāifā   (1) develop; (2) development [open emit]

24.1. Fēizhōu hái yǒu méi kāifā de dìfang ma?

80 Mǎ : Wǒmen xiànzài tántan guānyu Zhōngguode kuàngchǎn. Qǐng wèn ni, Zhōngguo chū shíyóude dìfang dōu zài nǎr?

Bái: Xīnjiāng、Gānsu dōu chū shíyóu.

Mǎ : Shénmo dìfang chū méi zuì duō ne?

Bái: Dōngběi、Héběi、Shānxi chūchǎn de zuì duō.

85 Mǎ : Nǐ zhǐdao shénmo dìfang chūchǎn gāngtiě?

Bái: Zhōngguode Dōngběi chū gāngtiě, Sìchuān gēn Héběi yě yǒu tiěkuàng.

Mǎ : Duìle.

Bái: Zhōngguo dì-dà-wù-bó, xiāngxìn yǒu hěn duō kuàngchǎn děngzhe kāifā ne?

90 Mǎ : Nǐ shuōde yìdiǎr yě bú cuò.

25.0. chūchǎnpǐn   products

nóngchǎnpǐn   agricultural products, crops

25.1. Nèige gāngtiěchǎngde chūchǎnpǐn shi quánguó zuì hǎo de.

25.2. Qiūtian shi nóngchǎnpǐn chéngshú de shíhou.

26.0. miánhua   cotton [cotton flower]

26.1. Zhòng miánhua zhǎng chóngzi shi yíge dà wèntí. (T)

27.0. fǎngzhī   (1) spin and weave; (2) textile

27.1. Zhōngguo cóng gǔlái jiu zhùzhòng fǎngzhī. Nà shíhou nánde yào
      zhòng dì, nǔde yào fǎngzhī.

28.0. bèi   times, -fold (M)

28.1. Jīnnián nèige xiǎoxué yòuzhìyuánde xuésheng bǐ qùnián zēngjiāle
      yíbèi. (T)

29.0. fēnpèi   divide up, distribute, ration [divide fit]

      pèiji   to ration [fit give]

29.1. Dǎzhàn de shíhou liángshi gēn rìyòngpǐn duōbàn shi yóu zhèngfǔ
      pèiji. Yīnwei dōngxi shǎo rén duō hěn bù róngyi fēnpèi.

30.0. gōngyìng   furnish, supply [supply respond]

30.1. Xiānggǎng rénmín chī de shuǐ, duōbàn shi yóu dàlù gōngyìngde.

Bái: Qǐng wen Mǎ Jiàoshòu, nóngchǎnpǐnlide miánhua Zhōngguo chūchǎn-
      de duō bu duō?

Mǎ : Chūchǎnde bù shǎo.

Bái: Zhōngguo fǎngzhī gōngyède qíngxing zěnmoyàng?

95 Mǎ : Zài zhànqián Zhōngguode fǎngzhī gōngyè jiu hěn fādá, jùshuō xiàn-
      zài bǐ yǐqián gèng fādá.   Bǐfang shuō bùde shēngchǎn bǐ yǐqián
      zēngjiāle jǐbèi.

Bái: Shuōdào fǎngzhī wǒ xiǎngqilai yíge wèntí. Shì bu shi zài Kàngzhàn
      de shíhou mǎi bù dōu shi pèiji?

100 Mǎ : Yǒude shíhou zài gōngyìngshang pà bú gòu, jiu ànzhe rénkǒu pèiji.

31.0. shìhé   suited (to), suitable [fit suitable]

31.1. Zài jīngjishang shuō nèizhǒng zhèngcè zài xiàndài shi bú shìhé le.
      (T)

32.0. mùxùyè   pastoral industry, animal husbandry [pasture keep enter-
                 prise]

32.1. Zhèige dìfang jiù chū cǎo, zhǐ shìhé mùxùyè. (T)

33.0. féiliào   fertilizer [fat materials]

33.1. Zhèizhǒng huàxué féiliào shi cóng guówài mǎilái de. (T)

33.2. Wǎng tiánli fàng féiliào zuì hǎode shíhou shi xiàguo yǔ yǐhòu. (T)

34.0. jīqi   machine, machinery [mechanism, tool]

34.1. Yìnshuā jīqi shi shéi chuàngshǐ de? (W)

35.0. tuōlājī   tractor [drag pull mechanism]

195 Bái: <u>Jūn</u> jiu shi <u>xiānsheng</u>de yìsi me? Wǒ kànjian yǒu rén xiě de
dōngxishang yǒu "Zhāng Jūn、Wáng Jūn、Mǎ Jūn."

Mǎ : Duìle. Jiu shi "Zhāng Xiānsheng、Wáng Xiānsheng、Mǎ Xiānsheng"
de yìsi. Hái yǒu <u>jūnzǐ</u> jiu shi <u>hǎorén</u>de yìsi. Bǐrú chùlǐ shìqing
hěn gōngpíng, bù jiānzhà, bú zuò huàishì jiu shi jūnzǐ.

SHĒNGCÍ BIǍO

1. Jīdūjiào
2. Tiānzhǔjiào
3. Jǐngjiào
4. xìnjiào
    chuánjiào
5. shénfù
6. Lì Mǎdòu
7. chuánrù (W)
8. tú*
    xìntú
9. mùshi
10. shìli
11. guānliáo
12. zūn
    zūnzhòng
    zūnchóng
13. dàodé
    <u>Dàodé Jīng</u>
14. zhuānzhì
15. xìn-shǎng-bì-fá (W)
16. yǐ-fǎ-zhì-guó (W)
17. Fǎjiā
    Mòjiā
18. Hán Fēizǐ
19. jūn
    jūnzǐ
    Shāng Jūn
20. jiān'ài
21. gōngji
22. dào

    Dàojiā
    Dàojiào
23. shǐzǔ
24. qīngjìng
25. wúwéi
    qīngjìng wúwéi (W)
    wúwéi ér zhǐ (W)
26. lún*
    wǔlún
27. chén
    jūnchén
28. fùzǐ
29. fūfù
30. fēngjiàn
31. zhū-zǐ-bǎi-jiā
32. zhǔtǐ
33. rén
34. shèng(rén)
35. fèng (W)
36. sì
37. Fójīng
38. chuàngshǐ (W)
39. chǎnwù (W)
40. tiánchǎn (W)
41. fánrǎo (W)
42. wúyíde (W)
43. yǒngjìn (W)
44. cháoshuǐ
45. zhuǎnlìdiǎn,

    zhuǎnlièdiǎn
46. dǎdǎo
    dǎdǎo Kǒng jiā
    diàn!
47. jūnfá
48. huódong
49. fǎnkàng
50. mínzhǔ zhǔyì
    shèhuì zhǔyì
    gòngchǎn zhǔyì
51. xīshōu
52. Mǎkesī
53. Lièníng
54. gémìng
55. lǐngxiù
56. wéiwùlùn
57. Shǐdàlín
58. zuòfēng
59. biàndong
60. shèngxíng (W)
61. shūrù (W)
62. chùlǐ

YŬFĂ LIÀNXÍ

(See note 3)

1. Tāde sīxiǎng hěn qiánjìn. Tā méi yǒu yìtiān bu gēn biéren tǎolùn shèhuì zhǔyì de.

2. Tā shi yánjiu gǔdài wénxué de. Tā zhǐ yào kànjian Chūnqiū、Zuǒ Zhuàn gēn Guóyǔ, nǎpà shi jiàqian hěn guì tā yě méi yǒu yìběn bù mǎi de.

3. Jiǎn mùshi zuòtian gēn wǒ yánjiu Lúnyǔ gēn Rúlín Wàishǐ. Tā shi zǎochen lái de, dàole yèlǐ shídiǎn zhōng cái zǒu de.

4. Zuótian wǎnshang nèige yīnyuè yǎnzòuhuì dàole yèlǐ yìdiǎn zhōng cái wán de.

5. Nèige yīnyuè xuéyuànde xuésheng yào dào èrniánjí cái xué zuòqǔfǎ.

6. Zhèige dìfang yào dào shínián yǐhòu jīngji cái néng fánróngqilai.

7. Nǐ rúguǒ xiǎng dào nèige dìfang qu chuánjiào, nǐ yào xiān xué nèige dìfangde yǔyán cái néng dào nèr qù. Yàoburán nǐ zěnmo duì nèige dìfangde rén chuánjiào ne?

8. Rúguǒ nǐ xiǎng cānjiā nèige Fójiào tuántǐ, tāmende bànfa shi nǐ yào xiān xué Fójīng nǐ cái nénggou cānjiā.

9. Zhènmo kànqilai tā duì piàntǐwén hěn yǒu yánjiu.

10. Nǐ shuō nǐ xuéguo diāokè. Zhènmo shuōqilai nǐ yě huì shíkè le.

11. Zài jūnfá lǐmiàn, xiàng Hú Dàwéi nèiyàng yǒu xuéwen de tài shǎo le.

12. Xiàng Mǎ Xiānsheng zhèiyàng zhùzhòng jiù dàodéde rén, zài zhèige niándài yǒu duōshao!

13. Xiànzài zuò fùmǔ de, zuò de xiàng Wáng Xiānsheng fūfù duì érnǚ nènmo zhuānzhì de hěn shǎo.

14. Yánjiu Chǔcí, yánjiu de xiàng nèiwèi Měiguo jiàoshòu nènmo hǎo de zài wàiguo rénli kǒngpà méi yǒu jǐge rén.

15. Lǎo Wáng, lí hái yǒu méi yǒu le? Wǒ zài lái yíge lí chéng bu chéng?

16. Zuótian wǎnhuì biǎoyǎn de shi wǔtáijù. Nèiwèi nǚ tóngxué biǎoyǎn de fēicháng jīngcǎi, yǎnwánle yǐhòu dàjiā dōu shuō: "Zài lái yíge."

17. Xiànzài yòng yù diāokè de dōngxi hěn shǎo, hěn nán mǎi.

18. Dàojiāde dàolǐ hěn bu hǎo dǒng, suǒyǐ yánjiu de rén fēicháng shǎo.

19. Jīnnián Xīyáng yuèqì cóng wàiguo láide hěn duō, fēicháng hǎo mǎi.

20. Lǎo Zhāng fùzǐ liǎngge rén dōu shi shíkè gōngren. Fùzǐ liǎngge měi yíge yuède gōngqián gāng gòu chī.

JIĂNGHUÀ

Zhūwèi tóngxué:

    Jīntian jiǎnghuà de tímu shi Zhōngguode sīxiǎng hé zōngjiào.

Zhèige tímu hé zhéxué hěn yǒu guānxi, suǒyǐ yě kéyi shuō shi yě shuōdao zhéxué.

5   Zhōngguode sīxiǎng hé zōngjiào ànzhe qǐyuán lái shuō kéyi fēnwéi
liǎngfāngmiàn. Dî-yī shi qǐyuán zài Zhōngguo, dì-èr shi cóng wàiguode
shūrù. Qǐyuán zài Zhōngguo de duōshù fāshēng zài gōngyuánqián wǔshí-
jǐ、sìshíjǐ de shíhou. Nà shíhou zhèng shi Zhōu Cháo mònián Chūnqiū
Zhànguó shídài. Yīnwei shèhuìshangde biàndong tài dà, suǒyǐ rénmende
sīxiǎng yě hěn huódong, "zhū-zǐ-bǎi-jiā" gè yǒu gède sīxiǎng, gè yǒu
10 gède xuéshuō. Qízhōng zuì zhǔyàode xuéshuō shi Rújiā、Dàojiā hái yǒu
Fǎjiā gēn Mòjiā.

      Rújiāde xuéshuō shi yǐ Kǒngzǐ hé Mèngzǐde xuéshuō wéi zhǔtí. Tā-
mende zhǔzhāng shi "rén." Shénmo jiàozuo "rén" ne? Zhōngguo gǔshūshang shuō "Rén zhě rén yě."* Jiù shi gàosu rén zěnyàng zuò rén, ye
15 jiù shi shuō rén yīngdāng dǒngde zuò rénde dàolǐ. Rújiā bǎ rén duì rén
de gèzhǒng gèyàngde guānxi fēnchéng wǔlèi, jiàozuo wǔlún. Wǔlún shi
jūnchén、fùzǐ、fūfù、xiōngdì、péngyou. Rén rúguǒ bǎ zhèi wǔlúnde guānxi
chǔlǐde hěn hǎo, nènmo jiu shi zuò rén zuì lǐxiǎngde le. Zhōngguo cóng
Hàn Cháo yǐlái yìzhí dàole Qīng Cháo mònián, dōu shi Rújiāde xuéshuō
20 zuì shòu zūnzhòng. Rújiāde shū xiàng <u>Lúnyǔ</u>、<u>Mèngzǐ</u> děngděng chéngle
dú shū rén bì dú de shū, shènzhì zūnchóng Kǒngzǐ、Mèngzǐ wéi shèngrén. Kějiàn Rújiāde xuéshuō zài guòqu shi zhàn zhòngyào dìwei de.

      Dàojiāde xuéshuō shi Lǎozǐde xuéshuō. Hòulái yòu yǒu Zhuāngzǐ.
Lǎozǐ hé Kǒngzǐ shi tóngshíde rén. Tāde sīxiǎng hé Kǒngzǐ bùtóng.
25 Lǎozǐ xiěle yíbù shū jiào <u>Dàodé Jīng</u>, shi yíbù gāoshēnde zhéxué. Lǎozǐde zhǔzhāng shi "qīngjìng wúwéi." <u>Qīngjìng</u> jiu shi <u>méi yǒu fánrǎo</u> de
<u>yìsi</u>, <u>wúwéi</u> jiu shi <u>bú yào zuò shénmo</u>. "Qīngjìng wúwéi" de yìsi jiu
shi shuō "Wúwéi ér zhì."

      Fǎjiāde xuéshuō yě shi fāshēng zài Zhànguó shídài. Zhèipài xué-
30 shuō zhǔzhāng "yǐ-fǎ-zhì-guó," "xìn-shǎng-bì-fá." Fǎjiā zuì zhùmíngde
shi Hán Fēizǐ、Shāng Jūn děng.

      Mòjiāde xuéshuō zhǔzhāng "jiān'ài." Jiān'ài jiu shi rén yīngdāng
ài biéren xiàng ài zìjǐ yíyàng. Rén dōu néng zhīdao "jiān'ài" zìrán méi
yǒu zhēngduó le. Zhèipài xuéshuō shi Zhànguó shí Mòzǐde sīxiǎng.

35   Yǐshàng suǒ shuō de dōu shi qǐyuán zài Zhōngguode sīxiǎng. Zài

---

* See note 1 at the end of this lesson.

zhèixiē sīxiǎngli hòulái fāzhǎn chéngwéi yìzhǒng zōngjiàode zhǐ yǒu Dàojiā chéngle Dàojiào. Dàojiàode chuàngshǐ shi zài Dōng Hàn shídài, fèng
Lǎozǐ wéi shǐzǔ. Dàole Táng Cháo hěn shèngxíng. Xiànzài Zhōngguode
mínjiān yě yǒu hěn duō rén shi xìn Dàojiào de.

40   Xiànzài shuōshuo cóng wàiguo shūrù Zhōngguode sīxiǎng hé zōngjiào. Zhōngguo gǔshí duì wàiguode jiēchù bù duō, suǒyǐ zài sīxiǎngshang
yě bǔ róngyi cóng wàiguo shūrù.   Zhǐshi zài zōngjiàoshang hěn zǎo jiu
cóng wàiguo chuánrù Zhōngguo le. Chuánrù Zhōngguo zuì zǎode zōngjiào
shi Fójiào. Fójiào qǐyuán zài Yìndu. Zài Hàn Cháode shíhou jiu chuán-
45 dàole Zhōngguo, dàole Táng Cháo shi zuì shèng shíqī. Dāngshíde zhīshi
jiējí fānyì Fójīng. Yìbān rénmín xìn Fójiàode hěn duō. Zài Táng Cháo
mònián gèdì Fójiàode miào、sì dōu yǒu hěn duō tiánchǎn, chéngle dà dìzhǔ, zài dāngshí yǒu hěn dàde jīngji shìli. Cóng Táng Cháo yǐhòu yìzhí
dào jìndài, Fójiào zài Zhōngguo shi yǒu dà duōshù xìntú de.

50   Qícì shi Huíjiào. Huíjiào qǐyuán zài Xī Yàxīyǎ. Zài Táng Cháode
shíhou yóu Zhōngguo xīběibù chuándào Zhōngguo, suǒyǐ zài Zhōngguode
xīběibù xìn Huíjiào de rén zuì duō. Cǐwài zài gèdì yě yǒu yìxiē Huí-
jiàotú.

          Yòu qícì shi Jīdūjiào. Jīdūjiào qǐyuán zài Jìndōng. Yě shi Táng
55 Cháo de shíhou chuánrùle Zhōngguo, dāngshí jiàozuo Jǐngjiào. Hòulái
dàole shíliùqī shìjì Míng Cháode mònián, Yìdàlì rén Lì Mǎdòu lái Zhong-
guo chuánjiào, nà jiu shi Jīdūjiàolide Tiānzhǔjiào. Xiànzài zài Zhōngguode Jīdūjiào yǒu xīn-jiù liǎngpài. Xīnde shi Jīdūjiào, chuánjiào de rén
jiàozuo mùshi. Jiùde shi Tiānzhǔjiào, chuánjiào de rén jiàozuo shénfù.
60 Zhèixiē chuánjiào de rén búdàn bǎ Jīdūjiàode dàolǐ chuánrù Zhōngguo,
bìngqiě bǎ Xīfāngde wénhuà、kēxué yě chuándàole Zhōngguo.

          Zhōngguode sīxiǎng dàole jìndài yīnwei hé Xīfāng wénhuà jiēchù de
gèng duō le, tóngshí yòu shòule shídài cháoliúde yǐngxiǎng, suǒyǐ yǒule
zhòngdàde zhuǎnbiàn. Zhèizhǒng zhuǎnbiàn de zhuǎnlìdiǎn, wúyíde shi
65 Wǔsì Yùndong. Wǔsì Yùndong dāngshí yǒu yíge kǒuhào shi "dǎdǎo Kǒng
jiā diàn." Zhè shi duì Rújiā sīxiǎngde yíge dà fǎnkàng, tóngshí duìyu
guòqu de fēngjiàn sīxiǎng, shènzhì duìyu dāngshíde jūnfá、guānliáode
zhuānzhì zuòfēng yě gōngjide hěn lìhai. Zhè zhēn shi Zhōngguo sīxiǎng-
shangde yícì dà gémìng. Jiēzhe jiu shi cóng wàiguo lái de xīn xuéshuō

70 xiàng mínzhǔ zhǔyì, shèhuì zhǔyì, gòngchǎn zhǔyì shènzhìyú wéiwùlùn hé

Mǎkèsī, Lièníng, Shǐdàlín děngděng xuéshuō dōu xiàng cháoshuǐ yìbān

yǒngjìnle Zhōngguo.   Zhèixiē sīxiǎng suírán shi hé yìxiē shíjì zhèngzhi

hěn yǒu guānxi, dànshi zhè dōu shi shíjiǔ èrshí shìjì Xīfāng sīxiǎng

zhòngyào chǎnwù.   Zhèixiē sīxiǎng duìyu Zhōngguode yǐngxiǎng shi zěn-

75 moyàng? Xiànzài hái hěn nánshuō, kěshi jīnhòu Zhōngguo sīxiǎngde qū-

shì, yǒu rén shuō, yīnggāi shi yìfāngmiàn xīshōu wàiláide xīn xuéshuō,

yìfāngmiàn yào bú wàngle Zhōngguo mínzú yuányǒude sīxiǎng.

FÙSHÙ

Zhèipán lùyīndài shi Zhōngwén dì-yìzǔ dì-shíliùhào, shi yóu Bái

Wénshān fùshù de. Tímu shi Yìshu.

Zhèicìde Zhuāntí Jiǎnghuà shi qǐng Zhōngguo Yìshu Xuéyuàn yuàn-

zhǎng Zhāng Shàngwén Xiānsheng lái jiǎng de. Jiǎngtí shi Zhōngguode

5 Yìshu. Zhāng Xiānsheng kāishǐ shuō yíge guójiāde yìshu shi fǎnyìng

yíge guójiāde wénhuà rúhé.

Zhōngguo shi yíge gǔguó, suǒyǐ yìshu hěn zǎo jiu fādá le. Cóng

gǔshíhou chuánliúxialai de yìshu yǒu shíkè, táoqì, tóngqì, diāokè, jiànzhu

hái yǒu wénxué, shīgē, yīnyuè gēn wǔdǎo, zhè dōu shi yǒu gāodùde yìshu

10 jiàzhi. Tā shuō yìshude fànwéi bāokuò de hěn guǎng. Xiàndàide yìshu

kéyi fēnchéng bālèi. Dì-yī shi wénxué, dì-èr shi yīnyuè, dì-sān shi huì-

huà, dì-sì shi xìjù, dì-wǔ shi jiànzhu, dì-liù shi diāokè, dì-qī shi wǔdǎo,

dì-bā shi diànyǐng. Zhāng Xiānsheng shuō jiǎng Zhōngguode yìshu zài

hěn duǎnde shíjiān shi jiǎngbuwán de, suǒyǐ zhèicì zhǐ tándào yīnyuè,

15 wǔdǎo, huìhuà, xìjù.

Zhāng Xiānsheng shuō Zhōngguo shi lǐyuè zhī guó de guójiā. Gǔ-

shíhou yàoshi gōngtíngli gēn mínjiān yǒu shénmo yíshì, dōu yǒu yīnyuè

gēn wǔdǎo, suǒyǐ yīnyuè gēn wǔdǎo zài Zhōngguo wénhuàshang shi hěn

zhòngyàode. Tā shuō Zhōngguode yīnyuè gēn gēwǔ zài Táng Cháo hěn

20 shèng, yuányīn shi zài nèige shíhou guójiā hěn tàipíng, suǒyǐ jīngji fēi-

cháng fánróng, ér Táng Mínghuáng zìjǐ yòu fēicháng xǐhuan yīnyuè gēn

gēwǔ, kéyi shuō shi yíge gēwǔ shēngpíng de shíqī. Táng Mínghuáng zài

líyuán xùnliàn yīnyuè, wǔdǎode réncái, tóngshí Táng Mínghuángde fēizi

Yáng Guìfēi gēn líyuán zǐdìde gēwǔ dōu xiāngdāng hǎo, zài gǔshūshang
25 dōu shi yǒu jìzǎi de.

Zhāng Xiānsheng shuō Zhōngguo xiànzài shòule Xīfāng wénhuàde
yǐngxiǎng. Zhōngguo yíqiède yìshu dōu yǒu xīnde zhuǎnbiàn. Bǐfang yīnyuè ba, suǒyǒu zhōngxué丶xiǎoxuéde kèchéng dōu shi yòng Xīyuè dàngzuo
jiàocái le. Zhōngguode dàxuéli yǐnyuè xì yě fēn Zhōngyuè丶Xīyuè le.
30 Zhōngguode yuèqì yǒu hěn duō zhǒnglèi. Hézòuqilai yào hěn duō rén.

Zhāng Xiānsheng jiǎngdao huìhuà. Tā shuō Zhōngguo huàr yào suàn
Táng丶Sòng shi zuì shèngde shíqī le. Jìnlái yǒu rén fāxiàn Dūnhuáng bìhuà. Shénmo jiàozuo Dūnhuáng bìhuà ne? Jiù shi zài Gānsū Shěng Dūnhuáng Xiànde shíkūle yǒu hěn duō bìhuà. Dōu shi Liù Cháo hé Táng
35 Dàide huàjiā suǒ huà de. Hái yǒu yíbù zuì yǒumíngde huàpǔ jiào Xuānhé
Huàpǔ, shi yánjiu Zhōngguo huàr zuì yǒu jiàzhide zīliào.

Zhāng Xiānsheng yòu shuō Zhōngguo shūfǎ gēn huàr shi fēnbukāi
de. Xiě zì gēn huà huàr de jìqiǎo dōu shi xiāngtóngde. Zhōngguo huàr
yǒu rénwu丶shānshuǐ丶huāhuì děng tícái. Huàr yě shōudaole Xīfāngde
40 yǐngxiǎng. Jiānglái huàrde qūshì zěnmoyàng xiànzài hái bù néng xià pànduàn.

Zhāng Xiānsheng yòu shuōdao Zhōngguo xìjù. Tā shuō jīngxì gēn
dìfang-xì xìlǐde rén chàng hé shuō dōu shi yǒu qiāngdiào de. Wǔtáishang
yǎn xì de dòngzuò wánquán dōu shi yòng wǔdǎo lái biǎodá. Zǒu lù de
45 zīshi yě hé píngcháng rén zǒu lù de zīshi bùtóng. Xìjùli suǒ yòng de
dōngxi, zhēnde dōngzi yě hěn shǎo, dōu shi xiàngzhēng de. Bǐrú shǒuli
názhe biānzi jiu xiàngzhēng qí mǎ. Hái yǒu liǎnpǔ jiu shi huà huāliǎnde
yàngzi, yǎnyuán huà huāliǎn shi biǎoshì nèige rénde xìnggé. Zhāng Xiānsheng shuō cóng Mínguó yǐlái yīnwei Xīfāng wénhuàde yǐngxiǎng yòu
50 chǎnshēngle yìzhǒng xīnde xìjù, bú chàng, zhǐ shi duìhuà. Zhèizhǒng xìjù
jiàozuo huàjù.

Zhāng Xiānsheng zuìhòu shuō Zhōngguode yǐnyuè丶wǔdǎo gēn huìhuà
suīrán shi wǎng xīnde yìfāngmiàn fāzhǎn, ér rénmen háishi xǐhuan jiù
yǒu de. Jìnlái yǒu hěn duō rén tíchàng bǎocún Zhōngguode guócuì, fāyáng
55 Zhōngguo yuánlái yǒu de yìshu. Yīncǐ Zhōngguo yǐnyuè丶wǔdǎo gēn xìjù
háishi nénggou bǎocún érqiě yě zài jìnbùzhe.

WĒNXI

1. Zài yíge wénxué zuòtánhuìli yǒu rén tídao Xiān Qín wénxué, yòu yǒu rén tídao gǔshíde bǔcí yǐjí Yì Jīng、Zhànguócè、Hànfù、yuèfǔ děngděng. Zhèi liǎngge rén shuōle yòu shuō, hěn duō rén dōu méi xìngqu tīng. Yǒu rén shuō nà dōu shi hěn nán liǎojiě de yīnggāi dǎdǎo de dōngxi.

2. Yǒu yíge yīnyuèduì měicì yǎnzòu de qǔzi dōu hěn hǎotīng. Shēngdiào gèng shi xióngzhuàng.

3. Zhāng Xiānsheng shi yíge jūnren. Duì Rìběn dǎzhàng de shíhou fēicháng yīngyǒng, hòulái shòushāng le, xiànzài chéngle cánfèi rén le.

4. Wǔsì Yùndong zhīhòu quánmiàn tuīdòng báihuàwén. Qīngnián xuésheng duìyu wányánde cí、fù dōu bu yánjiu le.

5. Wǒ měitiān wǎnshang dōu zuò mèng. Zuótian wǎnshang mèngjian wǒ fēidao yíge hěn gāode shānshang. Zhèige shān shi yíge fēnshuǐlǐng. Wǒ kànjian yuǎnyuǎnde yǒu liǎngtiáo hé, yìtiáo wǎng dōngbiān liúdao hǎili qu le, yìtiáo wǎng xībiān liú, liúdaole shāmò.

6. Yǒu yíge xiǎoháizi yòng gèzhǒng yánsede qiānbǐ wǎng qiángshang huà. Tā huàle yòu huà, huàle yòu huà de. Qiáng běnlái shi bái de, hòulái biàncheng huāde le.

7. Zhōngguo duì Rìběn Kàngzhàn de shíhou, hěn duō rén táonàn qu dào Sìchuān. Sìchuānde mùqì hěn guì, guìdao pǔtōng rén mǎibuqǐ, duōshùde rìyòngpǐn shi yòng zhúzi zuò de. Dāngshí yǒu rén shuō: "Wǒmen xiànzài shi zhúqì shídài."

8. Wénxué zuòpǐn dōu yǒu shídàide bèijǐng. Xiànzài shi xīn shídài, yǒule xīn sīcháo yě yīngdāng yǒu xīnde chuàngzuò. Bù yīnggāi lǎoshi mófǎng Hóng Lóu Mèng、Lǎo Cán Yóujì nèizhǒng xiězuò le.

9. Nèiběn kānwù dēng de zuòpǐn yǐ zhèngzhìxìngde wéi xiàn. Hǎoxiàng yǒu shénmo tèshu shǐmìng shide.

10. Zhōngguo gǔren yǒu yíjù huà, dàyì shi: "Zuò gōng de rén yào xiǎng bǎ gōngzuò zuòhǎo, bìděi xiān yǒu hǎode gōngjù."

11. Yǒu yíge jiàoyuán zài shàngkè de shíhou duì xuésheng shuō: "Zhōngguo hé Yìndude biānjing dōu shi dà shān. Liǎngguóde biānjiè hěn nán huàfēn. Xiànzàide biānjiè shi shénmo shíhou huà de? Huà de shíhou shì bu shi liǎngguó dōu chéngrèn? Zhè shi hěn zhòngyàode yíge wèntí. . . . Xiànzài yīnwei xiànyú shíjiān děngdao xiàcì zài jiǎng."

12. Xiànzàide nánháizi yǒude tóufa liú de hěn cháng. Tóufade xíngshì kànqilai shènzhiyú xiàng nǚren. Zhèizhǒng fēngqì bù zhǐdào shi zěnmo kāishǐ de.

13. Fánshi zuòchéng yíjiàn shì yíbàn kào rénlì, yíbàn kào jīhui. Rúguǒ jīhui chéngshú le zài jiāshang rénlì yídìng néng chénggōng de.

14. Wǒ kànjian yìběn xiǎoshuō jiào Líyuán Wàishǐ. Shūli bǎ chàng xì de xiěde huàidao bù néng zài huài. Yóucǐ kějiàn yǒu rén háishi tuōbuliǎo jiù guānniàn, kànbuqǐ chàng xì de rén.

15. Dàojiāde xuéshuō shi <u>wúwéi</u>. <u>Wúwéi</u>de yìsi hǎoxiang shi shuō <u>bú yào zuò</u> de yìsi. Kěshi rúguǒ rénrén <u>dōu</u> bú yào zuò, shìjiè hái chéngle shénmo shìjiè? <u>Wúwéi de zhēnzhèng yìyì shi zài jiào zhǐ guó de rén bú yào zuò tài duō duì rénmín méi hǎochude shì. Zuì gāode lǐxiǎng shi wúwéi ér bǎ guójiā zhìhǎo le.

WÈNTÍ

1. Zhōngguode sīxiǎng hé zōngjiàode qǐyuán kéyi fēnwéi jǐfāngmiàn? Shi něi jǐfāngmiàn?

2. Chūnqiū Zhànguó shídài zhū-zǐ-bǎi-jiā gè yǒu gède xuéshuō. Qízhōng zhǔyàode xuéshuō shi něi jǐjiā?

3. Rújiā xuéshuō yǐ shéi wéi zhǔtǐ? Zhǔzhāng de shi shénmo? Rújiā bǎ rén hé rénde guānxi fēncheng wǔlèi jiàozuo wǔlún. Shénmo shi wǔlún?

4. Dàojiāde xuéshuō zuìchū shi shéide xuéshuō? Hòulái yòu yǒu shéide zhǔzhāng yě shi Dàojiāde xuéshuō? Lǎozǐ xiěle yíbù shū shi shénmo? Tāde zhǔzhāng shi shénmo?

5. Fǎjiā xuéshuō zhǔzhāng de shi shénmo? Zhànguó zuì zhùmíngde Fǎjiā shi shénmo rén?

6. Mòjiāde xuéshuō yǒu shénmo zhǔzhāng? Shi shéide zhǔzhāng?

7. Dàojiào chuàngshǐ zài shénmo shídài? Fèng shénmo rén wéi shǐzǔ? Zài shénmo cháodài hěn shèngxíng?

8. Fójiào qǐyuán zài shénmo dìfang? Shénmo shíhou chuánrùle Zhōngguo? Shénmo shíhou shi zuì shèng shíqī?

9. Huíjiào qǐyuán zài shénmo dìfang? Chuánrù Zhōngguo shi zài shénmo shídài? Zài Zhōngguo shénmo dìfang xìn Huíjiàode rén zuì duō?

10. Jīdūjiào zài shénmo shíhou chuánrù Zhōngguo? Dāngshí jiàozuo shénmo jiào? Jīdūjiào hòulái yǒu jǐpài? Dōu shi shénmo pài? Tiānzhǔjiàode chuánjiào rén jiàozuo shénmo? Jīdūjiàode chuánjiào rén jiào shénmo? Zhèixiē chuánjiào rén chúle chuánjiào yǐwài hái chuánlaile shénmo?

ILLUSTRATIVE SENTENCES (ENGLISH)

4.2. In the Ch'ing Dynasty there was a period when limitations were imposed on foreigners coming to proseletyze.

8.1. In this city the believers in Christianity are far less numerous than the believers in Buddhism.

12.1. In ancient times emperors were revered as if they were deities.

20.1. Some people like The Travels of Mr. Derelict, saying that it is very well written. Others attack it as being badly written.

25.3. Please say a written (style) sentence using "to govern by doing nothing."

27.2. Do all democratic countries lack lords and ministers?

35.1. Yǒu jǐge nóngren hé mǎile yíge tuōlājī.

Bái: Qǐng wèn nín, shì bu shì Zhōngguo xīběibù yǒude dìfang bú shìhé zhòngtián, ér shìhé mùxùyè?

Mǎ : Shìde. Zài xīběi gāoyuán yídài, yǒude dìfang zhǐ néng yǎng mǎ gēn yǎng niú, yáng.

105 Bái: Shì ... gni yīnwei tǔdìli méi yǒu féiliàode guānxi?

Ma : Wǒ xiǎng bìng bú shì méi yǒu féiliàode guānxi, shi yīnwei nèige dìfangde tǔdì hé tiānqi bú shìhé zhòng dōngxi.

Bái: Xiànzài Zhōngguo rén zhòngtián yòng jīqide duō bu duō?

Mǎ : Jùshuō duōshù háishi yòng rénlì. Búguò yǒude dìfang shǐyòng tuō-
110   lājī le. Xīwang jiānglái Zhōngguo nénggou zhěnggèr nóngyè jīxiè-
    huà, zhòngtián dōushi yòng jīqi, yìlái shi kuài, èrlái miǎnde nóng-
    ren nènmo shòukǔ.

36.0. nóngchǎng   a farm [agriculture arena]

36.1. Wǒmende nóngchǎng yīnwei hànzāide guānxi, jīnnián suǒ zhòng de nóngchǎnpǐn zhǎngbudà jiu sǐ le. (T)

37.0. jítǐ   collective (used before nouns) [collect body]

37.1. Nèiběn shū shi sānwèi xuézhěde jítǐ chuàngzuò.

37.2. Jīběn hézuòshè gēn jítǐ nóngchǎng dōu shi hézuò shìyè. (T)

38.0. hùzhùzǔ   mutual-aid team [mutually help group]

38.1. Cānjiā hùzhùzǔde rén yīnggāi bǐcǐ hùxiāng bāngzhu.

39.0. nóngzuòyè   farming [agriculture work enterprise]

39.1. Zhōngguode nóngzuòyè cóngqián dōushi shǐyòng rénlì, xiànzài zhú-
    jiànde shǐyòng jīqi le.

40.0. jīngyíng   carry on (a business), deal in, transact, develop [pass
            camp]

40.1. Nèige nóngchǎng shi guójiā jīngyíng de, bú shi sīren de. (T)

Bái: Zhōngguo dàlùshangde jítǐ nóngchǎng gēn Sūliánde yíyàng ma?

Mǎ : Wǒ xiǎng shi dàtóngxiǎoyì, méi yǒu duō dàde fēnbié.

115 Bái: Tīngshuō dàlùshang zài tǔdì gǎigé de shíhou xiān zǔzhile hùzhùzǔ,
    ránhòu cái yǒu jítǐ nóngchǎng.

Mǎ : Wǒ kàn bàozhǐshangde lùnwén cháng shuō zhèizhǒng zǔzhi duìyu
    nóngzuòyèshang shi hěn yǒu bāngzhu de.

Bái: Zhōngguo yǒu méi yǒu dà guīmóde nóngchǎng?

120 Mǎ : Wǒ tīngshuō Dōngběi yǒu, zhǐyú guīmo zěnmoyàng wǒ bu dà qīngchu.

Bái: Yàoshi sīren bàn yíge nóngchǎng shì bu shi hěn bù róngyi?

Mǎ : Bù róngyi.   Wǒ yǒu yíge péngyou bànle yíge nóngchǎng jīngyíngle
      bú dào sānnián jiu bú bàn le.

Bái: Nánchu shi shénmo?

125 Mǎ : Bǐrú zhòng cài zhǎng chóngzi, yǎng zhū、yǎng、jī zhǎngbudà jiù sǐ
      le. Wǒ nèiwei péngyou tā bàn nóngchǎng de dî-yīnián yǎngle wǔbǎi
      duō zhǐ jī, bù zhī zěnmode, hūrán yígeyígede dōu sǐ le.

41.0. guàngài   (1) irrigate; (2) irrigation (W) [pour irrigate]

41.1. Yǒude shuǐtián lîyòng hé shuǐ guàngài, yǒude shuǐtián zhǐ kào xià
       yǔ. (T)

42.0. yánzhòng   severe, serious [strict heavy]

42.1. Yánzhòng shi "hěn yàojǐn, hěn zhòngyào" de yîsi.

43.0. qiànshōu   have a bad harvest (W) [deficient receive]

43.1. Nèige dîfang jīnnián yǒu hànzāi, suǒyǐ nóngchǎnpǐn zhěnggèrde
       qiànshōu.

44.0. zàolín   (1) reforest, afforest; (2) reforestation, afforestation [make
       forest]

44.1. Zhèngfǔ tíchàng zàolín wèideshî shénmo, nǐ zhīdao ma?

Bái: Qǐng wèn guàngài zhèige cér cháng yòng ma?

Mǎ : Xiě dōngxi de shíhou cháng yòng. Nǐ kàn bàoshang yǒu zhèige lìzi:
130   "Jiǔ bú xià yǔ hànzāi xiāngdāng yánzhòng. Jìshǐ yòng réngōng
      guàngài, jīnniánde liángshi yě yào qiànshōu."

Bái: Shénmo jiào zàolín?

Mǎ : Jiu shi zhòng shù. Kě bú shi xiàng zài yuànzili zhòng shù, yìkē
      liǎngkē de. Shi zhòng hěn duōde shù.

45.0. zēngjiàn   increase the building of, construct in greater number (W)
                   [increase erect]

45.1. Zhōngguo jìnlái zēngjiànle hěn duō gāngtiěchǎng.   (W)

46.0. qiáo   a bridge

46.1. Wǒ jiāde qiánbiān yǒu yìtiáo xiǎo hé, héshang yǒu yíge xiǎo qiáo.

47.0. zhèngquán   political power

       quánshì   power and influence

47.1. Nǐ zhīdao xiànzài Zhōngguo zhǎngwò zhèngquánde shi shéi?

47.2. Tā suírán dìwei bù gāo, kěshi tāde quánshì hěn dà.

48.0. xiū   (1) build; (2) self-improvement

48.1. Zhèitiáo lù shi shéi xiū de?   Shénmo shíhou xiū de?

49.0. tiělù   railroad [iron road]

49.1. Zhōngguo zuì zǎode yìtiáo tiělù shi zài yī-bā-qī-liù nián Yīngguo rén zài Shànghǎi xiū de.

135 Bái: Zēngjiàn zhèige cér bìng bú shi shuō de ba?

   Mǎ :   Bú shi shuō de, shi xiě de. Bǐrú "zēngjiàn dà qiáo, zēngjiàn gāng-tiěchǎng."

   Bái: Shì bu shi Gòngchǎndǎng dédàole zhèngquán yǐhòu, xiūle bu shǎode tiělù, hái zàole yíge dà qiáo?

140 Mǎ :   Shìde. Tāmen tiělù xiūle bù shǎo. Tāmen zàole yíge zuì dàde qiáo jiào Cháng Jiāng Dà Tiě Qiáo.

50.0. dàyuèjìn   (1) advance in great leaps; (2) Great Leap Forward [big jump advance]

50.1. Dàyuèjìn shi Zhōngguo Gòngchǎndǎngde kǒuhào, yìsi shi jìnbùde hěn kuài.

51.0. jiāshang   (1) add, increase; (2) plus, moreover [add on]

    jiāzhòng   add weight (to) [add heavy]

51.1. Nèige guójiā gōngyè běnlái luòhòu, jiāshang wàiguo huò yǒngjìn, suǒyǐ gōngyè gèng bu róngyi fāzhǎn.   (W) (T)

51.2. Xīnde cáizhèng zhèngcè shíxíng yǐhòu rénmínde fùdān jiāzhòng le.

52.0. quēshǎo   be deficient (in), be in short supply [lack few]

52.1. Nèige guójiā quēshǎo miánhua. Yīnwei chūchǎnde bu gòuyòng, suǒyǐ bìděi cóng wàiguo mǎi.   (T)

53.0. xiāofèi   (1) consume; (2) consumption [consume waste]

53.1. Nèige guójiāde jīngji zhèngcè shi zēngjiā shēngchǎn, jiézhì xiāofèi. (T)

54.0. shuǐbà   dam, dike, breakwater [water dam]

    shuǐkù   reservoir [water storehouse]

54.1. Shuǐbàde gōngyòng shi zǔzhǐ shuǐ de.   Yǒule shuǐbà cái kéyi zào-chéng shuǐkù.

   Bái: Guòqu Zhōngguo dàlùshang yǒu yíge kǒuhào shi "shēngchǎn dàyuè-jìn." Shíjìshang shì bu shi dàyuèjìnle ne?

   Mǎ :   Jù wǒ suǒ zhīdao de, liángshi shēngchǎn yìfāngmiàn bìng bù lǐxiǎng.
145   Yīnwei zài nóngyède jihuashang fāshēngle cuòwu, jiāshang tiānzāi, liángshi qiànshōu, suǒyǐ liángshi quēshǎo, shēngchǎnde bú gou xiāo-fèi de.

Bái: Nèi jǐniánde tiānzāi xiāngdāng yánzhòng.

Mǎ : Yòu yǒu shuǐzāi yòu yǒu hànzāi.

150 Bái: Tīngshuō dàlùshang xīn xiūle jǐge shuǐbà gēn shuǐkù.

Mǎ : Xiū shuǐbà 、shuǐkù wèideshì fādiàn gēn guàngài.

55.0. yùn   transport, move about

       yùnhuò   transport goods

       yùnshū   transportation [transport transport]

       yùnhé   (1) canal; (2) Grand Canal [transport river]

55.1. Zhèixiē huòwu dōu shi yào yùndao Yīngguo qù de.

55.2. Yùnhuò yòng hángkōng bǐ hánghǎi kuài.

55.3. Cóngqián Zhōngguo nánfāng chūchǎn de mǐ yùndao Běijīng, shi yóu
       Yùnhé yùnshū de. (W) (T)

56.0. huòchē   vehicle for transporting goods, truck [commodity vehicle]

56.1. Yùnhuò de chē jiàozuo huòchē.

57.0. zǔchéng   organize, constitute, accomplish, achieve (W) [organize
                  form]

57.1. Xiànzàide Liánhéguó shi yóu yìbǎi duō ge guójiā zǔchéng de. (W)

57.2. Sān Yǒu Xiǎoxué shi jǐge xìnjiàode rén zǔchéng de. (T)

58.0. qǐyè   (business) enterprise [expectant enterprise]

58.1. Fánshi jīngyíng yìzhǒng shìyè xīwang dédào lìyi de jiu jiàozuo qǐyè.

58.2. Nèijiā qǐyè gōngsī zhuānmén jīngyíng tuōlājī. (T)

59.0. jīnshǔ   metals (W) [gold belong]

59.1. Jīn、yín、tóng、tiě dōu shi shǔyu jīnshǔ yílèi de.

60.0. zhōngchǎn jiēji   middle class

60.1. Zhōngchǎn jiēji bú shi qióngrén yě bú shi fùrén. Shi bù qióng gēn
       bú fù zhījiān de.

Bái: Zhōngguode Yùnhé shì bu shi zài Suí Cháo jiu yǒu le?

Mǎ : Yùnhéde gōngchéng dōu shi lìdài yíduànyíduànde xiū de. Jiāngsu、
       Zhéjiāng zhèi yíduàn shi cóng Suí Cháo xiūqǐ de, yìzhí dào Yuán
155   Cháo cái xiūhǎo.

Bái: Zhōngguode Yùnhé zài shìjièshang shi yíge hěn dàde gōngchéng.
       Jùshuō Yùnhé yǒu sìqiān sìbǎi sìshi gōnglǐ nènmo cháng.

Mǎ : Zài lìshǐshang shi zhènmo shuō.

Bái: Shì bu shi Zhōngguo hěn zǎo yǐqián, yùnshū huòwu dōu shi kàozhe
160   Yùnhé?

Mǎ : Búdàn yùnshū huòwu, érqiě nánfāng gēn běifāng rénmínde láiwǎng yě hěn fāngbian.

Bái : Yǐqián yùnhuò chúle shuǐlù yòng chuán yǐwài, zài lùdìshang yě yòng huòchē yùn ma?

165 Mǎ : Yě yǒu huòchē. Kěshi gēn xiànzàide huòchē bùtóng, dōushi yòng niú chē gēn mǎ chē.

Bái : Zǔchéng zài pǔtōng shuō huà de shíhou shi <u>zǔzhìchéngle</u> de yìsi, shì bu shi?

Mǎ : Shìde. Nǐ kàn bàozhǐshang zhèi yíduàn: "Jiǎ Yǐ èrrén zǔchéng yì-
170 jiā qǐyè gōngsī, zhuānmén jīngyíng gèzhǒng jīnshǔ."

Bái : Jīngyíng qǐyè de jiu shi zīběnjiā. Qǐng wèn, zhōngchǎn jiēji shi zhǐzhe něi yìzhǒng rén shuō de?

Mǎ : Zhōngchǎn jiēji shi zhǐzhe zhōngděngde zīchǎn jiēji, jiu shi bù hěn qióng yě bù hěn fùde rén.

61.0. gǎijìn   advance (N/V) (W) [change advance]

61.1. Yīnwei miánhua chūchǎnde hěn bù hé lǐxiǎng, suǒyǐ tāmen kāi zuòtánhuì yánjiu gǎijìn miánhua chūchǎn de fāngfǎ. (T)

62.0. yuánliào   raw materials, original matter [source materials]

62.1. Zhèige gōngchǎng yòng de yuánliào shi cóng nǎli lái de?

63.0. shōurù   income [receive enter]

63.1. Yǒude gōngren měitiānde shōurù lián chī fàn dōu bú gòu.

175 Bái : Qǐng wèn nín, <u>gǎijìn</u> zhèige cér shi shuō de ma?

Mǎ : <u>Gǎijìn</u> shi xiě wénzhāng huòzhě yǎnjiǎng yòng de. Bǐrú: "Mǒumǒu gōngchǎng chūchǎnpǐn yīnwei yuánliàode guānxi, yòu jiāshang gōngrende jìshu bu hǎo, suǒ zào de dōngxi bu hé lǐxiǎng, yīnggāi xiǎng fázi <u>gǎijìn</u>." Nǐ yě yòng <u>gǎijìn</u> shuō yíjù huà.

180 Bái : "Rú bù nǔlì gǎijìn wǒmende gōngyè shēngchǎn, nènmo zài shìjièshang yǒngyuǎn shi luòhòu de."

Mǎ : Hǎojíle. Cér dōu tǎolùnwán le.

Bái : Shíjiān dào le, xiànzài jiu qù tīng Biān Jiàoshòu jiǎng Zhōngguode Jīngji. Qián jǐtiān wǒ kànjian Biān Jiàoshòu le, tāde jīngshen hǎo-
185 xiàng hěn bù hǎo shide.

Mǎ : Tāde fùdān tài zhòng, shōurù yòu bù hěn duō, jiāshang tā tàitai shícháng shēngbìng. Tāde jīngji zhuàngkuàng jùshuō hěn bù hǎo.

Bái : Oh! Yuánlái shi zhèige yuányīn.

SHĒNGCÍ BIĂO

1. péngzhàng

2. tōnghuò (W)
   tōnghuò péngzhàng

3. huòbî (W)

4. wùjià

5. zhăng
   zhăngjià
   gāozhăng (W)

6. wĕndìng

7. fùdān

8. hŭnluàn

9. bēngkuî

10. cáizhèng

11. guójì

12. màoyì

13. zhèngcè

14. zībĕn
    zībĕnjiā
    zībĕn zhŭyì

15. hángyè

16. huīfu

17. huòwu

18. shìchăng

19. jīxiè

20. kuàng
    kuàngyè
    kuàngchăn

21. shíyóu

22. méi

23. gāngtiĕ
    gāngtiĕchăng

24. kāifā

25. chūchănpĭn
    nóngchănpĭn

26. miánhua

27. făngzhī

28. bèi

29. fēnpèi
    pèiji

30. gōngyìng

31. shìhé

32. mùxùyè

33. féiliào

34. jīqi

35. tuōlājī

36. nóngchăng

37. jítĭ

38. hùzhùzŭ

39. nóngzuòyè

40. jīngyíng

41. guàngài (W)

42. yánzhòng

43. qiànshōu (W)

44. zàolín

45. zēngjiàn (W)

46. qiáo

47. zhèngquán
    quánshì

48. xiū

49. tiĕlù

50. dàyuèjìn

51. jiāshang
    jiāzhòng

52. quēshăo

53. xiāofèi

54. shuĭbà
    shuĭkù

55. yùn
    yùnhuò
    yùnshū
    yùnhé

56. huòchē

57. zŭchéng (W)

58. qĭyè

59. jīnshŭ (W)

60. zhōngchăn jiēji

61. găijìn (W)

62. yuánliào

63. shōurù

YŬFĂ LIÀNXÍ

(See note at end of lesson)

1. Zhèli zhòngtián yòng tuōlājī cóng qiánnián jiu yŏu le.

2. Zhōngguode Yùnhé shi cóng Suí Cháo jiu kāishĭ zào de.

3. Wŏ jīntian yŏu shì, bú dào nóngchăng qù le.　Nĭ jiànle Mă Xiānsheng qĭng nĭ gĕi shuō yìshēngr.

4. Wǒ bù míngbai tōnghuò péngzhàng de yìsi. Qǐng nǐ gěi wǒ jiěshi jiěshi.

5. Wǒmen míngtian qu cānguān nèige dà shuǐbà qu. Yàoshi nǐ yuànyi qù ne, jiu gēn wǒmen yíkuàr qù. Bú yuànyi qù ne, jiu bú bì qù.

6. Hángyè gōngsīde gōngzuò, rúguǒ nǐ xǐhuan zuò ne, nǐ jiu zuò. Bù xǐhuan ne, nǐ jiu bú bì qu zuò.

7. Guójì màoyì gōngsīde Zhāng jīnglǐ, rén hǎozhe ne, búlùn duì shéi dōu nènmo héqi.

8. Kuàngyè gōngsī lí zhèr kě yuǎnzhe ne. Nǐ zǒudeliǎo zǒubuliǎo?

9. Wèile yào gǎijìn rúhé yùnshū huòwu zhèige wèntí, Zhāng Xiānsheng hé Lǐ Xiānsheng zhījiān jiu fāshēngle yìjian. (W)

10. Zài sīxiǎngshang, Rújiā hé Fǎjiā zhījiān yǒu hěn dàde fēnbié.

11. Zài zhèizhǒng hǔnluànde shíqī, shéi yě bāngzhubuliǎo shéi.

12. Búlùn zài shénmo shíhou, shéi yě bù gǎn shuō shéi yào gémìng.

13. Zhèiwèi xīn cáizhèng bùzhǎng yìxīnyíyìde yào xiǎng fázi bǎ huòbì wěndìng le.

14. Wǒmen fùjìn yǒu ge gāngtiěchǎng, suǒyǐ měitiān lùshang yìláiyìwǎngde dōu shi gōngren.

15. Tā bàn nóngchǎng háishi bàn qǐyè gōngsī zhè wǒ kě bù zhīdào.

16. Gāngtiě dōu zhǎngjià le zhè shi zhēnde ma?

17. Tā xìnshang méi xiězhe nèijiàn shìqing nènmo yánzhòng.

18. Biān Xiānsheng xiànzài bìng méi jīngyíngzhe nèijiā fǎngzhī gōngsī.

19. Zhèr chūchǎn de nóngchǎnpǐn, nǎr xiāofèi de duō wǒmen jiu wǎng nǎr yùn.

20. Wǒmen xiànzài tǎolùn liángshi qiànshōu de wèntí. Shéide yìjian hǎo wǒmen jiu cǎiyòng shéide yìjian.

JIǍNGHUÀ

Zhūwèi tóngxué:

Jīntian jiǎnghuàde tímu shi Zhōngguode Jīngji. Zhōngguo shi yíge nóngyè guójiā, jīngjide zhòngxīn yìzhí zài nóngyè. Zhèizhǒng qíngxing jǐqiānnián lái dōu méi yǒu duōdàde biàndong. Kěshi dàole shíjiǔ shìjì
5 Zhōng-wài tōngshāng yǐhòu, jiu yǒu dian bùtóng le. Yóuqíshi jìn jǐshí-nián lái biàndongde gèng dà. Jīntian suǒ jiǎng de jiu shi jìn jǐshínián lái jīngji yǎnbiàn de qíngxing.

Zài yī-jiǔ-sān-qī nián Zhōngguo duì Rìběn Kàngzhàn yǐqián, Zhōng-guode jīngji zǔzhi yǒu sānge tèdiǎn: Zài zhìdushang shuō, shi zìyóu jīng-

10   ji, bǎ shìchǎng gōngyìnggěi Zhōngguo hé wàiguode shāngren. Zài shèhuì-
     shang shuō, shi yǐ zhōngchǎn jiēji wéi zhǔ.   Zài guójiāde shōurù lái
     shuō, yǐ nóngyè wéi zuì zhòngyào de.   Zǒngkuò lái shuō, nèige shíhou
     Zhōngguode jīngji, nóngyè shi zhǔyào de, shāngyè shi zìyóu de, gōngyè
     shi luòhòu de.

15   Nà shíhoude gōng-shāngyè yǒu liǎng dà shìli.   Yìzhǒng shi wàiguo
     gōngshāngyède zīběnjiā. Tāmende zīběn duō, zǔzhī hǎo, hěn duō zhòng-
     yàode qǐyè xiàng hángyè、kuàngyè děngděng chàbuduō dōu zài tāmende
     zhǎngwòli. Lìngwài yìzhǒng shi Zhōngguo shèhuìshang yǒu quánshìde rén,
     tāmen zài yánhǎi dàde chéngshì jīngyíng gōng-shāngyè. Hòulái zhèi liǎng-
20   zhǒng shìli dōu shòu Kàngzhànde yǐngxiǎng, shìli yìtiān bǐ yìtiān xiǎo le.
     Zhōngguo zhěnggè jīngji qíngxing yě shòu Kàngzhàn de yǐngxiǎng, yìtiān
     bǐ yìtiān huài le. Hòulái gèng yīnwei nèizhànde guānxi jīngji qíngxing jiu
     gèng huài le.
          Tōnghuò péngzhàng shi duì Rìběn Kàngzhàn yǐhòu jīngji hǔnluànde
25   zhǔyào yuányīn. Kàngzhàn zhīqián zhèngfǔ wěndìngle huòbì, zài jīngjishang
     shi yíge hěn dàde chénggōng.   Zài zhànshí yīnwei shìchǎngshang huòwu
     quēshǎo ér zhèngfǔ wèile zhīchí Kàngzhàn zēngjiāle huòbìde fāxíng, yīn-
     ér xíngchéngle wùjiàde gāozhǎng. Hòulái nèizhàn kāishǐ, Zhōngguo jīngji
     hěn kuàide jiu tōnghuò péngzhàng, jiéguǒ jīngji bēngkuì. Zhè yě shi Guó-
30   mín zhèngfǔ zài dàlùshang shíbài yǐjí hòulái chénglìle Zhōnghuá Rénmín
     Gònghéguó de zhǔyào yuányīn zhī yī.
          Yī-jiǔ-sì-jiǔ nián Zhōngguo xīn zhèngquán chénglì yǐhòu, tāmende
     jīngji zhèngcè hé yǐqián wánquán bùtóng.   Tāmen shíxíng yǒu jìhua de
     jīngji, dì-yīge wǔnián jìhua zài yī-jiǔ-wǔ-sān nián kāishǐ.   Zhèige jìhua
35   yǐngxiǎngle jīngjide gè fāngmiàn rú nóngyè、gōngyè、màoyì、cáizhèng、
     yùnshū děng.
          Zài nóngyè fāngmiàn Máo Zédōng zǎo jiu qiángdiào fēnpèi nóngtián
     gěi nóngren, nà shi Zhōngguo gémìng yíqiè wèntíde jīběn chūfādiǎn, suǒyǐ
     Zhōngguo xiāngcūn gǎigé de dì-yībù jiu shi tǔdì gǎigé. Lìng yíbù jiu shi
40   hézuò shìyè. Hézuò shìyède chénglì yǒu sìbù: hùzhùzǔde chénglì、jīběn
     hézuòshède zǔchéng, jítǐ nóngchǎngde zǔchéng hé rénmin gōngshède shì-
     yàn. Tóngshí wèile zēngjiā nóngyède shēngchǎn jiu dàliàng shǐyòng féi-
     liào, yóuqíshi huàxué féiliào yòng de gèng duō, yòu zàole hěn duō shuǐ-

Jīngji

bà、shuǐkù yǐbiàn guàngài hé fādiàn. Yǒude dìfang, xiàng Dōngběi, nóng-
45 zuòyè kāishǐ shǐyòng tuōlājī.   Tāmen xīwang jiānglái zhěngge Zhōngguo
jīxièhuà.   Liángshi shi zhǔyàode nóngchǎnpǐn, miánhua yě hěn zhòngyào.
Zài bú shìhé nóngyè de dìfang jiu zàolín. Zài Měnggǔ děng dìqū mùxùyè
yě shi jīngjide zhǔyào bùfen.

Zài gōngyè fāngmiàn yě hěn zhòngshì. Yóuqíshi zhòng gōngyè zēng-
50 jiānle hěn duō gāngtiěchǎng, chūchǎn jīqi、yùnhuò de huòchē、tuōlājī děng.
Duìyu xiāofèide gōngyè rú fǎngzhī děng bú tài zhùzhòng. Wèile yào gōngyìng gōngyè yuánliào, suǒyǐ dàliàng kāifā jīnshǔ děng kuàngchǎn, yóuqíshi méi、tiě、shíyóu zhèi sānzhǒng kuàngchǎn dōu zēngjiāle shēngchǎn.

Yīnwei jīngji jìnbùde hěn kuài, suǒyǐ jiāzhòngle yùnshūshangde fù-
55 dān. Tāmen jiu xiū tiělù, zào dà qiáo, yě gǎijìnle yùnhéde yùnshū.

Zài guójì màoyìshang, zài wǔshi niándàili zhǔyào duìwài màoyi shi
duì Sūlián hé qítā shèhuì zhǔyì guójiā.   Hòulái duì Xīfāng zīběn zhǔyì
guójiāde màoyi yě zēngjiā le.   Dànshi Zhōngguo jīngjide fāzhǎn bù hěn
píngjūn. Zài 1957-1959 dàyuèjìn de shíhou, yǒude dìfang fāzhǎn le, yǒude
60 dìfang luòhòu le. Yuányīn shi jìhuàshangde cuòwu zài jiāshang tiānzāi hé
nóngchǎnpǐn qiànshōu, zàochéngle yánzhòngde liángshi quēshǎo, shènzhiyú
xūyào pèiji. Yī-jiǔ-liù-yī nián yǐhòu, jīngji cái jiànjiànde huīfu le.

FÙSHÙ

Zhèipán lùyīndài shi Zhōngwén dì-yīzǔ dì shíqīhào, Bái Wénshān
fùshù de Sīxiǎng hé Zōngjiào.

Zhèicìde Zhuāntí Jiǎnghuà shi zhéxué-xì xì zhǔrèn Qián Yǒuwén
Jiàoshòu jiǎng de. Tímu shi Sīxiǎng hé Zōngjiào.   Qián Jiàoshòu xiān
5 jiǎng sīxiǎng gēn zōngjiàode láiyuán. Tā shuō yǒu liǎngge láiyuán, yíge
shi cóng wàiguo ér lái de, yíge shi qǐyuán zài Zhōngguo de.   Tā shuō
Zhōngguode zhéxué sīxiǎng, kāishǐ shi zài gōngyuánqián sìshìjìde shíhou,
nèige shíqī shèhuìshangde qíngxing biàndongde hěn lìhai, suǒyǐ zhū-zǐ-
bǎi-jiā dōu huódongqilai, gè yǒu gède xuéshuō.   Suīrán suǒ jiǎng de
10 dōngxi gè yǒu gède dàolǐ, dànshi zuì zhǔyàode xuéshuō shi Rújiā、Mòjiā、
Dàojiā gēn Fǎjiā.

Qián Jiàoshòu xiān cóng Rújiā jiǎngqi de. Tā shuō Rújiāde xuéshuō
shi ná Kǒngzǐ gēn Mèngzǐde xuéshuō zuò zhǔtǐ.   Kǒngzǐde xuéshuō ná
rén zì zuò jīchǔ. Rénde yìsi jiu shi zuò rénde dàolǐ.   Rújiā bǎ rén gēn

15 rénde guānxi fēnchéng wǔzhǒng, jiàozuo wǔlún, jiu shi jūnchén、fùzǐ、fūfù、

xiōngdì、péngyou. Rúguǒ bǎ wǔlúnde guānxi wéichíhǎo le, nà jiu shi zuò

rén zuì lǐxiǎng de. Zhōngguo cóng gǔ dào xiànzài yìzhíde zūn Kǒngzǐ

shi shèngren, kějiàn Rújiā xuéshuō zài Zhōngguode zhòngyào.

Qián Jiàoshòu shuō Mòjiāde xuéshuō shi jiān'ài, yìsi shi ài zìjǐ yě

20 yào ài biéren. Bìxū zhèiyàng cái néng hépíng.

Tā yòu jiǎngdào Dàojiāde xuéshuō. Dàojiā wúwéi ér zhǐ shi Lǎo-

zǐde xuéshuō. Tāde zhéxué shi qīngjìng wúwéi. Lǎozǐ xiěle yìběn shū

jiào Dàodé Jīng, shi yíbù hěn gāoshēnde Zhōngguo zhéxué lǐlùn.

Qián Jiàoshòu yòu shuōdao Fǎjiā. Tā shuō Zhōngguo gǔshíhou zuì

25 yǒumíngde Fǎjiā shi Hán Fēizǐ gēn Shāng Jūn. Fǎjiā xuéshuō yě shi

Zhànguó shídàide chǎnwù. Tāmen zhǔzhāng "xìn-shǎng-bì-fá, yǐ-fǎ-zhì-

guó."

Qián Jiàoshòu shuō yǐshàng tā suǒ jiǎng de jǐjiā zhǐ yǒu Dàojiā

hòulái yǎnbiànchéngle yìzhǒng zōngjiào. Dàojiào kāishǐ shi zài Dōng Hàn

30 shíqī. Zūn Lǎozǐ shi Dàojiàode shǐzǔ.

Qián Jiàoshòu yòu jiǎng cóng wàiguo shūrù de sīxiǎng hé zōngjiào.

Tā shuō wàiguode zōngjiào hěn zǎo jiu chuándao Zhōngguo le. Tā xiān

shuō de Fójiào. Tā shuō Fójiàode qǐyuán shi Yìndu, cóng Hàn Cháode

shíhou chuándaole Zhōngguo de. Fójiào zài Zhōngguo zuì shèngde shíqī

35 shi Táng Cháo, nèige shíhoude zhīshi jiēji fānyì Fójīng, rénmín xìn Fóde

hěn duō. Dàochu dōu yǒu miào. Fójiàode shìlì hěn dà, xìntú yě duō.

Yìzhí dào xiànzài Fójiào xìntúde rénshù háishi zhàn dì-yīwèi.

Qián Jiàoshòu shuō Zhōngguo xìn Huíjiào de rén yě bù shǎo. Huí-

jiào yě shi cóng Táng Cháo chuándao Zhōngguo de. Xìn Huíjiào zuì duō

40 de dìqū shi Zhōngguo xīběibù.

Qián Jiàoshòu yòu shuōdao Jīdūjiào shi zěnmo chuánjìn Zhōngguo

de. Tā shuō yě shi zài Táng Cháode shíhou chuánjìn Zhōngguo de. Dāng-

shí jiàozuo Jǐngjiào. Dàole Míng mòde shíqī yǒu Yìdàlìde shénfù Lì Mǎ-

dòu dào Zhōngguo lái chuánjiào. Nà jiu shi Tiānzhǔjiào. Jīdūjiào hòulái

45 fēnchéngle xīn jiù liǎngpài. Jiùde jiu shi Tiānzhǔjiào, xīnde jiu shi Jī-

dūjiào. Tiānzhǔjiàode chuánjiào rén jiào shénfù, Jīdūjiàode chuánjiào rén

jiào mùshi. Tāmen búdàn bǎ zōngjiào chuánrù Zhōngguo, tóngshí yě bà

Xīfāngde kēxué、wénhuà yě chuánrùle bù shǎo.

Qián Jiàoshòu yòu shuōdao sīxiǎng yìfāngmiàn. Tā shuō guānyu
50 sīxiǎng yìfāngmiàn jìnlái yīnwei gēn Xīfāng guójiā jiēchù de jīhui duō le,
yòu yīnwei shídài cháoliúde yǐngxiǎng, yǒule gèng dàde zhuǎnbiàn, dōushi
shòule Wǔsì Yùndongde yǐngxiǎng. Yìxiē xīnde xuéshuō xiàng mínzhǔ
zhǔyì、shèhui zhǔyì、gòngchǎn zhǔyì、wéiwùlùn gēn Mǎkesī、Lièníng、Shǐ-
dàlínde zhèngzhi xuéshuō dōu chuándaole Zhōngguo.

WÉNXI

1. Yǒu rén gōngji Zhāng Shìzhǎng, shuō tā shi fēngjiàn sīxiǎng、guānliáo
    zuòfēng, yòu shuō tā zūnzhòng yǒu quánshìde rén, zhīchí zīběnjiā. Tā
    duì rénmín yǒu zhǒngzhǒngde fánrǎo, cóng tā dāng shìzhǎng yǐlái tā bǎ
    rénmínde fùdān jiāzhòngle yíbèi.

2. Zhōngguo zìcóng Hàn Cháo yǐlái jiu zūnchóng Kǒngzǐde xuéshuō. Lìdàide
    huángdì duōbàn yòng zhèizhǒng xuéshuō zhīchí tāde zhèngquán, shíxíng
    zhuānzhì. Zài zhuānzhì shídài shènzhiyú jūn jiào chén sǐ, chén bìděi
    sǐ, jiǎnzhí shi bù néng fǎnkàng. Kěshi dàole Mínguó chūnián, Xīfāngde
    xīn sīxiǎng xiàng cháoshuǐ shide yǒngjìnle Zhōngguo, Zhōngguo jiu qǐle
    géxīnde yùndong. Yìbān qīngnián zhǔzhāng "dǎdao Kǒng jiā diàn," "dǎdǎo
    jiùde dàodé." Zhèizhǒng yùndong shi Zhōngguo sīxiǎngshang yíge zhuǎn-
    lìdiǎn.

3. Dàojiā suǒwèi dào shi yìzhǒng hěn gāoshēnde zhéxué sīxiǎng. Wǒmen
    kànkan Dàojiāde chuàngshǐ rén Lǎozǐ suǒ xiě de Dàodé Jīng jiu kéyi zhī-
    daole. Zhìyú Dàojiāo fèng Lǎozǐ wéi shǐzǔ, shi zài Lǎozǐ yǐhòu hěn duō
    nián cái shèngxíng de.

4. Yǒu rén wèn wǒ Dàojiàode miào shi bu shi jiàozuo sì? Wǒ gàosu ta,
    Fójiàode miào duōshù jiàozuo sì, Dàojiàode miào hěn shǎo jiàozuo sì.

5. Tā shi zhèige dìfang rénmínde lǐngxiù. Tā shuō zhèige dìfangde kuàng
    hěn duō, yīngdāng kāifā. Tā yòu shuō kāi kuàng suīrán xūyào hěn duō
    zīběn, kěshi rúguǒ yóu dāngdì yìxiē yǒu tiánchǎnde rén náchu qián lai,
    zīběn shi bù chéng wèntí de.

WÈNTÍ

1. Zhōngguode jīngji wèi-shénmo yǐ nóngyè wéi zhōngxīn? Cóng shénmo
    shíhou qǐ cái yǒu diar biàndong? Shénmo shíhou biàndongde zuì dà?

2. Zhōngguo jīngji zài duì Riběn Kàngzhàn yǐqián yǒu sānge tèdiǎn. Qǐng
    nǐ shuōshuo nèi sānge tèdiǎn shi shénmo?

3. Zhōngguo zài duì Rìběn Kàngzhàn yǐqián, gōng-shāngyè yǒu liǎng dà shìli.
    Shi něi liǎngzhǒng shìli? Zhèi liǎngzhǒng shìli hòulái zěnmoyàng le?

4. Zhōngguo duì Rìběn Kàngzhàn yǐqián, zài jīngjishang yǒu hěn dàde chéng-

gōng, shi shénmo?   Hòulái yīnwei shénmo dōngxi zhǎngjià, shènzhiyú jīngji bēngkuì?

5. Zhōngguo xīn zhèngquán zài yī-jiǔ-sì-jiǔ nián chěnglì yǐhòu, tāmende jīngji zhèngcè hé yǐqián xiāngtóng ma?   Tāmen shíxíng shénmo zhèngcè?

6. Máo Zédōng wèi-shénmo qiángdiào zhǔzhāng fēnpèi nóngtián gěi nóngren? Zhōngguo xiāngcūn gǎigé dì-yībù shi shénmo?   Lìng yíbù shi shénmo?

7. Hézuò shìyède chénglì yǒu sìbù.   Shi něi sìbù?

8. Zhōngguode nóngzuòyè shì bu shi yǐjing jīxièhuà le? Tāmen zài shénmo dìfang kāishǐ shǐyòng tuōlājī?

9. Zhōngguo zhǔyàode nóngchǎnpǐn chúle liángshi yǐwài hái yǒu shénmo? Zài bú shìhé nóngyède dìfang zuò shénmo? Zài Ménggǔ děng dìqū shénmo shi jīngjide zhǔyào bùfen?

10. Zhōngguo zài gōngyè fāngmiàn zhòngshì něizhǒng gōngyè?   Duìyu xiǎofèide gōngyè zěnmoyàng? Zài guójì màoyìshang cóngqián dōu hé shénmo guójiā màoyì? Hòulái ne? Zài suǒwèi dàyuèjìnde shíhou, wèi-shénmo bù néng píngjūn fāzhǎn?

ILLUSTRATIVE SENTENCES (ENGLISH)

9.1. If currency is continuously inflated unquestionably the economy will collapse.

12.1. All modern states place great emphasis on foreign trade.

15.1. The expansion of shipping is one of China's economic policies.

19.1. Some countries still use human power in the agricultural sector, other states have already become mechanized.

26.1. In the raising of cotton, insects [lit. growing insects] are a big problem.

28.1. This year the kindergarten children in that elementary school have doubled over last year.

31.1. Economically speaking, that policy is no longer suited to the present.

32.1. This region produces nothing but grass and is suited only to animal husbandry.

33.1. This chemical fertilizer is purchased from abroad.

33.2. The best time to apply fertilizer to the ground is after a rain.

36.1. On our farm because of the drought the crops which we planted died without being able to grow to maturity.

37.2. The basic cooperatives and the collective farms are all cooperative enterprises.

40.1. That farm is state-managed, it isn't privately owned.

41.1. Some paddies use river water for irrigation, some simply depend on the rain.

51.1. Industry in that country is backward to begin with.   Add to this the influx
of foreign goods, then it is even more difficult for industry to develop.

52.1. That country is deficient in cotton. Because it doesn't produce enough, it
must buy from abroad.

53.1. The economic policy of that country is to increase production and to re-
strict consumption.

55.3. In the past the rice produced in the south of China was transported to Peking via the Grand Canal.

57.2. The Three Friends Elementary School was established by several religious
people [lit. people who believed in religion].

58.2. That business enterprise deals solely in tractors.

61.1. Because the production of cotton was far from ideal, they called a conference to study means of advancing the production [of cotton.]

NOTES

The following miscellaneous usages are illustrated in the exercise <u>Yǔfǎ Liànxí</u>
in this lesson:

a (1-2). N (V) cóng TW jiu V   'N V'd from TW':

Zhèige xuéxiào xué Zhōngwén yòng pīnyīn cóng qùnian jiu yǒu
le   'This school has used the Chinese Phonetic Alphabet in the
study of Chinese since last year.'

b (3-4). gěi (N) V   'V (for N)':

Zhèige zì wǒ bú huì. Qǐng ni gěi niànnian.   'I don't know this
character. Please read it (for me).'

c (5-6). V_1 ne, jiu V_2; bu V_1 ne, jiu V_3 'If V_1 then V_2; if not V_1, then
V_3':

Xǐhuan ne, jiu mǎi; bù xǐhuan ne, jiu bù mǎi.   'If you like it,
buy it; if you don't like it, don't buy it.'

d (7-8). SVzhe ne   'very SV':

He! Jīntiande çér kě duōzhe ne!   'Gosh! There sure are a lot
of (new) words today!'

e (9-10). N_1 hé N_2 zhījiān   'between N_1 and N_2':

Zhōngguo hé Rìběn zhījiānde quānxi zěnmoyàng?   'What are
relations like between China and Japan?'

f (11-12). shéi V shéi?   'Who V's who?':

Dàjiā dōu qióng. Shéi néng bāngzhu shéi?   'Everyone's poor.
Who can help whom?'

g (13-14). yī A yī B   (where AB is a fixed combination, emphasizes single-
ness or completeness of AB):

Nǐ yì rén yì kǒu de hěn róngyi shēnghuó. 'It's easy for you all by yourself (i. e. having no dependents) to make a living.'

h(15-16). A sentence functioning as the subject or preposed object of a verb phrase is often recapitulated by zhè 'this' or nà 'that':

Tā bù lái nà wǒ bù zhīdào. 'I didn't know that he wasn't coming.'

i (17-18). The negative form of the continuous aspect with zhe uses méi (yǒu), not bù:

Shūshàng xiězhe míngzi ne ma? . . . Méi xiězhe míngzi. 'Is there a name written in the book? . . . There's no name written in it.'

j (19-20). Paired question-words (See Beginning Chinese, p. 375, note 1):

Nǐ dào nǎr qu, wǒ yě dào nǎr qu. 'I'll go wherever you go.'

Dì-Èrshi'èrkè. Lìshǐ

Bái: Mǎ Jiàoshòu zǎo.

Mǎ : Zǎo. Zhèikuài túzhang gěi ni.

Bái: Nín yǐjing kēhǎo le?

Mǎ : Kēde bù dà hǎo. Zhèikuài yù hěn bù hǎo kē, yòu jiāshang wǒ hǎo-
5 jǐnián méi kē le.

Bái: Hǎojíle. Nín zěnmo shuō kēde bù hǎo ne? Xièxie nín. Jiānglái
yǒu jǐhui wǒ gēn nín xué kē túzhang ba.

Mǎ : Hǎo a. Kē túzhang bìng bù nán. Nǐ dǒngle tāde jìqiǎo hěn róngyi.
Zuótian guānyu jǐngjide jiǎnghuà nǐ lùyīn fùshùle ma?

10 Bái: Méi yǒu. Zhèi liǎngtiān wǒ yǒu diar shāngfēng, zuótian wǎnshang
shāode hěn lìhai, hǎn zǎo jiu shuì le, lián wǎnfàn yě méi chī.

Mǎ : Zhèi jǐtiān tiānqi bù hǎo, yìhuěr lěng yìhuěr rè. Hěn róngyi shāngfēng. Yào bu yào xiūxi xiūxi?

Bái: Búbì, méi guānxi, jīntian hǎode duō le.

15 Mǎ : Jīntian Zhuāntí Jiǎnghuà jiǎng de shi Zhōngguo Lìshǐ. Wǒmen xiànzài tǎolùn tǎolùn shēngcér.

Bái: Hǎode.

1.0. fén-shū-kēng-rú   burn books and bury Confucian scholars

1.1. Qín Cháo fén-shū-kēng-rú wèideshì shénmo, nǐ zhīdao ma?

2.0. (Qín) Shǐhuáng   First Emperor (of Ch'in)

2.1. Qín Shǐhuángde shíhou gōngtínglide fēizi duōde bùdéliǎo.

3.0. huómái   bury alive

3.1. Zhōngguo shénmo cháodài céngjīng huómáile xǔduō niàn shū de rén?

4.0. tǒngyī   (1) unify, centralize, standardize; (2) unity, unification, cen-
tralization, standardization [unify one]

4.1. Zhànguó yǐhòu Qín Cháo tǒngyīle Zhōngguo.

5.0. yǐnqǐ   lead to, attract   [attract rise]

5.1. Qīng Cháo mònián yīnwei zhèngzhi bù hǎo yǐnqǐle gémìng.

Mǎ : Nǐ zhīdao něicháode huángdi céngjīng fén-shū-kēng-rú?
Bái: Shi Qín Shǐhuáng.

20 Mǎ : Shénmo jiào fén-shū-kēng-rú?

    Bái: Fén-shū jiu shi bǎ shū shāo le. Kēng-rú jiu shi bǎ niàn shū de
          rén huómái le.

    Mǎ : Qǐng nǐ shuōyìshuō fén-shū-kēng-rú de jīngguò.

    Bái: Qín Shǐhuáng bǎ Zhōngguo tǒngyīle yǐhòu, tā tīngle yíge dà chénde
25   huà, wèile tǒngzhì sīxiǎng fánshi yǒu zhū-zǐ-bǎi-jiāde shū dōu děi
          shāo le. Tóngshí yīnwei Qín Shǐhuáng nèizhǒng zhèngcè yǐnqǐ niàn
          shū rén de pīping, suǒyǐ tā bǎ niàn shū de huómáile sìbǎi liùshí
          duō rén.

    Mǎ : Duìle.

    6.0. (Hàn) Gāozǔ   Emperor Kao-tsu (of Han)

    6.1. Hàn Gāozǔ shi Hàn Cháo dì-yíge huángdì.

    7.0. fēng   enfeoff

    7.1. Hàn Gāozǔ fēng hěn duō rén wéi wáng. (W) (T)

    8.0. Shèng Táng   Glorious T'ang (designation for a particularly brilliant
                        period, 713-766) [flourishing T'ang]

    8.1. "Shèng Táng" shi shuō Zhōngguo Táng Cháo shi zuì shèngde shíqī.

    9.0. gǎi-cháo-huàn-dài   change the dynasty [change dynasty exchange
                               generation]

    9.1. Gǎi-cháo-huàn-dàide zhǔyào yuányīn shi zhèngzhi bù hǎo.

    10.0. fǔbài   corrupt [decay defeated]

    10.1. Zhèngzhi fǔbài jiu yào yǐnqǐ gémìng.

    11.0. shī   lose

          sǔnshī   loss, injury, casualty [damage lose]

    11.1. Tā shīle yíge niàn Zhōngwén de jīhui.

    11.2. Dūnhuáng shíkūlide bìhuà huàile hěn duō, zhè shi yìshushang yíge
          hěn dàde sǔnshī.

    12.0. mínxīn   popular sentiment [people heart]

    12.1. Zhèngfǔ yīnwei shícháng jiāzhòng rénmínde fùdān, suǒyǐ shīqule
          mínxīn. (T)

30 Bái: Shì bu shi Qín Cháode shíhou qǔxiāole fēngjiàn zhìdu, zài Hàn Cháo
          yòu huīfu le? Wèi-shénmo yòu yào huīfule ne?

    Mǎ : Yǒu liǎngge yuányīn. Dì-yīge shi Hàn Gāozǔ dāngle huángdì yǐhòu,
          tā xiǎng Zhōu Cháo shi fēngjiàn zhìdu, zuòle bābǎi niánde huángdì,
          ér Qín Cháo qǔxiāole fēngjiàn zhìdu, cái yǒu shíwǔniánde lìshǐ. Dì-
35   èrge yuányīn shi Hàn Gāozǔ suīrán běnlái shi ge píngmín, dànshi

tā hái tuōbuliǎo fēngjiàn sīxiǎng, suǒyǐ tā yí zuòle huángdì jiu xiān fēng tāde tóngxìng.

Bái: Shì bu shi Hàn Cháo shi Zhōngguo zuì shèngde shíqī?

Mǎ : Táng Cháo yě shi Zhōngguo zuì shèngde shíqī.   Lìshǐshang yǒude
40   shíhou tándao Táng Cháo jiu shuō Shèng Táng.

Bái: Zhōngguo lìdài gǎi-cháo-huàn-dàide zhǔyīn dōu shi yīnwei zhèng-zhi fǔbài ma?

Mǎ : Chàbuduō dōu shi zhèngzhi fǔbài, shīqu mínxīn.

13.0. zhūhóu   feudal princes [all marquis]

13.1. Zài fēngjiàn shídài zhūhóude quánshì hěn dà.

14.0. jūnzhǔ   sovereign, monarch

14.1. Yīngguo hé Rìběn dōu shi jūnzhǔ guójiā.   (T)

15.0. wángshì   royal house, royal family (W)

15.1. Zhōu Cháo mònián wángshìde quánshì yìtiān bǐ yìtiān xiǎo le. (W)

16.0. xīng   flourish

      xīngqǐ   rise, begin [flourish rise]

16.1. Míng Cháo xīngqǐ de yuányīn nǐ zhīdao ma?

17.0. miè   (1) extinguish; (2) be extinguished

17.1. Zhànguó shídài dàole hòulái Qín Guó bǎ biéde guó dōu miè le, Zhōngguo jiu tǒngyī le.

18.0. wáng   perish (of nations)

      mièwáng   destroy

      xīngwáng   rise and fall (W)

18.1. Qīng Cháo yīnwei shénmo wáng de?

18.2. Qín Cháo mièwáng yǐhòu jiu shi Hàn Cháo.

18.3. Guójiāde xīngwáng rénrén yǒu zéren de.   (T)

Bái: Qǐng wèn zhūhóu shi shénmo?

45 Mǎ : Jiu shi fēngjiàn shídài huángdì suǒ fēng de gè dìfangde lǐngxiù.

Bái: Dōu shi huángdì yǒu guānxi de rén ma?

Mǎ : Shi zhèiyàng.   Shǒuxiān fēng tóngxìng.   Rúguǒ duì guójiā yǒugōng de, bú shi tóngxìng de yě fēng.

Bái: Jūnzhǔ shi huángdìde lìng yíge míngchēng, shì bu shi?

50 Mǎ : Shì.   Xiànzài Yīngguo、Rìběn hái shi jūnzhǔ guójiā.

Bái: Wángshǐ shi shénmo yìsi?

Mǎ : Wángshǐ běnláide yìsi shi huángdìde jiā. Yīnwei gǔlái guójia shi
shǔyú huángdì de, suǒyǐ yě yǒu guójiāde yìsi.

Bái : Xīngwáng zhèige cér shi wényánde ba?

55   Mǎ : Duìle. Xīng jiu shi xīngqǐ, wáng jiu shi mièwáng.

19.0. zhìshì   peaceful era (W) [manage world]

19.1. Zhōngguo lìshǐshang suǒwèi zhìshì jiu shi guójiā zhìlǐ de hěn hǎo
érqiě méi yǒu zhànzhēng de shíhou.

20.0. luànshì   period of disturbance, time of anarchy [disordered world]

20.1. Nǐ shuō xiànzài shì bu shi luànshì?

21.0. fēnliè   rent asunder, divided [divide split]

sì-fēn-wǔ-liè   badly split, fragmented [four divide five split]

21.1. Yuènán zài yī-jiǔ-wǔ-sì nián fēnliè le, fēnchéng Nányuè Běiyuè.(T)

21.2. Yíge guójiā rúguǒ sì-fēn-wǔ-liè nèige guójiā jiu yào wáng le.

22.0. hú*   foreigners, barbarians

Húrén   Tartars

Wǔhú Shíliù Guó   Five Barbarians and Sixteen Kingdoms

22.1. Jùshuō Húrén dōu néng qí mǎ, qí mǎ de zīshì hěn yīngyǒng.

22.2. Wǔdài Shíguó zài Wǔhú Shíliù Guó yǐqián háishi yǐhòu ne?

Mǎ : Zài lìshǐshang kàn, cháng yǒu zhìshì gēn luànshì. Qǐng nǐ shuōyì-
shuō shénmo jiào zhìshì, shénmo jiào luànshì?

Bái : Zhìshì jiu shi méi yǒu zhànzhēng, shèhuì hěn āndìngde shíqī. Luànshì jiu shi guójiā sì-fēn-wǔ-liè, shèhuì hǔnluàn rénmen shēnghuó
60   bù āndìng de shíqī.

Mǎ : Duìle.

Bái : Zài lìshǐshang kàn, luànshìde shíqī hěn duō.

Mǎ : Shìde. Bǐrú Chūnqiū Zhànguó、Wǔhú Shíliù Guó、Wǔdài Shíguó dōu
shi luànshì.

65   Bái : Qǐng wèn nín, Wǔhú shi shénmo?

Mǎ : Zài Cháng Chéng yǐwàide wǔge mínzú jiàozuo Wǔhú.

Bái : Shíliù Guó dōu shi Wǔhú ma?

Mǎ : Bù. Yǒude shi Wǔhú zǔzhi de, yǒude shi Hànzú zǔzhi de, yígòng
shi shíliùge guójiā.

23.0. wàihuàn   trouble from the outside (e. g. foreign invasion) [outside
disturbance]

23.1. Qīng Cháo mòniánde wàihuàn tài duō, jiǎnzhí shi méi fázi dǐkàng
le.

24.0. Xiōngnú   Northern Barbarians, Huns

24.1. Hàn Cháode shíhou yǒude Hànrén hé Xiōngnú jiēhūn.

25.0. wèi(le) . . . qǐjiàn   with a view to (W) [for . . . rise see]

25.1. Wèile shíhé guójī xūyào qǐjiàn, Zhōngguo gāngtiě chūchǎnpǐnde shuǐpíng yě tígāo le. (W)

26.0. wǔlì   military power

26.1. Nèige guójiā yǒule xīnde jūnduì yòu jiāshang xīn wǔqì, suǒyǐ tāde
wǔlì bǐ cóngqián zēngjiāle hǎojǐbèi. (T)

27.0. qīnrù   invade (W) [invade enter]

qīnlüè   (1) invade; (2) invasion, aggression [invade invade]

27.1. Cóng shénmo shíhou qǐ Xiōngnú qīnrùle Zhōngguo?

27.2. Wénhuà qīnlüè bǐ wǔlì qīnlüè hái lìhai.

70 Bái: Qín Cháode shíqī, zuì dàde wàihuàn shì bu shi jiu shi Xiōngnú?

Mǎ : Shì. Qín Shǐhuáng zào Cháng Chéng, jiu shi wèile Xiōngnú. Xiànzài
qǐng nǐ yòng Xiōngnú shuō yíge̞ xiě de jùzi.

Bái: "Qín Shǐhuáng wèile pà Xiōngnú wǔlì qīnrù qǐjiàn ér zào Wànlǐ
Cháng Chéng."

75 Mǎ : Zhèige jùzi hěn hǎo.

Bái: Xiōngnú yě shi Húrén ma?

Mǎ : Shì. Xiōngnú jiu shi Wǔhú lǐtoude yìzhǒng.

28.0. shēngwēi   prestige (W) [sound prestige]

28.1. Zhōngguo shēngwēi zuì dàde shíhou shi Yuán Cháo, qícì jiu shi Hàn
Cháo gēn Táng Cháo.

29.0. kuà   bestride

29.1. Sūliánde lǐngtǔ kuà Ōu-Yà liǎngzhōu.

30.0. shuàilǐng   lead, take with one (W) [lead lead]

30.1. Nèige guójiā tōnghuò péngzhàng, wùjià gāozhǎng. Yǒu rén shuō shi
gōngyòng shìyè shuàilǐng zhǎngjià de. (T)

31.0. shuāiruò   become debilitated, feeble [decay weak]

31.1. Tāde shēntǐ yìtiān bǐ yìtiān shuāiruò.

32.0. guóshì   national strength

32.1. Qīng Cháo mònián yīnwei wàihuàn tài duō guóshì zhújiàn shuāiruò
le.

Bái: Shēngwēi zhèige cér wǒ zhīdao shi xiě dōngxi de shíhou yòng de,
kěshi wǒ bú dà huì yòng. Qǐng nín gěi wǒ jǔ ge lìzi.

80 Mǎ: Wǒ jǔ ge lìzi. "Yuán Cháode huángdì shuàilǐngzhe jūnduì zhēngfúle
hěn duō guójiā. Nèige shíhoude lǐngtǔ kuà Ōu-Yà liǎngzhōu, suǒyǐ
shēngwēi hěn dà."

Bái: Wǒ míngbai le. Shuāiruò shi qiángde duìmiàn ma?

Mǎ: Shì. Bǐrú shuō: "Nèige guójiā shícháng fāshēng zhànzhēng, suǒyǐ
85 guóshì yìtiān bǐ yìtiān shuāiruò."

33.0. pài   depute, despatch, appoint

33.1. Zhèngfǔ pài tā dào wàiguo yánjiu yuánzǐnéng.

34.0. Zhāng Qiān   Chang Ch'ien (2nd century B.C.)

34.1. Zhāng Qiān shi Zhōngguo lìshǐshang yǒumíngde rénwu.

35.0. Xīyù   Western Regions

35.1. Zhōngguo gǔshí suǒwèi Xīyù jiu shi xiànzàide Xīnjiāng.

36.0. (Hàn) Wǔdì   Emperor Wu-ti of Han (140-86 B.C.) [martial emperor]

36.1. Hàn Wǔdì yǐ wǔlì zhēngfú Xīyù.   (W) (T)

37.0. shòukǔ   suffer, receive bad treatment (VO) [suffer bitter]

37.1. Zhāng Qiān bèi Xiōngnú liúxia le shì bu shi shòukǔ le?

Bái: Pài Zhāng Qiān dào Xīyù qù de shi Hàn Cháo něige huángdì? Wǒ
wàng le.

Mǎ: Shi Hàn Wǔdì.

Bái: Lìshǐshang jìzǎi, Zhāng Qiān wǎng Xīyù qù de shíhou, lùguò Xiōng-
90 núde dìfang, bèi Xiōngnú gěi liúxia le, yǐ zhù jiu shi shíjǐnián.

Mǎ: Duìle. Jùshuō zài nèi yíduàn shíjiānli, Zhāng Qiān shòule hěn duō
kǔ.

Bái: Shì bu shi cóng nèicì Zhāng Qiān dào Xīyù, Zhōngguo xīběi hěn
duō dìfang cái gēn Hàn Cháo yǒule láiwǎng?

95 Mǎ: Shì.

38.0. Nányáng   Southern Seas [south ocean]

38.1. Nèixiē huòwu dōu shi cóng Nányáng yùnlai de.

39.0. qúndǎo   archipelago [crowd island]

Nányáng Qúndǎo   South Seas Islands

39.1. Yǒu yìxiē dǎo bǐcǐ jùlí hěn jìn jiu jiàozuo qúndǎo.

39.2. Nányáng Qúndǎo zài Zhōngguode xīnán, lí Zhōngguo bù yuǎn, suǒyǐ
zài nàli yǒu bù shǎo Huáqiáo.

40.0. Zhèng Hé   Cheng Ho   (Ming Dynasty admiral)

40.1. Míng Cháode shíhou Zhèng Hé shuàilǐng hěn duō rén qùguo Nányáng
Qúndǎo, érqiě qùle hěn duō cì. Zài lìshǐshang jiu jiào "Zhèng Hé
xià Xīyáng."

41.0. cùchéng   stimulate [hurry become]

41.1. Yǒu jǐge yīnyuèjiā xiǎngyào zǔzhi yíge yīnyuèduì, hěn jiǔ yě méi
zǔchéng, hòulái háishi wǒ bāngmáng cùchéng de.

42.0. yìmù liǎorán   understand at a glance [one eye clear so]

42.1. Yìmù liǎorán shi yí kàn jiu míngbai de yìsi.

Bái: Qǐng wén nín, zài Míng Cháode shíhou suǒ shuō de Xīyáng shi zhǐzhe xiànzàide shénmo dìfang?

Mǎ : Jiu shi Nányáng Qúndǎo.

Bái: Zài Míng Cháode shíhou pài Zhèng Hé xià Xīyáng, mùdì shi shén-
100   mo?

Mǎ : Yǒu liángge mùdì. Yíge shi Míng Cháo dì-èrge huángdì táozǒu le,
dì-sānge huángdì yàoxiǎng zhǎozhe ta. Yīnwei nèige shíhou Nányáng
Qúndǎode Huáqiáo hěn duō, tāmen xiǎng kěnéng shi táodao Nányáng
Qúndǎo qu le. Háiyǒu yíge mùdì shi dāngshí xiǎngyào cùchéng duì-
105   wàide màoyìde fāzhǎn.   Wèile zhèi liǎngjiàn shì, suǒyǐ pài Zhèng
Hé xià Xīyáng.

Bái: Zhèng Hé dào Nányáng qùle qīcì, bù zhīdào yígòng yòngle duōshao
shíhou?

Mǎ : Qiánhòu yígòng yòngle èrshiqīniánde shíjiān.

110 Bái: Shì bu shi Zhōngguo Dàshì Niánbiǎoshang dōu yǒu?

Mǎ : Dōu yǒu. Něicháo něinián dōu fāshāng shénmo shìqing quándōu yǒu
jìzǎi. Biǎoshang kéyi yìmù liǎorán.

43.0. xuānyáng   publicize (W) [proclaim raise]

43.1. Wǒman bù kě xuānyáng biérénde duǎnchu.

44.0. hòushì   later ages, posterity (W) [rear generation]

44.1. Xuānhé Huàpǔ yǒu gāodùde měishù jiàzhi, suǒyǐ néng liúchuándao
hòushì. (W)

45.0. túqiáng   seek to be strong (W)

45.1. Túqiáng jiu shi "xiǎng fázi yào qiángqilai" de yìsi.

46.0. jí   very (W) (prefix before stative verbs, equivalent to jíle after a
stative verb in the spoken style)

46.1. Zuótiande yīnyuèhuì yǎnzòude hěn hǎo, tīng de rén jí duō. (W)

47.0. kōngjiān   space, interval (W) [empty interval]

47.1. Lìshǐ shi yóu shíjiān hé kōngjiān zhīchéng de. (W) (T)

Bái: Mǎ Jiàoshòu, <u>xuānyáng</u> gēn <u>fāyáng</u> shi tóng yíge yìsi ma?

Mǎ : Yìsi chàbuduō. Lìrú <u>xuānyáng wénhuà</u>、<u>fāyáng wénhuà</u> dōu kéyi.

115 Bái: <u>Hòushì</u> kǒuyǔ jiu shi <u>jiāngláide shìjiè</u>, duì ma?

Mǎ : Duìle.

Bái: Qǐng wèn nín, <u>túqiáng</u> shi shénmo yìsi?

Mǎ : Jiu shi "xīwang guójiā chéngle yíge qiángguó" de yìsi.

Bái: Qǐng wèn nín dāndú yíge <u>jí</u> zì zěnmo yòng? Shi wényánde ma?

120 Mǎ : <u>Jí</u> zài xíngróngcí qiánbiār jiu shi wényánde. Bǐrú <u>jí dà</u> jiu shi <u>zuì</u>
<u>dàde</u> yìsi, <u>jí shèng</u> jiu shi <u>zuì shèngde</u> yìsi.

Bái: Shēngcí biǎoshang <u>kōngjiān</u> zhèige cér shì bu shi jiu shi zài Kàngzhàn de shíhou yǒu yíge kǒuhào yìsi shi ná <u>shíjiān</u> huàn <u>kōngjiān</u>
de nèige <u>kōngjiān</u>?

125 Mǎ : Shì.

48.0. yǎpiàn   opium

48.1. Yīngguo yùn yǎpiàn dào Zhōngguo lái. Zhōngguo bǎ zhèixiē yǎpiàn
dōu gěi shāo le, bìngqiě bù zhǔn zài yùn.   Yīncǐ yǐnqǐ zhànzhēng.
Lìshǐshang jiu jiàozuo Yǎpiàn Zhànzhēng. (T)

49.0. nèiluàn   internal disturbance, civil war [interior disordered]

49.1. Yíge guójiā yǒule nèiluàn rénmín jiu yào shòukǔ le.

50.0. Xīnhài Gémìng   Revolution of 1911 (see Intermediate Chinese, p. 346,
note 2)

50.1. Xīnhài Gémìngde shíhou yǒu rén xià pànduàn shuō gémìng yídìng
néng chénggōng de.

51.0. hàozhào   summon, rouse [signal summon]

51.1. "Qīqī" yǐhòu Zhōngguo zhèngfǔ jiu hàozhào rénmín quánmiàn duì
Rìběn kàngzhàn. (T)

52.0. qǐyì   raise a righteous revolt [rise righteousness]

52.1. Xīnhài gémìng yǐqián rénmín jiu yǒu hǎojǐcì qǐyì le.

Bái: Yǎpiàn Zhànzhēng, Zhōngguo sǔnshī hěn dà a?

Mǎ : Xiānggǎng jiu shi cóng nèige shíhou zuòle Yīngguode zhímíndì.

Bái: Shì bu shi nèicìde zhànzhēng yě yǐnqǐle Zhōngguode nèiluàn?

Mǎ : Shì.   Cóng nèige shíhou qǐ yìzhí dào Xīnhài Gémìng shícháng yǒu
130   nèiluàn.

Bái: Xīnhài Gémìngde shíhou yòng shénmo hàozhào rénmín?

Mǎ : Gémìng kāishǐ de shíhou, Sūn Zhōngshān Xiānsheng yòng <u>Sānmín Zhǔyì</u> lái hàozhào.

Bái: Shì bu shi Xīnhài Gémìng qǐyìle jǐcì cái chénggōng le?

135 Mǎ : Shìde. Qǐyìle hǎojǐcì, sǐle bù shǎode gémìng fènzǐ.

53.0. zhèngtǒng   orthodox [upright unify]

53.1. Zhōngguode sīxiǎng yǐ Rújiā xuéshuō wéi zhèngtǒng shi cóng Hàn Cháo kāishǐ de. (W) (T)

54.0. chénjiù   stale, obsolete, old-fashioned (W) [stale old]

54.1. Tāde sīxiǎng tài chénjiù, gēnbushàng shídài le.

55.0. yādǎo   (1) upset, overturn; (2) excel, surpass [press collapse]

55.1. Nèikē líshù jiào qiáng gěi yādǎo le.   (T)

55.2. Zhōngguo Gòngchǎndǎng yǒu yíge kǒuhào shi "dōngfēng yādǎo xī-fēng." (T)

56.0. zǒngjié   (1) conclude, sum up; (2) conclusion, summary [general knot]

56.1. Wǒ bǎ zhèicì zuòtánhuìde tánhuà zuò yíge zǒngjié.

57.0. biànfǎ   reform [alter method]

57.1. Qīng Cháo mònián zhèngfǔ suírán yǒu yìsi biànfǎ kěshi nèicìde biànfǎ shi shībài le.

58.0. Tángrén   men of T'ang, Chinese

58.1. Zhōngguo rén wèi-shénmo yě jiào Tángrén ne?

59.0. xià*   (1) summer; (2) Hsia Dynasty; (3) (a surname)

       xiàtian   summer

59.1. Jù Zhōngguo gǔshūshang jìzǎi Shāng Cháo yǐqián shi Xià Cháo.

59.2. Yǒu yíge chéng měinián xiàtian dōu quē shuǐ. Rénmen bùdébù cóng hěn yuǎnde dìfang qu yùn shuǐ.

Bái: Mǎ Jiàoshòu, <u>zhèngtǒng</u> zhèige cér zěnmo yòng?

Mǎ : Wǒ jǔ ge lìzi: "Zhōngguo gǔshíhou zhǐ chéngrèn Rújiāde xuéshuō shi zhèngtǒngde sīxiǎng.

Bái: <u>Chénjiù</u> jiu shi <u>gǔlǎode</u> yìsi, shì bu shi?

140 Mǎ : Bǐrú "Xiànzàide xīn wénxué shi yādǎole chénjiùde gǔ wénxué."

Bái: <u>Zǒngjié</u> shì bu shi shuō huà <u>zǒng'éryánzhī</u> de yìsi?

Mǎ : Shìde. Wǒ xiànzài wèn nǐ yíge cér. <u>Biànfǎ</u> nǐ zhīdao shi shénmo yìsi ma?

Bái: Jiu xiàng Qīng Cháo zuì hòude shíqī yǒu xiē dà chén kàn guóshì
145   yuè lái yuè ruò, suǒyǐ xīwang Qīng Cháo huángdì gǎigé zhèngzhi.
         Nà jiu shi biànfǎ.

Mǎ : Nǐ zhīdao wèi-shénmo guǎn Zhōngguo rén jiào Tángrén?

Bái: Shi zhǐzhe Táng Cháo shuō de. Yīnwei Táng Cháo shi Zhōngguo
      zuì shèngde shíqī, suǒyǐ hòulái guǎn Zhōngguo rén jiào Tángrén.

150 Mǎ : Duìle.

Bái: Shēngcí biǎoshangde <u>xià</u> jiu shi <u>xiàtiande</u> <u>xià</u> ma?

Mǎ : Shì. <u>Xiàtian</u>、<u>Xià Cháo</u> dōu shi zhèige <u>xià</u>.

Bái: Yě yǒu rén xìng Xià shì bu shi?

Mǎ : Shì. Yě shi ge xìng.

60.0. jiāoliú   interflow, interchange (N/V) [join flow]

60.1. Zhōng-Měi Xuéhuìde zǔzhi wèideshì Zhōng-Měi wénhuà jiāoliú.

61.0. wùzhǐ   (1) matter, substance; (2) material, materialistic [thing sub-
        stance]

61.1. Zài wùlǐxuéshang shuō wùzhǐ shi yǒngyuǎn bú miè de.

62.0. dōng*   winter

        dōngtian   winter

62.1. Rìzi guòde zhēn kuài. Yòu shi qiū qù dōng lái le. (T)

62.2. Wǒ xiǎng yǐ "dōngtiande nóngchǎng" zuòwei huìhuà de tícái. (W)(T)

63.0. jìyì   (1) remember, recollect; (2) recollection (W) [record re-
        member]

        jìyìlì   memory [record remember strength]

63.1. Ànzhe wǒde jìyì, tā chūguó yǒu sānnián duō le. (W)

63.2. Zuótiande shì, wǒ jīntian jiu wàng le. Wǒde jìyìlì zhēn bù hǎo.

64.0. téng   hurt (IV)

        tóu téng   headache (N/V)

64.1. Wǒ xiě zì tài duō le, xiěde wǒ shǒu dōu téng le.

64.2. Wǒ xiànzài tóu bù téngle. Wǒmen chūqu zǒuzou qu, hǎo bu hǎo?

155 Mǎ : <u>Jiāoliú</u> zhèige cér nǐ zhīdao zěnmo yòng ma?

Bái: "Liǎngge guójiā bǐcǐ fǎngwèn, mùdì shi cùchéng liǎngguóde wénhuà
      jiāoliú."

Mǎ : <u>Wùzhǐ</u> nǐ míngbai tāde yìsi ma?

Bái: <u>Jīngshēn</u>de duìmiàn shi <u>wùzhǐ</u>. <u>Wùzhǐ</u> jiu shi <u>dōngxi</u>.

160 Mǎ : Duîle.

Bái : Mǎ Jiàoshòu, wǒ xiǎngqi yíjiàn shîqing lái. Zài qián xiē rìzi nín
shuō ràng wǒmen wàiguo xuésheng zài dōngtian zǔzhi yíge guóyuè
yánjiuhuî, yuányīn shi yīnwei yǒu hǎojǐge wàiguo tōngxué duî Zhōngguo yīnyuè yǒu xìngqu. Bù zhīdào shénmo shíhou cái zǔzhi?

165 Mǎ : Duîbuqǐ, zhèijiàn shîqing wǒ gěi wàng le. Yàoshi nǐ bù tí, wǒ yìdiǎr yě bú jîde le. Wǒ jìnlaide jìyìlî fēicháng huài. Shuōguo de
shîqing, bìděi yòng bǐ jîxialai, yàoburán jiu wàng le. Wǒ xiǎng
děng wǒmende Zhuāntî Jiǎnghuà wánle yǐhòu, qǐng jǐwèi duî guóyuè
yǒu xìngqude tóngxué, dàjiā zài yíkuàr tǎolùn yíxiàr.

170 Bái : Wǒ yě cānjiā.

Mǎ : Jiu shi nǐ bù cānjiā wǒ yě qǐng ni. Hǎo, jīntiande cér dōu tǎo-
lùnguo le. Yǒu shénmo wèntî méi yǒu?

Bái : Méi yǒu.

Mǎ : Hái yǒu shíjǐfēn zhōng cái xià kè ne. Nǐ yào bu yào xiūxi yìhuěr?

175 Bái : Yě hǎo. Wǒ hái yǒu yìdiǎr tóu téng.

SHĒNGCÍ BIǍO

1. fén-shū-kēng-rú

2. (Qín) Shǐhuáng

3. huómái

4. tǒngyī

5. yǐnqǐ

6. (Hàn) Gāozǔ

7. fēng

8. Shèng Táng

9. gǎi-cháo-huàn-dài

10. fǔbài

11. shī
    sǔnshī

12. mínxīn

13. zhūhóu

14. jūnzhǔ

15. wángshî (W)

16. xīng
    xīngqǐ

17. miè

18. wáng
    mièwáng
    xīngwáng (W)

19. zhìshî (W)

20. luànshî

21. fēnliè
    sì-fēn-wǔ-liè

22. hú*
    Húrén
    Wǔhú Shíliù Guó

23. wàihuàn

24. Xiōngnú

25. wèi(le) . . . qǐjiàn (W)

26. wǔlî

27. qīnrù (W)
    qīnlüè

28. shēngwēi (W)

29. kuà

30. shuàilǐng (W)

31. shuāiruò

32. guóshî

33. pài

34. Zhāng Qiān

35. Xīyù

36. (Hàn) Wǔdî

37. shòukǔ

38. Nányáng

39. qúndǎo
    Nányáng Qúndǎo

40. Zhèng Hé

41. cùchéng

42. yímù liǎorán

43. xuānyáng (W)

44. hòushî (W)

45. túqiáng (W)

46. jí (W)

47. kōngjiān (W)

48. yǎpiàn

49. nèiluàn

50. Xīnhài Gémìng	56. zǒngjié	61. wùzhǐ
51. hàozhào	57. biànfǎ	62. dōng*
52. qǐyì	58. Tángrén	dōngtian
53. zhèngtǒng	59. xià*	63. jìyì (W)
54. chénjiù (W)	xiàtian	jìyìlì
55. yādǎo	60. jiāoliú	64. téng
		tóu téng

YǓFǍ LIÀNXÍ

(See note 1)

1. Yǒu jǐge huàjiā zài Dūnhuáng zhùzhe ne . . . Zài Dūnhuáng zhùzhe jǐge huàjiā.

2. Yǒu yíge huòchē cóng qiánbiār kāiguolai le . . . Qiánbiār kāiguolaile yíge huòchē.

3. Yǒu jǐge yīnyuèjiā cóng táishang zǒuxialai le . . . Cóng táishang zǒuxialaile jǐge yīnyuèjiā.

4. Yǒu hěn duō lí dōu cóng Shāndong chūkǒu le . . . Cóng Shāndong chūkǒule hěn duō lí.

5. Nǐ tīngwánle yīnyuè yǐhòu hái dào nǎr qù ma?

6. Nǐ xuéwánle wǔdǎo yǐhòu hái dào chéng lǐtou mǎi shénmo ma?

7. Yǎnzòuhuì wánle yǐhòu nǐ hái kàn shéi qù ma?

8. Yīhuěr kāiwánle guānyu tígāo chūchǎn gāngtiěde nèige huì yǐhòu, nǐ hái yào gēn zhǔxí shuō shénmo ma?

9. Nèige yùnhuò de gōngrén tiāntian bùyánbùyǔde jiu shi zuò gōng. Nǐ kàn ta yīhuěrde gōngfu bǎ nènmo duōde huòwu dōu yùnwán le.

10. Nǐ kàn zhèi liǎngge zì nǐ xiě de bùqīngbùchǔde, nǐ xiě de shì bu shi qúndǎo liǎngge zì a?

11. Zhèlide tiānqi yǒngyuǎn shi bùlěngbúrède, zuì shìhé mùxùyè.

12. Tā guǎn cáizhèng guǎn de bùmíngbùbáide.

13. Zuótian wǎnfàn zài Xīyù Lóu chī fàn wǒ chīle sì dà kuài hóngshāo yángròu.

14. Jīntian shàng lìshǐ kède shíhou, xiānsheng jiào wǒ zhànqilai, niàn cóng Qín Cháo xīngqǐ dào mièwáng nà yí xiǎo duàr lìshǐ.

15. Nà yí dà chē yuánliào dōu shi gōngyìng féiliào gōngchǎng zào féiliào yòng de ma?

16. Wáng Xiānsheng yào xiě yíbù Qīng Dài xīngwáng shǐ, suǒyǐ ta yì zhěng zhuōzi dōu shi cānkǎo shū.

17. Xià Xiānsheng xīn hǎo, tā chángcháng bāngzhu biéren.

18. Wǒ zuì bù xǐhuan tiàowǔ, wǒ yì tīngshuō yǒu rén yào qǐng wǒ tiàowǔ wǒ
    jiu tóu téng.

19. Rénmínde fùdān yòu yào jiāzhòng le. Tīngjian zhèige xiāoxi, shéi néng
    bù tóu téng?

20. Wǒ xiànzài tóu bù téng le, kéyi dào yīnyuèhuì qù le.

JIǍNGHUÀ

Zhūwèi tóngxué:

    Jīntian jiǎnghuàde tímu shi: "Zhōngguode Lìshǐ." Jiǎng zhèige tímu
zhèng xiàng Zhōngguo yíjù súhuà suǒ shuō de: "Yíbù Èrshisì Shǐ bù zhī
cóng nǎli shuōqǐ." Yào jiǎng de zīliào jìrán yǒu zhènmo duō, suǒyǐ jiu
5 bùdébù xuǎnzé jǐge yàodiǎn lái jiǎng. Wǒmen xiànzài suǒ xuǎn de yàodiǎn shi cóng liǎngfāngmiàn kàn. Yìfāngmiàn shi cóng shíjiānshang lái
kàn. Zhōngguo lìshǐ yǒu sānqiān duō nián. Zài zhèi sānqiān duō niánli,
yíge cháodài jiēzhe yíge cháodài. Jiūjìng yǒu duōshao cháodài? Dōu shi
xiē shénmo cháodài? Zhè shi yánjiu Zhōngguo lìshǐ zuì jīběn zhīshi, yě
10 shi wǒmen shǒuxiān yīngdāng zhīdao de. Lìng yìfāngmiàn shi cóng kōngjiānshang lái kàn, jiu shi zài měi yíge cháodài dàngshí yǒu shénmo dàshì, yóuqíshi nénggou yǐngxiǎngdào hòushìde dàshì. Zhè shi lìshǐde zhōngxīn, gèng shi wǒmen yào yánjiu de. Zhèixiē dōu shi jīntian yào jiǎng de
fànwéi.
15   Zài Zhōngguode lìshǐshang yǒu zhìshì hé luànshìde fēnbié. Zhìshi
jiu shi guójiā tǒngyī、shèhuì āndìng de shíqī. Luànshì jiu shi guójiā fēn-
liè、shèhuì hǔnluàn de shíqī.
    Wǒmen xiān shuō zhìshì shíqīde cháodài. Yìbān jiǎng gǔdài lìshǐ
dōu shi cóng Xià Cháo kāishǐ shuōqǐ, dànshi yīnwei Xià Cháo méi yǒu
20 shìshíde gēnjù, suǒyǐ wǒ xiànzài cóng Shāng Cháo shuōqǐ. Cóng jǐyuánqián yìqiān duō niánde Shāng Cháo, yǐhòu jiu shi Zhōu Cháo. Zhōu Cháo
zhīhòu jiu shi Qín、Hàn、Jìn、Suí、Táng、Sòng、Yuán、Míng、Qīng yìzhí
dào xiànzàide Zhōnghuá Mínguó yǐjí Zhōnghuá Rénmín Gònghéguó. Zhèixiē cháodài jiù zhèngzhide zhìdu lái shuō, zài Zhōnghuá Mínguó yǐqiánde
25 dōu shi jūnzhǔ zhuānzhì de. Jiù shèhuìde guānxi lái shuō, dōu shi fēngjiàn shìli de. Jiù tǒngzhì de rén lái shuō, dà duōshù dōu shi Hànrén,
zhǐ yǒu Yuán Cháo shi Měnggǔ rén, Qīng Cháo shi Mǎnzhōu rén.

Zhōngguo lìshǐshang luànshìde shíqī kéyi
shuō shi yǒu sìge. Dì-yī shi Zhōu Cháode

30 mònián Chūnqiū Zhànguó shíqī. Dāngshíde
Zhōngguo fēnchéng hěn duō xiǎo guó, hòulái
chéngle qīge bǐjiǎo dàde guójiā. Dì-èr shi
Hàn Cháo mònián Zhōngguo fēnchéng Sān Guó.
Dì-sān shi Jìn Cháo mòniánde Wǔhú Shíliù

35 Guó hé Nánběi Cháo. Nà shi Zhōngguo zuì
hǔnluànde shíqī le. Búdàn guónèide xiǎo guó
hùxiāng dǎzhàng, érqiě guówàide Xiōngnú děng
zú yě qīnrùle Zhōngguo. Dì-sì shi Táng Cháo
zhīhòu yǒu Wǔdài Shí Guó yě shi yíge hǔn-

40 luàn shíqī. Xiànzài wèile róngyi jìyì qǐjiàn,
ànzhe cháodàide xiānhòu huàle yíge cháodài
tú. Zhūwèi kàndao zhèizhāng tú duìyu Zhōngguode cháodài jiu yímù liǎorán le.

Xiànzài jiǎngjiang Zhōngguo lìshǐshang-

45 de dàshì. Zhōngguode lìshǐ jìrán yǒu sān-
sìqiānnián le, gèzhǒng dàshì dāngrán hěn duō.
Zhèli suǒ jiǎng de zhǐ shi duì hòulái yǒu
yǐngxiǎng de jǐjiàn dàshì.

(Yī). Shāng Cháode jiǎgǔwén. Shāng

50 Cháode wénzì shi Zhōngguo zuì gǔde wénzì,
zài gōngyuán yī-bā-jiǔ-bā nián zài Zhōngguode Hénán Shěng dìxia bèi fājuéchulai. Yīnwei zhèixiē wénzì dōu shi kèzài guījiǎ hé
niúde gútoushang, suǒyǐ jiu jiào jiǎgǔwén. Jiǎ-

55 gǔwénde fāxiàn, zài yánjiu gǔdài wénhuà hé
lìshǐshang dōu yǒu hěn dàde jiàzhí.

(Èr). Fēngjiàn zhìdu. Zhōngguo cóng
Zhōu Cháo qǐ shíxíng fēngjiàn zhìdu. Fēngle
hen duō hé wángshì tóngxìng de rén zuò zhū-

60 hóu, bǎ tǔdì fēngěi zhūhóu. Zhūhóu yào fúcóng wángshì. Zhèizhǒng zhìdu yìzhí dàole
Qín Cháo cái bú yòng le.

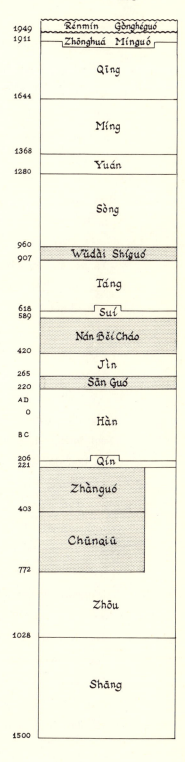

4

94 Dì-Èrshi'èrkè. Lìshǐ

(Sān). Wànlǐ Cháng Chéng hé fén-shū-kēng-rú. Qín Shǐhuángde
shíhou zài Zhōngguode běibù zhùle yídào hěn chángde chéng. Cháng Chéng
65 shi cóng Héběi Shěngde dōngbiān yìzhí dàole Gānsu Shěng xībiān, cháng
yǒu qīqiān duō lǐ, yīnwei tài cháng le, suǒyǐ jiàozuo Wànlǐ Cháng Chéng.
Zhù Cháng Chéng wèideshì bú ràng Xiōngnú jìnlai. Xiànzài zhèige Cháng
Chéng hái cúnzài ne. Dāngshí hái yǒu yíjiàn jīngréndede dàshì shi fén-shū-
kēng-rú. Qín Shǐhuáng bǎ gǔdàide shū dōu shāo le, yòu bǎ xǔduō niàn
70 shū de rén dōu huómái le. Qín Shǐhuángde xiǎngfǎ rúguǒ méi yǒu shū yòu
méi yǒu niàn shū de rén, rénmin jiu méi yǒu zhīshi, jiu bú huì fǎnkàng
ta le.

(Sì). Píngmín huángdì. Hàn Cháo dì-yīge huángdì shi Hàn Gāozǔ.
Tā běnlái shi yíge píngmín, zhè shi Zhōngguo lìshǐshang dì-yīge píngmín
75 huángdì. Hàn Cháo dàole Hàn Wǔdìde shíhou duìnèi shi zūnchóng Rújiā.
Cóng zhèige shíhou qǐ Rújiāde sīxiǎng jiu chéngle Zhōngguode zhèngtǒng
sīxiǎng. Hàn Wǔdì duìwài tā zhēngfú Xiōngnú, yòu pài Zhāng Qiān dào
Xīyù qù, suǒyǐ Hàn Cháo zài Zhōngguo lìshǐshang zhàn hěn zhòngyàode
dìwei.

80 (Wǔ). Shèng Táng shíqī. Táng Cháo zài Zhōngguo lìshǐshang shi
yíge jí shèng shíqī, suǒyǐ lìshǐjiā jiào ta shi Shèng Táng. Zài Táng Cháo
zuì shèng shíqī búdàn guónèi gēwǔ shēngpíng, wénhuà fādá, érqiě guótǔ
yě hěn dà, lián Cháoxiǎn Ānnán hé Yàzhōu biéde hěn duō xiǎo guó yě
dōu fúcóng Táng Cháo le. Suǒyǐ yìzhí dào xiànzài hái yǒu rén jiào Zhōng-
85 guo rén shi Tángrén.

(Liù). Lǐngtǔ kuà Ōu-Yà. Yuán Cháo shídàide wǔlì zuì qiáng, búdàn tǒngzhìle Zhōngguo, bìngqiě zhēngfúle Ōu-Yà liǎngzhōu hěn duōde
guójiā. Tāde lǐngtǔ kuà Ōu-Yà, shi gǔ-jīn Zhōng-Wài dì-yīge dà guó.
Dāngshí yīnwei Yuán Cháo jūnduì dǎdào Ōuzhōu, suǒyǐ cùchéng Zhōng-Xī
90 wénhuàde jiāoliú. Zhōngguode huǒyào、yìnshuāde fāngfǎ děng dōu shi nèi
shíhou xiānhòu chuándàole Xīfāng de. Tóngshí Xīfāngde wénmíng yě jiànjiànde chuándàole Zhōngguo. Zhè shi Yuándài zài lìshǐ wénhuàshang yíge
hěn dàde gòngxiàn.

(Qī). Zhèng Hé xià Xīyáng. Míng Cháode shíhou céngjīng pài Zhèng
95 Hé dào Xīyáng qù. Nà shíhou suǒwèi Xīyáng jiu shi xiànzàide Nányáng
Qúndǎo yídài. Zhèng Hé cóng gōngyuán yī-sì-líng-wǔ nián qǐ dào yī-sì-

sān-èr nián yígòng qùle qīcì. Měicì dōu shi shuàilǐng hěn duō chuán hé hěn duō rén, wèideshì xuānyáng Zhōngguode shēngwēi. Zhè zài Zhōngguo lìshǐshang shi yǐqián suǒ méi yǒu de shì.

100   (Bā). Yāpiàn Zhànzhēng. Zài gōngyuán yī-bā-sān-bā nián Qīng Cháode shíhou Zhōngguo wèile jìnzhǐ Yīngguo yùn yāpiàn dào Zhōngguo, jiu yǐnqǐle Zhōng-Yīng liǎngguóde zhànzhēng. Zhè jiu jiàozuo Yāpiàn Zhànzhēng. Zhèicì zhànzhēng duì Zhōngguode yǐngxiǎng hěn dà. Zhàn-zhēng zhīhòu Xīfāngde sīxiǎng hé wùzhì wénmíng yādǎole Zhōngguo chén-
105 jiù sīxiǎng. Zhōngguo rén suírán yě xiǎng biànfǎ túqiáng, kěshi guóshì hái shi yìtiān bǐ yìtiān shuāiruò le.

    (Jiǔ). Xīnhài Gémìng. Qīng Cháo mònián guóshì yìtiān bǐ yìtiān shuāiruò, wàihuàn nèiluàn dōu hěn duō. Yúshi yǐnqǐle rénmínde gémìng. Guómíndǎngde lǐngxiù Sūn Zhōngshān Xiānsheng yòng tā xiě de <u>Sānmín</u>
110 <u>Zhǔyì</u> lái hàozhào gémìng. Zài yī-jiǔ-yī-yī nián jiu shi yīnlìde Xīnhài nián gémìng de, suǒyǐ jiàozuo Xīnhài Gémìng. Zhèicìde gémìng chéng-gōngle zhīhòu jiu chénglìle Zhōnghuá Mínguó. Zhè shi Zhōngguo lìshǐ-shang huà shídàide dàshì. Guòqu jǐqiánnián lái de jūnzhǔ zhuānzhìde zhì-du cóngcǐ méi yǒu le, xīnde mínzhǔ zhèngzhi yě jiu cóngcǐ kāishǐ.

115   (Shí). Guó-Gòng wèntí. Zhōngguo lìshǐ dàole xiàndài, fāshēng yí-jiàn zhòngdàde shì, jiu shi Guó-Gòng wèntí. <u>Guó</u> jiu shi <u>Guómíndǎng</u>, <u>Gòng</u> jiu shi <u>Gòngchǎndǎng</u>. Zhèi liǎngdǎngde zhèngcè shi dà bù xiāng-tóngde. Yǒushíhou hézuò, yǒushíhou bù hézuò. Gòngchǎndǎng zài yī-jiǔ-sì-jiǔ nián zài Běijīng chénglìle Zhōnghuá Rénmín Gònghéguó Rénmín
120 Zhèngfǔ. Tóngshí Zhōnghuá Mínguó Guómín Zhèngfǔ jiu bùdébú qùdao Táiwān. Zhè jiu xíngchéngle Guó-Gòng liǎngge zhèngfǔ. Zhè búdàn shi Zhōngguode zhòngdàde wèntí, yě yǐngxiǎngle shìjiè, chéngle guójìjiānde dà wèntí.

    Xiànzài zǒngjié lái shuō, Zhōngguo zhěnggè lìshǐ dōu shi jìlù lì-
125 dàide xīngwáng dàshì. Wǒmen yánjiu měicì gǎi-cháo-huàn-dàide yuányīn, dà duōshù shi yīnwei zhèngzhi fǔbài, rénmín shòukǔ, zhèngfǔ shīqùle mín-xīn. Suǒyǐ zhìguó de rén bìxū dé mínxīn. Yíge cháodài shīqù mínxīn, rénmín jiu yào qǐyì gémìng le.

FÙSHÙ

Zhèipán lùyīndài shi Zhōngwén dì-yīzǔ, dì-shíbāhào, shi Bái Wénshān fùshù de Zhuāntí Jiǎnghuà "Jīngji."

Zhèicìde Zhuāntí Jiǎnghuà shi wǒmen xuéxiào jīngji-xì Zhāng Jiàoshòu gěi wǒmen jiǎng de. Tā suǒ jiǎng de zhèng shi wǒmen xūyào zhī-
5 dao de. Tóngshí yīnwei Zhāng Jiàoshòu shi Běijīng rén, tā shuō de shi
chúncuìde Běijīng huà. Wǒmen búdàn zhīdaole bù shǎo guòqu gēn xiànzài
Zhōngguo jīngjide qíngxing, érqiě yě děngyú shàngle yíkè Guóyǔ.

Zhāng Jiàoshòu shǒuxiān gěi wǒmen jiǎng, Zhōngguo jǐqiānnián yǐlái
dōu shi yǐ nóngyè wéi zhōngxīnde guójiā.   Tā shuō Zhōngguo jìrán shi
10 nóngyè wéi zhōngxīnde guójiā, dāngrán jīngji zhōngxīn yě shi nóngyè le.
Kěshi cóng shíjiǔ shìjì gēn wàiguo tōngshāng yǐhòu, qíngxing jiu gǎibiàn
le.

Zhāng Jiàoshòu shuō zài yī-jiǔ-sān-qī nián Zhōngguo duì Rìběn
Kàngzhàn yǐqián, jīngji zhìdu shi yìzhǒng zìyóu jīngji, shìchǎng dōu shi
15 yóu Zhōngguo shāngrén gēn wàiguo shāngrén zìyóu zuò shēngyi. Zài nèige
shíhou, guójiāde jīngji zuì zhǔyàode shi nóngyè.   Gōngyè shi luòhòu de.
Zhāng Jiàoshòu shuō dāng nèige shíhou Zhōngguo gōng-shāngyè yǒu liǎng
dà shìli.   Dì-yī shi wàiguode dà zīběnjiā.   Tāmende zīběn duō, suǒyǐ
Zhōngguode zhòngyào qǐyè xiàng hángyè、kuàngyè dōu zhǎngwòzai tāmen
20 shǒuli. Dì-èr shi Zhōngguo shèhuìshàng yǒu shìlide rén, tāmen zài yánhǎide dà chéngshi jīngyíngzhe gōng-shāngyè. Zhèi liǎngzhǒng shìli shòule
Kàngzhànde yǐngxiǎng, hòulái tāmende shìli cái yuè lái yuè xiǎo le.

Zhāng Jiàoshòu yòu jiǎngdào tōnghuò péngzhàng de yuányīn.   Tā
shuō zài Zhōngguo Kàngzhàn yǐqián, huòbì shi wěndìng de. Yīnwei Kàng-
25 zhàn de yuányīn, zhèngfǔ xūyào yòng qiánde dìfang tài duō, zhǐ yǒu dàliàng fāxíng huòbì cái néng zhīchí Kàngzhàn.   Huòbì yì duō le, wùjià jiu
zhǎng le.   Děngdào nèizhàn yì kāishǐ, Zhōngguode jīngji hěn kuàide jiu
tōnghuò péngzhàng. Jiéguǒ jīngji bēngkuì le.

Zài yī-jiǔ-sì-jiǔ nián Gòngchǎndǎng dédào zhèngquán yǐhòu, jīngji
30 zhèngcè jiu gǎibiàn le. Tāmen yǒu yíge xīnde jīngji jìhua, zài yī-jiǔ-wǔ-
sān nián kāishǐ dì-yīge wǔnián jìhua.   Zhèige jìhua yǐngxiǎngle zhěnggède Zhōngguo jīngji, xiàng gōngyè、màoyì、yùnshū děngděngde.

Zhāng Jiàoshòu shuō Máo Zédōng zài nóngyè fāngmiàn tā zhǔzhāng bǎ nóngtián fēngěi nóngren, zhè shi Zhōngguo gémìngde jīběn chūfādiǎn.

35 Zhōngguo nóngcūn gǎigéde dì-yībù shi tǔdì gǎigé, dì-èr shi bàn hézuò shìyè, jiu shi bàn hézuòshè, hùzhùzǔ, jítǐ nóngchǎng, háiyǒu rénmín gōngshè.   Tóngshí wèile yào zēngjiā nóngyède shēngchǎn, tíchàng zhòngtián shǐyòng huàxué féiliào.   Yòu zàole hěn duō shuǐbà gēn shuǐkù, wèideshì guàngài hé fādiàn.

40 Zhāng Jiàoshòu jiǎngdao nóngyède gōngjù tuōlājī.   Tā shuō zài Zhōngguo Dōngběi, nóngzuòyè yǐjing yòng tuōlājī le.   Tāmen xīwang zhěnggè Zhōngguode nóngyè jiānglái dōu shi jīxièhuà.

Zhāng Jiàoshòu shuō Zhōngguo nóngchǎnpǐnli liángshi shi zhǔyàode nóngchǎn.   Miánhua zài nóngchǎnpǐnli yě zhàn hěn zhòngyàode dìwei.   Jìn-

45 lai zhèngfǔ yě tíchàng zàolín.   Tāmen yě zhùzhòng mùxùyè, yīnwei mùxùyè zài jīngjishang yě shi zhòngyàode.

Zhāng Jiàoshòu shuō, Zhōngguo dàlùshang duìyu zhòng gōngyè fēicháng zhòngshì, zēngjiànle hěn duō gāngtiěchǎng, yǐjing chūchǎnle bù shǎode gèzhǒng jīqi, xiàng huòchē, tuōlājī děngděng.   Duìyu fǎngzhī gōngyè

50 gēn qítā xiāofèi gōngyè, bìng bú zěnmo zhòngshì.   Tāmen hěn nǔlì kāifā kuàngchǎn, yóuqíshi méi, tiě gēn shíyóu.   Wèile jiāotōng hé yùnshū, zào dà qiáo xiū tiělù, tóngshí bǎ yùnhé yě gǎijìn le.

Zuìhòu Zhāng Jiàoshòu jiǎngdao Zhōngguo duì guójì màoyìde wèntí. Tā shuō Zhōngguo kāishǐ shi duì Sūlián hé lìngwài jǐge shèhuì zhǔyìde

55 guójiā màoyì.   Jìnlai duì zīběn zhǔyi guójiāde màoyì yě jiànjiànde zēngjiā le.

Zhāng Jiàoshòu yòu shuōdao dàyuèjìn.   Tā shuō zài yī-jiǔ-wǔ-qī dào yī-jiǔ-wǔ-jiǔ nián dàyuèjìn de shíhou, yǒude shi chénggōng le, yǒude shi shībài le.   Yuányīn shi jìhuashangde cuòwu, jiāshang tiānzāi, liángshi

60 qiànshōu.   Suǒyǐ zài dàyuèjìn yǐhou nèi liǎng sānnián lǐtou liángshi shēngchǎn bú gòu, shènzhiyú rénmín xūyào de liángshi dōu děi pèiji.

WĒNXI

1. Yǒu yíge huàjiā zuì xǐhuan huà huāhui.   Zhǐ yàoshi yǒu rén qǐng ta huà huàr, tā jiu gěi rénjia huà huāhui.   Tā shuō: "Zhǐ yǒu huāhui cái shi chún měishù."

2. Zuótiande wǎnhuì, xiān shi yīnyuèhuì, shi Xīyuè hézòu. Zài yuèqìli yǒu jǐjiànde yàngzi hěn tèbié, zhèizhǒng yuèqì wǒ cónglái méi kànjianguo. Jùshuō zhèicì yǎnzòu shi yǐ zhèi jǐjiàn yuèqì wéi zhǔ. Hòulái shi wǔtáijù, yǒu xiē rén biǎoyǎn gēwǔ, dòngzuò hěn měi. Zuìhòu shi tiàowǔ, hěn duō rén bǎ liǎn dōu huà huā le. Wǒ kànjian hěn duō huāliǎn tiàolái tiàoqù. Yǒu rén shuō: "Zhèige wǎnhuì fǎnyìng rénmen xīnlide kuàilè, zhēnshi gēwǔ shēngpíng a!"

3. Táng Mínghuáng hé Yáng Guìfēi dōu hěn xǐhuan gēwǔ xìjù, Táng Mínghuáng jiu xùnliànle xǔduō Líyuán Zǐdì. Suǒyǐ hòulái guǎn chàng xì de dìfang jiào Líyuán, chàng xì de rén jiàozuo Líyuán Zǐdì.

4. Zhōngguode lǐjié duōbàn qǐyuán zài Zhōu Cháo. Zhōu Cháo hěn zhùzhòng lǐyuè, yě zhùzhòng jì shén de yíshì.

5. Zhōngguo jīngxìli yòng gèzhǒng xíngshìde dòngzuo xiàngzhēng gèzhǒng shìqing. Bǐrú zhànzai zhuōzishang jiu shi biǎoshì dēng shān, jǔqǐ biānzi jiu biǎoshì qí mǎ.

6. Nèige dìfang yǒu hěn duō chūchǎnpǐn, érqiě hái yǒu jīnshǔde kuàng. Cóngqián yīnwei quēshǎo gōngren, yòu yīnwei yòng jiùde fāngfǎ fēnpèi gōngzuò, suǒyǐ bù néng dàliàng kāifā. Jìnlai gǎijìn hěn duō. Bǐrú shǐyòng jīqi, zēngjiàn tiělù děngděng, suǒyǐ nèige dìfang hěn kuài jiu fánróngqilai le.

7. Yǒu yíge lǎonián rén shuō, jù tāde jìyì zài liùshi duō nián qián zhèige qúndǎo yǒu shíjǐge xiǎo dǎo. Zài yícì dà fēng zhīhòu hūrán shīqùle yíge xiǎo dǎo. Yīnwei hěn duō rén dào nèige dǎoshang qù lǚxíng, suǒyǐ sǔnshī hěn dà.

8. Jīngxìlide liǎnpǔ shi xiàngzhēng rénde xìnggé. Rúguǒ yào biǎoshì yíge jiānzhàde rén, jiu bǎ tāde liǎn huàchéng báide. Kàn xì de rén yí kànjian báiliǎn jiu kéyǐ pànduàn zhèige rén yídìng bú shi hǎorén.

9. Yǒu rén shuō: "Jìnlai shèhuìde fēngqì bǐ cóngqián zhuǎnbiànde tài dà le. Jiù ná xuéxiàode xuésheng lái shuō ba. Nǐ rúguǒ wèn cóngqiánde xuésheng 'Chúle shàngkè zhīwài nǐ dōu zuò shénmo?' tāmende huídá duōbàn shi shuō, kànkan shū, liànxi liànxi shūfǎ. Xiànzài ne, duōbàn shi chàng gēr, tiàowǔ. Chàng gēr de qiāngdiào hěn tèbié, fēicháng nántīng. Yàoshi jiào tāmen zuò shì shénmo yě zuòbulái. Zhè zhēnshi yíge yánzhòngde wèntí. Dàjiā yīnggāi mìqiè zhùyì."

10. Wáng Xiānsheng yǒu yìzhǒng bìng, yí dào dōngtian jiu tóu téng. Tā shuō: "Wǒ wèile zhì bìng yòngle hěn duō qián, hǎojǐnián yě méi zhìhǎo. Wǒ jiā yǐqián suírán shi yíge zhōngchǎn jiējí, kěshi jìnlai měiniánde shōurù zhǐ gòu wéichí shēnghuó, nǎr yǒu qián cháng zhìbìng ne?"

11. Zhōngguo yǒu yíjù cháng shuō de huà: "Miè biéren guójiā de, rénjia yě bì miè tāde guójiā." Zhèijù huà shi gàosu wǒmen rén bú yào yòng wǔlì miè biérende guójiā. Kěshi wǒmen cóng lìshǐshang kàn yíge guójiāde mièwàng duōbàn shi yīnwei xiān shīqù mínxīn. Rúguǒ bù shī mínxīn guójiā bú huì wàng. Suǒyǐ yíge guójiā bú pà biéren lái miè, jiu pà shīle mínxīn.

12. Yǒu rén wèn wo: "Zài lìshǐshang yǒu shíqì shídài, shì fǒu yǒu táoqì hé yùqì shídài?" Wǒ gàosu ta gǔshí suírán yě yǒu táoqì, yùqì dànshi méi yǒu táoqì shídài, yě méi yǒu yùqì shídài.

13. Tā zuòqǔ shi yòng Xīyáng zuòqǔfǎ. Yǒu shíhou hái bǎ Xīyángde qǔzi yě bú yìchéng Zhōngwén, jiu yòng zhèixiē qǔzi zhíjiē zuò jiàocái le. Suǒyǐ yǒu xiē yào bǎocún guócuìde rén dōu shuō bù yīngdāng yòng zhèizhǒng qǔzi zuò jiàocái.

14. Yǒu yíge rén zuì xǐhuan yánjiu gǔdàide jiànzhu, diāokè, shíkè. Tā shuō cóng zhèixiē gǔdàide dōngxili kéyi zhīdao dāngshí yìshude zuòfēng.

15. Wǒ jiā yòng de mùqì dōu shi wǒ zǔfù liúchuánxialai de, yòu yǒu jǐjiàn zhúqì jùshuō shi zǔfù cóng nánfāng mǎilai de, suǒyǐ quánjiāde rén duìyu zhèixiē dōngxi dōu rènwéi shi hěn bǎoguì.

WÈNTÍ

1. Zhōngguo lìshǐshang yǒu zhìshì hé luànshì. Shénmo shi zhìshì? Shénmo shi luànshì? Cóng Shāng Cháo dào xiànzài, zhìshì shi něixiē cháodài? Luànshì yǒu jǐge shíqī? Shénmo shíqī zuì hǔnluàn?

2. Zhōngguo lìshǐ jiù zhèngzhide zhìdushang hé shèhuìde guānxishang yǐjí tǒngzhì de rén lái shuō shi zěnyàng qíngxing?

3. Shénmo jiào fēngjiàn zhìdu? Cóng shénmo cháodài kāishǐ? Dào shénmo cháodài jiu bú yòng le?

4. Qín Shǐhuáng wèi-shénmo zào Cháng Chéng? Wèi-shénmo fén-shū-kēng-rú?

5. Zhōngguo lìshǐshang dì-yīge píngmín zuò huángdì de shi shéi? Nèige cháodài duìnèi duìwài yǒu shénmo dàshì?

6. Lìshǐjiā wèi-shénmo jiào Táng Cháo shi Shèng Táng shíqī? Shèng Táng shíqī guónèi guówài shi zěnyàng qíngxing? Xiànzài hái yǒu rén jiào Zhōngguo rén shi shénmo rén?

7. Yuán Cháo lǐngtǔ kuà Ōu-Yǎ. Tā zài wénhuàshang yǒu shénmo gòngxiàn?

8. Míng Cháo wèi-shénmo pài Zhèng Hé xià Xīyáng? Shénmo shíhou kāishǐ qù de? Qùle duōshao cì?

9. Shénmo shi Yāpiàn Zhànzhēng? Tā duì Zhōngguo yǒu shénmo yǐngxiǎng?

10. Qīng Cháo mònián wèi-shénmo yǐnqǐ rénmínde gémìng? Wèi-shénmo jiào Xīnhài Gémìng? Yòng shénmo lái hàozhào? Zhèicì gémìng wéi-shénmo shi huà shídàide dàshì?

ILLUSTRATIVE SENTENCES (ENGLISH)

7.1. Emperor Kao-tsu of Han enfeoffed many persons as kings.

12.1. Because the government constantly added to the burden of the people, [therefore] it lost popular support.

14.1. England and Japan are both monarchies.

18.3. Everyone is responsible for whether a country rises or falls.

21.1. Vietnam was split up in 1954, being divided into South Vietnam and North Vietnam.

26.1. That state acquired a new army plus new military equipment, so its military power increased several fold [compared to the past].

30.1. That country experienced an inflation and a rise in prices. Some people say the public utilities led the rise in prices.

36.1. Emperor Wu-ti of Han used military power to subjugate the Western Region.

47.1. History is made in [lit. woven from] time and space.

48.1. England transported opium to China. China burned the opium and forbade its future importation. This led to war. In history it is called the Opium War.

51.1. After the Marco Polo Bridge Incident of July 7, 1937, the Chinese government summoned the people to an all-out war of resistance against the Japanese.

53.1. The establishment of Confucian ideology as the orthodox in Chinese thinking started in the Han Dynasty.

55.1. That pear tree was crushed [lit. overturned] by the (falling) wall.

55.2. The Chinese Communists have a slogan "The Eastern wind will surpass the Western wind."

62.1. Time has gone by very fast. Again autumn is past and winter has come.

62.2. I plan to use Winter Farm as the subject of a painting.

NOTES

The following miscellaneous usages are illustrated in the exercise Yǔfǎ Liànxí in this lesson:

  a (1-4). Sentences containing indeterminate subjects in the pattern yǒu V N can often be transformed into equivalent sentences with the pattern V N:

        Yǒu liǎngge kèren láile . . . Láile liǎngge kèren.   'Two guests have come.'

  b (5-8). In sentences containing both a question particle and a question word the latter is used in an indefinite sense:

        Nǐ dǎo nǎr qu ma?   'Are you going somewhere?'

  c (9-12). The construction bù A bù B signifies 'neither A nor B' if A and B are opposite in meaning, and adds emphasis to the negation if A and B have the same or similar meaning:

        Jīntian cér bù duō bù shǎo, zhěng èrshige.   'The words today are neither (too) many nor (too) few. There are exactly twenty.'

        Bùzhībùjuéde yòu shi qiūtiān le.   'Without our becoming aware of it, it's already fall again.'

d (13-16). A few words such as dà 'big,' xiǎo 'little,' zhěng 'whole' can be inserted before a numeral and a measure (including nouns used as measures):

> yí dà kuài dòufu 'a big chunk of beancurd'

> yì zhěng zhuōzi shū 'a whole tableful of books'

e (17-20). Some subject-predicate clusters can serve as predicates to other subjects placed in topic position with or without an intervening de:

> Nèige rén xīn hǎo. 'That man is kind' [lit. That man is heart-good.]

> Nèige rénde xīn hǎo. 'That man is kind' [lit. That man's heart is good.]

In most cases the negative is placed before the verb; in a few cases, before the subject-predicate cluster as a whole:

> Wǒ tóu bù téng.
> Wǒ bù tóu téng. } 'My head doesn't ache.'

Dì-Èrshisānkè. Wényán hé Báihuà

Bái : Mǎ Jiàoshòu zǎo.

Mǎ : Zǎo. Zhèi liǎngtiān hěn lěng, hǎoxiang dōngtian shide.

Bái : Kěbushìma. Zuótian wǒ dào Gāo jiā qù le. Gāo Xiānsheng fūfù wèn nín gēn Mǎ Tàitai hǎo.

5 Mǎ : Tāmen dōu hǎo ba?

Bái : Dōu hǎo. Gāo Xiānsheng shuō xiàyuè yào dào Nányáng qù yícî.

Mǎ : Qù duōshao shíhou ne?

Bái : Tā zìjǐ méi shuō. Měiyīng gàosu wo tā dàgài yào qù liǎngge yuè.

Mǎ : Tāmen shūdiànde shēngyi hěn hǎo ba?

10 Bái : Kàn qíngxing shi bú cuò. Tóngshí Gāo Xiānsheng yě shuō shūdiàn tài máng le. Hái xūyào zài zhǎo yíge rén bāngmáng. Zuótian Gāo Xiānsheng sòng wǒ liǎngběn shū, dōu shi xīn chūbǎn de. Yìběn Zhōngguo Jìndài Shǐ, yìběn Wénzìxué Jiǎnyào. Zhèi liǎngběn shū wǒ hěn xūyào, yóuqíshi Zhōngguo Jìndai Shǐ. Nà shàngtou guānyu Qīng

15 mò Yǎpiàn Zhànzhēng、biànfǎ gēn Xīnhài Gémìng dōu xiěde hěn xiángxi. Wénzìxué Jiǎnyào gèng yǒuyòng, yīnwie wǒ xiě de lùnwénli wǒ xiǎng xiě yìdiǎr wǒmen zěnmoyàngr qu yánjiu wénzìxué, suǒyǐ nèiběn shū yě hěn yǒuyòng.

Mǎ : Sān Yǒu Shūdiànde shū hěn duō. Cóngqián wǒ shícháng qù. Zhèi

20 yì liǎngnián yīnwei tài máng le, lǎo yě méi qù le.

Bái : Nín zhēn máng.

Mǎ : Zuótiande jiǎnghuà lùyīnle méi yǒu?

Bái : Lù le.

Mǎ : Zìjǐ tīngle juéde zěnmoyàng?

25 Bái : Háishi yǒu xǔduō cuòr.

Mǎ : Wǒ xiǎng mànmānde jiu huî hǎo le. Jīntiande Zhuāntí Jiǎnghuà shi Wényán hé Báihuà. Xiànzài wǒmen jiu tǎolùn tǎolùn zhèi xiēge shēngcér.

Bái : Zhuāntí Jiǎnghuà jīntian shi zuìhòu yícî le.

30 Mǎ : Kěbushìma!

1.0. jiǎntǎo (1) review, examine; (2) a review, an examination [inspect ask]

1.1. Wǒmen jiǎntǎo lìdài xīngwáng de yuányīn, duōbàn yóuyu dé mínxīn huòzhěshi shī mínxīn.

502

2.0. xīndé   a gain [heart get]

2.1. Nǐ yánjiu wéiwùlùn yǒu shénmo xīndé?

3.0. xiàndu   a limit [limit standard]

   zuìdī(de) xiàndu   at least [most low limit]

3.1. Zhèngzhi huódong shi yǒu xiàndu de. Rúguǒ chūle xiàndu jiu biàn-
     chéng fǎnkàng zhèngfǔ le.

3.2. Wǒ niàn shū zuìdī xiàndu yào niàndao zhōngxué bìyè.

4.0. yī   according to

   yīkào   depend on, trust   [according to lean on]

4.1. Zhèijiàn shì jiù yī nǐde yìjian qu bàn ba.   (T)

4.2. Táng Cháo mònián yǒu rén yīkào Húrén chénglìle yíge xiǎo guó.

5.0. gǔlì   (1) encourage; (2) encouragement [drum encourage]

5.1. Gòngchǎn zhǔyì gǔlì rénmín yào yǒu shòukǔ de jīngshen.

Bái: Mǎ Jiàoshòu, wǒ zìjǐ jiǎntǎo zìjǐ, wǒ juéde suírán zài gōngke yì-
     fāngmiàn duōshǎo yǒule yìdiǎr xīndé érqiě wǒ yě hěn yònggōng,
     kěshi zhīdao de háishi bú gòu. Zuìdīde xiàndu yīngdāng bǐ xiànzài
     hái dǒngde duō yìdiǎr.

35 Mǎ : Yī wǒ kàn, nǐ zhīdao de xiāngdāng duō le, érqiě nǐde chéngji, gēn-
     ju xuéxiàode tǒngjì, shínián yǐlái nǐ shi wàiguó xuéshengli zuì yōu-
     xiùde yíge.

Bái: Zhè shi nín gǔlì wǒ de huà.

Mǎ : Zhè shi shízài de.

6.0. Sòng Lián   (Ming scholar-official, 1310-1381)

6.1. Sòng Lián shi Míng Cháo rén, tāde zhùzuò hěn duō.

7.0. Wáng Miǎn Zhuàn   Biography of Wang Mian (a Ming Dynasty paint-
                                               er)

7.1. Sòng Lián zuò de Wáng Miǎn Zhuàn wǒ méi kànguo.   Jùshuō shi
     wényánde.

8.0. huí   chapter (in a book)

8.1. Hóng Lóu Méng yígòng yǒu yībǎi èrshihuí. Qián bāshihuí shi yíge
     rén xiě de, hòu sìshihuí yòu shi lìngwài yíge rén xiě de.

9.0. miáoxiě   describe, depict [depict write]

9.1. Hóng Lóu Mèngli bǎ jǐbǎige nánnǚ lǎoshàode yàngzi hé xìnggé dōu
     miáoxiěde xiàng huóde shide.   (T)

10.0. shēngdòng   lifelike, lively, animated [life move]

10.1. Zài nèipiān xiǎoshuōli miáoxiě fùzǐ liǎngge rénde duìhuà shífēn shēngdòng.

11.0. gùrán   of course, to be sure, unquestionably [solid thus]

11.1. Fǎjiāde xuéshuō gēn Mòjiā gùrán bù yíyàng, kěshi zài sīxiǎngshang lái shuō dōu shi yǒu jiàzhi de.

40 Bái: Qǐng wèn nín, Sòng Lián shi shénmo shíhoude rén?

Mǎ: Shi Míng Cháo yíwèi hěn yǒu xuéwende rén. Wáng Miǎn Zhuàn jiu shi tā yòng wényán xiě de.

Bái: Wényánde Wáng Miǎn Zhuàn wǒ méi kànguo. Rúlín Wáishǐshangde dì-yīhuí yě shi Wáng Miǎn Zhuàn. Nèige wǒ kànguo le. Nà shi
45 báihuàde, miáoxiěde shēngdòng jíle. Wényánde zěnmoyàng?

Mǎ: Wényánde gùrán yǒu wénxué jiàzhi, kěshi wǒ rènwei háishi báihuàde hǎo, rénrén dōu kàndedǒng. Nèipiān wényánde duōshù rén kànbudǒng.

12.0. yuē   say (used for introducing a direct quotation) (W)

12.1. Zài Sì Shūshang cháng yǒu "zǐ yuē" liǎngge zì. "Zǐ" shi zhǐzhe "Kǒngzǐ," "yuē" jiu shi "shuō." "Zǐ yuē" jiu shi "Kǒngzǐ shuō" de yìsi.

13.0. yǐnyòng   (1) use, bring forward for use; (2) cite (W) [lead use]

13.1. Tā zài lùnwénli yǐnyòng Mǎkèsī、Lièníng yǐjí Shǐdàlínde shuōfǎ.

14.0. xiàoguǒ   result, outcome (W) [efficacy result]

14.1. Tā suīrán chīle yào, kěshi xiàoguǒ zěnmoyàng xiànzài hái bù zhīdào.

15.0. jūzhù   reside (at) (W) [reside reside]

15.1. Yìlián jǐnián dōu yǒu nèiluàn. Shāole bù shǎo fángzi. Hěn duō rénde jūzhù dōu yǒule wèntí. (W)

16.0. héchù?   where? (W) [what place]

16.1. Wáng Xiānsheng zuìjìn xiěle yìpiān wénzhāng, tímu shi "Héchù shi Wǒ Jiā?"

Bái: Zài wényánlide "yuē" jiu shi báihuàde "shuō," zhèige wǒ zhīdào.
50 Nèige "yuē" zì hái néng zuò biéde jiěshi ma?

Mǎ: Dà duōshù shi "shuō" de yìsi.

Bái: "Yǐnyòng" zhèige cér, qǐng nín gěi wǒ jǔ ge lìzi.

Mǎ: Bǐrú "Tā nèipiān wénzhāng suīrán xiě de shi wénxué, kěshi yǐnyòngle bù shǎo Fójīngshangde jùzi."

55 Bái: "Xiàoguǒ" shi "chéngji" de yìsi ma?

Mǎ : Yào kàn zài nǎr yòng. Yǒu shíhou shi "chéngji" de yìsi, yǒu shí-
        hou yě shi "jiéguǒ" de yìsi.

Bái : Wǒ míngbai le.

Mǎ : Wǒ wèn nǐ yíge jùzi nǐ kàn shi shuō de hái shi xiě de: "Fǔshang
60   jūzhù héchù?"

Bái : Shi xiě de. Rúguǒ zài kǒuyǔshang shi "Fǔshang zhùzai nǎr a?"

17.0. bàle   (1) Enough of that! (And) that's that!; (2) just, no more than
              [used at end of sentence]

17.1. Nǐ bú qù jiu bàle, bú bì zài duō shuō huà le. (T)

18.0. nénggan   be capable [able do]

18.1. Tā shi yíge hěn néngande rén, suǒyǐ tā zuò de shì dōu hěn hǎo.

19.0. cāozòng   manipulate, control [drill release]

19.1. Wùjià hùnluàn shi yīnwei yǒu rén cāozòng.

20.0. jiědá   (explain and) answer (W)

20.1. Nǐ xiěchulai de nèi jǐge wèntí, wǒ xiànzài méi fázi jiědá.

21.0. xìng*   fortunate

       xìngkuī   fortunately [fortune deficiency]

       xìng'er   fortunately [fortune and]

21.1. Tā běnlái méi qián niàn dàxué. Xìngkuī déle jiǎngxuéjīn cái niàn
        de dàxué.

21.2. Qián jǐniánde nèiluàn wǒmen xiāngxia sǔnshī hěn dà. Xìng'er dāng-
        shí wǒ bāndao chéngli qù le.

Bái : Mǎ Jiàoshòu, <u>bàle</u> zhèige cér, wǒ zǒngshi yòngde bù hěn duì. Qǐng
        nín jǔ ge lìzi.

Mǎ : Hǎo. "Wǒ yìdiǎr yě bu nénggan, búguò shi wèile shēnghuò nǔlì
65   gōngzuò bàle."

Bái : <u>Cāozòng</u> zhèige cér wǒ bú dà dǒng.

Mǎ : "Jìnlái wùjià yǒu zhènmo dàde biàndong, dōu shi yìbān shāngrénmen
        cāozòng de."

Bái : <u>Jiědá</u> gēn <u>jiěshì</u> yíyàng ma?

70 Mǎ : Yǒu yìdiǎr fēnbié. <u>Jiědá</u> shi zhuān wèi jiěshi wèntí shuō de. Bǐrú
        "Zhèige wèntí wǒ bù néng jiědá." <u>Jiěshì</u> shi rènhé shìqing bu míng-
        bai, dōu kéyi jiěshi.

Bái : Zuótian yǒu yíwèi tóngxué gēn wo shuō, tā zǒuzài lùshang chà yì-
        diǎr ràng chē gěi pèng le, xìngkuī shi chē zǒude màn. Tā shuō de
75   nèige <u>xìngkuī</u> jiu děngyu <u>xìng'er</u>, shì bu shi?

Mǎ : Shì. X̱ìngkuī gēn x̱ìng'er shi yíyàngde yìsi.

22.0. chú cǐ zhīwài   apart from this (W)

22 1. Wǒde jìyìli zhǐ jìde wǒ xiǎode shíhou céngjīng zài Shànghǎi niàn-
       guo xiǎoxué. Chú cǐ zhīwài wǒ shénmo yě bú jìde le.

23.0. biànlì   (1) serviceable; (2) profitable; (3) convenient; (4) convenience
               (W) [convenient profit]

23.1. Wèile shàngxué biànlì qǐjiàn wǒ bìděi mǎi chē. (W) (T)

24.0. jǐngchá   police (N) [warn observe]

24.1. Nǐ zhīdao jǐngchá hé jūnren yǒu shénmo fēnbié ma?

25.0. zhìxu   order(liness) [order order]

25.1. Nànmín xiàng cháoshuǐ yíyàng yǒngjìn chéngli. Xìngkuī yǒu jǐngchá
       wéichí zhìxu, fǒuzéde huà chéngli jiu hǔnluàn le.   (W)

26.0. zhǎnlǎn   to exhibit [unfold view]

       zhǎnlǎnhuì   exhibition [unfold view meeting]

26.1. Nèige xuéxiào zài měinián xiàtian dōu kāi zhǎnlǎnhuì, zhǎnlǎn de
       dōu shi xuéshengde chéngji.

Bái : Xiě dōngxi de shíhou cháng yòng "chú cǐ zhīwài." Yàoshi shuō huà
        de shíhou bù cháng yòng ba?

Mǎ : Yǎnjiǎng de shíhou kéyi shuō.   Píngcháng shuō huà dōu shi shuō
80   "chúle zhèige yǐwài."

Bái : Ḇiànlì jiu shi f̱āngbiàn.

Mǎ : Shì. Bǐrú "Jìnlai zhèlǐde tiělù bǐ yǐqián zēngjiāle sānfēnzhī-yī,
        suǒyǐ jiāotōng fēicháng biànlì."

Bái : Wǒ míngbai le.

85 Mǎ : Qǐng nǐ yòng j̱ǐngchá、ẕhìxu gēn ẕhǎnlǎnhuì shuō yíjù huà.

Bái : "Zhèicì wùchǎn zhǎnlǎnhuì cānguān de rén tài duō le, suǒyǐ
        zhìxu hěn luàn, lián jǐngchá dōu wéichíbuliǎo."

Mǎ : Hěn hǎo.

27.0. jiànkāng   (1) health; (2) healthy [healthy peaceful]

27.1. Tāde shēntǐ cóngqián hěn jiànkāng. Jìnlai yìtiān bǐ yìtiān shuāiruò
       le.

28.0. shūfu   (1) comfortable; (2) comfort [relax yield]

       bù shūfu   (1) uncomfortable; (2) in poor health, indisposed.

28.1. Néng shòukǔ de rén jiānglái bù yídìng shòukǔ. Xǐhuan shūfu de rén
       jiānglái bù yídìng shūfu.

28.2. Wǒ zhèi jǐtiān shēntǐ yǒu yìdiǎr bù shūfu.

29.0. jiāoshe (1) negotiate; (2) negotiations; (3) mutual relations [join involve]

29.1. Qīng Cháo mònián duì wàiguo de jiāoshe dōu shi shībài de. (T)

30.0. zhēnglùn wrangle, dispute (N/V) [argue discuss]

30.1. Tāmen fūfù wèile háizimen shàngxué de wèntí fāshengle zhēnglùn.

Mǎ : Jīntian xiàwǔ wǒ hái děi dào yīyuàn qu kàn péngyou qu.

90 Bái: Nínde péngyou shēngbìngle ma?

Mǎ : Shìde. Běnlái zhèiwèi péngyoude shēntǐ fēicháng jiànkāng. Yǒu yìtiān hūrán gǎnjué yǒu diar bù shūfu. Búdào liǎngtiān jiu bìngde
hěn lìhai. Biéde péngyou mǎshàng sòng ta dào yīyuàn qù, kěshi
yīyuàn bù shōu yīnwei bìngrén tài duō, méi dìfang le.

95 Bái: Nà zěnmo bàn ne?

Mǎ : Nèiwèi péngyou jiāoshele bàntiān, yīyuàn cái bǎ ta liúxia le.

Bái: Nínde péngyou xiànzài hǎo diar le ma?

Mǎ : Qiántian wǒ kàn ta qu, shāowéide hǎo yìdiǎr. Wéixiǎn shi méi yǒu
le, búguò tā děi xiūxi yíge xiāngdāngde shíqī.

100 Bái: Tā jiāli yǒu biéren ma?

Mǎ : Jiù tā yíge rén. Běnlái tā tàitai yě zài zhèr. Yīnwei fūfù liǎngge
gǎnqíng bù hǎo, shícháng wèile yìdiǎr xiǎo shìqing jiu zhēnglùnqilai
le. Yǒu yícì fūfù liǎngge bù zhīdào wèile shénmo, zài yǔyánshang
yòu qǐle chōngtu. Tā tàitai yì shēngqì, shōushí xíngli dàizhe háizi
105 huí lǎojiā le.

Bái: Nènmo tā hěn jìmo le.

Mǎ : Kěbushìma!

31.0. fèizhǐ annul, abolish [abolish stop]

31.1. Wǔlúnlide jūnchén shì bu shi xiànzài yǐjing fèizhǐle ne?

32.0. jīliè violent, radical [incite ardent]

32.1. Zài huìyìde shíhou tāmen liǎngge rén zhēnglùnde hěn jīliè.

33.0. yōushì superiority, ascendance, ascendancy [superior tendency]

33.1. Shāng Jūn zhì Qín Guó de shíhou yǐ-fǎ-zhì-guó, xìn-shǎng-bì-fá,
suǒyǐ dāngshí Fǎjiāde xuéshuō zuì zhàn yōushì. (T)

34.0. jiélùn conclusion [knot discuss]

34.1. Dàjiā tǎolùnle bàntiān yě méi dédào yíge jiélùn. (T)

Mǎ : Zuótian xiàwǔ wǔdiǎn zhōng wénxué zuòtánhuî kāi huî.

Bái: Nín cānjiāle ma?

110 Mǎ : Wǒ qù le.

Bái: Zuótian tǎolùn de shi shénmo tímu?

Mǎ : Tímu shi "Gè Xuéxiàode Zhōngwén Kèchéng Shîfǒu Yīngāi Fèizhǐ
Wényénwén?"

Bái: Tǎolùn de qíngxing zěnmoyàng?

115 Mǎ : Yǒu fǎnduî de, yǒu zànchéng de. Dàjiā zhēnglùnde hěn jīliè.

Bái: Fǎnduî de zhàn yōushî, háishi zànchéng de zhàn yōushî ne?

Mǎ : Huî kāile bàntiān, shǐzhōng yě méi dédào yíge jiélùn.

35.0. xūzî   (grammatical) particle [empty word]

35.1. Wényánli suǒ yòng de xūzî zài báihuàli bù yídîng dōu yǒu yòng.

36.0. zǐxi   minutely, carefully [careful fine]

36.1. Xīn sīxiǎng suǒyǐ nénggou yādǎole chénjiùde sīxiǎng shi shénmo
yuányīn, nǐ zǐxi yánjiuguole ma?

37.0. yángé   strict, narrow [strict category]

37.1. Tā shuō huà yǒu diar Shāndong kǒuyīn, yángéde shuōqilai tā bù
néng jiāo Guóyǔ.

38.0. chūbù   (1) first step, introduction; (2) initial

38.1. Cóngqián wàiguo rén dào Zhōngguo chuánjiào, tāmen chūbùde gōngzuò shi bàn xuéxiào.

39.0. shízhǐ   physical, real, solid, substantial [solid matter]

shízhǐshang   in reality, actually

39.1. Yào zhùzhòng shízhǐ, bú yào zhùzhòng xíngshì.

39.2. Yòng wényán xiě de Wáng Miǎn Zhuàn hé yòng báihuà xiě de Wáng
Miǎn Zhuàn zài shízhǐshang dōu shi xiě de Wáng Miǎnde shîqing.

Mǎ : Shuōdao wényán hé báihuà, wǒ wèn nǐ yíge wèntí. Nǐ zhīdao wényánlide zhī、 yě、 hū děngdengde zì yǒu yíge míngchéng jiào shénmo?

120 Bái: Jiào xūzî.

Mǎ : Duîle. Xūzî zài wényánli hěn bù róngyi yòng. Yǒu rén cháng bǎ
xūzî yòngcuò le. Suǒyǐ yào zǐxi yánjiu, yào yángéde fēnqīngchule.

Bái: Yánjiu xūzîde chūbù yīnggāi shi shénmo?

Mǎ : Chūbù yào míngbai xūzîde yîsi, érqiě yào zhīdao zài shízhǐshang
125   dōu děngyu báihuàde shénmo zì.

Bái: Zhī děngyu de, hū děngyu ma, yě děngyu ya.

Mǎ : Duìle.

40.0. shuāngyīnjié   two-syllable expression

40.1. Yǒu rén shuō: "Gǔ shíhou méi yǒu shuāngyīnjiéde cí." Zhèizhǒng shuōfǎ shì bu shi kěkào ne?

41.0. húdiè   butterfly

41.1. Zài Zhuāngzǐshang shuō, Zhuāngzǐ zuòle yíge mèng, tā huàle yíge húdiè. (T)

42.0. qíngkuàng   condition, circumstances [condition state]

42.1. Wǒ méi qùguo Nányáng Qúndǎo. Wǒ bù zhīdào nèige dìfangde qíngkuàng.

43.0. biàn   distinguish, discriminate

    biànbié   distinguish, discriminate [distinguish other]

43.1. Nèitiān wǎnshang tiān hěn hēi, wǒ méi fázi biànbié lái de rén shi shéi.

Bái: Yǒu rén shuō gǔwénli méi yǒu shuāngyīnjiéde cér. Nín rènwei zěnmoyàng?

130 Mǎ : Wǒ rènwei nèige shuōfǎ bú duì. Xiàng Zhuāngzǐshang húdiè nèige cér jiu shi shuāngyīnjié me.

Bái: Duìle. Húdiè shi shuāngyīnjié.

Mǎ : Nǐ kéyi shuōshuo Zhuāngzǐ biàn húdiède gùshi ma?

Bái: Zhuāngzǐ cóngqián céngjīng zuòguo yíge mèng, mèngjian tā zìjǐ
135 biànchéng yíge húdiè le. Tā hěn gāoxìngde fēizhe. Zài dāngshí nèige qíngkuàngli, tā biànbiébuchūlái tā shi Zhuāngzǐ ne hái shi húdiè ne.

44.0. fàn   offend, violate (the law)

    fànfǎ   break the law (VO)

    fàn (. . . de) máobing be guilty (of . . .) (lit. offend by the defect of . . .)

44.1. Tā yòu fànle bú ài shàngxué de máobing le. (T)

44.2. Rénren dōu shuō ta shi jūnzǐ, tā bú huì fànfǎ de.

44.3. Tā shi yíge xìnjiào de, tā bù yīnggāi zuò fànfǎ de shì.

45.0. zuì   crime, sin

    fànzuì   commit a crime (VO) [offend crime]

45.1. Shénfù duì xìntú shuō: "Rénrén yǒu yuánshǐde zuì."

45.2. Zūnzhòng dàodé de rén yídìng bú huì fànzuì de.

46.0. zhìqi   will, ambition, inclination [will air]

46.1. Tā shi yíge yòu yǒu zhìqi yòu hěn nénggande qīngnián.

47.0. xiěqì, xuěqì   vigor [blood air]

47.1. Xīnhài Gémìng zhīqián yǒu qīshí'èrge yǒu xiěqìde qīngnián qǐyì, kěshi méi chénggōng dōu sǐ le.

48.0. yōnghù   protect, uphold [support protect]

48.1. Tā shi zhèige tuántǐde lǐngxiù. Hěn duō rén dōu yōnghù ta, kěshi yě yǒu rén gōngji ta.

Bái: Mǎ Jiàoshòu, qǐng wèn fànzuì gēn fànfǎ shi yíyàngde yìsi ma?

Mǎ : Chàbuduō yíyàng. Bǐrú "Nèige rén fànle shénmo fǎ le?" yě kéyi
140   shuō "Nèige rén fànle shénmo zuì le?"

Bái: Qǐng nín zài shuōshuo zhìqi gēn xiěqì zhèi liǎngge cérde yìsi.

Mǎ : Wǒ jǔge lìzi: "Fánshi yǒu zhìqi de dōu yīnggāi yōnghù zhèizhǒng àiguó yùndong." "Tā dāng bīng qu le, tā zhēnshi yǒu xiěqìde qīng-nián."

49.0. huópo   lively, quick, bustling [live spill]

49.1. Nèige xiǎo nǚhái yòu hǎokàn yòu huópo.

50.0. yǎnjing   eye(s)

50.1. Wǒde yǎnjing tài dà. Tāde yǎnjing bú dà yě bù xiǎo.

51.0. biǎoqíng   (1) express emotions, express feelings; (2) expression of emotions

      biǎoqíng dáyì   express emotions and state meanings

      dáyì biǎoqíng   state meanings and express emotions

51.1. Yǒude rén néng yòng yǎnjing biǎoqíng lái dàibiǎo shuō huà. (T)

51.2. Yǔyán wénzì dōu shi biǎoqíng dáyì de gōngjù.

52.0. hùnzá   mixed (together) [confuse mixed]

52.1. Nèige dìfang shèngxíng wán zhǐpái, érqiě shi nánnǚ hùnzá zài yíkuàr wán. Nǐ shi xǐhuan qīngjìng de rén. Nǐ bú yào qù.

53.0. gàiniàn   concept, idea [general ponder]

53.1. Gàiniàn shi xīnlǐxué hé lùnlǐxuéshang cháng yòng de míngcí. Tāde yìsi jiu shi yǒule hěn duō gǎnjué yǐhòu de nèige guānniàn.

145 Bái: Huópo shi yònglái xíngrong rén de. Bǐfang "Nèige xiǎoháizi hěn huópo." Yě kéyi xíngróng biéde ma?

Mǎ : Yě kéyi xíngrong yǔyán wénzî. Bǐrú "Nèipiān wénzhāng xiěde fēi-
      cháng huópo shēngdòng."

Bái : Yàoshi xíngrong yíge rénde yǎnjing, néng bu néng yòng huópo ne?

150 Mǎ : Nà děi yòng línghuó lái xíngrong.   Wǒ jǔ ge lìzi: "Nèige yǎnyuán
         hěn huî biǎoyǎn, biǎoqíng hǎojile.   Yóuqíshi tāde liǎngzhǐ yǎnjing,
         xiāngdāng línghuó."

Bái : Hǔnzá jiu shi bù chúncuî le, shî bu shi?

Mǎ : Shi.

155 Bái : Gàiniàn jiu shi guānniàn ma?

Mǎ : Bú shi. Gàiniàn shi xīnlǐxuéshangde míngcî. Yìsi jiu shi yǒule hěn
      duō gǎnjué yǐhòude nèige guānniàn jiàozuo gàiniàn.

54.0. chāo*   surpass

        chāoguò   surpass, go beyond

54.1. Jīnnián zhǎnlǎnhuî zhǎnlǎn de dōngxi bǐ qùnián duōqilai le. Jīnnián
        cānguān de rén kěnéng chāoguòle qùniánde rénshù.

54.2. Tā shuō de huà chāochule wǒmen suǒ tǎolùn de fànwéi. (T)

55.0. máodùn   (1) inconsistent; (2) inconsistency, contradiction   [spear
        shield]

55.1. Zuótian tā shuō tā zuî xǐhuan shuàilǐng xuésheng qu cānguān zhǎn-
        lǎnhuî. Jīntian tā yòu shuō tā zuî bù xǐhuan dài xuésheng chūqu.
        Tā qiánhòude shuōfǎ tài máodùn le.   (W)

56.0. bào   hold, embrace   (literal and figurative)

56.1. Zài dǎzhàng de shíhou, zuî kǔde shìqing shi bàozhe xiǎoháizi táo-
        nàn.

56.2. Fánshi xué yìzhǒng dōngxi, bǐděi bào yídìng yào bǎ ta xuéhǎo de
        mùdî.   (T)

56.3. Tā shícháng bàozhe yìzhǒng shībài de xiǎngfǎ, suǒyǐ tā shénmo shî
        yě zuòbuchénggōng.   (T)

Mǎ : Nǐ xiànzài zhīdao de cér yǐjing chāoguo sānqiān le ba?

Bái : Wǒ xiǎng chāoguò le, kěshi quèshíde shùmu wǒ yě bù zhīdào.

160 Mǎ : Wǒ xiǎng xiě yìběn pǔtōng chángyòng cí huòzhě chángyòng zî de
         shū, kěshi xīnli hěn máodùn, bù zhīdào xiě shénmo hǎo?

Bái : Zhèi liǎngzhǒng dōu hěn yǒuyòng, zuî hǎo nín dōu xiě.

Mǎ : Wǒ shi bàozhe ràng xuéshengmen néng zài kèwài duō zhīdao yì-
      diǎr de mùdî, suǒyǐ wǒ yào xiě zhèizhǒng shū.

57.0. jùjué   (1) break off relations; (2) refuse, repel; (3) refusal [refuse break]

57.1. Yǒu yíwèi mùshi jiào wo xìn Jīdūjiào, ràng wo gěi jùjué le.

58.0. qǔdé   to gain, make a profit [fetch get]

58.1. Tā yǒu yìzhǒng túqiáng de zuòfēng, suǒyǐ tā néng qǔdé rénmínde yōnghù.

59.0. è   evil (N/SV)

       shàn'è   good and evil, good or evil (N/SV) (W)

       zuì'è   evil, sin, wickedness

59.1. Nèige rén tài è le. Kànjian xiǎohár, bú shi dǎ jiushi mà.

59.2. Tāde mùdì shi jiù rén. Búlùn biéren shàn'è tā dōu jiù.

59.3. Rénrén dōu shuō jūnfáde zuì'è tài dà le.

60.0. chōngtu   clash (N/V) [rush suddenly]

60.1. Nèi liǎngguóde jūnduì zài biānjìngshang chōngtuqilai le.

60.2. Tā zhèi jǐtiān yòu fànle lǎo máobing le. Yì gēn rén shuō huà jiu gēn rénjia chōngtu. (T)

61.0. jì*   season

       sìjì   four seasons

       chūnjì   spring (W)

       xiàjì   summer (W)

       qiūjì   fall (W)

       dōngjì   winter (W)

61.1. Yìnián yǒu sìjì. Wǒ zuì bù xǐhuan dōngtian, yīnwei dōngtian tài lěng le.

61.2. Zhèlide tiānqi, chūnjì gēn qiūjì zuì hǎo, xiàjì gēn dōngjì tiānqi zuì huài.

165 Mǎ : Xiànzài hái yǒu sìge shēngcí. Wǒ xiǎng nǐ dōu huì yòng. Qǐng nǐ yòng <u>jùjué</u> shuō yíjù huà.

    Bái : "Tāmen ràng wǒ cānjiā nèige xuésheng yùndong, wǒ jùjué le."

    Mǎ : Duìle. <u>Qǔdé</u> zěnmo yòng?

    Bái : "Jiǎ Yǐ liǎngguó dǎzhàng. Yīnwei dìshìde guānxi Jiǎ guó qǔdé yōu-
170 shì."

    Mǎ : <u>Zuì'è</u> zhèige cér zěnmo yòng?

    Bái : "Nèiběn xiǎoshuō wánquán shi miáoxiě Mínguó chūnián guānliáo hé jūnfáde zuì'è."

    Mǎ : Qǐng nǐ yòng <u>chōngtu</u> shuō yíjù huà.

175 Bái: "Zhāng Xiānsheng gēn Lǐ Xiānsheng bù zhīdào wèi-shénmo liǎngge
rén shuōzhe shuōzhe jiu chōngtuqilai le.

Mǎ: Duìle. Jǐ shi shénmo yìsi?

Bái: Jǐ jiu shi sìjǐde yìsi. Bǐrú "Tiānqi zhèn hǎo. Suírán dōngjǐ le,
hǎoxiang shi chūnjǐde yàngzi."

180 Mǎ: Shuō dōngjǐ wǒ xiǎngqilai le, cóng xià xīngqīyī qǐ, wǒmen shàngkè
yào àn dōngjǐ shíjiān le.

Bái: Shì.

Mǎ: Xiànzài cér dōu tǎolùnwán le, shíjiān yě dào le. Jīntian shi wǒ hé
wàiguo tóngxué jiǎnghuà, tímu shi "Wényán hé Báihuà."

185 Bái: Hǎojíle. Wǒmen hěn zǎo jiu xīwang nín gěi wǒmen jiǎng yicì. Nínde
xuéwen nènmo hǎo, érqiě jiāoxuéde jīngyan nènmo fēngfù, suǒ jiǎng
de yídìng gěi wǒmen zēngjiā xuéshi bu shǎo.

SHĒNGCÍ BIǍO

1. jiǎntǎo

2. xīndé

3. xiàndu
   zuìdī(de) xiàndu

4. yī
   yīkào

5. gǔlì

6. Sòng Lián

7. <u>Wáng Miǎn Zhuàn</u>

8. huì

9. miáoxiě

10. shēngdòng

11. gùrán

12. yuē (W)

13. yǐnyòng (W)

14. xiàoguǒ (W)

15. jūzhù (W)

16. héchù? (W)

17. bàle

18. nénggan

19. cāozòng

20. jiědá (W)

21. xìng*
    xìngkuī
    xìng'er

22. chú cǐ zhīwài (W)

23. biànlì (W)

24. jǐngchá

25. zhìxu

26. zhǎnlǎn
    zhǎnlǎnhuì

27. jiànkāng

28. shūfu
    bù shūfu

29. jiāoshe

30. zhēnglùn

31. fèizhǐ

32. jīliè

33. yōushì

34. jiélùn

35. xūzì

36. zǐxi

37. yángé

38. chūbù

39. shízhǐ
    shízhǐshang

40. shuāngyīnjié

41. húdiè

42. qíngkuàng

43. biàn
    biànbié

44. fàn
    fànfǎ
    fàn (. . . de) máobing

45. zuì
    fànzuì

46. zhìqi

47. xiěqì, xuěqì

48. yōnghù

49. huópo

50. yǎnjing

51. biǎoqíng
    biǎoqíng dáyì
    dáyì biǎoqíng

52. hǔnzá

53. gàiniàn

54. chāo*
    chāoguò

55. máodùn

56. bào

57. jùjué

58. qǔdé

59. è
    shàn'è (W)
    zuì'è

60. chōngtu

61. jì*
    sìjì
    chūnjì (W)
    xiàjì (W)
    qiūjì (W)
    dōngjì (W)

YǓFǍ LIÀNXÍ

(See note at end of lesson)

1. Dōngjì fànzuì zhě duōyu xiàjì . . . Dōngtian fànzuì de bǐ xiàtiande duō.

2. Zhèige értóngde yǎnjing dàyu nèige értóng . . . Zhèige háizide yǎnjing bǐ nèige háizide dà.

3. Nèige húdiè xiǎoyu zhèige húdiè . . . Nèige húdiè bǐ zhèige húdiè xiǎo.

4. Tāde jìyìlì hǎoyu wǒ . . . Tāde jìyìlì bǐ wǒ hǎo.

5. Zhōngxuésheng yánjiu Hán Fēizǐ de jì shǎo . . . Zhōngxuésheng yánjiu Hán Fēizi de shǎojíle.

6. Yōnghù Wáng Xiānsheng zhě jì duō . . . Yōnghù Wáng Xiānsheng de rén duōjíle.

7. Zhōngguo Yuán Cháo shíqī, guóshì jì shèng . . . Zhōngguo Yuán Cháode shíqī guóshì shèngjíle.

8. Qīng Cháo mònián Zhōngguozhi zhèngzhi jì fǔbài . . . Qīng Cháo mònián Zhōngguode zhèngzhi fǔbài jíle.

9. Nèige yùndong yǐ mínzhǔ zhǔyì wéi hàozhào . . . Nèige yùndong shi ná mínzhǔ zhǐyì zuò hàozhào.

10. Nèige tuántǐ yǐ xīshōu qīngnián wéi mùdì . . . Nèige tuántǐ ná xīshōu qīngnián zuò mùdì.

11. Nèige xuéshù yánjiuhuì yǐ Rújiāzhi xuéshuō wéi zhǔtǐ . . . Nèige xuéshù yánjiuhuì ná Rújiāde xuéshuō zuò zhǔtǐ.

12. Xuéxiào zhèicìde lǔxíng shi yǐ Nányáng Qúndǎo wéi mùbiāo . . . Xuéxiào zhèicìde lǔxíng shi ná Nányáng Qúndǎo zuò mùbiāo.

13. Nèixiē jūnfá dōu wéi zhōngyāng zhèngfǔ suǒ dǎdǎo . . . Nèixiē jūnfá dōu ràng zhōngyāng zhèngfǔ gěi dǎdǎo le.

14. Wényánzhi <u>Wáng Miǎn Zhuàn</u> wéi Míng Cháo Sòng Lián suǒ xiě . . . Wényánde <u>Wáng Miǎn Zhuàn</u> shi Míng Cháo Sòng Lián xiě de.

15. Nèi liǎngguóde wénhuà jiāoliú wéi mǒumǒu rén suǒ cùchéng . . . Nèi liǎngguóde wénhuà jiāoliú shi mǒumou rén cùchéng de.

16. Qín Cháo wéi Hàn Cháo suǒ miè . . . Qín Cháo jiào Hàn Cháo gěi miè le.

17. <u>Yuē</u> zhě <u>shuō</u> yě . . . <u>Yuē</u> jiu shi <u>shuō</u>.

18. <u>Héchù</u> zhě <u>nǎlǐ</u> yě . . . <u>Héchù</u> jiu shi <u>nǎlǐ</u>.

19. <u>Xuānyáng</u> zhě <u>xuānchuán</u> yě . . . <u>Xuānyáng</u> jiu shi <u>xuānchuán</u>.

20. <u>Jí</u> zhě <u>zuì</u> yě . . . <u>Jí</u> jiu shi <u>zuì</u>.

JIĂNGHUÀ

Zhūwèi tóngxué:

Wǒmende Zhuāntí Jiǎnghuà yǐjing jiǎngle shíjiǔcì. Jīntian shi dì-
èrshicì, yě shi zuìhòude yícì. Zài méi jiǎng běntí zhīqián, wǒmen xiān
bǎ guòqu suǒ jiǎng de zuò yíge jiǎntǎo, kànkan cóng zhèixiē jiǎnghuàli
5 dédàole shénmo xiàoguǒ, zhūwèi yǒu shénmo xīndé? Rúguǒ yǒu yìxiē xiàoguǒ, yǒu yìxiē xīndé, dàzhì bú huì chāochu xiàbiān suǒ shuō de liǎngdiǎn:
Dì-yī shǔyu shízhǐ fāngmiàn de, jiu shi wǒmen cóng zhèixiē jiǎnghuàde
nèiróngli suǒ dédào de hǎochu. Wǒmen cóng nèiróng fāngmiàn zuìdī xiàndu yǐjing zhīdaole Zhōngguode mínzú、jiàoyu、lìshǐ、dìlǐ、zōngjiào、yìshu、
10 jīngji yǐjí Zhōngguo rénde fāmíng hé fēngsu xíguan. Huàn yíjù huà shuō,
jiu shi duìyu Zhōngguode wénhuà yǒule chūbùde rènshi. Dì-èr shǔyu yǔwén fāngmiàn de. Wǒmen cóng zhèixiē jiǎngyǎncíli xuéxíle bù shǎode cí,
zhīdaole yìxiē yǔfǎ, duō liànxile bù shǎode huìhuà. Huàn yíjù huà shuō,
jiu shi duìyu Zhōngguo yǔwén yǒule xiāngdāngde jìnbù. Zhè dōu shi zhíde
15 wǒmen gāoxìng de.

Chú cǐ zhīwài wǒmen zài zhèixiē jiǎngyǎncíli, kànchulai dōu shi
yòng de báihuà, zhǐ yǒu yí xiǎo bùfen yǐnyòngle wényán. Yīncǐ jiu yǐnqǐ
yíge xīn wèntí, nà jiu shi "wényán hé báihuà" de wèntí. Nènmo wǒmen
jīntian jiu tǎolùn zhèige tímu.

20 Zhōngguo zài jǐshinián qián, duìyu wényán hé báihuàde wèntí céngjīng yǒuguo yíge hěn jīlièide zhēnglùn. Nà jiu shi Wǔsì Yùndong yǐhòude
yíduàn qījiān. Dāngshí tíchàng báihuàde yǒu Hú Shì、Chén Dúxiù děng.
Tāmen shuō báihuà shi huó wénxué, wényán shi sǐde. Yōnghù wényán de
gèngshi duōde budéliǎo. Tāmen shuō wényán shi guócuì, yīngdāng bǎo-
25 cún. Hòulái báihuà qǔdéle yōushì. Búdàn xiǎoxuéde jiàokēshū dōu gǎiyòng báihuà, jiùlián zhōngxué jiàokēshū dà bùfēn yě yòng báihuà, érqiě
zài shíjì yīngyòngshang xiàng xiě xìn、xiě lùnwen、xiě xiǎoshuō děngděng
yě duōshù yòng báihuà le. Suǒyǐ wényán hé báihuàde wèntí dào xiànzài
yǐjing shi yíge bù chéng wèntí de wèntí, yě jiu shi yǐjing chéngwéi yíge
30 bú zài zhēnglùn de shìshí. Zhè shi wǒmen shǒuxiān yīngdāng zhīdao de.

Qícî wǒmen yào zhīdao de shi wényán hé báihuà yǒu shénmo fēnbié? Yǒu xiē rén shuō wényán hé báihuà shi Zhōngwénde liǎngzhǒng tǐcái,
zhèi liǎngzhǒng tǐcái wǎngwǎng hùxiāng hǔnzá, wényánli yě cháng yòng
báihuà, báihuàli yě cháng yǒu wényán, hěn nán yán'gé huàfēn. Zhèizhǒng
35 shuōfǎ gùrán shi shíshí, dànshi jìrán shi liǎngzhǒng tǐcái, jiu yídìng yǒu
bùtóngde dîfang.   Xiànzài wǒmen bǎ xiǎnzhù bùtóngde dîfang zài xiàbiān
shuōyishuō.

Dî-yī, yòng zî hé yòng cí shang. Jǔ lîzi lái shuō: Wényán suǒ shuō
de "kǒu" zài báihuà jiu jiàozuo "zuǐ." Wényán suǒ shuō de "yuē" báihuà
40 jiu shi "shuō." Wényán suǒ shuō de "mù" zài báihuà jiu jiàozuo "yǎnjing." Wényán suǒ shuō de "biàn shàn'è" báihuà jiu shi "biànbié hǎo hé
huài." Wényánde "yǒu zhî zhě" zài báihuàli jiu shi "yǒu zhîqide rén."
Wényánde "zài héchù jūzhù?" zài báihuà jiu shi "zài shénmo dîfang zhù?"
Hái yǒu wényánlide xūzî shi yòng "zhī, hū," zài báihuàli jiu yòng "de,
45 ma" děngděng.   Bǐfang shuō zài Zhuāntí Jiǎnghuà dî-yīkèli yǒu Kǒngzǐ
shuō de yíjù huà "Yǒu péng zî yuǎn fāng lái bù yî lè hu?" Zhèijù huà
shi wényán wǒmen zǎo jiu zhīdao le.   Rúguǒ zài cóng wénfǎshang lái
kàn, "bù yî lè hu" de "hū" zî shi yíge yíwèncí, děngyu báihuàlide "Nǐ
hǎo ma?" de "ma" zî. Wǒmen yí kàndao yòng de shi "hū" zî jiu zhīdao
50 zhèige jùzi shi wényánde.

Dî-èr, wénfǎshang.   Wǒmen yě jǔ lîzi lái shuō.   Zái dî-èrshikèli
yǒu "Rén zhě rén yě" wǒmen yě zǎo jiu zhīdao zhè shi yíjù wényán.
Zhèizhǒng "A zhě B yě" de jùzide yîsi yòng báihuà lái jiǎng shi "A jiu
shi B." Yàoshi zài cóng wénfǎshang lái kàn, tā zhǐshi zài wényánshang
55 yòng, nènmo yí kànjian zhèizhǒng wénfǎ jiu zhīdao zhèijù huà yídìng shi
wényán le. Yòu bǐfang shuō: "Dōngjì fànzuî zhě duōyu xiàjî." Zhèijù huà
rúguǒ yòng báihuà lái shuō jiu shi: "Dōngtian fànzuî de rén bǐ xiàtiande
duō." Wǒmen zài zhèi liǎngjù huàli kéyi kànchulai dî-yíjù wényánlide
wénfǎ shi "A duōyu B," zài dî-èrjù báihuàlide wénfǎ shi "A bǐ B duō."
60 Zhè yě shi wényán hé báihuà zài wénfǎshang de bùtóng.

Cǐwài yǒu rén shuō: "Zài yǔyīnshang yě yǒu bùtóng." Zhèizhǒng
shuōfǎ shi shuō wényán shi gǔrénde yǔyán, báihuà shi xiàndài rén suǒ
shuō de huà; gǔdàide yīnjié duō, xiàndàide yīnjié shǎo; gǔdài dōu shi dānyīnjiéde cí, xiàndài yǒu hěn duō duōyīnjiéde cí.   Yǐ wǒ kànlái zhèizhǒng

65 shuōfǎ bù wánquán zhèngquè. Gǔdài yīnjié zuì duō yě bú huì chāoguò sìqiānge.   Suírán bǐ xiànzàide yīnjié duō liǎngbèi duō, kěshi réngrán bú
   gòuyòng. Wèi-shénmo ne? Yīnwei Zhōngguó zìcóng yǒule wénzì, dāngshíde
   shèhuì qíngkuàng yǐjing hěn fùzá le, suǒyǒu rìcháng shēnghuóshangde gàiniàn zuì shǎo yǒu jǐwànge. Yòng sìqiānge dānyīnjié yuǎn bú gòu dàibiǎo
70 jǐwànge gàiniàn. Háiyǒu, bù néng shuō zài gǔshūshang suǒyǒu yòng de cí
   dōu shi dānyīnjié de. Jǔ yíge lìzi lái shuō, zài Zhuāntí Jiǎnghuà dì-shíqīkè hé dì èrshikèli dōu tídaole Zhuāngzǐ.   Zhuāngzǐ yǒu yíge gùshi
   "Húdiè Mèng," bù zhīdào shi Zhuāngzǐ huàle húdiè, háishi húdiè huàle
   Zhuāngzǐ. Zài zhèige gùshili suǒ yòng de "húdiè" jiu shi shuāngyīnjiéde
75 cí. Wèi-shénmo gǔdàide Zhuāngzǐ yě yòng "húdiè" zhèige shuāngyīnjiéde
   cí ne?   Kějiàn suǒwèi gǔdài dōu shi dānyīnjiéde cí de shuōfǎ shi bú
   zhèngquède le, zhèiyàngde duōyīnjié zài gǔshūshang yǒu bù shǎo ne.

   Zǒngkuò lái shuō, wényán hé báihuà dōu shi dáyì biǎoqíng de yìzhǒng gōngjù. Zhèizhǒng gōngjù dōu suízhe shídàide biànhuà ér biànhuà.
80 Biànhuà de jiéguǒ shi něi yìzhǒng gōngjù zuì biànlì dāngshíde yīngyòng,
   něizhǒng xíngshì jiu zuì shòu duōshù rénde huānyíng. Zài Zhōngguó jìndài yǒumíngde wénxué zuòpǐnli yǒu liǎngge Wáng Miǎn Zhuàn, yíge shi
   Míng Cháode xuézhě Sòng Lián yòng wényán xiě de, yíge shi Rúlín Wài-
   shǐli dì-yīhuí yòng báihuà xiě de.   Rúguǒ bǎ zhèi liǎngge zuòpǐn bǐjiǎo
85 bǐjiǎo, jiu kěnéng yǒu liǎngge jiélùn. Dì-yīge jiélùn shi duōshù rén yídìng rènwei Rúlín Wàishǐlide Wáng Miǎn Zhuàn xiěde hǎo. Tā bǎ Wáng
   Miǎn miáoxiěde shi yíge yǒu xiěqì, yǒu gǎnqíng, néng shuō huì xiào,
   shēngdòng huópode rén. Dì-èrge jiélùn shi Sòng Lián xiě de Wáng Miǎn
   Zhuàn yǒu hěn duō rén kànbudǒng.   Zhè jiu kéyi zhèngmíng wényán shi
90 shǎoshù rénde wénxué, báihuà shi dàzhòngde wénxué.

   Zuìhòu wǒmen suǒ yào zhīdao de shi wàiguo rén yánjiu Zhōngwén
   duìyu wényán hé báihuà yào bàozhe yìzhǒng shénmo tàidu ne? Wǒ xiǎng
   zhèige wèntí shi hěn róngyi jiědá de.   Wǒmen jìshǐ bù zìxìde xiǎng yě
   néng hěn kuàide shuōchu, wǒmen yào xiān cóng báihuà zhuóshǒu, yě yào
95 xuéxí yìxiē cháng yòng de wényán. Yìlái shi yīnwei báihuàli cháng yǐnyòng wényàn, yìlái shi Zhōngguo xiànzài hái méi fèizhǐ wényán.

FÙSHÙ

Zhèipán lùyīndài shi Zhōngwén dì-yīzǔ, dì-shíjiǔcìde lùyīn.　Shi Bái Wénshān fùshù de Zhuāntí Jiǎnghuà "Lìshǐ."

Zhèicìde Zhuāntí Jiǎnghuà shi Wén Jiàoshòu gěi wǒmen jiǎng de Zhōngguo lìshǐ.　Wén Jiàoshòu shuō, jiǎng Zhōngguo lìshǐ ná shíjiān lái

5　shuō, Zhōngguo shi yǒu sānqiān duō nián lìshǐde yíge guójiā le.　Zài jǐ-qiānniánli gǎi-cháo-huàn-dài bù zhī yǒu duōshao cì le.　Zài kōngjiānshang fāshēng de shìqing yě tài duō le.

Wén Jiàoshòu shuō, Zhōngguo lìshǐshang yǒu zhìshì gēn luànshì. Zhìshì jiu shi guójiā āndìngde shíqī.　Luànshì shi guójiā sì-fēn-wǔ-liè

10　shèhuì hǔnluànde shíqī.　Tā jiēzhe yòu shuō, Shāng Cháo yǐqián jiù lì-shǐshang shuō hái yǒu Xià Cháo, kěshi méi yǒu shénmo zhèngmíng, suǒyǐ wǒmen jiu cóng Shāng Cháo jiǎngqǐ.

Shāng Cháo yǐhòu yǒu Zhōu Cháo.　Zhōu Cháo yǐhòu yǒu Qín、Hàn、 Jìn、Táng、Sòng、Yuán、Míng、Qīng yìzhí dào xiànzài.　Zhèixiē cháodài

15　zài Xīnhài Gémìng yǐqián dōu shi jūnzhǔ zhuānzhì de.　Zhōngguo lìdài yǐlái dōu shi Hànren tǒngzhì Zhōngguo, zhǐ yǒu Yuán Cháo shi Měnggǔ rén, Qīng Cháo shi Mǎnzhōu rén.

Wén Jiàoshòu jiǎng, Zhōngguo gǔlái luànshì yǒu sìge shíqī.　Dì-yíge shíqī shi Chūnqiū Zhànguóde shíhou.　Běnlái yǒu hěn duō xiǎo guó, hòulái

20　chéngle qīge dà guó.　Jiéguǒ zhèi qīguólide Qín Guó bǎ qítā liùguó gěi tǒngyī le.　Dì-èrge shíqī shi Hàn Cháo mònián, yòu fēnchéng sānge guó-jiā.　Dì-sān shi Jìn Cháo mònián yòu yǒu Wǔhú Shíliù Guó gēn Nánběi Cháo.　Dì-sì shi Táng yǐhòu yòu yǒu Wǔdài Shíguó.　Yǐshàngde zhèi sìge shíqī dōu shi zuì luànde shíqi.

25　Wén Jiàoshòu jiǎngdao zhèli jiu zài hēibǎnshang huàle yíge Zhōng-guo cháodài túbiǎo, bǎ Zhōngguo lìshǐshangde cháodài xiěde hěn qīngchu. Tā huàwánle yǐhòu jiēzhe jiǎng.　Tā xiān jiǎng Shāng Cháode jiǎgǔwén. Guānyu jiǎgǔwén céngjīng yǒu rén gěi wǒmen jiǎngguo yìdiǎr, shi shuō: Kǎogǔjiā zài Hénán Shěng Ānyáng nèige dìfang cóng dìli juéchulai de

30　guījiǎ、niú gútou.　Yīnwei Shāng Cháo bǎ wénzì xiě huòzhě kē zài jiǎgǔ shàngmian liúchuándao xiànzài, suǒyǐ jiàozuo jiǎgǔwén.　Jiǎgǔwén duì yán-jiu Shāng Cháo wénhuà yǒu hěn dàde jiàzhi.　Wén Jiàoshòu shuō de dàzhì hé yǐshàngde chàbuduō.

Wén Jiàoshòu yòu ;iǎngdao Zhōu Cháode fēngjiàn zhìdu. Zhōngguode
35 fēngjiàn zhìdu shi cóng Zhōu Cháo kāishǐ de.   Fēngjiàn jiu shi huángdi
fēng tā tóngxìngde shi zhūhóu, bǎ tǔdi fēngěi zhūhóu.   Zhōu wángle yǐhòu dào Qín Cháode shíhou jiu qǔxiāole zhèizhǒng fēngjiàn zhìdu.

Wén Jiàoshòu yòu jiǎngdao Qín Shǐhuáng zào Wànlǐ Cháng Chéng
gēn fén-shū-kēng-rú liǎngjiàn dàshì. Qín Shǐhuáng zào Wànlǐ Cháng Chéng
40 shi pà Xiōngnú qīnrù Zhōngguo.   Fén-shū jiu shi bǎ suǒyǒu zhū-zǐ-bǎi-
jiāde shū dōu shāo le.   Kēng-rú shi bǎ niàn shū de rén gěi huómái le.

Wén Jiàoshòu yòu shuōdao Hàn Cháode dì-yīge huángdi jiu shi Hàn
Gāozǔ. Tā shi yíge píngmín zuòle huángdi. Dào Hàn Wǔdìde shíhou duìnèi yīnwei zūnzhòng Rújiāde xuéshuō, suǒyǐ cóng nèige shíhou qǐ Rújiāde
45 sīxiǎng jiu chéngle Zhōngguo zhèngtǒngde sīxiǎng le.   Duìwài zhēngfúle
Xiōngnú, pài Zhāng Qiān dào Xīyù yě shi Hàn Cháode dàshì.

Yòu jiǎngdao Táng Cháo jiu shi Shèng Táng shíqī.   Wén Jiàoshòu
shuō Táng Cháo zuì shèngde shíhou búdàn guónèi shi gēwǔ shēngpíng,
érqiě guótǔde fànwéi yě hěn dà.   Cháoxiān、Ānnán dōu fúcóng Táng Cháo.
50 Wén Jiàoshòu shuō Yuán Cháode wǔlì zuì qiáng. Yuán Cháode lǐngtǔ kuà Ōu-Yǎ liǎng dà zhōu.   Yīnwei nèige yuángu, suǒyǐ Zhōngguo zào
huǒyào、yìnshuā děngděngde fāngfǎ dōu chuándào Xīfāng qù le.   Tóngshí
Xīfāngde wénmíng yě shūrù Zhōngguo lái le.   Kéyi shuō duì Zhōng-Xī
wénhuàde jiāoliú Yuán Cháo shi yǒugōng de.

55 Yòu jiǎngdao Míng Cháo pài Zhèng Hé xià Xīyáng.   Xīyáng jiu shi
xiànzàide Nányáng Qúndǎo.   Pài Zhèng Hé xià Xīyáng zhǔyào mùdì shi
xuānyáng Zhōngguode shēngwēi gēn fāzhǎn duìwài màoyì.

Yòu jiǎngdao Yāpiàn Zhànzhēng.   Nà shi Zhōngguo gēn Yīngguode
zhànzhēng.   Yuányīn shi nèige shíhou Yīngguo rén bǎ yāpiàn yùndao Zhōng-
60 guode tài duō le.   Yǒu yícì Zhōngguo jìnzhǐ tāmen bǎ yāpiàn jìnkǒu.   Wèile
zhèijiàn shì liǎngguó jiu chōngtuqilai le. Cóng zhèige shíhou qǐ Zhōngguo
guóshì yuè lái yuè shuāiruò.   Suīrán Qīng Cháo zhèngfǔ xiǎng biànfǎ、
túqiáng yě bù xíng le.

Wén Jiàoshòu shuō Qīng Cháode zhèngzhi yuè lái yuè fǔbài, zài jiā-
65 shang wàihuàn, guóshì yìtiān bù rú yìtiān, suǒyǐ jiu yǒu àiguó fènzǐ qǐyì
gémìng. Zài yī-jiǔ-yī-yī nián, jiu shi yīnlì Xīnhài nián, gémìng jiu chénggōng le. Nà jiu shi Xīnhài Gémìng, yě jiu shi Sūn Zhōngshān Xiānsheng
yǐ Sānmín Zhǔyì zuò hàozhào de gémìng.

Zuìhòu Wén Jiàoshòu shuō, zài lìshǐshang kàn, lìdài gǎi-cháo-huàn-
70　dài dà duōshù shi yīnwei zhēngzhi fǔbài, shīqù mínxīn.

WÉNXÍ

1. Yǒu yíge wàiguo rén yánjiu Zhōngguo Dàojiāde xuéshuō hé Dàojiào.　Tā
   shuō: "Dàojiā xuéshuō chuàngshǐ de shi Lǎozǐ.　Tā zhǔzhāng qīngjìng wúwéi, wúwéi ér zhǐ.　Wúwéide yìsi jiu shi bù fánrǎo.　Tā xiě de shū yǒu
   <u>Dàodé Jīng</u>.　Zhìyú Dàojiào shi zài Dōng Hàn shíhou cái fèng Lǎozǐ wéi
   shǐzǔ.　Yǒu xiē rén bǎ Dàojiào kànzuo Lǎozǐ chuàngshǐ de.　Wǒ xiǎng
   zhèizhǒng shuōfǎ shi yǒu wèntí de."

2. Mòjiāde xuéshuō zhǔzhāng "jiān'ài."　Kǒngzǐde xuéshuō zhǔzhāng de shi
   "rén."　"Rén" yě yǒu "jiān'ài" de yìsi, "jiān'ài" yě yǒu "rén" de yìsi,
   suǒyǐ zhèi liǎngzhǒng xuéshuō bìng bù chōngtu.

3. Zhōngguo cóng Hàn Cháo yǐhòu lìdài dōu bǎ Rújiāde xuéshuō kànwéi bǐ
   shénmo xuéshuō dōu hǎo, zūn Kǒngzǐ wéi shèngren.　Wéi-shénmo zài
   Wǔsì Yùndongde shíhou yào dǎdǎo Kǒngzǐ, shènzhìyú yǒu "dǎdǎo Kǒng jiā
   diàn" de kǒuhào ne?

4. Zhōu Cháo chūnián quán guó tǒngyī, zài lìshǐshang shi yíge zhìshì.　Hòulái dàole mònián wángshì shuāiruò, guónèi fēnlièwéi hěn duō xiǎoguó.
   Zhèixiē xiǎoguó cóng xīngqǐ dào mièwáng, shíjiān dōu bú tài cháng.　Gè
   xiǎo guó zhījiān cháng yǒu zhànshì, suǒyǐ zài lìshǐshang shi yíge luànshì.

5. Tiānzhǔjiào zuìchū chuánrù Zhōngguode shíhou jiàozuo Jǐngjiào.　Dāngshí
   xìn Tiānzhǔjiàode rén hěn shǎo.　Hòulái Lǐ Mǎdòu dào Zhōngguo lái
   chuánjiào.　Tā shi yíge hěn nénggande rén.　Tā búdàn chuánjiào bìngqiě
   bǎ Xīfāngde kēxué chuánrùle Zhōngguo.

6. Zài zhuānzhì shídài, yǒu quánshì de rén jiùshi dǎle rén shènzhìyú shāle
   rén yě bù yídìng suàn shi fànle fǎ huòzhě shi fànle zuì de.

7. <u>Jūnchén</u> de <u>chén</u> shi zhuānzhì shídài zuò guān de rénde míngchēng.　Mínzhǔ guójiā shi méi yǒu zhèizhǒng míngchēng de.

8. Rúguǒ pànduàn yíge rénde shàn'è, bù néng zhǐ cóng tāde shuō huà shang
   lái xià pànduàn.

9. Tián Xiānshengde shēntǐ běnlái hěn jiànkāng.　Zuótian tā bìng le.　Wǒ
   wèn ta shénmo dìfang bù shūfu?　Tā shuō, tóu yǒu dian téng.　Wǒ gěi ta
   nálai zhǐ tóu téng de yào, ràng tā chī.　Tā jùjué chī, tā shuō: "Búguò
   yǒu dian tóu téng bàle.　Jiùshi bù chī yào yě huì hǎo de."

10. Zuótian cānguān zhǎnlǎnhuì de rén tài duō le, xìngkuī dàménwài yǒu jǐng-
    chá wéichí zhìxu, ràng cānguān de rén yī cìxu cóng dàmén jìnqu.

11. Xiànzài zhèngfǔde zhèngcè shi gǔlì rénmín zēngjiā shēngchǎn yǐbiàn cù-
    chéng jīngji fánróng.

12. Wèi-shénmo guǎn Zhōngguo rén jiào Tángrén ne?　Zhè wúyíde shi yīnwei
    Táng Cháode shíhou guójiāde shēngwēi hěn dà, suǒyǐ yìzhí dào xiànzài
    hái guǎn Zhōngguo rén jiào Tángrén.

13. Zhōngguo cóngqián zhǐ zhùzhòng wénxué, bú zhùzhòng kēxué, gèng bú zhùzhòng wùzhǐ wénmíng. Zìcóng Yāpiàn Zhànzhēng yǐhòu cái zhīdao wùzhǐ wénmíng shi yǒu shíyòng de, yúshi kāishǐ xuéxí, suǒyǐ shuō Yāpiàn Zhànzhēng shi Zhōngguo zhùyì wùzhǐde zhuǎnlìdiǎn.

14. Fójiàode miào yǒude shíhou yě jiàozuo <u>sì</u>. Cóngqián yǒu yíge sì yǒu bù shǎo tiánchǎn, zhèngfǔ dǎsuàn chùlǐ zhèixiē tiánchǎn. Sìlide rén hé zhèngfǔ jiāoshe, hòulái sìlide rén shènglì le. Sìlide rén shuō: "Xìng'er jiāoshe shènglì le, fǒuzé wǒmen jiu méi yǒu fàn chī le."

15. Wǒ bǎ Zhōngguo lìláide cháodài huà yìzhāng tú. Wǒ yí kàn zhèizhāng tú lìdàide míngchēng jiu yímù liǎorán le.

16. Jūnfá hé guānliáo dōu shi jiù shídàide chǎnwù. Tāmen hùxiāng lìyòng, cāozòng zhèngquán, wúyíde shi duì guójiā rénmín dōu búlìde.

17. Qín Cháode xīng hé Qín Cháode wáng, zài hòushìde rén kànlai zhēnshi tài kuài le.

18. Tā xiě de zhèipiān wénzhāng dàzhǐ shuōlai hái bú cuò, dànshi fànle yíge zuì dàde máobing, shi zài zǒngjié de jǐjù huàli hǎoxiang hé qiánbiān suǒ shuō de yǒu dian máodùn.

WÈNTÍ

1. Wényán hé báihuàde wèntí, zài shénmo shíqī zhēnglùnde zuì jīliè? Tíchàng báihuà de shi shénmo rén? Tāmen wèi-shénmo tíchàng báihuàwén?

2. Wényán hé báihuàde zhēnglùn, báihuà qǔdéle yōushì, yǒu shénmo shìshíde zhèngmíng?

3. Wényán hé báihuà zài yòng zì hé yòng cí shang hěn yǒu fēnbié, qǐng nǐ jǔ jǐge lìzi lái shuōshuo.

4. Wǒmen cóng wénfǎshang yě kéyi kànchu wényán hé báihuàde fēnbié, qǐng nǐ jǔ jǐge lìzi lái shuōshuo.

5. Yǒu rén shuō wényán shi gǔrénde yǔyán, báihuà shi xiàndài rén suǒ shuō de huà. Gǔdàide yīnjié duō, xiàndàide yīnjié shǎo, gǔdài dōu shi dānyīnjié, xiàndài yǒu hěn duō duōyīnjié. Zhèizhǒng shuōfǎ shì bu shi wánquán zhèngquè? Gǔdài yīnjié zuìduō bù chāoguò duōshao ge? Bǐ xiànzai duō duōshao?

6. Qǐng nǐ shuōshuo <u>Zhuāngzǐ</u> "Húdiè Mèng" de gùshi. Zhèige gùshilide <u>húdiè</u> shì bu shi shuāngyīncí? Cóng <u>Zhuāngzǐ</u>shang <u>húdiè</u> zhèige cí kéyi zhèngmíng shénmo?

7. Wényán hé báihuà dōu shi dáyì biǎoqíng de yìzhǒng gōngjù. Zhèixiē gōngjù shì bu shi suízhe shídài biànhuà? Biànhuà de jiéguǒ shòu huānyíng de shi něi yìzhǒng?

8. Zài Zhōngguo jìndài yǒumíngde wénxué zuòpǐnli yǒu liǎngge <u>Wáng Miǎn Zhuàn</u>, zhèi liǎngge <u>Wáng Miǎn Zhuàn</u> yǒu shénmo bùtóng? Shénmo shíhou shénmo rén yòng wényán xiě de? Zài shénmo shūshang yǒu yòng báihuà xiě de <u>Wáng Miǎn Zhuàn</u>?

9. Bǎ wényánde <u>Wáng Miǎn Zhuàn</u> hé báihuàde <u>Wáng Miǎn Zhuàn</u> bǐjiǎo yí-
    xià, jiu néng dédào liǎngge shénmo jiélùn?

10. Tīngle zhèi èrshicîde Zhuāntí Jiǎnghuà yǐhòu wǒmende xīndé kéyi cóng
     něi liǎngfāngmiàn lái shuō? Zài shízhǐshang yǒu shénmo xīndé? Zài
     yǔwénshang yǒu shénmo xiàoguǒ?

ILLUSTRATIVE SENTENCES (ENGLISH)

4.1. Then let's handle this matter in accordance with your view.

9.1. In <u>Dream of the Red Chamber</u> the appearance and temperment of several
      hundred people—men and women, old and young—are so described that
      they seem to be alive.

17.1. If you're not going, that's that. There's no need to keep on expatiating at
       length.

23.1. With a view toward convenience in getting to school I must buy a car.

28.2. I've been a bit indisposed.

29.1. Negotiations with foreign countries at the end of the Ch'ing Dynasty were
       invariably unsuccessful.

33.1. When Lord Shang ruled the state of Ch'in he made use of law to rule the
       country and established the inevitability of rewards and punishments, with
       the result that the theories of the legalists gained quite an ascendancy at
       that time.

34.1. Although everyone talked for a long time they did not succeed in reaching
       any conclusion.

41.1. In <u>Zhuàngzǐ</u> it is stated that Zhuangzi had a dream in which he was trans-
       formed into a butterfly.

44.1. He's again been guilty of not wanting to go to school.

51.1. Some people can use their eyes to express what they would say.

54.2. What he says is outside the scope of what we're discussing.

56.2. Whatever you study you must have the aim of wanting to master it.

56.3. He always has a defeatist attitude, so he never succeeds in doing anything.

60.2. The past few days he's repeated his old offense.   As soon as he talks to
       people he clashes with them.

NOTES

The Grammar Drill in this lesson consists of pairs of sentences which illustrate
contrastive syntactical patterns in classical and contemporary Chinese.   The
pairs are as follows:

   a (1-4): A SVyu B → A bǐ B SV 'A is more SV than B':

            Zhōngguo rén duōyu Měiguo rén → Zhōngguo rén bǐ Měiguo rén
            duō   'There are more Chinese than Americans.'

b (5-8):   jí SV → SV jíle   'extremely SV':

    jí dà → dà jíle   'extremely large'

c (9-12): yǐ A wéi B → ná A zuò B   'take A as B':

    Tā yǐ bāngzhu biéren wéi mùdì → Tā ná bāngzhu biéren zuò mùdì
    'His aim is to help other people.'

d (13-16): A wéi B suǒ V → A ràng/jiào B (gěi) V   'A is V'd by B':

    Chǔ wéi Qín suǒ miè → Chǔ Guó ràng Qín Guó gěi miè le   'Chu
    was destroyed by Ch'in.'

e (17-20): A (zhě) B yě → A jiù shi B   'A is B.'   This pattern is used especially often in dictionary definitions.   The particle zhě in literary Chinese is often equivalent to the subordinating particle de or to de rén 'person who' in spoken Chinese:

    Gǔ zhě jiù yě → Gǔ jiu shi jiù   'Ancient means old.'

Dì-Èrshisìkè. Wēnxi

FÙSHÙ

Zhèi yìpán lùyīndài shi Zhōngwén dì-yīzǔ dì-èrshihào, shi Bái Wén-shān fùshù lùyīn dì-èrshicìde Zhuāntí Jiǎnghuà, tímu shi "Wényán hé Báihuà."

Wǒmende Zhuāntí Jiǎnghuà zhèicì shi zuìhòu yícì le. Shi Mǎ Jiào-
5 shòu gěi wǒmen jiǎng de. Xiànzài wǒ bǎ Mǎ Jiàoshòude jiǎnghuà fùshù yícì.

Mǎ Jiàoshòu shǒuxiān duì women shuō, Zhuāntí Jiǎnghuà jiǎngguo de yǐjing yǒu shíjiǔcì le, dédào shénmo xiàoguǒ le? Dàjiā dōu yǒu shén-mo xīndé? Wǒ xiǎng zuìdī xiàndu dàjiā zhīdaole Zhōngguode mínzú, jiào-
10 yu, lìshǐ, dìlǐ, zōngjiào, yìshu yǐjí Zhōngguo rénde fāmíng hé fēngsu xí-guan děngděng. Zài yǔyán yìfāngmiàn, dàjiā xuéle bù shǎo cér le, yě huìle hǎojǐzhǒng yǔfǎ le, huìhuà yě xuéle bù shǎo. Tóngshí wǒmen zài yǎnjiǎngcǐli kéyi zhīdao wǒmen duōshù yòng de shi báihuà, yǒu shíhou yě

yǐnyòng yìxiē wényánde cér gēn jùzi. Yīnwei wǒmen xué de dōngxili yě
15 yǒu wényán de, suǒyǐ jīntian jiu ná "Wényán hé Báihuà" zuò tímu hé dàjiā
tányitán.

Mǎ Jiàoshòu shuō guānyu wényán hé báihuà zhèige wèntí, cóng Wǔsì
yǐlái dàjiā zhēnglùnde hěn jīliè. Tíchàng báihuàwén de jiu shuō báihuàwén
shi huó wénxué, wényánwén shi sǐ wénxué. Zàncheng wényánwénde jiu
20 shuō wényánwén shi guócuì, yīnggāi bǎocún. Jiéguǒ shi báihuàwén zhànle
yōushì. Yuányīn shi báihuàwén rénrén dōu dǒng, shi dàzhòng wénxué.
Xiànzài yìbānde xiǎoxué jiàokēshū dōu shi báihuàwén, ér zhōngxuéde jiàokēshū xiǎo bùfen shi wényánwén, dà bùfen dōu yòng báihuàwén. Zài yīngyòng yìfāngmiàn, xiàng xiě xìn、 zuò lùnwén duōshù shi yòng báihuàwén
25 le.

Mǎ Jiàoshòu jiǎngdao wényán hé báihuàde fēnbié. Tā shuō wényán
hé báihuà běnlái shi bùtóngde tǐcái, dànshi yǒu rén zài xiě wénzhāng de
shíhou jiu bǎ wényán hé báihuà hǔnzázhe yòng le. Báihuàli yǒu wényán,
wényánli yě yǒu báihuà. Zhè shi hěn bù róngyi yán'géde huàfēn. Tā jǔle
30 jǐge hěn jiǎndānde lìzi, bǎ shénmo shi wényán, shénmo shi báihuà gěi
wǒmen fēnxìle yíxiàr.

Mǎ Jiàoshòu shuō bǐrú 'zuǐ' wényán shi 'kǒu,' 'yuē' jiu shi 'shuō,'
'yǎnjing' wényán shi 'mù.' 'Biànbié hǎo hé bù hǎo' wényán shi 'biàn
shàn'è,' 'Yǒu zhìqide rén' wényán shi 'Yǒu zhì zhě.' 'Zài nǎr zhù a?'
35 wényán shi 'zài héchù jūzhù?' Hái yǒu xūzìlide 'zhī' gēn 'hū' jiu shi
báihuà 'de' gēn 'ma.'

Mǎ Jiàoshòu yòu shuō zài dì-yīcì Zhuāntí Jiǎnghuà xiàozhǎng
jiǎnghuàli yǐnyòngle yíjù Kǒngzǐ suǒ shuō de huà, shi "Yóu péng zì yuǎn
fāng lái bù yì lè hu?" Zhèijù huà shi wényán de. Cóng wénfǎshang kàn,
40 'bù yì lè hu' de 'hū' zì shi yíwèncí, 'hū' jiu děngyu 'ma.' Wǒmen yí kàn
jùwěi yíwèncí yòng de shi 'hū' jiu zhīdao shi wényán de. Zài dì-èrshíkè
lǐtou yǒu "Rén zhě rén yě" yě shi wényán de. Zài wénfǎshang kàn shi
"A zhě B yě." Báihuà jiu shi shuō "A jiu shi B." Zhèizhǒng jùzi yí kàn
jiu zhīdao shi wényán de.

45   Mǎ Jiàoshòu yòu shuō, wényán hé báihuà yǒu rén shuō zài yǔyīnshang yě yǒu hěn duō bùtóngde dìfang. Wényán shi gǔrén suǒ shuō de
huà, báihuà shi xiànzài rén suǒ shuō de huà. Yǒu rén shuō gǔrén shuō

huà dōu shi dānyīnjiéde, xiànzài shuō huà dōu shi duōyīnjiéde. Zhèizhŏng
shuōfǎ kŏngpà bù yídìng quèshí. Tā shuō wŏmen cóngqián jiǎngguo Lǎozǐ
50 gēn Zhuāngzǐ. Zhuāngzǐ yŏu yíduàn gùshi shi Zhuāngzǐ huà húdiè. 'Húdiè' jiu shi duōyīnjié, suŏyǐ yào shuō gǔdàide yǔyán dōu shi dānyīnjié
zhèi huà bù hěn duì.

Mǎ Jiàoshòu yòu shuōdao yīnjié. Tā shuō gǔdàide yīnjié yŏu chàbuduō sìqiānge, suīrán duōyu xiànzài liǎngbèi, kěshi nálai zuò dānyīnjiéde
55 cér réngrán shi bú gòuyòng. Yuányīn shi Zhōngguo zìcóng yŏule wénzì
zhīhòu, shèhuìde qíngkuàng jiu yìtiān bǐ yìtiān fùzá le, zài rìcháng shēnghuó gàiniànshang yŏu hǎojǐwàn. Jǐqiānge yīnjié zěnmo huì gòuyòng ne?

Mǎ Jiàoshòu yòu shuō, búlùn wényán huò báihuà dōu shi rén yǔ rén
zhījiān dáyì biǎoqíng de gōngjù. Suízhe shídàide biànhuà, něi yìzhŏng
60 gōngjù biànlì, něi yìzhŏng gōngjù jiu shōu dàzhòngde huānyíng. Mǎ Jiàoshòu shuō bǐrú Wáng Miǎn Zhuàn yŏu liǎngge rén xiě de, yíge shi Míng
Cháo Sòng Lián suŏ xiě wényán de, yíge shi zài Rúlín Wàishǐ dì-yīhuíde
Wáng Miǎn Zhuàn. Rúlín Wàishǐshangde Wáng Miǎn Zhuàn shi báihuà de.
Bǎ Wáng Miǎn yíqiè yíqiè miáoxiěde fēicháng shēngdòng yŏu gǎnqíng ér-
65 qiě huópo yŏulì.

Zuìhòu Mǎ Jiàoshòu shuō, suīrán báihuàwén róngyi dŏng, kěshi wényánwén yě yīnggāi xué yìdiǎr. Wàiguo xuésheng kāishǐ xué Zhōngwén,
gùrán yào xiān cóng báihuàwén xuéqǐ, dànshi yì yŏule Zhōngwén jīchǔ
zhīhòu, yě yào xuéxí yìdiǎr wényánwén, yīnwei wényánwén bìng bù néng
70 wánquán fèizhǐ bú yòng, érqiě gǔshū yě dōu shi wényánwén de.

WÈNDÁ

I.   Nǐ wèi-shénmo . . . ?

(dì-shíjiŭkè)

xué wǔdǎo   shuō zhèizhŏng fēngqi hǎo
bǎ zì xiězai qiángshang   bǎ yìsi zhuǎnbiàn le

(dì-èrshikè)

zūnchóng Dàojiào   yánjiu Jǐngjiào
shuō dǎdǎo Kŏng jiā diàn   gōngji ta

nènmo zūnzhòng ta   fănkàng zhèngfŭ
bú. zuò zhèngzhi huódòng   bú xìnjiào

(dì-èrshiyīkè)

shuō shōurù bú gòu   bù xiū chē
măi shíyóu   fănduì tōnghuò péngzhàng
niàn cáizhèng   yòng măchē yùnhuò
niàn guóji màoyì   yào xué jīxiè
fănduì zhèige zhèngcè   yào yánjiu făngzhī

(dì-èrshi'èrkè)

bù xĭhuan xiàtian   yào qĭyì
shuō zhèngfŭ fŭbài

(dì-èrshisānkè)

bú zìjĭ jiăntăo   yŏule zhèige gàiniàn
yīkào ta   yòu fànle zuìle
bù gŭlì ta niàn shū   bú zhùyì shízhĭ
bù yĭnyòng gŭwén   gēn ta zhēnglùn
méi yŏu biăoqíng

II. . . . zài năr?

(dì-shijiŭkè)

Mĕishù Yánjiusuŏ   nĭ yùbei de jiàocái
huār   juéchulai de shíqì
huàpŭ   Dūnhuáng shíkū
tāmende yuèqi dōu   Xuānhé Huàpŭ
wŏde biānzi   nèikuài yù
bìhuà

(dì-èrshikè)

Wáng shénfu   tāde tiánchăn
Dà Fó Sì

(dî-èrshiyīkè)

xīn kāi de méi kuàng   nǐ mǎi de nongchǎnpǐn

Yùnhé   mǎilai de yuánliào

tā jīngyíng de gōngsī   nèige qǐyè gōngsī

zuî dàde gāngtiěchǎng

(dî-èrshi'èrkè)

Xīyù   Xiōngnúde běntǔ

Nányáng

(dî-èrshisānkè)

zhǎnlǎnhuî   húdiè

III. . . . báihuà zěnmo shuō?

(dî-shijiǔkè)

huîhuà   zhújiàn

yǐ tā zuò zhǔ   gēwǔ shēngpíng

(dî-èrshikè)

qīngjìng wúwéi   yǐ-fǎ-zhî-guó

xìn-shǎng-bî-fá   wúyíde

(dî-èrshiyīkè)

huòbî   zēngjiàn

tōnghuò   guàngài

(dî-èrshi'èrkè)

jí dà   hòushî

xīngwáng   yìmù liǎorán

qīnrù   túqiáng

(dî-èrshisānkè)

dōngjî   chú cǐ zhīwài

jūzhù   biànlî

héchù   dáyî biǎoqíng

xiàoguǒ

IV. Nǐ zěnmo zhīdao . . . ?

(dì-shíjiǔkè)

tā hěn jiānzhà

tā bú huì tiàowǔ

Táng Cháo hěn fánróng

tāmen hěn mìqiè

tā pànduànde bú duì

zhè bú shi yùqi

tā huì zuòqǔ

tā hěn yīngyǒng

tā jiù huì huà huāhuì

nà shi chún wénxué

tāde jìqiǎo bù hǎo

tā huì diāokè

tāde xìnggé

nà shi zuì shèng shíqī

nà shi xiàngzhēng yìshu

(dì-èrshikè)

tāmen shi zhǔtǐ

tā shi Fójiào xìntú

tāde shìli hěn dà

tā shi gémìng lǐngxiù

tāmen fūfù dōu lái

tā wàihào jiào shèngren

xiànzài shi zhuǎnlìdiǎn

cháoshuǐ yào yǒngjìn

tāmen fùzǐ dōu lái

tā jìnlaide zuòfēng

báihuàwén shèngxíng

shi tā chuàngshǐ de

(dì-èrshiyīkè)

nèr bù wěndìng

pèijide bù gōngpíng

chūchǎnpǐn bú gòu

tā fǎnduì dàyuèjìn

tā yào zhēngduó zhèngquán

zīběn bú gòu

shuǐbà xiūhǎo le

nóngzuòyè luòhòu

wùjià yào gāozhǎng

fùdān yào jiāzhòng

shìchǎng hěn hǔnluàn

wùjià yào yǒu biàndong

jīngji yào bēngkuì

zīběn zhǔyì shībài

tā shi zīběnjiā

nàli yǒu kuàngchǎn

yào huīfu hépíng le

rénkǒu zēngjiā yíbèi

shi tā fēnpèide

shi tā gōngyīng wǔqì

zhèlǐ shìhé zàolín

tāde bìng hěn yánzhòng

nà shi jīnshǔ

(dì-èrshi'èrkè)

tā mǎi yāpiàn	guóshì shuāiruò
tā hěn néng shòukǔ	shi wǒ shuàilǐng de
zhèngfǔ shīle mínxīn	shi wǒ cùshéng de
guóshì yào shuāiruò le	tāde sīxiǎng chénjiù
yào biànfǎ le	wùzhǐ bú miè
tāde sǔnshī hěn dà	tāde jìyìlì hǎo
tā shícháng tóu téng	nà shi wénhuà jiāoliú
néng yǐnqi gémìng	Yuán Cháo shēngwēi zuì dà
jiù yào gǎi-cháo-huàn-dài	Yuán Cháo bú suàn zhèngtǒng
díren jiù yào mièwáng	tā bù néng hàozhào
guójiā bú huì fēnliè	

(dì-èrshisānkè)

qiūjì bǐ chūnjì lěng	tā yōnghu zhèngfǔ
tā shi jǐngchá	tā chāoguò shíbāsuì
tāde yǎnjing bù hǎo	biānjìngde qíngkuàng
wǒ yǒu xīndé	tā méi fànfǎ
tā hěn nénggan	tā shi hěn ède rén
tā méi fázi jiědá	lǚguǎn nánnǚ hǔnzá
tā bù hěn jiànkāng	wǒ yǒu chūbù jīchǔ
tā bù shūfu le	nà shi xūzì
wényán bù néng fèizhǐ	tā bú biànbié shàn'è
tā fànfǎ le	jūnfámende zuì'è
zhēnglùnde hěn jīliè	tā yòu fànle máobing
tāmen sīxiǎng chōngtu	tāde wénzhāng máodùn
tā jùjué hézuó	tā xǐhuan shūfu

V. Nǐ shenmo shíhou . . . ?

(dì-shíjiǔkè)

yòng liǎnpǔ	yòng táoqì
chī lí	bǎ shū yìcheng Yīngwén
qí mǎ	gēn ta hézòu
xué shūfǎ	

(dì-èrshikè)

qù kàn Wáng mùshi   chǔlǐ zhèige wèntí

xīshōule xīn sīxiǎng   zūn ta shi lǎoshī

(dì-èrshiyīkè)

mǎi méi   dào shìchǎng qu

zhòng miánhua   qù kàn shuǐkù

guò qiáo   mǎide nèixiē huòwu

yòng féiliào   cānjiāle hùzhùzǔ

xiū zhèibù jīqi   jiāshangde féiliào

(dì-èrshi'èrkè)

dào Nányáng Qúndǎo   shuōshuo Xīnhài Gémìng

jiǎng Wǔhú Shíliù Guó

(dì-èrshisānkè)

zǐxì kànguo   qǔdéle xuéwèi

gēn ta jiāoshe de

VI.   . . . gēn . . . yǒu shénmo bùtóng?

(dì-shíjiǔkè)

fēizi, guìfēi   yīnyuèjiā, yīnyuèhuì

huāliǎn, báiliǎn   pànduàn, xià pànduàn

guóyuè, Xīyuè   líshù, líyuán

zhúqì, mùqì

(dì-èrshikè)

Fǎjiā, Mòjiā   Rújiā, Dàojiā

Tiānzhǔjiào, Jīdūjiào   shénfu, mùshi

Dàodé Jīng, Fó Jīng   chuánjiào, chuánrù

(dì-èrshiyīkè)

nóngyè, mùxùyè   nóngchǎng, gōngchǎng

hángyè, kuàngyè   yùnshū, shūrù

tuōlājī, qìchē   gǎijìn, dàyuèjìn

(dì-èrshi'èrkè)

zhìshì, luànshì   Húrén, Xiōngnú

Tángrén, Hànrén   kōngjiān, shíjiān

wàihuàn, nèiluàn

(dì-èrshisānkè)

dōngjì, xiàjì   huí, cì

zhìqi, xuěqì   xiàndu, xiànzhi

jiélùn, zǒngjié

VII. . . . de duìmiar shi shénmo?

(dì-shíjiǔkè)

huā yīfu   guóyuè

bǎoguì

(dì-èrshikè)

chén   jūn

zhuānzhì zhèngfǔ

(dì-èrshiyīkè)

quēshǎo   qiànshōu

(dì-èrshi'èrkè)

xīngqī   wáng

dōngtian

VIII. . . . shi shénmo rén?

(dì-shíjiǔkè)

Yáng Guìfēi   nèi jǐge rénwu dōu

Táng Mínghuáng   wǔtáishangde rén

Líyuán zǐdì

(dì-èrshikè)

Mǎkèsī	Shāng Jūn
Lièníng	jūnfá
Shǐdàlín	zhū-zǐ-bǎi-jiā dōu
Lǐ Mǎdòu	guānliáo dōu
Hán Fēi Zǐ	Dàojiàode shǐzǔ

(dì-èrshiyīkè)

zhōngchǎn jiēji	kāifā kuàng de
zīběnjiā	zǔchéng hùzhùzǔ de

(dì-èrshi'èrkè)

Hàn Gāozǔ	fén-shū-kēng-rú de
Qín Shǐhuáng	huómái niàn shū de
Zhāng Qiān	zuìchū fēng zhūhóu de
Hàn Wǔdì	miè Qín Cháo de
Zhèng Hé	zhèngfǔ pài de

(dì-èrshisānkè)

Sòng Lián	wéichi zhìxu de
cāozòng wùjià de	bàozhe hěn duō shū de
jiǎngyǎn zuì shēngdòng de	

IX. . . . yǒu shénmo tèdiǎn?

(dì-shíjiǔkè)

wǔtáijù	Zhōngguo jiànzhu
Zhōngguo lǐyuè	tāde zuòqǔfǎ
tā tiàowǔ de zīshi	jīngxìde dòngzuò
tāmen xùnlian wǔdǎo	Zhōngguo rénde lǐjié
gōngtíng lǐde shēnghuó	

(dì-èrshikè)

mínzhǔ zhǔyì	wéiwùlùn
shèhuì zhǔyì	Dàojiào
gòngchǎn zhǔyì	fēngjiàn shèhuì

(dì-èrshiyīkè)

jítǐ nóngchǎng   nèitiáo tiělù

(dì-èrshi'èrkè)

zhūhóu zhèizhǒng jiēji   Shèng Táng wénhuà

jūnzhǔ guójiā

(dì-èrshisānkè)

báihuàde <u>Wáng Miǎn Zhuàn</u>

FĀYĪN

1. qiāngdiào, qiángdiào   8. yōushì, yǒu shì

2. dǎdǎo, dǎdào   9. xīngqǐ, xīngqī

3. shìli, shílǐ   10. yíshì, yìshi

4. xiāofèi, xiǎofèi   11. bǐhuá, bǐhuà

5. huòchē, huǒchē   12. shíqī, shíqì

6. tǒngyī, tóngyì   13. tícái, tǐcái

7. wǔlì, wùlǐ

HUÌHUÀ: XUÉXĪN HÉ WÉNSHĀN

Xué: Wénshān, zǎo. Nǐ qián jǐtiān bù shūfu xiànzài wánquán huīfule ma?

Bái: Wánquán huīfu le. Xièxie ni.

Xué: Jiànkāng dì-yī. Chīle zǎofàn yǐhòu wǒmen dào Quánguó Wùchǎn Zhǎnlǎnhuì qu cānguān cānguān, hǎo bu hǎo?

5 Bái: Hǎo a. Tīngshuō zhǎnlǎnde dōu shi nóngchǎnpǐn, shì bu shi?

Xué: Nóngchǎnpǐn búguò jiu shi miánhua、màizi、shuǐguo shénmode. Hái yǒu kuàngchǎn gēn fǎngzhīpǐn děngděng.

Bái: Kuàngchǎn shì bu shi jiu shi méi、gāngtiě、jīnshǔ?

Xue: Bùzhǐ zhèi sānzhǒng, hái yǒu qítā biéde kuàngchǎn.

10 Bái: Wǒmen shénmo shíhou qù?

Xué: Chīwánle zǎodiǎn wǒmen jiu zǒu. Yào bu yào wèn Měiyīng qù bu qu?

Bái: Tā zǎoshang yǒu shì, wǒ xiǎng tā bú huì qù de. Wǒ jīntian xiàwǔ hé Měiyīng jiànmiàn. Wǒ zhèige yuèli hěn shǎo jiànzhao ta.

15 Xué: Nǐ tiāntian gēn ta shuō diànhuà bú shi yíyàng ma?

Bái : Zhèi jǐtiān jiu gěi ta dǎguo yícî diànhuà.

Xué : Zhēnde ma?

Bái : Dāngrán shi zhēnde le.

20 Xué : Yàoshi wǒ yǒu nǚ péngyou měitiān zhǐshǎo yě gěi ta dǎ liǎngcî diànhuà.

Bái : Xìngkuī nǐ méi yǒu nǚ péngyou, fǒuzé fǔshangde diànhuàfèi kě bùdéliǎo. Wǒ xiǎngqilai le. Nǐ lǎo shuō nǐ méi yǒu nǚ péngyou, zhèige huà shi zhēnde ma?

Xué : Nǐ qiáo wǒ xiàng yǒu nǚ péngyoude yàngzi ma?

25 Bái : Yàoshi yǒu nǚ péngyou hái yǒu shénmo tèshūde yàngzi ma?

Xué : Zuìdīde xiàndu yīfu yào chuān de piàoliang yìdiǎr, xiàng nǐ yíyàng.

Bái : Wǒde yīfu bǐ nǐ piàoliang ma?

Xué : Dāngrán le.

30 Bái : Zhēn shi xiàohua. Wǒ shi yíge méi yǒu biéde shōurù kào jiǎngxuéjīn niàn shū de qióng xuésheng, nǎr yǒu piàoliang yīfu. Yìnián sìjì zhǐ yǒu liǎngtào yīfu. Bié shuō xiàohuar le. Wǒmende Zhuāntí Jiǎnghuà, zuótian shi zuìhòu yícî.

Xué : Wǒ tīngshuō zuótian shi Mǎ Jiàoshòu gěi nǐmen jiǎng de.

35 Bái : Duìle. Zhuāntí Jiǎnghuà zhèige kèchéng, duì wáiguo xuéshengde bāngzhu fēicháng dà. Xiànzài yǒu jǐge wàiguo tóngxué tāmende chéngdu dōu kéyi yánjiu zhuānménde xuéshù le. Yǒude rén duì jīngji yǒu xìngqu, jiu kéyi niàn jīngji-xì, yàoshi xǐhuan zhéxué jiu kéyi niàn zhéxué le.

40 Xué : Nǐde cōngming gēn yònggòng dōu chāoguò biéren. Wǒ xiǎng nǐ duì gèzhǒng xuéshù dōu yídìng hěn yǒu xīndé le.

Bái : Wǒ yǒu shíhou zìjǐ jiǎntǎo yíxiàr, wǒ shāowéi yǒu yìdiǎr xīndé, dōu shi jiàoshòumende gǔlì hé péngyoumende bāngzhu. Tóngshí dédao nǐde hǎochu yě bù shǎo.

45 Xué : Hái shi kào nǐ zìjǐ nǔlì de jiéguǒ. Wǒmen xiànzài gāi zǒu le. Wǒmen dào zhǎnlǎnhuì qu ba.

(Bái Wénshān cānguānwánle wùchǎn zhǎnlǎnhuì yǐhòu, yòu dào Gāo jia qu kàn Gāo Měiyīng Xiǎojie)

Bái : Měiyīng hǎo. Hǎojiǔ bú jiàn le.

Měi : Zhēnshi hǎojiǔ bú jiàn le.

50 Bái : Qíshí yě búguò jiu yǒu jǐtiān méi jiàn, hǎoxiang yǒu hěn duō rìzi shide.

Měi : Nǐ lián diànhuà yě hěn shǎo dǎlai le. Wǒ běnlái xiǎng gěi nǐ xiě yìfēng xìn, kěshi náqi bǐ lái méi huà kě shuō de, suóyǐ yě méi xiě.

Bái : Yīlái shi tài máng, èrlái shi shāngfēng le, bù shūfule jǐtiān.

55 Měi: Shāngfēng shāng de hěn lìhai ba?

Bái: Xiāngdāng lìhai. Měitiān tóu téngde bùdéliǎo.

Měi: Guàibude nǐ hǎoxiang shòule shide.

Bái: Shòu dào bú shi shāngfēng de yuányīn, shi yīnwei zhèixiē rìzi tài
máng le.

60 Měi: Xiànzài wánquán hǎole ma?

Bái: Wánquán hǎo le.

Měi: Nǐmen qu cānguān zhǎnlǎnhuì yǒu yìsi ma?

Bái: Hěn hǎo, zhíde qu kànkan. Zhǎnlǎn de dōu shi quánguó gè dìfangde
chūchǎnpǐn. Zhōngguo zhēnshi dì dà wù bó, chūchǎn de dōngxi shí-
65 zài fēngfù, nǐ zhēn bù yīnggāi bú qù.

Měi: Qíshí wǒ zhēn xiǎng qù, kěshi qīnqi jiēhūn yídìng děi qu bāngmáng
a.

Bái: Nǐ yào bu yào qù? Wǒmen xiànzài qù hǎo bu hǎo?

Měi: Nǐmen zǎoshang qù rén duō bu duō?

70 Bái: Jīntian rén tài duō le, zhìxu hěn huài.

Měi: Méi yǒu jǐngchá wéichí zhìxu ma?

Bái: Yǒu shi yǒu. Cānguān de rén tài duō le, jǐngchá bù néng wéichí
le. Hòulái méi fázi, fánshi yǐhòu qù de rén dōu jùjué tāmen jìnqu
cānguān.

75 Měi: Yàoshi nènmo luàn wǒ kě bú qù.

Bái: Nènmo wǒmen qu kàn diànyǐngr qu?

Měi: Kànkan bàozhǐshang, něige diànyǐngryuànde piānzi hǎo.

Bái: Nǐ xǐhuan kàn lìshǐ piānzi, xiànzài Zhōngguo Diànyǐngryuàn zhèng
yǎn "Luómǎ Xīngwáng Shǐ" ne.

80 Měi: Wǒmen jiu dào Zhōngguo qu kàn ba!

Bái: Wǒmen xiànzài jiu zǒu, xiān mǎi piào, ránhòu zài qu chī fàn qu.

Měi: Hǎo.

Bái: Měiyīng, wǒ cóng xià xīngqī qǐ, jiu bú huì xiàng yǐqián nènmo máng
le. Wǒmen kéyi shícháng yǒu jīhui zài yikuàr wárwar le.

85 Měi: Zuìdǐde xiàndu nǐ kéyi cháng dào zhèr lái dàjiā tántan.

Bái: Kěbushìma! Jīntian qiàqiǎo Gāo Xiānsheng, Gāo Tàitai bú zài jiā,
yě méi kànjian tamen.

Měi: Tāmen yìhuěr jiu huílai. Wǒmen kànwánle diànyǐngr huílai nǐ jiu
jiànzhe tāmen le.

90 Bái: Kànwán diànyǐngr wǒ hái yào huílai ma?

Měi: Mǔqin zài chū mén yǐqián gàosu wo le, shuō wǒmen búlùn dào nǎr
qu wár, wǎnfàn yídìng děi huílai chī. Nǐ xǐhuan chī de cài tā dōu
yùbeihǎo le.

Bái: Nènmo wǒmen yídìng děi huílai chī fàn le.

DUĂNWÉN

1. Wǒmende xiàozhǎng niánji tài dà le, zǎo jiu yīnggāi tuìxiū le. Kěshi tā
hái bù kěn xiūxi, hái tiāntiān dào xuéxiào lái.   Dànshi tā yìtiān bànbuliǎo duōshao shì le. Zai xíngshìshang tā shi xiàozhǎng, shízhìshang tāde
shì dōu shi jiàowuzhǎng gěi bàn le.

2. Wǒmen shi xiāngxia rén, shi zhōngchǎn jiējide jiātíng, jiu shi xiǎo zìgēngnóng le.   Wǒmende tiándì dōu shi zǔzong liúchuánxialai de.   Fùqin
měitiān zài tiánli zhòngdì, měitiān hěn zǎo jiu chūqu, tiān hēile cái huí
jiā.   Zhōngwǔ shi mǔqin gěi ta sòng fàn. Wǒmen dìxiōng wǔge rén.   Wǒ
zuì dà, wǒmen jǐge rén dōu zài yíge sīshúli niàn shū, suǒyǐ měitiān
mǔqin mángde bùdeliǎo, chúle guǎn háizi gēn guǎn jiāshì yǐwài, hái děi
bāngzhu fùqin zài nóngchǎngli zuògōng.   Bǐrú wǎng tiánli fàng féiliào
děngděng dōu shi mǔqinde gōngzuò.   Wǒmen shícháng wèile yìdiǎr xiǎoshì dìxiōng jǐge jiu chōngtuqilai.   Yǒu yícì mǔqin yòu yào dào tiánli qu
gōngzuò.   Zǒu de shíhou bǎ cài、fàn dōu gěi wǒmen yùbeihǎo le, ràng
wǒmen jǐge rén zài yíkuàr chī. Chīzhe chīzhe wèile chī ròu dàjiā dǎqilai le, bǎ pánzi dōu dǎpò le. Mǔqin huí jiā yí kàn hěn shēngqì. Tā shuō:
"Yǐhòu chī fàn wǒ fēnpèi gěi nǐmen chī, yào gè chī gède." Yúshi mǔqin
gěi women shuōle yíge gùshi.   Tā shuō zài Sān Guóde shíhou yǒu yíge
xiǎohár cái sìsuì, dàjiā zài yíkuàr chī lí, tā zài pánzi lǐbiār nále yíge
zuì xiǎode lí. Biéren wèn ta wèi-shénmo ná xiǎode bù ná dàde? Tā shuō
tā niánji zuì xiǎo, yīnggāi chī xiǎode. Mǔqin shuōwánle zhèige gùshi, duì
wǒmen shuō: "Nǐmen dōu bǐ nèige háizi dà, wèile chī ròu dǎqilai duómo
ràng rénjia xiàohua."

3. Yǒu yíge guójiā jìnlai tōnghuò péngzhàng, wùjià gāozhǎng. Tónghuò suǒyǐ
péngzhàng de yuányīn shi yīnwei nèige guójiā yǒu zhànshì ér zhèngfǔ fā-
chu de zhǐbì tài duō le, yòu jiāshang yìbān zīběnjiā cāozòng wùjià. Rúguǒ zhèngfǔ bù xiǎng yíge bànfǎ yángé guǎnlǐ, kěnéng nòngdao jīngji bēngkuì, shèhuì hǔnluàn. Wǒ yǒu yíge péngyou jiu zài nèige dìfang. Zuótian
gěi wo lái xìn shuō tāmen nàlǐde zhànshì xiāngdāng jīliè. Tā běnlái zài
nàlǐ jīngyíngle yíge qǐyè gōngsī, shēngyi fēicháng bù hé lǐxiǎng. Tā xiǎng
zài biéde dìfang gǎnkuài lìngwài zhǎo ge shìhé ta de gōngzuò, quánjiā jiu
dōu líkai nàli le.

4. Zhōngguo dàlùshang yǒu yíge shíqī yīnwei tiānzāide guānxi, niánnián qiànshōu, nóngzuòyè hé mùxùyè shòule hěn dàde sǔnhài, suǒyǐ yǐngxiǎng tāmen dàyuèjìn.

5. Zhōngguo yǐqián nánběi huòwude yùnshū quán kàozhe Yùnhé.   Tíqi Yùnhéde lìshǐ, shi xiāngdāng cháng le.   Suīrán shuō shi Suí Cháo zào de,
kěshi shíjìshang zhǐshi Jiāngsu、Zhéjiāng zhèi yíduàn shi Suí Cháo zào
de.   Yùnhé búdàn yùnshū huòwu, tā duì nán-běi wénhuàde jiāoliú yě yǒu
hěn dàde gòngxiàn.

6. Nèige guójiā zìcóng xīn zhèngquán zhízhèng yǐlái, kāifāle bù shǎode
kuàng, bǐrú jīnshǔ kuàng、shíyóu kuàng děng. Tóngshí yě xiūle bù shǎode

shuǐbà gēn tiělù. Yòu zēngjiànle jǐge gāngtiěchǎng. Zài hángyè yìfāngmiàn tāmen yě hěn zhòngshì. Tīngshuō zuìjìnde jiānglái tāmen yě yào
fāzhǎn guójì màoyì.

7. Wǒ dìdi jīnnián suírán niánji bù xiǎo le, kěshi hěn bù dǒng shì. Cháng-
    cháng búshi gēn rénjia dǎqilai jiùshi gēn rénjia màqilai le. Dànshi tā
    hěn nénggan, yǒu zǔzhī nénglì. Zài xuéxiàoli tóngxuémen dōu tīng tāde
    zhǐhuī. Tóngshí tā yě yǒu hàozhàode nénglì, yàoshi tā fābiǎo yíge yìjian
    dàjiā dōu yōnghù ta. Tāde zuòfēng, wǒ fùqin fēicháng bú zànchéng. Yǒu
    yícì tā yòu fànle máobing gēn rénjia dǎqilai le, jǐngchá yào bǎ ta dàizǒu,
    tā gēn jǐngchá shuō: "Wǒ méi fànfǎ, nǐ wèi-shénmo yào bǎ wǒ dàizǒu?"
    Xìng'er fùqinde lǎo péngyou kànjian le, gēn jǐngchá shuōle bàntiān hǎo
    huà, jiéguǒ jǐngchá méi bǎ ta dàizǒu. Yòu yǒu yícì tā gēn fùqin shuō, tā
    yào dāng bīng qu, tā shuō fánshi yǒu xiěqìde rén dōu yīnggāi qu dāng
    bīng. Yúshi dàshēng shuōle yíge kǒuhào "Hǎo nán yào dāng bīng!"

8. Wǒ yìjiā bākǒu rén quán kào wǒ zài gōngchǎng zuògōng shēnghuó, suǒyǐ
    wǒde fùdān hěn zhòng. Xiàge yuè wǒ nèiren yòu yào shēng háizi le.
    Wǒde fùdān gèng jiāzhòng le. Xìngkuī wǒ zuògōng de nèige gōngchǎng
    gōngyìng wǒmen gōngren fángzi zhù, érqiě rìyòngpǐn gēn liángshi duo shi
    ànzhe rénkǒu pèiji. Tóngshí gōngchǎngli yě yǒu xiāofèi hézuòshè, mǎi
    dōngxi yě bú guì. Suǒyǐ shēnghuó suírán kǔ yìdiǎr hái suàn wěndìng.

9. Zuótian Wáng Xiānsheng gěile wǒ yìběn huàcè, shi wǔwèi huàjiāde jítǐ
    chuàngzuò. Yǒu jǐzhǒng bùtóngde tícái, yǒu huāhuì、húdié、shānshuǐ shén-
    mode. Wǒ zuì xǐhuan de shi yìzhāng "Xiāngcūn Fēngjǐng Tú," shàngmiàn
    huà de shi nóngren. Yǒude zài zhòngtián, yǒude zài guàngài, huàde shēng-
    dòng jíle. Wǒ kànle zhèizhāng huàr zhēn xiǎng qu dāng nóngren. Huàr
    huàde nènmo hǎo. Zhè huàjiā yídìng shi yǒu hěn gāode yìshu shuǐpíng le.

10. Yíge yǒu qián de rén shuō tā diūle hěn zhíqiánde dōngxi, zhǎole hěn duō
     jǐngchá lái. Zhèijiàn shìqing kànzhe hǎoxiang hěn yánzhòng. Jǐngchámen
     lái diàochá hǎojiǔ yòu zǐxìde yánjiu, yě bù míngbai tāmende dōngxi shi
     zěnmo diū de, shǐzhōng débudào yíge jiélùn. Hūrán yǒu yìtiān tāmende
     dōngxi zhǎodào le. Yuánlái shi tā tàitai bǎ dōngxi shōuqilai le, kěshi
     tā wàngle shōuzai nǎr le.

11. Yǒu yíge luòhòude guójiā, zìcóng mǒu zīběn zhǔyìde guójiā zài cáizhèng
     jīngji yìfāngmiàn bāngzhule ᴛamen, yúshì tāmende huòbì jiu wěndìng le,
     shìchǎngshang yě mànmān fánróngqilai le. Tāmen hé mǒu gōngyè guójiā
     mǎile hěn duō jīqi, xiàng tuōlājī、fǎngzhījī děngděng. Tāmende zhèngcè
     shi zàolín hé tíchàng mùxùyè. Chú cǐ zhīwài yě yào gǎijìn tāmende jiāo-
     tōng gōngjù, xiū shuǐkù, zào shuǐbà. Tāmen hái yǒu yíge kǒuhào shi
     "nóngzuòyè yào jīxièhuà." Hòulái tāmende gōngshāngyè yě dōu jiànjiàn
     fādáqilai, tāmende nóngyè chǎnwù yě yìtiān bǐ yìtiān duō. Tāmende zhèng-
     fǔ hé guān dōu bàozhe yìzhǒng bìdìng chénggōng de sīxiǎng, suǒyǐ tāmen
     chénggōng le.

12. Wǒ xiànzài xīn lǐtou hěn máodùn. Yuányīn shi běnlái wǒ xiǎng xué yìdiǎr
     Fàwén, dào Fàguo qu niàn shū, xīwang zài Fàguo qǔdé yíge xuéwèi, kě-
     shi wǒ duì Zhōngwén yě fēicháng yǒu xìngqu ér Zhōngguo wénxué、yìshu
     yǒu jí gāodù wénhuà jiàzhí. Zuótian hé wo fùqin yánjiu, yī tā lǎorén-
     jiāde yìsi shi jiào wǒ dào Zhōngguo qù. Tāde yìsi shi Zhōngguode wén-
     huà hǎo dào bù néng zài hǎo le, suǒyǐ nòngde wǒde xīnli fēicháng máo-
     dùn.

13. Zhèlide hézuòshè zuìjìn zǔchéngle yíge shēngchǎn hùzhùzǔ. Hùzhùzǔde yìsi shi zài zhòngtián de shíhou yàoshi quēshǎo rénlì huòzhě shi gōngjù shénmode, dàjiā dōu bǐcǐ bāngzhu.

14. Yǒu yíwèi lǎo xiānsheng cónglái bù chuān Xīzhuāng. Rénjia wèn ta wèishénmo bù chuān Xīzhuāng, tā shuō shi bǎocún guócuì. Tā jiànzhe qīngnián rén lǎo shuō wényán, zuǐli búshi "Zǐ yuē" jiushi "Biàn shàn'è." Yǒu yìtiān wǒ gēn ta zài lùshang zǒuzhe, tā hūrán shuō "Héchù shi wǒ jiā?" Wǒ méi míngbai tāde yìsi. Wǒ shuō: "Nǐde jiā bú jiu zài qiánbiān ma?" Hòulái wǒ cái míngbai, tāde yìsi shi tāde lǎojiā zài nǎr.

15. Yíge dà qǐyè gōngsī, zài mǒu gōngchǎng dìngle hěn duō gōngyè yuánliào. Bǎ huò yùnlái zhīhòu jīngguò jiǎnchá, jiéguǒ hé yuánlái dìng de yàngzi bùtóng. Jīngguò jǐcìde jiāoshe, qǐyè gōngsī xīwang bǎ huò quánbù tuìle ràng tāmen yùnhuiqu. Nèige gōngchǎng fù zéren de rén shuō: "Yuánlái dìng de jiù shi zhèizhǒng huò, wǒmen bù néng yùnhuiqu. Háiyǒu, zhènmo yuǎnde lù, xiànzài jiāotōng yòu zhènmo kùnnan, rúguǒ wǒmen yòng huòchē yùnhuiqu, jiu shi zài yùnhuò zhèi yìfāngmiàn wǒmende sǔnshī yě xiāngdāng dà le."

16. Pǔjí jiàoyu shi xiāngdāng zhòngyàode. Zài shínián yǐqián zhèli fànfǎ de rén zhàn rénkǒu zǒngshùde bǎifēnzhī-èrshí. Zìcóng pǔjí jiàoyu shíxíng yǐlái, tāmen chūbùde diàochá jiéguǒ, jìn shínián lǐtou zhǐ yǒu bǎifēnzhī-sānde rén fànfǎ.

17. Wǒmen niàn zhōngxué de shíhou guówén lǎoshī Zhāng Dàwén Xiānsheng shi yíge fǎnduì báihuàwénde rén. Tā cháng duì wǒmen shuō, báihuàwén yán'gé shuōqilai bù néng ná ta dàngzuò wénxué zuòpǐn, zhǐ néng yòng ta xiěxie tōngsú xiǎoshuō bàle. Tā měicì ràng wǒmen zuò wén dōu shi ná wényánwén zuò zhǔtǐ. Xiàng xiě rìjì shénmode cái kéyǐ yòng báihuàwén. Tā jiāli gòng Kǒngzǐ. Tā shuō: "Niàn shū de rén yīnggāi fèng Kǒngzǐ shi shén."

18. Zhōngguo rén yǒu yíjù súhuà shi "Guǐ pà è rén" jiu shi shuō yíge rén yàoshi tài lìhai le lián guǐ dōu pà ta. Kěshi shìjièshang yǒu guǐ méi yǒu, shéi yě bù néng jiědá zhèige wèntí.

19. Rúlín Wàishǐshang dì-yīhuí jiu shi xiě de Wáng Miǎnde gùshi. Suīrán tímu bú shi Wáng Miǎn zhuàn, kěshi shízhǐshang jìzǎi de shi Wáng Miǎn. Lìngwài hái yǒu yíge Wáng Miǎn Zhuàn, shi Sòng Lián xiě de. Suīrán tǐcái shi wényán de, kěshi gùshi shi dàzhǐ xiāngtóng de.

20.   Měiyīng:

Zuótian wǎnshang líkāi fǔshang, dào jiāli yǐjing shí'èrdiǎn zhōng le. Xiěwánle rìjì wǒ jiu shuìjiào le. Zuótian wǒmen zài yíkuàr tánde hěn gāoxìng, Gāo Tàitai gěi women zuòle nènmo hǎochīde cài, tóngshí wǒmen kàn de nèibù diànyǐng yě xiāngdāng jīngcǎi. Nǐ kàn Luómǎde jiànzhu duómo xióngzhuàng. Hái yǒu miáoxiě gōngtíng lǐjié yíshì, yǐjí shēnghuóshangde zhǒngzhǒng fēngsu, hái yǒu xíngróng zhànzhēngde zuì'è. Wǒ suīrán méi qùguo Luómǎ, wǒ xiāngxìn Luómǎ zài dāngshí quèshí xiàng diànyǐng suǒ yǎn de nèizhǒng qíngxing. Luómǎ běnlái shi yǒu jí gāodù wénhuàde gǔguó. Yīnwei zhànzhēng bǎ nènmo hǎode jiànzhu dōu shāo le. Gǔdài Luómǎde jiànzhu shi yādǎo rènhé yíge guójiā de.

Běnlài wǒmen míngtian yòu kéyi jiànmiàn le. Kěshi wǒ juéde hǎoxiang
yǒu hěn duō huà hái méi gēn nǐ shuōwán shide, suǒyǐ yòu náqi bǐ lái xiě.
Wǒmen cóng xiànzài qǐ, yòu kéyi cháng zài yíkuàr wár le.   Wǒ néng
cháng hé nǐ zài yíkuàr wár wǒ fēichángde gāoxìng.   Nǐ ne? Zhù

Hǎo.

Wénshān

Shíyue jiǔrì

COMPARATIVE TRANSCRIPTION TABLE
Pinyin—Yale—Wade-Giles

Pinyin	Yale	Wade-Giles	Pinyin	Yale	Wade-Giles
a	a	a	ceng	tseng	ts'eng
ai	ai	ai	cha	cha	ch'a
an	an	an	chai	chai	ch'ai
ang	ang	ang	chan	chan	ch'an
ao	au	ao	chang	chang	ch'ang
			chao	chau	ch'ao
			che	che	ch'e
ba	ba	pa	chen	chen	ch'en
bai	bai	pai	cheng	cheng	ch'eng
ban	ban	pan	chi	chr	ch'ih
bang	bang	pang	chong	chung	ch'ung
bao	bau	pao	chou	chou	ch'ou
bei	bei	pei	chu	chu	ch'u
ben	ben	pen	chuai	chwai	ch'uai
beng	beng	peng	chuan	chwan	ch'uan
bi	bi	pi	chuang	chwang	ch'uang
bian	byan	pien	chui	chwei	ch'ui
biao	byau	piao	chun	chwun	ch'un
bie	bye	pieh	chuo	chwo	ch'o
bin	bin	pin	ci	tsz	tz'u
bing	bing	ping	cong	tsung	ts'ung
bo	bwo	po	cou	tsou	ts'ou
bou	bou	pou	cu	tsu	ts'u
bu	bu	pu	cuan	tswan	ts'uan
			cui	tswei	ts'ui
ca	tsa	ts'a	cun	tswun	ts'un
cai	tsai	ts'ai	cuo	tswo	ts'o
can	tsan	ts'an			
cang	tsang	ts'ang	da	da	ta
cao	tsao	ts'ao	dai	dai	tai
ce	tse	ts'e	dan	dan	tan
cen	tsen	ts'en			

Pinyin	Yale	Wade-Giles	Pinyin	Yale	Wade-Giles
dang	dang	tang	gai	gai	kai
dao	dau	tao	gan	gan	kan
de	de	te	gang	gang	kang
dei	dei	tei	gao	gau	kao
deng	deng	teng	ge	ge	ke, ko
di	di	ti	gei	gei	kei
dian	dyan	tien	gen	gen	ken
diao	dyau	tiao	geng	geng	keng
die	dye	tieh	gong	gung	kung
ding	ding	ting	gou	gou	kou
diu	dyou	tiu	gu	gu	ku
dong	dung	tung	gua	gwa	kua
dou	dou	tou	guai	gwai	kuai
du	du	tu	guan	gwan	kuan
duan	dwan	tuan	guang	gwang	kuang
dui	dwei	tui	gui	gwei	kuei
dun	dwun	tun	gun	gwun	kun
duo	dwo	to	guo	gwo	kuo
e	e	e, o	ha	ha	ha
ei	ei	ei	hai	hai	hai
en	en	en	han	han	han
eng	eng	eng	hang	hang	hang
er	er	erh	hao	hau	hao
			he	he	he, ho
fa	fa	fa	hei	hei	hei
fan	fan	fan	hen	hen	hen
fang	fang	fang	heng	heng	heng
fei	fei	fei	hong	hung	hung
fen	fen	fen	hou	hou	hou
feng	feng	feng	hu	hu	hu
fo	fwo	fo	hua	hwa	hua
fou	fou	fou	huai	hwai	huai
fu	fu	fu	huan	hwan	huan
			huang	hwang	huang
ga	ga	ka	hui	hwei	hui

Pinyin	Yale	Wade-Giles	Pinyin	Yale	Wade-Giles
hun	hwun	hun	la	la	la
huo	hwo	huo	lai	lai	lai
			lan	lan	lan
ji	ji	chi	lang	lang	lang
jia	jya	chia	lao	lau	lao
jian	jyan	chien	le	le	le
jiang	jyang	chiang	lei	lei	lei
jiao	jyau	chiao	leng	leng	leng
jie	jye	chieh	li	li	li
jin	jin	chin	lia	lya	lia
jing	jing	ching	lian	lyan	lien
jiong	jyong	chiung	liang	lyang	liang
jiu	jyou	chiu	liao	lyau	liao
ju	jyu	chü	lie	lye	lieh
juan	jywan	chüan	lin	lin	lin
jue	jywe	chüeh	ling	ling	ling
jun	jyun	chün	liu	lyou	liu
			long	lung	lung
ka	ka	k'a	lou	lou	lou
kai	kai	k'ai	lu	lu	lu
kan	kan	k'an	luan	lwan	luan
kang	kang	k'ang	lun	lwun	lun
kao	kau	k'ao	luo	lwo	lo
ke	ke	k'e, k'o	lü	lyu	lü
ken	ken	k'en	lüe	lywe	lüeh
keng	keng	k'eng			
kong	kung	k'ung	ma	ma	ma
kou	kou	k'ou	mai	mai	mai
ku	ku	k'u	man	man	man
kua	kwa	k'ua	mang	mang	mang
kuai	kwai	k'uai	mao	mau	mao
kuan	kwan	k'uan	mei	mei	mei
kuang	kwang	k'uang	men	men	men
kui	kwei	k'uei	meng	meng	meng
kun	kwen	k'un	mi	mi	mi
kuo	kwo	k'uo	mian	myan	mien

Pinyin	Yale	Wade-Giles		Pinyin	Yale	Wade-Giles
miao	myau	miao		pan	pan	p'an
mie	mye	mieh		pang	pang	p'ang
min	min	min		pao	pau	p'ao
ming	ming	ming		pei	pei	p'ei
miu	myou	miu		pen	pen	p'en
mo	mwo	mo		peng	peng	p'eng
mou	mou	mou		po	pwo	p'o
mu	mu	mu		pou	pou	p'ou
				pi	pi	p'i
na	na	na		pian	pyan	p'ien
nai	nai	nai		piao	pyau	p'iao
nan	nan	nan		pie	pye	p'ieh
nang	nang	nang		pin	pin	p'in
nao	nau	nao		ping	ping	p'ing
ne	ne	ne		pu	pu	p'u
nei	nei	nei				
nen	nen	nen		qi	chi	ch'i
neng	neng	neng		qia	chya	ch'ia
nong	nung	nung		qian	chyan	ch'ien
nou	nou	nou		qiang	chyang	ch'iang
ni	ni	ni		qiao	chyau	ch'iao
nian	nyan	nien		qie	chye	ch'ieh
niang	nyang	niang		qin	chin	ch'in
niao	nyau	niao		qing	ching	ch'ing
nie	nye	nieh		qiong	chyung	ch'iung
nin	nin	nin		qiu	chyou	ch'iu
ning	ning	ning		qu	chyu	ch'ü
niu	nyou	niu		quan	chywan	ch'üan
nu	nu	nu		que	chywe	ch'üeh
nuan	nwan	nuan		qun	chyun	ch'ün
nuo	nwo	no				
nü	nyu	nü		ran	ran	jan
nüe	nywe	nüeh		rang	rang	jang
				rao	rau	jao
pa	pa	p'a		re	re	je
pai	pai	p'ai		ren	ren	jen

Pinyin	Yale	Wade-Giles	Pinyin	Yale	Wade-Giles
reng	reng	jeng	shuo	shwo	shuo
ri	r	jih	si	sz	szu
rong	rung	jung	song	sung	sung
rou	rou	jou	sou	sou	sou
ru	ru	ju	su	su	su
ruan	rwan	juan	suan	swan	suan
rui	rwei	jui	sui	swei	sui
run	rwen	jun	sun	swun	sun
ruo	rwo	jo	suo	swo	so
sa	sa	sa	ta	ta	t'a
sai	sai	sai	tai	tai	t'ai
san	san	san	tan	tan	t'an
sang	sang	sang	tang	tang	t'ang
sao	sau	sao	tao	tau	t'ao
se	se	se	te	te	t'e
sen	sen	sen	teng	teng	t'eng
seng	seng	seng	ti	ti	t'i
sha	sha	sha	tian	tyan	t'ien
shai	shai	shai	tiao	tyau	t'iao
shan	shan	shan	tie	tye	t'ieh
shang	shang	shang	ting	ting	t'ing
shao	shau	shao	tong	tung	t'ung
she	she	she	tou	tou	t'ou
shei	shei	shei	tu	tu	t'u
shen	shen	shen	tuan	twan	t'uan
sheng	sheng	sheng	tui	twei	t'ui
shi	shr	shih	tun	twun	t'un
shou	shou	shou	tuo	two	t'o
shu	shu	shu			
shua	shwa	shua	wa	wa	wa
shuai	shwai	shuai	wai	wai	wai
shuan	shwan	shuan	wan	wan	wan
shuang	shwang	shuang	wang	wang	wang
shui	shwei	shui	wei	wei	wei
shun	shwen	shun	wen	wen	wen

Comparative Transcription Table

Pinyin	Yale	Wade-Giles	Pinyin	Yale	Wade-Giles
weng	weng	weng	zan	dzan	tsan
wo	wo	wo	zang	dzang	tsang
wu	wu	wu	zao	dzau	tsao
			ze	dze	tse
xi	syi	hsi	zei	dzei	tsei
xia	sya	hsia	zen	dzen	tsen
xian	syan	hsien	zeng	dzeng	tseng
xiang	syang	hsiang	zha	ja	cha
xiao	syau	hsiao	zhai	jai	chai
xie	sye	hsieh	zhan	jan	chan
xin	syin	hsin	zhang	jang	chang
xing	sying	hsing	zhao	jau	chao
xiong	syung	hsiung	zhe	je	che
xiu	syou	hsiu	zhei	jei	chei
xu	syu	hsü	zhen	jen	chen
xuan	sywan	hsüan	zheng	jeng	cheng
xue	sywe	hsüeh	zhi	jr	chih
xun	syun	hsün	zhong	jung	chung
			zhou	jou	chou
ya	ya	ya	zhu	ju	chu
yan	yan	yen	zhua	jwa	chua
yang	yang	yang	zhuai	jwai	chuai
yao	yau	yao	zhuan	jwan	chuan
ye	ye	yeh	zhuang	jwang	chuang
yi	yi	i	zhui	jwei	chui
yin	yin	yin	zhun	jwun	chun
ying	ying	ying	zhuo	jwo	cho
yong	yung	yung	zi	dz	tzu
you	you	yu	zong	dzung	tsung
yu	yu	yü	zou	dzou	tsou
yuan	ywan	yüan	zu	dzu	tsu
yue	ywe	yüeh	zuan	dzwan	tsuan
yun	yun	yün	zui	dzwei	tsui
			zun	dzwen	tsun
za	dza	tsa	zuo	dzwo	tso
zai	dzai	tsai			

GLOSSARY AND INDEX

Entries are arranged alphabetically by syllables. Thus jĭhua (jĭ + hua) precedes
jiātĭng. References after each item are to lesson and subsection. Thus 1.50 refers to
Lesson 1, Item 50 among the new terms, and 1 N 2 refers to Lesson 1, Note 2 at the end
of the lesson.

A duĭ/gēn B (de) guānxi   connection,
    importance of A to/with B 2.43
A shi shuō B   A means B 5.2
A yĕ xiàng B yíyàng V   A, like B, V
    16 N
A yìsi jiu shi shuō B   A means B 5.2
ài   love, love to, like 11.13
àiguó   love one's country, be patriotic
    (VO) 11.13
àn   by the . . . ; according to 5.22
ān-tŭ-zhòng-qiān   be content in one's
    native place and consider moving
    a serious matter 5.1
ànzhào   according to 5.22
ànzhe   according to 5.22
ànzhe A lai suàn   calculate according
    to A 16 N
Ào   Australia 4.17
Àozhōu   Australia 4.17
aspect, negative form of continuous 21 Ni

Bā Jĭn   Pa Chin 17 N 4
bàle   Enough of that! (And) that's that!
    just, no more than 23.17
Bāyuejié   Mid-Autumn Festival 11.7
băi   display, arrange, spread out 11.31
bài   bow to; call on; worship 10.11
bài   be defeated (also used as postverb)
    11.14
băihuò gōngsĭ   department store 10.40
báiliăn   white-painted face 19.2
bàinián   pay New Year's calls (VO)
    10.11
bàishén   worship the gods (VO) 10.11
bān   move, shift 5.3
bàn   arrange, manage, handle 2.3
bàndăo   peninsula 4.26
bànfă   way of handling a matter, way to
    manage 2.3
bàn gōng   transact official business
    2.3
bàngōngchù   office 2.8
bàngōngshĭ   office 2.38
bànhăo   do, manage (a job satisfactorily)
    (RV) 2.3
bānjiā   move, change residence (VO)
    5.3

bàn shì   manage an affair, transact
    business 2.3
bànshìchù   office 2.8
bànyè   midnight 10.42
băngyàng   (human) example, model,
    pattern 13.23
bāo   to wrap; package, bundle 10.64
bào   hold, embrace (literal and figura-
    tive) 23.56
băocún   preserve, keep safely 9.45
bàodăo   announce, report; announce-
    ment, report 15.15
băoguì   precious, valuable 13.42
bāokuò   include; including (especially
    after a parenthesis) 1.36
băoshŏu   protect, defend, conserve,
    preserve; conservative 9.16
băozhàng   safeguard (N/V) 8.52
bàozhú   firecracker, fireworks 9.29
bèi   by, at the hand of (CV) 5.35
bèi   times, -fold (M) 21.28
bèi   the back 14.4; learn by heart 14.35
bèijĭng   background; ulterior motive
    17.59
bèi shū   learn the contents of a book by
    heart; recite from memory 14.35
bĕnbù   China Proper 4.49
bĕnshēn   one's own body; (one's) self
    3.19
bĕntĭ   this topic, the topic in question
    2.60
bĕnxiào   our school, this school 1.28
bĕnyì   basic meaning 14.28
bēngkuì   collapse (N/V) 21.9
bĭ
    in A bĭ B SV   'A is more SV than
        B' 15 N 1
    in yìtiān bĭ yìtiān   'day by day, one
        day after another' 4 N 3
    in bĭ QW dōu SV   'more SV than QW'
        8 N 4
    in bĭ QW dōu V 'to V more than QW'
        9 N 1
bĭ   currency 9.53
bĭcĭ   mutual(ly), reciprocal(ly), one an-
    other, between or among themselves,
    yourselves, ourselves 7.50

chúncuì   pure, unadulterated; purely,
    simply 13.36
chūnjì   spring 23.61
Chūnjié   Spring Festival 10.8
Chūnqiū   Spring and Autumn Period
    (770–475 B.C.); Spring and Autumn
    Annals 17.19
chūntian   spring 10.6
cí   poem of unequal lines with fixed tonal
    pattern 17.36
cí bù dáyì   words do not make one's
    meaning clear 13.35
cídiào   (word) tone 16.36
Cíhǎi   15 N 5
cíhuì   word-list, vocabulary 15.7
císù   smallest meaningful element,
    morpheme 16.50
cítáng   ancestral hall 8.23
cítóu   prefix 16.31
cǐwài   besides this, apart from this
    2.28
cíwěi   suffix 16.31
cìxu   sequence, scheduled order of
    events 10.58
Cíyuán   (book title) 15.17
classical style 23 N
cóng   in N (V) cóng TW jiu V   'N
    V'd from TW' 21 N b
cóng . . . ér   from 7 N 1
cóng . . . lái shuō   speaking from . . .
    3 N 3
cōngshū   collectanea, collection of books
    published in a set 15.30
cùchéng   stimulate 22.41
cūn   village 5.41
cúnzài   exist, survive, continue 8.39
cūnzi   village 5.41
cuòwù   mistake 13.21

dá   to answer 5.64
dà   big (used between numerals and
    measures) 22 N d
dǎbài   defeat; be defeated (RV) 11.14
dáchéng   attain, achieve 1.51
dáchéng yípiàn   become one, form a
    group 17.47
dádào   attain 1.34
dǎdǎo   knock down, overturn; Down
    with . . . ! 20.46
dǎdǎo Kǒng jiā diàn!   Down with Con-
    fucianism! 20.46
dàfēng   big wind; typhoon 15.44
dàhù   great family, rich family 8.7
dǎhuài   smash, beat 10 N 5
dà jiātíng zhìdu   big-family system 2.9
dàliàng   large quantity, large number
    5.59
dàlù   mainland 4.27
dàlüè   in outline, in general 11.60

dǎ májiàng   play mahjong 10.31
dǎpò   smash (RV) 11.59
dàren   an adult 10.36
dásao   to sweep 11.32
dǎshèng   fight and win (RV) 11.21
dàtǐ   in general, in the main 3.20
dàtóngxiǎoyì   much alike, not very dif-
    ferent 3.51
Dàxīyáng   Atlantic Ocean 11.27
dáyì   make one's meaning clear 13.35
dáyì biǎoqíng   state meanings and ex-
    press emotions 23.51
dàyuē   probably, most likely 7.14
dàyuèjìn   advance in great leaps; Great
    Leap Forward 21.50
dǎzhàng   fight a battle or war (VO)
    5.8
dǎzhēn   inoculate (VO) 9.38
dàzhǐ   in general 4.6
dàzhòng   the masses 14.30
dàzhōu   continent 4.16
dǎ zuǐba   slap the cheeks 16.49
dài   belt, strip (M); carry, take, bring
    2.39
dàimíngcí   pronoun 16.32
dàizi   belt 2.39
dān   single, singly 2.24
dānlìrér   'single standing man' 15.55
dānyīn   single sound 14.17
dānyīnjié   monosyllable 14.17
dānyīnzì   monosyllabic character 14.17
dānzì   single character 2.24
dǎng   political party (N/M) 11.50
dǎngpài   faction, party 11.51
dǎo   island 4.26
dào   contrary to expectation, yet, never-
    theless; after all, yes of course
    but . . . , to V all right, but . . . 2.1
dào   'to' (with stative verbs) 15 N 2
dào   The Way 20.22
dào   in yào dào . . . cái V   'will not
    V until . . .'
dāochā   knife and fork 9.26
dàodé   morality, virtue 20.13
Dàodé Jīng   Morality Classic 20.13
dàodǐ   to the end; finally, after all 14.27
Dàojiā   Taoist(s) 20.22
Dàojiào   Taoism 20.22
dàoshi   contrary to expectations, yet,
    nevertheless; after all, yes of
    course but . . . , to V all right,
    but . . . 2.1
Dé   Germany, German language 7.42
de   (as sentence particle) 2 N 1
    (at end of adverbs and adverbial
    phrases) 2 N 3
definite N   15 N 3
Déguo   Germany 7.42
de huà   if 8.30

Déwén   German language 7.42
dēng   lamp, light 10.7
dēng   mount, ascend 11.1
dēng   publish 17.13
děng A B   to B after A 16 N
děngdao A zài B   to B after A 16 N
dēnggāo   ascend to a high place 11.1
Dēngjié(r)   Lantern Festival 10.8
dēng shān   ascend a mountain 11.1
děngyú   equivalent to 7.62
děngzǎi   publish 17.13
dǐ   low 4.50
dǐ   bottom; end 14.27
dì   hand over, pass to 8.43
dì = dìfang   'place' 1 N 4
dì-dà-wù-bó   large in territory and rich
    in natural products 4.2
dǐkàng   resist 7.38
dìqū   region, area 16.8
díquè   really and truly, certainly 8.42
díren   enemy 17.56
dìshì   physical feature 4.63
dǐxia   underneath; next in order 14.27
dìxiong   (older and younger) brothers
    8.18
diànbàojú   telegraph office 11.44
diànnóng   tenant farmer 8.6
diànshì   television 11.56
diào   fall, drop; fall to, fall into; (post-
    verb); lose (by dropping from
    clothes, etc.) 13.19
diàochá   investigate, check up on; in-
    vestigation 5.23
diāokè   carve, sculpt, engrave; carving,
    engraving, sculpture 19.17
dǐng   D 14.1, 14 N 3
dìng   order merchandise; subscribe to
    a periodical 15.29
diū   lose 13.29
diūdiào   lose 13.29
diū liǎn   lose face, be embarrassed
    13.29
dōng   winter 22.62
dòngcí   verb 16.28
dōngjì   winter 23.61
dòngluàn   disturbance, upheaval 5.42
dòngtài   activity, mobility 5.10
dōngtian   winter 22.62
Dòngtíng Hú   Tungting Lake 4.43
Dōngyǎ, Dōngyà   East Asia 4.20
dòngzuò   action, movement 19.34
dōu
    used with question words 17 N 1
    used with nǎpà 19 N 1 a
    in lián V dōu bù/méi V 'not even V'
        11 N 3
    in construction S₁ dōu S₂   4 N 2
    paired with fánshi 2 N 4
    used with zhǐ yào or zhǐ yàoshi 2 N 2

in bǐ QW dōu SV   'more SV than any
    other' 8 N 4, 9 N 1
dú   read; study 8.41
dú   alone 11.36
dù   degree, extent 5.27
dúlì   independent 11.36
dúshū   study (VO) 8.41
dútè   particular, special 14.14
dúwù   reading matter 15.26
dúzì   alone, independently, by oneself
    11.36
duān   exactly 11 N 5
duàn   satin 9.3
duàn   segment, section, paragraph,
    period 13.30
duǎnpiān xiǎoshuō   short story 15.3
duǎnqī   short period 3.30
duǎnwén   short essay 5.65
Duānyáng   Dragon-Boat Festival 11.7,
    11 N 5
Duānyángjié   Dragon-Boat Festival
    11.7, 11 N 5
duànzi   satin 9.3
duàr   segment, section, paragraph,
    period 13.30
duì   a group (M) 14.44
dùn   (measure for meals) 14.61
Dūnhuáng   Tunhuang (in Kansu Province)
    19.12
duōchulai   be in excess (of an expected
    amount) 10.20
duōma SV (a)!   how SV! 9.20
duōyīnjié   polysyllable 14.17
duōyú   surplus; superfluous 10.17
duōyúchulai   be left over, be superfluous;
    has as surplus 10.20
duō-zǐ-duō-sūn   (have) many sons and
    grandsons 5.17
duration of time, expressions of 5 N 3

Ē, É, È   Russia; Russian language 4.22
è   evil (N/SV) 23.59
Ēguo, Éguo, Èguo   Russia 4.22
enumerative comma   p. 15
ér
    and, and yet, but, whereas, while on
        the other hand 7.35, 7 N 1
    in yóu A ér V   'to V from A, to V
        because of A; be V'd by A' 8.15
    in yóuyu A ér V   'to V from A, to V
        because of A; be V'd by A' 8.15
Ēwén, Éwén, Èwén   Russian language 4.22
érhuàyùn   retroflex sound 16.43
értóng   children 15.25

fà   law 2.37
fācái   become rich 10.14
fādá   develop, advance, prosper; developed,
    advanced, prosperous; development 4.56

huá   stroke (of a Chinese character) (M)
      3.22
huà   demarcate 17.34
huà   -ize, -fy 3.27
huàfēn   demarcate 17.34
huāhuì   flowers and plants (as a branch
      of painting) 19.9
huàjù   (spoken) drama 15.2
huāliǎn   painted face (of actors in gen-
      eral); non-white painted face (rep-
      resenting a heroic character) 19.2
huàpǔ   book of paintings 19.7
Huáqiáo   overseas Chinese 5.33
huāyuán   (flower) garden 9.64
huài   bad; (used as postverb) 10.52,
      10 N 5
huàihuà   slander (N) 10.52
huàirén   an evil person, a bad egg 10.52
huàishì   evil deed 10.52
huàn   change, exchange 5.15
huánjìng   environment, circumstances
      2.45
huàn jù huà shuō   in other words 5.15
huàn nǎozi   switch to another subject,
      take up something else 16.55
huàn yíjù huà shuō   in other words 5.15
huáng   yellow 4.11
huángdì   emperor 7.4
Huáng Hǎi   Yellow Sea 4.11
Huáng Hé   Yellow River 4.11
huángjīn   gold 9.19
huángluàn   be in confusion, be in disorder,
      be upset 13.55
huángyīng   oriole 13.6
huār   flower 9.64
Huí   Mohammedan, Moslem 7.11
huí   chapter (in a book) 23.8
huì   collection 15.7
huìbiān   compendium 15.7
huídá   answer (that) 5.64
huīfu   recover, revive 21.15
huìhé   join together, come together,
      merge 14.43
huìhuà   draw and paint; drawing and
      painting 19.8
Huíhui   Mohammedan, Moslem 7.11
Huíjiào   Moslem religion 7.11
huìyì   compound ideograph 14.9, 14 N 1 C
huìyì   conference; hold a conference
      11.62
huìyìshì   conference room 11.62
Huízú   Chinese Moslem nationality 7.11
hǔnluàn   confusion, chaos 21.8
hǔnzá   mixed (together) 23.52
huò   calamity 5.5
huòbì   currency 21.3
huòchē   vehicle for transporting goods,
      truck 21.56
huódong   movable; active; flourishing;
      activity 20.48

huómái   bury alive 22.3
huópo   lively, quick, bustling 23.49
huòwu   (articles of) merchandise 21.17
huǒyào   gunpowder 9.27
huózì   movable type 9.37

indefinite N   15 N 3
indeterminate subjects   22 N a

jí   hurried, hasty, urgent; worried, ex-
      cited, upset 11.35
jí   very (prefix before stative verbs,
      equivalent to jíle in spoken style)
      22.46, 23 N b
jì   offer sacrifices (to) 10.23
jì   since, because 10.51
jì   season 23.61
jīběn   foundation; fundamental 3.28
jīchǔ   foundation, base 8.21
Jīdūjiào   Christianity; Protestantism
      20.1
jígé   qualify, pass an exam, pass a course
      2.12
jīhū   nearly, almost, practically, vir-
      tually 7.65
jìhua   plan, figure out; plan, proposal,
      plan of action 1.42
jījihū   nearly, almost, practically, vir-
      tually 7.65
jīlěi   accumulate, pile up 13.3
jílì   lucky, auspicious 10.15
jīliè   violent, radical 23.32
jìlù   make a formal written record of,
      take minutes of; records, minutes
      2.58
jímáng   worried, flustered 11.35
jìmo   lonesome 1.54
jīqi   machine, machinery 21.34
jìqiǎo   ingenious, skillful, expert; skill,
      expertness 19.47
jìrán   since, because 10.51
jìshí   when; some time or other 10.33
jìshǐ   even if, supposing 13.13
jìshi   since, because 10.51
jìshu   technique, skill; technology 8.49
jítǐ   collective (used before nouns) 21.37
jīxiè   machinery; mechanical, machine
      21.19
jìxu   continue (doing something) 1.5
jìxude   continue (doing something) 1.5
jìyì   remember, recollect; recollection
      22.63
jìyìlì   memory 22.63
jìzǎi   record (N/V) 19.49
jìzào   make offerings to the Kitchen God
      (VO) 10.23
jízhōng   concentrate 5.16
jiā
      family 8.10
      measure for homes, stores, etc. 8 N 5

Kàngzhàn   War of Resistance (i.e. anti-
      Japanese War of 1937–1945) 7.38
kào   lean on, depend on; be due to;
      border on, be located at; veer in a
      certain direction 4.41
kàodezhù   able to rely on, reliable 4.41
kǎoqǔ   select by examination 2.17
kàozhe   lean on, depend on; be due to;
      border on, be located at; veer in a
      certain direction 4.41
kē   carve, engrave 9.35
kē   (measure for trees and plants) 11.3
kě   see also méi yǒu N kě V de 'not
      have any N that one can V' 10 N 2
kècheng   curriculum (M: mén) 1.41
kèfú   conquer, subdue 13.20
kējǔ   select by examination 3.8
kěkào   reliable, dependable 4.41
kèshǐ   classroom 2.38
kètáng   classroom 3.15
kētóu   to kowtow 10.16
kěxī   be unfortunate, too bad (that . . .)
      14.41
kéyi búbì   not have to 5.57
kē zì   engrave characters 9.35
kěn   be willing (to) 11.47
kōng   empty, unoccupied 9.39
kōnghuà   empty talk 9.39
Kǒng Jiā diàn   the shop of the Kong
      family 20 N 2
kōngjiān   space, interval 22.47
Kǒngjiào   Confucianism 7.1
Kǒngmiào   Confucian temple 8.25
Kǒngzǐ   Confucius 1.56
kū   cry, weep 10.57
kǔ   bitter (literally and figuratively),
      hard 8.35
kǔgōng   hard physical labor; laborer,
      worker (engaged in hard physical
      labor) 8.35
kuà   bestride 22.29
kuàiji   accounting 14.57
kuàilè   happy, joyful 1.55
kuàng   a mine; ore 21.20
kuàngchǎn   mineral product, mineral
      production 21.20
kuàngyè   mining industry 21.20
Kūnmíng   Kunming (in Yunnan) 16.12
kùnnán   difficult, troublesome; a diffi-
      culty, a trouble, distress 2.33
kuòdà   enlarge, widen, expand 7.39
kuòhú   parentheses, brackets 15.36
kuòzhǎn   develop, expand 7.36

Lādīng   Latin 14.47
Lādīnghuà   Latinize; Latinization 14.47
Lādīngwén   Latin language 14.47
Lǎma   Lama (priest) 7.8
Lǎmajiào   Lamaism 7.8

làyue   twelfth lunar month 10.25
lái N   bring N, cause N to come 20 N 3 h
lái
      double use to indicate purpose p. 14
      in ànzhe A lai suàn 'calculate ac-
            cording to A' 16 N
      in ná . . . lái shuō 3 N 3
      in nǎr láide N V 'where would one
            find the N to V?' 19 N 1 b
      used with de and bu to form resulta-
            tive verbs 8 N 1
láiyuán   source, place of origin 11.8
Lǎo Cán Yóujì   Travels of Mr. Derelict
      17.3
láo-ér-wú-gōng   work to no avail 15.46
Lǎo Shè   Lao She 17 N 4
lǎoye   old gentleman (polite form) 10.24
le
      in V₁ le jiu V₂ 'to V₂ after having
            V₁' 16 N
      in V le yòu V 'keep on V-ing, V
            over and over again' 11 N 2
lè = kuàilè 'happy' 1 N 4
lèi   kind, sort, category (M); used as
      suffix, e.g. tānglèi 'soups' (in a
      menu) 8.47
lèisì   similar, alike, like 16.57
lěng   cold 4.60
lí   pear 19.29
lǐ   gift, present 10.45
lǐ   etiquette 19.22
lì   establish, set up 3.4
lì   calendar 10.2, 10 N 3
lì   profit 14.46
lìhai   severe 15.63
lǐjié   etiquette, formality 19.22
lìjù   illustrative sentence 1.8
Lì Mǎdòu   Matteo Ricci 20.6
lìrér   'standing man' (radical) 15.55
lìrú   for example 7.48
lìshǐ-xì   history department (similarly
      for other departments) 2.34
líshù   pear tree 19.29
lìwài   exception; be an exception 14.36
lǐxuéyuàn   college of science 2.57
lìyì   advantage, benefit 4.62
lìyòng   use for one's own ends, make a
      tool of; utilization 9.57
líyuán   pear garden 19.28
lǐyuè   etiquette and music 19.22
lìzi   example, sample, illustration 1.6
lián   with dōu or yě 4 N 2
lián V dōu/yě bù/méi V 'not even V'
      11 N 3
liǎn   face 13.15
liánchuàn   string together 16.54
Lián-Dà   (abbreviation for) Southwest
      Associated University 5.13
liánhé   join with, federate with 5.13

nónggōngyè   agriculture and industry 2.53

nònghuài   spoil, put out of order 14 N 5

nóngmín   farmers, peasants (usually collectively) 2.53

nóngren   farmer, peasant 2.53

nóngtián   agricultural land 2.53

nóngxuéyuàn   college of agriculture 2.53

nóngyè   agriculture 2.53

nóngyè hézuoshè   agricultural cooperative 2.53

nóngzuòyè   farming 21.39

nǔlì   exert great effort, strive hard 1.32

numbers

    used in recapitulating items in a series 17 N 3

    same measure with two different numbers 19 N 1 d

occupations, names of 8 N 3

Ōu   Europe 4.19

Ōuhuà   Europeanize 4.19

Ōu-Měi   Europe and America 4.19

ǒurán   by chance, occasionally 9.56

ǒurán yíge jīhui   by a chance encounter, (on) an unexpected occasion 9.56

ǒuránde yíge jīhui   by a chance encounter, (on) an unexpected occasion 9.56

Ōuzhōu   Europe 4.19

pái   signboard; trademark; brand, make; playing cards, dominoes, mahjong pieces 10.30

pài   faction, party, group (M) 11.51

pài   depute, despatch, appoint 22.33

páiliè   arrange in a series 15.52

páizi   signboard; trademark; brand, make; playing cards, dominoes, mahjong pieces 10.30

pán   measure for dishes, reels of tape 2.40

pànduàn   judge, give a judgment, determine; judgment, decision 19.58

pánzi   dish, plate 2.40

páng   other, others; side; from the sidelines, as a spectator 11.19

pàng   fat, stout 13.52

pángbian(r)   side 11.19

pángmén   side door 11.19

pángren   other people 11.19

pángtīng   audit (a course), sit in as an auditor 11.19

pàngzi   a fat person 13.52

pàozhang   firecracker, fireworks 9.28

pèiji   to ration 21.29

péng = péngyou   'friend' 1 N 4

pèng   to knock, bump 13.24

pèngjian   meet with, run into 13.24

péngzhàng   swell, expand, inflate; expanded, swollen 21.1

pīping   criticize; criticism 8.67

piān   section, chapter, book (e.g. Book I) (M); (measure for articles and essays) 8.58

piàn   sheet, slice (M) 17.47

piàntǐwén   literature characterized by balanced sentences 17.42

pīn   spell out, represent speech-sounds in writing 7.23

pǐn   goods, stuff, article 9.5

pīnyīn   spell out (VO); spelling 7.23

píngjūn   level, even; on the average 2.27

pò   break, broken, worn out (also used as postverb) 11.59

pòhuài   spoil, destroy (literally and figuratively), slander 11.59

Póyáng Hú   Poyang Lake 4.44

pù   store (N) 15.42

pǔbiàn   general, prevailing, widespread 3.29

pǔjí   (make) widespread, (make) universal 3.29

pūren, púren, pǔren   servant 8.20

pǔtōng   common, ordinary 8.40

pǔtōnghuà   common speech, general speech 8.40

pùzi   store (N) 15.42

qī   period 3.30

qí   flag (M: ge, miàn) 7.52

qí   ride (astride) 19.19

qícì   next, second(ly) 7.45

qìhuài   be terribly angry 10.52

qilai

    in zènmo Vqilai   'in so V-ing, V-ing in this way, from what is V'd' 20 N 3 e

    see also SVqilai 9 N 2

qǐshēn   start out, start on a journey 3.19

qíshí   actually, as a matter of fact 7.2

qítā   the rest, the others (PR) 7.26

qǐyè   (business) enterprise 21.58

qǐyì   raise a righteous revolt 22.52

qíyú   the remainder, the remaining, the leftover 10.17

qíyúde   the remainder, the remaining, the leftover 10.17

qǐyuán   beginning, origin, source 7.6

qízi   flag (M: ge, miàn) 7.52

qiàqiǎo   just at that moment, precisely (then), just; accidentally, by coincidence 15.45

qiànshōu   have a bad harvest 21.43

qiántú   prospects for the future 11.57

qiānzhēnwànquè   completely authentic 13.59

qiáng   powerful; preferable, better 11.54

rìlì   calendar 10.2

rìyòngpǐn   article of daily use 9.5

rú   be like; for example; such as 15.62

rú   scholar; Confucian 17.2

rù   enter 4.67

rúguǒ yào yǒu   if have 2.47

rúhé   how? be like what? 15.62

Rújiā   scholar of the Confucian School 17.2

Rúlín Wàishǐ   The Scholars 17.2

rùmén   introduction, primer (in book titles) 4.67

ruògān   quite a number (of), quite an amount (of), a certain (number of); how much? how many? 7.59

sài   compete (in) 11.17

sàibuguò   unable to compete successfully with (RV) 11.17

sài chuán   to race boats; a boat race 11.17

sāndiǎn shuǐ   'three-dot water' (radical) 15.59

Sānmín Zhǔyì   Three People's Principles (of Sun Yatsen) 8.65

sǎnwén   prose; essay 15.34

Sān Zì Jīng   Three Character Classic 3.1

sǎo   to sweep 11.32

sǎomù   sweep the graves (of one's ancestors) 11.39

shā   kill, murder 5.44

shā   sand 48

shāmò   desert 4.48

shāsi   kill 5.45

shàn'è   good and evil, good or evil (N/SV) 23.59

shāng   commerce 4.31

Shāng   Shang (Dynasty) (ca. 1500–1028 B.C.) 9.42

shāng   injure, wound; injury, wound 15.45, 15 N 5

shǎng   reward, grant, bestow; enjoy, appreciate 11.28

shāngfēng   catch cold (VO); a cold 15.45

shànggòng   make offerings (VO) 10.44

Shànggǔ Hànyǔ   Archaic Chinese 16.16

shānghuì   chamber of commerce 14.58

Shāng Jūn   Lord Shang 20.19

shǎngqián   bestow money (VO); a tip 11.28

shāngren   merchant 4.31

Shàng Shū   Book of History 16.18

shàng tiān   ascend to heaven 10.29

shāngyè   commerce 4.31

shàngyóu   upper reaches (of a stream) 5.12

shǎngyuè   enjoy the moon 11.28

shàngzuò(r)   seat of honor 10.62

shāo   burn; roast 10.27

shǎoshù mínzú   minority nationality, national minority 5.38

shāowēi   slightly, somewhat 15.18

shàoye   (your) son (polite form) 10.24

shè   establish, set up 3.5

shèhuì zhǔyì   socialism 20.50

shèlì   establish, set up 3.5

shéi   in shéi V shéi   'who V's who?' 21 N f

shēn   deep, profound 3.39

shēn   body 3.19

shén   spirit, deity, god 10.26

shénfù   (Catholic) priest 20.5

shénhuà   myth 10.26

shénmo yě bù/méi V, jiù V N   V nothing but N 5 N 2

shēnqǐng   apply, make a request (to a superior) 2.31

shēntǐ   body 3.20

shēn-xīn   body and mind 3.19

Shěnyáng   Mukden (in Manchuria) 16.14

shènzhì   even to, even as far as to, culminating in 8.31

shènzhìyu   even to, even as far as to, culminating in 8.31

shēng   initial (sound) 14.25, 15 N 5

shēng   used in yìshēng 'once' 11 N 6

shěng   save, economize 3.23

shèng   victorious; victory 11.21

shèng   a sage 20.34

shèng   flourishing, prosperous, glorious 19.23

    in yǐ A wéi shèng   'A was the most flourishing' 19 N 2

shēngchǎn   produce; production 8.22

shēngcí   new word, vocabulary 1.1

shēngcí biǎo   word list, vocabulary list 1.1

shēngdiào   tones; tune 16.9

shēngdòng   lifelike, lively, animated 23.10

shěnghuì   provincial capital 14.58

shěnglì   provincial (i.e. established by a province) 3.4

shènglì   victorious; victory 11.21

shèngrén   a sage 20.34

Shèng Táng   Glorious T'ang (designation for a particularly brilliant period, 713–766) 22.8

shēngwēi   prestige 22.28

shēngwù   biology 2.36

shēngwùxué   biology 2.36

shèngxíng   flourishing; practice extensively 20.60

shēngyù   to bear, rear 5.21

shī   poem, poetry 8.54

shī   lose 22.11

shí   stone 4.55
shí   eat; food 14.38
shǐ   cause to 3.37
shǐ   use (V) 9.22
shǐ   room 2.38
shì   scholar (W) 8.38
shì   municipality 5.30
shì   look at 11.56
shì   form, style 8.11
shì   clan name 14.21, 14 N 4
shì
        used in joining a sentence with a noun
            17 N 2
shíbài   be defeated, fail 11.14
shìchǎng   market, marketplace 21.18
shìdàfū   gentry 8.3
Shǐdàlín   Stalin 20.57
shìdàifū   gentry 8.3
shìfǒu   is or is not 13.14
shīgē   poems and songs 17.25
shìhé   suited (to), suitable 21.31
shíhou   in yàoshi A de shíhou   'if and
            when A' 16 N
Shǐhuáng   The First Emperor (of Ch'in)
            22.2
shíjì   actual, factual, practical 5.55
shìjì   century; age, period 7.41
shíjìshang   as a matter of fact, in fact
            5.55
shìjiè   world 3.24
shìjiè dàzhàn   world war 5.7
Shī Jīng   Book of Odes 16.17
shíkè   stone engraving 19.16
shíkū   stone cave 19.14
shìli   strength, power, influence 20.10
shǐmìng   task, mission 17.58
shíqì   articles made of stone 19.54
shìqián   before an event, beforehand
            1.27
shīren   poet 8.54
shítou   stone 4.55
shīwàng   lose hope; be disappointed
            10.59
shīyì   poetic quality, lyricism 13.10
shǐyòng   use (V) 9.22
shìyòng   sufficient for use, answers the
            purpose, usable, applicable, applied;
            application, applicability 15.21
shíyóu   petroleum 21.21
shīyùn   rhyme in poetry; (book title)
            14.24
shìzhǎng   mayor 5.30
shízhǐ   physical, real, solid, substantial
            23.39
shízhǐshang   ... in reality, actually, in
            fact 23.39
shǐzhōng   (from) beginning to end, the
            whole course of an affair 11.26
shǐzǔ   first ancestor, founder, founding
            father 20.23

shōu   receive, accept, collect 4.66
shòu   receive, suffer, endure 3.33
shòu   thin (of people) 13.51
shòukǔ   suffer, receive bad treatment
            (VO) 22.37
shōuqilai   set aside, gather up and put
            away 4.66
shōurù   income 21.63
shòushāng   be wounded, be injured 15.45
shǒuxiān   first of all, in the first place
            13.1
shǒuxu   procedure 11.46
shū   writing; calligraphy 14 N 1, 19.10
shǔ   belong, pertain to 3.52
shù   tree (M: kē) 11.2
shūfǎ   calligraphy 19.10
shūfu   comfortable; comfort 23.28
shùlínzi   forest, woods 11.2
shūrù   import (N/V) 20.61
shǔyu   belong, pertain to 3.52
shuàilǐng   lead, take with one 22.30
shuāiruò   become debilitated, feeble
            22.31
shuāng   double, pair (M) 15.40
shuānglìrér   'double standing man'
            15.55
Shuāngshíjié   Double Tenth (i.e. Oct. 10,
            national day of Republic of China)
            15.40
shuāngyīnjié   two-syllable expression
            23.40
shuì   to sleep (VO) 10.41
shuǐbà   dam, dike, breakwater 21.54
shuìjiào   to sleep (VO) 10.41
shuǐkù   reservoir 21.54
shuǐzāi   flood 4.7
shuō
        in A yìsi jiu shi shuō B   'A means
            B' 5.2
        in A shi shuō B   'A means B' 5.2
        in ná . . . lái shuō   'speak of . . . ,
            speaking of' 3 N 2
shuòshi   M.A. 2.22
Shuōwén   (book title) 14.20, 14 N 6
sī   private 3.3
sī   (raw) silk 9.1
sǐ   die 5.45
sì   temple, monastery (Buddhist) 20.36
sīcháo   flood of ideas 17.60
Sìchuān   Szechuan 5.9
sìdiǎn huǒ   'four-dot fire' (radical)
            15.59
sìfāng   square 4.64
sìfāngde   square 4.64
sī-fēn-wǔ-liè   badly split, fragmented 22.21
sìjì   four seasons 23.61
sīlì   private(ly established) 3.4
sīrén   private person 3.3
sǐshāng   die and be wounded; dead and
            wounded 15.45

wùchǎn   product 4.3

wǔdǎo   dance (N) 19.21

Wǔdì   Emperor Wu-ti of Han (140-86 B.C.) 22.36

Wǔhú Shíliù Guó   Five Barbarians and Sixteen Kingdoms 22.22

Wǔ Jīng   Five Classics 3.1

wùjià   commodity prices 21.4

wǔlì   military power 22.26

wùlǐ   physics 2.35

wùlǐxué   physics 2.35

wùlǐxuéjiā   physicist (similarly for some other disciplines) 2.35

wúlùn   no matter (= búlùn) 8.32

wǔlún   five human relationships 20.26

wǔqì   military equipment 9.30

wǔsèqí   five-color flag (used in 1912 by the Republic of China) 7.52

Wǔsì Yùndong   May Fourth Movement 17.11

wúsuǒwèi   be of no importance, make no difference, not matter 8.32

wǔtái   stage, theater (literal and figurative) 19.21

wǔtáijù   stage play 19.21

wúwéi   do nothing, remain passive; inaction, quietism 20.25

wúwéi ér zhì   govern by doing nothing 20.25

wúxiàndiàn   radio 9.10

wúyíde   unquestionably, doubtless 20.42

Wúyǔ   Wu dialect 16.4

Wǔyuèjié   Dragon-Boat Festival 11.7

wùzhì   matter, substance; material, materialistic 22.61

wūzi   room (in a house) 10.37

xī   sparse, thin, diluted 5.31

xí   banquet 10.18

xì   course, department (in a college or university) 2.34

xì   a play 15.1

xíguàn   be used to; habit, custom, tradition 5.52

xìjù   drama, play 15.2

Xīkāng   Sikang 7.21

Xīnán Liánhé Dàxué   Southwest Associated University 5.13

Xī-Ōu   Western Europe 4.19

xīshǎo   few, scarce 5.31

Xīshì   Western style 8.11

xīshōu   absorb 20.51

xìtǒng   system 7.47

Xīyáng   the West 11.27

Xīyù   Western Regions 22.35

Xīyuè   Western music 19.20

Xīzàng   Tibet 4.36

xì zhǔrèn   chairman of a department 2.34

Xīzhuāng   Western-style dress 11.41

xià   used in yíxià 'once' 11N6

xià   summer; Hsia Dynasty; (a surname) 22.59

xiàjì   summer 23.61

Xiàmén   Amoy (in Fukien) 16.7

xià pànduàn   reach a conclusion 19.58

xiàtian   summer 22.59

xiàyóu   lower reaches (of a stream) 5.12

xià yǔ   be raining 4.53

xiàn   thread 9.10

xiàn   limit (N/V) 17.41

xiān V₁ hòu V₂   'first V₁ then V₂' 16N

xiàndu   a limit 23.3

Xiānqín   pre-Chin 17.16

Xiānsheng   Mr. 14N4

xiànyu   limited to, limited in 17.41

xiànzhi   impose a limitation 17.41

xiǎnzhù   obvious 16.40

xiāng   the country (versus the city) 4.47

xiāng   perfume, incense 10.28

Xiāng   monosyllabic name for Hunan 16.2

xiàng   toward 3.57

xiàng   article, section (of a document); item, matter 13.61

xiàng
in A yě xiàng B yíyàng V   'A, like B, V' 16N
in Vde xiàng N₁ SVde N₂   'an N₂ who/which V's as SV as V' 20N3g

xiāngchù   get along (with someone) 7.61

xiāngchùbulái   unable to get along (with someone) 7.61

xiāngcūn   village; rural 5.41

xiāngdāng(de)   suitable, suitably; fairly, quite, rather 2.19

Xiānggǎng   Hong Kong 3.62

xiànglái   hitherto 3.57

xiàngshēng   phonetic character 14.5

xiàngshì   simple ideograph 14.22

xiāngtóng   (very) similar, almost, identical 3.43

xiángxi   detailed 2.52

xiāngxia   the country 4.47

xiāngxìn   believe, be convinced that, have trust in 1.33

xiàngxíng   pictograph; pictographic 14.5, 14N1a

Xiāngyǔ   Hunan dialect 16.2

xiàngzhe   toward 3.57

xiàngzhēng   symbol; symbolize 19.33

xiǎo   used between numerals and measures 22Nd

xiāofèi   consume; consumption 21.53

xiàoguǒ   result, outcome 23.14

xiǎohù   poor family 8.7

zhŭxiūkē   major (course of study) 13.41

zhŭyì   principle, idea, theory, ism 8.65

zhúzi   bamboo 9.24

zhū-zĭ-băi-jiā   all classes of philosophers 20.31

zhuā   scratch; grasp, seize 9.21

zhuān   special(ly) 1.17

zhuǎn   revolve, evolve, change; pass on 14.12

zhuàn   biography 15.32

zhuǎn bài wéi shèng   change defeat into victory 14.12

zhuǎnbiàn   change (N/V) 19.59

zhuǎnchéng   change, evolve into 14.12

zhuànjì   biography 15.32

zhuānjiā   a specialist, an expert 1.18

zhuǎnlìdiǎn   turning point 20.45

zhuǎnlièdiǎn   turning point 20.45

zhuānmén   special(ly) 1.17

zhuāntí   special topic 1.19

zhuānzhì   despotic, autocratic 20.14

zhuǎnzhù   derive; derivative character 14.12, 14N1f

zhuāng   style of dress 11.41

Zhuàng   Chuang nationality 7.18

zhuàngkuàng   circumstances, state of affairs 5.11

zhuàngtài   situation, status 5.10

Zhuāngzĭ   Chuang Tzu 17.22

Zhuàngzú   Chuang nationality 7.18

zhŭn   permit, allow, grant 14.34

zhŭnbèi   prepare, get ready 15.41

zhuō   a table; (measure for banquets) 11.30

zhuōzi   a table; (measure for banquets) 11.30

zì = cóng   'from' 1N4

zīběn   capital 21.14

zīběnjiā   capitalist 21.14

zīběn zhŭyì   capitalism 21.14

zĭdì   sons and younger brothers, sons and heirs, one's juniors 19.30

zìgēngnóng   peasants who farm their own land 8.33

zìhuì   list of characters, vocabulary 15.7

zìjīngnóng   peasants who farm their own land 8.33

zīliào   materials 14.6

zĭmèi   sisters 13.53

zìpáng(r)   side of a character; side radical 15.37

zìrán'érrán(de)   natural(ly), spontaneous(ly), of course 3.58

zìshā   kill oneself, commit suicide 5.44

zīshi   carriage, deportment, bearing, manner 19.35

zĭsūn   sons and grandsons; descendants, posterity 5.17

zìtóu(r)   top of a character; top radical 15.37

zìxi   minutely, carefully 23.36

zìxíng   form of a character 14.23

zìyì   meaning of a character 14.23

zìyīn   sound of a character 14.23

zìyóu   free; freedom 8.64

zìyóu zhŭyì   liberalism 8.65

zìzhìqū   autonomous region 4.9

zìzhuàn   autobiography 15.32

zŏng   always, invariably 2.41

zŏng'éryánzhi   to sum up, to put it briefly 5.38

zŏngjí   comprehensive collection, general collection 17.28

zŏngjiào   religion, religious denomination 7.1

zŏngjié   conclude, sum up; conclusion, summary 22.56

zŏngkuò   bring together; generalize; comprehensive 14.42

zŏngkuò yíjù   to sum up in a word 14.42

zŏngshi   always, invariably 2.41

zŏngshù   sum, total, amount 2.41

zŏngzhi   to sum up 3.38

zòngzi   dumpling made of glutinous rice 11.12

zōngzú   clan 8.29

zú   people, nationality, nation 5.38

zú   clan 8.29

zŭ   group, unit, series (M) 1.3

zŭ   ancestor 8.17

zŭchéng   organize, constitute, accomplish, achieve 21.57

zŭfù   father's father, grandfather 8.17

zŭmŭ   father's mother, grandmother 8.17

zŭxiān   ancestors 8.17

zúzhǎng   clan head 8.29

zŭzhĭ   impede, obstruct, stop 17.24

zŭzhi   organize, form; organization 2.42

zŭzong   ancestor 8.24

zuĭ   mouth 16.49

zuì   crime, sin 23.45

zuĭba   mouth (Shanghai dialect); cheek 16.49

zuìdĭ xiàndu   at least 23.3

zuìdĭde xiàndu   at least 23.3

zuì'è   evil, sin, wickedness 23.59

zūn   to honor 20.12

zūnchóng   to worship, reverence, respect 20.12

zūnzhòng   honor, respect (N/V) 20.12

zòu   perform (music) 19.37

zuò
    as postverb 3N2
    in ná A zuò B   'take A as B' 23Nc

zuò   seat 10.62

zuòchénggōng   achieve success (RV) 4.65